Zine Scene

amous Monsters-

ALL ABOUT TIME AFTER TIME

MONSTERS

The origi[...] [...]TERS which was o[...] [...] redu level of th[...] [...] J. A fault, or a[...] [...]sing sually blam[...] [...] othe are involved. First and foremost is its trendy attitude that veloped since the release of STAR WARS. Instead of giving th rare information, star biographies and interesting filmbooks once found in the mag, we now are inundated with commonly se and boring info on any one current "blockbuster" that comes WARS was featured in nearly 14 consecutive issues. Next came [...]UNTERS which got considerable coverage in 4 consecutive issues. MOON-[...]AKER could be found in 3 issues. BATTLESTAR GALACTICA tallied 5 dull [...]eature articles. SUPERMAN got 3 equally uninteresting pieces of cov-[...]rage. And currently ALIEN is getting the saturation treatment, with 5 [...]eatures so far and more to follow. Still, FAMOUS MONSTERS has survived [...] long, long time. The earlier is[...] [...]est J. [...]kerman. The newer ones are sim[...] [...] on-[...] good thing about any new issue[...] [...] stills [...]d some interesting information [...] [...]s fun [...]r the younger set, but the seri[...] [...] to [...]ave it, and will sometimes put i[...] [...]pen-[...]g it. With the price currently [...] [...] mag, [...] just isn't worth it anymore.

Sta

Above FAMOUS MONSTERS in qualit[...] [...] magazine t[...]self with a lot more science fa[...] [...] has a few a[...]er FM: 1) Glossy pages 2) Extensi[...] [...]erviews 4) A[...]pproach 5) Fewer advertisements. [...] FM in all a[...] [...] any [...]ende[...] [...]er" [...]his

# XEROX FEROX

## The Wild World of the Horror Film Fanzine

### by John Szpunar

I don't find sci[...] [...]e folks at a knack for maki[...] [...] of rather d the magazine does concern itself with the fantastic cinema, when to quit relating to any one particular film. Though ext was given to ALIEN, most of it was in the form of interviews scenes shots and other items of this sort thus making the ar worthwhile. The horror side of STARLOG has been replaced by

angoria-

magazine of its type ever to be published on the horror cine[...] FANGORIA, which is published by the group that brings you ST[...] [...]robably the most similar magazine to DEMONIQUE available on the stands, FAN[...] [...]uperbly done publication that, as late as issue #4, has only improved in qua[...] [...]ariety. Each issue contains in-depth interviews with various make-up artists [...]nd writers usually not seen anywhere else. For example, in recent issues FA[...] [...]nterviews with David Cronenberg, Tom Savini, Richard Matheson, Caroline Mun[...] [...]nd Don Coscarelli. As well as covering the latest films, FANGORIA recalls o[...] [...]ccasionally gives histories of various characters and celebrities. Their la[...] [...]overed the "Wizard of Gore" Hirschell G. Lewis, and for a bit of contrast t[...] [...]ad a well written summary of Godzilla's illustrious screen career. One thin[...] [...]s a more adult approach, though they cater to a level of intelligence well [...] [...]AMOUS MONSTERS youngsters. Pictorally and artistically the magazine seems t[...] [...]here nudity or violence are concerned, there are a few too many reservation[...] [...]irschell Lewis [...] [...]e scenes. But most of [...]overed in depth [...] [...]ience. Articles on th[...] [...]ING KONG are to[...] [...], as well as the feat[...] [...]n the STAR TREK film which was adequately covered in both STARLOG and FUTUR[...]

A HEADPRESS BOOK

# CONTENTS

XERO
FEROX



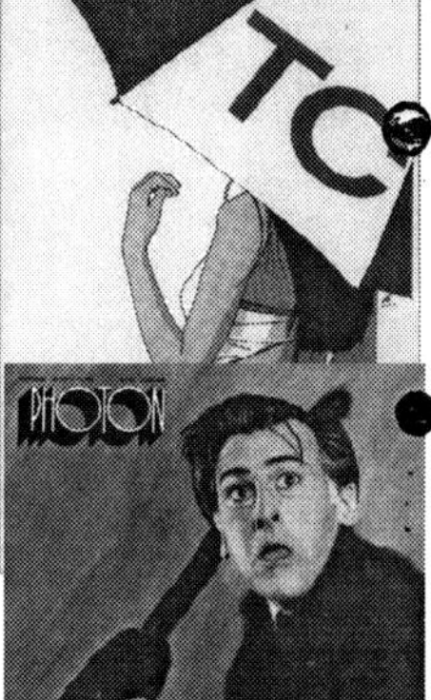
PHOTON

WORLDS OF HORROR

GIALLO PAGES
Volume 1

# CONTENTS

**WAR OF THE COLOSSAL BEAST**

A monster of the Atomic Age! A towering terror from Hell! The story of a man trapped in the blast of a plutonium bomb—and the terrible events that followed. Only $6.20

**THE BLOB**

Teenagers see what looks like a shooting star blaze to earth. At its landing spot they find an old man writhing in pain, his hand covered with a strange substance. They rush him to a doctor, who watched the substance spreading before his eyes. The Blob continues to spread, & terrorize the town. Only $6.20

**IT CAME FROM OUTER SPACE**

WHAT HAPPENS WHEN A SPACE SHIP loaded with stellar monsters goes out of control! They land on earth and battle a brave scientist trying to save the earth. Is he successful? This scary film tells you what really happens. 160 feet, 8mm. $6.20.

**ABBOTT & COSTELLO MEET DR. JEKYLL & MR. HYDE**

AMERICA'S MOST MIRTHFUL COMEDIANS meet the world's most monstrous Monsters . . . and that's where the fun begins. Dr. Jekyll gives Costello a drug, turns him into a monster. Everything goes crazy and Scotland Yard goes mad. Monsters can be fun, and this film is the funniest! 8mm, 160 feet, $6.20

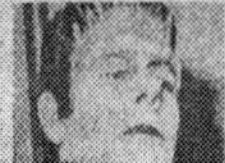

**ABBOTT & COSTELLO MEET FRANKENSTEIN**

THE WHO'S WHO of the MONSTER WORLD team up in the funniest monster film ever made. Imagine Frankenstein, Dracula, The Wolf Man and The Invisible Man combining their eerie talents to trap Abbott & Costello. They even suggest using Costello's brain for the Monsters. Great fun! 8mm, 100 feet, $6.20

**ABBOTT & COSTELLO IN ROCKET & ROLL**

THE FUNNIEST COMICS in Hollywood double up for a crazy rocket trip through outer space. Beauties and cuties in Venus tempt them. The runaway rocket ship scares the life out of them. And through it all Abbott & Costello give a hilarious performance that will make you "die" laughing. 8mm, 160 feet, $6.20.

**NOW FOR THE FIRST TIME— THE 3 STOOGES IN 3D**

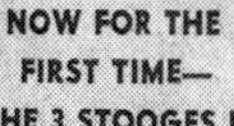

Aside from the special color-filter viewers supplied with the film, no special equipment is needed. No special screen . . . no special projector. Just watch the startling action! Sixty feet of film.

The Stooges in a hilarious slapstick romp . . . funnier than ever in 3-D. So real they seem to jump right out of the screen. When something is thrown . . . you duck! Only $5.25

This 3-D Stooge comedy is a wild tale that takes place in an old haunted house. Our 3-Dimensional Stooges are mixed up with all sorts of deadly weapons . . . Only $5.25

**EAST SIDE KIDS MEET BELA LUGOSI**

YOU'LL DIE LAUGHING as the East Side Kids match their side-splitting stunts with Bela Lugosi's terror-filled action. Featuring Bela Lugosi and the original East Side Kids. Only $6.20

**WE WANT OUR MUMMY**

Hired as detectives, our 3 friends take a hilarious taxi ride to Egypt. And when they enter the tomb . . . WOW! Only $6.95

Please rush me the following, for which I enclose, $............ plus 25¢ postage & handling for each film checked.

CAPTAIN COMPANY,
P.O. Box 5987, Grand Central Station
New York, New York 10017

- ☐ The 4-D Man, $6.20.
- ☐ War Of The Planets, $6.20.
- ☐ War Of The Colossal Beast, $6.20.
- ☐ The Blob, $6.20.
- ☐ It Came From Outer Space, $6.20
- ☐ A. & C. Meet Dr. Jekyll & Mr. Hyde, $6.20
- ☐ A. & C. Meet Frankenstein, $6.20
- ☐ A. & C. in Rocket and Roll, $6.20
- ☐ East Side Kids Meet Bela Lugosi, $6.20
- ☐ We Want Our Mummy, $6.95
- ☐ Spooks in 3-D, $5.25
- ☐ Tales Of Horror in 3-D, $5.25

NAME.......
ADDRES...
CITY.....
STATE...

CAPTAIN COMPANY: "UPON THIS ROCK, THEY BUILT THEIR FANDOM."

# INTRODUCTION

BY JOHN SZPUNAR

RECORDED & INDEXED

DRAFT

## FANZINES A-Z

BY CHAS. BALUN

**THE BEWILDERBEAST**
**Dennis Fischer/336 N. Spaulding Ave. No. 12/Los Angeles, California 90036/$2.25 per issue**

*Knowledgeable, intelligent interviews, articles and reviews; published bi-annually. Respected by other 'zine editors for its frankness.*

**BLACK MARKET**
**Carl Schneider/405 W. Washington Street/Plot 212/San Diego, California 92103/$8 for 4 issues**

*Look out for this mother! Full color covers, square bound, and mighty thick; crammed with an eclectic mix of splatter topics, Deathrock bands, and hardcore, guttersnipe ramblings about such things as: "Real Movies from Hell," "Chamber of Gorrors," "The Mass Murderer's Coloring Book," the Butthole Surfers, and all sorts of mean and nasty stuff. Plenty of violent graphics and comix; this mag goes for the throat.*

**BLEEDERS DIGEST**
**Paul Higson/63 Geoffrey Street/Chorley, Lancashire/PR6 OHF/England/Suggested price $1.50 per issue**

*Fantasy, terror trivia, and recent releases reviewed and dissected from a unique "Brit" point of view.*

**CHILDREN OF THE NIGHT**
**Derek Jensen/7450 Village Drive/Prairie Village, Kansas 66208/$3.00 single issue**

*Horror from America's Heartland! Published irregularly, but worth the effort to track down some back issues. Features interviews with such genre names as Tobe Hooper, in-depth treatment of zombie, alien, and maniac classics of the past. Get one before they're snowed in for the winter.*

SCIENCE FICTION, FANTASY & HORROR IN FILMS

**CINEFAN**
**Randall D. Larson/Fandom Unlimited Enterprises/P.O. Box 70868/Sunnyvale, CA 94086/$3.50 single issue**

*Published "every so often," this journal is devoted to the review and analysis of sci-fi, fantasy, and horror films. 74 pages crammed to brimming with all sorts of neat stuff: "Fantastic Cinema 1980-85," "Contemporary Directions in Horror," and "The Horror Anthology Film." Reviews of books, soundtracks, and recent releases, as well as in-depth treatments of the old classics of the 40's and 50's.*

**CINEMACABRE**
**George Stover/P.O. Box 10005/Baltimore, Maryland 21204/$2.50 per issue**

*Published on an irregular basis, this 60-page, slickly-produced 'zine covers sci-fi,*

I started thinking about this book back in 2006. I had recently interviewed *Deep Red* editor Chas. Balun and fanzine veteran Steve Bissette. My idea at the time was to conduct and assemble a collection of interviews with some of the key people involved in the old fanzine scene. Not just any zine scene—I wanted to talk to the guys behind the horror film rags. Dirty little things like *Subhuman*, *Slimetime*, and *Sleazoid Express*.

I began working on things in earnest, but I quickly realized that I had started to spread myself way too thin. I was working a day job as a technical writer for General Motors and trying to keep my DVD label (Barrel Entertainment) out of debt. I started shelving a lot of the projects that I was involved with, and *Xerox Ferox* was one of them.

By 2007, I was mentally and physically drained. It was time to take a break from things. I said goodbye to my old life, spun a much needed cocoon, and eventually resurfaced with new wings. I started working at

JOHN AND JOEL M. REED (LEFT) AT SAM'S, 1998. PHOTO BY DAVID SZPUNAR.

one of the finest museums in the world—The Henry Ford in Dearborn, Michigan. The time that I spent there was essential and rejuvenating. All of my colleagues were in love with history, and I embarked upon a five year tenure as a both a student and teacher of early American agriculture.

Working at a museum can be relaxing and maddening at the same time. When things were good, it seemed as if I was on a paid vacation. When things were bad… well, let's just say that I began to seek solace in a long lost love—exploitation films of every shape and size. Films and fandom suddenly became fun again. This wasn't something that I did for a living. It was something that I did to relax. I started watching movies again. I started reading about them again. And I started to write about them again. Another very personal metamorphosis was about to take shape.

When David Kerekes (the publisher of the book that you're now reading) wrote and asked me if I had any of the old files from my lengthy (and sadly aborted) book about the exploitation director Joel M. Reed, I pinched myself. Perfect timing. I went directly to a long locked vault and started searching. Sure enough, there they were. I set about editing a few chapters together, and what do you know? I enjoyed it. I enjoyed it so much that I started excavating some other artifacts from my past.

In 2011, I stumbled upon some ancient floppy discs and cassette tapes that had been patiently waiting in a box that I thought was long gone.

# INTRODUCTION

BY JOHN SZPUNAR

The dust covered thing was labeled (in rather crude printing) "Xerox Ferox." I decided to give the contents a once over.

Before I knew it, the past became a big part of my present. I started making plans with myself to begin climbing the mountain that would eventually become *Xerox Ferox*.

I started out by transcribing the tapes. Shit, this stuff was good. Really good. But would anyone else be interested in a book about old fanzines? Would I be able to track down the people that I wanted to interview? And if I did manage to track them down, would they even care about the old boxes in their closets? Only one way to find out. I started making some phone calls.

One of the first people that I talked to was Jim Morton, the editor of *Trashola*. He lives in San Francisco, and I live in Detroit. By the time I finished talking to him, it was very early in the morning, but I didn't care. Jim was great—thoughtful, funny, and full of wonderful stories. I quickly transcribed the interview and made some more calls. Before long, I was talking to a lot of the old gang, and they were actually talking back—pages and pages of taking back. If I didn't have the contact information for a potential interview, it was almost guaranteed that somebody within my newfound circle would. Before long, I was looking at twenty, thirty, forty interviews. And that was only the beginning.

Actually, this is probably a good time to address my beginning. I was born in 1973 in Warren, Michigan, a suburb of Detroit. Most of my earliest memories involve watching horror movies. Like many of the people interviewed in this book, I was mesmerized by the fuzzy UHF signals that came to life on the family television. I was addicted to a show called *Chiller Double Feature*. It aired on Saturday afternoons, and a man who called himself Sir Graves Ghastly administered my first dose of horror films from the sixties and seventies. I'll never forget seeing Eugenio Martín's *Horror Express* for the first time. The glowing eyes of the creature scared the shit out of me, as did John Cacavas' haunting score.

Shortly after, I discovered comic books. One day, my grandfather

brought a big box down from his attic. It was filled with coverless pre-codes, and I instantly fell in love with them. I started making weekly trips to the library, scouring the shelves for any information that I could find about the things. Before long, I was reading about Fredric Wertham and his attack on what I had recently identified as the ECs. I'm fairly certain that I was the only sixth grader in my neighborhood that had an axe to grind with the man.

And then, I discovered *Famous Monsters of Filmland*. I had seen ads for the magazine in the back pages of *Creepy* and *Eerie* and I really wanted to read it. I finally found a few tattered copies at a flea market and I took them home. As a child of the eighties, I wasn't really impressed by the content. *Famous Monsters* was talking about "old" movies, and by this time, I was hip to the splatter craze that was just beginning to blossom. What did make an impression was the other-worldliness about it. As with the ECs, *Creepy*, and *Eerie*, reading *Famous Monsters* was very much like stepping into a time machine. I was enamored by the history and nostalgia of it all, but where was the voice of my generation?

Suddenly, it hit. On a routine trip to the local pharmacy, my young eyes saw *Fangoria* for the first time. I was still too young to buy it (and my mother yanked it away before I could turn to page four), but I knew then and there that it was something very special. My father had the ECs, my older cousins had the Warren mags, and I had *Fangoria*. A few years later, I was a proud member of the *Fango* Family, and my life would never be the same.

Before long, I was sneaking into R-rated horror flicks with my friends. That was always a thrill, even if the film that we saw was less than stellar. It was almost as if we were breaking the law. We were doing something taboo, something forbidden. And when a VCR finally hit my household, all bets were off.

It was around this time that I discovered the fanzines. I remember seeing ads for a comic book shop called FantaCo in the back pages of

RECORDED & INDEXED

# INTRODUCTION

BY JOHN SZPUNAR

DRAFT

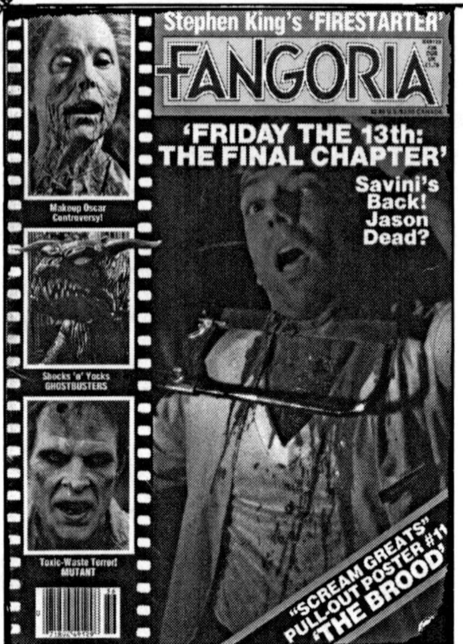


*Fangoria*. It was kind of like seeing the ads for *Famous Monsters* in *Creepy* and *Eerie*, but this time the ads were current. I quickly sent away for something called the *Gore Score*. Soon after that, I purchased my first copy of *Deep Red*. On page thirty-eight of issue number 2, was an article called "Fanzines A-Z."

I sat down with a pencil in my hand and made out a list of the zines that I wanted to read. *Cinemacabre. Crimson Celluloid. Demonique. Gore Gazette. Sleazoid Express*. I didn't get my hands on them all at once, but as the years went on, I built up a solid collection.

Those zines led to others, and I soon became a full-fledged bloodhound: I was sniffing out fanzines from every corner of the earth and I was always on the lookout for more. When I read in *Incredibly Strange Films* (the seminal book from RE/Search) that guest editor Jim Morton had once published a fanzine called *Trashola*, I knew that I had to track it down. Before long, I was a part of a network of zine and tape traders, and the goods kept rolling in: *Stink*. The *Splatter Times. Fatal Visions. Hi-Tech Terror.* I was coming of age with the help of a new generation, and I was having the time of my life.

The fanzines were different than the mainstream magazines like *Fangoria*. They had nothing to lose, and the results were both serious and sleazy. Nothing beat getting down in the dirt with Rick Sullivan as he ranted and raved in the pages of *Gore Gazette*. There was something mysterious and fascinating about *Sleazoid Express*—Bill Landis and Jimmy McDonough were wading knee-deep in filth, but there was real poetry to be found in their words. Stefan Jaworzyn's *Shock Xpress* took genre criticism to an entirely new level. And J. Adler's *Grindhouse* was just plain out there!

When I was a kid reading fanzines, I had a theory. I figured that all of the guys who wrote, edited, and published the things were kind and kindred spirits. A wonderful network of fans connected in those days, be they readers or writers. I was a reader who wanted to become a writer, and as I made headway with my research for this book, I realized that I

FANTACO ENTERPRISES PRESENTS

# SPLATTER HEAVEN

IF YOU DON'T HAVE THESE BOOKS.....THEN YOU MUST ALREADY BE DEAD!

COME WALLOW WITH US....DEEP....DEEPER STILL....INTO THE RED AND BEYOND!

RED ALERT!

"I have seen the future of horror and its name is... DEEP RED." *******

VOLUME 1. Quarterly journal of horror film commentary; interviews with David A. Hess (LAST HOUSE ON THE LEFT), James Karen and Tom Fox (RETURN OF THE LIVING DEAD), and new FX artist Steve Patino (FROM BEYOND, PREDATOR, MONSTER SQUAD) with photo tour of his studio and featuring his extensive FX prop collection, features on Lucio Fulci, Argento's INFERNO, TEXAS CHAINSAW; Movies with Guts; Horror Hotline; Gore Scoreboard; more!

VOLUME 2. Exclusive interview with Mark (FROM BEYOND, EVIL DEAD 2, NIGHTMARE ON ELM 2-3) Shostrom and photo tour of his FX studio; celebrity guest writer Gunnar (Leatherface) Hansen's "Post Chainsaw Dating Etiquette"; lunch with Forrest J. Ackerman.

SPECIAL ZOMBIE ISSUE also includes Foreign and Domestic dead; obscure European Gore Films; complete horror fanzine list (U.S. and foreign); interview with Jeffrey (RE-ANIMATOR, FROM BEYOND) Combs; L.A. Monster Makers Annual Halloween Makeup Contest. I could go on and on...

ZOMBIES • MUTANTS • BRAIN EATERS
CANNIBAL CARNAGE

"Top contender for 'must-have' splatter book of the year! We'll give 'em an A+!"
FILMFAX MAGAZINE

Reviews over 300 recent splatter epics with a unique dual-rating system...

"This little masterpiece...is hilarious. The man is a genius...every review is witty and some are downright hysterical. Balun tells it like it is. You gotta like this guy."
FANGORIA MAGAZINE

FantaCo Enterprises, Inc., 21 Central Ave., Albany, New York 12210

Please send me:

___copies of HORROR HOLOCAUST @ $9.95
___copies of THE GORE SCORE @ $6.95
___copies of DEEP RED, Vol. 1 @ $3.95
___copies of DEEP RED, Vol. 2 @ $3.95

Name __________
Address __________
City ________ State ____ Zip ____

ADD $2.50 POSTAGE PER ORDER (FOREIGN: ADD 5.00)

# INTRODUCTION

BY JOHN SZPUNAR

RECORDED & INDEXED

DRAFT

## LIKE INVESTING IN A GHOUL MINE!

#56 KARLOFF

BACK ISSUES of FAMOUS MONSTERS for YOUR PRIVATE COLLECTION!

#57 GREEN SLIME

#58 MALTESE BIPPY

1969 YEARBOOK

#49 NEW COMIC STRIP

#50 GORGO!

COLLECTOR'S RARE EDITION FAMOUS MONSTERS PAPERBACK

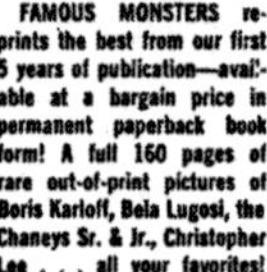

FAMOUS MONSTERS reprints the best from our first 5 years of publication—available at a bargain price in permanent paperback book form! A full 160 pages of rare out-of-print pictures of Boris Karloff, Bela Lugosi, the Chaneys Sr. & Jr., Christopher Lee . . . all your favorites!

#51 WOLFMAN SPECIAL

#52 BARNABAS

#53 HAMMER'S HORRORS

#54 CHRISTOPHER LEE

MONSTER MAKE-UP BOOK

#55 DRACULA 2000

1963 YEARBOOK ($1.20)
1964 YEARBOOK ($1.20)
1965 YEARBOOK ($1.20)
1966 YEARBOOK ($1.20)
1967 YEARBOOK ($1)
1968 YEARBOOK ($1)
1969 YEARBOOK ($1)
☐ #28 ($1)
☐ #31 ($1)
☐ #32 ($1)
☐ #33 ($1)
☐ #34 ($1)
☐ #35 ($1)
☐ #36 ($1)
☐ #37 ($1)
☐ #38 ($1)
☐ #39 ($1)
☐ #40 ($1)
☐ #41 ($1)
☐ #42 (70¢)
☐ #43 (70¢)
☐ #44 (70¢)
☐ #45 (70¢)
☐ #46 (70¢)
☐ #47 (70¢)
☐ #48 (70¢)
☐ #49 (70¢)
☐ #50 (70¢)
☐ #51 (70¢)
☐ #52 (70¢)
☐ #53 (70¢)
☐ #54 (70¢)
MAKE-UP BOOK ($1)
MONSTER PAPERBACK (75¢)
☐ #55 (70¢)
☐ #56 (70c)
☐ #57 (70c)
☐ #58 (70c)

SORRY NO CANADIAN OR FOREIGN ORDERS

FAMOUS MONSTERS BACK ISSUE Dept.
Box #5987 Grand Central Station
New York, N. Y. 10017

☐ I enclose $________ for the back issues.
☐ I enclose $3.00 giving me the next 6 issues.

NAME..................................................
ADDRESS..................................................
CITY..................................................
STATE....................ZIP CODE NO....................

65

was slowly becoming a part of this wild and crazy bunch. The interviews went on for hours into the night. At times, I was asking questions. And at other times, I was simply talking to fellow fans. To paraphrase something that Dennis Daniel said in the pages of *Deep Red*, we were friends shooting the "horror shit." We were brethren. We were one.

As much as I'd like to call this book the definitive study of its subject, I have to acknowledge two glaring omissions. I made every effort to interview *Psychotronic*'s Michael Weldon and Rick Sullivan of the *Gore Gazette*. Both publications were seminal zines that paved a road that is still widely traveled. Alas, those interviews were not meant to be. I'd like to take this moment to thank both men for all of their hard work and inspiration. Perhaps we'll get the chance to talk one day.

With that out of the way, let's get on to the meat of things. The book that you hold in your hands is the result of a lifetime obsession with monster movies. That obsession is not just mine. Everyone interviewed within this book's pages shares the same love of the genre, and their enthusiasm and passion shines through with every word. I'm sure that you share these sentiments as well, and I dedicate this book to all of the fans who once sat spellbound in front of the television, marveling at the monsters that seemed to live inside it. We are brethren. We are one.

I've held these interviews close by my side for a very long time. The time has finally come to let them loose…

**John Szpunar**
***Detroit, Michigan***
***The last days of January, 2013***

# THANK YOU:

David Kerekes, Chris Poggiali, Steve Bissette, Jan Bruun, Kris Gilpin, Greg Goodsell, Tim Ferrante, Dennis Daniel, Graham Rae, David Szulkin, Tom Skulan, Keith Crocker, Tim Paxton, Donald Farmer, Cecil Doyle, Ant Timpson, Jimmy McDonough, Bruce Holecheck, Larry Treadway, George Maranville, Tom Stockman, Mike Howlett, Jamie Chimino, Sadie Wutka, Mark Critchell, Graeme Cuthbert, and David, Walter and Rosemary Szpunar. Your, assistance, support, and contributions have meant the world to me.

The title of this book was inspired by David Slater's article, "Xerox Ferox—The Joys of Copy Shops," which appeared in *Headpress* 3.

For Chas.

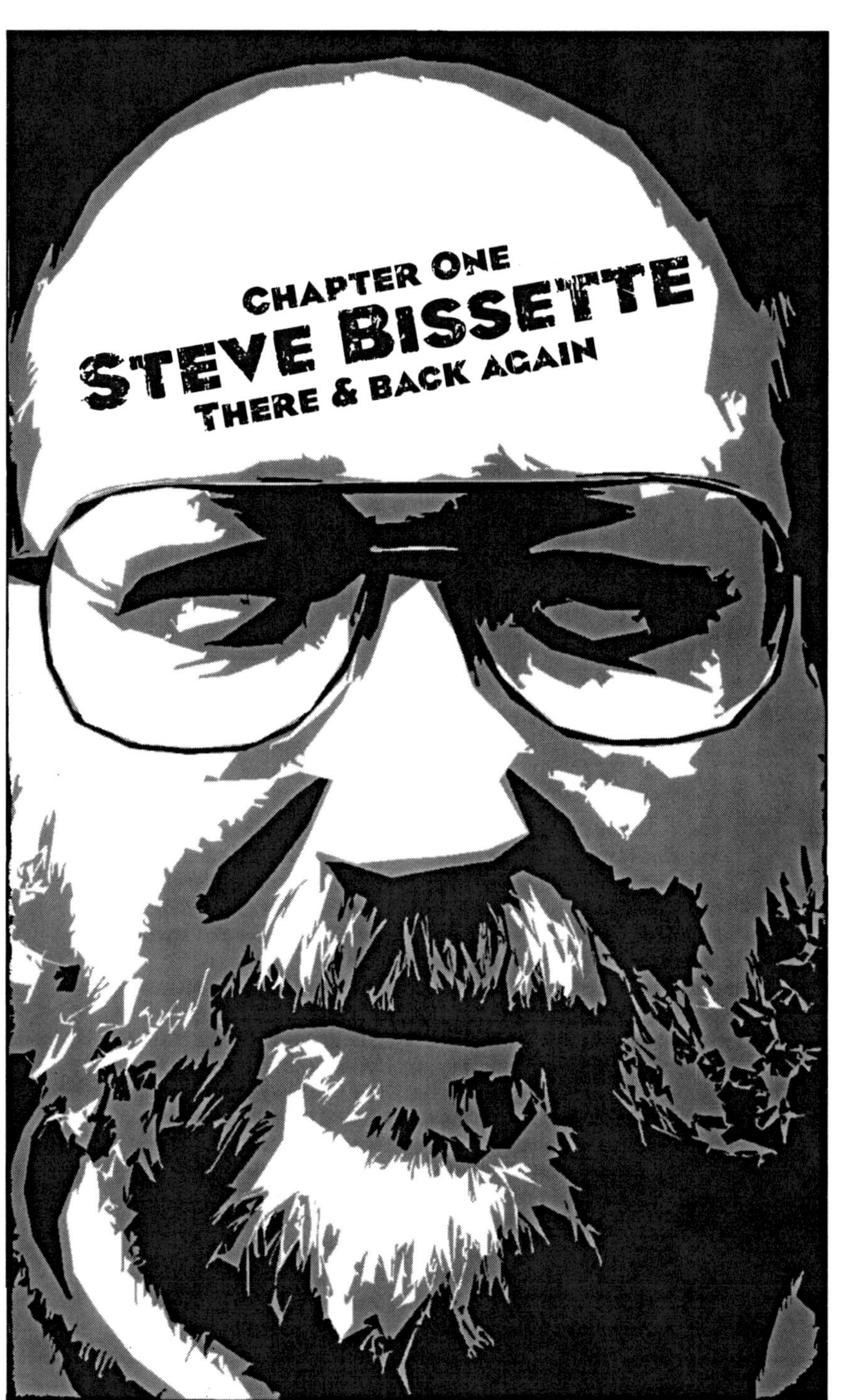
Chapter One
Steve Bissette
There & Back Again

# STEVE BISSETTE

## THERE & BACK AGAIN

RECORDED & INDEXED

DRAFT

STEVE BISSETTE. PHOTO © JOSEPH A. CITRO.

I first met Steve Bissette on a cold Halloween night, many, many years ago. One of my neighbors was passing out comic books, and I ended up going home with something called *Swamp Thing*. As a sheltered monster fanatic, I was thrilled; a quick glance at the cover told me that this was something that would normally be out of my reach. I stashed the book under my pillow and waited for bedtime.

That night's reading proved to be different. *Swamp Thing* was different. It was adult in nature and it was nothing like the other comics I'd seen before. Not sure what to make of it, I read the thing again and again as the clock on my nightstand slowly ticked its way toward November. The clock (its face lit up green, as I recall) is long gone, but I still have that issue of *Swamp Thing*.

I next encountered Bissette in a magazine called *Deep Red*. I was about to enter high school, and was hell-bent on horror films. In his "Reditorial", editor Chas. Balun mentioned that *Swamp Thing* artist Steve Bissette had joined the *Deep Red* fold. I couldn't believe it. It seemed like this Bissette guy was showing up in all of the right places.

I was at those places, too. We next met in the pages of FantaCo's *Gore Shriek*, and then in an issue of *Death Rattle*. By this time, I was a full-fledged Bissette fanatic. And by the time *Taboo* hit, I knew exactly what to expect.

But it didn't stop there. Bissette contributed an avalanche of essays and

reviews to many of my favorite magazines, including *Gorezone*, *European Trash Cinema*, *Ecco*, and *Video Watchdog*.

I could go on and on about Bissette's fine hand as an artist. About his encyclopedic and obsessive essays and film reviews. About his current work as a teacher at Vermont's prestigious Center for Cartoon Studies. I could go on, but I don't have to. If you're reading this book, you've met the man somewhere along the line. You know him, too.

I will, however, say this.

I had the chance to work professionally with Steve a few years back (hell, it's been more than a few years now; who's this old boy trying to kid?) and he was one of the nicest people I've ever met. And when I first started work on the book you're now reading, he was the first person I contacted for an interview.

So, hurry on up to bed and lock your door. Pull down the windows and dim the lights. Smell that cold October air? Hear that clawing at the door? Recoil in terror, you fool!

Urm... Aw hell, enough of *that*! No need to panic. After all, it's only Steve Bissette...

The following interview was conducted via telephone in August, 2006; edited & revised November, 2012.

---

**JOHN SZPUNAR: You mentioned to me that you still remember the first issue of *Famous Monsters of Filmland* that you saw.**

**STEVE BISSETTE:** Oh yeah. It was number 28, the one with Bela Lugosi on the cover—the portrait of him as the leader of the Manimals in *Island of Lost Souls*.

**JS: Was that the first time you'd seen a magazine like that?**

**SB:** Yeah, pretty much. I was born in 1955, so aside from occasionally stumbling onto coverless horror comics from the fifties, all that I really saw were the code-approved comic books of the sixties. *Tales to Astonish* and that kind of stuff. I didn't dream that monster magazines even existed. *TV Guide* and *True Confessions* were the only film magazines that I'd seen before.

And the scariest thing I'd ever seen was the *National Enquirer*.

**JS: Seriously?**

**SB:** When I was a kid, the *Enquirer* was very different from what it is now. It was a really disturbing tabloid newspaper. I still remember visiting an aunt's house, and there was a cover photo of Jayne Mansfield's fatal accident with this little white arrow pointing to a clump of hair on the ground. It was her head.

**JS: Interesting...**

**SB:** I didn't imagine that there was anything like monster magazines. But I already had a deep and abiding love for monster movies and I caught them whenever they were on television.

**JS: Do you remember the first horror film that had an impact on you? I'd imagine that you were pretty young.**

**SB:** Yeah. I grew up in northern Vermont. We essentially had three TV stations to choose from. WMTW from Poland Springs, Maine had a package of films that included *The Beast from 20,000 Fathoms*, *Them!*, and *The Thief of Bagdad*. I got to see those movies over and over again. At that time—the late fifties and early sixties—the TV stations leased their film packages. And they'd repeat them fairly constantly. The first of the three films that I saw was *The Beast from 20,000 Fathoms*. I was so young that I tried to talk my dad into driving us to Coney Island before they killed the monster. I don't know how I knew it, but I knew that Coney Island was a real place. I knew that what I saw on TV was sometimes "the news". I knew that I was only watching a movie. But still, on the off-chance... Anyway, my dad didn't have a clue as to what I was asking or what I was talking about. I must have been three years old. And that's the film that sold me for life.

**JS: Were you aware of dinosaurs at the time?**

**SB:** Oh yeah. Dinosaurs were my first love. I was one of those little kids who, when my mom would read dinosaur books to me, she couldn't pronounce their names. She'd stop at that part of the book and I'd pronounce them.

That's pretty much how I learned to read. I copied those drawings and I had the little plastic Marx dinosaur sets that came out in the late fifties. That was a real important part of my childhood. So dinosaurs, yeah, they were big. No wonder *The Beast from 20,000 Fathoms* was the movie that caught my eye. Ray Harryhausen was the first filmmaker that I was aware of. And that was thanks to *Famous Monsters*.

**JS: Were there any fan magazines going prior to *Famous Monsters*?**

**SB:** Fan publications about horror films followed *Famous Monsters*. The two magazines that existed when I was a kid were *Famous Monsters of Filmland* and *Castle of Frankenstein*. There were many others, including the Charlton monster magazines (which were hard to come by and lame), including some good ones like *Modern Monster* and Russ Jones' *Monster Mania*, but those came a bit later; for me, *Famous Monsters* and *Castle of Frankenstein* were it. This was before I saw or ever heard of a fanzine dedicated to horror movies. Now, what both of those magazines did from early on was list the addresses of other monster movie fans. There were sections dedicated to that. And as the fanzines began to appear, I first heard of them there. Specifically in *Castle of Frankenstein*. They would actually reproduce the covers of some of the monster, comics, and serial fanzines that were coming out.

**JS: What year are we looking at?**

**SB:** That was a little later in the sixties. 1963 to 1965.

**JS: I sort of assumed that horror fans would have been writing and publishing about monster movies before that, considering the whole science fiction fan network that had started much earlier.**

**SB:** The science fiction fanzines existed first. And some of the people involved with the science fiction fanzines were later editors at comic companies like National Periodical Publications, now known as DC Comics. People like "Julie" Schwartz . Forrest J Ackerman occasionally wrote columns about science fiction films. If you're tracking the origin of horror film fanzines, you have to go back to those publications. Although, that's in the context of fanzines that were actually dedicated to literary science fiction, with the exception of Forrest J Ackerman's "ScientiFilms" columns, which date back to 1934.

**JS: The pulps.**

**SB:** Yeah. The pulp era of *Weird Tales* and *Amazing Stories*. Fantasy and science fiction. And then, in the early fifties, you had the first wave of comic fanzines.

**JS: The EC Comics fanzines?**

**SB:** Those were the first, as far as I'm aware. Now, I don't know how many of the terms I'm about to use will make sense to your readers, but most of those magazines were either done as carbon copies or with mimeographs. That was an early form of printing where you'd actually have to type onto these stencils. And if you wanted to draw on the stencils, you'd have to use

cutting tools that were specifically designed for them. I used those in grade school and a little bit in high school. At that time, schools were still using mimeo for papers.

**JS: Did you ever try to draw with one?**

**SB:** I did get to play with trying to do a comic on a mimeo. It was hard. You couldn't draw the way you'd normally draw; you couldn't use a pencil or paper. You had to draw on this opaque blue-black surface that was sort of like a messy sheet of carbon paper. You'd have to carve into that to leave an impression on the mimeo master. And that's what you'd run your copies from. It had this very specific smell to it—I can smell it right now, as we're talking.

**JS: I've often wondered why those early fanzine drawings looked so crude.**

**SB:** That kind of thing, seen today, is beyond archaic. You just can't picture the process of what mimeography was about. But that's how most of the early fanzines were done. The cost of printing was expensive. You didn't have photocopiers; they didn't exist yet. That kind of technology didn't emerge until the late sixties. You certainly didn't have the equivalent of a photocopy shop in every town the way you do today. And typesetting was still done the old way where you actually set the type in these large flatbeds. The type was metal slugs. All of that was beyond the reach of any kid. You'd have to be a really devoted adult fan to do something like that. So, the first fanzines that I actually saw printed were in the late to mid-sixties.

**JS: The Warren magazines played a big part in the evolution. How did *they* evolve?**

**SB:** Jim Warren was a young independent publisher and there were a lot of strange adult magazines being published back then. This was way before there were hardcore adult magazines. There was nothing like *Penthouse*, and *Playboy* was brand new. Most of the men's magazines emerged from the men's "joke" magazines. That's where Jim Warren began. He did a magazine called *After Hours*, and he printed an article by Forrest J Ackerman [issue number 4—JS]. It was a pun-filled photo-illustrated article on monster movies with an adult twist. I'm assuming the photos included buxom babes with little on. That article was the catalyst for *Famous Monsters*.

**JS: *Famous Monsters* emerged in 1958.**

**SB:** Right. That was the thing that put Warren on the map with the distributors. Nobody had ever done a magazine like that before. It was surprisingly successful. Like most publishers of the time, almost everything else he had done had been an imitation of something that already existed. *After Hours* looked like thirty other softcore magazines. I've since gone back and scoured the flea-markets. I've found artifacts from the pre-Warren period. Certain issues of *Popular Mechanics* and *Popular Science* would have an article on the special effects in a science fiction movie. I've tracked

down copies of science and invention magazines that had cover stories on George Pal's *Destination Moon*. There's a great one with a cover story from *The Creature from the Black Lagoon*. I've also tracked down some of the men's magazines from that era.

**JS: What were they like?**

**SB:** They were about the size of the men's magazines now, but they didn't have slick paper and they didn't have full nudity. There were breasts inside, but never a shot of pubic hair. Certainly no sexual activity. And those magazines would occasionally have articles with guys wearing Frankenstein monster masks or ghoul masks. Little two- or three-page articles that weren't even articles; just photo sessions of semi-nude models and a guy with a monster mask. And those magazines would occasionally have an article on horror films. I've stumbled upon a few. I've also found these digest-size magazines—they were like a weird cross between an adult magazine, a tabloid news publication, and an entertainment magazine. Very strange little things.

CONTAINS FORRY J ACKERMAN.

**JS: They were published in the 1950s?**

**SB:** Yep. And in them, I've found individual photos and articles about horror films. But there was no scholarly angle to them. They were just selling pages. The reason I'm going on about this is because when Jim Warren and Forrest J Ackerman introduced *Famous Monsters*, it was a wholly new kind of publication. There had never been anything like it before. It wasn't like the EC horror comics; it wasn't like the black and white magazines that Bill Gaines created to emulate *Mad*. And it wasn't like *Mad*. *Mad* was a completely different creature. So, that's what put Jim Warren on the map. And a quarter of *Famous Monsters*' contents was devoted to advertisements for Captain Company, which was Jim Warren's mail order business.

**JS: I look back at those advertisements and wish that I could order some of that stuff.**

**SB:** For fifty cents! But that was a whole new thing. I've seen copies of the trade magazines that were designed for newsstand distributors. There was a cover story in 1963 or '64 about *Famous Monsters*, bringing it to the attention

RECORDED & INDEXED

DRAFT

of distributors—here's the new hit. Warren hit at the right time with the right thing. There was that whole wave going through our pop culture. The Shock Theater packages were on late-night TV in urban and rural markets, and had been since 1957. A whole generation of kids was being exposed to the black and white Universal horror films for the first time. You had a science fiction and monster boom going on in the drive-ins, thanks primarily to American International Pictures and Allied Artists. And horror comics had been banned. But the appetite for that kind of thing never goes away. There was an entire generation that wasn't able to satisfy the craving for horrific entertainment via comic books and *Famous Monsters of Filmland* was tapping into that whole thing. *Creepy* and *Eerie* followed.

**JS: How did you first stumble across *Famous Monsters*?**

**SB:** I discovered it through the Aurora model kits. When the first Aurora monster model kits hit—Dracula and Frankenstein—there was coupon inside the box for a sample copy of *Famous Monsters of Filmland*. I sent in for one and so did my next door neighbor, Mitch Casey. We each got a different issue.

**JS: Was it easy to find on the newsstands?**

**SB:** Not until later. Obviously, after we saw our first issues, we started scouring the newsstands for it. We ordered back issues through our sample copies. That's how we first started getting our hands on the magazine. *Famous Monsters* wasn't really available in our part of Vermont until the big monster boom hit in 1964.

**JS: Why do you think the big boom happened at that particular period in time?**

**SB:** That's a good question. Firstly, there's the obvious answer that these things run in cycles. It had been a full decade since the 1953-'54 horror comics boom had been shut down. What goes around comes around, and there was a new generation—my generation—that was hungry for that stuff. But, the monster boom of the early sixties was, in part, a carryover of the exploitation and drive-in boom of the late fifties. And it definitely was an offshoot of what was happening on television.

**JS: You mentioned Shock Theater.**

**SB:** The Shock Theater thing never went away. It just got bigger and sort of rippled out. When Zacherley was no longer the staple of the urban market, the little boon dock stations, like the ones I got, had their Shock Theaters. We got it on Channel 5 in the mid-1960s, which was the NBC affiliate out of Plattsburgh, New York. And the evening weather guy—a guy with a wig, some Halloween makeup, and a Dracula cape—he was the host for the first late-night monster movie program that we had direct access to. So, first of all, you had that ripple effect of what had been big at the drive-ins throughout the fifties. Those boom years, as you know, were 1957 and 1958. And then, the Hammer movies hit and they never stopped. I mean, the Hammer films were running all throughout my childhood and

HAMILTON'S INVADERS—NOT CONNECTED TO ANYTHING.

teenage years. I was part of the generation that got to see *Dracula, Prince of Darkness*, *Plague of the Zombies*, and everything that followed as they hit the theaters. But the biggest monster boom was from 1962 to 1965, and part of what nurtured it was network TV. Network TV finally embraced things. We had *The Outer Limits* and *The Twilight Zone*. *Alfred Hitchcock Presents* had been going since the mid-fifties. There were the comedy shows, the monster sitcoms. *The Munsters* and *The Addams Family* really pushed it. And then there was Irwin Allen and *Voyage to the Bottom of the Sea*. That was a monster of the week program, no question about it. We'd watch it just to see what the monster was going to be on Sunday night.

**JS: You mentioned the Aurora model kits.**

**SB:** Those were a major part of it, too. They were like the monster magazines; we could put our hands on them and bring them into our homes. They were ours. There was definitely the tactile possession part to it. We could build them and paint them. The *Mars Attacks!* cards came out around then, too. I still remember when those hit. We thought they were amazing, but there was no way that we could see all of them because they were yanked off the shelves, almost immediately. But that just made them all the more precious. The Sears Christmas catalog arrived, and suddenly there were these weird monster and science fiction toys. There was something called Hamilton's Invaders. It wasn't connected to anything—there wasn't a show called Hamilton's Invaders. It was just this huge green bug with bloodshot human-like eyes. It came with these little plastic tanks and army guys. The jaws of the bug would close around them. This was in the Sears catalog! You could ask for it for Christmas! So, that was a really exciting time to be a kid.

**JS: Were you drawing comics at the time?**

**SB:** Yeah. By the time Mitch Casey and I saw our first issue of *Famous*

RECORDED & INDEXED

DRAFT

BISSETTE'S *SPIDER BABY COMIX*: RANDOM ACTS OF CARNAGE!

*Monsters of Filmland*, we were already drawing our own comics. You'd take three sheets of paper, fold them, and staple them. There was no way to reproduce it; we didn't have access to the mimeo machines at elementary school. Early on, we tried to do Basil Gogos-like covers with colored pencil and crayon. So in terms of monster magazines, we were already making our own one-of-a kind fanzines. This would have been in 1963.

**JS: Did that progress into wanting to write about movies?**

**SB:** Not really. Actually, what it progressed into was that we started ordering the fanzines that we read about in *Castle of Frankenstein*. I saw a cover of somebody's fanzine reproduced in "The Graveyard Examiner" section of *Famous Monsters*. I saw a cover for *Gore Creatures* in another magazine. That was the first fanzine that I ever ordered, Gary Svehla's *Gore Creatures*. I also remember seeing the cover of another magazine in *Monster Mania*.

**JS: What was *Monster Mania*?**

**SB:** It was a short-lived magazine that Russ Jones edited. It was dedicated to Hammer films. I think they did four issues. That would have been around 1966 or 1967. Anyway, I remember seeing a cover of a zine reproduced in the letters column—it turns out that it was John Carpenter's fanzine.

**JS: The filmmaker?**

**SB:** Yeah. I didn't know that at the time. Nobody knew it at the time. Not even he knew it! Anyway, Mitch was a little older than me and he got into organized sports and girls. He and I weren't getting together anymore, and that led to my not drawing comics. There was nobody to do them with. I won't bore you with all of that. I started ordering fanzines. And that's kind of my entry point into what this book is about.

**JS: How did the fanzines stack up to the prozines?**

**SB:** It's interesting. Once I was exposed to *Famous Monsters*, I wanted to buy all of the monster magazines that I could get my hands on. And within a year or two, there were a bunch of them out there. In the early sixties, the

RECORDED & INDEXED

DRAFT

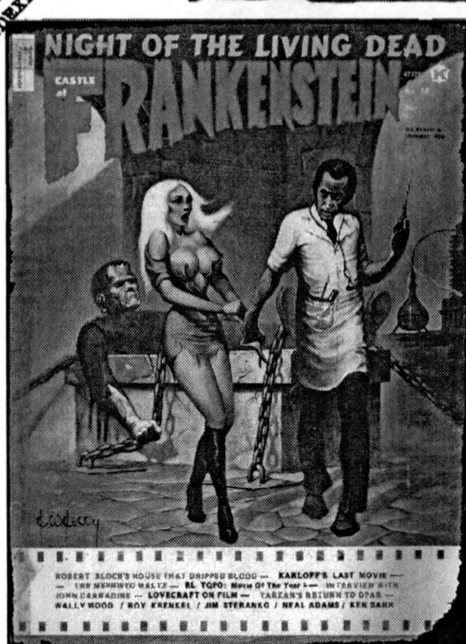


Charlton monster magazines like *Mad Monsters* were the worst. They were badly printed and would have one picture on a page, sometimes two. No articles, just stupid captions; they were just thrown together. I didn't know anything about production, but I definitely knew that those were cheesy magazines. And then, there were these interesting, short-lived magazines that would pop up. There was one called *Modern Monsters*. It had a really high level of writing—that's the first place I read about *Invasion of the Body Snatchers*. That was one of the first scholarly essays I'd ever read about a movie. It tried to describe what it was like to see the film and what the impact was; it hinted that there was a political dimension to it. That was something new to me. But, the top tier of all the monster magazines, from when I first laid eyes on it, was definitely *Castle of Frankenstein*.

**JS: That was partially inspired by *Cahiers du Cinema*.**

**SB:** Yep. *Castle of Frankenstein* wrote at an adult level. They still had the stupid puns and the dumb captions, but one of the first issues that I saw had one of those reprints that [publisher] Calvin T. Beck did—completely illegally—of a serialized article from either *Sight & Sound* or *Films and Filming*. He just reprinted this article verbatim, and it was a great little history of horror movies. It was fully illustrated, but it was written for the adult British film magazine reader. That was something new to me. The capsule reviews that Joe Dante and Bhob Stewart wrote were really amazing. They had an attitude and sassiness to them, and they were very well informed. They weren't just reviewing the obvious horror and science fiction films; they were writing about Fellini's *Juliet of the Spirits*, *The Fool Killer*, and all of these odd movies that I suddenly wanted to see. I found out that they existed and I found it interesting. So my point is that *Castle of Frankenstein* was the high-end of the magazines. As for the fanzines, *Gore Creatures* wrote at a very high level. Gary Svehla's writing today is pretty close to how he wrote then. If you've read any of the *Midnight Marquee* magazines or books, that's pretty much the level that Gary was writing at

for *Gore Creatures*. Some errors would pop up, but that was true of all the newsstand magazines. It wasn't until *Castle of Frankenstein* that things started getting more sophisticated.

**JS: Bhob Stewart edited *Castle of Frankenstein*.**

**SB:** Bhob was also writing the blurbs for *TV Guide*. He was one of the first Manhattan sophisticates to tap into this kind of junk pop culture. He brought that sensibility to his work for *Castle of Frankenstein*. And Joe Dante, from the time he was a teenager, had that appetite too. I still have the *Famous Monsters* with "Dante's Inferno", which was his list of the worst horror movies. That was something new, a new sensibility. *Gore Creatures* fell between those camps. It was as good as *Modern Monsters* in its writing, but not as sophisticated as *Castle of Frankenstein*. And it was heads and tails above what *Famous Monsters* was doing, with the exception of the [*Famous Monsters*] filmbooks. The writing in the filmbooks was always great.

**JS: The early issues of *Gore Creatures* were very crude.**

**SB:** If you want to bridge the gap between what was happening in the mid-sixties to the seventies, *Gore Creatures* is a good zine to chart. That was one of the magazines that went from a pre-photocopy mimeo-zine format to offset printing. Gary was very conscientious about putting together a professional package. But, without listing every fanzine that came out around that time, the class-act of the day was *Photon*. It was edited by Mark Frank and it was the best of the current fanzines, bar none. It had the best writing, the most sophisticated articles, and the most mature orientation to the genre and to the films. It printed the first retrospective article on *Curse of the Demon*— just wonderful, wonderful stuff.

**JS: And after that?**

**SB:** The one that made the jump from fanzine to prozine in production and writing quality was *Photon*, and the first of the high-end zines that finally hit the newsstand was *Cinefantastique*. Tim Lucas can get into that more, because he actually wrote for Fred Clark. The first time I read Tim's work was in *Cinefantastique*.

# STEVE BISSETTE

## THERE & BACK AGAIN

RECORDED & INDEXED

DRAFT

ON THE HORIZON.

**JS: That started publishing in the early seventies, right?**

**SB:** *Cinefantastique* actually started in the late sixties. I have a couple of copies of the early format, when it was just a mimeo-zine. By 1971, I could find it at a college bookstore up in Burlington, Vermont. I believe that the first issue I bought was one of their first newsstand distributed copies. The issue with the *Andromeda Strain* cover. And then I subscribed; I never stopped buying them. I still have a complete collection. That was probably the transitional zine. It was written and packaged at a much higher level than anything since *Photon*.

**JS: Was *Castle of Frankenstein* still kicking?**

**SB:** By then, *Castle of Frankenstein* kind of disappeared. I bought the last issue that ever came out off the newsstand in Johnson, Vermont when I was in college. And by that time, *Famous Monsters* was just a jumble of new material and reprints. They had some good writers like Randy Palmer, but it just wasn't an imperative to me anymore. I would buy it occasionally if there was an article or a cover that I liked, but that was just out of nostalgia.

**JS: *Fangoria* was on the horizon.**

**SB:** I was a member of the first class of the Joe Kubert School of Graphic Art. I started in September of 1976 and I graduated in May of 1978. That's when *Fangoria* hit. We'd never seen anything like it. The first issue of *Fango* looked like any other science fiction knock-off. But when they did the spread of the exploding head from *Dawn of the Dead*, that was it. It was like, "Whoa!" We'd never seen anything like that in a magazine before. That was the kind of thing Forry wouldn't have touched with a ten-foot pole.

**JS: Yet alone print in color.**

**SB:** Right. So, I have to point to *Fangoria* as the beginning of the wave of the gore, exploitation, and sleaze zines.

**JS: I first saw *Fangoria* in the early eighties. I remember wishing that I could buy a copy without getting in trouble at home.**

**SB:** Well, luckily I was old enough to buy it by then, so I didn't have to

worry about that. But you know, that is an issue that you'll probably be talking about with somebody. I never hid my magazines from my mom, but I vividly remember coming home from school one day. There was a stack of magazines on my bed and my mom was upset about one of the covers. The *Famous Monsters* covers were almost never gory. They were just those amazing Basil Gogos covers. But she didn't like them.

**JS: The stories I could tell!**

**SB:** That's a part of all of our existences [laughs]. I couldn't have gotten away with bringing something like *Fangoria* into the house in the sixties. I mean, I just couldn't have.

**JS: I had no idea what it was. All I knew is that I wanted to read it.**

**SB:** And if it's forbidden, you'll want to read it even more.

**JS: Let's talk about some of the fanzines from the late seventies and early eighties.**

**SB:** That's when *Sleazoid Express* popped up. Suddenly, there was a whole new wave—*Sleazoid Express*, *Gore Gazette*—they were down and dirty exploitation magazines. Journals, in a way—they really were more diary-like. And they flaunted their homemade aspect. They were all written with a punk attitude and they reflected the residue of the punk era of the seventies.

**JS: A New York attitude.**

**SB:** Oh yeah. Bill Landis from *Sleazoid* didn't give a fuck. And that's what made it so appealing to read. I wanted to read about what was playing on 42nd Street because when I was at the Kubert School, I was going to 42nd Street. And, back home in Vermont, I missed that world.

**JS: This would be during the *Taxi Driver* era of New York.**

**SB:** It was dangerous to go there. Times Square was a real nasty part of Manhattan. On one side of the street, there was nothing but exploitation and horror films. And on the other side, there was nothing but XXX films. I didn't really care about the XXX films, I just wanted to see the bizarre Italian/Spanish horror films that were playing. I finally got to see a couple of Andy Milligan movies on 42nd Street. I'd read about them, but I'd never seen them before.

Rick Sullivan's

GORE GAZETTE

A much-needed vacation as well as an attempt to expand the G.G. into a larger, glossier format has caused the long delay between issues. In that time, the summer gore draught has subsided, leaving us with a bountiful autumn bumper crop of sleaze fare. The sheer number of films released since the last G.G. forces us to adopt a capsule review format for this edition only. The G.G. will be back on its regular fortnightly schedule in full review format with issue #62.

THERE & BACK AGAIN

RECORDED & INDEXED

DRAFT

**JS: What was the scene like?**

**SB:** The marquees were incredible. 42nd Street, at that time, still had the prominent marquees above the theaters. I never gravitated toward one theater or another. I would just take the bus into New York, usually to go to a job interview. I was hoofing the pavement, trying to get gigs with magazines. Illustration jobs from comic publishers—anything I could get my hands on. And I would build my trip around the movies. When I left Port Authority, I'd walk across 42nd Street to Broadway and I'd scope out what was on the marquees. I'd decide what I was going to see after the job interview, before I got on the bus to go home. And I'd see three, four, five movies, if I could figure out a way to get the timing right. The last bus didn't leave until 12:30, sometimes not until one in the morning. And the movies ran all night long. But they came and went. I'll tell you, there was more than one time when the movie title on the marquee had changed before I got back. It was already gone, and there was another film playing. Some of those programs turned around in one day. If you missed what you wanted to see, you were out of luck.

A STABBING NIGHTMARE BECOMES A LIVING TERROR!

JOSEPH BRENNER PRESENTS

EYEBALL

A blinding vision of horror.

JOSEPH BRENNER PRESENTS

"EYEBALL"

Starring JOHN RICHARDSON · MARTINE BROCHARD · INES PELLEGRIN · SILVIA SOLAR · GEORGE RIGAUD
Directed by UMBERTO LENZI · Executive Producer JOSEPH BRENNER
A JOSEPH BRENNER ASSOCIATES, INC. RELEASE · IN COLOR

**JS: That must have made for some interesting viewing.**

**SB:** It was weird. You never really knew what was what. I remember going to see a double bill of *Eyeball* and *Almost Human*. I knew *Eyeball* was a giallo because Lenzi's name was on it, but I didn't know what *Almost Human* was. It turned out to be one of the Tomás Milián gangster films. So there was a weird mix on 42nd Street, and that's what *Sleazoid Express* was all about. Bill would write up everything that was playing there. It was kind of like having somebody keeping the finger on the pulse of one of my favorite film havens on planet Earth. *Sleazoid Express* and *Gore Gazette* were just the tip of the iceberg. There were tons of different magazines

like that. Donald Farmer was doing *Splatter Times*. I subscribed to everything I could get my hands on. And none of those guys, at that point in time, were being proprietary about things. They would cross-promote each other's magazines, put the addresses in, and tell you what they cost. It would be eight bucks for a year and they showed up every two weeks. It was great.

**JS: Where did *Deep Red* fit in?**

**SB:** Well, you sort of had a split happen. You had the attitude of the Rick Sullivans, the Bill Landises, and Donald Farmers; it kind of distilled (a little later in the eighties) into the distinctive brand of writing that Chas. pursued, once *Deep Red* was introduced. Chas. had a partner that he did the first *Deep Red* with.

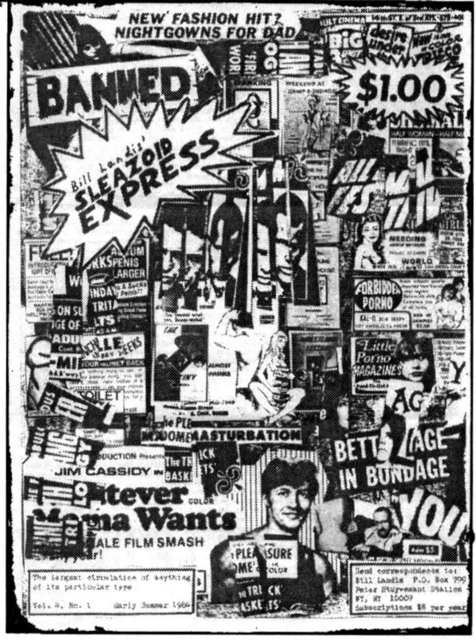


**JS: Chris Amouroux.**

**SB:** Yep. Chris and Chas. had a specific take, and Chas. ran with it. It was a fresh voice to most people, but if you track it back, the precursors were definitely the New York/New Jersey/Chicago magazines that were coming out. And they all went through their little arcs. *Gore Gazette* kind of disappeared after Sullivan lost his job for using the photocopier late at night. In the case of Landis and *Sleazoid*, 42nd Street was starting to go through its final phase, before it got Disneyfied. Bill got heavily into gay hardcore films. He started writing about that in *Sleazoid*, but those weren't the kinds of films that were interesting to his readers. It wasn't so much homophobia; they just wanted to read more about the exploitation, horror, and violent films. And that's not what Landis was into anymore.

**JS: Things were about to change again.**

**SB:** You had the real scholarly stuff that popped up like *Shock Xpress* and Tim and Donna Lucas' *Video Watchdog*. There were really diverging forks in the road at that point: Chas. and his school of writing going in one direction and then Stefan Jaworzyn and his peers—you know, *Shock Xpress*, *Eyeball*, and the more genre-specific magazines. You started

# STEVE BISSETTE

## THERE & BACK AGAIN

RECORDED & INDEXED
DRAFT

seeing magazines that were only about Italian horror films. And then you started seeing magazines that were only about Eastern European horror films [laughs].

**JS: How did you meet Tim Lucas?**

**SB:** Tim wrote for *Fangoria*. And *Fangoria* ran a two-part article that he wrote about Mario Bava. Now, Mario Bava had been, and still is, one of all time favorite filmmakers. I was one of those kids in the sixties that had been traumatized by *Black Sunday*. I mean, that movie was probably the first film that I saw that scared me in an adult way. I became addicted to Mario Bava, but it was hard to identify his movies; his real name wouldn't always be listed.

**JS: He was credited as "Mickey Lion" on a lot of films.**

**SB:** Yep. Once I was sixteen and had a driver's license, I'd go to the drive-in and see anything that sounded even vaguely like it might be a European horror movie because it might turn out to be a Bava film. That's how I lucked into stuff like *Kill, Baby, Kill* and *Twitch of the Death Nerve*, which first played in Boston as *Carnage*.

**JS: Who released it?**

**SB:** It was released by Hallmark; they put it out as the second film rated V for violence (because *Mark of the Devil* was the first)! I saw an ad for *Carnage* in a Boston paper, and it said, "Mario Bava's *Carnage*." It had the image of that woman lying on the ground after her throat was cut. *Carnage* disappeared; it never played anywhere else. Then, the ad for something called *Twitch of the Death Nerve* appeared in a New York paper. I recognized the graphic from *Carnage*, and I said, "That's it!" It played a couple of weeks later at our local drive-in. So, I was into Bava and *Fangoria* came out with the first article that I'd ever seen on him. The only writing that had existed about Bava before that were the capsule reviews that Joe Dante wrote in *Castle of Frankenstein*. When the article appeared in *Fangoria*, I wrote to Tim, via Starlog Press. They forwarded the letter to him, and Tim wrote back to me. We struck up a correspondence and we've been friends ever since. I had written a paper on Bava's films for college,

Attachment

and had amassed some clip files; I offered whatever I had to Tim, once he let me know he was working on a book about Bava, and I could just let go of that pipedream. I mean, Tim was so far beyond anything anyone had ever written about Bava, and clearly would get his book done, however many years that might take. So we initially corresponded in the 1980s. That's around the time that I started connecting with Chas., as well. We're talking late eighties here.

**JS: What was your first published work in a fanzine?**

**SB:** I sent some sketches to Greg Shoemaker, in Ohio. He did a fanzine called *Japanese Fantasy Film Journal*. His was one of the few fanzines that I really stuck to until it ended its run [in 1983—JS]. I loved it. His obsession was just with Japanese science fiction films. When his magazine started, it was done with a mimeo or with crude offset printing of some kind. It got slicker, issue by issue. Greg was very serious about what he was doing—he began to strike up correspondences in Japan, and so on. So, I drew some of the Japanese monsters and sent the originals to him. This was before photocopiers. The first one published was a photo that I copied from *Famous Monsters of Filmland* number 28 of *The Manster*. He ran it, and that's when the bug bit. Well, wait a minute, my memory is a little shaky here. I also sent some art to other zines, one of which—Gary Heilman's *Crypt of Horrors*—actually published one of my drawings, a few years before Greg did, so I reckon *Crypt of Horrors* was actually the first of my fanzine art to see print. Then Greg ran my *Manster* sketch in *Japanese Fantasy Film Journal*, and I later contributed some artwork to Ted Rypel's *The Outer Limits* fanzine, which was published, too. I sent a lot of art out that never saw print and that I never got back, which is one of the hazards of the zine scene. I was lucky: some of mine saw print. The first writing I ever had published was a letter in *Take One*, which was a terrific Canadian film magazine. They ran this pretentious, scholarly article

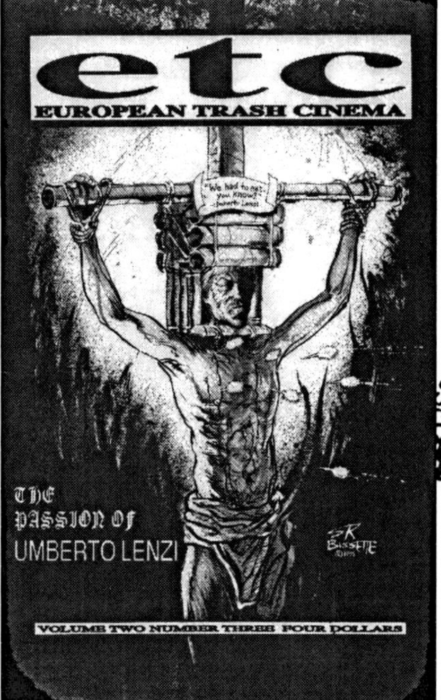


STEVE BISSETTE COVER ART.

STEVE BISSETTE COVER ART.

about *Godzilla* and whoever wrote it got the chronology completely wrong. I wrote a letter clarifying things, and they published it.

**JS: I first became aware of your critical writing via *Deep Red*.**

**SB:** I've got to say that the person who really opened the door for me was Chas. Balun. I was really impressed with the first issue of *Deep Red* when I saw it. I wrote Chas. a fan letter, and he immediately said, "Well, why don't you submit some stuff?" The first big piece that I was really happy with was my interview with Buddy Giovinazzo about *Combat Shock*. I was the first or second person to do that. I think it had gotten some good press in *Shock Xpress* over in the UK and I was the first person in the US to give the film some attention. I thought it was just a tremendous film; that's when I thought I was doing something worthwhile.

**JS: You also started writing for zines like *European Trash Cinema*.**

**SB:** Yep. *ETC*, for Craig Ledbetter. That was around the same time. I also did work for [Charles Kilgore's] *Ecco*, and for Tim and Donna Lucas for *Video Watchdog*—I was in on that from their first issue, and was in fact one of the folks who convinced Tim and Donna to pursue self-publishing. I really felt a sense of camaraderie and loved a lot of the work that was coming out at that time. And some of the folks who were doing the magazines were just good, good people. Craig Ledbetter was a wonderful guy. We only met once, but we talked on the phone a lot; he was based in Texas and I was up here in Vermont. I started writing reviews and submitting them to Craig and he almost always ran them. When I was working on *Taboo* number 4 and reprinting (for the one and only time in America) the *Eyes of the Cat* (written by Alejandro Jodorowsky and drawn by Mœbius), I got to spend two days with Jodorowsky in Boston. They were showing *Santa Sangre* at the Boston Film Festival that year. I got to have dinner with Alejandro and his producer, Claudio Argento.

**JS: What were they like?**

**SB:** They were completely unlike one another [laughs]. Alejandro was like

this amazing gesticulating madman and Claudio was as cool as a cucumber. They were very nice, both of them, and we did a formal interview during the meal. And then, I turned around and I found as many places as I could to sell the interview. I loved the movie so much and I wanted to help promote it. I sold a portion of the interview to the *Valley Advocate*, which is an alternative newspaper that serves Massachusetts and southern Vermont. I sold a section of it to *Gorezone*, which was the briefly-published magazine that *Fango* did to knock their competitors off the newsstands. That was in the early nineties, when *Slaughterhouse* and a lot of other full color gore/horror zines came out. So, I did the interview and I sold a portion of it to Tony Timpone. And then I went to Craig. There were chunks of the interview that I couldn't include in the other publications because of what Alejandro was talking about. It was either so outrageous or so specific to something that the readers of the other publications wouldn't know or care about. I knew Craig would love it, and he was like, "Oh yeah, great!" He ran the section of the interview that I couldn't run elsewhere. Alejandro was either making sexual references or he was talking about Juan López Moctezuma, the guy who did *Alucarda*. Alejandro was outraged when I mentioned Moctezuma's name; he just went ballistic. He spit out his food: "That bastard! He stole my money! All my money he stole to make his films!" Craig loved that [laughs]. He ran with it, no problem. And then, I started doing some covers for Craig.

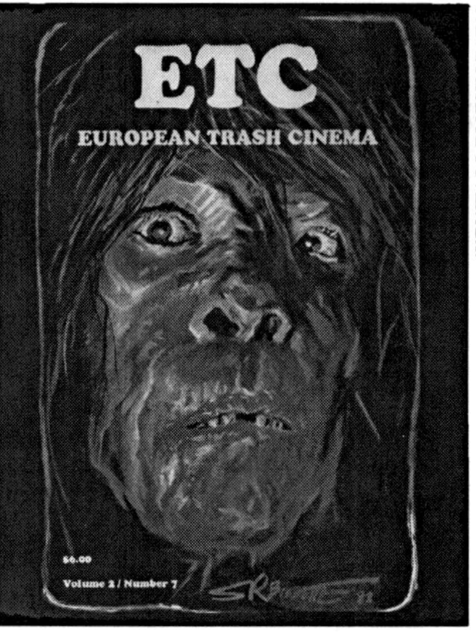


STEVE BISSETTE COVER ART.

**JS: You also did some covers for Charles Kilgore's *Ecco*.**

**SB:** Charles Kilgore is terrific. I was going to talk about him, as well. *Ecco* was going around the same time as *ETC*, and I loved it; I started doing covers for him, early on. I did a swamp-trash cover for his article on hillbilly movies. I think I did five or six covers, including one of Abel Gance's *J'accuse*. At that time, there was no money in it for any of us. It was just exciting to be able to write about the films that I loved and to see the stuff published. And with very few exceptions, Tim and Donna, Craig, Charles, and Chas. ran just about everything that I put together. So, that was a real

DRAFT

RECORDED & INDEXED

# BISSETTE Draws The Line

BY CHAS. BALUN

Oh, excuse me, but when publisher Tom Skulan mentioned to me a year or so ago that a horror connoisseur by the name of Stephen Bissette would like to meet me and perhaps contribute to our fledgling magazine, I replied with a rather noncommittal, "Oh, sure. Okay." Shit, howdy! I didn't know Steve Bissette was a C-O-M-I-C-S L-E-G-E-N-D! Revered by many and acclaimed by some as "comics' next superstar" and the "best horror illustrator of the decade," this dude, Bissette, came armed with a heavy arsenal of credentials. And, pity poor me, not knowing jack shit about it either. So kick me. I immediately established an attitude; I always do when someone's work makes me feel as though I'd never progressed past Freehand Drawing 101A. Bissette has a fine, fine hand. Consider his work as Berni Wrightson's successor in the popular Swamp Thing comic books, his contributions to House of Mystery,

21

BALUN INTERVIEWS BISSETTE. *DEEP RED* NUMBER 6.

exciting time.

**JS: Things would eventually wind down.**

**SB:** Yep. Around the mid-nineties, for a variety of reasons. It was all tied in with distribution; some of the distributors began to go under and every one of these folks was burned in one way or another. Distributors went out of business and owed them money. And when you're doing a low print run fanzine that has nothing to do with your day to day income, that's just a loss. That's quite a blow. What happened was interesting. A few people like Tim and Donna stayed focused on *Video Watchdog*. They really put together an economically viable model. Donna still worked freelance in the computer business in the Cincinnati area, but by in large, their whole life became tailored around the *Watchdog*. There were a few diversions; Tim's written a couple of wonderful novels, but they kept their focus on the magazine. Other people got pulled in other directions. Craig Ledbetter sort of got yanked in a few directions with the success of *ETC*; he got pulled into *Asian Trash Cinema* for a brief time, but whatever happened there (and I don't know what happened) was a bad experience. He just retrenched and got out of it. So, it's interesting. I've seen different people achieve a certain level of fanzine success and if it started pulling them away from the fanzines that got them that attention, it would start to dissipate their energy. They would just sort of drop it. And when they dropped it, they tended to drop it completely.

**JS: Craig went from *ETC* as a magazine to *ETC* as a mail order service.**

**SB:** Right. And in the case of *Deep Red*, Chas.' fortunes were pretty tied up with FantaCo Enterprises, Tom Skulan's company in Albany, NY. Tom was a retailer, ran conventions, and was publishing a lot of great stuff, including comics. When FantaCo closed up shop, Chas. sort of closed up shop for a time. He took a few stabs at doing other issues or books in that vein, but he was burned by those experiences. They weren't happy experiences, in every case. That gets tough. It really gets to a point of, "Why am I doing this?"

**JS: Most of the zines that we're talking about right now made their mark, took a bow, and went out strong. They didn't slowly fade away or repeat themselves.**

**SB:** I think part of what made that whole period of fanzines so compelling is that there was a real candor and honesty about them. *Deep Red*, for instance, existed for as long as Chas. kept his enthusiasm for what was out there. And that enthusiasm was about being as candid and honest about how crappy some of the stuff was, as well as being as candid and honest about saying, "Hey, why are you paying attention to that bullshit that Paramount's putting out? Look at these movies!" Chas. did it for as long as it kept his interest. That meant he wasn't perpetuating some sort of front.

**JS: Yep.**

**SB:** You could tell in *Famous Monsters* when Jim Warren, as publisher, was just saying, "OK, we're going to do a reprint." As a reader, you could just

# STEVE BISSETTE

## THERE & BACK AGAIN

feel that laziness. And that was never an aspect of the magazines you're talking about. They were real labors of love. And, as is the case of a labor of love, when you fall out of love, you put no labor into it.

**JS: What's your take on the state of things today?**

**SB:** A number of things have happened. We'll start out by talking about the internet. The impulse that once led to somebody making a physical magazine no longer exists for the new generation. I have a blog. I use it as a writing exercise in the morning to warm up, before I work on my other stuff. Now, years ago, if I'd had the internet—why fuck around with submitting stuff to an editor? You put it up, and it's out there. If you're doing it for free, which a lot of us who were writing for these zines by in large were... Well, actually, I don't want to stand with that perception. There was usually an economy of barter that drove the writing for the fanzines. You got copies of the magazine you were in. The person you were submitting to was also sending you bootleg videos of things that you wouldn't otherwise see.

**JS: Right.**

**SB:** The internet has changed that. The impulses that once led to the publications that we've talked about (going back to the first science fiction fanzines in the thirties and forties, right up to *Deep Red*, *Ecco*, and *Video Watchdog*) are now, by in large, channeled into the internet. There are still a lot of interesting magazines and fanzines out there, but a lot of that energy, I have no doubt, is spent online. You and I could name, off the top of our heads, sixteen people each who come across as experts in various aspects of the genre... and we've never read them in print. So, that's a major change.

**JS: The printed fanzine has started to disappear.**

**SB:** Another major change happened. The fanzines worked their way up from a mail order and subscription-only basis and started to appear on the newsstands. Newsstand distribution opened up for a little bit in the nineties. Some of that involved the direct sales market. But then, the alternative distributors who were supporting this collapsed, owing a ton

of money to all these little publishers.

**JS: *Psychotronic* was a casualty.**

**SB:** Yeah. And we should mention *Psychotronic*. That was one of the great ones. I was a subscriber since the first issue. I even have some of the newspaper tabloid issues that Michael did back in his New York City days. But anyway, my point is that the fanzines were burned by distribution throughout the nineties. There's case history after case history after case history.

**JS: And, now—**

**SB:** And now, you have a wave of what would have been fanzine publications manifesting as one of two things. Publishers like FAB Press and Headpress are yielding wonderful full-size books. That's the kind of intensity, passion, research, and hard work that used to go into fanzines. And then, there's the independent DVD labels. No longer do you have to dedicate all your time and energy to a magazine that will somehow be a testimonial to a film (in the vicarious manner that print is). Now, you can put all of that energy into actually releasing a restored edition of the film itself. The extras—the interviews, the commentaries, the booklets, the what-have-yous—have become the fanzine.

SIN'S BREAKFAST. BISSETTE'S *TABOO* NUMBER 1.

**JS: I think about that from time to time. When I was putting together the *Last House on Dead End Street* DVD, I really wanted it to be a love letter to *Deep Red*.**

**SB:** You did it, man [laughs]!

**JS: It's kind of crazy, when you think about it. A lot of people who started out buying bootleg tapes and reading fanzines eventually became a part of the DVD industry.**

**SB:** When you were a kid and first getting into this stuff, I was an adult, aching to see the movies that were not available on television or via any theatrical distribution method, including 16mm rental. Video changed all of that. There suddenly were bootleg tapes on the tables at conventions all around the country. And those tables have now become DVD labels. The entire market for the European horror films—from the giallos to the Bava films to the Franco films—would not exist on DVD today if it had not been for ten years of video bootleg marketing. We wouldn't have anime labels.

# STEVE BISSETTE

## THERE & BACK AGAIN

ALIENS! CREATURES! THINGS!

"SING A SONG OF SUSPENSE
A POCKET FULL OF EYES,
FOUR AND TWENTY MONSTERS
BAKED IN A PIE..."

MONSTER PIE

*MONSTER PIE*—PERSONAL COLLABORATIVE MONSTER ZINE.

And we wouldn't have Disney owning all of Miyazaki's films and releasing them in sterling editions on DVD, had it not been for twenty-five years of bootleg anime marketplace. All of this is an outgrowth of fanzine culture.

**JS: That's a pretty wonderful thing.**

**SB:** It's mind-blowing. And it shows just how far the culture has come. And now, things are coming back around. Internet activity—websites, discussion boards, blogging (which I did daily from 2005 until January of 2012)—sort of sucked up a lot of that energy and oxygen. My son Daniel got me back into drawing comics and zines, when he did his own odd little one-shot zine, *Hot Chicks Take Huge Shits*, in 2006. Teaching at the Center for Cartoon Studies since 2005 has gotten me back into zines big-time; our first Fellow, who joined the faculty, was Robyn Chapman, this amazing cartoonist, creator, and zine editor/publisher who absolutely loves comics and all zines, and her enthusiasm got me back into print zines over time. Robyn's love for the zine form and freedom was and is contagious. Given the fact that CCS has its own fully operational production, print, and binding lab in the school's basement, all the students and many of the faculty make their own zines. Robyn scored with a comic zine about wearing glasses entitled *Hey, Four Eyes*, and others. I also teach with Alec Longstreth and Jon Chad, and they've been doing this marvelous pinball zine, *Drop Target*—just

terrific stuff. The students and alumni are constantly creating their own zines, and its fantastic, stimulating stuff.

**JS: What do you think of the recent activity of some of the old fanzine guys? Dan Taylor has started up *Exploitation Retrospect* again, and Tim Paxton and Brian Harris have launched *Weng's Chop*.**

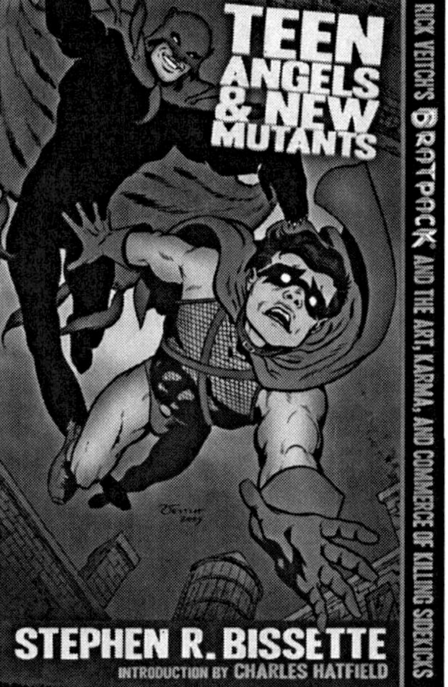


**SB:** Well, I'm sort of guilty of getting Tim Paxton going again, according to Tim. Since 2002, I've been experimenting with print-on-demand, and as of this year [2012] have been gearing up to do my own eBooks, all of which are extensions of zine culture, or a synthesis of DIY zine culture and book publishing. I guess you could call my first original print-on-demand book with Black Coat Press a zine: it was entitled *Green Mountain Cinema*, and it was the first of a planned series of book-format publications about Vermont films and filmmakers. I did it with my friends Jean-Marc and Randy Lofficier's Black Coat Press. Jean-Marc handled all the digital production, and we published it in 2002, and I self-distributed over 1,000 copies to Vermont bookstores—a regional filmzine, if you will, in book form. I then collected all my weekly newspaper video review columns from 1999–2001 into a four-volume book series, *S.R. Bissette's Blur*, with and for Black Coat Press, and kept working with Jean-Marc, Black Coat, and the print-on-demand format, eventually doing truly odd books like *Teen Angels & New Mutants* (400+ pages on Rick Veitch's graphic novel *Brat Pack* and the whole of teen pop culture and comic book sidekicks).

Among the many books I've labored over now for quite some time are collections of all my horror zine and magazine writings, and I'm working up new material and excavating unpublished material for those. For one of them, I convinced Tim Paxton (whose zines I've always loved) to write an article on his 1960s correspondences with Paul Blaisdell, the pioneer effects and monster maker who created *The She Creature*, the *Saucer Men*, the Venusian for *It Conquered the World*, and so on. Tim

came through in 2010–2011, excavating his original letters from Paul, and we put it together for one of my upcoming books. Tim told me recently that resurrected his passion for doing zines, and he began collaborating with another friend, Brian Harris, on what has become *Weng's Chop*, and I contributed to number 1 and number 2 (and will likely continue to, as long as Tim and Brian keep going).

It's great seeing this happening. I've never given up on zines—as I said, Robyn Chapman reawakened that enthusiasm, and I've been a regular subscriber to comics zines like *Mineshaft*, Rob Imes's *Ditkomania*, and so on, and contributed to a few over the years. I never stopped reading, and occasionally contributing to, *Video Watchdog*; I love Tim and Donna, and what they do. It's still a great medium, and the internet hasn't supplanted what zines are, what they do. I'm now expanding my activities into eBooks, and I'm currently working with Crossroad Press, and I do see the eBooks in part as fat zines.

**JS: I'd also like to hear a little bit about the genesis of *Horror Boo!M* and *Monster Pie*. Comic zines kind of bring things full circle.**

**SB:** Among my tightest friends in the circle of CCS alumni and colleagues is Denis St. John, who this past year completed his first horror graphic novel *Amelia* (serialized, over five years, in his own comics zine *Monsters & Girls*, and most highly recommended). Denis was part of a "horror host" monster movie scene in Indiana called Atomic Cinema before he came to CCS as a student, and we clicked with all the shared enthusiasm for the genre in all media. Denis graduated from CCS a number of years ago but stayed, geographically and actively, with the CCS community, and we've continued doing things together, showing movies every week to the CCS students and so on. That led to our doing some odd one-off fun things for film and comics events near us—we did a couple of minicomics, a "survival guide" for a double-feature showing of *The Killer Shrews* and *Night of the Living Dead* that we did a couple of years ago

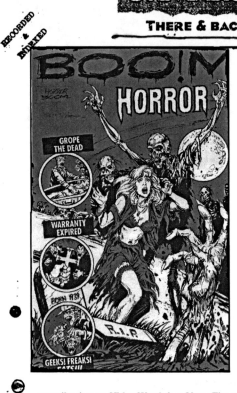

with fellow CCSers (now alumnus) Tim Stout, a "Killer Klowns" perverse poetry minicomic we did this Summer for the Keene, NH Saturday Fright Special "horror host" Spooktacular 35mm theatrical showing of the Chiodo Brothers' *Killers Klowns from Outer Space*. I'd also contributed a couple of "pinup" drawings to his *Monsters & Girls*. We enjoy working together, we're into the same crazy shit—at some point, I proposed we do a zine together to have something new and weird for a then-upcoming Keene NH comics shop appearance in conjunction with the Saturday Fright Special Spooktacular for Halloween 2012, showing a 35mm print of the Amicus *Tales from the Crypt*. So we pulled together two zines, *Monster Pie* and *Horror Boo!M*, and had fun with the process and were pretty happy with the results. We're going to keep going—*Monster Pie* is our personal collaborative monster zine, and with *Boo!M* we're going to devise theme issues: *War Boo!M*, *Six-Gun Boo!M*, and so on. We've sold a few, but mind you, per usual, there's no money in it. There never is with zines. It's another labor of love, is all. As long as it's fun, we'll keep going, I reckon.

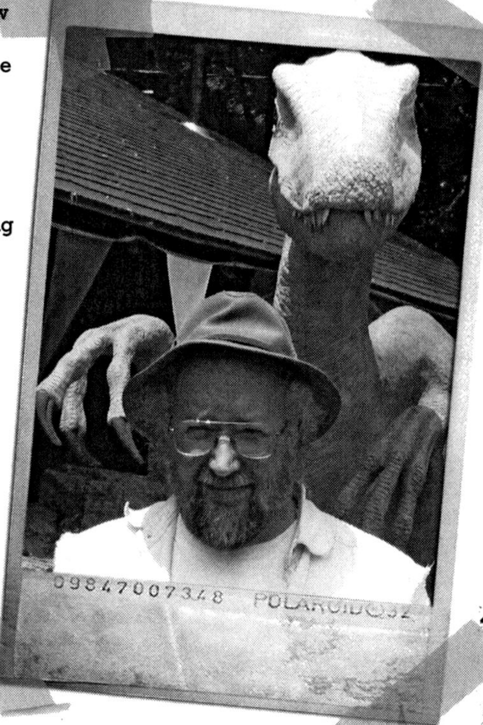


PHOTO © JOSEPH A. CITRO

Also bringing this conversation full circle is one of my print-on-demand/eBook projects which is nearing completion, which tracks the "secret history" of monster magazines, John—all the way back to those science fiction fanzines of the early 1930s. I've got stuff nobody has ever written about, that I know of, and some nobody's ever put together in terms of historical importance and chronologies. I'm hoping to have that done and out in 2013, so—hey, I'll race you to the finish line!

## Chapter Two

# Bhob Stewart

## Of Fanzines and Frankenstein...

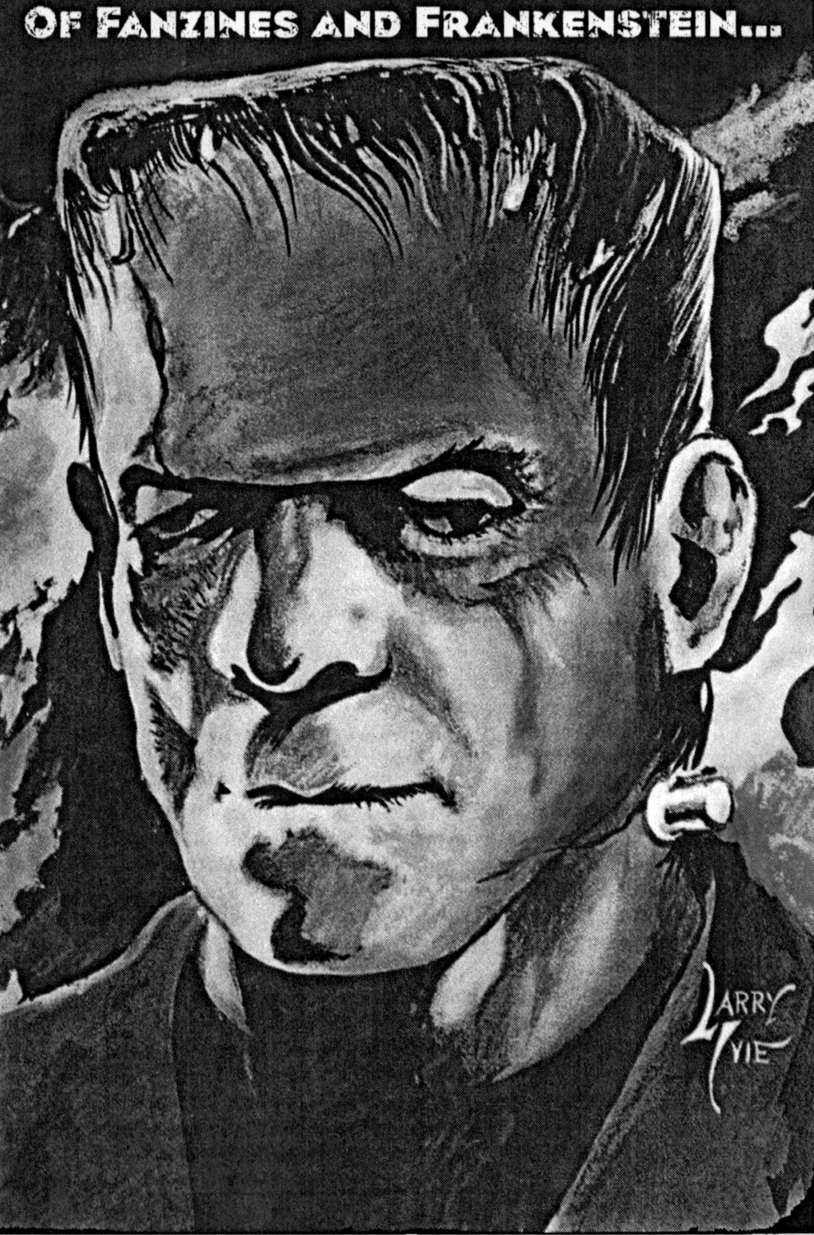


*CASTLE OF FRANKENSTEIN* NUMBER 1. ARTWORK BY LARRY IVIE.

he fact is undisputable: Bhob Stewart has gathered enough feathers for his cap to last him a lifetime. An incessant fan of comic books and science fiction, Stewart published the first EC Comics fanzine, the *EC Fan Bulletin* back in 1953. In 1954, he collaborated with fellow comics scholars Ted White and Larry Stark on *Potrzebie*, a groundbreaking fanzine that again focused on the old ECs. In 1962, he and John Benson interviewed Bernard Krigstein. The piece still stands as one of the most detailed studies of a comic book artist's work that has ever seen print.

In 1963, Stewart began his long tenure as the editor of Calvin T. Beck's seminal magazine, *Castle of Frankenstein*. Originally edited by Larry Ivie and Ken Beale, *Castle of Frankenstein* is widely regarded as the thinking man's *Famous Monsters of Filmland*. Stewart came on board with the third issue and he stayed with the magazine until the early 1970s.

Stewart went on to co-author *Scream Queens* with Calvin Beck in 1978, and has written for *TV Guide*, *Publishers Weekly*, and *Heavy Metal*. 2003 saw the publication of *Against the Grain: Mad Artist Wallace Wood*. His most recent writing can be found online on his blog *Potrzebie*.

Bhob Stewart has enough memories and information swimming around in his brain to fill an entire series of books. In this interview, we discussed the science fiction pulps, the early days of fanzine culture, EC Comics, and the origins of *Castle of Frankenstein*…

The following interview was conducted via telephone on May 22, 2012.

---

**JOHN SZPUNAR: When did you first get involved with fanzines?**

**BHOB STEWART:** I started with fanzines when I was in high school. In the forties, I was really caught up with Fawcett comic books. *Captain Marvel*, *Mary Marvel*, the *Marvel Family*—I really loved that stuff. But as I got older, there came a time when I was about to totally drop it.

**JS: I guess it's safe to say that you didn't.**

**BS:** When EC comics started 1950, I decided to continue reading them.

**JS: How old were you at the time?**

**BS:** In 1950, I would have been thirteen.

**JS: What was it about the ECs that held your interest?**

**BS:** Well, I could see that what they were doing was kind of similar to what I had been listening to on the radio. I listened to *Suspense*, *Escape*, and *Inner Sanctum*. It was pretty clear that they were coming from the same area. I'd also been reading science fiction magazines—you know, *Astounding*, *Galaxy*, and the *Magazine of Fantasy & Science Fiction*. I think there was a photo of Johnny Craig in the EC offices that showed an entire shelf of *Astounding Science Fiction* behind him. So, it was pretty clear to me that the people who were putting out these publications were very familiar with everything that I liked. At the same time, the NBC radio show

# BHOB STEWART

## Of Fanzines and Frankenstein...

RECORDED & INDEXED

*Dimension X* had begun. In fact, in 1950, everything sort of took off. There was *Sunset Boulevard*, *Young Man with a Horn*, *Destination Moon*, *Rocketship X-M*, and the ECs. It was almost as if everything exploded, and I was absorbing every aspect of it.

**JS: There was an article about old radio shows in *Castle of Frankenstein*. What effect did they have on your imagination?**

**BS:** Basically, I'd say that I listened to the radio every day. I grew up listening to those shows and I continued to listen to them, even when they were coming to an end in the early fifties.

**JS: It's fascinating to me that *Mad* parodied things like *The Shadow* and *The Lone Ranger* before they appeared on TV. There was only a radio reference—the artists had to create their own images of the characters.**

**BS:** It's funny—in 1949, they came out with this thing called Frontier Town. I don't know if you got it in certain boxes of General Mills cereals or what, but what you would get was a sheet of paper. You'd unfold it, and it would spread across the entire living room floor. You'd have these little cardboard buildings that you'd put together from the different cereal boxes. You'd set them around on the landscape—your entire living room was transformed into the old west. You'd reach over, turn on the radio, and listen to *The Lone Ranger*. You actually could see where his horse was running, right on your living room floor. What do you think of that?

**JS: Well, it sort of reminds me of the storybook records that I used to listen to when I was a kid. And it sounds as if it might have been a good selling point for General Mills [laughs].**

**BS:** It's surprising that no one else ever did this, as far as I know. It was a very complicated marketing idea—I guess you had to keep buying boxes of cereal to populate the American West [laughs]. They had a great gimmick on *The Lone Ranger*—when he would ride across a wooden bridge, the sound effect would change to the sound of hoofs galloping across a bridge. And right in front of you, you were seeing the bridge that he was riding across.

**JS: When did you start reading the sci-fi magazines?**

**BS:** I started reading *Astounding Science Fiction* with either the April or May issue of 1950. I picked up my very first issue of *Fantasy and*

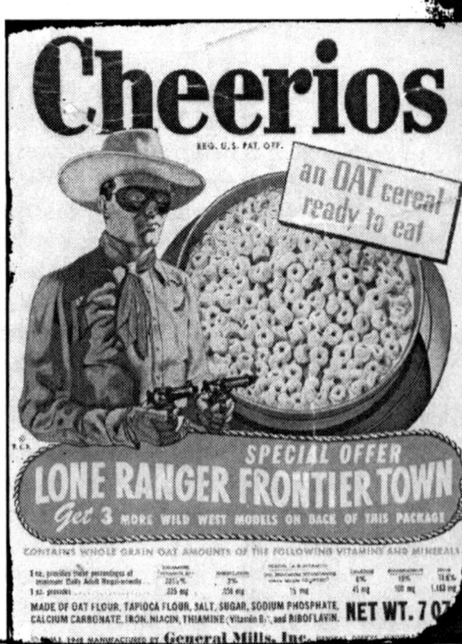


FRONTIER TOWN IN A BOX.

*Science Fiction* in the Summer of 1950. And at the end of the Summer, the very first issue of *Galaxy* came out. Each of these magazines had its own distinct personality. At the same time that I was reading all of this, I would go to the library. They had the giant Groff Conklin anthologies—I was reading every book of science fiction they had. One day, I went there and said, "I think I've read everything here." The guy said, "Oh, yeah? Follow me." He pulled *Out of the Silent Planet* off of the shelf. That was my introduction to C.S. Lewis.

**JS: Why did you start writing?**

**BS:** It was almost like a way of life. I was interested in the whole idea of how you could express yourself, and I began putting out my own handwritten publication. I passed it around to the other students when I was in the sixth grade. This was before I even thought about doing a fanzine.

**JS: Didn't you call that the *Nutty Newspaper*?**

**BS:** [stunned] Where did you get *that* information?

**JS: I did a little research. What was it like?**

**BS:** Well, I was a kid. I just opened my notebook, took a out pencil, and started imitating the newspaper format. Are you a reader of science fiction?

**JS: Yeah. My family had a pretty big stack of books, and I got my start there.**

**BS:** In the early fifties, I was really big on Heinlein and Bradbury. I don't think that EC Comics really realized that they had a lot of readers who recognized that they were swiping the Ray Bradbury stories. We all read *The Martian Chronicles*, and we knew where they were getting their story ideas.

**JS: My first experience with Bradbury was reading the EC adaptations. Again, from my family's library.**

October 1953 · 35 Cents
Astounding
SCIENCE FICTION
The Gulf Between BY TOM GODWIN

# BHOB STEWART

## OF FANZINES AND FRANKENSTEIN...

RECORDED & INDEXED

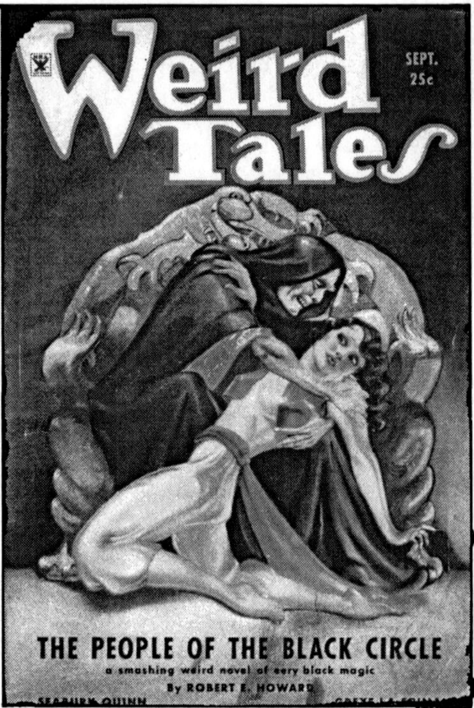

**BS:** Did you get to read any of the science fiction magazines?

**JS: No. I had access to a lot of old paperbacks.**

**BS:** You have to realize that things were sort of in transition. By 1954, *Weird Tales* and the other pulp magazines were collapsing. What you were seeing was a transition from pulp magazines to digest magazines and paperbacks. You would walk into a newsstand and it would all be there. Mainstream magazines, a whole section of digests and paperbacks—there would be comic books up to the ceiling. I would sit on top of a stack of Collier's and read comic books.

**JS: What did you think of the EC imitations?**

**BS:** I lost interest in them pretty fast. I remember reading certain issues of *Adventures Into the Unknown*. I'd read the stuff that had Basil Wolverton—*Weird Tales of the Future*, and that kind of thing. But for the most part, I didn't really pay much attention to them.

**JS: What led up to your publishing of the *EC Fan Bulletin*?**

**BS:** I was working with a guy on a science fiction fanzine, and I started to think, "Why don't I do something that I'm more interested in?" There had never been a fanzine about EC comics before.

**JS: Was that in 1954?**

**BS:** That would be in 1953 or '54. It lasted a couple of issues, and that led to the idea of doing *Potrzebie* with Ted White and Larry Stark. After one issue, Ted turned the publication over to somebody else.

**JS: What was your goal with *Potrzebie*?**

**BS:** I originally intended *Potrzebie* to be not so much of a fanzine as a literary publication. Larry Stark had just graduated from Rutgers with a degree in Library Science, and I knew that he had written these letters to Bill Gaines. Gaines felt so highly of them that he gave Stark a lifetime subscription. Once I got in contact with Larry, I said, "The criticism that you're writing is fascinating. We should actually do a publication where the main point is your writing."

**JS: How did you meet Ted White?**

**BS:** Ted White put out one of the very first comics fanzines. I guess I had ordered it. It was called the *True Story of Superman*. Every time he got some new information about Superman, he would retitle it—the *True Story of Superman, Third Edition*. He was also doing a fanzine called *Zip*. I think I might have contributed to that. But basically, we shared certain interests. We both had an interest in EC Comics, and it just seemed logical that Larry Stark, Ted White, and I would get together to do *Potrzebie*.

**JS: How approachable were the EC guys?**

**BS:** Well, I was in East Texas, so there was no real way to approach them. However, one day I got a postcard from Jerry DeFuccio, and another day I got a postcard from Bill Gaines. So actually, I was in contact with them. What they didn't know was that I was in contact with Marty Jukovsky, who would visit their office. They didn't quite understand where I was getting certain news items from. Similarly, Larry Stark would come down to visit the office, but again, I was more interested in what he was writing as criticism. This was a brand new thing—nobody other than Larry Stark had ever said, "Hey, I think I'll write a very serious critical commentary on these comic books." This led me to write a fanzine article about Bernie Krigstein. That particular article was read by Krigstein. Years later, when I went to interview him, he was fully familiar with what I had written some years before.

THE FIRST EC COMICS FANZINE.

**JS: It's fascinating to me that guys like you were taking this stuff seriously at a time when the majority of the world really wasn't.**

**BS:** That's a good point. You would find that people such as teachers and librarians really despised anything connected to pop culture. I had an English teacher in

RECORDED & INDEXED

high school. She told the class that if she was reading the newspaper and saw an editorial cartoon, she would—quote—avert her eyes.

**JS: I guess that eliminates Thomas Nast...**

**BS:** I'll leave it up to you to figure out whether this woman was totally demented [laughs]. And in college, I had a very good teacher in contemporary literature. I tried to get him interested in Lovecraft, but he totally dismissed the idea as not being worth his time. There was a long period where these people would not acknowledge any of this stuff.

**JS: How were you doing research?**

**BS:** There was no place to do research. As a matter of fact, there weren't even any books about movies back then. If you wanted to read about them, the only things that existed were the fan magazines. There was one book called something like "Remember When." It was kind of like, "Well, there used to be these silent movies..." It was totally barren territory. James Agee's *Agee on Film* wasn't published until a few years later—that was the first collection of film reviews.

**JS: It's almost hard to believe, in this day and age...**

**BS:** You know, years passed before there was even a book about film noir. Everybody knew about film noir, but there were no books about it until *The Film Noir Encyclopedia* was published in 1979. The only thing prior to that had been a magazine article in *Film Comment*, or something. It's kind of interesting—all of these people were paying attention to this stuff and then years later, they began to write about it.

**JS: I'd like to talk a little about the mechanics of putting out a fanzine in the early days. What was working with a hectograph like?**

**BS:** Well, it wasn't very pleasant. Every time you brought out a page and moved over to the next one, things would be a little bit dimmer. You began to realize that you were never going to be able to push the thing past fifty copies—anything after that would just be fading away. And when it was all over, you'd have all of this alinine ink on your hands. You couldn't get rid of it, no matter how many times you washed them. Everything about it was wrong. That's why we switched to mimeograph when we did *Potrzebie*.

**JS: For a youngster like me, could you explain the difference between hectograph and mimeograph?**

**BS:** With a mimeograph, you'd take a stencil and wrap it around a drum. The ink came through the stencil letters as you turned the handle. With a hectograph, you'd put the master face down on a gelatin pan and pull it off. The image was now in the gelatin, and you'd put individual sheets of paper on top of that and pull them off. There was absolutely no advantage to hectograph, other than the fact that you could get red and blue illustrations.

**JS: Let's hear a little about that...**

**BS:** Well, I have a defective eye—I can't really see artificial 3-D movies,

magazines, or comics. But, I got the idea that it would be interesting to do a 3-D drawing and put it into a fanzine. It turned out that hectographs were perfect for that because the colors red and blue worked perfectly with the 3-D glasses.

**JS: How could you tell?**

**BS:** I didn't know what I was doing, but I'd show my experiments to my brother. He'd say, "This one's a little better." I began to understand the mechanics of 3-D, even though I couldn't see it. With that in mind, I began to produce full page 3-D drawings, and I put out the world's first 3-D fanzine.

**JS: Wasn't that called *Fansciful*?**

**BS:** Yes. I did that with a fan writer named Bobby Gene Warner. I haven't seen a copy in many decades, so I don't remember much about it. I do remember one thing that we did—I contacted Jim Harmon. Do you know who he is?

**JS: Yeah. At the time, he was writing short stories for *Rare Science Fiction* and things like that.**

**BS:** Right. I contacted him and I said, "I would like you to write a parody of this ad that's on the back cover of *Galaxy Science Fiction*." He said, "OK." and he did it. I met him later at a science fiction convention and apologized for putting it out with a hectograph [laughs].

**JS: Let's hear some more about mimeography.**

**BS:** Well, as the years went on, there was a huge upgrade in mimeograph technology. If you get into reading about it, it's kind of interesting. There was the Gestetner company—they came out with an extremely high-tech mimeograph machine. With that, it was possible to do something with electronic stencils. There were places that you could take the stencils to and get an image burnt into them. So, let's say you wanted to do a photograph. You would take it to this place, and they would burn it in. You could take that to a Gestetner machine and actually get a fairly high quality image. In the olden days, you had to put down a photograph and trace around it with a stylus.

**JS: Let's get back to the prozines. What were your impressions of *Famous Monsters* when you first saw it?**

**BS:** Well, you have to realize that Ackerman had been doing this years earlier. When I was in junior high school, he was writing a column for *Imagination*. It was essentially the same sort of stuff—he wrote about one movie after another, and occasionally there would be some bad puns. So to me, *Famous Monsters* was really just the final expression of what he'd been doing years earlier. I wasn't particularly interested in it. A lot of people thought that *Castle of Frankenstein* imitated *Famous Monsters*, but I had very little interest in it.

**JS: On that note, let's move on to *Castle of Frankenstein*. How did you meet Calvin Beck?**

**BS:** I went up to Calvin at a convention in Philadelphia. I was interested in the

RECORDED & INDEXED

idea that maybe I could do some kind of work there, because he seemed to be an independent kind of guy. I got very little response from him. Now, time passed—maybe a year or so—and Larry Ivie had been putting the magazine together for him. Ken Beale phoned me up and said, "Calvin's afraid that the new issue won't get finished because Larry isn't here." I guess he'd gone on a Christmas vacation or something. I didn't see what the big deal was—why not just wait until he got back? But, I went out to New Jersey and saw what was left, which was very little, actually. It was just sitting there and it didn't take very long to finish things up. We sent it to the printer. After that, I said, "Let's get to work on the next issue." That was how it all began.

**JS: You came in with issue number 3.**

**BS:** Yes. Meanwhile, Larry Ivie had returned. I said to Calvin, "Look, it would be great if Larry does his comic strip. I'll continue to put the magazine together." Calvin said, "No." For some reason, he didn't really want to run Larry's comic strip.

**JS: Why was that?**

**BS:** I don't know. I was trying to get a lot of comics into the magazine when I could. Larry went off and launched his own magazine. By turning him down, Calvin basically created his own competition. *Monsters and Heroes* was born because Calvin said, "We don't need you anymore."

**JS: I haven't seen any issues of that.**

**BS:** It was distributed by Kable News. It was totally written, produced, created, and assembled by Larry Ivie.

**JS: What's Ivie up to these days?**

**BS:** He's vanished. We're trying to figure out just what the hell happened to him.

**JS: Wow...**

**BS:** He was living in California. Last year, some people tried to contact him and nobody could get a response. Somebody went to his house, and it was empty. Nobody has heard from him. So, let's get the word out and see if we can hear from Larry Ivie.

**JS: What was it about *Castle of Frankenstein* that made you want to be a part of it?**

**BS:** Well, I was working at *TV Guide*. And of course, I was

# BACK ISSUE DEPT.

#1

—SPECIAL COLLECTOR'S EDITION—**THE MUMMY THROUGH THE AGES; THE BORIS KARLOFF STORY;** picture-stories on **TIME MACHINE, WOMAN EATER, JACK THE RIPPER, SEVENTH SEAL, PIT AND THE PENDULUM, FRANKENSTEIN 1970, TINGLER, GIANT BEHEMOTH, MYSTERIANS, ALLIGATOR PEOPLE, DARBY O'GILL AND THE LITTLE PEOPLE, HOUND OF THE BASKERVILLES** and **HAVE ROCKET WILL TRAVEL;** Portfolio of monster cartoons; **TV JEEBIES;** Japanese monsters; **BRITISH HORRORS.**

#2

—**VAMPIRE**—a 6-page horror comic story written and illustrated by Larry Ivie; **THE MANY FACES OF CHRISTOPHER LEE;** picture-stories on remakes—the 1957 **HUNCHBACK OF NOTRE DAME,** the 1962 **PHANTOM OF THE OPERA** and the 1962 **CABINET OF CALIGARI;** American-International hits; **EARLY YEARS OF FRANKENSTEIN,** a screen history plus analysis; Larry Ivie on super heroes—**THE DAY MEN FLEW;** Charles Collins on **Lilith.**

#3

—The first **FORGOTTEN FRANKENSTEIN;** conclusion of **BORIS KARLOFF STORY;** beginning of **LON CHANEY JR. STORY;** Larry Ivie on more super-heroes; picture-stories on **WHAT EVER HAPPENED TO BABY JANE?, DAY OF THE TRIFFIDS, THE RAVEN, CAPTAIN SINBAD** and **NIGHT CREATURES;** Mary Shelley and the **BIRTH OF FRANKENSTEIN;** Charles Collins on Shirley Jackson and Ray Bradbury, Larry Byrd as **FRANKENSTEIN; TWILIGHT ZONE, TEEN-AGE MONSTER MAKERS.**

#4

**SPECIAL VAMPIRE ISSUE:** picture-stories on **NOSFERATU, KISS OF THE VAMPIRE, BLACK SUNDAY** and **BLOOD OF THE VAMPIRE;** Mike Parry on historical, literary and filmic vampires; Bram Stoker's autograph; foreign vampires in **CONTINENTAL CREATURES;** part 2 of **LON CHANEY JR. STORY; OUR FEATHERED FIENDS**—birds in horror films; **LEGEND OF THE MUMMY;** picture stories on **FREAKS** and **THE HAUNTING;** Charles Collins on Lovecraft; **WONDERFUL WORLD OF GEORGE PAL;** Al Hirschfeld caricature of **DR. NO; FRANKENSTEIN RADIOGUIDE;** first **FRANKENSTEIN MOVIEGUIDE.**

#5

—Noted film historian William K. "**Silents Please**" Everson recalls his personal encounters with Lorre in **THE PETER LORRE STORY**—with checklist of all Lorre films; picture-story review of **EVIL OF FRANKENSTEIN;** leading Burroughs expert Dick Lupoff describes **MONSTERS OF EDGAR RICE BURROUGHS**—with illustrations by Frank Frazetta, Reed Crandall, Larry Ivie and Al Williamson; **OUTER LIMITS;** interview with Arthur Lubin, director of 1943 **PHANTOM OF THE OPERA;** first CoF **OLDIES BUT GOODIES;** fantastic films of **JEAN COCTEAU; OUT OF THIS WORLD WITH BORIS KARLOFF; ADDAMS FAMILY;** rare photo autographed by Karloff in 1914; lengthy movie reviews; Al Hirschfeld caricature of Lorre in **M.**

FRANKENSTEIN
RADIO
HORRORS!!
HITCHCOCK!
LON CHANEY JR.'s
MONSTERS—


#6

—The second **FORGOTTEN FRANKENSTEIN; FANTASY FEST**—report on 2nd Trieste Science Fiction Film Festival; **HORROR ON THE AIR**—nostalgic memories and rare photos of **The Shadow, Inner Sanctum** and other great radio fantasies; part 3 of **LON CHANEY JR. STORY;** questions and answers with Hitchcock at **A HITCH-COCKTAIL PARTY;** amateur **FRANKENSTEIN** film; Charles Collins on Robert E. Howard; **MUNSTERS;** four year's worth of **CHRIS LEE** films; **MASQUE OF RED DEATH; UNDERDOG;** part 1 of **FRANKENSTEIN TV MOVIE-GUIDE** listing all horror on TV.

**JOURNAL OF FRANKENSTEIN**—Extremely limited supply available of this rare one-shot, published in 1959. History of European horror films from 1895 to present. Boris Karloff as seen by different writers; picture-stories on **7TH VOYAGE OF SINBAD** and **HOUSE ON THE HAUNTED HILL;** animated fantasy films; **FRANKENSTEIN AT LARGE;** review of Le Fantastique au Cinema; biography of horror host **JOHN ZACHERLEY;** parody horror screenplay—**RETURN OF THE BRIDE OF THE SON OF FRANKENSTEIN;** detailed report on horror films of '58. No back issues of this one will be around soon—so first come, first served.

**For Back Issues ($1.00 each . . . 5 for $4.00)**

**JOURNAL OF FRANKENSTEIN ( )**

**CASTLE OF FRANKENSTEIN: #1 #2 #3 #4 #5 #6**

**(Check off copies you want.)**

NAME ..............................

ADDRESS ..............................

CITY ..............................

STATE .................. ZIP CODE ..............

**Mail all cash, checks or money orders to:**

**GOTHIC CASTLE – Box 43 – Hudson Heights**

**North Bergen — New Jersey — 07048**

## DID YOU MISS ANY?

RECORDED & INDEXED

CASTLE of
FRANKENSTEIN
35c
RADIO
HORRORS!!
CHRISTOPHER LEE RETURNS IN THE
GORGON!
INTERVIEW WITH ALFRED
HITCHCOCK!
LON CHANEY JR.'s
MONSTERS--
DRACULA AND
THE WOLFMAN
PLUS ANOTHER LOST FRANKENSTEIN!

a cog in a big, huge juggernaut. The idea that I could go to New Jersey on the weekends and do an entire magazine on my own, without anybody telling me what to do, was a lot of fun. I worked seven days a week for about four years. I would leave New York on Friday, go to New Jersey, and spend the entire weekend working on *Castle of Frankenstein*. I'd come back to the city on Sunday night and go back to work at *TV Guide* the next morning. I did that week after week and month after month.

**JS: I've read that you were very meticulous.**

**BS:** I built up whole systems of organizing all of the files—everything was systemized. I even had a concept of how you could storyboard a magazine by putting pictures up and deciding what was going to go where. One of the key factors in this was an article that had appeared in *Esquire*. Jim Warren had been interviewed, along with Gloria Stavers of *16* magazine. I read that article over and over again, and it gave me all of these ideas of what I should be doing.

**JS: Such as?**

**BS:** Gloria Stavers said, "We try to make the magazine look like the readers have actually done it." I said, "Hey, that's an interesting idea." Jim Warren said, "We're trying to reach the eight- to twelve year old market." I said, "Hey—why not eight to sixty-five? Why are you eliminating all of these people?" The article really kicked me into thinking about what I was doing. I was trying to put out a magazine for an adult audience, and I don't think that's what Jim Warren and Forry Ackerman had in mind.

**JS: A lot of the people I've talked to really appreciated that.**

**BS:** Another point here is that there were no magazines devoted to B movies. In fact, there were no books devoted to them until *Kings of the Bs* was published.

**JS: That would have been in the mid-seventies.**

**BS:** Right. That was an important book. Nobody had ever covered that subject before—it had never been done.

**JS: *Castle of Frankenstein* seemed to cover everything. You even ran capsule reviews of Jess Franco movies in 1965...**

**BS:** That was probably due to Joe Dante. He wrote almost all of those

# CASTLE OF FRANKENSTEIN



INSIDE FRANKENSTEIN



Vol. 2 No. 2

INSIDE FRONT

Yet another forgotten Frankenstein! Lon Chaney Jr. as Frankenstein on ABC-TV's TALES OF TOMORROW (1952). This test makeup was created by Vincent J-R Kehoe.

BACK COVER

Lugosi stalks!—on the same staircase seen in the Frankenstein Monster scene used on the back cover of CoF#3. Save these back covers for a complete staircase collection.


CHARLES F. KANE
Editor & Publisher

BHOB STEWART
Managing Editor

NICHOLAS MORGAN
Associate Editor

JOHN BENSON
Editorial Asst.

CHRIS STEINBRUNNER
Editor, Special Projects

MICHEL PARRY
European Editor

CONTRIBUTING EDITORS
Joe Dante, Jr. — Leroy Kennedy
Charles M. Collins
Richard ("Bojak the Bojar") Bojarski

CORRESPONDENTS
Jim Harmon
Victor Wiscovitch
Ramon Delgado



ACKNOWLEDGEMENTS

Milton Livingston, Universal-International; Vic Ghidalia, ABC-TV; Pat Crinnion, Sylvia Kline, CBS-TV; Jerry Cutler, Ruth Palage, American International; Arnold Friedman, Eve Siegal, Embassy; Mort Sunshine; Harvey Chertok, Seven Arts; Jim Harmon; Ron Haydock; Wm K. Everson; Jean-Claude Romer, Midi-Minuit Fantastique; John Newfield, Columbia Pictures; Fred Espy, Myrna Jacobs, NBC-TV; Christopher Lee; Marty Jukovsky; Vincent J-R Kehoe; Charles Michelson; Bert Grey; Max Stratyner; Phil Ressequie; Eddie Reicher; John Oken.

CASTLE OF FRANKENSTEIN, published quarterly by Gothic Castle Publishing Co. Editorial, subscription and Advertising offices: Box 43, Hudson Heights Station, North Bergen, New Jersey 07048. Contents © copyright 1965 by Gothic Castle Publishing Co. Volume 2, Number 2 (whole #6). 2nd Class Entry Pending, North Bergen, N. J.

SUBSCRIPTION RATES: $2.00 for 6 issues; $3.00 for 10 issues in the U.S.A. and Canada. Elsewhere: add $1.00 more. NOTE TO POTENTIAL CONTRIBUTORS: While your contributions are always welcome, please enclose sufficient postage at all times, with an envelope whenever possible. Care will be given to all works, but no responsibility can be assumed for any unsolicited material.

Printed in the U.S.A.

## OF FANZINES AND FRANKENSTEIN...

RECORDED & INDEXED

miniature reviews. Calvin and I did around ten per cent of them, but he did the rest.

**JS: I have to ask about Joe Dante—how did he come into the fold?**

**BS:** I believe he was writing similar kind of stuff for a magazine in Philadelphia. How he made contact with Calvin, I do not know.

**JS: Matt Fox (of *Weird Tales*) did some artwork for *Castle of Frankenstein*.**

**BS:** Correct. He wanted to sell horror posters, and he thought that *Castle of Frankenstein* would be a good place to advertise. He came over one day; I wrote about meeting him in my blog. It didn't work out—he didn't get any orders for the posters like he thought he would and he never turned up again. I might have seen him twice in that period of time.

LATEST FILM NEWS FROM *CASTLE OF FRANKENSTEIN*.

**JS: Wally wood also contributed some artwork. How did that happen?**

**BS:** That was a trade off. He was starting his magazine *Witzend*. He said, "Run my ad, and I'll send you a free picture."

**JS: What was Wood like?**

**BS:** You know, a lot has been said about Wood's problems, but they weren't all that apparent. There were a couple of things a little later on, but he wasn't hitting the bottle while he was working. Work was getting done, and work was getting out. It wasn't that much of an issue in '67 and '68—he was very productive. But on the other hand, you could look at things this way: Why wasn't he a success like Jack Davis? I think a lot of that had to do with the fact that Jack Davis was a very social kind of a guy. Wood was very withdrawn—it was all in the artwork.

**JS: How and why did your tenure with *Castle of Frankenstein* come to an end?**

**BS:** Cal wanted to switch from zines to books. I assembled a full issue that he never printed. I then began writing *Scream Queens* with him.

**JS: These days, things seem to be heading into cyberspace. Can you tell me a little about your blog?**

**BS:** *Potrzebie* combines memoir with pop culture observations. Have you read it?

**JS: Yeah. I really enjoy it.**

**BS:** If you search *Potrzebie* for "Weird Tales", you'll find an article that

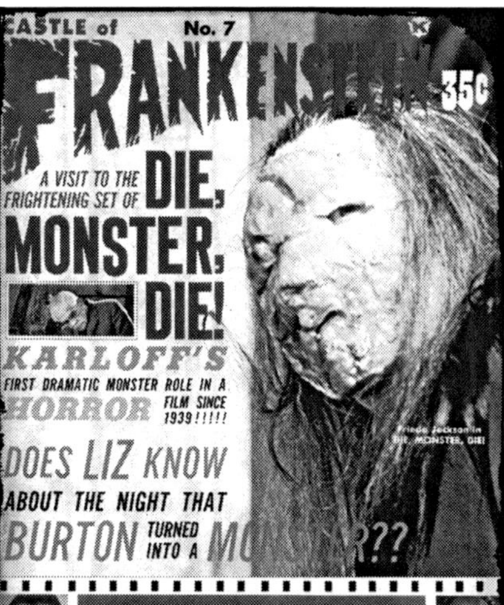


I wrote about the history of *Weird Tales*, which is related to these publications that were almost like fanzines. And the humor publications of the 1920s were very much related somehow to *Weird Tales*. I was curious about this, and the whole point of the article was to find the connection between *Weird Tales*, cartoon magazines, and comic books. You'll find it interesting, because I put in illustrations of *Home Brew* magazine, which is where Lovecraft started. *Home Brew* was apparently very close to being like a fanzine.

CASTLE of FRANKENSTEIN
No. 7
35¢
A VISIT TO THE FRIGHTENING SET OF
DIE, MONSTER, DIE!
KARLOFF'S FIRST DRAMATIC MONSTER ROLE IN A HORROR FILM SINCE 1939!!!!!
DOES LIZ KNOW ABOUT THE NIGHT THAT BURTON TURNED INTO A MO...???
LUGOSI VS. LEE
SCENES FROM DRACULA, PRINCE OF DARKNESS

**JS: In a way, the fanzines are still flourishing in the form of blogs, although I'd imagine that it must have taken a little more time and money to churn something out in the mimeo days.**

**BS:** I don't know. The cost of a stack of mimeograph paper wasn't that much. And in some cases, a person might have been able to produce a fanzine by having access to a mimeograph machine in a school, a church, or some other place. I don't know of any examples, but some people must have done that. A person who puts out a blog today is not any different than a person who put out a fanzine in the 1950s…

Some day it may become impossible to get early back numbers from our already dwindling stock. In fact, The International Society For Rare Magazines has found that some collectors have asked as much as $5 or more for a copy of CoF or JoF. To avoid the ... and humiliation of consorting with bootleggers or various shady characters in the future trying to sell you rare back copies (most likely in inferior condition), you can do probably one of two things: (1) Develop the power to cloud men's minds and, thus, avoid paying high prices. (2) Take advantage of our Back Issue Service, like below . . . okay?

Back issues: Only $1.00 a copy . . . Any 5 for $4.00

PARTIAL LIST OF CONTENTS:

#5: THE PETER LORRE STORY . . . THE EVIL OF FRANKENSTEIN . . . BURROUGHS MONSTERS . . . JEAN COCTEAU . . . INCREDIBLE MR. LUBIN . . .

## SubsCryptions

Did you like the idea of going to a newsstand the last time you wanted an issue of CASTLE OF FRANKENSTEIN, and perhaps having one of several loathsome things happening to you? To avoid such disorders, and whether you're over 35 or under 15, take the easy way . . . use the coupon below (if you do not wish to cut up the page, you can write up your order on a piece of paper instead). Each issue comes to you neatly in a protective wrap.

For Future Issues

( ) $2.00 for 6 issues ( ) $3.00 for 10 issues

For Back Issues ($1.00 each . . 5 for $4.00)

( ) JOURNAL OF FRANKENSTEIN ( )

CASTLE OF FRANKENSTEIN: #1, #2, #3, #4 #5

(Check off or put a circle around issues you want.)

NAME ..........

ADDRESS ..........

CITY ..........

STATE .......... ZIP CODE ..........

Mail all cash, checks or money orders to:

GOTHIC CASTLE – Box 43 – Hudson Heights

North Bergen — New Jersey — 07048

Midnight Marquee's

# Chapter Three
# Gary Svehla
## Gore Creature!

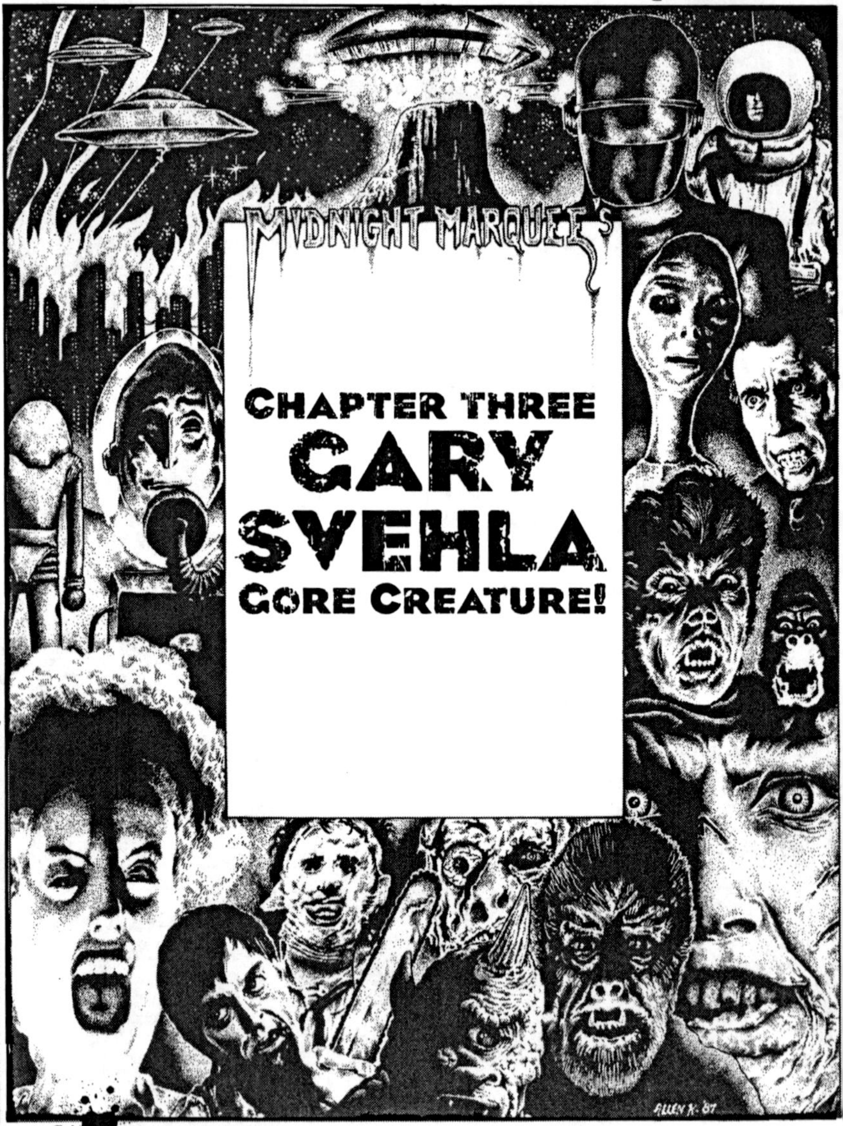

Allen K. '87

ALLEN KOSZOWSKI ARTWORK FROM *MIDNIGHT MARQUEE* NUMBER 36.

Gary Svehla began publishing *Gore Creatures* in 1963, at the age of thirteen. In 1976, he changed its name to *Midnight Marquee*, and it's been going strong ever since. *Gore Creatures/Midnight Marquee* will always remain the longest running monster magazine in the history of fandom. Gary was there from the beginning, and he certainly shows no signs of stopping.

I was introduced to *Midnight Marque* with issue number 37, the twenty-fifth anniversary edition that FantaCo distributed in 1988. I started searching for back issues shortly after that, and was amazed at the transformation that had taken place: what had started out as a quintessential homemade fan publication was now a squarebound, glossy, beautiful thing. *Midnight Marquee* was added to my list of must-haves, and I've been reading and enjoying it for nearly twenty-five years.

Today, Gary Svehla runs Midnight Marque Press with his wife Susan. I thought it would be a good idea to talk to him about the early days of fandom, the influential monster mags of the 1960s, and about the evolution and future of *Midnight Marquee*.

The following interview was conducted via email, July, 2012.

---

**JOHN SZPUNAR: What are your earliest memories of watching a film?**

**GARY SVEHLA:** When I was five years old, my mother took me to see Disney's *Lady and the Tramp* in 1955. By the middle of the movie I was totally bored and vocally complained, so she had to take me home before the movie ended. When I was seven years old my father Richard and older brother Dick took me to a neighborhood movie on a school night. Boy, that was extra special! They wanted to see a movie called *Bop Girl* because of the music (both my father and brother played saxophone in bands), but the co-feature was *The Monster that Challenged the World*, and I wanted to stay and see the monster feature twice. Even watching the onscreen terror behind clinched hands covering my eyes, I knew these monster movies were for me.

**JS: What were you reading when you were growing up?**

**GS:** As a child I was into 1950s and 1960s classic science fiction. The idea of going into outer space and finding other planets with life was always exciting to me. When the US gave up on the space program of sending people into space, I felt this was a major mistake. I loved all the DC comics, mainly *Superman* and *Batman* and *Justice League*. I also liked *Archie* comics and *Little Lulu* and the classic Walt Disney stuff. While EC and the classic horror comics were gone by 1957 when I started buying comics, I loved all the monster comics that were available. But when I discovered *Famous Monsters of Filmland*, I was hooked on monsters forever.

**JS: What was your childhood like?**

**GS:** I was the luckiest kid in the world. My mother supported my hobby, but it was my father who actually enjoyed the classic horror movies and told me stories of when he first saw *Dracula* and *Frankenstein* in the theaters, when he was about eleven years old.

I watched all the classic horror movies on late-night TV, making my mother adjust the antennae in the backyard, even during Winter snows ("Mom, a little more to the left!"), so I could get the best broadcast signal to see *Bride of Frankenstein*. I bought and assembled all the monster model kits, chewed a wad of gum to get all the monster non-sports cards and had to get every single issue of every monster magazine ever produced. And of course, inspired by *Famous Monsters* and *Castle of Frankenstein* magazines, I started my own fanzine *Gore Creatures* at the tender age of thirteen in the Summer of 1963.

**JS: Let's talk a little about *Famous Monsters of Filmland*.**

**GS:** A boy in school brought in issue number 11 of *Famous Monsters* and I was awestruck. At the first opportunity, I walked half a mile to the drugstore that had the largest magazine rack in the area, looking for that monstrous cover. When I found it, I eagerly thumbed carefully through its pages and headed to the nice lady at the register. I would come back every week or so to buy my comics and monster magazines. It was one of the most exciting times I ever experienced in my life, not knowing what I would find on the magnificent magazine rack.

**JS: What was your initial reaction to *FM*?**

**GS:** Being a horror film fan, I learned that a community of monster movie lovers existed around the country. I knew this through all the letters and fan ads placed in the front and back of *Famous Monsters* and *Castle of Frankenstein*. While none of my buddies were into monsters (except my good pal Dave Metzler), I developed long-distance friendships with other budding monster fans. We did not have email, Facebook or Twitter, but we wrote long letters to one another regularly and even made cassette tapes where we spoke to one another and shared our passions. The sci-fi and movie conventions were the places for all of us to eventually meet.

**JS: When did you first meet Forry Ackerman?**

**GS:** Around 1965 my father Richard took me up to LunaCon, the major

*GORE CREATURES* NUMBER 2: BIRTH OF A MONSTER KID.

fantasy, horror and science fiction convention held in New York City. New York hosted the World Science Fiction Convention in 1967. And I believe it was there at Nycon 3 that I first met Forrest J Ackerman. We posed for photos with each one of us proudly displaying our own monster magazines. It was magical finally meeting this living icon.

ALEX SOMA'S *HORRORS OF THE SCREEN*.

**JS: What kind of impression did he make on you?**

**GS:** Forry was the fountainhead of horror film fandom. He was the adult who made all our monster passions legitimate. He validated all of our obsessions and made us feel like a worthy community of Monster Kids who were normal and not weird. Forry made it cool to love horror and science fiction.

**JS: You remained friends...**

**GS:** I do not know if anyone was truly Forry's friend. Forry always was about Forry, self-promoting himself and his magazines, books and movies. He was a great figure and fan, but he always told the same stories in the same ways year after year. Forry was wise enough to know that being an icon to children meant a great deal of his personal life should remain private. I believe Forry was rather shy and that he crafted his persona to help him emerge from his shell. I hosted Forry at my house for dinner once and saw him socially in Baltimore when he attended the FANEX film conventions that we sponsored. One of the best times was when Forry attended the Thursday night 16mm movie screenings at the home of good friend George Stover, who has hosted these classic movie nights at his home for over forty years. Forry was truly in his element there. But Forry never really let his hair down or allowed fans to get past his Uncle Forry persona. He always remained an enigma. Fans were only allowed to see the tip of the iceberg.

**JS: When were you introduced to fanzines?**

**GS:** From 1961 to 1962 I studied the "Haunt Ad" pages of *Famous Monsters* and similar sections in *Castle of Frankenstein*. I loved to write and seeing amateur versions of the great horror magazines inspired me to try the same. The fanzine that really rocked my world was Alex Soma's *Horrors of the Screen*. I studied the paper, the layout, the position of the text, the percentage of text to graphic image, etc. I never dreamed that an amateur

# GARY SVEHLA

## GORE CREATURE!

magazine could acquire such a high degree of quality. I knew I had to do my own fanzine, and in 1963, at age thirteen, I did.

**JS: How did your peers react to your monster obsession?**

**GS:** My peers always thought I was strange so it did not matter whether I did a fanzine or read monster magazines or collected comic books. I was a marked man. So I kept my small circle of friends and continued to indulge in all my passions. There are always a few friends around who share your mad obsessions.

My friend Dave Metzler loved the monster stuff and many of my friends went to see horror movies with me, but other than Dave, none shared the obsession with monsters and vampires that I had. All kids love genre cinema but not all kids take it to the next level. That's the difference.

**JS: What are your memories of *Castle of Frankenstein*?**

**GS:** For me this was the greatest monster magazine of all time. *Famous Monsters* sparked the fires of the child within; *Castle of Frankenstein* provided the adult horror film education. *Famous Monsters* was written for kids but it never spoke down to its audience. And let's face it, the classic era of *Famous Monsters* actually existed for only its first thirty-three issues or so… a relatively short stretch. After that, the magazine deteriorated. But as we matured, we had *Castle of Frankenstein* and Calvin Beck to latch on to and continue our education in the grotesque. *Castle of Frankenstein* provided my primary education in horror and science fiction cinema.

**JS: When and why did you start publishing *Gore Creatures*?**

**GS:** I started publishing *Gore Creatures* because, being shy and not knowing die-hard monster lovers locally, I wanted to reach out and provide a beacon for horror movie lovers across the USA. Just as Forry Ackerman and Calvin Beck inspired me, I now wanted to reach out and provide a forum to inspire others, to bring us all together as the children of Ackerman and Beck.

**JS: How did you settle on the name? Did you have any alternate titles for your publication?**

**GS:** Remember, I was twelve or thirteen at the time, and every fanzine was a variation of the title *Famous Monsters of Filmland*. I do not remember any alternate titles, to be truthful. But the word "gore" was not commonly used at the time, so something called *Gore Creatures* seemed to fit the bill just fine.

**JS: What did you feel that you could bring to the table?**

**GS:** At the time, as a thirteen year old, I did not think philosophically or psychologically. For me it was like joining the band. I was the East Coast USA version of the newly emerging monster mania. After my crude beginning, what I thought I was bringing to the table was the personalized touch of being able to share my personal and private love of monster movies with the world. I was Monster Fan Number One and my obsessions could become yours. Also, I focused on using original art in the magazine and reached out to attract some fantastic artists such as David Ludwig and Bill Nelson to draw for my little fanzine. Also I wanted to provide a forum to review other fanzines published around the country, and I tried to spark an interactive letter column that could become a "message board" for horror movie fans to express their views.

**JS: How was it produced?**

**GS:** The fanzine was first produced, typed, with carbon paper copies; soon we went high tech by being printed on gelatin sheets; then we switched to mimeograph; then we went offset; and finally we added professional saddle-stitch binding to the offset printing. Today we are print-on-demand with our magazines manufactured by CreateSpace. Next stage will most likely be digital and paperless.

**JS: How did production change as the issues went on?**

**GS:** We could get

## GORE CREATURE!

about twenty copies from a carbon copy. With the ditto produced from the gelatin sheets, we could get forty to seventy-five readable copies. With mimeograph we got a few hundred copies. With offset the sky's the limit. In other words, as our sales increased we needed to find a method of reproduction that could handle increased print runs. And with magazines such as *Photon* going very slick and glossy, we had to follow their lead. I still thank my late father Richard for going out to A.B. Dick Company to buy the latest machine to produce the latest issues. He was there for me all the time.

**JS: How did you distribute?**

**GS:** Based in Baltimore as we were, Diamond comics picked us up to distribute to comic book shops very early on. Many independent distributors also carried us, but most of them went bankrupt, belly-up, often filing bankruptcy still owing us lots of money. Many independent bookstores and comic shops carried us. And primarily we took out ads in some of the pro magazines and many of the fanzines. Remember, fanzines were primarily published as a labor of love, not to make a profit. However, Gene Klein (soon to be Gene Simmons of KISS) always busted my chops because I dared charge a quarter for my fanzine while he insisted that fanzines should be given away for free. Gene's philosophy did slightly change over the years! The KISS ARMY never gave anything away for free!

**JS: Do you have any favorite issues/articles from the *Gore Creatures* days?**

**GS:** I have fond memories of all the issues, but you are right, the extra special issues were the ones from issue 18 through issue 25. At this time the magazine was the focus of my life and these issues demonstrated the evolution of technology where the improving look of the magazine matched the improving quality of articles and artwork. We were growing by leaps and bounds and earning the respect of the fanzine-loving public. It was great being a big fish in a small fishbowl.

**JS: When and why did *Gore Creatures* become *Midnight Marquee*?**

**GS:** Ronald V. Borst, a writer for *Photon* and the number one horror movie poster collector in the country at the time, hated the title *Gore Creatures*, calling it juvenile and childish. So, in 1976 *Gore Creatures* number 25 was followed by *Midnight Marquee* number 26. We never started from scratch

*MIDNIGHT MARQUEE* FORMERLY *GORE CREATURES* NUMBER 37.

because the magazine was absolutely the same—the same writers, the same artists, the same editor and publisher. But issue 26 was the only issue of ours to be printed on glossy stock. To be honest, I never liked it all that much because the glare of the paper did not favor the reproduction of photos. Funny thing, a few years after I changed the magazine's title, splatter and gore films became the rage. If I had only held out a few years longer, *Gore Creatures* would have become a cool title once again for the new age of emerging horror. But I foolishly listened to Ron Borst.

**JS: You've been publishing since the early 1960s; how do you deal with burnout?**

**GS:** I deal with burnout by stepping back and chilling. I taught high school English for forty years (I recently retired), got married and became devoted to Aurelia Susan, my wife. We sponsored the FANEX horror film conventions (including Monster Rally and Classic Filmfest) for nineteen years. And in 1995 we started Midnight Marquee Press, INC., our niche book publishing company. So if I became burned out from doing the magazine, I could focus more on the books or my personal life or the conventions. Diversify! If I wanted to publish two issues a year I could, or even one. For me it is all about longevity, not the amount of issues published.

**JS: How did you start working with artist Bill Nelson?**

**GS:** Bill wrote me and wanted to see a copy of *Gore Creatures*. From there of course I asked him to do some artwork for us, and he did. Bill was always a gentleman and true fan, always willing to help another fan. He was busy with his university teaching job but he always had time to do some art for my magazine. In fact when our fiftieth year anniversary issue is published next Summer, guess who volunteered to do our cover? Of course, none other than Bill Nelson. He's a wonderful man and an absolutely fantastic talent.

**JS: I remember ordering the twenty-fifth anniversary issue of *Midnight Marquee* from FantaCo as a kid. It was the first issue I saw, and I was blown away. Can you tell me a little about what went in to producing that issue?**

**GS:** Tom Skulan was an avid fan of our magazine and was selling many

# GARY SVEHLA

## Gore Creature!

COVER ARTWORK BY BILL NELSON AND [NEXT PAGE] ALLEN KOSZOWSKI.

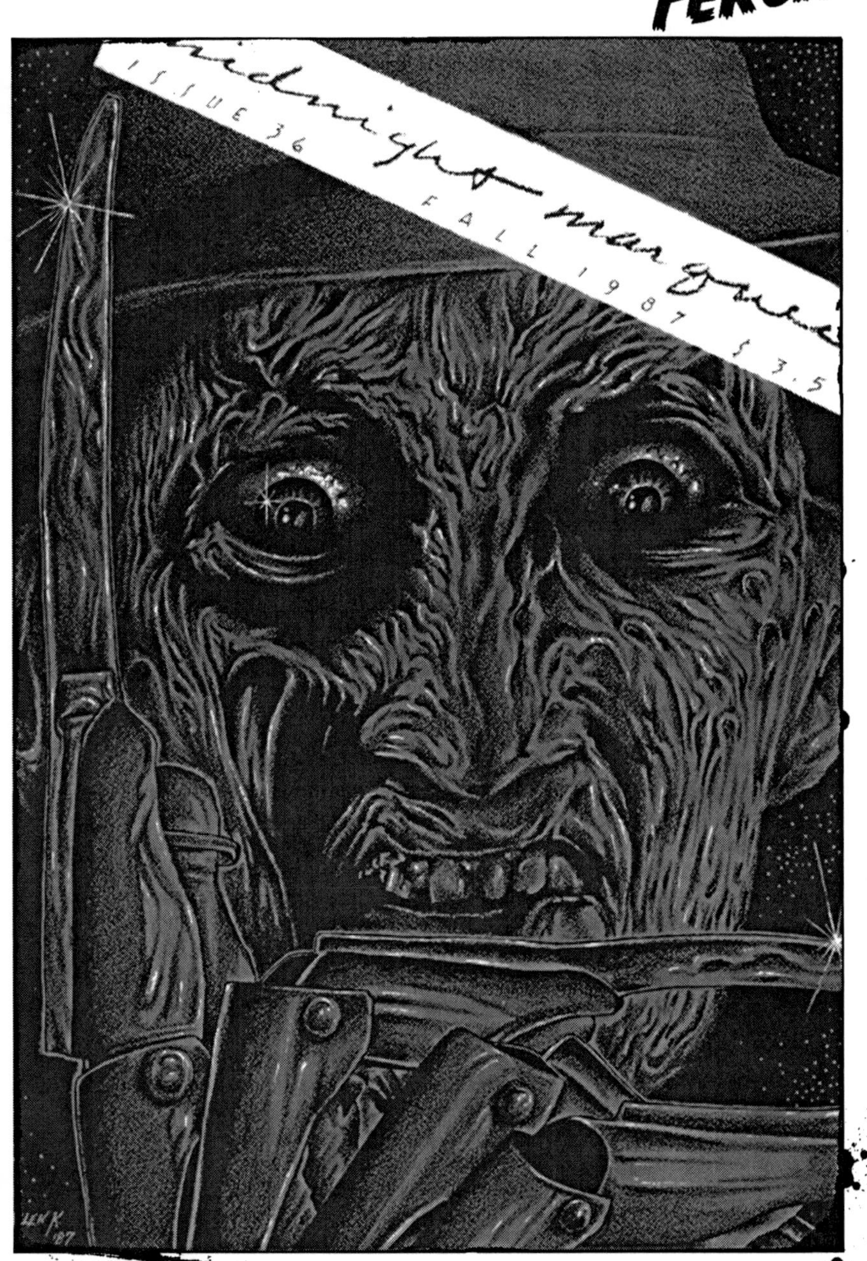
midnight marquee
ISSUE 36
FALL 1987
$3.5

DRAFT

RECORDED & INDEXED

copies through his FantaCo distribution company. He had the idea of doing something special for the twenty-fifth anniversary issue. He would pay for the book-size anniversary issue and he wanted me to be a special guest at his annual FantaCo convention, and the anniversary issue would premiere at his show. It was a great experience to relive twenty-five years of publishing the magazine and to be honored as special guest at the Albany, New York convention. For my father, Susan and me, it was the thrill of a lifetime. I will never forget Skulan's kindnesses.

**JS: What was your relationship with Tom Skulan of FantaCo like?**

**GS:** Absolutely perfect! Perhaps it remains our finest issue ever, but without the participation of Tom Skulan, the anniversary issue would have been an ordinary issue. He was a gem!

WE BELONG DEAD
FRANKENSTEIN
ON
FILM
Revised
Edited by
Gary J. Svehla and Susan Svehla


ONE OF THE MANY BOOKS FROM MIDNIGHT MARQUEE PRESS.

**JS: What can you tell me about the FANEX conventions?**

**GS:** My wife Susan wanted, as her way of doing something special for me, to bring the pages of *Midnight Marquee* to life. Instead of horror film experts writing articles, we could finally meet one another socially as friends and share our knowledge and expertise at panel discussions. Instead of writing about our love of celebrity genre giants, we could bring stars such as John Agar, Ray Harryhausen, Roger Corman, Christopher Lee and hundreds more to Baltimore and show them our appreciation. FANEX was entirely Sue's concept and her legacy to horror film fandom. And she did it to bring the pages of my magazine to life.

**JS: How is *Midnight Marquee* produced today?**

**GS:** With all our business responsibilities, Susan always insists that I devote time to *Midnight Marquee* the magazine. It never was a moneymaker; as I said, the magazine was always a labor of love. We now produce the magazine once or twice a year, even though I wish I could publish it more frequently. We experimented with going digital, but most classic monster movie fans are old school and want to be able to hold, sniff, and display their monster magazines. We experimented with doing a totally all-color issue (interior and exterior) but sales did not justify the added expense. In other words, with fifty years of publishing upon us, we are still growing,

trying new things. As Bob Dylan said, he who is not busy being born is busy dying.

MIDNIGHT MARQUEE MONSTERS
Issue 60
Summer/Fall 1999
$6.00 U.S.A.
$7.00 Canada
David Manners; The Invisible Man; Malibou Lake;
Michael A. Hoey—Navy vs. the Night Monsters;
The Art of the Low-Budget Horror Film;
The Blair Witch Project

**JS: How has distribution changed throughout the years?**

**GS:** Distribution for fifty years has always caused the biggest headache and created the most problems for niche magazine publication. At first the independent distributors latched on to a good thing, but they suddenly stopped paying us or went belly up, sometimes overnight. Great companies such as Diamond, who supported us for decades, now require a higher minimum pre-order than a niche product can provide, so we are dropped after decades of working together. Websites, Facebook and having a presence on Amazon.com certainly help, but it has always been an uphill battle for the little guy to get noticed and survive.

**JS: How and when did Midnight Marquee Press start up?**

**GS:** We incorporated [Inc.] in 1995 when Sue suggested we expand our market by publishing trade paperbacks and not only magazines.

**JS: How do you go about selecting titles?**

**GS:** Susan and I suggest topics to our stable of professional writers and the ones that garner the most interest became published books. Just like any other publisher, most of our books result from authors approaching us to publish their book. We sometimes say no, but when we say yes, we put our heart and soul into each project. We are a totally open shop and encourage first-time authors to approach us.

**JS: What does production involve?**

**GS:** Today, every writer feels he or she can self-publish and they can cut out the middleman, the publisher. And their final product suffers as a result. When an author approaches us with their book, being fans, we know the subject matter. We help authors shape their books and suggest ways to improve an already good concept. When the book is submitted, we do a pre-edit as we gather up photos, posters, graphics, etc. Authors are encouraged to submit graphics for consideration as well. Then we lay out the manuscript. After the layout stage, the book goes to one of our professional editors, and they do the final edit. At this point, the book, laid out, goes back to the author for one final check, or to do the index.

RECORDED & INDEXED
DRAFT

When everyone is satisfied, the book goes to Create Space for digital manufacturing. After publication, we help the author promote the book. Besides having a well known website presence, we have a mailing list of 5,000 active names. And we have a presence on Amazon.com and many independent bookstores across the US. With Hemlock Books in the United Kingdom, we have a presence in Europe and beyond. But with any niche publication, the success or failure of any book depends in large part on the efforts of the author to promote his or her book.

**JS: Where do you think print media is headed?**

**GS:** Print media is dead. Well, to be honest, print media will become a niche product for people resistant to technological change. With the barrage of iPads, Kindles, Nooks and beyond, digital publishing is the wave of today, as well of the future. As I said, I wanted to take *Midnight Marquee* digital years ago but our customers would not have it. Print media will continue to fade away, slowly at first, then more rapidly, as e-publications become the latest wave. To me this new technology is exciting and fuels creativity. And that is always a good thing.

**JS: What's your take on internet fandom?**

**GS:** In the old days one reader would write a publisher a letter and that would take a week. It would take another week to respond. That's two weeks for one communication cycle. Today, on message boards or the internet, it takes minutes to deliver the same result. So, in one sense internet fandom is fantastic, making communications a keystroke away. However, this can also be a bad thing. People sometimes respond rapidly without thinking things through and they might come to regret the venom they spread. Sometimes immediate communication is not as effective as well thought out communication where people carefully pick and choose their words. Sometimes message boards become a boys' club meaning cliques form and we once again have an in and out group. When anyone among the in-group publishes, everyone pats the person on the back and gushes. If someone in the out-group publishes something just as worthy, he or she receives far less attention, let alone a pat on the back. It's as though the schoolyard playground has been transported to the internet.

COVER ART BY BILL NELSON.

But human nature is human nature and the habits of youth sometimes follow us into adulthood. But maintaining the fandom network via the internet is overall a wonderful thing.

**JS: The state of fandom today?**

**GS:** I wish I saw more fresh young blood in the hobby, but the state of fandom is the best it has ever been. It has never been easier to communicate with likeminded individuals via the internet, Twitter, Facebook, etc. In 2012 more horror movie magazines are being published than ever before. And this pertains only to print publications. When it comes to webzines, they are exploding upon the scene. Conventions are held practically every month. We have podcasts and blogs. For anyone interested in any type of niche hobby, it is happening now on the internet. Fandom has never had so many technological tools by which to share one's obsessions and passions. And while flame wars and petty attacks bring everyone down, such negativity appears to be the exception, not the rule. So I believe the state of fandom today is thriving. More power to fandom! Long may it continue to prosper.

# CHAPTER 3.5
# THE SZUREK ZONE
## AN INTERVIEW WITH FANZINE LEGEND DAVID SZUREK

*WEIRD CITY* NUMBER 2. ARTWORK BY JEFF SMITH.

**JOHN SZPUNAR: When were you born?**

**DAVID SZUREK:** In 1948. I'm sixty-three now.

**JS: You grew up in Detroit...**

**DS:** Yeah. When I was little, I lived on the west side. There were a lot of macho kids that belonged to street gangs. Some of the parents were employed and some weren't. My father worked in a factory. My mother was what you'd call a housewife. Later on, I lived in what became notorious part of Detroit called the Cass Corridor. That's when I was in my late teens. At that point, that neighborhood was kind of like the Midwest version of Haight-Ashbury.

**JS: Was your father supportive of your interests?**

**DS:** I guess he was supportive of what I was into, but he was not supportive of a kid basing his life around movies and reading. You were supposed to go out and play ball all the time.

**JS: I'd imagine that it would make you want to push the envelope a little further.**

**DS:** It probably did. At least when I got into my teens. And I was the world's youngest completist, at one time. I took to seeing films, even though I knew that I wasn't going to like them. It was strange. I started writing about them. When I was in high school, I started doing a fanzine called *Demons Unlimited*. That was originally for this monster club that I had formed in the neighborhood. After the first issue, I decided to advertise it in *Famous Monsters*—I wanted to make it into a regular magazine. I'd send it to whoever wanted to see a copy, as long as they paid. And the payment was only something like thirty-five cents.

**JS: What was your club called?**

**DS:** Monsters of Detroit.

**JS: [laughs] That's great! What was *Demons Unlimited* like?**

**DS:** A lot of the articles were actually reprinted (with my name on them) from *FM* [laughs]. It was mostly reviews and sometimes, just plain synopses, which really bored me a few years later. I know there were a couple of guys who put out fanzines that were nothing but synopses. And they bored the hell out of me, you know? No kind of content or review.

**JS: Were you aware of *Famous Monsters* from the start?**

**DS:** Yeah, but the funny thing is that *FM* came to Detroit a little later than it did everywhere else. I'd say the first issues hit Detroit in 1960. And actually, I saw three magazines before *FM*—*World Famous Creatures*, *Monsters and Things*, and *Monster Parade*. *Monsters and Things* and *Monster Parade* were published by the same guy. He never gave his name, he just called himself Dr. Headstone.

**JS: What did you think of those mags?**

**DS:** They were pretty bad. I recognized that as a kid.

**JS: Those magazines are very scarce these days. How hard was it to find them back then?**

**DS:** At that time, they were kind of limited to a few stores. Like the way some movies are limited to grindhouses, you know? It was the same way. There were a few stores that carried them, and a lot that didn't. Including *Famous Monsters*. In the beginning, they weren't distributed everywhere.

# The Szurek Zone

## An Interview with Fanzine Legend David Szurek

**JS: Do you remember the first horror film that you saw?**

**DS:** I'm not sure if it was *Them!* or *Creature from the Black Lagoon*. I went with my mother and she went to see something else. I know it was one of the two. You can't really tell by the release date, because everything was kept in reissue, until it hit television.

**JS: Was it a common thing for you to go out and see movies?**

**DS:** Yeah. Oh, yeah.

**JS: What do you remember about the theaters in Detroit at that time?**

**DS:** When I was a kid, there were at least two theaters in my neighborhood. I usually went to the Senate—that was within walking distance from home. And there was one called the Kramer. It was the first one to take what I consider the suburban fare. It played one movie at a time. It never had a double-bill or a triple-bill, even. It charged a little more and everything. So, I thought it was kind of poetic justice when, a few years later, it became one of the ultimate grindhouses in Detroit. They'd show a G, an R, and an X rated film, all on the same program. They didn't even list the films in the paper—they advertised themselves, with handbills. Later on, I walked about three miles to a theater called the Lincoln. Later, after I'd been around the country, I went back to see what had become of it. It's now one of the city's DHSS offices.

**JS: You've been involved in fandom for a very long time.**

**DS:** Since the sixties. Comic book, film, and science fiction fandom.

**JS: Who were your favorite science fiction writers as a kid?**

**DS:** At that time, I'd say Bradbury and Heinlein. Now, if there are any, I'd say it would be Harlan Ellison. But I don't really read that much any longer.

**JS: Did you ever get the chance to talk to any of those guys?**

**DS:** I met Harlan Ellison once. But that was before he was big. I think he had one or two stories published.

**JS: What kind of comic books were you reading back then?**

**DS:** Mostly superhero and horror comics. And I always thought that too much attention was paid to the ECs and not to the other horror comics. The ECs were the best, I have to admit, but it's like the others are almost ignored—things like *Chamber of Chills* and *Tomb of Terror*.

**JS: Did you ever think that the horror comics went too far?**

**DS:** No. Somehow I always knew that

RANDOM PAGES FROM "DETROIT GRINDHOUSE BLUES".

the comic books and movies were fictional. But one time, just after I saw *Them!*, there were all of these crickets outside of our house. They were chirping, and I remember thinking, "These are giant ants!"

**JS: Let's talk a little about the first Detroit Triple Fan Fair convention.**

**DS:** I was one of the originators of that—me and a guy named Bob Brosch, from Allen Park. It started out as just a gathering of fans. The next thing I knew, he wanted to rent a hotel and everything. I didn't really think it would go through, but it did. He had big ideas. I was sixteen years old. That was in 1964. We held it at the Tuller hotel. I don't even know if it exists any longer.

**JS: It's long gone. How did you go about organizing the convention?**

**DS:** Well, we contacted all these fans, and we contacted some people to be the guests—they never showed up [laughs]. We rented *Things to Come*, which was not often seen at the time. We also rented a *Flash Gordon* serial. Or was it a *Captain Marvel* serial? I don't remember—it was so long ago [laughs]. I know that eventually, the same convention showed both. Anyway, after the second convention, I wasn't really involved with it. I attended it, sometimes. One year I had a choice of attending that or something called Autoclave, which was one of those science fiction conventions. I ended up going to Autoclave instead. They were both on the same weekend. I don't know if there was intentional competition there or not.

**JS: How did you meet Bob Brosch?**

**DS:** In those days, there was a network going on. Whenever somebody had a letter in *FM* or something like that, all these people in the same area would look up their number in the phone book. You'd call them up and sit and talk for a while. That's how I met Bob. I had a letter in *FM*, and all of the sudden, I got a call from him.

**JS: It seems like the fan community was pretty big.**

**DS:** It was, at the time. At least in Detroit and in some cities like New York and Philadelphia.

**JS: Did you ever have anything besides a letter published in *Famous Monsters*?**

**DS:** No. It's a funny thing—I sold a review of *Curse of the Demon* to a thing called *Fantastic Monsters*. They paid me, but then they went out of business right before it would have been published.

# THE SZUREK ZONE
## AN INTERVIEW WITH FANZINE LEGEND DAVID SZUREK

**JS: Wasn't Ron Haydock involved with *Fantastic Monsters*?**

**DS:** Yeah. *Fantastic Monsters* was him, Paul Blaisdell, and Jim Harmon. I get the impression that they were a lot like the Detroit fandom guys, except somebody had enough money to put out their magazine professionally. And they called it *Fantastic Monsters of the Films*. I mean, how close to *Famous Monsters of Filmland* can you get [laughs]? But it was a halfway decent magazine. I wouldn't call it great, but they were better than some of the others that came out.

**JS: I meant to ask you this earlier—were you active in any journalism programs in school?**

**DS:** I wrote for the school paper for a while, but I never got anything printed. The principal would inspect it before it could go out. I know that's not supposed to happen, but that's the way they did it at my school. And after all, that was in the early sixties, and he was a real super-conservative. I was writing articles about ending the war and legalizing marijuana. He decided that he didn't want to see any of that in the paper.

THE SZUREK ZONE!

A zone unknown to man. Dave's waiting for you, right around the corner, next to the Dairy Queen.

"Entertaining! Programmer to round out triple bills!"
-Szurek Zone
"Suspense! Sex! Mayhem! Unusually Erotic!
-Variety
"Scary as Hell"
—Flick

**JS: It sounds like you were a rebellious kid.**

**DS:** Well, the so-called counterculture was beginning to happen. There had been no social progress of any kind for most of my life. I just figured that I'd become… well, basically a weirdo. I really identified with the Beat culture. I fantasized about that a lot, but I was still in high school. Mostly, what we did was go out and smoke dope.

**JS: What gave you the drive to self publish?**

**DS:** It was a creative drive, I guess. I don't really know where it comes from. It's just something that's built into you. As I mentioned before, I did *Demons Unlimited* when I was a kid, and more recently *Weird City* and *Weirdness Before Midnight*. Actually, *Weirdness Before Midnight* was about the same magazine as *Weird City*. I hadn't done an issue for about two or three years, so I decided to change the name. Both of them were mostly written by me and they were pretty general—I wrote about whatever I felt like writing about. The mainstay was film, but there would be other articles about my personal experiences.

**JS: Your taste in genre films seems to be all over the place.**

**DS:** Well, I eventually dropped the

Toho and Santo films, but my interest in films didn't change much over the years. The first director I was interested in was Corman, but there were directors that I liked a lot better later on.

**JS: Such as?**

**DS:** Romero, Larry Cohen, and Mario Bava. But I still can't get into some of those other Italian directors like Dario Argento. I only really liked a couple of his pictures—*Suspiria* and *Deep Red*. I thought the other ones were very overrated.

**JS: I think *Suspiria* and *Deep Red* are two of his more lucid pictures... if you can even use the word lucid and Argento in the same sentence.**

**DS:** He's too much into style and not enough into story.

**JS: What was it about Mario Bava that grabbed you?**

**DS:** The cultivation of atmosphere. And Larry Cohen always seemed to make his stories seem at least halfway plausible. Romero did the same thing. I really liked the atmosphere of *Night of the Living Dead*. When I first saw that, it hardly had any advance publicity, or anything. When I went to see it and saw the name Romero, I figured that it was a foreign picture. And of course, I didn't know anything about it. It was the lower half of a double-bill, and it had what I considered one of the worst posters that I'd ever seen at the time. I went in, and it broke all of the clichés.

**JS: Where did you see it at?**

**DS:** At the Fox Theater in Detroit. It was a real obscurity and an unknown film at the time.

**JS: [laughs] The Fox has since been restored and it blows my mind to think that *Night of the Living Dead***

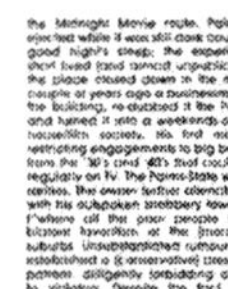

**once played there on a double-bill!**

**DS:** It was a big old grindhouse. They mostly played triple-bills [laughs]! When it closed down, the Adams Theater kind of took its place. You know the Adams, don't you?

**JS: Yeah. It closed in the late eighties. You know, I have to say that I really loved your article about the old Detroit movie houses in *Magick Theatre* number seven. "Detroit Grindhouse Blues" is one of the only documents of that era that I've come across.**

**DS:** The theaters in Detroit tended to almost be like the ones in New York. They were showing just about everything—even things that most people thought were direct-to-video.

**JS: You're very well known in the fanzine world. You've been published in just about everything.**

**DS:** Yeah. It wasn't done by design or anything [laughs]. It just sort of happened.

**JS: I remember reading your stuff in things like *Temple of Schlock*, *Subhuman*, and *Wet Paint*. You seemed to explode from there. Were you on some kind of crazy mission to appear in every zine known to man?**

**DS:** Yeah [laughs]. But not until I'd seen them first. I was writing just about every day, for a while.

**JS: It also seemed like you were reading everything. Even if you didn't contribute to a zine, you always seemed to have a letter published in the letters section.**

**DS:** Yeah, I think I was reading everything. And for a little while, I didn't keep the same address for very long. I'd just write to people, and they really didn't know if I was writing to them form a mailing address or a park bench!

**JS: This is kind of a weird question, but did you ever encounter any peer-backlash for being involved in fandom when you were growing up?**

**DS:** I didn't encounter that so much. I did encounter some people in fandom that were kind of down on people who weren't. But there were some people who would get down on anybody who was obsessed with anything, you know? And there were people who were down on anybody who had any sort of intellect. But those were guys who were more like my father. They were playing sports all the time, and all of that. But the majority just kind of took it as, "You have your interests and I have mine." It was a coexistence sort of thing.

**JS: When I was growing up, I was sort of an outsider.**

**DS:** I ended up having two kinds of people that I'd hang out with. There were the "mundanes" (as we called them) and the people more like me. I got along with both.

**JS: Another thing about my childhood—when I was growing up, *Fangoria* was sort of the "new" *Famous Monsters*. What did you think of *Fango*?**

**DS:** Well, it changed the definition of what horror was. They made little

# DETROIT GRINDHOUSE BLUES

By Dave Szurek

claims that were certainly their own to make them sound like they were the general attitude. They were always calling certain movies cult films. There was never a *Last House on the Left* cult until they started to talk about it. Craven's original reputation was based more on *The Hills Have Eyes* than on *Last House*. And *Last House on the Left* was a movie that a lot of people ignored before *Fangoria* started talking about it. I didn't think it was a very entertaining movie at all. I didn't even like it when I finally saw it. It was one of those movies that you see and sort of forget.

**JS: That's an interesting take on things. What other films (and cults) rubbed you the same way?**

**DS:** Well, there's the cult thing about Andy Milligan. But I kind of *like* Andy Milligan's movies.

**JS: So do I.**

**DS:** They have a sense of enthusiasm to them. But I assume a lot when I think that most pictures have some kind of system of enthusiasm to them. Otherwise, they wouldn't even exist! Some people express it better than others.

**JS: Milligan is an interesting case. In a way, I think it goes back to the outsider thing. The fact that his films actually played in theaters is amazing to me. I'm really glad that he got some recognition. Now that we're talking about cult films, what was your take on Ed Wood?**

**DS:** Off and on. At least there was a sense that he liked what he was

ticipated argument, just because **most** fans are relatively affluent, that doesn't mean that **all** are. There are potential fans who were easily discouraged from participation only because they lacked the money. Unfortunately, we live in a material world, but for God's sake, why make it any more that way than it already is? There's also an attitude — it's the meat of the Reagan administration — which pretends that the less affluent don't even exist; and by its very nature, that's even **more** offensive than the overt brand of economical bigotry. **(c)** It certainly does nothing to encourage experimentation by newcomers — and **everybody** started out as a newcomer. **(d)** It inadvertantly perverts the publishing brotherhood into a rivalry, transforms it into an unhealthy form of competition as readers are literally forced into picking and choosing the two or three zines they like best. The fourth may also be a worthy product, but it is financially crowded out, and after some time may be forced to fold entirely due either to unreasonable loss of revenue or lack of readership, or both.

On a personal level, I'd been attracted to **MkT** for quite a while, but the truth of the matter is that I **did** cop a relatively negative attitude and was very turned off at the stipend. **(Which means you don't buy anyone's magazine — Ed.)** This inspired

PART OF A LETTER FROM DAVID SZUREK IN *MAGICK THEATRE* NUMBER 7.

**DAVE SZUREK**

# THE SZUREK ZONE

## AN INTERVIEW WITH FANZINE LEGEND DAVID SZUREK

Views and reviews by the one and only DAVE SZUREK

doing, for more than the money. Which is the opposite of Herschell Gordon Lewis and his partner Dave Friedman. They both admitted that they were basically making films for money.

**JS: I've always had a soft spot in my heart for H.G. Lewis.**

**DS:** Actually, I did like *Two Thousand Maniacs*. I didn't like the other ones so much.

**JS: Why do you think that was?**

**DS:** There seemed to be a little bit more of the same thing that I was talking about with Milligan. There was an enthusiasm behind it. It didn't even seem like his other movies. And I kind of liked *The Wizard of Gore*, despite the fact that it had one of the dumbest titles I'd ever heard in my life [laughs].

**JS: What did you think of Ted V. Mikels?**

**DS:** I thought he had a sense of enthusiasm, too. But I didn't think that *The Astro-Zombies* had much of it. And the sequel to it certainly didn't. That was just boring.

**JS: When I was in college, I worked with a guy who saw *The Corpse Grinders* when it first played in Detroit. He told me that he was pretty disappointed with the thing. What's the expression? All sizzle, no steak? I don't know if I'm some kind of idiot, but I really enjoyed it when I finally saw it.**

**DS:** I did, too [laughs]!

**JS: He told me that he walked into the theater and there was a big display. You know the drill—"Do you know what this is? This is a corpse grinding machine!"**

**DS:** Well, *The Corpse Grinders* only showed at the things that they called grindhouses, anyway! And that was one of those films that didn't get much publicity, except in the fanzines. A lot of those films didn't have much going for them, other than the camp element. And some of them didn't even have that!

**JS: OK, here's the final question: Are you aware of just how important your writing was to the zine scene?**

**DS:** Well, I don't know if it was important or not. There were a lot of others from that era. Your friend Greg Goodsell is one of them. He was in everything. And then, there was Jeff Smith from *Wet Paint* and Cecil Doyle from *Subhuman*. There was Kris Gilpin. There was Brian Johnson. He did a zine called *They Won't Stay Dead*. There were a lot of guys, and they were writing about everything. It wasn't just me...

SZUREK ZONE LOGO DESIGNED BY THE EVIL TWIN.

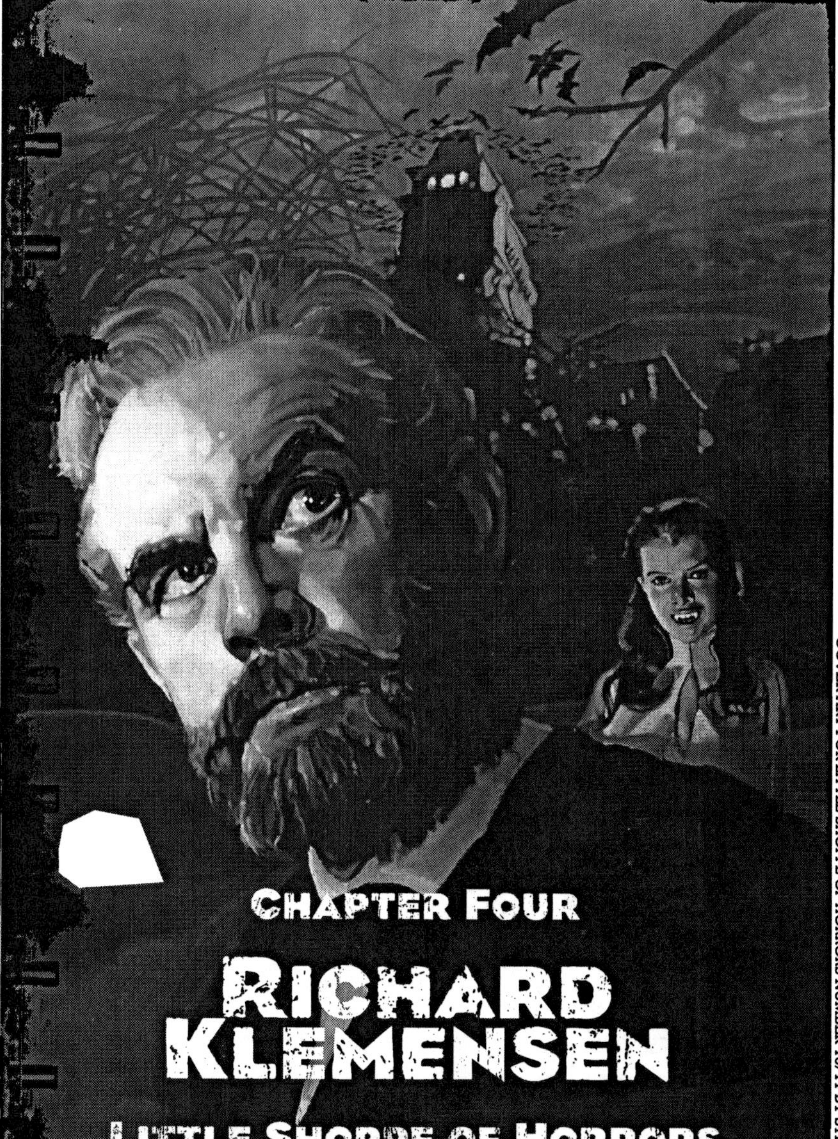


COVER ART FOR *LITTLE SHOPPE OF HORRORS* NUMBER 10/11 BY STEVE KARCHIN.

# Richard Klemensen

## Little Shoppe of Horrors

RECORDED & INDEXED

DRAFT

The world would be a considerably duller place without the grace of *Little Shoppe of Horrors*, for which the epithet "old school" might well have been invented. The stalwart Hammer films zine, edited and published by Richard Klemensen, and expanded to other reaches of British fantasy cinema, has been around forever. Well, since the seventies, anyway, which is much the same thing.

The format has barely changed over the years, with perhaps the exception that the quality of contributor artwork is now nothing short of astonishing.

There's not an awful lot I feel I can add to the story that follows. So I venture instead a meeting with a friend of mine called Graeme Cuthbert, who has confessed more than once to a tenuous connection with *Little Shoppe of Horrors*. As a British teenage Hammer fan in the early 1980s, Graeme attended the proto Hammer film conventions in London, organised by Hammer International. Richard Klemensen had also been in attendance at the first of these, and possibly the others, too. Richard writes about his experience in the debut issue of his scarce side project, the *Hammer Journal* (abandoned due to pressure from the studio, concerned that it might be construed as an official vessel for Hammer).

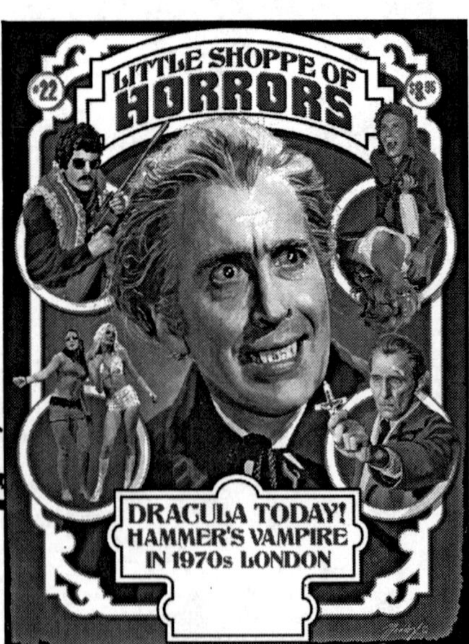

Little SHOPPE of HORRORS
AMICUS: "TWO'S A COMPANY"


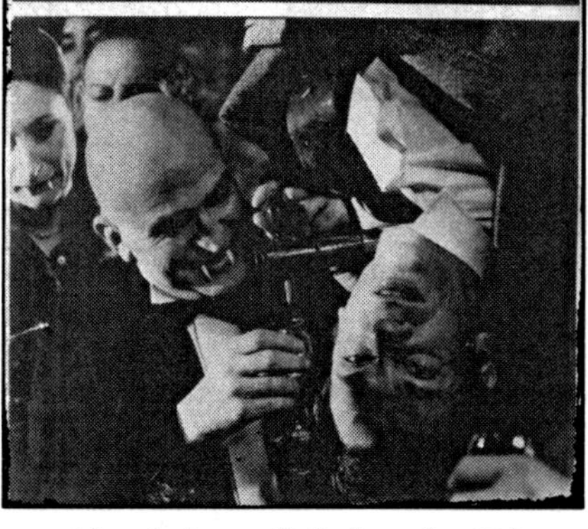

Recalling the Hammer movies screened at the convention and the personalities in attendance (Roy Ashton, Michael Ripper, Ralph Bates and Ingrid Pitt among them), Graeme says that the studio already appeared relegated to history, despite new inroads into television at the time.

In *Little Shoppe of Horrors* number 7 (December 1982), he has a photo published. It shows Oakley Court, the old manor house next to Bray studios as featured in many Hammer films. He doesn't recall any actual correspondence with Richard Klemensen. But rather he sent the photo unsolicited as a fan. This was followed likewise by a bunch of photographs taken in the Palladium Cellars; a relatively short lived London attraction with famous movie characters rendered as wax animatronics. The exhibition had a section with Hammer monsters, including Oliver Reed as a werewolf who growled and rattled his cage. Alas, these photographs never reached their intended destination and are lost.

What goes around, comes around. Today Graeme works in post production for a company called Deluxe that restores movies for release on blu-ray—among them some of the Hammer classics. His office on Wardour Street is located opposite what was once Hammer House, the old Hammer films office. I imagine Graeme's story is typical of *Little Shoppe of Horrors*.

The following interview with Richard Klemensen was conducted by email in March 2011.

---

**DAVID KEREKES: How did *Little Shoppe of Horrors* come about?**

**RICHARD KLEMENSEN:** I was always a fan of horror and science fiction movies, and always had a little thing for self publishing (my first attempt was a humor magazine done during the ninth grade—not very funny though—called *Fleabit*). But my interest in the films, and Hammer in particular, came together during a trip to the drive-in theater in 1969 (after just recovering from a Summer bout of "mono") to see *The Valley*

RECORDED & INDEXED

DRAFT

COVER ART BY JEFF PRESTON.

LITTLE SHOPPE OF HORRORS

NO. 14

$7.

THE BRIDES OF DRACULA

Hammer's Greatest Horror

LITTLE SHOPPE OF HORRORS
NUMBER 3
$1.50
THE LEGEND OF THE 7 GOLDEN VAMPIRES (HAMMER-SHAW BROS. 1973)


*Of Gwangi*, *Godzilla Vs. The Thing* and Hammer's *Dracula Has Risen From The Grave*. I was knocked out by it, rushed home very early in the morning—even though I had to get up to go to work in a few hours—and dug out my old copies of *Famous Monsters of Filmland* and *Castle of Frankenstein*.

Writing off for back issues of those prozines, I also discovered amateur titles like *Photon* and *Gore Creatures* listed. And ordered copies of those, too. Much more than the professional mags, the fanzines really struck a chord with me. I soon realized I would like to publish a similar magazine. But finishing my first four years of college, in May 1970, I immediately received my draft notice. The Vietnam war was going on, and all of us who were able were being taken. My two best friends saw serious combat, but I never left the States, being stationed in Richmond, Virginia my whole tour.

On discharge in January 1972, I was back in college and also started laying the groundwork for my own fanzine (early on I took the name of *Little Shoppe of Horrors*, after the Roger Corman horror comedy). I had stayed in contact with other publishers like Gary Svehla of *Gore Creatures* (soon to be *Midnight Marquee*) and had made a number of friends in England. Mainly Gary Parfitt (still a big time collector) and the late writer, Alan Dodd. That first issue in Spring 1972 had a definite British tinge to it.

Through the first three issues, it was apparent that while striving to be a general interest horror film zine, my interests really were heavily into the British horror films. So after my massive history of Hammer in 1978 (Hammer producer, Anthony Hinds, called it the best thing ever done on Hammer), I decided that if I was going to keep doing this, the emphasis would be totally Hammer. Even now, although we have expanded into other areas of British horror—Amicus, *The Blood On Satan's Claw*, etc—Hammer remains the ultimate focus of *Little Shoppe of Horrors*.

**DK: How were those early issues were put together, in terms of editorial content, as well as the physical layout and production?**

**RK:** As today, sometimes the contents would be a combination of

# Richard Klemensen

## Little Shoppe of Horrors

RECORDED & INDEXED
DRAFT

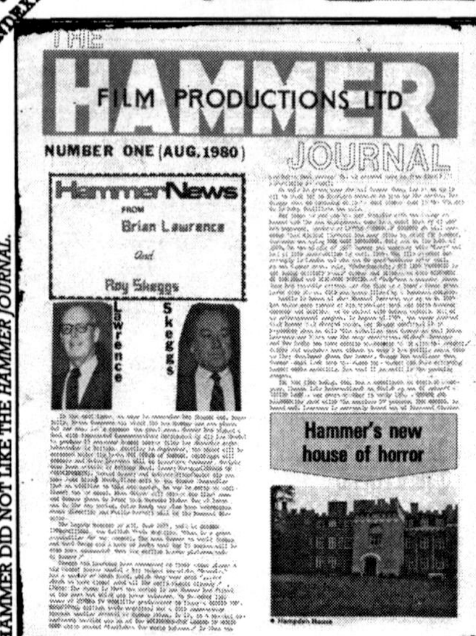
THE HAMMER FILM PRODUCTIONS LTD JOURNAL

NUMBER ONE (AUG.1980)

HammerNews
FROM
Brian Lawrence
and
Roy Skeggs

Lawrence
Skeggs

Hammer's new house of horror

Hampden House

HAMMER DID NOT LIKE THE *HAMMER JOURNAL.*

dumb luck and someone approaching me with an idea. Those first three issues were individual pages printed by a small firm (actually their house) in Janeville, Iowa (near my home of the time in Waterloo, Iowa) by two crippled brothers. Another smaller printer would do the page photos, and then I'd type the text working around those photos (I typed everything on an electric typewriter, which is why the joke is still around how I would do hand corrections to the text rather than start from scratch again! Even then, the issues tended to be huge in the sense of page count). My mother and I would spread the pages around my bed at home—I was still in college and living at home to save money—and together, we'd sort them by hand. As *Little Shoppe of Horrors* number 3 was 104 pages and by then we were up to over 1,000 copies, it was a monumental amount of *boring* work.

Between issue numbers 3 and 4, I got married for the first time, so there was a four year gap in issues—something until very recently that happened quite often. Divorces, moves, job losses. All would put paid to an issue for a number of years. With number 4, I decided to go all out—color cover, professional typesetting, slick enamel paper. And with the help of many friends in England—especially Susan and Colin Cowie—I put together what is still considered the Bible of Hammer magazines, *Little Shoppe of Horrors* 4. From that, for one issue, I thought I would do a four time a year Hammer newsletter called the *Hammer Journal*, but a tussle with the Hammer owners of the time made me decide to go back to *Little Shoppe of Horrors*.

Up to issue number 8, each issue tended to be a hodgepodge of articles and interviews. With number 8, I decided to focus on one particular film or group of films (but not excluding other features or interviews). In this case, in 1984, we did the Karnstein trilogy. And we've had a central focus on all issues since then. I think I've been the one who has come up with the subject matter idea for each issue, although once I get an idea, it seems like related articles and interviews just seem to materialize once I get out the word to our contributors. For example, in

XERO
FEROX

our upcoming *Little Shoppe of Horrors* number 26, I decided to go with *Hands Of The Ripper*, because (1) it is an extremely good film and (2) there was research materials available to say something new. No need to just rehash the same stuff over and over. From there, I was able to find someone to interview Angharad Rees and Peter Sasdy. David Taylor had actually seen the uncut film in the Phillipines and we had an article on the "Ripper cuts." It seems to have worked out that way for all the issues.

LITTLE SHOPPE OF
HORRORS
ROMAN POLANSKI REMEMBERS THE MAKING OF
DANCE OF THE VAMPIRES AKA
THE FEARLESS VAMPIRE KILLERS

In the case of our Amicus issue, where we turned over a complete mag to what is really a book-length feature, I had been aware of Phil Nutman's eighties research into Amicus, and always reminded him that the article had a welcome home in *Little Shoppe of Horrors* if he ever decided he wanted it published. I think that issue is wonderful and maybe the best thing we have ever done.

Our Terence Fisher tribute issue was a personal goal for me. Of all the film people in the world, the only one I ever *really* wanted to meet was Fisher. For many years, a bio of Fisher by Alan Frank has been mooted. So far it has not appeared, and I wanted to give tribute to this great director while people who remembered him, and worked with him, were still around. Fisher's daughter thought the issue was great,

LITTLE SHOPPE OF
HORRORS
DANIEL RADCLIFFE on
THE WOMAN IN BLACK
HAMMER'S NEW GOTHIC HORROR

RECORDED & INDEXED
DRAFT

LITTLE SHOPPE OF HORRORS
NUMBER TWO (JULY 1981) - formerly "THE HAMMER JOURNAL"
(LSoH 6)
TERENCE FISHER 1904-1980
"ONE OF A KIND"

which was the ultimate compliment.

It has gone where the two daughters, and brother, of Alan Gibson of the modern day Hammer *Dracula* films, helped us put that together. Or that John Gilling had been interviewed in depth by Gilbert Verschooten and I was finally able to convince him to let us publish the interview in our *Plague Of The Zombies/The Reptile* issue. Anyway, you get the idea.

Now, with the wonders of the computer age, where it used to take me two- three- four years, using snail mail and back and forth letters and telephone calls to put one issue together, we can put out two in one year's email attachments. InDesign computer programs. The improvements sometimes seem like dreams.

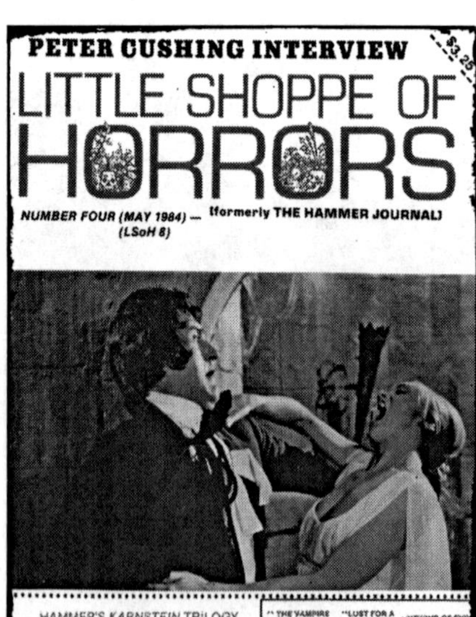
PETER CUSHING INTERVIEW
$3.25
LITTLE SHOPPE OF HORRORS
NUMBER FOUR (MAY 1984) — (formerly THE HAMMER JOURNAL)
(LSoH 8)
HAMMER'S KARNSTEIN TRILOGY
"THE VAMPIRE LOVERS"
"LUST FOR A VAMPIRE"

**DK: What was the fan base for Hammer and horror films like back in the early days and how does it differ now?**

RK: There was a good fan base out there in 1972 when I started. The problem always being how did one reach them? In those days, everything was word of mouth, reviews in other related fanzines and putting little ads in them. So things grew slowly.

With the advent of distributors who would get you into related shops, and comic book stores, sales really blossomed. The 1990s were the golden

A DINNER FOR HAMMER CHIEF, MICHAEL CARRERAS, IN APRIL 1994. [L–R:] PRODUCER KENNETH HYMAN, HAMMER BUSINESS MANAGER BRIAN LAWRENCE, RICHARD KLEMENSEN, HAMMER PRODUCER ANTHONY HINDS AND MICHAEL CARRERAS. CARRERAS WOULD DIE OF CANCER TWO WEEKS LATER.

years of distribution where you could move thousands of copies. But the distributors, one by one, fell away and Diamond Comics Distributors took over the market. Two years ago, they had a bloodletting where they dropped hundreds of magazines and comics, *Little Shoppe of Horrors* included. What was ironic is the year before they had voted *Little Shoppe of Horrors* one of the ten best media magazines of that year. But the hard dollars and cents meant we just didn't sell enough copies.

The audience for classic horror films is much older now, and shrinking rather than growing. What makes it possible for a magazine like *Little Shoppe of Horrors* to survive is the internet. There are still a few shops in the UK and the States that give us presence, but we are mainly sold online. My son set up a website for me with issue number 16 in 2004 and it has been the godsend to keep *Little Shoppe of Horrors* going.

We were young and full of enthusiasm in the seventies. Access to the research and info just wasn't there, but we were eager to find it. Now in this digital age, everything is at your fingertips. But I never see *Little Shoppe of Horrors* as a digital online mag. We'll live and die as a real magazine. From that simple one-page-at-a-time rag of 1972 to the slick pages now, with covers by some of fandom's greatest artists. Quite a journey.

This could be you! Send us your B & W makeup photo and list of materials used. If we print it, you win a coupon worth 40% DISCOUNT on your next Blood Boutique order!

*FANGORIA*'S BLOOD BOUTIQUE AD WITH UNCLE BOB MARTIN.

# Chapter Five
# Uncle Bob Martin
## Enter Fangoria

Many of the people interviewed in this book remember well the first time they saw an issue of *Fangoria*. I certainly remember mine.

There was a little store called Beacon Drugs that my mother used to shop at. It was the usual small town America kind of place—part stationary store, part candy store, part druggist, and part gifts and trinkets. The only thing missing was the soda counter. My brother and I were born too late for that.

But the place had a magazine stand, and that's where we would gravitate to whenever our mother wasn't paying attention. I was always on the lookout for the latest issue of *Mad*. Sometimes they'd have some old issues lying around, and sometimes I'd spot a few *Mad* paperbacks that I desperately needed to complete my collection. My mother had no problem with *Mad*, but she did have a problem with *Fangoria*.

I can remember it, as clear as day. My brother and I had gotten loose once again, and we made a break for the newsstand. Before long, something caught our eyes. My brother made a grab for it first.

"What is that?" I asked, while trying to wrench the thing from his hands.

My brother is two years younger than me, and I snickered as he mispronounced the title.

"Fang-or-a."

We stood there underneath the fluorescent lights, paging through the magazine, laughing and gasping in amazement. I knew right then that I wanted to take "Fang-or-a" home with me. Unfortunately, my mother had other plans.

In an instant, she had tracked us down and she put the first issue of *Fangoria* that I ever laid eyes on back on the shelf. At that moment, I made a pact with myself. I was going to read this magazine one day. I didn't know what it was, but I was going to find it, buy it, read it, and collect it. And as the years went on, I did.

*Fangoria* became a staple of my youthful reading and I savored every issue that I was able to sneak into my house. The mag was subversive, gory as shit, and it was mine.

Many of the zine editors and writers interviewed in this book cite *Fangoria* as a major influence, and there's no question as to why—the magazine made a giant ripple throughout the mainstream press that was all but impossible to ignore. If Uncle Forry was the voice of his generation, *Fango*'s first editor, Bob Martin was surely the voice of mine.

So, gather 'round, kids. Here he is—our one and only Uncle Bob Martin. Make sure to dim the lights for his arrival. And make sure to leave your bedroom window halfway open. No telling what kind of guests might come a knocking in the night.

And, oh yeah...

Keep yer eyeballs peeled for your mothers...

# Uncle Bob Martin

## Enter Fangoria

The following interview was conducted via telephone, April 25, 2012.

**BOB MARTIN:** To start with, can I just ramble for a little bit about the subject?
**JOHN SZPUNAR: Sure.**
**BM:** OK. At the time that *Fangoria* started, New York had a lot of stuff going on. There was Michael Weldon's *Psychotronic*. There was Bill Landis and his rather notorious *Sleazoid Express*. And there was Rick Sullivan's *Gore Gazette*. As far as I could tell, everything else was sort of in the shadow of those three guys. They were the giants of the zines, as far as I was concerned. And, I think all three of them started around the same time as *Fangoria*. I don't know to what extent *Fangoria* encouraged them, or to what extent *Fangoria* was a product of them. I do know that I was looking at what they were doing. And, to some extent, I was copying my approach from them, especially Michael Weldon.
**JS: Did you know Michael back then?**
**BM:** Yes. He was a really good friend. When I broke up with the girl I was supposed to marry, Michael gave me his apartment for a while. He was out of town. You're aware that he's now a DJ, right?
**JS: Yeah.**
**BM:** What a collection of records the man had! Absolutely magnificent. I was there for maybe two or three weeks, and I spent the whole time filling up tapes with stuff from his collection. But anyway, at the time we met, we were still pretty much kids, and he was a great influence. He had scrapbooks that were filled with things that he had cut out (and organized) from magazines like *Famous Monsters* and *Castle of Frankenstein*. Has anyone talked to you about Ann Magnuson yet?
**JS: Not yet.**
**BM:** She used to have a counterculture salon on St. Mark's Place. And once a week, the Monster Movie Club was held at her space.
**JS: I've heard of that. They screened horror movies, right?**
**BM:** Yes. It was run by Tom Scully and Susan Hannaford (who was later an actress, herself). I think Rick Sullivan was somewhat involved in their screenings. Michael used to attend them, Frank Henenlotter was frequently there, and Bill Landis was part of that circle, too. There was this whole off-the-page, real-world warm-body culture that was going on. It was a real sausage fest, of course [laughs]. Girls weren't into it. But, nevertheless, it was very influential to *Fangoria*. There were a lot of guys involved, either directly or tangentially, who contributed to the whole cultural stream. Anybody who had an opinion could say something, and the next thing you knew, it might be repeated in the fanzines or in *Fangoria*. Those get-togethers gave things a life that couldn't be reproduced today.

**JS: Why do you think that is?**

**BM:** Well, there's no such scene anymore. And, I don't know if a scene like that could happen again today, because it's so much easier to turn on the computer. But anyway, let's get into your questions.

**JS: OK. First of all, I'd like to get an idea about what the years leading up to the Monster Movie Club scene and *Fangoria* were like.**

**BM:** Sure. When I was a teenager, I left home. I was an extremely sheltered kid. I basically had to leave home, in order to become unsheltered. But, when I was at home, I read a lot and didn't feel comfortable around a lot of people. I kept to myself—I used to think that I'd maybe become a priest. But, I lost religion hard at around eleven or twelve. My father died when I was twelve and that didn't encourage me to become religious. I guess I should really concentrate on my high school years, because that's where most of the readership of *Fangoria* was at.

**JS: Sure. Let's get into that...**

**BM:** Well, my high school years were very bitter. Absolutely awful. When my father was alive, he used to volunteer for transfers within the corporation he worked for.

**JS: Where did he work?**

**BM:** He worked for Sears. When he transferred, he would go to a new store to break in the new team. That meant that he would get some quick advancement within the company. He would constantly volunteer for these new positions and we would move every couple of years. So, I didn't really develop relationships. I was always the new kid. And the habit of always being the new kid kind of cures you of trying to make attachments to other people—I'm the new kid and I'm going to be the new kid again, someplace else. Why bother? But, I had books that I could carry with me to the next location. I was an incredibly voracious reader of *everything*.

**JS: You mentioned that you lost faith in religion.**

**BM:** I became an enthusiastic agnostic—I wasn't an atheist, but I took up doubt rather anxiously. I also became very politically orientated. This was just after the civil rights years—it was right around the time that the

RECORDED & INDEXED

DRAFT

UNCLE BOB IN THE CLUTCHES OF TOM SAVINI.

'DAY OF THE DEAD' • 'HOUSE ON HAUNTED HILL'

FANGORIA

K49129 #43 DGS UK £1.95

$2.95 U.S./$3.50 CANADA

Toxic Monster Makeup!

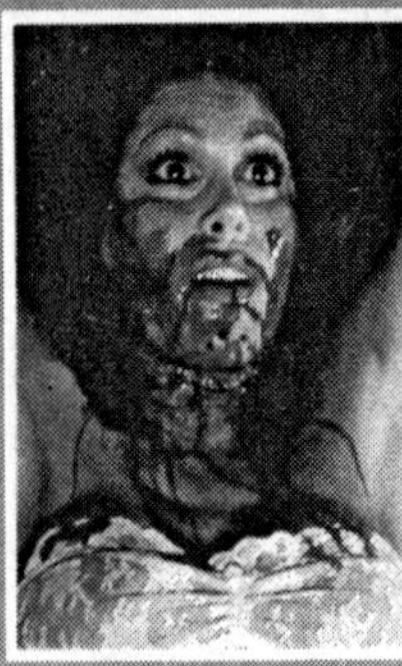

Mike "Mannix" Connors vs. Slasher
TOO SCARED TO SCREAM

New Stephen King Movie!
CAT'S EYE

On the Set: I Was a Zombie in
'DAY OF THE DEAD'!

Makeup Man
Tom Savini and
a Zombie Editor

"SCREAM GREATS"
PULL-OUT POSTER #18
'CREEPSHOW'

Kennedys and King were killed. That hit me emotionally, and I became a political cynic. I was very anti Vietnam. I wasn't at the draft age, but I knew that we had people out there, and that the war was slowly being escalated.

I worked for LBJ's reelection. Even though I was only twelve or thirteen, I went out canvassing and shit. And when Johnson turned out to be booster of the war, I was very disappointed. I became very cynical about that.

**JS: A minute or so ago, you said that you moved away from home at an early age. What led up to that?**

**BM:** One evening when I was sixteen, I told my mother that I'd be staying late after school to take an aptitude test. It was being given by the armed forces. I just wanted to take the test to find out something about my aptitude—I didn't know what I was going to do as an adult, and I was worried about it. My mother thought that it was a step toward winding up in the armed forces, and she forbade me to do it. So, I took the train from Queens to the lower east side of Manhattan. I went to this apartment building that had a sign saying, "Vacancy. See superintendant." A big fat black guy answered the door, and said, "What do you want?" I said, "I'm looking for an apartment." He said, "You got money?" I said, "I have eighty dollars," which was true. He laughed at me, and then he said, "Are you prejudiced?" I told him no, and he said, "You can stay here for a while." For the following three months, I lived with Bobby, a black guy who happened to be a marijuana dealer and the superintendent of four buildings. He put me up in a vacant apartment.

**JS: What was that scene like?**

**BM:** It was pretty weird. For about three months, I had no communication whatsoever with the white world. I basically spent all my time with the fat guy. People called him Big Bobby because his cousin, Little Bobby, also lived there. He had a good friend who everybody called Spanish Bobby. I became White Bobby [laughs]. Now, Big Bobby forbade me to have any reefer. He said, "That white boy will go crazy and kill us all in our sleep!" So, I was forbidden to have any, but Little Bobby would pass

RECORDED & INDEXED

DRAFT

me the J, anyway. After about a month, it was broken to Bobby that I'd been smoking and that I hadn't killed anyone, so he said, "OK." So, basically, that was my introduction to the New York underground.

**JS: Where did you go from there?**

**BM:** I ended up running into a guy in the Village who had been as much of a friend as I'd ever had in high school. His name was Terry, and he had moved into a one-room apartment on MacDougal Street in Greenwich Village with his girlfriend. And they were running out of money. I had a little bit of money, on account of having stolen some drugs. I won't go into detail about that, because it's not a story to be admired. But it was something that I had done. I was selling the drugs off, bit by bit. Eventually, I got ripped off for the vast majority of them. But for a little while, I had a little money and I was able to cover the rent. I wound up living on MacDougal Street in the Summer of 1966. That was my heyday as a hippy—that year and the next. I was in San Francisco for the Summer of love in '67, which was another weird trip. So, those were my hippy years, which had nothing at all to do with eventually finding out how to make a living [laughs].

**JS: What kind of a job did you end up getting?**

**BM:** I got a couple of jobs in the publishing industry. They were boring office jobs that I do not wish on anybody. And when I was writing for *Fangoria*, I would think about the fact that my readers were going to have to grow up, get a job, and be slaves to the nine to five for most of their lives. I tried to encourage them to find some other way to live. Whether it's making movies or making music, or whatever, there's got to be something that you can do to avoid the nine to five.

**JS: How did *you* get out of the grind?**

**BM:** I got so fed up with things that I took a shittier job (as far as pay goes) as a clerk in a little occult bookstore on Broadway.

**JS: What was the store called?**

**BM:** Samuel Weiser. It was an interesting shop that specialized in the kind of books that most bookstores didn't carry. Stuff on astrology, yoga, Buddhism, what have you. It had a very interesting clientele. Patti Smith was always in there, buying flying saucer books and the like. Todd Rundgren was a regular customer. I sold Kareem Abdul-Jabbar a Koran. Anyway, that's the kind of place it was, and that was the kind of crowd that we catered to. And it was a very interesting job for me because while I was there, I also explored my spiritual side a bit. I became somewhat involved in a workshop that involved the teachings of a Russian mystic named G.I. Gurdjieff. And through that, I came into touch with some people who were rather successful with writing. One of them was Henry Beard.

**JS: From *National Lampoon*?**

**BM:** Yeah. The other was Tony Hiss. His father was the famously imprisoned Alger Hiss—he was accused of trading our secrets to the communists by Nixon. Anyway, Tony and Henry had a writer's workshop that I participated in, and I got a lot of encouragement from both of them. And, I got my first writing job from someone who was in the same group. Her name was Melissa Lande. Her family owned a magazine, and she was working for the family company.

**JS: What was the company called?**

**BM:** North American Publishing. One of their organs was called *Marketing Bestsellers*. It was about newsstand sales—paperback books and magazines. It was basically a trade magazine that had capsule reviews of new paperback books, outlines on new magazines, etc. My very first writing job was writing something like fifty reviews of paperback books each and every month. While I was doing that, I was also reading manuscripts for Dell Books, which was a paperback imprint. They're probably better known as Delacorte now. I read the manuscripts, and wrote reports on whether or not I thought Dell should reprint them in paperback. I don't why they thought I would know, but there you go. And through that, I also wound up writing paperback copy. I wrote the jacket copy for *Islands in the Net*, by Bruce Sterling. I saw it some years later, and it was terrible. Anyway, with all of these book reviews, book jackets, and manuscripts, I was reading about 200 books per month, for a period of two years. After those two years, I was incapable of finishing a book. It really robbed me of the pleasure of reading. I had been an addictive reader, but after that, you couldn't get me to crack a book for anything. I've only recently been able to finish books again. Anyway, Melissa, the editor of *Marketing Bestsellers*, became the publisher of the magazine and needed a replacement as editor. She asked me if I would like to do it. I said, "Sure, why not?" I took her job.

JACKET COPY BY UNCLE BOB.

**JS: What was that like?**

**BM:** It was terrible, for reasons that I won't go into. But Mellissa told me that the publishers of *Starlog* were starting a new magazine and were looking

## ENTER FANGORIA

RECORDED & INDEXED

DRAFT

for an editor. Now, by telling me this, she basically left herself high and dry, but she went ahead and did it. So, this was the third big favor that this woman did for me. I went to the *Starlog* offices and was interviewed by various people. And I told them the huge lie that I had a Bachelor of Arts in English from Brown University. I was a high school dropout and I never went back to any form of school after that. I got the equivalency diploma, and that's it. But, I told them that I was a graduate from Brown, and that helped put me over.

**JS: Did they ever find out the truth?**

**BM:** I told everyone the truth a year later, but by then it was too late. *Fangoria* was a success [laughs]. So, that's my life up until then. I can give you more detail on any part that you want.

**JS: Were you aware of *Starlog* before your interview?**

**BM:** Well, let's see. I was aware of it, but I wasn't a reader of it. I had been a reader of *Monster Times*. I was a regular purchaser of it, right until the end. Before that, I read *Castle of Frankenstein*. I never did get into *Famous Monsters*—I thought it was very childish, let's face it.

**JS: That's true, but when I look at it through adult eyes, I can appreciate what it meant to people.**

**BM:** Yeah, as an adult, you can respect it more than you would as a child. When you're a child, you want to be grown up. You don't want to be talked to like you're a kid.

**JS: That's exactly the way that I felt when I was growing up.**

**BM:** Me, too. I had that eagerness to be a hipster beatnik, even though I was a little kid. I was too much of a beatnik when I first saw *Famous Monsters*; this Uncle Forry guy was talking to me like I was twelve. Damn it, I'm fourteen [laughs]! Now the thing about *Castle of Frankenstein* was that Cal Beck and Bhob Stewart made that magazine for themselves. They weren't thinking of an audience that was somebody different from them. They were thinking of an audience that was just like them, that had the same interests. Somebody like Joe Dante would read it and say, "Yeah, this is for me." Joe Dante didn't do much writing for *Famous Monsters*, although

I'm sure he read it. I think he was much more enthused about *Castle of Frankenstein* because it talked about film. I didn't talk about the subjects of the movies as if you were telling stories around a campfire. And it didn't matter if you were twelve, *Castle of Frankenstein* was dealing with you as if you were an adult. And when you're twelve years old and want to forget that you're twelve—you want to be treated like a human being—that means a lot. I always tried to use the same approach in *Fangoria*, even though I was well aware that there weren't many thirty year old people reading the magazine. I tried to make it as readable for me as it would be for anybody else.

**JS: What was the genesis of *Fangoria*? How did the magazine start?**

**BM:** OK... in the last issue of *Marketing Bestsellers* that I edited, there was a little blurb about this new magazine that was coming from the publishers of *Starlog*, called *Fantastica*. It was going to do for the world of fairies, elves, dwarves, and magical creatures exactly what *Starlog* did for the world of spaceships and distant galaxies. This was in part due to the interests of Kerry O'Quinn. He was very interested in fantasy art, as practiced by the Hildebrandt brothers and others of that ilk. There was a feeling among the publishers (given that *Star Wars* had blown science fiction sky high) that there was going to be something that would do the same thing for fantasy. They thought it might be the *Conan* movie that at that time was being planned, but wouldn't see the light of day for another three or four years. They were looking to the *Conan* movie as possibly being the comet that they could tie their magazine to. I don't think that they were aware that Robert E. Howard was a little more manly than the type of elf art

**TOO FAR?**

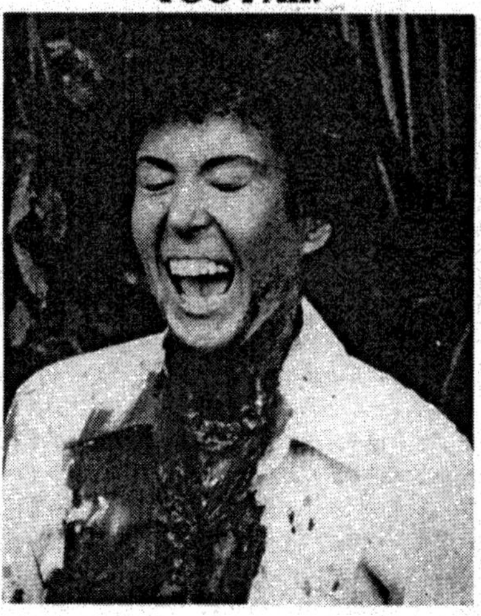

... Okay, you went way overboard in issue #7. I mean the *Friday the 13th* scenes in #6 were okay, but those *Maniac!* scenes were totally repulsive! What makes you think that any normal person wants to see that scalping effect! In the movie, fine—if anyone wants to shell out money for that garbage they can see it. Keep showing such totally sick scenes and I'll stop buying FANGORIA. I'm sure many people will agree. Well, I've said my piece. Hopefully, you'll take this into consideration when *Zombie* or some other such garbage comes out.

Don Hicks
Carson City, NV

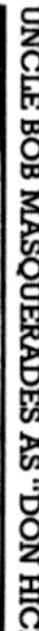
UNCLE BOB MASQUERADES AS "DON HICKS".

RECORDED & INDEXED
DRAFT

they were looking at. Anyway, that was the plan—to get the magazine going before *Conan* hit. They figured that the movie would take it through the roof.

**JS: The magazine didn't quite go that way.**

**BM:** There were a couple of things that got in the way. The first thing was the lawsuit that stopped it from being published for six months. I was hired to be the editor. They had already put together an initial issue, which was sitting in boards. It was on the shelf in the office where I worked for six months, while worked a little bit on *Starlog* and a few other projects. They certainly had enough work for me to do without *Fangoria* around.

**JS: What was the court case about?**

**BM:** There was another magazine in business called *Fantastic Films*. Now, *Fantastic Films* was established long after *Cinefantastique*, which was still in print at that time. As everyone knows, in French, *Cinefantastique* means fantastic film. But *Fantastic Films* felt that a magazine called *Fantastica* was messing with their trademark and would confuse their potential audience. It was a rather ridiculous case that I think we should have won with no problem, but we lost it. The judgment was in favor of *Fantastic Films*. And so, I got to work one morning and was told that the boards that had been sitting on the shelf for six months needed to be gone over. Certain things that had aged beyond the pale needed to be pulled out, new stuff had to be created to make it seem more timely, and we needed to come up with a new title and send it out to press within twenty-four hours. So, Ed Naha and I worked on it. Now, Ed had been the primary guy on the first issue—he had basically put *Fantastica* together, as the editor. He had chosen not to put his own name on it. He chose the name Joe Bonham. So, if you look at the first issue of *Fangoria*, you'll see my name as associate editor because I did work on those pages before they were shipped out. But Joe Bonham is credited as the editor of that issue, and that's Ed Naha's pseudonym.

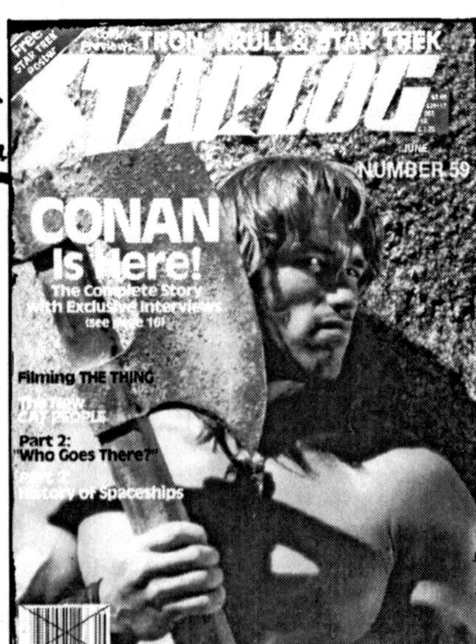


**JS: Do you know where the name came from?**

**BM:** It came from a novel by Dalton Trumbo. Dalton Trumbo is the man who

wrote the screenplay for *Spartacus*, and he also wrote a novel called *Johnny Got his Gun*. It's a pacifist novel about a paraplegic, and it's told from the point of view of Joe Bonham in his hospital bed. Anyway, that's the name that Ed Naha chose to use for his pseudonym. And so, the first editor of *Fangoria* was Ed Naha.

**JS: How was the first issue received?**

**BM:** The first issue and the eight issues that followed failed miserably, largely because the magazine's focus wasn't where people expected it to be. Part of the reason for that was the name of the magazine. If you see a magazine named *Fangoria*, you don't think that it's going to be about elves. You don't know what it's going to be about—you're going to say, "What the fuck?" It's a complete nonsense word out of left field, and it had no meaning until we gave it one.

**JS: Who came up with the name?**

**BM:** There's a whole story about that. Again, it was a matter of these pages that had to ship out the next day. We needed a name for the magazine. Now, the editor of *Starlog* at the time was a guy named Howard Zimmerman. Howard wanted the two of us to sit down and see if we could come up with something. And so, I sat down with him in his office. We were throwing around words, and he made a list. One thing that I thought of was the rather long word, "fantasmagoria." Richard Corben did a self-published magazine called *Fantagor* that was mined from that word, and I went back to that well, myself. Howard thought *Fantasmagoria* was way too long. I said, "I know, but let's play with it a little bit." I don't know if it was him or me, but one of us tried the shortened word "fangoria". He wrote it down, which was something that I would not have done. Looking over his shoulder, I said, "Do me a favor. Don't show that to Norman Jacobs, because if you show it to Norman, when I come into work tomorrow morning, I will be the editor of a magazine called *Fangoria*." Howard betrayed me [laughs]. He showed the list to Norman. Norman fell in love with it and said, "*Fangoria* it is." And so, there we were.

RECORDED & INDEXED

# UNCLE BOB MARTIN

## ENTER FANGORIA

DRAFT

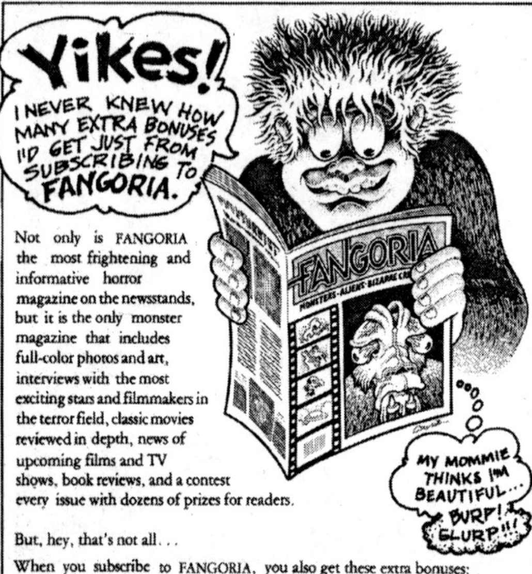

Yikes!
I NEVER KNEW HOW MANY EXTRA BONUSES I'D GET JUST FROM SUBSCRIBING TO FANGORIA.
FANGORIA
MONSTERS · ALIENS · BIZARRE CR
MY MOMMIE THINKS I'M BEAUTIFUL... BURP! SLURP!!!


Not only is FANGORIA the most frightening and informative horror magazine on the newsstands, but it is the only monster magazine that includes full-color photos and art, interviews with the most exciting stars and filmmakers in the terror field, classic movies reviewed in depth, news of upcoming films and TV shows, book reviews, and a contest every issue with dozens of prizes for readers.

But, hey, that's not all . . .

When you subscribe to FANGORIA, you also get these extra bonuses:

BONUS #1—You save money off the regular newsstand price; actually over 15%! Yearly subscription is just $9.98.

BONUS #2—You receive the bi-monthly Castle Fangor Newsletter absolutely FREE. And it's filled with all the last-minute news and reviews that no true horror fan should be without. *Only* for subscribers!

BONUS #3—FANGORIA subscribers receive special private mailings, discount offers not available to anyone else. Special-interest merchandise for creature lovers.

BONUS #4—When you subscribe (or extend your present subscription) you can get a Count Fangor T-Shirt at HALF-PRICE! This colorful original art work is 100% cotton and regularly sells for $7.98—yours for just $3.99.

BONUS #5—Our newest bonus is your own personal 3-line listing, FREE of charge, in the FANGORIA Classified Ads. You can list your address and meet new pen-pals, or tell others what you have to trade, or write any kind of non-profit, non-commercial message. Your personal listing, a $15.00 value, is FREE!

### SEND YOUR ORDER NOW!

All these bonuses are for a limited time *only*! Subscribe TODAY, just $9.98, and get all these extra FREE things! At last, an offer you really *can't* refuse . . .

Send cash, check or money order to:
**FANGORIA, Dept. OF, 475 Park Ave. South, New York, NY 10016**

☐ Send me a Count Fangor T-shirt at HALF-PRICE: $3.99 (Size: S · M · L · XL) We pay postage & handling!!!

Enclosed: **$9.98** (for subscription or renewal)
**$3.99** (for T-shirt option)
$12.25 One year foreign surface
Total: $ ..........

NAME

ADDRESS

CITY

STATE ZIP

☐ This is a renewal of my current subscription, and I have enclosed my mailing label along with payment.

FREE CLASSIFIED LISTING: (3 lines)
(limit: 35 characters per line)
(Non-commercial, non-profit only!)

NOTE: Your free listing will appear in the next available issue of FANGORIA. Space limitations may force late listings into next issue. First come, first served.

appeared in issue nine of FANGORIA. This reader complained about the gore that is depicted in your magazine, in particular the scalping scenes from *Maniac*. The reader wrote: "What makes you think that any normal person wants to see that scalping effect!" Now, this person is saying that anyone who enjoys visceral films like *Dawn of the Dead*, *Zombie* and *Maniac* (to name a few) is abnormal!

Well I am *quite normal* and I found the scalping effect very interesting. I truly enjoy your magazine's pictorial content and articles explaining the conception of filmdom's special effects, bloody or otherwise. After all, what does the "Gor" in FANGORIA stand for anyway?

In closing, I would like to say that whether or not you tone down your gore, you'll always have thousands of hardcore readers like me to back you up and keep your magazines alive and kicking!! So, to FANGORIA and staff, a long and prosperous life!

Jim Korloch
309 West High
Jackson, MICH 49203

Dear Fang,

. . . In response to the many letters requesting that you cut down on gore in your magazine, I say that if they don't like it, they shouldn't look at it. It looked as though your *Motel Hell* article in #9 was watered down to suit these people. I like gore and I'm proud of it. One of the reasons I buy the magazine is because you often print such pictures in it. If you're going to cover Monsters, Aliens and Bizarre Creatures, it is almost required to show gross pictures from gross films. That's the whole point, right?

Marshall B. Crist
1604 9th Street
Manhattan Beach, CA 90266

*It may not be the whole point, but grossness and the art of excess will always have a special place in our hearts and in the pages of FANGORIA. Rest assured that every blood-stained film we've covered has been represented by the most disturbing photos we can get our grubby little fingers on. If our policy ever changes, we'll be sure to let you know.*

To (Yecch!) FANGORIA,

. . . Gory is bore-y. Try scaring me with nothing but yecchs will ya?! I have been looking at your magazine and many others since I was in second grade and you think gore is my weakness? You must be mad! You think you can gore me and many others to death?! You're wrong!! You only get bored, not gored! I once looked at your issue with that *Zombie* on the cover, then ate two hot dogs!!!

I close this letter hoping your magazine will be forced into bankruptcy.

David Fargason
Huntsville, AL

*David, letters like your's make life worth living.*

Editors of FANGORIA

. . . I want to start off by saying that I'm a big fan of your magazine and a big fan of horror movies "true" horror movies. What I mean is, I'm not a fan of the "blood-and-guts" type film that seems to get a lot of publicity in your magazine. The

*FANGORIA* NUMBER 7, THE BREAKTHROUGH ISSUE.

**JS: You came into work the next morning as the editor of magazine called *Fangoria*...**

**BM:** [laughs] I told you earlier about being a slave to the nine to five. As the editor of the magazine, I was never enslaved by that. People would have liked to see me come in at nine. I had a tendency to come in at eleven or noon, even when I was in trouble. On that particular day, I came in around 11:30 in the morning. They had a logo already, which is the familiar logo that you can see on the first thirty or forty issues. There it was, on my desk. I can't say that I hated the title—well, no I will say it. I hated it. Day to day, what I had to do was tell publicists who were representing filmmakers and films that I needed to talk to their director or that I needed to get stills from their film, and that I wanted to put them in a magazine named *Fangoria*. They'd ask me how to spell it, I'd tell them, and they'd still sound doubtful. For a long time, they would be very reluctant—it was like pulling teeth. It took a long time before people realized that *Fangoria* was where you had to have your stills and you had to have your story for fans of horror to see that your movie might be something to contend with. I'd say that wasn't even close to happening until issue 7. That was our breakthrough issue—it was the one with Jack Nicholson from *The Shining* on the cover, and it was pretty much the first magazine that had its focus together.

**JS: When did sales improve?**

**BM:** Well, the sales were *not* improving over the first five or six issues. As the magazine continued to falter, Kerry O'Quinn started to maintain his distance. Nobody wants to be associated with a failure. But, the further away from it he got, the more successful it became.

**JS: Did that give you more free reign to do what you wanted?**

**BM:** Yes. Basically, I was able to take the lead of the readers. I was able to use the readers as my excuse for doing what I wanted to do. I wanted to make it a magazine that dealt with horror films without being dainty about it. *Famous Monsters* was a little bit shy of covering the type of film that was being made at the end of the twentieth-century. We were ready to cover late twentieth-century horror films and to move forward into the twenty-first. No other magazine was going to do that. Even *Monster Times* had always been somewhat shy and not ghoulish. When they covered gory films, they indicated, "Well, you know, instead of using real horror, this thing is exploiting gore." Like that's a bad thing [laughs]. We didn't say, "This movie is just exploiting gore—what a horrible thing to do!" I would say, "Hey, here's one that's exploiting gore. That's a basic interest of ours. There's no shame in exploitation."

**JS: The word "exploitation" carried a certain stigma for quite a while.**

**BM:** Right. And it took me a while to get used to the idea that there's no shame in using the word. I'd kind of test the waters of some of the filmmakers I dealt with by using the term exploitation with them. If they reacted negatively, I wouldn't mention it again. The fact is, the vast majority of them reacted negatively because that's the way we were all conditioned. Before there was *Fangoria* and before there was Stephen King and Quentin Tarantino, we were all pretty much conditioned to regard anything that used real graphic horror as being exploitation. And exploitation was beyond the pale. It was something that unfair people did in order to take unfair advantage of something. But, there's nothing unfair about exploiting gore. I mean, who does it hurt? Nobody gets cheated, except maybe the people who are told that something is going to be gory and it's not. They go in and say, "Where's the gore?" Those are the only people who get cheated. But, at that time, there was just this overwhelming cultural conditioning that exploitation was a bad thing. *Fangoria* was one of the first cultural waves against that. And we owed that, more than anything else, to the zines like *Gore Gazette* and *Sleazoid Express*. And personally, I owe that to Frank Henenlotter. He's the first guy to say, "Yeah, I'm an exploitation filmmaker." He was the first guy who said it with relish and who wasn't at all defensive about it.

**JS: What can you tell me about David Everitt?**

**BM:** David was my co-editor. He had equal billing with me—I made sure of that, because I wanted him to work just as hard [laughs]. First, though, I have to give due credit to Robert Greenberger. Before there was David Everitt, the only guy really helping me out was Robert. And his help was priceless. Without him, I would have drowned; I would have had to quit a lot sooner than I did. He went on to have a great career at DC and Marvel as an editor. But, he started out with me on *Fangoria*, and he did a great job. He never tires of telling people about the day that P. J. Soles came to our office to take him out to lunch to thank him for interviewing her. But anyway, after Robert left, David Everitt was hired. Not to replace him, but more or less as a free agent to work on various projects that needed help. Everything at *Starlog* was always understaffed because they were so damn cheap. Everitt was there to lighten the load for the people who were swamped, which included me. I noticed that he had an encyclopedic knowledge of film. He could sit down and type out publishable copy on first draft. And, he was about the funniest guy I'd ever spoken with. We got along really well, so I went to my boss and made a devil's deal. David and I lived to regret it, but not entirely.

**JS: What was the deal?**

**BM:** Basically, the deal I made was this: I told Norman Jacobs that this guy David Everitt was good. I said, "If you put him on *Fangoria* full-time, make him my co-editor, and give him equal pay with me, I will be able bring in the magazine at half of its current budget." OK. That was crazy. First of all, by the fact that I extorted salary equal to what I was getting, for the rest of the time that I was at *Starlog*, I could never again really ask for a raise. I had used all of my juice to get Everitt this equal money. Also, because we were going to be producing the magazine at half the budget, David and I were sold into the slavery of writing half the magazine each and every issue while we paid our freelancers what was remaining in our budget. David and I respected writers

FORRY WRITES. *FANGORIA* NUMBER 25.

**Fango: Choice of Noted Film Authorities!**

Dear David Everitt,

Now that I am no longer bound to *Famous Monsters* I feel like Fredric March in *Dr Jekyll & Mr Hyde* exulting, "Free! Free at last!" While Editor of *FM* it would have been inconceivable for me to write a letter to FANGORIA: I would have been stomped like Bambi beneath the foot of Godzilla.

I want to express my sincere appreciation to you for dedicating the Nov. 1982 issue to me. November 24 was my 66th birthday and I consider this a very nice present, especially the surprise Editorial, which was also read by my wife Wendayne with great gratification.

I have followed FANGO from the first, often regarding you with envy because of your better stock of paper, your color, your decency in always giving credit where credit is due (i.e., bylines), your Classified Ads dept. for fans, your features by Alex Gordon, your say-something editorials instead of the pablum I was perennially required to prepare.

As you may or may not be aware, thru the years visitors to my Ackermuseum of Filmonster Memorabilia have from time to time abused my hospitality and made off with prized possessions from my collection. It is a sad statistic that any time there are about 25 strangers in the house, somebody (or some *thing*) has sticky fingers and something disappears. Spock's ears. The mate to the claw of the Thing from Another World (original version). The horrid little manikin that chased Karen Black around the kitchen in the TV *Trilogy of Terror*. Every speck of Startrekiana I ever owned. A raygun from *Forbidden Planet*. Stills, posters, lobbycards, books. (Some of the crooks, of course, have been caught: in less than a week I had Bela Lugosi's Dracula Ring back.) But now—are you ready for this? —*my entire file of FANGORIA has disappeared!* I expect your editorial response will be, "Obviously, when they steal from Forry, they steal nothing but the best!"

Cordially,
Forry Ackerman
1313 Dracula Drive
Hollyweird
Karloffornia
UFA 124C4U

Attachment

UNCLE BOB'S HEAD, RENDERED BY TYLER SMITH FOR THE MOVIE, *GEEK MAGGOT BINGO*.

too much to screw them. That meant we were going to pay our writers fairly, but we couldn't buy much stuff. We had to produce as much as possible in house. It instantly became tougher for all of the freelancers to sell stuff to us. And the freelancers, of course, weren't happy with that change. But, because David and I knew the magazine so well, we were able to tighten the focus even further. We made it stronger, and that helped it's sales. So, actually, although it was stupid crazy of me to make this deal, it was the best thing possible for the magazine.

**JS: What kind of effect did it have on your workload?**

**BM:** It freed me, to a certain extent. I stopped slaving quite as hard as I had been, and saw a lot of the slack being picked up by Everitt. But of course, to the extent that I relaxed, that's the extent to which Everitt became more enslaved. There was sometimes a weird and uncomfortable dynamic between us. He lost patience with me a few times when I was just a bit too lazy. As you know, my habit was to come in at eleven in the morning and leave sharply at five.

**JS: Why was that?**

**BM:** I did a lot of work at home. At home, I had a computer with a word processor—everything was publishable in its first draft. I didn't have to retype shit. I just had to make a few revisions here and there. At work, I had to use a typewriter. Everyone else was typing things over and over again.

**JS: I'm curious as to how you met Frank Henenlotter.**

**BM:** In New York City in the late 1970s and early eighties, public access television was full of filth, which I used to watch for kicks. There was Al Goldstein's *Midnight Blue*, but before that there was an interview show with naked people. It was bizarre. Anyway, I used to watch these filthy programs, and before they came on, there was a show called *The Nikki Haskell Show*. Nikki Haskell was a socialite-type who had married a stock broker. I believe he died young and left her very well off. So, finding herself fairly young and with lots of money, she started buying time on public access TV to do a fabulous show about nightlife and such. On one movie and says, "Yeah, right, life sucks. I should just blitz out and take what little pleasure I can from drugs."

**Henenlotter:** I don't think the film says that at all. I really don't.

**Fang:** But some people might interpret it that way.

**Henenlotter:** There are people who will interpret anything any way they want it to be. If I planned to portray drugs as pleasurable, Brian wouldn't have lost everything that had meaning to him: his girl friend, his life, all of it. If he's left alone with his pleasure, then what's the point? I can't see anybody perceiving this film as pro-drug. The moment you see him accept Elmer's deal, you know it's suicide.

But I don't see *Brain Damage* relating to any real-life drug issues in that way because it's not a pro-drug film and it's not an anti-drug film. It's a monster movie. If I had any desire to make a movie about drugs, then Brian would have picked up a needle and injected himself, or smoked some crack, and there would be no doubt as to what the film was about. This film is about a monster.

At one point in the writing of the script, I became aware of how druggy the story was getting. I said to myself, "Let's put an end to this real fast." I tried to write around it, to avoid having Elmer inject Brian with drugs and so on. I tried several ways around it, and it just wouldn't

**You saw it here first: Writer/director Frank Henenlotter (left) receives a grant from the late William J. Casey, former CIA head (and victim of brain damage).**

work. So I had to come back to it and said, "Instead of skirting around it, let me embrace that." And that worked. It gave me that great withdrawal scene.

**Fang:** Drugs are the carrot on the stick that makes the cart move. They're not the cart itself.

**Henenlotter:** Right. But as far as my opinions go on issues like that, I don't really feel that my opinions should matter to anyone else, and I don't need to explain those opinions to anyone.

**Fang:** It's certainly not necessary to the enjoyment of the film.

**Henenlotter:** Right.

**Fang:** But there's never *anything* in FANGORIA that's *necessary* for the enjoyment of a film. *(laughter)* We simply enhance the reader's enjoyment.

**Henenlotter:** FANGORIA never delves into topical politics, either. I'll give you a nice political slant on this: Who do you think was the first person to invest in any of my films, way back before I was doing anything commercial?

**Fang:** Ronald Reagan?

**Henenlotter:** Nope.

**Fang:** Joe McCarthy?

**Henenlotter:** Nope. It was William J. Casey, former CIA director and

*(continued on page 68)*

**"A rare event; Martin has translated Henenlotter's screenplay into first-rate horror fiction, as unsettling as it is entertaining!"**

— T.E.D. Klein, Author of *Dark Gods* and *The Ceremonies;* Founding Editor of *Twilight Zone* Magazine

**BRAIN DAMAGE**

signed and numbered limited first edition 1000 copies, illustrated with photographs

Who and what is Elmer? What strange destiny does he weave for those who fall prey to his whims? The answers to these questions, and many others, are to be found in *Brain Damage*, the novella by Bob Martin, based upon the original Frank Henenlotter screenplay.

THIS EDITION IS AVAILABLE ONLY THROUGH THIS ADVERTISEMENT AND WILL NOT BE DISTRIBUTED TO STORES

**Special Pre-Publication Price: $15, includes postage**
**After February 10: $25**

The first 100 copies sold through this ad will be signed by both Bob Martin and Frank Henenlotter.

**WARNING:** This book is based upon the complete, uncensored screenplay and deals frankly with drugs, sex and violence.

Broslin Press, P.O. Box 1711, Hoboken, NJ 07030

**Yessiree,** here's my fifteen bucks, in check or money order made out to Broslin Press! (Unless, of course, it's after February 10, in which case I've enclosed twenty-five.) Rush me *Brain Damage* upon publication with all due haste!
I certify that I am over 18 years of age.

Name ______

Address ______

City, State, Zip ______

Broslin Press, P.O. Box 1711, Hoboken, NJ 07030

particular occasion, she decided to take her show to the Cannes Film Festival. She encountered Rex Reed at poolside, and started interviewing him. He was very clearly drunk. I don't know whether he was kidding her or if he was trying to play a cruel joke, but when she asked him if there was any film in Cannes that she absolutely had to see, he said, "Nikki, you must see the film I saw this afternoon, *Basket Case*." Now, months later when the film opened in New York, Rex Reed would famously give *Basket Case* a terrible review. He tore it apart. But before his review ever appeared, he did give a quote that was used in advertisements.

**JS: "The sickest movie I've ever seen."**

**BM:** Right. But it wasn't necessarily part of a bad review. You can take that however you want. Later, his review came out and it was very negative. But here at poolside drunk, he told Nikki Haskell she had to see it. I didn't know what he was driving at. I just heard the title, and I said, "This is something that might help *Fangoria* to establish a different sort of identity." The next day, I went wading through all the trade magazines and there was a thick *Variety* issue for Cannes. I was finally able to find one tiny little item that said the film *Basket Case* was being represented by a company called Analysis Film Corporation. Analysis was a company that, like a lot of New York film companies, had its start with porn. It had sort of slowly moved out of that with things like Bob Guccione's *Caligula*. That was still porn, but it was porn of a different level, I guess. They later handled Bill Lustig's *Maniac*. Anyway, I tracked them down, got a little bit of information about the film, and wrote it up in the "Monster Invasion" section of *Fangoria*. I knew precious little about the film, but enough to make one little entry that there was such a film in existence. I also asked the people at Analysis if they could please put me in touch with the filmmaker Frank Henenlotter. I never heard back from them, but through the same grapevine that I was talking about earlier, I

THE TENANT IN ROOM 7 IS VERY SMALL, VERY TWISTED, AND VERY MAD

BASKET CASE

an IEVINS / HENENLOTTER production starring KEVIN VanHENTENRYCK TERRI SUSAN SMITH BEVERLY BONNER Director of Photography BRUCE TORBET Music GUS RUSSO Executive Producers ARNIE BRUCK TOM KAYE Production Executive RAY SUNDLIN Produced by EDGAR IEVINS Written and Directed by FRANK HENENLOTTER

RUGGED FILMS INC.

MISCELLANEOUS

**BRAIN DAMAGE—THE NOVEL:** Critically praised novelization by former Fango editor Bob Martin. Copies still available, but going fast. For current price info, send S.A.S.E. to: Broslin Press, P.O. Box 1711, Hoboken, NJ 07030.

got Frank's phone number. I called him up, and as usual it rang through to his answering machine. To this day, if you somehow find Frank Henenlotter's phone number and dial it, it will ring through to his answering machine. You leave a message, and he may or may not get back to you. So, I left him a message and told him that I represented *Fangoria*. He called me back, and said he'd be delighted to speak to us. He told me that he practically had a heart attack when he saw the name *Basket Case* in "Monster Invasion"—he thought that someone had stolen their title [laughs]. So, that's how Frank and I first got together.

**JS: How did you start collaborating with him?**

**BM:** Well, I did a couple of interviews with him about *Basket Case* because nobody else was doing it. Like I said, I thought it was the type of film that would help to establish who we were. I wanted to identify with that movie as much as possible by mentioning it as much as possible. And, when you're nice to a filmmaker and his films, the filmmaker tends to be fond of you. We developed a friendship, and I think Frank saw an opportunity to make *Fangoria* a better magazine by educating me a little bit. I think Frank made me watch more Ray Dennis Steckler movies than I had ever watched before. The same is true for Jess Franco and a number of different filmmakers. He was a huge influence on our attitude. Anyway, our friendship was there first, before there was any collaboration. Now, what happened was that I had a series of personality crises that culminated in my leaving the magazine. It was the best job I ever had, and I still think I was crazy to leave, but I really didn't have any choice but to do it for my own well being. I left *Fangoria*, and some time later, I got a call from Frank. He asked me to come by and he said, "I've got another movie coming called *Brain Damage*. The screenplay is right here and I'd kind of like there to be a book based on it." I read the screenplay and told him, "Yeah, I think

RECORDED & INDEXED
DRAFT

there's a book there. I could write it myself. And I'd like to publish it myself." My plan was to write the book and put an ad in *Fangoria* for a limited edition hardcover based on the screenplay by Frank Henenlotter and written by Uncle Bob. I had already priced out what it would cost to do a hardcover book.

**JS: What was the cost?**

**BM:** It would cost me about four dollars per unit. It would cost me $4,000 to do a thousand copies that I would sell at $20 each. If I didn't get $4,000 in responses I'd sent all of the checks back at my own expense. I went ahead with this Ralph Kramden "get rich quick" scheme, and it actually worked. The sales kept me afloat for approximately a year. And the next really big paycheck that I got was from working with Frank on *Frankenhooker.* My collaborations with Frank got me through a couple of very tough years.

**JS: Did you ever imagine that *Fangoria* would become such an institution?**

**BM:** I knew that what we were doing and the way we were doing it was very different, because nobody else had dared to. And I was always thinking to myself, "When are the parents going to raise a squawk? When are they going to boycott the newsstands? When are they going to say, 'This is a sickness entering our homes? We need to do something about this!'" The craziest thing about that is that it never happened until after I left *Fangoria*. I went to work down the hall in the same offices for another magazine out of the same company.

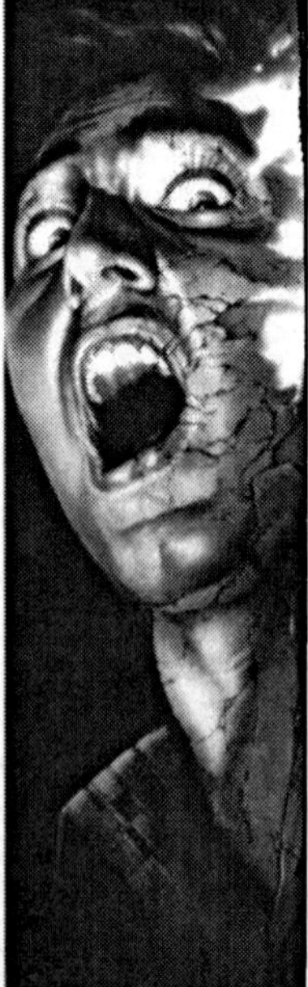

By Robert Martin
from the screenplay by Frank Henenlotter

**JS: What magazine was that?**

**BM:** It was called *Rock Video Idols*, which is an awful name. Part of my going over to it was the deal that we would change the name. I wasn't happy with the way the name was changed, either. It became *Hard Rock Video*. We were the first magazine to put Metallica on the cover and we were the first magazine to cover Anthrax. We were poised to take advantage of the way rock was going to change. If we would have hung on until Nirvana broke, our magazine would have done very well. Anyway, one Sunday, I

FANGORIA

October 1985 Issue #48

Business and Editorial Offices:
FANGORIA Magazine
475 Park Avenue South
New York, New York 10016

**Editors**
R.H. MARTIN
DAVID EVERITT

**Editorial Consultant**
ALEX GORDON

**Art Director**
EMILY SLOVES

**Assistant Art Director**
DENNIS M. DOYLE

**Designers**
JESSICA RUBIN
CHRIS HARDWICK

**Photographic Effects**
JOHN CLAYTON

**Editorial Assistant**
ANTHONY TIMPONE

**Medic**
DR. CYCLOPS

**Editor At Large**
DAVID SHERMAN

**British Correspondent**
PHILIP NUTMAN

**Literary Associate**
STANLEY WIATER

**Contributors**
TOM WEAVER
JOHN WOOLEY
VINCENT KEHOE
DAVID HUTCHISON
BOB STRAUSS

**Financial Manager**
JOAN BAETZ

**THANK YOU:** Stephen King, Richard Rubinstein, Tyler Smith, Peter Haas, Richard Edlund, William Stout, Paul Sammon, Daniel Attias, Tom Phillips, the cast & crew of *The Supernatural*, Bill Blair, Jeff Hogue, Joe Wolf, Dave Powell, Robert Brewer, George Romero, Joe Pilato, Gene Corman and you.

Dedicated to Vincent Kehoe.

Production Assistants: Ed Berganza, Chris Kwath, Andrea Passes.

**For Advertising Information: (212) 689-2830.**
**Advertising Director: Rita Eisenstein**
**Classified Ads Manager: Connie Bartlett**

# Imagination Inc.

UNCLE BOB SAYS GOODBYE. *FANGORIA* NUMBER 48.

## Uncle Bob: The Final Chapter!

What can I say? It's been great. Helping to bring this magazine into the world, and giving it shape in its first years, has been the most exciting, wonderful thing I've ever done, and I've enjoyed sharing it with you.

But Fango is no longer in its first years. It is, on its own level, a successful magazine, and various reasons for its success have been contemplated, formularized and memorized by all concerned; as a result, a lot of my work here has been a matter of fulfilling expectations: yours, mine and everyone else's. I'd much rather surprise people.

Some time ago, I told the publishers of this magazine that I was feeling restless, and that I would be interested in a new challenge. That challenge has arrived.

*Rock Video* is no doubt a familiar title to many of our readers, at least from the ad that's frequently appeared in our pages. The next issue of that mag to hit the stands will bear the title *Hard Rock Video*, and with that issue I'll be joining Danny Fields as his co-editor. There are other changes in store for the future, with the title some indication of its new direction. I hope that all of our readers who enjoy loud, fast, guitar-based music (whether it's called hard rock, metal, or hardcore) will consider joining us there.

Before I go, some thank yous: to Mick Garris, who was of more help to this book at the beginning than anyone but the two of us will know (I'll be applauding your *Amazing Stories* credit *loudly* every week, Mick); to everyone whose name has ever graced an article, particularly to Alex Gordon, Michael Weldon, Tim Ferrante and Johnny Legend; to my former managing editors, Bob Woods and Robert Greenberger, whose energy allowed me freedom; to publicity folk Tom Phillips of Paramount, Barbara Pflughaupt of England-Strohl-DeNegris, Gery Herz of New Line, and every other publicist who never asked me how to spell "Fangoria"; and to all the "Hall of Famers": Baker, Carpenter, Craven, Cronenberg, King, Hooper, Romero, Savini, Smith; plus folks like Frank Henenlotter, Craig Reardon, Don Coscarelli, H.G. Lewis, Sam Raimi, the Coens, Joe Dante, Steve Miner, Brother Theodore, Ed French, Steve Johnson, Randy Cook, David Miller (I could go on all day); all of our efforts would have been a bad joke if you guys weren't around.

And thanks, of course, to David Everitt. In the last year, as I've battled my case of dry rot, David has worked tirelessly to keep the magazine fresh. The challenge is still here for him, and I'll enjoy seeing *Fangoria* thrive under his care.

As always, final thanks go to (who else?) you, the readers. Couldn't have done it withoutcha. If we ever run into each other in the street, ask me to tell you the story about Spielberg and the Sword of Conan.

For the last time,
Your Uncle Bob

P.S. It doesn't have to be the last goodbye! If you're into hard rock, write and let us know what you'd like to see happen in *Hard Rock* magazine; include an S.A.S.E. and you'll get something or other back: Bob Martin, O'Quinn Studios, 475 Park Avenue South, New York 10016.

actually watched Jimmy Swaggart on television for some amusement. And that day, Jimmy was talking about rock mags. He was telling his audience that rock magazines were filth. He wanted everyone to band together and let all the chain stores know that they did not want this rock'n'roll filth coming into their homes. He went on like that for a good hour—he was really exhorting his crowd to do something. The next day—and again, I'm coming into work at 11:30 in the morning—I got the news, much like I got the news that our name was *Fangoria*. *Hard Rock Video* had been dropped by the distributor that handled us in six southern states. We had also been dropped by Walmart and 7-11. The magazine was killed in a day. That totally disgusted me.

**JS: Where did you go from there?**

**BM:** I continued to work in the magazine field for another ten years, but it put a bad taste in my mouth that lasted forever. When I finally quit the business, I think that was the biggest reason—what Jimmy Swaggart did to me.

**JS: What can you tell me about *Toxic Horror*?**

**BM:** I had gone on in the magazine business and worked for a few different companies. I got to thinking, "You know, my old boss Norman Jacobs wasn't such a bastard after all [laughs]. I could probably come up with another magazine idea that I could make work for him." So, I went to Norman's office and I pitched him a magazine called *Toxic*. Not *Toxic Horror*, just *Toxic*. I told him that it would be about social irritants—things that rubbed society the wrong way like sand getting into your shorts when you go to the beach. Things that are there to annoy society and wake it up a little bit. I'll tell you—what comes closest to the idea that I pitched to Norman was a book that came out around that time. It was edited by Adam Parfrey.

**JS: *Apocalypse Culture*?**

**BM:** Exactly. I was driving at something like that. At the same time, I was talking to a friend of mine about possibly doing a fanzine that we would call *Countdown to Millennium*. We would number it according to the number of months between the year and date of the

JIMMY SWAGGART DOES NOT LIKE IT.

year 2000. The magazine would be all about how much crazier things were going to get as we approached year zero. And *Toxic* was my idea of trying to make *Countdown to Millennium* more commercially acceptable and viable to somebody like Norman. Anyway, I put together a magazine. I contacted Miriam Linna from Norton Records. She also did a rock fanzine called *Kicks* and was well known as a collector of paperbacks. Miriam did a portfolio and an essay about teen delinquent fiction for the first issue of *Toxic*. I interviewed Ivan Stang from the Church of Subgenius. I did an article about zines where I talked to Donna Kossy from *Kooks*. Do you have both *Toxic* one and two?

**JS: Yeah. I think I have all of them.**

**BM:** If you have number one and number two, you have the magazine that I put together. They cut my magazine in half and filled the empty pages with Freddy Krueger and Jason. They did a first and second issue based on the material that I put together for issue number one. I gave them a complete first issue, but they tore it apart and diluted it. I quit that day. I said, "I understand why you're doing this, but the magazine that you're making this into is not something that I want to have anything to do with."

**JS: I always thought that *Starlog* launched *Toxic Horror* to eliminate the competition on the newsstand.**

**BM:** That might have been in the back of Norman's mind. I know he's done things like that in the past. Take *Gorezone*, for instance. *Gorezone* was a good magazine in its own right, thanks to the people who worked hard on it. But it really came about because Norman wanted to be his own competition. But by the time that *Toxic* came around, I think we'd pretty much wiped it out. All I was trying to do was put out my dream magazine.

**JS: You interviewed Joe Coleman for *Toxic Horror*.**

**BM:** Joe was my upstairs neighbor. I lived in an basement apartment on East 10th Street, just off of Second Ave. Joe lived in the first floor apartment directly above me. I was shocked as hell to be sitting on the steps one day. He walked into the building, and I recognized him. I don't know how many people would, but

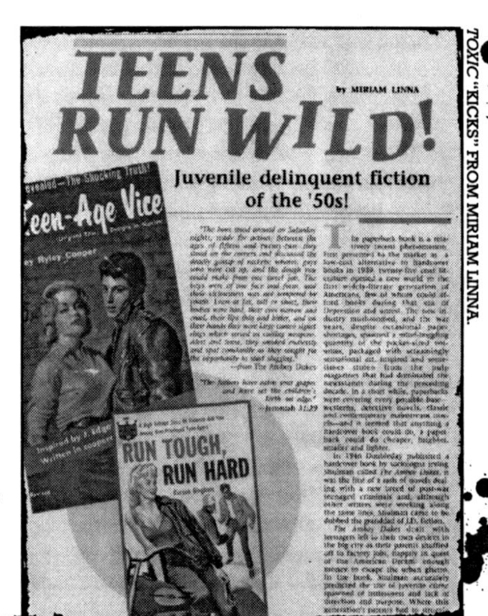
TEENS RUN WILD!

by MIRIAM LINNA

Juvenile delinquent fiction of the '50s!



*TOXIC* "KICKS" FROM MIRIAM LINNA.

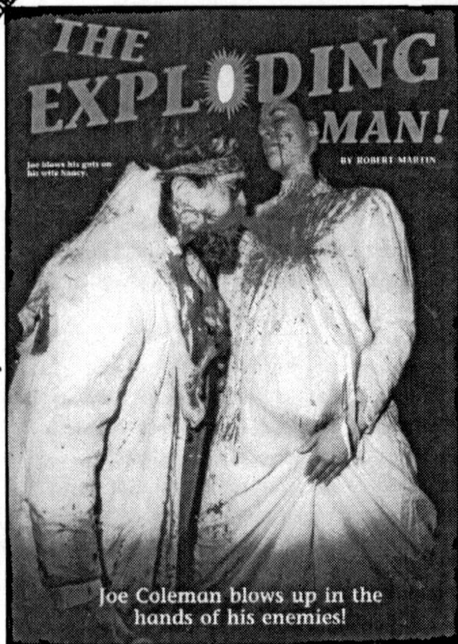

Joe Coleman blows up in the hands of his enemies!

UNCLE BOB INTERVIEWS UNCLE JOE IN *TOXIC HORROR*.

I did. I was stunned. Then I noticed that if you looked in the window on the right hand side of the building, there was this dummy head that looked pretty weird. It was part of his odditorium. I wish I'd been sick enough to show a real interest in that, but at the time I was so disgusted with the way my career was going that I was distracted from the wonder that was right above me. But, I did strike up a friendship with Joe and I interviewed him for the magazine. He certainly fit right in with what my concept of *Toxic* was. That was supposed to be one of the real gems in the first issue. And by the way, I also wrote a review of *Apocalypse Culture* in the first issue. I had to say something unpleasant about it, because Adam had gone out of his way to insult Howard Cruise, who was a good friend of mine. He said that the way Howard blended the Disney style with homosexual themes gave him a sense of vertiginous nausea [laughs]. I had to defend him, so I made a remark about that. Other than that, I gave it a good review. It certainly was a groundbreaking book.

**JS: What did you think of the way *Fangoria* went after you left?**

**BM:** The fact is, no matter what I thought of particular editorial choices that were made, I have to thank Tony Timpone every day for keeping the magazine commercially viable. He did that for twenty-five years. I only did it for five. Now, OK I gave him a great start. I'll take credit for that, sure. But, a great start is not twenty-five years. He kept it going, and I won't say anything bad about him. My baby is still out there, and people are saying it's better than ever. I've heard that Chris Alexander is doing a great job, and I tend to believe what people tell me.

**JS: What have you been doing lately? I know that you were writing stuff for the *Dread Central* website for a while.**

**BM:** I've been plotting and planning my next move. I'm not over as a writer, in my opinion but I'm not entirely sure what is coming next. I have a couple of strange ideas—they aren't all writing, but they're all creative in one way or another. Anyone who pals me up on Facebook will certainly be informed.

**JS: Are you still writing for *Dread Central*?**

"GO SEE THE STUNT MAN." *FANGORIA* NUMBER 11.

FANGORIA

FEBRUARY 1981 #11

**Business and Editorial Offices:**
FANGORIA Magazine
475 Park Avenue South New York,
New York 10016

**Publishers**
NORMAN JACOBS
KERRY O'QUINN

**Associate Publisher**
RITA EISENSTEIN

**Editor**
BOB MARTIN

**Managing Editor**
ROBERT GREENBERGER

**Art Director**
CHEH N. LOW

**Senior Designer**
BOB SEFCIK

**Designer**
LAURA O'BRIEN

**Photographic Effects**
JOHN CLAYTON

**Contributors**
JAMES H. BURNS
HOWARD CRUSE
DOUG FINCH
ALEX GORDON
DAVID HIRSCH
MARK THOMAS McGEE
DAVID P. NICHOLS
RANDY PALMER
RICHARD JAY SILVERTHORN
AL TAYLOR
STANLEY WIATER

**THANK YOU:** Stephen Lack, Mick Garris, Tom Schwartz, John Boorman, Dolores Hudson, Roberta Burrows, Charles Griffith, Craig Reardon, Rick Baker, Fredell Pogodin, Rob Bottin, Joe Dante, Harvey Bernhard, Richard Scott, Jimmy Sangster, Keith Dudley, Anthony Hinds, Richard Gordon, Peter Kuran, George Mihalka, Ed Egan, David Cronenberg, Jim Wynorski, John Carpenter, Miller Drake, Priscilla McDonald, James Cummins, Vic Ghidalia, Steven Paul Leiva, Andrew Helfer, Eric Bloom and especially YOU!

This issue is respectfully dedicated to **Harlan Ellison**

**Production Assistants:** Eileen Dempsey, Cindy Levine, David Gitman and Nancy Reichardt.

**For Advertising Information:** Rita Eisenstein (212) 689-2880

FANGORIA is published six times a year by O'Quinn Studios, Inc., 475 Park Avenue South, New York, NY 10016. This is issue #11 Volume 2. (ISSN 0164-2114) Entire contents is copyright © 1981 by O'Quinn Studios, Inc. All rights reserved. Reprint or reproduction of any material in part or in whole without written permission from the publisher is strictly forbidden. Subscription rates: $9.98 for six issues delivered in the U.S. and Canada; foreign subscription $14.98 in U.S. funds only. **New Subscriptions:** send directly to FANGORIA, 475 Park Avenue South, New York, NY 10016. Notification of **change of address** or **renewals:** send to FANGORIA, Subscription Dept., P.O. Box 142, Mt. Morris, IL 61054. Authorized to mail at controlled circulation rates in Sparta, IL. FANGORIA accepts no responsibility for unsolicited manuscripts, photos, art or other materials, but if freelance submittals are accompanied by a self-addressed, stamped envelope, they will be considered and, if necessary, be returned. Printed in the U.S.A.

# Imagination Inc.

## Thanks!

Very few people are lucky enough to have a job like mine. Not just that working on FANGORIA is fun, which is rare enough. But also that, after a lot of worry and sweat, every two months, I get to see the product of all our labors summed up in 68 pages (counting covers), and can enjoy the feeling of accomplishment that it brings.

But, before that moment when I have the fresh issue in my hands, there's a period of self-doubt that begins when we send the issue off to the printer, and continues until three weeks later when we receive the first bound issue. Usually this consists of a gnawing conviction that we've just done the worst issue of any magazine the world has ever seen. At the same time, I plunge into a dark mood that makes me one of the least likeable guys on earth, and I lie on my bed at night, staring at the ceiling, going over the entire issue page by page and wondering what went wrong.

Then I receive my advance copy, and recognize all the little signs of extra effort that are in each issue. It's not so bad after all, I think—and a week later I'm convinced that the newest issue is our best, never to be improved upon. And the cycle begins again.

As I write this, we're still in the thick of it. There's only one more article to be written, but we're still waiting for some photos to come in, and Kerry and Norman and I have yet to get together to plan our cover. But, even so, I already know that this issue is a bit different from the others. Already, I have a certainty that this is the best issue of FANGORIA that we've ever done.

Of course, we don't want to break our arms in patting ourselves on the back—that's not what I'm trying to do. You may notice, at the left of this editorial, on our masthead, there's a list of names that begins with the words "Thank You," and these are the people I'm talking about. Publicity people and filmmakers whose contributions allow us to publish this magazine. This issue, there's a few people in particular whose special help make this issue very exciting to me—and I expect most of you reading this will agree.

First of all, there's John Boorman. You'll have a hard time finding a film director with such a great sense of commitment to his own personal vision, even as the film industry becomes, more and more, enslaved to marketing statistics and economic expedience. He's worked for ten years to bring *Excalibur* to the screen, and only when moviemaking trends caught up with his imagination was he enabled to do so. He lives in Ireland, and was only in New York for *six hours* to discuss the marketing of the film with Lloyd Leipzig of Orion Pictures. Still, he found the time to talk with us about *Excalibur*, and to express his appreciation of our work. I have never been so gracefully flattered in my life. Thanks also go to Mr. Leipzig and to Dolores Hudson, who were of great assistance in our coverage of this film.

We didn't plan on interviewing Rick Baker for this issue (though we had always planned on getting to it, someday). But it just so happened that a few gaps in our story on *The Howling* required that we get in touch. Rick is now fully occupied in preparing effects for *American Werewolf*, and it wasn't easy distracting him from that. But, once we did, our efforts were paid back severalfold, with news about current Baker activities that you'll find in various parts of this issue. And we also received the pleasure of learning what a nice human being Hollywood's greatest ape can be!

We also had the great pleasure of speaking with another special makeup man of the Dick Smith school for this issue. Like Baker, Craig Reardon merits a lengthy article in these pages detailing his entire career. This time, however, he graciously stepped in when our plans to interview Tobe Hooper fell through. Fortunately, we reached him just prior to his departure for Nova Scotia(!) for location shooting on a forthcoming suspense film. Keep warm, Craig!

And then there's Rob Bottin. It doesn't happen often that you start out doing an interview and end up making a friend. Rob is a friend of ours, now, and that's part of the reason why I think that our *Howling* coverage is one of the best pieces we've ever run. Both Rob and director Joe Dante should be thanked for going to unusual extremes for us.

The list of "Thank Yous" contains quite a few other names that should be mentioned here as well, and it goes on forever, to include everyone who has helped us on past issues, and all the people who will be helping us in the future—and, most of all, every one of our readers (that's you!) The list is there, to the left. Please read it, in every issue.

In a way, it's the most important part of the magazine.

—Bob Martin

P. S. – It's not fantasy or horror, so we didn't cover it – but go see 'The Stunt Man' – a great movie!!

**BM:** It kind of petered out. Here's the deal—for a blog to be effective on *Dread Central*, it has to be really regular and clockwork. That draws more and more people from month to month. People say, "Are you reading Uncle Bob's blog? It's not bad and it comes out every third Thursday. You should log into *Dread Central* and check it out." But, if you don't do it regularly like that, it's not worth a cent. They were paying me more generously than they could afford for somebody who is just too temperamental to be able to write like clockwork. I can't be burdened by a deadline right now—I've got too many other things to do in my life than to wrack my brain for copy that has to be due by the third Thursday. So, while I enjoyed writing and working for them, I was too just expensive for them, and they were too demanding for me. Not that they were demanding of me. For the money they were paying me, they deserved to get more than they got. I knew that I wasn't bringing them the eyeballs that a regular blogger can. I was too infrequent and I knew that it wasn't going to work out. If what I were to do next would be some kind of a blog thing, it would be my own blog on my own site. That's something I've considered doing and might yet do. It's one of a whole field of possibilities that I've thought about. And, certainly one ambition of mine is to write a decent novel of some sort.

**JS: One last question—where did the nickname Uncle Bob come from?**

**BM:** Well for one thing, in *Famous Monsters* Forry Ackerman was known as Uncle Forry. The fellow who was most aware of that was David Everitt, who was a *Famous Monsters* reader as a youth. But it was actually a way for David to mock and attack me [laughs]. There were times when we were asked to do things in a certain way, and I felt like we were cheating the readers. I'd say, "Norman, I can't do that. It wouldn't be fair." David started calling me Uncle Bob because of my avuncular attitude. I was really concerned about the readers getting the magazine that they deserved.

**JS: Well, thank you so much, Uncle Bob. You did a great job.**

**BM:** [laughs] You're welcome.

### Chapter Six

# Bill Landis & Michelle Clifford

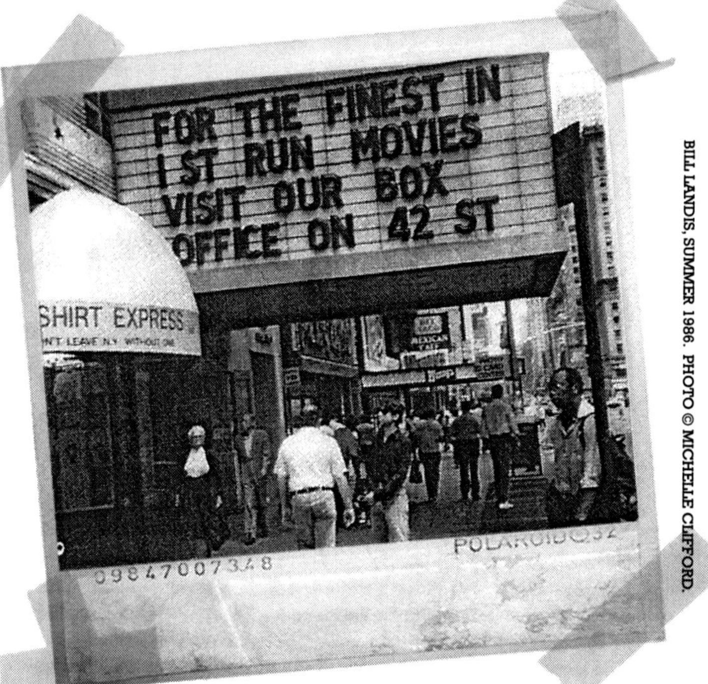


BILL LANDIS, SUMMER 1986. PHOTO © MICHELLE CLIFFORD.

## Watch Your Wallets and Stay Out of the Bathroom!

By Jan Bruun

# Bill Landis & Michelle Clifford

## Watch Your Wallets and Stay Out of the Bathroom!

LANDIS INVADES THE MAINSTREAM IN THE SUMMER 1984 DOUBLE ISSUE (426–427) OF *ROLLING STONE*. PHOTO © NIGEL DICKSON.

Bill Landis, deep into the Deuce lifestyle. 'We go for the stuff that really makes people angry.'

I never got to know Bill Landis. I wrote to him years ago, but that was a strange affair. My plan was to interview him about Times Square—the old Times Square that had once festered with every sin and vice imaginable. Bill had once pounded the beat, recording what he saw on the streets and in the run-down theatres for his legendary fanzine *Sleazoid Express*.

I wanted to know Bill Landis. I shot him a letter. But before I was granted access to the man, I had to talk to his wife, Michelle. "Must be some kind of screening process," I thought. "Makes sense, I guess. Never know what kind of crazy fans you'll run into these days..."

I played along, but after a week or so, our correspondence ended. I received fewer and fewer replies to my letters and soon, they stopped coming altogether. I decided to bide my time. "Let's not be too overeager," I thought. "I'll try again someday."

That "someday" never came. Bill Landis passed away on December 22, 2008, the victim of a heart attack.

I never got to know Bill Landis. I only knew him through his writing.

Make no mistake about it; Bill Landis could write. The pages of *Sleazoid Express* were filled with his unique vision of a world gone to hell. Of course, hell is what you make of it, and Bill seemed to be having a fine time trawling the streets of Times Square, ducking into theatre after theatre, taking in some of the most disgusting and depraved films known to man. The theatre experience became a part of his reviews. Soon, Bill was not only reviewing the films he saw, but the theatres he saw them in. He seemed to have become one with their inhabitants... both human and otherwise.

Bill was no longer just an observer. He was as much a part of the seedy trappings that surrounded him as the films he was writing about. *Sleazoid Express* broke new ground in the fanzine arena. The style was fresh, funny, and degenerate; others soon took note.

As much as we'd like it to, the carnival can't go on forever. There comes a time when the fun and games are forced to move on. The carnys emerge from their tents, gloves in hand, to pull up the stakes and rip down the canvas. By 1985, the first attempts to sterilize Times Square had taken hold. You could almost see each light bulb on the theatre marquees break and go dark as the years marched on. Times Square's star was fading and so was *Sleazoid Express*.

I never got to know Bill Landis. I only knew him through his writing. A hand reached down from the sky to turn on the lights of the Empire Theater one last time as Mr. Sleazoid slowly walked home.

The following interview was conducted by Jan Bruun. It originally appeared in *Creeping Flesh: The Horror Fantasy Film Book, Vol. One* (Headpress, 2003).

---

**JAN BRUUN: Where were you born? I assume it wasn't in Times Square?**

**BILL LANDIS:** This takes a bit of time: Nearly forty-four years ago, I was born of American parents in Landes de Busac, France. Hence, the name Landis—Landes is the Euro spelling—like Corleone in the *Godfather* movies—it's a taken name from where I was born. I grew up until age five at a full service hotel in Christine Keeler-era London. Fun reading about her in the scandal sheets, though I didn't comprehend all the "mechanics" then. It was 66 Lancaster Gate, for American military personnel. The location of the hotel changed when I was last in London in 1972. Interestingly, my cousin Patti Pallidin—of Johnny Thunders notoriety (she sang with him and produced some of his records and was in the Cale group Snatch with Judy Nylon)—is an American expatriate in London.

I first set eyes on the Deuce when returning to NY around 1965. To a little kid, it was a neon palace. Sexually driven. It was still the era of the "midnight cowboy", so they were around, looking weird and delusional, like something dropped off of Hollywood Boulevard.

**MICHELLE CLIFFORD:** I was born in Boston, Massachusetts. Little Ireland. Moved at seven years old to Fort Lauderdale, Florida. Moved then at nineteen in with Bill, on 14th Street, NYC.

**JB: Do you have any education pertaining to movies, journalism or anything else, or did you just learn as you went along?**

**BL:** I had been writing critiques of movies since age ten or so, with the encouragement of some neighbourhood girls. We'd trade tips on movies after seeing them on creature features—late-night TV, where the censorship was low. "That was Jane Fonda's tit just now in *Circle of Love*!" they'd shout. And that movie was playing theatrically with *Murmur of the Heart*.

Some movies had simultaneous theatrical and edited TV runs, like *Mondo Cane*. By the time I was fourteen, PBS (public broadcasting in the US) ran all the great Euro-movies like *La Dolce Vita*, *L'Aventurra*, all the Bergmans (I liked *Sawdust and Tinsel* best), great Japanese ones like the *Burmese Harp* and *Hara-kiri*. So I got an early education in art movies by the time I was fourteen, which were stodgy by the time *Sleazoid* came out in 1980.

In high school, I was the paper's film critic, as I was in grad-school. A self-taught one. In fact, ironically, Michelle found a note from a teacher saying I should expand beyond reviews. I think I got a B in the required expository writing—the classes were in huge auditoriums and often taught by a grad student who found it an annoyance to their own studies. I got sick of it early. Just read the books, passed the test, then went to 42nd Street all the time to catch new movies since I was sixteen. I was in a perpetual state of competition—how many new flicks could I see a week? Ten, fourteen, more even? John Friday [contributor to the early *Sleazoid Express*] went on the ride for some, and got shocked by *Last House on Dead End Street*, though we both thought the race-hate *Black Gestapo* was hilarious, well paced, and delivered roughie elements.

**MC:** It's passion. What I write about is my religion. I try to tell the truth. Truth is my religion.

**JB: What were the first movies you saw in Times Square, and when? What kind of impact did it have to go there for the first time?**

**BL:** Oh, it's been so long ago. The streets were lined with neon... the theatre marquees were a virtual umbrella over the Deuce, which was tiny considering it is just one block— 42nd between 7th and 8th. Sex stores abounded for every preference. Everything from the Serena S&M classic loop *Girls Behind Bars* to bestiality Color Climax coded ones were ubiquitous.

In terms of movies, cannibal vomitorium; *Carnivorous (Last Survivor)*—that was a shocker billed with *I Drink Your Blood*... Andy Milligan's *Torture Dungeon* (didn't live up to the title and the Milligan aesthetic is hard to take the first time you accidentally see it), Bob Cresse's *Love Camp 7* (did live up to the title), as did *Slaves in Cages*. My intro to Jess Franco was *Barbed Wire Dolls*, which showed how much further Euro movies went than US ones—not quite hardcore, not quite softcore. Of course, fave women-in-prison movies like *Big Doll House* and *Black Mama White Mama*. Among the hundreds of kung fu, I liked *Streetfighter* for the violence, *Hammer of God* for originality and visuals, and *Master of the*

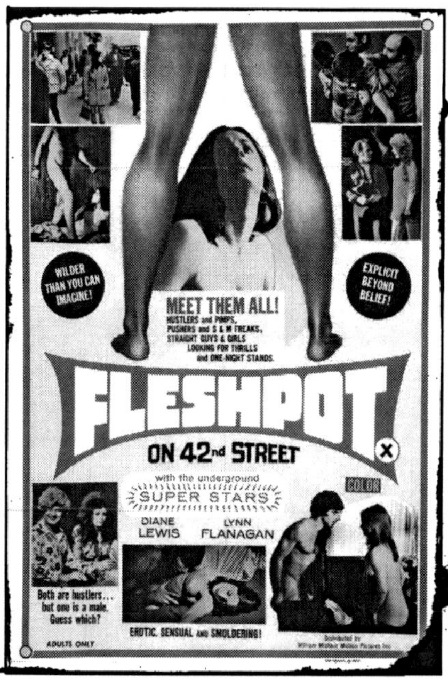

*Flying Guillotine* because the guillotines looked like those little fans sold to hot commuters on NY subways. Saw the edited-down version (R-rated) of *Ginger* with the heavy giallo *Girl in Room 2A*—that impressed me with its action and relentless sadism. Eventually, I did catch up to the uncut *Ginger* and it was everything I'd hoped it would be.

The cut versions of *Devil in Miss Jones* and *Deep Throat* played at the Mini Cinema for at least a year after *Animal Lover* was busted. Eventually, I saw the uncut versions of them. "Porno chic" flicks I liked included *800 Fantasy Lane*, Alex De Renzy's *Femmes De Sade*, *Waterpower* and a weird one called *The Naughty Victorians*.

**MC:** *Mountainside Motel Massacre* and *Girls for Sale*—my first date with Bill; my first day in NYC. I thought it was like a wee tiny street for such a big reputation.

**JB: Did you enjoy the slightly dangerous and half-criminal feeling of the old 42nd Street/Times Square days?**

**BL:** Loved it, participated in it, was part of my life as a projectionist/ theatre manager there.

**MC:** The crime never scared me, it entertained me. I was never harmed there. The old Times Square reminded me of my mother. My childhood. In the old Times Square, you could be yourself. For good or ill.

**JB: How does the clean-up completed in the last ten–twelve years make you feel?**

**BL:** Well, I took my kid to the Toys R Us there for a small ferris ship ride and kept remembering that it used to be the Loews Fiveplex. The topography keeps changing all the time… it's not the same. Took her to see *Thomas the Tank Engine*, and it made me sad because it used to be the Empire, where I saw *Blind Rage*, *Battle of the Amazons*, many great triple bills. You go over to 9th Avenue, 10th Avenue; no theatres there, but the Hispanic population has stayed since the 1950s, with some Irish holdouts.

**MC:** The cleanup is "progress". Life changes. The world changes. The values of the world change. Change hurts. But, now we bring our daughter to the

RANDOM PAGES FROM *SLEAZOIDS* PAST.

multiplex and tell her a book was dedicated to her about how it used to be, a long, long time ago. A history book we wrote… when mom and dad met a long time ago.

But let me add, when Times Square closed, it broke our hearts. Bill stopped writing about the films because there were no more playing. Video companies like Something Weird had yet to acquire their stocks. He was heartbroken that it was demolished. I took photos of its death there. Some are in the book. Some we have of Bill standing in front of places being torn down. It just killed him. It hurt him to see other mags ape his style and claim to have been there when they were lame imitators. He stopped writing for a couple years, then I got him to go back to record "all that hath occurred", as Crowley, I think, put it.

The last film we saw there was *Falling Down*, appropriately enough. The audience was so sad. Everyone knew the end had come. America had changed. And we and our kind especially were not wanted. Film mags, periodicals, we couldn't write for because the Deuce wasn't "timely" anymore. We were a figment of the past. And one that NYC was glad to get rid of. They let the buildings rot until, like decayed teeth, needed to be extracted. Which was their plan. The owners of the theatres got rich. Millionaires.

**JB: Did the cinemas in the Times Square area show a mixture of porn and horror, or was that always in separate theatres?**

**BL:** Always separate, with one funny example. On US holidays, the Victory—a porn theatre right off 7th Avenue north near subway—would have a horror triple bill! Things like the *Curse of the Living Flesh* thing (an old Mario Bava movie, an Anita Ekberg vehicle), *Kingdom of the Spiders*, *Frogs*, real horror oldies that Aquarius Pictures either got a hold of or had prints lying around.

**MC:** Sometimes the theatres changed what they showed like the Roxy went hardcore, changed to exploitation, then back to triple X.

**JB: When was the original version of *Sleazoid Express* published?**

**BL:** Summer 1980, on a manual typewriter. 8 x 11.5 inches, offset printed.

**JB: That was just a couple of sheets in each issue, wasn't it? How often did that come out?**

**BL:** It came out every other week, literally telling what was good, bad or indifferent on the Deuce. A one-sheet bulletin. It was also distributed at Club 57 where friends of mine like Kenny Scharf, Basquait, and Keith Haring also encouraged my interest in Times Square. We did performance art pieces—like one where I gave Kool Aid to an audience tripping on LSD pretending I was Jim Jones. I also gave out *Sleazoids* at Artforum parties at the Hellfire Club, record and bookstores. We also did a thing called the Times Square Show, where all these artists did their raunchiest projects and I gave out hundreds of *Sleazoids*. Beth and Scott B were involved—I later played a small part in their movie *Vortex*. Then, it grew to 11 x 17, offset printed with a cover price of fifty cents. That let me examine genres, directors, and campaigns more explicitly.

**JB: Why did you decide to restart it as a thicker zine a few years ago?**

**BL:** After the success of Michelle's *Metasex*, and seeing how many people copied the *Sleazoid* formula without even venturing to 42nd Street. The latter factor is one factor in my depression—all these imitators. That made me stop putting out the magazine. And Michelle encouraged me to be myself more with the new one (I had always wanted it magazine length). The love of Eurosleaze films, old chestnuts from the Deuce, obscure films, all together. With the background of the vice there—*Metasex* handles that in-depth.

**JB: Did you arrange special screenings of films during the old *Sleazoid* period?**

**BL:** Yeah. A throwback to the smoker era with rented or owned 16mm prints at Club 57. All my faves like *Big Doll House*, *Manson* (I had a Manson impersonator and the *LIE* album play), *Villain* with a drunk Richard Burton as a gay S&M gangster, the sleaze classic *Toys Are Not For Children*, *Caged Heat*, Paul Bartel's best movie *Private Parts*, Warhol's *Flesh*, *Paranoia* with Carroll Baker, Larry Cohen's *God Told Me To* (aka *The Demon*), and, of course, *Mondo Cane*.

**JB: You portray the director of *Mondo Cane*, Gualtiero Jacopetti, as a lying racist paedophile in *Sleazoid*, but that film remains one of my**

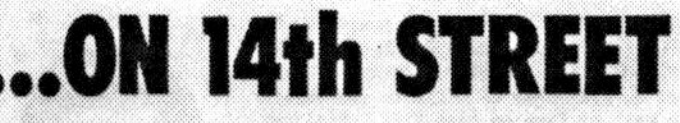

# ...ON 14th STREET

By Mr. Sleazoid and Buggin' Out

If you ever wondered what happened to those baggy bell bottoms with high cuffs and unlikely plaids, platform shoes, white imitation leather slip-ons, ultra-suede and vinyl jackets and overcoats (the fly imitation of burburries), all the leftover tams mixed in with broadrimmed fedoras, taxi driver's caps and the ubiquitous knit stocking caps in any weather at any time of the day or night, check out--

14th St. between 2nd and 3rd Aves. Former home of Movie Star News and present locale of the most notorious shooting gallery in the city (Sahara Hotel), only cuchifritos between 14th and Sutton Place on the east side, Varieties, Metropolitan and Cinema 14 Theaters, the old Jefferson Theater which hosted a nightclub above in a residence loft after hours some years back. Before that, the theater showed 3rd run porn and Spanish films, probably to the same people who haunt this turf today.

By day, it's Koreans and a few Arabs selling jewelry, produce, shoes, clothes and studded leather--anything--making their money to spend or lose around Times Square later. Mostly white streetwalkers hang during the day in front of the now closed 200 East 14th, a massage parlor which has been around since the 60s and was the last to remain open in the city, surviving vice busts and the board of health. 15 years of hooking on the same corner has turned girls who may have once been attractive into grotesque drones of women, undoubedly serving black and Spanish pimps. Narcotics show on many faces.

Up and down the block the familiar hawk of "sense sense" can be heard a dozen times. Black guys in the latest flash clothes (expensive name brand running suits; anything nylon; labels like LEE and Sergio Valente; Nike, Adidas or Puma sneakers; plastic baseball caps; in winter, much leather and fur). These guys are sharp and streetwise, and their faces have an eerie savageness J McD compared to the bowler-hatted hard black faces in dusty 30s photos. Their reefer is sometimes good, more often OK, but you have to deal with 4 of them shoving bags in your face. Don't even give them the time of day. In spite of frequent patrol cars and cops with big guts joking about the Miss America issue of Penthouse walking beats often, these boys are undaunted and are up any time of the day or night to make their cash.

Variety on 14th St. is incredible. The sense salesmen with perhaps $500 of cash money in their pockets exist peacefully with bums, Ones, Crazy Niggers, and the folks who proudly wear their colors (clothes mentioned earlier)--Pappos.

MR. SLEAZOID and GUMS.

Ones--newest entry into the Sleazoid Life Casualties. Their god is Stretch, a tall, thin black man dressed in a cross of velour styles adding up to a decayed Ike Turner. A black Golem head, with stitches on both cheeks making it seem really shrunken, mumbles beneath a porkpie hat. Stretch is by some reports a numbers runner, procuror of drugs and part time pimp, and a permanent fixture on the Lower East Side. Ones must believe that this man is the most fly among them and the elements of style he possesses are the elements of their aspirations. Since your average One isn't hooked up with any moneymaking venture other than a monthly welfare check, it's quite certain that they are far from the mostly down Stretch. Stretch walks confidently into the brown door and orders 8 cokes. Ones push their way to the front of a line, permeating the air with the aroma of wine, sweat, piss and filthy polyester, holding the only money they've made all day ($5), blurting out "ONE!!!" "WUUUUUNNN!!!" Yes, ONE and only ONE small foil with not enough coke to give the big rush is all these poor fellows can afford. Big black palm stuck out with a demanding, desperate look on that lined, frowned face... "ONE!" They'll often give their buddies a taste of the spoon, sharing works used enough to make them dull as a butter knife. Watch where you step for Ones are known to defecate or urinate without warning in a gamut of places--lots, busy streets, tenement rooftops, dopehouse stairwells... you name it, they've left it, the mark of One. Works salesmen are several steps above Ones economically, so don't let appearances fool you.

"ONE!"

SUPER C, SENSE SALESMAN

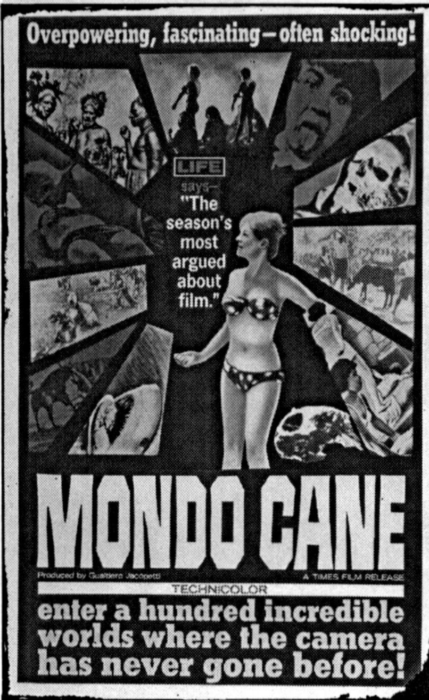
Overpowering, fascinating—often shocking!
LIFE
says—
"The season's most argued about film."
MONDO CANE
Produced by Gualtiero Jacopetti
A TIMES FILM RELEASE
TECHNICOLOR
enter a hundred incredible worlds where the camera has never gone before!

**favourites. I had the local Cinemateque in Oslo dig the film out of their archives to show it for a full house in 2002, with lots of media coverage. It was probably the first time that print had been shown since the sixties... Do you still show movies?**

**BL:** I did it again in 1981. I was the first to revive Herschel Lewis' *Blood Feast* in a decade, since the demise of the Elgin Theater, at the now defunct 8th Street Playhouse, which had a midnight movie a night. *Blood Feast* was a midnighter. Then I talked the owner into having a month-long sleaze festival—the only constraint that the rental of the movie had to be below $250.

That was March, 1983. We had *Pink Flamingos* and *Female Trouble*; a gay triple of *The Back Row* with George Payne and Casey Donovan, *Wanted: Billy the Kid* (freakish straight scene) and *Demi Gods* (an animated short, very rare, with the heads of Sal Mineo, Marlon Brando et al in various positions); *The Big Doll House* and *Big Bust Out*; *Night of the Bloody Apes* and *The Last Survivor*; Russ Meyer's *Good Morning and Goodbye* and *Common Law Cabin*, *Finders Keepers* and *Cherry Harry & Raquel*; *I Spit on Your Grave* (the one Ebert hated) with the extraordinary *Axe*; *Ilsa She Wolf* and *Harem Keeper* (uncut); *The Love Butcher* (great Deuce find) with Cresse's *Love Camp 7*; *The Ghastly Ones* (one of Milligan's best) with *The Headless Eyes* (a fave crazy loner horror, X for violence); *Fight For Your Life* and *Black Shampoo* (race hate mixed with blaxploitation); *Drive In Massacre* and *I Dismember Mama*; *I Drink Your Blood* and *Don't Look in the Basement*; the tranny documentary *The Queen* (supposedly staged).

Years ago, it took legwork to find out who had these films—the Meyers weren't yet on Cable TV; I got to know a lot of Deuce distributors through this project other than ones I already knew, like Ava Leighton of Audubon Films. Another trip—it was fun arranging this festival from the pay phone at the Bryant Theater, where I was the projectionist.

**MC:** We started showing movies again in 1999—did a *Sleazoid* Festival at Yerba Buena Center for the Arts in San Francisco in 1999 showing *Last House on Dead End Street* (its first theatrical showing in years; people were getting sick!), *Pets*, *The Candy Snatchers*, *Sweet Savior* (Troy Donohue as Charlie Manson) and *Back Row.*

We just met with the owner of the Pioneer Theatre/Two Boots on 3rd Street and Avenue A, a nice hipster venue and are planning a *Sleazoid/Metasex* Festival, similar to that at the 8th Street Playhouse. They have capacity for video projection, which opens up the floodgates for many obscure films (like *Pets*) that are just on tape and the rights are floating in limbo. Also, they are reviving some hardcore movies, so we're looking at *Behind the Green Door* and Bill Lustig's *Violation of Claudia*—we will be doing DVD notes for Lustig's company Blue Underground. So we're back in the swing of doing film festivals; they're far from a thing of the past for us.

**JB: Did you make notes continually or do you remember all these details regarding the look and smell of the sleaze theatres, the patrons, the movies, the directors, distributors etc?**

**BL:** Both. And the first *Sleazoid*s were so immediate I just went home and typed them down. Whatever was remarkable—the patrons, the film, whether Joe Brenner had slipped a horror title on a stupid Italian crime movie... whether the theatre was packed or empty, freezing or not... Some movies it was worth noting the details, others I couldn't give a damn... like when *Mad Max* first opened it took second place to *Let Me Die A Woman* in the first *Sleazoid* because (1) It wasn't sleazy enough and (2) I didn't like the dumb dubbing or Brian (*Queen*) May music.

Another funny thing—I hated the Romero adaptation of *Creepshow* (I felt he totally sold out by then) and someone got stabbed to death while watching it. So I took note of that—that piece of garbage was the last thing the person saw with his dying eyes.

**MC:** I remember from memory the smell, the look, the floor, toilet, patrons, meeting actors.

**JB: Were the theatres open twenty-four hours?**

**BL:** Some were: The Harem (all porn, "balcony for couples only"; people would go in there and change into drag), and the

# Bill Landis & Michelle Clifford

## Watch Your Wallets and Stay Out of the Bathroom!

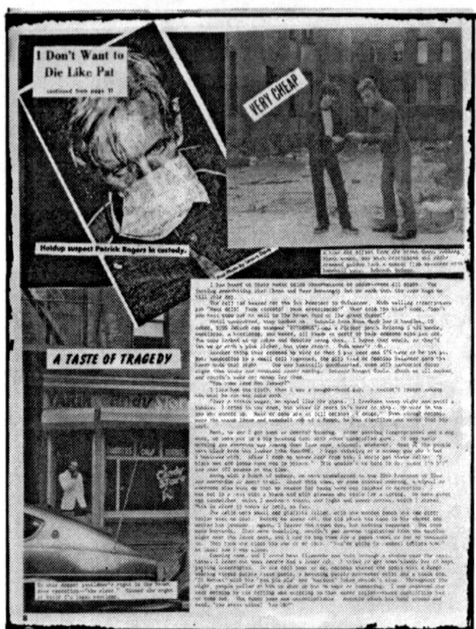


Roxy, after it became an exploitation grindhouse. Some of the regular Deuce grindhouses I remember leaving at 3:30 AM. They were open pretty late.

**JB: Did bums "move in" to sleep? Any sex or violence or anything out of the ordinary when you were working as manager or projectionist at the theatres?**

**BL:** Oh, you haven't seen (sub) humanity until you've seen 8th Avenue around the time the bars close at 4:30 AM. There was a curtain behind the Eros theatre that made people adjust their eyes for a minute to get used to the light... and they'd stand and get pickpocketed there. The Eros was open from 10 AM to 5 AM.

The Venus had a lot of sleepers—it was open 10 AM to 7 AM. And that's where you had a lot of crazy outbursts. Like in *Metasex* number 1—real interesting one reeler XXX films. But more of a closety black street clientele than the all-male Eros next door. And the whites that sought them out. Most remarkable scene at the Venus: a dusthead ripped his clothes off, declaring "IT'S ORGY TIME"—the EMS lady who showed up later with an ambulance said "all that trouble for that little thing"... and then the guy would go in again and we'd just hope he wouldn't start it up once more...

There was the problem of the mad shitters at the Venus... a black guy in thick glasses with a *M*A*S*H* Army T-shirt—he got nervous and everyone said, "Don't let him in!" It turned out he was defecating in the aisles.

Stabbings—a common Summertime thing on 42nd Street. I saw my first stabbing when I was around sixteen. Some guy went nuts in front of a massage parlour, then there were cops following bloody footprints to the subway. We describe this in the book. Black robbers often assumed Asian men had hidden sums of gambling money or that Indian men were easy marks. They'd take each side of the victim, flash a small sharp pocket knife or object and rob them. The victim would be too terrified to even leave the front of the theatre, fearing the assailants were still out in the throngs of Deuce Street.

One of Chelly Wilson's girlfriends, the obnoxious one named Angela

who was paying off some "medical debt" was so nasty to the Venus customers that one night they pistol whipped her. Same thing for Mae. Mae was from Hell's Kitchen, but moved to Brooklyn and continued to take the train at the ungodly hour or 5 AM. When she'd close the Eros, she'd end up being beaten up or pistol whipped, too. Mae was about eighty. Blonde wig, very sweet. Why her kids were letting her work there is beyond me. She used to have an apartment on 42nd and 9th; a real old time Hell's Kitchener.

Chelly Wilson's 8th Avenue Theaters had poor security. The Avon chain had a million people ready to stop a disturbance, from a live show team to a bouncer, so there were no problems like that at the Doll. Only that Phil Prince was a murderer!*

**MC:** Phil Prince was the director of the notorious roughie Avon films like *Kneel Before Me*. All starring George Payne.

**BL:** You could—in a way—conceive of 42nd Street/Times Square as Marco Vassi's ideal of the "metasexual"—except, like many things in human execution, it got way, way distorted from its idealization.

**JB: Did you work at making movies as well, writing scripts? You mention some of this in your Andy Milligan article in *Sleazoid*'s Spring 1999 issue. Tell me some of the movies you've worked on and what you did.**

**MC:** I never worked in film.

**BL:** I did scriptwriting anonymously for certain infamous people under very phoney names… and I was paid but I have no idea what happened to them!

**JB: In your Andy Milligan article you mentioned working as "focus finder"…**

**BL:** Oh yeah, that's how antiquitated Andy was—a focus finder! They

**Phil Prince had a wife with whom he worked in the live sex shows. The police suspected him of killing her to get the life insurance money. Suspect number two was Phil's best friend (and possibly homosexual lover) Pat Rodgers, a fellow employee at the Avon Theatre. The whole story is in* Metasex *number 2.*

never use 'em on regular flicks any more—and general gofer, I guess, for that production he did *Carnage*—a haunted house thing that went right to video and isn't half bad.

**JB: What other magazines have you written for over the years?**

**MC/BL:** Many articles for *Film Comment*, *Carbon 14*, *Screw*, *Swank*, *Hustler*, *Jersey Voice*.

**BL:** Many for the *Village Voice*. One article I wrote for them got reproduced in two books, an ACLU handbook and a book called *Beyond Crisis*—it was about the needle exchange program by ACT-UP. I wrote for *SoHoNews* when it was in existence—I had a weekly column on what was playing on the Deuce.

**JB: Bill, I find it very interesting that your wife seems to share a lot of your interests re: the sleazy films and the industry. How did you two meet?**

**BL:** She wrote me a letter after *Film Comment* did a profile of me.

**MC:** I wanted to be a writer. I read Bill's articles and respected his writing. I saw it in a mag in the library in Florida. I was a high school dropout. My mother had been shot in the head by a police officer and I was taking it easy in the library. Reading for my education. Not much to learn in Florida. I would go to the library every day and read a book or two a day. I wrote to him. Moved in with him as a teen. I knew what he wrote was real. He taught me much.

**JB: I appreciate your ongoing effort to document these areas of popular culture that most others would scorn or regard with contempt or disinterest. I think it's important to remember and preserve, especially in the light of the clean-up of NYC.**

**MC:** Vice is my area. I document this area because of my mother bringing me to the Combat Zone as a child and to grindhouses to see films. She took me to see *Taxi Driver* when it came out and *The Godfather*. She loved film. She was a tough Irish Mick criminal. *Reservoir Dogs* style crimes. Violent crime and killings, I saw one once… at six years old. She was a Madame as

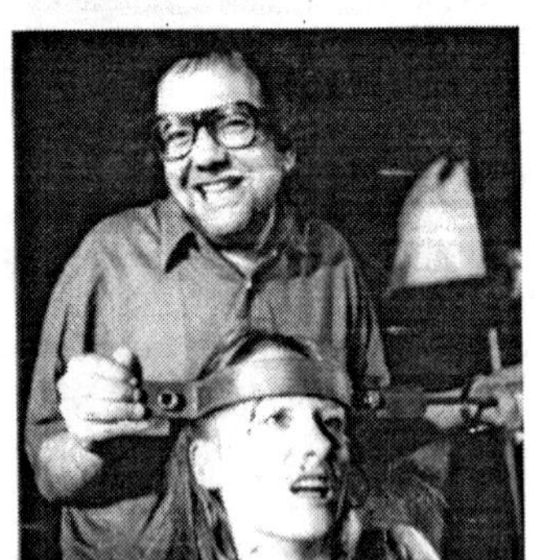
SLEAZOID EXPRESS

SPECIAL ISSUE:
THE BIOGRAPHY OF JOEL M. REED
DIRECTOR OF "BLOODSUCKING FREAKS"
...or "Games Con Men Play"

SLEAZOID EXPRESS ANEW.

well… I didn't grow up with her. I visited. I visited her in jail once. She gave me my first 8mm camera and Polaroid. She was a violent criminal. She would tell me the inner workings of the vice arena. Her friends, pimps, etc, would treat me like a princess and tell me very personal stories and let me Polaroid them as a kid. I document like John Grisham tried to, what I knew to be truth. Inner workings of a secret society. Not a friendly one. One that doesn't like outsiders.

**JB: Is it hard to maintain an interest in these movies for such a long time?**

**BL:** You know, some of the movies I can live without seeing again like *Carnivorous*. Or *Farewell Uncle Tom*, or anything by Jacopetti. Others like *Black Emmanuelle* are perennial faves. Or anything with Alice Arno. I think *La Comptesse Perverse* is her best role—along with the faithful adaptation of *Justine* where she plays the lead. Alice is like the *Sleazoid* Marilyn Monroe—her image is on the website and there's the snuff scene hyperlink with her in *La Comptesse Perverse* mentioned in issue number 3. There are the old Times Square chestnuts I love, such as *Barbed Wire Dolls*, although I've taken a liking to more Eurosleaze. *La Punition* with Karin Schubert is pretty unforgettable and it would be hard to make a movie like that in the US. Same thing for *Eden & After*; I like the image so much I made it one of the covers for *Sleazoid*.

**JB: I just rented the TV movie *Rated X* with Charlie Sheen and Emilio Estevez, about the brothers Jim and Artie Mitchell, who made *Behind The Green Door* and started the O'Farrell Theatre in San Francisco. Artie used even more coke than his brother, became violent and threatening, so Jim brought over a shotgun and killed him.**

**BL:** Actually, the Sheen Brothers didn't do a bad job, all things considered. There are two books about the Mitchells—*Bottom Feeders*, which is very, very good, and *Rated X*, which is more about their legal trials.

Personally, I have nothing against Jim… when we had the film festival in San Francisco he donated a brand new 35mm of *Green Door* for the screening—people went nuts, loved it. It was all young couples turning up.

The Mitchell Brothers Present
the all-American girl
MARILYN CHAMBERS
in
Behind the Green Door
adults only
mitchell brothers film group/san francisco


But I think the tragedy of the Mitchells—apart from the obvious of what happened—is that they turned into peepshow pimps instead of developing as filmmakers. *Green Door, Resurrection of Eve, Reckless Claudia*—the early movies—they are very interesting semi-outgrowths of underground movies mixed with the stag mentality. Quite unique and often aesthetically very good. I assume they just made more money running a dirty bookstore and didn't develop as filmmakers. The later big budget ones like *Insatiable* are pretty dull compared to the early seventies' ones.

**MC:** With the survivalist mentality Jim had, the attitude was if you are being physically threatened, you hurt or kill the aggressor. No questions asked. So I understand why Jim would do this if the brother kept acting nuts and threatening his girlfriend.

**JB: I was in San Francisco recently and lived around the corner from O'Farrell Street, so I walked by their cinema, still owned by Jim, I suppose. It's a strip club now. I didn't go in, though.**

**MC:** When I was in SF for the *Sleazoid* Film Fest, I went into the Mitchell Theater. It's a very friendly place. We were running *Behind The Green Door* at the museum, Yerba Buena. Although a crazy stripper did start a fight with our driver right outside the theatre while we were inside, saying it was her "handicapped parking zone"...

**JB: When you did the *Anger* book, did you ever talk to Kenneth Anger or get any co-operation at all at any point, maybe early in the process?**

**BL:** I was friendly with him when I got him on the cover of the *SoHo News* in 1980. Then by the end of the year I started seeing why people thought he was a jerk and a leech—though he never got to leech off me. This is the difference between art and exploitation—the guy's been on the scam and he's only made two-and-a-half hours worth of film in his life! Exploitation is a one-time sale, but the filmmakers are so, so, prolific.

**JB: I've heard that Anger is quite difficult to have anything to do with.**

**BL:** This is true. Even when you're attempting to help or be friendly with him. So after the last straw—the Danceteria incident—I turned him into a subject for ridicule for a while. He was supposed to read from his then current book *Hollywood Babylon 2* and he was on acid and freaked out and ran down the street like a nut. He refused to go on. The incident is all in the *Anger* book.

ANGER RAN DOWN THE STREET.

**MC:** I was co-author, but didn't take any credit on that book. I was an odd duck. Shy. *Anger* wrote to me. After appealing to me to stop the book, he cursed me, in a ridiculous scroll letter which Bobby Beausoleil, designed years before.* Kenneth Anger didn't know I was friends with Bobby, so the "curse" was useless to scare me. Big red lettering. Ooga booga… I had a pleasant time working with him and wish him the best.

**JB: I just saw a video copy of Paul Morrissey's *Forty Deuce*, which is about hustlers around Times Square…**

**MC:** That film sucks. It's like a filmed high school play. Terrible, and Kevin Bacon played an excellent hustler in the film *JFK*. So it was the director, not the actors.

**JB: Do you have any memories of Hubert's Museum and freak shows on 42nd Street?**

**BL:** By the time I was there, Hubert's Museum was a sleazy hustler arcade in the process of turning itself into Peepland, the thing with the giant quarter.

**JB: What kind of movie is Russ Meyer's *Steamheat*? I saw it mentioned in one of your articles.**

**BL:** It's a nudie. And a rare one, because William Mishkin put it out. Supposedly the idiot son who died of brain cancer could have melted that down for the silver content too. It was made before Russ was big, meaning it could have been a one-time sale to Mishkin. He made it four years after *The Immoral Mr Teas*.

**JB: How did the deal for the *Sleazoid Express* book come about?**

**MC:** We were approached by an editor at Simon and Schuster, through our wonderful agent, Craig Nelson. The book is all original….all about

**Michelle interviewed Bobby Beausoleil for the* Anger *book. The letter is some stationary that Beausoleil designed for* Anger.

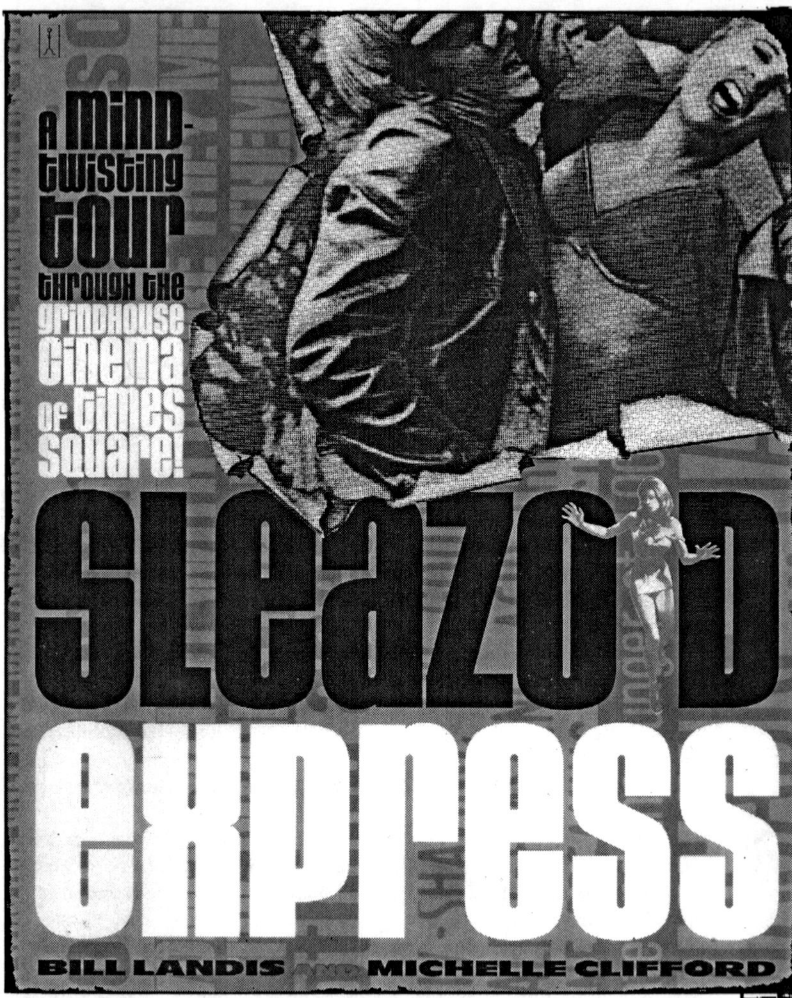

A MIND-TWISTING TOUR THROUGH THE GRINDHOUSE CINEMA OF TIMES SQUARE!

SLEAZOID EXPRESS

BILL LANDIS AND MICHELLE CLIFFORD

theatres, films, genres.

**BL:** There's lots of unpublished stuff, all within a historical/grindhouse/etc. context. You can think of the book as both magazines with new material and new outlooks on some of it.

**JB: Will the *Sleazoid* and *Metasex* zines continue to come out?**

**MC:** Both mags continue. We'd like to do a documentary and maybe another book...

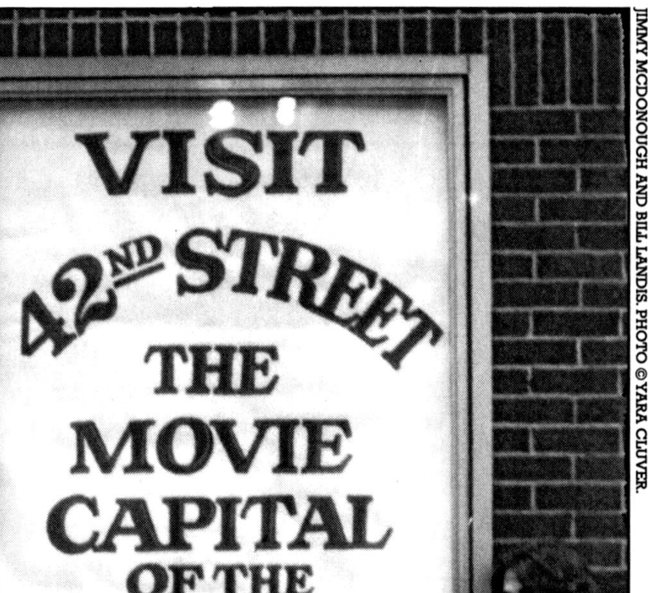

JIMMY MCDONOUGH AND BILL LANDIS. PHOTO © YARA CLUVER.

## Chapter Seven
# Jimmy McDonough
## All Aboard the Night Train!

# ALL ABOARD THE NIGHT TRAIN!

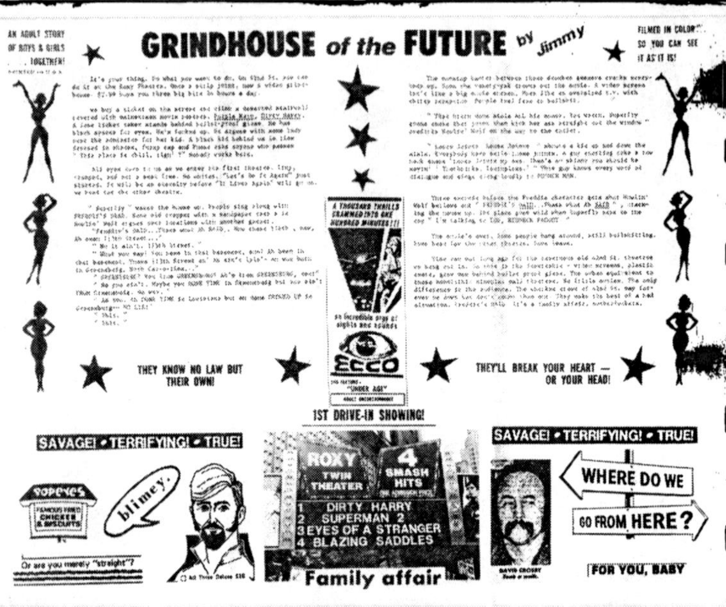

RECORDED & INDEXED

DRAFT

AN ADULT STORY OF BOYS & GIRLS . . . TOGETHER!

## GRINDHOUSE of the FUTURE by Jimmy

FILMED IN COLOR SO YOU CAN SEE IT AS IT IS!

A THOUSAND THRILLS CRAMMED INTO ONE HUNDRED MINUTES!!!

an incredible orgy of sights and sounds

ECCO

"UNDER AGE"

THEY KNOW NO LAW BUT THEIR OWN!

THEY'LL BREAK YOUR HEART — OR YOUR HEAD!

1ST DRIVE-IN SHOWING!

SAVAGE! • TERRIFYING! • TRUE!

POPEYES FAMOUS FRIED CHICKEN & BISCUITS

blimey.

Or are you merely "straight"?

ROXY TWIN THEATER 4 SMASH HITS

1 DIRTY HARRY
2 SUPERMAN 2
3 EYES OF A STRANGER
4 BLAZING SADDLES

Family affair

SAVAGE! • TERRIFYING! • TRUE!

DAVID CROSBY

WHERE DO WE GO FROM HERE?

FOR YOU, BABY

RANDOM PAGES FROM *SLEAZOIDS* PAST.

I wasn't sure if I'd get the chance to talk to Jimmy McDonough. Well, that's not entirely true. Getting a hold of him was easy enough—I sent him a letter outlining my intentions for this book and he wrote me back within the hour. His response was sympathetic and encouraging, but it left me anxious. I knew from the start that there might still be some rancor between McDonough and Bill Landis, and JM's response confirmed my fears. It wasn't that McDonough was afraid of what Bill might say in rebuttal; Landis died of heart failure in 2008. Rather, McDonough wasn't so sure that he wanted to revisit that particular chapter of his past.

"The history is a tortured one. I've never really spoken about it and don't know if I want to. It can only bring me grief. I'll think it over. I hope you're not in a hurry."

My heart skipped a few beats as I wrote him back. I thanked him for his frankness and honesty and asked him to take his time.

I first read Jimmy McDonough's work in Bill Landis' *Sleazoid Express*. *SE* made an instant impact on me, and McDonough's writing played a big part in that. His words seemed effortless, and they painted *Sleazoid*'s pages with the rancid sights, sounds, and smells of old Times Square. The picture was far from pretty, but it was alluring, just the same. McDonough and Landis were creatures of the night, and they documented everything

they encountered—good, bad, and ugly—in a way that no "legitimate" journalist would ever dare. The two made an amazing team before things went south.

But, as they say, all good things must come to an end. The streets of Times Square were eventually swept clean and conflicts of personality caused McDonough and Landis to part ways. Luckily, that didn't keep either of them from writing.

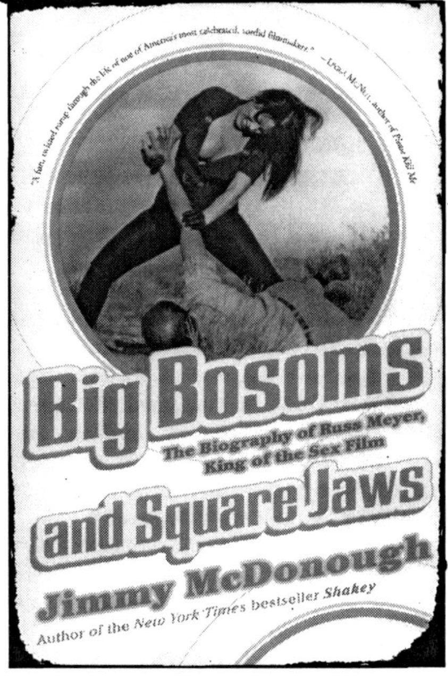


Landis went deeper and deeper underground, but eventually surfaced with a biography of Kenneth Anger in 1995. In 1999, he and his wife Michelle relaunched *Sleazoid Express*. 2002 saw the publication of a full-fledged book, *Sleazoid Express: A Mind-Twisting Tour Through the Grindhouse Cinema of Times Square*. Then, sadly and suddenly, the hand of fate came knocking, and Bill Landis left this world far too soon.

McDonough tried his hand as a biographer and the words that poured out of him were even more fluid and focused than what he had written for *Sleazoid Express*. With relentless obsession, he laid the lives of Neil Young, Russ Meyer, and Tammy Wynette bare. *The Ghastly One: The Sex-Gore Netherworld of Filmmaker Andy Milligan* (2001) stands as one of the most exhaustive and heartbreaking biographies ever written. The book's dedication is haunting in itself: "For Landis—Arrivederci."

Nine days after writing to Jimmy McDonough, an encouraging letter appeared in my inbox: "Send me questions. I'll do my best to answer."

I sent the man a cautious wave of questions, and they were promptly answered with the addendum, "JS... Send more questions. Go for broke."

Far be it from me to turn such an offer down. I took the bait and went down deep. And when I finally came up for air, the following exchange surfaced with me.

So, how about it, kids? You wanna go down deep, too? There's only one train running this late at night. JM told me about it. Things might get dirty. Things always get dirty when you go down that far. But don't worry. Jimmy McDonough's been there, and he can teach you a trick or two. Get your

tokens out of your pockets—the next stop is Port Authority. All aboard the night train…

The following interview was conducted via email, May–October, 2012.

---

**JOHN SZPUNAR: I just read *The Ghastly One* and *Big Bosoms and Square Jaws* again, in preparation for this interview. You've recently published *Tragic Country Queen*. How do you go about choosing the subjects for your biographies?**

**JIMMY McDONOUGH:** I have to be moved by them. That's it.

**JS: I can only imagine the amount of work it must take to be so exhaustive. How much preparation and research do you do on somebody before you decide to take the plunge?**

**JM:** Usually, I've thought about it a few years or more. That first phone call to somebody in the story is always the most interesting. It sort of predicts how things will go.

**JS: Have you found that gaining access to interview subjects has gotten easier over the years?**

**JM:** No. If anything the opposite. Everybody is so aware of everything these days. And they want to control the end result.

**JS: Let's back up for a second. Where were you born and raised?**

**JM:** Born in New York. Moved to Chicago, then New Jersey, then Indiana. My childhood is a weird blend of *Happy Days* and *Hee Haw*. Left home at sixteen or so. Moved to NYC when I turned twenty.

**JS: Were you always a reader?**

**JM:** Yes, and I was always obsessed by something, even as a little kid. Dinosaurs. Abe Lincoln. Leonardo Da Vinci. When I'm interested in something I have to know everything I can about it. Everything. Always been that way.

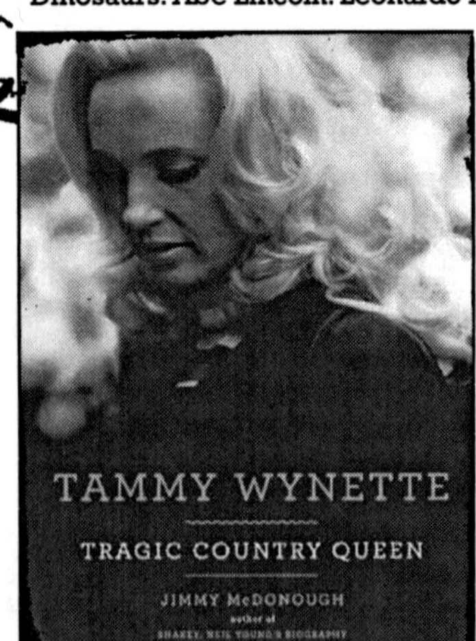


**JS: A broad question, but what was your childhood like?**

**JM:** I don't recall too much about it, to be honest. My wife Natalia's always saying, "How can you write these books? You can't even remember what happened an hour ago!" Maybe that's why I'm so interested in the lives of others. I was off in some dream world most of the time. My father was a salesman. He was a funny guy, grew up on the wrong side of the tracks. I have a great picture of him shaking

**by Landis and McDonough**

ahhh...time bandits...

GREEK SEX
24 hours
I Like It Up The Rear Or Anyway. Call
ANGELA
(212) 15-3 73

4-COCK RATING

FIGHTIN' GALS
WRESTLERS, BOXERS, STRONG WOMEN. FILMS & FOTOS FROM ALL THE WORLD. WRITE FOR FREE LIST.
PEERLESS SALES, BOX 171-E
CANAL ST. STATION · NEW YORK 13, N.Y.


CHINESE FORTUNE COOKIE
FOR DESSERT
call Suzy Wong
7 days a week from 11am-2am
at WN 8-8873

Yes, we have Mistresses, Black, white or Spanish. Come explore the erotic joys of light dominance, body worship, spankings & golden showers.
(212) 15-3 2

ATTRACTIVE GIRLS
WANTED

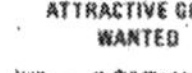


OPPORTUNITY TO EARN
FANTASTIC MONEY
IN PLUSH CLUB

hands with Perry Como at some convention. I guess it was in the blood. Whatever moxie I have came from him.

**JS: When did you become interested in journalism?**

**JM:** I don't know that I ever was. I just wrote. Even as a kid. It was just something I did. There was no plan.

**JS: When did it hit you that you had a talent for words?**

**JM:** It still hasn't hit me. None of it comes easy. I can remember when Landis and I were each invited to write an article on 42nd Street for *Variety*. That was a big thrill for us. I wrote and rewrote, huffed and puffed. As usual, Landis left it to the last possible minute. Finally he showed up at my Hoboken apartment zonked out of his skull. In between nods, cig hanging from his lip, he scribbled something down in one shot. The end result? His was great. Mine was crap.

**JS: Where were you first published?**

**JM:** Free hippy paper in Bloomington Indiana. *Primo Times*. A review of Neil Young's *Comes A Time*, which I also illustrated. It was a pan.

**JS: Your work really holds a mirror up to its subjects and the reflection isn't always pretty. That said, you paint a very human portrait of them. How does this impact your relationship with the people that you research?**

**JM:** Some get a big kick out of it. Some want to kill me. It's not my

# Jimmy McDonough

## All Aboard the Night Train!

GETTING DIRTY AT THE ROXY. [L–R:] JIMMY MCDONOUGH, UNKNOWN, AND BILL LANDIS. PHOTO © YARA CLUVER.

concern. Biography may be an art; it can also be an illness. I think that's never far from the surface in my books.

**JS: Most of the films that I love today were the product of another generation. What was it about the films of Milligan, Meyer, Sarno, and Lewis that made that era so special and memorable?**

**JM:** They were handmade. When the budget is $1.50, the personality can't help but bleed through. As well as a grimy reality. If you want to know what a certain year feels like, find an exploitation film from that time. You can smell the hot dogs. These days, slickness is available to everyone for that same $1.50. Not so exciting, if you ask me. But that's the way of the world. You can't go back. I'm just glad I was there to see some of it, even if it was only the death rattle.

**JS: That brings us to Times Square. What initially attracted you to that circus?**

**JM:** I was working in the film business and walked down 42nd street day and night. Joke shops and knife stores and porno bookstores and record shops and back-issue magazine joints and greasy spoons... dubious characters of every stripe wherever you looked. I loved the carny atmosphere of it all. Any movie fan had to gravitate to the place. You could bounce like a pinball from theatre to theatre not knowing just what you might encounter next. A movie-based fantasyland. It was delirium. Now, 42nd Street was the final destination for Bill Landis. Turns out I was just passing through.

**JS: How much of a feeling was there of the neighborhood's past? I'd imagine that walking into a once grand, now deteriorating theater would conjure up a lot of ghosts...**

**JM:** Oh yeah. Back in the day, Landis and I used to hit these two decrepit NYC porno theatres—the Met on 14th street and the Variety a few blocks down. These joints had been around since Stonehenge. Sticky floors, shadowy clientele, grunts in the darkness... Every once in a blue moon they'd show some ancient sexploitation/exploitation picture. Without warning—you had to be a fucking detective to deduce what they'd slipped onto the bill. Believe me, there was no advertising or coming soon, nothing. At the Met you'd have to read what was scrawled on the paper in the ticket taker's window, pay your $1.99 or whatever it was and take your chances. You'd have to call up the Variety and ask Hector what was playing and hope you could decipher the mumble. Sometimes you'd go by and the poster was just a title in magic marker hastily written on the back of another poster. I remember telling Dave Friedman one of his movies was playing the Variety. News to him. Smoke was practically coming out of his ears as he ran to call his sub distributor. No wonder we could never find out what was showing. It was free money to whoever physically possessed these prints at the time. They just wanted to pocket the flat rental, which had to be next to nothing. These were movies nobody

cared about being showing to an audience that wasn't watching anyway. They had other things on their minds, haha. But being the cineastes William Z and I were we actually came to watch the film. It's kind of amusing, actually. You should've seen the look on the faces of the poor working stiffs in the box office when we inquired as to what was playing and when. It was as if we were asking to read their toilet paper.

**JS: Why do you think the vice nested and settled in Times Square?**

**JM:** Location is everything. You had the Port Authority and the subway right there. Passersby with loot in their wallets. A never-ending stream of rubes hungry for cheap thrills.

**JS: Do you think that element was always there? Did it just change to reflect the times?**

**JM:** Well, I'm no historian of Times Square but I can tell you when crack came in, everything changed. You knew the end was near. Everybody had gone loco. *Dawn of the Dead*, but starring Disco Tex and his Sex-O-Lettes.

**JS: How did you meet Bill Landis?**

**JM:** I had read his rag and was fascinated. None of the alleged competition moved me. Only Landis and *Sleazoid*. You sensed it wasn't a hobby with this guy. He'd show movies at Club 57 and I'd attend. At the time, he was this pudgy mama's boy in a leather jacket—it was only later that he developed a peculiar style all his own. Bill was blessed with the most obnoxious, most annoying, room-clearing Staten Island accent, and he'd host these movie nights, trying to be real serious and in charge, shushing all the hipsters as the picture was starting. And they'd all laugh at him. I remember the night at Club 57 *I, Burr* went on. This was Bill's Raymond Burr exposé, which starred ex-Warhol "superstar" Ondine. Ondine was tripping, and he started making fun of the play—while he was performing it. I felt for Bill that night, like I did most of the time. He wanted to be a tough guy, a cool customer, and he was anything but. I started talking to him and was amazed by his encyclopedic knowledge of movies and the way his mind worked. Bill had odd ideas on everything. We hit it off. He was an extreme character, as was I.

A TERRIBLE IDEA—*SLEAZOID* REBORN.

**JS: How did you end up writing for *Sleazoid Express*?**

**JM:** I found Bill and his real interests a bit more fascinating than a lot of what was in *Sleazoid* then. Review after review—who cares? I encouraged him to make it more

personal, much to the disgust of some fans. Nobody wanted to hear about Toby Ross or similar subjects at the time. Bill took a lot of flak for that—"What's with all the fag stuff?" I was also on his back to make it look a bit better. I have to hand it to Bill, he went for it. And he encouraged my participation. We started writing together. A lot.

That said, I could be as much of a minus as I was a plus. The material I wrote on my own was often the worst crap in the magazine. Like an ape with a crayon, I was. I literally didn't know how to form a sentence. I wish I could torch it all. But Bill gave me a chance. He let me contribute to the *Sleazoid* articles in mainstream magazines and I can tell you none of those big shots wanted me included. They just thought I was another dope fiend maniac he hung out with, which was only half true. It was a big surprise when I started doing things on my own, let me tell you. It never would've happened at all if it hadn't been for Landis. And that's why *The Ghastly One* is dedicated to him. That's my best book. And that one's for Bill. As far as I know, he never read it.

**JS: Those old issues of *SE* are amazing time-capsules. Were you aware at the time that your writing and reportage would be such an important cultural artifact?**

**JM:** Oh, I knew it was original. Not like anything else. I'd get a shiver in my blood every time an issue was finished. I saved everything—the original art, fliers, manuscripts, even the glassine bags. I wish somebody would put together a book of the original run, I'd be all for it if it were done right. I have all the material. I doubt it'll ever happen. Too bad. Nobody knows this, but Landis called me before he started the magazine again. We hadn't spoken in years. Apparently, Bill wanted me on board. I thought it was a terrible idea and told him so. We'd shot our wad on the first go round and it was perfecto, a little jewel of a thing. So what if only seventeen people knew? At the end of that first run, every issue was something you waited for, something you had to see. A real cliffhanger—what's gonna happen with this bunch next? We felt we had to up the ante

RECORDED & INDEXED

DRAFT

SLEAZOID EXPRESS

ECCO ECCO ECCO ECCO

ECCO ECCO ECCO ECCO ECCO ECCO

ECCO ECCO ECCO ECCO ECCO ECCO

ECCO ECCO ECCO ECCO ECCO ECCO

THE STORY OF A FAKE MAN ON 42ND STREET

THE LAST ISSUE OF THE ORIGINAL RUN. DESIGN BY JIMMY MCDONOUGH.

each time, and we did. Very few things in life come together like that. So why go back? Obviously he felt differently.

As I've said before, the last issue of the original run was my baby—"Ecco: The Story of a Fake Man on 42nd Street." For me, that issue was the culmination of it all. And it was personal. I thought Bill was going down with the ship and told him so. All the subscription money was going to nickel cokes. I paid for that one to be finished. To say Landis wasn't happy with the end result is an understatement, haha. I'm told in later years he refused to send out copies if people requested it. To this day, I think it was the best thing we ever did. How I slaved over every detail, including the crazy layout. I'd love to see an oversized 11 x 14 reprint of that one just as it is. On the very last page in the bottom right corner were the words "all Me Back". It was supposed to say, "Call Me Back"—just a bit of type I lifted from some fifties pulp magazine, God knows why. I can remember using a black Sharpie to add the C to every copy.

**JS: What can you tell me about Buggin' Out? I've always wondered about him.**

**JM:** Buggin' Out was a roommate of Bill's for a spell. I won't reveal his identity without permission. Haven't talked to that guy in decades. He contributed a lot.

**JS: What did he do for a living?**

**JM:** B.O. was a musician and worked as cook. Somewhere I have a tape of him and Landis jamming. William Z on vocals. Bill, the frustrated rock star. Buggin' Out did a couple of the all-time great *Sleazoid* covers. Old ads all cut up, very crude and raw.

**JS: I always enjoyed reading his stuff.**

**JM:** Buggin' Out was an important part. He was another one that got erased from the dirty canvas that was *Sleazoid*. They had a falling out. What else is new? Bill fell out with everybody sooner or later. That side of things got increasingly tiresome to me. Bill had to have an enemy. And the harassment of that enemy became a twenty-four hour a day obsession. The extreme nature of it was amusing—until you were on the receiving end. Then came the phone calls and the hang-ups and the emails from seven addresses. There was a reason Bill loved Chuck Connors in *The Mad Bomber* or Nicholas Worth in *Don't Answer the Phone*. He was that guy. What did all the harassment really amount to? I think his mother never let him throw water balloons or toilet paper a house. The puny and penny-ante nature of it all... sooner or later dealing with Bill became like swatting a fly. A very annoying, insistent fly. The vibe could be so down around that guy. Great for the magazine, but exhausting if you were living it. Everything was hate, hate, hate. Even hate becomes boring after awhile.

**JS: How closely did you and Bill work as a team? A lot of *SE* articles are credited to both of you.**

**JM:** How closely? Like Lennon and McCartney, Jagger and Richards, Shields and Yarnell. We could finish each other's sentences. It was like that. Together, we added up to something we weren't on our own. Bill and I hung out day and night. A lot of stuff came out of what I call routines—stuff we'd talk about while walking to this theatre or that. We came up with a whole lingo that went along with it—popeyes, bodybuilding grannies, velour soul, Friday the Sensuous John. We'd talk these things into the ground. The more vicious or juvenile the sentiment, the more he enjoyed it. I could do a pretty fair impression of Joel Reed. Bill loved that. He even had me call Reed while I was impersonating him. That was odd. Imagine Joel Reed having an angry conversation with himself. Bill had everybody calling that poor slob, and I do mean everybody. He got calls from around the world! George Payne made the best ones. He'd use that low, nutty psychopath voice of his. At one point, we were going to write a book about the calls simply entitled *The Caller*. A treatment exists for that somewhere. There were so many things we never got done it was frustrating. Bill and Joel. Funny. I always thought Bill had more in common with Reed than he cared to admit.

Later on, Bill sold copies of the mag with my byline erased. Suddenly I was no longer part of the tiny history of *Sleazoid Express*. I mean, can you imagine physically obliterating somebody's credit? It's like the KGB

RECORDED & INDEXED

DRAFT

taking Oswald out of the photo. After all I had been through with this guy. We had created this stuff together. I could handle the trash talk and the denigrating of my contributions, but that was the lowest of the low. Bill found out what would hurt you the most and then stick the knife in. He could be a real bum, Landis. Look, I loved the guy and I defended him to the death, but that was William Z, unfortunately. I'm far from the only one who feels this way. Maybe in later years he changed and shazam, turned into Gandhi. I couldn't tell you, I didn't know him then. And maybe I deserved it all for the "Ecco" issue. Couldn't help myself, I had him in the sights of my love gun. They call me the hunter/And that's my name...

I'll tell you a funny story. Just to annoy me, Landis used to do an impression of my then-paramour Carole. This "impression" consisted of Landis slipping on her high heels, her blonde wig, then taking his schlong out and prancing around whilst in a very high voice shrieking "Yoo-HOO! Jimmy, I'm HOME!" He looked like one of those grizzled queens in *Bloodthirsty Butchers*. Now, I would rather watch the blu-ray of *Zaat* than see Bill mincing about with that tired tallywacker flapping in the wind, but it was funny. Once. Thirty-six times later, not so amusing.

So one day she came home and I said, "Carole, guess what? Bill does an impression of you. C'mon, Bill. Show Carole your impression." Well,

A SLICE OF JIMMY'S "ECCO" LAYOUT.

Bill turned green. And started stuttering and sputtering. Presto! No more impressions.

**JS: What was Bill like back then?**

**JM:** Bill was a perverse character. He would've humped Hitler just to see what would've happened. Or Bea Arthur. Or even the family pooch. He was too degenerate for Andy Milligan, which is saying something. Landis claimed that he made a pass at Michael Weldon one night. Now, I didn't know Weldon at all, but he struck me as a pretty reserved guy. That's like pinching Hal Holbrook on the ass. The fact that Bill did that—if he did—cracked me up. Bill was shameless. Anything to provoke.

Understand this: Bill Landis was a walking exploitation movie. Some people grow up on the Bible or the Beatles. Bill grew up flipping the pages of the big red *American Film Institute Feature Films 1961–70* books studying the date, place and time *White Slaves of Chinatown* opened. That's what made him fascinating, unique. And maybe that was his downfall.

I was down in the catacombs the other day and found those AFI books in the archives. They're bloodstained, the binding's shot and they are generally beat to shit. We got a lot of use out of those two volumes, Landis and I. It kind of choked me up to see them, actually. I live in a land of ghosts, boo-hoo for me. I miss them all, even that little bastard.

**JS: Can you describe a typical night out in Times Square?**

**JM:** Better you crack open an old issue of *Sleazoid* and get a contemporaneous account. That part of my life is long over and I'd be faking it now. I could give a shit if I ever see another exploitation movie. Stephen Thrower certainly got the vibe right in that book of his. [*Nightmare USA*, 2007.] And he's the only one I know of. Too bad he didn't hang out with us in the bad old days. He would've fit right in.

**JS: What was the most notorious theater in those days?**

**JM:** The Harem was a real armpit. Twenty-four hour porno theater. Dimestore transsexuals. There was a murder in the theatre once. The Roxy was a favorite of mine. I believe that was the first all-video exploitation theatre. Just a fuzzy blown-up VHS tape blaring in a crappy little room with rows of plastic seats that were every bit as uncomfortable as the ones at the Port Authority. No frills grindhouse. Climbing the barren stairwells in that hellhole was a bit daunting. There were a lot of homeless people who just stayed all day watching *Shaft's Big Score* over and over. Whatever happened at the Roxy, you knew you were on your own. It seemed like nobody worked there.

By far the most extreme theatre I've ever been in was in downtown Los Angeles. A cavernous dump called the Cameo. Imagine Calcutta with four walls and a movie screen. Hazy smoke rose from the audience... there seemed to be constant wheezing, hacking and moaning. It was hard to tell if some audience members were alive. A guy actually went around with a stick and rousted people to make sure they were conscious. Ancient

prints of Harry Novak's stuff were still playing there in the late eighties or whenever it was.

**JS: A lot of people who are my age look back on the *SE* era of Times Square with nostalgia for something they never experienced. Why is there still a fascination for those days?**

**JM:** Because it doesn't exist anymore. People can romanticize anything once it's gone.

**JS: I probably wouldn't have lasted a week.**

**JM:** A lot of it wasn't great, I'll tell you. It was misery and burning hell. The "Ecco" issue covered that. I can remember being in Bill's 14th Street apartment one day. It was a great joint—dingy, dirty and an always unforgettable line-up of exploitation posters he'd put together hanging in a long row on the brick wall. I was sitting there staring at a vinyl copy of Lou Reed's *The Blue Mask* that had been jettisoned to the floor. Across the cover was a big spurt of blood from a hypo. And I thought, "I gotta get outta here. Or I'll turn into a wax dummy." Bill was smitten by all that Johnny Thunders, Lower East Side, dyed-black-hair, nodding-off-in-dirty-black-leotards crap. I thought that number had been done to death, no pun intended. That's when I decided to go hang out with honky-tonk singer Gary Stewart, who was living like Dracula in a Florida trailer with the windows blacked out. My idea of healthy, haha.

But you couldn't stop Bill. The worse it was, the more Landis wanted it. He was a man possessed. Tough luck. For everybody.

Who knows if it's true, but I've been told that one of these well-known potentates who spews forth all the exploitation crap out on DVD puts down *The Ghastly One* because it doesn't represent the "fun" side of exploitation. Yeah, 42nd Street, just like a ride at the carnival. Well, I saw what it did to Bill. I saw what it did to Andy. And many others. There's a reason it's called exploitation, right?

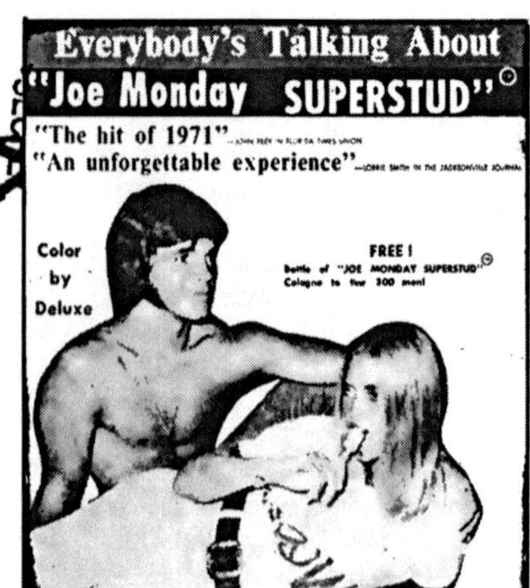

Everybody's Talking About
"Joe Monday SUPERSTUD"
"The hit of 1971"
"An unforgettable experience"
Color by Deluxe
FREE!
Bottle of "JOE MONDAY SUPERSTUD" Cologne to first 300 men!


I loved hearing that comment, by the way. Loved. I don't blame the guy, he probably has children he has to justify himself to, haha. It's amazing the shit people forward you these days. Everybody's an expert, everybody judges everything. You can't escape it now. Like when I sold Andy's prints. Putting them on eBay was one of the best things I've ever done. It led me to Nicolas Winding Refn, the absolute perfect person to have Andy's stuff. I'm sorry it took so long to get it released. I tried but it

XEROX
FEROX

Make BIG MONEY in Your Own
RESTAURANT
Diner or Drive-In
FREE BOOK
HOW TO
LOVE
and be LOVED!
YOU/THE JURY
What would your verdict be?
MONUMENTS
EASY TERMS
LOW DOWN PAYMENT
Learn—
FINGERPRINTING
and IDENTIFICATION
ALABAMA SCHOOL OF FINGERPRINTING
Box 185-O, Fairfield, Ala. 35064

# 8. THE BEGINNING OF MY END

It was late when Joe left the set. He took a cab to Spanish Harlem and another cab to the Lounge Theatre. Big Wally was in the box. Joe asked him if he could use the bathroom. Wally frowned. Fuck him, Joe thought, and pulled back the turnstyle. Joe got off in the bathroom.

When he came to he was in another theatre. It took Joe a few minutes to realize it was the Haven, a 24-hour joint on the deuce. Joe couldn't remember how he got there. The last thing he remembered was arguing with Wally at the Lounge.

He looked up to the big screen. There was Joe Monday, naked and fucking some woman on top of a car. A few queens in the balcony applauded his money shot. Jesus. Joe Monday in Tight Pants. Joe shut it off. He didn't like seeing his own movies.

Joe puked on the street after leaving the theatre. A Spanish lady started screaming. "That man, Officer, he make a PUKE! He make a PUKE!"

Somehow Joe made it home. Bags of coke fell out of his pocket as he took off his jacket. Where the fuck had they come from...had he gone out again? He didn't remember going out again. Had he gone out again?

Joe went to the suitcase and got out his works. The book was in there too, the red leather book. It meant nothing to Joe now. Neither did the still collection sitting on the table in a folder. The "Off-Beat Still Collection". Joe gave the folder a tap and the pictures cascaded to the floor. The pictures made him sick. So did the book. Bald men and innocent women. It reminded him of porno sets. Sometimes you have fantasies...they wear out.

Rose was on the set today. She wanted to come over. That wouldn't do. What was he gonna do — bring her home to meet Jumbo? Introduce her to his [illegible]? Better they see the real man on the porno set than the fake one at home.

Joe cleaned the works and got some water. There was a noise at the window. O'Leary on the fire escape, no doubt. Come and get me, Joe thought. I'm ready. Joe thought of Jumbo and how paranoid he'd get of cops when he did the coke. There would be Jumbo, naked and sweating, peering through the keyhole and muttering "[illegible]...[illegible]..." Where the fuck was Jumbo, anyway? Oh right. Joe had thrown him out 'cause they had been doing too much drugs. What a joke. Jumbo would be back. Tomorrow, or the next day.

Joe absently stared at the yellowing posters on the wall as he grabbed a rig from the paper bag full of them on the floor. That fucking poster for [illegible]. Thor pinched ass with the goatee pushing a needle through his neck. Joe blinked and saw himself on the poster, pushing a needle into his arm instead. [illegible]

Joe heard that old song he liked, that one by the [illegible]. Where was it coming from? Was it the radio? The radio didn't look on. Was it the radio?

Joe took off his shirt and sat in the chair. He lined up the bags on the table. Then he disconnected the phone. There was a lot of work to do tonite. He wanted no interruptions.

After all, he deserved it. He was Joe Monday. He had been in thirty movies, and he came in every one of them.

Be a Detective!
WORK HOME OR TRAVEL
DETECTIVE Particulars FREE
Write GEORGE S. P. WAGNER
125 West 86th St., New York
Name
Address
JOBS ON SHIPS
SELL Advertising Book Matches
FULL OR PART TIME!
SUPERIOR
SUPERIOR MATCH CO.
HELP WANTED—SPARE TIME
NO MONEY DOWN!
FLORIDA
1/4 ACRE
Only $395
FULL PRICE

CALL ME BACK

just never worked out. It had to be done with respect and admiration for Andy, not some crap release just chucked out there. And Nicolas has accomplished that, I'm happy to say. Andy Milligan on blu-ray released by the BFI? I laugh every time I think about it. Refn's got balls. Although just today I got the DVD and NWR's notes are wrong: he only paid 15K for the Milligan bounty. I mean, twenty-five...that would've been larceny, haha.

**JS: You said that you slaved over your work for the first *Variety* piece and Bill waited until the deadline. Was this dynamic always the case between the two of you?**

**JM:** It always came easy for him. Not for me. Landis was great under pressure, I was in awe of the way he could just spit it out. The flip side of that coin was the fact that Bill was lazy as hell when it came to research. When he was doing the Anger biography, I gave him a ton of leads. He never followed up. Bill had a very narrow vision of things and he didn't want it to be sullied by anything unexpected. That's a powerful stance to take. And that attitude served *Sleazoid* well. We were arrogant punks who thought we ruled the world, and all because of a badly typed mimeographed rag thirty-seven people read, haha. So crazy. I remember one night I was pissed off by something one of these queer-haters had written in his fanzine about Bill and the "new" *Sleazoid*. We drove out to the suburbs high out of our minds and papered his lawn with copies of *Sleazoid*. A particularly homosexual

DRAFT

RECORDED & INDEXED

issue, I might add.

**JS: Actually, how did the *Variety* gig come about?**

**JM:** We were friendly with the reviewer who covered exploitation, Lawrence Cohn. Great guy. They gave us a shot.

**JS: Did writing for bigger publications change your style, or the way you approached things as a writer?**

**JM:** Hopefully not, at least in the long run. Got a little excited the first couple of times we wrote for the *Village Voice* and *Film Comment*, but that wore off fast. After *Sleazoid*, I just did it my way, for better or worse.

**JS: Why did *Sleazoid Express* end when it did?**

**JM:** The volcano had erupted. We shot our load.

**JS: What did you think of the relaunch of *Sleazoid Express*?**

**JM:** I'm the wrong guy to ask. Didn't read it.

**JS: Bill did that with his wife, Michelle.**

**JM:** If memory serves me correctly, I introduced those two lovebirds. She used to write us from Florida. I knew she was just what the doctor ordered. Michelle became the gatekeeper to all things Bill and *Sleazoid*. A thankless task. I'm sure she did her best.

**JS: Do you recall the last time that you talked to Bill?**

**JM:** I got a screwball "I'm the Greatest" email from him shortly before he died. I chose to ignore it.

**JS: What led up to your decision to become a biographer?**

**JM:** There was no decision. I just started doing it.

**JS: Was Neil Young your first choice?**

**JM:** Everything I write about is my choice. I can't manufacture enthusiasm.

**JS: What was the genesis of that book?**

**JM:** Young made three albums that had a big influence on me as a kid. I was writing profiles for the *Voice* at the time and a pal at Warner Brothers said, "Who do you want to write about? Anybody on the label— anybody."

"'Well, there's one guy. You don't want to hear his name. And I want to

tell him his albums have sucked for the past ten years."

"C'mon, who is it?"

"'Neil Young."

Long pause. But he got me there. Nine months later, there I was in the passenger seat one of Young's million-dollar vintage cars. It was intense. I got in his face, told him what I thought. He spilled his guts about a few things. What a good sport he was. Little did I know I was just one more in a long line of opinionated assholes that he'd collected. Anyway, I did the interview and never thought I'd see him again.

Some months later, I got a call inviting me back into his life. I remember a little devil and a little angel were sitting on my shoulder, one going, "Don't go back—you already did the interview, leave it at that!" and the other saying, "Do it, DO IT!" I chose to listen to the devil, of course.

**JS: What was Neil like to work with?**

**JM:** Neil gave me the freedom to do the book, yet made it as difficult as possible. And Neil Young is a master at making things difficult, believe me. There are days I'd like to take a croquet mallet to his skull. But he taught me a lot about creativity, Mr. Young.

**JS: How did you deal with the stress?**

**JM:** By taking 3-D photographs of naked broads. My only remaining vice. Using mostly vintage cameras from the fifties. There are hundreds, if not thousands of them. Very few people have seen 'em. One day, it'll all be a book. My wife Natalia took a bunch of them, it's a collaboration. Here's one below, although not in 3-D, of course. That's Annie eating a popsicle and Natalia. Let me know if it reduces your stress.

**JS: What's it like dealing with celebrities?**

**JM:** Dealing with celebrities of that stature is like dealing with General Motors. They have a phalanx of henchmen whose job it is to tell you what not to do. And they don't like anybody getting too close to the

REDUCING STRESS IN 2-D.

RECORDED & INDEXED

DRAFT

# MIXED COMBO by Joe Monday.

Towards the end of last summer, I got cast in yet another one day video wonder. It was shot somewhere in Queens. On the train out there, what stuff I'd have to do with whoever crossed my mind, since the call time was the only info I was given.

The director was one of the better ones. The set was full of new faces. A trashy blonde girl, a blockhead. A big black buck. There was this black chick, Liz, a little daffy but friendly. The director said we'd be working together, making this my first "mixed combo" scene. It was her second movie.

This thing was supposed to be a naked [illegible] i.e. a bunch of people fucking on the [illegible]. I can usually work with anyone or anything but it helps to have something about the person to groove on. In Liz's case, it was that she looked like a transsexual. I kept thinking of a story in Love magazine, "I Fell in Love With a Boy With Tits," because she looked so much like the photo.

We pulled off the scene great, doing a whole slew of positions Kama Sutra style. We even looked like we enjoyed it. In the back of us was a threesome featuring the Frenchman who could never come, a porno regular. A guy in search of an erection, let alone an orgasm. I had to hear him talk [illegible] fuck me garbage in a thick accent while he fondled his limp dick. The director was really pleased with us. We felt comfortable with each other.

Afterwards, we took turns using the set's shower. Notch, my first thoughts about what to do later was to get high. Having just gotten arrested on the Lower East Side for possession, I wasn't too anxious to cop there. I knew this woman liked to get high and that she used me, too. She was keen on getting C, but didn't say much about the D side. I went along with it.

On the train back to the city, I found out a few things about Liz. She was a stripper, mostly at the Harmony on 49th St., the last place in the city that has the semblance of traditional burlesque. [illegible], a disgusting porno star who could suck his own dick, had brought her into the biz. She worked with him in her first flick. Her real first name wasn't Liz. [illegible] because it made her full name the same as a 40s star.

We went to a bar in Times Square. Liz ran into a dealer she knew and got a 20. Sniffing coke is one of my least favorite ways to get high. It leaves me depressed with a nervous head I can't get rid of. Hurts the nose and lungs, too. This coke was cut with head shop garbage. It was clearly Liz's way of getting high. She talked alot, much of her conversation indecipherable. Before any playing around happened, she split, most likely to get more C from the bar. She left her number and encouraged me to call her.

NOW...
THE NAKED TRUTH
for all the world to see!
TEMPTATION THRU THE AGES
...from the unashamed Adam and Eve to the shameless man & women of today's sinful world!

MALE AND FEMALE
since ADAM and EVE

HERE'S LITTLE RICHARD

LONG TALL SALLY
MISS ANN
SLIPPIN' AND SLIDIN'
TUTTI FRUTTI
—WHAT IS HIS THEORY??

I knew it would be trouble, but I gave Liz a buzz. An ancient guide answered the phone. This was Sal, her "roommate" i.e. sugar daddy. We got together again, sure enough to spill something. Toni, another stripper, joined us. Toni was also a veteran of the Lower East Side dope and coke scene. [illegible] caused her to become a full fledged coke fiend. [illegible] my apartment, we all engaged in more indecipherable yakkety yak. My roommate Buggin' Out came home [illegible] Liz's incessant talking as "crazy nigger [illegible] cocaine."

Liz was never straight. Next date, we saw The Female Bunch with some friends. Pretty good for Al Adamson. A bunch of independently minded gals brand Russ Tamblyn on the forehead. Lon Chaney Jr. walks around in an alcoholic stupor. Liz kept going in and out of the bathroom sniffing and babbling the whole time.

She spent less and less time at Sal's place in the Bronx and most of her time at mine. Pretty soon, I had a third roommate.

In the entire time she lived with me, we slept in the same bed but had sex only about four or five times. This is true of alot of drug addicts; you just lose interest in it. When we did fuck, she surprised me by being the passive one. Liz liked it doggie style. That [illegible] stereotype of blacks and assfucking came up—"someday, Joe, you'll fuck me up the ass"—though I never did. One time, she said "you sleep like the dead" because even one of her [illegible] couldn't arouse me out of a deep nod. Both of our eyes were closed during sex, our minds in other places.

To alot of Times Square people, I'm another sort of stereotype—"white freak." At the time I [illegible] with Liz, I was much more homosexually [illegible] she interested me in terms of the Little [illegible] Which is that if you have a goodlooking [illegible] the straight guys will come like bees to honey. [illegible] how all the minority guys like the [illegible] salesmen [illegible] to her. There were a few Spanish guys in the neighborhood that seemed likely prospects but Liz and [illegible] were [illegible] dick. She really had it in for black guys. Maybe it's "yo, yo, Liz, lemme fuck dat brown eye." She had an affair with a South American black that resulted in an abortion. "I don't know why I remember these things."

Admit it or not, Liz also dug the same sex. She always admired the woman instead of the man in photos or movies. An older woman, another former "roommate," apparently kept her for a couple of months. The "[illegible] money" rationalization came up. In one movie, she did a lez scene. On the Harmony stage, she ate this Amazonian stripper's pussy, causing them to get in trouble with the management. The Yuppies in the audience had [illegible], throwing dozens of dollar bills at the action. To hear Liz insist she was straight was like listening to those Times Square hustlers who say they don't suck cock.

merchandise. Naturally, I don't get along with these people. Such dopey authority figures are meant to be kicked. The whole thing became a nightmare. And that was when Neil was on my side!

**JS: How long did it take you to research and write *Shakey*?**

**JM:** Eight years. Another three years were spent battling to get it published, which was exhausting. The time spent I regret. Once I start something I stay with it until it is done—whatever the odds. As usual, good for *Shakey*, bad for everything else. I lost a few projects close to my heart. Mr. Young would be happy if I was locked in a box somewhere still working on it. Everything about that book was lunacy. I'm glad people seem to like that one, but I think it's my worst book. Too much monkey business.

**JS: When did you decide that you wanted to write a book on Andy Milligan?**

**JM:** From the moment I saw one of his posters hanging on Bill's wall. I was staring at that poster, and a bolt of lightning hit. I had to know everything about the guy. That was a very hard book to sell, haha. The advance didn't pay for the blank tape.

**JS: What was your initial reaction to his films?**

**JM:** I just couldn't believe it. They seemed like broadcasts from another dimension. Everything about them was unusual, off in some way.

**JS: I was sort of re-introduced to Andy Milligan's films when Tim**

**Lucas did those long articles in *Video Watchdog*.**

**JM:** He did a great job. His knowledge of film is something else. Way out of my league. Facts are great, but I'm more interested in emotions.

**JS: *The Ghastly One* is a very personal book. How difficult was it for you to write?**

**JM:** That one was easy. Everybody had kicked the bucket. I'd thought about it a long, long time. After the endless interference that came with *Shakey*, it was a vacation. It happened faster than a speeding bullet. Nine months.

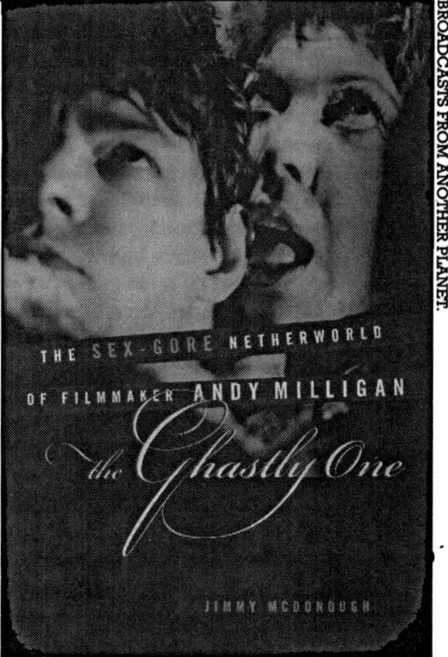


BROADCASTS FROM ANOTHER PLANET.

**JS: I'd imagine that writing a book on Andy Milligan is as strange of an experience as writing a book on Neil Young. What was the general reaction of your interview subjects when you approached them about talking to them about Andy?**

**JM:** "ANDY MILLIGAN?!? You MUST be JOKING." People laughed in my face. Some of the snobbier members of Caffe Cino reached for the smelling salts. They didn't want the Cino legend defiled. One or two people really blocked my efforts. But they gave up; I couldn't be stopped. There is more of the Cino story revealed in that book than anywhere else.

**JS: You're as much of a character in the book as Andy Milligan. Do you feel that you could have written the book any other way?**

**JM:** No. I do what the book tells me to do and ignore everything else.

**JS: I'm glad of that. When do you know that you've done enough research on a subject?**

**JM:** When people start asking me, "Isn't this enough? You've interviewed Neil Young's Phys Ed teacher, can you just quit it now?" Research is the fun part, you can never do enough. Look at that Caro guy and Johnson. I would've loved to have been able to apply that approach on Milligan. Four 500-page volumes on Andy. Just imagine.

**JS: How do you go about turning your brain off after such a ride?**

**JM:** Turning the brain off is something I've wrestled with my whole life. Not easy. I've tried everything. I get obsessed. What's that epigraph of Selby's? "A man obsessed/Is a man possessed/By a demon." I agree.

# JIMMY McDONOUGH

## ALL ABOARD THE NIGHT TRAIN!

**JS: When I first read that you were working on a book about Russ Meyer, I was very excited. The book didn't disappoint! What led up to your work on *Big Bosoms and Square Jaws*?**

**JM:** I don't know. It was just one of the names in the hat. There aren't very many names in that hat, I'll tell you.

**JS: What was it about Russ Meyer that attracted you?**

**JM:** The guy was driven by an absurd fetish and based a career around it. RM gave the world the finger, did whatever the fuck he wanted, and sat on his pile of money. There was an utter disregard for anything else, namely reality. We should all be so lucky. Of course, it didn't end well. He thought he had all the answers, Russ. When he needed help nobody was there.

**JS: How difficult is it to research and get personal with someone who you don't have direct access to?**

**JM:** I don't know, I zeroed in on RM's vibe right away. I started talking like him in my head, seeing things his way. He had such a deathly serious attitude, even when mailing a letter. He reminded me of Sterling Hayden in *Dr. Strangelove*.

**JS: How did the lack of personal interaction affect the way you wrote the book?**

**JM:** Makes you try harder. And sometimes it can give you freedom.

**JS: Russ Meyer and Andy Milligan were both artists who had very unique and personal visions. How do you feel that their work differs?**

FRIDAY ... THE SENSUOUS JOHN

"FRIDAY.... THE SENSUOUS JOHN," BY LANDIS AND MCDONOUGH. *SLEAZOID EXPRESS* NUMBER 146.

**What's the link that they have in common?**
**JM:** RM was all about making fantasy reality. Andy was, "Make reality even grimmer." They both spoke a language that was wholly and completely their own. They were almost childlike—and somewhat puritanical. Awfully obsessed with their mothers, those two, haha. And both were more than a little nuts. I'd love a film festival where they alternated between Meyer and Milligan. Probably cause seizures.

JIMMY MCDONOUGH AND LITTLE JIMMY SCOTT. PHOTO COURTESY OF JIMMY MCDONOUGH.

**JS: You've recently written about Tammy Wynette. What was it about her that made you want to tackle her life as a subject?**
**JM:** A great singer that never got her biographical due. Again, she had a big impact on me as a kid. Tammy and her husband George. George Jones that is, the greatest living country singer. I'm a sucker for a sad song. I'd love to write a book with that title—Sucker for a Sad Song. The slower, the sadder, the better. Oh, how I can pontificate on that subject. I have a vast collection of southern soul and country ballads. So this was a chance to immerse myself in the country side of it, tell the world why I love this music so. Tammy was fatally romantic. She wanted life to be the cover of a romance novel. That's an attitude I can appreciate. I like writing about women. Next stop, Golda Meir.
**JS: Your work as a biographer covers a very diverse section of people. What do you think links them all?**
**JM:** Obsession. A certain yearning, a certain melancholy.
**JS: What can the world expect next from Jimmy McDonough?**
**JM:** I wish I could tell you. I've spent the last few years in Nightmare City. I'm amazed that I'm still ambulatory, to be quite frank. Hopefully it will lead to something creative. Not thus far. So here I sit, waiting for Whatever to happen. One can't force these things. The important thing is that I got a new pair of snakeskin shoes today. Italian. Loud, sinister, questionably stylish. Like me.

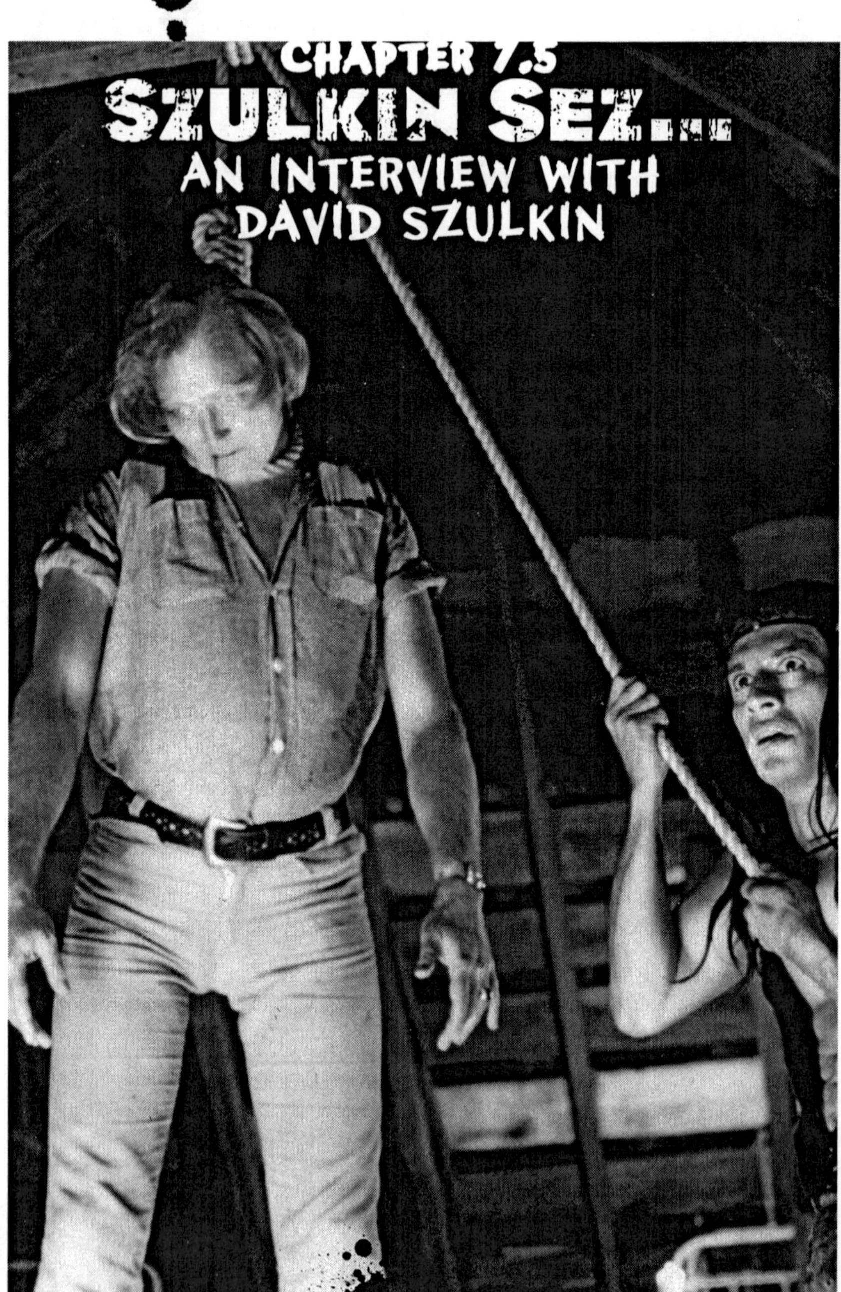

# CHAPTER 7.5
# SZULKIN SEZ...
## AN INTERVIEW WITH DAVID SZULKIN

**JOHN SZPUNAR: When did you start reading zines?**

**DAVID SZULKIN:** The first horror zine I got my hands on was Barry Kaufman's *Demonique*—this was at the height of the slasher/gore movie craze, maybe 1981 or '82.

**JS: How instrumental were they in turning you on to films that you'd never heard of?**

**DS:** Fanzines were absolutely crucial to my discovery of movies (and music, too). At the time, there was no other access to information about many of these forgotten, weird, and obscure films. I couldn't see most of these movies; even if I'd had a VCR, most of them were not commercially available. The commentary and images in the old zines sparked my fascination with horror and exploitation movies; fanzines were also the gateway for collectors who sold or traded bootleg videos. The zines fueled the obsession with finding this stuff; they were generally written by obsessed characters (who else would make the effort?) and that appealed to my own obsessive nature. It's been said that the posters and ad campaigns for most exploitation flicks were more memorable than the films themselves; I'd add that the reviews in horror fanzines by guys like Chas. Balun, Michael Weldon, Rick Sullivan and Bill Landis were often more entertaining than the actual experience of watching the movies they wrote about. A one-paragraph, matter-of-fact summary by Michael Weldon saved you ninety minutes of living death by boredom. And a zine like Craig Ledbetter's *European Trash Cinema* was vital for us in the States where the movies he wrote about were completely unavailable. There was a mystique, a kind of intrigue surrounding these bizarre, low-down, dirty and overlooked movies at a time when there was no instant access to them...or even to information about them. You had to seek it out—you had to send letters to other likeminded weirdos and trade tapes, and the zines were at the center of all that. Donald Farmer's *Splatter Times* and Hugh Gallagher's *Draculina* were important fanzines, too... I read all of them that I could get my hands on. These days, all the mystery is gone—all the info is a mouse-click away, nothing is obscure or overlooked...and it's not quite as interesting. On saying that, *Ultra Violent* are the heirs/keepers of the horror zine flame; they are continuing the tradition of doing the print zine and they do good work. Same with Dave Kosanke whom I met not long ago. He still doe a print zine.

**JS: What are your memories of *Sleazoid Express*?**

**DS:** A friend of mine named John Donaldson loaned me his complete collection of *Sleazoid Express* when I was in college. It was fascinating. I was more of a *Gore Gazette* guy in high school, but the *GG* was sophomoric by comparison. Deliberately so, I think—as I understood it, Rick Sullivan started the *Gore Gazette* as a reactionary response to Landis. Anyway, I was late to the party with *Sleazoid*, but thanks to my friend John I caught up with the back issues maybe around 1989. (Not sure if Bill was still publishing at that point, but I don't think so.) *Sleazoid Express* was dangerous, creepy, highly intelligent, and hip. Bill was among

the first writers to delve into the lower depths of exploitation cinema. He really walked that beat, not as an academic studying the genre but as somebody who lived the life. He hung out in 42nd Street grindhouses where no respectable film critic would set foot and he brought that experience to his readers. For that reason, his writing is without peer. Those zines felt feverish, they had all the menace of the territory they covered. *Sleazoid* wasn't just about the movies, it was about Times Square, the underworld of porn and drugs and prostitution; most of the other zines came off nerdy by comparison. As I recall, the issues got more intense as the magazine neared the end of its run—Bill's writing got very personal as he became a part of the whole scene he was writing about (which is probably where Rick Sullivan reacted against it). I remember thinking Bill's "Led Zeppelin: Faggots?" article about *The Song Remains the Same* was pretty funny. And I love Led Zep. By the way, Larry McMurtry was a *Sleazoid Express* subscriber. He's written about it in his essays (see his book *Film Flam*).

**JS: What did you think of Bill and Michelle's book? The newer issues of *SE*?**

**DS:** The book was great. I'd put it at the top of a very short list of essential works about exploitation cinema. The later issues of *Sleazoid* (and *Metasex*) were great, too. Some of the trivia-obsessed fans complained that Bill played loose with the facts—but those detractors don't know the "facts" in the first place, and even when they think they are right, they miss the point. Bill Landis captured a cinematic netherworld in his writing. He really got the stickiness, the rancid allure of those movies; he understood the shady people who created them and the audience that consumed them. The tall tales carry more truth than the "facts". Bill more than earned the moniker of Mr. Sleazoid.

**JS: Let's talk about Rick Sullivan's *Gore Gazette*.**

**DS:** The *Gore Gazette* had an *enormous* impact on me! I can't stress that enough; more than any of the other zines, the *GG* had the attitude that really grabbed me. Rick Sullivan became a personal hero to me. I was a proud subscriber for years. When each new issue arrived (folded in a handwritten envelope) I ordered videotapes of rare movies from Rick, exchanged letters, and years later, I met him. I think Rick is the person that made me want to write about movies, the one who made it seem cool... though of course I was also immersed in all of the other writing I could find about horror and exploitation movies, particularly Chas.

The largest circulation of anything of its particular type

Vol. 2, No. 9 January 1982

**50¢**

THE *SLEAZOID EXPRESS* MASTHEAD LAYS IT ON THE LINE.

Balun and *Deep Red*, Michael Weldon's *Psychotronic Encyclopedia of Film* (the Bible!), the old issues of *Fangoria* (the great Uncle Bob Martin and Dave Everett), and Richard Meyers' book *For One Week Only*. All of that stuff was scripture to me: I pored over it, memorized it, lived by it...I was more interested in that stuff than I was in any of the normal high school interests. Rick was the Right Reverend in the church of exploitation. I looked up to his zine persona. Like Bill Landis, Rick took you to the scum-infested theaters of 42nd Street; unlike Landis, he was very anti-artsy (or anti-"lobster", in the *GG* argot). That rubbed off on me. I really enjoyed the sophomoric humor, offensive rants, and politically incorrect editorial slant of the *Gore Gazette* and still do—it actually influenced my personality... much to my detriment!

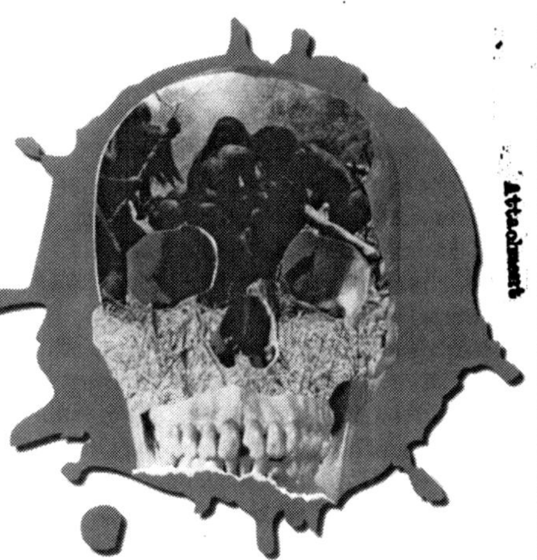

SKULL ART FOR GRINDHOUSE RELEASING'S *CANNIBAL HOLOCAUST*.

**JS: How did you meet Rick?**

**DS:** At NYU, one of my Cinema Studies instructors was a super-cool guy named Chuck Stephens. He happened to be a personal friend of Rick's. So when Chuck announced that he would be bringing Rick in to give a talk on campus, that was like winning the lottery to me. Rick was very laid-back in person, very nice guy and as cool as I imagined him to be. I was the only student at the event who even knew about the *GG*, I think—I brought up all the jokes and lingo from back issues he'd probably forgotten already. As mentioned, I'd corresponded with Rick before, and he was very helpful in getting me copies of movies I was looking for. I wrote about a lot of those movies I got from Rick in my *Last House on the Left* book. He also gave me a tenth anniversary *Gore Gazette* T-shirt; one day, I was wearing that while walking through (fittingly enough) Times Square and I got hassled by cops because the shirt said "TEN FUCKING YEARS AND STILL MAKING ENEMIES!" on the back. I also want to mention one of my favorite stories from the pages of the *Gore Gazette*—about the black "video terrorist" who rented *Out of Africa* from a local video store, put the tape into a camcorder, and strategically taped over parts of the film with his own homemade scenes. As the story was told in the *GG*, the guy's image would pop up right in the middle of this Meryl Streep film, saying, "You enjoyin' the movie, you white asshole?"

**JS: You mentioned Chas. Balun's *Deep Red*...**

**DS:** *Deep Red* was one of the best horror zines—the writing and the graphics, too. Chas. was a

talented artist, and I think his was the best-looking of all the zines. And of course, Chas. was an evangelist when it came to horror... he wrote with passion and conviction, and he got a lot of kids excited about movies. He encouraged his readers to go out there and do it themselves, whether it was writing, moviemaking, special effects, etc. He was down to earth, didn't suffer pretentiousness or foolishness. And he was an old hippy who loved Blue Cheer—gotta love that about him! (I remember a bio of Chas. in one of his books that listed one of his hobbies as "chainsaw chooglin'"!) Chas. believed in the genre, and his fervor came through loud and clear. He wrote in a colorful, lively and irreverent style, and most of all, he was sincere. He was all about shooting from the hip; oftentimes his negative reviews were the most enjoyable ones. On the positive side, when Chas. got behind a certain movie, he really pushed it. Like I said, he was an evangelist—if not for Chas., I don't think certain films/directors would be so revered (or even known) by fans today. He's much missed.

**JS: How did the idea for your *Last House on the Left* book come about?**

**DS:** I was fascinated with the movie as a kid in the seventies, when I was too young to see it. I grew up in Massachusetts and the distributors/financial backers of *Last House* also owned movie theaters in my area, so the movie often played at those theaters and drive-ins during the seventies and early eighties. The newspaper ads made a big impression on me—my brother had a collection of movie ads he cut out of the local paper, including some of those images I used in the book. So that was the seed of my obsession with *Last House*. The idea for the book came about when I went to see Roy Frumkes' movie *Document of the Dead*. Roy was showing a 16mm print of *Document* at a bar called Chet's Last Call in Boston, and he brought along his infamous reel of outtakes from *Last House*. He had met Wes Craven not long after the release of the film, and Wes gave him a collection of materials related to it. That reel just hypnotized me! And as he screened those missing scenes from the movie, Roy told some behind-the-scenes stories about the making of *Last House*. This was all fascinating to me, and that's when I started thinking about the book. I sold my first article to *Fangoria* magazine a year or two later, started writing for

them regularly and they published an advance excerpt from the book. That got a great response, a ton of mail—this is back when people wrote letters, not emails!—and I stuck with it.

Years before I did any serious work on the book, I remember drawing a mock-up of the cover...actually, it was a fake ad for FantaCo, the company that used to sell books such as John McCarty's *Splatter Movies* (another influence) and Chas. Balun's the *Gore Score*. They used to advertise in *Fangoria*. About a decade later, that imaginary ad I drew became a reality, because FantaCo was the US distributor of my book and they did in fact take out a full-page ad for it in *Fangoria*! I willed that dream into being!

**JS: How long did it take you to write it?**

**DS:** I spent years gathering the material and researching it, on and off during the early 1990s. The actual writing of it took about six months.

**JS: What was the biggest challenge in your research?**

**DS:** I did most of the research before the internet, so it wasn't like I typed something into Google and got my instant "expertise". It was a challenge just to find some of the people involved with the movie at that time.

**JS: Was anyone less than amiable about being approached?**

**DS:** Some of the people who put up the money to make *Last House* weren't eager to be interviewed! But I did eventually talk to them.

**JS: You mentioned Roger Watkins by name in the book. How did you come across this information?**

**DS:** Through Chas. Balun, of course!

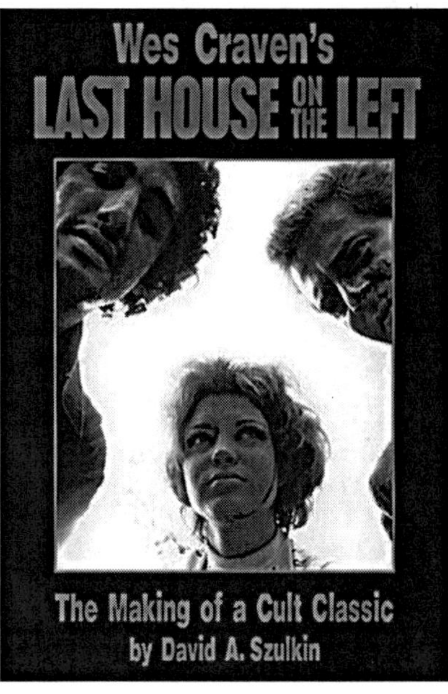

Wes Craven's
LAST HOUSE ON THE LEFT
The Making of a Cult Classic
by David A. Szulkin


**JS: *Wes Craven's The Last House on the Left* was one of the first books to be published by FAB. What was your relationship with them like?**

**DS:** Very good. Harvey Fenton of FAB Press did an excellent job with my book in every way. I visited him in London after the book came out when a British zine publisher named Paul Brown [*Is it Uncut?*] put together a film festival that included *Last House*.

**JS: You've worked a lot with Grindhouse Releasing. How did that come about?**

**DS:** I got involved with Grindhouse Releasing after I moved to Los Angeles in 1999. One of the first people I met on my initial trip out to LA was Bob Murawski, who co-founded Grindhouse with Sage

Stallone. They had released Fulci's *The Beyond* a couple of years before I met them, and they'd put out *Cannibal Ferox* (aka *Make them Die Slowly*) back in the days of laserdisc! Bob and I met through Eric Caiden at Hollywood Book and Poster, hit it off right away, and he introduced me to Sage, who became one of my closest friends throughout my time in Los Angeles. Bob was working on a DVD release for one of my favorite movies: David Durston's *I Drink your Blood*. I ended up coming on board as a co-producer of that release. Bob, Sage and I all had the same interests and the same sensibility as far as movies, music, and yes, the old horror zines.

**JS: Steve Bissette said that the niche labels like Synapse and Grindhouse could be considered the new fanzines. What's your take on that?**

**DS:** I'll take that as a compliment! I can see Steve's point in that these are DVD labels run by fans, for the fans. I can vouch for the fact that Grindhouse Releasing co-founder Bob Murawski and I both read all the horror fanzines. It's still hard for me to talk about Sage in the past tense, but I have to say that Sage Stallone knew more about movies than anybody I've ever met. He didn't even need to get information from a fanzine—when it came to films, he was just a walking encyclopedia unto himself. Sage showed me movies that nobody has ever heard of, or probably ever will! And I give him a lot of credit for pursuing his interest in offbeat cinema the way he did, instead of being some lame Hollywood conformist.

Grindhouse Releasing is the only one of these (now dwindling) labels that is purely a labor of love—it's a hobby, not a full-time business, and the reverence for the movies comes before the profit motive. The amount of time and money and hard work that goes into producing the Grindhouse Releasing discs is staggering—and ironically, the label gets a lot of grief from the fans for not putting out the movies quickly enough. It's also worth mentioning that Grindhouse Releasing has made a point of hiring the great horror fanzine editors to write liner notes, including both Chas. Balun and Bill Landis. We'd love to get Rick Sullivan to contribute something to one of our releases.

**JS: Any thoughts on fandom today?**

**DS:** With the advent of DVD came this sense of entitlement among the fans—and with the internet, everyone became an instant expert. A lot of fans seemed to become focused on the minutiae of technical specs, digital transfers, running times, etc. The whole Tim Lucas/*Video Watchdog* approach. But whereas Tim Lucas is a very thoughtful, intelligent guy who

genuinely loves film, the digital-age fanboys reduced movie-watching to a mechanical exercise in comparing screen captures and spouting technical jargon. I wonder how these people even enjoy movies when they're sitting at their computers and looking for flaws in an audiovisual presentation to prove their own eagle-eyed superiority. Their great pleasure appears to come from announcing on the internet that they own the Region 7 dual blu-ray release of Jess Franco's worst cinematic excretion and that they find the color correction lacking. Now that the DVD craze is all but dead, that phase of "fandom" seems to be waning... but at its worst, that mentality really sucked the fun out of things for me.

I've focused instead on theatrical releases—bringing these movies back into theaters the way they were meant to be experienced. And that's been very gratifying for a zine kid like me; from clipping movie ads out of the newspaper as a teenager, I've gone on to place some of those same movies I loved back into theaters. I've worked with Bill Lustig releasing *Maniac* and *Zombie* in theaters all over North America. With Grindhouse Releasing, I've released *Evil Dead*, *I Drink your Blood*, *Pieces*, *Cannibal Ferox*, *The Beyond*, *Gone with the Pope*, *Cannibal Holocaust*, and others. Knowing that there's some kid getting to see these movies for the first time in a packed theater full of gorehounds is a great feeling. I feel like we're at least striking a symbolic blow against the lameness that permeates the world today!

LYNN LOWRY GETS A HAND IN *I DRINK YOUR BLOOD*.

PHOTO COURTESY OF JIM MORTON.

## Chapter Eight

# JIM MORTON

## Incredibly Strange Culture

ithout Jim Morton, the world would have waited a lot longer for the films of Ray Dennis Steckler, Ted V. Mikels, and Herschell Gordon Lewis to achieve wide recognition, let alone critical analysis. *Incredibly Strange Films*, first published in 1986 by RE/Search, was as much of a pioneering force as the filmmakers it celebrated. Written and edited by Jim Morton and Boyd Rice (with assistance from V. Vale and Andrea Juno), *Incredibly Strange Films* took a serious approach to the films that had once lined the bottom of the cinematic barrel, concentrating not only on the works of said directors, but also on their personalities, obsessions, and place in a largely forgotten chapter of American pop culture.

Morton began his writing career in San Francisco, self-publishing *Trashola*, an offset printed fanzine that covered the schlock films that graced the city on a weekly basis. After editing *Incredibly Strange Films*, he went on to publish *Pop Void*, a one-shot journal (which survives today as a website) focusing on an esoteric assortment of cultural oddities. In a similar vein, he co-authored *What a Character!: 20th Century American Advertising Icons* (1996) with Warren Dotz and John William Lund. Most recently, Morton's writing can be found on his *East German Cinema Blog*, in which he concentrates on the films of DEFA, the official film studio of East Germany.

The following interview was conducted via telephone on November 11, 2011.

---

**JOHN SZPUNAR: What kind of films did you watch as a child?**

**JIM MORTON:** Anything and everything. My mom worked at the train station in Tucson and she used the downtown movie theaters to babysit me. It was cheaper to just give me a quarter, or later, fifty cents, and have me sit and watch the same movie for a few times before she came back when she got off work.

**JS: And what kind of movies made an impact on you back then?**

**JM:** Well, I was always a big fan of horror movies, from a really early age. The first movie that I remember seeing by myself was *The Deadly Mantis*. I tended to like the horror movies; I went to them more often. I was also completely fascinated by the "sin-films"—I don't know what you'd call them. The black and white films like *Baby Doll* and *Walk on the Wild Side*. By modern standards, they're pretty tame, but back then they were considered very shocking. Completely wasted on a ten year old kid, though!

**JS: You're a native of Tucson?**

**JM:** Yeah, I was born and raised in Tucson.

**JS: When did you move to San Francisco?**

**JM:** Well, first I moved to New York and lived there for about a year and a half. From 1974 to the first part of '75; kind of right before punk

RECORDED & INDEXED

DRAFT

broke, actually. I should have stayed a little longer; things were about to get interesting. But at the time, New York was really dead. CBGB's wasn't cracking yet. I moved to Denver. New York was a little too crazy for me, but Denver was too boring. I spent a couple of years there, moved to San Francisco, and I've been here ever since.

JIM MORTON'S
TRASHOLA
The Newsletter for the Fan of the Grotesque
Send correspondence to: Jim Morton, Suite 583
109 Minna St., San Francisco, CA 94105
SCHLOCK,
SLEAZE,
AND HORROR
FREE!
Subscriptions:
to cover postage

**JS: San Francisco was about to get its first taste of punk...**

**JM:** I first encountered punk in Denver. There were maybe ten of us who were interested in it, and my girlfriend and I were two of the people! There was Wax Trax in Denver, which was a really great record store that was promoting punk music pretty heavily. I think we decided to move to San Francisco one night while we were at a party. I put on the Stranglers and somebody came by, said they hated it, and put on Buffalo Springfield or something. I said, "OK, we gotta get out of this town!"

**JS: What was a typical night out like in San Francisco back then?**

**JM:** Well, you would either go to the Mab, and then later to the Deaf Club, which I actually kind of enjoyed more. Or to Temple Beautiful—those were kind of the three main places. And there was Club Foot, in the early eighties. That was about the time I started *Trashola*.

**JS: I take it that you were reading a lot of the punk fanzines that came out at the time.**

**JM:** Oh yeah. And *Trashola* was spawned by an article in *New York Rocker* by Bill Landis (he had been doing *Sleazoid Express* for about a year at that point). He wrote an article called "From Tack to Gore"—it was kind of an overview of things. This was stuff that I knew really well, because I'd seen so many horror movies. There was that whole "do it yourself" aesthetic of the times. I was like, "Yeah, that's what I like to talk about! I like to talk about sleazy, trashy horror movies!" So I started *Trashola*.

**JS: Didn't you publish something earlier called the *Horror Show*?**

**JM:** I did have something called the *Horror Show*, but that's hardly known. *Horror Show* was my first fanzine. It came out in 1978—it was really early. That was all handwritten and xeroxed—a lot of collage stuff. But I didn't distribute it, I just sent it to my friends. I actually printed up a couple hundred copies of *Trashola* and left them in little coffee shops around San Francisco. And then, I commandeered a newsstand at the corner of Second and Market. I used to put them in there, too.

**JS: You were seeing films in movie theaters...**

**JM:** There were a lot more theaters back then. The main places were along Market, between 8th and 5th. There was the St. Francis, which was

a duplex theater. They would usually show one of three things: First-run movies that weren't quite good enough to make it in the bigger theaters; the guy who owned it had some deal where he was showing Hong Kong films dubbed into English—those were kind of fun. And then, just trashy horror movies for my people.

**JS: When you started *Trashola*, did you figure that there would be an audience for what you were writing about?**

**JM:** You know, I really didn't care. It was more of a case of, "OK, I'm really interested in this stuff. I'm going to put it out there—let's just see what happens." I'm kind of doing the same kind of thing with the East German cinema stuff. I've never really worried about whether there was an audience for what I did. This is what interests me. It's nice if there's some other people who are interested in it, but you can't plan on what you do to please anybody else.

**JS: *Trashola* did find an audience...**

**JM:** Oh yeah, I got people from all over the country. I went back and was sort of surprised at some of the names of the subscribers who have gone on to become pretty well known film reviewers and filmmakers. It's kind of funny.

**JS: Care to name any?**

**JM:** Well, I know that Joe Dante used to get it. Chuck Stephens was reading it—that kind of surprised me.

**JS: How did you distribute the thing outside of San Francisco?**

**JM:** The way I got national interest was thanks to Bob Martin of *Fangoria*. If you were a subscriber, they had a wrap on the magazine; it was a like a little newsletter. Bob mentioned *Trashola* on one of those, and he told people how they could get it. Bill Landis gave me a plug, too.

**JS: You said that *Sleazoid Express* inspired you to do *Trashola*. Your sensibilities were a little different than Bill's...**

**JM:** *Trashola* was more about horror stuff and low budget filmmaking. *Sleazoid Express* had a stronger bent for really sexual stuff. Straight and gay. That kind of Deuce culture really appealed to Bill. I was more horror-oriented and I was also trying to explore the area between really badly made movies and experimental movies. What makes it acceptable and artistic for Godard to film somebody's feet while they're talking, and yet Doris Wishman would be mocked for doing the same thing? I was sort of exploring that. I wanted people to say, "Look, there's more here than meets the eye."

RANDOM IMAGES FROM *TRASHOLA*.

RECORDED & INDEXED

DRAFT

JIM MORTON'S

# TRASHOLA

The Newsletter for the Fan of the Grotesque

Send correspondence to: Jim Morton, Suite 583
109 Minna St., San Francisco, CA 94105

SCHLOCK,
SLEAZE,
AND HORROR

VOL. 1 NO. 6

FREE!

Subscriptions: $3.00 to cover postage

No shortage of movies lately. Here are the best, along with the rest:

LEGEND OF THE BAYOU: Dir: Tobe Hooper. Neville Brand, Marilyn Burns, Mel Ferrer, Carolyn Jones, Stuart Whitman, William Finlay. A mad hotel owner feeds his guests to his pet crocodile. Don't let the title fool you, this film is none other than the infamous EATEN ALIVE, made by Tobe Hooper shortly after TEXAS CHAINSAW MASSACRE. MPM Releasing has picked ip the distribution rights and, in usual MPM fashion, tacked a new title on it. Not that this film is any stranger to alternative titles, It has, at various times in it's existence, been known as EATEN ALIVE, STARLIGHT SLAUGHTER, and DEATH TRAP. Whatever the title, LEGEND OF THE BAYOU is the best horror movie to hit town this summer. Neville Brand plays the hotel owner with lunatic gusto. He is matched by perennial weirdo William Finlay (SISTERS, PHANTOM AT THE PARADISE, etc.). Marilyn Burns, who was terrorized so well in CHAINSAW, is again on hand to scream and run. The film appears to have been shot entirely on sets, which gives the outdoor scenes a strange surrealistic atmosphere, reminiscent of HORROR HOTEL. The gore is graphic and painful looking and, like CHAINSAW, the horror doesn't let up for a minute. If you haven't seen it, by all means, don't miss it this time around. RATING:

HERCULES: Dir: Lewis Coates. Lou Ferrigno, Sybil Danning, Ingrid Anderson, Mirella D'Angelo. Lewis Coates is a pseudonym for Luigi Cozzi, an Italian director of little repute and absolutely no shame. His specialty is the grade Z ripoff. After STAR WARS, Cozzi gave us STARCRASH, a truly awful film starring Marjoe Gortner as a space cadet. After ALIEN, Cozzi came forward with ALIEN CONTAMINATION, which managed to combine the original ALIEN with IT CONQUERED THE WORLD and several James Bond films. In his latest effort, Luigi takes on CONAN and the results are mind boggling. Several critics have called HERCULES a bad movie, but HERCULES is beyond all such defamatory descriptions. It transcends bad. If camp is unintentional humor, then this flick is hypercamp. The script (written by Cozzi) is the closest thing to a grade school history play that has ever been commited to celluloid. Cozzi has thrown in elements from everything from JASON AND THE ARGONAUTS, and CLASH OF THE TITANS to INFRA-MAN and BARBARELLA. Lou Ferrigno tries valiantly to play the mythical strongman, but Steeve Reeves he ain't. Almost totally deaf, you could occasionally catch a glimpse of Lou's hearing aid peeking through his hair. Sybil Danning is on hand as the evil woman (natch!), and Ingrid Anderson and Mirella D'Angelo provide the love interests. The audience I saw this film with laughed uncontrollably all the way through it. HERCULES stands out as one of the funniest movies to come along in some time. It is far funnier and more enjoyable than nine out of ten recent comedies, and that is worth something. RATING:

NIGHTMARES: Dir: Joseph Sargent. Cristina Raines, Emilio Estevez, Richard Masur. This film is a quartet of horror stories. Originally it was intended as a TV movie rip-off of TWILIGHT ZONE, but the producers decided to release it theatrically instead. Like most TV fodder it is as bland and unexciting as tofu. The first story is based on an actual event. It concerns a woman out alone at night while an escaped murderer is roaming the hills. It is all punchline and no story. The second tale is an obvious attempt to cash in on the popularity of video games. It stars Martin Sheen's son and Frank Zappa's daughter and features some TRON like effects and an obvious outcome. The third story is a cross between DUEL and THE CAR without adding anything new to either concept. The forth and final episode is about a giant rat invading a suburban home. It is supposed to be the coup-de-grace, but the story is too dopey and badly handled to suspend our disbelief. The giant rat is so obviously matted into the picture even Bert I. Gordon would disown it. All in all, NIGHTMARES adds up to nothing more than a bad evening on NIGHT GALLERY. RATING:

MORTUARY: Dir: Howard Avedis. Mary McDonough, Bill Paxton, Lynda Day George, Christopher George. A young woman is tormented by a hooded spectre that is somehow connected to her father's death. Meanwhile, strange things are going on at the local funeral parlor. Let me preface this review by saying that this film has not received a single good review in any magazine or newspaper, nor has anyone I have talked to liked it either. I wasn't expecting much from this film, but I actually found it mildlyentertaining.The killer, slinking through the midnight fog in a monk's cowl and white face paint was a strange, stylized effect. Unlike many recent slasher flicks that try to keep the killer's identity a secret, MORTUARY clues you in early as to who the killer is and saves the twists for the subplots. The gore is minimal and what there is isn't particularly realistic. Christopher George (bad actor non pareil) is on hand, along with his wife, but never gets much of a chance to chew up scenery. The most surprising thing about MORTUARY is the way it manages to evoke sympathy for the killer. The shy apprentice embalmer is quirky, intelligent, sensitive and likable. He resembles David Byrne as a psychokiller. The "hero," on the other hand, is a typical, dumb, blond, Southern California jock with about as much personality as an MTV veejay. The disparity between the two characters is so great I cannot help but suspect Director Avedis wanted the audience to side with the killer (of course, in many recent slasher flicks the audience has cheered the killer on, but it is not because the killer is a sympathetic character, but because the victims are always such assholes). Still, the odds are you won't enjoy this movie as much as I did so approach it with caution. RATING:

NEXT ISSUE: THE ANNUAL HALLOWEEN SPECIAL ISSUE! DON'T MISS IT!

**JS: Were you aware of Rick Sullivan?**

**JM:** Well, once I started doing *Trashola*, I heard from a lot of the others. Although, interestingly, they were all from the east coast. *Gore Gazette* was one of them. There was always some sort of animosity between Bill and Rick Sullivan. I never understood that. Actually, Sullivan's zine was in some ways closer to mine; he was really horror-orientated. I was somewhere right between *Gore Gazette* and *Sleazoid Express*.

**JS: How were you producing *Trashola*? Were you photocopying?**

**JM:** I worked at a print shop back then, so it was actually offset printing. I went through a few typewriters and eventually a dot-matrix printer for the last issue. But, most of it was done on this old IBM Executive. I did it on a larger sheet and then most of it was reduced to 8.5 x 11. I got a big discount because I worked there, so I was essentially just paying for the printing. And everybody at the print shop read it.

**JS: Vale and Andrea must have read it.**

**JM:** I was doing *Trashola* and Vale and AJ [Andrea Juno] at RE/Search got a hold of some copies. They thought it was really cool and they introduced me to Boyd Rice, who was into a lot of the same films that I was. He knew about these films—I mean, there was some stuff that I was talking about that very few other people knew about. *The Incredibly Strange Creatures Who Stopped Living and Became Mixed Up Zombies!!?*, and stuff like that. Boyd was really into all that stuff. It was like, "Finally! Somebody actually knows these films!" Vale and AJ came over to my place; I had just gotten a VCR.

**JS: VHS or BETA?**

**JM:** I eventually had both. I think at that point, I just had a VHS. This was about a year before the end of *Trashola*. Anyway, they called me and I showed them—I don't know, it might have been *Incredibly Strange Creatures*. I showed them a film every Saturday night. Around the same time, I met Marcus Hu, who runs Strand Releasing. We rented videos from the same guy who really liked John Waters films. This was back in the very beginning of video rental. This guy had this service where he would deliver the video rentals to your house, which I thought was great. I gave him some of my newsletters and he'd put them in with his newsletters that he'd mail to his clients. So, Marcus contacted me and he was a wealth of information. He knew people from all over the place.

**JS: Was Marcus instrumental in helping you track down some of the people that you covered and interviewed in the book?**

**JM:** He wasn't instrumental in tracking down the people, but he was instrumental in tracking down some of the films. He was instrumental in tracking down some of the Herschell Gordon Lewis films at a time when they just weren't available to anybody. And then, my friend Lory Ringuette had a copy of *Spider Baby,* which, back then, was like gold. He was an actual film collector. We'd go to his house and he would show us movies; he'd

screen them in his living room.

**JS: A lot of people take the availability of these films for granted these days.**

**JM:** Some of the stuff that we were trying to write about—we just assumed that *The Curse of Her Flesh* was gone. Nobody would ever get to see it. But Something Weird Video has it now. Everything was still out there, it just needed some light shone on it.

**JS: There's mention of the *Incredibly Strange Films* book as forthcoming in the Boyd Rice interview in *Industrial Culture Handbook*. Whose idea was it to do the book?**

**JM:** That's a good question. I don't really know who came up with the idea. At some point, Vale, I think, said, "You and Boyd should do a book on these movies." Whether he had discussed that with Boyd before me, I don't know. That was the way I first heard about it.

**JS: Was researching the book an equal effort between all of you?**

**JM:** It was a little bit of everybody, really. When we first started the project, AJ knew about films from going to university. But she'd been trained in the classic film stuff— this was all new to her. Vale was a complete innocent—everything was new to him. So they were mostly just following our leads. We'd say, "We really need to interview Ray Dennis Steckler," and they would say, "OK." But then, later, they started adding their own interviews as they talked to people. They would go traveling; they did more traveling than I did back then. I couldn't afford that; I was working at a print shop for just a little bit more than minimum wage. When I interviewed David Friedman, I took an overnight Greyhound bus to LA, interviewed him, and took an overnight bus back to San Francisco. That was a grueling schedule!

**JS: I can imagine. How did you track these guys down? Were they listed in the phone book?**

**JM:** Yep. I worked at Blueprint Service, which back then was at Second and Market. The AT&T building was a block away, back before they broke up the telephone company. Just off the lobby of the building was a phone book for every city in America. I would go to the California section and

just look in all of the Los Angeles area phone books. You would be amazed at the people who were in the phone book. Sometimes I would go, "I can't find this director—who produced the movies?" That's how we found Ray Dennis Steckler. He wasn't in the phone book, but the guy who produced his films was. Ray had already moved to Las Vegas and was doing movies there.

**JS: What was the usual reaction to your calls?**

**JM:** Most people were really happy. It was like, nobody had ever done that before. Nobody had ever asked Ray Dennis Steckler or T.V. Mikels for an interview; certainly since the mid-sixties. Every one of them was really nice, especially David Friedman. He was such a sweet guy; I was so sorry when he died. The only one who was prickly was Doris Wishman. I had tried to get a hold of her back when I was doing *Trashola*, and she would not respond to me. She was in the phone book. I knew her address, but she would not contact me. She eventually let AJ interview her. Russ Meyer was a little prickly, too. But, he let me interview him.

**JS: You actually went to his house.**

**JM:** Yes, I did.

**JS: Out of curiosity, what was it like?**

**JM:** Well, on the outside, it was just one of those normal ranch-style houses; nothing special. But the inside was filled with all of his posters and photos, so it was pretty cool. He was a little cantankerous; he didn't like what I wrote about him, which totally shocked me. I mean, I said that *Faster, Pussycat!* was the greatest movie ever made and that *Beyond the Valley of the Dolls* was a great American film. Those are quotes from the book. You would think that that would be enough for one person. You would think they would just take those high levels of praise and go home with them. But, I also said that I thought that his earlier movies were better than his later movies. That's all he saw. He was so used to being praised at that point. The idea that anyone would offer any criticism at all would just send him to paroxysms of anger. He sent all the books back.

**JS: Wow...**

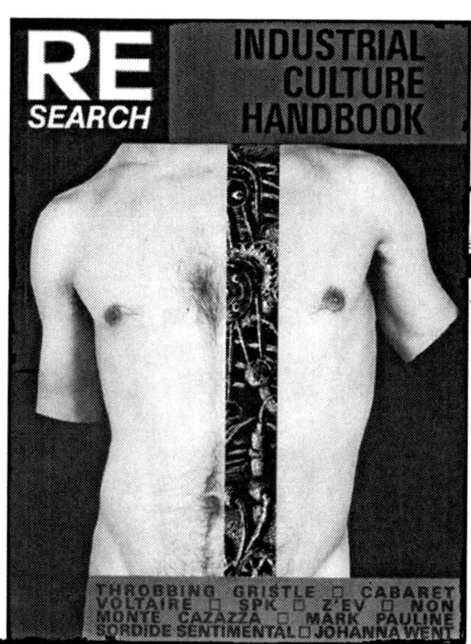

RECORDED & INDEXED

DRAFT

**JM:** And then, there were people we wanted to interview that we just couldn't find. Herschell Gordon Lewis, for instance. He was one of life's little mysteries—he was really hard to find for a long time. And then, all of the sudden he showed up in the direct mail marketing stuff. But, when we first started that book, he was invisible. He had completely divorced himself from his past.

**JS: Was there anybody you wanted to interview that you couldn't find?**

**JM:** Let's see. Michael Findlay was dead by then. It would have been nice to interview Roberta Findlay, but that was more of a case of not getting a chance to. At a certain point, we just sort of had to wrap it up.

**JS: How did you know when it was time to do that?**

**JM:** We had been working on the book for two years. We just realized that we could do this forever; it's theoretically never going to end. Let's just put the book out; maybe we'll try to do a second one later.

**JS: Were there ever plans to actually do a second book?**

**JM:** Well, there was some discussion. There were topics that we wanted to cover that we didn't even talk about. We wanted to cover blaxsploitation, but we didn't really get to it.

**JS: A Rudy Ray Moore interview would have been hilarious.**

**JM:** It would have been wonderful. An interview with Melvin Van Peebles would have been great, too.

**JS: Back to working with Vale—I went to visit him at the RE/Search office back in 2002 and was really impressed with the sheer amount of books, records, and everything else that lined the walls. I could have explored it for days. What was the place like in the mid-eighties?**

**JM:** It was about the same, except they had Compugraphic typesetters in there [laughs].

**JS: Really?**

**JM:** *Incredibly Strange Films* was all done on a Compugraphic typesetter. In fact, I've been busy scanning some of the pages to turn them into text again because it's all gone now, you know? The machines are gone, and the book was done on 5½ inch

Cannibal Film. These films are all extremely gory and are often banned in several countries. The plots are mainly devices to get a group of westerners into the jungles so the natives can chow down on them. Often the films include scenes of actual animal death and dismemberment. They are weird cross-breeds; a combination of MONDO CANE and DAWN OF THE DEAD. So far, the Cannibal Films have fared quite badly in the United States. CANNIBAL HOLOCAUST played very limited engagements here under the title THE LAST SURVIVOR. QUEEN OF THE CANNIBALS fared even worse; after having sizable portions removed, parts rearranged, and totally unrelated new footage added, it was released here as DR. BUTCHER M.D.; a film only a gorehound could love. Like it's predecessors, MAKE THEM DIE SLOWLY is cut a bit. Some of it's gore has been removed, but not much. It remains essentially intact. Unlike most Italian gore films, this one actually has an interesting premise at it's roots. Umberto Lenzi seems to take more pride in his work than most of his fellow Italian hack directors. MTDS is no work of art, but it is fairly well mounted and pays more attention to details than most spaghetti horror films. People with weak stomachs are warned to stay away. Most gorehounds are gonna love it. RATING: ☠☠½

FORCED ENTRY: Dir: Jim Sotos. Ron Max, Tanya Roberts, Nancy Allen. A weirdo rapes and kills women. This flick was made a few years back, but has only recently received much distribution. It was made back when slasher flicks were still going strong and features a pre-"Charlie's Angels" Tanya Roberts. Nancy Allen, who gets third billing is in it for about ten minutes as a hitchhiking victim. FORCED ENTRY has been available on video tape for a couple years now. It is by the same man who gave us SWEET SIXTEEN, and like that film, it is utterly forgetable. The murders are brutal and sexual and dopey voiceovers at the beginning of the film set the killer up as a stereotypical mass murderer (nice, quiet guy, loner at school, eats lots of junk food--hell, it sounds like me!). Sotos manages to keep all of the characters from displaying anything remotely resembling personality. The result is a film as bland and lifeless as overcooked spaghetti. There must be a better way to spend an hour and a half. RATING: ☠

REVENGE OF THE POPCORN EATER: THE STUDIO ONE THEATRE: Studio 1 is in the Fruitvale district of Oakland. It's schedule is not listed in the San Francisco papers, but it is listed in the Tribune under "Kung-Fu Studio 1." The Kung-Fu in the title is because the first two films on their triple bills are always chop-sockey flicks; the third feature is inevitably a horror movie. All horror fans should know about this theatre. Several of the films they show are movies that rarely show on the west coast, or anywhere outside of midtown Manhattan. Recent screenings include BLOOD-THIRSTY BUTCHERS, MS. 45, and NIGHT OF THE BLOODY APES. It is a medium size theatre that looks like any grindhouse from the outside, but is surprisingly clean inside. The audience is young, predominately hispanic and black, and surprisingly well behaved. This is probably because every ten minutes the aisles are patrolled by a man the size of a warehouse who does not look like somebody you would want to upset. The lobby is cramped and the snack bar selection is uninspired, but adequate. They are also one of the only theatres I've been to in a long time that plays a concession stand trailer after the movie. If snack bar food is not your cup of tea, there is a Kentucky Fried Chicken next door and plenty of good Mexican restaurants down on 14th. The theatre is close to Bart and fare from downtown San Francisco is $1.35 each way. The price of admission to the theatre is always $1.50. The films play one week, and the horror films are usually shown at four on weekdays and at one-thirty and six-thirty on weekends. They are closed Mondays and Tuesdays. Upcoming films include THE SLASHER (starting Feb. 10), THE RATS ARE COMING! THE WEREWOLVES ARE HERE! (Feb. 24), THE FEMALE BUTCHER (Mar. 2), and TORTURE DUNGEON (Mar. 16).

The Studio 1 is a sleaze fan's dream come true and a trip to this marvelous establishment is highly recommened to anyone who claims to like TRASHOLA kind of movies.

BACK ISSUE INFORMATION: I receive a lot of requests for back issues of TRASHOLA. Most of the early issues are long gone. From the first year (volume one) issues number 6, 7, 9, 10, 11, and 13 through 17 are still available. All of Volume Two is still available as well. Back issues are 50¢ each, or $6.50 for the complete set of volume two. Offer good while supply lasts! Make checks payable to J. Morton.

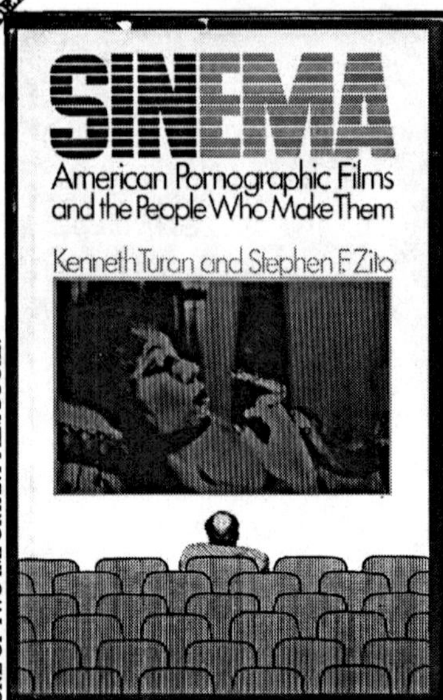

SINEMA
American Pornographic Films and the People Who Make Them
Kenneth Turan and Stephen F. Zito

ONE OF TWO IMPORTANT FILM BOOKS.

floppies in whatever code that particular machine used.

**JS: The book deserves to be in print. Did you have any idea that *Incredibly Strange Films* would be such a watershed when you were working on it?**

**JM:** I kind of did; I didn't know to what extent. For me, at that point, there were really only two books that were as important as *Incredibly Strange Films* seems to have become to a lot of people. Those were *Kings of the Bs* and *Sinema*.

**JS: I've never heard of *Sinema*.**

**JM:** That's a good one. Turan and Zito wrote it. Those are great books—huge sources of inspiration and ideas. But, I knew that there wasn't really anything out there. I knew that Michael Weldon was working on something, but that it was more of an encyclopedia. He wasn't doing the same thing; I knew there wasn't anything out there like our book. So yeah, I thought it was actually pretty important. No false modesty there.

**JS: I probably wouldn't have even cared about Ted Mikels if it wasn't for your book. His films never seemed like they'd be my cup of tea, but after reading those interviews, I had to track them down.**

**JM:** Yeah, that's one thing I've discovered in everything I've written. You can just take some subject—even if it doesn't sound that interesting—you just start to dig into it, and all of this interesting stuff pops up. That's kind of the story of my writing career.

**JS: I was able to find his films via video, but that was a few years after the book had come out. What was actually available to you? Was there grey-market stuff floating around?**

**JM:** Oh, just the beginnings of it. It was very, very minimal. There were a few things, but it was a little hard to get stuff at first. That's changed. Even within that last year of *Trashola*, it was already changing pretty dramatically. Once VHS and Betamax machines became cheap enough that almost anyone could afford to have one, you saw this explosion of stuff. I would tape stuff off of late-night TV and somebody would be wanting *Tales of Hoffman*. I would have recorded that. I'd trade it for *Two Thousand Maniacs*.

**JS: That's a good trade! Video made things more accessible, but did**

**you miss the theater experience?**

**JM:** Video was pretty cool, but I've always preferred watching movies in a theater. It was part of my impetus for doing "The Revenge of the Popcorn Eater" in *Trashola*. Which, ironically, turned out to be the most valuable thing about *Trashola*. Most of the movie stuff is all available now, and my synopses were so brief that they really didn't add much to that. But my reviews of the movie theaters are something that you can't find anywhere else. I was just putting them in to fill up space, but it turns out that they were actually the thing of real value.

**JS: So... movie theaters, San Francisco. Describe one, if you would!**

**JM:** Of all of "The Revenge of the Popcorn Eaters," the one that made me the happiest was the one about the St. Francis. It was a wonderfully sleazy place. The audience there was primarily young black kids; very loud and boisterous. They would scream at the screen when somebody would do something really stupid. "Don't go in there! Don't go in there!" Then, after the girl goes in there in gets killed, they'd say something like, "White people are so stupid!" It was kind of fun to be in there. I was in there one day with Stefan Hammond, who writes about Hong Kong films. He's the guy who wrote *Sex and Zen* & *A Bullet in the Head*. He and I went to see *Evil Dead 2*. The St. Francis was packed! A big, raucous crowd. About a half-hour into the movie, a rat decided to run up through the aisles. The whole audience went ballistic—people were crawling on each other and screaming and crying! Complete pandemonium in the movie theater! You don't get that at home [laughs]!

**JS: Not unless you live in a really bad home!**

**JM:** The Strand was always a fun and sleazy experience, too. But my favorite theater, I think, was the Embassy. It unfortunately was destroyed in the '89 earthquake. It's now just a big pit in the ground. That was the most fun of all the theaters. They would show triple, sometimes quadruple bills of movies with no particular order to them. It would be like, *The Eyes of Laura Mars* with *Trouble Man* with *Bring Me the Head of Alfredo Garcia*. Some weird

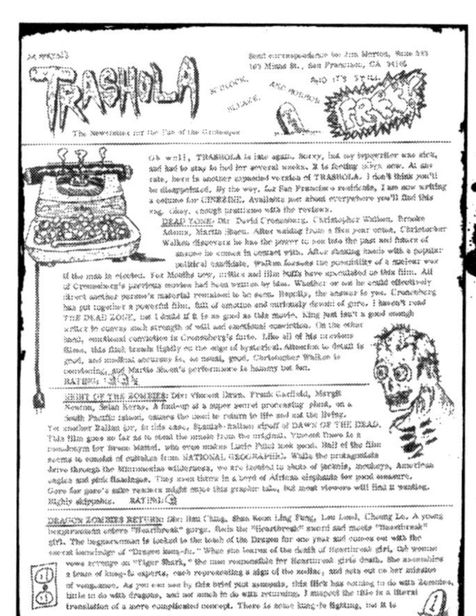

TRASHOLA

Send correspondence to: Jim Morton, Suite [illegible] [illegible] Minna St., San Francisco, CA [illegible]

SCHLOCK, SLEAZE, AND HORROR

AND IT'S STILL FREE!

The Newsletter for the Fan of the Grotesque

Oh well, TRASHOLA is late again. Sorry, but my typewriter was sick, and had to stay in bed for several weeks. It is feeling [illegible] now. At any rate, here is another expanded version of TRASHOLA. I don't think you'll be disappointed. By the way, for San Francisco residents, I am now writing a column for CINEZINE. Available just about everywhere you'll find this rag. Okay, enough prattling with the reviews.

DEAD ZONE: Dir: David Cronenberg. Christopher Walken, Brooke Adams, Martin Sheen. After waking from a five year coma, Christopher Walken discovers he has the power to see into the past and future of anyone he comes in contact with. After shaking hands with a popular political candidate, Walken foresees the possibility of a nuclear war if the man is elected. For Months now, critics and film buffs have speculated on this film. All of Cronenberg's previous movies had been written by him. Whether or not he could effectively direct another person's material remained to be seen. Happily, the answer is yes. Cronenberg has put together a powerful film, full of emotion and curiously devoid of gore. I haven't read THE DEAD ZONE, but I doubt if it is as good as this movie. King just isn't a good enough writer to convey such strength of will and emotional conviction. On the other hand, emotional conviction is Cronenberg's forte. Like all of his previous films, this flick treads lightly on the edge of hysterical. Attention to detail is good, and medical accuracy is, as usual, good. Christopher Walken is convincing, and Martin Sheen's performance is hammy but fun.
RATING: [illegible]

NIGHT OF THE ZOMBIES: Dir: Vincent Dawn. Frank Garfield, Margit Newton, Selan Karay. A foul-up at a super secret processing plant, on a South Pacific island, causes the dead to return to life and eat the living. Yet another Italian (or, in this case, Spanish-Italian) ripoff of DAWN OF THE DEAD. This film goes so far as to steal the music from the original. Vincent Dawn is a pseudonym for Bruno Mattei, who even makes Lucio Fulci look good. Half of the film seems to consist of outtakes from NATIONAL GEOGRAPHIC. While the protagonists drive through the Minnesotan wilderness, we are treated to shots of jackals, monkeys, American eagles and pink flamingos. They even throw in a herd of African elephants for good measure. Gore for gore's sake readers might enjoy this graphic tale, but most viewers will find it wanting. Highly skippable. RATING: [illegible]

DRAGON ZOMBIES RETURN: Dir: Hau Chang. Shan Kuan Ling Fung, Lau Lund, Cheung Lo. A young beggarwoman enters "Heartbreak" gorge, finds the "Heartbreak" sword and meets "Heartbreak" girl. The beggarwoman is locked in the tomb of the Dragon for one year and comes out with the secret knowledge of "Dragon kung-fu." When she learns of the death of Heartbreak girl, the woman vows revenge on "Tiger Shark," the man responsible for Heartbreak girl's death. She assembles a team of kung-fu experts, each representing a sign of the zodiac, and sets out on her mission of vengeance. As you can see by this brief plot synopsis, this flick has nothing to do with Zombies, little to do with dragons, and not much to do with returning. I suspect the title is a literal translation of a more complicated concept. There is some kung-fu fighting, but it is combination like that. Action films and stuff for the masses. And the snack bar, besides serving the usual stuff, also served liverwurst sandwiches.

**JS: How much would a sandwich set you back?**

**JM:** It went for like five dollars [laughs]. But my favorite thing was this: Before the 8:00 film, they would pull this giant wheel out on the stage. They would spin it and give away money. The first time I went to the Embassy, I actually walked out with more money than I came in with. I was hooked from that point on.

**JS: What kind of runs did the films have?**

**JM:** Usually, at the Embassy, they'd show the same film for a week. The same three films. But they'd cycle through, and stuff would show up again. If you missed *Bring Me the Head of Alfredo Garcia* one week, you could wait a month or two and it would show up again.

**JS: Did the audiences differ from theater to theater?**

**JM:** It was pretty different. The St. Francis, like I said, was mostly young black kids. The Embassy had a fair number of homeless people. The Strand was this weird conglomeration of street people and artsy-types; film lovers. The Roxy was a little more intellectual; they tended to show more serious stuff. So yeah, each theater kind of had its own vibe going. It was interesting that way; it wasn't uniform by any means.

**JS: *Incredibly Strange Films* was published in 1986. When did you start working on *Pop Void*?**

**JM:** I started working on that as soon as I finished the *Incredibly Strange Films* book. *Pop Void* took a little while to put together, too.

**JS: You were painting on a larger canvas. What gave you the urge to start that project?**

**JM:** Curiously enough, it was a guy named William James Sidis. He was this kid—his father (Boris Sidis) was a really well-respected psychologist in New York. His kid was named after William James, the psychologist (who was Henry James' brother). Boris Sidis had this belief that kids are never too young to learn; if you get to them really young, you can make them geniuses. He wanted

to prove this with his own son. So, by the time the kid was five, he could speak several languages. He could translate books from Greek and Latin. It's just insane. I think he was accepted to Yale at the age of eleven, but he didn't go until he was around thirteen. He was like this total whiz-kid. All of the newspapers were following him; it was like a "This kid is smarter than any of us!" kind of thing. He worked for a while teaching higher mathematics, but when he turned eighteen, he was kind of a free man. He completely dropped out of sight; nobody knew what happened to him. What happened was this: He would go to a town where nobody knew him, get the most menial job he could—accounting in some factory—and spend his days collecting street transfers off the ground. He sorted them in boxes.

**JS: Why?**

**JM:** That's the question! He eventually wrote this massive, 350-page book called, *Notes on the Collection of Transfers*. The single most boring book ever written. It's just about collecting street car transfers. It just fascinated me that somebody could do this. I thought, "What a great idea! I'll find a subject that people find completely boring—of no value, whatsoever—and write about it. That was sort of my impetus for *Pop Void*.

**JS: I kind of want to find his book now!**

**JM:** [laughs] Whatever subject you take, if you kind of look at the other side of it, there's all kinds of interesting stuff going on.

**JS: OK—you got the idea. Where did you go from there?**

**JM:** Well, then I just started thinking, "What are the things that I don't really like to write about?" I said, "OK, I wouldn't really want to write about Rod McKuen, so Rod McKuen should be in there." Or those big-eyed paintings of kids. "OK, the Keane paintings are in." Kraft Macaroni and Cheese dinners—they're pretty boring. It kind of went like that. But then, as soon as I started writing about something, it got interesting [laughs]!

**JS: How did you go about producing *Pop Void*?**

**JM:** Two things happened: My dad died, and the place that I was working at closed. That gave me enough money to not work for a little while

As some of you readers know, I am currently working on a book with Boyd Rice (of *Non*). We are working diligently on it and, if we're lucky, will have it completed by the end of the year. All subscribers to *Trashola* will receive information in the mail on this and any other projects I come up with. If you do not get *Trashola* in the mail, but wish to be on my mailing list, just drop me a line. Future projects include *The Last Trashola Magazine*, Fun With Forensics, The History of Jell-O and An In-depth Look at Macaroni and Cheese Dinners.

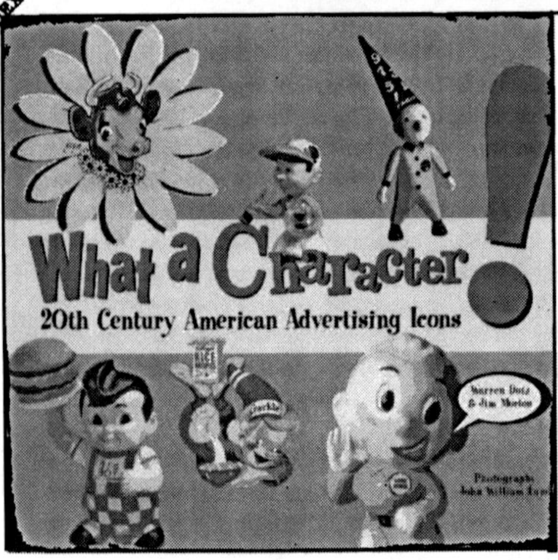


and to buy myself this new computer called a Mac Plus. I started working on this new computer with a program called PageMaker. I realized that the world had just changed. I went and told Vale and AJ, "Quick! Sell your typesetting equipment!" They eventually did.

**JS: This was the start of desktop publishing.**

**JM:** Yeah, *Pop Void* was one of the first desktop published books. Although, there were no scanners then, except for this little thing called a ThunderScan. I did put that to some use, but I still had to shoot halftones for the photographs.

**JS: You co-authored a book called *What a Character!* (about American advertising icons) in 1996. It includes more than a few *Pop Void*-like subjects.**

**JM:** I had an idea for an article about Funny Face. It was this drink that General Mills put out in the sixties to compete with Kool-Aid. Each flavor had its own character. I thought that would be a good thing to put in *Pop Void*. I went over to the Museum of Modern Mythology, which unfortunately no longer exists.

**JS: The Museum of Modern Mythology?**

**JM:** That was a museum that was devoted to advertising characters and our modern myths. We don't have fairies, Zeus, and Hera anymore. We have Tony the Tiger and Speedy Alka Seltzer. They represent powers in our life; they can fix things for us. It was a fairly high concept, but it was a great little museum. I met Ellen Weis, who was the person who ran it and started to work with her. Then, I met this guy named Warren Dotz; he was one of the collectors who liked to come to the museum. He contacted me about doing a book about characters, based on his collection. It's really pretty much based on what Warren collected at that point.

**JS: Why do you think you're fascinated by this kind of thing?**

**JM:** I don't know. I think that on some level, everything either does or can fascinate me. I tend to try to find things to study that I haven't thought about studying before. I do that a lot. *The East German Cinema Blog* is kind of a case in point. That came about because I started to learn German, which

*THE MURDERERS ARE AMONG US*. SOME OF THEM ARE LOOKING OUT OF A WINDOW.

was something that I had never considered doing in my life.

**JS: What made you decide to study the language?**

**JM:** I was working at a trade show in Germany and I learned a few things in German. They said, "You speak pretty good." So, I figured, "Aw, what the heck. I'll learn German." Word of advice to anybody: Do not learn German! It's a hard, hard language [laughs]! But I really got into it. I think it was because it was so difficult—that made it more appealing to me. You do have to work a lot harder to master the language. It was through that that I encountered those East German films. At first, it was sort of a case of, "Oh my God! I can't believe this movie exists!" And then, "This movie was made behind the Iron Curtain? Are you kidding me?"

**JS: Nowadays, the fanzine has all but metamorphosed into the "blog".**

**JM:** Yeah, absolutely. The thing about blogs is that anybody can do one fairly easily. And that means that there's a lot of crap out there. But I believe that if you write well, and your writing engages people, it's going to find an audience. And if it's serving some function other than just stroking your own ego—Like, when I write about the East German films, I always try to pick up information that hasn't been put in one place before. I do that for people who really are going to want to do something more serious with it, like in school or something.

**JS: You can't really discuss those films without discussing East German history.**

**JM:** Every time they made one of those films, something was going on with Walter Ulbricht or Erich Honecker, or whoever was in charge at that point. There was always something involved with that; you always have to refer back.

**JS: What's the earliest film that you've seen?**

**JM:** Well, the earliest film (and this is kind of what it is) is *The Murderers are Among Us*. That was the first East German film; in fact it wasn't even East Germany yet. It was still in the Soviet occupation zone, at that point. But, that was the first film made by the studio that would eventually become DEFA. DEFA made all the films for East Germany.

**JS: What was the last?**

**JM:** The last film is a little harder to say; there were a few in the can that were distributed after the wall fell. But, the film that premiered the same

RECORDED & INDEXED

DRAFT

Jim Morton's

TRASHOLA

The Newsletter for the Fan of the Grotesque

Send correspondence to: Jim Morton, Suite 5[illegible] 1[illegible] Minna St., San Francisco, CA 94105



THE ANNUAL AUTUMNAL & HALLOWEEN ISSUE OF TRASHOLA! (A LITTLE LATE AS USUAL.)

Yes, it's time again for the annual TRASHOLA Halloween issue. Yes, I know Halloween is over but once you take a look at the insides of this issue you'll see what took me so long. Besides, if you're like me (and God help you if you are), then every day is Halloween. There is a newspaper in San Francisco called the Bay Guardian that regularly publishes a list of what they call "Best Bets"--places or things that their readers would like but might not know about. For those of you with a taste for the macabre, I print the following list of places and things for your enjoyment and edification.

1. COLMA, CALIFORNIA. I want all of my San Francisco readers to put down whatever you are doing and immediately head for this garden spot on the west coast. Colma is a town that is comprised entirely of cemeteries. The best in Colma: Cypress Lawn.

2. FAMOUS MONSTER MODELS. Remember those wonderful models put out by Aurora back in the 60s? Well these are. Monogram is making them this time around. But they're using the original molds so nothing has changed. Also available are the Big Daddy Roth-like creations called "Weirdos." Only now they're calling them "C[illegible]dies."

3. STACY'S BOOKSTORE. Have you ever wanted a skull? I don't mean a plastic one. I mean the real thing. If so, then check out the medical section in the basement of Stacey's Bookstore at Second and Market. They have a wide variety of human skulls, varying in price from $[illegible]0 to $1[illegible]0.

4. SLEAZY TABLOIDS. Granted, The National Enquirer is not what it use to be, but there are alternatives. The most accessible is the wonderful WEEKLY WORLD NEWS. Available at newstands everywhere. For only 5[illegible]¢, this rag gives you articles like "I died and Rose From the Dead as a Zombie," or "Vampire Murders Sweep the Nation." The editorial policy of this paper is so right wing they recently called Reagan a wimp. If you speak spanish, three intensely gory rags from Mexico called, ALARMA, ALERTA and BOMICHBO might be of interest. Another tabloid I have been told about but have not been able to find is a paper called CLOSE-UP ON CRIME; a rag so gory and revolting that many newstands refuse to carry it. Any info on this one would be greatly appreciated. In the mean time, I'll keep looking.

AND NOW! ON WITH THE SHOW!

1

night that the wall came down was a film called *Coming Out*, about gay men in East Germany. It was sort of a pro-gay film.

**JS: Are you planning on doing a book?**

**JM:** Yeah. At some point, all of that East German stuff will end up in a book. It won't be like the blog; the blog's just, "Here's a movie." It's very straightforward. I've already started working on the book, and it's more of a rolling history of East Germany. I see it as kind of a history of East Germany, told one frame at a time.

**JS: Are you still on the lookout for "Incredibly Strange" films?**

**JM:** I keep finding new ones every day. I just saw a Japanese film from 1960 called *The Warped Ones*. Unbelievable. It's about wild and crazy youths in Japan— mostly about this guy who needs to listen to loud jazz music all the time and jiggle around, or else he sort of goes berserk. It's insane [laughs].

**JS: I take it that it has a pretty wild musical score?**

**JM:** Yeah. It's a wonderful movie. In fact, it was actually released by Radley Metzger. Probably heavily cut and badly dubbed; I'm sure he butchered it. But they just released the original version on DVD in a box set. So, that was a recent discovery that may well become one of my favorites. It's pretty mind boggling. From the Eastern side, I love *In the Dust of the Stars*, sometimes referred to as the East German *Barbarella*. And then, of course, *Hot Summer*, which is sometimes referred to as the East German *Beach Party*. Except the beach is on the Baltic Sea. It's pretty wild. The songs are actually better in *Hot Summer*. You can watch *Beach Party* and you won't come away humming anything from it, but I guarantee you'll be humming those damn songs from *Hot Summer* for the rest of the week.

**JS: That's a totally different culture tackling a very American genre. Did they copy it?**

**JM:** The girls are wearing two-piece bathing suits and the guys are wearing swim trunks. They kind of copy things, but without admitting it. It's got a very proletarian theme to it. It's not about the individual, it's about the collective. The bad girl is the one that's not doing what the collective needs to be done—that kind of thing. But, there's stuff from East Germany—I'm still finding stuff every day. I recently saw a film called *The Baldheaded Gang*. It's a film about skinhead bikers made in 1963. That's two years before *The Wild Angels*.

**JS: You're kidding!**

JM: There was stuff going on over there that we didn't know anything about.

**JS: What's next for you?**

JM: I don't know what I'll do after I finish this. Maybe I'll look at Czechoslovakian films [laughs].

**JS: There's a whole world of things out there to discover.**

JM: There really is. There's so much out there. And I've tried to do as good a job as I can of chronicling and examining. In the end, it's all about the joy of discovering things. Who knows where I'll go next…

THE FINAL ISSUE OF *TRASHOLA*.

# THE COMPLETE GUIDE TO GORE AND SLEAZE!

I have, in the past, reviewed several worthy newsletters and magazines. For those of you who missed them, here are the addresses and brief descriptions of all of those publications, plus a few I never got around to. Contrary to the title, this list is, by no means, complete. But it does contain the best, the best-known and the ones most *Trashola* readers would enjoy.

**SLEAZOID EXPRESS** (Bill Landis, P.O. Box 799, Peter Stuyvesant Station, N.Y.C., N.Y., 10009. Subscriptions: $8 per year) What can I say that I haven't already said? If there wasn't a *Sleazoid Express*, there would not be a *Trashola*. Bill will teach you that everything you know is wrong. Buy it!

**GORE GAZETTE** (Rick Sullivan, 73 N. Fullerton Ave., Montclair, N.J., 07042. Subscriptions: $13 per year) Entertaining and flippant, Rick Sullivan reviews most of the sleaze that hits the New York City area, and that is most of the sleaze, period. I usually agree with this guy, and that is a rare treat.

**CONFESSIONS OF A TRASH FIEND** (Richard Green, P.O. Box 32, Old Bridge, N.J., 08857. Subscriptions: $7 per year) Certainly one of the best! Richard Green covers the whole field of low budget films; from gore and sleaze to teenpix and softcore. Very well informed and informative.

**CHICAGO SHIVERS** (Ron Carlson, 4443 Grace Street, Schiller Park, Illinois, 60176. Subscriptions: $6 per year) Although Ron Carlson is a subscriber from way back, I only recently discovered he puts out his own newsletter. I only have one copy of his rag, so I can't say much. Chicago is certainly a city worthy of this sort of review. Good luck Ron!

**THE SPLATTER TIMES** (Sordid Publishing, P.O. Box 2733, Cookeville, Tenn., 38501) A terrific magazine. The first three issues were tabloid-style, but the latest issue is a full-fledged magazine. Publisher Donald Farmer has more knowledge of publishing and graphic arts than most of the others in this field, and it shows. *The Splatter Times* is well layed out and put together. So far, all of the issues have been excellent. Get them all!

**ZONTAR** (Brian Curran, 29 Darling St., Apt. 2, Roxbury, Mass., 02120. $2 per issue) A better magazine than first appearances would lead you to believe. Editor Brian Curran mixes humor, drivel and parody, but in it all are some really *good* articles. Worth buying.

**SCAREAPHANALIA** (Michael Gingold, 55 Nordica Drive, Croton-on-Hudson, N.Y., 10520. Subscriptions: $6 per year) Unlike most of the other newsletters reviewed here, this one does not concern itself with sleaze, porn, or sexploitation. It is strictly devoted to horror. For those who collect movie soundtracks and novels, Michael Gingold provides a list of books and records currently in print, and he updates the list with every issue.

6

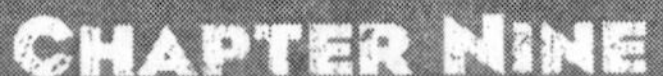

# Chapter Nine

# Tim Mayer

## Fear of Darkness

By Chris Poggiali

vol.2 issue 5

$1.50

Fear of Darkness

MAD MAX

George Kuchner

Screaming Mimi

Bizarre And Unusual Cinema Today

My introduction to the world of fanzines was the "Recommended Reading" section of Michael Weldon's trailblazing and indispensable the *Psychotronic Encyclopedia of Film*, which I didn't get my hands on until almost a full year after its November 1983 publication date. There on page 804, under the subheading of "Magazines," were newsstand known quantities such as *Fangoria* and *Cinefantastique* sharing space with titles that were new and exciting to my fourteen year old brain, including *Sleazoid Express*, *Gore Gazette* and a few with questionable post-publication postmortem dates that seemed to be telling me I may have just missed the boat: *Trashola*, (1980–1984), *Confessions of a Trash Fiend* (1982–1984), and *Fear of Darkness* (1982–1983). My suspicion was confirmed a few months later when Jack Barth's "Fanzines" article in the April 1985 issue of *Film Comment* referred to all three in the past tense.

I caught up with *Trashola* and *Confessions of a Trash Fiend* by the start of the 1990s, thanks to a friend with an extensive collection of fanzines, but it took another fifteen years after that for me to get my hands on an issue of *Fear of Darkness*. In early 2005, while reading posts on the message board *AV Maniacs* (née *DVD Maniacs*), the name of a recently registered board member jumped out at me from the past: Tim Mayer. Could this be the same Tim Mayer who edited the elusive *Fear of Darkness* so many years earlier? It was, and we were soon corresponding through email and swapping old fanzines for rare Lee Frost movies on DVD-R. I learned that Mayer's zine was indeed officially pronounced dead by the end of 1983. I also learned that unlike many of its counterparts, *FOD* was printed offset and is a real magazine (with advertising!) rather than a photocopied fan sheet or two-page newsletter.

Speaking of fan sheets and newsletters, the debut issue of *FOD* not only boasts "A Look at Movie Gimmicks" by *Trashola*'s Jim Morton, but an excellent interview with John Waters by *Sleazoid Express* founder/editor Bill Landis. Talk about instant street cred! Two more articles by Morton and Landis—"With My Tombstone and Guitar: A History of Rock'n' Roll Horror Movies" and "Essays in Sleaze," respectively—appear in the sophomore issue, along with a Paul Naschy profile written by *Gore Gazette* founder Rick Sullivan. For number 3, Brian Curran of *Zontar, The Magazine from Venus* chimes in with "Art and Aleination: The Bad Horror Movies of Larry Buchanan," with an essay on LSD movies by Morton and a look at mondo documentaries by Landis also included. Issue number 4 contains goodies like "The Movie's the Thing: Good Acting in Horror Films" by *Cygnus* and *Wet Paint* editor Jeff Smith, ubiquitous zine contributor Dave Szurek's "Bombastic Bikers, Hairy Hippies and Cinematic Sleaze," and a letter from *Fangoria*'s Uncle Bob Martin. Szurek's "All Night at the Grindhouse," from *FOD* number

## FEAR OF DARKNESS

RECORDED & INDEXED

5, offers a detailed remembrance of two long-gone twenty-four hour grindhouses in Detroit, the Fox and Colonial, and is an excellent warm-up for his masterpiece, "Detroit Grindhouse Blues," published a few years later in *Magick Theatre* number 7 (1986). Other highlights of issue five include a Harry Medved interview by Kris Gilpin (reprinted from the Canadian zine *Yeech!*), "Screaming Mimi: Forgotten Psycho Flick from the Fifties" by Roger Berrian, and "Mad Max: One View" by *Confessions of a Trash Fiend*'s Richard Green.

At about the same time I brought my own fanzine back from the dead in blog form, Tim resuscitated *Fear of Darkness* as an online presence (www.gammaone.blogspot.com) and then expanded the brand with *Z7's Headquarters* (www.z7hq.com), his blog dedicated to "pulp, mystery, science fiction, fantasy, crime and horror novels." He's also a member of several movie message boards, and is very much a part of the fan community, so disregard that tombstone inscription on page 804 of the *Psychotronic Encyclopedia of Film*: Tim is still here, and the fear of darkness never goes away!

The following interview was conducted via telephone on July 5, 2012.

---

**CHRIS POGGIALI: When I first approached you to do an interview about *Fear of Darkness*, your response was "Sure! If nothing else, future zine editors can learn how not to lose their shirt."**

**TIM MAYER:** Things were different thirty years back. You didn't have the internet, for one. You didn't have a lot of digital printing options like you do today. So if you had a burning desire to get a magazine out, you were going to have to invest a significant amount of capital on it. Then you had to find a distribution outlet. And so forth. And if you didn't know the first thing about printing, like me, you were in for a nice sharp line curve. It could get really expensive. I ended up supporting a lot of printers!

**CP: I miss the cut and paste aspect of doing a fanzine, but not the photocopying, the collating, the mailing...**

**TM:** Things are better now. You don't have to go to print physical media if you want to get something out. If you've got some burning desire to give your opinion on a film, it's much easier just setting up a web page. But the problem with "anybody can do it" is, in fact, sometimes everybody does. Then you've got to sort who's got something worthwhile to say. So I think the fact that it was a difficult barrier did mean the people getting into it were pretty dedicated. Or they found out they were going to be dedicated after the first issue, when they were trying to figure out how to pay for a second.

**CP: And once the issue was done and printed, they still had to find an audience for it.**

**TM:** Distribution was a big problem. You do 1,000 copies of the

magazine. Well, how do you get it out there? Do you just put 'em in your car and drive around? I tried that. It doesn't work that way. You find a dis–trib–u–tor. They'll take some and then pay when the next one comes out. There's kind of a delay factor there. That's why a lot of people just did a little newsletter they could slap into an envelope and mail out.

**CP: Like *Sleazoid Express*.**

**TM:** Exactly. For somebody like Bill Landis, that was perfect, because he's right next to 42nd Street, he goes out, sees all the great movies that nobody else can see—because we don't live in New York—he writes about them, bangs out a little newsletter on his typewriter... It worked fine for him for years. Same thing with Jim Morton in San Francisco.

**CP: So you were familiar with the photocopied zines before you first issue of *Fear of Darkness* was done.**

**TM:** Yeah, I subscribed to *Sleazoid Express* and the one Jim used to do, *Trashola*. I think there was one out of Chicago [*Chicago Shivers*]. It was a small group of people who were just starting.

**CP: Was the first shot fired by *Psychotronic* or *Sleazoid Express*?**

**TM:** The thing that kicked it off was Bill's article in *New York Rocker*, called "From Tack to Gore." It was a 1980 issue of *New York Rocker*. It was a really, really neat article. I must've read the thing over about ten times. It was about exploitation films. Basically, he listed types of movies that no one seemed to even know about because they had vanished from the face of the earth after being released [laughs]! Like the black and white adult stuff from the sixties that never made it into the seventies. I think it kind of woke people up, thinking "Here are hundreds, maybe thousands of films that people have just completely forgotten about."

**CP: 1980 was also the year Lawrence Cohn started covering the 42nd Street beat for *Variety*. What do you think brought on this new wave of fandom and interest in exploitation movies?**

Fear of Darkness
vol.1 issue 4 $1.50
BIZARRE AND UNUSUAL CINEMA TODAY

BOMBASTIC BIKERS, HAIRY HIPPIES AND CINEMATIC SLEAZE
by
Dave Szurek

## FEAR OF DARKNESS

RECORDED & INDEXED

**TM:** A lot of things were happening at the same time. The drive-ins were shutting down, the city theaters were starting to close, and people were realizing that a lot of these films might be lost. People started checking out what's at the drive-ins. I had a group of friends who'd call me, "Hey, did you see what's at the drive-in this weekend?" It was a combination of people feeling that part of the culture was being lost and we better get together and preserve it, and at the same time people were kind of connecting in some ways.

**CP: What inspired you to start *Fear of Darkness*?**

**TM:** Back in 1980, if you wanted to see some really cool films, you had to live in a big city... or, get some friends together and rent some 16mm stuff. So I had this film society I was running. It was called the Exploited Film Society [laughs]. Then I thought, wouldn't it be nice if we had a magazine to go along with the film society? That would be really cool. I had seen a do-it-yourself fanzine called *Magic Lantern* sometime in the late seventies that covered all kinds of different film media and I thought: "This looks really neat! I should do something like this." I couldn't come up with a title, but I had a cassette tape playing of a local punk band and the song that was playing was "Fear of Darkness." I thought, okay, there's my title!

**CP: Did the Exploited Film Society have a consistent venue for its programming?**

**TM:** We kind of floated around. We got kicked out of one place. We showed *Faster, Pussycat! Kill! Kill!* And people didn't like that. It got nasty. At one point, somebody had won the use of a balcony at some movie theater, and they were showing a John Waters movie [*Polyester*] so we all got together to sit in the balcony, eat popcorn and watch the John Waters movie. It wasn't very organized! So, we moved around, and finally found a home at a local art gallery.

**CP: How long were you in charge of the Exploited Film Society?**

**TM:** I did it for about a year, and then I turned it over to some other people. It was a case of "Oops, we're going to have to pay for that film. Well, there goes my paycheck!"

**CP: It sounds like you were more interested in publishing the magazine than running the film society.**

**TM:** It's hard to get enough people to show up and pay admission. The people who took it over after me, I think they did a better job. It was always pretty much who was running the show was who could pay the bills [laughs]. I can remember going to a couple of showings at this art gallery that they had organized. At one point, the film was introduced by somebody who was "one of our fourteen chairmen." It was kind of ad hoc.

**CP: The home video boom was still a few years away.**

**TM:** Video was just coming out at the time. At one point we found out we could get really great stuff on video, so I went out and found a place

I could actually rent a video from. I got everybody together and we invaded somebody's house, cos he had a videotape machine, and we all watched it there. That was a shadow of things to come.

**CP: You did five issues of *Fear of Darkness* in two years.**

**TM:** I kind of had an erratic publishing schedule. Again, whenever I could pay off the bills for the last one was when the next one would generally get published.

**CP: You got off to a great start with that John Waters interview in issue one.**

**TM:** Yes, Bill Landis had done that interview, and the *SoHo Weekly News*—which was kind of the rival of the *Village Voice*—was going to run it, and I think they went belly-up right about that time. I had gotten to be friends with Bill, about as best as anybody could've been friends with him at the time. We even flew him in to introduce a film. He was an interesting guy. God rest his soul. So Bill told me "You can have the interview for your magazine."

**CP: In the second issue there are full-page reproductions of one-sheets for movies like *The Body Beneath* and *Alabama's Ghost*. Were those your posters?**

**TM:** They were part of a collection I had, and I'd bought them from the Great Southern Hotel Theater in Columbus, Ohio. It had shown all those movies before it finally closed down. They showed *Nightmare in Blood* and things like that all the time, and they kept the posters. The poster for *Alabama's Ghost*, which you can now find just about anywhere on the internet, is just astounding, such beautiful colors and it was printed on uncoated stock. I became kind of obsessed with the film just based on the poster. I think I did a few "in search of" type articles in *Fear of Darkness*. Then occasionally I would find a lobby card for the movie. Finally it came out on VHS, and I remember making a

RECORDED & INDEXED

special trip to a video store in St. Louis because I'd heard they had a copy of it. And it was kind of a letdown! I don't think anything could've matched my expectations!

**CP: I really enjoyed the George Kuchar interview in *Fear of Darkness* number 5.**

**TM:** Pat Hollis sent that to me. [The Kuchars] were not that well known outside New York City and maybe San Francisco. And they're still not that well known. The weird thing is, I think it's Mike Kuchar—the one with the moustache—who's still creating these little mini epics, but now he's doing them all on video. He's still going strong, making some of the most gosh-darned bizarre things you ever saw! More power to him!

**CP: How many regular contributors did you have?**

**TM:** I probably had five. I thought I could get a bunch of people to write for me. I thought, "Well, these guys are good writers. I'm sure they'll want to knock out something." Sometimes yes. I wrote things under pseudonyms. We all did that, to try and beef it up.

**CP: So you did the five issues and threw in the towel?**

**TM:** There was one more issue that never got published, number 6. Everything was all cut up and laid out on boards. It was all set up and ready to go to the printers, but I just had no money to get it printed. I sent it off to somebody who said they'd take it over, and they never did. They could never get it out. I've contacted him a few times over the years and he thinks he may have lost it. It's too bad. It would've been a nice issue. It had a whole history of Florida's independent horror movies, written by Fred Olen Ray.

**CP: Was he doing his own fanzine at that point?**

**TM:** No, but he had done one in the early seventies, I think. He'd gotten into TV broadcasting and had made a black and white movie called *The Brain Leeches*. Somebody had given him all this free film he could shoot on, and that was the genesis of it. I think he was able to put *The Alien Dead* together a little bit after that.

**CP: How did Fred become a contributor?**

**TM:** That was kind of funny. I got a real nasty letter from him after the first issue. He just tore the first issue to pieces. And then I found out he was a filmmaker. I thought, "Oh yeah, this is just too perfect." [laughs] So I called him up and did an interview. I did this whole preamble about "No, we don't get mad! We do the interview!"

**CP: Did you trade zines with other editors?**

**TM:** Oh yeah, everybody did that. I never really had enough subscribers to make much of a difference. That was always the goal, to get a big subscriber base. But it's kind of hard to get people to put money out for something they don't have, or they don't know if you're going to be around afterwards [laughs].

**CP: You told me once that you met up with Bill Landis during a trip**

**to New York.**

**TM:** Yeah, I had taken a job up there and thought I would try it for about a month. It was in north New Jersey. It didn't work out. Bit of a cultural shock. I'm an Ohio boy and getting dumped into north Jersey in the early eighties was just horrible. But it was nice because I could then go over and check out 42nd Street, and that was when 42nd Street was in its glory. I would call up Bill and we would get together and walk around. He was busy. He had quit his corporate job and was trying to make it, I don't know, doing various things wherever he could. But he was nice enough. He showed me around. I remember walking down 42nd Street with him. I was just amazed by it, and he said, "They've cleaned this up a lot" and I'm looking around, "Oh really?" "Oh yes, it used to be a lot worse than this." "No kidding?" [laughs]

**CP: How about the other New York editors?**

**TM:** I hung out with Rick Sullivan a few times. I met Michael Weldon, too. He was a really nice guy. I showed up on his doorstep one day. He was living in some efficiency apartment filled with catalogs and files of all kinds. He was a soft-spoken, quiet guy—just a really nice person.

**CP: Did you ever get out to San Francisco to meet Jim Morton?**

**TM:** No, but occasionally we would talk on the phone. Jim's a great guy. He writes extensively now on East German cinema. He's found a perfect niche!

**CP: One of the great things about *Fear of Darkness* is that it brought fanzine editors like Bill Landis, Rick Sullivan, Jim Morton, and Richard Green together under one roof. Otherwise, there was never a really strong sense of community among early eighties zine editors.**

**TM:** It's too bad. You'd think at some point somebody would've said "Let's all get together and try to work on common interests," but I think also it would've turned into some case of "Battle of the Egos." It takes a certain amount of ego to think you can actually crank something like this out.

**CP: In the case of Landis, Sullivan and Michael Weldon, I think they were too busy watching movies and banging out issues to have much time for correspondence. They were basically paving the way for the rest of us.**

**TM:** They were real close to where everything was going on, so I think that helped them a lot. When you're right next to the action, which is basically where they were in those days—until it just kind of diffused everywhere—you can get a ground view of what's really going on. If you were living out in the Midwest at that time, hopefully you had enough drive-ins open in the Summer that would show some interesting things. But you couldn't get to the drive-ins if you didn't have a car or you were under sixteen.

**CP: So that left late-night or Saturday afternoon TV.**

**TM:** Some places, like Dayton and Cincinnati—I'm from Dayton, Ohio—would actually have all-night movies on Friday night. Once the network

RECORDED & INDEXED

movies would go off they'd run three more movies until the farm report would come on. We didn't have videotape at the time, so you'd set your clock to 4:30 so you could get up and watch *The Vulture* or something like that. That's just what you had to do. I remember going to bed early one time and getting up at 3:00 because *Lake of Dracula* was on and I wanted to see it really bad. It made finding obscure things worthwhile. You really truly had to work at it.

**CP: When I interviewed Richard Blackburn a number of years ago, he told me that he had heard a story about a guy who drove 100 miles with a VCR and checked into a motel in order to record *Lemora* from a late-night TV broadcast.**

**TM:** I've heard that story. It's true, you had to travel. It wasn't unusual to drive a hundred miles to see a good movie back in those days. It wasn't so easy to get, so it created a more hardcore fan.

**CP: If only we had time machines...**

**TM:** I'm not going to say that I want to go back to that, for God's sake [laughs]! I like the fact that I can see all these obscure things with the click of a button.

**CP: Still, when you have to go through almost as much trouble finding a movie as the filmmakers did getting it finished you become more forgiving of even the most cheapjack homegrown efforts.**

**TM:** That's why I think I'm still primarily interested in obscure movies before 1980—because somebody really, really had to bust their ass to make that movie. Granted that sometimes, like *Manos, The Hand of Fate*, it just fell apart on them. But at the same time, somebody really had to make an effort! Even if it was with a wind-up 16mm camera!

**CP: When I put up the blog post about the Beatles Meet Star Trek on *Temple of Schlock*, you wrote a comment about seeing similar mashups at midnight movies.**

**TM:** That's the kind of stuff you would occasionally see back in the seventies and wonder, "What the hell?" There was a series of midnight movies that was playing around the country called Underground Cinema 12 that would play in small theaters, usually adult theaters. It was very hip to go to movies at midnight back then and watch all the cool short films. There was a place in Columbus, Ohio that used to do it. It might be a John Waters movie one night, a series of educational films another night—you never knew what was going to be there. You would see things like "Tonight! The Rolling Stones Meet Punk Rock!" and they'd have a short of the Rolling Stones matched up with one of Devo. I thought: "Who comes up with these things?!" But it was kind of fun to see that stuff, even if half the time I could never make it out there.

**CP: A lot of the single screen and independent theaters that ran midnight movies began to disappear in the 1980s, along with the XXX houses that didn't convert to video.**

VOL 1 ISSUE 1
FEB MAR APR [illegible]

$1.50

# Fear of Darkness

BIZARRE AND UNUSUAL CINEMA TODAY

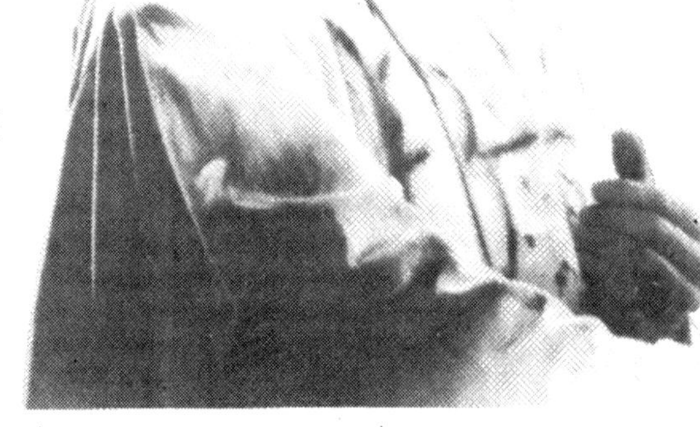

JOHN WATERS

GODZILLA

EDGAR ALLEN POE

## Fear of Darkness

RECORDED & INDEXED

**TM:** Jack Stevenson, who had a zine about that time [*Pandemonium*], he wrote a book called *Land of a Thousand Balconies* (Headpress, 2003), about film collecting. He writes a lot for *Bright Lights Film Journal*. He did a series of articles about the decline of the adult theaters, how these things were falling into ruin. Basically the owners had squeezed every last dime out of them they could possibly get. It reminded me a lot of the city theaters that you could visit at the time. Just looking at the places, you knew they weren't going to be around for very long.

**CP: What fanzines, if any, did you read once you stopped publishing *Fear of Darkness*?**

**TM:** *Scareaphanalia* was a great little zine I used to get. A guy out of Illinois, Jeff Smith, used to send me *Wet Paint.* There was a guy in St. Louis who did *Vidiot*, or something like that. It was pretty funny. But I didn't follow a lot of the zines. I just didn't have the time. This goes back to the VHS explosion. I used to joke that in 1984 I bought a VCR and spent the entire year just watching all the stuff I had wanted to see [laughs]!

**CP: That was a great time, wasn't it? We suddenly had access to so many offbeat, unknown movies!**

**TM:** Because all the low budget stuff was coming out and there were mom and pop video stores that had to have stuff to put on their shelves. Many times it would be a drive-in movie that you'd vaguely heard about that somebody had popped into a clamshell. "Oh my God, there it is! I can't believe I'm seeing this!" There were some funny stories about that.

**CP: I had memberships to half a dozen different video stores and I knew what rare titles were stocked in all of the other rental places around town.**

**TM:** I used to be really good friends with a Filipino family that owned a video store near where I lived in St. Louis. They were always good at getting the really obscure stuff. I don't know if they just wanted to fill up the shelves or what, but you could find some of the most obscure titles in their store. They had every single kung fu movie known to humanity. Anyway, there's a movie called *I Dismember Mama* with Zooey Hall, but the same company also put out *Mantis in Lace*, which I had always wanted to see. I grabbed *Mantis in Lace* because they had it on the shelf, I took it home, I popped it in, and lo and behold they'd spliced off the credits and it's *I Dismember Mama*, which they also had in the store, but under that name. So I took it back, I showed [the storeowner] the two movies and I said, "You've got the same movie under two different titles." She popped both of them in, saw that they are indeed the same movie, and she turned to me and said, "No one ever complained before!" [laughs]

**CP: I would get a lot of movies through tape trades. Did you get into that at all? With some traders it would be a tape-for-tape trade, but other folks preferred to get two blank tapes for every title you wanted from their list.**

**TM:** When I moved to Wichita in the late eighties, somebody said that you get all these obscure Distribpix films on a video trade. I said, "You've gotta be kidding me! That stuff's been lost to history!" "No, no, somebody's got 'em!" So I wrote off to this guy, and you'd send him two blank videocassettes and he'd send you one back with whatever movie you wanted. I remember going over that list and it was almost like the Holy Grail! I thought: "I don't believe what this guy's got! Oh my God, he's got stuff from the Ormond family! I can't believe this!" Somebody at some point had gotten access to a film vault and just started making copies of them.

**CP: I think it's great that, twenty-five years later, there are still so many rare films being found and released.**

**TM:** Look at *Nightbirds*, that Andy Milligan movie that was considered lost. Now it's out on DVD. That just blows my mind. I thought nobody was ever going to see that again.

**CP: A few years ago you brought back *Fear of Darkness* as a blog.**

**TM:** I tried, but I didn't have anything left to say. I was finding out there were all kinds of things you could download and look at that were cool. But once you've seen *The Stone Tape* and *Terror in the Jungle* in one week, what else is left to watch?! I mean, I'm not that interested in anything after 1980.

**CP: You also have a book blog called *Z7's Headquarters*.**

**TM:** Yeah, but that's just basically whatever I read. That started out when I thought: "Wouldn't it be kind of fun if you could blog about all those *Operator 5* books and do commentaries?" Well, that lasted for about two books. But then I found a list of essential books that Karl Edward Wagner, the horror writer—he passed away in the nineties—published in the old *Twilight Zone* magazine. At the time you couldn't find them. People were scouring book stores and libraries trying to find these things, but Karl had a very refined taste. Some of that stuff was just impossible to find. The R.R. Ryan stuff is still very collectible. But again, now stuff's been coming out. Now it's coming out under print on demand, so it's a lot easier. So at one time I was just trying to review all of the books on that list. I've even got a little shelf here in my library just dedicated to Karl Edward Wagner's list. I ran out of things that are kind of easy to get. The stuff remaining on the list may eventually come out, maybe not. Every now and then when I get around to it, I'll review a book and throw it up there [on the blog].

**CP: There's always interlibrary loan.**

**TM:** Yep. You've gotta go to a little bit of an effort to do that. As a matter of fact, I've gotten copies of stuff that was on Karl's list from somebody who went through interlibrary loan. I got *The Fire-Spirits* by Paul Busson, the German writer, which was actually translated into English in the 1920s in, as far as I know, one edition only. A guy found it in a library, got

RECORDED & INDEXED

it through interlibrary loan and was able to get me a copy.

**CP: I've gotten a few very hard-to-find books through interlibrary loan, including one or two that should never have left a rare book room.**

**TM:** I remember in college I got to see an original Edgar Allan Poe edition in a rare book library at Ohio State. I asked for it, and the librarian basically positioned himself between me and the door of the library until I finished looking at it!

**CP: Are there any other lesser known science fiction authors you can recommend?**

**TM:** I was very interested in the science fiction and fantasy writer Margaret St. Clair. I was able to get her books in used copies through Amazon. All knowledge of her seems to have gone, yet she was probably one of the major writers of short story fiction in the fifties and sixties. A lot of her stories are still considered classic, but she was a very private person and just didn't do the convention circuit. She passed away in the early nineties and her writings just don't seem to get reprinted anymore.

**CP: There are still plenty of really interesting books and films waiting to be discovered or rediscovered.**

**TM:** It's amazing how many people knocked things out and they never went anywhere. Just last Summer I found out about a movie shot in Philadelphia in 1975 called *2076 Olympiad*. The guy who directed it has a copy of it, and apparently that's the only copy. It's like one of the other shot in Philadelphia movies, *Malatesta's Carnival of Blood*. I first heard about that in the early eighties. John Donaldson put out a zine called *Crudezine*, which was just full of movies like that. He basically slapped together *Variety* reviews of movies that had vanished. The only reason *Malatesta* ever came out on DVD is because the guy who shot the movie found a copy of it.

**CP: Did you go to conventions when you were publishing *Fear of Darkness*?**

**TM:** The only one I used to go to was a local film buff convention in Columbus. I knew a guy who owned a theater and he had a lot of memorabilia to sell. But they were all 16mm collectors back then, so that was a whole different breed [laughs]. These were guys who lived in houses that were sealed up, like in the book *Land of a Thousand Balconies*. Jack Stevenson talks a lot about these people. Basically they lived in houses that were sealed; they had a projector, a home theater and their circle of friends. Most of the time they were divorced or never married because their collection was their wife. Those were the type of people who went to that convention. They'd sit there and trade-off copies of 16mm prints. They had little rooms set up where they had a projector and they could look at the films. I actually got a copy of David Durston's *Stigma* that way. That's an excellent movie. But when I explained to them what I was trying to do, they treated me like I was somebody's

idiot kid brother. They couldn't believe somebody was actually interested in these films.

Now we've got things like Monster Mania down in Cherry Hill, and Chiller Theatre, which is humongous. I went there a few years ago and had to wait on a line for an hour, and I wasn't even going into the celebrity area! It kind of astounds me that these things have grown so big. I couldn't get enough people to pay for a 16mm film rental or sell 'em a copy of my magazine, but they'll pull these huge numbers for these events. So I do some conventions occasionally if I've got nothing better to do. I got to meet 42nd Street Pete. This was when *Grindhouse* had just come out. We were joking about all the twenty-something guys who are now grindhouse experts [laughs].

**CP: Meanwhile, we lost the ultimate grindhouse expert, Bill Landis, in December of 2008.**

**TM:** Bill had a lot of personal issues, but he was such a good writer. He was the first. He was the guy who got out there and told everybody, "Look, all these little drive-ins and theaters, what's playing there is just as good as what's at your big screen art theater." He was the first, and I'm really sad that he's gone.

**CP: Do you have any closing thoughts on doing a fanzine?**

**TM:** It was fun at the time. There's nothing quite equal to the thrill of getting that first copy in your hands and thinking, "Wow, I've done it! I actually produced this thing!" It's kind of exciting. That's probably why most of us did it. We wanted to feel like we were adding something, helping preserve culture, thought we had something to say... Some of the same mentality you see in the late seventies punk zines kind of carried over. "Just get out and do it! Do it however you can." Towards the end I was doing it on a mimeograph machine that I had found somewhere—anything to keep the project going. I don't think anybody in the long run really felt they were going to make a lot of money. Most people hoped they could quit their day job, but in most cases that never happened. I think we just did it mostly for the love of doing it.

Due to the abnormal
subject matter of this motion picture,
absolutely no children will be allowed
with or without their parents.....special
uniformed police will supervise admissions
M.A. Ripps
PRODUCER "POOR WHITE TRASH"


## Chapter Ten

# Richard Green

## Confessions of a Trash Fiend

By Chris Poggiali

In October of 1980, a second one-page, bi-weekly review guide to the 42nd Street movie scene appeared in the New York/New Jersey area, barely four months after the debut of Bill Landis' trailblazing *Sleazoid Express*. This second serving of sleaze was named the *Gore Gazette*, and it was created out of editor Rick Sullivan's frustration with Landis' heady film reviews, which he felt "were becoming increasingly critical and unfairly analytical of a genre of films that just don't hold up to that style of criticism and were never made to." The final straw was *Mother's Day*, which Landis had supposedly "trashed" in the previous issue of *Sleazoid* but Sullivan referred to as "probably the best gore flick and comedy of 1980." Not only was Landis' review fair and balanced ("Still, there are some good, jarring, gruesome scenes, and the film is relatively well shot and edited"), it wasn't even all that negative in its summation ("I wouldn't say that I liked *Mother's Day*, but I will say it isn't boring"). As far as being the catalyst for a meat-and-potatoes rebellion and a symbol of his zine's raison d'être Sullivan's example of anti-intellectual genre cinema is a curious one; *Mother's Day*—love it or hate it—is exactly the type of genre film that invites critical analysis.

"Now," to quote Bill Cosby from one of his classic Fat Albert routines, "I told you that story to tell you this one."

A few nights ago, I scanned the "Best and Worst Trash of 1983" lists from *Confessions of a Trash Fiend* and posted them on the official Facebook page of the book you're now holding in your hands, just to see what the reaction would be. For the uninitiated: *Confessions of a Trash Fiend* (1982–1984) was the second review sheet to emerge from the New York metro area in the wake of *Sleazoid Express*. Like Sullivan, *Trash Fiend* editor Richard Green was based in New Jersey and covered many of the same horror and exploitation flicks released to theatres at the time, but the similarities between the two publications end there. Green was a devoted follower of Landis' writing and shared a similar critical viewpoint, and as a result, his reviews both in *Trash Fiend* and his later zine, *Grind* (1988–1990), were sometimes dismissed as the opinions of a contrarian. That was pretty much the consensus on Facebook the other night when beloved fan favorites like *The Evil Dead*, *Xtro*, *The Last American Virgin* and *Basket Case* suddenly appeared on a "Worst" list, while the obscure mid-seventies Troma acquisition *Feelin' Up* topped the "Best" list, supported by such equally offbeat choices as *Christmas Evil*, *Midnight*, *Pink Motel*, *Powerforce*, *Just Before Dawn* and *Teen Lust*. None of the expected fallout seemed to bother Richard at all. "Seventeen responses in less than twenty-four hours," he wrote in an email to me the next morning. "That's more people than saw those lists originally!"

Notice how he's more concerned with the circulation numbers than he is with the half dozen incensed readers waving their fists at his lists? That's because he still thinks like a fanzine editor. It's something you never

forget—like riding a bike. Say what you want about Rick Sullivan and his taste in movies, but when Richard disagreed with the critical direction *Sleazoid Express* was taking, he started his own damn zine and stuck with it for 106 issues and fourteen years. No one ever started a horror movie zine just so they could push a purposely unpopular agenda; it's way too much trouble to go through for no reward whatsoever. The zine editors I knew did it because they loved movies and felt a need to express their opinions, no matter how unpopular they were. It took a lot more time, money, thought and effort for Richard Green to get that "worst of '83" list out into the world than it did for anyone online to respond they way they did.

It is fitting, then, that the one person who came to Richard's defense on Facebook was Ant Timpson, a former zine editor (*Violent Leisure, Filmhead*) turned film producer (*The ABCs of Death*), who wrote the following: "RESPECT! Richard Green never towed the line. He was the Pauline Kael of xerox. BOW to his exquisite taste. He was a pioneer in trash commentary." I smiled when I noticed that Richard had clicked "Like" under Ant's comment, so I clicked it as well—our way of bumping fists. There was no way Ant could've known that Richard described Bill Landis as "the Pauline Kael of zine writers" in the interview you're about to read.

Respect indeed.

The following interview was conducted via telephone on July 22, 2012.

---

**CHRIS POGGIALI: You were one of the few genre reviewers in 1983 who gave *The Evil Dead* a really negative review.**

**RICHARD GREEN:** Oh, I thought it was obnoxious! Everybody was talking like it was the greatest thing in the world! OK, the second one had a lot of energy, there's no way around it, and the third one was just goofy and a throwaway and edited to pieces, who cares. But no, I didn't like it at all. I think by then emphasis was changing and it was becoming gore for gore's sake. Another movie I despise is *Cabin Fever*. That, I think, is one of the worst films I've seen in my life, and I haven't seen another of Eli Roth's movies to this day. To me, that was like *The Evil Dead*. The same mindset that made *The Evil Dead* made *Cabin Fever*. It's gore for gore's sake. I don't get it.

**CP: That was not popular opinion in 1983.**

**RG:** Look, by the time *The Evil Dead* came out, everything had changed. It was all over with. I guess you can make the analogy to punk rock: as soon as it became popular, it was over. When *Halloween* hit it big, they started to drag out a lot of junk. The old stuff they were reissuing was interesting, but the new stuff coming out that was copying *Halloween* had a fanboy mentality that was not. "Isn't this shocking? Isn't this outrageous?" No, it's not.

**CP: This year marks the thirtieth anniversary of your fanzine debut.**

Richard Green's

# CONFESSIONS OF A TRASH FIEND

Vol.2 No.6

Or: I COVER THE DRIVE-INS. Published twice a month, mailed out on Fridays. Subscriptions: $7.00 per year (24 issues) to help cover postage and printing expenses only. Correspondence and subscriptions should be addressed to: Richard Green, P.O. Box 32, Old Bridge, N.J. 08857. Back issues 50¢ each. This issue is dedicated to Bob Walker.

## The Stupid Dead

No other film has spawned as much reader response as New Line Cinema's latest release, The Evil Dead, probably for the following reasons: 1) It was given way too much coverage in way too expensive horror-oriented magazines. 2) Advance company hype labeled it as the sickest, bloodiest film ever made. 3) New Line chose to release it unrated with all the blood and guts intact (further hyping #2.) 4) It opened in Trash Fiend's back yard first, so everyone wanted to know if it was as good/gross as they had been told. Well: 1) It is as bloody as you've heard, 2) there's been no blood cut - it is unrated (though I've heard rumors it will be cut to a safer R rating for wide release) and 3) that's it. There's nothing else to The Evil Dead, it's just blood, and it's silly looking blood at that. Filmed under a very low budget and in 16 mm, it's the first effort by Sam Raimi, a young filmmaker from Michigan. It's obvious that he was probably influenced by those awful Hammer films rather than say, a George Romero, and that's no compliment. I've said it once and I'll say it again: gore with nothing behind it equals nothing. It's sad to think that the independent horror/blood and guts genre has become the place for young idiot directors to get their start. I mean let them go to Hollywood, Hollywood deserves them. Anyway forget about the gore, The Evil Dead has a boring airhead story behind it: Young idiot couples go to a deserted cabin in the woods (Lord, not again) and unwittingly unleash a whole bunch of pissed-off demons by fooling around with a silly plot device they find in the cellar. Also in the cellar is a ripped up one sheet for The Hills Have Eyes. Do you think Raimi is trying to show us his love for the genre? Ha Ha Ha Ha Ha. He's probably just trying to earn the respect of naive "horror" fans. Wonderful. Oh well, one by one demons possess the idiot characters and the only way the one survivor can kill them (wanna bet?) is via total dismemberment. That's right, arms, legs, heads, ears, everything has to come off. I mean, they had to get tons of gore in some way. How else could Raimi make a name and lots of money for himself? He may not be in Hollywood, but he's been trained there. There is a certain percent of carnage that is laughable, but after one gross-out (and if there's one, there's hundreds) it's just dead meat. What is hilarious are Raimi's over-obvious attempts at serious filmmaking/art: Scenes that

Wishful thinking

RECORDED & INDEXED

# RICHARD GREEN

## CONFESSIONS OF A TRASH FIEND

DRAFT

WILD PARTIES, HOT MUSIC, SEXY GIRLS.
THESE KIDS WERE NEVER LATE FOR SCHOOL!

LADIES

LET'S CHECK OUT THE MEN'S ROOM NEXT!

MY TWO TIGHT ENDS!

R

YOUNG GANGS FROM WILDWOOD HIGH

DOCTORED ADS IN *TRASH FIEND*.

**RG:** When you first wrote to me, I was thinking about how different I am now than I was back then. I was so obsessed. I would go to see four movies a day. Now, if I get something from Netflix and watch it within a week it's a miracle, for God's sake [laughs]!

**CP: Did you spend a lot of time in New York movie theaters as a kid?**

**RG:** I was a suburban kid. If I did go to New York, I would go to the art houses because I was very much into foreign films. I had gone to a progressive high school and they had a film class, and we were only allowed to take the film class once, but they allowed me to take it for all four years. We watched *Jules and Jim* and other classics. The teacher was a big influence on me. So I started going to New York to see foreign films when I was a teenager.

**CP: When did you become interested in offbeat horror and exploitation films?**

**RG:** I was always interested in films that were lost and obscure. When I was a teenager, there was a series on PBS from the Museum of Modern Art—I think it was called *Lost Films*—where they would find old movies, silent movies, and broadcast them on PBS. They would talk about how they found each one. They had to go to a lab, go through a storage bin, and that fascinated me. I wrote to the woman who was the curator at the Museum of Modern Art, which was pretty nervy, and I said "Oh my God, this is wonderful! This is what I want to do! How do I do it?" She was a very nice lady. She wrote back, "Graduate from high school, go to college, and then think about it." [laughs] And then, with all of the horror and exploitation films that were being dragged out that nobody had heard of at the time, I think that kind of fueled the interest.

**CP: Who gets the lion's share of the blame for turning you into a trash fiend?**

**RG:** I think what inspired me most was Michael Weldon's *Psychotronic*, which I read about in the *Village Voice*. There was a little blurb about this guy who was doing a weekly guide to movies on TV in New York. I was in my mid- to late teens, and I started to get *Psychotronic* immediately

because of one little line in the *Village Voice*. This was when the local channels were playing movies from the early seventies that were starting to show up in TV packages. You would see *Children Shouldn't Play with Dead Things*, *The Crazies*, and *Deep Red* show up on Channel 9—all cut to ribbons, of course. So once I got into Michael Weldon I started to watch everything that was on Channel 9, and those movies just blew my mind. *Horror Express* with Telly Savalas, remember that? They used to show that a lot. And then Michael Weldon led me to Bill Landis.

**CP: What attracted you to Landis' writing?**

**RG:** In *Sleazoid Express*, you weren't just reading about films, you were reading about him, and that's what I thought was interesting. After a while, with *Gore Gazette* and zines like that, it was all about, "Look at the gore, look at the girls, look at this, look at that"—it wasn't interesting. Landis was writing about his life, about himself, about his reactions. He was so brilliant. My God, he could encapsulate so many ideas into one sentence. His writing was very dense. I'm hoping there will be some kind of anthology. I know he did the book, but I mean a collection of his newsletters. If you read them, one thing builds on top of another. He'll reference different things from earlier issues.

**CP: How did *Sleazoid Express* affect you?**

**RG:** I wanted to see the things that Landis was writing about, so I made my first trip to 42nd Street, this little suburban teenager, scared out of my mind, to go to big bad 42nd Street. Well, it turned out I was right to be scared out of my mind! Back then, it was really rough! So I started going to 42nd Street to see movies, and I would plan it out. I would get the show times from the *New York Post* and get the bus, go right to 42nd Street, see three or four movies a day, get the bus and go the hell home [laughs]. It was a great education. Seeing something like the mondo

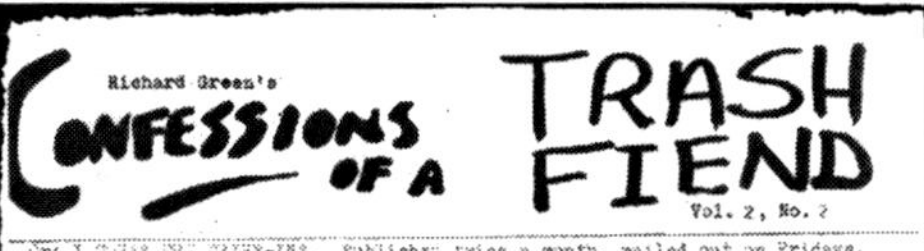

Richard Green's

CONFESSIONS OF A TRASH FIEND

Vol. 2, No. 2

Or: I [illegible] DRIVE-INS. Published twice a month, mailed out on Fridays. Subscriptions: $7.00 per year (24 issues) to help cover postage and printing expenses only. Correspondence and Subscriptions should be addressed to: Richard Green, P.O. Box 32, Old Bridge, N.J. 08857. Back issues 50¢ each.

Soft

Greydon Clark, the notable exploitation director who's given us items such as Black Shampoo, Without Warning, and Satan's Cheerleaders makes his welcome return with Joy Sticks, a teen sex comedy set in a video arcade. It's no surprise that someone would (eventually) attempt to capitalize on the videogame craze (especially Clark,) but it seems like this one's about 6-8 months too late. Commercially, it's not a bad idea to combine the successful elements taken from the successful king-of-the-teen sex-comedies (Porky's) with a craze (like the just-released Valley Girl (coming soon).) but no matter how fond you are of Clark, you must admit that Joy Sticks just doesn't cut it. (To those who have seen it: I know I'm being way too kind, but after the glorious Without Warning, can you blame me?) The most interest is sparked not by the horny teenage cast, but by the several neat exploitation scenes that Clark manages to unobtrusively sneak in. They're the only things that bring any life to Joy Sticks and Clark should be thanked for at least this much. There's bondage, fantasy, lots of T and A - you get the picture. The plot? Forget it - it's right out of countless other movies - instead of, say, "We've got to save the camp!" (from Summer Camp (Vol.1, No.1),) it's now "We've got to save the arcade." The worst element present is Joe Don Baker (of Walking Tall fame,) who's turned into a true horror - fat, old and bloated. Let's face it, most people will hate Joy Sticks, and looking at it on the surface it should be condemned to play in only Southern California Drive-ins. (There's even a Valley girl thrown in and her dialog is completely unintelligible.) But if you look a little more closely you'll find one or more Trash elements to keep you occupied. Maybe. Whatever the case it's nice to see that Clark still has something left in him. It's just too bad that this is so damn rotten and boring. Maybe next time he'll have more luck.

From Outer Space

Time Walker, yet another release from New World Pictures manages what I thought would be the impossible - taking a very intriguing story line and turning it into a crashing bore. New World? No surprise. Time Walker nobly tries to resurrect the old mummy bit which, with the exceptions of The Awakening and the largely unseen Dawn of the Mummy hasn't been tried in years. Hopes were high, but were crushed by Corman (please, no more letters.) Set in current times, a mummy is unearthed only to have it rise and terrorize various university types. Aha! This isn't really a mummy but an alien that was trapped in King Tut's tomb. When a student steals some power crystals from the sarcophagous, the alien gets up and searches for them - you see, they're part of

documentaries with a full audience on 42nd Street was just amazing. The rest of the time I was watching this stuff in New Jersey, at multiplexes.

**CP: Do you have any 42nd Street stories you'd like to share?**

**RG:** I'll tell you one. I was crazy over Ulli Lommel, and he had a movie out called *Warbirds*, which was a *Top Gun* rip-off. The second feature was *The Accused*, with Jodie Foster. I swear to you it was sold out, and it was a 99 per cent male, 99 per cent black audience. When the rape scene came on in *The Accused*, everyone in the theater started cheering and screaming the most horrible things! "Rape that whore!" Things like that. It was mind-blowing. But wait, it gets better! The movie goes on, and at the end when the rapists are convicted? The whole audience cheered [laughs]! They were doing the exact same thing! They were encouraging the rapists, and then at the end they cheered when they were convicted! You can't make that up!

Richard Green's

CONFESSIONS OF A TRASH FIEND

FREE

Meatball Surgery

First we had The Fan and The Seduction which both dealt with famous people being stalked by admirers-turned-madmen and now along comes Visiting Hours a Canadian production with basically the same thing on its mind. A TV newscaster (Lee Grant,) known for her outspokenness arrives home to find her maid brutally slain and the killer waiting for her in the hall closet. Grant survives and the balance of the film takes place in a hospital where she's recovering. The killer starts (easily) knocking off everyone on the same floor, while all Grant can do is scream about the lack of security around her. While the film (thankfully) wastes no time getting started, it can't raise itself above the simplistic and slasher mentality that has ruined many a film before it, despite some surprisingly intelligent direction by Jean-Claude Lord. Michael Ironside, so good in Scanners plays the killer to the hilt and overshadows everything and everyone involved, which is not necessarily good. Ironside is so intensely compelling and fascinating to watch he eclipses the male tedious plot and you actually start wanting him to come back on screen. The rationale for his stalking Lee Grant is right out of Don't Go In The House and just like that film, when you finally realize what his problem is, all you can do is yawn. His strange habit of photographing his victims before killing them and what he does with those photos isn't explained or brought out enough. It's as if they just wanted to make him seem sicker. Another big problem is that Grant is all too colorless, whiny, serious and just plain boring in her role to elicit any kind of necessary sympathy. It's as if we're supposed to feel for her simply because she's a hard-nosed reporter who stands up for what she believes. Compared with Ironside's dynamic, intense performance, the film seems to be over one off. If they were trying for some kind of symbolic contrast, they missed. You really have to reach to think of something good to say about Visiting Hours, but it did have a few clever, if unbelievable plot twists during the last half hour. There are even several surprises to make you jump, although about five seconds after each one you'll be planning on what to have for dinner, as it fails to sustain any tension. Also starring Linda Purl as a sympathetic nurse and William Shatner as Grant's boss/love interest (he must have had a free lunch hour, he's only on screen for about ten minutes.)

The Snag Always Rings Twice

What promised to be the movie of the year (after the late Great White) finally landed in town and we should all give it the heave-ho and throw it back. Isle of the Fish Men starring Barbara Bach, Joseph Cotten and Richard Jordan was a very mild science-fiction (if you could call it that) film from 1978 along the lines of The Island of Dr. Moreau. That is, until trash master Roger Corman (I, unlike many others, have no respect for this grub.) got hold of it and added a super-gory prologue with Cameron Mitchell and Mel Ferrer to qualify it for the horror market and a sure R-rating. He retitled it Something Waits In The Dark and it did quite badly. Mr. "Never-say-die" retitled it again under the new moniker Screamers and gave it a new ad campaign featuring the now famous line "Be warned: You will actually see a man turned inside out!" Of course we never really see someone turned inside

**CP: How did you come up with the name *Confessions of a Trash Fiend*?**

**RG:** When I started college I was in charge of the film committee. I was always trying to show edgy, interesting things like John Waters' films. I almost got fired from the committee because I tried to show *Female Trouble* and *Pink Flamingos*. Because they knew they were rated X, they had to have a screening for the board before they allowed them to be shown. And they wouldn't let them be shown. I was trying to show edgy, interesting things and some exploitation, and one of the other people on the committee said, "You really are a trash fiend! Did you know that?" So that's how I got the name *Trash Fiend* [laughs]. Because this guy wanted to show Hollywood musicals!

**CP: I consider *Trash Fiend* to be the suburban "bridge and tunnel" cousin of *Sleazoid Express* and *Gore Gazette*.**

**RG:** It was more New Jersey because the stuff was in my backyard. I lived at the time, and still do, in this multiplex area—what they call "Whitelandia"—[laughs] I forgot who called it that, but it's true. Big giant multiplexes and drive-ins. There were a lot of drive-ins in the area that would show this stuff. I started going to drive-ins as a teenager. I remember they showed *Dracula and Son*, a French movie, and I ran to see

See? See? I'm not kidding!

that when it came out. *When Women Had Tails*—remember that? That showed up as the co-feature to the Bo Derek *Tarzan* movie, of all things.

**CP: *When Women Had Tails* was reviewed in the first issue of *Trash Fiend*.**

**RG:** It was [laughs]?!

**CP: At the Route 35 Drive-In.**

**RG:** Long gone! It's a Costco and a multiplex now.

**CP: You called *When Women Had Tails* "the find of 1981."**

**RG:** [laughs] Well, we were kids, we were at the drive-in just out of our minds with this ridiculous movie that had no business being shown in 1981, for goodness sake, because it was older than dirt!

**CP: Around that time there were a lot of older horror and exploitation movies being released for the first time in the New York area, or re-released under different titles by local sub-distributors.**

**RG:** Again, this is post-*Halloween*. After *Halloween* became a big hit, every distributor in the world was looking for old, junky horror movies that they could throw out onto fifty or sixty screens, make some money and then disappear. So in the suburbs you'd have eight–, nine–, ten-screen theaters—back then ten was a lot—and there would be great big Hollywood movies on nine screens and on the tenth one, because they needed to put something in there, they'd play a *Porky's* rip-off or a *Halloween* rip-off from Italy or *Night of the Bloody Apes* [laughs]! How that thing ever got released, I don't know! But I saw it on a giant suburban multiplex screen!

**CP: Multiplexes would also run double features, another thing that's unimaginable today.**

**RG:** I remember seeing *Invasion of the Blood Farmers* with *The Coed Murders* in a theater that must've had 1,000 seats. They had it in the big theater, and it was packed because everyone thought "Oh, it's a new scary movie! Let's go!" On a Saturday night there were 1,000 people watching *Invasion of the Blood Farmers* from 1970-whatever, this old crappy movie, and just howling at it! Well, I couldn't believe my eyes. I dragged my friends to it a few days later, and here were 1,000 seats that were completely empty [laughs]. A big cavernous theater and this totally weird movie, and absolutely nobody there. Very strange.

## Confessions of a Trash Fiend

**CP: *Teen Lust*, which was number seven on your "Best Trash of 1983" list, was also a few years old by the time it reached New York.**

**RG:** Yes! What about *Making Out*, do you remember that one? That opened in something like eighty theaters [in the New York area]! It was one of those movies that had no business playing at a suburban multiplex. I remember sitting there in the afternoon, and it was no one but me—I was a kid—and a sea of businessmen in business suits on their lunch hour thinking they were going to see some softcore porn thing. Who knew what the hell it was?

**CP: I found out later it was *Schoolgirl Report 13*.**

**RG:** But who knew at the time? The posters gave no clue.

**CP: That was released by SRC Films—their posters never gave a clue. The names were all bogus and the prints usually had a new title card and no other credits...**

**RG:** But that was the fun of it, not knowing what you were seeing! I vaguely remember it was European and there were little vignettes and lots of little sex things that went a little too far and then they stopped and went on to another vignette. The other one that blew my mind was when Troma released *Feelin' Up*, which was this little experimental film from the seventies and they dragged it out into the eighties. That just blew my mind when I saw that on the screen.

**CP: It was made in 1975 by the experimental film cooperative Total Impact, under the title *Getting Together*.**

**RG:** And then Troma had the nerve to release it like it was another *Porky's* [laughs]! We sat there in the multiplex with our mouths open because we couldn't believe this movie—we had no idea what it was—this movie with such a sixties mindset was showing in the eighties! And people were expecting a sex comedy with teenagers, and instead they got this radical experimental film commune project! Amazing. I still have a VHS of it because it's just so wonderful.

**CP: You were always pretty forgiving of Troma. You gave *Waitress!* a glowing review and wrote that it was funnier than *Airplane!***

**RG:** [laughs] The Comcast Network has some of the old Troma movies on demand this month. *Waitress!*, *Squeeze Play*, I can't remember the others. I sat here and watched *Squeeze Play* twice all the way through! Because it's free and it's on demand [laughs]! It's just amazing to go back to that period. I was trying to figure out the locations for *Squeeze Play*, where it was filmed, and I would've bet money it was in south Jersey. I was trying to identify the town. I had to look it up on the IMDb and no, it was way north Jersey, right across the river.

**CP: I have to thank you for introducing me to the wonders of *Powerforce*.**

**RG:** Oh, that thing! Yeah! That was another one that, again, showed in a big super multiplex because they needed filler. That's the only reason. It was mostly showing in the inner cities, like Jersey City and places like that.

Richard Green's

# CONFESSIONS OF A TRASH FIEND

#3 FREE

## Golden Gate

Beyond The Gate (originally released as Human Experiments) barely lasted a week at local theaters last January and that's a shame because Gate is one of the two or three best films I've seen all year. Although it's a women-behind-bars prison film, it's not quite along the same exploitative lines as Wanda, Wicked Warden or even the 3-D Prison Girls. While it does have flashes of the usual prison movie cliches (menacing guards, tough lesbians etc.) the film (surprisingly) doesn't dwell on these for very long and digs right in to the meat of its story. Linda Haynes plays a down-on-her-luck-out-on-her-own country and western singer who accidentally stumbles upon the scene of a mass murder, is accused and convicted of the slayings and sentenced to life in prison. Enter the prison's mad doctor (Geoffrey Lewis, veteran of all those God-awful Clint Eastwood movies) who besides performing his regular duties is also conducting a kind of mind control experiment on many of the lifers. Haynes quickly falls victim and for the rest of the movie we're left wondering if she'll be the one to escape. A wonderfully paranoid film, everyone except our heroine is totally corrupt, from the people on the outside who take advantage of her to the police and prison officials and even the prisoners themselves. What other choice do we have but to root for her? She's the only one left and more put upon than Yvette Mimieux in Jackson County Jail and more worthy of our hopes of escape than Indiana Jones. Many scenes will stay in your mind for months - the one where Haynes finds the victims she's later accused of killing is so creepy, it alone is worth the price of admission (I had nightmares over that one for weeks.) The many scenes of the brainwashing process she's put through are very disturbing but also fascinating, working on an emotional as well as a gut-wrenching level. All of this works beautifully thanks in part to a great cast - besides Haynes and Lewis there's also trash regulars Aldo Ray, Jackie Coogan and Ellen Travolta. This was the second time this masterpiece has been put up to bat. Let's not let it strike out a third time. If it ever returns, go see Beyond The Gate right away. Released by Essex Distributing whose main releases are hard-X.

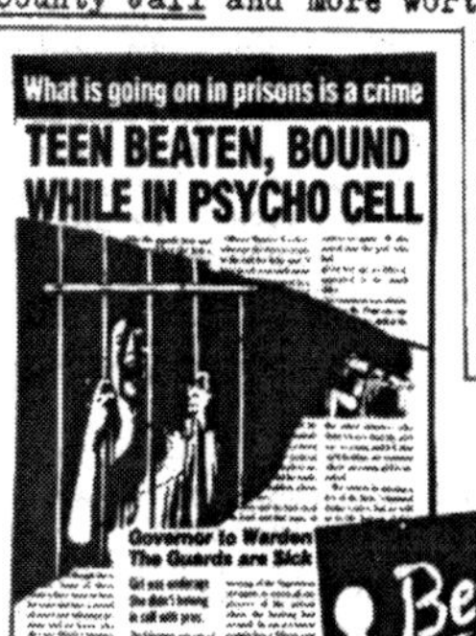

What is going on in prisons is a crime
TEEN BEATEN, BOUND WHILE IN PSYCHO CELL
Governor to Warden: The Guards are Sick
YOUR KEY TO SHOCKING BRUTALITY
Beyond THE GATE
LIFE! A WOMEN'S PRISON WITH NO ESCAPE
Starring ALDO RAY
LINDA HAYNES GEOFFREY LEWIS

# RICHARD GREEN

## CONFESSIONS OF A TRASH FIEND

Sometimes they'd skirt the suburbs and that's when I'd see the kung fu stuff.

**CP: There were a couple of issues of *Trash Fiend* that were written entirely by Tim Ferrante and Craig Ledbetter.**

**RG:** [laughs] Yes, those issues were gifts!

**CP: Tim didn't think that he had ever met you, even though he wrote for *Trash Fiend* and you guys only lived about seven miles from each other.**

**RG:** I did meet him at a convention in New York. I don't remember where or when, but I did meet him. He was very nice. He offered to continue *Trash Fiend* for me, and I was horrified because I had so few subscribers back then, they were all comps, and I didn't want him to know!

Richard Green's CONFESSIONS OF A TRASH FIEND Vol. 1, No. 22

Or: I NEVER MET DRIVE-INS. Published twice a month, mailed out on Fridays. Subscriptions: $7.00 per year (24 issues) to help cover postage and printing. Correspondence and Subscriptions should be addressed to: Richard Green, P.O. Box 32, Old Bridge, N.J. 08857.

Flyzirl Returns

Madman finally made it to the NY/NJ metro area after playing all over the place for nearly a year. This release had garnered largely mediocre to poor reviews and the prospects of yet another rotten "mad slasher" movie were not exactly uplifting. Hell, the thought alone of another one of these was more horrifying than anything any producer, director or writer could dream up. Surprisingly, Madman turned out to be O.K. The biggest plus is the surprise presence of Gaylen Ross ("Francine" from George A. Romero's classic Dawn of the Dead,) she's hiding under the new name of Alexis Dubin. What happened? Was she embarrassed to be in this? Is that why she had it changed? She was plain old Gaylen Ross in Creepshow. It makes no sense. Madman's not that bad. Whatever the case, Madman is another counselors and kids at camp being terrorized by an unknown killer movie. Can you name all the other recent films that have utilized that same plot line? Let's see - there's Friday the 13th Parts 1, 2 and 3, The Burning - need I go on? Madman opens up quickly and startlingly with the group sitting around the campfire while a counselor sings an old traditional campfire song about the legend of one Madman Marz, a local cutent/mass murderer. The catch is never to say his name above a whisper or he'll come and kill you. That's the twist in Madman - it's no legend. Really. It's actually an ancient monster. It's neat because you're kept wondering if the killer is one of the group, or if they really had the guts to do something like that. Granted, Madman has more than its share of rotten genre cliches and a weak and unbelievable final quarter, but there are several interesting aspects that make it worthwhile and watchable. Included are a neat chase scene where a girl hides in a refrigerator (I haven't seen that done before) and there's lots of creepy nighttime atmosphere present. It's imaginatively filmed and Gaylen Ross (or whoever) is great. Add these few things to the bad parts and you get a mixed bag indeed, but overall, it's a cut above the average. Released by Jensen Farley Pictures. Written and directed by Joe Giannone.

They thought they were alone. MADMAN

Dust, Dusher, Dustbust

The new 3D film Treasure of the Four Crowns is 1) a terrible rip-off of Raiders of the Lost Ark and 2) the most incredibly boring film I've seen in

**CP: I think he did take over *Hi-Tech Terror* for Craig temporarily…**

**RG:** No, he wanted to buy my newsletter. I think he wanted to give me $100 for the title and the rights to it—not that there were any rights to transfer, I was a kid, for God's sake, doing it out of my basement!—but for $100 he wanted the title, the rights, and my subscription list and he would take it over. And I was like… "Why?" [laughs] I had no subscribers! Everything was free, pretty much! I was scraping money together to put the thing out every month.

**CP: Craig was very supportive of *Temple of Schlock* from the start. I think he's the only editor who saw the first issue.**

**RG:** Whatever happened to him? He was a good friend of mine for a little bit, and then, I don't know… Is he still *alive* [laughs]? We used to write long letters to each other back and forth about things we were doing and we were really good friends and then we just lost contact. I'll have to look him up.

**CP: He still runs *European Trash Cinema* as an online business.**

**RG:** He became obsessed with finding everything he could possibly find from every European director. That was his thing. And he was cataloging everything he could find.

**CP: After two years and almost fifty issues, *Confessions of a Trash Fiend* ended its run.**

**RG:** I had to stop because I was going to school and I had a lot of

problems going on in my family. It was just too taxing to do it. I had a really crazy screwy family relationship, and it was just too much to handle at the time. I wanted to keep going, but I just couldn't, and I had no confidence in what I was doing. I didn't think it was any good. I would write this stuff and think, "God, this is terrible!" [laughs] Because then I would read Landis and he'd be so brilliant, and I'd think, "I have no business doing this, I'm a kid from New Jersey, if Landis is living the life what have I got to say?" I had a lot of insecurities about it. I was a kid, I was screwed up.

NOTHING CAN PREPARE YOU FOR WHAT HAPPENS WHEN SHE FIGHTS BACK.
THE HOUSE ON SORORITY ROW
WHERE NOTHING IS OFF LIMITS
R

**CP: Michael Gingold always says that it was *Trash Fiend* that inspired him to start *Scareaphanalia*.**

**RG:** When anybody even remembers or writes about *Trash Fiend*, I'm just shocked, because to me it was junk. I absolutely hated it. I look back on it to this day, and if I re-read some of it—which I haven't in a long time—I actually cringe and think, "God, how could I have written that and not edited a little or something?" But that's just me.

**CP: That one little mention in *Film Comment* has guaranteed you a spot in fanzine history.**

**RG:** That blew my mind! *Film Comment* was like my Bible when I was in high school, because I was a foreign film person, so to actually get a little blurb in *Film Comment* blew my mind. It also made me very insecure, like "Oh my God, I don't deserve this because it's so *bad*!" And then there was *Rolling Stone*, too. I got a little mention in that great article that had Michael Weldon on the front page.

**CP: Weldon listed *Trash Fiend* in the bibliography of *The Psychotronic Encyclopedia of Film*.**

**RG:** Yes he did. I think I was lucky to have started *Trash Fiend* at just the right time to still get mentioned with *Sleazoid Express* and *Gore Gazette*. After I started, the floodgates opened, probably because of the video boom, when kids in the suburbs could see all the things we were writing about. I also got a quote on the box cover and the advertising for the VHS of John Russo's *Midnight*. That was surprising.

**CP: A few years after *Trash Fiend* folded, you came back with a similar zine called *Grind*.**

**RG:** Around that time, the multiplexes were starting to grow from six screens to eight screens, ten screens, sixteen screens, twenty-five

RICHARD GREEN

CONFESSIONS OF A TRASH FIEND

A Year With A View

Best Picture 1988

19th SMASH WEEK!
"HAIR-RAISING FUN!"
—Janet Maslin, NEW YORK TIMES
An All American Comedy by John Waters
HAIRSPRAY

| Best | | Worst | |
|---|---|---|---|
| 1. | Hairspray | 1. | A Nightmare on Elm Street Part 4: The Dream Master |
| 2. | High Tide | 2. | Arthur 2 on The Rocks |
| 3. | The Thin Blue Line | 3. | Sunset |
| 4. | Working Girl | 4. | D.O.A. |
| 5. | The Lair Of The White Worm | 5. | Die Hard |
| 6. | Aria | 6. | Dead Heat |
| 7. | Mélo | 7. | Rented Lips |
| 8. | The Telephone | 8. | Rent-A-Cop |
| 9. | Beetlejuice | 9. | Poltergeist III |
| 10. | Tucker: The Man And His Dream | 10. | Dead Ringers |

screens! And I would go to see these junky Hollywood movies that nobody else would go see. There would be a thousand seats and nobody there. I thought that was interesting. So I started to write about junky Hollywood movies that nobody went to see, and why they were bad or why they were good. But I wasn't interested in *Batman* or anything like that. I was interested in the junk Hollywood would just throw out. That's when I started to do *Grind*.

**CP: That was a unique idea for a fanzine.**

**RG:** Right, but here's the problem with that: nobody cared! There was no audience to read it, because no one cared about those movies! And for most of them, they shouldn't have [laughs]! I remember seeing a movie called *Second Sight*, with John Larroquette, and again, it was this terrible movie, every piece of dialogue was stilted, nothing made any sense, and there was nobody there. I was in this 1,000 seat theater and there was no one else there watching this movie that must've cost several million dollars to make, and I could hear it echoing throughout the entire multiplex. I said, "OK, now this is interesting! These things are showing to NO ONE! They contractually have to show them to NO ONE!" But again, who cares [laughs]? No one. That was the problem.

**CP: Still, *Grind* had a pretty good run, with twenty-three issues produced in two years. Why did you stop?**

**RG:** Life got in the way again. I started working and didn't have time to do it.

**CP: Do you still read any movie magazines or fanzines?**

**RG:** The only thing I pick up anymore is *HorrorHound*, because they have articles on the bygone days of the video business that are interesting.

"A YEAR WITH A VIEW," *GRIND* NUMBER 8.

Sometimes I get *Shock Cinema*. I haven't seen *Fangoria* in ages. I have been so out of the scene, I didn't find out Bill Landis died—what, four years ago?—until last year, and when I did find out, I sat here and cried.

**CP: Surely he had to be one of the top five most influential movie critics of the 1980s, don't you think?**

**RG:** To me, it was Landis and that was it. I would say that I became a little bit obsessed with him. He wrote me a letter when I started *Trash Fiend*. I sent him the first issue and he wrote back and said I'd done a great job. I should get the letter framed, because to me that was like getting an Academy Award [laughs]. He was the Pauline Kael of zine writers.

**CP: If you can point to one film that represents your philosophy, what would it be?**

**RG:** There are actually two films that are representative of my work.... philosophy... whatever... and I still watch them every few months, sometimes every month, and they make me constantly turn over in my head the me that was twenty years old vs. the me that is fifty. One is Charlie Ahearn's *Wild Style*. There is no reason why a suburban kid with no love—or dislike, for that matter—of hip hop should love this movie so much. I re-watched it recently and had a revelation: just like the characters in the movie, I think the writers of newsletters and horror zines were all in the same mind frame. Hip hop, like low budget exploitation filmmaking, came from the same roots. It's something from nothing, a voice in the wilderness, seeing beauty in the nondescript, what normal society passes over and dismisses.

**CP: Is there an example that comes immediately to mind?**

**RG:** The Frederick Friedel film *Axe*. There is so much sadness and beauty there. To others it's an exploitation film, a gore film, a video nasty, period. I think the reason it's so revered among zine people is that they're able to see beyond its mainstream limitations. They're able to see the sadness, the emotion, the torture in every frame.

**CP: Friedel is one of those low budget auteurs I wish had made two dozen movies instead of just two. What's the other film you feel is representative of your philosophy?**

**RG:** The other is more personal. It's George Romero's *Knightriders*, a shining rocket of nonconformity about a troupe that eschews society and redefines the terms on their own, through argument and a struggling birth process. In some ways, and I may be waxing too poetically here, it was a last hurrah, a beacon before all was lost. The idealism in that movie is beyond amazing. To me, it was the last of Romero's films before he lost his own personal vision. There is nothing in his canon afterwards that I am particularly interested in, although I admit I haven't seen any of his post-*Day of the Dead* sequels. They are in my Netflix queue though [laughs]! Good God, go back to *Dawn of the Dead*. Making that revolutionary film in a huge multimillion dollar shopping mall? What does that say about

# RICHARD GREEN

## CONFESSIONS OF A TRASH FIEND

RECORDED & INDEXED

life and art in an abstract sense?

**CP: *Dawn of the Dead* was the hit that made *Knightriders* possible.**

**RG:** It's interesting that *Knightriders* was such a box-office failure, because it ran at my local theater for three months. On one screen, in one small suburban enclave, it found its audience. This was in central New Jersey. Was it bikers who kept it playing? The horror crowd? Or was it slowly finding an appreciative audience? The distributor never found out. The Christmas movies came in and shoved it out of the way.

**CP: I'll have to watch both of those movies again, now that I have your analysis fresh in my mind.**

**RG:** It really hit me watching *Wild Style*. The idealism was startling. I think that's what zine writing was—idealistic, optimistic, hoping to find a voice, to say "Hey, look, this is art. Wake up. Hear my voice. I may be an inner city heroin addict, I may be a suburban kid, I may be a guy just trying to find his voice, but my voice has value. I have something to say." It was born out of punk rock as much as out of hip hop and 42nd Street sleaze.

**CP: So, what Troma classics do you have lined up for tonight?**

**RG:** No, you have to recommend some movies to me. Here's what I've got to watch: I have *Black Swan*, which I've never seen, and *The Muppets Take Manhattan* on the top of my queue. If someone had told me when I was eighteen that I'd be sitting here with a Muppet movie when I was fifty years old, I probably would've said "Kill yourself." [laughs] "What happened to you, man? You're fifty years old and watching *The Muppets Take Manhattan* because you think it might be cute?!"

Richard Green's

# GRIND

<u>Grind</u> • April 1989 • Vol.1, No.11 • Published monthly by Richard Green, P.O. Box 32, Old Bridge, NJ 08857. All text (c) 1989 and may not be reproduced without written permission. Subscription rates: $5/year (12 issues). Back issues: 50¢/each. "<u>Grind</u> welcomes you to the exciting, wonderful world of the movies."

I was rooting for either <u>Working Girl</u> or <u>Dangerous Liaisons</u> to take the Oscar, but <u>Rain Man</u> won (all together now: "Time for Judge Wapner! Time for Judge Wapner!,") so the only way to clear out all this unpleasantness is to trash four new releases. Well, three are rotten and one's not so bad. Next time I'll find something really worth your time, promise. (Personal to F.P. : Yes, I know they used "Iko Iko" in <u>Rain Man</u>, but they also used it in <u>Satisfaction</u>, so what does that prove?)

<u>Nightmare Valley</u>

DREAM A LITTLE DREAM

1989 is only four months old and already we've got a candidate for the worst movie of the year. I've been wrong before, but I seriously doubt that anything could top the effort put forth by <u>Dream A Little Dream</u>. The Coreys, Feldman and Haim, star, and they've become their own high-concept; put them together and who cares if it's the <u>fifth</u> body reversal rip-off to come out in the last year and a half? It's got the Coreys! The surprise is that two old pros like Jason Robards and Piper Laurie have been suckered into the proceedings. Let's hope they just wanted to have fun playing to a younger audience - surely they weren't attracted to the project as a whole. Robards is an ex-scientist, professor, or voodoo priest (I was never sure,) who, with his wife (Laurie,) attempts a bizarre physics experiment that involves the scientific act of touching a finger to one's nose under a starry sky. So much for physics! What it's supposed to accomplish is never clear since the only thing it resembles is a drunk check. Corey Feldman is nearby, racing somewhere, when he accidentally slams into his would-be girlfriend (Meredith Salenger, an unappealing young actress with a nightmarish set of teeth - appropriately she was last seen in the horror film <u>The Kiss</u>.) Whammo! and the two sets are transposed etc., etc., etc.. But forget about the story, because as rendered by director Marc Rocco, it's as bad as the others. The opening scenes are played so softly they barely register, there is no pace to speak of, and he lets the Coreys run rampant, their drug-fed real-life rich and famous teen angst coming to the surface. And by the 10th rendition of the title song I was ready to retch. The only interesting moment comes when the director lets his real-life father (Alex Rocco, a grotesque supporting actor,) play a grotesque supporting role, Feldman's uncaring father, who can't even remember his son's name. A cry in the dark, Marc?

<u>Queen's Reich</u>

"Here, king...here, king..." Yes, <u>Farewell to the King</u> is a dog, but not easily dismissed; the amount of psychic energy poured into this film is herculean and schematically bizarre. Who else but the repressed John Milius could've come up with a fable that manages to be closety, ridiculous, overblown and incredibly dull at the same time? As the king of Borneo (!) Nick Nolte gives a surprisingly engaging and entertaining physical performance of a badly written character, basically a 60's mind-rotted hippie in disguise, which is probably Milius' ego-

DONALD FARMER'S EDITORIAL PHOTO, THE *SPLATTER TIMES* NUMBER 4.

# DONALD FARMER

## The Splatter Times

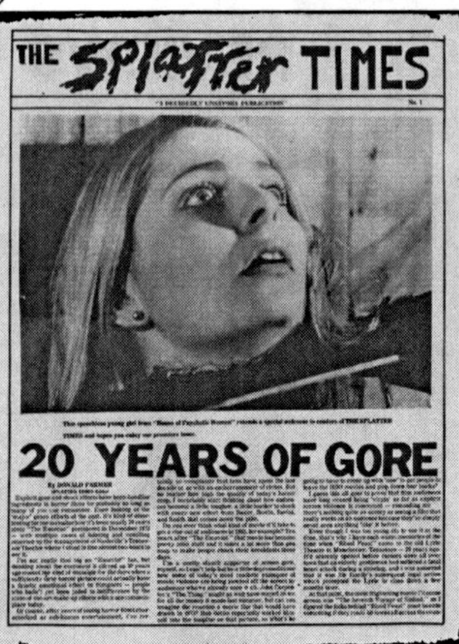
THE Splatter TIMES

20 YEARS OF GORE

A TABLOID FOR THE FIRST THREE ISSUES.

When I finally got my hands on a few issues of Donald Farmer's *Splatter Times* (courtesy, I think, of a fellow fanzine collector from somewhere out west), I couldn't believe my eyes. I was used to the usual look of the horror zines, but this was something different. Printed on newsprint, the *Splatter Times* resembled the entertainment insert in my local paper. I carefully unfolded the things and gave them the once over. Right off the bat, I knew that I was in for something special.

What sold me right away were the interviews. Donald Farmer made it a point to go in-depth, and his chats with the likes of Fred Olen Ray, Herschell Gordon Lewis, Joel M. Reed, and Richard Johnson were filled with information that was very hard to come by. One mustn't forget that the premier issue of the *Splatter Times* was published in 1983. Donald was tracking these guys down and picking their brains long before it was a commonplace practice.

With the fourth issue, the *Splatter Times* changed its look. No longer a tabloid, it now looked like a magazine. And as the years rolled on, the world was treated to interviews with Mary Woronov, Lynn Lowry, and an excellent behind the scenes look at Dan O'Bannon's *Return of the Living Dead*.

In 1986, Donald made *Demon Queen*, his first commercial film as a director. He has since gone on to become an accomplished and prolific filmmaker, directing such cult classics as *Cannibal Hookers*, *Savage Vengeance*, *An Erotic Vampire in Paris*, and *Chainsaw Cheerleaders*.

The following interview with Donald Farmer was conducted via telephone on February 22, 2012.

---

**DONALD FARMER:** In 1958, I saw a preview on TV for AIP's movie *The Spider*. Ever since then, I've been obsessed with going to genre movies. My parents wouldn't take me to see horror films, but they would take me to see fantasy and science fiction movies. A lot of those movies had

horror movie previews, so I have fond movies of horror films before I was old enough to go see them. And every time we'd go to the drugstore, I'd see *Famous Monsters* on the shelves. A few years later, I started seeing *Castle of Frankenstein*, and some of the cheaper imitations, like *Mad Monsters*. You would always see three or four of them in the same section of the drugstore. I was desperate to get some of these monster magazines, but again, my parents refused to buy them for me.

**JOHN SZPUNAR: When did you finally get your hands on one?**

**DF:** I had a very conniving plan to get my first issue of *Famous Monsters*. We had a gift exchange at school. I found the person who drew my name and said, "Here's what I want for my gift—you have to get me the new issue of *Famous Monsters*." That's how I finally got my first issue.

**JS: How old were you?**

**DF:** That would have been around 1965. I was ten or eleven. After that, I just sort of clandestinely started getting issues. Fortunately, we lived within walking distance from a drugstore, so I would take whatever money I could get together, wander down the street, and get them. I would hide them in my room—if my parents saw them, they would throw them all out.

**JS: What was your favorite title of the bunch?**

**DF:** I vastly preferred *Castle of Frankenstein*. I liked the fact that it wasn't just a printed press-kit, fawning over every movie. It was way more critical and was also much more comprehensive. It went into detail. That's how I became aware of so many European horror movies that weren't even getting any kind of US theatrical release.

**JS: When did you actually start seeing horror films?**

**DF:** Well, the first horror film that I ever watched was *Return of Dracula*, which I saw on the late show in the early sixties. And again, I saw the previews. I remember my mother took me to see the Doris Day movie, *Lover, Come Back*. All I remember about it is seeing the preview for *House*

SPARTA DRIVE-IN
THEATRE
SPARTA, TENN.
GATE OPEN 6:30 NIGHTLY
PHONE 738-5501

ATTEND
CHURCH
OFTEN

1972 DECEMBER 1972
Subject to Change Without Notice

SUN MON TUE WED THU FRI SAT

NOV 26 | 27 | 28 | 29 | 30 | 1 | 2

YOUR KIND OF BLACK FILM
MELINDA

DOUBLE FEATURE

PLUS

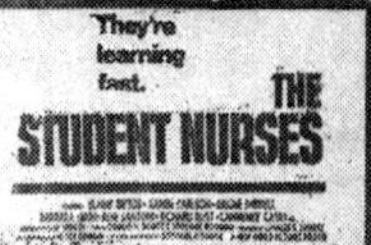


FOUR BIG NIGHTS

3 | 4 | 5 | 6 | 7 | 8 | 9

DOUBLE FEATURE

PLUS

FOUR BIG NIGHTS

10 | 11 | 12 | 13 | 14 | 15 | 16

FOUR BIG NIGHTS

Four young flowers that bloomed after they were picked.

Here and Now
There is the time and the place in every young girl's life!

17 | 18 | 19 | 20 | 21 | 22 | 23

DOUBLE FEATURE

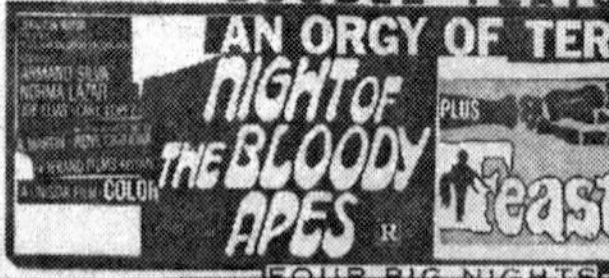

FOUR BIG NIGHTS

24 | 25 | 26 | 27 | 28 | 29 | 30

FOUR BIG NIGHTS

No Husbands... No Wives
Only Lovers
Mutual Mates—Carnal Companions
Group Marriage

The Stewardesses
THE UNPUBLISHABLE NOVEL IS NOW AMERICA'S MOST CONTROVERSIAL FILM!
R

DIXIE LITHO CO., INC. P.O. BOX 882 ATLANTA, GA. 30301

*of the Damned*. I became obsessed with seeing that movie, and I didn't see it until many years later. My family took me to see *20,000 Leagues Under the Sea*, and all I remember about it was the preview for *Tales of Terror* with Vincent Price. I don't think I actually saw a horror film in the theater until 1968. I finally got my father to take me to the local drive-in when I was fourteen. They were showing a double feature of *Berserk!* and *Torture Garden*, the Amicus anthology film with Jack Palance and Peter Cushing.

**JS: Why do you think your parents were against you seeing horror films?**

**DF:** They probably thought they were shielding me from something, but the fact was, it just made me want to see them all the more. In fact, if they would have let me see them, I might not have been such a fan. I think being denied them for so many years just made me obsessed with them.

**JS: You mentioned that you were reading about European horror films in *Castle of Frankenstein*. Did you ever think that you'd get the chance to see any of that stuff?**

**DF:** The first Italian horror move I ever saw was due to the fact that my parents had an 8mm projector. They would buy movies to watch on it. For some reason, they didn't object to me seeing horror movies on Super-8. They figured that the horror movies on Super-8 were the old ones, and they didn't mind me seeing the movies from the thirties, like the Universal series with Karloff and Lugosi. It turned out that an early sixties Italian horror movie called *The Vampire and the Ballerina* was released on Super-8, in a 200-foot digest version. They bought that for me, thinking that it was one of those super-tame Universal movies. It was a nice surprise for me to find out that it was very erotic. It also had a fairly graphic disintegration scene at the end—it was even more graphic than *Horror of Dracula*. It would be years and years later before I'd finally see it uncut.

**JS: Where were you buying these films?**

**DF:** All through the sixties, every major department store in America would always have a Super-8 department with a rack of movies that you could buy. Every time we would go to a department store, I would always go directly to the Super-8 rack to drool over the new releases. I could usually get my parents to get me one. Then, when I started earning money, I started buying them myself. My parents just assumed that everything on the rack was from the thirties. They had no idea that they were gradually releasing more recent films that were a little bit more graphic. And I made it a point not to show them the more graphic ones, so that they wouldn't be any the wiser.

**JS: I take it that there was a big market for horror and science fiction films on Super-8.**

**DF:** It was very much slanted toward horror and science fiction. The main distributor in America for those films was Castle Films. The second biggest distributor was called Ken Films. All of the classic Universal

Attachment

horror movies were put out by Castle Films. They also put out Super-8 versions of the Abbot and Costello films and some of the comedies. Ken Films put out stuff like *Mighty Joe Young* and *The Hunchback of Notre Dame*. Then, later, as you moved toward the seventies, some of the prints were in color, and they started to have sound. Columbia got into the act, and started putting out a Super-8 line. They put out *Revenge of Frankenstein* with Peter Cushing in color. Anyway, the Super-8 collecting sort of culminated in the mid-seventies. There was a company from England called Derann Films, and they would put out the entire movie in sound on several reels. They started putting out all the Hammer movies, like *Scars of Dracula*, *Twins of Evil*, and *Vampire Circus*. I used to have the Super-8 version of *The Texas Chain Saw Massacre*. It was completely uncut. So, by the mid-seventies, you could get a really good variety of movies on Super-8.

THE BLOOD-BROTHERS OF HORROR AND TERROR!
TOGETHER IN THE MOST TERRIFYING MONSTER SHOCK SHOW OF THE YEAR!
ALL NEW! NEVER BEFORE SEEN!
BOTH IN SPINE-TINGLING COLOR!
HORROR OF FRANKENSTEIN
starring RALPH BATES KATE O'MARA VERONICA CARLSON and DENNIS PRICE
SCARS OF DRACULA
starring CHRISTOPHER LEE
STARTS TOMORROW
R
PARAMOUNT Theatre

**JS: How expensive were they?**

**DF:** They were really expensive. You're talking an entire movie, Super-8 color sound. Right through the mid-seventies, I was spending $150 a pop to get an entire movie on Super-8.

**JS: How did the films look on Super-8?**

**DF:** They were reasonably presentable. What I really liked to get were the color Super-8 sound trailer reels. There was actually an H.G. Lewis trailer reel that had the trailers for *Blood Feast* and *Two Thousand Maniacs*, paired together with some other stuff. I remember a Christopher Lee and Vincent Price trailer reel.

**JS: Did you get the chance to fool around with any 8mm cameras as a kid?**

**DF:** Oh, sure. I made a whole string of Super-8 movies, starting in '67, when I was twelve. At the time, there was a movie in the theaters called *In Cold Blood* with Robert Blake. Even though I hadn't seen it, I thought it would be good to do a parody of it. So, my very first movie was a little four-minute movie called *In Cold Blood*. It basically just had some of my friends killing each other. In 1974, I did a movie called *The Summoned*

which was a forty-minute horror movie about an incubus character that was seducing women and killing everybody. I got a lot of my friends to be in that. We had to make our own special effects—we were trying to make it as gory as we could. We went to the local butcher shop, got a bunch of animal guts, and created our own autopsy scene. We made squibs by taping firecrackers to the actors' chests, with a little piece of cardboard below the firecracker to supposedly protect them. We put a condom full of blood on top of the firecracker. We were just making our own effects, whatever way we could.

**JS: Speaking of splatter, how did the *Splatter Times* get going?**

**DF:** Well, all through the seventies, I was seeing all of these obscure movies and I always wanted to do a fanzine of my own. *Little Shoppe of Horrors* was my favorite fanzine, but I was always intimidated by how great it was. I thought it would just be hopeless to put out my own—there was no way that I'd ever be able to come within a mile of what they were doing, even if I was covering a different genre area. I thought that it was just as good or better than a lot of the so-called pro magazines. So, even though it was my favorite, I think it delayed me from entering the fanzine world for many years. But then, in the early eighties, you started seeing more and more xeroxed fanzines. You had *Sleazoid Express*, *Scareaphanalia*, and *Gore Gazette*—they were just xeroxed and stapled together. When everybody started doing that, I said, "I can do something on that level." In fact, I thought that I could do something a little bit better, because at the time, I was working for a newspaper. One of my jobs was to put out a weekly entertainment magazine, which was in tabloid format. I figured that I could use the same layout sheets and put together my own fanzine. There was nobody out there doing that—in fact the only publication that had done something in a newspaper style was the *Monster Times*. I thought that this would give me a little niche—I didn't want to do it if I thought I was doing the same thing that everybody else was doing. I wanted to be a little bit different.

It also allowed me to follow

DONALD FARMER

THE SPLATTER TIMES

DRAFT

RECORDED & INDEXED

ART CORNER

THE BRUTAL BEYOND BELIEF "ART CORNER" IN *DEMONIQUE* NUMBER 4.

The circumstances accompanying the 1977 American release of *Salo, or the 120 Days of Sodom* were almost as unusual as those depicted in this, the final film of Italian director Pier Paolo Pasolini. Advance word in *Film Comment*, *Film Quarterly* and particularly *The Village Voice* indicated that *Salo* features extremes of sadism, violence and scatology then unheard of in a major picture, and the publicity mills were scarcely hampered by the fact that Pasolini himself had been brutally murdered on November 2, 1975 – nearly six months after his film's completion.

When the critical verdict returned from the picture's fall 1977 showing at the New York Film Festival, however, it was clear that the usually softened reception given a posthumous work had been abandoned for an overwhelmingly negative, often vicious backlash.

Attacked as both nauseating for its frankness and depressing for its bleak ideology, *Salo* has since garnered a reputation as one of the screen's darkest works. At least in terms of shock value, the intervening

## Salo, or the 120 Days of Sodom:
# Pasolini's Sadistic Work of Art
### By Donald Farmer

years have seen its violence outdone by the current wave of explicit gore films, but even in 1977 the gore scenes were hardly as disturbing as one in which 16 captives are forced to eat their own excrement.

Anyone familiar with the Marquis De Sade's *The 120 Days of Sodom* knows that the exhaustive catalog of tortures and sexual perversities found therein would seem doubtful material for a major film production, much less one by a director who had previously won praise from as unlikely an admirer as Billy Graham for *The Gospel According to Saint Matthew.* But just as De Sade's work was intended more as literary rebellion

than exploitation, so Pasolini's approach to this material took a similar intent – with a special emphasis on political allegory.

The worst possible frame of reference for a viewer to approach *Salo* would be with comparisons to films where sadism is the main attraction. To quote Pasolini from an interview conducted during the filming by Gideon Bachmann, "My film is planned as a sexual metaphor, which symbolizes, in a visionary way, the relationship between exploiter and exploited. In sadism and in power politics human beings become objects."

Pasolini conceded that he was not indifferent to whatever salacious appeal the finished film would have and said, "I am surely not planning to create an aesthetically political, puritanical film. Obviously, I am fascinated by these sadistic orgies in themselves. So there you have two basic dimensions: the political and the sexual."

Both the film and De Sade's novel have a particular numerical emphasis, an aspect which Pasolini amplified with some revisions. For example, the book features four symbols of French authority: a bishop, a president, a banker and their leader, the Duc de Blangis, of whom De Sade writes, "He may be regarded as the repository of every vice and every crime. He has killed his mother, his sister, and three of his wives."

Pasolini transformed this group into four equally sadistic Italian fascists who abduct 18 teenage boys

*Page Six—Demonique #4*

up my agenda—I had always wanted to meet as many of my idols as possible—the people who had made the movies that I was obsessed with. When I saw *Blood Sucking Freaks*, I became obsessed with everything about it, and wanted to meet Joel Reed. But, when you're just a fan, you don't have any right to pester them. If you're a writer for a magazine, it gives you a legitimate reason. So, the *Splatter Times* gave me a legitimate excuse to meet the people from the exploitation side of the industry that

I wanted to meet. That was one of my main agendas—it gave me some sort of an excuse to meet these people and pick their brains. And I had it in the back of my head that I wanted to get into the filmmaking. I thought the best education would be to pick the brains of as many filmmakers as I could.

And then, at the time, there was an explosion of obscure horror films playing the drive-ins in my area. It had been going on all through the seventies, and it was still going on very hot in the early eighties. Lucio Fulci and Paul Naschy films were playing in the drive-ins. The drive-ins in Nashville were playing all night quadruple-features. I wanted to document it—I wanted to have a historical document of what was happening at the drive-ins in my area. A lot of the New York based fanzines were saying that a movie didn't really count, unless you saw it on 42nd Street. They were worshiping the grindhouses. I thought the experience was more special if you saw it at one of the drive-ins.

**JS: You were covering a lot of exploitation films, but you were also covering a lot of art films.**

**DF:** That was always my dual-interest. But the art films that I'm interested in are exploitation films. It fascinated me that a director like Pasolini, Marco Ferreri or Andrzej Zulawski could make a film that would satisfy the checklist of everything you'd want to see in an exploitation movie. And when you'd read interviews with these directors, they would always deny that they were trying to appeal to a prurient interest. They would always come off as being very high-minded. The ultimate example of an art film that works perfectly as an exploitation film is Pasolini's *Salò*. It gives you everything and more you'd find in something like *Ilsa, She Wolf of the SS*. Of course, Ilsa is looked down on by serious critics, while the same critics think *Salò* is a masterpiece. When you look at those films side by side and analyze their content, one film is just as sleazy as the other. Pasolini would always bristle at the thought that he was trying to make an exploitation movie. He would always say that he was trying to make an analogy about fascism or about the state of consumer society today.

**JS: I always thought that some of those guys were working with exploitable elements in order to draw a crowd.**

**DF:** They can say what they want, and deny, deny, deny, but I don't think most people were going to see those movies for high-minded reasons.

**JS: Can you tell me a little about your job at the newspaper?**

**DF:** I was actually working for two newspapers. I was working for a daily paper in Cookeville, Tennessee, which is a medium sized town. I was also the state correspondent for the *Nashville Tennessean*, which is the biggest daily newspaper in Tennessee. I was covering the police beat—I was covering all the murder cases and violent accidents. I was also doing life features and human interest sorties. I was doing political stories and interviewing politicians. Walter Mondale came through once when he was

THE Splatter TIMES

More gore to come from H.G. Lewis?

ANOTHER TABLOID ISSUE: THE *SPLATTER TIMES* NUMBER 2.

running for president, and I interviewed him. The height of it was when the local TV station started recruiting me to interview politicians on one of their TV shows. I did a thirty-minute public affairs show with Al Gore. He made it very easy because he gave such long answers. I only had to ask him three or four questions. I was doing all that at the same time I was doing the *Splatter Times*. Sometimes, I'd stay at the newspaper late at night, after I'd already clocked out. I'd work on the layout for the *Splatter Times*, at least for the first three issues that were done as a tabloid. I would typeset it on their typesetting equipment. But after the third issue of the *Splatter Times*, I got a bigger job with Simon and Shuster, and they moved me to Florida to work at one of their branches. I was making more money, but I no longer had access to the newspaper presses. I had to find another means to get the *Splatter Times* published, so I did four issues in standard magazine format.

**JS: You mentioned Bill Landis. When did you first become aware of him?**

**DF:** I think around 1982. I read about *Sleazoid Express* somewhere, and I started subscribing to it. Once I subscribed to that, I started subscribing to a few other fanzines. And when I started putting out my own fanzine, other fanzine editors would trade subscriptions with me. I was getting most of the major fanzines of the time.

**JS: Did Bill Landis get you in touch with Joel Reed?**

**DF:** I can't remember how I got in touch with Joel Reed. I know that I interviewed him in '82, because that's when I started work on the *Splatter Times*. The first thing I did for the first issue was my Joel Reed interview.

**JS: Did you interview him by phone?**

**DF:** Yes. A few years later, when I went to New York, Joel invited me over to his apartment. I went over there and got to meet him in person. He took me out and showed me around. It was really exciting to finally meet him in person.

**JS: Where was he living at that time?**

**DF:** He was living in a rent controlled apartment, not very far from

Times Square.

**JS: What were your impressions of Reed?**

**DF:** I had nothing but admiration for him. I wanted to see *Blood Sucking Freaks* from the first time I became aware of it. I became aware of Joel and that film through the *New York Times*. In the late seventies, they ran a very large display ad in the Arts and Entertainment section for the film under its original title, *The Incredible Torture Show*. I thought it had the most incredible poster art I'd ever seen—it looked very demented and very wrong. Finally, when *Blood Sucking Freaks* came out, I found out that it was *The Incredible Torture Show* under a new title. I saw it two or three times the week it opened. It became my mission to track down Joel and get an interview with him. That was another strong contributing factor for starting the *Splatter Times*. *Fangoria* had no interest in an interview with Joel at that time. In order to contact him for an interview, I needed to tell him that I had a magazine that I could put it in. If I had my own magazine, it made it all seem a little more legitimate. There only a couple of times I called a celebrity out of the blue to gush over them as purely as a fan. In the mid-seventies I made a transatlantic call to producer/director Michael Carreras at Hammer films to bend his ear about how I loved Hammer. I still can't believe how he talked to me for at least fifteen minutes when I was basically just calling to say Hammer was the greatest. Then a few years later, after seeing Mario Bava's *House of Exorcism*, I called the Screen Actors Guild, requested the agency number for star Robert Alda, and asked them for Alda's home number. Five minutes later I was pumping Alda for any tidbits about making *House of Exorcism* and working with Bava. Alda was happy to accommodate me and probably spent half an hour answering my questions. And it never even occurred to me to tape the interview and offer it to a magazine!

**JS: You interviewed Richard Johnson. How did you get in touch with him?**

**DF:** That sort of fell into my lap. That was in '83 when I was doing the *Splatter Times*, and working for *Fangoria* and the newspaper. One of my jobs was to look for local events that were of interest to the area. Our newspaper was contacted by Sandy Howard, the producer of *A Man Called Horse* and *Island of Dr. Moreau*, and invited to attend a local press junket for his current production with Richard Johnson. Howard had started out as a fairly big budget, prestige producer, but sort of degenerated into doing

the ultimate orgy of evil...

CANNIBAL HOOKERS

trashier films like *Avenging Angel* and *Hollywood Vice Squad*.

**JS: What film was it for?**

**DF:** It was originally called *Secrets of the Phantom Caverns*, but it ended up being retitled *What Waits Below*. Howard was shooting in Cumberland Caverns just an hour from my town. So I jumped all over that—I knew instantly who Sandy Howard was and let him know that I would definitely be at his press junket. Hey, this was the man who produced *The Devil's Rain*! When I got there, I was ushered into the courtyard of a local motel. There were tables sitting around, and there was a celebrity at every table. The main three were Robert Powell, Timothy Bottoms, and Richard Johnson.

**JS: Was Don Sharp there?**

**DF:** Unfortunately, he had to stay in his room to work on the breakdowns for the next day's filming. Anyway, they said, "Let us know who you'd like to interview for your local newspaper." I said, "I want Robert Powell and Richard Johnson." That was the first and only time a press junket like that has happened in my area. I immediately contacted *Fangoria* and said, "Hey, I asked Richard Johnson questions about working with Fulci on *Zombie*." I went out of my way to make the interview of interest to *Fangoria* readers. That was how I broke in with *Fangoria*. I pitched them an article that I had already written.

**JS: Another guy I wanted to ask you about is Tim Ferrante.**

**DF:** Tim was one of my contributors. In 1984, I made my very first trip to New York at the invitation of Buddy Cooper, an attorney who produced and

directed *The Mutilator.* Buddy had heard about the *Splatter Times*, and he sent me a press kit. I covered it, and he invited me to come to the premier on 42nd Street. He said that I could stay with his editor, who lived in Queens. I'd never been to New York before, and I thought, "Wow! A horror director is inviting me to be his guest and he's giving me a free place to stay. Sounds good to me." I went up there, and they somehow knew Tim Ferrante. That's how I met him. Tim took us to ABC where he worked as an editor and gave us a quick tour. A few years later when I was living in California, he came out there to do a documentary called *Drive-In Madness* with Forrest Ackerman and Linnea Quigley. Tim had me help out his crew, which was great because it gave me my first visit to Forrest Ackerman's house.

**JS: What did you think of that?**

**DF:** It was fairly big house. It must have cost millions in LA real estate prices. But even with such a large house, Ackerman was not allowed to have any of his collection on the main floor. Apparently, that was his wife's rule. He had to cram the entire collection into the basement. And you couldn't take a step without narrowly missing something old and priceless! One wrong step, you could crush a one-of-a-kind movie prop. It was a little frustrating that I was there to work… I could happily have spent all day browsing through Ackerman's book shelves and display tables.

**JS: You interviewed Herschell Gordon Lewis at a time when was pretty much forgotten. How did you get in contact with him?**

**DF:** I interviewed Herschell Lewis when I was still living in Tennessee. I was taking my girlfriend to Florida for Spring break. I coordinated it so I'd drop her off somewhere for the afternoon where she could do whatever she wanted to do with her friends. Then I hightailed it over to Herschell Gordon Lewis' house and spent the whole afternoon with him. I can't remember exactly how I got his phone number, but somehow I did. I made arrangements with him, and he was very open to the idea of me coming down. I went there, and he gave me a tour of his place and introduced me to his wife, Margo. At the time I interviewed him, the only films of his I'd seen were *How to Make a Doll* and *Just for the Hell of It*. I didn't even see *Blood Feast* until it came out on video in the mid-eighties. It had played my local theatre in 1964, but there was no way my parents would take me to a movie called *Blood Feast*!

**JS: Do you know if Jim Morton had interviewed him prior to you?**

**DF:** I'm not sure. The only major article that I'd read about him was in the *Monster Times*. At the time that I went down and interviewed him, he told me that mine was the most detailed interview that he'd ever given. A few years later, I did another interview with him for *Fangoria*, when I was on the set of *Blood Feast 2* in Louisiana. By this time I was good friends with *Blood Feast* producer David Friedman, who I met while I lived in Los Angeles in the mid-eighties. I'd been invited to a party for Lewis at the home of Hollywood Book and Poster owner Eric Caiden, and that's where I first met Friedman. Russ Meyer was also at the party. At the time, I was dating one of Fred Olen Ray's actresses from the movie *Star Slammer*. I introduced her to Russ Meyer and Dave Friedman but I don't think she had any idea who these people were [laughs]. She was totally oblivious. For me it was a huge thrill to meet Russ Meyer; I was a very big fan of his since seeing *Beyond the Valley of the Dolls* and *Vixen*. This was a filmmaker who made sleazy films that I really admired. He made them with all the production value and skill of any A-list filmmaker. In fact, even though I liked Herschell Gordon Lewis, I was always a little sad that his movies looked so shoddy and sloppy. I was looking at him standing next to Russ Meyer and thinking, "Why can't Lewis make films that look as good as Russ Meyer's?"

**JS: Why do you think that was?**

**DF:** Well, when I worked on *Blood Feast 2*, I could sort of see why his films looked like that. He pretty much wants to go with the first take of everything. He had a very professional crew on that movie—the same crew that had just shot the film *Bully* for Larry Clark. It was a way more professional crew than Herschell had ever had before, and they wanted to light everything meticulously. He just was not having that. During the filming, there was kind of a constant back and forth between the crew wanting to make things look professional, and him just wanting to shoot everything as fast as possible. He was concerned with content, but not so much with presentation.

**JS: What gave you the push to start making feature films?**

**DF:** Well, I'd been making my own Super-8 movies all through the seventies. Then, for about ten years, I just concentrated on writing. I got back into movies in the eighties because the video companies were open to distributing direct-to-video product. I thought it was something I should try because I had a friend who ran a video production company and he was willing to do everything for aper centage of the movie. And I had access to horror makeup effects through Rick Gonzales, who had worked with Romero's crew on *Day of the Dead*. I figured I had these two key things I need to make a horror movie: I have a state of the art makeup guy and a production company that will shoot and edit. All I need to supply is the script. We got most of the actors for free. We were able to make *Demon*

*Queen* for around two grand.

**JS: You shoot on video for budgetary reasons...**

**DF:** If given the choice, I would always prefer to shoot on 35mm. But I shot *Demon Queen* with the resources that were available to me. After doing a few of these shot-on-video movies, I started getting hired to work on crews for larger movies. I worked on the crew for this one movie that was a 35mm theatrical release called *No Justice*. That's the only movie that I worked on that actually played theaters. After I did that, I got an invitation to work on another crew down in Georgia. Once I got down there, I hit it off with the producer and convinced him to hire me to write and direct three movies in a row for him. He gave me a $750,000 budget to do them. We were able to shoot on film and get some cheap celebrities. We got Dana Plato and Brigitte Nielsen.

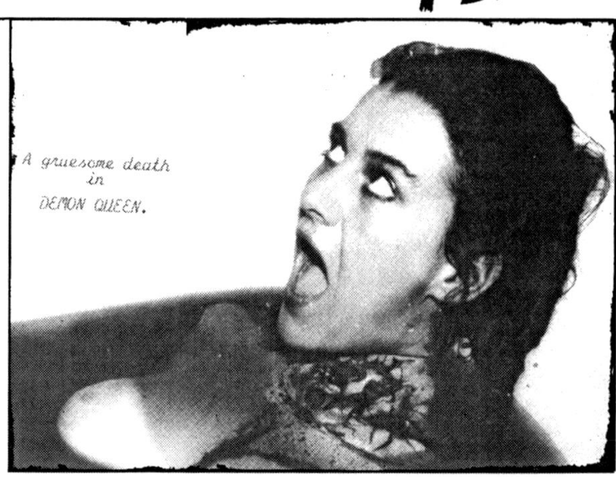

A gruesome death in DEMON QUEEN.

VERY TRUE... *DRACULINA* COMMENTS ON *DEMON QUEEN*, ISSUE NUMBER 10.

**JS: Were you aware of any other shot-on-video films when you were starting out?**

**DF:** The first one I became aware of was *The Ripper*, with Tom Savini. I saw that one. There was another one I didn't see called *Boardinghouse*. So I thought, "Well, it's now OK to shoot a movie with your video camera. I should give it a try." I was also friends with a lot of the people in acquisitions from independent distribution labels through the *Splatter Times*. I knew people from Aquarius Releasing, who put out *Make Them Die Slowly*. I was very close friends with the vice president of Motion Picture Marketing, the company that put out Fulci's *City of the Living Dead* under the title *The Gates of Hell*. And when I moved to LA, I was making more and more contacts. I was convinced that if I made something, I could get someone to put it out. As it turned out, I had two companies fighting over my first movie. Mogul immediately made me an offer, and right after I signed the contract Motion Picture Marketing stepped in and offered me ten times as much. But unfortunately it was too late to go with them.

**JS: How did you finance your early films?**

**DF:** *Demon Queen* was all my cash. I just paid for it with my income from

Simon and Shuster. It didn't take much. For *Cannibal Hookers*, I was able to get most of the actors for free. The first time I ever got a serious investor was when I made *Scream Dream* and *Savage Vengeance*. I made those as co-productions with a local video production company who again agreed to do all of the services for free in exchange for a piece of the movies. So again, my only cost was for certain actors and for makeup effects. By doing it that way, I was always able to keep my budgets under five grand. It wasn't until *Vampire Cop*, my first movie shot on 16mm, that I needed a bigger budget. I found an investor—these people were friends with one of Elvis' step brothers. I had a meeting with them, and the plan was to get Elvis' step brother in the movie for celebrity value. They would also put money into the movie. The Elvis stepbrother thing fell through—he ended up not being interested. But, they still invested in the movie and put about ten grand into it. I put in about five, and that gave us a little more money than we had before. And then, after we shot the movie, we got the interest of this New York company called Panorama Entertainment. They paid to have even more scenes shot to make it more commercial. They ended up paying for all of the editing.

**JS: Let's talk a little about Camille Keaton. How did you meet her?**

**DF:** I met her through an actor on *Cannibal Hookers*. After we did that film, he wanted me to come up with another movie that he could be in right away. He decided to be very proactive about it—he decided to find celebrities that would make the movie more viable. He very proudly announced to me one day that he was friends with Camille Keaton. I hadn't heard about her for years. I asked, "How did you meet her?" He said, "I work with her." He worked for Amtrak on their LA to Seattle train line, and she was a hostess. He said, "I see Camille every day at work. If you want her to be in one of your movies, or if you just want to meet her, I'll tell her." At the time, I didn't have anything to put her in, but I decided right then that I would make it my mission to find a movie for Camille to

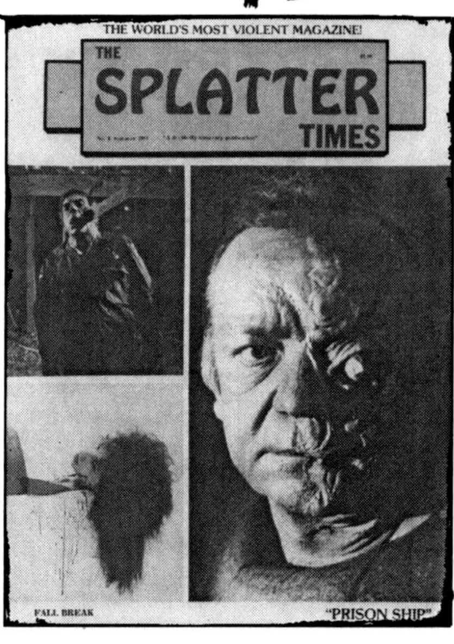


do. The very next year, when I moved back to Tennessee, I immediately got hired onto this *No Justice* movie, and they put me in charge of celebrity casting. I said, "I'm friends with Camille Keaton. I can get her for the movie. I'm also friends with Cameron Mitchell." I'd interviewed him for the *Splatter Times*, and I'd even gotten him a job with Fred Olen Ray. Before the producer put me in charge of the celebrities, he had tried to do it himself, and he failed miserably. He tried to hire Charles Napier, and had gotten off on the wrong foot with him. Then he tried to hire William Sanderson from *Blade Runner*, and again got nowhere. He basically figured that hiring a celebrity was some mystical art that was beyond his reach. He didn't know how to talk to them, and he no clue how to go about doing it. Apparently, he said something to Charles Napier that made him very pissed.

**JS: How were you negotiating with people?**

**DF:** It wasn't hard to get the people for *No Justice* because I was already friends with them. A few years later when I did *Compelling Evidence* with Dana Plato and Brigitte Nielsen, I just went through their agents. It was very easy to get a hold of them. You just call the Screen Actors Guild and tell you that you need the agency listing for such and such a star. You can't just come out and say, "How much will this star cost?" you have to make them an offer. So, you make them a low ball offer and negotiate.

**JS: What was it like working with Dana Plato?**

**DF:** Rod Dailey, the guy from *Cannibal Hookers* who introduced me to Camille Keaton also reached out to Dana Plato for me. He was a very industrious fellow. Right after Dana Plato was in trouble for robbing the video store in Las Vegas, he decided to make it his mission to track her down and let her know that his friend Donald would put her in a movie and help her rebuild her career. I had not asked him to do this—he did this all on his own. One day, out of the blue, he presented me with a photo of him and her sitting on her front porch. He tracked her down, and found out where she lived. He must have been a good amateur detective. All the tabloids were trying to find her—everyone in the world wanted an

interview with her about the robbery. He said, "I talked to Dana, and she's very willing to do one of your movies." So I talked to her probation officer and told him I was going to give Dana a job, and I got him to sign off on it. That's the only time I've had to sweet talk a probation officer to hire a star. I must say that I expected the worst. I expected her to be drugged out of her mind, and that it would be hell to work with her. It was just the opposite. She was so professional and nailed everything on the first take. I gave her a lot of dialogue, and Dana was word perfect—a complete dream to work with. I was actually shocked at how professional she was.

**JS: How has low budget filmmaking changed since you started out?**

**DF:** Well, on one hand, it's easier to make low budget movies that look presentable because nowadays, inexpensive cameras give you such a high resolution. You can do HD for not too much money. When I was making ¾ inch video movies, they did not look good at all. They were barely passable. Nowadays, you can make something that looks fairly presentable on a low budget. The problem is that there are fewer companies that will pay the same money that they did in the eighties for movies that are made in this budget range. People were making insane money back then, and I really don't see that nowadays.

**JS: What are your favorite films that you've made, and why?**

**DF:** *Cannibal Hookers* is a favorite for lots of reasons. It had lots of discoveries in the cast who went on to big careers like our effects guy, Brian Sipe, who now works for Ridley Scott, David Fincher and J.J. Abrams. Plus we got to film in Ted Mikels' "castle" in Los Angeles, and the title

nabbed the movie way more publicity than such a no-budget film should expect. I loved putting together my version of an "all star" female cast for *Compelling Evidence*, with Brigitte Nielsen, Dana Plato, Lynn Lowry and Melissa Moore. *An Erotic Vampire in Paris* is a favorite for giving me a chance to film in France and shoot at amazing locations like Notre-Dame cathedral and Père Lachaise cemetery.

**JS: Are you still writing about films?**

**DF:** The last article I did for *Fangoria* was two or three years ago, when I covered the Tiffany Shepis/Bill Moseley movie *Home Sick* for them. Now I'm working on a long article about the making of *Barbarella*.

THE WORLD'S MOST VIOLENT MAGAZINE!
THE SPLATTER TIMES
THE RE-ANIMATOR THE TOMB

**JS: Is there anything you'd like to add?**

**DF:** As much as I still love the films that inspired me to launch the *Splatter Times*, I wonder if I would have been so motivated if I'd seen these movies on VHS or DVD and not first run in theatres and drive-ins. The big screen experience has always been that X factor for me that pushes a movie from great to unforgettable. Almost all the movies I wrote about in my early issues were films actually playing theatrically in my area around Nashville and Knoxville, and seeing them in theatres or drive-ins, with their titles on a marquee and big posters framed around the snack bar… all that fueled my fascination. It's that whole package, the movies *and* the venues, that inspired me to start my own zine. I can remember exactly where I was when I saw Argento's *Deep Red* or [Mel Welles'] *Lady Frankenstein* or [Don Edmonds'] *Ilsa, She Wolf of the SS* in a theatre for the first time—the theatre is a huge part of that experience. But do I remember anything about the first time I watched *Suspiria* on video or even a great recent movie like *Dead Girl* on DVD? Not really. I remember the movies but that's it.

# Chapter Twelve
# Tim Ferrante
## Drive-In Madness

TIM FERRANTE

IMAGE © 1992, IMAGINE, INC.

K, show of hands. How many of you have heard of a guy named Tim Ferrante? His work has graced the pages of a multitude of genre publications, the list of which includes the *Splatter Times*, *Hi-Tech Terror* (he edited the zine for a short while when Craig Ledbetter was on sabbatical), *Fangoria*, *Starlog*, and *Gorezone*. In 1983, he founded the acclaimed spaghetti western fanzine *Westerns... All'Italiana!* Are your hands in the air yet? Good. I thought you might know him.

Tim was also the vice president of Imagine, Inc., the publishing house responsible for Tom Savini's monumental *Grande Illusions*, *Forrest J Ackerman: Famous Monster of Filmland*, and *Drive-In Madness! The Video*. In 1987, Tim became the first and only person to interview the elusive Duane Jones, the doomed hero of George A. Romero's *Night of the Living Dead*. With credentials like those under his belt, I made it a personal mission to track him down for an interview.

It became apparent right away that Tim Ferrante is a hell of a nice guy. When I mentioned that I was in need of a few publications for research purposes, he offered to send them to me. And once we started talking, I found it hard to stop. Tim's infectious laugh and amazing stories made my head spin, and before long, close to three hours had passed.

These days, Tim's writing regularly appears in Joe Kane's *VideoScope* and online at Chris Poggiali's *Temple of Schlock*. His enthusiasm for the genre is still as strong as ever, as the following interview certainly attests.

The following interview was conducted via telephone and email, May 2012–January 2013.

---

**JOHN SZPUNAR: What first got you into horror movies?**

**TIM FERRANTE:** What lit the fuse was the original *Invaders from Mars* when it was on TV. I couldn't have been more than five or six years old. It just frightened me to death. That was followed by memorable events such as the night when *The Outer Limits* premiered in 1963. Imagine an eight year old monster lover's excitement seeing the very first episode, "The Galaxy Being"! I vividly recall going to see *Two on a Guillotine* in 1965 at a kiddie matinee. It scared me so badly that I begged my father for another fifty cents to go see it again the next afternoon—I had to confront that fear. I went back and watched it again, so I wouldn't be so scared. Then one day I discovered a stack of comic books and magazines next to my cousin's bed. Tucked amongst it all was a copy of *Famous Monsters of Filmland* and I went nuts. It was those kinds of childhood experiences that drew me in.

**JS: When you're a kid, your imagination can go into overdrive. I remember being frightened by *From Hell it Came* because my grandfather told me the Tabanga was real.**

DRAFT

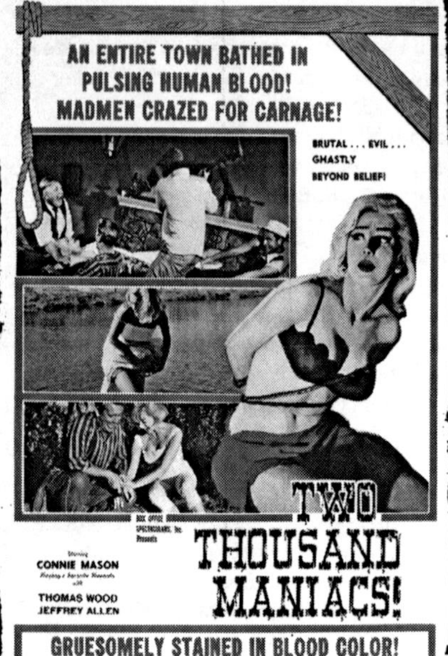
AN ENTIRE TOWN BATHED IN
PULSING HUMAN BLOOD!
MADMEN CRAZED FOR CARNAGE!
BRUTAL . . . EVIL . . .
GHASTLY
BEYOND BELIEF!
TWO
THOUSAND
MANIACS!
CONNIE MASON
THOMAS WOOD
JEFFREY ALLEN
GRUESOMELY STAINED IN BLOOD COLOR!

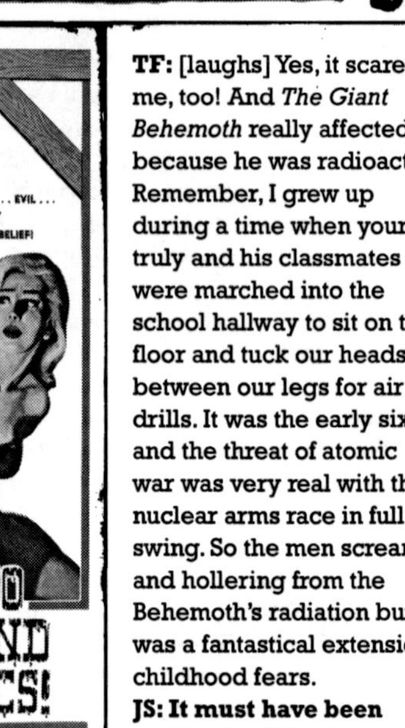

**TF:** [laughs] Yes, it scared me, too! And *The Giant Behemoth* really affected me because he was radioactive. Remember, I grew up during a time when yours truly and his classmates were marched into the school hallway to sit on the floor and tuck our heads in between our legs for air raid drills. It was the early sixties and the threat of atomic war was very real with the nuclear arms race in full swing. So the men screaming and hollering from the Behemoth's radiation burns was a fantastical extension of childhood fears.

**JS: It must have been pretty shocking to see a magazine like *Famous Monsters of Filmland* for the first time.**

**TF:** Finding that magazine was the triggering mechanism for a lifelong fascination with movie monsters. It was proof that I wasn't alone. Forry Ackerman was sending out a "correspondence course" with each issue. He was teaching thousands of us all at the same time while forging personal relationships from afar.

**JS: You were reading *Famous Monsters of Filmland* and *Castle of Frankenstein*—did you ever go to the library to find information about movies?**

**TF:** Oh, sure. And every time I went to a bookstore I headed straight for the film section and pull down whatever I could find and stand there and read it. Today you can sit, read, drink a latte and take smartphone pictures of pages that interest you so can read them again later. I've done it! Here's a perfect example of how difficult things were to find information: I saw *Two Thousand Maniacs* for the first time in 1971. It was on a double bill with *Night of the Living Dead* which I'd already seen multiple times and *Two Thousand Maniacs* was a total unknown. So naturally I had to know all there was to know about it. But how? Who in the hell is Herschell G. Lewis? I'd never heard of this person. Who is David F. Friedman? Where did this movie come from? The credits said it was made in St. Cloud, Florida.

Shortly after I'd seen it, my parents were taking a trip to Florida to visit my brother. I begged them to go to St. Cloud and ask anyone they could about *Two Thousand Maniacs*. Can you believe that? That's like getting information by smoke signal technology.

**JS: So, what happened?**

**TF:** They went to St. Cloud! And one woman had some sketchy memories of the main street being closed on a Sunday for filming or something. That was like getting the inside scoop. So I kept digging through movie memorabilia catalogs—anything where I could purchase material related to that film just to find out who these people were. I eventually got a pressbook, a one-sheet and some still photographs, some of which featured the cheesy gore scenes. I even sent away for the paperback novelization that was hyped in the pressbook. This was several years after the film was originally released, but I sent for it anyway from the Chicago publisher. Instead of a book, a letter came back stating it was no longer available. Basically, you were researching and learning like a detective who relies on good old-fashioned legwork to get the facts. That's how difficult it was to get any meaningful information on your niche interests. It was frustrating, but very, very satisfying when you succeeded.



**JS: We now have DVDs and blu-rays of those films. Does that surprise you at all?**

**TF:** I come from an era when you had nothing, so I doubly appreciate today's technology and availability of product. You're talking about blu-ray—someone's found the original camera elements for *Manos: The Hands of Fate* and plans a blu-ray release. There's a website devoted to it. *Manos: The Hands of Fate* on blu-ray? Are you kidding [laughs]? Never would have dreamed...

**JS: When did you first put pen to paper to write about films?**

**TF:** The first published article was called "The Most Valuable Record in the World". It was about *The Caine Mutiny* soundtrack album in issue number 4 of a tabloid publication called *Nostalgia World*. *The Caine*

RECORDED & INDEXED

DRAFT

LAYOUT BOARDS FOR *FANGORIA*.

*Mutiny* was on the RCA Victor label and is one of the rarest soundtrack LPs ever pressed. I used the pseudonym of Noel Harrison for no particular reason other than it was Rex Harrison's son's name. A friend had made a vinyl re-pressing that he was marketing at the time and I was hoping the article would generate some sales.

**JS: What year are we talking about?**

**TF:** That was in 1978. The first thing published that was horror-related was in the second issue of Donald Farmer's the *Splatter Times* in the Summer of 1983. It was an interview with John (Jack) Russo who, of course, is one of the creators of *Night of the Living Dead*.

**JS: That was a good one. How did you meet Donald Farmer?**

**TF:** I'm not sure how we met, but it was that interview that got me started writing professionally thanks to my friend Gary Dorst. Gary's fandom profile dates back to the early sixties. He's an original 'monster kid' whose interests were wide-ranging. He'd been writing for fan publications before I knew such things existed. He was a beautiful person who, unfortunately, died in January 2013. Anyway, he liked the Russo interview and said, "Why don't you send it to *Fangoria*?" I argued back saying, "No way, that's *Fangoria*, for heaven's sake. They're not going to publish anything by me." It was an automatic reaction—I held the magazine in such high regard. But Gary was very convincing so I contacted David Everitt who was co-editor with Bob Martin. He said, "Sure, send it and we'll take a look." I did and it was accepted. Gary was right! It appeared in issue number 32 and I was paid $200. Bear in mind that I was working for ABC Television during this entire period and I wasn't consciously looking to be a writer. It just kind of happened.

**JS: What were Bob Martin and David Everitt like?**

**TF:** Bob emulated the Forry Ackerman tradition to a degree. His magazine persona was like a mixture of John Zacherle and Forry Ackerman. David was the straight man, if you will. He certainly had the comedic chops, but he knew where to draw the line. Their combined personalities were perfectly suited for *Fangoria*'s pages. They worked in office space that was no bigger than a tiny bedroom and were constantly under deadline pressure. Extremely tight quarters—two desks and that was about it. Fun story: In those days, everything was done "old style" with paste-up mechanical layout boards. One day I was walking out of the office and to my left is garbage piled outside in the hall. Only it wasn't garbage per se. The original mechanical layout boards from the magazine were being discarded! I began digging through them and started to find the boards for my articles. I took as many of my own work that I could find. As far as I know, the only existing mechanical layout boards from *Fangoria* are the ones I rescued and perhaps one or two that Tim Lucas might have gotten from Tony Timpone.

**JS: That's a nice piece of history.**

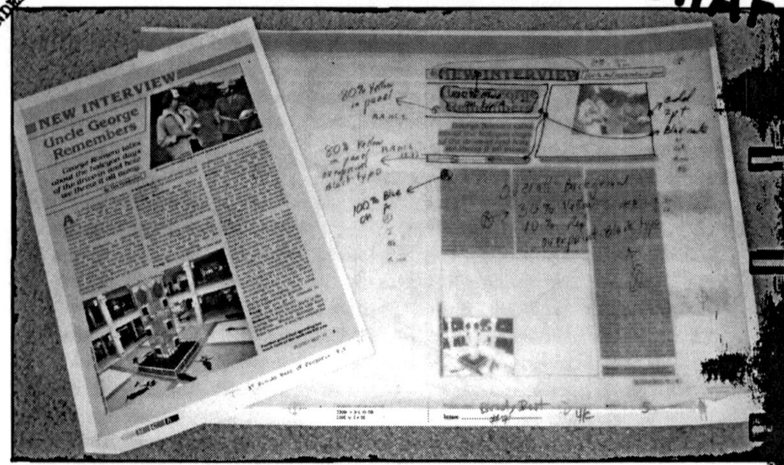


**TF:** Absolutely. Imagine if someone today said he had layout boards from *Famous Monsters of Filmland*!

**JS: What was more satisfying to you as an up and coming journalist—the fanzines or *Fangoria*?**

**TF:** They were both legitimate venues for expression. The fanzines permitted writing about things the prozines didn't, unless you pitched it and they said yes. For example, the second piece published in *Fangoria* was pitched. It's an interview with actor James Karen. They were like, "Who's James Karen?" At the time, James Karen was the Pathmark Man in the northeast. He was doing the region's TV, print and radio spot ads for a supermarket chain—he did them for twenty years. I said, "That's the Pathmark guy, but look at his credits. Look at all the movies he's done." They said, "OK." So, I got in touch with James Karen and he was happy to oblige. Up to that point he had no fan activity. He certainly had a flourishing career, but there was nothing going on at the fan level.

**JS: It was the exact opposite for me. I knew about his films, but I had no idea that he was doing commercials.**

**TF:** There were a couple of reasons for wanting to interview James Karen. One was that I'd first seen him in *Frankenstein Meets the Space Monster* in 1965. That movie experience stuck with me. I remember thinking—this is a ten year old, mind you—it was strange that the star's first name was a man's and his last was a woman's. I never forgot it or him. So now we skip from 1965 to the Spring of 1972 where I'm attending a Broadway play called *The Country Girl*. And who in the hell comes out on stage? James Karen. I couldn't believe it! I looked in my *Playbill* program and sure enough, there he is. I got home and I wrote him a fan letter, gushing about his performance in *Frankenstein Meets the Space Monster* and

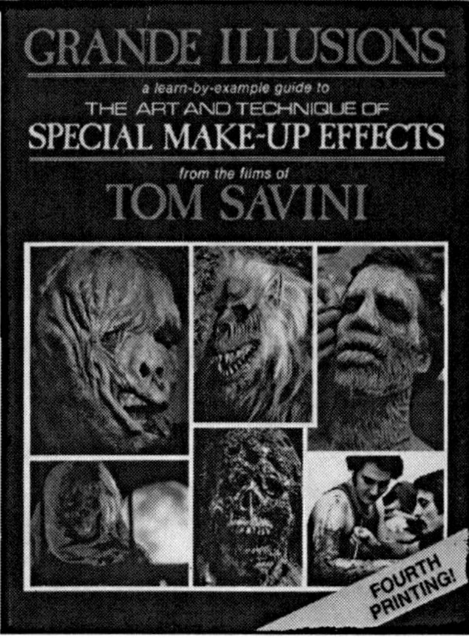


how much I enjoyed him in *The Country Girl*. He responded some months later with a letter thanking me for thanking him, and so forth. Handwritten—it was just wonderful. Now we skip from 1972 to 1983 when this fan geek contacted him for a *Fangoria* interview. We became friends and met up during one of his trips to New York to shoot Pathmark commercials. I presented the letter he'd written in 1972. I said, "Do you want to see some history between us?" He said, "I think I remember writing this." And I believed him. How many fan letters could James Karen have replied to by that point in his career in 1972? Now here's a fun aside to all of this… I married my wife in 1988 and come to learn that her father knew James Karen. How did he know him? He was the props guy on *The Country Girl*! I was a teenager sitting in that theatre in 1972 watching James Karen and my future father-in-law was working backstage. Crazy.

**JS: I've always been curious—how lucrative was writing for *Fangoria* in those days?**

**TF:** I've kept every pay stub. As I said, I was paid $200 for the Russo interview which was about average. It ticked up a little over time… $225… $250. Or, if you supplied photos or wrote a sidebar you were paid extra for those. I also used to get $50 residual checks when an article was translated and used overseas. Writing for *Fangoria* was never about the money because I had a very good job at ABC-TV. It was for the enjoyment, the friendships and all else that went with it.

**JS: When I was growing up, I'd read all of the bylines and think, "These guys have got the best job in the world."**

**TF:** The majority of the time it was pure pleasure so your childhood perception was correct. I always felt privileged to be there and in the company of such engaging people. I recall when the writing process changed a bit. After David Everitt left, Dave McDonnell—who was *Starlog*'s editor—began co-editing *Fangoria* with Tony. Prior to then you were basically on your own. Now if you were going to do an article, assignment sheets were issued that contained specific questions and angles you should pursue. Even though you'd have researched the topic yourself, you also had their questions and guidance. I liked it because you had specific

[L-R:] JOE KANE, TIM FERRANTE, TONY TIMPONE, AND THOMAS C. RAINONE. TAKEN AT TIM FERRANTE'S KEYPORT, NJ HOME IN 1992. PHOTO © 2013, TIM FERRANTE.

direction, but it meant more work for them to write it up. After Dave returned to *Starlog* full-time, J. Peter Orr joined Tony and later Michael Gingold.

**JS: So, how did your assignments work? How often were you able to successfully pitch ideas?**

**TF:** It was a mixture. When Bob Martin left, Tony came on board as co-editor with Everitt. I remember inviting Tony out to lunch. We became friends—in fact, I'm going to see him tomorrow. He already knew what I was capable of doing. I'd get a call, "Hey Tim, Troma's doing *The Toxic Avenger II* or whatever and we'd like someone to go out to the set." And other times, I'd say, "I love *Frankenstein Meets the Space Monster*. Can I do a full-blown retrospective?" You basically knew what you could reasonably suggest as an article to the get the go-ahead. One time I was asked to do a new George Romero interview for *The Bloody Best of Fangoria*. Instead of talking to Romero the idea was to cull his remarks from some press releases and then fashion an "interview" in Q&A format. I also used outtake commentary from—and even some that appeared in—his interview footage shot for a video that I produced and directed called *Drive-In Madness! The Video*. So while I never spoke directly with George for this new interview, his comments were genuine and fresh. I simply created the questions and edited the flow and structure.

**JS: Didn't another guy named Ferrante once write for *Fangoria*?**

**TF:** [laughs] Yes, there was! Anthony C. Ferrante's byline started to

THE NONEXISTANT FILM SOCIETY
PRESENTS
FREE
DAMN-FINO
THE PRE-ZINE
CRUDE AND RUDE
SCHIZOPHRENIC
ISSUE # 1

*DAMN-FINO*, VIRTUALLY UNKNOWN.

appear somewhere along the line. A friend said, "So, how long are you and Tony Timpone going to write under that pseudonym?" Can you believe it? There were some who thought we were collaborating and writing under a pen name. I said, "No, that's a real person and he's good!"

**JS: Wait a minute...**

**TF:** You're not confusing me with someone else, are you [laughs]? I never met the other Ferrante, although I would have liked to. His appearance wasn't too long before I stopped writing for *Fangoria*. Here's something you don't know: If you look back, there's an article about Bill Hinzman's and Jack Russo's movie called *The Majorettes*. It's written by Vinnie Johns. That's me [laughs]. Being close to Jack, I didn't want it to seem like a shill job by writing about his movie. I also created some letters to the editor under pseudonyms that Dave Everitt and Bob Martin published. The letters page had the occasional phony one that they'd write themselves. I'm not sure many people know about that.

**JS: You're a New York guy. What did you think of the New York fanzines that were coming out?**

**TF:** The beautiful thing about the east coast fanzines was that each had its own voice. You knew that if you read two or three, you got the skinny on something—they covered the 42nd Street beat, the neighborhood theaters and even some local TV. There were still sub-distributors in those days, which were small regional companies supplying screens with marginal movie product. 42nd Street was just a goldmine for that kind of thing. It was a wonderful time. I always looked forward to *Gore Gazette* because of Rick Sullivan's personality. Rick was—and I say this with admiration—out of his mind with balls of brass.

**JS: I love the time capsule element that those old New York zines have today.**

**TF:** There was no other way to communicate or to express oneself, so to speak. They were the printed blogs of their day with typewritten pages and sometimes completely handwritten! The only way to disseminate that material was by fax or mail. That was it. You had no other way of communicating unless you read it to somebody over the phone. Those fanzines are legitimate documents of record. They did fashion themselves around an era when these kinds of films were very important to us. And still are.

**JS: How did *Westerns... All'Italiana!* get started?**

**TF:** I created an Italian westerns fanzine called *Westerns... All'Italiana!* in 1983. I originally called it *Westerns All' Italia* until a friend in Italy corrected it. Thank heavens no issues were published with that cockeyed title. The first issue was mailed in April 1983. It was a niche interest for which there was very little—there was a book or two published overseas, but that was about it. The hope was to provide a place for likeminded enthusiasts to meet and share information about a dead genre for which there were still fans. Gary Dorst liked the idea so I recruited him. He's credited as co-editor in the first four issues and also contributed material. I just didn't want to do it entirely alone. After a while he was like, "You're doing most of the work and I'm sharing in the credit. You don't need me, you know what to do!" Those who responded went crazy—they couldn't believe there was someone else who liked Italian westerns. Several friendships were forged as a result. There were only fifty hand-numbered copies of the first one and I overprinted some as file copies and freebies. I'd already done two single issues and a double issue for numbers 3 and 4 when Tom Betts wrote me and said, "Hey, I love this stuff. How about if

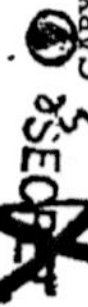

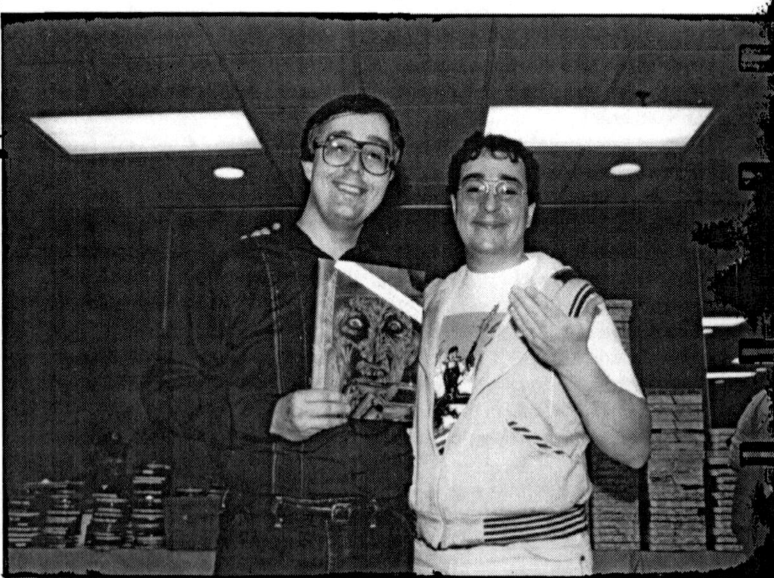

GARY SVEHLA [LEFT] AND TIM FERRANTE, CIRCA MID-EIGHTIES © 2013, TIM FERRANTE.

we do this together and put the issues out faster?" That sounded good to me so we alternated doing them. Every other issue would be mailed by me from New York while the others would be mailed from Tom in California. He took it on full-time in 1987 and is still doing it, only now it's a blog that's updated daily. Yes, daily. God bless him because *WAI!* would have died years ago had been left up to me.

**JS: How were you finding the films at the time?**

**TF:** It was difficult, but there were instances where some of the common titles were available on videocassette like *Bad Man's River* and *God's Gun*. 16mm film was important and it was through that medium we found things that were very obscure such as *My Name Is Pecos*. There were film collector shows for that sort of thing. You'd find all kinds of odd movies, posters, pressbooks and stills, which was just the type of material I needed for illustrating the zine. I don't know if you're familiar with a person named Jerry Beck, the animation historian. He worked at the MGM building which was a block up from the ABC building where I worked. Sometimes he would get 16mm prints out of the MGM library and I would run after-hour screenings of Italian westerns at ABC for my friends. Everyone's gone home, and I'm running stuff like *The Ugly Ones*. As the worldwide home video market expanded and more and more movies were cropping up we'd get copies of westerns that were only available overseas. It was an exciting time of discovery and learning. Today, the genre and its participants are revered and have been integrated into popular culture. From fifty copies of the first *Westerns... All'Italiana!* thirty years ago to Quentin Tarantino's *Django Unchained* on movie screens worldwide. Amazing, isn't it?

**JS: What did you think of what Craig Ledbetter was doing?**

**TF:** I've known Craig for a very long time, although we've been out of touch for a good twenty years or more. Craig is an incredibly driven and smart man. I've always admired him and everything he was able to accomplish. As you know, he published *Hi-Tech Terror*. There was a three-issue period where he dropped out of it and I published those.

WESTERNS ALL' ITALIANA

Volume 1
Number 1
no. FREE COPY of 50

FIFTY COPIES ONLY... UNLIKE *DJANGO UNCHAINED*.

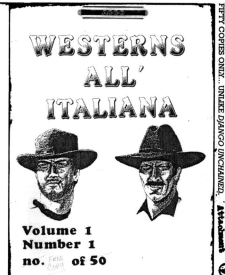

RECORDED & INDEXED

# TIM FERRANTE

## DRIVE-IN MADNESS

DRAFT

A TIM FERRANTE ISSUE OF *HI-TECH TERROR.*

Established in May 1985 at Richardson, Texas by Craig Ledbetter, Editor Emeritus and Contributor.

HI-TECH TERROR is published every six weeks at – P.O. Box [illegible], Keyport, NJ [illegible] Editor: TIM FERRANTE. Subscription rates are $[illegible]-(USA & Canada) $10.00-(overseas) for twelve (12) issues. This is issue # 15 – September 1986.

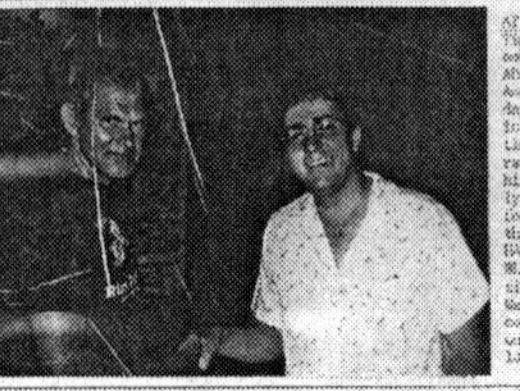

AT LEFT: HI-TECH TERROR honcho Tim Ferrante (on right), hob-nobs with the legendary AL ADAMSON on a recent trip to Los Angeles. Adamson is busy these days tending to his [illegible] in Hollywood and spending most time in Utah where he owns a ranch. Adamson, best known for his ability to shoot films quickly and under budget, chatted [illegible] about the days of making those drive-in naturals like [illegible], ANGELS WILD WOMEN, BLACK SAMURAI, and the thrice-titled BLOOD OF GHASTLY HORROR. We here at H-TT wish Al the continued success he has achieved outside the film business and look forward to his return!!!

Thanx go out to everyone who kindly dropped a letter of welcome and back-patting. I appreciate all the good wishes and hope you enjoy this H-TT installment as much as you did my first go-round. As of this writing, Craig Ledbetter tells me he misses doing this 'zine but is fighting back more everyday to wrestle this bugger away from me. Thankfully he has found some time to devote to fandom during this period of economic turmoil and has a fab review this edition on [illegible]!!

Everyone may take notice that I did not include the selling price this time of the tapes reviewed. Since vid companies are constantly playing yo-yo games with list prices, I thought it useless to list them. If anyone finds it bother to not have the retail price listed along with the review, let me know and they'll be back next issue!

And much success to contributor [illegible] who reports he is currently writing a horror – made for home video – movie. [illegible] there'll be lots of skin & blood!! [illegible]

Enclosed once again is an IMAGINE, INC. flyer. The advertised book has gone into 2nd printing and is IN STOCK! Hey! I gotta make some money outta this ... !

**JS: How did that come about?**

**TF:** *Hi-Tech Terror* was coming out fast and regular… and then something happened. My recollection may be wrong, but I think it had to do with Craig changing jobs. He was going to postpone or give up doing any new issues. I said, "Don't do that. Everybody loves it." He said, "I can't do it anymore. Not now, anyway." I told him that I'd fill in until he was capable of coming back because it was just too good to lose. So I did three issues. Then he said, "Hey—I'm free. I can do it again." He came back but ran into a small problem; the readership perceived my issues as being better than his were and complained about it. See, Craig put together whatever he had to in order to get out an issue. They weren't pretty, but no one cared. Mine were better graphically, but that was all. The subject matter and the writers were still the same. So all of a sudden a prettier fanzine was more important than content, which made no sense! I was always this "it has to look nice" freak. And I was putting pictures of myself in it at the *Amityville Horror* set in Toms River, NJ and stupid stuff like that. [laughs] Who knew that it was undermining Craig? I treated it as if it were my own, but still knowing he would return at some point. So he got complaints from people because it was back to what they originally liked and now decided they no longer liked. He said, "Look, this is what it is. I can't do it as nice as Ferrante!" It didn't affect our friendship in the slightest. I felt terrible about it though. But the joke was on everybody because Craig just continued on and on and reached greater successes. As a result of all it, I separately published a one-issue zine called *Awe-Filled Clunkers Funzine* which I sent to all of the *Hi-Tech Terror* subscribers for free.

**JS: I've never seen that!**

**TF:** I'll send you an issue. I know one fanzine you don't have documented—*Damn-Fino The Pre-Zine*. There was only one completed issue. It was published by John W. Donaldson in New York City. John was also the film editor on *Raiders of the Living Dead*. He made me a copy and perhaps a dozen others. Few saw and read it—it was so limited. And

good! John has an enormous knowledge of movies. There was a second issue, but only half the pages were finished and it was never distributed, although I do have a copy. *Damn-Fino The Pre-Zine*, yes indeed. It was a New York fanzine, virtually unknown.

THE NONEXISTENT FILM SOCIETY PRESENTS
DAMN-FINO
THE PRE-ZINE
ISSUE 2
'Joey, what the hell happened?'
NEW YORK POST
MORE REVIEWS
MORE ADS
MORE BULLSHIT
SINGING SATAN'S SONG
ASSASSINIO AL CIMITERO ETRUSCO

**JS: You were the last person to interview Duane Jones. Could you tell me a little about that?**

**TF:** More like the only person! Duane Jones was never formally interviewed about *Night of the Living Dead*. He wouldn't grant any. There's a very brief mid-eighties video interview that he had done for *Entertainment Tonight* as I recall, but it wasn't specifically about *Night of the Living Dead* and it's ridiculously short. He didn't discuss that film with anyone for publication. If he did, I'd love to know when and where it was published because nothing else has ever surfaced since 1968.

**JS: What was your impression of him?**

**TF:** It's a Sunday afternoon, December 13, 1987, and my wife and I were at his home on the campus of the College at Old Westbury on Long Island. Duane walked into the room—I describe it in Joe Kane's *Night of the Living Dead* book—he walked into the room, and his presence was immediately felt. It was remarkable. He had a way of carrying himself, presenting himself—you sensed you were in the presence of a unique human being. And it didn't have a damn thing to do with him being in the movie. He was a lovely, gentle man. It's sad that he died so soon after interviewing him although we did have a second phone conversation about a month later. It wasn't related to the movie, though. We were just talking. We really liked him and we knew he liked us. It was such a memorable afternoon, John.

**JS: Why do you think he was so guarded about talking about *Night of the Living Dead*?**

**TF:** As I said, whenever he was approached to do interviews he always refused. To give this some context, I'd just written a series of articles called "Where The Living Dead Are Buried" and interviewed many of its actors. *Fangoria* published the first color photographs from *Night of the Living Dead* thanks to slides I got from Bill Hinzman. But Duane was a key missing

RECORDED & INDEXED

DRAFT

piece... like trying to find the Ark of the Covenant. Then Tony learned where he was because another *Fangoria* writer was trying and trying to get an interview. Tony said, "Duane Jones is out on Long Island, but he won't grant an interview." So I called Jack Russo who was my business partner at the time in Imagine, Inc. If anyone could sway Duane, Jack could. He said, "Well, I'll call him and ask. I haven't talked to him in a long time." He called and Duane agreed. The only reason that interview ever happened was thanks to Jack's relationship with him and his vouching for me. Now, why was he so guarded? He didn't want his entire life's work to be defined by being Ben from *Night of the Living Dead*. It came through in everything he said—he was Duane Jones, a person with so much more to offer this world than the fact that he portrayed Ben. He refused to suffer anyone who perceived him as only that. The movie was a sliver of time in his life. Nevertheless, he knew his contribution to it was important. He said, "I know what this movie means to people." He appreciated and understood it, but expected people to relate to him as a person, which they did because that's how he carried himself. He had a high regard for himself and other people as complete human beings. He was so intelligent and such an arresting man.

**JS: With that in mind, how did you approach the interview?**

**TF:** Well, I had several questions ready and the only thing I could do was play it by ear and see where things went. I mean, I didn't know him. I'd no idea what kind of a person he was and it could have gone downhill pretty

"AWE-FILLED CLUNKERS"

[illegible]

Pictured here is your humble editor (on right, natch) with the man who uttered those words of deep wisdom, "They're coming to get you, Barbara!" Yup, that's Russell Streiner, better known as 'Johnny' in Night of the Living Dead.

Currently heading up a production facility in Pittsburgh, Streiner is active as ever in television and motion picture development projects. Soon to be seen in The Majorettes, he's optimistic that production in Pittsburgh will continue to flourish.

A true gentleman, Russ Streiner is the person to watch in months to come!

Good seeing you, 'Johnny!'

As promised some months back, this free issue of a fanzine by Tim Ferrante is now in your genre-hungry hands. No, we're not Hi-Tech Terror this time out. My good friend Craig Ledbetter is back to pumping out that baby. While I intended to produce a 'zine on a regular basis ... charge subscriptions ... do all the things you'd expect, I discovered that time is so short these days that I would probably not be able to handle it. Common excuse with 'zine publishers. The fact remained that I did promise you all a fanzine in my farewell issue of H-TT. And here it is.

This is the only issue you folks will receive of AWE-FILLED CLUNKERS. It is a o-t-o (one-time-only) offering to fulfill what I said I would do. I simply hate 'zines that promise something ... and don't deliver. I ask that you enjoy this sure-fired collectors edition as you would any other oddity that claims to be a sure-fired collectors edition!

Might as well give Imagine, Inc. a plug here. Our book Drive-In Madness is in the process of typesetting and production is going strong. This much-awaited volume will certainly satisfy your unholy cravings for degenerate reading. We are also putting the finishing touches on a neat merchandise catalog tailored for the cheesy horror/sci-fi/fantasy/lunatic crowd. There's more to tell, but why spoil the damned things. By the way, this 'zine you hold is not a product of Imagine, Inc. While I may be the Vice-President, I am also a fan of high magnitude.

Let's get on with whatever you'll find in here. Again, don't expect anything of razor-edged brilliance. Don't expect fandoms top writers. And don't expect to get another issue of this [illegible]! It's free, you [illegible]!

Fondly,

Tim

AWE-FILLED VIDEO MAYHEM TO COME!

Vidmark nails the release of John Russo's horror gem, MIDNIGHT! A hefty $79.95 price tag for you vid tappers! .... FRIDAY VIDMARK LIVES is among us from Paramount ... VidAmerica gutsily releases the plodding documentary, IN SEARCH OF NOAH'S ARK. This snooze-inducing crapper purportedly shows an actual photo of what may be the real Ark .... MCA scores some points with the home appearance of CURSE OF THE WEREWOLF, 1962 PHANTOM OF THE OPERA and THE EVIL OF FRANKENSTEIN .... [illegible] back, Magnum dumped SHOCKING ASIA II on the vid market but the diamond that had gone un-noticed by many was an imported Italo-war pic called THE DESERT TIGERS! Eric Mache reports that this title is heavy on nazi perversities and slim on battle scenes! Claims that Gordon Mitchell steals the show! .... Video City Prods. adds WAR VICTIMS to their vastly twisted catalog. It's a look behind enemy lines during WWII. They'll also have on the shelves S.S. LOVE CAMP #27 and [illegible] PLANET .... Fangoria topper Kerry O'Quinn takes the SCREAM GREATS vid line and plunges full tilt away from the fantasy side of the genre by releasing SCREAM GREATS VOL. II, SATANISM AND WITCHCRAFT. Excerpts from themed films like THE OMEN and ROSEMARY'S BABY are included in real-life studies of cult followers. Big disappointment after the terrif VOL. I on Savini .... And applause to [illegible] Electronics of New York for the commercially available Video Copyguard Killer! They've developed a handy device to eliminate the annoying Macrovision from rented tapes so we can make our jail term deserving dubs. Price for this legal "black box" is a smooth $199.95 (sugg. retail) .... [illegible] instructional release, HOW TO [illegible] ON YOUR DADDY'S [illegible] due out soon.

"Uh...let me guess. That was the two-by-four...no, wait. The baseball bat! No...no! I got it! The axe handle, right?!"

We all agree on certain things in this crowd. Sure, Ed Wood was a miserable filmmaker. BEAST OF YUCCA FLATS is a piss-poor film ... as is CREEPING TERROR. They're all in league with the MONSTER FROM THE OCEAN FLOOR, BLOOD OF GHASTLY HORROR and Larry Buchanan messes. However, a little viewed stinker titled MANOS, THE HANDS OF FATE rarely is listed with this group of genre rejects. Has anyone out there ever seen MANOS? If not, you owe it to yourself to take a peek. It is, hands down, THE WORST FILM I HAVE EVER SEEN! FREAKING, THE WORST!! I assure every one of you that it beats CREEPING TERROR and the rest of 'em by a country mile! I'd like to hear from anyone who has seen MANOS. It's available from SINISTER CINEMA, Box 777, Pacifica, CA 94044. Or I can supply one to whoever is curious for a minor fee. Believe me gang, this is one film that you won't sit through all at once. Let's hear from all you MANOS devotee's!

*AWE-FILLED CLUNKERS* NUMBER 1 IN A SERIES OF 1.

THE GUARDED DUANE JONES IN *NIGHT OF THE LIVING DEAD.*

quickly. Even though I was nervous, the primary goal was not to blow it because that interview was a very big deal. As it turned out, we were able to discuss anything and everything. He was gracious, funny, sincere… oh, it was just as wonderful as you could imagine. There are several places in the tapes where he asked that I shut off the recorder which I did, of course. I regret not recalling what "off the record" comments we made. You know, I could be wrong, John. I could be completely wrong. Maybe he knew he was terminally ill and this was an opportunity for him to at last discuss the movie. Maybe he wanted to share what he knew before it was too late. That's a possibility, knowing how insightful he was, but again, it's personal conjecture. Unfortunately, he didn't allow any photographs to be taken of him. A very disappointing development, although he did sign a *Night of the Living Dead* lobby card that I'd brought along.

**JS: I first heard the audio excerpts on the Elite Entertainment laserdisc.**

**TF:** Vini Bancalari from Elite said, "Tim…you have that interview. We'd really like to include it on the laserdisc." So I sat down with the cassette tapes. Now, bear in mind that I'm the only person who has this content… two hours and fifty-some minutes of conversation with Duane Jones. I set about cutting it down to forty minutes or so of bits and pieces. What you hear on that laserdisc and subsequent DVD releases is about seventeen minutes of those bits. It's as much as I've publicly released and licensed of that interview. I've often thought of making a few hundred CDs of the complete interview and just selling them to whomever was interested. It would need to be a three CD set because it's so long!

**JS: You were business partners with Russo for a long time. How did that happen?**

**TF:** I was introduced to him through my friend Sam Sherman at

RECORDED & INDEXED
DRAFT

When the DEAD
Drink the BLOOD of the LIVING!
MIDNIGHT
If You Have a Weak Stomach - Don't Come!
an Independent-International presentation

Independent-International Pictures. Sam and his partner, Dan Kennis, were the executive producers and distributor of Jack's movie *Midnight*. Shortly thereafter Jack and I became friends as a result of the *Splatter Times* interview. Imagine, Inc. was co-founded by James Aiello and Bob Michelucci. It specialized in publishing genre movie books. It had four titles in release when Aiello announced he wanted a $15,000 buyout of his majority share. So, Jack said, "Tim—if you and I each put in five grand and my attorney Andy Schifino puts in five grand, we can buy Aiello's controlling interest in Imagine, Inc." I knew of the company, of course, and thought, "Wow! For five grand, I can own a piece of a publishing company!" So I did.

**JS: What kind of involvement did Tom Savini have with Imagine, Inc?**

**TF:** He was given ten per cent of Imagine, Inc. if my recollection is correct, as part payment for *Grande Illusions*, the company's very first and most successful book. He wasn't involved in the day to day business. He was too busy making movies, anyway. He was always there for us whenever we needed him, though. Whether it was the company marketing his brand or making himself available when he could. I didn't have much interaction with him because I didn't live in Pittsburgh and he was always busy. Imagine, Inc. was owned by five people during this period and today it sounds like a cast list for *The Sopranos*: Russo, Ferrante, Michelucci, Schifino and Savini. Anyway, we'd all become partners in a publishing company that had existing debt, but it also had a book that was ready to be printed—*Forrest J Ackerman: Famous Monster of Filmland*. Bob was the art director for everything we did and he had already laid it out so it was just sitting there waiting for us. Forry's book was the first one published under the new ownership.

**JS: How did Imagine, Inc. grow and evolve?**

**TF:** Imagine, Inc. never really got out of the red from the time I bought

"ADIÓS, SABATA"
COLOR United Artists
SELMUR PICTURES
"a minute to pray, a second to die!"
EASTMAN COLOR
fast guns finish first...
dead out!
ANY GUN CAN PLAY
EASTMANCOLOR and SCOPE
BYRNES-ROLAND-HILTON
and introducing KAREEN O'HARA
Presented by GOLDEN EAGLE FILMS, LTD
Released by RAF INDUSTRIES, INC.
"UP THE MACGREGORS!"
A COLUMBIA PICTURES RELEASE
"THE UGLY ONES"
COLOR by Deluxe
United Artists
VOLUME 1
NUMBER 2
No. of 50.
WESTERNS ALL' ITALIANA
JUST TURNED SEVENTEEN!!! JUST TURNED KILLER!! AND RUNNING FOR HIS LIFE!!!
A FEW BULLETS MORE
TOTALVISION and EASTMANCOLOR
VAN HEFLIN • GILBERT ROLAND
KLAUS KINSKI • GEORGE HILTON
SARAH ROSS
THE RUTHLESS FOUR
TECHNICOLOR TECHNISCOPE
FINALLY THEY MEET and THE HILLS RUN RED
TECHNICOLOR TECHNISCOPE
UNITED ARTISTS
CAMERON MITCHELL is
Minnesota Clay
The sightless gunman... who killed by sound!
TECHNICOLOR & WIDESCREEN
ANTHONY QUINN
FRANCO NERO
'DEAF SMITH & JOHNNY EARS'
TECHNICOLOR
A bullet doesn't care who it kills!
A Bullet For The General
IN COLOR
AN AVCO EMBASSY FILM
TODAY WE KILL ...TOMORROW WE DIE!
COLOR
RICHARD HARRISON
VENGEANCE
PG
JOSEPH COTTEN
ALBERT BAND'S Production of
THE HELLBENDERS
IN COLOR

into it to the time I left, which was about five years. We always owed someone money… including ourselves! That's not said with any rancor or embarrassment because that's common for many businesses. You carry the debt and when receivables come in you manage the money to pay some debt, pay some rent and so on. You do what you have to do. We put out trading card sets, more books and the *Drive-In Madness! The Video* on VHS. We even had a store for a while in the Green Tree section of Pittsburgh called Just Imagine. I was extremely fortunate to have been involved with a group of such talented people.

**JS: Could you tell me a little about the *Drive-In Madness!* video?**

**TF:** Bill George had written a portion of and compiled material from other authors for a book entitled *Drive-In Madness! The Jiggle Movies*. It was the most anticipated book that never happened even though it was laid out—twice! It was being delayed for a variety of reasons. We felt we had to do something to get people off of our backs asking about *Drive-In Madness!* We had to put something out and decided on a feature length video program which I wrote, produced and directed. It featured trailers and TV spots that I had in my personal collection as well as newly shot interviews. I enlisted help from everyone and anyone I knew. James Karen did the narration and you'll see Donald Farmer's name on the credits—he provided a crew of three guys to shoot the Forry Ackerman, Bobbie Bresee and Linnea Quigley segments at the Ackermansion. It was a wonderful group of people and friends who helped out and did things for nothing or next to nothing. Most of the production money was spent for travel and

MORE FROM *AWE-FILLED CLUNKERS.*

editing. It cost less than $10,000 to make. Anyone interested in more of the history about *Drive-In Madness! The Video* will find it at www.timferrante.com.

**JS: Do you mind saying a few words about Forry Ackerman?**

**TF:** What I admired most was that he completely understood the seriousness of his presence in the pages of the Warren magazines. He was speaking primarily to children and teens, and he earned their respect, admiration and trust. We didn't call him "Uncle Forry" for nothing. And best of all? If you ever did have the chance to meet him, he never disrespected the relationship he'd created from afar. He didn't disappoint you and was everything you expected and hoped him to be. I mean, you loved him before you met him and you loved him even more after you met him! How rare is that in our lives… that our perception of a person actually matches the reality? His passion for the fantastic was genuine and he projected it wherever he went. I loved being around him and was fortunate to have shared in a very small portion his life.

**JS: What are you doing these days?**

**TF:** I'm mostly writing for Joe Kane's the *Phantom of the Movies VideoScope*. We co-founded the magazine with our wives, Nancy and Jacqueline, in September 1992. The first issue went out in January, 1993. We published fourteen bi-monthly editions as a twenty-page newsletter. In June 1994 Joe and Nancy assumed full ownership and have turned it into the vastly improved product that you see today. I occasionally write for some online sites such as Chris Poggiali's *Temple of Schlock*. I do voiceover work for the coin-operated amusement game industry and recently did the narration for a documentary on Italian western actor Craig Hill for a DVD company called Wild

DRIVE-IN
MADNESS!
The Video
HOSTED BY...
James Karen
George A. Romero
Bobbie Bresee
Tom Savini
Linnea Quigley
Sam Sherman
Forrest Ackerman
Russo
Popcorn
THE MOST FUN YOU'LL EVER HAVE IN THE BACKSEAT OF YOUR LIVING ROOM!

DRAFT

Original WAI! Art: Richard Landwehr Photo copyright 2013 Tim Ferrante WAI! artwork copyright 2013

East Productions. It's owned by my friend Eric Mache and his partner Ally Lamaj. I've also produced two horror soundtrack CDs in recent years: *Dracula vs. Frankenstein* and *Mad Doctor of Blood Island*. I stay busy with fun things.

**JS: Joe Kane edited the *Monster Times*.**

**TF:** That's another beautiful thing. I used to read the *Monster Times* during my high school years and see Joe's name all the time. So, we fast forward to the mid-eighties when he's a columnist at the *New York Daily News* writing as the Phantom of the Movies. I would read every column, of course. We happened to have a mutual friend named Mike Maimone who is the audio engineer on Rush Limbaugh's radio program. Mike introduced us and that launched a friendship that's lasted over twenty-five years [laughs]! He and Nancy live right down the highway. What boggles the mind is that Jack Russo, Joe Kane, Sam Sherman, Tony Timpone, and all of the other folks I've mentioned… they're all personal friends. But I'm a fan of them, too! How wonderful is that?

# Chapter Thirteen

# Chas. Balun

## A Deeper Shade of Red

DEEP
RED
Delivers

Deep Red Delivers
THE OFFICIAL DEEP RED SWEATSHIRT!

FANTACO ENTERPRISES, INC.
21 CENTRAL AVENUE
ALBANY, NEW YORK 12210
TELEPHONE: (518) 463-3667 FAX: (518) 463-0090

# Chas. Balun

## A Deeper Shade of Red

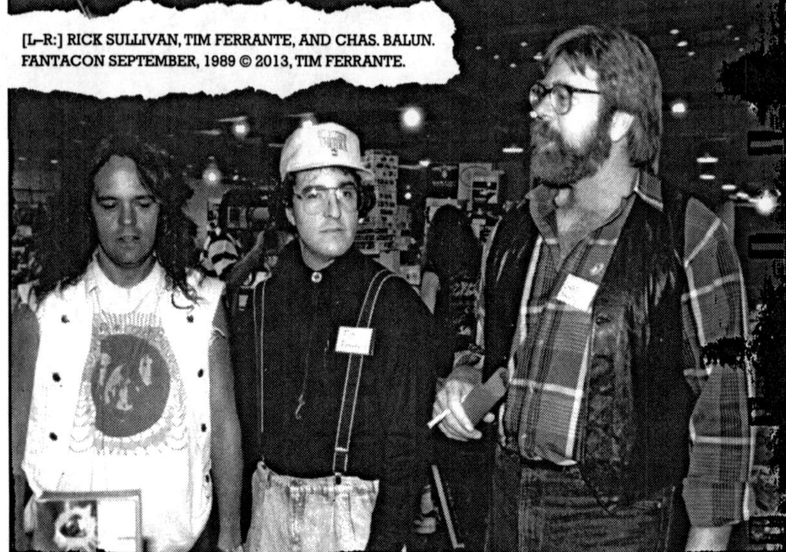

[L–R:] RICK SULLIVAN, TIM FERRANTE, AND CHAS. BALUN. FANTACON SEPTEMBER, 1989 © 2013, TIM FERRANTE.

Let's go back a little bit, shall we? In 1988, I was obsessed with horror movies. My friends and I would take everything in. We snuck into theaters to see the latest horror shit (and a lot of it was), and even suffered through the opening credits of *Salsa* before the ushers turned their backs and left us with a do-or-die run to the next screening of *Evil Dead 2*. You know the drill: Buy a ticket to the latest PG-13 slopfest and then scurry into the darkness of the neighboring room without being seen.

Sometimes we got caught, sometimes we didn't, but I don't ever remember being turned away when we were. The ushers would simply shrug, smile, and let us in. One afternoon, we sat hidden in the dark for two hours before *The Horror Show* began its first matinee screening. The movie sucked, but hell—at least it starred Brion (*Blade Runner*) James.

The Summer of 1989 will remain special to me for two reasons: I met my first "real" girlfriend, and (more importantly) I discovered a magazine called *Deep Red*. *Deep Red* was edited by a guy named Chas. Balun, a name I'd recognized from the pages of *Fangoria* and *Gorezone*. I'd seen an ad in *Fangoria* for the thing and decided to order a few back issues. Let's just say that I was completely blown away. As the kid in *Shogun Assassin* so eloquently stated, "That's when everything changed."

I didn't know it then, but every word, every sentence, every issue of the magazine was slowly worming its way into my brain. Balun was a damn fine scribe, and he assembled an amazing crew of writers and artists and let

them have their way with the page.

There was Steve Bissette, who is interviewed in these very pages. I was aware of him through his artwork in *Swamp Thing*. Who knew that he was a journalist as well? His mammoth interview and essay on Buddy Giovinazzo's *Combat Shock* sent me searching through every video store in (and out of) town until I finally found a copy. There was Dennis Daniel (also interviewed within), who would later write the definitive history of *Famous Monsters of Filmland* magazine. These people were my heroes. *Deep Red* had Italian correspondents, Dutch correspondents, German correspondents! There was coverage on Jörg (*Nekromantik*) Buttgeriet, Jim (*Street Trash*) Muro, Ruggero (*Cannibal Holocaust*) Deodato—none of it written in a pandering PR-suck-up style. Hell, the general public wouldn't even have a clue what to do with this stuff. These were our movies, and Chas. was there in front of us all, leading the charge. The writing was real, rough, and ready. And it was revolutionary; nobody else was even bothering trying to spell Dario Argento or Lucio Fulci, yet alone attempting to dissect and analyze their films.

I'd literally stare at every issue for hours on end. I loved the attitude, the mystery of the films discussed, and the bold sense of, "You're one of us, so hop on board and enjoy the ride!" Most of all, I loved Chas. Balun's writing.

The years went on and *Deep Red* folded. Balun's work became scarcer and scarcer, but every time he published something, I snapped it up right away. And even when he was at his most cynical, the underlying message was crystal clear: We're all in this together, and the seeds have been sewn. It's your turn to go out and do something.

DEEP RED
NO. 6 MARCH, 1989
£ 2.50 U.K. $3.50
GOBLIN: MUSIC TO BLEED BY
SPLATTER ART
DIRECTOR'S FORUM
FOREIGN GORE
SPAWN 2
NINTH & HELL STREET
FantaCon 88
Cruelty, Carnage & Christianity


Fast forward to the cold Winter of 2010. I got the bad word that Chas. Balun passed away on December 18, 2009. Cancer. He lost his final battle with a beast that had hunted him for many, many years. I just sat there, stunned. A towering mountain seemed to have been leveled, just like that. Or had it been?

I first read the following paragraph way back in high school. I've read it again and again hundreds of times throughout the years:

"So get started, kids. Write it. Draw it. Film it and believe it.

## A DEEPER SHADE OF RED

We're a hyper-enthusiastic, devoted, ofttimes fanatical bunch who need to discover the hidden powers lurking within ourselves. Gustave Flaubert said, 'Nothing great is ever done without fanaticism. Fanaticism is religion. It is faith, burning faith, the faith that works miracles.' We've got the former in spades, my friends, but where is our faith? Must it always lie with others?"

You heard the man. Let's show some fuckin' guts and paint this town *RED*.

The following interview was conducted via telephone in August of 2001.

---

**JOHN SZPUNAR: What came first, the writing or the drawing?**

**CHAS. BALUN:** Well, I was always a painter and illustrator who wrote—not the other way around. The art always came first. I just sort of got into writing because I was always a witty smart-ass and it was just way easier to write than it was to paint or draw.

**JS: And when did the drawing start?**

**CB:** Oh, around kindergarten [laughs]. I started right off. That's what I did—that was always my little thing, right from the get-go.

**JS: Portrait of the artist as a young man: Who were your major influences?**

**CB:** I usually fell back into the old masters school of art and painting. That classical, realistic approach to things. Whether it was a Rembrandt or Vermeer, or a da Vinci. All of the top-level talents were an inspiration to me as a kid because they could just draw so well! I was just so impressed with that. Anyone who could just really draw in a realistic manner… But, I started off with the "learn to draw" courses on television. I bought one of those kits and sat in front of the TV set with my charcoal stick and eraser. You know, I followed the lessons.

CHAS. BALUN'S MONSTERFOLIO

**JS: This eventually led to some underground comix work.**

**CB:** Oh yeah. I used to go to the San Diego comic convention over here. It's been going for over thirty years. I was going to it

back in the hippy days, essentially. I'd go down and get stoned with the *Zap Comix* artists and meet all of those guys. Rick Griffin and Victor Moscoso. So, some friends and I came out with our own comics. What was cool was that all of us worked in the graphics section at Golden West College at one time. Besides Jack Lewis and myself, one of our other co-conspirators was Mike Gabriel. He went on to direct *Rescuers Down Under* and *Pocahontas*. He turned into Mr. Disney superstar! But we did a bunch of issues of *Mighty High Comix* and *Spaz Comix*. We contributed to some other stuff, as well.

**JS: All self-published?**

**CB:** Actually, George DiCaprio was an old friend of ours. He was one of the major distributors of *Spaz Comix*. Of course, he's the father of Leonardo DiCaprio. He probably isn't pushing underground comics out of the trunk of a beat up '59 Dodge anymore…

**JS: Leonardo DiCaprio said that his father inadvertently turned him on to S. Clay Wilson.**

**CB:** Oh, shit yeah! He was one of the major comix distributors on the West Coast.

**JS: What were your impressions of the underground guys?**

**CB:** Well, I met Rick Griffin, Gilbert Shelton, Victor Moscoso, Paul Mavrides… they were just fun guys. Sure, they were party-hearty type guys, but shit! They could also wield a mean pen.

**JS: A lot of those guys have cited EC Comics as a major influence. Did they have a similar affect on you?**

**CB:** Well, I used to buy them. But I don't think they made that big of an impression on me. Except for Jack Davis, who drew the best. You know, the stories… as cool as they were, you'd read the first two panels and you could always guess how the ending would be. I appreciate them in a historical context. They were an important step in the pulp fiction/exploitation cinema link. Stuff like *Creepshow* and *Tales from the Crypt*. The anthology series that spawned in movies

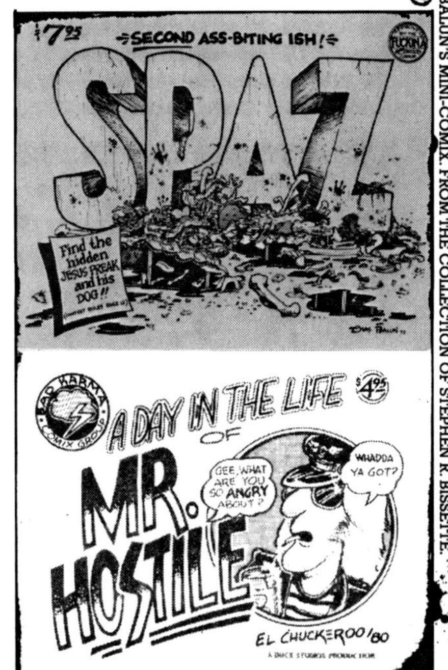


TWO OF BALUN'S MINI-COMIX. FROM THE COLLECTION OF STEPHEN R. BISSETTE.

## A Deeper Shade of Red

sort of came from a comic book source. They were hugely influential. Whether they were really good or not is another matter.

**JS: Where did your obsession with horror films come from?**

**CB:** Oh, *King Kong*, of course. I saw that so many times that my nose would be bleeding. I grew up in the early days of television. There weren't that many stations. Here in LA, there was the Million Dollar Movie on Channel 9, which was one of the major local stations. In those days, they didn't show, like, fifteen movies a week. They showed one movie every night at 7:30. And then twice on Saturday and once on Sunday. They got maximum mileage out of the films they showed. And *King Kong* was one that I would watch every night. Three times on the weekend! I would just be utterly amazed. That's just a magical film. It's held up for seventy years. It creates its own special world, where you go, "Yeah! Punch my ticket! Count me in here!"

**JS: So that led to your initial fandom—**

**CB:** Well, it was a circuitous route there, John. It didn't just go from *King Kong* to splatter films. I had a long side trip in the sixties and early seventies. That's when I came of age, when the pigs were coming onto the campus and thumping your professors. So monster movies and comic books kind of took a back seat to overthrowing the government and getting ready for the revolution. All of that shit. The revolution didn't come and Pig Nation wasn't overthrown… I got back into horror movies.

**JS: You've said that things really started to open up for you with *Dawn of the Dead*, *Friday the 13th*, and *Alien*.**

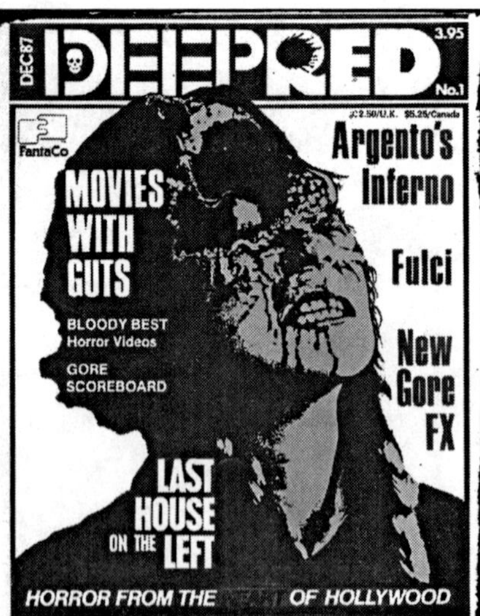


**CB:** Well, I was always a fan of *Texas Chain Saw Massacre*. That was always the big influence. But I think things broke open in '79 and eighties. That's kind of when things really turned. *Alien* and *Dawn of the Dead* really showed us something that we hadn't seen before. *Dawn of the Dead*—that was just so extreme when it came out. I was fairly shocked by the explicit violence that it had. So you could obviously see that the tide was turning. Then, when *Friday the 13th* came out, it was just this mainstream phenomenon. But it actually worked. I

mean, the ending is terrific. The first time you see it—it's just a great chair jumper. It's set up and manipulated so well. So you could see that people were putting a new spin on the old stories. *Friday the 13th* was nothing but a rehash of Mario Bava's *Bay of Blood*. But it worked. It wasn't an Italian film, it had recognizable stars… I think it just tapped into a nerve and into something that was waiting to happen. Maybe it was a barrage of films. It was *Halloween*, *Friday the 13th*, *Dawn of the Dead*, it was *Alien*. And now, when you look at how many films are the bastard progeny of them… it would be triple figures. How many films were spawned from *Friday the 13th*, *Halloween*, and *Nightmare on Elm Street*? That's like thirty films right there! Yet alone all the Prowlers and the Grad Nights! They kind of just found the template in 1980. And then refused to let go of it.

**JS: You mentioned Mario Bava. When did you first become aware of the Italians?**

**CB:** After I started to get really bored with American horror films. They were just repeating themselves. I just started getting back to the roots. I saw *Suspiria*, *Bay of Blood*, found Ricardo Freda—even our humble Joe D'Amato. Theirs was a product that seemed more directly aimed at horror film fans.

**JS: Why do you think that was?**

**CB:** I don't think the Italians have the pop sensibility about the horror film that we do.

**JS: Well, we're talking about two totally different cultures.**

**CB:** Right. We have to have hip cultural references, hip pop music, TV stars, and movie stars. Whereas, they took the plot dynamics and realized all the things you could do with a simple stalk and slash formula. They originated the giallo cinema, which came from all those books. They evolved into movies. I think things were bouncing back and forth across the Atlantic, between stalk and slash films and the Italians inventing a certain genre. The Americans copied it and then the Italians copied it back again, upping the ante a little bit. I think things were bouncing back and

forth there for a while.

**JS: What do you say to John Carpenter's claim that *Halloween* was a tip of the hat to the giallo?**

**CB:** I don't think so... Because *Halloween* is such a straightforward stalk and slash number. If he thinks he's bringing in any supernatural overtones to it... I don't think that really holds any water. It's just a masked, unseen, unknown killer who's frightening because you don't know his motivation or where he's coming from. That seems like an archetypal boogeyman type of thing. It's not in the direction that Argento has with his multi-layered plots. I mean, there was no doubt from the get-go who was doing the killing in *Halloween*. And that's always the root of the giallo: Who's doing it and why? In *Halloween*, they just strip it down to the original motivation: He just kills because he's such a bad dude!

**JS: Why did you start writing film reviews?**

**CB:** Because I don't think anyone ever did it right for horror films. Horror films always seemed to be looked down on as a bastard child of real cinema. They always got the short end of the stick. And I don't think you can judge horror films with the overall template of major cinema. In a lot of cases, at least. A lot of consideration has to be given to the conventions of the genre—whether it's a horror film or a western. There are going to be things that turn up again and again. Which is not necessarily a bad thing. In a war movie, you've got to have a war. You've got to have people who die, heroes, the coward, the love interest. But when it's really done well, you don't resent the access to those conventions. You welcome them.

FIRST REAL CRACK AT THINGS.

**JS: The *Connoisseur's Guide to the Contemporary Horror Film* was your first real crack at things.**

**CB:** Yeah. And when you go back to that, it's more serious and scholarly. I didn't really joke around that much. So I was going through the phase where I said, "Horror films certainly deserve some kind of

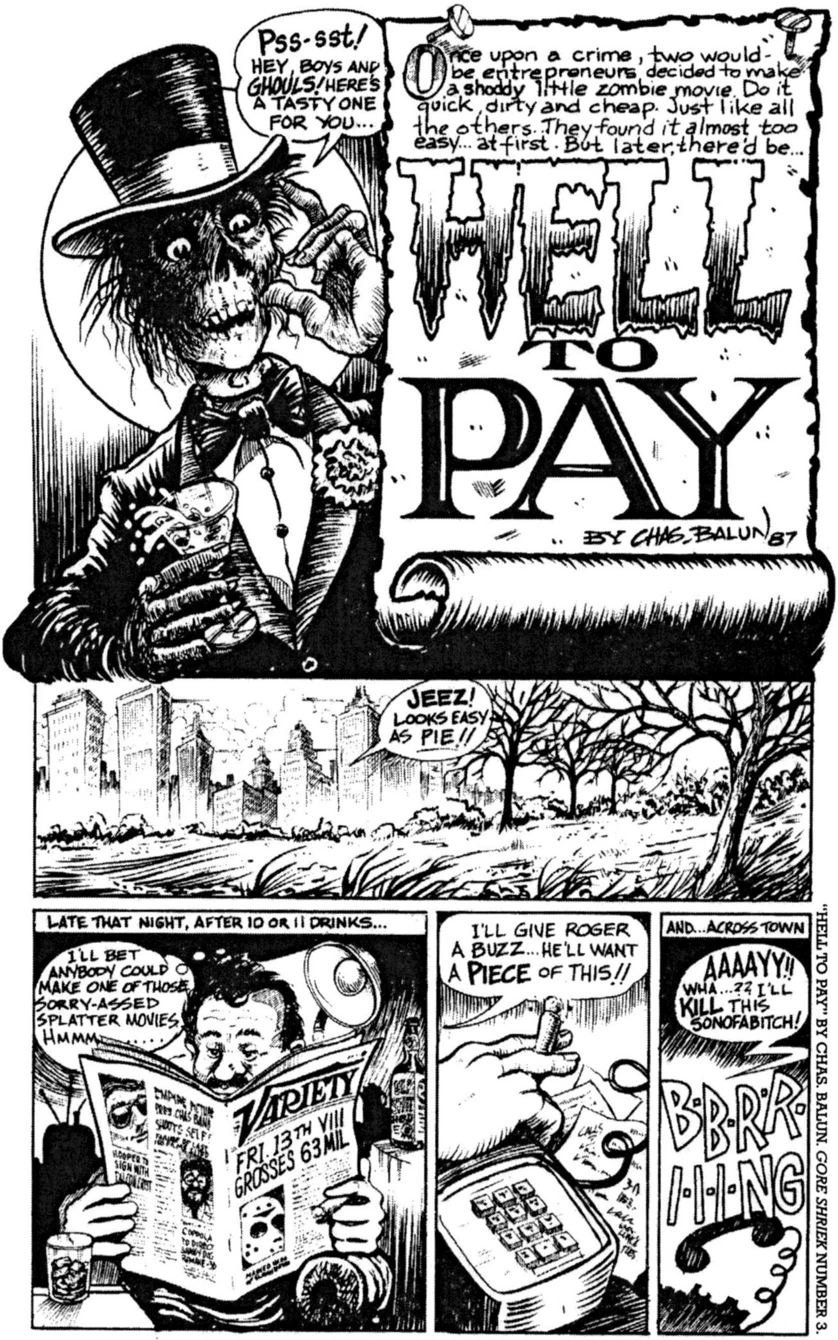

Pss-sst! HEY, BOYS AND GHOULS! HERE'S A TASTY ONE FOR YOU...

Once upon a crime, two would-be entrepreneurs decided to make a shoddy little zombie movie. Do it quick, dirty and cheap. Just like all the others. They found it almost too easy... at first. But later, there'd be...

# HELL TO PAY

BY CHAS. BALUN '87

JEEZ! LOOKS EASY AS PIE!!

"HELL TO PAY" BY CHAS. BALUN. GORE SHRIEK NUMBER 3.

THESE BOYS SEEM NONE TOO PLEASED...
I CAN'T BELIEVE IT! LOOK AT THOSE ZOMBIES!! BOGUS! TOTAL BOGOSITY!!
YEH... LOOK AT THE ONE DUDE! BAD PROSTHETIC WORK!
SAVINI IS GOD

FINALLY... THE CLIMACTIC ASSAULT!!
BOOO! THE PASTA LAND CHUNK BLOWERS ARE WAY BETTER!
CHECK OUT THE PHONY GUTS!! COULDN'T THEY'VE GOTTEN SOMEBODY GOOD TO DO FX? THIS SHIT IS PATHETIC!!!

MAN, WHAT A BURN! THOSE "FILMMAKERS" CAN ROT IN HELL! WHAT A RIP-OFF!!
CHEER UP! LET'S HIT THAT BOOKSTORE OVER THERE... MAYBE THE NEW FANGORIA IS IN!!

WHY BOTHER? NOTHING OVER THERE IS GONNA MAKE ME FEEL ANY BETTER!
YEH, FUCK IT! WE'D PROBABLY MISS OUR BUS ANYWAY...
METRO EDITION
Los Angeles Times
FILMMAKERS GUILTY! FACE DEATH PENALTY
ELECTRIC CHAIR FOR BIZARRE CEMETERY SLAYINGS!!

SUCH A PITY, NO? KIND OF RENEWS YOUR FAITH IN THINGS, HUH? ZOMBIES AND HORROR FANS ARE NOT TO BE FUCKED WITH! YOU'VE BEEN WARNED!!!
THE END

serious treatment, so I'll try this approach." That was only after watching X amount of films. But after watching ten times as many, I realized that I really needed to have a sense of humor to go on! Most of them blew homeless goats! And unless you were just a completely anal retentive fanboy, you could not accept some of this stuff. Most of them weren't done by people who had any love or affinity for the genre. They were made by people who were lazy. They could make a film with no story, no actors, no budget and it would still be a success. I mean, if ice skating movies were a big hit, they would have made those. But they made horror films because *Friday the 13th* made so much damn money.

**JS: Jack Ketchum recently compared your writing to that of Lester Bangs. How do you feel about that?**

**CB:** I'm flattered! I think that's terrific! I appreciate the comparison. And the fact that Jack Ketchum wrote an introduction for me—just the fact that he did that is enough! That someone who I've respected for years would say those kinds of things. The fact that he compared me to anybody was just an honor. But Lester Bangs… I mean, that's quite a notable designation there, for crying out loud. Because I liked that guy's attitude! I liked that someone could say, "That Led Zeppelin album blew!" or, "That hot shot is copping riffs from some old Muddy Waters record." You could just blow the whistle on people. And… when do you ever find honest critics who will go against the stream? And go against what the fans deem to be sacrosanct? Just to have someone say, "Well fuck it! I don't owe anything to anybody. I'll call things the way I see them and let the chips fall where they may!" But Lester's was one of those lives that ended way too soon, for chrissake. You've got to pace yourself and find a drug that you can use for fifty years! Not one that you can abuse for fifty seconds and say, "Whoops! I'm dead!"

JULY86
DEEP RED
2.50
HORROR FROM THE HEART OF HOLLYWOOD
PREMIER ISSUE!
Savini Video
MEAT MARKET MAYHEM
EXPLODING HEADS
In Praise of RE-ANIMATOR
CANNIBAL HOOKERS
ZOMBIES
BLOODY BEST Horror Videos
GORE SCOREBOARD
GODZILLA VS. JOE DANTE


**JS: Back to the *Connoisseur's Guide*… How did you find distribution for that?**

**CB:** I folded, stapled, and collated it on my kitchen table. Then I bought every horror film magazine that ever came out and mailed it out to all of them. I figured that I'd hit on something, somewhere. I'd put an ad in *Fangoria*; I was just my own public relations, shipping

and receiving dude. I'd go to conventions and pass them out, mailed them to every fanzine and editor that I could find. I just got hip to the world and found out who was doing what. A lot of my inspiration for self-publishing came from Rick Sullivan, who used to do the *Gore Gazette*. I give him all kinds of credit for opening up the gates of gore and for having a real opinioned, sarcastic approach to things. And also, one that was funnier than hell! I'll always give him credit for coining the word, "chunkblower." That was never mine. I just used it more than anyone else, so there was an association made there.

**JS: Was Steve Puchalski doing *Slimetime* at the time?**

**CB:** That was kind of around the same era. The other one I read at that time was Craig Ledbetter's *Hi-Tech Terror*. It was a little xeroxed zine from Texas.

**JS: When did you first start to freelance?**

**CB:** Well, *Fangoria* called me up when I was writing *Horror Holocaust*.

**JS: *Horror Holocaust* was published by FantaCo.**

**CB:** FantaCo picked up on some of my stuff and they started to distribute it. They always had a full-page ad in *Fangoria*. That really opened it up. FantaCo would say, "We need 160 copies!" Then, "We need another 200!" I always believed in self-publishing. If you were a writer and graphics artist like I was, you could essentially put together everything. All you needed was to get it printed.

**JS: How did you get involved with FantaCo in the first place? Did Tom Skulan call you up?**

**CB:** Yeah, he sent me a letter and called. I'd sent him copies of *Connoisseur's Guide* and he kept reordering them. They did pretty well selling it. Then I did my self-published *Gore Score*. That really got a good review in *Fangoria* [laughs]. So, Tom wanted me to do *Horror Holocaust*. He saw that I was doing something good and that I could be gotten cheaply. I was the cover artist, the writer… I was a one-man army.

**JS: What kind of a guy was Tom?**

**CB:** A complex individual [laughs]! I always thought of him as a good friend—a best friend, but I never really understood him. And I think he lost the fun and the joy of being involved in the scene too soon. It became

more of a labor to him. It wasn't fun anymore. I think that's what really wrecked it for him.

**JS: The first issue of *Deep Red* was self-published.**

**CB:** Yeah. We only printed around seven or eight hundred of those.

**JS: You did that issue with a woman named Chris Amouroux...**

**CB:** Yeah, Chris. She used to work with Eric Caidin at Hollywood Book and Poster. Eric was always selling my stuff and Chris was always there. She always had an interest in horror films and funky ass shit. Plus, she looked like this hip, cool, goth chick before that movement had a name. She was doing a fanzine at the time, so we just kind of combined forces. It was a nice connection with Hollywood Book and Poster; one of the regular employees was right there with all of the directors who came in all the time. So we thought we could put something together and have a good outlet for it. And Chris was cool! She got Joe Dante to write an article for us... she had some good Hollywood connections. And since she worked at Hollywood Book and Poster, we got all of the visual graphics that we needed.

DEEPRED

HORROR FROM THE HEART OF HOLLYWOOD JULY86

EDITORS
CHRIS AMOUROUX
CHAS. BALUN

CELEBRITY GUEST
JOE DANTE

CONTRIBUTORS
ERIC CAIDIN

TYPOGRAPHER · PAT PETRIC

Your Editors...Trust Us.

P.O. BOX 703 • 1765 N. HIGHLAND • HOLLYWOOD, CA 90078

A PAGE FROM THE RARE FIRST ISSUE, AKA *DEEP RED* NUMBER 0.

**JS: Who were the contributing writers for the first issue?**

**CB:** Probably just Chris and me [laughs]. There might have been somebody else, but I think it was just us.

**JS: You mentioned that you did some underground comics work with Jack Lewis. He turned up as one of the graphic artists for *Deep Red*.**

**CB:** Yeah. I've known Jack for thirty years. He was my original boss at Golden West; he was the first guy who hired me as a graphic artist. We go way, way back. We were painters together, comic artists together... best friends for thirty years. He was a great artistic inspiration to me—somebody who's just a great fucking painter.

**JS: What did you hope to accomplish with *Deep Red*?**

**CB:** Oh, to bring a more eclectic approach to horror films to the public. And to fill in the blanks that *Fangoria* was missing. *Fangoria* was just too slick. They liked everything—there were no shitty horror films. There was always something fascinating about this shoot, or this crew... this catering company. I wanted the bubbling effervescence of the frothing fan boy.

But I also wanted some sarcasm and some black humor. A jaundiced look at things; a highly personal look at things. I wanted to give all kinds of people a voice to say what they had to. And there were all kinds of people out there who were good writers; they just needed a forum for it. I just wanted to do a grass roots, people's horror zine.

**JS: You collected a bunch of notable contributors, including Denis Daniel and Steve Bissette. How did you get a hold of them?**

**CB:** They just got a hold of me. And Tom Skulan was on the East Coast, while I was over here in fucking California. So he knew a lot of these guys and he had a big store in Albany. A lot of these guys would ask him how to get a hold of me. Bissette was one of them; Tom published some of Steve's comic art. I don't know what Denis Daniel is up to now. He was a radio disc jockey back in those days. I think he wanted to do a radio interview with me on *Halloween* and one thing led to another.

**JS: You also had a lot of foreign correspondents, like John Martin.**

**CB:** John was writing for *Samhain*. Once the first couple of issues came out, I hit a nerve with people. We had letters come in; I remember David Schow writing in about what a refreshing change the magazine was. I followed up on some of those letters and got people to put their money where their mouth was. John Martin was one of them—I always liked his stuff in *Samhain*. He knew a lot of English blokes that I wanted to do some interviews with. That interview with Sean Hutson… I'd have never been able to have done that. And Loris Curci wrote some stuff for *Deep Red Alert*. He was neighbors with Lucio Fulci and Giannetto De Rossi. So all of these people sort of knew what we were trying to do and wanted to contribute. I think that's why the magazine had any success or popularity. It was the voice of the people, not some film studio or corporation dictating to the people what movies we had to say good things about. We had self-motivated individuals who wanted to do this because they felt passionately about it.

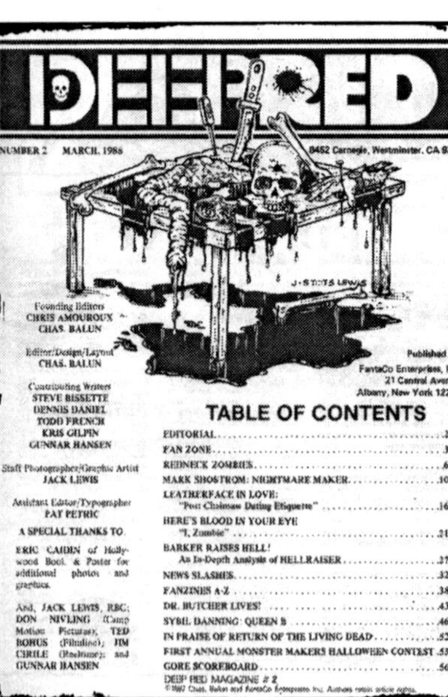

DEEP RED

NUMBER 2 MARCH, 1988

8452 Carnegie, Westminster, CA 92683

Founding Editors
CHRIS AMOUROUX
CHAS. BALUN

Editor/Design/Layout
CHAS. BALUN

Contributing Writers
STEVE BISSETTE
DENNIS DANIEL
TODD FRENCH
KRIS GILPIN
GUNNAR HANSEN

Staff Photographer/Graphic Artist
JACK LEWIS

Assistant Editor/Typographer
PAT PETRIC

A SPECIAL THANKS TO

ERIC CAIDEN of Hollywood Book & Poster for additional photos and graphics.

And, JACK LEWIS, RBC; DON NIVLING (Camp Motion Pictures), TED BOHUS (Filmline); JIM CIRILE (Reeltime); and GUNNAR HANSEN

Published By
FantaCo Enterprises, Inc.
21 Central Avenue
Albany, New York 12210

TABLE OF CONTENTS



DEEP RED MAGAZINE # 2

©1987 Chas. Balun and FantaCo Enterprises Inc. Authors retain article rights.



**JS: But there was a time when you started to feel**

**disillusioned with the way things were going.**

**CB:** Oh yeah. I didn't want to become like *Fangoria*, where I had issues coming out and there was nothing to say. I wasn't going to become part of that. I wasn't going to put out a magazine unless I really had something to say. Not just to fill pages and meet a deadline. I had other things going on in my life and I didn't want to waste the time putting together something that I wasn't proud of. I decided to wait for this time to pass; maybe it would be cool again, maybe it would be exciting again… which of course hasn't happened yet.

**JS: In its own way, *Deep Red* was a shot in the arm. You covered a lot of films that a lot of people wouldn't have known about. I know Buddy Giovinazzo credits *Deep Red* for exposing *Combat Shock* to its audience.**

**CB:** Yeah. We were shamelessly biased in promoting something that we thought we'd discovered. A buried treasure or a hidden gem that we thought we'd polish up a bit and throw on the table. So many films get lost. I thought enough was written about the popular films. How many articles can you write about Jason and Freddy Krueger before you just want to see something like *Combat Shock*, where some fucking junkie is baking his baby in the oven—and unapologetically so! You see that and say, "Gosh, this is kind of grotesque. I kind of like this. This has a point of view, this has an attitude."

**JS: You wrote about *Last House on Dead End Street* in the *Deep Red Horror Handbook*. You were about the only person at the time who knew that Victor Janos was really Roger Watkins. How did you know that?**

**CB:** Roger asked me that too! Well, I was the editor of a horror magazine and I got mail from all over the place. I just happened to get mail from someone who had maybe eight different versions of *Last House on Dead End Street*; he knew how many minutes and seconds each version was—how much was cut out of this one, he knew about the alternate title as *The*

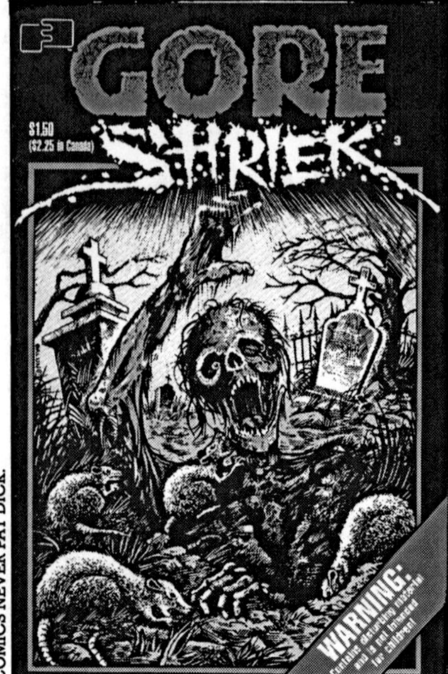


*Fun House*. And he knew that it was made by students and that Victor Janos was really Roger Watkins. He just thought that I would benefit from that knowledge. I used it and probably got that film more promotion than it had ever gotten before!

**JS: Around the time that FantaCo was publishing *Deep Red*, you did some artwork for their comic book, *Gore Shriek*. What was it like doing comics again?**

**CB:** *Gore Shriek*… as a comic, it was fine. I tell you though, after I realized how long it took to draw a comic, that sort of turned me off to whole experience. It took way, way too long. And comic books never pay dick. I've talked to Bernie Wrightson and he said, "Chas., I felt like I was really smoking if I could just ink a page a day." And at a time when people were paying between $40 and $100 a page… I mean jeez! You might as well go mow lawns or wash cars or something! Drawing is just too hard. And there's no way to do it quickly. I can count the number of people on no fingers and no hands who can just grab an ink pen and start inking in things without penciling it in first. But I don't mind telling a story. I'll either draw stuff without the words or write the words without the pictures.

COMICS NEVER PAY DICK.

**JS: You were once slated to work on a film called *Butcher's Pride*. What can you tell us about that?**

**CB:** Well, that was one of those situations where everybody said, "We're going to make a film, we're going to do this, we're going to do that." I had a lawyer friend who wanted to do something. And I knew Gunnar Hansen, so we thought we could work together on it. Gunnar would be involved, I would direct… it was one of those things that never worked out. I think I got fired from the project. I had such a bad attitude. I was supposed to come up with the story and Gunnar would do the screenplay. I could just tell that we weren't all on the same page. And I'm one of those people who does not work and play well with others. I would just be insufferable to work with on any kind of film project. So, kind of mercifully, that project never really got

past its embryonic stages.

**JS: Was this kind of experience the kind of thing that made you want to write fiction?**

**CB:** Why did I want to write fiction... Well, I thought, "Gee, I've read so much horror fiction and most of it just blows. I don't care about these characters, I don't care what they had for lunch, what car they drive, or if their uncle drinks too much..." Come on, if you're going to write a good splatter novel, there's got to be a lot of guts, you've got to kill a lot of people, and there's got to be a lot of horror. If you want the important shit, read the other books. But, if you just want to get off on some mayhem, deliver! That was my motivation. Why can't more books be like Jack Ketchum's *Off Season*? For 192 pages, that's a fucking killer read. It's got everything you want in a horror novel. The only other person I found who was writing balls-out horror all the time was Sean Hutson. And everybody hated him. "He's just a hack, he wrote *Slugs*." But I've yet to read one of his books that I thought didn't deliver the goods or was a pretentious bore. And that wasn't over 400 fucking pages long!

Pure horror... as hard as it comes.

Chas. Balun

JUST PUBLISHED!

NINTH & HELL STREET

Faith and Fury. Meat and Madness.

ONLY 9.95

"Balun joins the splatter punk ranks ... a vicious, disturbing and unsettling piece of horror fiction." — Anthony Timpone, FANGORIA Magazine

"Pure, unrelenting, no-holds-barred horror from the master. This is Chas. Balun at his best." — Gunnar (Leatherface) Hansen, THE TEXAS CHAINSAW MASSACRE

"A splatterfest of gore ... uniquely depraved. Ninth and Hell Street — my kind of neighborhood." — Buddy Giovinazzo, Director, COMBAT SHOCK

"Rips the guts right out of you!" — Eric Caidin, Hollywood Book & Poster Co.

NINTH & HELL STREET, Chas. Balun's first horror novel, is presented as an oversized Quality Trade Paperback in a SPECIAL LIMITED EDITION. Each book is personally hand-signed and numbered by the author.

**JS: Quick Gore Score review: What did you think of the J.P. Simon adaptation of *Slugs*?**

**CB:** Um... not as good as the book, but good enough! I mean, it's just stupid exploitation cinema, but the slugs and shit falling in the salad, heads blowing up... that couple crawling across the floor that's teaming with slugs and snails... That filled the bill for me! "Oh, there wasn't a serious psychological subtext to this about a fear of invertebrates that developed in the home of a dysfunctional family..."

**JS: You told me that Jim VanBebber was once interested in doing something with your novella, *Director's Cut*.**

**CB:** That got as far as a phone call. You know how movie things are. Again, that's why I just started shying away from the film business. I can write books, do paintings, and illustrations on my own. Just me. I don't have to call up other people to get their approval or money. I need to do something that I can do in my own house, unadulterated on my own terms. And movies aren't the pathway for that.

**JS: In 1987, you wrote an article called "Movies with Guts." It listed ten or twelve films that you thought were about as rough as they came. Things like *Freaks*, *Peeping Tom*, *The Devils*, *Blood Sucking***

## GORE SCOREBOARD

**THE RATING SYSTEM**

- bow-wow
- nearly worthless
- ordinary
- solid & scary
- hard core horror

**The Gore Score**

This evaluation then, deals with nothing but the **quantity** of blood, brains, guts and assorted precious bodily fluids, spilled during the course of the film. It's quite simple really, "The Bad News Bears Go To Japan" would get a big, fat zero in the Gore Score category while "Dr. Butcher M.D." and "Maniac" would most likely receive juicy nines or tens.

 Mary Poppins, Dumbo and Terms of Endearment

10 "Bloodsucking Freaks," "The Evil Dead" and "The Gates Of Hell"

***Freaks*, *The Conqueror Worm*... How would that list change today?**

**CB:** Movies with guts... now I think they're just happier to gross you out. Just to break some taboos—and they think that's ballsy. You look at some of this stuff and say, "Where's the story?" It's just, "Here, we can gross you out!" And, you know, today, there's this edgy neuroses thing that people are working out, which I'm sure Nacho Cerda was working out in *Aftermath*. I think a lot of people are using film as their personal forum, to rid themselves of certain issues that they need to address. It's not necessarily interesting to someone outside their circle. No one has a good fucking story to tell.

**JS: Not to say that personal issues shouldn't be addressed.**

**CB:** Right. But give me a story there! Just watching all of these aberrant, psychological anomalies that this person has... that doesn't necessarily make for entertaining cinema. Put it in the context of *Texas Chain Saw Massacre*, where you have cannibalism, someone works in a slaughterhouse, somebody's a psychotic... you wrap it up in that kind of cool story. Then you've got something.

**JS: It's always fun when something springs out from nowhere. What films in the last ten years have restored your faith?**

**CB:** That's a tough call. The only thing I've really gotten behind and enjoyed a whole lot was Peter Jackson's *Braindead*. That was almost an anomaly there; it didn't even belong where it did. And then it just disappeared. No one is going to do something like that again. And now Peter Jackson is doing *Lord of the Rings*. Good bye, Peter. Good to know ye... it was too short. There haven't been those kinds of films that came out in the seventies and early eighties, whether it's an *Evil Dead*, a *Dawn of the Dead*, a *Texas Chain Saw Massacre*... films that got all that grass roots support. *Braindead* was one of those horror films for the people.

**JS: The last one that really got me in that way was *Street Trash*.**

SHOCK

VOMIT BAG

you'll be petrified!

INTENSE TERROR!

IT WILL SHATTER YOU!

BRAVE NEW HORRORS

MORE GORE SCORE

WARNING!

WILD
BITING
SAVAGE
BIZARRE

CHAS. BALUN

RECORDED & INDEXED

DRAFT

**CB:** Uh-huh. And that's really not a horror film, it's a splatter film. I think that what one can gleam from *Street Trash* is this: Jimmy Muro directed it. And I thought, "God, this guy's got an incredible career ahead of him." But then you realize that he probably learned a whole lot about making movies and how it works. Isn't it odd that he hasn't ever directed another movie, yet he appears in the credits of some really high budget films as a steadycam operator? I think he really got a full-on blast of what low budget filmmaking is all about with *Street Trash*. "Gee, it's great to be in all these magazines and get popular accolades… but that doesn't pay the rent. Maybe it's time to do something that utilizes my skills, but also has some kind of payback to it."

**JS: With that in mind, what's it going to take for a new renaissance in the horror film?**

**CB:** Unfortunately, I don't see much hope at all because all of the major horror directors either burned out or went on to other things. And I don't think that anyone's come up to take their place.

**JS: Well, we have people like Jim VanBebber… although it doesn't look like we'll be seeing a nationwide release of *Charlie's Family* any time soon.**

**CB:** It's such a political arena when you enter into filmmaking. You have to worry about who's going to distribute, what the content's going to be—we'll give you money if you do this, if you do that. I think the era of the independent filmmaker is just going to rapidly erode… as far as getting distribution and making money on a little film, you've got to play the game. You've got to produce a viable commercial product. Come on, nobody's going to give you a million dollars to just be an artist. Fuck that, it's called showbusiness. And there is no show without the business. So these days of these people making a film for 80,000 bucks, by accident—that's not going to happen.

**JS: Why do you think that things are different today?**

**CB:** Because everyone is more self-conscious about what product they're putting

out. And there's always going to be a bottom line. Is it going to open big, is it going to play theatrically, is it going to play foreign, is it going to be R or PG-13… There's so many more business considerations in it, whereas I think back in those days, it was kind of the last of the "pull yourself up by your own bootstraps" era. You could just be fucking nuts, you could get some dentist or lawyer who had a few bucks to back it. It's more of a corporate thing now. I don't think anything's done by accident. It's all pretty well calculated. And it's even more sad when you see a movie that cost 100 million dollars and you go, "Jeez, why didn't they spend more than $500 on the script?"

**JS: You know things are bad when they're planning to remake *Dawn of the Dead*. It's insulting.**

CHAS. BALUN'S *RED INK* (BLACKEST HEART MEDIA, 1999).

**CB:** Sure [nervous laughter]. But look at all the ridiculous things that have been happening. Look at all the bad TV shows that are being remade… that's saying something. That's saying, "Hey, we've got nothing to say."

**JS: So is the state of the genre better or worse than you thought it would be ten years ago?**

**CB:** Oh, it's worse. It's no fun. A lot of the fun is gone because every horror film that comes out is so self-conscious. Look at all that self-referential shit they have in the *Scream* movies. Everybody's got to be so hip to everything. You've just sort of lost that innocence where you could drop people into an intense situation and manipulate them. We've passed that certain point where we can look back and see what happened there, but I don't think it bodes well for the future. There's not enough passion, there's not enough dedication to the right way of doing these things. A lot of people think that they have to follow the formula. And a lot of people won't admit that they peaked twenty-five years ago. It was a flashpoint and it will never happen again. It's like the way they keep throwing these Woodstocks. In 1969, things were happening in a certain direction, and that tapped into it. You can't just dredge into the past and try to

manufacture an experience again.

**JS: A lot of directors are repeating themselves.**

**CB:** I think that it's really unfortunate that people like John Carpenter and Tobe Hooper can't come to grips with the fact that they got it dead on, one of their first times out of the chute. And after tens of millions of dollars, and God knows how many opportunities, they can't recapture that. They can't go back, they can't make it better. And I think that must really grate on their asses. It's like, "Gee, maybe you guys ought to write your memoirs or something."

**JS: How do you feel about the way that Dario Argento has gone?**

**CB:** Well, Argento's such a passionate true believer that he's just going to keep making films until he gets it right again. He's going to remake the same film over and over again [laughs]. But… he's going to make another *Deep Red*, another *Opera*, another *Tenebre*, because he just tries so hard and he believes so passionately. It's his religion. It's his faith; it's his reason to believe. I realize he's fucked up a bunch of times, he's just put out stuff that's just numbing at the best. But he won't quit. He's one of those passionate believers in things.

**JS: That's what we need, I guess. True believers.**

**CB:** Uh-huh. Some people are so self-delusional and will never understand the kind of stuff that we're talking about. But the fans do. And luckily, there will always be the true believers and the watchdogs like ourselves out there to call them on it.

# Chapter Fourteen

# Tom Skulan

## The FantaCo Man

ART BY LARRY MCDOUGALL

# TOM SKULAN

## THE FANTACO MAN

**TOM SKULAN**
Story and dialogue. Layout and design. Co-scripter. Corrections. Promotion.

**JOHN M. HEBERT**
Artwork and design. Additional dialogue. Corrections. Continuity.

**ROGER GREEN**
Co-scripter. Additional dialogue. Corrections. Continuity. Order supervision.

**ANDREA P. MOSSEY**
Lettering. Corrections. Continuity.

**AUGUSTUS MATTICK III**
Co-scripter. Additional dialogue. Corrections. Continuity.

**HANK JANSEN III**
Corrections. Continuity. Order Processing.

**JOELLE C. MICHALKIEWICZ**
Archaeological consultant. Long name.

**not pictured:**

**MARY CLARE**
Promotional layouts. Typesetting.

**BRUCE SPAULDING FULLER**
Front and back cover layout and design.

**SOLD OUT # 1** is published by
FantaCo Enterprises, Inc.
21 Central Avenue, Albany, New York 12210 - 1391
This is the first printing ($1500 cover price)
November 1986

THE FANTACO GANG.

Tom Skulan has always been a bit of a mystery to me. As the president of FantaCo Enterprises, Inc., Albany, New York, he was the man responsible for publishing Chas. Balun's *Deep Red* magazine (and its many offshoots), as well as a multitude of horror related books and comics.

Mail order ads for FantaCo graced the pages of *Fangoria* and *Gorezone* regularly, offering everything from horror zines to monster masks and props. *Gore Shriek*, FantaCo's extremely graphic horror comic, was a splatter-fan's dream, featuring artwork from the likes of Steve Bissette, Bruce Spaulding Fuller, and a then-unknown Greg Capullo. FantaCon, FantaCo's annual convention, was a thing of legend, offering gorehounds the opportunity to meet with Clive Barker, Dario Argento, and Tom Savini in a much more intimate environment than the bigger (and, truth be told, downright generic) cons. Where else could you find Roy Frumkes (the writer/producer of *Street Trash*) and the crazy cartoonist Gahan Wilson

under the same roof?

I ordered from FantaCo regularly as a kid, checking off the days on a makeshift calendar as I waited for the mail to arrive. The *Horror Yearbook*, FantaCo's annual catalog, became my personal *Consumer Reports*. If FantaCo didn't stock it, it wasn't worth getting.

Still, just who was Tom Skulan? Outside of the credits on the FantaCo publications, I could never gather much information about him. Was he an artist, as well as a writer? A fan, as well as a businessman? Could he possibly be all four? A trip to FantaCo itself in 1994 offered no leads; the man wasn't at the store (as I naively assumed he'd be), and I had to head back home to Michigan the next day. I left Albany with an armful of books and a mission: "One day," I decided, "I'll talk to him and get the answers."

The answers finally arrived on a fine November evening in 2011, when I dialed Tom Skulan's number. As the phone rang, I couldn't help but think of a square on my childhood calendar that had long gone unchecked. A friendly voice answered, and soon we were talking like old friends. Here then, at last, is Tom Skulan, the FantaCo Man...

The following interview was conducted via telephone on November 27, 2011.

---

**JOHN SZPUNAR: Let's start out with a fairly simple question. Or maybe not so simple. How did FantaCo get started?**

**TOM SKULAN:** Well, the idea for FantaCo happened while I was in college. I had always been interested in horror films, horror comics, regular comics—just the whole thing about it. I was an art studio major in school. I did a lot of paintings and illustrations, and stuff like that. And even though it was not popular with the teachers, I always ended up reverting back to a comic-type style. Whether it was from EC Comics or whatever—something in that style would revert back. It was probably around 1973–1974 or so that I started getting the idea for FantaCo. While I was in school, I worked at The Crystal Cave, which was one of the first comic book stores.

THE FANTACO 1991 HORROR YEARBOOK

**Editors**
Eric Hausmann
Sandra Stokey

**Additional Assistance**
Tim D'Allaird
Hank Jansen
John Moore
Tom Skulan
Jason Slutsky

**Thanks to**

Dennis Daniel, Rita Eisenstein, FantaCo customers, Mike Gunderloy, Richard Klemensen, Dave MacDowell, Kelly Meeks, Mikrotek Scanners, Dan Murtagh, Dave Peck, Gurchain Singh, Tony Timpone

Extra special thanks to Chas. Balun for kicking ass when deadlines were flying from all directions and for the incredible oil painting he did for the cover.

The FantaCo Horror Yearbook is published annually by FantaCo Enterprises, Inc., 21 Central Ave., Albany, New York 12210 U.S.A. The FantaCo 1991 Horror Yearbook is copyright © 1991 by FantaCo Enterprises, Inc. No part of this book may be copied or reproduced without written consent from the publisher. To order any of the products in this book call FantaCo's mail order service at (518) 463-3667 twenty four hours a day. To obtain a price list for any of the enclosed products send a self addressed stamped envelope to the address above.

HORROR'S *CONSUMER REPORTS*.

## THE FANTACO MAN

RECORDED & INDEXED

DRAFT

**JS: What city was that in?**

**TS:** That was in New Paltz, New York. It was owned by Peter Maresca, who now owns the *Sunday Press*. They do those huge books on *Little Nemo* and other Sunday page comics. They're just gorgeous, gorgeous books. I worked there and got introduced to all of the comic book personalities, like Phil Seuling, really early. I think the second year Bud Plant was in business we were dealing with him. The idea came from my past and from my situation at the comic store. So, that's a long answer to your short question [laughs]!

**JS: You were always attracted to the horror genre?**

**TS:** Yes. I have always been fascinated by horror. I loved Edgar Allan Poe when I was really young. Scared me half to death but I read every story. I got the original *Mars Attacks!* cards when they came out, and nearly wore them out from reading the backs. I actually found a near complete set of them in the road near my house when I was about nine. They terrified and intrigued me at the same time. For weeks I would look at them and read them under the covers at night with a little flashlight! I could *feel* the pain in those images! I was repulsed and hooked all at once. I have never forgotten those cards, ever.

My first memory of a horror film was watching (with my hands over my eyes—it was really scary to me) *The Blood of Dracula*. It's about this girl who goes off to a girl's school and the teacher is hypnotizing them into becoming vampires. At the time, it just seemed unbelievably scary and I remember my father was watching it with me because I was so terrified. Those are some of the earliest memories I have.

21 PRIZE CAPTIVE

A MARTIAN ATTACKS IN *MARS ATTACKS!*

**JS: You also mentioned the EC Comics...**

**TS:** I wasn't aware of the EC Comics when I was younger; the very tail end of EC would have been around then. I got into EC Comics when I was around eighteen. My earliest horror comic memory is this: I was staying with my parents in Maine at a cabin. We had arrived when there was absolutely nothing to do. It was too late to go outside or anything; I was totally bored out of my

mind. I was in bed and I reached my hand up the wall. I couldn't believe it—I found, stuck in a hole in the wall, a copy of *Fantastic Giants*, the Steve Ditko comic. Man, that was just great! Not only did I have something to do, but something really cool to do. I read it from cover to cover for the entire week we were there.

**JS: When did *Famous Monsters of Filmland* come into your life?**

**TS:** My earliest memory of printed horror stuff is that copy of the *Fantastic Giants* comic, which I think came out in 1962. I didn't read or find a copy of *Famous Monsters* until 1964. So it was a couple of years later, and I was like, "Wow!" That was really cool. And when I first found *Famous Monsters*, it was actually not at a newsstand. I bought some trading cards, and the back of the cards had an ad for *Famous Monsters*. I ordered my first couple of issues directly from Captain Company. It wasn't until around 1965 that I actually found it at a newsstand, and the newsstand was ten miles from my house. I had to get a ride to get there. It was hit or miss—I remember going there one day; I got *Famous Monsters* and *3-D Monsters*. I think I might have gotten *3-D Monsters* before *Famous Monsters*, actually. It was a really weird magazine. They photographed Aurora model kits in 3-D; they set them up in these weird poses and everything. It was really disappointing and really thrilling at the same time. It was in 3-D, which was cool, but I had the model kits already.

**JS: Were there any other magazines that caught your eye?**

**TS:** Like I said, I was going to newsstands that were hit and miss. The only other thing that was there (periodically) when I picked up *Famous Monsters* was *Weird* magazine. That really twisted me.

**JS: From Eerie Publications?**

**TS:** From Eerie Publications. The first couple issues were there at the same time that I was picking up *Famous Monsters*. I had a moral dilemma in buying the things. It was like, "This is just absolutely sick beyond belief!" I would read a copy of *Weird* and just be absolutely appalled at the stories and the artwork. I remember one story, to this day. It was about an orphanage. The owner of the orphanage made

*FANTASTIC GIANTS*: EARLIEST HORROR MEMORY.

a deal with these underground ghouls to come in at night to steal and eat the children. *Weird* weirded me out so much that I actually ended up burning my copies.

**JS: Seriously?**

**TS:** Yeah. That story just got me so disturbed I couldn't take it.

**JS: How old were you?**

**TS:** I was probably around twelve years old.

**JS: I found my first issue of the *Haunt of Fear* in my grandfather's attic when I was around eleven. Soon after that, I tried to draw my own.**

**TS:** I did a lot of illustrations when I was little. The earliest thing that I did was with my friend Jeff Williams. This was in fourth grade or something. I don't remember what our "publication" was called. We did three issues, and it had stuff for monster movies and TV shows—*Get Smart*, *The Man from U.N.C.L.E*, and stuff like that. We handed them out in class. That was the first thing that I ever put out.

**JS: I did the same thing.**

**TS:** Really? What did yours have in it [laughs]?

**JS: Horror comics and movie reviews. We did two issues. I think my friend Matt got sick of me ordering him to draw things, so we "folded" [laughs].**

**TS:** We got shut down by the teacher! We did three issues and then the teacher said, "No, you can't distribute that in class!"

**JS: That's great! Might as well distribute worldwide! Actually, did FantaCo start out as mail order or as brick and mortar?**

**TS:** Well, I started my own mail order company under my name in the Summer of 1967. I sold coins (I was heavily into coin collecting), back issue comic books and albums. Those were the only three things that I sold. I started the company when I was really young and I kept it all the way through college. I ended up going through six years of school without taking out a student loan and without any financial aid. And that turned into FantaCo. It was on August 28, 1978, that I changed it to an S corporation. We opened with a retail store on 21 Central Ave. in Albany, NY.

**JS: When did you actually start publishing through FantaCo?**

**TS:** The first publication that we did was for our first

convention in August, 1979. We published a magazine-sized program. The first nationally distributed publication was in 1980.

**JS: How did your distribution work?**

**TS:** Well, it was really simple in those days [laughs]! It was: get an idea and call up Phil Seuling and see what he thought of it. If he was interested, I would tell the artist that we were going to do the book. After we went over how I wanted the book set up, how many pages we wanted, and everything like that, I'd contact the two or three other distributors that existed and see what they thought of it. You'd usually send out some kind of promotional thing—maybe a cover or something. You'd take it from there; it was down and dirty distribution. Real back-bone stuff.

**JS: How well were your initial publications received? You worked with Fred Hembeck...**

**TS:** The first thing we did was *Smilin' Ed* number 1. That was in January of 1980. We did Fred's book in February, which was *Hembeck 1980*. We took that over from Eclipse. The *Smilin' Ed* book did OK—it didn't do great. It was virtually supported by Phil; he took enough to make the book possible to publish. I mean, we were doing a totally unknown character and putting it in its own comic book. It was like, here's a black and white comic book that costs eight times as much as a color comic book from a company you've never heard of. We were lucky to be able to do it. Now, Fred's book did very well out of the gate. He was a known commodity; he had put out the *Dateline* book with Eclipse. We pretty much went through about 5,000 copies of that, which at the time, was a phenomenal number.

**JS: I'm one of those guys who became familiar with FantaCo through *Deep Red* and *Gore Shriek*. I knew that it was a comic store, but to me, it was always more of a horror store. When did that aspect start to creep into things?**

**TS:** Actually, the store itself always carried horror stuff. It was something I was interested in; the store pretty much reflected my personality. Now, in terms of coming into publishing, the first horror thing that we

did was in 1981. It was fairly early in our publishing career. We did the *Splatter Movies* book with John McCarty.

**JS: How did you get involved with him?**

**TS:** Well, he was a local guy who came into the store. He lived around six miles from me. Then, we did the Herschell Gordon Lewis book in 1983. That was solely based upon my interest in doing that book. This was somebody who had terrified me as a kid at the drive-in—the trailers alone terrified me. And I couldn't find anything about the guy. I picked up the movie guide books and they didn't even list his movies. I looked around for someone to do that book and John ended up taking it on. He found Herschell's cameraman, Daniel Krogh. The two of them put together the book; Daniel had a tremendous collection of behind-the-scenes stills, so I was really happy. That was a big project.

**JS: Speaking of Herschell Lewis, you also reprinted two of the novelizations of his movies.**

**TS:** Yep. We reprinted *Blood Feast* and *Two Thousand Maniacs*. We got the rights to do the novelizations for a one-time printing. Bruce Spaulding Fuller, who was big in *Gore Shriek*, was the person who designed the books.

**JS: How big of a print run did they have?**

**TS:** Those two novels each had a print run of 5,000.

A FANTACO DOUBLE FEATURE
IF YOU DARE—READ THE SHOCKING, UNEXPURGATED* NOVELIZATIONS OF AMERICA'S FIRST SPLATTER FILMS!
THE NOVEL
BLOOD FEAST
Written by HERSCHELL GORDON LEWIS
Designed by BRUCE SPAULDING FULLER
Produced by TOM DAVID SKULAN
THE NOVEL
TWO THOUSAND MANIACS!
Written by HERSCHELL GORDON LEWIS
Designed by BRUCE SPAULDING FULLER
Produced by TOM DAVID SKULAN
WARNING:
A BLOOD SPATTERED ORGY OF WANTON GORE!
FROM THE GODFATHER OF GORE, HERSCHELL GORDON LEWIS!
AVAILABLE AT YOUR FAVORITE SPECIALTY SHOP
OR CALL: (518) 463-3667 AND CHARGE IT!
GRUESOMELY STAINED IN BLOOD COLOR!
"Shocking. . . Sexual. . . But with Social Significance."
—THE NATIONAL INSIDER Newspaper


AD FOR H.G. LEWIS NOVELIZATIONS.

**JS: And how did you track down the rights holders?**

**TS:** Through a guy named Jimmy Maslin, from California. To tell you the truth, the path to him was a very long one. I can't even remember all the steps it took to find him. But we did find him, and he sent us the original negatives from the films. We used the frames for the stills and the covers—they were as good of pictures as you could get.

**JS: Jimmy's pretty involved with Mike Vraney from Something Weird Video.**

**TS:** That doesn't surprise me, because he was really into the exploitation films and everything else. He was a real pleasant person to deal with.

THE COMIC BOOK·SCIENCE FICTION·HORROR·FANTASY CONVENTI

SATURDAY & SUNDAY · SEPTEMBER 10 &

EMPIRE STATE PLAZA CONVENTION CENTER · ALBANY NE

STEP INTO THE FUT

★ DEMONSTRATIONS!

★ FILMS! ★ DEALERS!

★ SPECIAL GUESTS

SHOW REPORT '88

## THE FANTACO MAN

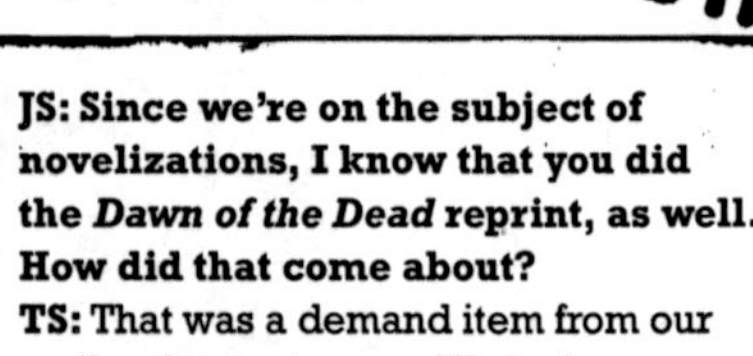

When there's
no more room in HELL
the dead will walk the EARTH
GEORGE A. ROMERO
SUSANNA SPARROW
FANTACO
DAWN
OF THE
DEAD

**JS: Since we're on the subject of novelizations, I know that you did the *Dawn of the Dead* reprint, as well. How did that come about?**

**TS:** That was a demand item from our mail order customers. We had a very large mail order business—for most of the time of FantaCo, it was many times the size of the retail store. In the mid-eighties, the number of requests for the *Dawn of the Dead* novel was overwhelming. We would track down one or two copies, but they were really expensive for us to get. We would have to buy them from collectors. And for every copy that we found, we had fifty people who wanted one. So, we contacted the original publisher and, fortunately for us, it was St. Martin's Press. We had ordered a lot of books from them, and we had a relationship with them from when they published the revised edition of *Splatter Movies*. So, that was how that came about; we didn't actually have to talk them into it. We just said, "We're very interested in doing the book and we'd like to do a printing of it." They said, "Yeah. How many copies do you want to print?" We got that going fairly quickly.

**JS: How many print runs did that go through?**

**TS:** Well, there was the St. Martin's hardcover, which is still a very expensive item. I have one copy of it, myself. And then there was the St. Martin's Press softcover. I don't know if they did multiple printings of that. Unless somebody out there is sitting on stacks of them, it's not something that we found that many copies of. Everyone wanted it, and every copy that I found was a first-printing copy. I never really had a discussion with them about how many printings they had done. We got the rights to do a single printing with them. And it sold very well.

**JS: You also sold fanzines through FantaCo.**

**TS:** Oh yeah. We were grabbing all of them. I mean, we were ordering just about anything that we could find to sell through our mail order company. I was pretty familiar with all of them. We were ordering stuff that had—we would talk to people, and they'd say, "We're printing 300 copies." And we'd say, "Well, we need 200." What we would do is this: if we could get ten-, fifteen-, or twenty copies of something, we would probably put it in the store. If we could get fifty or more, we'd sell it through mail order. It's not like now where you have a website and put something up; once

it's gone, you take it down. If we had a full page ad in Fangoria and spent thousands of dollars to list something, we didn't want it to sell out in the first day.

**JS: What were some of your favorites?**

**TS:** Oh, man…there are just so many. My first love was *Gore Creatures*. I picked that up with the fourth mimeographed issue. And I really liked *Shock Xpress*. And of course, I just loved Chas.' stuff. He had done a number of things before we hooked up with him. He'd done an issue of *Deep Red*, he'd done the *Gore Score*. I was really impressed with his work. When he sent us copies of the *Gore Score*, I said, "Hey, we want to carry all of your stuff. And we want lots of copies, not just a few." We ended up deciding that we were going to publish *Deep Red* and his other things. We wanted to move along in a series and put things out together. That worked out great for everybody. We had this brand new material in enough quantity that we could supply everyone who wanted a copy with one. And also, at the same time, distribute it to stores. That was something that Chas. hadn't been able to do that well. He'd done it with individual stores, particularly in the California area, but we got him international distribution.

**JS: *Horror Holocaust* was the first thing that he published with FantaCo.**

**TS:** It was *Horror Holocaust*, yeah. When Chas' book came out, I went to London to talk to Titan Distributors; they'd ordered a bunch of books. I went by a couple of Forbidden Planets, and they had a window display of FantaCo publications. *Horror Holocaust*, the Herschell Gordon Lewis book, *Splatter Movies*; all kinds of horror stuff. It was pretty exciting for me.

**JS: I can imagine! Now, Chas. told me that that he was pretty much a one-man army when it came to design…**

**TS:** Oh, I'll tell you something—he was a pretty amazing factory. He did the design, the artwork, the articles, the covers. And his wife [Pat Petric] was cranking it all out of their house on an old typeset machine. I would get the finished boards, set up an appointment with the printer, and print up however many copies that had been pre-ordered, plus about twenty to thirty per cent. Pat is sort of the

THE 1991 *HORROR YEARBOOK*. ARTWORK BY CHAS. BALUN.

RECORDED & INDEXED

DRAFT

unsung hero in this. The amount of work that she had to do—the way she was doing it—was phenomenal. I mean, it was just astonishing. I had been to their house many times, and they had this old, one-letter-at-a-time, type machine. Just doing strips of this and pasting that in. She's the one who cranked that all out. We got boards that had halftone artwork in place. If there was a movie still that had to be inserted, it was sent in and it was marked with positioning. All of the type was in place, all the headlines were in place. We'd get a huge package from [Chas. and Pat], and it would totally be ready to go to the printer. Every issue was like that.

**JS: I'd imagine that *Deep Red* was immediately successful.**

**TS:** Oh yeah, it was a success right off the bat. The sales on number 1 were really good, and the sales on number 2 were better. But, as *Deep Red* went on, more and more titles came out from all over the place. When we got to issue numbers 5 and 6, the sales started to drop off to a lesser quantity than the first four.

**JS: You published the *Deep Red Horror Handbook* around this time.**

**TS:** It was an economic thing to change the format and start doing things like the *Deep Red Horror Handbook*, which was wildly successful. I mean, that thing sold so fast that it was completely out of print in record time. We literally had an entire floor underneath our building, not just the store. It was twice the length of the store and the entire width of the store; it was chock-full of publications. We'd go down there whenever we ran out of something and grab up a stack. We went running down so many times for the *Deep Red Horror Handbook* that one day, it was just like, "Hey! This is the last copy!" We actually surprised ourselves; we had no idea that we had completely run out of the book.

**JS: I have to tell you, I ordered the book through the mail and then I went to a comic shop near my house. The *Deep Red Horror Handbook* was there, in that store. And this was a small little store in the middle of nowhere. I was actually kind of mad because I wanted to read it that day, but I had to wait the six to eight weeks for it to arrive in the mail. And it was behind a glass counter, so I couldn't even page through it!**

**TS:** Yeah, if there's one thing we were responsible for, it was getting a lot of publications that would ordinarily not be carried by comic shops into comic shops. Today it's different, but that wasn't something that would normally be carried in a comic shop.

**JS: That comic shop also had *Gore Shriek* for sale. How did *Gore Shriek* come about?**

**TS:** Well, *Gore Shriek* came about for a couple of reasons. The first was just my interest in doing a horror comic. We had done a lot of comics, but we hadn't done a horror comic. The second thing was— which I'm sure you'll remember—that this was the absolute peak of everybody buying 100 copies of a black and white comic books because it was going to be

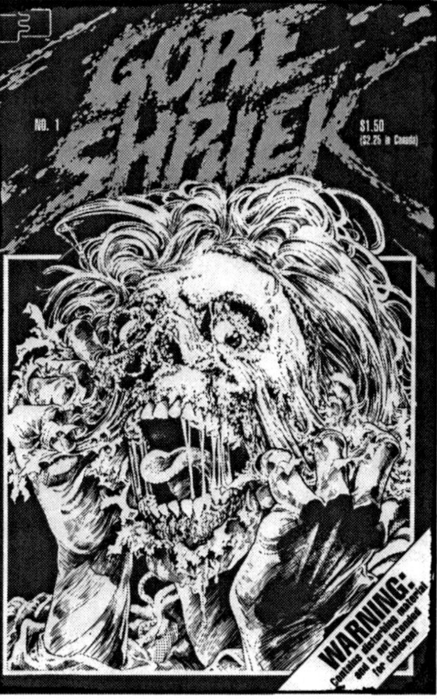
GORE SHRIEK
NO. 1
$1.50
($2.25 in Canada)
WARNING:
Contains disturbing material
and is not intended
for children!

worth $100 in a week. And one of the things at the time was, the weirder the title, the better the book sold. So there was "Radioactive Black Belt Hamsters". Take a string of adjectives, plug in an animal, and that book was out. I wanted to do something completely different from that. And with a completely different title. So that's how *Gore Shriek* started. I was just thinking of titles for a couple days and I came up with *Gore Shriek*. It was short, and if you were reading down a list of comics and hit *Gore Shriek*, it was going to stand out. I wanted something to stand out in the completely saturated crowd of black and white comic books. Also, at the time, there wasn't a whole gamut of horror comics coming out.

**JS: Where did you get your pool of talent from? There was a lot of great artwork in *Gore Shriek*.**

**TS:** There were three ways that we got our talent for *Gore Shriek*. One base was the actual customers from the store. There was Bruce Spaulding Fuller—he's in California now, but he was local throughout the first run of *Gore Shriek*. The second group came from people who had sent in artwork; they had read the earlier issues. People were also sending Steve Bissette artwork, as well. He would send us stories that he thought would work well in *Gore Shriek*.

**JS: How did you and Steve meet?**

**TS:** I'm pretty sure that the first time I met Steve was during a comic that we did in 1980 called *Alien Encounters*. Do you know the title?

**JS: Yeah. Pacific—**

**TS:** It was later put out by Pacific, but we did issue number 1. The editor was Larry Shell and the cover was done by George Chastain. That was the first piece of art that he had done. Excellent cover and a great guy too. Anyway, Steve Bissette had a story in *Alien Encounters* number 1 and that was the first time I met him.

**JS: He went on to edit *Gore Shriek* numbers 5 and 6.**

## THE FANTACO MAN

**TS:** Steve turned into a good friend and when I started becoming overwhelmed by everything that was happening I turned to Steve to edit those two issues. I'll always love issue 1, but 5 and 6 are my favorites just because they are so packed. Steve did a wonderful job on them.

**JS: One of my favorite *Gore Shriek* stories was "Circular File".**

**TS:** Oh really! That was a recurring dream I had for about a month—a really stressful month of talks with banks and printers. I told Greg Capullo my dream and he really interpreted it perfectly. I was very happy with how that story turned out without a single word.

**JS: Was *Gore Shriek* successful as a comic?**

**TS:** Yes. The first issue was swept up in the black and white craze and sold a ridiculous number of copies. Like all crazes, the black and white thing had completely died out by the time issue two came out. So, the second issue only sold twenty per cent of what number 1 had sold. Issue 2 actually had the lowest print run of the first wave of *Gore Shriek*s.

**JS: Did you ever consider moving on to color comics?**

**TS:** Well, we had priced out color well before *Gore Shriek*. It might be difficult to believe now that you can do separations in your bedroom on a computer—but, back then, to do a color comic and actually make money on it, you had to have an enormous print run. You had to have a print run of at least 100,000.

ARE YOU PREPARED TO EXPERIENCE
ALIEN
ENCOUNTERS
No. 1
$1.25
SPECIAL
FLYING SAUCER
ISSUE


**JS: One thing that's always bothered me, as far as my collection goes, is something called the *Gore Shriek Poster Book*. I saw it advertised, but I never found a copy.**

**TS:** It never came out. Instead of that, Bruce Spaulding Fuller put out a portfolio of *Gore Shriek* art. Did you ever get one of those?

**JS: You know what, I never did, but I know exactly what you're talking about.**

**TS:** Yeah. He put that out himself, it wasn't done by FantaCo. What happened with the poster book is that it really came down to numbers. We had solicited the poster book three separate times and the

numbers never came in high enough that we would be able to give the artist any appreciable amount of money; it would just go into the printing bill. We decided not to do it. That's basically what it came down to.

**JS: You also published a comic anthology called *Shriek*.**

**TS:** When the whole black and white market settled down and normalized, we were up to issues 5 and 6 of the first run of *Gore Shriek*. There was a contingent of stores that weren't carrying *Gore Shriek* because of the word, "Gore". Basically, we decided to do a more fantasy/surreal magazine. There was a horror element to it, but *Shriek* wasn't a hardcore horror book. It had a lot more to do with surrealism. It was basically an experiment, just to see what would happen. We put it out, and the first issue did well. It didn't go off the charts, but it did a good, solid number. The second issue did around the same as the first. And then, the third issue dropped off because the black and white market had crashed again. The third issue actually broke even—it didn't lose money, but it wasn't enough to carry the magazine any further. So, basically, *Shriek* was an experiment. Let's see these people put their money where their mouth is. If they're not going to carry something because it has "Gore" in the title, let's see if they'll carry *Shriek*. But basically, no comic could hold against the second big crash that came against black and whites. So, it quietly disappeared.

**JS: I actually never saw the third issue of *Shriek*.**

**TS:** Yeah, a lot of stores didn't carry the third issue. The sales of that one were a little less than half of issue 2.

**JS: What was the cover like?**

**TS:** It was a marvelous cover by Mark Martin of a little boy with a white shirt on going to the doctor. The doctor was holding a huge mosquito like a syringe; he was inserting it into the kid's arm. It was a color painting, and it was absolutely fantastic. It was a real work of art.

**JS: Along the same lines, what was *Strobe*?**

**TS:** Well, *Strobe* was my little pet project. I had always been a big fan of

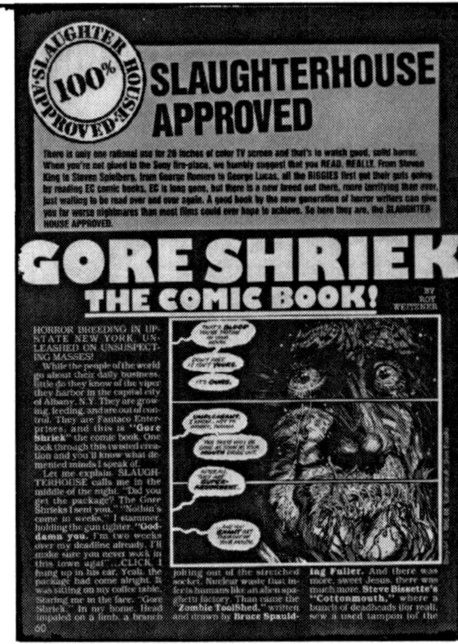

100% SLAUGHTERHOUSE APPROVED

SLAUGHTERHOUSE APPROVED

There is only one rational use for 26 inches of color TV screen and that's to watch good, solid horror. When you're not glued to the Sony fire-place, we humbly suggest that you READ. REALLY. From Steven King to Steven Spielberg, from George Romero to George Lucas, all the BIGGIES first got their guts going by reading EC comic books. EC is long gone, but there is a new breed out there, more terrifying than ever, just waiting to be read over and over again. A good book by the new generation of horror writers can give you far worse nightmares than most films could ever hope to achieve. So here they are, the SLAUGHTERHOUSE APPROVED.

GORE SHRIEK THE COMIC BOOK!

BY ROY WEITZNER

HORROR BREEDING IN UPSTATE NEW YORK, UNLEASHED ON UNSUSPECTING MASSES!

While the people of the world go about their daily business, little do they know of the viper they harbor in the capital city of Albany, N.Y. They are growing, feeding, and are out of control. They are Fantaco Enterprises, and this is **"Gore Shriek"** the comic book. One look through this twisted creation and you'll know what demented minds I speak of.

Let me explain. SLAUGHTERHOUSE calls me in the middle of the night. "Did you get the package? The Gore Shrieks I sent you." "Nothin's come in weeks," I stammer, holding the gun tighter. **"Goddamn you.** I'm two weeks over my deadline already. I'll make sure you never work in this town agai"...CLICK. I hung up in his ear. Yeah, the package had come alright. It was sitting on my coffee table. Staring me in the face. "Gore Shriek." In my home. Head impaled on a limb, a branch jolting out of the stretched socket. Nuclear waste that infects humans like an alien spaghetti factory. Than came the **"Zombie ToolShed,"** written and drawn by **Bruce Spaulding Fuller.** And there was more, sweet Jesus, there was much more. **Steve Bissette's "Cottonmouth,"** where a bunch of deadheads [illegible] sew a used tampon [illegible] the

60

TS: Yeah, a lot of stores didn't carry the third issue. The sales of that one were a little less than half of issue 2.

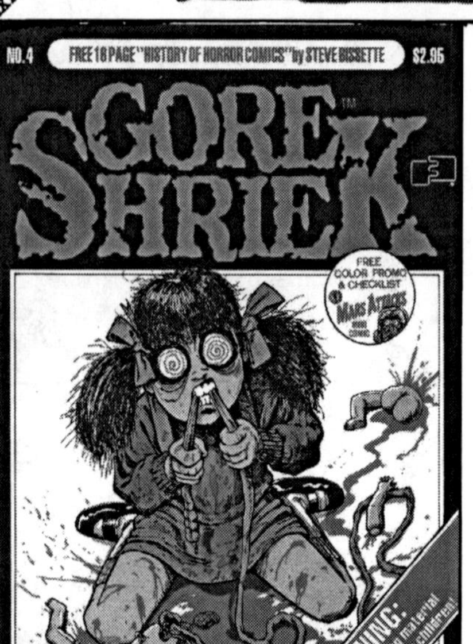

NO.4
FREE 16 PAGE "HISTORY OF HORROR COMICS" by STEVE BISSETTE
$2.95
GORE SHRIEK
FREE COLOR PROMO & CHECKLIST
MARS ATTACKS
WARNING:
Contains disturbing material and is not intended for children!


Dalì. One of the things that he eluded to was that anything could be a piece of art, it was just a matter of how much creativity you put into it. A creative studio, person, or team could do a number of projects that could all be considered part of a series. I came up with this idea that I was going to do *Strobe* and each "issue" would be something completely different. Number 1 could be a piece of woodworking. Number 2 could be a magazine. Number 3 could be a single painting. Number 4 could be… whatever. Just something creative. So, *Strobe* was obviously something completely lost on the distributors and everyone else. It was kind of an oblique idea [laughs]. It was something that I really wanted to do and end up with a series of 100 items that were all part of *Strobe*. And, maybe as a reader or collector, you could only get about ten of them [laughs]. You know what I mean? Things could be limited to one or two, and then there would be a magazine. Then something that was limited to five copies. I don't know how to explain it any better. It was just this idea that really ran counter to making anything successful. It was just a creative idea, that's all.

**JS: You know, the other thing I wanted to ask you about was the *Mars Attacks!* mini-comic.**

**TS:** Yes! Oh, how I wish that would have continued. That was a brain child of Mario Bruni. He was another customer of the store. He got the idea from the *Mars Attacks!* cards that we carried. He did a phenomenal amount of work. He never told me about this until it was completed, and I couldn't believe that he had done it. These days, Joe Blow can go license a movie title from a company and put it out. It's still work, but it's not what it was then. Mario was so impressed by the cards that he contacted Topps. He came up with this whole idea that he pitched them about how he was going to turn the *Mars Attacks!* cards into a comic book series. And he was going to market them as though they were trading cards. As far as I know, no one's ever tried to do that. Mario's idea was completely unique. He got the approval from

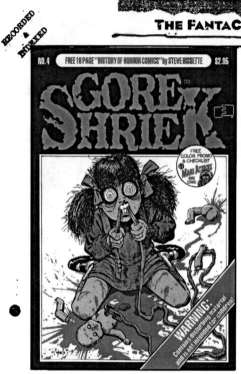

Tops and I actually saw the original proofs and separations from the cards. Mario had them at his house.

**JS: That's crazy!**

**TS:** I know, isn't that nuts [laughs]?

**JS: So, how did FantaCo get involved?**

**TS:** Mario was and is a graphic designer; that's what he does for a living. He set up the whole licensing contract and got everything set up in terms of percentages, and things like that. He had all the artwork shipped up. The thing that he didn't know how to do was how to distribute anything. He had no contacts for that. He came to us to do the distribution of the series. I knew that this was going to be huge, and we just went nuts on it. We put that center spread in *Gore Shriek* number 4 and did all kinds of advertising in the horror magazines. We racked up 100,000 orders for the first two issues. We filled those, and the re-orders completely sold it out. I own two boxes that are sealed and I don't know of any other sealed boxes around. Everyone opened them up to see what this thing was. It was so weird.

**JS: Could you describe what a customer would see?**

**TS:** It was a counter display with twenty-five copies of number one on one side and twenty-five copies of number 2 on the other side. It was just so unique—it was a fantastic marketing idea. So, I went to Mario and said, "OK, here's the orders we got for the first two issues." Box one had issues one and two, and box two would have issues three and four. There was going to be twenty-five boxes, right? Well, the orders came in on box two, and because of the way the comic market is, the orders for number two came in before people had seen number one. Know what I mean? They didn't know of the sales of number one yet, so the orders were way less. I mean, way less. We sold 100,000 of the first one, and I want to say that we sold 42,000 of the second. In terms of doing a color comic and color promotional boxes, separation, and advertising, it was just a precipitous drop. I went to Mario and I said, "Look, this is not representative of what the numbers are going to be. The numbers on box three are going to be much better." He said, "Nope. Can't do it. I'm just going to cancel it now." And that was that.

**JS: That's a shame.**

**TS:** It was just something I never expected. He had put so much time, effort, and design into this. He had to go to companies to get die-cuts

made for the boxes; all of this stuff had been paid for in advance. He wouldn't have to pay that cost again. But he just decided to cancel it. There was nothing I could do; it was Mario's project.

**JS: Want to talk about the FantaCons?**

**TS:** Sure.

**JS: You said that the first convention was held in 1979. How did you go about organizing things?**

**TS:** Well, it was sort of guerilla tactics because there just weren't many conventions. What we would do is contact as many stores directly as we could and let them know about the show. FantaCo, in people's minds (as a company), had only started in '78. So here's a company we've never heard of doing a convention we've never heard of in a place called Albany, New York. People were like, "Where's that?" Well, it's only the capital [laughs]. So, it was like pulling teeth to get people to sign up. We did have a good response from people that were in a fifty-mile radius of Albany, so we actually did have a pretty good show that year. Fortunately for us—and this has always been the case with FantaCon—there's a tremendous pool of talent that's semi-local to the Albany area. There was the Bernie Wrightson Studio in Saugerties—only forty miles away. We had no problem getting Bernie and people from there. We got Wendy and Richard Pini. There were a lot of people who we got to come up, mainly because, hey—it was a one-hour drive for them. It was no problem. They all ended up having a really good time and they came back for later shows. There was a very upbeat atmosphere. We didn't have a lot of people from out of town like we did in the later years, where we had people from all over the place, but it was a nice, friendly show. And boy, when that show was over, I collapsed! I was just so tired.

**JS: I can imagine. I get tired just attending conventions. How did you get Dario Argento as a guest in 1989?**

**TS:** His friend Luigi Cozzi was doing these model kits and magazines that Dario was financing in Italy. He contacted us to see if we wanted to carry them in our mail order department. We did carry a number of things, and in the Spring, before the convention, I just mentioned to him, "You know, it would be great if you and Dario came to the convention this year." Well, it happened. It all worked out. Dario and Luigi were there, and people were just shocked. It was just one of those things where it was perfect timing that it happened.

**JS: I visited the store in 1994 and things seemed to be going well. I've always wondered why FantaCo came to an end.**

**TS:** The plan for FantaCo was always a very sound business plan. We started out with the retail store, but that was always backed up by the mail order company. The mail order company made more money than the store, so if the store lost money for a while, it could stay afloat. And then later, when we added publishing, there was a good block of years (from 1983

to 1991) where that made quite a bit of money. So, publishing became another building stone of backup. And once the convention was established, it became a very big thing. That was another block. Basically, what happened was, we lost all the blocks; the fail-safe failed. As we got into 1996, the horror fans had disappeared from the mail order company—sales had dropped ninety per cent. The store was supporting the mail order company; this was something that had never happened before. If you remember the late nineties comic market, we were just totally out of it. I haven't lived through all of the comic market, but I've lived through a lot of it, and that was the worst implosion of comics that I've ever encountered. Sales were plummeting on everything. The Marvel and DC sales were plummeting—books that had always sold over 100,000 copies were selling 40,000. Black and white sales plummeted to nothing. So, we lost the publishing segment.

**JS: How about the conventions?**

**TS:** There was nothing that hurt the convention, other than lack of interest. There wasn't enough interest for us to do a convention. As we started soliciting ahead, it was like twenty per cent of the normal response. So, that stone was gone. We were left with the store, and the store was trying to support the staff that worked at the publishing, mail order, and conventions. You can't do that for very long. I decided to close down the business on August 28, 1998. We had started on August 28, 1978. I held the business open until that exact day.

**JS: That's a wonderful run, I have to tell you that.**

**TS:** Yeah. It was a solid twenty-year run.

**JS: And now, FantaCon 2013 in order. What can you tell me about that?**

**TS:** Basically, this is something that totally came about from people's interest in FantaCo. I've gotten a lot of wonderful emails from people over the years. To some people, FantaCo was only a store. To some people, FantaCo was only a publishing company. For some people, FantaCo was only a convention. And for some people, FantaCo was only a mail order company that they ordered from for years and years. It's funny—it's all segmented. But, it was all one company, and there's been a ton of interest

in FantaCo and having another convention. So, I thought, "Well, while I'm still alive and kicking, I might as well throw a nice big party for everybody." Let the old guests come back up and get a bunch of new guests who've never done the show before. It's sort of half nostalgia and half party. I started working on FantaCon 2013 in 2009.

**JS: Wow.**

**TS:** Yeah. To me, I've been living with this thing for years. I wanted to do it in the convention center where we'd done all of the other shows. But, since 9/11—see, the convention center is owned by New York State. The procedures that we'd have to go through to hold the convention there now, you would not believe. They want to do a background check of each person as they enter the facility. Can you imagine that? We would have to start the show a week before the show just to get the show together. For dealer load-in, they want to run a complete check on the vehicle before the merchandise is offloaded. The sad part is that the convention center really wanted us to have the show there. It was like a tradition. It really would have been nice, but I can't put people through all that.

**JS: I don't blame you.**

**TS:** In my mind, doing another FantaCon was simply turning on a switch. It suddenly became, "Holy cow, now I've got to find a place to do the show!"

**JS: What did you do?**

**TS:** I started searching! There's only a limited number of spaces in the Albany area that could hold the show. I started contacting them, one by one. After I went through the loop of all the locations, I had to go back and start negotiations again because one would have some term that wasn't acceptable and another would

TOM SKULAN AND THE FANTACO STOREFRONT.

PHOTO COURTESY OF ROGER GREEN.

be offering something that the first one wasn't offering. I constantly had to do a loop. That's taken all of this time, since 2009. It was only around six weeks ago that I got the finalized contract for the convention.

**JS: This is going to be at the Marriott?**

**TS:** Yeah, it's a wonderful facility and the Marriott staff is really into hosting the show. We're taking over the entire building. We took every single guest room, the restaurant and every single inch of convention space that they have. It's going to be a massive party!

**JS: You know, I always wanted to attend a FantaCon, but I was pretty much just a kid when they were happening. I had no real way of getting to New York. I did manage to save up my shekels for the mail order, though. My friends and I used to call the UPS driver "The FantaCo Man."**

**TS:** [laughs] I have a favorite FantaCo mail order story. We shipped everywhere. I mean, we shipped to every country that you can think of. But… there was this poor guy in Canada. He had ordered a book and a Creature mask. He sent us a letter and he said, "I had to go down to the customs office because of my order" We were like, "Why?" We called him on the phone and he said that the Creature mask was seized by customs as an obscene item!

**JS: A Creature mask? You mean *The Creature from the Black Lagoon*?**

**TS:** Isn't that nuts? His mask was destroyed. And they returned his book to us that went with the mask. They said that the order had been refused by Canadian Customs.

**JS: [stunned] A Creature mask? The gillman?**

**TS:** We never found out why the mask was considered obscene. But, one of the printing companies that we used was in Montreal. I was going up there to put in a new book, and I took this guy's book with me (I didn't want to take a chance with the Creature mask if I was going to end up in a Canadian customs station). I found out that he was only about forty miles outside of Montreal. So, I drove the book to his house and I delivered it to him in person.

**JS: That's great!**

**TS:** This poor kid, he was there! His mother answered the door. I didn't know if he was going to be forty or ten —I mean, we had people of all ages who ordered from us all the time.

**JS: How old was he?**

**TS:** He was about fourteen years old, and he just about fainted. There I was, hand-delivering his book to him.

**JS: Well, I can't top that with another question!**

**TS:** [laughs] Well, listen, if you have any more questions, just shoot me an email and we'll set up another thing.

**JS: Will do. And hey, from all of us Creature fans, young and old, thanks for everything!**

## Chapter Fifteen

# Graham Rae

## Trans-Atlantic Terror Tales

GRAHAM RAE WITH A KNB PROP FROM *BRIDE OF RE-ANIMATOR*. PHOTO COURTESY OF GRAHAM RAE.

I first met Graham Rae on a warm Summer evening in 2004. I had travelled to Chicago to meet up with Jim VanBebber upon the theatrical release of his magnum-opus, *The Manson Family*. VanBebber's first feature, *Deadbeat at Dawn*, had been a cause célèbre in the horror fanzine scene, and his long awaited follow-up was scheduled to open the eleventh annual Chicago Underground Film Festival. I had been in Los Angeles a year or so earlier when Jim was doing the sound design for *Manson*, and I was excited to finally see the finished film.

After the film had played, the theater emptied into the streets and we all started walking toward a bar. Suddenly, a Scottish accent boomed out from somewhere behind us. Jim looked up, paused for a second, and let out an enthusiastic howl: "Damn, Graham!" I turned around to see an amiable looking guy of about my age. Turns out that the two had met before, and they immediately started talking. I was thusly introduced to Graham Rae.

I first read Graham Rae's work in Chas. Balun's *Deep Red* magazine. As a foreign correspondent, his blistering attacks on the censorship laws in the UK rattled the pages with white-knuckled urgency. I was fed up with the MPAA in the United States, but this was something else entirely. Battling the odds (and the threat of legal action), Graham gave stateside readers the first reviews of toxic films like Jörg Buttgereit's *Der Todesking* and Peter Jackson's *Meet the Feebles*.

Shortly thereafter, I noticed Graham's work in the pages of *Film Threat Video Guide*. His coverage of the Edinburgh Film Festival really struck a chord with me—here was a mad movie fan shifting through the drivel in order to give the reader the honest goods on the films that actually mattered.

I followed Rae's writing through the pages (and later, website) of *Film Threat*, and our brief meeting at the 3 Penny was much like saying hello to an old friend. Today, Graham Rae continues to write, and is a noted scholar and lecturer on the works of William S. Burroughs and J. G. Ballard. His first novel, *Soundproof Future Scotland* was recently published by Creation Books. No stopping this boy. Damn, Graham, indeed!

The following interview was conducted via several email exchanges, October 2011–November 2012.

---

**JOHN SZPUNAR: Could you give me some brief background information about yourself?**

**GRAHAM RAE:** I'm alive, I breathe, I sleep, I shit. Is that brief enough? Too vague you say? OK. I am a self-taught writer from Falkirk in Scotland who now lives in Chicago, and have done since July 2005. I have written for a lot of websites but, for your purposes, I wrote for the horror fanzines *Deep Red* (and its 1989 offshoot the *Deep Red Horror Handbook*), *Deep Red Alert*,

RECORDED & INDEXED

*Viscera View*, *Samhain*, *Neros/*the *Last Movie Zine*, *Nothing Shocking*, and *Sludgefeast*, in the late eighties/early nineties. I have also written for *Film Threat*, *Cinefantastique*, and *American Cinematographer*. I am a self-taught writer who served his time in the horror/alternative zine trenches learning how to write right. I think I managed passably well, because Creation Books (which allegedly turned out to be run by a scumbag fraudster who never pays his writers, but that's another story altogether) published my first novel, *Soundproof Future Scotland*, which contains horror fandom traces in it.

**JS: How So?**

**GR:** Well, the main characters in the book, Johnny Certex and Ratsoup, are young twenty-second century splatter film (or holos, as I call them) fans. Shit, the name Ratsoup comes from a line from *Dolemite* with Rudy Ray Moore, a hero of mine, and Certex comes from the name of my favorite video shop (or store to Americans!) for a couple of years in the early eighties in my old Scottish home town of Falkirk, which closed down in 1983. I will always remember that—I took out *Blood Simple* one day, came back the next… and the place was on a different floor in the same building with new owners! They never even bothered telling us it was changing hands, and it felt like the end of an era. I used to love that place. I used to hang around sometimes with my brother Tony waiting for stuff like *The Thing* or *The Evil Dead* or *Creepshow* to come back in if they had been rented out, talking about movies to Colin and Tiger, the owners, and playing the videogame *Dragon's Lair* (which we finished). I rented many a shady or stupid movie (many a Charles Band piece of low-to-no-budget shite was viewed) during Summer holidays from that great place, who didn't give a damn how old you were (I was only thirteen or fourteen when it closed) and let you take out whatever you wanted. It was only years later that I realized that Certex was a weird way of spelling 'Certificate X,' and that made it even cooler, if such a thing was possible! In *Soundproof Future Scotland* I have a good few lines from splatter and exploitation movies serving as dialogue from my characters (I even have a line from *Xerox*—sorry, *Cannibal—Ferox* during a poignant emotional chapter!) in slightly changed form, and have them talking about splatter films and their fave sleazesploitation directors ("Crash Flagg" is one of them, a pretty obvious Ray Dennis Steckler riff) and suchlike through the whole book.

**JS: What writers first interested you?**

**GR:** When I was a youngster I grew up reading science fiction stuff like *Doctor Who* novels and suchlike. I loved the late seventies/early eighties post-*Star Wars* science fiction starburst that Charles Band effectively killed off by the mid-eighties with his terrible Empire Pictures movies. You know the names, I won't repeat them. The first novel I can actually recall reading by myself is *Prophecy* by David Seltzer which they made a shite movie out of in 1979 with Talia "ROCKEE!!!" Shire. I spent five years when I was a kid in South Africa and got the book for my tenth birthday. I don't know what my parents were thinking buying me such stuff, but I'm glad of it! The old paperback cover had a strange deformed bigtooth monster fetus in an amniotic sac on it. I still remember page 166 of the South African (dunno if it was the same as the American/European) version, cos it's where two kids are eaten by the mutant creature, which "ate lazily" as it stands eating a kid over the boy's sibling, dripping blood on the kid's face. This made a huge impression on a young boy (for some reason), as did the "vanilla twist" scene from the original *Assault on Precinct 13* (where a young girl of around eight is shot to death by a cold uncaring murderer standing in an ice cream van) when I saw it around age twelve or thirteen. At that age you simply have no frame of reference or defense against such things, no logical or emotional way of processing them. I remember just sitting in horrified shock as the wee lassie looked at the blood spattered on her shattered ice cream cone and slowly slumped to the ground with a weird confused look on her face. I'll never forget that moment. Remember reading that the MPAA asked John Carpenter to take that moment out, so he simply took it out of the version he gave them and released the street versions uncut. Good on him!

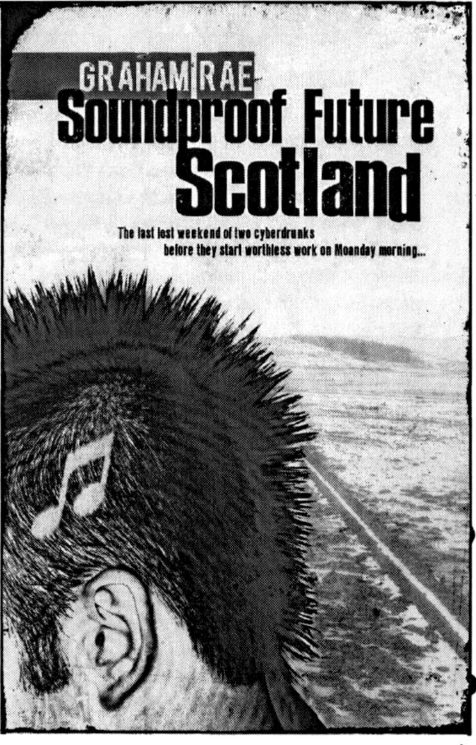

GRAHAM RAE
Soundproof Future Scotland
The last lost weekend of two cyberdrunks
before they start worthless work on Moanday morning...

**JS: When I was a kid, one of my favorite writers was Stephen King.**

**GR:** When I was eleven, I discovered Stephen King, and the first novel I can remember buying was *Cujo* (from an old branch of the John Menzies chain in my old Scottish home town that now no longer exists) which, when I think about it, has another bloody dead kid in it (at least in the book version)! Jesus! What fun fond childhood memories! I am chuckling here. I became a huge Stephen King fan from ages eleven to eighteen (he and Romero were the inspiration and impetus for me to write an unpublished-but-finished zombie novel entitled *Grave Business*, which I toiled over from ages sixteen

RECORDED & INDEXED

to eighteen), even joined the Castle Rock fan newsletter he put out when I was sixteen, so that I could write to Stephanie (the sister of King's wife Tabitha), his assistant, and ask her nonsense about whether or not King liked George A. Romero movies ("he watches them over and over"—DUH!), important stuff like that. And talking of George Romero, I discovered *Dawn of the Dead* at age eleven, but that's another, life-changing story.

**JS: I always wanted to join the Castle Rock fan club, but somehow never managed to get around to it.**

**GR:** Well, I can't even really remember where I heard about that; maybe in *Fangoria*, maybe in the back of a King novel, who knows; time kills lucidity on some details, and we're talking about over twenty-five years ago now. I just recall getting it monthly(?) for a year maybe. It had ads for rare editions of King books that you couldn't get elsewhere, and King would go on about his radio station and how his DJs would tell him that maybe the very early morning wasn't the right time to play stuff like AC/DC, which he was a huge fan of. It had interviews with King, and book reviews. I remember one time somebody writing in asking him why there was racism in his books (think he was a high school kid; it's a pretty naïve question) and him replying that while there was racism and racist language used in his books, the ones who used it were the ones who got punished by being horribly killed. Moralistic stuff! It was the size of a full newspaper, if slightly smaller, and the name of the publication on the front was written in *Creepshow*-like letters. I just cheated by checking briefly on the net for that last memory-lost detail; everything else is my own vague recall. But my interest in King eventually petered out as I got slightly older, after that banner year, 1987, when he put out four books and I bought them all in hardback. Which, on a Youth Training Scheme "wage" was no easy thing, trust me!

**JS: Were you reading Clive Barker at the time?**

**GR:** I discovered Clive Barker around age seventeen, after reading a review in *Fangoria* of the *Books of Blood* (which I can still recall demanded you walk into a bookstore and "talk loud. Eat an onion sandwich" to make sure they got Barker books in stock!), and that beautyfuel "poetry of the perverse" stuff seemed far more sophisticated and interesting and intellectual and aesthetically pleasing to me than King's much simpler work. I still love the *BoB*, and "Jacqueline Ess: Her Last Will and Testament" is still one of my all-time favorite stories: "Common waters made of thought and bone," lovely. I think he's an excellent painter. Met Barker a couple of times, once with Michele Soavi at a horror film festerville (joke spelling!), and he's always cool and easy to talk to. When I hit nineteen, I got into Hunter S. Thompson and Lester Bangs, with everything that fandom of these two writers entails.

**JS: How long did your horror-phase last?**

**GR:** The whole period of time we're talking about only runs for me from 1988 to 1992, ages eighteen to twenty-two; by then I had stopped writing for horror zines. I was really young, and my interests just changed as I

grew older. On the King front though, ironically, I just recently went back and re-read the first two Bachman books, *Rage* and *Roadwork*, from the now-banned American volume, and found them thoroughly enjoyable and want to get back into King's work again! I've come full circle! I guess you never forget your first literary love!

**JS: What got you interested in horror films?**

**GR:** No real idea, to be perfectly honest. Bear in mind I was a child in the seventies, when horror material was a lot easier to come by; there was a big horror boom back then for some reason. Maybe my horror fandom is due to my early childhood love of *Scooby-Doo*! Who knows? Tell you one thing though. When I was in South Africa, January 1976–December 1980, exactly five years, we used to rent out a 16mm projector and screen the films on the wall of our Edenvale home. That was a *real* home entertainment system. The last film I saw like that was years ago in Los Angeles on the living room wall of Bob Murawski, the guy who won the Oscar for editing *The Hurt Locker*. We watched *Bring Me the Head of Alfredo Garcia*; great stuff. I remember stuff like the *Mighty Mouse* cartoons being rented in Suid Afrique, but one that made a real impression was John Carpenter's old version (shit, every fucking film I talk about will be an old version, I don't watch the tedious remakes!) of *The Fog* ("Don't go into the fog! There's something in the fog!"), especially the part where the undead pirate Blake came back in the dark at the end with the red glowing eyes and cut the priest's head off. That is still evocative to me of the double-glazing-muted cry of crickets in a balmy South African childhood evening, and it sends shivers up

# NEVER APOLOGISE, NEVER EXPLAIN

## Hunter S. Thompson on Trankfantasy, Journalism and Psychoactive Etiquette

By GRAHAM RAE

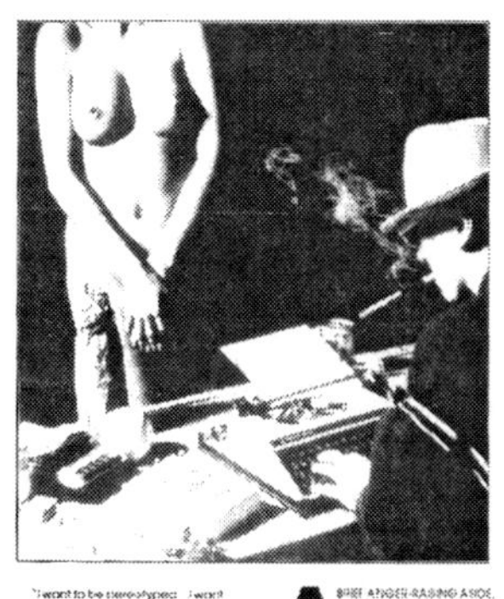

"I want to be stereotyped. I want to be classified"
*The Descendents*

28

Psychotic Reaction Issue 1

PSYCHOTIC REACTION NUMBER 1.

RECORDED & INDEXED

SPLATTERFEST '90

SATURDAY, FEBRUARY 24TH, 1990.

SCALA CINEMA, LONDON. (PENTONVILLE ROAD – KINGS X)

ADMIT ONE ONLY. DOORS OPEN 12.00pm. THIS TICKET IS NON-TRANSFERABLE.

NOT TO BE RESOLD. ANY QUERIES, TELEPHONE THE SCALA (01)-278-3052 (10am - 6pm)

UNFORTUNATLY, NO REFUNDS. £20

my spine for more reasons than one.

**JS: You were first published in *Deep Red*...**

**GR:** I was indeed. 1988. I was eighteen years old. It was (if you don't count a letter in issue number 4 I wrote to them as being published: "Loved the Savini interview, now how about one with Romero?") for an article entitled "All Cut Up" about UK censorship and cutting up (hence the oh-so-clever title, because I was—cough—all cut up about what they were doing to my fave graverave flickershows) horror movies for general release. I just loved the fact I got to say 'FUCK THE CENSORS' in print. I even told Chas. if he had a problem with that he could leave it out. Yeah right, like Chas. would have a problem with swearing! I am chuckling here. It's incredible to think back on it. Here I was, this wide-eyed teenage horror movie freak (I grew up during the well-documented "video nasties" ludicrous hysteria of the eighties in the UK) who still lived with his parents in Bainsford (a Falkirk suburb), and I wrote a letter sitting on the floor to Chas. Balun on my old lightweight manual portable typewriter asking if I could be a "foreign correspondent"—with absolutely no contacts in the movie industry whatsoever!—and he wrote back saying, well lad, go for it! I went to a festivile (another bad pun crock title) called Shock Around the Clock 2 at the now-sadly-defunct Scala Cinema in Pentonville Road in London (it was the UK's only grindhouse—Kubrick sued when they showed *A Clockwork Orange* without his permission after he withheld it from being screened in the UK, and the legal costs shut the place down) (fuck you, Kubrick!) (guess that would be homosexual necrophilia now, mind you) (moving swiftly on…) and (speaking of necrophilia) I saw *Nekromantik* (you and I certainly had fun taking Jörg Buttgereit to Ed Gein's grave in Wisconsin in July 2012, didn't we? I will never forget that truly bizarre experience) there, was blown the fuck away, and

Attachment

wrote the first ever American review of it for *Deep Red*. And the rest, as they say, is (personal) history. I must admit I will never forget when the *Deep Red Horror Handbook* came out. Each writer got five contributor's copies (some of which had blurred pages or tended to fall to pieces, unfortunately; they were not well bound) and I got a check for something like $80 (first check I ever got from Chas. was for $40, and I couldn't believe I was being paid to write about this stuff!), but it was the thrill of seeing my teenage work in a book that just blew me away, for obvious reasons. I mentioned all my friends in it at the end of my article. One of them, Fenn, is dead now from multiple sclerosis, died horribly in his twenties, and it's slightly sad to think about. The writer bios at the end were the best: everybody else in the book was some professional writer or other, having been on TV or radio or, with people like Stephen Bissette (a fine man—we keep in constant touch on Facebook), in multiple media venues—and my bio just said that I had an axe to grind with the BBFC and lived in Falkirk! Classic!

**JS: How did you become aware of *Deep Red*?**

**GR:** Italian pseudonymous slash-and-hackmeister Vincent Dawn came to me in a bloodred wet dream and told me of its erection-raising writing-career-starting existence. No, not buying it? Okay, lemme see… to be perfectly honest I don't exactly remember exactly how I came to hear about it. I remember reading about the *Gore Score* in *Fangoria* in 1987 (I read the mag for a few years from my early to late teens and used to thoroughly enjoy it, what with "The Pit and the Pen of Alex Gordon" and Dr. Cyclops and Bob Martin's sterling editorship—I got my name in an editorial in issue 72 for a letter I wrote to them about… yeah you got it, it's a cliché… censorship) and such. They wrote a review of this wild review chapbook by some guy called Chas. Balun, and I thought it sounded hysterical.

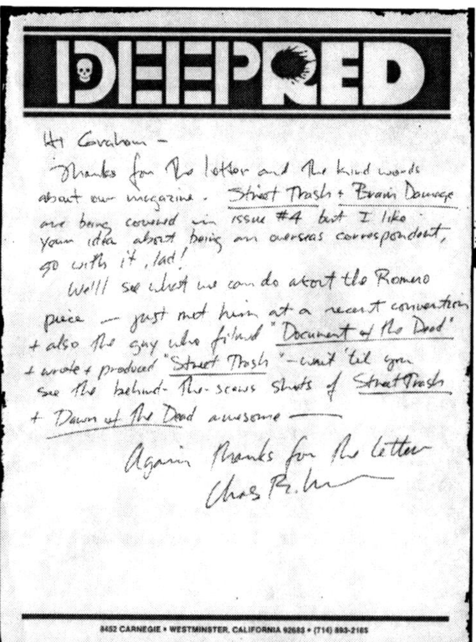

DEEP RED

Hi Graham –

Thanks for the letter and the kind words about our magazine. Street Trash + Brain Damage are being covered in issue #4 but I like your idea about being an overseas correspondent, go with it, lad!

We'll see what we can do about the Romero piece — just met him at a recent convention + also the guy who filmed "Document of the Dead" + wrote + produced "Street Trash" – wait 'til you see the behind-the-scenes shots of Street Trash + Dawn of the Dead awesome ——

Again thanks for the letter

Chas B.—

8452 CARNEGIE • WESTMINSTER, CALIFORNIA 92683 • (714) 893-2185

GRAHAM RAE: FOREIGN CORRESPONDENT.

RECORDED & INDEXED

HORROR TALES FROM CHAS. BALUN

NO.1

Hi Graham —
Great work, lad! You did a fine job - just what I was looking for - send a quick note for a short bio I want to include in the book on each of the writers. OK?
So... let's swap "Document of Dead" for "Nekromantik"
Mine's a pristine print on VHS NTSC - what's yours?
Thanks again for the terrific work! Chas—
P.S. I liked your story.. alot.

8452 CARNEGIE AVENUE • WESTMINSTER, CALIFORNIA 92683

WORDS OF ENCOURAGEMENT FROM CHAS. BALUN.

I remember them quoting the review for *Humungous*: "Wretched crap about some weird cannibal asshole in diapers. This one's got puke for brains." (this is all done from memory, folks, without a safety net!) I have always had a pretty decent sense of humor, even about things I hold dear, and really liked the demented irreverent sound of it. I went through to the now-sadly-defunct Science Fiction Bookshop in West Broughton Street in Edinburgh (which was a fifty mile round trip I used to make by myself when I was seventeen or so) and found the *Gore Score* and bought it. I took it home and loved it! There was one review in there for *Monster Dog* with Alice Cooper that is really easy to remember: "Title tells all. With Alice Cooper. Fuck it."

**JS: That review is timeless.**

**GR:** If a film was a 'dog' they printed a graphic of a dog, but for this one they printed a BIG dog. It was hilarious. I distinctly remember thinking, at age seventeen, shit, anybody could write that! That review literally changed my life. So I wrote to Chas. and he wrote back. Maybe he told me about *Deep Red*, I truly can't quite remember, despite my much-vaunted super-impressive memory. Maybe *Fangoria* mentioned it again or something. I still have all the back issues of *Deep Red* back at my parents' house in Scotland, I believe. I actually got fan letters about my writing from people in the UK—Chas. would send them to me. He always wrote in red on his envelopes—I still have a load of letters from him.

**JS: What other horror magazines were you reading at the time?**

**GR:** *Fangoria* was pretty much it, though I liked the first few issues of *Gorezone* when it came out, and can remember buying it in Edinburgh and being literally blown away by a two-page color spread of a headshot from

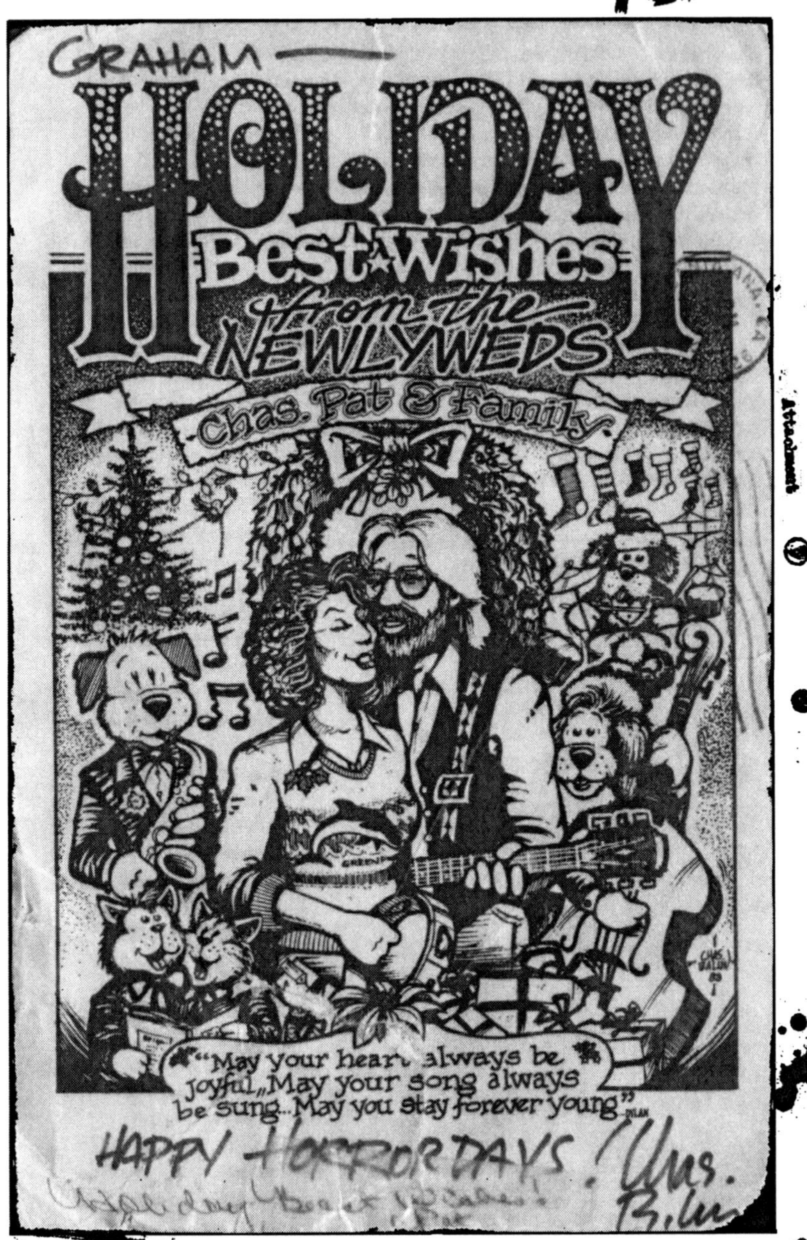
GRAHAM —
HOLIDAY
Best Wishes
from the
NEWLYWEDS
Chas. Pat & Family
"May your heart always be joyful.. May your song always be sung.. May you stay forever young."
HAPPY HORRORDAYS!

RECORDED & INDEXED

Pete Jackson's *Bad Taste* as I read it in a model store I was visiting with my pal Stephen 'Scanny' Scanlan. (And let me tell you a brief tangential story about wee Stevie. I met him because I had just purchased issue 72 of *Fangoria*, the one with my name in the editorial, and had it in my hand as I took back a copy of some cheapjack splatter movie to a video shop in Callendar Square in Falkirk. He noticed it in my hand, started talking to me about it being a good mag… I showed him my name in the editorial—I keep thinking of Chas. calling it a "Reditorial"—and we have been friends ever since, for a quarter of a century). There wasn't anything else, really, that I can recall. As I say, I had to make a bloody fifty mile round trip to even get *Deep Red*! *Film Threat* was the only other zine-cum-mag I read as a teen, from 1987 onwards, issue 12; I have long since stopped reading the website, or writing for it. I remember when I was seventeen they had the name Harlan Ellison on the grey cover and I looked at it cos Stephen King had mentioned him in *Danse Macabre*, and he sounded interesting. So I picked up the mag… and once again my life was changed. The spiky mad spunky punky rude crude attitude of that mag fit my teenage anger like a glove, and I took to it instantly. Would be years before I wrote for it, or its "mutant twin" (as Chas. Balun, I think though I may be wrong, named it) the *Film Threat Video Guide*.

**JS: When did you start writing for other fanzines?**

**GR:** Not until after I wrote for *Deep Red*, then it was for the others I mentioned. *Viscera View* (you get it? *Viscera Review*? Genius!) was my own one-shot photocopied (on my dad's home photocopier for his business, which ran out of toner! He was not happy!) fanzine in August 1989, punted at Shock Around the Clock 2 for 50p, done with Scanny, with a Jörg Buttgereit interview in it I'd done by mail, and a red

SPECIAL NECROPHILIA ISSUE - INTERVIEW WITH JÖRG (NEKROMANTIK, HOT LOVE) BUTTGEREIT, NECROPHILIA IN FILM, NEKROMANTIK PICTURE GALLERY, NECROPHILIA SHORT STORY - ALL IN VISCERA VIEW - IN TESTS, EIGHT OUT OF TEN UNDEAD GHOULS PREFERRED IT FOR GORY NEWS.

*VISCERA VIEW*—PUNTED AROUND SHOCK AROUND THE CLOCK 2.

plastic spine holding the pages together! A timeless crass sick classic. I don't even own a hard copy myself now, though I do have it on a PDF as Scanny found one in 2012 and sent it to me. It was weird as hell to see it again after all these years, and it wasn't nearly as bad as I thought it might be, but some of it was just cringeworthy, with us going all-out to try and just be as offensive as possible. Teenage nonsense, but fun in retrospect. Looking at it I can't even believe we had heard about all this stuff in the pre-internet days, and can't really remember how we did it. Probably through other zines, as there are pieces from a few other zine people in there. It amazes me how much we were into that scene back then, and it's oddly poignant too, meeting your rabid frothing hyper-excited teenage self in middle age. That long-forgotten gem also resurfaced in *Soundproof Future Scotland* as a splatter webzine. Had to be done.

MARIO BAVA: NEVER MIND THE PLOT, IT'S THE MURDER THAT COUNTS BY BILLY BALLANTYNE

Mario Bava is one of two great exploitation directors who came to prominence in the 1960's (he is second only to Seijun Suzuki, a Japanese exploitation director who made some of the most dazzlingly violent and stylish movies ever, movies which are still unreleased in the U.K.). Like many of the most interesting Italian directors, Bava took his movies seriously as a craft as well as a profession. Other directors, many Italian, also do something that is becoming increasingly rare in movies from the U.S. and U.K: when it comes to the real meat, the gore, the violence, they really deliver the goods. Most Italian directors do/did one of these things. Mario Bava did both.

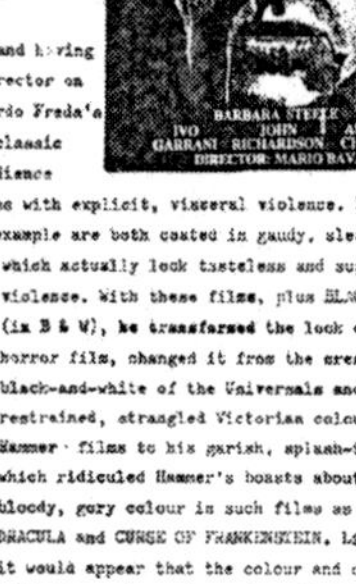


Progressing from cinematographer, and having proved himself more than a capable director on the few weeks of work he did on Riccardo Freda's I VAMPIRI, Bava began to direct some classic horror movies which mesmerised the audience with atmospheric visuals and kicked ass with explicit, visceral violence. BLACK SABBATH and BLOOD AND BLACK LACE for example are both coated in gaudy, sleazy colours which actually look tasteless and suggest violence. With these films, plus BLACK SUNDAY (in B & W), he transformed the look of the horror film, changed it from the creaky old black-and-white of the Universals and the restrained, strangled Victorian colours of the Hammer films to his garish, splash-it-on style, which ridiculed Hammer's boasts about its bloody, gory colour in such films as HORROR OF DRACULA and CURSE OF FRANKENSTEIN. Like Suzuki, it would appear that the colour and overall look of Bava's early movies such as BLACK SABBATH were an exact result of them mostly being shot in the studio. They look artificial, unreal, and that is what gives them their atmosphere. In this respect, Bava's influence can be traced to other directors like Dario Argento, John Carpenter and now Gianfranco Giagni, director of the recent SPIDER LABYRINTH (see review this issue).

(34)

VISCERA VIEW.

**JS: What was your first impression of *Deep Red*?**

**GR:** I fucking loved it. It was the best thing I had ever seen at that time, much looser than *Fangoria* and ready to riot. It seemed to me a natural extension of all these weird and wonderfuel films that *Fango* had talked about in its pages that I knew I'd never see (especially with censorshit so bad in the UK back then) but I always wanted to see, the more obscure the better; stuff like the Cinema of Transgression or Joe Christ stuff in the back of *Film Threat* too. I will still watch anything, no matter how obscure, and judge it all equally. Growing up swapping bootlegs with people all over the world, if it was the only way you could get to see a film, uncut or not, really helped foster a democratic attitude in me towards the visual and sonic quality of films, even today. I couldn't care how bad the picture on something on YouTube is; at least you can see it without having to write

# GRAHAM RAE

## TRANS-ATLANTIC TERROR TALES

RECORDED & INDEXED

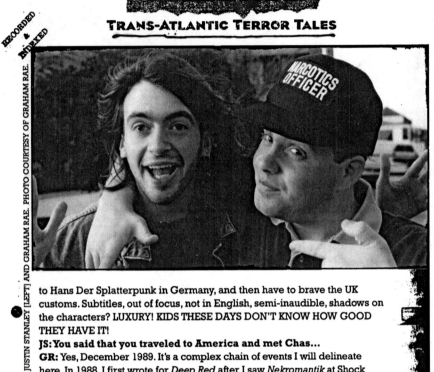

JUSTIN STANLEY [LEFT] AND GRAHAM RAE. PHOTO COURTESY OF GRAHAM RAE.

to Hans Der Splatterpunk in Germany, and then have to brave the UK customs. Subtitles, out of focus, not in English, semi-inaudible, shadows on the characters? LUXURY! KIDS THESE DAYS DON'T KNOW HOW GOOD THEY HAVE IT!

**JS: You said that you traveled to America and met Chas...**

**GR:** Yes, December 1989. It's a complex chain of events I will delineate here. In 1988, I first wrote for *Deep Red* after I saw *Nekromantik* at Shock Around the Clock and reviewed it. I went to the same festival for the second (and last) time in August 1989 at the Scala. This eighteen year-old kid came up to me and asked me if I was Graham Rae. I was wary and replied yes, ready for a fight. Turns out the guy was (and still is!) named Justin Stanley and had a wild idea of organizing a festival of his own, Splatterfest '90, to be held at the Scala in February 1990. He knew who I was through *Deep Red*, of course. He asked me if I wanted to help. I said yes, though to be perfectly honest I didn't do much apart from give him Chas.'s phone number, as I recall. He called Chas., told him his plans, said he needed more phone numbers, and for some reason Chas. gave him the numbers of people like Scott *Intruder* Spiegel; why he would give these sort of numbers out to an English teen saying he wanted to run a fest is anybody's guess. We both went across to Los Angeles in December 1989 (after a brief abortive trip to Pittsburgh to meet Tom Savini, which never happened, but we did get to go to the Monroeville Mall, so it evened out) and stayed at Chas.'s house for a few days. When he picked us up opposite Disneyworld in Anaheim he was appalled that I was drinking a can of Budweiser from a twelve pack we'd got a friendly black woman to buy us, telling her that this trip was a twenty-first birthday present for me. It wasn't. I was twenty. In America five minutes and breaking the law already! I am chuckling here.

**JS: How did you and Chas. get along?**

**GR:** Chas. didn't get on all that well with Justin and me, to be perfectly honest. He was twice our age and we were just young goggle-eyed guys in America for the first time getting drunk and having fun; we had nothing much in common with him except a love of horror movies. He showed us a clip of Bud Dwyer, the Penn State Treasurer, shooting himself in the head, and kind of gloated at our appalled reaction: "You can see when he hits the floor there's no soul there or anything." Justin was so upset and disgusted and sickened he had to go lie down. He goosed us with a snuff movie without telling us what we were going to see (I never watch any real-life death stuff on the net—I don't want the last moments of these poor dying people being used for entertainment, or in my mind for the rest of my life—never really ever been into that mondo shit), and it was an antagonistic and unpleasant thing to do. But then you recall that he would write about taking great pleasure in driving people out of his house by showing them stuff like *Doctor Butcher: Medical Deviate*, so he obviously had this wee juvenile slightly sadistic streak in him. But I guess that goes with splatter film fandom, to a degree, to be perfectly honest. He was meant to be a guest at the fest, but gave us his ticket back. I guess that's what happens when a forty-odd-year-old ex-hippy hangs around with shy drunk foreign people half his age. Still, he did give me my writing start, and I can never forget that. We didn't talk much after that, though I did contribute a couple of reviews to *Deep Red Alert* number 1 in 1991; nothing after that. I did tell him about my impending set visit to *Land of the Dead* (for *Cinefantastique*) in Toronto in 2004, and he told me to "make the beast" of it—it was only then, with the benefit of distance and time, I realized that some of his wordplay tendencies had been inherited/nicked from Forrest J Ackerman, whose work I had and have never read, but knew of. When I heard that he died I was sad—it was like an important part of my youth dying.

**JS: Didn't Chas. introduce you to some of the *Evil Dead* guys?**

**GR:** He introduced us to the cool-as-hell Scott Spiegel, who took us to get drunk on vodka and orange with Sam Raimi at his minimally decorated Silverlake house, where we recognized the old yellow car from *Evil Dead* sitting outside! I remember Justin pointing to the script for *Evil Dead 3* on a shelf; a weird and unbelievable memory now. I remember sitting there at twenty years old thinking shit, I am drinking with the director of my all-time fave youthful horror films how the fuck did this happen and what did I ever do to deserve this? I wonder if Raimi even remembers all these years later. And the amiable and all-round great guy Greg Nicotero (whom I still occasionally trade emails with—he was another Splatterfest '90 guest) took us round the (called at that time) KNB FX labs, which were full of stuff from *Dances With Wolves* and *Tales From the Darkside*, horror stuff as beautiful and cool as you can imagine. And in a roundabout way this is all due to Chas. (and Justin, of course), so I can't knock the man too much. Not that I

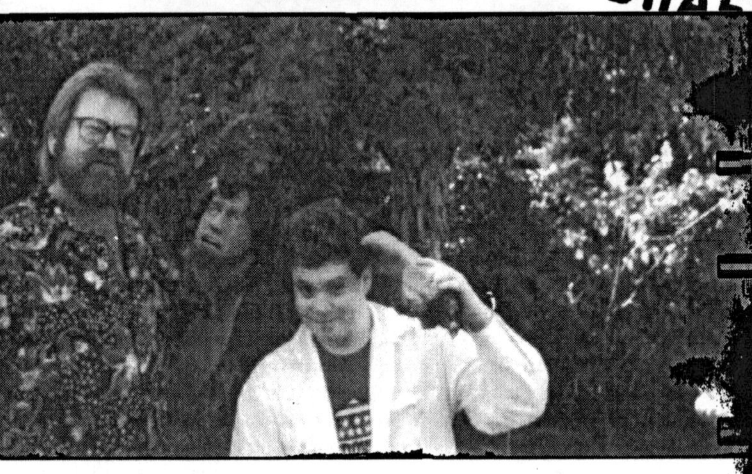

CHAS. BALUN [LEFT] AND GRAHAM RAE. PHOTO COURTESY OF GRAHAM RAE.

would want to anyway. You don't speak ill of the dead, and any problems between us were long finished with and forgotten by the end of his life.

**JS: I've always wondered what the Chunkblow Chateau was like...**

**GR:** It was just a normal looking Orange County house from the outside. In the inside he had loads of his own paintings (I remember a big one of a capuchin monkey, I believe it was, that I complimented him on, on his living room wall) and fake horror props and posters from loads of different horror films. I have some photos I'll have to see if I can dig some out for you to illustrate this piece. I remember he made us massive burgers on his BBQ in his back garden, and swore that nobody could eat two of them. I don't recall if either Justin or I proved him wrong; I doubt it. His wife Pat was lovely. I wonder how she's getting on. Hope she's well.

**JS: Was this the same trip that you met Jim VanBebber?**

**GR:** No, I actually met Jim in England a few years later, though Chas. did show us Jim's work (he would go to bed at night and I would stay up, with his blessing, and watch stuff like *Deranged*, digging through his collection for the juiciest-sounding stuff) for the first time—he had the grim *Roadkill* short and the *Charlie's Family* (as it was known at that time) trailer. We thought it was great. My best friend Davey Blair and I got a hold of a bootleg copy of this selfsame material around 1990 or 1991, including a Skinny Puppy video and a trailer for some Chas.-scripted thing called *Chunk Blower* ("There is no why!") that never got off the ground, and we became big Jim fans. We finally met him in Northampton in England in 1992, at a festival called Nothing Shocking, and we hit it off with him straight away. I'll never forget Davey's opening gambit to the director: "Jim! Jim! Here's a wee tinny tae yersel!" He handed a confounded VanBebber a can of cheap lager without ever actually having met the man

before, and it actually freaked the director out slightly. Later on we took him to a pub across the road (hidden in a shopping mall for some weird reason—the cinema was in the same building as a leisure center, you had these mothers walking past with their kids and moving them away from the suspicious-looking horror fans!) (I remember we met the bass player from the Spencer Davis Group in that pub, working as a barman, and it impressed Jim and Davey no end, though I had never heard of the combo before) and bought him loads of pints of Beck's and sat talking to him about horror movies. He was there with *Deadbeat at Dawn* and was the main guest of the fest. I am laughing here as I recall this. We got him so totally drunk (not that we were particularly sober by any means—Davey nearly knocked over the extremely expensive video projector screening a Charles Manson documentary—it wobbled and wavered but thankfully never hit the floor) that he got up on stage to do a Q&A with the audience. "Are you guys as drunk as I am?" was all he said to the crowd before trying to do a backwards kick for some reason and falling flat on his back! End of Q&A! Mission accomplished! I met Jim a few more times over the years. Very intense man, very talented, but very angry. His excellent work, of course, reflects his personality and personal intensity. He was inspired by the raucous reaction his work got at Nothing Shocking to make *My Sweet Satan*, which is a fine film I reviewed and interviewed him about for the *Film Threat Video Guide*. We don't speak anymore, though.

**JS: What was the horror/zine scene like in Scotland in the late eighties?**

**GR:** There was no horror/zine scene in Scotland back then—it's as simple as that. As I said, a friend and I did a one-shot fanzine called *Viscera View*, and we met a couple of teenage weirdos through advertising it in John Gullidge's excellent *Samhain* (I got a quote on the *Santa Sangre* quad poster from a review I did for that zine of the film), but there was never anything organized, anything coherent. There was a community of likeminded people round the country that we corresponded with here and there, but the main hub of all that stuff was London. And the London (ob)scene cognoscenti were pretty arrogant, ignorant guys, some of them—naming no names cos I am not interested in over-two-decades-old feuds—and thought that anything outside London was not even worth noting. There was a lot of petty name-calling and backstabbing in that scene back then—when the Splatterfest was getting put on, we even had people physically threatening us for some reason! Needless to say, nothing happened, despite toilet graffiti in the Scala that said that "blood will flow" at the Splatterfest. It was all very parochial and tiresome, in retrospect, worse at the time, and hardly worth discussing any further. We did meet some great guys from England, mind you, like Paul Mallinson of *Sludgefeast*, or Tony Cotterell of *Neros* (which he jokingly told me was spelled that way because he couldn't spell 'neurosis'!), guys we would hang out with at festivals and who occasionally

RECORDED & INDEXED

DRAFT

GREG NICOTERO OF KNB AND GRAHAM RAE. PHOTO COURTESY OF GRAHAM RAE.

would come to Scotland to visit us. This is actually making me nostalgic for those times. It was such great fun.

**JS: What was the process of getting uncut tapes like in the UK?**

**GR:** Well, Scanny and I got our first one from a guy I met in the line for Shock Around the Clock 2 who was handing out lists of bootleg splatter videos. We sent off for—I'll never forget this—a tape with both *The Texas Chainsaw Massacre 2* (which was banned in the UK at that time) and *Blood Sucking Freaks* on it—and the last few minutes of *BS* (an appropriate acronym—I parody the title in my novel as *Bloodfucking Shrieks*) was cut off when the tape ran out! Nightmare! But we thought this was great and Scanny built up a pretty big list of banned and cut titles, trading tapes with people up and down the British Isles and going to the occasional festival to get even more lists from people. Scanny was a big Fulci and Argento fan, but I was much more into the whole trash aesthetic thing—films like *Mad Foxes* (to this day a fave of mine) and *For Your Height Only* and *Suffer Little Children* and such horrible intolerable shite. I recall trading with one guy from Germany (they cut a lot of things over there too), though I don't think we had any American contacts—our system was PAL and yours was NTSC, so there was that barrier, and some of the stuff would have been a bit iffy—and pricey!—to get converted from one format to the other. I did import both *Dawn* and *Day of the Dead* from FantaCo though, from the pages of *Fangoria*, and paid to have them converted in Edinburgh (*Day* had an annoying slightly greenish tint to it), because no way in hell was the British

Board of Film Classification (aka the BBFC for short—I used to call them the British Board of Fucking Cunts) (such rapier-like youthful wit) going to stop me seeing Romero zombie genius uncut. Some of the old pre-censorship tapes were quite easy to find in Scotland from old video shops and could be bought cheaply, then sold down in England at fests for a lot of money—there were a pair of weird splatter collector brothers in Wales (I remember their name, but am purposefully leaving it out) who could be relied on to pay far over the odds for what something was really worth. It was kind of funny; we used to joke about how tragic a house fire would be with their extensive expensive collection!

**JS: The nasties campaign was clearly something that you railed against.**

**GR:** Yes, I had a real bee in my bonnet about censorship at the time, and would rail against it to an incredibly boring degree. My friends and I just hated the idea of the BBFC dictating what we could and couldn't see—it was so condescending and infantilizing. The fascistic Customs clowns you had to brave to get some tapes into the country were unbelievable; they would sometimes catch VHS videotapes coming through the post from some random correspondent you met at a horror film festival, and send you a letter ("NOTICE OF SEIZURE UNDER THE CUSTOMS AND EXCISE ACT 1979"—talk about melodrama!) saying you know, we have this tape of yours we have caught you trying to bring into the country (something bloody totally innocuous and surrealistic like, say, the uncut *Re-animator* or something), you're more than welcome to claim it from us… but there was a catch. The (in their subjective opinion) "indecent or obscene articles" could be claimed for up to a month after the letter's date, but (and I quote from one reproduced in the twentieth anniversary edition of the much-confiscated *Nekromantik*) "If you make such claim within the time aforesaid, legal proceedings will be taken for the condemnation thereof"! So yeah, you can have your tape back, just come and get it from us… and we'll prosecute and persecute you if you do! Brilliant *Catch 22*! They even raided people's houses all over the UK and confiscated tapes and prosecuted people; how I never got hassled back then I'll never know, cos I had correspondents all over the UK top to bottom. I'm glad I didn't though! Guy I knew through my zine in Glasgow, twenty-five miles away from where I lived, had his house raided and got a huge fine of thousands of pounds—he was only fifteen years old and his dad tried to kill himself. People's lives were literally destroyed. A disgusting disgrace from the "moral guardians" that is very well explained in the excellent, anger-making English documentary *Video Nasties: The Definitive Guide*. It's almost funny now that "video nasty" is now a reverent term (much like the hilarious and pathetic "suffering erotica" euphemism for "torture porn") that tiresome splatter fans use in the USA when talking about that period of time, wistfully romanticizing something they would have utterly despised had they been there!

RECORDED & INDEXED
DRAFT

**JS: I thought the MPAA was bad at the time, and then I started reading about that.**

**GR:** Be thankful you weren't there! I mean, these were only uncut cheapjack splatter movies! Most of them weren't worth the half-chewed blurry-picture tape they were spooled on!

**JS: And today—**

**GR:** Many of the "indecent or obscene" films have actually been released uncut in the UK now, with a loosening up of the censorship rules, so all that pain and misery people went through being raided was really, tragically, in vain. I must admit, though, knowing you were defying the government with these illegal tapes made things that wee bit more exciting when you traded them, like taking drugs is made more exciting by being taboo.

**JS: How did you start writing for *Film Threat*?**

**GR:** That's a good question, and one I'm not entirely sure of the answer to. Justin went across to America after the Splatterfest to stay with Scott Spiegel for a while. I think Justin was introduced to Chris Gore by Spiegel; Spiegel had been interviewed by *Film Threat* years earlier and those guys knew each other from back in Michigan. So I think I met Gore and Dave Williams, of the *Film Threat Video Guide* (I got on well with Dave at the time and did a lot of writing for the *FTVG*; I never dealt much with Gore, and the only thing that I wrote that was actually used in the *Film Threat* magazine—as opposed to the *FTVG*—was a reprint of the aforementioned interview I did with Jim VanBebber about *My Sweet Satan*) through Justin at the end of 1990; that was when I met Quentin Tarantino at Spiegel's house (Justin and I watched *The Dead Next Door* with him) before he had even made *Reservoir Dogs*. A truly bizarre memory.

**JS: What was Tarantino like?**

**GR:** Well, he was everything that you would now expect him to be, and I'm not imposing any retrospective perspectives on him; I genuinely remember him very well, for obvious reasons. He was a motor-mouthed film geek who never stopped going on all the time, constantly, about anything and everything, but mostly about cinema. Talking to him was like sticking your finger into an electric socket, but that's not necessarily a good thing. I remember him going about "What if there was a bomb in the house and it was a clap-on bomb and you clapped and the house exploded!" I don't know why I retain that random piece of specific dialogue; it's just one of those things. I don't know why he said it either; he's Tarantino, and that's enough explanation. I vividly remember quoting dialogue to him from *I'm Gonna Git You Sucka*, the blaxsploitation parody. The reason I remember it is because it was Antonio Fargas' dialogue about the "Pimp of the Year" and I still (pathetically) know that dialogue. "My bitch better have my money! My ho better have my dough!" I remember us somehow getting onto the subject of this great film (think Spiegel had a videocassette that was commented upon; he had a huge collection of tapes lining the walls)

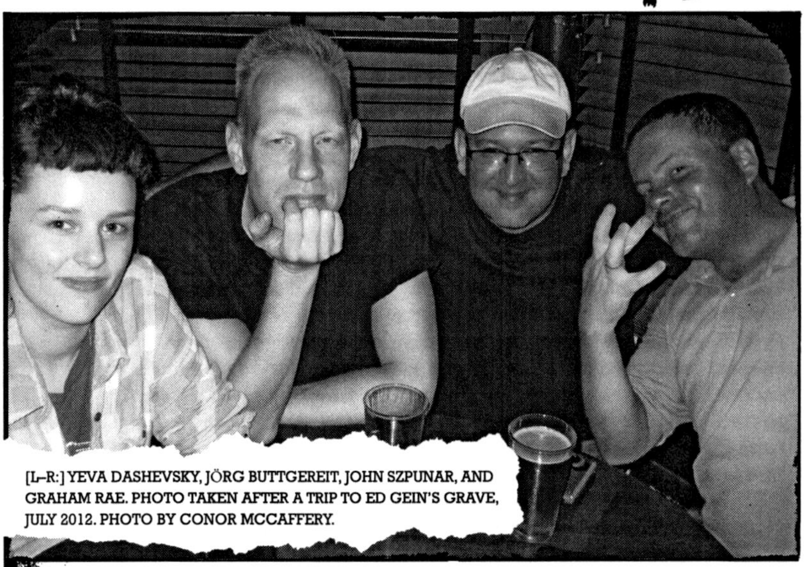

[L–R:] YEVA DASHEVSKY, JÖRG BUTTGEREIT, JOHN SZPUNAR, AND GRAHAM RAE. PHOTO TAKEN AFTER A TRIP TO ED GEIN'S GRAVE, JULY 2012. PHOTO BY CONOR MCCAFFERY.

and me quoting it and Tarantino laughing. Which is absolutely perfect in retrospect, because of his much noted notorious proclivity for racist blaxsploitation-alike dialogue. It's just a random weird memory. He left Spiegel's house the night after I met him after spending half the night getting the low-down on Hollywood filmmaking as I tried to sleep on the couch next to him as he sat on the floor, wishing he would just shut the fuck up! I distinctly remember asking Justin who the hell that irrepressible guy was! He told me and said that he was just about to direct his first film, *Reservoir Dogs*, and that Hollywood was raving about it. He showed me the script and I remember noting that the dialogue was very good. I saw the movie at the Edinburgh International Film Festival when it came out and was totally blown away. I remember when I saw Tarantino at the Oscars a year or two later I thought shit, that's that guy from Scott Spiegel's house who kept me awake that night talking to him.

**JS: What's your take on today's horror films?**

**GR:** Well, I'm not going to lie, I really don't watch horror films anymore very much, and I'm not well informed about them anymore. They, like every other cinematic subgenre, just come off, to me, as pale irritating remakes of seminal works by far better and more interesting filmmakers. I really can't forgive, or want to see, subpar remakes of Pete Jackson or Sam Raimi or George Romero films; if I want the classics I'll just watch them again, not some no-life geek's interpretation of them. I'll give you a couple of examples. People raved about *Shaun of the Dead*; Romero himself loved

RECORDED & INDEXED
DRAFT

it. I grew up on Romero, and *Dawn of the Dead* is my all-time favorite film. I got to be a zombie in *Land of the Dead* in 2004 in Toronto, made up by Greg Nicotero, and it was one of the absolute high points of my life, second only to the birth of my beautiful daughter Fiona. I wrote a story for *Film Threat* about it that anybody who's curious can read to this day on their site. However, I watched *Shaun of the Dead* and it just annoyed the hell out of me. The reason it did was because, although I got implicitly from start to finish what Simon Pegg and those geeks were doing, making their own wee Romero zombie fanboy homage epic, it just wasn't interesting to me because I'm not interested in seeing a regurgitation of scenes done far better by somebody far more talented (though I must admit I loved *Hot Fuzz*) and original. Most cinema these days to me is just warmed-over crap as seen through the lens of the director, who grew up loving the source material; film geeks are often shut-ins who know nothing about real life, so their lack of existential experience comes through in their sorry soggy plagiaristic works. *Dead Snow* was another piece of shit I abhorred.

**JS: I wasn't fond of it, either.**

**GR:** I actually reviewed that film for *Film Threat*'s site, and their butchery of the review made sure I never wrote for them again. But again, all you have is some obnoxious fanboy wank who grew up obsessed with Raimi and Jackson, and is putting his own lame perversion of their vision onscreen… and who cares? I mean, that movie even had a character wearing a T-shirt for the movie *Braindead* (*Dead Alive*) by Pete Jackson! That New Zealand film happens to be one of my all-time faves, and I could tell you a stunningly funny story about my friend Davey Blair and I getting kicked off the bus drunk at three in the morning drunk 200 miles from London when we went down to see it in 1992 at the Prince Charles theater… but who cares about some geek's slavish irritating imitation of his genre hero's best work? And I mean, Nazi zombies, shit… that pathetic riff's been done to death a million times by everybody from Jean Rollin to Jess Franco! So this stuff just doesn't interest me.

**JS: Any final thoughts?**

**GR:** Let me finish by saying this. Horror movies were a youthful phase for me, as they are for many people. You get older, you move on. My life has been a much better place for having horror films in it—and my fandom of such; I will always think this. I have seen and done some incredible things because of it. I'm probably the wrong person to ask about the current horror scene; sure if Chas. was still alive he would have given you a much more upbeat (as opposed to beat-up) answer about the genre. I really don't want to denigrate it all that much, but, you know, even when I was around twenty-three I genuinely found it stale and was mocking the same old conversations about Argento and Fulci and such in the pages of *Psychotic Reaction* fanzine as I moved on. I just outgrew it. But that's just me…

# Chapter Sixteen

# Dennis Daniel

## "Here's Blood in Your Eye!"

DENNIS DANIEL [LEFT] MEETS UNCLE FORRY. PHOTO COURTESY OF DENNIS DANIEL.

# DENNIS DANIEL

## "HERE'S BLOOD IN YOUR EYE!"

RECORDED & INDEXED

DRAFT

Dennis Daniel was a member of what I like to call the Splat Pack—a crazy group of guys who wrote for Chas. Balun's *Deep Red*. When I read Daniel's words in those pages, I felt as if he was talking directly to me. Most of my peers weren't into the same things that I was, and my parents were concerned about my bizarre taste in music and movies. I was looking for an adult voice, any adult voice to reassure me that my childhood loves didn't have to come to an end as I grew older.

I got a lot of guidance from the boys at *Deep Red*, but Dennis Daniel's words really struck a chord with me. Here was a Clio Award-winning radio personality who was in love with the same things that I was. Here was an adult who could wax poetic about something as ridiculous as Andrea Bianchi's *Burial Ground* without shame or pretence. Here was an adult who was writing about these things because he loved them. When Daniel offered a hearty handshake to his fellow horror brethren in the pages of *Deep Red*, I instantly took him up on his offer.

The years went by as they do, and I somehow managed to become a "respectable" adult. Still, I have never forgotten the lesson that Dennis Daniel taught me. The sparks that are born out of childhood obsessions never have to die (this book is a testament to that!). With that in mind, let's sit down and have a little talk with a true blood brother...

The following interview was conducted via telephone, on May 12, 2012.

---

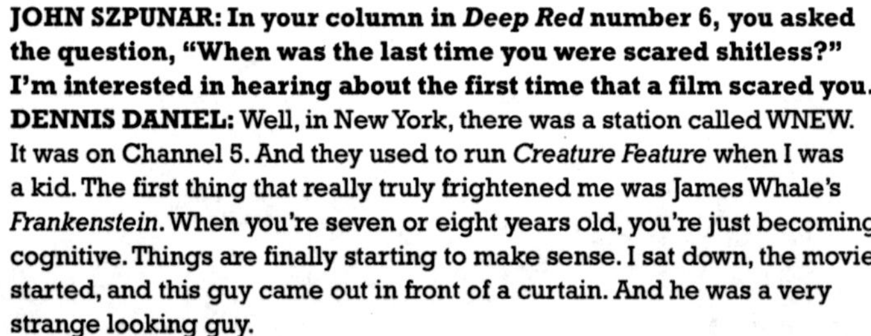

**JOHN SZPUNAR: In your column in *Deep Red* number 6, you asked the question, "When was the last time you were scared shitless?" I'm interested in hearing about the first time that a film scared you.**
**DENNIS DANIEL:** Well, in New York, there was a station called WNEW. It was on Channel 5. And they used to run *Creature Feature* when I was a kid. The first thing that really truly frightened me was James Whale's *Frankenstein*. When you're seven or eight years old, you're just becoming cognitive. Things are finally starting to make sense. I sat down, the movie started, and this guy came out in front of a curtain. And he was a very strange looking guy.
**JS: Edward Van Sloan.**
**DD:** Yeah. He was very weird looking, and his manor of speech was theatrical. Film was still very young, and not everybody had mastered what it was like to act in front of a camera. They tended to overact, the way you would on a stage. There was just something about the way he came out. "You are about to see the story of *Frankenstein*. A man of science..." He went through that whole thing, and I just remember being utterly captivated. And at the end when he said, "I think it will thrill you. It may shock you. It might even... horrify you.," I was like, "Holy shit! What the hell is coming up, man?" Then, *Frankenstein* started, and it was absolutely

gruesome from the very get-go. It was an incredible experience and I remember being very frightened by it. To this day, when I watch *Frankenstein*, I place myself back into my young mind and the first time I saw it.

**JS: The film must have had a serious effect on you.**

**DD:** It did. And then, when they added the extra scene (when I first saw it, they didn't have the scene of the monster throwing the girl in the water) it really brought it home. *Frankenstein* is a gruesome, horrific story with the murder of children. Heavy! A guy puts a body together and brings it back to life! All of those scenes where he's reaching up for the light… everything about it just really got me. So, I always feel that *Frankenstein* was the first thing that made me say, "Hey! There's something to this!" And I wanted to know more about it so I wouldn't be frightened by it.

**JS: When I was growing up, I was never really frightened by the Universal stuff because the monsters had become so iconic. Did you ever feel any sort of distance to them as a kid?**

**DD:** No. The first impression always stayed with me. I've always had reverence for it all. *Frankenstein* was my introduction, and I connected everything that was wrought after it to that initial birth. It had a different meaning for me. I know that the films have become iconic. My goodness, have they become iconic. But, there's so much depth to them—there's a lot going on there. And learning the history of it all was great.

**JS: So, were you reading books about movies as a kid?**

**DS:** You know, it's funny. When I was growing up, I really got into reading books about cinema, but I also got into true crime. One time, when I was ten or eleven years old, I went to my local public library. There was this huge encyclopedia sitting on the table. It was called *Blood Letters and Badmen*. It was an encyclopedia about all kinds of crime. Everything from the old west to serial killers. It was just incredible, and it really warped my young mind. To this day, I'm still interested in all of that.

RECORDED & INDEXED

DRAFT

INTERVIEW WITH ARGENTO. *PSYCHOTRONIC* NUMBER 18.

# DARIO ARGENTO

Interview(s) by Dennis Daniel and Michael Will

*Dario Argento is the most stylish and consistently interesting director of suspense (and horror) movies working today. His movies have broken new boundaries in the use of unflinching violence (he loves violence), dazzling cinematography, bright colors and rock music. Unlike many Italian directors who grind out copies of bigger- budgeted hits, Argento is an original whose movies are studied and copied. After nearly 25 years of directing he's still younger than most of his contemporaries and looks more like an underfed former rock star than a typical director. And unlike many of the people covered in PSYCHOTRONIC, Argento has been the topic of many articles and even whole books and documentaries. One feature can't do his career justice, but we hope if you're not already a fan, this might encourage to see his movies.*

Dario Argento was born the son of producer Salvatore Argento in 1940, the year the Allies entered Italy and Mussolini was replaced as premier. As a young man he wrote film reviews for a Rome daily and appeared in an Alberto Sordi movie (SCUSI, LEI E FAVOREVOLE O CONTRARIO? - 66) that starred Anita Ekberg. Soon, he was writing scripts and by 1968, he already had seven screen credits. The most famous is ONCE UPON A TIME IN THE WEST, Sergio Leone's epic all star classic follow-up to his three Clint Eastwood movies. Argento is credited with director Bernardo Bertolucci (THE LAST EMPEROR), Leone and Pino Donati. ONCE UPON A TIME IN THE WEST is in many ways the ultimate western, and had a great Morricone soundtrack. It was a hit around the world but not in America when it was first released (by Paramount) cut to 144 mins. It's now available in its uncut 168 mins. glory on tape. "It was beautiful. First thing that I did." Viewers often wonder what inspired the script. The writers started by studying westerns. "I remember especially two or three pictures, JOHNNY GUITAR and THE SEARCHERS." Among others, Argento contributed to the famous hanging flashback (during the Charles Bronson and Henry Fonda shootout) and wrote the opening scene with the dripping water and the fly. "Some ideas were mine. Also the beginning with the fly is mine. I wrote. Me and Bernardo, we write it, because Sergio only says, 'It's Okay', or 'It's no good'. This part in the beginning. I write. The waiting and the obsession with the train don't arrive. I was never on the set. I started to write my pictures." Argento has stated that he received $1000. for co-writing ONCE UPON A TIME.

Argento co-wrote two other westerns released that year. TODAY IT'S ME, TOMORROW YOU was written with director Tonio Cervi. Since Cervi was primarily a producer, some think Argento co-directed too. American actor Brett Halsey starred as a stranger dressed in black with Tatsuya Nakadai, William Berger and Bud Spencer. The plot resembles THE SEVEN SAMURAI (and THE MAGNIFICENT SEVEN). CEMETERY WITHOUT CROSSES was made in France. It was written by Argento and director/star Robert Hossein (and Claude Desailly). Hossein plays a gunfighter out for revenge. Michele Mercier co-starred and the theme was sung by Scott Walker of The Walker Brothers. Sergio Leone also appeared in his only bit part.

COMMANDOS was a WWII movie, written with director Armando Crispino (and others). It starred Americans Jack Kelly and Lee Van Cleef, plus Marilu Tolo and Joachim Fuchsberger. American Henry Silva starred in ZERO PROBABILITY, written with director Maurizio Lucidi. Argento wrote the story and screenplay for LA RIVOLUZIONE SESSUALE (or "Sexual Revolution"). Laura Antonelli had her first starring role in the feature directed by Riccardo Garrone (using the name Ghione). Argento also co-wrote the sex comedy METTA UNA

**JS: Why do you think that is?**

**DD:** I guess because it's a dark side of human nature. It's like the yin and yang of life. When you know the dark side, you appreciate the light side more. That's the way I look at it. Some people say, "Why are you so hung up on horror? Is there something in you that wants to harm people? Are you attracted to it because you want to do it yourself?" That's nonsense. It's an exorcism when you look at that stuff. I think it cleanses you.

**JS: I guess it's no surprise that everyone I've interviewed for this book was attracted to horror—be it comics, books, or films—from a very early age. I was terrified by a lot of that stuff as a kid, but I was fascinated by it, just the same. Horror ended up becoming my lifelong obsession.**

**DD:** Sure. And what determines the direction in life that someone gets into? What made me get into horror films, when the guy next door got into the Yankees? Everybody has their point of discovery, and I think that it all happens in youth. Most of the things that I reminisce about now—and I'm fifty-two—are from my youth. I could forget what I did yesterday, but I can remember a lot of things from my childhood that affected me and stayed with me. Take my love of the Beatles, for example. I still love the Beatles as much as I did when I was a kid. And it's funny to me that there are actually people walking around the earth who don't even know who they are. I was on a movie set once, and I asked one of the young guys there if he knew who Groucho Marx was, and he said no. That means he's fading away. If *Dracula*, *Frankenstein*, and all of those guys still exist in their iconic form, but people still know who they are, it's better than nothing.

**JS: I know that you're a big fan of *Godzilla*.**

**DD:** That's another film that frightened the hell out of me. I mean, *Godzilla* is really relentless. He's murdering millions of people. It's an astonishingly horrific idea, even though it's a giant monster movie. There's all this death—it's incredible. And then when you see the Japanese version, he's even more ruthless. When it comes to *Godzilla*, the more ruthless the better, for me! Whenever they make *Godzilla* really evil, I really love him. I don't like it when he's friends with children [laughs].

**JS: I also know that you were a huge fan of *Famous Monsters of Filmland*.**

**DD:** Yep. I'm almost positive that the first issue I saw was the one with Jonathan Frid as Barnabas Collins on the cover. It jumped out of the magazine rack. There was a little stationary store near where I lived, and I'd ride my bike over. I'd buy *Mad* and *Cracked*—I loved all of that stuff. One day I rode my bike over there, and *Famous Monsters* was on the rack. How could you not notice it? I mean, I already liked monsters, so it was a done deal. And the great thing about it was that it was filled chock full of pictures of things that I was just dying to see. There were stills of test makeups—I remember a test makeup of Bela Lugosi from *Island of Lost Souls*. He didn't originally look the way that he ended up. And then there

## "HERE'S BLOOD IN YOUR EYE!"

RECORDED & INDEXED

DRAFT

DANIEL AND BISSETTE'S "BURIED TREASURES". *DEEP RED* NUMBER 5.

BITING, GNAWING TERROR CLAWS AT YOUR BRAIN!

By Steve Bissette and Dennis Daniel

# BURIED TREASURES

## GREAT BLOOD-HORRORS TO RIP OUT YOUR GUTS!

SO WEIRD!.. SO SHOCKING! Do YOU dare see it!
Half woman–half snake!
THE REPTILE
Starring NOEL WILLMAN · RAY BARRETT · Also Starring JENNIFER DANIEL · JACQUELINE PEARCE
Produced by ANTHONY NELSON KEYS · Directed by JOHN GILLING
Screenplay by JOHN ELDER
A Seven Arts-Hammer Production Released by 20th Century-Fox
COLOR BY DELUXE


### All That Glistens Is Not Gold

These are our "Buried Treasures," films we can watch almost any day of the week, endlessly. Many of them had

But, first a few ground rules.

works by Dario Argento, Brian DePalma,

were pictures from all of those lost movies, like *London after Midnight*. I was always a big Lon Chaney guy. I saw all of those incredible pictures of Lon Chaney as the vampire, with all of those teeth. You'd sit there thinking to yourself, "Wow. It's gone. The movie's gone! It's a lost film! No one can see it. All we can look at are the pictures!"

**JS: Did you ever order any of the models from Captain Company?**

**DD:** The homemade monster kits? Oh, yeah! We used to blow them up with firecrackers in front of the house [laughs]! One day, after having them for the longest time, me and my friends were like, "Let's do something with these!" We took *Godzilla* and *Frankenstein*, put them out in the street, and put some firecrackers in them. We stood back, hummed a little Universal theme music and watched them explode [laughs]! But I got a lot of stuff from Captain Company. I got that big Jack Davis *Frankenstein* wall hanging, which was awesome. And talk about iconic. The way Jack Davis draws is iconic, period, let alone his *Frankenstein*!

**JS: Speaking of *Frankenstein*, let's talk a little about *Castle of Frankenstein*.**

**DD:** Oh, God. I gotta tell you something, John, you just made my heart skip a beat. I haven't even thought about *Castle of Frankenstein* for thirty

years, maybe more. And now that you bring it up, I'm really racing back. I loved that magazine. Loved that magazine. The thing was, it was very hard to find. I was very proud of the fact that I had every issue of *Castle of Frankenstein*, especially because the people who wrote for it were fans.

**JS: When I finally got my hands on an issue, I was really impressed with how seriously it took the genre.**

**DD:** It was like the adult *Famous Monsters*—the writing in it was magnificent. *Castle of Frankenstein* was a major influence, and it led me to other pursuits in reading about horror. It was journalism of the highest order. They knew what they were doing, they knew what to say—you learned so much from it. My God, you've really got my brain spinning. I loved those magazines. I treated them with utter reverence. And I had friends who were into the same stuff, too. I had this one friend named Howard who had every issue of every *Famous Monsters*. I was so envious of him—he had every freaking issue, man [laughs]! At least I got to look at some of the ones I didn't have. But, what's the point of having them if you can't share them? That was cool.

**JS: When did you start writing about genre films?**

**DD:** Well, my career was in radio. It still is, by the way. But... I had seen *Halloween*, *Friday the 13th*, and some of the other films that were coming out. They were very interesting to me, and I ended up picking up an issue of *Fangoria*. In that issue, there was a little article about Chas. Balun's the *Gore Score*. Chas. was a great artist, and the cover had his drawing of a guy with an arrow in his head. It was a little red booklet. It got this nice little write-up, so I ordered it. I contacted Chas.—I decided that it would be great to interview him on this radio show that I did called *People, Places, and Things*.

**JS: What kind of a show was that?**

**DD:** It was a half-hour radio show that we did for public service. All radio stations have to do a certain amount of public broadcasting—that's why you hear all those talk shows and stuff on Sunday morning. But anyway, I thought, "Let me interview Chas. We'll talk about what it's like to publish your own pamphlet and how you go about doing it. We'll talk a little about the films, and I'll give him a little publicity." So I contacted him, and we did the interview. To make a long story short, we became friends. He called me up and told me that he was going to be publishing his own magazine called *Deep Red*, and he asked me to be one of its writers. We had talked a lot about film together, so he obviously knew that I knew my stuff. And I was already a writer; I was producing and writing radio commercials. I was also writing for various publications in the radio industry. So, I was very used to writing, and I thought that I had a voice that was mine.

**JS: What writers influenced you?**

**DD:** I would say that the biggest influence on my writing is Harlan Ellison, who I got to meet, hang out with, and be friends with. He's a great guy, and his style of writing is something that I really admire. Especially in his movie reviews. So, with him as an inspiration, I tried to find a way of speaking in

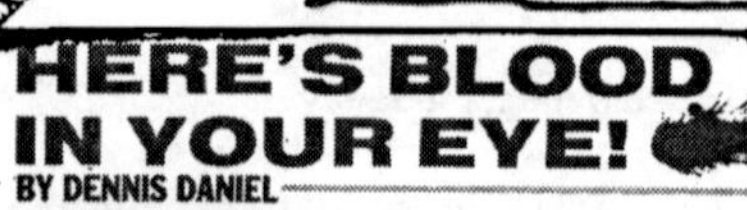

HERE'S BLOOD IN YOUR EYE!

BY DENNIS DANIEL

WHEN WAS THE LAST TIME YOU HAD THE SHIT SCARED OUT OF YOU?

28

my own voice. I suggested to Chas. that I write a column called "Here's Blood in Your Eye."

**JS: So, you came up with that title?**

**DD:** Yeah. With an influence like Chas., it wasn't hard too to come up with [laughs].

**JS: What's the story behind the picture of you as a zombie that always appeared in your byline?**

**DD:** When I was working for the radio station in 1985, we were involved with this huge promotion for *Day of the Dead*. We were giving away tickets and all this other stuff. I was in the absolute apex of things—the fact that what I did for a living and what I did on the side were now meshed together was just too much for me. My head exploded. It was the best of both worlds! I contacted this makeup artist that I knew and he dressed me up as a zombie to go to the premiere of *Day of the Dead*.

**JS: What was that like?**

**DD:** It was unbelievable. I don't think there will ever be anything like it again. All of these people who loved *Dawn of the Dead* were sitting in a theater to see *Day of the Dead*. Everybody was primed and ready. Savini's doing the effects—there was just this incredible build-up. There was no internet then, so nothing had been given away. To make a long story short, it was just incredible. With every effect—with every leg that was chopped off or gut that was spilled, the crowd went wild. Wild! And Savini was in the audience. So was Romero. They got to have a viewing of the film with all of these people who were just so happy to be there. So, the picture of me from the column was taken on the day that I went to that.

**JS: What do you think about Romero's recent films?**

**DD:** Well, that's an interesting question. *Night of the Living Dead* is such an entity, in and of itself. It was the king, forever. I remember being younger—you would just say the name to people and they would be freaked. *Night of the Living Dead* and *The Texas Chain Saw Massacre*—those two movie titles put the fear of God in you. You knew that they were really heavy duty things. *Night of the Living Dead* was such a benchmark. And then, of course, *Dawn of the Dead* was another benchmark. It always seemed to me, that

from that point on, he was cruising on the benchmarks. I think it would have been great if he got to do what he wanted. He even had a much greater vision for *Day of the Dead*. So, what happened is a sort of "we've got to take what we can get" kind of thing. And I think it's great that George is making movies. It's great that he's trying new and different things. That's wonderful, and I'm glad they're there. I never thought in my life that there would be six *Living Dead* films. And when you think about it, every single zombie movie made since *Night* has pretty much done the same thing. There's all sorts of variations of what they've done with things, but they all come from the same source. It's nice to see the guy who created the genre see what kind of stories he can tell from what he's spawned. The only thing that's not cool about it is the CGI.

**JS: You can spot it a mile away.**

**DD:** Oh my God, don't even get me started. CGI has wrought a lot of wonderful things, but it's also wrought a lot of shitty things. You know CGI blood when you see it [laughs]. The artistry—the incredible, unbelievable artistry of creating makeup effects and animatronic figures has been lost. The first shot of *Day of the Dead* is a perfect example of what I'm talking about. That shot of Dr. Tongue in the beginning of *Day* is animatronic, and when you see it, it looks unbelievable. That kind of artistry was one of the things that turned me on to the horror films of the eighties to begin with. Special effects were getting better and better, and by the time I interviewed Tom Savini, he was a god.

**JS: What was Tom like?**

**DD:** When I interviewed Tom Savini, he was absolutely at the apex of his makeup thing. The reverence that people had for him was incredible. He was the most gracious and nicest guy. And he still is. He likes the fans, he likes the genre, and he always considers himself lucky to be a part of it. Talking to him was great. And when I got to go to his house? Oh my God!

**JS: How did you get the interview with him in the first place?**

**DD:** I believe that I was able to do it through Tony Timpone at *Fangoria*. I called him up and asked him if he could make a connection for me. Also, Roy Frumkes knows so many of the Romero people. I'm sure that he had something to do with it. It might have been a combination of those things. But anyway, there I was talking to Tom. It was surreal.

**JS: Did you interview him in person or over the phone?**

**DD:** It was over the phone. It was one of the most monumental things in my life that I'd ever done at that time. I was very proud of it.

**JS: I have to say that it's one of my favorite interviews with him. It still stands up today.**

**DD:** Well, thank you. You're very kind to say so. I haven't read it in quite a few years [laughs]. But, I know that when I did it, I did it with my whole heart and soul. I loved it, and I was enthralled by it all. It's weird because when I was working in rock radio, I got to meet a lot of very famous people all the

DENNIS DANIEL [LEFT] AND LAWRENCE TIERNEY AT HOLLYWOOD BOOK AND POSTER. PHOTO COURTESY OF DENNIS DANIEL.

time. The thing that was cool was that they soliciting us. We were helping them by playing their music. It's a whole different relationship when you meet somebody who's famous and they're coming to see you. You're an equal to them—you're all part of this big machine. That was a very nice thing, and the same thing happened when I interviewed Savini and all of the other people. I felt so utterly and completely comfortable with them. We were on the same level. I was a writer, and people had read me. They had read me. Many of the people that I eventually talked to knew who I was. That was kind of nice.

**JS: You and Chas. did a lot of interviews together.**

**DD:** Oh, yeah.

**JS: How often did you go to California?**

**DD:** I only went to California once. I stayed with Chas., and we went to interview Forry Ackerman and James Karen. Everything else I ever did was at a convention or over the phone.

**JS: What was Chas. like?**

**DD:** Oh, man [laughs]. I don't know exactly how tall he was, but he was monstrous. If you told me he was seven feet tall, I'd say, "OK." He was a big, big guy. And he was as much of a California hippy dude as you could ever imagine. He was the embodiment of it. I say that with reverence and love—I think that's what made him so cool. He was very mellow and open. His wife was a very nice person, too. All of the people that I met out there were wonderful people. It was very fun. I got to go to Hollywood Book and Poster. When I went there, Lawrence Tierney was sitting outside the door,

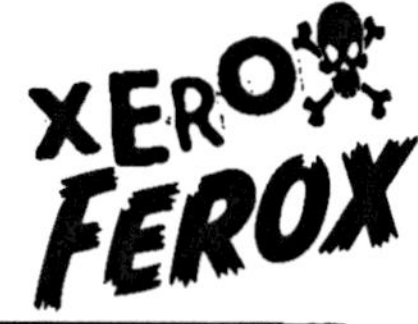

reading a newspaper like he owned the place [laughs]. I was walking in, and I said, "Lawrence Tierney?" He said, "Yeah. How you doin'?" I said, "Can I take a picture with you?" He said, "Sure, kid. Take a lot of 'em." I went in and I bought a couple of pictures of him and he signed them. Eric Caidin, the guy who owns Hollywood Book and Poster, said, "Yeah, he just hangs out here." He wasn't rich. I think he lived in an apartment complex or something like that. Whatever movies he was doing got him by. He was quite a character.

**JS: Let's talk a little about some of the other magazines that you wrote for.**

**DD:** I wrote for *Psychotronic*, *Film Threat*, and *Filmfax*—I did a whole bunch of interviews for *Filmfax*. I also wrote for the *Comics Journal*, *Comics Buyer's Guide*, *Gorezone*, and *Fangoria*. The *Psychotronic* gig came about because I was a tremendous fan of the *Psychotronic Encyclopedia*.

**JS: What was your favorite?**

**DD:** I'd have to say *Deep Red*, because it was the first. And *Deep Red* really allowed me to be me. It was also the purist. When I wrote for some of the bigger magazines, there was a lot of editing. You know, I really wanted to write for *Video Watchdog*. I thought it would be a real miracle if I could get into *Video Watchdog* because of the tremendous intelligence of the writing. In my mind, Tim Lucas is a genius.

**JS: Do you know Tim at all?**

**DD:** Yeah. We became friends. You know, you'd meet that whole circle. I remember that I tried to write an article *Video Watchdog*. I really tried with all my heart to get into the style and intensity of it.

**JS: Did you make it in?**

**DD:** He rejected it [laughs]. Again, Tim was my friend. I never thought that the rejection was a purposeful or hurtful or anything like that. I know how much I struggled to write it. Maybe I wasn't at that level, which is fine by me. If I have a certain style that works a certain way, OK. You can't write everything. The same person who wrote *The Godfather* probably couldn't write *Finnegan's Wake*.

**JS: When I read your stuff in *Deep Red*, I felt like I knew you. It was almost as if you were an old friend.**

**DD:** Well, thank you.

**JS: I'll always remember reading this passage from one of your columns: "Are you really into it? Then the word 'horror' must be a daily part of your vocabulary, as well. Put 'er there, pal!" I was like, "OK, man. You got it!"**

**DD:** [laughs] I forgot all about that. It really falls in line with what my philosophy was. I was being myself, and I felt like I really was talking to kindred spirits. That's why *Deep Red* was so much fun. I remember writing an article about *Return of the Living Dead Part II*. I hated that film. I thought it was terrible, and I remember writing a really vicious article where I was

RECORDED & INDEXED
DRAFT

saying things like, "I don't like people fucking with my zombies!" I'd love to read that again, because I wrote it in such anger [laughs].

**JS: I never bothered to see the film after reading that.**

**DD:** Good for you [laughs]! You saved yourself some very precious minutes of your life that would have been wasted.

**JS: I wanted to ask you about the article that you wrote with Steve Bissette in *Deep Red* number 5. It was called "Buried Treasures".**

**DD:** Steve Bissette and I got along very well. We just hit it off. He was part of the whole Chas. Balun crew. I loved his writing, and I loved *Swamp Thing*. We got along tremendously well. I spent time at his place in Vermont. He's a very sweet and creative guy, and he's very intelligent. We were talking one day, and we thought, "Wouldn't it be fun to write an article together?" He and I always loved the really obscure stuff, the stuff that you just couldn't find. Bissette always had ways of finding it. He'd send me tapes, and I'd be, "Bro, where the hell did you get this?" There was a lot of incredible stuff that we shared, and we decided to write the article to let people know about it. The article became so big that it was like a book. It could have been a book, but we had too many other things going on in our lives.

**JS: How did the *Famous Monsters Chronicles* come about?**

**DD:** Well, we have to talk a little bit about Tom Skulan. As the *Gore Score* got more famous, Chas. became partners with Tom from FantaCo. They published and distributed it. I was working with Chas, so I had contact with Skulan. I went up to Albany and met him. We got along great. He was a really great guy who was in love with the genre and he was very pure-hearted about it all. I guess he became comfortable with me—he saw that I met deadlines and that I had the enthusiasm. He was the one who proposed it to me. He called me up and said, "Look, we've been doing this 'chronicles' series about several different magazines." I think most of them were about comic books. Anyway, he wanted to do one about *Famous Monsters*. He wanted to know if I was interested in writing it. I'm thinking, "Well, Howie has every issue. So, whatever issues that I don't have, Howie has." I knew that I could see every issue. A lot of people wrote for *Famous Monsters*. A lot of people had written about *Famous Monsters*. A lot of people were influenced by *Famous Monsters*. I thought, "A lot of people would really want to talk to me if they knew I was doing a book like this." It just took off from there. I got to speak with and correspond with some pretty heavy hitters. Vincent Price, Ray Bradbury, Ray Harryhausen—even Peter Jackson wrote something for the book. That's when he was doing all the gore films. I got to the point, though, where I realized that I had bitten off more than I could chew. Cataloging the magazine was the really torturous part of the job.

**JS: I can only imagine.**

**DD:** What do you mention and what do you not mention? Do you know what I mean? There were all of these incongruities, if that's the proper word. And then, also, for what it's worth, I came to the realization that *Famous Monsters* was made for kids. I was an adult who was looking at this magazine that was made for ten year olds. And Forry's writing style—not that I didn't love it— was like having too much chocolate. I love chocolate, but it got to the point where I couldn't eat anymore. I had to get some friends to help me finish it. I got this guy named Jim Knusch who was a genre fan that I had met, and Steve Morrison, who was a writing partner of mine in radio. But, the fun part about it was definitely doing the articles and interviews. It was such a pleasure to get to talk to all of those people.

*FAMOUS MONSTERS CHRONICLES.* TOO MUCH CHOCOLATE.

**JS: Let's talk a little bit about the FantaCons. What were they like?**

**DD:** Very simply, the gathering of the tribes. I used to address people as "brethren" because we really were like this army of lovers of this stuff. We were all very much the same. FantaCon was great because it was home turf. It was Tom Skulan, and being a guest at a FantaCon convention was like coming home. It was great, and he always had great guests. I mean, I got to talk to *Dario Argento*. You've got to be fucking kidding me [laughs]! Who in a million years would have ever thought I would be able to talk with him?

**JS: Is that how you landed the interview with him for *Psychotronic*?**

**DD:** Yes. I've been lucky enough to be able to get more than one publication interested in certain interviews, yet I don't repeat anything. So, the Dario piece in *Deep Red* was different than in *Psychotronic*. Man, what a thrill it was to hang out with him! A great guy too! Very real... personable and fun.

**JS: What led up to you being on the set of *Two Evil Eyes*?**

**DD:** Again, that was Roy Frumkes. I had interviewed Roy for *Deep Red* and we became friends. He was about to shoot some new footage for *Document of the Dead*, and he asked me to come with him to be the still photographer. He also thought that it would be fun for me. It was wonderful, and that's also how I got to go to Tom Savini's house. I guess you must know, but the *Two Evil Eyes* DVD includes the footage that I shot there.

# DENNIS DANIEL

## "HERE'S BLOOD IN YOUR EYE!"

DENNIS DANIEL AND DARIO ARGENTO, FANTACON 1989. PHOTO COURTESY OF DENNIS DANIEL.

**JS: Yeah. Is there any more footage, or is everything on there?**

**DD:** They got everything. It's interesting, because they also used some of the footage that I shot on the documentary about it. A guy from Blue Underground found out that I had the footage. He called me, and I let him use it. But, as you can see, just from the way Tom is, that's Tom. He's just a friendly, cool guy that loved his stuff and loved sharing it with people. The other thing that was really interesting was watching George Romero direct. He was shooting the scene in the movie where the pendulum lands in Ramy Zada's chest. In the documentary, you see a lot of footage of George directing that. They kept on doing it over and over because the pendulum wasn't landing the right way. With CGI, you wouldn't even worry about that—"We'll do it later!" But, they kept doing it and doing it until they got it right. I remember that the pendulum was held up by a vacuum. When they shut the vacuum off, it would drop. It was interesting. Romero had all of these clothespins on his scarf and he was playing with a yo-yo. He looked at my camera and said, "Smoking substitute."

**JS: What can you tell me about being on the set of Savini's remake of *Night of the Living Dead*?**

**DD:** *Night of the Living Dead*. My God, what a memory. Washington, Pennsylvania was the name of the town that they were shooting it in. It was an incredible thing because there was a certain amount of hope involved in it. All of the original people were there. It wasn't like somebody else was taking the reins. George wrote the screenplay and Tom Savini was directing it. All of the guys were involved, in one way or another. They

were really trying to get their copyright back.

**JS: You appeared as a zombie in the film.**

**DD:** It was incredible. Here's a question for you, John. If you had the chance to appear as a zombie in the remake of *Night of the Living Dead*, which scene would you want to be in?

**JS: The first thing that comes to mind is the gut-munching scene.**

**DD:** Of course! If you're going to be in *Night of the Living Dead*, and you're going to be a zombie, you've got to be in the only flesh-eating scene! Fuck walking around like you're drunk, I want to be eating somebody! So, when we all got there, we were all in this big church. There were about 100 of us—we were going to be the zombies. We all had to sit in these chairs, and they did it like an assembly line. First, you got the powder. Then, you got the first coat. And then, they made you an individual-looking zombie. The ones who got the real cool makeup would go and see Everett Burrell and John Vulich. They would really do you up. Well, I got done up by John Vulich, so I was as happy as a pig in shit. Then, they said, "Go pick a costume." My brain just went, "Look for a gas station attendant costume." Who's going to be near a gas station when it explodes?

**JS: A gas station attendant [laughs].**

**DD:** Right! So, I found the costume, with a hat and everything! I was thrilled! Now, right outside the church, was this old graveyard. A real graveyard! It was awesome! I mean, it made for some great pictures. Everyone was taking pictures of themselves around these old seventeenth century stones. Anyway, we were all standing out there, and this guy was standing on a chair. He said, "OK, we're going to shoot this scene." I didn't even have to raise my hand. He just pointed at me and said, "OK, you, for sure." So, I lucked out there. I got to be in a lot of scenes. They're not all in the film, but you can see me in that flesh-eating scene, as clear as day.

**JS: What were you really eating?**

**DD:** Turkey, roast beef, and karo syrup blood. It was surreal. And there were around 150 people watching and cheering us on. It was great! And the thing that got me the most, is when you look at the scene, I'm the only zombie whose face you can see. Everybody else was digging their head so deep into the body that you can't see their faces.

**JS: Gahan Wilson was in that scene with you.**

**DD:** Gahan Wilson is the real deal. I got to be very close to him. I went to the movies a couple of times with him—horror movies, you know? He must have been in his early sixties in those days, and he had his popcorn and soda pop—he sat there and watched the movie like a little kid. It was unbelievable. And, he never cursed, except at a point where it really demanded it. That's what made it so funny—he was the kind of guy who would usually go, "Oh, golly gee! Gee, that's swell!" He was like Jimmy Stewart—that's how he talked. And then, he was so fucking brilliant with his cartoons and macabre humor. He's right there with Charles Addams, if not superior to him. He's still

RECORDED & INDEXED

DRAFT

doing it, so I guess he must be winning in the department of getting work done [laughs]. I was able to interview him for the *Comics Journal*, which is one of my favorite things I've ever done in my life.

**JS: At what point in your life did you decide that you didn't want to write anymore?**

**DD:** Well, it goes back to *Night of the Living Dead*, unfortunately. That was the beginning of it. Being on that set was amazing. I remember watching a scene being shot. We were in this barn, and there was all of this hay in bails. I was in between John Skipp and Craig Spector—they were in the film, as well. There were around thirty zombies in front of us, and they started walking forward. We were all looking at each other, going, "Can you fucking believe where we are?" It was an awe inspiring and wonderful thing. But unfortunately, there was also a lot of negative stuff going on—people who drank, people who were doing drugs—people who had major personal problems that were affecting their performance. And because we were led into the arena open heartedly by these people, we were also exposed to some of the negative things. Some of these people didn't go to sleep, or they'd have temper tantrums and throw shit—it was just bizarre. It really soured me. I was like, "My God… these people are miserable!" Seeing these unhappy people and the depth of their unhappiness affected me. I don't know what happened. All of the sudden, something hit me and I said, "You know, I've done enough. If this is where things lead to, I'd rather go back to loving it. I'd rather go back to not being involved with it and just enjoying it for what it is." I don't know—does that make sense?

**JS: Yeah. You got a glimpse of the faces without the makeup on.**

**DD:** You always hear that when it comes to entertainment. Whitney Houston just passed away. People think that she had the most idyllic life in the world, but she fucking killed herself. She destroyed herself with drugs. What a stupid thing to do. I feel sorry for her, don't get me wrong. Whatever happened to her happened to her because she needed to deal. Everybody deals in a different way.

I don't know, there was just something about it that put me off. It just stopped for me. It stopped. I think that Chas. wasn't going to be doing *Deep Red* anymore, anyway. He was moving on to other things. It felt like an era was ending, in a lot of ways. It felt like something was dying, and not in a good way. And, I think the other thing that really fucked things up was that whole *Guinea Pig* episode. That really bent my head.

**JS: Could you go into that a little bit?**

**DD:** Well, being horror fans and friends, Chas. and I always mailed each other tapes. Chas. had sent me *Guinea Pig*, which is basically a movie with this Samurai—he's tearing this woman apart on a table. It's all done in that very weird Japanese way. I remember sitting down to watch it with my friend Steve Morrison. Before we put it in, we looked at each other and said, "Do we really want to watch this? What's wrong with us?" Well,

GERORGE ROMERO AND DENNIS DANIEL. PHOTO COURTESY OF DENNIS DANIEL.

the only reason we watched it was because we wanted to see the makeup. And let me tell you, it looked pretty damn real. Chas. had told me that there was a series of *Guinea Pig* films and he even had this documentary called *The Making of Guinea Pig*, where you could see the girl laughing while she was getting her arm cut off.

Then one day out of the blue, the phone rang. The guy on the other end of the line told me he was a Special Agent. "Oh, Mr. Daniel? This is Special Agent Sam Sneed," or whatever his name was. He started asking me questions about this tape because after I saw it, I mailed a copy to Chris Gore. And Chris Gore lent it to another friend of his. And this friend of his was friends with Charlie Sheen. So, Charlie Sheen and his friend were now watching this tape that had originally been sent to me by Chas. Sheen's looking at it, and he's saying, "This shit is real, man! I've got a friend in the FBI—let me have him check this out!"

**JS: What did the FBI guy say to you?**

**DD:** He told me that sending the tape was a felony or something. "You're going to be in a lot of trouble, sir." I was like, "Holy shit! It's fake!" The sad part was that I had to call Chas. I'm thinking, "There's no harm in saying I got the tape from Chas.—it's not real. Chas. can show him *The Making of Guinea Pig*, and we're all done."

The day I called Chas, of all days, was his birthday. He was having a party at his house. He was like, "Dude... why are you hitting me with this now? I'm going to go back to my party, bro." And, that was the end of that. Nothing ever came of it.

**JS: If I got a call from the FBI about a *Guinea Pig* movie, I would have assumed that it was some kind of joke.**

**DD:** Can you see why all of the sudden I wasn't into horror anymore [laughs]? The fucking FBI is calling me about a tape? I'm out of here [laughs]! Fuck this, I'm going to watch Disney films—I'm not going to get into this shit anymore!

**JS: A few years ago, I read some of your reviews on Roy Frumkes' *Films in Review* website.**

**DD:** Yeah. But, it's been around twenty years since I've done any honest to god horror journalism. I have written some stuff for *Films in Review*. I wrote a review of *King Kong*, and I wrote a review of *The Devil's Rejects*. But, those were just labors of love.

**JS: Do you ever regret stopping when you did?**

**DD:** No. And, that's the cool thing about it. I don't regret it. I don't say to myself, "Oh shit—I wish I would have kept going." Because now, it really is more fun. I wanted to get back to that feeling of riding a rollercoaster again. It's fun discovering things again, and not necessarily being in the loop.

**JS: You mentioned a little while ago that you felt as if an era was ending with the death of *Deep Red* and the fanzines.**

**DD:** It's an era that's gone, but that's OK. Things are supposed to go. Things are supposed to evolve and change. And now, everything you'd ever want to know (right up to when Rick Baker's taking a shit) can be found on the internet.

**JS: There's almost an overflow of information available.**

**DD:** Yeah. But that's what makes those magazines so coveted today. That's what makes them mean so much. And if you live long enough, you have the opportunity to look back and say, "Oh my God… it's not like that anymore. But, boy am I glad to have been a part of it." When you called me and said that you were interested in talking to me—you've got to imagine, this shit's been dormant for twenty years. I was like, "Wow! Somebody read this stuff and actually gave a shit?" What a gift that is.

**JS: Believe me—I gave a shit [laughs].**

**DD:** Let me ask you a question. I don't know if you'll put it in your book or not but, if could turn the tables on you. You said that the thing that you liked most about *Deep Red* was that it made you feel like you were talking to a friend. Could you explain that to me a little bit more? What was your mindset when you first discovered it, and why did it affect you in that way?

**JS: Well, when I was growing up, I always knew that I was a little different than most of the people around me. I always gravitated toward a lot of things that my peers didn't know much about—horror movies, old comic books, and old music. I had no one to share it with. When I discovered *Deep Red*, a whole new world opened up for me. I realized that there were other people who were just like me. And they weren't just fans of the stuff, they were going the extra**

**mile and writing about it. You guys didn't talk down to me. Your writing was intelligent. It was immediate, adult, and it was personal. I remember thinking, "Hey, I finally found my club, and it's the coolest club in the world!" It's actually kind of hard to explain...**

**DD:** No, I don't think it's hard to explain at all. I understand completely what you're saying, and I think it's beautiful. The fact that you were moved enough to even want to talk to me, or any of the other people that you're talking to, makes me feel that I did something with my life that affected people. I mean, I still do it today—as a writer for advertising, I'm always affecting people. But the stuff I wrote for *Deep Red* was different. It was from the heart. It wasn't done to make money, it was done to share. And the fact that you're doing this... I just wish Chas. was alive. I think that he would really appreciate it.

**JS: I do, too. I had the honor of interviewing him a few years ago. It was one of the greatest afternoons in my life.**

**DD:** That's great. So, Chas. is here, too?

**JS: Yeah. And this book is dedicated to him.**

**DD:** That's a beautiful, beautiful thing. You know, when I wrote my book *Tales of the Tape*, which is about my years in radio, I dedicated it to the person who influenced me most in life, my best friend Mickey. My dedication for that was, "To Mickey—a teacher." That has so much meaning to it. And it's nice that you can dedicate your book to somebody who made such an impact to you.

**JS: I only got to meet Chas. in person once, but his words sure played a big part in my life.**

**DD:** What a big presence he was...

**JS: Hey, listen— I really want to thank you for taking the time out to talk to me. This has been great. And I'd really like to sign off by saying something that I've wanted to say to you for years: "Put 'er there, pal!"**

**DD:** [laughs] You got it, John! Put 'er there!

PHOTO COURTESY OF KRIS GILPIN.

# Chapter Seventeen
# Kris Gilpin
## Shit Flick Serenade!

I first noticed Kris Gilpin's name in the pages of Cecil Doyle's *Subhuman*. I distinctly remember reading his review of a movie called *Get Out of My Way, Man, I Really Mean It!* The thing was obviously a review of a film that didn't exist—no sane person would ever waste their time or money making it, and I couldn't imagine anyone actually paying to see it. The plot was rude and ridiculous: a heavy duty "Bud Spencer type" guy gorges himself at a sleazy Mexican restaurant ("belching and farting all the while") before stumbling outside. He then runs through the streets, terrorizing everyone in his path before ultimately exploding, "spewing viscera and excrement high into the air." The 'review' ended thusly: "This is the first film to be distributed by the new Superb Films, Inc. Co., and let's hope there aren't any more of its ilk to follow." A sound assessment to be sure, but luckily for us, Kris Gilpin had plenty more weird productions waiting in the wings.

The pages of *Subhuman* soon gave way to some of the sleaziest writing imaginable, and a good deal of it was penned by Gilpin. I'll always remember his interview with the mysterious porn film cinematographer known only as Mr. X. And who could ever forget *Imbecilicus*, his science fiction screenplay satire that was sporadically serialized in *Subhuman*?

Next thing you know, I recognized Gilpin's byline in Chas. Balun's *Deep Red*. Wow! There he was again, interviewing the likes of David Hess, Sam Raimi, and Sybil Danning. Before long, I was enjoying Gilpin's work in almost every fanzine that showed up in my mailbox. It was as if the man himself was lurching through the streets of an unsuspecting city, threatening to shower everyone in sight with… well, whatever his twisted mind could come up with!

Today, Kris lives and writes in Salt Lake city, Utah, where he plots and pens the superb Movie Crossword Puzzle for the website BestCrosswords.com. I finally got the chance to speak to the man in January, 2012. Generous, funny, and a hell of a nice guy, we talked in length about movies, American pop culture, and his impressive career as a film journalist.

The following interview was conducted via telephone and email, January–February, 2012.

---

**JOHN SZPUNAR: Where did you grow up?**

**KRIS GILPIN:** I grew up in Miami and hated it. It was humid as hell and boring— white trash and guns everywhere, bugs in the air, and an occasional snake in your front lawn. I always hated Top Forty culture, the insipid music on the radio, and the same old fashioned Hollyshit movies—thank God I always hated that stuff! So, somehow I discovered my own music and films.

**JS: Such as?**

DRAFT

95¢
Barry N. Malzberg
Winner of the John Campbell Award for the Year's Best Science Fiction Novel
BEYOND APOLLO


A BLEAK MASTERPIECE.

**KG:** Well, somehow I discovered Fripp and Eno, King Crimson, prog-rock, and the early Peter Gabriel Genesis albums. Selling England by the Pound is a note by note masterpiece. I got into Brit groups like Godley and Creme, early 10CC, and Stackridge. Some people actually thought they were the Beatles, but they weren't.

**JS: And what were you reading?**

**KG:** Anthony Burgess, Harlan Ellison (I love his nonfiction commentaries even more than his fiction) and Harry Crews. His early novels kick ass! I read Sir Arthur Conan Doyle, early Richard Laymon, and Barry N. Malzberg. I've always suffered from depression because of my dysfunctional, semi-hateful family and something about Malzberg's mordant stories really clicked with me. *Beyond Apollo* novel is a bleak masterpiece.

**JS: Where were you seeing films?**

**KG:** There were two theaters in Miami that saved my life; one of them was called the Cinematheque. They showed imports, and I got into Antonioni films, early Wim Wenders films.

**JS: How old were you at the time?**

**KG:** Well, I had a car, so I was sixteen. I was there every night. They had these beautiful old airline seats that you could stretch out and sleep on. They were really comfy, like a couch. If the movie was boring, you'd just stretch out and go to sleep.

**JS: What was the other theater like?**

**KG:** It was a hippy thing in the Coconut Grove area. Two brothers ran a theater called the Grove Cinema. They changed movies around every three days. Once a month, they showed *Harold and Maude* and *Where's Poppa?* as a double feature. I saw those films dozens of times—they're still favorites. So, as an adult, I look back and I realize that if it wasn't for those two theaters, I would have never known about a lot of stuff.

**JS: I take it here wasn't a lot of "artistic culture" happening in Miami.**

**KG:** Yeah, that's what I'm saying. There were just those two theaters, and I was lucky to have them both. Robert Downey, Sr. made a lot of underground films. They showed those kinds of things—*Putney Swope* was huge at the time. I was always in these theaters watching anything and

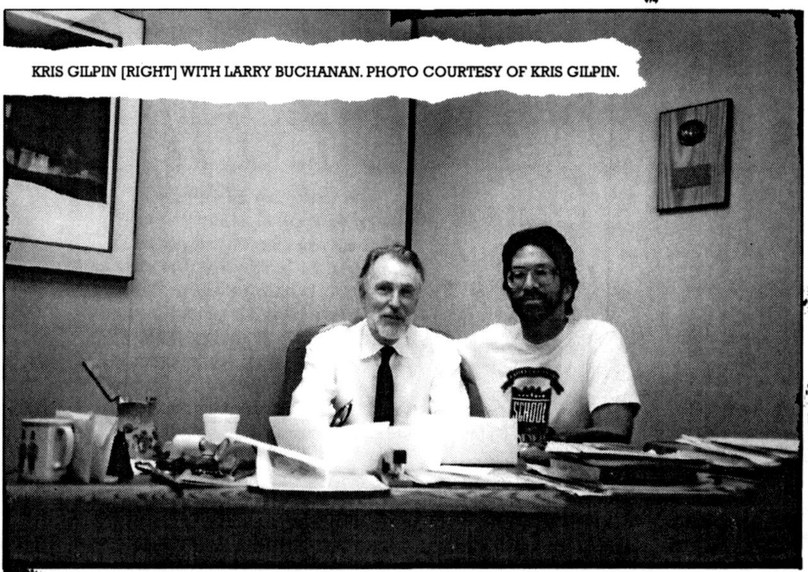


KRIS GILPIN [RIGHT] WITH LARRY BUCHANAN. PHOTO COURTESY OF KRIS GILPIN.

everything they had.

**JS: What were the drive-ins like?**

**KG:** The drive-in in North Beach actually got some weird obscure shit. That's where I discovered Herschell Gordon Lewis. I went there, saw *Blood Feast*, and laughed my ass off. Sleaze has always made me laugh. They played my favorite, *The Wizard of Gore*. I saw *The Gruesome Twosome* there. It was great. My friends asked me how I could sit through a Bergman film one afternoon and then go to a drive-in that night to laugh my ass off at a Herschell Gordon Lewis shit flick, but like Stephen King said, "There's good shit and there's bad shit." I said, "Well, you had your typical McDildos for lunch, and then Italian for dinner, right?" That shut them up.

**JS: [laughs] Let's hear about the shit flicks...**

**KG:** I'd stay up until 1:00 AM on Saturday nights and squint my eyes at Channel 12 from West Palm Beach. It was a county away. The picture was always tons of snow, but I'd see Larry Buchanan films like *Zontar* and *It's Alive!* and I'd laugh my ass off at all the cheese in them.

**JS: Bergman and Buchanan! There's an education! Now, this was during the sixties and seventies.**

**KG:** Right.

**JS: A lot of non-Hollywood films were being made. What do you think it was about that time that caused American culture to change?**

**KG:** I think it started with Vietnam. We were fighting a war that had nothing to do with us, but we were still getting sent over there to get

RECORDED & INDEXED

DRAFT

PROFILE ON H.G. LEWIS FROM THE *DEEP RED HORROR HANDBOOK.*

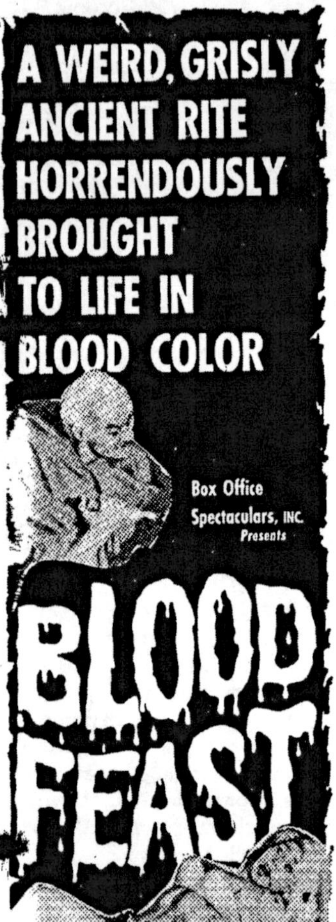

A WEIRD, GRISLY ANCIENT RITE HORRENDOUSLY BROUGHT TO LIFE IN BLOOD COLOR

Box Office Spectaculars, INC. Presents

BLOOD FEAST

Introducing CONNIE MASON YOU SAW HER IN PLAYBOY

Adult HORROR!

PROFILE BY: KRIS GILPIN

# H. G. LEWIS

The Godfather of Gore who ushered in Mutilation Movies years before anyone else. If you still don't know who he is, why did you buy this book? In his own words: "There was a script I had for years called The Music of Mr. Mundy, a children's picture about a grade school orchestra so bad they're a smash. I found it completely charming but couldn't see it as a commercial enterprise so I never made it."

"Nudies were lots of fun to make. BOIN-N-G was my favorite because it had a sense of humor. When David Friedman and I made THE ADVENTURES OF LUCKY PIERRE [chuckles], we were the whole crew. We cut no film out of that shoot, we used every foot we bought. It was a smash, which made me very cynical toward filmmaking. I felt LIVING VENUS was a good, well-made picture, with a union crew and it cost six or seven times as much as PIERRE, which was in color. In the entire life span of PIERRE, I think we made eleven prints, playing them mercilessly. We'd splice around the horrible tears and send them out again. Karen Black played herself, literally, in THE PRIME TIME. I notice she still does. It was her first picture; she was still a student [1960]. I shot BLACK LOVE for a fellow who owned a bunch of ice cream parlors in Chicago, supplying only the technical aspects of filmmaking. I also put the campaign together, pairing it with my own MISS NYMPHET'S ZAP-IN (a soft-core rip

45

fucked up or killed. And the young folk were protesting this; I grew my hair halfway down my back.

**JS: I was born at the very end of that. I can only imagine what things were like.**

**KG:** My brother called us once from his Illinois college, and we could hear guns going off in the background. On a fucking college campus. It was insane! The whole culture changed then; Hollytrite was pissing away millions. And then, Corman figured out he could appeal to the young crowd with violence and sex at the drive-ins. *Deep Throat* and *Easy Rider* appeared and they made a mint. I remember thinking at the time, "Thank God! The world has changed; we'll never go back to the tight-ass, square, Republican way of life!"

**JS: [laughs] That was back by the time I was ten years old.**

**KG:** I was shocked to see Reagan and *Rambo* come back full-force in the eighties. I like Sly, but you know what I mean! Kids were cutting all their hair off instead of letting it grow. And then, of course, it was followed by that rich, white, uncaring, imbecilic prick Bush. So I guess life really does go in circles.

**JS: Where were you working in Florida?**

**KG:** I managed a couple theaters in Miami and basically hated it. See, I fucked up my whole life. I should've been a character actor. I always wanted to act, but sucked at first. I'm kind of scarred up because of bad acne. That's haunted me my whole wife, especially with women. Anyway, I always wanted to be a character actor, and one dead Sunday in Miami I was running *La Cage aux Folles*. Up walked Ernest Borgnine and his wife!

**JS: Nice!**

**KG:** I was stunned, but I walked them in for free. The company had scheduled a forty-five-minute break between shows (they'd walked up in the middle of a showing) and I went in and talked with him about acting.

**JS: What was he like?**

**KG:** He was the nicest guy in the world. He told me go follow my dream and told me to contact Irwin Allen if and when I got to LA. I did, and nothing came of it, but I knew then I had to get the fuck out of horrible Florida. So first I went to New York and roomed with an old buddy Gary Goldstein.

**JS: Where were you living?**

**KG:** In Hell's Kitchen. It was a shithole. I passed out resumes for a couple months and nothing happened, so I ended up writing what we called "romance" novels, if you know what I mean. They wanted a sex book hacked out every four days. I collected $128 a book (for four books) and bought a ticket for LA, my last hope.

**JS: How did you like Los Angeles?**

**KG:** I felt more at home in LA than I ever did in Florida, but that was because of the movies. All the women there looked like starlets. I had no plan as an actor, so I hit all the networks with my resume. The ABC

## Shit Flick Serenade!

Film Services department just had an official order come down that they couldn't just hire someone off the street or somebody's nephew anymore. The head of the film department went through a stack of resumes and mine was the first one that had a college education on it—I'd gotten a BFA in Cinema from the University of Miami. So they called me in, and I all but begged them to let me start there. I thought, "ABC's a good a place to start as an actor." What did I know? Anyway, I was an assistant film editor in LA for twenty-two years.

**JS: So how did all of this lead to zines?**

**KG:** One day, I came across *Starlog Communications Handbook* number 1. There was an ad in the back for a Creeping Terror fan club. I got a laugh over that and joined, telling them I thought the Creeping Terror was a stunning shitter. They told me, "We also have a fanzine on bad movies called *Yecch!* out of Canada." So, I wrote to *Yecch!* and asked if I could review B-movies for them. I always wanted to be a writer and wanted to see my name in print wherever I could get it. They said, "Yes."

**JS: I'm not familiar with *Yecch!*...**

**KG:** It was run by two young guys. I named my column "Shit Flicks." I'd sit there in the dark and scribble notes as the movies were going on. People around me would whisper, "He's a film reviewer! Maybe for TV!" When I got home, I never recognized half my notes because my handwriting sucks.

**JS: You told me that you interviewed Harry Medved for *Yecch!*...**

**KG:** The World's Worst Film Fest came to New York's Beacon Theater in 1980. I saw and reviewed lots of great sleaze. *Plan 9*, *The Incredibly Strange Creatures...*, *Reefer Madness*, and the original *Maniac*, where the mad guy pokes out a (phony) cat's eyeball and eats it. It was being run by Harry Medved, who'd just co-written *The Golden Turkey Awards*. The *Yecch!* boys said, "Hey, see if you can get an interview with him too, yuk, yuk!" I thought, "Why not?" So, I got a long, clunky, double-headed tape recorder and asked Medved if I could interview him. He said "Sure," and we walked up to the balcony where it was empty and a lot less noisy. We spoke for just a few minutes, but it was my first interview and I liked it a lot more than just reviewing a flick. Like someone said—Einstein, I think—"Opinions are like assholes, everybody has one." Harry told me it was his first interview, too.

**JS: How did you spread your byline around? Did other zine editors write you?**

**KG:** You know, I don't remember how I came across more zines, but back then most of them had a section that advertised other zines. You'd read a brief description of them, send in a stamp (or a buck or two), and then that guy would send you his own zine. Nobody made money on these things. They were just great labors of love.

**JS: What came next?**

**KG:** Well, I came across a book for writers that listed mags and zines accepting submissions. I started with the As and saw that *Antithesis* (later called *Bifrost*), a fantasy fan-fiction zine, was looking for a film reviewer. I reviewed for them for a while. I was able to interview Frank Doubleday for them. He was the blond creep in Carpenter's *Assault on Precinct 13* who nonchalantly shoots little Kim Richards while she's eating an ice cream cone.

**JS: A great scene!**

**KG:** Yeah! He was a nice guy; almost everyone I ever talked with was very nice. He said he improvised the long hiss that came out of him when he got killed in one of the Carpenter films. "It's like the life force was escaping my body." I got Herschell Gordon Lewis for *Antithesis*, and when they ran it, they put the names of their fan fiction on the cover and didn't even mention him. So, I thought that it was a lot of work for nothing. They either didn't know about him—this was about the time when *Blood Feast* came back into fandom—or they just didn't care. I quit them and somehow came across Jason Simon's *Dungeon 13* next.

"The INCREDIBLY STRANGE CREATURES WHO STOPPED LIVING AND BECAME MIXED-UP ZOMBIES"

TO KRIS, ENJOY THE SHOW TONIGHT R. D. Steckler 3-19-88

A sinister gypsy fortune-teller named Madame Estrella, with the help of her sleazy sister Carmelita (a stripper) and her grossly disfigured hunchback servant Ortega, victimize innocent people who come to the midway. They scorch their victims faces with acid, thereby making them look like hideous monsters. Estrella then locks them in cages like abused pets. Anyone who discovers their secret must die a brutal death!

The film is jam-packed with action, songs and dancing, including the popular 'Mixed-up Zombie Stomp'!

JERRY . . . CASH FLAGG
MARGE NEILSON . . . CAROLYN BRANDT
HAROLD . . . ATLAS KING
MADAM ESTRELLA . . . BRETT O'HARA
ORTEGA . . . JACK BRADY
. . . JAMES BOWIE
ANGELA'S MOTHER . . . JOAN HOWARD
DRUNKARD . . . WHITEY ROBINSON
BARKER . . . NIEL STILLMAN
CARMELITA . . . ERIN ENYO
DANCER . . . BILL WARD
NIGHT CLUB MANAGER . . . GENE POLLOCK
POLICEMAN . . . SON HOOKER
HOBO . . . TITUS MOEDE

PG RATED

CAMP VIDEO

GILPIN MEETS RAY DENNIS STECKLER.

**JS: I've never seen a copy.**

**KG:** It was a very friendly zine. I did some shorter, capsule reviews for him. My column was called "Deadly Capsules." I interviewed Fred Olen Ray for him. I always begged Fred to give me a one-line speaking part in one of his films, but he never did. He said something funny to me back then. This was fairly early in his directing career. I'm guessing his latest film was *Armed Response*—I think he's made more flicks than anyone. Anyway, he said, "I don't love the B-movies I've made. I wish I had more money to make better movies. Hell, I wouldn't pay money to see one of my films!" I thought that was very funny.

**JS: He must have had some great stories.**

**KG:** He told me what could be the most perfect anecdote about making B flicks. It went basically like this: He said he was reading the trades one morning, and saw that some major studio was making Poe's *The Tomb*. He found out that the story was in public domain, so he called the studio and said

## SHIT FLICK SERENADE!

RECORDED & INDEXED

DRAFT

that he was already planning to shoot *The Tomb*. This wasn't true. The studio gave him some money to buy him out. They could afford it, and they weren't going to let a minor studio make one of their projects. Anyway, the studio *Tomb* film was never made. Fred took the money they sent him to not make *The Tomb* and then made his own *Tomb*. That did eventually get released, somewhere. I laughed my ass off over that!

**JS: Living in LA must have lead to some great chance-encounters with celebrities...**

**KG:** Yeah. One day, when I was working in the shipping department at Universal, I walked in and a big guy was talking and laughing with the boss. I froze, looked at him, and said, "Nicholas Worth?" My boss was thrilled that I knew who he was. His finest moment, of course, was as the psycho star of *Don't Answer the Phone*. I got him for *D13* and a couple other times after that. We stayed close friends until I left LA in 2003.

**JS: I always wanted to meet him.**

**KG:** He was the nicest guy in the world. He and the boss were Christians, as I am. He'd always say, "How's Mary? You guys call me Uncle Nick!" He'd always ask about my ex-wife every time I saw him.

**JS: Do you have any stories about him that you'd like to share?**

**KG:** This is a great Nick story: He'd eat lunch every day he wasn't working at a Burbank family restaurant. When I found that out, I'd go in there now and then and eat with him. Once we were talking, and Whitney Houston's song "I Will Always Love You" came across the restaurant's sound system. When she hit that nail-scraping high note, our faces scrunched up and Nick said disgustedly, "Listen to that! It sounds like two cats fucking!"

**JS: [laughs] You said you're Christian, how do you...**

**KG:** I know what you mean. You can be into sleaze and be a Christian, too. I'm just a nice, hard R-rated guy. I just finished reading Alice Cooper's autobiography, and toward the end he says that he's a Christian. First of all, I'm my own worst enemy. I've suffered from very low self esteem my whole life, and every time something good happens to me, I feel... well, I know I couldn't have done it myself. I've always believed in God, anyway, since I was a kid. It's just a feeling I've always had—that's why they call it blind faith. I'll just have a few questions to ask Him when I see Him.

**JS: Such as?**

**KG:** Well, if He doesn't cause stuff like 9/11, Hitler, and Bin Laden to happen—which I don't believe He does—then He must sit back and allow it to happen. Why? Anyway, Nick told me once that he had friends who asked him, "How can you believe and play such evil people?" And he said, "Listen, I prayed to be an actor and God made me one, and I'm gonna be the best actor I can be in any part I can get, so butt out!"

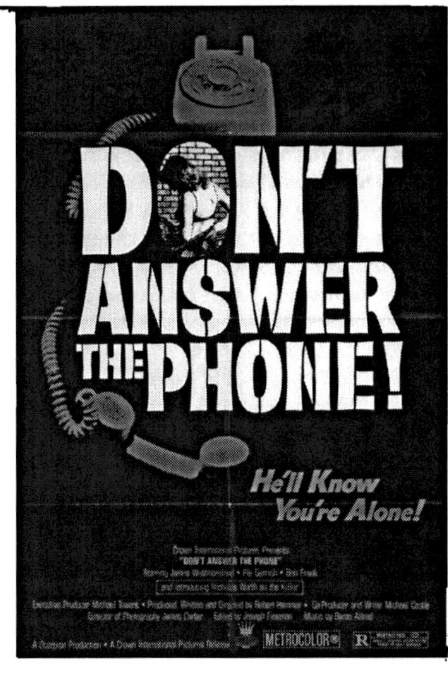


TWO CATS FUCKING.

**JS: Fair enough!**

**KG:** Woody Allen once asked Billy Graham, "Well, what if you're wrong and God doesn't exist?" Graham answered, "I don't think I am wrong." And Woody said, "Yeah, but what if you are?" Graham just answered, "Well if I am wrong, which I don't believe I am, then it'll just mean I lived my life the best way I possibly could." Allen said, "Well, I couldn't argue with that, so that was the end of our conversation." I've had many long talks about this over the years with my dear, sweet, Christian friend, C.K.

**JS: So, what happened after Nick Worth?**

**KG:** I came across a comedy zine out of New York called *Inside Joke*, by Elayne Wechsler. We'd talk about our love of The Firesign Theatre. I've always collected their stuff—funny "Movies of the Mind," as they called them. I got Eddie Deezen for her, and I covered an LA. Andy Kaufman tribute event, too. I read that Kaufman was at a dinner theater once and he just sat there onstage and ate dinner until the audience walked out [laughs]!

**JS: How seriously do you think people took Kaufman back then?**

**KG:** I think they never really knew if he was kidding or not. For a while after he died, people really wondered if he was actually dead! He got lung cancer and he'd never smoked a cigarette in his life.

# KRIS GILPIN

## SHIT FLICK SERENADE!

RECORDED & INDEXED

DRAFT

**JS: You mentioned that you lived in New York for a while. I meant to ask—do you have any 42nd Street stories?**

**KG:** It was incredibly sleazy. I was sitting in a theater once, and a fuckin' rat ran across the top of the seat in front of me. They actually had house cats living in the theaters to keep the rat populace down [laughs]! I went to the can in one once—big mistake!—and there was a businessman getting blown through a glory hole in it! And you didn't go into a porno theater; who knows what kind of scum was in there? I walked to a theater with a buddy once and he was gonna buy a joint. Another guy walked along with us for two seconds and then we got to the theater. "You gonna buy your shit?" I asked him and he said, "I just did." In the blink of your eyeball!

**JS: By the time I got to New York, all of that was pretty much gone. There were a few bookstores, but that was it.**

**KG:** I did check out a few of the XXX bookstores; I found my "romance" books in there. Professor Irwin Corey, an old comedian who called

# DRACULINA CINE

Due to poor picture quality and lack of story line, our previous videos..."Whip the Flesh" - "Pretty Girls Snuffed" - "Doors of Darkness" and "The Green Terror" have all been discontinued. Now we are offering three new videos with several more to follow in future issues. All tapes are available in VHS and BETA II, and soon in the *PAL system. Now available: HARPIES (see ad on front inside cover), VIRUS (see ad on back inside cover) and SEXPLOSION (see ad on back cover). All videos are $17 each, postage paid.

*For more information about the availability of the above videos on the PAL system: Please notify DEMENTIA HORROR stating your interest in the tapes and you will be notified by them when they are available. Write to: DEMENTIA HORROR - c/o H. BAGENHAMMAR - P.L. 3016 - 57400, VETLANDA - SWEDEN.

# Back Issues

DRACULINA 1 & 2 ARE SOLD OUT!

DRACULINA 3: Gang Games, Playmates of Terror, Final Cut (editing gore of TV), Wendy O' Williams, Video Vixen, Necrophilia in the Movies, Horrifying But True, Bit's 'n Pieces................$5.00

DRACULINA 4: Toxic Torment, Video Vixen, Heroes in Drag, Hilary Lipton, Glen or Glenda, William Sanderson, Horrifying But True, Memories of Mishkin, Bit's 'n Pieces................$4.00

DRACULINA 5: The Diabolical Doctor Fetus, Memories of Mishkin 2, Barbara Crampton, Tracey Walter, Brain Pain, Bit's 'n Pieces, Lamberto Bava, Sergio Stivaletti, Horrifying But True, Joe Bob Briggs................$4.00

DRACULINA 6: Herschell Gordon Lewis, Dyanne Thorne, Sex Crimes, Nathan Schiff, Bit's 'n Pieces, The Shuddering, God's Only True Prophet, Shipment of Heads................$3.25

"MANIAC SHOPPER," *DRACULINA* NUMBER 7.

himself the World's Foremost Authority, hung out in them and he'd be telling jokes to all the embarrassed men who frequented the places. And in the back, there were tiny jerkoff booths, where you'd watch thirty-second hardcore clips for a quarter or so. I looked in one once and there was, uh… spunk wiped on the walls. Disgusting! My buddy Gary told me an incredible story. He had a friend whose job was to mop up floors of the jerkoff booths— the worst job ever [laughs]! Once he went into one and someone had just taken a large bowel movement on the bench! He told his boss about it. The boss said, "What do you expect me to do about it? Clean it up!"

**JS: I would have quit on the spot.**

**KG:** Well, he said, "I don't wanna touch it!" The boss answered, "You clean that shit up or look for a new job!" He almost cried and took a long time getting the cleaning stuff together. When he finally shuffled back into the booth, someone had stolen the turd! Now who's sicker? The guy who takes a dump in public, or the guy who sees it and thinks, "Oh boy, fresh shit!" and takes it home [laughs]?

**JS: [laughs] Tell me about *Draculina*.**

**KG:** Hugh Gallagher and his wife were on a road trip once and they stopped by the house. My ex-wife and I were surprised; most of us nerds don't look very good, but Hugh looked like a cross between a young Mel Gibson and Kevin Costner. He was a surprisingly soft-spoken guy for the hardcore comix he drew for *Draculina*. I was able to get a lot of cool guys for him: William Sanderson, Tracy Walter—it turned out that they were old friends with Nick Worth.

**JS: What was Tracy Walter like?**

**KG:** I sat with him in his humble Beverly Hills home and the first thing he did was run his famous "Plate of Shrimp" speech from *Repo Man* for me. It didn't come across as pretentious; it was more like he knew that it was his claim to fame, and it was fun to watch it with him. Of course both those guys were just as cool as you'd think they be to meet and talk to.

**JS: What else did you do for *Draculina*?**

# KRIS GILPIN

## SHIT FLICK SERENADE!

**KG:** I got to cover Russ Meyer, John Waters, Sean Cunningham, and Dave Friedman. I did some LA film fests for Hugh too, in which they also took questions from the crowd. Man those were great nights! Then, I covered a huge film fest—it spread over two nights, I think—with films and live talks by Ted V. Mikels, Al Adamson, Doris Wishman and Ray Dennis Steckler. A lotta funny shit flicks there!

**JS: I've heard some strange things about Doris Wishman.**

**KG:** She was a real weirdo! She made very funny shitters, which she apparently thought were real films. People asked her questions and were "laughing along with her" at her answers—although she wasn't laughing at all. Someone asked her about the bizarre, funny close-ups of her actresses' huge fuck-me pumps, and she just stared at them, not getting her own jokes. She just said, "I think I'm being laughed at here and I don't like it. I'm going to leave!" She walked off the stage while everyone sat there, stunned. What a pretentious, humorless person!

**JS: Didn't you have something to do with *Cannibal Hookers*?**

**KG:** Donald Farmer called me and asked if I could be location manager for his flick. I asked him what a location manager does, since I always wanted to get a film credit. He said, "I wanna use your apartment for the shoot." So, there were a couple topless chicks in our old place for a day. One of them picked up my ex's Calico and ad libbed, "Isn't that right, Esmeralda?" So, one of her cats got into the movie.

**JS: Do you have any other memories about the shoot?**

**KG:** I remember one of Farmer's lines. The jock-type actor just didn't like it. I said, "What if he says (after a girl takes her top off), 'Stick around and I'll give you a standing ovation!'?" I can't remember if I ripped that off from a Woody Allen film, but that that's what it reminded me of at the time. So, I got a line into the flick too.

**JS: Speaking of Donald Farmer, you did some work for the *Splatter Times*...**

**KG:** Yeah, it was one of only three times I got to be on a set as a writer. It was a night shoot on the great *Return of the Living Dead*. It was great fun for me, and when they broke at midnight for lunch, I got to interview Dan O'Bannon as we ate.

**JS: What was the set like?**

**KG:** Dan was keeping his cool, even though it was his first directorial film. In fact, some of the actors told me that the first week of the shoot was kind of crazy, but once O'Bannon got into the swing of directing, the next two weeks had gone much smoother.

**JS: You did a lot of work for Donald...**

**KG:** Farmer had also co-written a magazine/book with Bill George called *Invasion of the Scream Queens*, and he wanted me in that too. I got Cheryl "Rainbeaux" (*Caged Heat, Lemora*) Smith for that, and it was the first time I had to conduct an interview through the mail. Like every other male back then, I was totally knocked out by her. She was ethereally lovely, with the face of an angel and I was pissed because I couldn't meet her in person. But, she sent back my questions with lots of smiley faces drawn on the pages along with her answers. She was such a sweetheart.

**JS: I've read some sad stuff about her.**

**KG:** Yes, it broke my heart when I read that she had overdosed at forty-seven! She should've had a sweet life, but I think it was very hard for her. She'd even been to prison twice for something. A real shame. Uh, you wanna here a sick story?

**JS: Of course!**

**KG:** Someone in fandom introduced me to this guy once. Let's call him "Mr. G." He showed me one of the films he shot. He said that old sick fucks would hire him to shoot perverted vids for them. One of them had a little boy crying in it. Then, it cut to his two totally obvious rubber Halloween monster feet, which Mr. G. was torching with a hand-held blowtorch. Although it was obviously 100 per cent fake, the concept was sick as shit! Well, as I heard it, the cops were coming after him for these films, and even though I don't think they could've done anything legal to him—even a kid could see that these "torture" flicks were totally bogus—he stupidly fled the cops. And whenever a dude wanted to get out of LA for a day or two, he'd just drive down to Tijuana. The cops went down there, walked around and simply found him drinking in some shithole. I heard they took him to jail for a while. He probably wouldn't have been arrested for anything if he'd just stayed in his LA apartment, but he ran like a dummy. That's where he fucked up. I have no idea where he is now.

**JS: One can only guess! How did you get into Jeff Smith's *Wet Paint*?**

**KG:** I don't remember, but Jeff is a very good artist, and I've stayed friends with him ever since. I got divorced around that time and became clinically

RECORDED & INDEXED
DRAFT

depressed—thank God for Paxil!—and once, just for the hell of it, I flew from LA to Bangor and took a lot of pictures of the outside of Steve King's house, with the cool iron gargoyles on his fence.

**JS: What was Bangor like?**

**KG:** It was an incredibly clean, pretty little town. At that time, they only had one multiplex theater. A girl inside said that King and his family watched the new films there all the time. I didn't wanna run back to LA yet, so I went to Fort Collins and saw Phil Dick's gravestone. He was buried next to his twin sister, who died when she was like six days old or something. Anyway, I wrote about those trips and it was printed in *Wet Paint*. Jeff Smith had an offshoot zine called *Forbidden Zone*. I did a Nick Worth update for that one.

**JS: Your IMDb page says you did a few acting jobs as an extra...**

**KG:** Yeah, that was during a few months when I was laid off for the Summer. I was a terrorist in *Terminal Entry*.

**JS: I've never seen it.**

**KG:** It was a thriller—I think it was eventually just a direct-to-video production. I only found it once on a shitty VHS tape that was recorded on the slow, six-hour mode!

**JS: What did you do in that?**

**KG:** I was beaten to death by Yaphet Kyoto! I said, "Uh, I've never done a fight scene, Mr. K. How do you want to work this thing?"

**JS: That's a reasonable question!**

**KG:** [laughs] He said, "Oh man, I'm just gonna mess with ya!" When the time came, he just pulled some punches while I spastically jerked around. When I finally fell to the ground, the crew laughed. I always thought they were laughing at my ragdoll movements. Oh, and one strange thing happened. Apparently, Edward Albert (the film's other star—he seemed like a nice guy when I introduced myself to him) went up to an actor who was lying on the ice cold ground during the night shoot and shot a blank round near the guy's head! It was loud and scary and everyone froze and looked at Albert like, "What the fuck?" Albert was just laughing. A gun tech walked up to Edward and just gently took the gun from his hand.

**JS: Wow.**

**KG:** But then, I did one film that finally did come out and it was good. Kyle MacLachlan's *The Hidden*. I wrote about that in *Wet Paint*. After the first fifteen minutes, as the camera pans inside the diner, you can just see me through the big window, walking with and talking to a woman outside. My blink-and you'll-miss-it friggin' acting career! After that, I reviewed more films and vids for Craig Ledbetter's *Hi-Tech Terror*. And then, somehow Mike Helms and I touched base.

**JS: He edited *Fatal Visions*.**

**KG:** Yeah. It was a very cool Aussie zine. I had a fun talk with Charles Napier for that one. I asked him about that shocking, horrendous scene

where he stabs and then stomps that woman to death in the bathtub in *SuperVIXENS*. He said that Russ Meyer said, "I wanted to make a film with no social redeeming values whatsoever, so I made *SuperVIXENS*!"

**JS: I wanted to ask you about *Nudist Colony of the Dead*.**

**KG:** That was another Super-8 epic by Mark Pirro, who'd directed Eddie Deezen before in *A Polish Vampire in Burbank*. *Nudist Colony* was supposed to be the best looking feature ever shot on Super-8, but he said the lab fucked it up. It did have some nice blood and makeup and some funny acting in it, though. I was the second assistant director on it, to get a crew credit on a movie.

**JS: What did the job entail?**

**KG:** Basically, I directed traffic and asked people to be quiet. Once, I had to go to some guy's house when we were shooting. I said, "Hi. Excuse me, but we're shooting a movie on this street, and I wondered if you could please turn off your car's engine for me for a couple minutes?" The guy looked at me and said, "Go fuck yourself!" I said, "Yes sir, I'll do that." [laughs] But my favorite *Nudist Colony* time came when I was asked to bring a couple of young women in the makeup area onto the set. They were both in robes, with white, undead, full-body makeup on. They started to giggle and they flashed each other over and over again. I'm sure they were just fucking with me since I was standing right between them, but I just smiled and looked back and forth at these two beautiful naked girls. That was a fun day! Oh, and I was also a zombie victim in a field in one shot, though all you can see is my foot.

**JS: Let's talk about *Subhuman*.**

**KG:** Oh man, I loved *Subhuman*!

**JS: It was one of my favorites.**

ONE OF THE DEAD IN *NUDIST COLONY OF THE DEAD*.

# KRIS GILPIN

## SHIT FLICK SERENADE!

RECORDED & INDEXED

DRAFT

**KG:** I loved getting into every zine that I could and did get into, but there was something wonderful about *Subhuman*. Cecil and Dawn Doyle were sweethearts when I talked to them on the phone, and the zine seemed to get sleazier as it went on, which I loved.

**JS: You did quite a few interviews for them.**

**KG:** Yeah. I interviewed Steven Poster, who shot one or two H.G. Lewis films and Don Gordon from *Bullitt* and *The Last Movie*.

**JS: What did he have to say about that?**

**KG:** He said it was truly as insane a shoot as its legend said it was. In fact, when I was at Universal, I found out that an editor there had been an assistant editor on *The Last Movie*. He said that Hopper and his buds would send in tons of footage every week from Peru, and none of it was in the script or made any sense. He said, "By looking at it all, we couldn't even begin to guess where the fuck it was supposed to go into the work print, it was just one big clusterfuck of film!" Hopper went down there, got wasted and just shot and shot and shot.

**JS: You know, *Subhuman* did get pretty sleazy.**

**KG:** I thought it was very funny— I'd keep sending them as much scum as I could and Cecil would just say, "Sure, thanks!" [laughs] One day, while I was an assistant editor on *In the Heat of the Night*, another worker just happened to mention in passing that he'd once shot a disgusting John Holmes porn loop. I said, "Whoa, we gotta talk over lunch!"

**JS: I remember that interview!**

**KG:** I taped him for Cecil. The guy wanted me to call him "Mr. X" . He said that there was a bunch of scagged out people in one room, including some poor, gross post-op transsexuals. "I had to shoot them close-up between their legs, and I nearly gagged! Their vaginas were horrible botch jobs, kind of jagged instead of vertical, with pieces of skin and shit hanging out of 'em. I felt like I needed to shower afterwards!" He claimed that Holmes did women and men both, and he called Holmes "a big prick," in both senses of the word. That was surely the grossest piece I ever wrote. [laughs]

**JS: Speaking of strange things that you wrote for *Subhuman*, I wanted to ask you about "Get Out of My Way, Man, I Really Mean It!" You reviewed a fake movie.**

**KG:** [laughs] I'd write some short comic pieces and tiny scripts for zines sometimes, and I sent two of them to *Subhuman*. They were bogus film reviews, and I think that one was about a huge bastard who goes on a McDonald's pig-out binge, then rolls out on the street yelling, "Get out of my way, man, I really mean it!"—which was the stupidest title I could think of—before exploding and spewing guts and shit all over the people in the crowd.

**JS: You did two of these things?**

**KG:** The other review was called *The Scum People*, about a white trash couple who didn't know exactly how many children they had shat out

GILPIN'S FINAL INTERVIEW. *DRAMA-LOGUE*, 1990.

PAGE 4 DRAMA-LOGUE SEPT. 6-12, 1990

# The King of Science Fiction

# Ray Bradbury

## May also prove to be the master of musical comedy

**BY KRIS GILPIN**

Ray Bradbury. Man, woman or child, if you've never read any of his over 500 short stories, published in magazines as diverse as *Weird Tales, The New Republic, Gourmet* and *Playboy*, chances are you've heard his name. His books of fantasy and science fiction (which include *The Golden Apples of the Sun, A Medicine for Melancholy, The Machineries of Joy* and *I Sing the Body Electric*) have been translated the world over while being reprinted scores of times.

How does it feel to be a living literary legend and the inspiration for generations of readers and writers? "Super," replies Bradbury." I go to France, Italy and England, and all over America, and all the young students—and the old ones, too—[know my work]; as a result, when people interview me I rarely have any static because they're all kids who read me in high school. I feel very fortunate." Bradbury is a very nice man, friendly to all who have approached him in public and at conventions. He's a modest man as well; he still lives in the same home he purchased 30 years ago.

In addition to his 25 collections and novels, he's sold over 200 poems and countless essays (some published in his recent *Zen in the Art of Writing*), television scripts (see USA Cable's current *Ray Bradbury Theatre*) and screenplays. He also worked with Jimmy Webb, composing lyrics for a musical version of his *Dandelion Wine*, and Bradbury's produced his own plays *The World of Ray Bradbury* and *Falling Upward*, a comedy about writing the *Moby Dick* screenplay in Ireland for director John Huston. Another play of the author's, *The Wonderful Ice Cream Suit*, opens soon in the most ambitious production ever mounted by the 73-year-old Pasadena Playhouse.

The play was first produced, along with *A Medicine for Melancholy* and *The Pedestrian*, as one of three one-acts performed at the old Desilu Theatre Workshop in the early '60s. "Lucille Ball was our landlady," Bradbury recalls. "We had a lot of good people, including Harold Gould, who was starting his career, and this director named Charles Rome Smith did the best directing of the three people who directed those plays." Consequently, Smith is back at the helm for the Pasadena's new production. "We all worked free back then; the entire production cost $200 for all three plays—$100 for a policeman and $100 for a night watchman, and that was the expense for the play." The author then rented L.A.'s Coronet Theatre for $500 a week in 1964, where his *Ice Cream Suit* ran for half a year.

The tale began life as a short story in a 1957 issue of *The Saturday Evening Post* and was then produced as a television comedy/drama half-hour the following year starring a young Peter Falk. The Coronet production featured Talia Shire (then called Coppola) and Henry (*High Chaparral*) Darrow—who's also in the new show—among other future notables. "On the last night of the production 26 years ago, the entire cast all signed one of the suits and gave it to me as a gift," the writer says, "and I put it away in the closet for over 20 years. And on the night of the Academy Awards four years ago, when they were handing out the Best Actor award, I said to my wife, 'Wait here!' I brought the suit out and as they handed the Oscar out, I opened the suit, and under the left armpit it read, 'F. Murray Abraham.' I wept with joy," he smiles, "because it was like having a son graduate from Harvard."

As *The Wonderful Ice Cream Suit* was produced over the years in cities like Chicago (where it starred Joe Mantegna), New York and Lincoln Park, Bradbury and company kept adding music to it. "It was just natural, and I'd say to myself, 'Someday, this'll be a musical because it's moving that way all on its own.'" Now, today's the day, as popular singer-guitarist Jose Feliciano has penned 16 songs for the new staging, with lyrics by him and his wife, Susan. The book itself needed no additional material. "There's no need, because I've been writing the darn thing for 32 years; if it isn't ready now it never will be. Just mainly a little cutting here and there to allow room for the songs."

The play concerns five Hispanic youths from East L.A. who spend their last dollars on a beautiful white suit, which they each get a turn to wear during their first night out. But the suit has magical powers and comes to offer all of them new hope for the future. The Bradburys had moved to L.A. in 1934, where the young Ray would make best friends with two Chicano (as they were called then) students, spending more time at Eddie Barrera's house than at his own. "So I sort of grew up in that Hispanic family and got to know all the traditions. And in the years before that, I lived in Tucson, Arizona and Roswell, New Mexico, again with a lot of Hispanic friends, so my background, all the way through, has been as Hispanic as anything else. Then, in the '40s, I lived in and out of a tenement at the corner of Temple and Figueroa, and I've written a novel about that tenement and the people I knew there.

"The suit represents, on an individual level, the thing we all need; we all need clothing," he explains; "we all grew up with our sibling's hand-me-downs. I was in my twenties before I had any clothes of my own. So the theme is very close to everyone's heart, and someone like myself was torn between buying books or a pair of pants. So the metaphor works on many levels; on the need to look neat and then the comradeship that comes with sharing the suit. So it's a suit of armor; it's Don Quixote going out in his suit of armor."

By now Bradbury has developed a great working relationship with his *Suit's* director, and his old friend, Charles Rome Smith. "He's wonderful; we've been together all these years and have done many plays—we did an Irish play two years ago—and our instincts are powerful," the writer notes. "We run on a track together. We can sit in a casting session not talking; 100 people can come through and at the end of the day we'll look at the lists we've made, and they'll be 80 percent the same. We'll pick the same people. So that's a wonderful friend and director to have."

Smith worked with the Felicianos on the songs much in the same manner as Bradbury has worked with artists who illustrate his pages and covers. "I give suggestions for metaphors to my artist friend Joe Mugnaini, who's done many of my covers, and I'm very careful not to nail him down; I just give him a simple metaphor and say, 'Now, do something with that,' and then back off. You get wonderful results. Same way with writing a song."

The author sees no difference between writing short stories or plays. "It's all the same; if it isn't fun you shouldn't do it. If it isn't great joy you should walk away and do something else. That's what's wrong with the world; there are a lot of people writing things they shouldn't be writing. That's why they write bad plays or stories or novels. You should just sit down and have fun, with the serious things as well. *Fahrenheit 451* was a very serious novel but I had a hell of a wonderful time writing it." Bradbury has recently turned that book into an opera, which premiered last year in Fort Wayne, Indiana; he hopes to take it to Czechoslovakia in 1991, since its President Havel is a long-time fan of the fantasist's works. "It's amazing how, suddenly, within the last 10 years, I've moved into the musical field," Bradbury states.

In the last few years, he has also turned to the mystery field, as his new novel, *A Graveyard for Lunatics*, is a well-received sequel to his recent mystery, *Death is a Lonely Business*. He has always loved mysteries as well as the fantasy genre, having grown up reading Chandler, Hammett, Cain and Sir Arthur Conan Doyle. Some of Bradbury's first stories sold to detective magazines; he's always wanted to pen a murder mystery, so five years ago he did. (He also had a collection of early mystery stories published years ago, but it was never reprinted, and is today a hard-core collector's item).

Both these mystery novels star the same character, who Bradbury patterned after himself. "I don't have to write my autobiography," he says; "if people want to find out about me they read my two murder mysteries. There's more of me and my friends and all the people I knew in the tenement in those [than in my other books]." He lived with his parents until he was 27 because he wasn't making enough money as a writer to afford to leave. "We all lived in Venice, California when we were poor and nowadays you *can't* live there if you're poor."

His great love of film plays a major role in his mysteries, especially the new one and, when he was 14, Ray Bradbury wrote some radio shows for Burns and Allen. "Of course they never *used* them," he chuckles; "I doubt if they ever read them but George was very kind to me and pretended to read them. And he actually used one of my jokes on the program—I think it was in February of 1935."

The two men would meet again some 30 or 40 years later, when Bradbury noticed Burns in the audience of a banquet held in Steven Spielberg's honor about 10 years ago. In the middle of the awards show Bradbury stopped the proceedings to give his own "award of love" to Burns for the affection he showed him as a boy. When the program ended Burns ran up to him, asking, "Was that *you*? I remember you!" And he embraced him for the first time in 40 years, which is why Burns is one of the Hollywood people to whom *Graveyard for Lunatics* is dedicated. In fact, the book was inspired by Bradbury's crazy days of hanging around Hollywood as an adolescent.

The author doesn't know what book will come next out of his subconscious; he doesn't like to force any genres from his mind and, God knows, he doesn't have to. It might be a mystery (though none is planned at the moment), or the science fiction novel he has started, or the 500-page book on Ireland—where he lived for a year—he's finishing, or the one he's writing about John Huston. He wanted to write the latter after reading what he thought were the less-than-complete recent bios on the late great actor-director. "I don't want to have a gossip book, which is what most of these other books are. I want to verify it."

He found working with Huston during the filming of *Moby Dick* to be very strange, since neither of them "knew what the hell we were doing; he didn't understand *Moby Dick* and neither did I. It took eight months of reading some sections 80 or 120 times so that it all got into my bloodstream; that's the only way you can adapt a book. And finally, when I'd been on the job for seven months, the day came when I understood the book. Huston was good as a ricochet board; I just bounced ideas off of him and he had enough taste, sense and perception to know when I'd hit something good, but we were both unprepared. I'd never read the novel until he came into my life and in the first month I suffered terrible depressions because I thought I might fail Herman Melville and my hero, John Huston. I'd always wanted to work for him." *Death is a Lonely Business* has been optioned as a possible overseas film project and, if *Graveyards* is turned into celluloid, Bradbury'd like to write the script himself. "It's fresh and I wouldn't be tired, whereas I worked on the first mystery novel for so many years I was exhausted with it." The first murder book took 30 years to write, the second only four.

Although he loves to write screenplays as much as stories or novels, he doesn't believe it to be a fulfilling profession for a writer. "You gotta be careful because you can't learn to write by writing screenplays," he says. "It's a totally non-educational way of writing. It's wonderful in its own way but you don't learn how to write narrative; you're learning to write dialogue and character. You can't turn that into a novel. You have to learn all the ways of writing first; short stories, novels and poetry, and *then* do your screenplays later in life, but if you start out that way you'll never grow. All the screenwriters I know are very vulnerable; if something happens to their careers they have no fall back."

Bradbury was a child of movies, born in Waukegan, Illinois. He claims total recall and can remember when his mother began to take him to movies at the age of two; 1923's *Hunchback of Notre Dame* and all those early Lon Chaney films are burned into his memory. He'd already begun to write by 1933, when he was madly inspired by *King Kong* and, by age 18, he'd formed a life-long friendship with special effects animator Ray Harryhausen, who was the author's best man at his wedding 43 years ago. *The Beast from 20,000 Fathoms* (1953) featured Bradbury's storyline and Harryhausen's dinosaurs. "The two of us are the luckiest people I've ever known."

He knew he wanted to write when he saw his first science-fiction magazine at the age of eight; he wanted to live in the cities of the future that he saw on the covers, and decades later he'd help do that as a creative architectural consultant for gallerias and EPCOT's Spaceship Earth in Florida's Disney World. "The best way to live in those cities was to write about them."

How does the great fantasist feel about turning 70 in August? "First of all, nobody feels their age; I still feel 14 and if I don't look too closely at myself when I'm shaving in the morning, I *look* 14," he smiles. "The only reason to think about 70 is to make you get more work out. The *Graveyard* novel was very important to me because it was one more gesture against the dark. So many of my friends've died in the last two years, it makes you say, 'I'd better get another book out,'"

In the future, Ray Bradbury would like to write "more operas, musicals, short stories, poetry and 12 more shows for my series; that'll put them up around 54 shows and then we'll quit and send them around the world. And who knows? I have files full of *hundreds* of stories I haven't looked at in 20, 30 years. So I may find something tomorrow that'll turn into a novel the day after." ☆

Basic Meisner Method
the John Parkinson School

Teachers/Photographers
STUDIO TO SHARE
PERFECT FOR CLASSES OR SHOOTS
PRESTIGIOUS HLLYD. AND VINE

SPEECH — VOICE BUILDING
FOR ACTORS & SPEAKERS
POWER, RESONANCE, DICTION, PROJECTION and

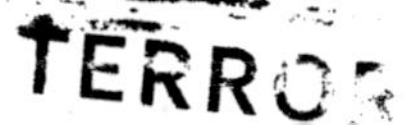

(around thirty-five). The stepfather would terrorize them by farting in their faces—close to, but not quite Algonquin Round Table material, there.

**JS: When did *Deep Red*, come into the picture?**

**KG:** I think it was next. That, of course, was a good looking zine and one of the best.

**JS: What are your memories of Chas. Balun?**

**KG:** He and his wife were one of the sweetest couples I ever met. Incredibly nice people. He had a *Deep Red* writers' party once and it was great fun. He had a gory Lucio Fulci shit flick on the TV in the background, and they made some great food. When everyone left, Chas. gave us all an extremely thoughtful surprise gift: a box of business cards. Mine had a raised drawing of a black, old fashioned camera on a white card, with "Kris Gilpin, Writer, *Deep Red*" printed on it. I was very touched and grateful to them, and I still have a handful of the cards. It was a big shock and incredibly sad when he died young—it really hit the whole horror community hard. He was like this big, *Gentle Ben* character who gave me a bear hug when I left that night. I hope his wife is OK now, wherever she is.

**JS: You interviewed David Hess for *Deep Red*...**

**KG:** Yeah, when I met him in an LA restaurant he had a salt and pepper beard. I said, "Oh, hi David, I didn't recognize you with your beard," and he said, "I didn't recognize you with your beard, either." He was pretty cool and he told me, "I gained twenty pounds for Deodato's *House on the Edge of the Park* to make myself look more physically repulsive as the rapist," which really cracked me up. At the end of our talk though, as we were leaving, he looked at me weirdly and said, "I also just played

DAVID A. HESS

SINGER SCHOLAR PSYCHO

BY KRIS GILPIN

Michelangelo in an eight-hour Italian mini-series." I smiled at him and said, "Really?" He looked at me, not smiling, and said, "Yeah, really." But I don't think that ever happened, so maybe I had somehow pissed him off with my comment about his beard and he was fucking with me. I dunno…

**JS: What did you think of the *Deep Red Horror Handbook*?**

**KG:** Man, that was a beautiful little book. One of the best zine publications, ever. Chas. asked me for a bunch of short interviews he could put in between the longer pieces in the book. I gave him a couple of shortened interviews I'd done before (which were in some of the more obscure zines), but I mostly got him fresh or updated stuff.

**JS: What did you think of *Starlog* and *Cinefantastique*?**

**KG:** I always liked *Starlog*, but for its last ten to twenty years or so it seemed to me to basically be an organ for *Star Trek*, which never did anything for me. But I always did wanna get in it—it looked so good—so I got my name in six issues in a row. That was cool because it was a paying gig. I remember though, at the beginning of my first piece, I starting writing it in the first person. "I didn't recognize so-and-so at first because she looked so different in person." I was trying to make it sound different and looser. I got a crazed postcard back from one of the bigwigs there saying, "What the *hell* do you mean writing a *Starlog* article in the first person?"

**JS: That would have ended my career over there…**

**KG:** That was kind of fucked up, I thought. And then, he bitched at me again for something else that happened later on. He wasn't the nicest guy out there, at least not to me. Then I also got my name in about six *Cinefantastiques* in a row. It was a big, beautiful mag, especially the huge double issues.

**JS: What was Fred Clarke like?**

**KG:** He seemed to me to be a weird dichotomy. On the phone, he was always very pleasant, but he was into some tabloid-like stuff in the mag sometimes, too. He published a photo of the deadly helicopter crash during the *Twilight Zone: The Movie* shoot that pissed a lot of industry people off. He paid by the word, and he would rewrite your stuff to bring your paycheck amount down. And once, he inserted some pseudo-negative comments about my subject into one of my pieces—I honestly don't remember who it was now, but their publicist called me up, all pissed off. I never made any subject in a pro or fanzine sound shitty, and it pissed me off a bit. I swore to him that I hadn't written that bit of info. Anyway, Fred would later say, "Gilpin,

KRIS GILPIN
Staff Writer
(818) 760-3063
8452 Carnegie Avenue Westminster, CA 9268[illegible]

Attachment

A PARTING GIFT FROM CHAS. BALUN.

# Kris Gilpin

## Shit Flick Serenade!

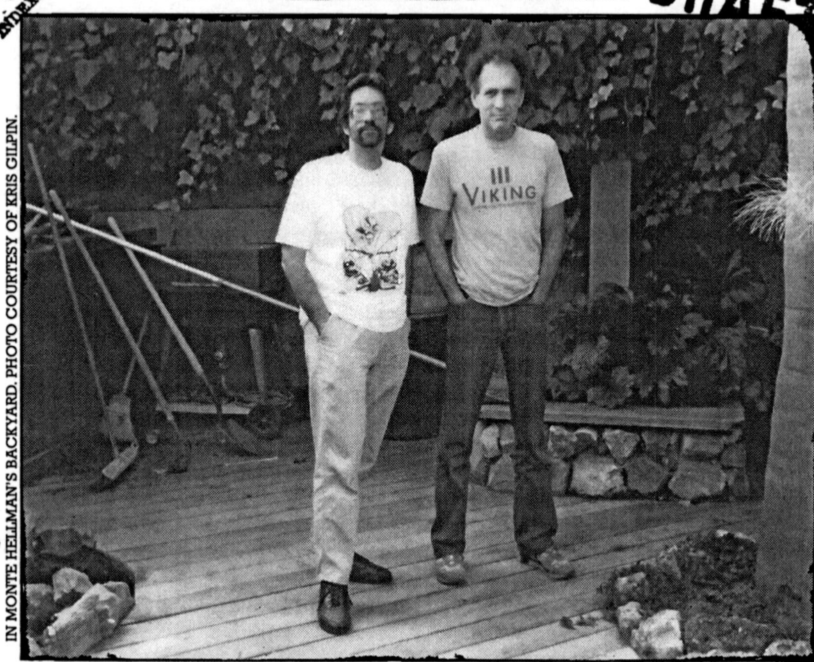


IN MONTE HELLMAN'S BACKYARD. PHOTO COURTESY OF KRIS GILPIN.

why don't you write something else for me?" I told him, "I like you, Fred, but so-and-so's publicist called me up, pissed off and yelling at me over something you inserted into my interview!" So, although the mag was a beauty, I didn't wanna chance writing something for him anymore. It was sad in the end, though because he suffered from depression so badly. He killed himself at fifty-one.

**JS: You did some stuff for *Shock Xpress*...**

**KG:** Yeah. Stefan [Jaworzyn] wanted my Larry Buchanan interview in there, and one night I interviewed Al Adamson for him, using questions written mostly by Jaime Pina. He knew Adamson's career better than I did, but he thought he was a big hack. I had to get that interview in a hurry and hadn't read all of his questions before I talked to Al, so I asked him a question which basically called his films shit. Adamson glowered at me and I said, "Oops! Sorry man, I didn't write that one." [laughs] Do you know the great film/counterculture journalist Jack Stevenson?

**JS: Yeah. He did some big zine-books called *Pandemonium*.**

**KG:** Right. He's a great guy, and he asked me to get Mary Woronov for *Pandemonium II*. That was awesome for me because she was always like Josephine Cool, you know? I got to talk to her in her place, which was full of her neat, abstract paintings. I went through her stills to send a couple to

Jack for the zine and came across a great one of her topless in a bath from *Sugar Cookies*. I said, "Oh, the editor would love this one!" And Mary said, "Yeah, I bet he would." "No?" I asked her. "No," she said [laughs].

**JS: You interviewed Monte Hellman for *Film Threat*.**

**KG:** That was one of the greatest talks for me, because I loved his stuff in the sixties and seventies. *The Shooting* is a great existential Jack Nicholson and Warren Oates western on a low budget, but it looks very good. Hellman has always been considered an American director with a European flavor to his work. I was thrilled because, along with Wim Wenders' *Kings of the Road*, Hellman's *Two-Lane Blacktop* was and still is my very favorite road film.

**JS: It's an amazing film.**

**KG:** When I saw it as a teen, I thought, "I can't believe someone got to make a film that goes nowhere." I fell in love with it more and more as it went along. That film got me into road films, existentialism, travel, and alternative cinema. The whole thing had this eerie, ultra-natural feeling to it—until I realized that it's one of the few films that has no musical soundtrack in the background, just some snippets of live, source music in certain scenes.

**JS: Like the music from the radio.**

**KG:** Yeah. That gave a very naturalistic, believable feeling to the film. And, when used to create a horror effect, that's also a reason why the original *I Spit on Your Grave* is so hard to take. It has no music. That's why I can't sit through some old films. The constant, shitty, syrupy music in the background bugs the hell out of me! And when you watch a film, even today, where sad music comes in under someone's sad speech, as if you're too fuckin' stupid to pick up on the mood of the scene by yourself without Hollytrite spoon feeding it to you. It's insulting to the viewer and it takes me right out of the film; it really distracts me.

**JS: Can you give me an example?**

**KG:** Well, I thought *A.I.* would've been so much more emotional without the constant sappy music in the background.

**JS: Gotcha.**

**KG:** Anyway, I said to Hellman, "What I got out of *Ride in the Whirlwind* was that sometimes in life you get screwed, even if you're a total innocent and there's not a fucking thing you can do about it." Hellman looked at me and said with a smile, "Oh, yeah? You got that out of it?" So maybe I didn't get it after all [laughs]. But, after the interview, as I got up to leave, he said, "Are you in a hurry? I have some buddies coming over and we're gonna watch my new film, if you're interested." Needless to say, there I was, for an extra two hours, watching a tape of *Iguana*. That was one of my best days...

**JS: Your writing appeared quite frequently in the pages of something called *Drama-Logue*. What exactly was that?**

**KG:** It was a... OK, first, quickly, I did a phone talk with Tobe Hooper for Derek Jensen's *Children of the Night*. Hooper was talking with me for an hour from his kitchen and I could hear kitchen noises and him holding

his kids in the background. When the issue came out. it looked very nice. It was his best-looking issue to date. Then, I'd noticed a local LA. actors' casting prozine named *Drama-Logue*, which also had great actor interviews in it. I sent the editor, a very nice guy named Lee Melville, that issue of *Children of the Night* with a resume, asking if I could write for him. He said yes, and that was the first of many character actor/director interviews I did for him.

**JS: What was your first interview for that?**

**KG:** The first one was Felton Perry, who was in *RoboCop* and the original *Walking Tall*. I let Lee know that I knew a lot of B-movie, character, and horror people. Every time one of their publicists would contact the mag, Lee would call me first. I got people like Paul Verhoeven and Sam Raimi. I was pissed later, because I'd spoken with them both the nights before *RoboCop* and *Evil Dead 2* opened, and I wished I'd gotten a chance to see the films first.

**JS: How often did they screen films for you before your interviews?**

**KG:** Surprisingly, not that often. The time that springs to mind first was *House II: The Second Story*, with that little puppet in it. I basically hated that flick, especially after loving the first one with William Katt. I slipped out before the director's friendly publicist asked me what I thought of it. And, of course, I never said anything bad about a film or its actor/director in a prozine piece.

**JS: Were you ever assigned to interview anyone whose work you weren't aware of?**

**KG:** Really early on, Melville told me, "You'll never guess who I got for you next!" My mind raced, and I finally asked, "Who?"

**JS: I'm going to ask you the same thing!**

**KG:** It was Jean-Claude Van Damme. I asked him, "Who the hell is Jean-

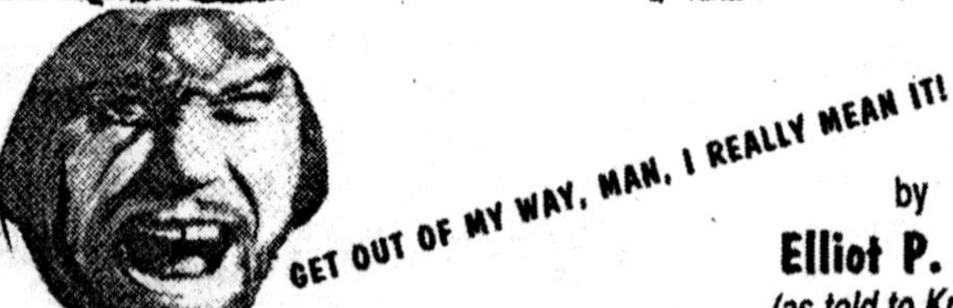


by
**Elliot P. Ness**
*(as told to Kris Gilpin)*

Get out of my way, man, I really mean it!! proves to be a film as stupid as its title. This Mexican/Canadian co-production stars Giraldo Pieyya (who?) as a constipated Bud Spencer-type who was severly traumatized as a child when his mother first caught him alone in the bathroom moving his bowels.

"I can't believe you did that!" she scolds him in an early flashback scene. "Sitting there, pinching turds! Grunting! Stinking up our beautiful home" (which had no walls, and was in a Mexican slum neighborhood)!! Consequently, the young Raoul could

Claude Van Damme?" He said, "Yeah I know. With that name he'll never go anywhere!"

**JS: When was this?**

**KG:** He was just starting out, and I was getting him for *Cyborg*. He was very nice, though, and he brought along his wife at the time. She was pretty and petite, but she was pretty buffed out too. He spoke in broken English then and kept saying, "Thanks God!" for his budding career.

**JS: As someone who does a lot of this myself, I'm curious about how you prepared for something like that.**

**KG:** The lazy kind of interview, where the host asks the subject, "So, who are you and what do you do?" is just a bunch of shit. It's just a piss off. The simple secret is to be as researched and prepared as possible. I'd ask every publicist to send me their people's most comprehensive resumes. This was before IMDb, of course. My memory sucks for most things, but for whatever reason I've always retained tons of movie trivia knowledge.

**JS: Which you must now use for your online movie crossword puzzles.**

**KG:** Right. Sometimes, an interviewee would say, "How did you find out about that film? Even I've forgotten about it!" Jeffrey Jones said he really appreciated my research and questions.

**JS: Wait a minute—Jeffrey Jones?**

**KG:** Yeah. He was the nicest guy in the world when I spoke to him, just like you'd figure he'd be. We ran into each other three times in the supermarket after our talk. He'd give me a bear hug and said, "Honestly, Kris, that was the best interview anyone's ever done with me!" I was shocked as hell when I heard he'd taken nude pictures of that fourteen year old boy. They say he never touched him, but that was some sick shit. I was shocked, surprised, and saddened that he did that.

**JS: When and why did you stop interviewing?**

**KG:** [Sighs] I was getting tired of transcribing the pieces, which always took me a few nights, for $60 a pop. Plus, I was getting somewhat depressed because I always wanted to do what these character actors were doing. But even then, I was torn. I was in one of these aging, very popular, and well-liked actor's apartments, and it was a small, bare, semi-bleak place. I thought, "Shit, I've been watching and loving this guy for decades, and I'm living better than he is now!" And another actor, who'd been working for decades, confided to me that, in all his time of acting, he'd made only $11,000.

**JS: [Stunned] What?**

**KG:** I got choked up and made him repeat the figure. I couldn't believe it. It was so fucking sad! So, I don't know, I was very conflicted inside. And then, Lee asked me to get the biggest name I'd ever gotten: Ray Bradbury.

**JS: Nice!**

**KG:** Yeah! He was talking about a play of his in LA. which had been adapted from his *The Wonderful Ice Cream Suit*—a film of the same name was made

by Stuart Gordon, by the way—and I'm sitting in his humble home, the same one he'd bought thirty years earlier, thinking, I can't believe I'm sitting in Ray Bradbury's living room! I said, "First off, Ray (as he insisted I call him), I loved and grew up on your stories!" He replied, "Yeah, you and a million others." Not in a mean way, but as if he'd heard it every day of his life. Then, I noticed a genuine Oscar sitting on his fireplace mantle.

**JS: I didn't know he'd won an Oscar.**

**KG:** That's the thing. I said, "Wow, Ray, I never knew you'd won an Oscar!" He said, "Nah, it's not mine. I wrote *Moby Dick* for John Huston in '56 and later on I told him, 'Hey John, you have two Oscars and I don't have any. Can I have one?' He said, 'Sure, kid!' So, I took one of John Huston's Oscars!" I quit the interviews after that, because I knew I could never top getting Ray Bradbury!

**JS: Are you still writing at all?**

**KG:** Oh yeah, I love to write. My movie crosswords keep me busy about half the time. I wrote an offbeat road movie script a few years ago, and now I'm outlining a novel about my late brother and myself. We had the same sense of humor and were like one. And I've been asking around for years if someone wants to publish a book of my old interviews. A lot of retro-film books are coming out now, including this one. Even if no one winds up reading these projects of mine, I'll still be happy after I knock them out. Like my late, beloved brother, who wrote five novels in his lifetime, I just love to write.

**JS: How do you feel about film blogs today?**

**KG:** Kevin Smith's is fun, and Ricky Gervais' is hilarious. Last year, two nice guys from *Death by DVD* contacted me and other old zine writers for some ninety-minute talks. That was great fun for me, especially knowing that a new generation, like you, has somehow discovered and loves these old labor-of-love zines. To me, that's cool and very flattering. And my old buddy Chris Poggiali has reprinted a handful of my old articles for *Temple of Schlock*.

**JS: Why do you think horror films have remained so popular?**

**KG:** I don't know. They've been around since before the beginning, as Firesign Theatre would say. For filmmakers, it's always been a cheap way to break into the biz. The ones who do something different with the little money they have really stand out. But, there must be something inside of us that's attracted to the dark side. These tales have been around in books, films, and campfire tales forever. I guess they always will be. Maybe it's a cathartic thing.

**JS: What do you think of today's films?**

**KG:** Thank God for indies! I'd be bored to death without them! Nine times out of ten these days, you see a trailer for the latest carbon-copy Hollyturd and you know how it's going to end. Why bother to go?

**JS: Who's your favorite filmmaker?**

**KG:** David Lynch. You can see his stuff countless times, and every time notice something new in it. Lately, there've been a lot of indies that have wonderfully ambiguous endings. They make you think for a change, and you can kind of imagine your own ending. Films like *Martha Marcy May Marlene*, *Take Shelter*, and *Meek's Cutoff*. Once in a blue moon we'll get a Hollyfilm which actually has some balls to it, like *The Grey*, *Fight Club*, *Bug*, or *Girl With the Dragon Tattoo*.

**JS: You've really got to dig deep...**

**KG:** In 1958, a great writer named Theodore Sturgeon said, "Ninety per cent of everything is crap," which, of course, is true and probably always will be. People can bitch about the internet, which has tons of time-wasting shit on it, but so do Hollymovies and books and music. The secret—and it's also the fun—is to find the interesting stuff amid all the offal...

## KRIS GILPIN'S MOVIE CROSSWORD

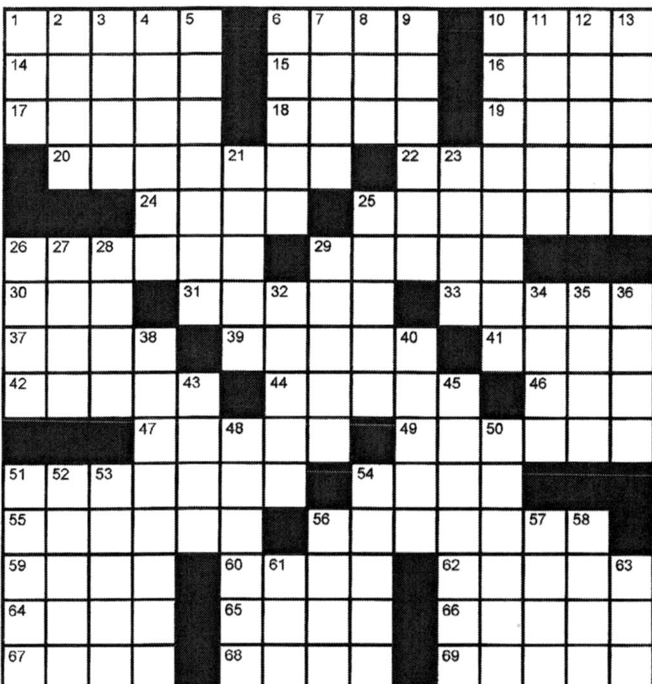

CLUES ON THE NEXT PAGE. SOLUTION ON PAGE 799.

## SHIT FLICK SERENADE!

RECORDED & INDEXED

DRAFT

Across
1. Safari sighting.
6. The li'l girl in Adventures in Babysitting thought Vinny D'Onofrio was he.
10. Fellow, often in a Brit film.
14. Milieu of Tobe Hooper's wonderfully sleazy, Eaten Alive.
15. A man knew when men would die by their (this), in a "Twilight Zone" episode.
16. Lovely Lucy, who played Sherrie in Scream 4.
17. William Smith had it back in our zine days, Jason Statham has it today.
18. Jerome, composer whose songs were in Mulholland Dr. & The Saddest Music in the World.
19. Pelvic parts.
20. Austin Powers did it in 1999.
22. A tray used for food & beverages, like for movie popcorn & Boone's Farm at home.
24. 1997 Jim Jarmusch docu on Neil Young, ____ of the Horse.
25. Like the hilarious, biting humor from the Sleazoid Express zine.
26. Like a cab in a Sherlock Holmes film.
29. Leg part.
30. Enjoy movies, u-all?
31. We have been (this) in many post-apocalyptic films.
33. A Cheech y Chong routine: "Blind _____ Chitlin."
37. The campus military organization in Taps.
39. Jaime Trujillo's zine out of Albuquerque, N.M., _____ Gore.
41. How many nuns ever subscribed to a fanzine?...
42. State in N.E. India.
44. King or queen.
46. Obsessive compulsive anonymous.
47. They go with the flow, in films like Dante's Peak.
49. Ed Rooney in Ferris Bueller..., "Tell ya what, dipshit...smooch my big ol' white butt..._______ up, buttercup."
51. Any substance that can stimulate the production of antibodies, as in a medical movie.
54. We all love the zines because we somehow ____ w/ the sweet, scummier aspects of life.

55. Mundanes don't share our love of Shit Flicks & consider them ______ movies (maroons).
56. Great, trippy 1966 Bergman film, in which Liv U. & Bibi A.'s identities meld.
59. Mr., in a Hindu movie.
60. Mr. Black, director of the cool Pretty Poison, w/ Tony Perkins & a beauty Tuesday Weld.
62. (Between us guys, what beauties like Jenny Agutter & Pam Franklin got us back in the day.)
64. Pretty, somewhat spacey album by This Mortal Coil: __'__ End in Tears.
65. Pot starter...
66. River in Hades.
67. Before Joe Carnahan directed the great, existential The Grey, he made 2010's ____ _-Team.
68. Sadly, I was destined to ____ some zines in my moves & it's haunted me ever since.
69. An archaic word for belated.

Down
1. Fade away.
2. Ballsy director of Dogville & Antichrist.
3. "Do we hate most rom coms, can I hear _ ___?"
4. Answers to "Did you see A Thousands Words?" & "Did you love Twilight?"
5. Jason Simon's fun zine from Pompano Beach, Fla., _______ 13.
6. The man/woman who tears your movie ticket--
7. AKA tinted, such as Georges Melies's films.
8. Pilot in Catch 22 (great book, good film).
9. The trailer for this 1996, Mel Gibson thriller played for weeks before every film I saw (!).
10. Derek Jensen's good Prairie Village, Kansas, zine (________ of the Night) got slicker as it went along.
11. A sweet, candylike confection seen in Turkish films (I loved the stuff as a kid!).
12. A Scott picture.
13. Neil, great drummer for Rush (long live prog rock! ;-).
21. Nicholas Worth (actually a big sweetheart!) ran the _____ of crazy in Don't Answer the Phone!
23. My old buds Nancy & Randy often sneak _ ___ & coke into their movies.
25. "I finally watched The Exorcist!" "So, whattta ya, want a _____?!"
26. Zeus's wife.
27. This John starred in Zombie Hamlet (oh, you didn't see it, either?).
28. Like Kathy Bates in Misery, say.
29. For creepy, disturbing, extreme horror, read Adam Pepper's Super _____! (from Eraserhead Press).
32. Holy text.
34. Back in the day, Nic Roeg's excellent Don't ____ Now scared audiences in 1973.
35. Hank Fonda was a great, evil bastard in ____ Upon a Time in the West (tough clue!).
36. I read that something sad & weird happened to ____ Dark's (1987) beauty, Jenny Wright.
38. Ultimate Porno is a book about the making of this Helen Mirren fiasco (to which porn was added).
40. A zombie could fall apart like a _____.
43. Like either Wizard of Gore (archaic).
45. Mr. Ken, one of the few A directors who loved sleaze (see Crimes of Passion & The Devils).
48. Belonging to or characteristic of youth.
50. The disease AKA St. Vitus's dance.
51. Monty Python: "Are you suggesting we eat my mother?" "Yes, sir" "Well, I __ a ___ peckish..."
52. As a kid, the monsters were often '______ your bed.
53. It's safe to assume that Andy Milligan never conducted _____ reads with his casts...
54. There's always one (or a dozen) in a horror film.
56. Cujo & the Monkey Shines monkey proved to be bad ones.
57. It's not gross...
58. 1941 3 Stooges short (w/ Curly, yay!), An ____ in Every Stake.
61. Most of the Beatles said, "Oh, no!" to her.
63. Mr. D., who became waterlogged in Creepshow.

Attachment

GREG GOODSELL AND CHAS. BALUN. HORROR FROM THE HEART OF HOLLYWOOD. PHOTO COURTESY OF GREG GOODSELL.

# Chapter Eighteen
# GREG GOODSELL
## Fanzine Babylon

## Making Your Adversaries' Life A LIVING HELL For Just Under $10!

*By Greg Goodsell*

I first encountered Greg Goodsell's writing in the pages of *Deep Red* and *Subhuman*. I'm not sure where I originally read him; his first published work for *Deep Red* appeared in issue number 4 (where he gave Jose Larraz's *Rest in Pieces* a justly deserved "dog" on the Gore Score), but I think that I'd gotten my hands on a copy of *Subhuman* by then. As time passes, these things blur together, especially when you take into account the haphazard publication schedules that most of the horror zines employed (not to mention the time that it took to receive them in the mail). Let's just say that I became a fan of Greg's work from early on, and I quickly started looking for any magazine that had his name on it.

I wanted to know about Greg's start in writing, about the personalities he met along the way, and what he thought of the current state of fandom. I sent him a letter, he wrote back, and before I knew it, I was dialing the phone for this interview.

I'm happy to report that Greg Goodsell was all that I'd hoped he would be. Opinionated, outspoken, and overflowing with anecdotes, Greg didn't flinch once when it came to calling things as he saw them.

Greg Goodsell still works as a journalist today; his most recent genre-related work can be found in the pages of *Screem* magazine and online at *Cinema Head Cheese* and *Angels in Distress*.

The following interview was conducted via telephone and email, January–March, 2012.

---

**JOHN SZPUNAR: Have you always lived in California?**
**GREG GOODSELL:** Yeah, I've always lived in California. I've lived in Bakersfield (my home town) my entire life. I'm over the hill from Hollywood. That gives me an ample opportunity to speak to film personalities, which I'm still doing, to this day. I'm still doing fan-related writing. Are you familiar with *Screem* magazine?
**JS: Yep. Daryl Mayeski.**
**GG:** I do a lot of writing for him. It's ironic that I now speak to and maintain relationships with a lot of the directors that I used to make fun of.
**JS: Has the benefit of time given you the chance to appreciate their work a little more?**
**GG:** I've always appreciated their work. I've always been entertained by their work for a variety of reasons. It if it's especially bad and inept (but they're very earnest and sincere), I have to give them credit. If they're earnest and sincere, it's like Edward D. Wood, Jr. He believed in what he was doing, which is not the same as a lot of Hollywood hacks who have no personal investment in their features; it's just a job. These independent filmmakers put their own vision and their own concerns into their films and it shows. You can't possibly walk away from an Andy Milligan film and not

*THE MUNSTERS*: BLUE-COLLAR.

say, "There's a deeper psychosis here at work! I must learn more."

**JS: Why do you think that is?**

**GG:** Independent filmmakers don't have any money; they use their friends as actors, etcetera. It's like when I was working at small newspapers and at large newspapers—if you're small, you can do what you please. You can bring your own neuroses, likes, and dislikes to a project. You can bring your own quirk and personality to it and no one is in the front office saying, "You can't do that." So yeah, that's the appeal about no-budget independent filmmaking.

**JS: The art film and the down-and-dirty exploitation film don't differ much, in that respect.**

**GG:** The bigger a project is, the more people you have with vested interests in it. They say, "You can't do that, you can't step on these toes, and you have to use this actor." It's just artistic freedom. The art film offers artistic freedom, and the low budget exploitation movie (which is ostensibly made to make money) offers the same sort of freedom.

**JS: What kind of movies did you enjoy as a kid?**

**GG:** Oh, I watched everything. I'm going to be fifty-two in March, so I fall within the realms and parameters of the *Famous Monsters*/monster-kid era. There was a steady stream of monster movies on independent TV channels, and so forth. That's what I was gobbling up.

**JS: Monsters were everywhere, even on the television sitcoms. There was almost a—I'm searching for the word...**

**GG:** Zeitgeist? Is that the word you're looking for?

**JS: Yeah [laughs]. Why do you think this happened in the sixties?**

**GG:** Well, there were shows like *The Munsters* and *The Addams Family* that addressed unconventional family units. You could always have the little argument that *The Munsters* best represented blue-collar east coast values, while *The Addams Family* embraced the avant-garde unconventional family. It wasn't a *Leave it to Beaver* setup, but they were both happy, functioning families. I think that was sort of acknowledging that America in the sixties was headed down a different path.

**JS: That's interesting...**

**GG:** There was the Eisenhower ideal, where mom and dad lived in the same house and little brother and sister got along and did well in school. There were a lot of divorces going on and there were a lot of single-parent

*THE ADDAMS FAMILY*: AVANT-GARDE AND UNCONVENTIONAL.

households then. I have very clear memories—I was very fortunate to have a mom and dad living at home, but that wasn't always the case. I had some friends who were living with their grandparents because their parents were spun-out on drugs. I think it was probably a reaction to the fifties ideal. Everyone can buy a house with a high school diploma and everyone has a car. It was just an acknowledgement that the family unit at the time didn't go up against that ideal. *The Munsters* and *The Addams Family* lived their lives as they chose, and they were still a happy functioning unit. I think that sort have had a pacifying effect.

**JS: What were you reading as a kid?**

**GG:** Well, the EC Comics had been stamped out, but there was *Mad*. That was very sharp, very satirical, and very adult. My parents were reading that. And of course, I was reading the Comic Code-approved books of the era—*House of Mystery* and *House of Secrets* by DC and stuff like that. As a child, everybody got Roald Dahl books, like *Charlie and the Chocolate Factory* and *James and the Giant Peach*. The one writer who really set my imagination alight was Ray Bradbury; he was very poetic. He's middle-brow today. Looking back, a lot of his stuff was very sentimental and obvious, but his stories were like pieces of candy that I would gobble up, one after the other.

**JS: I got into Ray Bradbury after reading the stories EC Comics adapted.**

**GG:** He was very poetic and accessible; he built a story around a very good executed idea. It was just very intriguing. You'd go, "Wow! What a

RECORDED & INDEXED



DRAFT

SHOCK XPRESS VOLUME 2 NUMBER 4.

# Cornpone Angst and Green Rubber Monsters:

## The films of Larry Buchanan

**By Gregory Goodsell**

The physical distance between Hollywood, California and director Larry Buchanan's Dallas, Texas, is a very long one. Both parties wish it to remain that way. Buchanan is by definition a fiercely independent regional director, whose films, when shown theatrically are distributed to the darker regions of the North American continent. In spite of the availability of obscure titles on videocassette, there are still plenty of films which go no further than the Drive-Ins of the deep South and the Northwest hinterlands. Lacking polish, these films have an undisputable purity about them; the isolated lumberjack has little time for the latest Dudley Moore comedy.

Director Buchanan's best known work, however, is seen on late, *late* night television on independent American stations. Johnny Carson has had his Las Vegas comedian do his schtick, David Letterman has shown his "stupid pet tricks," the late night news has informed the remaining insomniacs the world is getting worse, the only thing left is . . . *It's Alive!* (1968).

Buchanan's *It's Alive!* (not to be confused with the Larry Cohen mutant killer baby series) is the loony epiphany of the no-budget film-making he did in conjunction with American International Television. In summing up the Fifty Worst Fantasy Films of All Time, the late, great *Monster Times* tabloid of the early '70s declared that "this one is *so bad* TV doesn't dare show it before 1 o'clock in the morning!" All of this adds to the somnambulant nature of this creaky

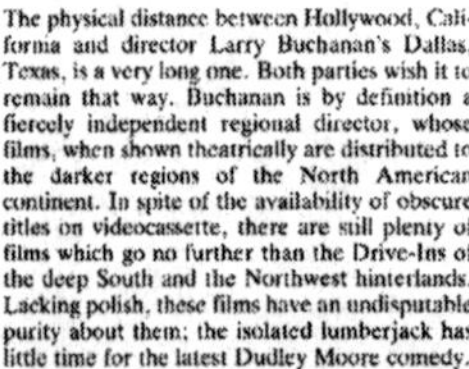

creature feature. One recalls seeing it, but scratches it off as a bad dream.

*It's Alive!* begins with a shot of a young couple motoring through the Texas wilderness, the white statues of dinosaurs peeking through the trees. In what sems to be an unbroken ten minute take, the car goes along the forlorn country road with no dialogue, no music, no soundtrack of any sort. It begins to sprinkle and the husband dutifully turns on the windshield wiper. A somber narrator sonorously intones, "They say when it rains when the sun is still shining, the devil is kissing his wife." The bleary-eyed monster movie completist knows that he's in for a winner.

They stop at a crazy old man's (Buchanan regular Bill Thurman, seen in Steven Spielberg's' *Close Encounters Of The Third Kind* as a radar technician) mansion for directions and a bite to eat. "Wanna see my caged animal collection?" he says. It's all a terrible trap, and the wimpy husband is fed to a ravenous gill man monster with ping-pong ball eyes, scissor-cut fins, and a skindiver suit torso. The wife is kept captive with a lachrymose paleontologist (Tommy Kirk) as they ponder the meaning of it all.

The crazy old man's housekeeper is a schoolteacher, also a captive in his house. She tells her story of being locked in her bland, sparsely furnished bedroom, her torture at the hands of the old man, her foiled attempts at escape, her repeated whippings by his vinyl and cardboard

belt, and laments "I was trapped. Helpless. Like the animals he kept in his cages."

The old lady gets killed, the gill monster kills the old man, and Tommy Kirk and the girl ponder the meaning of it all. All to the ceaseless accompaniment of dreary, muffled library soundtrack monster movie muzak. Is this a grade-Z effort thrown together in Texas for a contractual obligation or is it the real world . . . ?

Actually, a little of both. Whilst in Dallas in the mid-'60s, Buchanan was offered the opportunity to jazz up a syndicated film package deal by American International Television with new product. The provision being the films be in colour and have an approximate 90 minute running time, Buchanan set to work on projects that, according to one source, were from scripts "readily available." A more accurate scenario has Buchanan pressing a dime store tape recorder microphone to his television during an afternoon sci-fi creature feature and adapting the dialogue for his own aesthetic purposes.

The films L.B. made during this period were word-by-word, scene-for-scene remakes of old American International Pictures '50s monster pics. His *The Eye Creatures* (1965) is in reality a remake of *Invasion of the Saucermen* (1957), *Creature of Destruction* (1967) a take on *The She Creature* (1957), *In the Year 2889* (1966) a rip-off of Roger Corman's *The Day The World Ended* (1955), and *Mars Needs Women* (1966) a Buchananized adaptation of *Pajama Party* (1964). The aforementioned *It's Alive!* and *Curse of the Swamp Creature* (1966) are considered the series' originals, although the stories offered in both are highly derivative. The argued high point of the series is Buchanan's apocalyptic *Zontar, The Thing From Venus* (1966), a take on Corman's *It Conquered The World* (1956). Under the aegis of Buchanan's Azaela Productions, these remakes effortlessly transform the paranoid urgency of the Eisenhower era to the malign unrest of the Johnson administration in no time flat. The people in these films wait endlessly for the cleansing power of Woodstock in the city where Camelot was abruptly ended.

A Larry Buchanan monster movie knows it's going nowhere fast. Doomed to haunt late-night television programing, lousy remakes of already bad films, these pictures reek of malaise. While Tobe Hooper puttered in his father's hotel in kneepants and George Romero was shooting aspirin commercials to pay the rent, Buchanan was filming the invasion of Earth from his own backyard.

*Zontar, The Thing From Venus*, a domestic version of the end of the world, is arguably his best known work. A nerdy scientist communicates with a winged bat-thing from outer space via a shortwave radio in his hall closet. Flying creatures dispense spark plugs into the necks of the Dallas populace. World-wide power failures and panic grip the globe, or so the TV and radio tell us. All of this set in formica-lined houses with nary a trace of humanity or creativity anywhere. Is this the end of the world as we know it *or* the end product of the world as we know it – our friends and family transformed to alien cyphers because "Zontars wills it"?

Most science-fiction films throw in everything but the kitchen sink in order to make the audience suspend their disbelief. Larry Buchanan shows the audience a kitchen sink in *Zontar* (which runs hot and cold water because Zontar is our friend) and *that's all*. Through it all comes a harsh truth, exposing the romantic lie of all such "politically correct" alien mind-control movies: a gas station attendant's life *is worth* possession by superior forces from outer space.

Gas station attendants doubtlessly play a large part in filling out the casts of a Buchanan feature, evenly divided between non-actors, regional Texas performers, and one has-been Hollywood star to spruce up the package. Buchanan friend and associate John Agar appears in *Zontar* and

concept!" Unfortunately, I was quick to learn that most science fiction isn't like that. In fact, the hard science fiction, where everything has to go in line with physics—stuff like that doesn't lend itself to a compelling narrative. It doesn't make for a good story. I smattered around with science fiction, but I realized that it's rather inaccessible and not really geared toward my interests.

**JS: Where did you go from there?**

**GG:** I had a loving, supportive mom, and I began to read the works of Poe and Lovecraft. Another writer of that era, Fredric Brown, informs a lot of my own fiction. His stuff preceded flash-fiction; stories of 1,800 words, or less. All of his stories had a point and cleverness to them, a brevity and a wit. Fredric Brown was very good.

**JS: I'm a big fan of his stuff.**

**GG:** *Here Comes a Candle* was his first novel that I read. Karl Edward Wagner said that was like the second best novel of non-supernatural horror, preceded by *Psycho*. I said, "Hey! I gotta read this!" Of course, it all has a point. We have the young teenage hero with a neurosis. He's obsessed with a nursery rhyme and it's all a self-fulfilling prophecy.

**JS: Were you aware of Forrest J Ackerman as a kid?**

**GG:** Oh yeah. The thing is, my parents would become upset if I brought an issue [of *Famous Monsters*] into the house. They just could not handle it, for some reason. I had to sneak it into the house; they really had a bad time with it. My mother was more forgiving and she'd let me watch horror films. My father, being a highly educated man, at one time a defense lawyer and later a court commissioner, had an antipathy to genre literature anyway. However, one book that managed to turn both of my parent's heads around was this book in 1969 entitled *Horror!* By the pseudonymous author Drake Douglas, it introduced a lot of the main figures found in horror film and literature as well as an introduction to Edgar Allan Poe, H. P. Lovecraft and Arthur Machen. My father began to see the cultural and literary worth of this type of fiction, and he softened a bit. I was probably just young—my parents bought the *Monster Times* tabloid when I was a young teen, and *Monster Times* had all manner of radical politics and far more cynical worldview than the innocuous *Famous Monsters*. They figured I was just too young. Now, when I see hillbilly families drag their six and seven year old children into theaters to watch such films as Oliver Stone's *Savages*, I say to myself, "My parents raised me right!"

**JS: My parents did the same thing to me.**

**GG:** I do have to say that growing up, I did have monster paranoia. I loved to watch monster movies, but they stayed with me. When you're young and impressionable, you don't know any better. Like, after you've watched *The Birds* for the first time and you're only six years old, you're afraid to go out of the house because you think the ravens are going to pluck

your eyes out. I wasn't ready for a lot of this stuff. As I got older, it didn't become an issue. It all washes out in the end; I didn't become an axe-murderer. I did go through therapy, but it wasn't because of the monster movies [laughs].

**JS: That's good to know! When did you start writing?**

**GG:** I was writing as soon as I could. I will say one thing, and this will sound very stuck-up and immodest: A lot of the fanzine writers of my era—early eighties/early nineties—were fans and had enthusiasm for the genres they were writing about, but they didn't have good writing backgrounds. I wrote as a little child and I was involved with newspapers and journalism as a teenager. I was getting paid for my writing when I was about nineteen. I have a pretty strong writing background. It's still a big thrill to see my name in print. Everything is ego [laughs].

**JS: What was your first published work?**

**GG:** Well, discounting the junior high school newspaper, there was a small regional slick magazine called *Bakersfield Magazine*. They paid me for my film reviews. They didn't pay me a lot, but that was my first paid published work. Currently, I'm a web content provider for an online news agency, so I'm still writing to this day and getting paid for it.

**JS: How did you become aware of the fanzines?**

**GG:** The thing you have to remember is that we have fanzines dating back to the forties, fifties, and sixties. There was stuff like *Children of the Night*. You would get these odd publications; you'd read about them in *Famous Monsters* and send away for them. I was always aware that they were around. The thing that differentiated them from the ones that I was involved in was that they were trying to lend credence and legitimacy to the horror and science fiction genre. The stuff that I was doing was very irreverent. "Look at this inept piece of crap! Let's get drunk and laugh at this VHS piece of shit!"

**JS: What was your first brush with writing for fanzines?**

**GG:** In 1981, I tried to sell an article on Larry Buchanan to *Fangoria*. I interviewed John Agar. He was good, but he didn't know where Larry Buchanan was. I sent it to *Fangoria* and they said, "Hey! We'll print this if you get us some pictures!" I couldn't find pictures to save my life and that article went on the back burner. So, there was this fanzine called *Fear of Darkness* that had an article by Brian Curran about *Zontar, the Thing from Venus*. Are you familiar with Larry Buchanan?

IT CAME FROM HUNGER!
Tales of a Cinema Schlockmeister
LARRY ✦ BUCHANAN

**JS: Yeah. *Mars Needs Women*...**

**GG:** Brian hit Larry Buchanan's movies right on the head. They're just very dreary, tedious, boring science fiction movies that accurately reflect reality. That was the whole aesthetic. I said, "Hey, he got it, too!" I contacted Brian, who lived in Boston, and he sent me

THIS IS NOT JIM; THIS IS NOT JIMI. TWO OF THE STARS OF *DOWN ON US*.

some photos. I re-typed my article and sent it to *Fangoria*. Since this had been a period of two years, Uncle Bob Martin threw it back in my face, saying, "Get lost, kid!"

**JS: What did you do?**

**GG:** Well, Brian Curran had his own fanzine called *Zontar, the Magazine from Venus*. He offered to publish it, and the very month that Larry Buchanan finally granted an interview to *Fangoria*, my article came out. It was very embarrassing—I was using all these theories, and somebody had actually tracked him down; it just shot all of my theories out of the water. However, it all worked out for the better because my essays that appeared in *Zontar* were reprinted word for word by Larry Buchanan in his 1996 autobiography, *It Came from Hunger!* I befriended Larry later on and we stayed in touch.

**JS: What was he like?**

**GG:** Larry was very idiosyncratic. He admitted that the movies he did for AIP were utter crap, but he was dead serious about all his conspiracy theory movies. *Down On Us* and *The Trial of Lee Harvey Oswald*—he wouldn't budge on those; he believed all of the crazy crackpot theories behind them.

**JS: Where did you go from there, writing wise?**

**GG:** Well, I saw an ad for a fanzine called *Subhuman*. I sent away for it and I got a letter from Cecil Doyle. He said, "I'm so glad you wrote to me. I assume you are the Greg Goodsell who wrote the articles on Larry Buchanan in *Zontar*? Those are the best articles I've ever read in any small press fanzine." I just danced around the kitchen because someone had seen it and appreciated it. That was a big charge for me. That was very important and that was a turning point. I started writing for *Subhuman* and *Subhuman* opened doors. Chas. Balun liked my work and let me write for *Deep Red*. I met all these different people and I started writing for them.

**JS: You were a regular contributor to *Subhuman*...**

**GG:** I think many people would agree with me that *Subhuman* was probably the best fanzine that came after *Sleazoid Express*. When I was writing for *Subhuman*, I was working for Sears Roebuck—just wearing my polyester shirts and ties. I would come home, and if I was lucky, there'd be

DRAFT

RECORDED & INDEXED

# Bloody Ol' Blighty THE FILMS OF PETER WALKER

BY GREG GOODSELL

Odd commodities these horror flicks be.

Of the countless supply available on the video racks, the discerning viewer turns to critical reference books to sniff out a prospective title. But sometimes, criticism is not an accurate barometer of a horror film's worthiness. In order for this genre to succeed, they must ofttimes push buttons and emotions which are offensive and disturbing to their audience. It's funny just how reviled the original FRANKENSTEIN, Hitchcock's PSYCHO, the Hammer remakes, and THE EXORCIST were at the time of their release. We watch these films today with interest and enjoyment, having earned their "classic" status by succeeding all too well with the audiences of their day.

Such is the fate of the horror films of director Pete Walker. Condemned in his home country England, his work has been variously described as "nauseating," "vile," "derivative," "sadistic," and "grotesquely violent." All evidence that Walker does his job all too well.

Pete Walker is a definite, singular voice in horror cinema. All his films share distinct thematic threads and twisted views on modern life. Walker's films have gore aplenty, but not necessarily to fulfill the gorehound's expectations for splatter. He lures us into his stories with cunning and skill, only to bludgeon us unexpectedly and in such a way to make us feel sorry for having asked for it. Walker's movies make us squirm.

At all times, we feel a malign intelligence behind the camera. Gore is never featured decoratively and often only the sympathetic characters are murdered in coldly repulsive ways. The usual escape

MANY YOUNG GIRLS HAVE ENTERED THESE GATES
NONE HAVE YET COME OUT!
The story of a strange hobby and its victims, whose only crime was to be young and beautiful!
HOUSE of WHIPCORD
A Peter Walker Production

13

DEEP RED NUMBER 5.

a copy of *Subhuman* in the mailbox. A lot of people were complementary to my work in the letter columns. It was good to get positive feedback.

**JS: I first saw *Subhuman* mentioned in *Deep Red*. Actually, how did you become aware of *Deep Red*?**

**GG:** I saw it at a comic book store. Chas. gave *Subhuman* a rave review in *Deep Red* number 2. I wrote him a letter and he said, "Hey, come on board!" A short while later, I saw him at the 1988 *Fangoria Weekend of Horrors*. We hit it off from there.

**JS: You wrote a piece for the *Deep Red Horror Handbook* called "The Unwatchables". That actually made me go out and try to find some of the films that you mentioned. Was that your intent?**

**GG:** Oh, yes. I've met a few people who brag to me that they went out and saw all ten films on the list! There were some truly memorable and amazing films in that chapter that warranted viewing for sheer chutzpah alone.

**JS: Is there any value in truly bad films?**

**GG:** One of the magical things about movies is that absolutely terrible movies (that are no good whatsoever) are endlessly entertaining while, great, essential movies take on the joyless aura of "math homework" in order to view them. However—this argument comes up every now and then—do we reward "bad behavior" by writing about bad, inept movies? My reply is, not at all, as long as the films remain engaging, have a unique worldview, and are sincere in their attempts to entertain and tell a story.

More people can better relate to the struggles of an Edward D. Wood Jr. than a Joel Schumacher.

**JS: How did you divide up your work for the fanzines? I'm assuming that you would tailor your work to who you were submitting it to.**

**GG:** I had different approaches for all of fanzines I wrote for, due to my building a working relationship with their editors and publishers. In *Subhuman*, I was given free rein to be footloose and fancy-free—to be as irreverent as possible.

**JS: *Subhuman* spanned the map.**

**GG:** The films I covered in *Subhuman* covered a wide variety of genres, but there had to be something unusual or noteworthy about the films that I felt warranted attention. *Subhuman* went out to a wide variety of fringe folks who were into art, music and film. For *Deep Red*, I was also allowed to be footloose, but the readership for that publication was overwhelmingly male and malcontented. *Deep Red* was strictly for the teenage and older male gore fan. The films for that publication had to include blood and guts.

**JS: Why do you think that the readership for *Deep Red* was malcontented?**

**GG:** Chas. Balun was very upfront about his revulsion with the sort of people who would beg him for snuff videos and gang rape movies. The violence in horror films are supposed to have a cathartic effect, but they are only movies and special effects. Balun had no time for a lot of the stuff emanating from Japan, where schoolgirls are raped and are forced to eat their own intestines at knifepoint. But it was just par for the course for the type of magazine he had. There was one guy who would write all the fanzines and say, "I'm interested in films where women are raped, tortured and mutilated." Out of my sight, as Balun would say. This was around the time of Peter Sotos' *Pure*. We won't go there.

**JS: You wrote a piece on Regal Video's catalog for *Subhuman*. How difficult was it for you to track down and compare their titles?**

**GG:** The Regal Video piece was very simple to do. A downtown mom and pop video store had the run of the series, and I went through them, one-by-one. It was painfully obvious they were all re-titled with hasty, burned-in video titles. They were all pretty easy to identify. For example, *The Demon Lover* was easy to peg, as I had read an earlier review in *Cinefantastique* that mentioned that the star of the film was this rather heavy-set kung fu expert who went under the name of Christmas Robbins. Gunnar Hansen also had a featured role. I put one and one together, and voila! Out of that batch of releases was the mind-blowing *The Double Garden* from 1970, re-titled *The Revenge of Dr. X* on Regal Video, and *Venus Flytrap* elsewhere. It had many different names.

**JS: Didn't Ed Wood write that?**

**GG:** Yes. It's amazing that Ed Wood was still having his screenplays produced at that late a date! I appear in the documentary *Dad Made Dirty Movies*, about producer/director Stephen Apostolof, and he did a good job

RECORDED & INDEXED
DRAFT

of keeping Wood in liquor towards the very end. *Deep Red* alumnus Shane "Remo" Dallmann did a very thorough follow-up article on Regal Video, which revealed all the chicanery around that outfit, who were mostly in the furniture business.

**JS: You know, I really liked your "Confessions of a Would-Be Sleaze Screenwriter" piece for *Subhuman*. It really went beyond the standard zine fare...**

**GG:** I'm glad you enjoyed that, as it actually disappointed a lot of people.

**JS: How so?**

**GG:** To them, it lacked a punch line.

**JS: I thought the story was fascinating slice of life. Do you mind talking about it?**

**GG:** In short, I met this aspiring filmmaker named Jeff London who wanted to make an anthology horror film. He was rather slippery, not giving me a phone number or address. I wrote the script, and didn't hear back from him until months later. He said he was no longer interested in a horror film, but rather a story "about two friends, who've known each other their entire lives, who go through something over the course of a weekend that changes their lives forever." I lost interest, and I later saw London working shamefaced behind the counter at a ghetto video store. The punch line would come many years later after Jeff London became a very highly prolific director of straight-to-video gay films.

**JS: You're kidding!**

**GG:** Anyone who is interested in bad filmmaking in general—but is not interested in the prospect of viewing hot, sweaty man-on-man action should check out London's movies. The gay characters in his movies only hold hands, if that! Sure as shooting, all of London's movies are "about two friends, who've known each other their entire lives, who go through something over the course of a weekend that changes their lives forever." *And Then Came Summer*, *The Last Year*, *A Warm Wind*, *Regarding Billy*... all of them stink on ice. Oddly enough, he did go on to make an anthology horror film, *When Darkness Falls*.

**JS: Could you tell me a little about your experience with *Shock Xpress*?**

**GG:** For *Shock Xpress*, I had to craft my articles for a British and international audience. I had to explain to this audience—at a time when US films were hard to track down for these readers—why they were worthy and place them in an American context. A lot of US cult and horror films hinge on strictly American conventions.

**JS: *Shock Xpress* was a real class-act...**

**GG:** My contributions to the first *Shock Xpress* book were definitely a high point in my fanzine career. Glossy, color pages in a book in which I was rewarded financially—with residuals! Say what you will about Stefan Jaworzyn, but he always treated me very well and was very enthusiastic to have me on board. However, that wonderful relationship came to an

Greg Goodsell with Linnea Quigley: "This Polaroid is going out to all my friends at Femme Fatale magazine, isn't it?

FROM THE EDITORIAL OF *ANGELS IN DISTRESS III.*

end in 1993. My life had been upended at around that time after a period of wild excess, and I had promised Stefan an interview with director Rinse Dream (né Stephen Sayadian) of *Café Flesh* and *Night Dreams* infamy. The interview fell through after many false starts and Stefan and I lost touch. I wrote him and gave him a phone call every now and then, but received only stony silence. Jaworzyn reappeared in 2004 with *The Texas Chain Saw Massacre Companion*, but I haven't heard from him since. Stefan, wherever you are—cheers!

**JS: How do you think that the British small press differed from that of the US?**

**GG:** To be honest with you, the only exposure I had to the British fan press was *Shock Xpress* and the stray issue of *Ungawa!* here and there. I thought it was unusual that they seemed to be "US-centric," with most of the coverage on American films and directors. This was probably in reaction to the prevailing mood of the time that saw little worth in the films of Hammer and Amicus—which have since enjoyed resurgence in popularity. It tickled me that some people in the British press looked upon various genre personalities and actors with a certain amount of awe, whereas I live about two hours away from Hollywood—where I can see them pounding the streets eating chili dogs any day of the week!

**JS: You did some work for *Brutarian*...**

**GG:** *Brutarian* had very high literary standards, and I had to choose my words carefully and craft my sentences soundly. Dom Salemi is a great guy, but *Brutarian* was drifting more and more into alternative music coverage, which just wasn't my bag. Salemi paid me very well and had kind things to say about my work. Again, in 1993 my life was in a bit of a turnaround and my work for them began to decline, and we had a bit of a row. However, I published an article on Indonesian horror films in *Brutarian* in 2001, to which I was paid very well. I haven't heard from Dom in awhile, and like Stefan—if he's out there reading this—Hi Dom!

**JS: I wanted to ask you about a zine called *They Won't Stay Dead*. I never saw an issue, but Gene Gregorits had great things to say about the editor, Brian Johnson. Could you tell me a little about the mag and about your experience writing for it?**

**GG:** *They Won't Stay Dead* was sort of the last gasp for xeroxed fanzines,

RECORDED & INDEXED



DRAFT

# The Horror Film Trilogy of Alan Ormsby

## ARTICLE BY GREG GOODSELL

Modern day Hollywood could—and eventually will remake every single horror film made in the Seventies, and they still won't get it. Today's filmmakers relish technical skill and prowess over what made these films endearing in the first place, that elusive quality that can only be described as character. These reckless, go-for-broke features were made by indolent young pups without a background in conventional movie making, all intent on provoking, shocking and meeting the demands of the grind house and drive-in patron. *The Texas Chainsaw Massacre* (1974), *Night of the Living Dead* (1968), *Last House on the Left* (1972), countless others were made without the benefit of CGI, the internet and digital technology. There was an unspoken, tacit agreement between the movie makers and their target audience that their features would transcend their budgetary and technical limitations to give the crowds the frisson denied them in ordinary cinema.

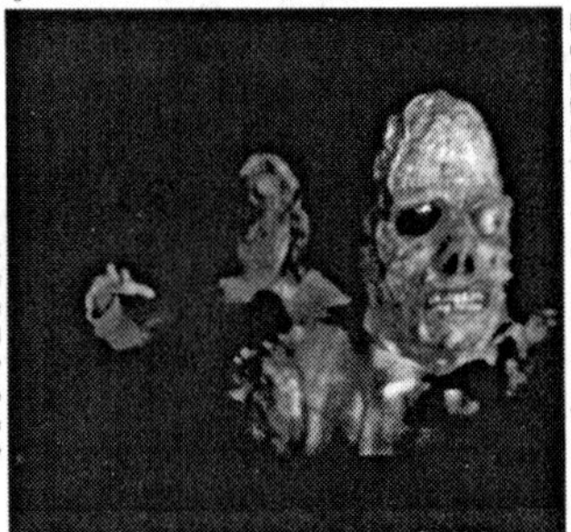

The undead run amok in *Children Shouldn't Play With Dead Things.*

A case in point are the three films associated with Alan Ormsby, *Children Shouldn't Play With Dead Things* (1971), *Deathdream* (aka *Dead of Night* 1972) and *Deranged* (1974). While Ormsby has worked as an actor (as in *Children*), a makeup man, and a director (*Deranged* with Jeff Gillen), he is primarily known as a screenwriter. His introduction to the world of low budget filmmaking was on *Children*, perhaps the world's first and certainly not the last "zombie comedy."

Ormsby was a drama student at the University of Florida in the early Seventies when he was introduced to director Bob Clark. "We were in college together," Ormsby says. Clark had already directed the incredible fetishistic transvestite opus *She Man* in 1967 (available from Something Weird Video).

Ormsby was a college student and doing paste-up and illustrations for a local black newspaper when *Night of the Living Dead* (1968) began to hit the midnight movie circuit heavily. Ormsby and Clark, along with several other interested parties, began to toy with the idea of making a low-budget horror film. "We consciously imitated *Night of the Living Dead*." Clark came up with the unforgettable title, and the group was in business.

"The budget was low . . . maybe 50 grand. I don't remember the shooting schedule." *Children* was shot on an island in Biscayne Bay in August and September of 1971, where the cast and crew had to contend with flesh-eating bugs and mosquitoes rather than the cannibalistic undead seen in the film. *Children* focuses on an insufferably pretentious theatrical group isolated on a Florida island as they perform a mock satanic resurrection ceremony. They get more than what they bargained for, with a mass uprising of the dead at the film's finale. Ormsby plays the troupe's leader under his real name of "Alan." Other members of the troupe include Ormsby's then-wife Anya Ormsby as "Anya," his ex-girlfriend Valerie Mamches, his then son-in-law Paul Cronin, and longtime associate Jeff Gillen. Director Clark insisted that the actors use their real first names to help in the editing stages, but went under the name of "Benjamin" Clark in the credits! Ormsby and Mamches had allegedly broken up under unhappy circumstances prior to shooting, perhaps explaining the pointed barbs she hurls at him throughout the film.

*Children* is remarkable for being among the first in a long string of zombie films that tried to capitalize on the success of *Night of the Living Dead*. Other outstanding aspects of the ragtag production are the highly effective living dead make-up created by Ormsby, constructed from latex and toilet paper. The scene where the corpses come tearing through the earth of the cemetery (a creation of Styrofoam headstones by art director Jeff Tremble) is straight from the pages of an EC horror comic.

The most written about aspect of *Children*, however, remain the costumes that Ormsby and his fellow thespians were forced to wear. On the tail-end of the hippie era in fashion, Ormsby says the clothes were bought straight off the rack from the nearby JC Penney. Ormsby is quite a vision in black, red and white striped jeans, orange shirt and red scarf. Macho Jeff Gillen wears a pink and white T-shirt and lime green pants, and poor Anya is reduced to wearing an orange and red sack dress!

Ormsby is upfront about *Children's* shortcomings . . . not enough action until the very end, and reams of risible dialogue hand-written by director Clark. In spite of some gore and scenes of implied gay necrophilia (!), *Children* squeaked by with a "PG" rating. The film did well theatrically, although it didn't translate into cash right away for the participants . . . "Profit? You're kidding, right?" Ormsby laughs. There was discussion of a sequel, titled *We Told You . . . Children Shouldn't Play With Dead Things*, which was never realized.

A young Alan Ormsby realizes that zombies don't have a sense of humor. From *Children Shouldn't Play with Dead Things.*

Spotted among *Children's* legion of undead is a Vietnam War soldier in full military regalia, which dovetails very nicely into Ormsby's follow-up horror script *Deathdream* (1972). Known under a plethora of titles, *Deathdream* was also called *The Veteran*, *Lazarus* and *The Night Walker* in scripting and pre-production. This unusually strong horror film follows the homecoming of a small town boy following his tour of duty in Vietnam. Andy (Richard Backus) returns to his mom (Lynn Carlin) and dad (John Marley) and sister (Anya Ormsby). (He literally looks a little green around the gills.) The tight-knit clan all too happily dismisses the official notice by the state department that their son was killed in action, while Andy takes to wearing gloves and dark sunglasses to hide his deteriorating flesh. Since this film features the debut of a young makeup artist by the name of Tom Savini, there's plenty of that red stuff to keep crowds happy.

They pretty much let me have my head—I had a lot of experimental pieces printed there. I was invited to write for the publication by Brian Johnson after I got burned big time by *Psychotronic Video*, and began to submit pieces that I wouldn't submit anywhere else. Kooky, experimental pieces that wouldn't fit anywhere else. My writings in that mag led me to long-term friendships with other fans, to which I am eternally grateful. The only clue that Johnson led a "wet and reckless" lifestyle was the time he wrote me about Desert Storm back in 1991. "Even drinking doesn't seem to help anymore." I was shocked to learn that he took his life later on.

**JS: A lot of the writing in the fanzines was exceptional—and most of the time much better than what was being published by the prozines. Why do you think this was?**

**GG:** The prozines had a much tighter focus. They didn't allow any wiggle room for "personal" writing. It was all very cut-and-dried. The only really personal stuff that I ever read in *Fangoria* was when Uncle Bob Martin began to have a very real middle-life crisis or nervous breakdown when he was covering *Videodrome* back in 1983. He was questioning what his purpose in life was by covering films that (at that time) hinged on practical, "bladder" special effects. He left the magazine shortly afterwards. This can go completely the other way, with some writers who just talk about their hangnails and how their cat has cruelly rejected them in lieu of talking about the films. No further comment, as the reader scrambles to fill in those blank spaces. Altogether, the best relationships I have had with editors—be it in fanzines, newspapers, websites, what have you—know what I can provide and let me take it from there. It's absolutely awful working with an editor or publisher who doesn't know what they want, but certainly doesn't want what you give them!

**JS: Let's talk a little about Bill Landis.**

**GG:** Oh, yes. A very, very complex individual, and that can be taken as both a bad and a good thing.

**JS: What was your take on him?**

**GG:** Bill kept my interest in writing for film alive. I was a subscriber to *Sleazoid Express*. We would exchange letters, and he would encourage my writing. He did the same for a lot of people, up until his death. However, it has to be said that Bill showed me both things that I should have done and things that I shouldn't have done. Bill kept an enemy list. He went after people like Kenneth Anger and Joel M. Reed. He would actively persecute them, and I said, "Hey! Bill is doing well and he's got all this publicity! I'm going to do the same thing. I'm going to attack innocent parties until I beat it into the ground." I followed in his footsteps rather closely and I did some stuff that I'd later regret. All of the positive things that Bill did were met with a negative. He was a big influence, and he turned a lot of eyes toward fanzine writing, but I'm not going to tell you he was a walk in the park.

I most quote the late Marilyn Monroe at this point: "I'm selfish, impatient

RECORDED & INDEXED

DRAFT

and a little insecure. I make mistakes, I am out of control and at times hard to handle. But if you can't handle me at my worst, then you sure as hell don't deserve me at my best." Which goes to show—a person can be a great person but a lousy artist, or a lousy person and a great artist. Human beings are highly complex mammals. This goes for me, Landis, everyone. I can be entertaining, genial and funny—as well as petty, vindictive and cruel. They're all essential stops on the tour.

The actions of his widow, however, Michelle Clifford, remain beyond disgraceful. Fearing litigation, I will defer to the Duchess in Lewis Carroll's *Alice in Wonderland*: ""That's nothing to what I could say if I chose," the Duchess replied, in a pleased tone." The only satisfactory bit to this story is that certain guilty parties are currently getting their comeuppance.

**JS: Well… I wanted to interview Bill a while back and she kind of… Let's just say that she put an end to it.**

**GG:** She gave me one of her patented email flames, and I learned from others that she sort of used a template. She did that with everybody—longtime friends, former advertisers. I don't know what Michelle Clifford's issue was that made her such an awful person.

**JS: The take I got was that she didn't want anyone to step on Bill's turf. Maybe it was a New York thing. I know that Bill really had it in for Rick Sullivan and *Gore Gazette*.**

**GG:** Rick was his own character. And towards the end, people were losing interest in that type of fanzine. He just started making all these phony prank phone calls to people like Mike Gingold and Tim Lucas. They were all bullshit; he just wanted to remain controversial.

**JS: I guess you could say that a lot of "fanzine wars" were going on…**

**GG:** That was one of the reasons that I dropped out for a long spell. Fanzines can make you friends from afar or mortal enemies through the mail. It's not worth it. I was stirring up bad feelings along with everyone else. There was really no point.

**JS: I wonder why that is, especially within the fan community…**

**GG:** There's a lot of jealousy going around. "He got this mentioned in this column and I didn't get this mentioned in that column." The people who put out and write for fanzines have very strong personalities. And if there's a clash, it's going to be big and colorful.

**JS: Do you mind talking about the old bootleg days?**

**GG:** No, go ahead. I'm an open book [laughs].

**JS: Well, OK. I know that *Film Threat* went after a lot of people. Chas. Balun, Donald Farmer, and Rick Sullivan, to name a few. What are your feelings about Chris Gore?**

**GG:** My dealings with Chris Gore were highly negative, even before he went after Chas. When my interview with Susan Tyrrell was stolen and published in *Psychotronic* number 6—you know about that, don't you?

**JS: Let's hear about it.**

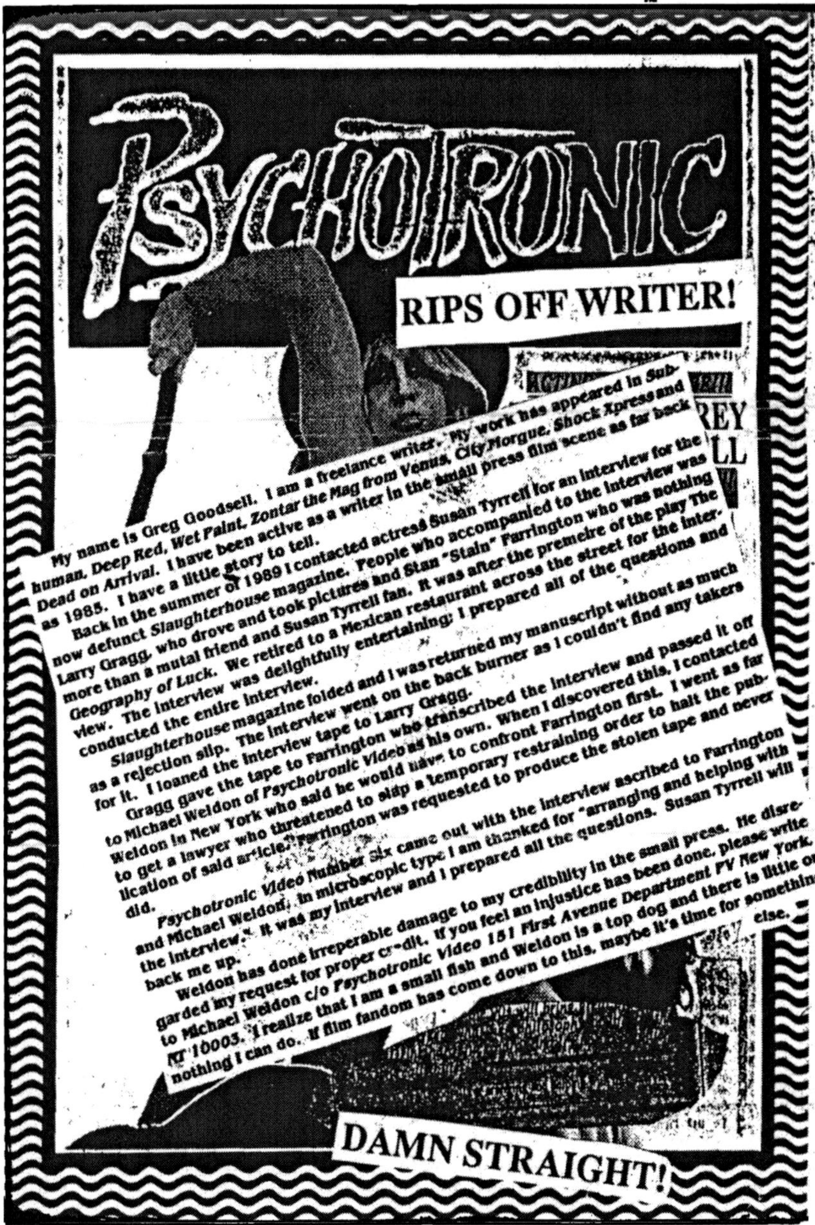

# PSYCHOTRONIC

## RIPS OFF WRITER!

My name is Greg Goodsell. I am a freelance writer. My work has appeared in *Subhuman, Deep Red, Wet Paint, Zontar the Mag from Venus, City Morgue, Shock Xpress* and *Dead on Arrival*. I have been active as a writer in the small press film scene as far back as 1985. I have a little story to tell.

Back in the summer of 1989 I contacted actress Susan Tyrrell for an interview for the now defunct *Slaughterhouse* magazine. People who accompanied to the interview was Larry Gragg, who drove and took pictures and Stan "Stain" Farrington who was nothing more than a mutal friend and Susan Tyrrell fan. It was after the premeire of the play *The Geography of Luck*. We retired to a Mexican restaurant across the street for the interview. The interview was delightfully entertaining; I prepared all of the questions and conducted the entire interview.

*Slaughterhouse* magazine folded and I was returned my manuscript without as much as a rejection slip. The interview went on the back burner as I couldn't find any takers for it. I loaned the interview tape to Larry Gragg.

Gragg gave the tape to Farrington who transcribed the interview and passed it off to Michael Weldon of *Psychotronic Video* as his own. When I discovered this, I contacted Weldon in New York who said he would have to confront Farrington first. I went as far to get a lawyer who threatened to slap a temporary restraining order to halt the publication of said article. Farrington was requested to produce the stolen tape and never did.

*Psychotronic Video Number Six* came out with the interview ascribed to Farrington and Michael Weldon. In microscopic type I am thanked for "arranging and helping with the interview." It was my interview and I prepared all the questions. Susan Tyrrell will back me up.

Weldon has done irreperable damage to my credibility in the small press. He disregarded my request for proper credit. If you feel an injustice has been done, please write to Michael Weldon c/o *Psychotronic Video 151 First Avenue Department PV New York, NY 10003*. I realize that I am a small fish and Weldon is a top dog and there is little or nothing I can do. If film fandom has come down to this, maybe it's time for something else. ■

## DAMN STRAIGHT!

GREG GOODSELL IS JUSTIFIABLY PEEVED—THE POWER OF A XEROXED PAGE, A HANDFUL OF STAMPS, AND A MAILING LIST…

**GG:** This so-called friend of mine stole my audiotape of Susan Tyrrell and he passed it off as his own in *Psychotronic*. This punk told Michael Weldon that it was his and Michael believed him. So, I made up all these fliers explaining my side of the story and I mailed them out to every single fanzine. Michael got phone calls and letters and death threats. Finally, Michael called up Susan Tyrrell, and she backed me up 100 per cent. So, in issue 7, he was supposed to give me a nice apology. It wasn't a nice apology. Chris Gore was whispering in my ear, "We'll print your interview if you write a letter denouncing Michael Weldon." So, I wrote the letter. They didn't publish my interview, and they didn't send me a copy. I sent Chris Gore a letter saying that he had a good future in politics. He called me up and screamed at me over the phone. The thing I learned most from fandom (and in general) is if you meet someone who is bragging about how he shafted it to the man, that's a warning that he's going to do it to you.

**JS: I could never really understand his take on bootlegs. It was one thing if a film was available for consumption, but in the case of most of the stuff... I mean, how else were you supposed to see *Cannibal Holocaust*? Or the stuff that was available, but cut to shit?**

**GG:** If you remember Chris Gore's early compilations, he was using stuff that he taped off the TV. He didn't pay those people royalties. Just the naked obviousness of that—he was taping copyrighted stuff of the TV and selling it. What is that? That was just a blind side to him. He didn't see the irony.

**JS: It can be argued that the fanzines and bootlegs gave a lot of directors their audience.**

**GG:** A lot of stuff was way out of the reach for most people. I never had a laserdisc player. Peter Jackson, Dario Argento—a lot of that stuff was only available on Japanese laserdiscs. Chas. was doing everyone a favor by introducing people to those movies.

**JS: And look what we've got now. Mainstream DVD and blu-ray labels that specialize in the stuff.**

**GG:** It all worked out in the end [laughs].

**JS: You mentioned *Screem* a while back. When did you start writing for them?**

**GG:** That's a real old publication. It went on hiatus for ten years. A while back, Darryl called me out of the blue and said, "Hey, Greg! Let's get the magazine going again!" I just made it my business to seek out and interview the filmmakers that I usually made fun of in my *Subhuman* days.

**JS: *Screem* printed your interview with Ray Dennis Steckler. It must have been one of his last.**

**GG:** Yeah, that was sort of a tragic interview. He called me after it was published and said, "You're the only writer to treat me as a serious filmmaker." He was crying on the phone. It was only belatedly that I

# JUST WHEN YOU THOUGHT IT WAS SAFE TO GO NEAR THE PARK . . . A CHAT WITH DIRECTOR LAWRENCE D. FOLDES

**By Greg Goodsell**

Filmmaker Lawrence D. Foldes takes it all in stride that the film he wishes to be remembered by, along with the film that he would rather forget are both making their debuts on DVD at approximately the same time. Foldes' *Finding Home* (2005), a soul-stirring drama starring Genevieve Bujold and Louise Fletcher has been winning praise at film festivals across the nation. When it comes to readers of this magazine, however, Foldes is more closely identified with the berserk horror thriller *Don't Go Near the Park* (1980), a haphazard mixture of grand ideas and technical incompetence that continues to stun viewers. Released to home video under myriad titles, Psychotronic Video's Michael Weldon warns against watching *Park* with a hangover.

Now out on DVD courtesy of Dark Sky Pictures, Foldes is amazed at the response that *Park* has gotten over the years. Foldes says the film is what it is, but makes no apologies for his directorial debut which he accomplished at the tender age of 19. More remarkable still is that *Park* is Foldes' second feature. *Malibu High* (1979), a rough and tough sexploitation film, served as his baptism into the world of film production. Other films in his filmography are of varying quality and radically different subject matter, but all keep their promise to surprise the viewer. In particular, his *Young Warriors* (1983) begins as an *Animal House* (1978) styled comedy only to turn into a rape-revenge melodrama, finally exploding in an apocalyptic finale.

Speaking from his Hollywood home, Foldes gave this writer a highly illuminating tour of his eclectic Hollywood career.

## A STUDENT OF FILM

Befitting an oeuvre that managed to employ tinseltown's highest and lowliest hands, Foldes was born and raised in Los Angeles. "Filmmaking was something that I wanted to do as far back as I can remember. I think it goes back to when I was in elementary school. I was born here in Los Angeles. My parents came here from Hungary in 1956 during the revolution. My grandfather, I remember, would come out and meet me every day after school. Instead of going home, the two of us would get on the 91 bus, and we would go down to Hollywood Boulevard, and I would go with him to at least two or three films a day before going home. What was neat about it was that he didn't speak any English at all, and he would go to any movie that I wanted to see. I could get in to see everything, any R-rated films, whatever. We would go and see anything and everything," Foldes says.

"We would sit in the back row because I would translate the film for him into Hungarian. Because he was hard of hearing, I used to do it kind of loud. So I would sit there with him and translate it, and when the movie was really bad or I got bored with it, I would just change the story and would just make something up, and he didn't know the difference! I maybe think I even made it better . . ." Foldes laughs.

Hoping to escape the sleaze in Hollywood, the Foldes clan moved to Lake Arrowhead when Lawrence was ready to start high school. "My father decided to move the entire family up there to escape the sex and drug scene in Hollywood. What he didn't realize was that at Lake Arrowhead, there was nothing to do but drugs and sex." With only one movie theater in town showing second or third-run features, Foldes went into serious withdrawal. As is the case with many souls faced with adversity, Foldes set his sights on entering the film world by any means possible.

"I only had one year of high school, and I took a proficiency exam and got the hell out of there." Foldes moved to San Bernardino, and got his general education classes out of the way. He then applied to several film schools. Foldes only lasted a month at the University of Southern California, with its overcrowded classrooms and students fighting over the meager equipment available. "All the undergraduates were expected to start in 8 mm, and the first things I shot were in 16 mm. I didn't want to take a step back."

Foldes had much better luck at the prestigious California Institute for the Arts, or Cal Arts. There were much smaller classrooms and ample equipment. More importantly, the instructors there acted as mentors. "My directing mentor was Alexander 'Sandy' Mackendrick, who directed Alec Guinness in *The Man in the White Suit* (1951)." Freed from the strictures of more basic classes, Foldes took nothing but film classes for his two years there.

"The only thing that was really disturbing at Cal Arts was the focus of a lot of the students, everything there was 'filmmaking as an art.' Business has nothing to do with it, this is an art form, and it was treated that way. They did stuff that was bizarre. They had screenings of some of the student films and I remember sitting in one, and it was dots on a blank screen, bouncing around. And then it was over and there was enormous applause and cheering, and I was 'what the hell is this?'" A similar scene pops up in Foldes' later epic, *Young Warriors*.

Foldes then transferred to the Brooks Institute of Photography in Santa Barbara, which was the polar opposite of Cal Arts. Brooks' emphasis in film classes was financing, budgeting and scheduling. Foldes graduated from Brooks when he was 18. Bound and determined, Foldes decided against starting at the bottom by working in an agency mail room or as a lowly go-for on a movie set. Foldes would produce his first film at the age of 18, the notorious sleaze-film epic *Malibu High* (1979).

## MALIBU HIGH

"I went and talked to every distributor that I could. And I went and I said, 'Look, I'm getting ready to do a low-budget exploitation movie. And I asked them what types of movies they were distributing. After talking to Sam Arkoff, Roger Corman and Mark Tenser, I found out that teen beach movies were really working at the time." A suitable script was found, and Foldes and company set out to make a beach movie. However, *Malibu High* was anything but a fun-in-the-sun film.

People who went to *Malibu High* expecting sun, silliness and sex, were instead confronted by an angry examination of teenage angst. "The original titles for the film were *High School Hit Girl, Death in Denim* and *Lovely But Deadly*," Foldes explains. *Malibu High's* heroine, high school senior Kim Bentley (Jill Lansing), has a bad attitude that grows increasingly worse. Jilted by her boyfriend and still smarting from the suicide of her father, she's flunking out of school until she hits upon the idea of seducing her teachers. Short of cash, she hooks up with two-bit pimp Tony (Al Mannino, aka Alex Mann of *I Drink Your Blood*) and begins pulling trains at construction sites. Buying a sports car and new clothes with her ill-gotten gains, she tells her mother (Phyllis Benson), "I tell you, I'm doing relief work!" She moves on to bigger and better things with an even bigger pimp, who then employs her for mob hits. Despite the connotations of the title, the beach only serves as the scene of a nasty triple homicide at the film's conclusion.

Directed by Texas regional filmmaker Irv Berwick (*Hitch Hike to Hell* and *Monster From Piedras Blancas*), *Malibu High* has many things in common with other exploitation film fare of this era. There are loads of unintentional hilarity and crude technical detail, and at one point, the theme song from TV's *The People's Court* yammers away in the background. But there's no denying the sleazy power it generates. The scene where a topless Patty taunts her school principal as he expires from a heart attack at her feet is as rough as any other film of its particular type. Director John Landis reportedly loves the film, and pronounced it "a film noir in broad daylight" and critic Kevin Thomas of the *Los Angeles Times* found *Malibu High* "compelling . . . calls to mind (Francois Truffaut's) *Adele H.*"

6

GOODSELL TALKS TO FOLDES. *SCREEM NUMBER 12.*

learned that he had just gotten the fatal diagnosis for his heart.

**JS: Man...**

**GG:** Yeah. He knew that he was on the way out and was very appreciative of the article that I wrote about him. He was a rough and ready filmmaker who took the camera and got the thing done; a very down to earth and nice guy. Are you looking for eccentric filmmaker stories?

**JS: Yeah. Do you have a few [laughs]?**

**GG:** Well... ask me about some of the people I've spoken to!

**JS: How about Lawrence D. Foldes?**

**GG:** He's a really good character and we've stayed in touch. Did you see his last film, *Finding Home*? He's trying to make a Douglas Sirk movie, and let's face it, Larry Foldes isn't Douglas Sirk. It's always fascinating. You'll see exploitation filmmakers try to make legitimate mainstream movies, like Herschell Gordon Lewis with *Suburban Roulette*. It just doesn't work. You have to have talent to make mainstream films. The trashy aesthetic works for exploitation, but if you have out of focus cameras and you're trying to tell a serious important story, it just doesn't go over well. If you have people pulled off the street as actors, it's not going to work. So, a lot of these filmmakers—I love them to death—but I see their inherent limitations.

**JS: What do you look for in a genre film today?**

**GG:** I go through phases. I will gobble up Indonesian fantasy films one month and old school Category III stuff from Hong Kong the next. There are a lot of elements in the films that I like that, when applied elsewhere, fail dismally. I have to say that even with my experience with *Deep Red*, the trend in "torture porn" has no appeal for me. If I want to wallow in disgust and despair, I can just go the twenty-four-hour supermarket down the street and see all the human flotsam wandering the aisles. I also have little time for nuevo grindhouse

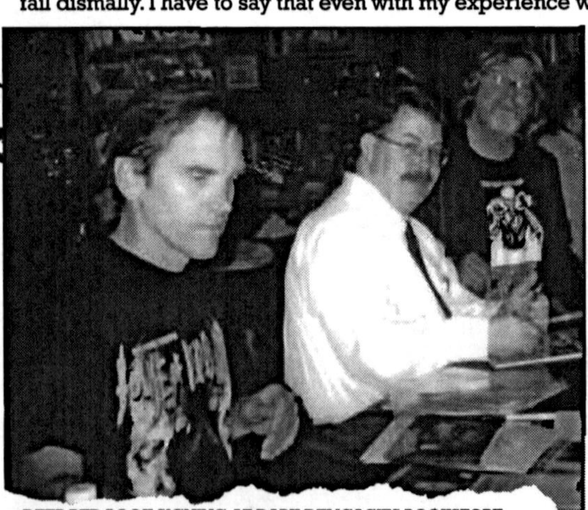

DEEP RED BOOK SIGNING AT DARK DELICACIES BOOKSTORE, HALLOWEEN WEEKEND, 2002. [L–R:] BILL MOSELEY, GREG GOODSELL, AND CHAS. BALUN.

features, where the filmmakers dumb everything down and wink and nudge the audience. Your film has to be heartfelt and sincere, or not at all. I won't mention a certain studio who has carved out a niche market by producing deliberately bad movies. Most movies are already pretty bad to begin with!

**JS: What are some of your recent favorites?**

**GG:** *Rubber, Devil, Orphan, Red White and Blue*, and the mind-melting game changer *After Last Season*. If there were to ever be a sequel to the *Deep Red Horror Handbook*, *After Last Season* would have its own chapter!

**JS: What would the chapter be named?**

**GG:** "They've Got Some Printers in the Basement You Can Use."

**JS: [laughs] I've always been curious about that film. Do you think that Mark Region's intent as a filmmaker was sincere?**

**GG:** Absolutely! Even in the age of the internet, where all secrets are laid bare, *After Last Season* has an incomprehensible aura of mystery about it. The one interview with Region online creates more questions than answers. There is not the slightest trace of irony in that film, anywhere. Where films such as *Dangerous Men*, *The Room*, and *Birdemic: Shock and Terror* fit snugly into the "What the fuck?" genre, *After Last Season* has its own genre: A single, extended f–u–u–u–u–u–u–u–u–u–u–uck.

**JS: What do you think he was trying to accomplish?**

**GG:** Region is obviously trying to tell a very simple story. Two parapsychologists are conducting experiments on a college campus where there has been a series of murders. Their experiments conjure forth one of the victims, who exacts his revenge on his killer. Because Region so totally disregards the syntactical rules of common filmmaking, the audience is left with an incomprehensible question mark, set in an alternate reality where all the surroundings and clothes are a drab light blue. There is the sound of a toilet flushing several doors down (probably due to bad audio looping) and the sets are rolls of butcher paper tied to columns. *After Last Season* is highly successful in that it takes the viewer and drops them into an almost alien

WITH LIZ RENAY AT THE CULT MOVIES CONVENTION IN HOLLYWOOD, 2000. PHOTO COURTESY OF GREG GOODSELL.

environment, with no guideposts.

**JS: To say the least! The eighties saw countless sequels. Now we've got remakes. What's your take on the recent "remake" craze?**

**GG:** What amazes me about the recent remake craze is that they are remaking all these classic movies and no one is going to see them. From best to worst, these films are flopping right and left at the box office. The recent remake of *Straw Dogs* played one week, if that, and bypassed the dollar theaters in my neck of the woods. Even the remake of *Let the Right One In*, which was Americanized to *Let Me In*, died a quick death. On a positive note, it proved that those who actually cared to see the film had sought out the Swedish original and passed on what was essentially a shot-by-shot remake. It's heartening that modern horror movie audiences, with the internet, illegal downloads, and active trading circuit are continuing to make intelligent choices well into the twenty-first century!

**JS: Do you think that the internet has "dumbed down" genre writing?**

**GG:** It takes nothing to throw up a blog. Crafting a publication takes thought and discernment.

**JS: True.**

**GG:** There is a lot of vital, important writing on film currently on the internet. But, strangely enough, there's a new breed of fan-writer who declines to work for print publications to concentrate solely on their online work. I don't know why! Then, there are those internet writers out there whose biggest ambition is to get an excerpt of their review used as a blurb on a DVD cover and will say the grandest things about the worst

GOODSELL SIGNS.

PHOTO COURTESY OF GREG GOODSELL.

films. They are rewarded in kind by a blurb that lists the website and not their names. Their reputations suffer for recommending lousy movies.

**JS: A corny question, but what the hell: Do you miss the good old days?**

**GG:** Not really. I had my fun, but this was during a time when I lived at home, had no car, only worked part-time, had very little money, and my only claim to fame was writing for small publications. I have since caught much larger fish to fry.

**JS: What are your thoughts on the state of fandom today?**

**GG:** It's really great that there is a continued sense of excitement and discovery over these films and films in general. People will see different things in different films, and share their readings with other people, forming bonds and camaraderie. One of my favorite sayings is, "The world is full of music geeks, record collecting geeks, movie geeks, video game geeks, drama geeks, toy geeks. In my humble opinion, the people with no interests whatsoever are the real geeks!"

# BAD MAGIC

by *Greg Goodsell*

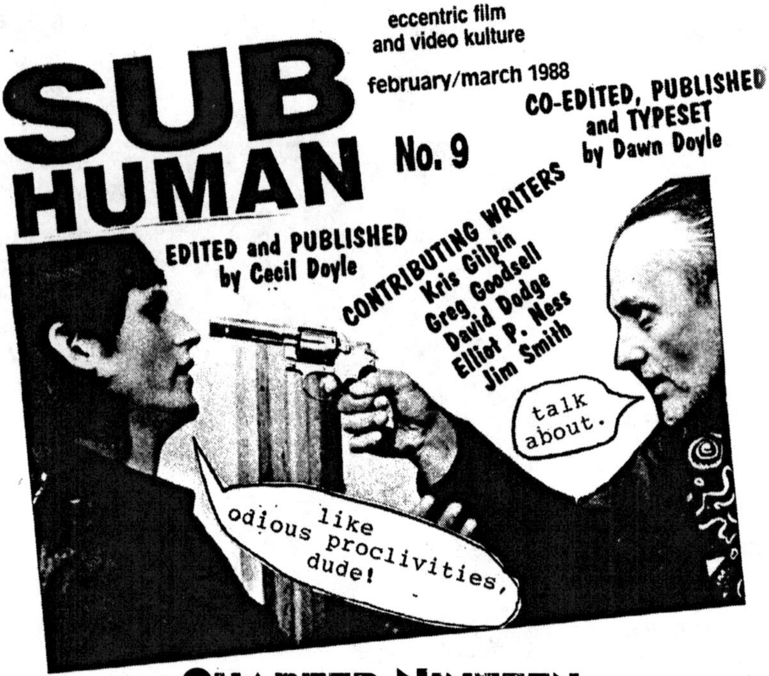

eccentric film
and video kulture

# SUB HUMAN

february/march 1988

No. 9

CO-EDITED, PUBLISHED and TYPESET by Dawn Doyle

EDITED and PUBLISHED by Cecil Doyle

CONTRIBUTING WRITERS
Kris Gilpin
Greg Goodsell
David Dodge
Elliot P. Ness
Jim Smith

talk about.

like odious proclivities, dude!

## Chapter Ninteen

## Subhuman!

SUBHUMAN

# CHAPTER NINETEEN

Cecil Doyle was the editor and publisher of *Subhuman*, a toxic little zine from Lafayette, Louisiana. Lasting only nineteen issues (1986–1990), *Subhuman* is still widely regarded as one of the most influential publications of its era. Kris Gilpin, Greg Goodsell and Dave Dodge made up the core of the *Subhuman* team and their writing, much in part due to Doyle's encouragement, soon morphed into something far different than the usual fanzine-fare. Doyle offered his writers free range and fertile ground to experiment and explore whatever approach they saw fit, resulting in some of the finest (and most unusual) film criticism ever published.

I first crossed paths with *Subhuman* the way most people did—through a review in another zine. *Subhuman* had already been going for a couple of years and was beginning to evolve into something delightfully sleazy. It was raucous, rambunctious, and in your face—not all that surprising, once I became aware of Doyle's roots in the early Louisiana punk scene.

Today, Cecil Doyle works as a music director at KRVS FM in southern Louisiana where he is the producer and host of *Medicine Ball Caravan*, *Jah Mon!*, and *Sounds Unusual*. We talked in length on a cold Winter's evening about schlock, sleaze, and, of course, *Subhuman*.

The following interview was conducted via telephone on February 6, 2012.

---

**JOHN SZPUNAR: Is Cecil there?**

**CECIL DOYLE:** Yeah, this is Cecil.

**JS: Hi. This is John.**

**CD:** Hey! How you doing, man?

**JS: Not too bad! First of all, I'd just like to thank you for taking the time for this. It's great to finally talk to you.**

**CD:** Well good, man. Thank you. I'm glad that you're doing this. There's still a few of us around.

**JS: My pleasure. Do you want to just jump into things?**

**CD:** Sure.

**JS: OK. I just want to get a feel for where you're coming from. I'll start with the stock question that I've asked again and again—where did you grow up?**

**CD:** Down here in Louisiana. I've never lived much farther than fifty miles from where I am right now. Southwest Louisiana—about an hour east of Baton Rouge.

**JS: What was life like when you were growing up? I mean, that's kind of a general question, but...**

**CD:** [laughs] It was just typical small town living. As far as movies are concerned, I grew up in a town called Opelousas. I grew up during the sixties and, in those days, the theaters switched out movies fairly often.

# CECIL DOYLE

## SUBHUMAN!

EARLY 3-D IN *THE MASK*.

I grew up a few blocks from the theater, so I was a regular movie-goer when I was a kid. It was sort of a golden age of interest in horror films and things like that. They just seemed to be everywhere.

**JS: I take it that you gravitated toward the monster films...**

**CD:** Yeah, certainly, because they showed a lot of them on the weekend. That's usually how I would spend my Saturday afternoons. In those days, they did a lot of double feature things. They showed a lot of the Roger Corman films. I got to see a double bill of *Little Shop of Horrors* with *A Bucket of Blood*—little did I know that they were basically being made at the same time! There were some really cool and creative double bills that I grew up on. I saw *I Was a Teenage Frankenstein* with *I Was a Teenage Werewolf*. I have a lot of childhood memories of going to see things like *The Mask*, one of the early 3-D movies.

**JS: What did you think of that one?**

**CD:** I was very impressed. As weak as it was, I'd never seen any sort of 3-D before. I still remember putting on those glasses and getting a semblance of that effect. So yeah, that's the kind of fare that I grew up with. Saturday was usually a monster movie or an Italian sword and sandal movie—*Hercules* movies, or something like that. No matter what was playing, I'd be there.

**JS: Were most of your friends into that kind of thing?**

**CD:** I suppose there were a few, but I don't know if we talked about movies as much as we talked about TV. School was more about talking about what was on *Lost in Space* and stuff like that. But I was pretty interested—I read up on the stuff and tried to see everything I could. I would get *Famous Monsters* at the newsstand just about every month. That's what was so great—that magazine was going on, and all the kids were watching those films. That's what was on TV and that's what was at the theater. The Universal monster movies played every weekend on some local channel. Growing up in the early sixties, it was hard to avoid.

**JS: Did you read a lot as a kid?**

**CD:** I wasn't much of a book reader. I read some books, but I was more of a comic book guy. Actually, I was a big fan of the *Classics Illustrated* series

[laughs]! Whatever literary knowledge I got was probably culled from them. The novels were probably a little over my head; I was only nine or ten at the time. But the comic books were another thing that really boomed during the sixties, with *Batman* and all of that. I remember buying *Creepy* and *Vampirella* from the newsstand. It seems like the whole monster/comic book/superhero thing kind of meshed together. Rock'n'roll and James Bond—it all kind of melded into one thing. It was everywhere. There was just something about that mid-sixties explosion of pop culture—I don't think I've ever encountered anything quite like it since.

CLASSICS ILLUSTRATED—LITERARY KNOWLEDGE.

**JS: When did you become aware of fanzines?**

**CD:** It was during the punk era. I was reading *Punk* and all the zines. In fact, I did a punk zine before I did *Subhuman*. It was called *Floating Turd*. I was kind of combining my interest in punk with my newfound interest in surrealism and dada.

**JS: You played bass in the punk band Toxin III.**

**CD:** Right. That was during the seventies. I played bass in a few bands and guitar in a few bands. I was reading a lot of rock zines that covered the glitter-era social scene. I remember reading about The Ramones two years before their first album was out. Reading about what The New York Dolls were doing in clubs and that kind of thing sort of took the place of what I was reading ten years earlier with *Famous Monsters*. Rock'n'roll was what loomed largest in my life. In those days, it seemed that everyone around the country who was punk or into the remnants of the glitter scene seemed to know one another. This was back before the internet—we were all just writing letters or calling one another. In 1978, I spent a month in Greenwich Village with some friends while the Sid Vicious murder thing was happening. I didn't know anyone in southern Louisiana who was into that kind of thing. I just kind of came back with the idea that I'd like to start a punk band.

**JS: What was your first band called?**

**CD:** The first one I started was called the Movie Stars, with my sister and her husband. We did mostly cover things. Before long, I ended up hooking

RECORDED & INDEXED

# CECIL DOYLE

## SUBHUMAN!

DRAFT

up with some other guys from around here who were also into it. One of the guys was writing his own punk songs—a guy named Chris Cart. He sort of asked me to come along, so I did Toxin III for a few years.

**JS: You guys were pretty infamous for your logo. Who came up with it?**

**CD:** Toxin III was totally the brainchild of Chris. All of the original material, as well as the sleeve's design, was his concept. A friend (underground comic artist Ray Weiland) inked the Felix the Cat with the switchblade front, while I'm sure the confederate swastika was Chris' design.

**JS: I'd imagine that it caused quite a stir. Were your politics misconstrued?**

**CD:** To this day, Toxin III are often interpreted as a skinhead band because of that EP cover. Certainly, there was absolutely no lyrical content to sustain any leanings in that direction. If anything, it was just the opposite. More like comparing the Confederacy's racist tendencies to those of the Nazi regime. There was no real trouble that I recall when the record initially come out, but it sure seems to be what most people think of, if they've ever even heard of the band.

**JS: It certainly stands out. You know, I'm curious—how many issues did *Floating Turd* last?**

**CD:** I think I did two or three issues, until I conked out on the band. *Subhuman* came right after that. It kind of coincided with the VHS era, when everybody was trading movies on tape. I got to see all these movies that I'd always heard about. I almost immediately stopped playing music and went directly into watching movies. I eventually wanted to make my own publication. Like punk, it seemed like a way for everybody to communicate.

**JS: Did you expect *Subhuman* to be as widely regarded as it was?**

**CD:** I didn't think it was going to be much. I just sent it to a few friends. The next thing I knew, I had people offering to contribute to the magazine. That's how the whole thing kicked off.

**JS: When did you actually start publishing *Subhuman*?**

**CD:** I think it was in 1986. It lasted until 1990. It was only around for four years—I must have started it early in '86. I haven't even seen the first two issues in a long time. The format for those was a little different, but by the time I got to issue number 3, my wife (Dawn Doyle) was working for a local newspaper. Instead of reducing the typewritten articles, she said, "Why don't I typeset them?" So, she started to do that in her spare time. At that time, *Subhuman* was one of the few zines that had actual typesetting. She designed the newspaper, so she had access to all of these different fonts. I was just like a kid playing. Everyone would send me their articles through the mail and I would edit them and give them to her. Then it was just cut and paste, bring it to the print shop, and print out as many as I needed.

**JS: It's interesting that your wife was involved. Were there many**

**women in the scene?**

**CD:** Oh no, not at all. In fact, I'm trying to think if there were any women that even did zines. It was pretty much male dominated. And Dawn would watch some of those movies—we'd have laughs over them—but she wasn't a big follower.

**JS: Why do you think the scene was so male dominated?**

**CD:** I don't know. That's hard to account for. Maybe because it was a male dominated industry, created by men for men. I would imagine that there's more female interest nowadays. But back then, I didn't have any female subscribers, that I'm aware of.

**JS: So, how much time did you typically spend on the layout?**

**CD:** Oh, I don't know. It just happened. I was always working on it a little bit by little bit. I only put out two or three issues a year. I did it in my spare time; it was sort of a continuous thing.

**JS: Where were you working at the time?**

**CD:** I was delivering for a local clothing store. I just drove around all day delivering stock. I stayed on the road all day, so that gave me the opportunity to stop in bookstores, shop, and kind of keep up with things. I'd also drop things off at the print shop.

**JS: I was going through some old zines that Greg Goodsell sent me, and I noticed that you did some writing for Herb Schrader's *Video Drive-In*...**

**CD:** Yes! In fact, I did that even before I did *Subhuman*—that's what prompted me. I'd totally forgotten about that. I remember reading *Video Drive-In* and I wrote in, offering to write something. I wrote two or three articles for him.

**JS: Other writers would soon be asking the same thing of you.**

**CD:** Yeah. I discovered Greg Goodsell through a zine called *Zontar*. He had an incredible Larry Buchanan article in there. I wrote to Greg because I thought it was sort of life-changing and eye-opening—really clever and well-written. Greg decided to subscribe to *Subhuman*, and after seeing one issue, he asked if he could start submitting articles. Kris Gilpin did the same thing. Dave Dodge—all those guys liked the zine and started to submit things. So, by issue number 4, I did very little. I was just sort of collecting stuff [laughs].

**JS: *Subhuman* wasn't strictly a horror zine. You seemed to cover**

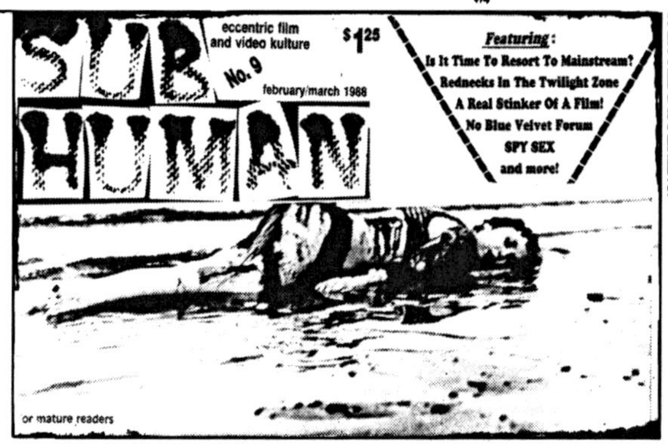


A LITTLE DIFFERENT.

**everything. What kind of criteria did you set for the movies you wanted to cover and for the articles that you wanted to run?**

**CD:** I didn't really have one. The majority of zines were doing horror, but there was the influence of *Sleazoid Express*. All of the sudden, people were trading movies by Roberta Findlay and people like her. I was finally getting to see all these different kinds of films. I covered what I was seeing and trading. I sort of gravitated toward the sleazy side of things. Then again, *Subhuman* was kind of dictated by what people contributed. I was putting in those cartoons by the Evil Twin. It was just sort of free-form. I didn't really have any set criteria. Just whatever I came across and found interesting. As things got closer to 1990, I was more interested in exploitation than horror.

**JS: Can you tell me a little about the fake movie reviews that Kris Gilpin was writing?**

**CD:** There was one article. I'm not sure if there were more.

**JS: I know of one called "*Get Out of My Way, Man. I Really Mean It!*"**

**CD:** [laughs] Yeah! That was an article that he wrote about an imaginary movie! I'm going to have to go back and look at it! That was Gilpin, man! I hadn't seen anyone in any other zines print things like that. Kris and Greg—their writing was getting really different. It wasn't your average review of a movie. They started getting into a total fantasy. In Greg's case, it was a personal reflection. I remember him writing an article about a time he was in a classroom and he started realizing that, "I am in control of my destiny. I am responsible for my actions. I am alive!" Things like that, all in the context of a review of some schlocky film! That was what I loved about those guys. They made *Subhuman* a little different. I wasn't seeing that kind of stuff anywhere else.

**JS: A lot of people regard *Subhuman* as being very influential.**

**CD:** Everyone always seemed to be pleased with it. I was surprised, because I was just jumping on the bandwagon with a few other people. I didn't feel like I was breaking any new ground. During the time it caught on, there wasn't a huge readership, but I think it really mattered to the people who did read it. I know Quentin Tarantino was a subscriber back when he was a video clerk

# CECIL DOYLE

## SUBHUMAN!

RECORDED & INDEXED

DRAFT

*SUBHUMAN* REVIEWED IN *DEEP RED* NUMBER 2.

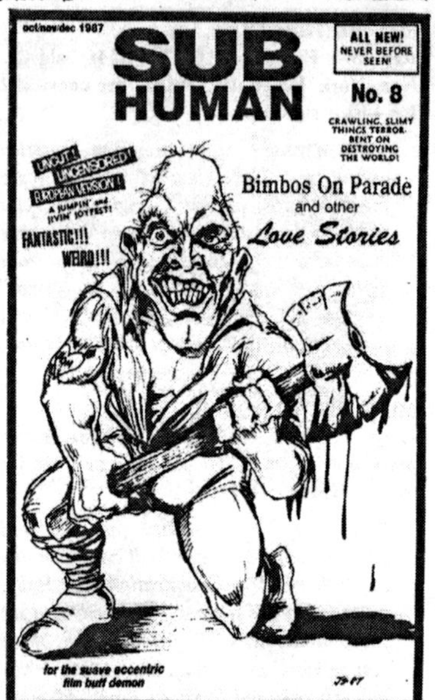


SUBHUMAN
Cecil Doyle/1509 W. St. Mary/Lafayette, Louisiana 70506/$3.00 for one year subscription (5 issues)

*Funky, irreverent and frequently hilarious, this "eccentric video and film" 'zine features nutzoid graphics, a rabidly opinionated viewpoint and very solid and skilled writing/reporting. Lots of bizarre ad mats and illustrations make this one an eye popping read.*

[laughs]. I think he sent in five bucks for three issues, or something like that. When he became famous, I thought, "I know that guy. He was on my list!" Lux Interior of the Cramps phoned me one afternoon. I guess he just called information and found me. He wanted to know if I had all the back issues. I didn't print back issues—that's why I did *Subhuman Confidential* (a collection of archival *Subhuman* material).

**JS: What year did he call you?**

**CD:** This was toward the end; he probably contacted me in 1989. Anyway, I did have one copy of every issue that I did. I ended up sending him my complete personal run of *Subhuman*. I don't even have issue number 1 or 2. He got those.

**JS: Did you have any other famous readers of note?**

**CD:** Rob Zombie was an early subscriber, and he was sending me homemade promotional things for White Zombie before anyone was talking about them.

**JS: I'm curious—how many copies of each issue were you printing?**

**CD:** I don't think I ever printed up more than 500 copies of any issue. So, only a few hundred people ever really saw *Subhuman*.

**JS: Dave Szurek certainly did. Do you have any memories of him?**

**CD:** All of us had, at the very least, letter encounters with Szurek. He would write the longest letters—handwritten letters that would just go on, front and back, for page after page. The guy gave you the impression that he did nothing but work, get home, and read and write. It seemed like everyone was in contact with him. We all had stories about his weird

parenthesis-riddled missives. There'd be a few words, and there'd be a parenthesis that would go on for about half a page. Then he'd continue. He was everywhere, in letter form.

**JS: I love reading the letters pages of old fanzines. Especially when people are talking about films that weren't widely known at the time. You can really feel the sense of discovery that was happening.**

**CD:** You had to try a little harder back then. There was a collective discovery between a core of fans. We'd all feed off of each other. Someone would hear about something and would let the rest of us know about it.

**JS: A trail was being blazed.**

**CD:** It was a fun era. You had to do a little work. But it's amazing how recordable video revolutionized an entire generation of people to go back and to see the things that had gone under their radar. And we started to dig deeper and deeper. We got into things like nudies and roughies. Educational films—all of the overlooked genres.

**JS: Most publications prior to the fanzines never took those films seriously.**

**CD:** In the fifties and sixties, magazines like *Film Culture* covered the underground films. They'd have a serious publication about something that most people didn't even know about. We were kind of akin to that. And nowadays, with the internet, everything's so instant. It's hard to say if that kind of camaraderie still exists. You don't have to be as dedicated to the journey or the cause.

**JS: Every zine had a distinct personality.**

**CD:** That was the fun thing. For me, it was fun to go to the mailbox every day. There'd rarely be a day when there was nothing there. I was getting great zines from all over the world.

**JS: We should talk a little bit about how difficult it was to see some of the films that you covered before the age of video.**

**CD:** In the early to mid-eighties, video rental became a big thing. Suddenly, there was an amazing amount of small companies putting out exploitation movies. You'd find them in grocery stores and the oddest little places. I'd just go about when I was delivering—as I said, I was driving all over the city.

RECORDED & INDEXED

DRAFT

SUBHUMAN
no. 15
Nov./Dec. 1989
eccentric film and video kulture
YOU'VE NEVER SEEN MORE ...LET US PROVE IT TO YOU.
INSIDE:
Necrophilia
3-D Surrealism
Animal Copulation
Pregnant Strippers
Horror Nerdism
Bovine Flatulence
plus
A Visit With Larry Buchanan
I demand you to get on your knees & be ready for the wild pleasure
MONSTERS MEET MODELS
$1.25
NEW MAILING ADDRESS INSIDE
ADULTS ONLY


PREGNANT STRIPPERS AND ANIMAL COPULATION.

I'd stop at these places and see things. That's how I first rented *Satan's Sadists*. I found these Al Adamson movies in some grocery store outside the city limits. Then, friends would be trading videos. I was lucky enough to hook up with Mike Vraney of Something Weird fairly early on. He used to send me tons of stuff. He liked *Subhuman*, so he would trade out for a little ad. I mean, he'd send me a box full of tapes. And one time, he sent a huge box of photocopied clippings of drive-in ads for me to borrow. We were all enthusiastic about it. Some of my favorite discoveries from that era were sent to me by people like Mike. Someone sent me a really bad copy of *Soul Vengeance*, and I was blown away. It was the most unique blacksploitation film that I'd ever seen.

**JS: *Subhuman* reviewed some strange porn films, as well.**

**CD:** I did a review of a porn video called *Chocolate Delight*. It was a slave and master tape of this gimp-type guy being abused. Basically, it was just this girl taking a dump on a paper plate or over these chairs into his mouth. Just shitting and pissing into his mouth. He was saying, "Oh, thank you mistress!" While all of this was going on, you could hear chickens in the room. But you never saw them. So, you're watching this, figuring that there were caged chickens somewhere in the house. It was so appalling that I wrote an article about it. Someone asked me, "Can I borrow this?" I said, "No… you can have it! I don't want to die and have someone find this in my collection!"

**JS: You never know what goes on behind closed doors. Did you ever think that *Subhuman* would become culturally relevant?**

**CD:** Culturally relevant [laughs]?

**JS: [laughing] Well… in an anthropological sort of way.**

**CD:** The only time I noticed that at least some people took notice of it was when mentioned in *Screen*. It's a very serious and long-running film journal. The writer, Jeffery Sconce wrote an article in 1992 called "Trashing the Academy". It was all about zines, and he made references to the scene. He quoted the cover of *Subhuman* number 15 where I was talking about pregnant strippers and animal copulation. All of this was written in a serious

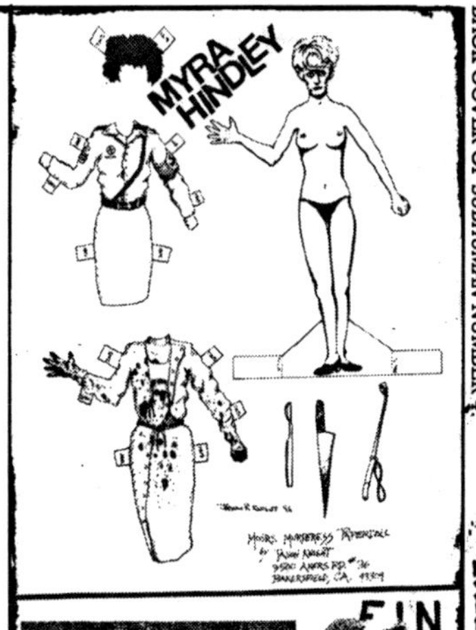


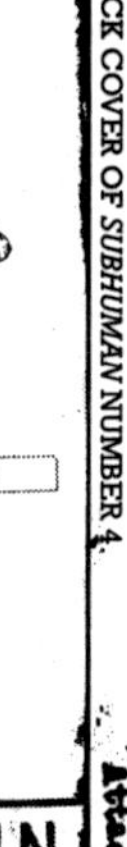
BACK COVER OF *SUBHUMAN* NUMBER 4

film journal [laughs]. That was the one time when I said, "Wow! *Subhuman* might have more relevance than I thought." It was fun when I ran across that.

**JS: I wanted to ask you about Mike Diana. He did some artwork for you.**

**CD:** [pause] That's right, he did! Mike had his own zine, too.

**JS: He was doing *Angelfuck* at the time.**

**CD:** I wasn't a fan of it. It was so simplistic that I kind of dismissed the guy and never paid much attention to him. But he's the guy who kind of hooked up with Nick Zedd and Kuchar. He actually got into the whole scene that I was championing.

**JS: What did you think of his trial?**

**CD:** That obscenity thing?

**JS: Yeah. In Florida.**

**CD:** I have a vague memory of hearing about that. But that could have happened to me. It could have happened to a lot of us—it just so happened that it happened to him.

**JS: On that subject, did you ever catch any flack for publishing the Myra Hindley paper doll?**

**CD:** Oh no, not at all. When I first printed it, I didn't totally get the Myra Hindley thing. I think it probably went over most people's heads. In fact, it probably caused a lot of people to look up Myra Hindley. But that was one of my favorite things ever, because it was such a unique idea. I liked little things like that.

**JS: Were you aware of pirated copies of *Subhuman* making their way across the globe?**

**CD:** Yeah, I figured that a lot of that happened. Through the years, people have told me that they saw it at this place or that place. Somebody told me that they bought it at a store in New York. In that sense, the readership went far beyond the people that I sent it to. All you had to do was run it through a copier. And that's fine with me. I'm glad that there was an interest in it.

**JS: Why did *Subhuman* come to an end?**

**CD:** I don't know. Maybe I was just getting tired of it. We had kids, and it was taking up so much time. My wife and I were married for ten years before we had kids, and I was doing *Subhuman* during that time. It just started to be a big slump on the free time that I had. It also kind of coincided with the internet, and all of that. Once that started happening,

RECORDED & INDEXED

# CECIL DOYLE

## SUBHUMAN!

DRAFT

STRIKING GRAPHIC DESIGN.

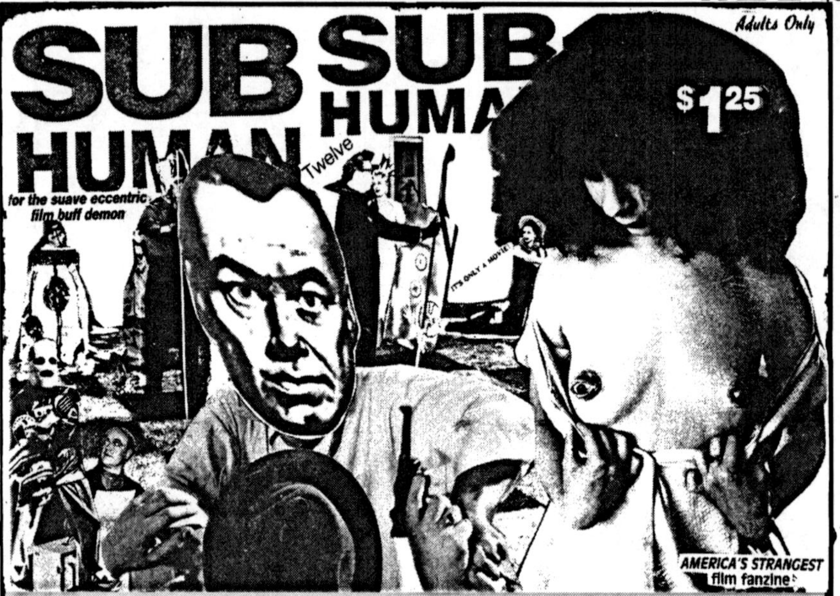

SUB HUMAN SUB HUMAN Twelve

for the suave eccentric film buff demon

Adults Only

$1.25

IT'S ONLY A MOVIE!

AMERICA'S STRANGEST film fanzine

things were more instantaneous. You could just put up a website. There was a brief flirtation with, "Maybe we should make a *Subhuman* website." I just sort of lost interest and didn't peruse it.

**JS: How many issues did *Subhuman* last?**

**CD:** I think I did nineteen issues. I was getting ready to work on number twenty, but it never happened. I had some really good articles from Kris and Greg. Kris did a really good interview with Don Gordon and I had that all ready to go. But, it never saw the light of day. I stopped publishing and things faded away much faster than they came together.

THE *ESSENTIAL SUBHUMAN* COMPENDIUM.

**JS: Well, at least you went out with a bang. *Subhuman* never got stale or repeated itself.**

**CD:** There was something about the eighties. There was the video revolution, and we could finally see these movies at home. In any other decade, you couldn't do that unless you had a projector. It all just sort of came from that. And it was a new concept to even look at some of these filmmakers. I'm sure a lot of those guys were surprised and impressed that there were any publications writing things about them. Whatever the zines covered at that time was lifted out of the underground.

**JS: It was an exciting time to be a film fan.**

**CD:** I have the fondest of memories of that time and of the way that scene made me feel. I've never quite experienced anything quite like it since…

!!NEXT TIME!!

SUBhuman begins it's second year with #6 featuring a close-up on Big Bucks Burnett, curator of Dallas'own Museum Of Bad Art and head of the Mr.Ed Fan Club; Blue Velvet Forum (hopefully) and of course, reviews and news from the world of eccentric video & film.

RECORDED & INDEXED

DRAFT

A LETTER FROM DAVID F. FRIEDMAN, THE TRASH-FILM KING!

July 12, 1991

Dear Cecil:

Your letter and sample copies Subhuman and Subhuman Confidential arrived this AM; for which many thanks. I'm gratified by your kind words, and enjoyed reading your publications, which are top-drawer 'zines.'

I'm dashing this off in haste, as am leaving in an hour for Las Vegas to attend the Video Software Dealers Ass'n. convention, where will intro the documentawdry, Sex and Buttered Popcorn. This is a compilation of about 25 of the old exploitation shlockers from the 20's thru the 50's. Dan Sonney and I are on camera for a good portion reminiscing about the derring-do days of the circulating salesmen of cinema sleaze. Ned Beatty hosts the show, adding the explanatory narration. It's fun, and a trash film memorabilia collector's must.

I'll see Mike Vraney in Vegas, and go on to L.A. with him. He's going to release some of my old B&W roughies, Defilers and Smell of Honey, Swallow of Brine as well as a reel of my trailers on video this fall. I'll also connect with Eric Caidin of Hollywood Book and Poster, who's my biggest Boswell, while in Vegas.

I'll be back in Dixie on July 19th, and it will be my pleasure to send you an autographed copy of A Youth in Babylon and some goodies from my pressbook files.

Again, thanks for writing and the copies. It's guys like you, Mike Weldon, Charles Kilgore, Don Metz, David Flint, Tony Binder and Eric Caidin who've made this and future generations aware of the celluloid carnage and carnality that shocked and tittilated their dads and granddads. You are all scholars who should be rewarded with seats on high in academies preserving the annals of human history.

Forty of my 68 years were spent in the exploitation business, most of them profitable, but money was just a way of keeping score, the real reward was in the fun and more than anything else, the razzle-dazzle.

All best.

Cordially, Dave

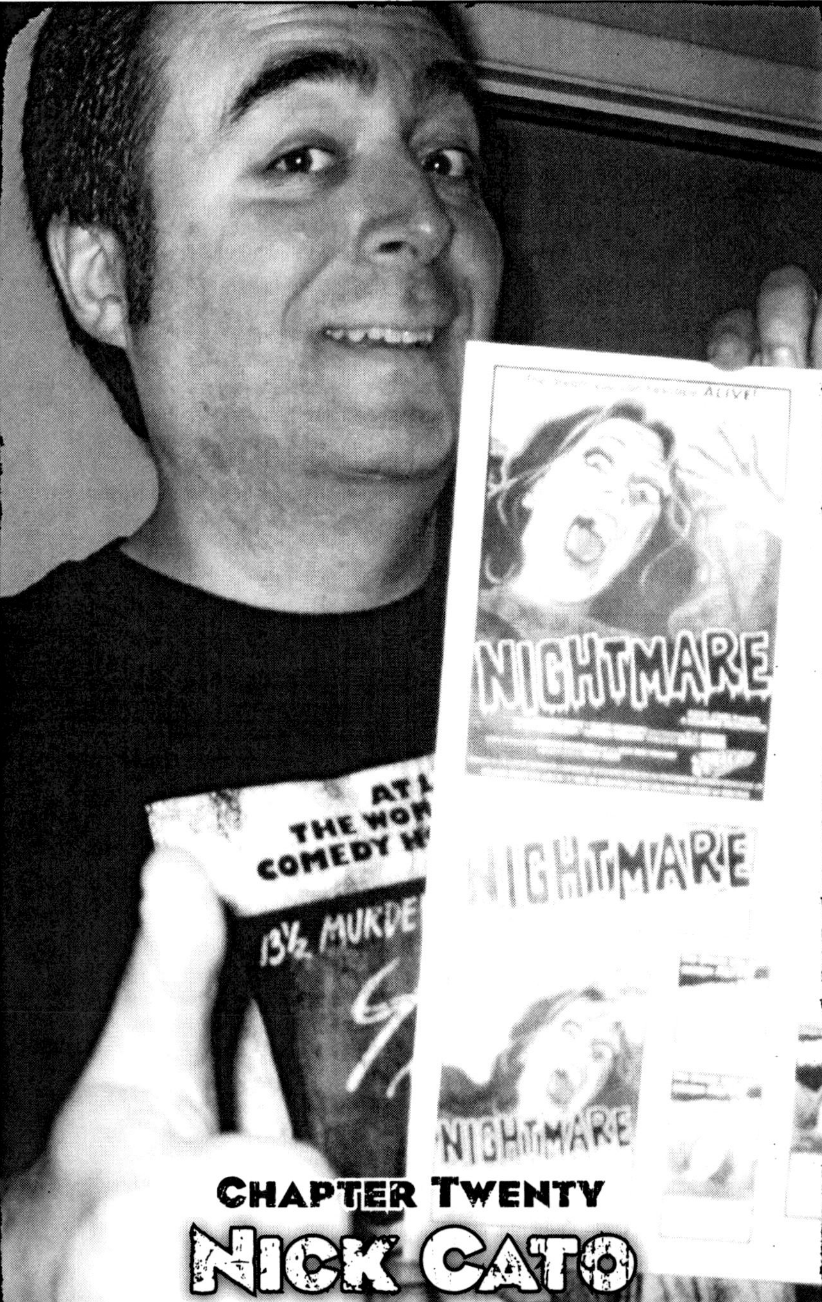


# Chapter Twenty

# Nick Cato

## The Yak Talks Back!

PHOTO COURTESY OF NICK CATO.

# Nick Cato

## The Yak Talks Back!

Nick Cato began publishing *Stink* in 1981. Inspired by Rick Sullivan's *Gore Gazette*, Nick soon found his own voice and *Stink* began making waves in the fanzine circuit. I got my first copy in 1989 and immediately fell in love with it. Nick wrote under the pseudonym Nick the Yak, and his writing was rude, crude, and funny as hell.

Much to my dismay, Nick ceased publishing *Stink* in 1991. But old habits die hard—in 2003, he started publishing the *Horror Fiction Review*. In 2008, the zine evolved into a website, and it is still very active today.

Nick began writing horror fiction in 1997 and has never looked back. His first novel, *Don of the Dead* was published in 2009, and 2012 saw the release of *Antibacterial Pope*, his first collection of short stories.

I interviewed Nick Cato in the early Spring of 2012 about *Stink*, the New York zine scene, and his work as a writer.

The following interview was conducted via telephone on April 4, 2012.

---

**JOHN SZPUNAR: Where did you buy monster magazines as a kid?**

**NICK CATO:** We had a local comic shop here called Paul's Sweet Shop. It was an old fashioned place with a great ice cream bar and everything. The guy carried all the comics and all the Warren magazines, like *Vampirella*. I saw *Famous Monsters* there, and I was addicted to it. This is when I was in the first grade, or something. I read that up until the end, until *Fango* knocked them out of business. The main horror comics we had in the seventies were things like *Tomb of Dracula* from Marvel. There was one from DC that I really liked called *Weird War Tales*. I don't know if it's true or not, but I heard a rumor that they're actually thinking about making a film about it, which would be awesome. As a matter of fact, there's a book out about Eerie Publications [*The Weird World of Eerie Publications*], the low budget imitations of *Creepy* and *Eerie*. One of them was called *Weird*. I loved those—they were twice as gruesome as the Warren ones. I liked the illustrations—they were really graphic. Whenever I could get my hands on one of those, it was like striking gold.

**JS: What were you seeing in the theaters?**

**NC:** I started going to the theaters by myself in 1981. I was in the sixth grade, and I actually had a mustache. I used to get everyone into R-rated movies. For some reason, they re-released everything in New York in 1981. I finally got to see *Dawn of the Dead*, *The Texas Chain Saw Massacre*, and *Shock Waves*—all of the classic seventies films. And that's about the time all the splatter stuff was coming out.

**JS: Were you mostly seeing this stuff in Staten Island?**

**NC:** Yeah, mostly in my home town. It wasn't until 1983 or 1984, when I was a sophomore in high school, that I started going to Times Square. I caught the

last three or four years of that whole 42nd Street grindhouse thing.

**JS: That must have been crazy.**

**NC:** I caught the tail end of it. A lot of the guys that I idolized, like Rick Sullivan from *Gore Gazette*—I was reading about their experiences, but I had no way of getting up there. I had a lot of cousins, but they weren't into that stuff. Then, one of my first girlfriend's friends said, "Yeah, I'll show you how to get up there." That was the end of it. We went up there every four days to see a movie. Triple-features… it was really just a great time.

**JS: Was it dangerous at all for a young kid like you to be in that area?**

**NC:** Well, me and my friends were into punk and metal, so we really didn't look like tourists. We kind of fit in [laughs]. That said, waiting for a movie in Times Square, especially on a Friday or Saturday night, was actually scarier than half the movies you were waiting in line to see. The prostitution was kind of kept down to the end of the block where the Port Authority was, but you had people offering you every drug available. You've heard the term "pusher"—you'd be waiting in line, and have these six-foot tall black guys come up to you and drop this white stuff in your hand and say, "You're buying it." That didn't happen to me, but I saw that happen to people.

**JS: Let me try to put things into context—how did you become aware of *Gore Gazette*?**

**NC:** In the West Village, there were a whole lot of record stores. There was one store called Bleecker Bob's—it's actually still there. I was in there buying whatever new stuff was out, and I saw *Gore Gazette*. I was totally attracted to how cheap it was. It was really bad looking [laughs]. When I saw that, I said, "Wow, this is cool. He's writing about the movies that *Fango* doesn't." That was in 1981, around the time that I started doing my fanzine. As a matter of fact, through his fanzine, I found out about Donald Farmer and all those guys. There were so many of them out back then, it was incredible. It seemed like every other week, somebody was trying to start up a fanzine.

**JS: Had you ever written anything before you started *Stink*?**

**NC:** When I was a kid, I was so into comics that I would attempt

EERIE PUBS: TWICE AS GRUESOME AS WARREN.

HARDCORE MUSIC ZINE.

to draw and write my own. That never went anywhere; it was just more for my own amusement. I didn't really consider trying to review films or anything like that until I got into reading *Gore Gazette*. And there was one called *Ecco*. It was written so intelligently that it was almost like reading college-level essays. I was like, "Man, this guy is writing about the dumbest films, and he's making them sound like classics."

**JS: When I started reading scholarly essays about schlocky films, I kind of felt vindicated. Somebody's finally taking this stuff seriously. Do you feel the same way?**

**NC:** Totally. Especially when I started meeting some of the guys. Michael Gingold is the managing editor at *Fangoria*. I was friends with him as a pen-pal, just trading fanzines. To see how high guys like him and Chris Alexander got—I just think that's so cool. They were street-level guys who just had this knack to write. I eventually found that I had a better talent at writing fiction, so I split off into that in the late nineties. But as far as back then, Rick Sullivan was very funny. He was a street-level guy like me, so I connected with him. And when I saw things like *Ecco* and *Sleazoid Express*, I was just like, "Wow this isn't just junk, it's actually an art form." It's a weird one, but it's definitely an art form. And I really respected everything that Mike Weldon did. That guy has been all over the place. Then there's the stuff like mine. I look back and read some of that stuff and I cringe [laughs]. Then again, it was supposed to be like that. I was a big collector of punk and metal fanzines. Those were just written like, "Yeah, I saw this band last night and they sucked." That's how I wrote, and a lot of people got a kick out of it. I just ran with it.

**JS: You started *Stink* in 1981...**

**NC:** Well, it was first called *Hardgore*. It was half hardcore album and show reviews and half movie reviews. It was a single two-sided sheet of paper that I folded into quarters. I did about six issues of it, and I started *Stink* toward the end of 1981/early 1982. I was around thirteen or fourteen. There were a lot of people doing hardcore magazines.

**JS: Which ones stuck out?**

**NC:** One of the most famous hardcore fanzines was called *Bullshit Monthly*. It was done by a guy named Mike Bullshit. He was one of those guys who

you'd always see hanging out. He used to handwrite the whole fanzine, and it was so freaking funny. I'd be hanging out in front of CBGB's, crying laughing at the way this guy reviewed gigs. A lot of people hated him, but he didn't bother me. In the early days of *Stink*, I would still review some hardcore shows but it was mainly movie reviews. Then of course, around 1983, when my family got our first VCR, that's when I really went haywire.

**JS: Let's talk a little about that.**

**NC:** We had a place here called Mike's Video. It was on Staten Island, but people came from Jersey, from as far north as the Bronx, and even Westchester because he had everything. It was five blocks from my house. By the time they closed, they had like 25,000 titles, and over 10,000 were horror, sci-fi, and fantasy. From reading the old *Fangos*, I couldn't wait to see the Herschell Gordon Lewis films—he had all of them. A lot of people don't remember this, but when VHS came out, brand new tapes were like seventy-nine bucks. Back then, everyone who was into this stuff had two VCRs and would trade tapes. Of course, now I cringe about that. I'm so against bootlegging, it's not even funny. But back then, it was the only way you could see certain films, unless you lived in New York, Los Angeles, or Chicago, where they had a decent video store.

**JS: I had to turn to the gray market to see things like *Cannibal Holocaust*.**

**NC:** I didn't get to see that until sometime in the mid-nineties. Back then, it was a pain in the ass to get on bootleg.

**JS: How did zines like *Stink* find their audience?**

**NC:** Well, this was all before there was the internet. There were a couple of fanzines that would advertise in the back of *Fangoria*, and if my memory serves it, in the back of *Gore Gazette*. It was mainly through word of mouth, through other fanzines. The big thing for me was when Chas. Balun did a fanzine article in an issue of *Deep Red*. It was between that article and an article that Mike Gingold did in *Gorezone*. I wasn't doing mail order; I was mainly selling them in a couple places in Manhattan. I was moving maybe thirty copies. But, after those two articles, my readership was over 200, which was really good for a fanzine. Especially since everybody was sending me one or two bucks an issue, which was pretty cool back then. I

## THE YAK TALKS BACK!

"BACK ISSUES"

ALL BACK ISSUES ARE JUST $1.00 UNLESS OTHERWISE NOTED.

SLIMEPIT #1-Sold Out
" #2-Sold Out
" #3-Sold Out
" #4-Sold Out
" #5-Sold Out
" #6-Sold Out
" #7-Sold Out
" #8-Sold Out
" #9-Sold Out
" #10-Sold Out
" #11-Sold Out
" #12-Sold Out
" #13-Sold Out
" #14-Sold Out
STINK #15-Sold Out
STINK #16-Sold Out
STINK #17-Sold Out
STINK #18-Sold Out
STINK #19-Sold Out
STINK #20-Sold Out
STINK #21-Sold Out
STINK #22-Sold Out
STINK #23-Sold Out
STINK #24-Sold Out
STINK #25-Sold Out
STINK #26-Sold Out
STINK #27-Sold Out
STINK #28-Sold Out
STINK #29-Sold Out
STINK #30-Sold Out
STINK #31-Sold Out
STINK #32-Sold Out
STINK #33-Sold Out
STINK #34-Sold Out
STINK #35-Sold Out
STINK #36-Sold Out
STINK #37-Sold Out
STINK #38-Sold Out
STINK #39-Sold Out
STINK #40-Sold Out
STINK #41-Sold Out
STINK #42-Sold Out
STINK #43-Sold Out
STINK #44-Sold Out
STINK #45-Sold Out
STINK #46-Sold Out
STINK #47-Sold Out
STINK #48-Sold Out

Recommended for fucked redders

STINK #49-Sold Out
STINK #50-Sold Out
STINK #51-Sold Out
STINK #52-Sold Out
STINK #53-Sold Out
STINK #54-Sold Out
STINK #55-Sold Out
STINK #56-Sold Out
STINK #57-Sold Out
STINK #58-Sold Out
STINK #59-Sold Out
STINK #60-Sold Out
STINK #61-Sold Out
STINK #62-Sold Out
STINK #63-Sold Out
STINK #64-Just Sold Out!!
STINK #65-Just sold Out!!
STINK #66-Plenty left/Frankenhooker, Death Nurse, loads of reviews and Sick Fiction.
STINK #67-Plenty left/HOLD Remake, Geek-Maggot [illegible], Sleepover [illegible]re, plus loads of surprizes.
STINK #68-Plenty Left/10 Year Anniversary issue with: The Immortalizer M-3D the movie, Multiple Maniacs, Luther the Geek, loads of cool articles & ads.
STINK #69-Plenty left/[illegible] Akira, Final chapter to [illegible] Fears sick story, loads of fun.
STINK #70-Order 'em now for just a buck!

Send all orders to: STINK FANZINE c/o Nick the Yak/27 Hillcrest Street/ Staten Island, N.Y./10308/USA

Please, CASH ONLY unless out of USA

All issues mailed flat in a protective brown wrapper to keep them from getting fucked up.

the 'zine Brinke likes!!

did Stink for fun—I wasn't thinking about making money off it. I got paid in other ways. Remember back in '88 when that movie *Nekromantik* was the big thing that everybody wanted?

**JS: Yeah.**

**NC:** Someone traded me that because I happened to have *The Wizard of Gore*. I sent it to him in an original hard-shell case because I had a couple of them. He sent me a beautiful copy of *Nekro*. I can't tell you how many films I got because I was able to trade that movie [laughs]. Everybody wanted *Nekromantik*.

**JS: I first read about *Nekromantik* in *Deep Red*. And I'm pretty sure that that's where I found out about *Stink*.**

**NC:** When Chas. reviewed *Stink*, he said, "It's free, but for chrissakes, send the guy something." You wouldn't believe what I got. One guy even sent me a cow's tooth—he was from Texas. My mom was flipping out, because every other day, I was getting packages. Guys were sending me pornos, and T-shirts of their bands and stuff. It was awesome.

**JS: Did you ever have any personal contact with Chas?**

**NC:** I spoke with him on the phone once. I had sent him a letter, thanking him for putting *Stink* in there. I put my phone number on the bottom, and he actually called. I didn't expect it. I just loved that man—to me, he was like the ultimate horror fan. I love guys who aren't ashamed of the genre. Chas. didn't give a crap what anyone thought. He was like, "I'm into horror, and that's it." Now you have all these pansies that say, "I don't write horror, I write dark fiction." There's a negative vibe that goes with being a horror writer or a horror filmmaker.

**JS: You were known as Nick the Yak. Where did that name come from?**

**NC:** That actually had a double meaning. I'm a Sicilian Italian, and my friends always called me "Yak" because I'm so friggin' hairy. The second thing is, when I was in high school, I worked part time in a supermarket. I was always quiet. Not because I was shy, I was like the least shy person that you ever met. But, I didn't know anybody—it was my first job. This guy Jerry and I became friends. I'd go around the store sweeping, and he'd go, "Hey, Nick the Yak." I'm like, "Where did you get that? That's what my friends call me." He called me that because I was quiet. It was funny that my new friend and my old friends came up with that name.

**JS: You know, when I think of Staten Island, I automatically think of Buddy Giovinazzo.**

**NC:** He was like a legend here. He taught at the College of Staten Island. As a matter of fact, I sat right behind him at the 1990 *Fango* con when they did a screening of *Combat Shock*. He shot all those early scenes of Vietnam in the marshlands right by the Staten Island Mall. Every time I drive past it, I just start laughing. He mixed it with stock footage, and it actually looked pretty authentic. But, yeah, he was pretty much a local legend to us film geeks.

**JS: Did you get to see *Combat Shock* when it premiered?**

**NC:** No. It premiered in Manhattan. I'm friends with one of Troma's actors, that big heavy guy, Joe Fleishaker. He told me that at the *Combat Shock* premiere, even for a Troma movie, people were pissed. It was advertised as a *Rambo* rip-off.

**JS: What did your readers think of *Stink*?**

**NC:** Some people loved it. I had readers from all over—people from Australia and Japan. They liked it more than anyone, because they couldn't get half of the movies that we could. But with *Stink*, I really tried to write the reviews like it was your friend telling you how the movie was. I know a lot of the people from the Troma movies, but I used to rip half of those films apart. A lot of them were terrible. I loved the first *Toxic Avenger*, but my friend Joe is in the sequels, and they're all horrendous. I loved the first *Nuke 'em High*, but he's not in it. He's in all the ones that sucked [laughs]. But, I don't know. I think people liked the average-Joe feel to *Stink*. They thought it was funny. When I hated a film, they always got a kick out of how I would write about it. And of course, I got all of that from Rick. Rick Sullivan had the greatest wordplay. I basically modeled myself after him. Eventually, I kind of developed a little bit of my own style.

**JS: When did you start to shift toward fiction?**

**NC:** Well, the last issue of *Stink* came out in early '91. That's around the time I got married. I started working full-time in '89—I didn't have the

time for it anymore. What I did have time for was reading. That's when I decided to try my hand at writing fiction. When you write, you've got to be totally focused on it. At least if you want to write halfway decent fiction. I've been writing fiction since '97 and I just started getting published in 2006. As a matter of fact, just this year [2012], I sold five stories, and I've had two books published. My first novel came out in 2009. It's a slow, tedious process.

**JS: Who are your influences, as far as fiction goes?**

**NC:** I read *The Stand* when I was in the fifth grade. People don't remember this anymore, but the original version of *The Stand* (which I think is the better version) was around 600 pages. It wasn't 1100 pages. I read the updated version, and I don't think it adds anything to the story. I think it wrecks it. But, I read Stephen King, Dean Koontz, and all those guys. In the mid-eighties, the girl I was dating gave me a stocking stuffer of this book called *Night Show* by this guy called Richard Laymon. That novel blew my mind. It had this cinematic style to it. Leisure Books reprinted all of his old eighties books in the 2000s, but for some reason, they didn't reprint that one. I don't know why, I think it's his best book. But really, Richard Laymon was my biggest influence. I thought, "This guy writes like movies. I think I can do this."

**JS: What did you think of the splatterpunk movement?**

**NC:** Splatterpunk was cool. John Skipp was one of the leaders of the splaterpunk movement and I've met him a few times. Great guy.

**JS: He collaborated with Craig Spector.**

**NC:** Yeah. John Skipp's kind of made somewhat of a comeback. He was really messed up on dope for a while. As a matter of fact, he just won a Bram Stoker award for an anthology of demon stories that he published last year. But Skipp and Spector's books were awesome during the whole splatterpunk thing. There was one author named Poppy Z. Brite. She wrote a book called *Exquisite Corpse*. It's considered the first extreme horror novel. Today, you've got guys like Edward Lee and this guy from Vegas named Wrath James White. They're like the modern splatterpunks. They write the extreme stuff now. Ed Lee wrote a book called *Header*,

## The Yak Talks Back!

RECORDED & INDEXED

DRAFT

FIRST PUBLISHED FICTION: "I ALMOST HAD A HEART ATTACK..."

which was made into a movie. It's the most brutal thing that I've ever read (I hear the film is quite intense, too). It's like the equivalent to ten *Nekromantik* films [laughs]. It's the fiction equivalent of, "How much can you take?"

**JS: What was the first story of yours that was published?**

**NC:** There's a magazine that's still going called *Hacker's Source*. It's a really low budget magazine that's based out of Texas. In 2004 or 2005, they bought a ghost story I wrote called "Non-Foods". It was about a supermarket. It got published in there. When it came out, I cringed because they were supposed to edit something and they didn't. It made the whole story look so amateur and I'm glad it's forgotten. The first pro-sale I had was a story called "Toes". It came out in 2006—it was in an anthology called *Deathgrip: Exit Laughing*. The reason that I'm very proud of that book is because I'm in there with William Nolan, the author who wrote all the *Logan's Run* books. I almost had a heart attack when I saw my name on the roster with him.

**JS: How many attempts did it take you to get something published?**

**NC:** A lot of people will tell you hundreds, but I must have submitted a good sixty times before I sold something. So, that's not bad. Then again, the competition's more fierce now, thanks to the internet. Now you've got people submitting who would never have submitted before. The slush pile is three times as high. My friend L. L. Soares and I did a humorous horror anthology called *Dark Jesters*, and we got over 200 submissions. It was brutal. I don't think I'll ever edit an anthology again. We were only picking ten stories, and we had some top-name guys. John Skipp and Ellen Datlow do several anthologies a year. I don't know how they read that much.

**JS: How did the *Horror Fiction Review* come about?**

**NC:** In 2003, I had hernia surgery and I was home for six weeks. After four weeks, I was sitting around, and I just had that itch to do a zine again. I looked at my bookcase—I had around 400 books that I'd never reviewed so I started to. I put out about seventeen print issues from 2003 to 2008. All of these publishers started sending me review copies. I can't even tell you the last time I paid for a book. And now, the thing is online. I've got around five people reviewing for the site. Right now, I've got a mountain

of books on my computer.

**JS: What are your feelings about converting to an eZine?**

**NC:** I went into it kicking and screaming, but one of my favorite fanzines in the eighties was called *Temple of Schlock*.

**JS: By Chris Poggiali.**

**NC:** Yeah. And right now, that is the best movie blog on the internet. And to me, it's even better because he puts new stuff up every week. To me, that's the best example of a zine that became a successful blog. For a while, Michael Weldon was doing it. He had an online presence somewhat, but I think he's vanished from the face of the earth.

**JS: Where did you get the idea for your first novel, *Don of the Dead*?**

**NC:** When I saw *Dawn of the Dead*, my friends and I were all Italian. We said, "We should make a zombie-gangster movie called *Don of the Dead*." Years later, they said, "You should write a book about that," so I did.

**JS: When did you make the decision to jump from writing short stories to novels?**

**NC:** Well, I'm still doing both. Most guys who write novels don't do shorts. Shorts are really a way to get your name out there. My favorite author is a guy named Bentley Little. He published shorts in several horror fiction magazines in the early eighties. He just built such a massive following—he was so off the wall and different. By the time his first novel came out in 1990, he already had a built-in fan base. As a matter of fact, I just bought his twenty-second novel yesterday. I'm still a big fan of his.

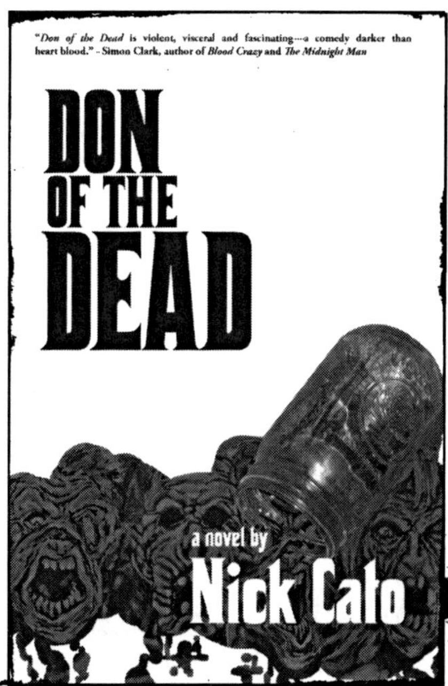

"*Don of the Dead* is violent, visceral and fascinating—a comedy darker than heart blood." – Simon Clark, author of *Blood Crazy* and *The Midnight Man*
DON OF THE DEAD
a novel by
Nick Cato


**JS: Do you prefer writing novels over short stories?**

**NC:** Believe it or not, I prefer doing novellas. My latest, *The Apocalypse of Peter*, was released in June, 2012. Novellas are basically like a quarter of the length of a novel. They're usually around 100 or 125 pages. Some of the best horror stories that I've read over the last fifteen years have been in novella form. When you write a novella, you can get a little more descriptive than you can in a short story, but you still can't have any filler in it because it

sticks out like a sore thumb. There's a writer from Ohio named Gary Braunbeck. He had a novella called *In the Midnight Museum*. It's one of the best books that I've ever read. I like working in that length. I'm lucky that I'm at the point now, where I was actually invited to write for six anthologies in the next year or two. I still submit stories to other places, but I'm at a decent level right now.

**JS: Where do your ideas come from?**

**NC:** Everywhere and anywhere. Most seem to just "pop" into my head at times when there's no paper handy…although now I can type them into my cell phone.

**JS: What's your writing schedule like?**

**NC:** I try to get in at least 2000 words a day, which some people think is hard. I have a minimum of 1500 a day. I really don't write fiction on weekends because I write a movie column for a website called *Cinema Knife Fight*. That takes up my weekend time.

**JS: You've got something new coming out called *Antibacterial Pope*.**

**NC:** Yeah, that was released in August, 2012. That was released as an imprint of my own press, so technically, it's a self-published book. By the way, there's this stigma. I've had guys tell me, from the time I started writing, not to ever self-publish, and I haven't. But now that all these main presses like Leisure Books have gone under, some of the biggest writers I know are self-publishing. I asked all of them, "Is this cool?" They were like, "Yeah, go for it." I'm really into this genre called bizarro fiction. Some of the biggest bizarro writers self-publish.

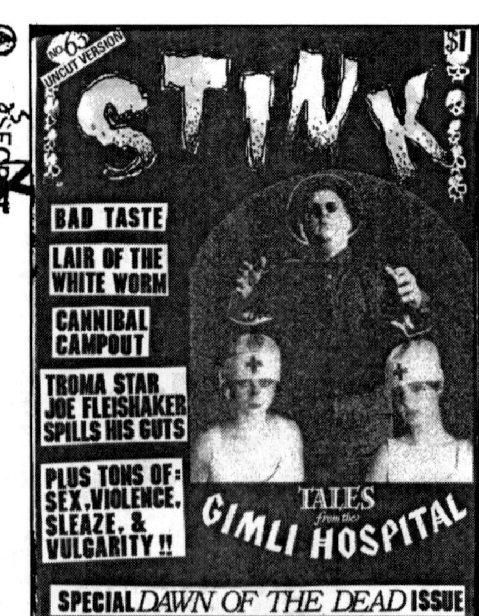


**JS: What is bizarro fiction?**

**NC:** A lot of it is horror oriented, but it's like David Lynch stuff. It's really strange. There's a guy named Tim Waggoner who writes horror, but it's considered bizarro. It's just so off the wall. But, *Antibacterial Pope* is a collection of super-short stories. Some of them aren't even a page long. The second half of the book is six stories, four previously published and two new.

**JS: Can you tell me a little about Novello Publishers?**

**NC:** It's a small press I

STINK
THE SICKEST SLEAZE-FILM 'ZINE IN THE WORLD
#68
FEB. '91
$1.00
WARNING!! Do Not store this 'zine in area's over 120°

1981 10 YEAR 1991
ANNIVERSARY

BROUGHT TO LIFE IN BLOOD COLOR
Box Office Spectaculars, INC. Presents
BLOOD FEAST
Introducing CONNIE MASON
YOU SAW HER IN PLAYBOY
Adult HORROR!

WE look Back at the films & theatres that keep us DROOLING for more!!

2ND TOXIC MONTH!
MIDNIGHT FRI. & SAT.
"WONDERFUL! A HOWLER!" —Village Voice
"HILARIOUSLY TASTELESS!" —N.Y. Daily News
THE TOXIC AVENGER

48th SMASH WEEK
BASKET CASE
Pink Flamingos
GEEK MAGGOT BINGO
a different set of jaws.
THE ROCKY HORROR PICTURE SHOW
8th Street Playhouse
A FEAST OF FIENDS!
"IF YOU ONLY SEE ONE MOVIE THIS YEAR, IT SHOULD BE FRANKENHOOKER!" — BILL MURRAY
FRANKENHOOKER
NIGHT of the DEMO

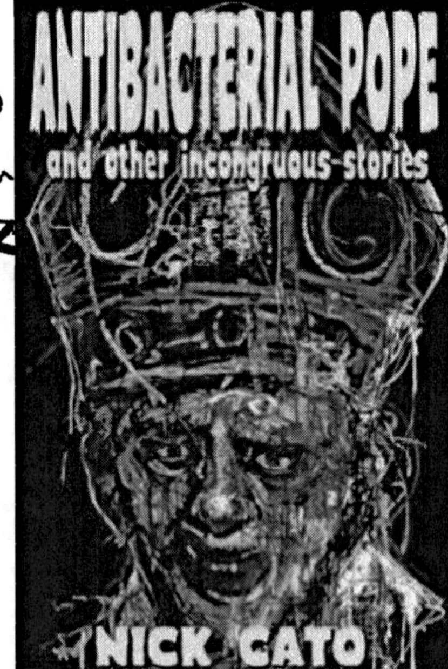

started in 2005 dedicated to humorous horror fiction. We haven't released too many titles, but the ones we have received good reviews. We have two or three titles coming out in 2013, including our first full length novel. We also branched out into bizarre fiction, and the novel we're releasing is along the lines of a literary tale, but at its core Novello Publishers likes the funny stuff.

**JS: What else do you have in the works?**

**NC:** I'm almost finished with my latest novella, titled *The Last Porno Theatre*, which will hopefully find a home before the Summer. I'm also just past the halfway mark on a collaborative novel titled *The House of Exorcism*, which I'm writing with author L.L. Soares. And of course there are plenty of short stories in the works.

On the nonfiction front, my column for the *Cinema Knife Fight* website, "Suburban Grindhouse Memories," may have its first fifty reviews collected as an eBook edition sometime in 2013.

*SHRIEK SPECIAL* NUMBER 3: "UPTOWN ZOMBIES" BY JIM WHITING AND STEVE NILES. PUBLISHED BY FANTACO ENTERPRISES, INC.

# Jim Whiting

## Slaughterhouse

RECORDED & INDEXED

DRAFT

In 1988, a strange magazine appeared on the rack at the corner store near my house. The place was within walking distance, and I'd make the trek every other day to see if they had anything new. I had my favorites: *Mad*, *Cracked*, and anything that was related to kung fu. The place on the corner—a liquor store called The Golden Rule— never carried *Fangoria*. I had to bike an extra mile or two for that. But it did carry a magazine called *Slaughterhouse*.

The magazine immediately caught my eye. John Carpenter's *They Live* was the hot movie of the day and it was featured on the cover. The mag also promised a "Horrifying Independent Section" as well as the latest on horror comic books. I bought the thing on the spot and took it home.

It was instantly apparent that *Slaughterhouse* was quite different than *Fangoria*. The editorial alone sent the message, loud and clear:

"They said we wouldn't. They said we couldn't. The other horror magazine even said don't, but we did it. The beast of horror magazines has been unleashed. Trick or treat..."

And shit howdy, what do you know? They were right! The *Slaughterhouse* boys told no lies and pulled no punches. For a mainstream mag, *Slaughterhouse* was a breath of fresh air. Not only did this issue have an interview with *Street Trash* star Vic Noto, it also had a feature on FantaCo's crazy horror comic book *Gore Shriek*. For a kid like me, this was heaven. I could literally walk down to the corner, saunter up to the newsstand, and buy the latest issue of *Slaughterhouse*, whenever it appeared.

And then, one day it was gone. I asked the man behind the counter if the new issue of *Slaughterhouse* had arrived, and he looked at me with blank eyes. "*Slaughterhouse*?"

"Yeah. You used to sell it here."

The guy obviously had no idea of what I was talking about, so I walked home.

Through the years, I often wondered what happened to the mag. Rumors were flying that the Starlog Group had launched *Toxic Horror* to knock it off the stands. It didn't seem fair to me. I really liked *Slaughterhouse*, as crude and strange as it was. It was almost as if a fanzine had gone pro. And I always loved their attitude: Oh, you mean there's *another* horror rag out there? Step up to the ring and bring it!

One of the editors for *Slaughterhouse* was a guy named Jim Whiting. From what I could tell, he was a comic book fan, and his artwork graced its pages on a regular basis. Shortly after the magazine's demise, I recognized his name and artwork in a number of FantaCo publications. And then... that was it. Jim Whiting disappeared, much like the magazine that introduced me to him. Who was Jim Whiting? What was the story behind *Slaughterhouse*? Where was he now? Let's take one more walk to that old corner store and try to shed some light on the subject...

The following interview was conducted via telephone on May 12, 2012.

**JOHN SZPUNAR: You grew up in New York, right?**

**JIM WHITING:** Yeah, in the Albany area. Actually, in the same city that FantaCo was located. I worked for them for around four years, or so.

**JS: Yeah, I was just talking to Tom Skulan about that the other day.**

**JW:** When I was a kid, I'd go there all the time and buy all of my comics there. Later on, I moved to New York City for about ten years. I got married and had a daughter, and in order to be closer to family, I moved back to Albany and started working in FantaCo's publications department. I was doing Clive Barker stuff, pitching comic book ideas and was bringing in new talent.

**JS: I get the idea that you were always a fan of comics and horror films.**

**JW:** Yeah. When I was four or five, there wasn't any cable, but we did have one station that ran *Chiller Theater*. It was on at 11:00 every Saturday night. They would show the old Universal movies and they'd throw in some schlock horror stuff. And at four or five years old, that was enough to scare the pants off of you. I had an older brother who would read *Creepy*, *Eerie*, and *Famous Monsters*, so I was exposed to that stuff at a young age. We'd go to the drive-ins quite a bit and see a lot of the Roger Corman films. It just perpetuated the whole genre for me—I loved it.

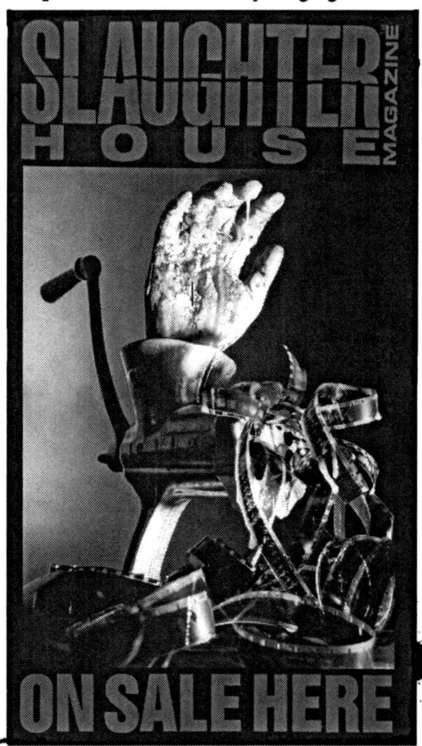


**JS: What other comics were you reading?**

**JW:** I loved the Marvel Comics stuff. A lot of the horror stuff that they were doing in the seventies was pretty good.

**JS: Can you tell me a little about how you got started in publishing?**

**JW:** Sure. I went to college at New York's School of Visual Arts and I didn't have a lot of money. I wanted to be a comic book artist. Well, everyone at SVA wanted to be a comic book artist. They all wanted to draw like Neal Adams, which was boring as hell. I switched to fine arts—it was the eighties, and things were beginning to happen with Frank Miller's stuff, and all that. So, I switched my major and ran out of money. I got a job doing plumbing and they gave me a free apartment. Little did I know that it was all mafia owned. I was living in a crack building. I had a friend who had a gallery in Chinatown. I called her and said, "I've got to get out of this place." She got me a loft in the Bowery—at the time, lofts were relatively inexpensive. She had a friend who published. He worked for Harvey Publications. I don't know if you're familiar with them.

**JS: Not really.**

**JW:** They were actually doing softcore porn. He used to work for them and then he started publishing on his own. I went to work for him while I was in school. He was a Chinese guy and he had a Jewish partner. They basically published softcore porn and wrestling magazines.

**JS: What kind of work were you doing over there?**

**JW:** I learned to do design. And a lot of time, you'd write the copy yourself. You'd send it off to the typesetter, they'd send it back, and you'd lay it out. After about four years working there, I pitched them the idea for *Slaughterhouse*, and they were fine with it.

**JS: You were stepping on *Fangoria*'s turf.**

**JW:** Yeah. But, I didn't want *Slaughterhouse* to be so much like *Fangoria*. I was influenced more by *Famous Monsters*. I wanted to update that, and to add a lot of the cheesecake stuff that was going on. And at the time, there were a lot of things that horror magazines didn't have—they didn't have comic reviews and they didn't do a lot of book reviews. And *Fangoria* didn't want to have anything to do with a lot of the underground stuff that we were reporting. That gave us an edge.

**JS: You had a co-editor named Mark Gibson.**

**JW:** Yeah. I was good with content and I was good with ideas, but I needed someone to help me who was a go-getter. I hired Mark to co-edit with me. He worked the phones to get things happening, and I worked on the creative end. He was good at getting through to people on the phone and setting up interviews with people like John Carpenter.

**JS: How did you go about putting together a staff of writers?**

**JW:** Well, in the beginning, we wrote it ourselves. I had a few friends who dabbled in writing and who were into the genre. I had a friend who read a lot of horror books. He wanted to write, so I asked him to write book reviews. But once we put the magazine out there, people started sending us stuff.

**JS: I'm guessing that names like Roy Weitzner and Nathan Stanes were pseudonyms...**

**JW:** Yeah, that was us. We didn't want to look like we wrote everything [laughs].

**JS: How did you work PR? Was it difficult to get interviews with the people you wanted?**

**JW:** In the beginning, it was pretty limited. Honestly, a lot of the low budget guys were willing to talk a little more than the bigger guys. But, the bigger studios were pretty hungry for promotion. They'd send us slides and press releases. You'd get a press agent's name, call them up, and keep bugging them—"Can you get me an interview?" We were trying to get on the press junket. So, in the beginning, it was hard, but after we had an issue in our hands, they'd say, "OK, they're not small- time. We'll send them some stuff." More doors began to open up.

**JS: You guys did an interesting article on Stephen King.**

**JW:** Stephen King wouldn't do an interview with us. We couldn't get him. My friend wrote an article about getting drunk and trying to get an interview with him. It was pretty much complete fiction. We really wanted to do a *Pet Semetary* story. We had all of these great pictures, but what could we do with them? We ran a story about trying to get the interview, but not being able to get it. If we couldn't get what we wanted, we would just find a creative way to use the material we had.

**JS: *Slaughterhouse* covered a lot of the New York independents. How close were you to guys like Roy Frumkes and Nathan Schiff?**

**JW:** Well, we got to hang out with them. They'd invite us over, and show us parts of their movies. I got to know a couple of the actors from *Street Trash*. Vic Noto was just as crazy as his character.

SLAUGHTERHOUSE

DRAFT

RECORDED & INDEXED

TRADE AD FOR *SLAUGHTERHOUSE*.

# AMERICA'S MOST NOTORIOUS MAGAZINE

CELEBRATES ITS FIRST YEAR IN PRINT WITH AN ALL STAR CAST, INCLUDING ARTICLES WRITTEN BY HORROR QUEEN'S LINNEA QUIGLEY AND BRINKE STEVENS!

"From film to fiction to comic books and beyond, modern horror has many faces... Slaughterhouse covers them all with enthusiasm, affection and–when needed–the occasional well aimed pie."
Archie Goodwin
Editor
DC COMICS

"I get a kick out of Slaughterhouse... I especially like the magazine's attitude."
Kim Thompson
Co-Publisher
FANTAGRAPHICS BOOKS

"Slaughterhouse is consistently one of our best selling magazines."
FANTACO ENTERPRISES

"Thick, glossy and professional."
MELODY MAKER MAGAZINE

SLAUGHTER
HOUSE
MAGAZINE
RESERVE YOUR COPY NOW...OR ELSE!!

He'd come up to the office and tell us all of these stories—he was going to do this and he was going to do that. I'd ask other people about it, and they'd say, "Oh, my God… who knows, with him?" He was quite the character. But, I hung out with a few of those guys. They were local, and you could just drive out to New Jersey and talk to them.

**JS: You mentioned earlier that you wanted *Slaughterhouse* to cover a lot of the cheesecake aspects of horror.**

**JW:** I was a big fan of that. I'd go out and I'd meet Linnea Quigley, Monique Gabrielle, and Brinke Stevens. It was fun.

**JS: You also mentioned that you wanted to cover horror fiction.**

**JW:** I was reading a lot of fanzines, and a lot of them were book-connected. And I got invited to some of the Stoker Awards, and got to meet Harlan Ellison and some of the other writers that were there. I just thought that if you're going to cover horror, why not cover everything? I liked the idea of finding young talent and giving them a place to go, so I started publishing fiction. Unfortunately, I didn't have a big budget to pay people a lot. All I could really offer them was a place to be published. The publisher didn't want to put out any money to pay anybody. He was publishing a magazine, and that was costing him a small fortune. Anytime I mentioned paying anybody to do anything, he would just freak out. He was a big, heavy guy who was connected to the Jewish mafia. If you mentioned taking any money away from him, he'd get pissed.

**JS: I always enjoyed the cover designs for *Slaughterhouse*.**

**JW:** We were trying to make the covers look really classy. We'd do two covers for every issue—when we sent out the color separations, there'd be two covers, and we'd decide which one we wanted to go with when we got things back. We did a Freddy cover, but we also had a Pinhead cover as an alternative. It looked incredible, but we didn't publish it.

**JS: What was the reasoning behind that decision?**

**JW:** The publisher insisted that Freddy would sell better. I pushed for the Pinhead cover, but we didn't get it.

**JS: Can you recall any of the other covers that didn't see print?**

**JW:** Well, let's see… The alternative to the Jason cover was something from an independent movie. Again, that didn't fly. I tried to make the cover of the first issue look like the cover of an old issue of *Famous Monsters*. It was sort of a nod to the way they looked during the middle of their run. Here's another thing—I had a friend who was a photographer. He would go out to slaughterhouses and take pictures. In one of our ads, we ran a picture of a hook coming down from the ceiling, along with a saw that was used to cut up the meat. That was taken in a real slaughterhouse.

**JS: No kidding?**

**JW:** Yeah. He was working with me on the design. He did some really interesting stuff—once, he recorded the sound of some pigs being slaughtered. I mixed it to music, and put some special effects over it. It

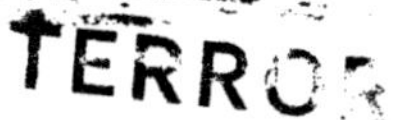

sounded like someone was screaming at the top of their lungs. I put it in the background of this thing that I recorded in my home studio. We actually took some promo pictures of a meat grinder with hamburger meat coming out of it. There was a rubber hand going into it. We'd do a lot of that stuff.

**JS: *Slaughterhouse* always seemed a little more reckless than *Fangoria*. Did you ever run into any censorship problems?**

**JW:** Yeah. We ended up getting banned on a couple of occasions. A couple of issues were sent back because they were too risqué. Again, we were trying to compete head-on with *Fangoria*. Their publisher was engrained in the publishing field, and when we started running cheesecake photos, they called up the distributor. They told them that we were running softcore material, and we got pulled off the stands.

**JS: Were they complaining about the picture of Linnea Quigley from *Hollywood Chainsaw Hookers*?**

**JW:** Yep. We ran full page photo of Linnea Quigley, and she had nothing on except paint. That almost put the nail in the coffin.

**JS: How many copies of that issue were returned?**

**JW:** Out of 100,000 magazines, 70,000 were sent back. The publisher was pretty pissed.

**JS: I've often wondered if the Starlog group launched *Toxic Horror* in order to kick magazines like *Slaughterhouse* off of the newsstands.**

**JW:** Oh yeah, they did. And a couple of other horror magazines came out around the same time. We were all fighting for space on the newsstands and we started racing each other to get cover stories. The studios would send us photos, and we wanted to make sure they were exclusive—no one else could have them. It started to get very competitive—we wanted to beat *Fangoria*. We wanted to squash them. Mark would say this to people over the phone, and I was like, "What are you doing? You can't tell people that!" The enthusiasm that opens doors can also shut them—it can

bring the hammer down on your head. We were pushing the envelope, and they squashed us. We put out the fifth issue, and that was it.

**JS: I'd imagine that you had already started working on the sixth issue.**

**JW:** Yeah. I still have the proofs for it. The cover was from *The Phantom of the Opera*, with Robert Englund. The whole issue was done. It was already color-separated and ready to go to press, but they pulled the plug.

UNPUBLISHED SIXTH ISSUE.

**JS: What did you do after *Slaughterhouse* folded?**

**JW:** Well, by that point I was working independently as a publisher. I wasn't a full-time employee anymore, I was contracting. I was basically working for a bunch of different publishers and designing their magazines. And by that point, I was working a lot with Steve Niles.

**JS: You eventually started doing a lot of comics work. Did your years at SVA help you to make any contacts?**

**JW:** When I first started in illustration, I went into one class and they wanted us to draw old *Nancy* cartoons. The teacher was just like, "*Nancy! Nancy! Nancy*'s great!" I was like, "I don't want to draw *Nancy!*" But, they were also big fans of Art Spiegelman and *Raw.* I had a friend who was interning with Art Spiegelman. He took me over to his studio and I got to hang out there. It was nice, but I probably got to meet more artists through *Slaughterhouse*. I got to interview Bill Sienkiewicz and go to his studio. And when I was working for FantaCo, they were partnering a lot with Kevin Eastman. At the time, the Ninja Turtles were making a lot of money, and he was doing Tundra Publishing. He would throw huge parties and all the artists would be there. You'd have everyone from Steve Bissette to Bill Sienkiewicz—they were all doing books for him. For me as a comic fan, it was like a dream come true. I got to hang out with these guys and get to know them.

**JS: Let's talk a little bit about your years with FantaCo.**

**JW:** I went to work for them in the early nineties. I was working a lot with Steve Niles. I met him through *Slaughterhouse*—he sent me a set of Clive Barker lithographs. He was a really cool guy and we became

RECORDED & INDEXED

UNUSED ALTERNATE ARTWORK FOR NUMBER 2.

really good friends. I'd go out to Washington and stay with him. Anyway, he was working with Barker at the time. He was also working for Eclipse; he was helping with the Barker adaptations that they were publishing.

**JS: The two of you did some comics together.**

**JW:** He wanted to write comics and we started working together—I was drawing most of them. We must have done seven or eight comics. I still have some unpublished stuff. Anyway, he helped me to reach out to Barker. The *Hellraiser* stuff was really hot, and Barker was really hot, too. He helped me set up some interviews. At the same time, I got a call from Mike Brown, who Clive had authorized to run his fan club. I helped him put together *Dread* magazine, and I helped him organize the fan club. So, when I went to work for FantaCo, I sort of took all that stuff over there. FantaCo was publishing *Dread*, and they were doing Barker T-shirts. In 1991, they sent me and Steve Niles out to FantaCon to negotiate Clive Barker doing the *Night of the Living Dead* adaption.

**JS: The *Night of the Living Dead: London* comic?**

**JW:** Right. We went out there and locked that down. I ended up lettering it, which was kind of fun. I also did the layouts, and I drew the logo by hand.

**JS: I've always considered those years to be the start of FantaCo's second wave in publishing.**

**JW:** By that time, FantaCo didn't have a relationship with Steve Bissette anymore. They were pretty much at odds with a lot of the old creators who had worked there. They had been out of publishing for a little while and they didn't want to publish anymore. But, I kind of talked them into it. We ended up doing a lot of stuff.

**JS: *Slaughterhouse* seemed to have pretty close ties to FantaCo.**

**JW:** When we started out, I called them up and said, "Look, do you want a free ad? We'll give you the back cover." That eventually led to a relationship with Tom. Like I said before, I always wanted to be a comic book artist. *Slaughterhouse* opened up a lot of doors.

**JS: Tell me about some of the other titles that FantaCo were putting out.**

**JW:** Steve Niles was doing the *King of the Dead* series. It was somewhat based on *Night of the Living Dead*, but this was a "king zombie" situation. He's smart, and he rules all the other zombies. It ran for four or five issues.

**JS: What about *Scab*? You did the artwork for that.**

**JW:** That was Steve's story. He had that floating around—I think he had the story done when he gave it to me. I went down to Washington, DC and I brought fifty rolls of film. I shot the whole DC area so I could draw the background. I wanted to get a feel of what things looked like—I took pictures of rooftops and things like that. Someone came out with another *Scab* and we had to send them a cease and dissect. It was a skateboarding hero or something [laughs].

**JS: What was *Shriek Special*?**

**JW:** I would get a lot of solicitations from people who had short stories. I tried to combine them into some kind of an anthology. FantaCo had already done *Gore Shriek* earlier, with Bruce Fuller and people like that. So, rather than doing a regular book, we did specials. We started doing a lot of stuff—I put one book out called *Kill Me Slowly*. It was all erotic horror. We did some anthologies of fiction pieces. It involved people from *Hellraiser*, at one point. I think it was a *Dread* special—it was all fiction written by the director of *Hellraiser 3*, Steve, Doug Bradley, and a couple of other people. Clive got mad because I ran a picture of a real mouse that

Attachment [TOP:] *SCAB*, COVER ART BY JAMES WHITING. [BOTTOM:] *KING OF THE DEAD*, THE SECOND WAVE OF FANTACO HORROR COMICS.

had been dissected. He didn't think that we should show real gore. My father was a photographer and I inherited a lot of his stuff. Some of it was moody and dark, and sometimes I'd throw it into the anthologies.

**JS: Why did you stop doing comics?**

**JW:** You know, one of the things that happened while I was working there was that the comic book market got so bad. Things kind of imploded. Basically, there was just one comic book distributor left. And the only way to sell books was to include sex. It was fun in the beginning; there was a little bit of a mix to it. But then it started going the other way, where it all had to be sex, sex, sex. I didn't like it, and I didn't like what I was doing. I was creating artwork to sell books, I wasn't creating artwork to do what I liked. I didn't want to do it anymore. I got a job doing graphic design and just got out of it.

**JS: What are you doing these days?**

**JW:** I'm still a full-time graphic designer. I still draw and I try to make some music—I try to stay creative. I still follow some horror stuff. I don't go too deep into it, but I keep my ears and eyes open to what's going on, particularly in music and movies. It's funny—I also teach yoga a couple times a week here in Albany. It's great stuff for de-stressing, particularly after spending all of those *Slaughterhouse* years staying up all night drinking coffee and smoking cigarettes for six hours straight, trying to meet deadlines. It's just a great way to de-stress...

# Chapter Twenty-Two

ART BY LYNDAL FERGUSON.

# TIM PAXTON

## MONSTER INTERNATIONAL!

im Paxton is a scholar in every sense of the word. A lifelong monster fanatic, he began his publishing career in the 1970s with a nifty little zine called *Photo Fiends*. In 1987, Tim (and co-editor Dave Todarello) upped the ante with *Video Voice*, and the pair was soon responsible for a plethora of wild and crazy monster mags.

With *Video Voice*, *Monster!*, and *Naked! Screaming! Terror!* going strong (and, for a short time, running simultaneously), Paxton seemed to be on a mad mission to write about every movie he came across. He raised the stakes yet again when he added *Highball* to the mix.

Alas, as Chaucer profoundly stated, "There is an end to everything, to good things as well." With rising printing costs knocking at his door, Paxton decided to pull the curtain down, shortly after publishing a beautiful double issue of *Monster! International/Highball*.

As we all know well, the things that we bury don't always remain dead. In 2012, Tim Paxton returned to the scene with *Weng's Chop*, a sharp and sturdy zine co-edited by Brian Harris.

As mentioned above, Tim Paxton is a scholar. His reviews and essays on Asian and Indian genre cinema are some of the most detailed that I've ever come across, and his love and obsession for said films rings true with every word that he types. That same sentiment rang true when I spoke to him last Winter.

The following interview was conducted via telephone on February 16, 2012; edited & revised January, 2013.

---

**TIM PAXTON:** I grew up in Oberlin, Ohio, which is about thirty miles west of Cleveland. I was born in 1962, and was basically influenced by an odd assortment of monster movie hosts. My mom was a big comic book fan, so that didn't hurt, either [laughs].

**JOHN SZPUNAR: Did she have a collection of old comics?**

**TP:** She used to, but the story is that her roommate in college tossed them all out. But she never would complain—she encouraged us to collect comics and books. She also loved old monster movies; growing up in the forties, she would watch monster movies in the theater. She was pretty much a hardcore media fan. So, that kind of fed into things. I was never one of these neglected media collectors.

**JS: Were any of your siblings fans of horror movies?**

**TP:** We are all, in one form or another, fans of fantasy films and monster films figure into that as well. Six kids and one big couch. When some Universal monster movie played on TV it was almost always a family gathering. So, yeah, it's in the Paxton genes.

**JS: Were there any Super-8 monster movies around your house?**

**TP:** Yeah. We would either watch them on 8mm or Super-8mm film that our family would buy when we would go on vacation. Almost every gift shop had them—you could buy 8mm movies of Niagara Falls, or whatever. They would also have regular movies—monster movies. And, growing up around Cleveland, we had five monster movie shows on TV every weekend. You could actually plop your butt in front of the television, starting on Friday night, and go until Sunday morning.

**JS: Who were your local horror hosts?**

**TP:** I barely remember this one guy named Ghoulardi. I'm more familiar with The Ghoul, who was more or less the follow up to Ghoulardi. We had a guy named Superhost, who was actually on for almost twenty years. We still have Big Chuck. The show used to be called *The Hoolihan and Big Chuck Show*, but now it's called *Big Chuck and Lil' John*. And then, we had this guy named Sir Graves Ghastly.

**JS: We had him in Detroit. I remember talking about him with the girl who sat next to me in kindergarten. I was really young...**

**TP:** He was on in the late seventies/ early eighties. I used to draw pictures and send them in to the guy. He was always willing to show your photos or drawings on his gallery. We had another guy who didn't last very long called Dr. Alucard. Then, there was *Creature Feature*. It always showed up after wrestling—that was a great lead-in [laughs]. Finally, we had something called *The Twelve Noon Monster Movie Show*. We would be sucked into TV-land for a good forty-eight hours.

**JS: Were they running the *Ultraman* and *Johnny Sokko* stuff in your area?**

**TP:** Oh, yeah. Cleveland was great for UHF stations. We had six of them, and three of them showed that sort of stuff. I grew up on *8th Man*, *Astro Boy*, *Marine Boy*, and *Johnny Sokko and his Flying Robot*. *Ultraman* was my favorite. We would always get into an argument—who would beat who, Ultraman or Johnny Sokko's robot? When I was in high school, I was heavily into *Star Blazers*. As an adult, I'll still sit and watch it if I can't find anything interesting when I'm flipping through the channels.

**JS: When I was a kid, all of my favorite TV shows were from Japan, but I was too young to make the connection.**

**TP:** I just turned fifty a couple of weeks ago, and I'm still sucked into shows like that. To me, monster movies and fantasy movies are all mythology. I grew up in a household that was equal parts Buddha statues and equal parts Christ hanging on the wall. It was a mish-mashed hippy/ Christian/Buddhist household. And Oberlin itself is an extremely liberal town—there was always weird stuff going on. When I look at these movies, they're like a whole different mythology. I mean, to me, the whole *Godzilla* thing is natural. It would be natural to have giant monsters running around. That's why I would never laugh at them. To me, they're the new gods.

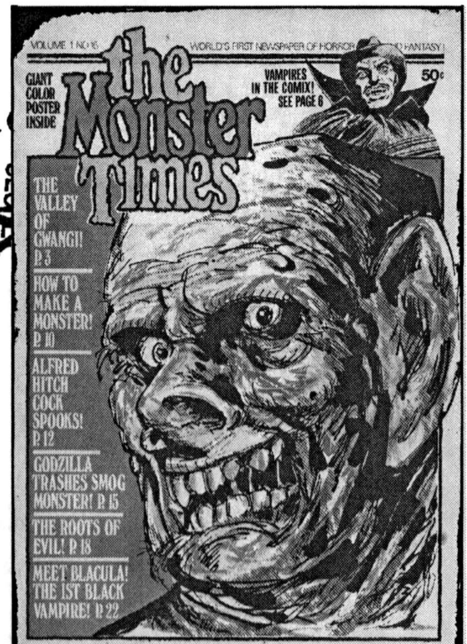


**JS: You mentioned comic books. What were your favorites?**

**TP:** I liked the *Hulk* and stuff like that, but I was a huge fan of Charlton Comics. Charlton had all of the ghost titles, and those were the things I liked. I loved the artists—I'm still a huge fan of Steve Ditko. He still puts stuff out independently. It's pretty weird, but it's

cool stuff. And of course, I liked *Famous Monsters of Filmland*. I had a subscription to that when I was in junior high school. And then, there was *Castle of Frankenstein* and the *Monster Times*. That was probably the best magazine—no one ever seems to remember it.

**JS: The *Monster Times*?**

**TP:** Yeah. The *Monster Times* was awesome. It went from '72 to '76. It covered everything—comic books and movie, and it had really intelligent book reviews. The *Monster Times* was great, but it did look like a mess. It looked like *Rolling Stone* did when it first came out. It was basically newspaper paper stock folded in half.

**JS: What were the newsstands like in your neighborhood?**

**TP:** We had two drugstores here, and they would compete with what they had on the racks. It was a smorgasbord. They also had wrestling magazines, *Creem* magazine, and all of that stuff. You know, another thing that was really influential to me was *Witches Tales* and all of the other horror titles that weren't from Warren. They were reprints from the fifties, and they had all of this really gross crap [laughs].

**JS: The Eerie Pubs. Tom Skulan was talking about those. He said that they disturbed him so much that he ended up burning his copies.**

**TP:** [laughs] I had nightmares, but I didn't burn them! I loved those things. And I was lucky—I was at a Chiller convention and I was talking to Steve Bissette. I noticed a table with some artwork on it. I went over to the table and discovered that it had the original covers to the Eerie stuff. I was wondering why they looked really weird. It turns out that they were paste-ups.

**JS: That's incredible.**

**TP:** Yeah. I'm sure they were from the later period. I wish I would have been on my game and taken photos.

**JS: What was your first exposure to fanzines?**

**TP:** That would be with comic books. I used to go to comic book conventions in the early seventies. We used to print up ditto comics—we'd draw our own superheroes and print them up. That was the first time that I saw any kind of comic fanzines. I was kind of aware of movie fanzines because the *Monster Times*

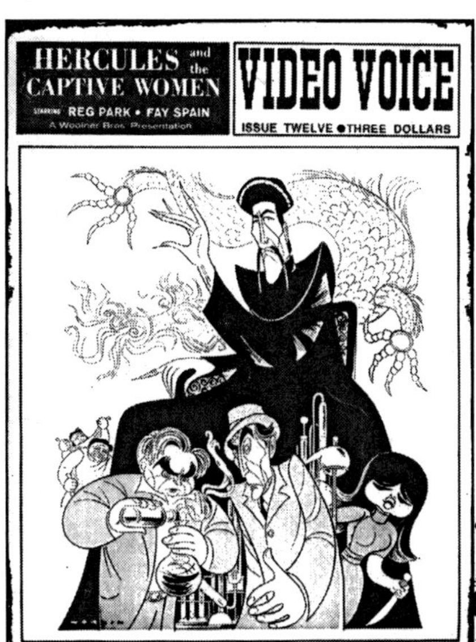

RECORDED & INDEXED

DRAFT

## INTRODUCTION:
### ARMED AND READY FOR BATTLE

Remember when I said that the last issue was the 100% reconditioned VIDEO VOICE? Well this issue is the NEW, IMPROVED and RE-VAMPED one! Dave and I have worked long and hard on this one to try and bring you, dear readers, something akin to our very flesh and blood. VIDEO VOICE #11 has to be our most thought-out and carefully constructed work to date. No, we haven't sold out our fanzine origins. We're just fan-ish examples of perfection.

**Our cover:** Paul Blaisdell as THE SHE CREATURE.

**NEXT ISSUE:**
Fanzine Editors speak out, suprise interviews, and crazed reviews. See you in October!

# TABLE OF CONTENTS



**VIDEO*VOICE** is published four times a year by KRONOS Productions, MPO Box 67, Oberlin, Ohio 44074-0067, USA.
Single copy cost - $3.00 (ppd) Subscriptions - $12.00/yr.
Please make checks and money orders payable to Timothy Paxton.
VIDEO VOICE is looking for contributors. If interested please contact us at the above address.
Poobah and Head Honcho: Tim Paxton.
co/publisher: Dave Todarello.
Copy Editor: Douglas Brooks.
Last-minute assistant Copy Editor: Jeff Francé
Staff: Lisa Waltz, GPA, Dave Szurek, and Mark Rollie.

**WARNING!**

When you come to see
"FRANKENSTEIN MEETS THE SPACE MONSTER"
We will furnish you with a
FREE SPACE SHIELD EYE-PROTECTOR
to shield you from the high intensity cobalt rays that glow from the screen and to prevent your abduction into Outer Space!
SEE! for the first time
Earth Horror vs. Space Terror!
"FRANKENSTEIN MEETS THE SPACE MONSTER"

**SPECIAL THANKS:** Leslie, Heidi, Grandma Dietlin, SINISTER CINEMA, CHILLER THEATRE, SOMETHING WEIRD, LOONIC VIDEO, SHEER FILTH/Cathal Tolhill, PSYCHOTRONIC VIDEO (M. Weldon), SUBHUMAN, SLIMETIME, FACTSHEET FIVE, BLOOD TIMES, Lisa Waltz, Craig Ledbetter, Cynthia Stewart, Nancy Black & COPIES, ETC., B&S PRINTING, and anyone else we may have forgotten! Love--Tim and Dave!

VIDEO*VOICE #11 is dedicated to the memory of Mike the Wolf.

had an article on them, but for some reason, I could never get my hands on some. There was a cool one called *Cyclops*, which was an early science fiction movie fanzine from the late sixties/early seventies. It's apparently hard to find now. There were a lot of mimeographed zines around. But, I really found out what was going on when I put out my fanzine called *Photo Fiends* in the seventies.

**JS: What was that like?**

**TP:** [laughs] It was horrible. It was my attempt to be like *Famous Monsters*, or something. This was pretty much before I even knew how to write. The best issue was number 3, where I got an interview with a monster maker named Paul Blaisdell. I was a pen-pal with him. He created the monsters for *The She Creature*, *It Conquered the World*, and *Invasion of the Saucer Men* and other films from the 1950s. When I was little, I thought those were some of the coolest looking monsters. They still are some of most novel creature creations. That issue became really popular, and I started trading with people after I put an ad in an early issue of *Starlog*. I started making connections with people.

**JS: When did you start publishing *Video Voice*?**

**TP:** I started that in 1987. It began as a publication that I ran when I worked at a video store—I'd hand them out to people. That didn't really take off until I sent a copy to a magazine called *Factsheet 5*. They listed thousands of fanzines.

**JS: Which zines did *Factsheet 5* introduce you to?**

**TP:** Well, *Slimetime* was one of them. There was Craig Ledbetter's

PHOTO FIENDS #3 "... undersized, slick paper, typset gem ... High point is a good interview with PAUL BLAISDELL, an effects man who was most prolific for AIP in the mid to late 50's. Great stuff." — THE HAMMER JOURNAL

PHOTO FIENDS

ISSUE THREE – LOST IN SPACE; PAUL BLAISDELL, creator of "It!, The She Creature," and other 1950's SF monsters; CRAWLING EYE filmbook; MARK PERSONS — a 'drone' from "Silent Running"; more! 3 COLOUR COVER, OFFSET! $2.75

Issue TWO – OUTER LIMITS; SPACE:1999; KRONOS [1957]; plus film reviews — offset! $2.35

Issue ONE – SPACE:1999; ROBOT FILMS; film reviews — offset! $2.25 ➡ LIMITED QUANITY ⬅

PRICES INCLUDES 1st CLASS POSTAGE!
KRONOS PRODS, c/o Tim Paxton, 386 E. 12th, Cols., OH 43201

*European Trash Cinema*, which started out as *Hi-Tech Terror*. There were so many of them out there. *Exploitation Retrospect*, by Dan Taylor. I started finding stuff from France and other countries. There was a lot of international trading back and forth.

**JS: How did you meet your co-editor, David Todarello?**

**TP:** I had come back to Oberlin after college, and he had rented some movies at the video store where I worked. He was a big fan of the same sort of stuff. Dave worked in the record department at our local college co-operative bookstore. I came in one day and asked him if he had any krautrock records.

**JS: This was in 1987?**

**TP:** This would be around 1986. He knew what I was talking about, and we became friends.

**JS: What kind of work went into the layout?**

**TP:** Dave and I used to lay out a lot of the early stuff with blue boards. A lot of it was just typing it up on a computer, cutting out the columns, and hand-pasting things up. Dave would hand draw many of the logos and article header. Later on, when I was able to afford it, we got a Mac and a scanner. I started scanning photos and putting stuff together.

**JS: Your zines are pretty famous for their design. Did you ever study graphic arts?**

*PHOTO FIENDS* NUMBER 3 WITH PAUL BLAISELL.

**TP:** Well, no, not really. I had always been drawing and making my own books since I can remember. Again, it was a family thing. Everyone in my family could draw, paint, and so forth. My dad could draw a mean stick figure. I did go to Ohio State University to study studio art—latex and oil painting and wood working. The graphic design elements of our magazines was something that Dave and I developed together.

**JS: You're one of the guys that published a lot of different titles.**

**TP:** Yeah [laughs]. There was a time when *Video Voice*, *Naked! Screaming! Terror!*, and *Monster!* were

all going out at the same time. In that period of my life, my brain was exploding, and I had to keep writing. I don't know if I had some odd form of OCD, or what—I just had to keep writing.

**JS: Which of your zines did you like the best?**

**TP:** My favorite is *Monster!* And that's also the one that got the most people interested in my writing and in what we were doing. For example, Steve Bissette did an illustration for my special "*Monster! Zero*" edition, and Tim Lucas wrote a couple reviews. I was lucky to strike up a friendship with this guy named Horacio Higuchi. He was the guy who did most of issue number 3, which was our special José Mojica Marins issue.

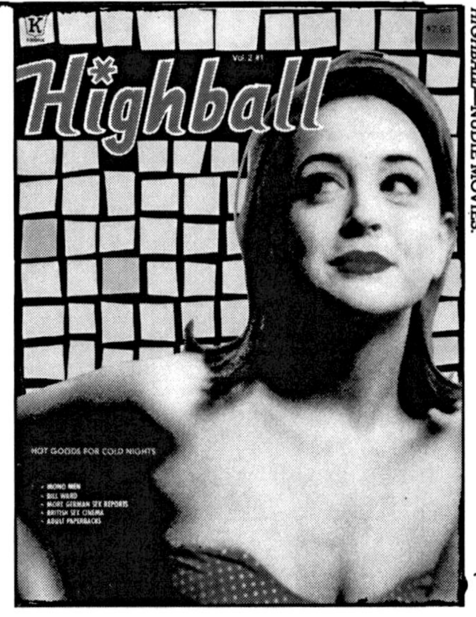


*HIGHBALL*—NUDIE MOVIES.

**JS: How did you meet Horacio?**

**TP:** Through *Monster!* We loved talking about all the weird international horror and monster films that are out there. He was a godsend for the zine. We had a pretty good friendship going and then something popped up, and I never heard from him again. I think there was some misunderstanding. Something really dumb on my part. He returned to Brazil and that was that. I think he does research in Belez. He's an ichthyologist.

**JS: You also did a magazine called *Highball*. Can you tell me a little about that?**

**TP:** That was about sixties nudie magazines. The first two issues were basically done by Betsy Burger and Dave Todarello. I designed them, but I was basically just the publisher. As much as I find nudie movies entertaining, I'm basically a more of a monster movie fan.

**JS: Are copies still available?**

**TP:** I only have one copy of each—we sold out really quickly on those runs.

**JS: How were you distributing your zines?**

**TP:** *Monster!* was published every two weeks. It was strictly a xerox zine at first. That was by subscription only. It got fairly big—I was mailing it out to 200 or 300 people every two weeks. But, our first big stab at distribution would be *Monster! International* number one. That was when we went off-set with it. Although the final few issues of *Video Voice* and all of *Naked! Screaming! Terror!* were offset as well.

## MONSTER INTERNATIONAL!

RECORDED & INDEXED

DRAFT

**JS: Who distributed that?**

**TP:** For the full magazine size *Monster! International*, we went through Diamond and Capital City. Luckily, Dave was really good at handling that end of things; he used to be a comic book buyer for the bookstore he where he worked. And things went fairly well until Capital City went out of business. And then, there was that entire magazine/fanzine implosion in the mid- to late nineties. Everything just fell apart. It was the same with the comic books. There were so many titles being pumped out that the distributors had a hard time moving them. Diamond suddenly got really stingy on how you would do returns. We didn't want returns where someone tore the cover off of the magazine. That's insulting and demeaning.

**JS: I agree. Especially for something that you spent so much time and effort to produce.**

**TP:** What can you do with the cover of a magazine? You'd have to pay the distributor back for what didn't sell. It was a real drag.

**JS: You covered a lot of Asian films in your zines.**

**TP:** Again, I grew up watching *Godzilla* movies and the samurai films that were on TV. My family has a long history of missionaries to the far east and Pacific Rim, so we had all this Asian stuff in the house. And also, Cleveland has a very small, but good Chinatown. One day when a girlfriend and I were driving into Cleveland, I noticed a Chinese grocery store. I wanted to get some tea, so we stopped in there. I saw that they had video tapes. This was probably in 1986 or '87. I started to rent ten to fifteen videos at a time, and I taped them. A lot of them were Taiwanese movies—if you're into Hong Kong movies, the Taiwanese ones are the most fucked up. They're the ones that deal with a lot of really bizarre natural realism.

**JS: How so?**

**TP:** Okay, maybe natural realism isn't the right wording. Magic and horror elements. Chinese Taoism and spiritualism. Really fun and messed up films. I was in heaven. Again, as with the *Godzilla* mythology business, I really love the entire ghost, zombie, hopping vampires, sympathetic

magic, weird wizards battling each other and so forth.

**JS: The whole Hong Kong thing really exploded in the early nineties...**

**TP:** *Naked! Screaming! Terror!* number 4/5 came out in 1989. Things were bubbling and ready to happen. All of that action stuff was coming out, and that was some of the hottest video stuff that was being traded between people. I had to sit through John Woo movies without subtitles—it was the only way to get them. I'd go to the Chinese grocery store and grab up as much Ringo Lam stuff as I could find. Anything that had explosions or chicks with guns. You'd go, "OK, that's the one I'm going to watch."

**JS: Why do you think the whole "heroic bloodshed" genre became so popular in Hong Kong?**

**TP:** I think it's the logical extension of the kung fu movies. There were cop movies made at the same time as the kung fu stuff, but there weren't a lot of them. I'm only talking about the stuff that I've seen. It's also really hard to get guns in Hong Kong and Japan. It's really illegal. And, those films were really fun to watch—you have Chow Yun-Fat jumping through the air with guns that should have broken his wrists when he shot them.

**JS: [laughs] I used to go to Asian markets to rent stuff, too. The tapes had xeroxed covers...**

**TP:** Oh, yeah. They were all like that. Most of the video tapes at our Chinese market were bootlegs.

**JS: Let's talk a little about David Szurek. He wrote a lot of stuff for your zines.**

**TP:** He's been in fandom for a long, long time. A couple of years ago, I was looking through an issue of *Fantastic Monsters*, the magazine that Paul Blaisdell put out after he left *Famous Monsters*. This was in 1963 or 1964. There was a letter in there from Dave Szurek.

**JS: That's great!**

**TP:** I loved it when he would write for us, but it would drive Dave Todarello up the wall—he couldn't stand the long reviews. I thought they were fun, but Dave just hated them. We actually once tried to get him on the phone to interview him. He was worse than I am about getting on the phone and talking to people [laughs].

NUMBER ELEVEN·$3.00
VIDEO VOICE
WILDER, MUCH WILDER!
AMAZING!
THE She-Creature
INTERVIEWS WITH:
JIM MORTON
SINISTER CINEMA

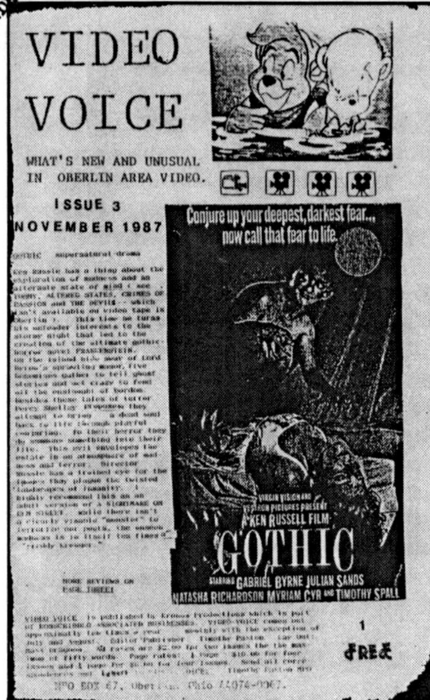

VIDEO VOICE

WHAT'S NEW AND UNUSUAL IN OBERLIN AREA VIDEO.

ISSUE 3

NOVEMBER 1987

Conjure up your deepest, darkest fear... now call that fear to life.

A KEN RUSSELL FILM

GOTHIC

STARRING GABRIEL BYRNE JULIAN SANDS NATASHA RICHARDSON MYRIAM CYR AND TIMOTHY SPALL

1

FREE

**JS: Szurek wrote a retrospect on old horror zines for you guys.**

**TP:** Yeah. He was great for that because he's been in it since the beginning.

**JS: You interviewed a lot of zine creators in *Video Voice*.**

**TP:** Yeah, we did Louis Paul, Jim Morton, and Craig Ledbetter. That was early on. It was fun—so much stuff was coming out then, with very different angles.

**JS: A lot of the guys like Jim Morton and Michael Weldon also did books. Did you ever want to do something like that?**

**TP:** To be honest, I never really thought of myself as a very good writer. I was more of an editor/idea guy. Like I said, my most popular issue was *Monster! International* number 3, the Coffin Joe issue. I asked Horacio Higuchi to put together an incredibly intense filmography of the guy. I don't now… I never really thought of writing any kind of book. There was a time back in the mid-nineties that Dave wanted to work on some kind of project with me for FAB Press in England. We never were ever to pin anything down because as soon as we started working on an idea, they came out with a book with the same sort of stuff. It was getting harder and harder to find things to write about. And then, when the internet came along, I was like, "Fuck it. I'm not going to publish anymore." Not to jump around, but in 1989 I actually tried to do an online magazine through CompuServe.

**JS: No kidding?**

**TP:** Yeah, it was based out of Columbus, Ohio. I went to school at Ohio State, and I knew about CompuServe when it was a bulletin board... pre-icon based internet. Pre-AOL.

**JS: Did it ever go anywhere?**

**TP:** I tried doing it, but it was really tough because it was dial-up [laughs]. It took forever to upload a graphic, and it never got much of a response. That was my first try at doing an online thing. It's probably still floating out

there, somewhere. It was called *Monster! Online*.

**JS: You have a pretty big collection of fanzines.**

**TP:** Yeah. Each of them has its own folder, and I have almost complete runs of some of them. Did I send you the link to the zine covers that I put online?

**JS: Yeah. You've got some amazing stuff.**

**TP:** I was really surprised—I found them in a crawl space in my house.

**JS: Wow!**

**TP:** The house I'm living in now is the house that I was living in when I started my magazines in the eighties. I looked in a crawl space upstairs, and there was a box that had been there since the end of the magazine days. That box had all of these magazines in it. I started xeroxing them and putting them up on the internet. Do you have the first two issues of *European Trash Cinema* when it went magazine?

**JS: Yeah. I was just paging through them the other night.**

**TP:** Dave and I put them together for Craig. Craig was really influential in the beginning of my magazines. He was always very encouraging. "Write about anything. Write about shit nobody's ever seen!" I wrote for Craig a couple of times, and it was a really good experience. We ended up doing his first two magazines. We designed them and tried to make them look somewhat professional. Then, he got hooked up with Tom Weiser. And Tom also helped out with *Naked! Screaming! Terror!* issue 4/5.

**JS: Craig and Tom eventually parted ways.**

**TP:** There was a huge falling out with Tom [Weiser]. My big head-banging with him was that he would make up the titles to Chinese movies. And he would just make up movies altogether. I would say, "I know that movie. That's not what it's about."

**JS: I've often wondered...**

**TP:** He made up shit, and that's where I was getting pissed off at him. And then, we had a falling out because we had more orders for the magazine and we needed to reprint it. He got it printed down in Florida,

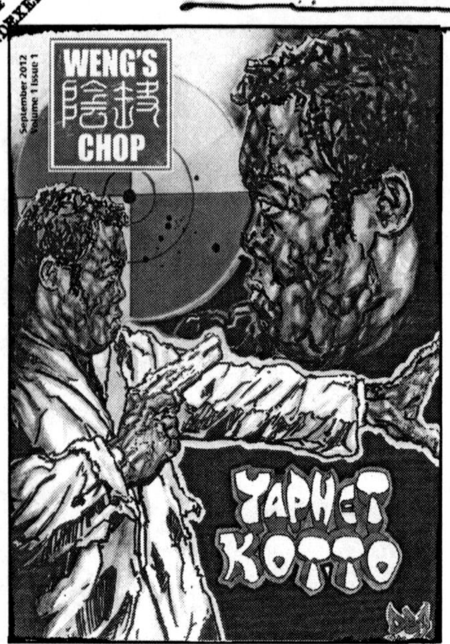


where it was cheaper. He wouldn't give back any or our original copies or any of the layouts. It was a big headache, which kind of soured me to the entire zine scene. I think Craig got tired of banging heads with Tom, as well.

**JS: I wanted to ask you about the artist Gary Dumm. He did some of the artwork for you.**

**TP:** Oh yeah, I like Gary. He contributed to the magazine through interior artwork and a comic for the *Highball/Monster!* double issue. The first time I saw his stuff was in an early *Outer Limits* fanzine from the late seventies called *Tolar*. That's Ted Rypel's *The Outer Limits: An Illustrated Review*. He did all the cover art and these free silkscreen prints that you would get with each issue. He did some stuff for us, and other fanzine people. I think he had a record store in Cleveland.

**JS: Speaking of records, what kind of an experience was putting out the Man or Astro-Man flexi-disc in *Monster! International*?**

**TP:** That wasn't bad. Man or Astro-Man was fine. The payment for that was sending them about fifty issues of my *Famous Monsters* collection, which I didn't mind doing. That's all we really had to do. They sent us a digital tape, and I designed the label. Apparently, Man or Astro-Man were fans of *Monster!*. I wasn't aware of that. Same thing with Buckethead. He apparently liked *Monster!* and I had no idea that he was a subscriber. I still can't figure out who he is. His alter-ego Throatrake wrote a long letter to *Monster! International*. That was exciting. It's fun when you get letters like that.

**JS: Why did you stop publishing *Monster! International*?**

**TP:** Well, I mentioned the internet. Also, the last issue with *Highball* almost bankrupted me. We had a four-color cover, and a four-color inside on some of it. We tried to go big, and unfortunately, that's right when everything started to melt down. Also, we made it a *Monster! International/Highball* double issue, where the cover would flip. They used to do that in the sixties.

**JS: *Mad* used to do that all the time.**

**TP:** Yeah. But, the distributors didn't know how to promote it. It was our worst seller—people would complain, "We don't know how to put it on the shelf. Which cover's what?" It doesn't matter! That's the whole point! And again... there was the internet. I kind of saw the writing on the wall—this is where everything's going. I did almost put out another run of *Monster!* as a newsprint zine. I contacted our local newspaper, and I was really close to doing it. Then, I just realized that the market was gone, even if I tried to do it as subscription-only, like I did before. Fandom was changing.

**JS: You've recently started editing and publishing a new zine called *Weng's Chop*.**

**TP:** Yes, it's a co-production with Brian Harris of Wildside.com. The title of the magazine comes from a series of Filipino action films starring this wee little guy called Weng Weng. Brian's a great guy, and he covers a great many genres of film on his websites. He has three volumes of his reviews published through Amazon called *Gimp: The Rapening*.

**JS: How did you meet Brian?**

**TP:** Through Facebook of all places. Facebook is how I got back in touch with folks. I didn't think I'd get back into the business, but after two radio interviews for Brian's podcast *Creep Show Radio*, we decided why not partner up for a stab at paper publishing? It's been a blast, and I gotta thank both Steve Bissette and Brian for kicking me in the pants so I'd finally get back to producing something.

**JS: How have things changed since you last published a zine?**

**TP:** Well, *Weng's Chop* is a print on demand publication through CreateSpace/Amazon.com. That's the only way I could ever afford to go back to publishing. I did publish a limited run xerox monster colouring book in 2011, but as far as magazines go, *Weng's Chop* is POD. And thanks to POD, I am considering assembling all my old issues of *Monster!* and publishing them as a three volume set through Creatspace. That will probably happen sometime late 2013.

**JS: Why do you think there's a sudden resurgence of print work from the old zine editors?**

**TP:** Not sure, other than maybe they got tired of the blogosphere. I for one have a blog, and it's fun to jot down stuff on a whim. But to hold a physical book in your hands... to smell the paper and ink, flip through the pages, cringe at your typos... that's all because it's something tangible, not digital. Maybe other old timers like myself feel it's time to return to paper publishing. The internet is getting boring. I'm doing it because I'm having fun.

**JS: Is there anything you'd like to add to wrap things up?**

**TP:** Buy *Weng's Chop*! Don't be afraid of paper. You bought this book, right?

# Chapter Twenty-Three
# Ant Timpson
## Violent Leisure!

I first met Anthony Timpson in Vancouver, British Colombia. We were both in town to experience a week of madness at Kier-La Janisse's (sorely missed) CineMuerte film festival at the Pacific Cinematheque. Kier-La had somehow pegged Ant as someone that I'd like to meet, and after a few missed connections, we ran into each other before a midnight screening of *Spider Baby*. As we introduced ourselves in the theater's lobby, I kept asking myself, "Ant Timpson—why does that name sound so familiar?"

It turned out that Ant had been the brainchild behind *Violent Leisure*, the only New Zealand sleaze-zine that I was aware of. Along with David Nolte (*Crimson Celluloid*) and Michael Helms (*Fatal Visions*), Ant taught my young brain an essential lesson: bad taste is good taste, and it's a universal disease. People from all over the globe—from the other end of the globe— were discussing and dissecting horror and exploitation films—publishing about them, even—with whatever means they had.

"Oh yeah," I thought, "*THAT* Ant Timpson!" A small and strange world, indeed!

Ant was one of the first guys that I contacted when I started putting this book together. Throughout the years (thanks to his tireless travels), he's run into just about everybody connected with the old zine-scene. And, as the director of New Zealand's Incredibly Strange Film Festival, he's seen more genre flicks than just about anybody you'd care to name.

I wrote to Ant in the Winter of 2012, and we wrapped up the following interview a few months later. As we exchanged letters, I got the same warm feeling that I experienced while talking to him in that theater lobby in Vancouver so many years ago. "One of us!" is an overused phrase in our circle, but it certainly applies here. So, before *Spider Baby* (or whatever it is that you're watching tonight) rolls, let's have a little chat with the one and only Ant Timpson.

The following interview was conducted via email, February-July, 2012.

---

**JOHN SZPUNAR: What kind of films did you gravitate toward as a child?**
**ANT TIMPSON:** I don't know if any child can gravitate towards a film. Most viewing is dictated by parents at an early age. You remember the ones you like more than those you didn't. I do remember enjoying those wilderness/wildlife movies at a young age. You know, things like *Born Free*, *Roar*, and *The Wilderness Family* series. Chronologically speaking, I loved adventure/wilderness movies, then fantasy/monster movies, then Terence Hill and Bud Spencer flicks and finally horror, which reigned for a long time. Oh, and anything with Charles Bronson in it. The fantasy movies (like *Robinson Crusoe On Mars*, *Light At the Top of the World*, *King Kong Escapes*, *The Seventh Voyage of Sinbad*, and *The Land That Time*

## VIOLENT LEISURE!

DRAFT

RECORDED & INDEXED

A film called LETHAL WEAPON, starring teen loin throb Mel Gibson, made 90 million collars. This film which was made a couple of years before it, probably grossed about 5. When in fact it appears that Lethal Weapon nearly lifted the script from DEADLY FORCE. When this happens it pisses me off, and it really makes me boil when I find out that the original movie is better. Well it is if your a fan of shlock-action, and unintentional laughs-a-plenty. WINGS HAUSER who I used to watch on the "YOUNG & THE RESTLESS", is one of those stars that people forget very easily, though his character in his films usually makes quite an impression on you. This is one underrated actor guys and girls. He plays an ex-cop (aren't there any left on the force?) who is hunting down a psycho, in this 1983 action extravaganza. The action scenes are right up there with the big boys, but what struck me was its' great sense of humour. Mostly intentional, but when the boom mike nearly steals the film, you know it's time to fire that mike-man. You'll wet yourself when you see it move back and forth between characters in one scene, like some omniscient observer. Hauser gets the shit knocked out of him, he gets hits by moving cars about 4 times. Not since Evil Dead 2, has the main character been abused so thoroughly by objects. Some other laughs come from, Hauser screaming at his wife to "GET OUT OF THE CAR!!!!", while it's travelling at 100 miles an hour. Another scene has him in the middle of a high speed car pursuit, to suddenly pull over, get out, fire a few bursts, get back in and continue. Paul Aaron the director must have been having a ball making this film, he breaks all the rules of logic and gets to abuse his lead. The most glaring mistake in this film hits the viewer hard, and that is that, Hauser plays his character to the extreme so well, that one starts to think that he should have been playing the psycho. Well if you are interested to see him in such a role, get out Gary Shermans' "Vice Squad", in which his performance is now used as the pinnacle of psychotic role-playing. Lots of fun, sure beats the shit out of all those preachy tv cop shows like Hill Street Blues.

# DRINKING GAME : FAMOUS FIVES

Basically a rendition of the campfire favourite " Scissors, Paper, Stone ", this liquid derivative has the gleeful participants sitting around and having a fun time. One person decides to start and calls for everyone to get ready. The starter holds out his hand as do the rest of the players, then start the count of three. Raising and lowering the closed hand as in "Scissors", when the Starter reaches three he holds out his hand with as many fingers he had decided on. All the other players who add up to " Five " with the starters' amount of shown fingers must then drink. Example : starter holds up 2 fingers, all players with three fingers showing drink. If no-one has three fingers up the starter drinks and the person to his left becomes the starter. When the Starter holds out no fingers (or thumbs) this counts as 0, and players who are holding up 5 (that kiddies is all your fingers and one thumb) lose and must consume. It sounds difficult especially after a few pints but it really is mind bogglingly easy, I saw it on " PLAY SCHOOL " and if five year olds can handle it so can you.

P.S (they weren't drinking)

P.S (see you next month with the immortal "Whizz, Bang, Bounce)

HOPE YOU ENJOYED THIS ISSUE, TIL NEXT MONTH, GET OUT THERE AND GET SLEAZY. LETTER AND COMMENTS ARE APPRECIATED. ON THE COVER IS LAUREL AND HARDY A GOOD SUBSTITUTE FOR FREDDY KRUGER... C'MON JOIN THE I HATE ELM ST FILMS CLUB. I HAVE!! P.11

VIOLENT LEISURE NUMBER 2, FRONT AND BACK COVERS.

*Forgot*) between the ages of seven and nine had far more impact on me than the standard Disney drivel like *Bedknobs and Broomsticks*. Those big-screen experiences built the foundations for a lifetime interest in genre film.

I still vividly remember many cinematic experiences to this day; the Albert Finney version of *Scrooge* scaring the nuts off my sac, staying up late and watching what I thought at the time was the greatest movie ever made, (actually *The Last Grenade*—and it only took me twenty-five-plus years to work that out). I know some have a tendency to romanticize their filmic history, but I really did see shit loads of films even from a very young age. I started going to the movies around eight or nine alone to watch spaghetti westerns and kung fu titles like *My Name is Nobody*, *My Name is Trinity*, and *Five Fingers of Death*. I was film obsessed from a very early age. I used to sneak into soccer clubs and see 16mm presentations of *The Wild Bunch*, *Straw Dogs*, and *Outlaw Blues* before I even got pubes. When I was eleven, we went to live in Los Angeles, I got paired off with the kids next door to see *Candleshoe*, the Jodie Foster flick. So the elder kid from next-door leans over to me five minutes into the film and says, "The treasure is in the suit of armor." I was so angry I punched him in the face for spoiling the film. Is that normal behavior for an eleven year old?

**JS: Depends on the eleven year old! What were the theaters like?**

**AT:** There were around fifty-plus suburban theatres in the city I grew up

in the seventies. Every suburb had a few and the city was lined with single screens. We didn't get multiplexes in New Zealand 'til quite late so it was a haven for loose independents; run down, grimy single screens in many locales. I have strong connections with many of those screens. Most are gone, but my dream one is still there. It was within a ten-minute walk from home and it was/is called the Crystal Palace. A beautiful massive single floor theatre built in the early twenties. It has a tiny candy bar out front and then just this enormous, beautifully decorated cinema inside with wooden floors for rolling sweets down. There was the Astor which was a real fleapit but it always had the most unusual marathons. I saw stuff like *Joy* and *The Ultimate Warrior* on double bills. At the PT Chev theatre, I caught two docs one day that blew me away for decades—*Blue Water White Death* and *The Hellstorm Chronicle*. I actually don't remember the first girl I kissed, but I remember my first kung fu film. When I stayed on my friend's farm, we sometimes journeyed to the Starlight which always had a fight outside the cinema. I remember once a Black Power guy just reaching over into the candy bar and eating everything in sight.

The suburban screens were filled with wildly diverse independent fare, away from the CBD [Central Business District] and with indie exhibitors the screens were awash with hundreds of unusual titles from all over the globe. The suburban theatres played all-nighters, five-, six-, seven-, eight films long. Taxi drivers would come and just sleep between shifts. The film line-ups in those marathons were just stupendous, an insane mix of exploitation and mainstream without any care or programming finesse. It was simply down to the deals the exhibitors had with certain distributors and what films could and couldn't play together.

**JS: This is going to sound uneducated, but were there drive-ins in New Zealand?**

**AT:** There were no official drive-ins in New Zealand. There was the odd temporary one that popped up here and there, but the unpredictable weather down here killed any chance they had for survival. New Zealand is heavy into car culture like Australia, so I'm unsure why it never took

RECORDED & INDEXED

# ANT TIMPSON

## VIOLENT LEISURE!

DRAFT

POST BAG

Hey Ant,

you gross little bugger!!!A special vomit issue?!!! You've outdone yourself boy. When's the bondage issue?? put me down for two. Anyway, many's the time I've had a drive of the porcelain bus, and Bob is right, A chuck chunder to the clear the system out and back into it. What's this beer shit though?? Don't you Kiwi's know that bourbon rules!!! Name change?? What about Nocturnal Emmissions that should get you a few more readers (only joking, stick to Violent Leisure). Well gotta go – I gotta see if I can find 'Black Gestapo' anywhere round town (you sure you don't make these movies up??)

party, party, party.... slash em up.

KAMI
DARWIN, OZ

"bourbons for people who have lost all hope, mate"

Dear Ant,

Hello there. Thanks for V.L #3 which, once again has changed format!! Glad you enjoyed The Barbarians, which I thought was okay, if a might slight. Loved (and laughed at) the vomiting article. Please tell me; it wasn't all true was it?? (puking up into mouths etc) No it couldn't have been all true, surely.... If only the Brit censors were as enlightened as good ol Arthur. What a guy!!! It's getting really silly over here, especially on video. SURF NAZIS MUST DIE can only be called SURF NAZIS, and HOLLYWOOD CHAINSAW HOOKERS can only be called HOLLYWOOD HOOKERS. Can you believe it!!! They're fucking censoring the titles. Anyway good luck with V.L #4,

regards,

KEN MILLER
HIGH WYCOMBE, U.K

"yes it was, maybe Thatcher should worry about Englands state of decline instead of video titles"

Dear Ant,

just recieved issue 3. I thought it was pretty cool except for the vomiting section (were the photos really necessary). SLAUGHTERHOUSE wasn't that bad, although I agree too much time was spent on the mainstream drek. REVENGE OF THE CREATURE FEATURE MOVIE GUIDE I think is one of the best resources for looking up horror movies. I find it indispensible. Change the title?? I think VIOLENT LEISURE is too obscure, how about VIOLENT MOVIES, simple and too the point. It is quite a shame moral bastards like to blame other's hobbies for anti-social behaviour. Dungeons and Dragons, fortunately, is too big for them to topple. It has been said the games promote Satanism and belief in the occult. Satanism, no. A belief in the occult, yes. But what is the occult, wasn't that Jesus supposed to have raised people from the dead (ressurection spell! heal people (restore health spell), yes the biggest occult figure of our time is Christ. People who live in glass houses..... Legend of the 7 Golden Vampires was a good film... for putting me to sleep. Ditto for the garbage, puss stain of a slasher film The Mutilator. That's it. I haven't been out to the video store for awhile, so please excuse my lack of knowledge of the films previewed. Censor Arthur Everard came across as a sensible enough guy, he seems pretty cool about the terrible job he has to do. I only wish he was our censor. They can get pretty rough over here. I heard every film in the U.S is cut at least once to obtain an R rating, no matter what value it may possess. Loved the article. Well gotta go and feed my tarantula,

take care,
JOSEPH OLSZEWSKI
PHILADEPHIA, U.S.A

"maybe I was a bit harsh on Creature Features, but I forked out $30 for it!!!. When I looked up some obscure movie, I still didn't have any idea whether I should get the movie or not. Just having a date and the stars, is not a great guide in my book."

"...MORE DYNAMIC THAN TRUE GRIT...
...SEXIER THAN I AM CURIOUS (YELLOW)..."
National Review
A WESTERN WITH THE SCOPE AND QUALITY OF THE LARGEST STUDIOS, AND THE BLATANT RAWNESS OF A SATURDAY NIGHT SMOKER FILM
HOT SPUR
ONE OF THE 10 BEST PICTURES OF THE YEAR!
R
FROM MUTUAL FILM DISTRIBUTORS

off—pretty sure it had something to do with excessive regulations. The government was always in fear that kids were out of control. They didn't show *The Wild One* uncut in NZ cinemas for decades for fear that it would cause society to breakdown.

**JS: Did your parents approve of your viewing habits?**

**AT:** Absolutely. Right from the start, we either went to movies as a family or I was left to my own devices. I remember going to see *The Towering Inferno* when I was eight with the family and my mother leaning over to me and asking if I wanted to leave during the first long burning death. I just nodded emphatically. Same thing happened with *Earthquake*, the Sensurround scared the shit out of me so much so that I had to go to the lobby to calm down. So, yes, very supportive. Right through my late teens, I was actually watching horror pics like *Alone in the Dark* with my mother. The only time I think I was embarrassed by what we were watching is when a mate and I were checking out *Boardinghouse* and my dad walked in and saw the lead in his leopard skin briefs and said, "Why are you guys watching gay porn on a Saturday afternoon?" After attending films together like *Outlaw Josie Wales* and *Pelham 123*, I kind of figured my parents felt I'd fallen off the path somewhere. Well, they definitely felt that when Customs raided their house (instead of my flat) years later and asked them where they kept their necrophilia and/or bestiality videos.

**JS: I have to know the story behind that!**

**AT:** The first I knew about being raided by New Zealand Customs was when I got an early morning wake-up call from my father. "Expect a visit from the cops in ten," is all he said. It was 1991 and I was living in a flat with five friends. I quickly got dressed and started hiding drug paraphernalia I thought they might confiscate. As I was throwing a jar of seeds into the depths of the fridge, there was a loud knock on the door. Opening the door revealed five men and two women. They were all dressed in uniform. They asked who I was and then proceeded to tell me, "We have it on good authority that you are in possession of bestiality, necrophilia, and snuff-type videos." Later, I would hear that this is what they asked my mother when they raided the wrong house. These doofuses didn't bother to check whether it was the father or son's place before they raided.

Realizing it was customs and not the cops, I replied that "They're all out at the moment." This flippant reply turned them into overdrive as they proceeded to storm the flat and wake all the flat mates up and began ransacking the house. A paper was waived in my face for the authority to do so and a microphone was put near my mouth from that point on, with one of the women recording everything I said.

They turned the place upside down. The flat mates were royally fucked off with me. Their private lives spewed all over the ground. They searched my room and found only a copy of Mike Diana's *Boiled Angel*

MORE FROM THE LETTERS PAGE.

that seemed to upset them. They said they knew I had the videos because they had personal correspondence stating exactly that. "What do you mean personal correspondence?" I asked, and one of them stepped up with the biggest ring binder I've ever seen and showed me copies of numerous letters I had received from friends, underground tape traders, and the like. It was the weirdest sensation seeing all those letters tagged and ordered chronologically. What was even weirder is that they had copies of letters I had sent to people. My letterhead was the *Combat Shock* baby, and the officer looked at me and said, "That baby seems to be in a great deal of distress. Why would you put that there, are you sick in the head?" It took me back that this guy thought that rubber baby was real and that's when I started to panic a little. Fuck! These guys are fucking clueless about this shit. This is not good.

**JS: How did they get your information in the first place?**

**AT:** I worked out how it all went down. Some fucking putz had kept writing to me, asking me to send him a copy of *Blood Sucking Freaks* while I was living in Australia. I eventually buckled and sent it to him. It was intercepted and the guy ratted me out. From that point on they kept a file on me.

Luckily, they found nothing to get jazzed about and were about to give me a stern warning when one of their posse asked, "What's in the garage?" My look spoke volumes, I'm guessing, as all of them promptly went around the back and opened it up. "Jesus, check this out!" I heard one of them say. The garage was lined with shelves—thousands of VHS stacked from floor to ceiling. Every conceivable video nasty and more all laid out in alphabetical order.

"Bingo!" said the boss one. They proceeded to search through the tapes, pulling anything with a fucked up cover or a strange title. "What's this one with 'Home Movies' on it about?" he asked. "Oh, that's just some crazy horror movies my brother and friends made." They quickly put it into the VHS and gathered around to watch the most embarrassing home movie horror of all time. They all just stared at it like it was *Salò* or something.

BAD NEWS

CCVL 2

CC/VL: TIMPSON AND NOLTE'S BASTARD CHILD.

They quickly gathered up their bounty and then took off saying they'd be in touch about possible prosecution.

**JS: How did things turn out?**

**AT:** In the end, it was all huff and no puff. They tried to make a case, but it was pathetic and none of the material I had actually broke any NZ laws. I wasn't distributing it and they were scrambling to make their big raid worthwhile.

I did have a run in again with the main boss from this elite outfit, but it was years later and it happened after 9/11. My moronic friend thought it'd be good to send me industrial fireworks from Florida in a box. These were insanely big explosives. He addressed it to "Udo Kier" and my PO Box. I had no idea about it until the crack squad stormed my next residence and this time armed with their hit TV show crew from *Border Patrol* behind them. This time it wasn't nasty vids, they wanted to find explosives. Once they realized I wasn't building bombs, the main guy sat down and had a cup of tea with me and talked about the earlier raid. He said he recognized me from all my film events I'd sprung up in the decade since the raid. He then asked if I had seen the movie *Cannibal Holocaust*.

**JS: You're kidding!**

**AT:** He told me he thought it "pretty amazing."

**JS: Let's get back to the more innocent years. Were you able to get hold of *Famous Monsters* as a kid?**

**AT:** Any kid into horror movies and is of the same age as me knew about *FM*. For many, it was a gateway drug for genre highs. Sure it was cheesy as all hell, but that same goofy charm created an air of accessibility for the very young and is a crucial reason for why the genre scene flourished as well as it did. I wasn't obsessive about it as some people my age were, I tended to mix it in with other mags like the incredible *Continental Films and Filming* and of course *Cinefantastique*, *Fantastic Films*, and *Fangoria* when they came onto the scene.

**JS: What's your take on *Famous Monsters* as an adult?**

**AT:** As much as I admired Ackerman's dedication to the scene and the encouragement he supplied to thousands over the years, I honestly think

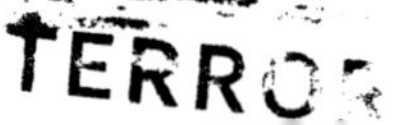

RECORDED & INDEXED

DRAFT

ANOTHER PAGE FROM *VIOLENT LEISURE* NUMBER 4.

CAMERON'S CLOSET

CHILD'S PLAY

that if *FM* didn't exist, something else would have and those movies and horror/science fiction fans would have continued to flourish. We can get overly nostalgic sometimes and tend to inflate the work of others to such historic heights that we feel that the scene would be diminished if not for their presence. The scene is always and should always be bigger than just one person. Some will say he created the scene, but that is history rewriting itself. He attended the first World Science Fiction con in 1939. He didn't create it. James V. Taurasi and Will Sykora did, but no one knows who they are. Sam Moskowitz was an inspiration for Ackerman and never gets enough recognition for the work he did to create the emergence of the fan communities. Ackerman took the baton and ran with it, and good on him for doing so. However, let's not forget it's the films that inspire, not the articles or photos about those films. I'd say TV horror hosts in regions who had them also deserve respect in spreading the love. I'm not taking anything away from Ackerman's legacy, he's intertwined with the scene on many levels. He was the ultimate fanboy. At the end of the day though, watching *King Kong* on late-night TV opened portals in my mind, not a photo of *Kong* with "Hairy and Scary" written underneath it.

**JS: *Fangoria* was my generation's *Famous Monsters*. When did you first encounter it?**

**AT:** At a mate's house after school one day. It was the *Saturn 3* issue cover. If it was the Spock cover, I probably would have never had continued reading it. Reading that issue was like doing a line of coke as long as a baby's arm. I was completely hooked. In fact, I started shoplifting that mag by putting it in a newspaper and buying it, as some of the early covers were so fucking nutso. *Zombie/Funhouse/Scanners* covers anyone?

*Fangoria* spoke to me like a new best friend who was both highly knowledgeable and interested in the same films I was. The early editors really helped establish that mag. Bob Martin did tremendous work in the

early days and helped cultivate a loyal following. And because of the shitty freight system back in those days, everything seemed so tantalizing close but so far away in terms of when I'd get to see the film. It was a complete tease. I mean, the mag was six to nine months old by the time we got it here, but even then, the films weren't available due to diabolically slow local release dates.

**JS: Fanzines couldn't have been far behind.**

**AT:** I saw the Andy Milligan article in *Fangoria* by Bill Landis. I think it credited *Sleazoid Express* at the end of the article but, I never followed. It wasn't until the late Chas. Balun published *Deep Red* number 2 (in 1988). It listed a whole bunch of zines and things really took off. That was the Rosetta Stone of fandom, for myself and many others. What happened was, I think I sent a note to Brett Garten (from the zine *Crimson Celluloid*) in Australia responding to a letter he wrote in *Deep Red*. That lit the fire. We ended up becoming good friends along with his buddy David Nolte. I think I even hired film prints off them for the first festival I worked on called the Bad Taste Film Festival in 1988, where we showed stuff like *Hot Spur* and *The Zodiac Killer*. I wrote to the zine addresses in the *Deep Red* article and became so inspired by ones like *Slimetime* and *Subhuman*, that I decided to start my own one called *Violent Leisure* in 1988. A friend helped me with the (now hideous) Apple 2 powered design of it, which resulted in one of the more unusual looking fanzines of the time. Even the images were fugly hand-created pixilation. My first issue had a large piece on *Bad Taste*, a film I had already covered for the German mag *Howl* by doing one of the first interviews ever done with Peter Jackson. It also had a drinking game that became a running gag in each issue.

**JS: How easy was it to come by zines in New Zealand?**

**AT:** Pretty much impossible. There were local music zines and comix back then, but there were no film zines. Mine was the first on the scene, but even then, we're only talking about a few hundred copies dumped in cinemas.

**JS: How instrumental were they in turning you on to films that you'd never heard of?**

**AT:** Zines were absolutely pivotal to opening up secret corridors of the cineverse to me. Without them, there's no way in hell would I have ever

EDITORIAL.

Short and sweet. Most of you reading this will have attended the festival at Charley Grays, hope you enjoyed it. With feedback from the public I'm sure there will be another. C'mon expand your horizons and get trashy, there are some fun times just waiting for you at the local cinema or video shop. People often ask me " but Ant, how do I find a cool movie ". Well all you do is look at the titles and if there is a label saying "contains sex and violence you know your're on the right track. look for covers with big breasted women and guys with enormous guns, stay away from ones with [illegible] and Harrison Ford. Don't be embarrassed about getting these films out, just walk up to the counter and say " I want Big Mama Jama part 2, you socialist money hungry pig-dog ", and you'll see results. They appreciate this up front attitude...and even if they don't, do we really care? Fuck no. This issue we cover some sick movies. Films dealing with un-[illegible] topics such as carnal lust, black 'n' [illegible] worship and cannibalism. What are yu waiting for...eat this shit up...yum..yum

VIOLENCE ON SUNDAY

A few words about violence on our t.v sets. Apart from the fact that there is not enough it amazes me where certain employees of TVNZ have drawn the line. Let me get this right, it's O.K to show sheep being butchered and left overs at bomb scenes being scrapped into plastic bags at 6.00pm but it is totally unacceptable to show 'Conan the Barbarian' punching a camel at 11.45pm. Yeah I know camels are an intelligent, rare race of creatures and that showing such a scene could cause controversy and strike actions by camels at zoos all over New Zealand, but guys I think it was a joke...you know ha..ha funny. I mean you see fit to show women being brought to Conan for sexual pleasure, showing Conan fondle their boobs. Lucky for us that they aren't as important as camels isn't it. Get your priorities right you maggots, show both or don't show it at all. Then we won't have nothing to get pissed off at. And while we are on the subject, can you please explain to the viewing public why whole scenes of the "Warriors" were hacked away. You kept all the fight scenes in but chopped out all the punches. PUNCHES!!!, and to top it off you cut the final scene where the Riffs close their circle on the bad guys. Yeah a circle of guys moving inwards is pretty horrific stuff, thanks for deleting it. It's fine to have the words "fuck, shit, bastard, prick, bitch, and have full frontal female nudity, but to show punches that's strictly taboo. Are you sure you guys/girls didn't start up the phone-sex lines here?. C'mon down TV3. O.K lets get on with the reviews.

IF YOU WANT VIOLENT LEISURE MAILED TO YOUR DOORSTEP RING 601-405 AND ASK FOR ANT

PAGE 1

A FEW WORDS ABOUT VIOLENCE ON OUR TV SETS...

# Ant Timpson

## Violent Leisure!

RECORDED & INDEXED

DRAFT

ANT TALKS WITH NEW ZEALAND'S CHIEF CENSOR..

CENSORSHIP IN NZ

A CHAT WITH CHIEF CENSOR ARTHUR EVERARD.

been exposed to so many rare and unusual films so early on. There were tantalizing mentions of titles that just seemed to crazy to be true. You have to understand that this was pre-Hong Kong hysteria, as well. It was the dark ages in terms of rare and eclectic titles. You either saw them in cinemas or were lucky enough to live in a country that put out gonzo shit on home video during the boom times. Otherwise, you had to become a detective and start hunting them down. Obviously in the early eighties, home video exploded and every country had a mountain of titles that were incredible, but the cool thing was the way distribution happened back then. What you had was a scenario in which certain countries had certain titles and the only way you could see this stuff is if you made a personal connection to someone in those other countries. So it became this underground network of tape traders who typed out lists of what they had and sent them to these contacts. You then agreed to dub what they wanted and exchanged tapes. This sounds prehistoric now, but it was an exciting and I think an underappreciated and important time. This hunting and gathering made you appreciate the films on a scale that no internet torrenter understands.

**JS: I'm curious—What were the censorship laws in New Zealand like?**

**AT:** It was dependent on the censor. When Chief Censor Arthur Everard amended the Classification Act to include hardcore pornography in '87, it was somewhat revolutionary. I was working at a video post plant when it happened, and I went from doing tourism and rugby videos to watching hundreds of seventies and eighties XXX films. What happened is that the censors office couldn't control the flood of titles coming in during the home video boom. Most were supposed to have ratings, but what happened was a long period of self-regulation with stores just slapping on any old rating certificate. Theatrically speaking, growing up in the seventies, we had the following ratings: G, GY, GA, R16, R18 and R20 and on the rare occasion R21. There were many cuts happening to horror

titles, but unless you had access to the classification notices, you didn't know what was happening. It was a glorious time for video hounds though, especially since New Zealand appeared to have titles distributed by tiny labels that weren't released anywhere else.

**JS: You started *Violent Leisure* in 1988?**
**AT:** The first issue was September, 1988. The main reason was to trade with better zines. It was sort of based on a similar earlier scenario when I'd pretended to be an Apple 2 software distribution company (Slot 6 Software) and wrote away to games companies for free sample copies of their upcoming games. Compared to other better written more interesting zines, I honestly couldn't compete. I was young, dumb and full of rum. I thought I had a unique voice and was opinionated enough to be humorous but looking back on them I failed utterly on both counts.
**JS: So, you were using an Apple 2?**
**AT:** It [*Violent Leisure*] was created on an Apple 2 using an early word processing program like Bank Street Writer, I think. I xeroxed them all on light blue paper at my dad's office.
**JS: How did you distribute?**
**AT:** Unloaded into a couple of cinemas and then sent to zine editors, *Factsheet 5* and the like. The silence was deafening. Actually, that's not totally true. There were fans from the very first issue and the crazy thing was I ended up meeting a lot of people locally through publishing it. Which wasn't what I expected at all. Some very cool people including graphic artists, musicians and future flatmates.
**JS: You mentioned *Sleazoid Express*. What was your initial reaction to it?**
**AT:** I'm guessing it's how certain people have epiphanies reading religious texts. Reading *Sleazoid* number 1 was like tooting on a Belushi bazooka. [Bill] Landis's unclassifiable mix of immersive behavior and erudition was simply jaw-dropping to me. It was unlike anything else I'd come across, and I felt the latter issues were the pinnacle of zinedom. It took the fannish obsessive qualities to dizzying new heights. You could feel that Bill was someone who wanted to always be swimming on the fringe and had a background that created the voyeur, who could only stand watching for so long before he needed to stop being passive and to make contact.

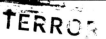

# ANT TIMPSON

RECORDED & INDEXED

## VIOLENT LEISURE!

DRAFT

VIOLENT LEISURE'S SLEAZE POLL, JANUARY, 1989.

TIME, IT WOULD HAVE TO BE, HANDS DOWN, KIM NOVAK. SHE TURNS ME ON NO MATTER WHAT SHE'S IN. SHE'S MORE BEAUTIFUL THAN MARILYN MONROE, AND IS A BETTER ACTRESS TO BOOT. (TODAY MARILYN COMES OFF KIND OF SILLY, WITH THAT STUPID MOANY/ GROANY/ RUBY-RED-LIPSTICK/ BUMP AND GRIND ROUTINE THAT WENT OUT THIRTY YEARS AGO) KIM NOVAK GAVE ME A HARD-ONS IN PUSHOVER, PAL JOEY, BELL, BOOK AND CANDLE . YOU'LL ALSO NOTICE SHE WAS PERHAPS THE ONLY ACTRESS OF THE 50'S AND 60'S TO GO BRALESS IN MOVIES, A FACT EXPLOITED BY HITCHCOCK IN VERTIGO FOR NOVAK'S "SECOND" CHARACTER.

2/ THE WORST MOVIE I'VE SEEN FOR AWHILE, IT WAS JOHN WATERS' MONDO TRASHO, AN UNWATCHABLE HUNK OF SHIT NO MATTER HOW MUCH OF A WATERS FAN YOU MAY BE. THERE'S NOTHING WORSE THAN A BAD MOVIE THAT'S BORING. BUT THE REAL WORST, LOWEST OF THE LOW, CAME IN 74. IT WAS RELEASED BY BRYANSTON PICTURES AND WAS THE CO-FEATURE TO PLAY NATIONALLY WITH THE TEXAS CHAINSAW MASSACRE. ITS TITLE THE MAD MAD MOVIE MAKERS (RETITLED THE LAST PORNO FLICK) IT'S NOT ONLY BAD, IT'S NOT ONLY BORING, BUT IT'S A G-RATED SKIN FLICK. AND THAT'S BAD!!!!!.

Ant says "has anyone sat through Ms Arquettes' performance in THE EXCUTIONERS SONG and not crossed their legs!!!! it made me nauseous watching pock face Tommy Lee Jones force her to give head. Agree 100% Ray she's a goddess.

NICK CAIRNS (EDITOR OF CREEPING UNKNOWN, U.K)
1/ WHAT, JUST ONE? OH HELL TRICKY ONE HERE. HAVE TO SETTLE FOR BARBARA CRAMPTON (BORING I KNOW BUT IT'S THE LEATHER GEAR IN FROM BEYOND THAT PERSUADED ME) PROBABLY BECAUSE SHE'S BEEN THROUGH ALOT WITH SEVERED HEADS/ EXTENDABLE FINGERS SHE'D BE GAME FOR ALSMOST ANYTHING ELSE.

2/ DOCTOR OTTO + THE RIDDLE OF THE GLOOM BEAM DR OTTO IS AN UNFUNNY GEEK WITH A XMAS TREE FOR A SUIT AND A LIVING HAND ON HIS HEAD. TRIES TO BE FUNNY BUT IS A PILE OF WORTHLESS SHIT. HE PLAYS LOADS OF CHARACTERS THAT ARE ALSO SHIT + UNFUNNY. ROBOT "ACID HOUSE" CREATURE IS ALSO UNFUNNY, DO I HAVE TO GO ON. JIM VARNEY IS UNFUNNY OKAY.

Ant says "why do we have to suffer through one joke comedians who are really only a success with the couch potatoes in their own country. Varney can fuck off back to U.S, Hogan can fry in cock on the bar-b back in Oz, and Tracey fucking Ulman!!!! can laugh all the way back to the U.K. New Zealand doesn't export our shit to your countries so give us a break.

CRAIG LEDBETTER (EDITOR OF HIGH TECH TERROR, U.S)
1/ BRIGETTE LAHAIE - WATCH THE FRENCH HORROR FILM FASCINATION + IT'LL EXPLAIN WHY.

2/ BLOOD SUCKING FREAKS ABOUT AS DISTASTFUL A FILM I'D EVER WANT TO SEE. I'LL BET JOEL REED HAS A BUNCH OF DEAD BODIES BURIED IN HIS BACK YARD.

Ant says " is she the one who gets her face pulled off in Jess Francos FACELESS? yeah agree with Freaks, it isn't too repulsive but you get the feeling that Reed would actually get a kick out doing that shit in reality.

DAIVD FLINT (EDITOR OF SHEER FILTH)
1/ MAMIE VAN DOREN ; IF YOU WANT CURRENT SEX KILLERS, WOULDN'T MIND RISKING LIFE AND LIMB WITH LYDIA LUNCH.

2/ THE DARK RIDE - THE CELLULOID EQUIVALENT OF HAVING A 6 INCH NAIL HAMMERED SLOWLY THROUGH YOUR SKULL FOR 90 MINUTES. THE KIND OF MOVIE THAT THINKS ENDLESS SHOTS OF COPS DRIVING ABOUT AND QUESTIONING PEOPLE IS ENTERTAINMENT. YOU'LL WANT TO PERFORM A HOME STYLE TRACHEOCTOMY ON YOUR VIDEO DEALER AFTER SHELLING OUT HARD EARNED CASH ON THIS SHITTER.

Ant says "expected as much from unscrupulous Dave, but after reading Sheer Filth I thought he would have gone for Chesty but that's what a sleaze poll is all about. Surprises!!!. Eager to hear more about the DARK RIDE.

PAUL DE CIRCE (EDITOR OF TEMPLE OF SCHLOCK)
1/ LINDA BLAIR. THIS OF COURSE DOESN'T MEAN I LIKE HER ACTING.

2/ IT'S A TOSS UP BETWEEN FAT GUY GOES NUTZOID & SAVAGE ISLAND. COME TO THINK OF IT, GHOULIES SUCKED TOO. OH, AND GI EXECUTIONER WAS AWFUL. OOH, WHAT ABOUT BLOODSUCKING FREAKS? HMMMMMN PUT ME DOWN FOR FAT GUY GOES NUTZOID I GUESS.

Ant says "Paul obviously cannot make up his bloody mind, methinks he has not watched enough trash. Christ if one more person writes in nominating LINDA I guess I'll have to run a photo."

DAVID R WILLIAMS. (EDITOR OF FESTERING BRAINSORE)
1/ SIGOURNEY WEAVER, NOT ONLY IS SHE BEAUTIFUL (THO NOT IN THE TRADITIONAL STARLET/ BITCH GODDESS WAY) BUT SHE'S GOT BRAINS AND COULD PROBABLY DRINK YOU UNDER THE TABLE. SHE STRIKES ME AS BEING THE TYPE OF BABE WHO CAN DISCOURSE ELEGANTLY ON THE ARTS AND SCIENCES AT ONE MOMENT, THEN TURN AROUND, SLAM DANCE HERSELF WET AT A LOCAL PUNK DIVE, THEN FUCK YOUR BRAINS OUT BIG TIME. (SHE'D BE ON TOP HER NIPPLES HARD AND ERECT - HER HEAD THROWN BACK TEETH CLUTCHED, HER CUNT GRINDING INTO YOU - RIDING LIKE A MADWOMAN!!.

2/ THE SHINING - KUBRICK HAS ALWAYS BEEN ONE OF MY FAVOURITES, FUCK ! ACTUALLY LIKED BARRY LYNDON!! THE SHINING (THE BOOK) IS THE ONLY ONE THAT

R TO KEEP BLACKMAIL FROM EVENTUATING — PLEASE SEND ME LOTS 'O' CASH PRONTO

**JS: What are your memories of Bill Landis?**

**AT:** Bill became a huge part of my life in film as well and for that I will always think of him with fondness. He played some of my 35mm prints at the rebooted *Sleazoid Express* Film Festival and the Music Box series. My Bill memories, however, started way back in the eighties, after reading the mind-blowing Milligan article in *Fangoria* and becoming somewhat obsessed with Milligan. When I eventually got the *Sleazoid* companion from *Pandemonium*'s Jack Stevenson, it was like some sort of exploitation holy grail. I remember Jack Stevenson being amazed that I wanted to learn as much about Landis as possible. I couldn't explain the reason for the fascination, but he kindly provided some interesting (and now obvious to everyone) back-stories that were intended to put me off but only ignited my interest. I eventually met Bill a couple of times over the years and we spent some time walking to some NYC haunts with him providing a ghostly travelogue. We ate Chinese food, talked about films and prescription drugs. I also met Michelle and their daughter Victoria when she was very young. The *Sleazoid* Film festival was put on by the talented Joel Sheperd in SF. It was attended by David Naylor from Alpha Blue Archives and *Flesh Gordon*'s Bill Ziehm and other assorted flotsam and jetsam. It was an unusual experience for various reasons. I eventually hooked Bill up with Tim League in Austin and he did a series for his book there, too. When I asked Tim how Bill enjoyed his visit, he said that Bill thought I was a drug dealer. I thought it pretty amusing, but it also confirmed what I had been feeling about Bill for a few years. That both he and Michelle's incredibly insular "them vs. us" mindset had increased their paranoia and bitterness to form an altered reality where everyone had a secret agenda against them.

They had a high burn ratio with all they encountered. I supplied rare 35mm prints for them to use and never received a thank you. It was just expected. I was another person that had something he needed. It's a weird feeling to be taken advantage of by an idol. It's simultaneously humiliating and liberating. It's freeing as you finally can severe whatever emotional connection you had with the person and eventually achieve some sort of closure.

Ultimately, I like to think a flawed character like Bill would never have left an impression on people if he was just another film nerd. He was affected by cinema in a way that very few are and thankfully for us, he

RECORDED & INDEXED

## VIOLENT LEISURE!

DRAFT

MORE RANDOM PAGES FROM *VIOLENT LEISURE.*

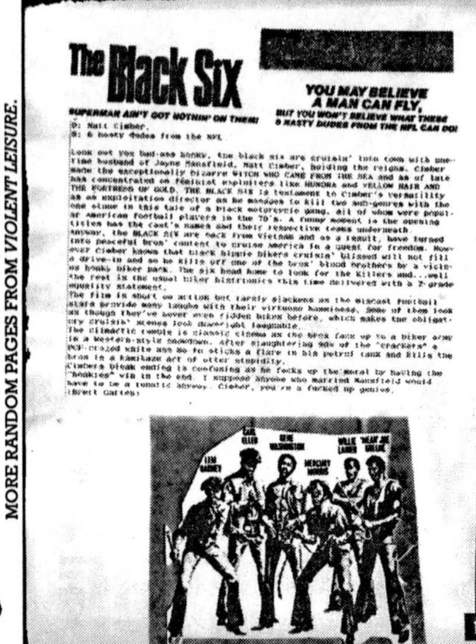


ZOMBIE BRIGADE

WAY TO GO BARRY!

17

TONY EGAN

managed to eloquently articulate his life on the film fringe. I hope there's some spectral *Variety Photoplays* that screens exploitation for eternity. And somewhere deep in the haze of smoke and shadows is Bill—sitting quietly in the dark with reflections of sex and violence flickering on his eyes.

**JS: Can you tell me a little about your experience with *Crimson Celluloid*?**

**AT:** Well, the first issue I saw was the one that both Dave Nolte and Bret Garten hated. It was their stab at a prozine and it kind of left a sour taste after publication. It was that issue that connected me to those guys in Australia that eventually led to me flatting with Dave and spending some time in Oz. I much preferred Dave's very personal xerox ones which, to me, were quintessential film zines.

**JS: When I think of a quintessential film zine, I think of *Subhuman*. What did you think of it?**

**AT:** One of the greatest. A phenomenal stable of talented writers and a design aesthetic that seemed very forward at the time made it one of the more rewarding zines out there. Everyone loved it. We all looked up to it, and I guess that's a tribute to Cecil who managed to just pull in the right people. Greg Goodsell and Kris Gilpin are both outstanding writers, and I was very jealous of their writing ability.

**JS: *Magick Theatre*?**

**AT:** A beautifully designed professional zine that was obviously a major labor of love. It was probably aimed at someone with more class than I had.

Back then, I found it kind of clinical and distant, but I think that's more due to where my headspace was at than the mag itself. Very irregular publication, so it never had any momentum or initiated a hunger to follow.

**JS: The other day, you mentioned Rod Sims of the *Gorefest* infamy. What are your memories of him?**

**AT:** Well, Rod brought out the worst in me, unfortunately. I picked on the guy because he was such an easy target. It felt like school all over again. A group of kids ganging up on the genuinely nice lunk and tormenting him. Even though Rod was older than me by nearly two decades, his taste and outlook on life seemed childlike and innocent. And it was this very individual at the controls of a horror zine that caused many to lob insults his way. He did nothing to provoke it, apart from being a terrible writer and unbelievable gore enthusiast. I felt people like him were keeping the perception of horror fans as morons alive and well. So, I parodied his writing style in our zine and wrote a review of the shot-on-vid shitter *555* in which I wrote a note perfect imitation of his gushing. The funny thing is Sim's reprinted it in a later *Gorefest* and said that even he thought it was funny. He kind of won me over with that, and I felt like a cock for being mean to the guy. He went out of his way to write a bizarre plea for kids reading *Gorefest* not to kill themselves (after a *Gore Gazette* reader's suicide) which many in zinedom tore apart viciously. None moreso than Rat and J from *Grindhouse*.

**JS: *Grindhouse* was that hand-lettered zine.**

**AT:** Yep. Handwritten. Nobody ever worked out who J Adler was.

**JS: How many issues did *Violent Leisure* last?**

**AT:** There were only five issues before it went onto merge with *Crimson Celluloid*, and finally becoming *Filmhead* in the nineties.

**JS: Why did you pull the plug?**

**AT:** I started becoming involved in distributing films and exhibition. It became full-time and there was suddenly very little time for producing a zine. I also started going to film festivals internationally and was traveling up to four months per year, leaving very little time to compile a zine. I was never a real zine guy, I purely did it to get free zines and meet other likeminded folks.

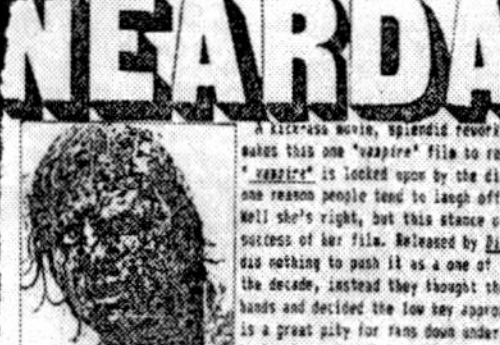

NEARDARK

A kick-ass movie, splendid reworking of a well used formula, makes this one "vampire" film to remember. The phrase "vampire" is looked upon by the director Kathryn Bigelow, as one reason people tend to laugh off or avoid such films. Well she's right, but this stance of hers backfired on the success of her film. Released by Dino de Dollarmstofs, they did nothing to push it as a one of the great horror films of the decade, instead they thought they had a turkey on their hands and decided the low key approach might be best. Which is a great pity for fans down under, I saw the film on video in America and its' release down here seems uncertain. With luck Charley Gray might eventually get it. So what's it about?, it has been described as a road/vampire movie. It involves a group of scabby/stinking bloodsuckers cruising through Americas heartland, picking on small towns and feasting on the local hicks. Believe me, whole towns could disappear in there, without people ever realizing. So using this rationale, script co-writer Eric (The Hitcher) Red, has developed an offbeat cast of weirdo characters as well as setting up some truly stunning visual episodes. The sympathetic main character who gets caught up in the bloodlust, due to some carried away love bites, goes through the rigors of becoming a child of the night. Near Dark offers some neat performances from the small cast, but the plasma drainer who gets the best of the script is none other than Wild Bill Paxton, who will probably be remembered for the most wankiest big brother of them all in Weird Science. Paxton who also stood out in Aliens, appears to get off on being the asshole character, his performance is a highlight in recent genre history. When he's about to chow down on a red-neck he turns and says " I hate it when they don't shave", then gobbles down anyway. This happens in the infamous bar scene which has now set the standard for blood letting in a vampire movie. (word has it that a new film called Waxwork has outdone this, will keep you posted.) The main theme is sort of Faustian, with the main character played by Adrian (Streets of Gold) Pasdar being pulled apart by contrasting emotions. Should he suck or not?. This has been used too many times and is the films only main flaw. I mean c'mon, the guy is shown that he's got all sorts of cool powers, he can stay up all night, have breakfast in bed, and so on. And he's just can't make his mind up. Another let down is having Tim Thomerson play the worried father, searching for his lost son, this guy is definetly not suited for this role. After seeing him in the comedys (Future cop, Cherry 2000, Zone Troopers ) it just didn't click. But these are minor pickings, the film has so many attractions it will amaze those who find it hidden in their local store. Forget those painty-waist vampire flicks Lost Boys, The Hunger, Vamp, see this one if you want to get down in the dust and grime. Photgraphy is splendid, the spacious landscapes where the film is set (Arizona?), are picturesque and one is reminded of scenes from Paris Texas, though I can't remember Harry Dean Stanton sucking the life out of anyone in that film. Since the film Rivers Edge has done very well here in N.Z, you'll be pleased to hear that the

# ANT TIMPSON

## VIOLENT LEISURE!

**JS: A lot of the writing in the fanzines was exceptional—and most of the time much better than what was being published by the prozines. Why do you think this was?**

**AT:** Zero pretense. The minute you're published in a real publication, you suddenly start over-writing to impress everyone. The wonderful casual style you might have had is smothered by this desperation to write something important. xerox allows you to experiment and not to be so precious. It allows you to really speak directly to the reader, without layers of respectability. I like going back now and then and reading all the zines. I find them very comforting. Not sure why they're so different to the zillions of film bloggers out there, but they sure seem to be.

**JS: A lot of the UK zines seemed to surpass their US counterparts, big time. Any thoughts on that?**

**AT:** The entire video nasties furor raised everyone's game in the UK. I think scarcity and that it was more lifestyle-based caused an intensity and focus way beyond US zines. That video revolution was a very real occurrence. There was panic, hysteria and the US only had that back in the Fred Wertham era with the comics code. History has shown that driving anything underground only creates loyalty and rebellion. And, from that crushing repression, comes great works of art.

**JS: How important do you think zines were to the new generation of monster kids?**

# filmhead

filmhead. volume 1, number1, March 1990. Published monthly by filmhead. Address all enquiries to P.O Box 5653 Wellesley St. Auckland New Zealand. Free to Aucklanders. Subs. $6 for six issues.

This newsletter is intended as a celebration of film. All types of film. **Filmhead** watches: comedies, westerns, horrors, pornography, thrillers, dramas, psychotronic, underground, cartoons, arthouse, homemade, mainstream, avant garde. **Filmhead** despises snobbery and elitism in cinema criticism, especially those who mock from afar. **Filmhead** will never turn it's head, no compromises. **Filmhead** can watch **Roger Rabbit & Faces Of Death** in a row and appreciate both. **Filmhead** revels in the shocking but also with the mundane. **Filmhead** liked **Parenthood** but hated **Back To The Future 2**. **Filmhead** loves **John Waters & Martin Scorsese** but thinks **Walter Hill & Tobe Hooper** are abject idiots. **Filmhead** thinks **Do The Right Thing** and **Roger & Me** should have scooped all the academy awards.

**Filmhead** realizes that the lack of quality entertainment in our town is cause enough for a new crop of couch potatoes to be harvested in living rooms everywhere. Their main source for pleasure being the idiot box and it's cousin the VCR. **Filmhead** uses this mode of viewing as a last resort, which with the state of cinema life in Auckland becomes a frequently used alternative. It's a crying shame when video offers the better film than the actual cinemas.

**Filmhead** does not know why there is such a heavy sexual content in these first few issues, but it could be a unsubtle warning to those who are expecting this newsletter to be the equivalent of the Herald's **Entertainment Section**.

**Filmhead** is amazed and frightened by the notion that people actually alter their viewing habits after reading a review in the local paper. Get a backbone and decide for yourself. Like someone said in the recent quirky yuppie fantasia, "don't take advice from someone you haven't had sex with". **Filmhead** agrees, so lets get intimate.

**Filmhead** laughs in the face of a woman from **Amalgamated Theatres** who said, quote "only bad films go straight to video without a theatrical release" aren't you glad that this sort of attitude, in the booking of films for Auckland, is alive and well.

**Filmhead** winces everytime **At The Movies** screens on the idiot box. The 3 puppets that helm the show have enough embarrassing characteristics to easily warrant the entire show being converted for radio, where these quirks of nature will lose their harshness. As it stands, it's a pastiche of boring behind the scenes footage and reviews which are either positive or negative, there is no in between in the world of television. The audience wants only **love or hate**.

**Filmhead** acknowledges it's forefathers: **Sleazoid Express 1980-85, Psychotronic 1980-1990, Crimson Celluloid 85-90, Trashola 1982-84, Grind 1988-90**.

**BILL AND TEDS EXCELLENT ADVENTURE**... is pure hokum from Critters director Stephen Herek. A hackneyed time travel farce that races through periods like a half hour sitcom. Bill and Ted are going to fail history unless they present a perfect presentation for the entire school. Unfortunately the wonderment of time travel has been reduced to something similar to a trip to Tangoville, Herek has no interest in what should be the most innovative aspect of the film, he's happy with lampooning famous figures from the past. If your idea of ball busting hilarity is watching Napoleon eat a mountain of ice cream, then catch this nerd apocalypse as soon as possible. Teen Beat hunk, Keanu Reeves proves that he's a second rate talent in these jove fests. For inspiration he's swiped Sean Penn's character from **Fast Times At Ridgemont High**, no class boyo.

the most exciting sport of all!
DON DORSEY'S
LOVE and KISSES
EASTMAN COLOR

**Shirley Valentine** is a **Ferris Bueller** for the middle aged set, replacing a wise ass Matthew Broderick with a more astute (but still a crude Oscar Wilde type) **Pauline Collins**, who supposedly did a marvellous job with the stage play of the same name. It's a shame that well crafted plays always end up with an inferior replay on the silver screen. There is absolutely no personal contact with the audience, something Shirley Valentine relys on. When Collins explains the logic about conversing with the kitchen wall, on film it's a one-liner, on stage it would be an insight into the character. Doesn't make sense huh? watch a play and see my point, the characters play off the audience, on film she's imposing her female logic to a piece of machinery, there's no real feeling and that becomes Shirley's biggest hurdle, one it never manages to elegantly achieve. The crowds at Devonport seem to differ though as they cackle to tell everyone near enough them. Judging by this I guess the majority of housewives do believe that they are trapped in their kitchens living out an uneventful life of boredom. I guess it's a case of, you're only as good as you feel.

**Little Vera** is a subtitled Russian entry from the post glasnost era, and if this is all we've got to look forward to then let us pray for a return to the Regime of old, cinematically speaking of course. I mean I'm glad to see Russia open it's first Mc Donalds, but do we need a film from the Pepsi generation as well? This awfully directed low budget teen tripe was ballyhooed as a revolutionary film, gimme a break, it's a dull, uneven and downright insulting piece of garbage. When are critics going to look past the 'foreign' aspects of a film and let it stand on it's own merits. **Come and See** was a film to be proud of, **Little Vera** is one to forget.

RECOMMENDED FOR THE ADULT MIND!

ANT TIMPSON'S *FILMHEAD*. *VIOLENT LEISURE* EVOLVES...

**AT:** To a very small niche it was hugely important, but that's really just a micro blip on the whole scene. I'd love to know real numbers, but when you're talking about most zines with print runs of anything between 200–800 copies max worldwide, it's pretty bloody tiny.

**JS: Films seem to get more and more extreme as the decades pass. Why do you think this is?**

**AT:** Today, I watched some cunt film his reaction to the Luka Magnotta sex-snuff killing video on YouTube. He sort of played it for laughs, with smirking faux horror on his face. I think back to when I heard about *Faces of Death* and was literally sweating when I put the VHS tape in. And now, here's some fifteen year old nerd laughing at a real snuff video showing the most horrendous shit imaginable. I think we were an innocent generation and I feel depressed about my kids and the future. I hope it's cyclical and that we're suddenly thrown back into some sort of ultra conservative hell, just so others can experience what it's like to come out of the tunnel.

The internet is a platform that allows anyone with fingers to operate from. We used to have natural filters in place, but now you can't escape from the stench of idiocy unless you disconnect. Their drivel is rammed home from all angles on news feeds, twitter—just everywhere. These annoying despicable fucking moronic cocksuckers that I once never had to acknowledge at are now everywhere I go. There are some great ones amongst the muck but who has the time to dig through all the shit?

**JS: I feel the same way. And I really miss the old zine days.**

**AT:** I wrote a piece for *Badass Digest* about the nature of film fans today and the gluttony that pervades them. They don't appreciate, they just consume. There's no discovery. There's no journey. It's all just a fucking click away. It's the reason why we have guys introducing *Boardinghouse* in a fancy NYC theatre and telling the audience it's a terrible film, like *Plan 9*, that you can laugh at. That just kills me. It's like giving a retarded child a loaded gun. I have really enjoyed reconnecting with many from the zine past and seeing that many of them are continuing to do outstanding work online and have become seasoned pros.

# Chapter Twenty-Four
# Michael Helms
## Fatal Visions

COVER TO *FATAL VISIONS* NUMBER 4. ART BY MARIA KOZIC.

ichael Helms was the editor and publisher of *Fatal Visions*, a fanzine from Australia that I stumbled upon in the late 1980s. As the old story goes, I knew a guy who knew a guy who had a pretty big movie collection. Introductions were made on a Summer afternoon and, after a dinner of beer and pizza, we got down to business. That is to say, we had a go at each others' lists of VHS dupes. After a while, we started talking fanzines.

I remember sitting at his kitchen table, slack jawed and in awe. The guy was a hardcore tape trader and he had it all—uncut tapes of *The Beyond* and *Cannibal Holocaust*, an address list of other collectors, and a stack of sleaze-zines that made my eyes tear up with envy. Laid out before me were fanzines from everywhere— Tennessee, Louisiana, Pennsylvania, and… Australia?

It was there, in a suburban Detroit kitchen (I was slightly drunk on the beer that I'd smuggled in—I couldn't have been a day over sixteen) that I first laid my eyes on *Fatal Visions*. I'd read about the mag in other zines, but I never dreamed that I'd stumble upon a copy so close to home.

*Fatal Visions* was a very important fanzine, and Michael Helms became a very important genre journalist. His name popped up in the pages of *Fangoria* and *Gorezone*. In fact, Michael's words still grace the pages of *Fango* today. He's also recently published *Fatal Visions—The Wonder Years,* a book that compiles the complete contents of the first two years of his pioneering mag. Time to break out a pizza and some beer and get all nostalgic, no?

Michael Helms took some time out of his busy schedule to answer a few of my questions via email. And I must admit that pizza and beer were most definitely involved (on my part, at least) when we finally made contact.

The following interview was conducted via email, June–August, 2012.

---

**JOHN SZPUNAR: When did you start publishing *Fatal Visions*?**
**MICHAEL HELMS:** Early 1988. I'd previously written for several local film mags including *Cinema Papers*, *Filmnews*, and *Metro*.
**JS: Why start doing a fanzine, then?**
**MH:** I knew from the above experience that I wasn't always going to be able to have subject choice or control over the finished piece. We managed to push out twenty-one issues, two calendars, a national film festival, and many screenings over ten years. I wanted to document the Australian situation—specifically that of Melbourne—with regard to trash cinema.
**JS: I've always been curious about Australian genre films. For the discerning reader at home, could you list some of your favorites?**
**MH:** *Pure Shit*, *Mad Dog Morgan*, *Going Down*, *Coming Of Age*, *Houseboat Horror*, *Marauders*, *The Howling III*, *Vicious,* and *Bloodlust*. And now, just

RECORDED & INDEXED

DRAFT

by writing this list, I seemed to have kick started some sort of unhealthy fascination for *Cosy Cool*, which is one of the worst films of any genre from any country in the world. That it's a biker film with Satanism thrown in just to elongate the running time makes it even worse.

**JS: That film takes place in a world of its own! Now then—I take it that you were born with an interest in horror films.**

**MH:** Yes.

**JS: What magazines caught your eye as a youngster?**

**MH:** As a sub-teenage kid with access to the great Space Age Bookshop, I was able to pick up copies of *Bizarre*, the *Monster Times*, *Gore Creatures*, and best of all *Photon*, which included a glossy horror 10 x 8, surely something that was key towards instigating the production of *Fatal Visions*.

**JS: I assume that *Fangoria* made an impact on you.**

**MH:** At first, I thought it was great that there was another English language *Godzilla* mag to join the superb *Japanese Filmmaker Journal* (another early model fanzine). Issue number 4 of *Fangoria* with Spock on the cover convinced me it couldn't be a real horror mag, though. I kept an eye on it, but it wasn't until issue 25 with the fake *Videodrome* cover that I really got into it. Immediately found a great mag under Uncle Bob and sought out all the back issues.

**JS: How did fanzines fit into the picture?**

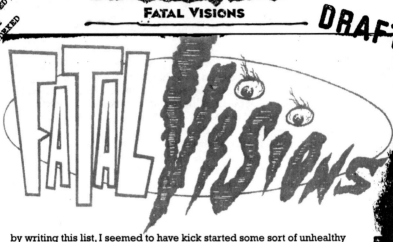

**MH:** At least four of the above-mentioned titles would have to be classed as zines: early to mid-seventies. As a ten year old, I picked up a copy of Richard Neville's *Playpower* and became fascinated with many activities of the underground, especially its various publications. Melbourne actually had a mag called *Ratz* that appeared regularly at my local newsagent. The teacher had to intervene just before I got up for "show and tell" to discuss a magazine that showed you how to knit penis mittens and had a naked rat centerfold!

**JS: I had a similar experience in school during "current events" when I walked up to the front of the class with a copy of the *National***

*Enquirer*! **Living in the suburbs of Detroit made it kind of difficult to find anything edgy to read, especially within biking distance.**

**MH:** In the major cities (Melbourne especially), there seemed to be opportunities for the eagle-eyed and persistent to come up with something. Au Go Go Records, Minotaur, the Gaumont Bookshop, Moviola, and Alternate Worlds in Melbourne carried many of the world's finest fanzines.

**JS: I got a lot of them through the mail. I'm guessing that's how you'd go about getting something like, say, *Sleazoid Express*?**

**MH:** Yes. And *SE* was incredible. I liked its attitude and how it not only talked about the films but about the audience, as well. Popeyes also shuffled the streets of Melbourne.

**JS: What were the theaters in Melbourne like?**

**MH:** The city had decaying picture palaces and small screens in basements. The suburbs had single screen hardtops and drive-ins.

**JS: Ant Timpson was telling me that Australia had many more drive-ins than New Zealand.**

**MH:** The west and north of Melbourne was littered with them. All these places were playing double bills. My favourite cinema was the Grand in Footscray (pronounce it: Foot-a-Scray) where on a weekend you could catch a pairing of something like *Four Flies on Gray Velvet* and *The Torture Chamber of Dr. Sadism*.

**JS: How were you distributing?**

**MH:** Initially by myself, then through a variety of distributors.

**JS: It must have been difficult to keep things on some sort of schedule.**

**MH:** It was shaky. It was a joke that I continually announced it as a quarterly but never producing more than three in any year.

**JS: Was *Fatal Visions* initially a xerox job?**

**MH:** First six issues were done on a photocopier. The rest were offset printing.

**JS: *Fatal Visions* started in 1988. The first Aussie horror zine that I'm aware of was *Crimson Celluloid*.**

**MH:** *Crimson Celluloid* was *the* seminal Australian horror film zine. Not happy

RECORDED & INDEXED

DRAFT

# FATAL VISIONS

MAY 1988 $2.50

VIOLENT MEDIA SCENE AND HEARD IN MELBOURNE

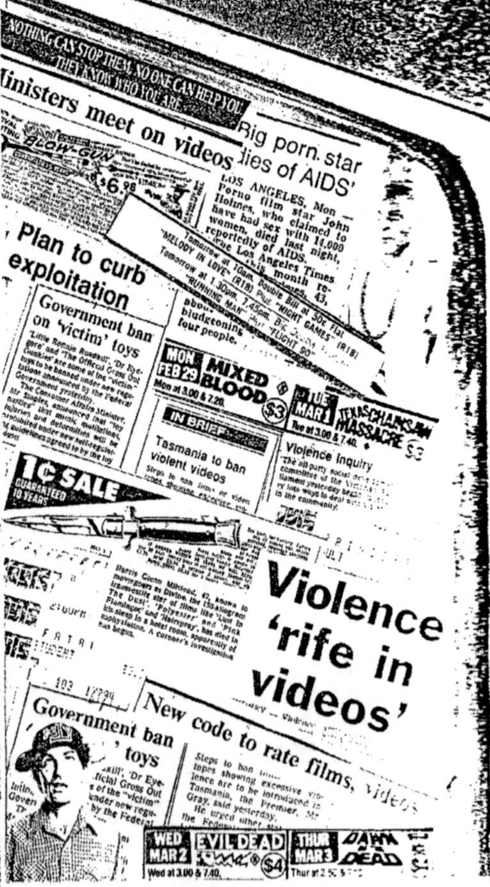

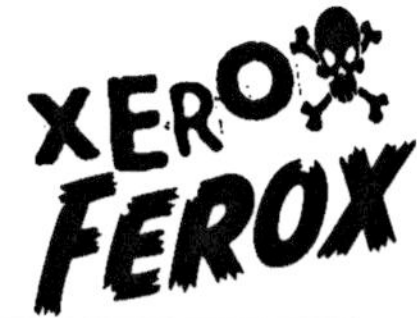

to just spew out reviews, but actually able to get out in the field and gather interviews and other insights. Basically, *Crimson Celluloid* led the way.

**JS: You worked with David Nolte for a time...**

**MH:** David is a great friend and not just because he's an excellent writer or Australia's foremost pen-pal to the most notorious serial killers. David is a kind and generous individual whose work is worthy of close attention on any day. I don't think we've really stopped working together yet.

**JS: I'm curious to hear about some other Australian zines. I've never seen a copy of *Visual Violence*.**

**MH:** *Visual Violence* was the second zine out of Sydney and it was just as snappy as *Crimson Celluloid*, which it bonded with. *Visual Violence* also demonstrated the importance of creating industry links in order to get review copies and graphics. Wally Ramborama's *Psycho in the Dark* from Melbourne was one of the best written zines ever produced in Australia and its editor eventually became a major contributor to *Fatal Visions*. *Mondo Gore* out of Queensland needs to get a mention, as should *Spraak!*, originally out of Darwin before relocating to Adelaide and later John Harrison and his own publishing empire that included *Strait-Jacket*, *Reel Wild Cinema* and *Hip Pocket Sleaze*.

**JS: How did you begin writing for *Fangoria*?**

**MH:** I walked in one day with the mail in my hand to the sound of the phone ringing. It was Mike [Gingold] from *Fangoria* and he was in Sydney visiting his grandparents. He wanted to know if I felt like coming over. As I've repeated to more than a few visitors to our shores (on more than a few occasions) Melbourne is not a suburb of Sydney. But as he talked, I began idly checking out the mail and just so happened to come across a letter from then little known New Zealand filmmaker Peter Jackson. Jackson, a fan of the early model *FV* wanted to see if I was interested in going to NZ to check out the making of this little zombie flick he was doing called *Braindead*. That became my first story for *Fango* (with a follow-up on the same topic in *Gorezone*) and I haven't stopped yet in this, the twentieth year of contributing stories.

**JS: You told me that you're going putting together a compilation of the first two years of *Fatal Visions*. What can we expect?**

**MH:** It's a 250-page book called *Fatal Visions—The Wonder Years (1988–89)*. It contains re-typeset versions of all of the first six issues minus the letters columns and retains many of the graphics that were ripped straight out of newspapers. It takes old trash and beautifully repackages it.

**JS: I can't wait to read it. A lot of the other zine guys seem to be returning to the fold these days. You can't keep the old guard down.**

**MH:** Lately, it's been hard to ignore the fond memories some folks seem to have cultivated and maintained for *Fatal Visions* and other zines of the eighties and nineties.

**JS: Do you think that fanzines are still vital in any way?**

# MICHAEL HELMS

## FATAL VISIONS

**MH:** Since the last issues of *Crimson Celluloid* or *Spraak!*, I can't say I've seen one. I still believe in dead tree technology and have a preference for their tactile nature and know there are people out there who share my view—so I still expect to see them from time to time just haven't got the energy to chase them let alone make them. The *FV* book is also a statement that supports that (but it's also going to be available as a PDF and *FV* is finally going to join the electronic world in other ways too…).

**JS: I've asked a lot of guys if they miss the good old days, but I've never really asked that of myself. And I've got to say that I miss them a lot.**

**MH:** They might be good old days now, but you're not going to know while you're living them—that is, if you were living them to the full.

**JS: That's true. And now we've got the internet. Does that even count?**

**MH:** The best zines always used to be the obvious products of talent and effort. The net just makes it very easy for too many to prove their basic lack of communication skills and presentation abilities. Undoubtedly internet zines count, but to whom I can't say. And, although online forums aren't without their uses, wading through them to find something meaningful amidst the armies of one-line sub-teenage heroes is often a great waste of time and cyberspace.

**JS: With that in mind, where do you think fandom is headed?**

**MH:** As a notoriously bad fan boy, I find it hard to gauge the state of fandom at any given time. However, I did notice that the first pro-horror convention to be held in Australia several years ago fell over not long after it was announced. Meanwhile, sci-fi conventions seem to be in state of constant expansion, and they do always seem to show some sort of tolerance for horror fiends. With genre film festivals also expanding, I'd estimate that fandom is doing pretty well.

$2.50

No.2

# FATAL VISIONS

VIOLENT MEDIA SCENE AND HEARD IN MELBOURNE

City sells drive-in for village

Ban pornography until it has been proved to be harmless

PANDEMONIUM

Get more out of life ...GO OUT to a movie.

Cult a threat — mother

Pay TV gets green light for start in early 1990s

Violence on TV may be curbed

IF YOU REALLY LOVE ME YOU'LL LET ME EAT YOUR BRAINS.

Booze, violence linked

Man stabbed victim and ate flesh, hearing told

Hail and farewell to Bangkok's Nazi Bar

'Bongs' left at kinder

Blood is our life, Darkness, our feeding ground And sunlight, our eternal damnation.

SNACK BAR

# Chapter Twenty-Five
# DAVID NOLTE
## Crimson Celluloid

FROM THE COVER OF *CRIMSON CELLULOID* NUMBER 10.

DAVID NOLTE AT THE MANDOLIN CINEMA IN SYDNEY. PHOTO COURTESY OF DAVID NOLTE.

David Nolte has been a part of the fanzine landscape for years. Inspired in part by Rick Sullivan's *Gore Gazette*, he began publishing *Crimson Celluloid* in the early eighties.

*Crimson Celluloid* was Australia's first horror film fanzine, and the impact that it made on the scene was tremendous. Nolte single-handedly blazed a trail for others to follow, and before long, Australia was home to a small but thriving fanzine community.

By the time an issue of *CC* made it into my hands, things were already in full swing. I read every issue of the mag that I could track down, and trust me, that wasn't an easy thing for a sixteen year old kid from Detroit to do.

David eventually put *Crimson Celluloid* on the back burner, but he brought the zine back in 1999. I finally caught up with the new *CC* with issue number 10. Nolte's in-depth interview with Andy Milligan star Hal Borske was just what the doctor ordered, and the thing sent me searching for back issues once again. Talk about déjà vu, eh kids?

In the Spring of 2012, I sent Nolte a letter of introduction, outlining my plans for this book. His response was enthusiastic, and I soon found myself engaged in a lengthy correspondence with the man.

So, here you have it. From Detroit to Adelaide, to wherever you may be as you read these words—I now present an exclusive interview with *Crimson Celluloid*'s David Nolte.

The following interview was conducted via email, April 6–13, 2012.

# DAVID NOLTE

## CRIMSON CELLULOID

VIDEO GRINDHOUSE
FRI 6 MAY 10PM–3AM
5 INCREDIBLE HOURS OF NON-STOP HI-QUALITY GIANT SCREEN VIDEO ACTION!!
A MIND BOGGLING BARRAGE OF GRINDHOUSE RARITIES OLD AND NEW... CULLED FROM THE BACKROOMS OF 42ND ST & PEEPSHOW ALLEY!!
INCLUDING:
• TITILLATING TRANSEXUALS
• MEXICAN MONKEY MUTANTS
• NAUGHTY ENGLISH NUDISTS
• CLASSIC TRASH/SCHLOCK/SLEAZE TRAILERS
• BACK YARD AUSSIE SPLATTER & SICKNESS
• VIDEO CUT-UPS, GIVEAWAYS, SURPRISES
AND MORE!! IN THIS UNIQUE NIGHT OF VIDEO ECCENTRICITY!!
LIVE SEX ACTS ON STAGE
NEW BIZARRE ACTION
GIRLS GUYS GIRLS
GOLDEN ROD & SHORTS


A *CC* SPONSORED LATE NIGHT HORROR/SLEAZE SCREENING AT THE MANDOLIN CINEMA IN SYDNEY.

**JOHN SZPUNAR: It seems that childhood obsessions have really fueled a lot of the zine guys over the years. I'm guessing that you're story isn't very different.**

**DAVID NOLTE:** It was all about the horror films. From cringing in terror at Christopher Lee's bloodshot eyes, through to *Godzilla* and weird made-for-TV fare. I used to take days off school, pretending to be ill, each time *The Norliss Tapes* and *Trilogy of Terror* were on the midday movie.

**JS: What kind of school did you attend?**

**DN:** I went to an English boarding school. I remember older students coming back one night after seeing *The Exorcist*, describing how terrifying it was, how people left the cinema in horror and threw-up. I vowed *never* to see this film… a vow I kept until I saw it was available on video. Still the scariest film I've ever seen. Being deeply Catholic at the time probably helped.

**JS: How big of a roll did your religion play in your reaction to these kinds of films?**

**DN:** Mum was in her own world and as a strict catholic probably wouldn't have approved of anything as nasty as horror films. Dad was a lifelong sci-fi fan. He once said that "Science fiction is horror with a brain." to which I replied, "Horror is science-fiction with balls." Dad would buy me books on Hammer films as a kid and I'd spend many an hour staring at the pictures and being equal parts revolted and excited (the same

feelings the women I have dated have felt!). Dad would always warn me that I'd get nightmares. I'd never listen and invariably wake up in the middle of the night in a cold sweat, haunted by what I had seen. Strangely enough, my grandfather wouldn't let me watch *Blacula* one night when he was babysitting because he read a description and saw that it featured homosexuals at the start.

**JS: I was kind of surprised to hear that you had TV horror hosts in Australia.**

**DN:** Yeah. Another major factor in my interest in horror was the Australian horror TV host Deadly Earnest. He had weird makeup, climbed out of a coffin, battled rubber bats and showed the cheesiest of cheesy horror films. I loved that guy. One of the saddest things in my life was endeavoring to hunt down Deadly for an interview many years later and meeting brick walls at every turn. I wanted to tell him how much he meant to me as a kid, how he had influenced me and how much entertainment he had provided. I then read an article on him in the local paper saying he had recently died and his one regret was that nobody cared about his legacy or remembered him as Deadly Earnest. It broke my heart.

**JS: Were you seeing films in theaters, as well as on TV?**

**DN:** Yes. As a preteen/teen growing up in South Australia I was lucky to have a twin cinema at the end of my street. It showed a lot of horror double-bills and I became friends with the manager. He used to let me go in for free and gave me any spare posters and lobby cards. I recall that the cinema was empty most of the time and it seemed like more of a labor of love than any kind of business proposition. It's long gone, but fondly remembered. I don't know why I had to look through the mountains of posters naked. "Security," he said, and who was I to argue when a pristine *Prophesy* poster was at stake!

**JS: I'm curious as to how difficult it was to find American magazines like *Famous Monsters* in Australia.**

**DN:** It was a rare occurrence when I actually managed to track down a copy. An issue here, an issue there. Naturally I loved it but, even at that young age, didn't think the "punny" nature of it was that funny. I loved the pictures and wanted to see as many of the films as I could, but I couldn't give a damn about Lon Chaney and the like.

**JS: *Famous Monsters* was almost a primer for things to come.**

**DN:** Forry was instrumental in exposing a world of kids to horror and he should be remembered for that.

**JS: Oddly enough, I didn't really appreciate the seminal aspects of *FM* until I got older, and when I did, it was sort of with a whimsical reverence. *Fango* was always more my speed.**

**DN:** The first issue of *Fangoria* I saw was probably number 3 or 4. I instantly knew I had found the magazine for me. As much as I dug *FM*, it seemed somewhat dated and I wanted to know about new films. This is especially true of the glorious Bob Martin days when the magazine was at its best. It

RECORDED & INDEXED

## CRIMSON CELLULOID

DRAFT

CRIMSON CELLULOID

#7

Ed Gein

*HANNIBAL*: The Fake Cannibal

FOR ONLY $1, you get:

Assorted Nuts: We make fun of crazy people, Chinese Movie Coverage, "Erotic Survivor", Extensive DVD and Video coverage and More sleaze than ever before.

opened my eyes to the world of gore and more extreme and violent horror.

**JS: I look at *FM* and *Fangoria* as stepping stones to the more eccentric world of the fanzines.**

**DN:** I have *Fangoria* to thank for this, too. I had absolutely *no* knowledge of zines at all 'till I saw a little ad in the classified section advertising Michael Gingold's *Scareaphanalia* and was intrigued. I sent off my money and got this xeroxed newsletter in the mail. I thought, "I can do this!" Not in an "I can do better" way but in a "fuck me… I want to do this!" way. Michael had access to all the cool films showing in NYC and I spent many an hour pouring over his zines. Being inspired by his zine opened the floodgates, leading to *Gore Gazette* and many other zines. *GG* changed my life. It showed me that I could review trashy films, be my obnoxious self and utilize my questionable sense of humor to great effect.

**JS: How easy was it to come by zines in Australia?**

**DN:** When *Crimson Celluloid* started, there were no other movie zines in Australia, certainly no other horror zines, and I'm proud of the fact that in our own small way we inspired many other zines to start up. I think a lot of people read *CC* and thought, "I can do better than that!" In a lot of cases, they were right, though I was first. The only way I got zines was to order them, mainly from the US. I'd put a few bucks in an envelope, send them my zine and hope they'd write back.

A lot of the films that were covered in the US zines at the time didn't make it down here, so it was at the same time frustrating and fun to read about them. This was in the days before the internet where all you have to do is point and click and any film you have ever wanted to see is available.

**JS: Were you aware that the Australian grindhouse films would make such an impression on the rest of the world?**

**DN:** No, we were pretty isolated, but it wouldn't take a genius to realize a film like *Mad Max 2* (*Road Warrior*) would have worldwide appeal. It's a great source of pride that we could export films like *Turkey Shoot*.

**JS: Who were your favorite Ozploitation directors?**
**DN:** Probably the same ones every Aussie mentions. George Miller. Tim Burstall. Bruce Beresford. I tend to think that a lot of the films that meant so much to me as a kid were very much of their time and a lot of them look like so much hot air today. I'm far more excited about the current crop of filmmakers and producers than I am when I look back at where we have come from. Today we have people like Ursula Dabrowsky directing quality films like *Family Demons* and *Inner Demon*. Richard Wolstencroft carrying the exploitation banner with his cult films and MUFF [Melbourne Underground Film Festival]. People like Mark Savage and Josef J. Webber continue to push the bounds and produce new and interesting genre films. Producers like Fiona De Caux are doing great work and we shouldn't forget mavericks like Dick Dale who runs the Trasharama Film Festival each year, bringing exposure to films that many times wouldn't otherwise see light of day.
**JS: What effect did the "video revolution" have on your shores?**
**DN:** The 1980s was a glorious period of time for those wanting to find weird and obscure films. We had many a "video warehouse" (clearing houses for new and secondhand videos) in Sydney, and weekends would be spent on hands and knees going through the discarded VHS and BETA films. We had many independent video labels who distributed all the "crap" (one man's crap was *our* treasure!) that the major labels had no interest in touching. Nothing can replicate the joy of discovering a copy of *Let Me Die a Woman* for the first time or *Night of the Warlock*, *Mantis in Lace*, *Switchblade Sisters*... the list is endless.
**JS: The UK had its video nasties. I've always been curious as to what the censorship laws in Australia were like.**
**DN:** It goes in stages and levels of repression and censorship. Every few years, a politician will brew a fondue in his pants about a certain film or video game and the "censorship debate" will flare up again. These days it's not as bad as it was, but not as good as it should be.
**JS: Was it hard to find the films that you wanted to see?**
**DN:** It was hard to see films on the big screen thanks to the narrow-mindedness of the distributors. But thanks to the video revolution the search would often yield films we'd long heard of but never had the chance to see.
**JS: When did you start *Crimson Celluloid*?**
**DN:** I started it in the early eighties. I was a seventeen or eighteen year old kid who had no knowledge of self-publishing, but was inspired to start up and foolish enough to think people would actually read the thing. And, more so, care what I had to say!
**JS: Had you written anything before that?**
**DN:** No, but at school, English was the only subject I ever excelled at. I have an English public school education to thank for my life-long

# David Nolte

## Crimson Celluloid

RECORDED & INDEXED

DRAFT

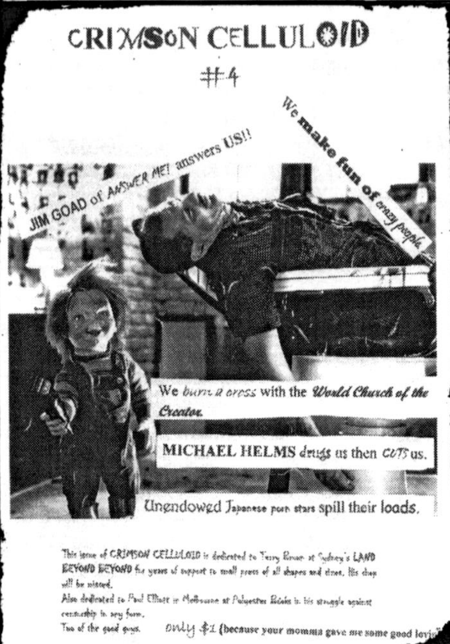


love of the English language as well as ritualized brutality and humiliation.

CRIMSON CELLULOID
#4
We make fun of crazy people.
JIM GOAD of ANSWER ME! answers US!!
We burn a cross with the World Church of the Creator.
MICHAEL HELMS drugs us then CUTS us.
Unendowed Japanese porn stars spill their loads.

**JS: Where did you find your inspiration?**

**DN:** *Scareaphanalia* and a love of genre films mainly, but also I was so keen to meet fellow horror movie fans. I was a pretty shy and reclusive kid and it was a *big* leap for me to put myself out there in such an overt fashion. Someone once said, "*Crimson Celluloid* isn't a fanzine, it's a cry for help." I tend to agree.

**JS: What did you feel that you could bring to the table?**

**DN:** I didn't think that far ahead nor had that much interest in self-analysis at the time; it was just a fun thing to do. Looking back at those early issues today, I think it always possessed a good sense of humor and was a fun read. I don't have copies of the earliest issues, I think they are lost to history, but I remember that as crude as they were, they were the most fun to produce. The first eight or nine issues had a bad hand-drawn logo and no illustrations, but they had enthusiasm behind them. I think I "borrowed" a lot of my writing style from Rick Sullivan at *Gore Gazette*, but nobody had seen that zine down here, so they all thought I was a comic genius rather than a plagiarizing hack. Strangely, I didn't feel the need to correct them. Later on, I was very lucky to meet Ken Taylor and he designed a cool and professional logo for us.

**JS: How was it produced?**

**DN:** I used to have this beat-up Brother word processor into which I'd use thermal paper. I used to print around fifty to 100 copies of those earliest issues. Like *Gore Gazette*, I also had a midnight grant, using the xerox machine at the office where I worked to do all my printing.

**JS: How did you distribute?**

**DN:** In Sydney, I would go to the legendary comic shop Land Beyond

Beyond, video shops, and the late, great Mandolin cinema to distribute *CC*. Funnily enough, I would leave *many* copies of the zine at the cinema and go back a few days later and usually find them all gone. It was only much later I would be told that a local musician would go in there, take all the issues and sell them on the weekend at the local markets. It didn't worry me; if he could make a buck on them, more power to him. I never put a cover price on the early issues, mainly because I didn't think people would pay for them and I was too lazy to chase up any money owing.

CRIMSON CELLULOID
#666
We go to the Arthouse!!!!
ANATOMIE
Manheim Jerkoff threatens life and limb.
"Dear Diamanda....you SUCK!"
Michael Helms answers our inane questions.
PO BOX 352
PLYMPTON, SA 5038
AUSTRALIA
crimsoncelluloid@hotmail.com
Guaranteed...at least 50% more half-arsed than normal and still only $1.


**JS: You had a co-editor as time went on.**

**DN:** It was at Land Beyond Beyond where I met my friend Manheim Jerkoff, who would go on co-edit the latter issues with me. The owner of LBB, Terry Brown, was a great supporter of *CC* back in the day. The link with the Mandolin Cinema would later provide us with the opportunity to screen a series of late-night horror and grindhouse films (again, ripping off an idea by Rick Sullivan). These were a great success while they lasted and enabled us to meet a lot of our readers (those on parole anyway). At one late-night screening, there was a young fellow sitting on the couch in the lobby bleeding from a knife wound. We suggested he had to go to the hospital to which he replied, "But I want to see the movie!" We'd run all-night sleaze marathons, do our best to imitate William Castle by having giant spiders crawl down the screen and tried to make it as much fun as it could possibly be.

**JS: What kind of publishing schedule did you have?**

**DN:** Anytime over the years I tried to work to a schedule it never happened. Best intentions and all that. I ended up publishing on an "it'll happen *when* it happens" basis.

**JS: How was *CC* received by its readers?**

**DN:** It seemed to be that the majority of people who bothered to write were usually other zine publishers, the people who understood the value of getting a letter in the mail. Over all the years I published *CC*, in its original incarnation or the more recent issues, I have probably received less than fifty letters. People would gladly take the zine (especially when it was free) but actually putting pen to paper and mailing a letter would prove to be too much for them. I'm not bitter about it, it just would have been nice to have heard from people, even if they said we sucked. That's why someone like Dave Szurek was so appreciated back then. Even if he hated what you were doing, he'd write these incredible letters, contribute reviews and keep the fire burning in you even when you were down to just ambers.

**JS: Dave was all over the place! How did you go about contacting people for interviews?**

**DN:** I'd usually (1) Exaggerate, (2) Stretch the truth, or (3) Outright lie. When approaching people for an interview, our circulation would mysteriously expand from fifty to 100 to several thousand. I'd usually purchase those big Cannes/Film Market issues of *Variety*, and go through them looking for genre films that looked interesting. Then, I'd try and scam stills out of distributors for "Australia's leading horror magazine" (the word "fanzine" mysteriously replaced).

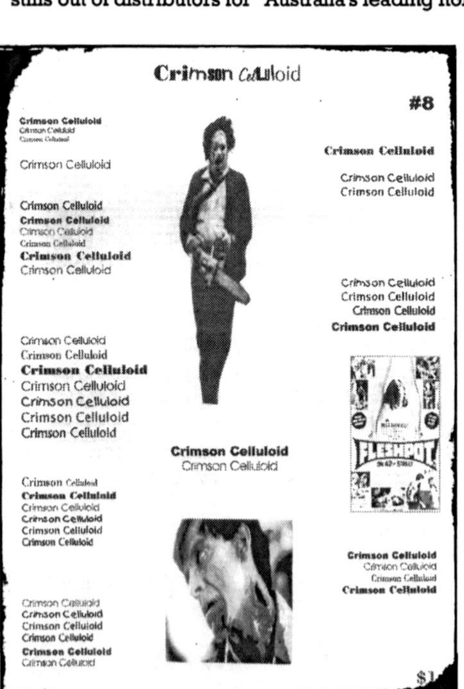


**JS: Did they usually accommodate?**

**DN:** Most people were actually really cool. Ringing someone in America from Australia back then probably added a bit of credibility. I did a phone interview with filmmaker Roberta Findlay that was a lot of fun. I went to H.G. Lewis' house in Florida and did a *long* interview with him. We spoke to Andy Milligan a few times but never got around to doing an interview. I learned to lie after approaching Australian filmmaker Brian Trenchard-Smith

for a set-visit to *Dead End Drive-In*. I spoke to him on the phone several times and he seemed keen and nice enough. Then I made the mistake of sending him some back issues of *CC*, after which he wouldn't return phone calls. It worked out OK; he's a hack and the film sucked anyway. We managed to scam our way onto the set of *Howling 3* and interview Philippe Mora.

**JS: What was he like?**

**DN:** Mora seemed nice enough. I don't think he had *seen* a copy of *CC*, otherwise we probably wouldn't have been invited. The film was shot outside Sydney and it was exciting seeing the machinations of film production up close for the first time. We saw a couple of scenes being filmed, chatted to a few extras and watched special FX artist Bob McCarron at work. Generally our time was spent trying to stay out of the way and not knock over props during shooting. We ended up featuring a pic of Mora signing autographs in *CC* and didn't really cover the film that much. In hindsight, after seeing the film, that was probably the *right* decision.

CRIMSON CELLULOID
David Nolte/312 Great Nth Road/Five Dock/
2046 NSW/Australia/$2.00 per issue

*Nifty 'zine from Down Under with editors who proclaim their love for "the lowest ebb of cinema" and their fondness for "foreign horror and sleaze films of the 1968-75 period--their perversity peak." Lots of films mentioned even your editor has never heard of. Good work, Lads!*

CHAS. BALUN REVIEWS *CC*. *DEEP RED* NUMBER 2.

**JS: Where did you usually source your stills from?**

**DN:** Some of the local video companies actually saw issues of *CC* and *still* wanted to contribute stills and would routinely invite us to media screenings. I guess they figured that even though we had a small circulation, we were still catering to a niche market and any publicity is good publicity. I can't remember the film, I think it was some Troma shitter, but a local film distributor put a fake quote on their video box "The *BEST* film of the year"—*Crimson Celluloid*. Obviously, since Troma was

RECORDED & INDEXED
DRAFT

CRIMSON CELLULOID
#12

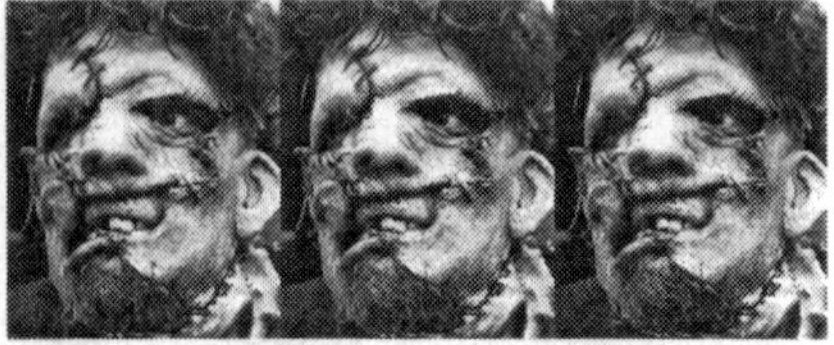

LEATHERFACE PRE-MAKEOVER
and

POST "QUEER EYE" 2003 MAKEOVER
ALSO IN THIS ISSUE:

CURTIS (BOOGER) ARMSTRONG
LARRY (*FRIDAY THE 13th PART 3*) ZERNER
KUNG FU *LEGEND* LEO FONG
TOKEN PORNSTAR ZENOVA BRAEDEN
DIGITAL DRUGS
HATEFUL PRANK E-MAILS

$1

involved, I had said no such thing. I rang them and told them it was bullshit, but didn't take it any further. I was amazed that they thought anyone would hire a film on the basis that *we* recommended it, anyway.

**JS: Did *CC* ever encounter any legal troubles?**

**DN:** We had one mother write in and say that she was upset her son was reading such trash. The only relatively serious legal issue came when *CC* was resurrected in South Australia many years later. A film company in the US took it upon themselves to send me a review copy of *Nekromantik*, which was promptly seized by our Customs department. This resulted in being visited by the authorities and threatened with a potential court appointment. Thankfully, they believed me when I told them that I had no control over what people sent me in the mail. Fuck 'em, I'd already seen the film anyway.

**JS: Did self-publishing lead to any pro jobs?**

**DN:** No, none of our female readers were ever so obliging…oh, *PRO* jobs.. no, none of those either.

**JS: On that note, let's talk about some of the seminal zines.**

**DN:** I thought *Sleazoid Express* was pretty good at the start, but only reached legendary status once Jimmy McDonough came onboard. Before that, it was somewhat dry. Though, having said that, I was never very au fait with drugs so the whole heroin thing was lost on me. I thought Bill's documentation of his drug addiction and descent into the world of porn was amazing, though, and lead to a quest at *CC* to find as many of his altar-ego's (Bobby Spector's) films as possible. If I had to choose between *Gore Gazette* and *Sleazoid*, I'd always take the former.

**JS: I always had a soft spot in my heart for *Subhuman*.**

**DN:** Cecil Doyle is one of the great writers of zinedom, and certainly

hasn't received the recognition he deserves (until *now*, hopefully). *Subhuman* was always a pleasure to get in the mail. He wrote lengthy and interesting articles and his reviewing style was unique.

**JS: In your opinion, was the fanzine network pretty close-knit?**

**DN:** Yes, the American zine publishers were very supportive of our efforts. Originally, there was nobody doing anything locally that was similar, so we didn't have a chance to compare. But once *CC* was out there and got known a whole bunch of Aussie zines sprung up.

**JS: Can you tell me a little about *Fatal Visions*?**

**DN:** Starting with issue number 1, Michael Helms did everything better than us, and on a much more professional and grander scale. I was a bit envious at the start, since he was doing everything we wanted to do, but didn't have the facilities and abilities to do. Michael has been the number one supporter of *CC* since day one, and without his support and encouragement, we would have folded a lot earlier.

**JS: When did you start writing for them?**

**DN:** I was still doing *CC* on and off, and during the *long* breaks between issues I'd get stuff in the mail to review. Rather than put this stuff to waste, Michael offered me a column which I called "DNA" (David Nolte Archives… a play on words and an egotistical way to keep my name out there). This gave me a chance to review the books, DVDs and other stuff that came my way. Also around this time, I was corresponding with any number of serial killers, and one of them was Gerard J. Schaefer who was incarcerated in Florida State prison. He wrote the disgusting *Killer Fiction* and I became an immediate fan of his work. He agreed to do some interviews on *FV*'s behalf with Ottis Toole, a convicted necrophile. I also contributed some reviews here and there and an interview with serial killer John Wayne Gacy.

**JS: What do you think the fascination with serial killers is all about?**

**DN:** When in doubt, blame your religious upbringing. Seriously though, despite my interest in violent movies and true crime I am probably the least violent person you'd ever meet. I have *never* had a fist-fight, never spent a night in jail, so I guess rocking back and forth in a dark room, fondling a knife *is* healthy and cathartic after all! I got into true crime around the mid-eighties. I had read a book about serial killer John Wayne Gacy and subsequently seen a painting he had done in a drug-addled abode in Sydney frequented my musicians and madmen. This dwelling, dubbed 'Gracelands', was the home of my friend Stu Spasm (of legendary Aussie punk band Lubricated Goat). We had met after his band had performed naked on a national TV show to much notoriety. Stu was an accomplished artist so I commissioned him to do a painting of Gacy surrounded by corpses (as you do). I noticed that another resident of the house had a painting from Gacy that was purchased from a store in the US. Up until then it had never occurred to me to write directly to the serial killers I had read about but Gacy was as good a person to start with as

any. I shot him a letter of introduction, mentioning I had recently broken up with a girlfriend and was interested in corresponding with him. I was thrilled to receive a letter back some weeks later that started with "Now you can quit jacking-off since your girlfriend dumped you..." Who knew that a serial killer could be so lacking in tact and diplomacy? Needless to say this opened the floodgates. I would continue to read true crime books and if the person seemed interesting I would drop them a line. Amazingly *most* wrote back. Hardly a day would go by when I would open my PO Box and it wouldn't be chock full of mail from many US prisons. So began friendships with Gacy, Bittaker, Doug Clark, Richard Ramirez, Henry Lee Lucas, Dahmer, Bill Bonin, Charles Ng, Herb Mullin, Phil Jablonski, Arthur Shawcross, Gerard Schaefer, Ottis Toole, Ed Kemper, Elmer Wayne Henley and many, many more. It was an expensive habit (especially if you were open to receiving collect phone calls) but fun. I mean, how many people have (or would want?) a collection of Gacy paintings (my fave is the *Pogo the Clown* that carries in the inscription, "To David Nolte. I hope you enjoy this painting as much as I enjoyed doing it with you." *WITH*??!!). How many people would chat late at night with Phil Jablonski and struggle to answer his question "When I get out of jail do you want to go on a kill spree with me?" *You* collect your stamps!

These days I only correspond with a handful of long-term fiends... and am planning a trip to San Quentin sometime soon to visit them one-on-one. It was a glorious time, and some of the more interesting individuals were preserved historically in the pages of *CC* and *Fatal Visions*.

**JS: I've always been curious about the zine scene Down Under. Were there any other zines from Australia that deserve mention?**

**DN:** *Visual Violence* was the brainchild of Darren Cole. It covered horror and pop

culture in an amusing and entertaining way. *Sepsis* was hardcore deviance, porn, and violence. *Shitfeast* was horror and sleaze. *Mondo Gore* originated in Queensland and was pretty similar to what we were doing. Dann Lennard's *Betty Paginated* was porn, wrestling, comics and sleaze all done in a very professional and (later) glossy way.

**JS: How did you come in contact with Anthony Timpson?**

**DN:** I'm assuming that the initial contact with Ant came about when he asked for a copy of *CC* to be sent to him in his native New Zealand. He started producing a zine called *Violent Leisure* and it was immediately obvious that we had a lot in common..

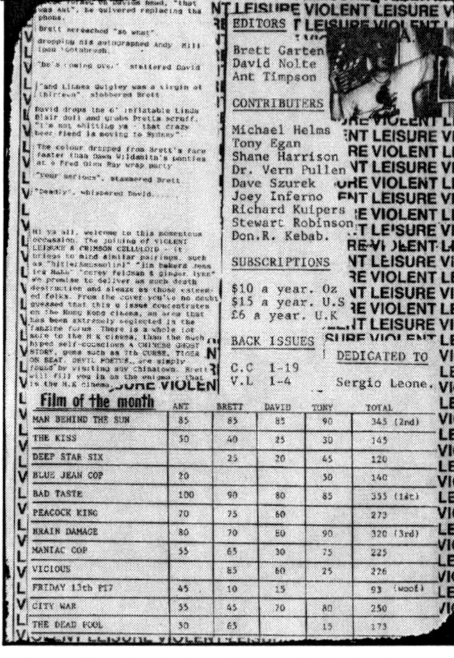

EDITORS

Brett Garten
David Nolte
Ant Timpson

CONTRIBUTERS

Michael Helms
Tony Egan
Shane Harrison
Dr. Vern Pullen
Dave Szurek
Joey Inferno
Richard Kuipers
Stewart Robinson
Don.R. Kebab.

SUBSCRIPTIONS

$10 a year. Oz
$15 a year. U.S
£6 a year. U.K

BACK ISSUES

C.C 1-19
V.L 1-4

DEDICATED TO

Sergio Leone.

| Film of the month | ANT | BRETT | DAVID | TONY | TOTAL |
| --- | --- | --- | --- | --- | --- |
| MAN BEHIND THE SUN | 85 | 85 | 85 | 90 | 345 (2nd) |
| THE KISS | 50 | 40 | 25 | 30 | 145 |
| DEEP STAR SIX | | 25 | 20 | 45 | 120 |
| BLUE JEAN COP | 20 | | | 50 | 140 |
| BAD TASTE | 100 | 90 | 80 | 85 | 355 (1st) |
| PEACOCK KING | 70 | 75 | 60 | | 273 |
| BRAIN DAMAGE | 80 | 70 | 80 | 90 | 320 (3rd) |
| MANIAC COP | 55 | 65 | 30 | 75 | 225 |
| VICIOUS | | 85 | 60 | 25 | 226 |
| FRIDAY 13th PT7 | 45 | 10 | 15 | | 93 (woof) |
| CITY WAR | 55 | 45 | 70 | 80 | 250 |
| THE DEAD POOL | 50 | 65 | | 15 | 173 |

EDITORIAL AND FILM OF THE MONTH. *CC/VL* NUMBER 5.

**JS: What was *CC/VL*?**

**DN:** Ant located briefly to Australia and, as luck would have it, moved into the house I was living in at the time. *CC/VL* (the initials of both our zines, obviously) came about as a result of both of us wanting to keep publishing and pooling our resources. We only churned out a couple of issues, but thanks to Ant's involvement, they were the best ones we ever did. They looked great and evolved to cover new genres like Asian horror films. Ant's enthusiasm and film knowledge more than made up for his rampant alcohol consumption and lingering beer farts.

**JS: You stopped publishing *CC* for a while and then started up again. Why did you stop, and what gave you the drive to jump back in?**

**DN:** *CC* had run its course, but I had also become somewhat jaded by the selfishness of some people involved in its production. I started *CC* alone and had done seven or eight issues before being contacted by my eventual co-editor Brett. He was a young kid, full of enthusiasm and knowledge about horror and cult films and I'll freely admit he bought a lot to the issues he was involved in. Unfortunately giving *him* credit for his contributions didn't seem to flow *both* ways. Time and time

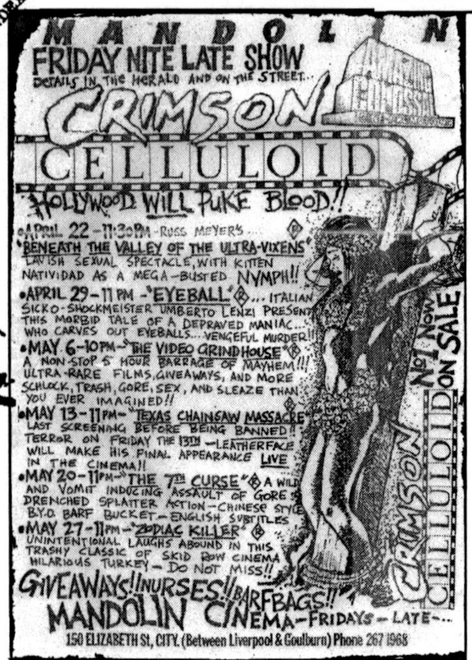


again Brett would do interviews about *CC* and when they were published I wouldn't get a mention, in fact there wouldn't be mention of a co-editor at all.. or worse still, *he* would be credited as the sole editor of the damned thing. Now I'm not a glory-seeker and was always more than happy to share whatever rare accolades came our way... but this started to rankle. Brett would always cite being "misquoted" but after it happened time and time again I began to get pissed off. The final straw for me was spotting him on the street dressed up in a suit. When asked where he was going he replied "to do an interview about *CC* for (some glossy magazine that came with the weekend edition of our largest newspaper)". I was annoyed about not even being told about it but, what the fuck, do you best and "make sure credit is given where it is due". I don't have to tell you that when the magazine came out, there's a full-color pic of Brett, smiling away as the "editor" of *CC* and no mention of me or any of the other many valuable contributors to the zine. I think *CC* went on for a little bit after that but I had lost interest. Eventually I moved back to South Australia and started up a whole new era of *CC* with the help of my co-editor Manheim Jerkoff and ably assisted by Michael Helms, Steve Jennings, John Harrison, and many others. *CC* could *never* be done alone, a fact that I am happy to admit.

**JS: Is *CC* still active in any form?**

**DN:** Like a rotting zombie you can't keep it down, though I haven't produced an issue in several years now. I tend to write online these days, mainly for the site located at www.cinemania.co.nz. I get the urge to put out a zine now and then, but then the meds kick in and I move onto something else...

# Chapter Twenty-Six
# MICHAEL GINGOLD
## Scareaphanalia

FANEX 4, AUGUST 11, 1990. [L–R:] DAN TAYLOR (*EXPLOITATION RETROSPECT*), DICK KLEMENSEN (*LITTLE SHOPPE OF HORRORS*), GARY SVEHLA (*MIDNIGHT MARQUEE*), NATHAN MINER (*BITS N PIECES*), DOM SALEMI (*ECCO/BRUTARIAN*), MICHAEL GINGOLD (*SCAREAPHANALIA*), STEVE PUCHALSKI (*SHOCK CINEMA/SLIMETIME*), CHARLES KILGORE (*ECCO*). PHOTO COURTESY OF NATHAN MINER.

Michael Gingold's

# SCAREAPHANALIA

No. 70, Oct. 1988

The monthly fanzine of horror film news and reviews. $7.50/year or trade for your fanzine. Send letters and subscription orders to Michael Gingold, 55 Nordica Drive, Croton-on-Hudson, N.Y. 10520. Single copies/back issues: 60¢.

Artwork: Webster Colcord.

HALLOWEEN IV

Why, oh why, did they do it?

Was it because the last film left some unexplored avenues that warranted a sequel? Was it because someone had a fresh or exciting new idea about approaching the story? Was it because no other films were around using the same kind of story? No, it was because Moustapha Akkad, who owned the rights, wanted to exploit a marketable property for a few quick bucks.

When I told some of my friends I was going to see Halloween 4: The Return of Michael Myers, they replied, "It's only up to four?" They evidently had the Halloween films mistaken for the Friday the 13th movies, and Halloween 4 will do nothing to alleviate the confusion. It's a stupid, gratuitous, and thoroughly unscary project that rips off and cheapens a classic of horror. The idiocy starts early in Alan B. McElroy's script, which tells us that Dr. Loomis (Donald Pleasence) and Michael Myers survived the explosion at the end of Halloween II, Loomis coming out with only a limp and some latex burn scars on his face. Mikey had a worse time; he's been in a coma for ten years, and in the opening scene, he's about to be transferred to a new hospital. After some of the most blatantly expositional dialogue of the year, he's packed into an ambulance for the trip, and any fan of Jason can tell you what happens next. After leaving the attendants dead and the ambulance to crash (apparently into a pool of dry ice, given all the mist around the accident site), Michael (George Wilbur) has a confrontation with Loomis that's lifted from The Hitcher's gas station scene, except in this one the fire happens to burn down the phone lines. Then the killer makes his way to Haddonfield, his hometown, where he walks into a store and gets a new mask, and the only person who notices is Jamie (Danielle Harris), his young niece. Wait a second; his niece? That's right, Laurie (Jamie Lee Curtis' character from the first two films), had a daughter, though she herself has since died, and now the Shape is after his last surviving relative. And if you think that's a ludicrous swipe from the first films, wait till the ending, when Jamie, having seen Michael murder several people and get blown away by shotguns, turns psychotic herself and is left standing in a clown suit, holding a pair of bloody scissors, in the final shot.

You'd hide your face too if you were in Halloween 4.

That's right; I just pulled a Gene Siskel and gave away the ending, but I did it for the same reason he did: to emphasize just how much I want people not to see this movie. Halloween 4 is an insult to the intelligence, taste, and most of all to the memory of the first Halloween. The script is full of stupid coincidences (Michael just happens to find Jamie's house and discover evidence of her relation to Laurie), ludicrous plotting (after Michael knocks out the power in town, no one but the main characters seems to notice), and scenes that would be unpleasant if they

# Chapter Twenty-Six

Ant Timpson once called Michael Gingold "the Kevin Bacon of fanzines." A clichéd analogy, to be sure, but his casual observation managed to hit the nail squarely on the head (ouch!). As the managing editor of *Fangoria*, Gingold has been dealing in the horror business for over twenty years—and that doesn't even count his long run as the editor and publisher of *Scareaphanalia*, the fanzine that he started when he was a sophomore in high school. From the photocopied reviews that he typed out as a kid to his set visits with the stars, Michael Gingold has been there and done that. Quite frankly, the guy has done and seen it all.

I first encountered *Scareaphanalia* a little late in the game. Michael was already working for *Fangoria* by that time, and I was amazed to find that he was juggling two publications. "This guy must never sleep!" I thought, and judging by the following conversation, I don't think that my assessment was too far off the mark. The man works very hard at what he does, but he clearly loves every minute of it.

Michael took time off from his busy schedule for the following interview, direct from *Fango* HQ, on a scalding July afternoon. I could almost feel the buzz at the office— the pending deadlines and fresh copy being passed around—as I dialed the phone and waited for an answer...

The following interview was conducted via telephone on July 17, 2012.

---

**JOHN SZPUNAR: Can you give me a little background information about yourself?**

**MICHAEL GINGOLD:** Sure. I grew up in Westchester County, New York, where I still reside, and where I started *Scareaphanalia* back when I was in high school.

**JS: Did you ever imagine that you'd become a journalist when you were growing up?**

**MG:** I never really studied writing or journalism; it was just sort of something that I did. I guess I found that I had a knack for it, very early on. I was actually writing for my local high school paper when I was still in junior high school. I had always wanted to write about film, and film reviews, and I got started about the age of eleven or twelve. There was no real professional outlet for them, so I just started contributing them to the high school paper. Then, of course, when I got to high school, I wrote for them a lot more. It was during my sophomore year of high school that I started *Scareaphanalia*.

**JS: I grew up with monster movies on TV.**

**MG:** My first love was *Godzilla* movies and Ray Harryhausen's stop-motion fantasy and monster films. I was huge into both of those when I was growing up. I would watch "Monster Week" on *The 4:30 Movie*, and

RECORDED & INDEXED

DRAFT

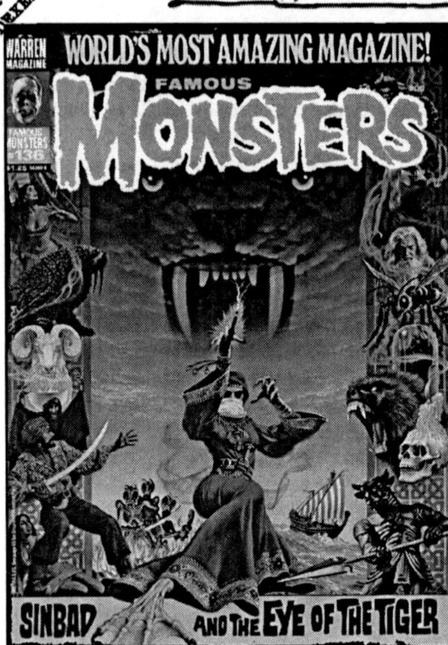


like a lot of kids of the period, I would scour every issue of *TV Guide*. They used to list every movie that would be airing on TV that week, and I'd go through that like a checklist and find out when the stuff was going to be airing.

**JS: Late-night shows?**

**MG:** Yeah, usually around one in the morning, or something; at a certain time of my life, they were on too late for me to stay up, but after a certain point I started watching all of that stuff. Then I remember when *Starlog* announced that it was going to be doing this new magazine called *Fantastica*. *Godzilla* was the first cover subject, so of course, I was way into that. Then, the well-publicized problems happened over the title. It got delayed for six months, and finally emerged as *Fangoria*. That was in 1979, right around the time that I was starting to see horror films in the theater. The first real horror film I saw in a theater was *Phantasm*, which came out around the time of the first issue of *Fangoria*. So, all of those things kind of coincided and transitioned me to being into harder-core horror, though I'm still a huge fan of both *Godzilla* and Harryhausen to this day.

**JS: Were you reading monster magazines before *Fangoria* hit the scene?**

**MG:** Oh, of course. I discovered *Famous Monsters of Filmland* in the Summer of 1977. Again, it was thanks to the cover. I was actually on vacation with my family. We were up in the Thousand Islands, and I walked into this pharmacy, or whatever store it was, and there was *Famous Monsters* with *Sinbad and the Eye of the Tiger* on the cover. Of course, I immediately snapped that up and became an instant fan. I read it and collected it for years after, right up until the time that the Forry Ackerman incarnation went out of business.

**JS: How old you were you discovered *Famous Monsters*?**

**MG:** I guess I was ten years old.

**JS: That's about the perfect age for it.**

**MG:** Oh yeah. I'm kind of surprised that I hadn't come across it before, because I had been into those movies before then. And it did turn out to be available in my area; it's just that I had somehow never found it. I immediately subscribed, started ordering back issues, and built up a little collection. I distinctly remember that I went on a trip to visit family in Australia in 1978, and my entire collection of horror and monster movie magazines fit in a backpack that I took with me on the plane. When I look at the size of my collection now, it's kind of funny.

**JS: Were there any fanzines in your backpack?**

**MG:** I wasn't really aware of too many fanzines at the time. I'd kind of heard about them, but I sort of assumed that they were professional magazines. I didn't really know about fanzines, as such, for a little while. It was only once I discovered what they were all about that I was inspired to do my own.

**JS: What zines inspired you?**

**MG:** It was kind of two-fold. I started going to the Lincoln Center Library for the Performing Arts. You could read movie magazines from around the world there, and they also had these big binders up on the top floor. They were scrapbooks, really, and they had clippings of movie reviews going way back to the beginning of cinema. I started going through those, looking up reviews of horror films, and I noticed that they had clippings from *Sleazoid Express* in there. *Sleazoid Express* was one of the first fanzines that I'd ever heard of, but, with limited information, I just assumed that it was at least a semi-professional magazine. Then I saw those clippings and discovered that it was a xeroxed fanzine. Around the same time, a friend of mine had put in a free subscriber ad into *Fangoria*. As a result, a couple of editors of xeroxed zines, like *Confessions of a Trash Fiend*'s Richard Green, sent him several copies in an attempt to get him to subscribe, and he showed those to me. At the time, I was growing up in a small town, and horror was not as big as it is now. I was pretty much the only die-hard horror fan that I knew, and I'd always been looking for a way to communicate with other fans. This, obviously, was well before the internet. So, the combination of discovering that *Sleazoid Express* (which had quite a reputation at the time) was a xeroxed zine and seeing these other zines that my friend had gotten inspired me to start my own.

**JS: For a long time, fanzines were the main way to get your voice out there. How did you come up with the title for yours?**

**MG:** I remember that I had two choices for the title. One was the *Terror Times*, which was kind of boring. Then, I came up with *Scareaphanalia*. I remember using this little printing outfit that I had gotten from school to make up some headlines. I made up one for the *Terror Times* and one for *Scareaphanalia*. I looked at them both and said, "It's got to be *Scareaphanalia*." I launched it in January of 1983.

**JS: A great time to be writing about horror movies. I'm just young enough to have missed a lot of great films when they were released**

# MICHAEL GINGOLD

## SCAREAPHANALIA!

Michael Gingold's **SCAREAPHANALIA** No. 60, Dec. 1987

**The monthly fanzine of horror film news and reviews. Published the third weekend of each month. Yearly subscriptions are $6.00, or in trade for a year of your fanzine. Send letters and subscription orders to Michael Gingold, 55 Nordica Drive, Croton-on-Hudson, N.Y. 10520. Single copies and back issues are 50¢ each.**

Artwork: Webster Colcord.

After seeing the all-too-tame film of V.C. Andrews' cult novel Flowers in the Attic and hearing about the incest and other sordid doings that were omitted in the page-to-screen transition, I decided to read the book to see what I'd missed. Surprisingly (or perhaps not surprisingly), the novel is almost as bad as the movie, an overwrought piece of Gothic silliness that reads like Stephen King for teenyboppers (teenage girls, in fact, comprised more than 60% of its readership). Some omissions and slight changes aside, the film follows the book pretty closely, telling the story of a family that is perfectly happy until one night when the father is killed in an accident. Mother Corinne (Victoria Tennant) has no way to support herself and her kids, and must turn to her parents, who disowned her when she married the man who was also her uncle, for help. She hopes to win back their favor (and their fortune), but there is a catch; Corinne's father never knew he had grandchildren, so the teenaged Cathy (Kristy Swanson) and Chris (Jeb Stuart Adams) and their little twin siblings are shut up in the attic of the family mansion by their stern, nasty Grandmother (Louise Fletcher).

Kristy Swanson after her long confinement in Flowers in the Attic.

The film makes a major mistake right at the beginning by never showing that the kids have a life outside of their original house. There's never a sense that they're missing anything by being shut up in the mansion, and not once do they mention friends, school, or anything else that they're being deprived of from their old lives. (This might have been less of a problem in a setting many years in the past, but some cops in the beginning and details in the rest of the film mark it as contemporary.) Mostly, the kids pine for their mother, who's busy getting in good with Grandmother and rather enjoying her life, and Chris and Cathy engage in a couple of very borderline flirtations while trying to figure out how to escape. It's another major blow to sympathy for them that they're exceptionally slow; it takes them a month to figure out that they might get out by tying bedsheets into a rope that can be lowered out an attic window, and four more weeks to realize that they might get out by removing the hinges on a door. Grandmother, of course, gets wind of their activities and chops off Cathy's beloved long hair; this seems to stunt its growth for good, because there's a transition that suggests that seasons pass, and when we return to Cathy, her hair is the same length as when we left her. And speaking of hair, how did Corinne and her children get to be so blindingly blond when both of her parents have dark hair? Must be a really recessive gene in there somewhere...

The one saving grace of Flowers in the Attic is the performance of Swanson (from Deadly Friend), an actress with angelic good looks and an unfortunate bad habit of getting stuck in lousy horror movies. Adams is earnest but mediocre, all of Tennant's character development takes place offscreen, and the youngsters who play the twins aren't even good enough to be cloying. The movie's worst acting, however, is that of Fletcher, who seems to be doing

theatrically.

**MG:** In the Fall of 1981, I made the remarkable discovery that you didn't actually have to be seventeen to get into R-rated movies without a parent. At least not in the theaters in my area. Four of us went to see *Halloween II* on Halloween night. We put masks on; we went in costume, figuring that if they couldn't see our faces, it would be easier for us to get in. Soon thereafter, we discovered that if you were fourteen or fifteen, most theaters would let you in without a parent. So, I'd been seeing horror films in the theater all through 1982.

**JS: The theaters discussed in *Sleazoid Express* must have been a revelation to you.**

**MG:** I was just reading those clippings of the reviews in those scrapbooks. I didn't really see a full issue of *Sleazoid Express* until several years later. That's when I got the sense of the Times Square ambiance and the history. So, I can't say that that inspired me too much. And at that point, I was still too young to go down to New York City without my family. That didn't come until a little later.

**JS: *Scareaphanalia* lasted for nine years?**

**MG:** Yeah, until a couple of years after I started at *Fangoria*. There was a period where I thought I could do both, but I obviously couldn't. *Scareaphanalia* kind of retired and I began devoting myself to *Fangoria*, and here I am. It's actually really funny that you're calling now. I'm writing up an interview with Dwight Schultz about *Alone in the Dark*, which was the very first movie I reviewed in *Scareaphanalia*.

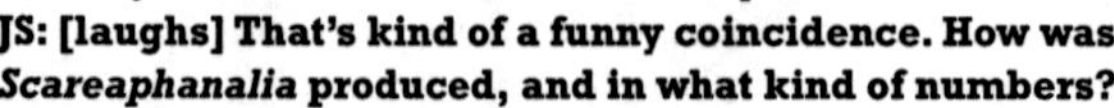

**JS: [laughs] That's kind of a funny coincidence. How was *Scareaphanalia* produced, and in what kind of numbers?**

**MG:** It was really just me typing it up, pasting it up, and taking it over to the copy shop to get it xeroxed. Like a lot of other people, I was mostly using ads that I'd clipped out of the newspaper to illustrate it. Every so often, I tried to do something a little creative with the layout. When

*Children of the Corn* came out, they had that great graphic with the hand with the sickle coming out of the cornfield. I cut around that and put that on the front. I actually put that in the typewriter and typed around the outline to give it a different look. Then, once I started going to college in New York, I discovered that publicists for distribution companies would actually take me seriously as a reviewer. This, again, was before the internet, so I guess they figured that this was their way of communicating with the youth or the grassroots, or whatever. So very quickly, once I got started in school in the Fall of '85, I got on a lot of press lists. I started getting into screenings and getting press kits. I started putting more photos in, in a very low-tech way: I'd cut a hole in the paper that the type was on and put that on top of the photos. I didn't want to cut the photos up! I remember going to Kinko's with these ridiculous legal-sized layout boards with halves of stills sticking out at odd angles. Again, a very low-tech way of doing it, but this was also before the golden age of desktop publishing and scanners. I actually retired *Scareaphanalia* right at the time that technology would have made it a lot easier to produce.

**JS: It's funny—I almost like the aesthetic of the cut and paste stuff better than a lot of the early computer layouts. Something about dot matrix printing made things look kind of cheap to me.**

**MG:** The quality of the early printers wasn't that great. I remember the day I was able to start using a laser printer. That made it so much more legible. I wish I could have gone back and run some of those early issues on a laser printer.

**JS: What kind of a reaction did you get from *Scareaphanalia*?**

**MG:** It was pretty positive. A lot of the reaction I got was from other fanzine editors. They were my most die-hard readers, in a lot of cases. I never went above 250 subscribers. Which, when you think about it back in the day, was a lot. You had 250 people willing to part with whatever it cost to read one person's rantings in a little xeroxed zine. I don't really recall anything too negative. Once in a while, I'd write a review that someone would take umbrage with, but for the most part, it was very positive. The great thing about the scene was that, in large part, it was very supportive. Everybody was kind of behind everyone else's zines and always wanted to plug everyone else's stuff. I actually put a free subscriber ad into *Fangoria*, advertising *Scareaphanalia*, and I got maybe half a dozen responses. When other fanzines would plug it, it got a much better response. The word really spread amongst other zines. We were all into the idea of exchanging ideas and opinions.

**JS: When did you start writing for *Fangoria*?**

**MG:** Well, I'd always been a reader. Like I said, I was with it from the very first issue. I was doing *Scareaphanalia*, going to conventions, and writing things up from there. I would always see Bob Martin and pester him about writing for them. I'm sure he saw me as just some kid—which I was. Then,

SPECIAL REPORT

By MICHAEL GINGOLD

# HOMEMADE HORRORZINES



*"The greater the oppression, the bigger the underground fan scene [that comes out against it]."*

If there's any doubt about the level of devotion that the horror genre inspires, all one has to do is look at the number of genre-oriented publications its fans produce. Fanzines, amateur newsletters and magazines born from typewriters and home computers, have embraced the horror genre like no other; only science fiction commands the same interest among fan editors. There are currently over 50 titles available by subscription—or, in some cases, in specialty shops—originating from all over the world.

The recent explosion of activity in the horror fanzine field began in the early '80s, spearheaded by Bill Landis' *Sleazoid Express*, the first zine to devote itself to the emerging trend of down-and-dirty horror. It was followed by a string of "review-zines," newsletter-sized publications devoted to coverage of current genre product. Many of these, like Jim Morton's *Trashola*, folded after a few years; among the survivors is my own *Scareaphanalia*, a monthly collection of theatrical and video horror reviews. If you've ever wanted to know what one of the Fango/GZ crew really thinks about the latest genre output, here's a chance to find out.

As the decade went on and video subsumed the horror market, it changed the way many fans saw genre films, and new publications sprang up devoted to terror on cassette. "Being located in Indianapolis, I don't get the chance to see theatrical screenings," says Rod Sims of *The*



54 GOREZONE #18

"HOMEMADE HORRORZINES," *GOREZONE*.

when I was in college, I went to interview for an internship. They were familiar with my *Scareaphanalia* work; I'd also been writing for some NYU papers. I got back to my dorm room and four hours later, they called and offered me an article writing job, as opposed to the internship. I started writing for them on a regular basis, and then I joined full-time in 1990.

**JS: What was your first job for them?**

**MG:** It was an interview with the director of *The Seventh Sign*. That turned out to be one of the most difficult *Fangoria* interviews that I ever did. He was one of those guys who kept insisting that his movie was not a horror film. That was the prevailing tone back in the late eighties. Horror was kind of looked down upon at that time, and people—even if they'd made a horror film—would say, "It's not a horror film, it's a supernatural drama," or some such silliness. So, that one was really difficult. But I guess they appreciated that I was able to pull an article's worth of comments out of the guy.

**JS: Horror films seem to get a little more respect these days.**

**MG:** I always say that *Buffy The Vampire Slayer* was kind of the gateway drug to a whole generation of horror fans, female as well as male. The wider the audience became, the more it started to become accepted. And once *Scream* came out, followed by *The Sixth Sense* and *The Blair Witch Project*, the studios started to see horror as something that could make money. A better class of filmmaker could be making horror films and not be ashamed to make them. Horror has kind of benefited from its own success.

**JS: What do you attribute the dark days of the early nineties to?**

**MG:** By the late eighties, most people associated horror with slasher films or franchise stuff like *Friday the 13th* and *A Nightmare on Elm Street*. It was kind of wearing out its welcome by that point.

**JS: I like slasher films as much as the next guy, but things were**

**getting stale.**
**MG:** There was just not a lot of good stuff coming out. I think it took a few successes to get horror into being a serious art form. And you know, you had filmmakers like Francis Ford Coppola doing *Bram Stoker's Dracula*, which certainly helped.
**JS: I was just starting to really get into horror films when the decline started. And I'd always look to fanzines to give me an education about films that I would have otherwise never have known about.**
**MG:** I think fanzines also fed on the fact that there was not a lot of critical attention being paid to these movies. There were a few critics who recognized good horror films when they saw them, but most of the reviews were very dismissive. It's funny—I was just talking to someone about *Friday the 13th*. It was screened at a local club on *Friday the 13th*, and I was talking to someone who's young enough not to have been around at the time it came out. And of course, now it's considered a classic. I was telling her, "You wouldn't believe the reviews that it got when it first opened." You look at the movie now, and it seems kind of tame compared to more recent films, but the reviews that came out at the time basically were equating it with pornography. I think part of the function of fanzines throughout the eighties was to alert the die-hard fans as to what the good stuff was. There were simply not too many places where you could get informed criticism or reviews of these things. A lot of critics just weren't taking them seriously.
**JS: You became the managing editor of *Fangoria* in 1990, right?**
**MG:** Associate editor to start, and then after about a year or so, I became managing editor.
**JS: Out of curiosity, what does a managing editor do?**
**MG:** Pretty much everything. That term varies with the publication. At this point, I'm practically doing everything that the chief editor does. Copy editing, assigning articles, and doing a lot of the writing myself. It varies. It's basically doing everything goes into putting the magazine together, without having the foremost responsibility for the content. Although, since we've changed editors and Chris Alexander's taken over (he's in Toronto and I'm over here in New York), I have a few more responsibilities. He still guides the overall tone of the magazine.
**JS: *Fangoria* is doing a lot of retrospectives these days.**
**MG:** Chris is very much into the retro stuff. I go to conventions, and there are actors there who have done interesting things in the past, and I can sit down with them for interviews. For example, the Dwight Schultz interview that I got about *Alone in the Dark*. There's a place for it in the magazine because Chris is as interested in celebrating horror's past as he is in what's in the present.
**JS: You know what, let me ask you a little about *Gorezone* and an article that you wrote about fanzines for that. It was called "Homemade Horrorzines".**

**MG:** One of the nice things about *Gorezone* was that it was kind of an outlet for some of the odder stuff that I was interested in doing. It was much more focused on the independents and the foreign films. The example I used when we recently did our special issue of *Gorezone* was that I had the idea, "We should talk to Dardano Sacchetti," who wrote (or co-wrote) pretty much every Italian horror classic in the seventies and eighties. *Gorezone* was a place where we could do that kind of thing. Anyway, at that point, I was trading with at least thirty or forty other zines. I thought, "Well, *Gorezone* is so devoted to the independents; we should do something on all these independent publications." It was also a way to give everybody a plug, with a little sidebar where I listed everybody's address and let people know where to subscribe. I basically sent out a form letter and asked everybody to put some quotes down and to comment about the scene, and got comments from pretty much everybody. It was my way of giving a little bit back to the fanzine community that had been so supportive of my efforts over the years.

**JS: That article turned me on to some good zines that I wasn't aware of.**

**MG:** Again, before the internet, there was no other way to let the people know. I remember a magazine that was a directory of fanzines called *Factsheet 5*, with whom I traded subscriptions. I remember when I got the first issue, just being blown away by the breadth of fanzines on all these different subjects. It had never occurred to me that you could have a political fanzine in addition to a movie or music fanzine. But they covered everything. Also, when I was in New York City, I would sell *Scareaphanalia* through a store called See Hear.

**JS: That was such a great place. It's gone now, right?**

**MG:** It's long gone, which is a shame. Obviously, with the decline of xeroxed

MORE "HOMEMADE HORRORZINES".

This week the Kernel Critics look at "The River Wild"

Interviews by Amy Kean

**Erik Estridge, 26, Manhattan:** It was really slow and disappointing. We have to wait 90 minutes to see any real action. The scenery was beautiful, which was the movie's only real strength. Meryl Streep was playing the same type of role that she always plays, but Kevin Bacon was great. I think young kids might like it. **5**

**Kerri Barbour, 22, Brooklyn:** It was a very good film. Meryl Streep was absolutely great, really athletic. I liked her in this role because it was different from some of the roles she's been taking lately, many of which I haven't liked at all. I was proud to see a woman in her mid-40s go out to get in shape. Sports-oriented teens might like it. **8+**

**Michael Gingold, 27, Manhattan:** I enjoyed it pretty much. Kevin Bacon was quite good as the villain. I could have done without the really corny ending. The romance was developed pretty well, but the action took center stage for most of the movie. If you are going to see it, you should see it on the big screen because it will lose a lot on video. **7**

**Chris Poggiali, 23, Manhattan:** The performances were really good, but the story was very paint-by-numbers. Meryl Streep was great as usual. Her character was pretty strong, but the script was just not up to par with her usual stuff. She is taking some parts now that are a little out of her usual range. I would recommend this movie only as a rental. **7**

**Meghan Jackson, 27, Manhattan:** It was great, really suspenseful. Meryl Streep was excellent. I liked this just as much as her other roles, because she always plays strong women; this one is just more athletic. Her character was really believable. I would have changed the sappy ending, though. **9**

*NEW YORK POST'S "POPCORN PANEL"* **Attachment**

zines, their bread and butter was pretty much gone. But, I would go in there every month with my new issue and see what else they had around and pick up a few things. That opened my eyes as to just how big things were.

**JS: You know, I meant to ask this earlier—what kind of impact did Michael Weldon's work have on you?**

**MG:** I got the *Psychotronic* book, and again, just assumed that *Psychotronic* was a professionally published magazine. Then I realized that while it was very slick, it was a fanzine, too. But you know, that's another thing—at the time, there were very few books being published about horror and exploitation films. You had the more scholarly books that talked mostly about the Universal movies and things like that. Today you have tons of books on all kinds of obscure horror, but at the time, you really didn't. That was another area where the fanzines filled in the gaps. I remember specifically that *Wet Paint* ran a story about *Manos: The Hands of Fate* years before it was on *MST3K*, years before anyone was paying attention to it. A lot of people today are part of the cult of *Manos*, but it should be acknowledged that Jeff Smith was there first with *Wet Paint*.

**JS: One of things that I liked about *Gorezone* was that it kind of bridged the gap between the fanzines and the prozines. You had writers like Chas. Balun, Steve Bissette, and Tim Lucas, and they were all doing excellent stuff.**

**MG:** That was another cool thing about it. *Gorezone* allowed for more opinioned columns than *Fangoria* did. *Fangoria* sometimes got criticized for not being critical enough of the films. That was due in large part to the fact that, because of lead times, we'd often not have seen the movies before we ran the coverage on them. With *Gorezone*, we ran more reviews, we had opinionated columns, and it was a little more like a fanzine. And then, once it folded, the nice thing was that we were able to take what had made *Gorezone* distinctive and kind of fold it into *Fangoria*. We started doing more coverage of the independents and the foreign stuff. A few years later, the rise of the internet and email allowed us much easier communication with

DRAFT

RECORDED & INDEXED

Michael Gingold's SCAREAPHANALIA No. 69, Sep. 1988

The monthly fanzine of horror film news and reviews. $7.50/year or trade for your fanzine. Send letters and subscription orders to Michael Gingold, 55 Nordica Drive, Croton-on-Hudson, N.Y. 10520. Single copies/back issues: 60¢.

Artwork: Webster Colcord.

Hi, everyone. As you've noticed, Scareaphanalia has become the Incredible Shrinking Newsletter; this is not the result of a radioactive cloud but part of my continuing struggle to keep costs down. It's also a cue taken from Paul DeCirce, whose Temple of Schlock zine also recently underwent a trip into the Reduction Zone. His prices and address have changed, too; it's now $9/year or 75¢ an issue ($1 each overseas) to Paul at 409 Hixson Ave., Syracuse, N.Y., 13206.

* * *

Jeremy Irons as the withdrawn twin Beverly Mantle in Dead Ringers.

Dead Ringers finds David Cronenberg at his most obsessive since The Brood; it's a bizarre melodrama with touches of the most unsettling kind of psychological horror. Not as accessible as his other mainstream work, it's still required viewing for all Cronenberg fans, and proves once again his skill with actors as well as shock. Jeremy Irons gives an excellent double performance as Elliot and Beverly Mantle, a pair of identical twins whose successful career as gynecologists has its roots in their obsession with the female sex. (It's no accident that their names have feminine-sounding diminutives, Ellie and Bev.) Neither one seems capable of fully dealing with women emotionally - Elliot's attitude toward them is cold and manipulative, while Beverly is shy and withdrawn - and their fascination has become a clinical one. "I've always thought there should be a beauty contest for the insides of women's bodies," Elliot tells Claire Niveau (Genevieve Bujold), an actress he has been treating, shortly before seducing her. He then, without her knowing, turns her over to Beverly, whom he has frequently set up with his conquests because he knows Bev will have no success on his own. What neither of them count on is that Beverly will wind up falling in love with Claire, and his struggle between his growing dependence on her and his continuing dependence on Elliot will lead to tragedy for both twins.

The movie is based on the novel Twins by Bari Wood and Jack Geasland, which in turn was inspired by the true case of twins Stewart and Cyril Marcus, who were found dead in their New York apartment several years ago. From this unusual story, Cronenberg and cowriter Norman Snider has fashioned a psychological mystery that's compelling, though somewhat confusing at times as the brothers both descend into madness. As Beverly's relationship with Claire deepens, he begins to pick up her drug habit, and when her work as an actress takes her away from him for ten weeks, his loneliness only makes the habit worse. Meanwhile, Elliot, who has always handled the business aspects of their clinic, can't help but be affected by his brother's deteriorating condition. When the twins' characters are being set up in the first third, Irons makes them remarkably similar-yet-distinctive, but as both begin to freak out, it's sometimes hard to tell which twin we're watching. Nonetheless, Cronenberg makes the situation and its development intriguing enough to keep one's interest throughout, and his visual style has never been stronger. The cold blue hues of the Mantles' environment and the silver of the tools they

other countries, and we were able to get more reporters in other countries in on it. One of them was Michael Helms, who was in Australia doing *Fatal Visions*. Even before email came along, I asked him if he wanted to cover local movies for us, and he started covering Peter Jackson and things like that. He was on the set of *Braindead*. It was nice to get more of that focus into *Fangoria*. I was able to bring a number of other writers from the fanzine

world to *Fangoria* as well.

**JS: I somehow managed to see *Braindead* theatrically in a suburb of Detroit, but I had to settle for a lot of films on video. I'd imagine that the VHS revolution was pivotal in the films that you had access to when you were doing *Scareaphanalia*.**

**MG:** Video was a big way that I started seeing a lot of movies in the early eighties. Also, cable TV was starting to air them. It was a way to see things that had never played theaters. I had a couple of special issues just devoted to VHS releases. That was actually the way I dealt with the fact that I was going off to camp for a couple of Summers [laughs]. I would watch a bunch of VHS movies and write up reviews and put together those issues early, so that the month I was away at camp, that would be the issue that would go out. It just kind of grew and grew until I was reviewing more VHS titles than theatrical films. That was back in the late eighties, when there were a ton of video titles coming out every month, but not too much in the way of theatrical horror.

**JS: The VCR pretty much tuned me into everything.**

**MG:** Well, it was cool that I was close enough to New York City to go in as a teenager, and that I was living in New York while I was in college. I was able to go to the theaters and see a lot of things that other people only discovered on VHS. I saw stuff like the first two *Silent Night, Deadly Night* films and a lot of the Italian horror stuff. There was a great advantage. Even some of the smaller obscure stuff that would only play in Times Square for a week—I'd get to see that.

**JS: Example?**

**MG:** I remember there was one weekend when *Boggy Creek II* and *Guardian of Hell* came out at the same time in New York. When and where else would you actually be able to run from one theater to another to see those two movies projected?

**JS: Did you appreciate the experience at the time?**

**MG:** Oh, absolutely. And it's funny to me that the same kinds of films that were playing in Times Square back then are now considered art films. A lot of foreign horror films are being imported by companies that otherwise release art cinema, and give them specialty bookings. But I do miss the days when you could see a lot more low budget and independent horror films on the big screen. I also miss the sense of mystery that came with not having the internet to look up information about them. For example, something like *Horror Planet* would be opening, and I'd see the advance listings and have no idea what this movie was. It was only once I went to the theater and saw the credits that I realized that this was the same movie as *Inseminoid*. And any movie is more fun to see in a theater than to watch on video. I guess these days, with eighty-inch flat screen sets, you can get a bunch of people together and kind of have the communal experience, but I can still remember how much fun it was just

## SCAREAPHANALIA!

RECORDED & INDEXED

DRAFT

to go to a theater and catch them. You took your life into your hands on occasion, depending on which theater you were going to, but still...

"A shocking tale of horror that takes you beyond fear."
ONE DARK NIGHT
"too late to escape"
PG PARENTAL GUIDANCE SUGGESTED

**JS: When and why did *Scareaphanalia* officially come to an end?**

**MG:** Well, I did it for about a year-and-a-half or two years after I started at *Fangoria*. And really, it was just a matter of where I wanted to concentrate my efforts. Being with *Fangoria* and *Gorezone* afforded me with a much wider audience than *Scareaphanalia* ever had. And it really filled the desire to communicate my enthusiasm for horror on a much bigger canvas. *Scareaphanalia* was great for all those years, and then once I got to *Fangoria*, I was speaking to such a much wider audience that the fire wasn't there to do *Scareaphanalia* the way it had been all those other years. I couldn't really serve two masters. With no regrets, I folded *Scareaphanalia* and dove into *Fangoria*. I had a couple of other freelance film reviewing jobs at the time, too. I wrote for the *Motion Picture Guide* while that was still in existence. That kind of satisfied the reviewing jones, again for a much bigger audience. But I can certainly say that without *Scareaphanalia*, I wouldn't have made it into *Fangoria*. They saw my enthusiasm and, I guess, whatever writing skills I have. I didn't have to say, "Well, here's some clippings from a newspaper that I did." This was something where I'd devoted years and years of my life to writing about and publishing horror. *Scareaphanalia* was my audition for *Fangoria*, without even knowing it.

**JS: What recent films have impressed you these days?**

**MG:** Well, my favorite horror film of this year is *Cabin in the Woods*. I loved that one. I'm actually going to head up to the Fantasia festival in Montreal in a week or so, which is where I usually discover a lot of cool and interesting stuff. Earlier this year, we had a lot of good mid-range horror films like *The Grey* and *The Woman in Black*.

**JS: Buddy Giovinazzo has a new movie that's coming out at Fantasia this year.**

**MG:** Yeah. That's one of the films that I'm really looking forward to seeing. I loved his segment of *The Theatre Bizarre*. I think this is his first true horror

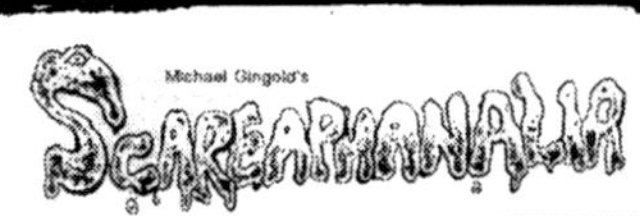


No. 109

The fanzine of horror film news and reviews. $7.50/year, $14 (U.S.) overseas, or in trade for your fanzine. Send letters and subscription orders to Michael Gingold, P.O. Box 489, Murray Hill Station, New York, N.Y. 10156-0489. Single copies/back issues: 75¢ ($1 overseas)

Artwork: Webster Colcord.

Hey, how 'bout those Academy Awards, huh? SILENCE OF THE LAMBS sweeping the top awards, TERMINATOR 2 nailing more technical Oscars than any other film (Stan Winston's gonna run out of space on his mantel real soon), and Ray Harryhausen getting a lifetime achievement award, complete with a great montage of his best work. After all that's already been written, no need to go into much detail about how cool this all is. But I think we could've done without all the "SILENCE is Golden" headlines.

One of the first things I learned at NYU film school was the difference between plot and story in a film. "Story" refers to the events that occur, or are even only referred to, in a film; "plot" refers to how these events are arranged in the screenplay. I thought of that disparity more than once during RAISING CAIN, director Brian De Palma's long-anticipated return to the psychothriller genre that helped make him famous. De Palma also wrote the script, and its story, at least, is fairly straightforward. Carter Nix (John Lithgow) is a child psychologist who's become obsessed with the rearing of his little daughter. To this end, he's adopted a stay-at-home lifestyle and even installed a video camera in the girl's room, the better to be able to check on her. But his obsession has grown into dementia, and he embarks on a campaign to kill women he

Is he for real, or is John Lithgow's mind just RAISING CAIN?

knows and steal their children. His intention is to deliver them to his father and brother Cain (both of whom are also played by Lithgow), who plan to conduct new psychological experiments on the kids, and who may also in fact be only in Carter's mind. Carter's wife Jenny (Lolita Davidovich) is slated to be Carter's last victim and his daughter the last subject, and when Jenny, sensing something weird about Carter lately, falls back into the arms of old lover Jack (Steven Bauer), the daffy doc realizes that Jack is the perfect frame for his crimes.

Like I said, that's the story of RAISING CAIN. The plot, however, is an utterly incoherent mish-mosh of flashbacks, dream sequences and voiceovers. Evidently, De Palma wanted to present different points of view and hallucinations, leaving the audience to slowly come to the realization of how they all tie together, but all he succeeds in doing is thoroughly confusing the audience as to what the hell's going on, and even how it falls into place chronologically. To make matters worse, all this cinematic bait-and-switching allows him no time to explain anyone's motivation or backstory in a visual manner, and so the audience is subjected to big, unwieldy chunks of expository dialogue that even gimmicks like a five-minute tracking shot can't make palatable. De Palma certainly lets all his visual stylistics hang out, but

feature, though *Combat Shock* had some horror elements to it. Speaking of which, I mentioned that when I got to college, I started getting on a lot of publicists' lists, and that allowed me to get into a lot of advance screenings. One of the benefits was that Troma was just starting to get into horror at the time with *The Toxic Avenger*, etc., and they would screen absolutely everything for the critics. Not just their own productions like *Toxic Avenger*, but these weird little pickups. I got on their list, and I would go to see all of these things—it's so weird to think that back then, I could be sitting in this upscale Times Square screening room watching *Student Confidential* or something like that. I grew up with the Troma theme music ringing in my ears. That's another thing that I miss—being able to go into a fancy screening room and seeing the lowest of the low budget. I don't know this for sure, but I think Troma screened everything because getting a review in the *New York Times* was cheaper than buying the equivalent amount of ad space.

**JS: [laughs] That's probably a good guess.**

**MG:** The *Times* would review everything of theirs, and sometimes favorably, too. I can still remember going to the screening of the first *Toxic Avenger* with about half the cast sitting in there with me.

**JS: You were in a few Troma movies.**

**MG:** Oh, yeah. Through going to all of their films, I got to know Lloyd [Kaufman] and that crazy bunch. They wound up shooting a few of their movies up near where I lived. I was very briefly in *Troma's War*. Then a year or so later, I came home for Summer break from college and went to a video store that I used to hang out at all the time. I was good friends with the owner because he loved these kinds of movies, too. It turned out that they had shot part of *Toxic Avenger III* in his store—actually, they shot *Toxic Avenger II* and *III* at the same time as one film, and then they decided to split it into two. They had another month to go, so I basically spent the first part of that Summer driving around to the various locations. I could probably write an entire magazine just about my experiences on that

Michael Gingold's

SCAREAPHANALIA

No. 86, Feb. 1990

The monthly fanzine of horror film news and reviews. $7.50/year, $14 (U.S.) overseas, or in trade for your fanzine. Send letters and subscription orders to Michael Gingold, 55 Nordica Drive, Croton-on-Hudson, N.Y. 10520. Single copies/back issues: 50 cents ($1 overseas).

Clive Barker's NIGHTBREED

BASKET CASE 2

Also in this issue:
FANGORIA Convention Report
PHANTOM OF THE MALL
And more!

Artwork: Dennis Lundberg

shoot. There was a lot of funny and crazy stuff that happened there.

**JS: I can believe it. OK, here's a question: In the eighties, we had sequels. Now, we've got remake after remake after remake. Do you think that horror films commercially have to cannibalize themselves to survive?**

**MG:** I always find it kind of amusing when people act like horror films having sequel after sequel is a modern thing. Back in the thirties and forties, you had all of the Universal monster sequels. They churned out one after the other—that was one of the first sequel syndromes in film history. Obviously, originality is to be supported, but sequels aren't necessarily a new blight on the horror scene.

**JS: That's true.**

**MG:** Sequels have always been with us, it's just a matter of whether they're well done or not. With remakes, there are people who—quite rightly, I think—are blasting last year's *The Thing* remake/prequel. They're basically saying, "How dare they?" forgetting that Carpenter's film was also a remake. And back then, a lot of fans from the 1950s were blasting it: "How dare Carpenter take this classic film and turn it into a gorefest?" To be sure, I don't like the whole remake/sequel trend as a whole, because I think original films should be supported. But, I also think it is possible to do a remake well if you come at it with the idea of taking an existing film and doing something new and interesting with it. I've been briefly attached to a couple of remakes myself as a screenwriter, so, obviously I can't be entirely against that idea [laughs].

**JS: What's your take on fandom on the internet? It seems weird to me that so much has happened in such a short space of time.**

**MG:** Well, I always say that the great thing about the internet is that it

gives everybody a voice, and the bad thing about the internet is that it gives everybody a voice. Back when we were doing fanzines, you really had to have the enthusiasm to make the effort to type them up and lay them out, copy them and send them. You really had to have a commitment to the genre and an interest in communicating. Nowadays, anyone can go on a message board and throw their comments up. I think it's given a lot of people who would never have had the opportunity to share their views a chance to do so. It encourages a lot of positive commentary and debate about things. But, it also allows a lot of people to throw a lot of gratuitous negativity out there, and the sad thing is that negativity tends to attract a lot of attention. There was just a little of that in the fanzine scene, too, where the most hostile voice attracted the most attention. But now, with the internet, you get a lot of people who aren't informed about what they're talking about. I've had some of that, too. I've written some films, and had some pretty negative things written about them online. Some of the criticism is valid, and some of it is just people spouting off and not getting it. Personally, as far as reviews of my own stuff, I try to let it roll over me. But looking at it as someone who's been writing reviews for all this time, there's a real distinction between someone who is a critic and loves film and someone who is doing it because they love the sound of their own voice.

As far as fanzines are concerned, the internet has really kind of taken their place, as well it should. If I would have had the internet when I started *Scareaphanalia*, I could have reached infinitely larger numbers of people. As I said, I published maybe 250 copies a month at the maximum, and I could have probably reached 100 times that many people if I'd had the internet. It's all part of the evolving technology, and it's all about how people use it. As I was saying, it can be used for good or for evil. *Fangoria* is still doing pretty well as a print publication because it's a niche publication. A lot of the more general movie magazines have folded, but a lot of the niche publications are still chugging along, including ours. I think the new direction has helped, because you get not only people who want to read about new movies, but people who really value the older films. I think it fits in very nicely that we have a little more of a retro emphasis in the magazine. To a certain extent, people who are nostalgic about print enough to buy a print magazine will also be nostalgic about the older films. They say vinyl is coming back, so who knows? Maybe more people will get back into buying print magazines, too.

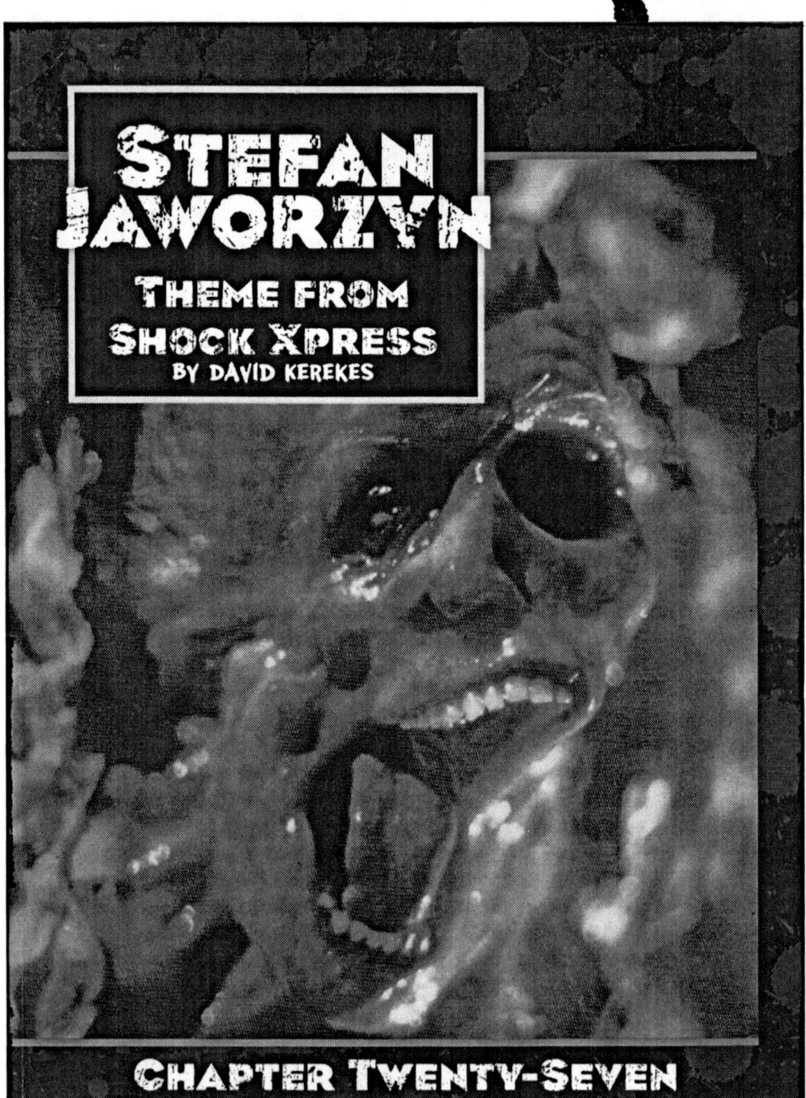
STEFAN
JAWORZYN
THEME FROM
SHOCK XPRESS
BY DAVID KEREKES
CHAPTER TWENTY-SEVEN

The climate in Britain in 1985 for fans of horror films was hostile. The government and the media had colluded to invent the concept of the "video nasty" in response to the home video explosion. The entrepreneurial wild west spirit that had prevailed with video was terminated with extreme prejudice under the Video Recordings Act, 1984. Consequently it became an offence to sell, distribute, exhibit or trade in some otherwise awful and dull movies that had a modicum of gore and some others that did not. The threat of the so-called nasties created widespread animosity, not to mention the actual ruination of careers and lives. The stigma attached to these films by the press correlated with hardened criminal activity. Any individual who watched them—god forbid *collected* them—faced being exposed like some squalid little nonce in a blather of media indignation. It happened often enough. We are talking about horror videocassettes like *The Driller Killer*, *The Evil Dead* and *Evil Speak* (uncut). These are some of the relatively innocuous titles on the original DPP list that had been prosecuted or were liable for prosecution under Section 2 of the Obscene Publications Act, 1959.

SHOCK XPRESS

INSIDE

JULY 1985

ISSUE ONE

THRILLING TO DRILLING



*SHOCK XPRESS NUMBER 1.*

It was at the height of the nasties panic that I stumbled upon the first issue of *Shock Xpress*. I remember it vividly, as I do this type of thing. It was displayed on a shelf in the squat comic store Odyssey 7, beneath the Corn Exchange in Manchester city centre. (Odyssey 7 doesn't exist now, but has become a part of the Forbidden Planet chain, located in the vaunted Northern Quarter.) *Shock Xpress* was special in that it was a British based fanzine—at a push we could call it a prozine—that spoke from within the belly of the beast itself to other British horror fans. Thus, a fairly common film to American zine writers took on a different mantle when viewed within context of the nasties panic. Kim Newman, talking about *The Driller Killer* on the front page of that first *Shock Xpress*, calls it "the most-criticised-by-people-who-haven't-seen-it film of all time." Which summed up the frustration that many fans felt about the whole nasties panic. There was a

# STEFAN JAWORZYN

## SHOCK XPRESS

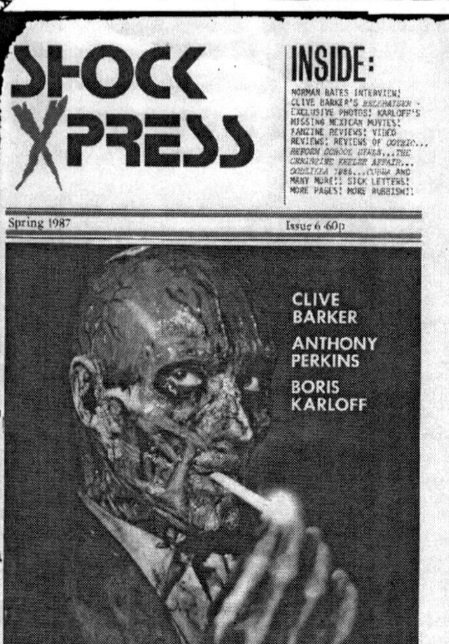


sense of underground camaraderie with *Shock Xpress* from the get-go.

A number of *Shock Xpress* writers had professional writing careers. This isn't common in the world of zines (certainly not in the world of Brit zines, anyway). The first issue had Philip Nutman, Dave Reeder, Neil Gaiman and the aforementioned Kim Newman, who was also writing about the nasties for the BFI flagship magazine *Monthly Film Bulletin*. The most prolific author however was Stefan Jaworzyn, who proved the exception in that he wasn't published elsewhere, not so one could notice anyway. Says Stefan: "I hadn't had any experience of writing that kind of material for anyone else beforehand. And, funnily enough, I was rarely asked to write for other people's magazines either [laughs]. I wonder why." He penned the "odder" pieces in that first issue. He deduced of *The Incredibly Strange Creatures Who Stopped Living and Became Mixed Up Zombies!!?* a film "difficult to criticise—it merely exists."

This statement seems completely in tune with nascent changes in pop culture in general, of which I feel *Shock Xpress* was an important part. I would say the same about Barry Kaufman's *Demonique* but for different reasons. RE/Search's galvanising book, *Incredibly Strange Films* was only a few months away from publication. While *Sleazoid Express* had already been there and done that. But *Shock Xpress*, to one in Britain, a post totalitarian video nightmare world, the concept of mere existence seemed good enough an argument and wholly prescient. In later issues of *Shock Xpress*, elements of "transgressive" forms of music and other interests combined with film for what seems now a sort of cultural entropy. It puts me in mind of a late-night roundtable discussion on serial killers, broadcast live on British terrestrial television in April 1991. Among the professional

guests was Stefan, who got in a spat with another guest, veteran film director Michael Winner, over the value of integrity.

As much as I loved the overseas zines, *Shock Xpress* operated on a different frequency. Low art wasn't high art, nor was it necessarily good or bad art. It was simply deserving of a dialogue on its own terms.

With issue 3 (January/February 1986), Stefan Jaworzyn became the editor of *Shock Xpress* and it is his name that is commonly associated with the zine. The reputation he has is that of a curmudgeon towards horror film fandom, a reputation instigated by his opinionated editorials and take-no-prisoners fanzine reviews of later issues. The small press did not like to be informed of its shortcomings and it railed for blood. Literally in some instances! At the inaugural Shock Around the Clock film festival, established with Alan Jones in 1987 and running annually for four years, Stefan was taking no chances and appeared bedecked in a heavy chain for "protection."

In its zine form, *Shock Xpress* lasted for a dozen issues through to Summer 1989. After this it appeared as three hefty trade paperbacks of all-new material published by Titan. But by the final book, titled simply *Shock* after Stefan's own record label, the writing was already on the wall. With *The Texas Chain Saw Massacre Companion* in 2004, that was effectively that for Mr Shock.

It is not without some bias that I approached this interview with Stefan Jaworzyn. After all, it was under the aegis of Stefan and *Shock Xpress* that I was first published (a review of *Last House on Dead End Street* in volume 2 number 1, 1987). I contributed regularly after that. But *Shock Xpress* holds its own. It remains a unique voice in the canon of British horror film culture.

SHOCK XPRESS

INSIDE:
CHUCK NORRIS SPEAKS!
RAMSEY CAMPBELL'S 10 FAVOURITE HORRORS!
SPANISH HORROR UNEARTHED!
AND MANY MORE; MOVIE RATINGS; SHOCKING CORRESPONDENCE! BITS & PIECES!

May-Jun 1986 | Issue 4·50p

EMASCULATING HORROR

by STEFAN JAWORZYN

HOUSE

I had met Stefan many times since the late eighties and would venture that we were pretty good friends. His library and music collection were an unending source of interest and amusement. (Books on electric shock therapy were somewhat unusual outside of a medical library in those days.) Slowly over time Stefan slipped

# STEFAN JAWORZYN

## SHOCK XPRESS

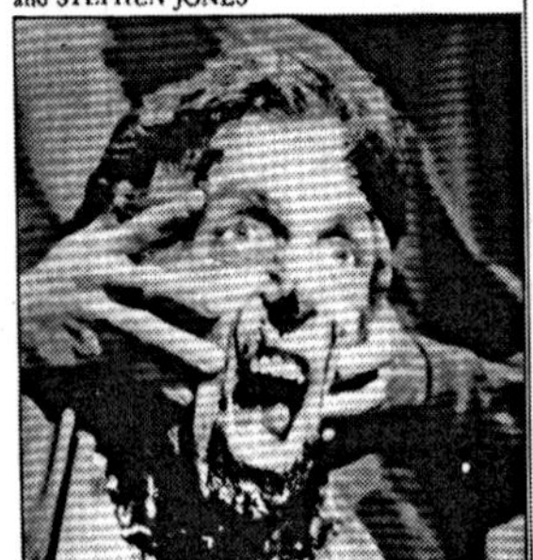

SHOCK XPRESS

INSIDE:
STUART GORDON INTERVIEW:
CLIVE BARKER'S BLOODY BEST:
WES CRAVEN INTERVIEW PART II:
BARRY FORSHAW REVIEWS VIDEOS:
REVIEWS OF *SPLATTER UNIVERSITY* ...*RE-ANIMATOR*...*FEAR CITY*... *UNDERWORLD*...*THE BOYS NEXT DOOR*...*CAFE FLESH*...*THE WOMAN IN THE ROOM*...*INVASION U.S.A.* AND MUCH MORE!!
MOVIE RATINGS: MINI-REVIEWS!
SHOCKING CORRESPONDENCE!!

Jan-Feb 1986 Issue 3 · 50p

LOVECRAFT RE-ANIMATED

by STEFAN JAWORZYN and STEPHEN JONES

from everyone's radar in a self imposed exile. I was among the last to go and by the mid-nineties he had effectively x-ed himself from the world. "When people ask me what I'm doing now," he said at one point, "I just tell them I drink."

The interview that follows was conducted in Stefan's home in London, on January 16, 2011. I avoided talk of music for the most part. (The record label; Whitehouse, Skullflower and Ascension, which he played in…) It wasn't for this interview. For this same reason a whole chunk debating the notion of cultural entropy is also gone. My overall impressions from that meeting: Stefan appeared tired but the caustic spirit hadn't dampened so one could notice. His three sons were all grown up, one of his neighbors was a "cunt," and the book on electric shock therapy was gone.

---

**DAVID KEREKES: How did *Shock Xpress* come about, and how did you get the job of editor, with issue 3?**

**STEFAN JAWORZYN:** Sitting in the pub, sometime in '84—Steve Jones, Kim [Newman], Dave Reeder, me… Maybe Neil Gaiman. Oh, Alan [Jones] must have been in on it from the word go. I think *Halls of Horror* had packed up, so there wasn't anything apart from *Starburst* in England. The idea was to produce a more undergroundish publication dealing with non-mainstream stuff. I can't recall whether there was any specific conceptual thing, though some of us were interested in the *Gore Gazette* and *Sleazoid Express* approach.

**DK: The first Shock Xpress came out in '85.**

**SJ:** Dave Reeder edited the first one, I think we printed 400 or 500, definitely a low run. Steve Jones actually edited the second cos Dave was

# SHOCK XPRESS

## INSIDE:

WES CRAVEN INTERVIEW! THE 50 MOST BORING FILMS OF ALL TIME! THE MAKING OF *THE BRIDE*! REVIEWS OF *A NIGHTMARE ON ELM STREET*...*LIFEFORCE*...*FRIDAY THE 13TH PART V*...*TONIGHT I WILL EAT YOUR CORPSE*...*THE TOXIC AVENGER*...*SILENT MADNESS* AND MUCH MORE!! INCLUDING A GREAT FREE COMPETITION...

Sep·Oct 1985 Issue 2 · 50p

# INTERVIEW: WES CRAVEN

by KIM NEWMAN

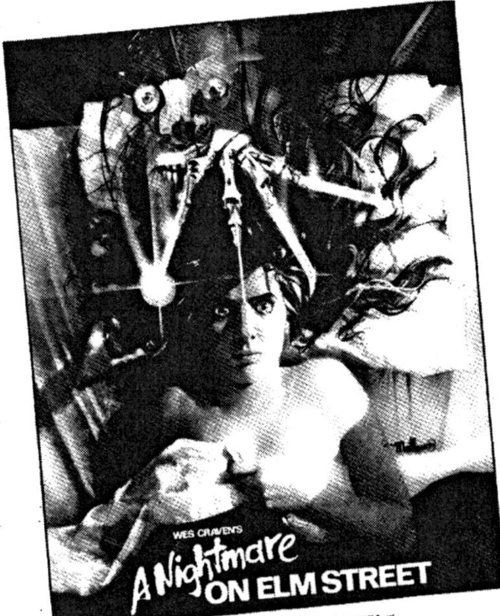


SX: What was the genesis of *Last House on the Left*?

WC: It was rather straight ahead. I had worked on a film before, as an assistant, and the producer was offered money to make a horror film. The producer asked me to be the writer/director/editor. The only guidance was that we had to make a horror film that pulled out all the stops.

SX: Did you expect *Last House* to have the kind of impact it did?

WC: Not really. We had a much more local viewpoint at that time, thinking maybe some people in New York might see it, and a few other states. It never occurred to us that it would take off like it took off. We didn't have experience. We just had this feeling we were making a film and having fun - sort of being naughty.

SX: You know it's illegal to distribute *Last House* in this country?

WC: It feels like Britain's a little bit restrictive in that way. There's a general tone to the country, sort of very nice and very repressed. Compared to the way that American culture seems wide open and whacky. There's a cap on things. I'm interested by British television, and how nice everybody is - the talk show hosts, everyone. After a while, you want to shake them. It's all so civilised. To me, the video censorship thing is like mucking about with things that shouldn't be mucked about with. I can see things being restricted for television, things that come into one's home without being invited. But with cassettes, where a person voluntarily goes out and gets it, or a feature film, I just don't believe in censorship.

SX: Any problems with *A Nightmare on Elm Street*?

WC: Yeah, we did. In America, it was

THE 50 MOST BORING FILMS!
by STEFAN JAWORZYN
and KIM NEWMAN

editing like five magazines a week for the Arab market, he didn't have time, though Steve still credited him. After that Steve talked about dropping it if Dave couldn't do it. I was hanging out with Steve a lot, so I said I'd co-edit it with Dave, attempt to push it along so it came out more often. I was really eager for it to appear regularly, to turn it into something with more of a profile. I got impatient and edited the third issue on my own.

**DK: You were already doing a lot of contributions, weren't you?**

**SJ:** I wrote a load for the first issue: The *Ilsa* movies, *The Incredibly Strange Creatures...*, *The Worm Eaters*—I was desperate to write about this crap, there wasn't any forum for it in England, certainly not to write about it at length. That was important to us from the outset: there needn't be any constraint on article length. If a writer interviews somebody interesting and only a third of it gets used in *Time Out* or wherever, then we'll run the whole transcript. Same with reviews: if you feel like writing a page and a half on something awful, then go ahead, fine!

**DK: Were you involved in any kind of film society or anything like that at university?**

**SJ:** I was at Sussex for a while, that's where I met Kim. No, I just used to go and see the stuff Kim put on. I came across him in the common room, handwriting posters for some old dark house dog he was showing. I approached him saying, "Why are you doing that by hand? Why don't you go and get a few printed?" He looked at me as though I was insane, you know, "No one's going to come anyway, why would I bother doing that?" And that got me interested straightaway. He used to put on all-night horror shows, he got lots of obscure black and white stuff, anything he could get cheap, basically. *She-Demons... The Incredible Petrified World... Teenage Zombies*...Tod Slaughter films...Old 16mm prints. We even showed a couple at Shock Around the Clock, got them from the same place Kim had. The guy was still active, some old guy in Wales with a houseful of 16mm prints of terrible old movies! We closed the first Shock Around the Clock

XEROX FEROX

with *She-Demons*. Then the second with *Nekromantik*!

**DK: Serious reviews of horror films and sex films had existed in the like of *Cinema X*, but that wasn't of my generation. It was quite a revelation to come across *Shock Xpress*.**

**SJ:** The closest I got [to *Cinema X*] as a youngster was *Films and Filming*. *Famous Monsters*, obviously, and *Castle of Frankenstein*. *Famous Monsters* was slightly frustrating because there wasn't that much text, so you saw great pictures that made you want to see the films, but a lot didn't actually have those pictures in when you saw them, certainly not the British versions…

**DK: Or they were fleeting.**

**SJ:** Ha, a microsecond of some dodgy makeup. *Castle of Frankenstein* made me realise it was possible to write intelligently about horror movies in a magazine actually dedicated to them. There didn't seem to be much of that around over here, apart from the odd article or review. Much later on, *Halls of Horror*/the *House of Hammer* and *Starburst* had their moments. In its early/mid-period *Starburst* was fantastic, Alan [Jones] was doing a lot of great stuff, the zombie issue, that really impressed me...

**DK: He'd infiltrated it with his reviews of Italian gore and American B-pictures, hadn't he?**

**SJ:** Yeah, and Fulci, when he discovered Fulci! Then there was *Fangoria*, that started turning up over here. I was living in Bristol, a friend brought me a bunch back from trips to London and the US. That issue with the Andy Milligan interview! But there wasn't much in England attempting to treat horror movies seriously. I wanted serious horror movies and serious criticism!

CITY LIMITS
'SHOCK AROUND THE CLOCK'

PROGRAMMING/LIAISON:
*STEFAN JAWORZYN*!

CO-ORDINATION:
*STEPHEN JONES & MATT PRESTON*!

PUBLICITY:
*KATE HUGHES*!

MEDIA LIAISON:
*KIM NEWMAN*!

Special Issue·10p

PROGRAMME

1st Session

1.00pm
*RETURN TO SALEM'S LOT*

3.00pm
*SURPRISE FEATURE*

5.00pm
*AMERICAN GOTHIC*

7.00pm
*HELLRAISER*

8.30pm
*CELEBRITY PANEL DISCUSSION*

9.30pm
*THE STEPFATHER*

2nd Session

11.45pm
*STREET TRASH*

1.30am
*SURPRISE FEATURE*

3.15am
*WITCHBOARD*

5.00am
*THE LAMP*

6.45am
*TRASH CLASSIC - SHE DEMONS*

(Times are approximate)

Attachment

SHOCK AROUND THE CLOCK FESTIVAL, AUGUST 1–2, 1987.

DRAFT

RECORDED & INDEXED

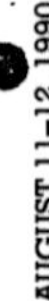

# SHOCK AROUND THE CLOCK 4

**Programmed by Stefan Jaworzyn and Alan Jones**

| | |
|---|---|
| 12.30pm | MEET THE FEEBLES |
| 2.30pm | BLUE STEEL |
| 4.30pm | CARNIVAL OF SOULS |
| 6.30pm | HIGHLANDER 2 - Exclusive preview reel |
| | MIRACLE MILE |
| 9.00pm | NIGHTBREED |
| 11.30pm | TWO EVIL EYES |
| | HARDWARE |
| | FRANKENSTEIN UNBOUND |
| | MANIAC COP 2 |
| | LEATHERFACE: TEXAS CHAINSAW MASSACRE III |

*Please note: Starting times are approximate. Please listen for announcements of time changes. The programme is subject to change without notification and at the whims of the programmers...*

**Guests include:**
**Dario Argento** (Director: *Two Evil Eyes*)
**Clive Barker** (Director: *Nightbreed*)
**Geoff Portass** (Make-up: *Nightbreed*),
**Richard Stanley** (Director: *Hardware*)
**Nick Vince** (Actor: *Nightbreed*)

AUGUST 11–12, 1990.

Early on with *Shock Xpress* I started to feel horror movies were becoming trivialised, which pissed me off beyond measure. You know, screaming teen retard crap like *House*, *The Return of the Living Dead*—especially the second...

**DK: That particular bug bear was one of your cover pieces, wasn't it? "Emasculating Horror."**

**SJ:** [laughs] It's kind of embarrassing in retrospect, but I was really tub-thumping about it. Troma, I had a particular fucking flea up my ass with Troma. I was really bothered by modern horror seeming to address the lowest common denominator, both in its target audience and its subject matter. Maybe it always had—certainly that's how horror movies were often perceived in the thirties and forties. But, obviously, it's all relevant to what you're seeing at a particular time. And when you started seeing shit like *The Toxic Avenger* and *Class of Nuke 'Em High* and blah, blah, blah, it just gave me the arsehole so massively. The idea that there always had to be humor—jock-type "yucks" in horror just freaked me out. "Spot the number of tits in this film, there's seven tits in this film." I wanted movies to be like *Day of the Dead*. But of course there were never many *Day of the Deads*.

**DK: You had interviews with Stuart Gordon, Wes Craven and Clive Barker. And then you've got Chuck Norris. [laughs]**

**SJ:** I was particularly pleased with that Chuck Norris interview. Three pages in issue 4! Putting Chuck Norris in there really, really tickled me. I loved the idea of having stuff that might piss off the punters or throw people, and Chuck Norris was the perfect example. It summed up *Shock*'s, um, irreverence quite early on, sort of, "Fuck you, we're not only about horror films!" And that irreverent attitude definitely did piss some people off.

I've got to give Steve Jones credit, as publisher he always backed me on

my "Fuck 'em if they can't take a joke" decisions. And though at first we argued a bit about what should be included, that argument progressed from 'Yeah, but is it a horror movie?' to "Yeah, but is it a *Shock Xpress* movie?" And ultimately pretty much anything became a *Shock Xpress* movie…

So yeah, my "attitude". Let's digress for a moment. When we did the first film festival, some fuckhead from *City Limits* phoned up and yelled at me for about an hour because I'd dared to program *Salvation!*, which wasn't a horror film, and apparently no one at *City Limits* liked it, therefore I didn't have the right to program it! It was called an "Xploitation Film Festival", not "Horror Film Festival" anyway! The fucking retard had no idea what it was all about! And he was saying stuff like "We've heard a lot of bad things about you, and you're proving it all true"! So I'm, like, Charles Manson for not letting some little puke push me around. Well, we showed the film, then dumped *City Limits* as partners. So it goes.

Another time Julian Grainger shows up acting all woeful because he'd been in LA having his ear bent by "someone" whose directorial abilities (and wife's acting abilities) I'd rather called into question. Apparently he was waving the offending issue of *Shock* around, saying I epitomised the absolute dregs of humanity/film criticism/fanzine fundom, and so on. So I'm like this vicious brute in a kingdom of evil, ruining fun for everyone, everywhere! Sitting in the pub with Steve deciding whose reputation to destroy next! Give me a fucking break.

Anyway, back to reality. One thing I wanted to do—I don't know that we did it as much as I'd have liked to—but I was reading John Waters recently, and there's a particular way of dealing with art movies as if they're exploitation films that I really enjoy. That always appealed to me, reviewing mainstream movies or art movies in a completely different context. Waters does it really well. I think it worked on a slightly different level by including Chuck Norris, something you wouldn't necessarily associate with *Shock Xpress*, but who we felt was part of exploitation cinema. I liked

# FANZINE FUN

by STEFAN JAWORZYN

the idea of sort of "gonzo" film criticism. *Film Comment* in the US got there sometimes. My *Shock Xpress* fantasy might have been Hunter S. Thompson, John Waters and William Burroughs writing about Bergman…

**DK: The more interesting zines always seem to manage to create their own dynamic with seemingly diverse material. Take the *Psychotronic Video Guide* and the notion of a "psychotronic" film, for example. You can see this happen later on with *Shock*. It's in here, so that means it's a part of something else.**

**SJ:** Yeah, putting *The Last Temptation of Christ* in really appealed to me. I think broadening your horizon ultimately builds up its own kind of weird atmosphere or conceptual approach. It struck me there were more and more areas we could touch on that enlarged our remit, and that would interest people who were into more esoteric aspects of horror and fantasy. Because if you like weird, arty horror movies, why wouldn't you like *The Last Temptation of Christ*? It fits in on a lot of levels with the more intelligent and unusual types of horror. Cronenberg became less viscerally horror-oriented and his movies became more arty, but they weren't any less terrifying. *Spider* is one of the most horrible films he's made, and you can't really call it a horror film as such. It's one of his most uncomfortable to watch, really gruelling, an incredibly unpleasant experience.

**DK: You've interviewed Cronenberg four or five times, haven't you? It's like "hang on, he's here again".**

**SJ:** [laughs] I think John Waters as well. Yeah, Cronenberg and Waters ended up in there more than anyone else. Cronenberg always gave interesting interviews. And God knows how many times we featured Clive Barker. He was always great, and a friend of *Shock* from the outset.

**DK: He wrote for *Shock* as well, didn't he?**

**SJ:** He was the first person to write about his top ten movies. I thought that was a good thing, getting horror and fantasy authors to pick their favourite movies, so again we moved slightly away from always having the same people writing similar pieces about the same type of films.

One thing that often crops up when I'm watching trash with the boys: *Shock Xpress* was probably there first. We'll be watching something and I'll say "You know, I think we showed this before anyone had even heard of it here" or "Yeah, we kind of discovered this director" or "Yeah, we reviewed that when it was still a 'lost' film"...We covered so much crap before anyone else or in more depth than had been done previously. Stuff like the list of Italian director pseudonyms. It's a throwaway piece but it was the most comprehensive I'd ever seen. I don't think there'd been an English language piece on [Riccardo] Freda...Your *Last House on Dead End Street* piece. And so on. Apart from *Lunchmeat* of course, where we got mightily cunted!

[*tape break*]

**DK: Issue 1 was 400 copies, you said. I'm assuming that it steadily increased thereafter?**

**SJ:** Yeah, we upped the page count and the print run each issue. We sold considerably more of issue 3, with "Lovecraft Re-Animated" and Stuart Gordon on the cover. Issue 4, Emasculating Horror, we actually had to reprint! I guess we printed maybe 1,500 or 2,000 copies of issues 5 and 6, it was doing pretty well by then. When we started with the glossy cover issues we did 5,000.

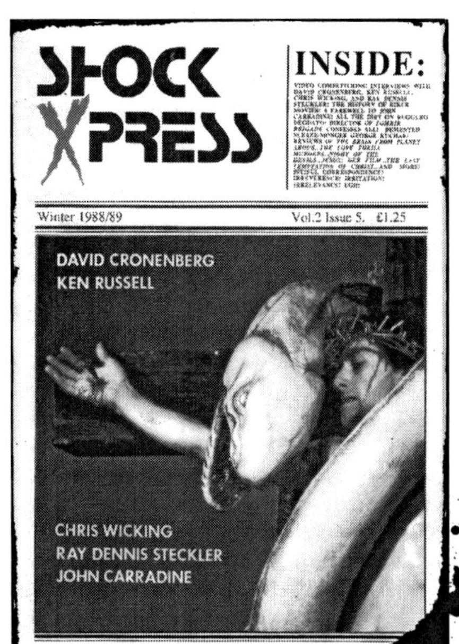

SHOCK XPRESS
INSIDE:
Winter 1988/89
Vol.2 Issue 5. £1.25
DAVID CRONENBERG
KEN RUSSELL
CHRIS WICKING
RAY DENNIS STECKLER
JOHN CARRADINE


**DK: Who was handling distribution?**

**SJ:** It was all over the place, which was a problem. Titan took some, Gold's, anyone we could sell to, basically. It was a classic fanzine scenario: sending out half a dozen here, a dozen there. It's then much harder collecting the money and putting it into the next issue. Small businesses can take five fucking years to pay or not pay at all! A major problem was trying to find one distributor to take enough copies so we could

# STEFAN JAWORZYN

## SHOCK XPRESS

SHOCK XPRESS

INSIDE:

JESUS FRANCO! AL ADAMSON! CLIVE BARKER! DAVID CRONENBERG! FRANK LALOGGIA! ERIC RED! PLUS: HALLUCINOGENS ON FILM! TRANSCENDENTAL NIGHTMARES! 'CAREER' RETROSPECTIVES ON: CHUCK VINCENT AND S.F BROWNRIGG! WEIRD FILMS REVIEWED: *2 FEMALE SPIES WITH FLOWERED PANTIES, DON'T SCREAM, IT'S ONLY A MOVIE...THE IMPURE...WHAT HAVE THEY DONE TO OUR DAUGHTERS...VOODOO MAN...* AND MORE! EXULTATIONS! EJACULATIONS! EXPOSTULATIONS!

Summer 1989 Vol. 3 Issue 1. £1.50

AL ADAMSON
S.F. BROWNRIGG

CLIVE BARKER
JESUS FRANCO

break even, then we didn't have to worry about when the small mail order people paid us. Chasing up money was something for which none of us really had time or inclination. It's pretty unpleasant and it stops you getting on with what you're supposed to be doing, which is producing the actual issues!

**DK: You got into [the high street chain] WHSmith's.**

**SJ:** Yes, it was in WHSmith's [laughs]. Gold's was actually getting it into WHSmith's, which is completely crazy when you think about it.

**DK: There was something about not being able to use the f-word in WHSmith's, wasn't there?**

**SJ:** Yeah, I did actually asterisk it out!

**DK: But *Metal Hammer* got around it.**

**SJ:** Fookin'. "It's fookin heavy"—remember that? [laughs] Now, well, even the *Guardian* has "fuck" in it regularly! I'd forgotten I didn't allow use of the word "fuck" in *Shock Xpress*. To a certain extent it might have been paranoia, having managed to get the bloody thing into WHSmith's—but they used to "spot check" stuff I believe.

**DK: Yeah, it was very difficult to get in there. Everything seemed to have to go before a committee.**

**SJ:** It must be that Gold's just kind of sleazed it in with a bunch of other crap, and they didn't realise what they'd bought. It was in regular newsagents too. People discovered it and they'd write and say "I was looking through the men's magazines in the local newsagent and I found this" [laughs]. And they'd stuffed it in with *Mayfair* and *Razzle*…

**DK: How many subscribers did you have, at your peak?**

**SJ:** When we packed it in, God Almighty, I sent out so many checks and refunds. It seemed like a lot, a couple of hundred probably.

**DK: That's healthy.**

**SJ:** Yeah, it was. But the thing with that is you get the money at once and it goes into the next issue, so with a three-issue subscription, by the time it's got to the third issue the money has been long spent. Everything needs to keep ticking over, and in the end it was not ticking over acceptably. Steve put in his own money, we put in our film festival money, but the turnover from distributors just wasn't happening fast enough or in large enough quantities to make it viable. And to get a constant turnover of cash from distributors you need to get issues out regularly…

**DK: Were contributors getting paid at this point?**

**SJ:** Yeah, once we started the glossy cover issues. Did we pay a bit

THE LETTER WRITERS ARE REVOLTING AGAIN. *SHOCK XPRESS* VOLUME 2 NUMBER 1.

# XPRESS MAIL

*Before we hit the mailsack to see what ravings we can dredge up this time round, let me say, once and once only (I'll doubtless have to repeat this every issue . . .) that you stand absolutely less than zero chance of receiving a reply unless you include a STAMPED ADDRESSED ENVELOPE. Got it? All letters received are liable to publication. I do occasionally reply personally to letters and am not actually averse to doing so, but if you want to know where to get hold of movies etc. a) it's highly unlikely I'll be able to tell you b) it's even less likely if you don't include return postage. On with the show . . .*

**ANGRY BLOCKHEAD WRITES**

Dear Stefan,

As much as I respect the opinions of both Ernest Harris *and* Barry Forshaw, is it really necessary to have *two* video columns? They both, thankfully, provide much-needed info/credits/dates etc for odd and usually unknown tapes, but I feel the space is being wasted on too much too soon.

There's plenty of time to do every video and the space should be used for the better articles – that characterise SX – such as (in last ish) 'Mexican Karloffs' and . . . well, that's it actually. Out of 24 pages, *10* are of a 'review' nature, including vids and zines, with two interviews – Perkins, Barker – that aren't really necessary. The glossies you moan at so much will, in time, cover these mainstream angles and I think you should get back to the spirit of ish 1, which had far more interesting and useful material in it . . . most of which I possessed no previous work on prior to the arrival of your rag.

Sorry if I upset anyone. Now to the second and main point of this letter. Since you demanded (and got) a video of *Beast In Heat* in your editorial, I was struck with the marvellously illegal idea of a video exchange column, or something like it. Surely swaps/copies/loans etc could be arranged through a column which could replace the much-slagged-off 'Review Round Up' (basically an excuse for you lot to piss us off by showing us how many movies you see a month – it's roughly £30 to see that lot on the back page every month. Some of us have to eat you know). It would also create more space in the letter column, junking the usual 'Where can I get . . .' type of question.

Pirate copies flying around may be corrupt but this is the only way some of us out here in the wasteland can see some things. This is what repressive legislation does to the people.

Vive le revolution!

Karl Maskell

PS. Oh, and if you're going to tell me that the point of the 'Review Round Up' is to put us off the shit so that we don't waste £30 then you can get lost – you know that we *have* to see *everything* . . .

*Who rattled your cage, peabrain? I couldn't care less if you think the video columns are a waste of time. As you think the majority of the magazine is a waste of space, I'd be interested to know exactly what you'd replace it with . . . 'Much slagged-off'? By whom? Your noble self, indeed . . . Don't eat. So watching videos is part of the revolution, eh? You urban guerillas terrify the hell out of me . . .*

**Q.E.D.**

Shock Xpress,

I am just writing to ask where I can get hold of a copy of *Mondo Sexualis USA* on video. Do you have an address where it is available from? It would be a good idea to put names of distributors where people could get hold of films esp. the more obscure ones. I feel this would be a good addition to your magazine, which I find v. good apart from the occasional tendency to dwell on mainstream stuff, information on which is easily available elsewhere. Still all tastes etc. I suppose.

Yours,

David Lloyd Jones

*No. We're here to review movies, not distribute them. Yes, all tastes etc. is just how I feel. Thank you.*

RECORDED & INDEXED

DRAFT

EDITOIRAL MASTHEAD.

# XPRESSWAY TO YOUR SKULL

before? I can't remember. Anyway, the guy who funded it had an inheritance. Steve knew him, he was "slightly" eccentric. He approached us and said if we wanted to do *Shock* as a professional magazine he'd be willing to fund four issues. Significantly, he was also supposed to handle distribution. We got a good quote from a typesetting company, so they did the typesetting and picture scanning, me and Steve worked on the layout and design.

The funding, well, after a short time he decided that he wasn't making any money from it, it was all some egotistical bollocks—I'm not sure whose—and jumped ship. We had an issue at the printers [volume 2 number 4], so Steve clawed around and got the money together. After, we cut the print run to save money and managed two more issues. I started doing the typesetting myself, over at a friend of Alan's who had a Mac. For the last one [volume 3 number 1], I got a Mac so I could do it at home. I got the pictures scanned at Titan, I did pretty much everything apart from the cover. But the rot had set in—we had virtually no advertising and a very slow turnover.

I remember mooching around Upper Street in the bookshops and stuff, having a really horrible time, thinking how the fuck are we going to do this? By the time I'd made my way from Highbury and Islington to the Angel, I realised we had to pack it in, which was, you know, one of the great shit

afternoons out.

**DK: You didn't want to pack it in?**

**SJ:** Oh, no, no, no. But in retrospect we did so much wrong; the price should have been twice as much to start with. If you're producing essentially an uncommercial niche publication, you have to price it higher. It was a big mistake keeping the price so low. It didn't generate enough money and it was crazy. The stupid margins we had to give distributors... A simple price rise would have solved so many problems! For some reason we never thought of it! And it was frustrating to work on the film festival then put the profits into the magazine straight away. It didn't add up. Steve had run out of goodwill as far as putting in his own money, and I wanted payment for working on the film festival—I didn't have any other income at the time!

**DK: I want to touch on the kind of fan base that you had.**

**SJ:** Hmm [laughs] yeah.

**DK: Following your "Fanzine Fun" column in *Shock*, the vitriol started to pour in.**

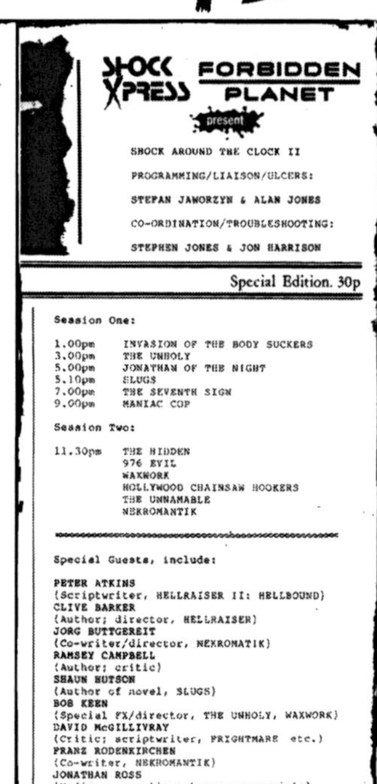
SHOCK XPRESS FORBIDDEN PLANET present

SHOCK AROUND THE CLOCK II

PROGRAMMING/LIAISON/ULCERS:

STEFAN JAWORZYN & ALAN JONES

CO-ORDINATION/TROUBLESHOOTING:

STEPHEN JONES & JON HARRISON

Special Edition. 30p

Session One:

| | |
|---|---|
| 1.00pm | INVASION OF THE BODY SUCKERS |
| 3.00pm | THE UNHOLY |
| 5.00pm | JONATHAN OF THE NIGHT |
| 5.10pm | SLUGS |
| 7.00pm | THE SEVENTH SIGN |
| 9.00pm | MANIAC COP |

Session Two:

| | |
|---|---|
| 11.30pm | THE HIDDEN |
| | 976 EVIL |
| | WAXWORK |
| | HOLLYWOOD CHAINSAW HOOKERS |
| | THE UNNAMABLE |
| | NEKROMANTIK |

Special Guests, include:

PETER ATKINS
(Scriptwriter, HELLRAISER II: HELLBOUND)
CLIVE BARKER
(Author; director, HELLRAISER)
JORG BUTTGEREIT
(Co-writer/director, NEKROMATIK)
RAMSEY CAMPBELL
(Author; critic)
SHAUN HUTSON
(Author of novel, SLUGS)
BOB KEEN
(Special FX/director, THE UNHOLY, WAXWORK)
DAVID McGILLIVRAY
(Critic; scriptwriter, FRIGHTMARE etc.)
FRANZ RODENKIRCHEN
(Co-writer, NEKROMANTIK)
JONATHAN ROSS
(Media personality; lager commercials)

JULY 30–31, 1988.

**SJ:** Er, yeah, that was unfortunate; I never saw that coming. In my naivety I thought I was just being honest about which magazines were shit and which were good. Fucking hell, I think there are still people who hold a grudge against me for that. And I'd rejected contributions from people, possibly not in the most kindly manner, some of whom became trolls but with typewriters! Anyway, I'd helped John Gullidge with *Samhain*, told him how to get started, pointed him in the direction of a couple of writers. But I couldn't believe what a pile of shit it was. So, well, I'm supposed to review it, so I said "it's a pile of shit!" [laughs] I kind of made peace with Gullidge years later, I did an article on him for David McGillivray's *Scapegoat* magazine. Gullidge had been singled out by local yokels for the sort of opprobrium and loathing that nonces get, just for producing a horror magazine. The retards wanted to burn him at the stake. I really felt sorry for the guy; it destroyed his fucking life at the time, he had problems with his job and so on. But yeah, [laughs] the fucking nutters that used to write into *Shock*... A lot were wind-up artists who just knew that they would get me pop-eyed with a well-phrased letter of abuse. Some I knew were fakes but

# STEFAN JAWORZYN

## SHOCK XPRESS

published them anyway because it was still a laugh. Carl Ford always used to like winding us up. One could never really tell whether his apoplexy was genuine or whether he knew exactly what buttons to push.

**DK: [Flipping through issues of *Shock Xpress*.] Here's an extract from one letter: "*Shock Xpress* has an attitude problem; it comes across as the most unfriendly mag in fandom."**

**SJ:** [laughs] Yeah, there were plenty of negative reviews, basically following the issue with the Fanzine Fun page. The *Deep Red* dingleberry [Chas. Balun] set into us over our bad attitude on several occasions. He was kind of the embodiment of everything I hated. We considered ourselves serious writers, many *Shock* contributors were serious writers! So when I see someone say "this movie sucks farts out of dead cats", I didn't feel that was proper criticism. It might be the kind of thing I'd say now—many years have passed and I'm into my second infantile phase, it seems like a valid criticism! At the time it seemed outrageous to have people trivialising horror movies by writing about them in an infantile manner. I gave the impression of being dour and despotic, but it didn't do *Shock Xpress* any harm, and tough shit if it upset anyone. People still had to buy it because they knew they'd find stuff in there they wouldn't find anywhere else. They knew the writers could spell the directors' names properly, that they'd actually watched the movies and cared about what they were writing. That, to me, was what made us different. If that makes me an elitist, I'm happy to be an elitist. Being a moron with a video machine and a typewriter did not automatically entitle people to call themselves a "critic" or whatever, certainly not to contribute to my fucking magazine or plague me with their drivelsome opinions! We cared about getting our fucking facts right. "Oh, I missed the 'the' off the

title, it doesn't matter." It does matter; it's got "the" in the fucking title. I was mortified when Kim pointed out I'd spelt Martin Scorsese's name wrong, I felt like a fucking idiot!

I was talking to Doug Winter once about a young horror author and Doug said, shaking his head, "He's got a lot of rage in him." I had a sudden realisation, "Shit, he's not the only one"... And, let's face it, one of the reasons *Shock* had a "personality" was because my bad attitude and rage shaped it, sort of "informed" the overall feel of it. And I was a very hands-on editor. I interfered with pieces, interjected comments—but that never stopped contributors submitting material. People wanted to write for *Shock*... They knew they were getting their work published in a magazine people respected, regardless of their antipathy towards me.

**DK: Did you meet many of these fans? At the first *Shock* festival, you'd had a suspicion that they may turn up and do you in, or something.**

**SJ:** You mean the particularly rabid haters? When we saw *Talk Radio*, Kim said something like "That's going to happen to you one day," which at that point only seemed half funny. It was weird. People would regularly write in, either to tell me I was a cunt or that *Shock* was the greatest thing ever, one extreme or the other, and they'd order tickets for the film festival. Then like a day after the festival I'd get a letter from them saying, "oh, it was great to be there," but ninety per cent of them never came over to speak me. I was taking tickets—they had their fucking chance to bottle me! Somehow I never encountered the most, um, agitated fans. But there were some sane fans! And Alan knew loads of people, they would flock to him, whereas they'd mostly keep away from me.

**DK: Not like the old Forbidden Planet days then! I was down in London for a break [circa the late eighties] and had popped into the shop to say hello. It was your day off. We'd not met at this point and I thought Alan was perhaps you. He struck me over the head with a**

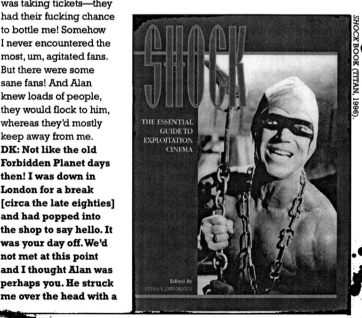

SHOCK
THE ESSENTIAL GUIDE TO EXPLOITATION CINEMA
Edited By
STEFAN JAWORZYN


*SHOCK* BOOK (TITAN, 1996).

RECORDED & INDEXED
DRAFT

# FANZINE ZONE

By Stefan Jaworzyn

***I Drink Your Blood/I Eat Your Skin* t-shirt!**

**SJ:** [laughs] Back in the old Forbidden Planet, freaks would just come in and talk about crap for hours. I remember Alan saying the first time a mutual friend appeared, he sleazed up to the back of the shop and said "Got anything on *Last House on the Left*?" and Alan immediately realised this was a partner in crime... There was a sense of discovery, the same with old bookshops, record shops and the video library. That delight in turning up *Absurd* or *Anthropophagous*, you name it, all that shit we used to blunder across before the VRA.

You'd get talking to some freak or the freakish owner of the video shop, maybe they'd steer you onto *SS Experiment Camp* or whatever. When I was at university a girl from London told me "You'd really like John Waters films, *Pink Flamingos*; they show it at the cinema in London sometimes." I never managed to see any Waters films until they started turning up in video shops. I had these things in the back of my mind—I remember in the seventies Lux Interior from the Cramps talking about Herschell Gordon Lewis, maybe in the *NME*, and thinking "God, I've got to see these". It's probably just old man talk, but tracking that legendary stuff down, I guess that's never going to happen again—maybe it's great from a different perspective, because as soon as you find out about something, you can watch everything by the fucking director off Netflix.

**DK: So you've got a different kind of kick.**

**SJ:** Well, I don't think internet kicks are as valid as the kind of kicks we got, but that's partly because it seems a bit sad when you do everything from home. But I do it now; I can't remember the last time I bought a record in a record shop. I know there's no point going into the west end of London—I'm not going to find a copy of *Simon: King of the Witches*, I'm not going to find whatever the fuck it is on vinyl, I'm going to have to order it from the States.

Going back to the video libraries, plenty would sell you their shitty movies for a fiver—they thought it was Christmas. Who wanted a copy

of *Blood Rites* (*The Ghastly Ones*) or *Frozen Scream* sitting around in their racks? Once word got out about those films, they couldn't rent them for 50p! I think *Blood Rites* was one of the first videos I bought [laughs]. Owners didn't want those fucking films in their clubs; they knew punters felt burned when they saw them.

**DK: And then, with the VRA, they had to burn them literally.**

**SJ:** Or go to prison…

**DK: Do you think the kind of censorious climate in which we were operating motivated us?**

**SJ:** It made it seem like we were trying to do our bit against the forces of oppression. But the whole situation was ludicrous. I went on a TV program about movie censorship with Alan, James Ferman and members of "the public", including a frothing self-righteous nutter who wanted to murder us. Afterwards a woman who'd been pro-censorship came over, she was really surprised how reasonable we were. She said "I never realised people took these films seriously, that you guys aren't mental cases and it doesn't always turn you into axe-wielding maniacs". Because that was what they'd been trying to propagate, particularly after the Hungerford massacre and the Jamie Bulger murder. Post-Bulger, the madness actually appeared to escalate. A lot of ignorant people got on moral high horses, none of them knew what they were talking about and hadn't seen any of the movies, but obviously, that's what a climate of censorship does. And of course in the case of the Hungerford massacre, Michael Ryan never even owned a video machine, despite the press claiming he'd been influenced by repeat viewings of *First Blood*! So yeah, we really did feel we were trying to do something against that kind of garbage. But I don't know if we were achieving much other than preaching to the converted. Going on that program with Alan was, I suppose, a step in the right direction. But there weren't enough forums for us to make any difference. The climate in the country was so bad, so horrible. Ten years of genuine fucking horror: Tory horror.

SHOCK XPRESS

INSIDE:

Aug-Sep 1986

Issue 5-50p

ALIENS

ALIENS. G.B./U.S.A. 1986. Dir: James Cameron. With: Sigourney Weaver, Carrie Henn, Michael Biehn, Paul Reiser, Lance Henriksen. 20th Century Fox.

RECORDED & INDEXED

DRAFT

# COLD PRINT

By Stefan Jaworzyn

**DK: Did you encounter any of that moral fallout with *Shock Xpress*?**

**SJ:** Well, one of the contributors phoned me and said he'd fallen in love with an ex-witch and they'd been Born Again, so as a devout Christian he had to disassociate himself from *Shock*! That was nuts. And we had a babysitter quit [laughs]! I stupidly told her what the *Shock* book contained, and she's, "Oh, I can't handle that, I can't be having anything to do with that" and quit! I never really got that, I mean, it is only a movie. People really didn't seem to engage with the fact that it's not real—including the BBFC, including Parliament. The business about imitatable violence in horror films is just so absurd. Has anyone ever imitated a fucking cannibal movie, or a vampire movie, or a zombie movie? The people who claim they were influenced by movies have been told to do so by their defense counsel, and it's always been disproved. Even after all these years it amazes me that people bring up crap about "But people could imitate it". Well, they fucking well haven't. The video nasties period in Britain makes about as much sense as the McCarthy period in America. People went to prison and a lot of people went to court… It's easy to forget how demented it was. That vague feeling of paranoia whenever you ordered a video through the post that not only would it not turn up, but you might also get a visit from the police, who'd take your fucking videos away and you'd possibly spend the night in the cells. I mean, blokes with wives and kids and a horror video collection got nicked, the fucking pigs came round to their house! Taken down the station and grilled for having a bunch of stupid horror videos on the shelf in their lounge! Like they're drugs or guns!

But the excitement at seeing a Herschel Gordon Lewis film for the first time! It's almost impossible to explain to somebody now that it was exciting to see a Herschel Gordon Lewis film [laughs]. When a friend got *The Gruesome Twosome* and *The Gore Gore Girls* from the States, it was like

going to see Prince at Wembley! I'm going to watch the fucking *Gruesome Twosome* down at Mick's, on his NTSC player, on his tiny little monitor! Sitting there, a couple of fucking inches away from the screen, taking notes, busily taking notes. It doesn't really make sense, does it?

**DK: There was a compulsion to take notes. I was the same: you had to document things now, because you never knew when you'd need it.**

**SJ:** Yeah, because it seemed it was going to be taken away from you as well. Seeing a lot of those imports and zero-quality bootlegs really was like peering into another world. Stuff you'd read about in *Sleazoid Express* and *Gore Gazette* and whatever weird fanzines you managed to get hold of. The issue of *Demonique* with *Horror Hospital* on the cover—that was another touchstone—I wanted to see every movie reviewed in it. That was definitely one of those magazines that wormed its way into my consciousness. Finally finding copies of some of those films was like a magical experience! Now, there's no, uh, sense of occasion, I think that's the main problem with DVD. You don't feel you're opening a treasure chest—or a fucking Pandora's box… But it's great to finally see good prints, it's made me reconsider my opinions of a lot of movies, seeing them intact, in their correct aspect ratio, with an audible soundtrack—with subtitles even! The amount of information we were missing on videos of Italian movies, those panned and scanned prints—it's inconceivable now. People talked about those films being incomprehensible—of course they were fucking incomprehensible! They were cut by ten minutes by the British censors, then more by distributors, you were only seeing the middle third of the picture, the dubbing was terrible or inaudible. How could you know some of those movies were actually good?

The TEXAS
CHAIN SAW
MASSACRE
Companion
Stefan Jaworzyn
Foreword by Gunnar Hansen


Now I don't have to slog around the country trying to watch shit in fleapit cinemas or sleeping on someone's floor with a bunch of perverts after sitting through five virtually watchable bootlegs of stuff that was absolutely unbearable—yet somehow I feel that was part of the attraction, oddly enough.

CHAPTER 27.5
NIGEL BURRELL
MIDNIGHT MUSINGS

**JOHN SZPUNAR: When did you start your career as a journalist?**
**NIGEL BURRELL:** Journalist! Wow, that sounds almost professional! I still consider myself a fan who happens to write. My true roots as a fanzine writer lay in the British punk rock scene of the late 1970s—I edited a punk fanzine called *Into the Void* from 1979 to about 1981, covering the local music scene in Cambridge mainly, but also other bands from all over.
**JS: Was it widely distributed?**
**NB:** Rough Trade sold it in their shop in London, the rest I distributed myself locally. I would get promo freebies sent to me from UK bands for review, but I once got a seven-inch single from a band in Sweden, so my lowly zine got around!
**JS: A lot of the people I've spoken to got their feet wet with the punk scene.**
**NB:** Punk rock gave me the drive to start writing. Pure and simple. I'd always loved horror films since I was a nipper, but I was only galvanized to write about films when the video recorder and video stores entered my life.
**JS: I'm guessing that *Into the Void* was photocopied—**
**NB:** It really was a xerox publication! Looked crap to be honest, but it was my baby and I was proud of it. Still am. Then, I wrote film and music reviews for a left-leaning local newsletter/ magazine (the title of which escapes me) in Cambridge in the mid-1980s. My crowning moment with them was reviewing the uncut *Re-Animator*, which got a one-day/two screenings outing at the Cambridge Arts Cinema in 1985 (on loan from the London Film Festival). It was heavily cut for regular cinema/ VHS release soon after. I also recall writing an article on the video nasties, attacking censorship, which drew the ire of local feminists!
**JS: Going back a bit—you're not originally from the UK...**
**NB:** I was born in Nigeria longer ago than I'd care to put down here, lived there for the first four years of my life, then lived and schooled in Tanzania until I was nine years old. I was sent to a UK boarding school at the age of ten and left there at the age of eighteen. While at school, I holidayed in Uganda and later Kenya. I'm quite the white African!
**JS: I'm curious about the genre films that were playing in Africa. What kind of things were you exposed to?**
**NB:** Whatever was showing at the local hardtop cinemas in Tanzania and Uganda. A lot of violent Italian sword and sandal epics, the early *Sinbad* films, Disney (of course), sci-fi, and whatever monster movies screened. We had no TV and, of course, no home video in those days. Later in Uganda, I caught a few mild horror films, of which *The Fearless Vampire Killers* made the biggest impression. At the same time (aged eleven or twelve), I was just being allowed to sit up late on my own at my grandmother's house during the school holidays to watch the horror/ thriller films they would screen every Friday night.
**JS: This was during the seventies?**
**NB:** Yes. This allowed me to discover Hammer films, a smattering of weird 1950s flicks, and some great 1960s genre offerings. Up until this point, my only access to "real" horror films was through imported US horror magazines

such as *Monster World* and *Famous Monsters of Filmland*, which I'd flicked through in fascination in Tanzanian bookstores as a young kid, but had never been allowed to purchase, as my mother disapproved of such rubbish.

**JS: How did your viewing habits change as you got older?**

**NB:** I began to see a larger selection of horror movies via TV screenings throughout the 1970s—also, such great British TV horror series such as Brian Clemens' *Thriller*. As the 1970s unfolded, the films being screened on TV got more graphic, both in the violence and nudity stakes—I can well remember my first viewing of *Blood on Satan's Claw*! One of my favourite cinema memories, though, was catching Bob Clark's creepy *Black Christmas* in a cinema in Nairobi, Kenya, just before Christmas 1975!

THE BLOOD ON SATAN'S CLAW

DENNIS FRIEDLAND AND CHRISTOPHER C. DEWEY PRESENT "THE BLOOD ON SATAN'S CLAW" STARRING PATRICK WYMARK AND LINDA HAYDEN • EXECUTIVE PRODUCER TONY TENSER PRODUCED BY PETER L. ANDREWS & MALCOLM B. HEYWORTH • DIRECTED BY PIERS HAGGARD A TIGON BRITISH / CHILTON FILM PRODUCTION • COLOR • A CANNON RELEASE

R

Then came the classics such as *Dawn of the Dead*, *Alien*, *Halloween*, and *Friday The 13th*, which I saw in my late teens just prior to the home video explosion.

**JS: I think the earliest work of yours that I've seen was in *Fantasynopsis*.**

**NB:** That was indeed when I began to get my writing out in a semi-professional publication.

**JS: How did you start writing for them?**

**NB:** I got in touch with [*Fantasynopsis* editor] Paul Brown via a message left with the manager of the Cambridge branch of Forbidden Planet that there was a local guy looking for people to write for a film fan magazine he was planning to edit. I left my phone number, Paul phoned me, popped around, and nearly fell over when he saw my VHS collection and left clutching my uncut copy of *Dawn of the Dead* after a few beers in my local pub. This would be round about 1988.

**JS: Why do you think Britain was so uptight about everything? I can think of much worse things to do than watching something like *Dawn of the Dead*...**

**NB:** Britain has always been a tight-arsed, control-freak country on so many levels, though we have always been somewhat hypocritical, criticizing sexy films/stories whilst secretly loving them, for example.

**JS: I find the entire video nasties phenomena to be a bit baffling. Was the British public really that paranoid about these films?**

**NB:** The average person on the street had little concern about video nasties—it was the politicians, moralists, and church leaders "protecting" us from moral harm. It was

a dreadful era to be a British horror fan. You could be raided, arrested, and imprisoned for collecting/importing uncut horror videos. We were made to feel like serious criminals. Horror videos were butchered by the BBFC in a more brutal manner than anything the killers in the much-maligned slasher films could have done to their onscreen victims! It was no wonder that a whole underground fan network emerged. We felt under constant siege from the authorities, and the tabloid rags were labeling such films as Deodato's grisly *Cannibal Holocaust* and Joe D'Amato's cheesy *Anthropophagous the Beast* as snuff films.

**JS: Speaking of the British underground, which UK horror zines did you first run across?**

**NB:** I actually never got to see very many examples of the original homemade lo-fi British horror zines. They really didn't get any kind of wide distribution that I can recall. It was only when I met Paul Brown of Midnight Media, who was getting hold of zines from the UK and the US that I saw a smattering of UK titles.

**JS: What did you think of them?**

**NB:** I remember being largely unimpressed, to be honest. I did have a soft spot for Trevor Barley's fanzine *Cold Sweat* and also liked *In the Flesh*. British horror zines got a little better towards the end of the 1980s, and into the 1990s.

**JS: I was always impressed by the serious tone that the UK zines gravitated toward. Why do you think the British zines evolved in the direction that they did?**

**NB:** It's just a case of your educational background and general outlook,

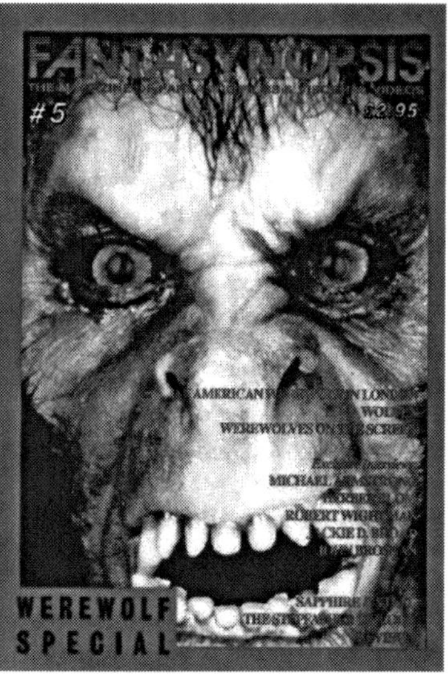


*FANTASYNOPSIS* NUMBER 5.

I guess. Also, it might have been a deliberate attempt to get out of that whole dribbling gorehound/video nasty collector scene, where films were often rated on how bloody or cheaply offensive they were (I was as much guilty of that mentality myself at the time). Sometimes I think they took things *too* seriously, as when *Shock Xpress* described the uncut *Toxic Avenger* as "fast food fascism!"

**JS: Speaking of Trevor Barley, I remember wishing that I could travel to the Everyman cinema in London to attend the Eurofests. What are your memories of them?**

**NB:** Well, Paul Brown co-organized many of the Eurofests, so I got to attend all of them! Too many good memories to put down here, but I'd have to say that the two best Eurofests were the ones attended by Jörg Buttgereit of *Nekromantik* infamy and gore maestro

Lucio Fulci. I have a happy, surreal memory of sitting next to Fulci in a London curry house discussing *Don't Torture a Duckling* after that two-day Fulci-Fest! They were great days for sure. I feel blessed to have met so many key genre figures over the years.

**JS: Could you give me a little background information about Midnight Media?**

**NB:** It was originally a part-time mail order-only company supplying British horror fans with imported horror zines that were not easy to find here. In the early 1990s, Paul decided to turn his hobby into a real company, working full-time from his home, mail order and selling through UK film fairs.

**JS: I'm assuming that things were pretty grass-roots in the old days.**

**NB:** You assume correctly! From 1983 to the late 1990s, British horror fans were treated generally as undesirables, so we formed our own networks for collecting films on VHS, as well as horror mags, both domestic and imported.

**JS: How big of an operation is it these days?**

**NB:** Still pretty much a one-man show! I help out from time to time in an editorial/writing capacity, but that's it. It's Paul Brown's baby.

**JS: How did *Is It... Uncut?* come about?**

**NB:** Almost as a joke in response to the irritating chorus of, "Is it uncut?" one heard at UK film fairs from VHS collectors. However, after Paul had folded *Fantasynopsis* a few years previously, he was getting itchy to get back into the publishing/writing side of things. The time was right.

**JS: It certainly was. The magazine was a hit.**

**NB:** The magazine fed directly into the whole rabid film collector/nasties fan mentality in the UK, plus Paul has a great way of packaging/designing the visuals for his magazines. The magazine soon grew a fan base in the US, as well as other parts of the world. Not bad, given the small numbers printed and largely self-distributed.

**JS: How big of a readership do you have these days?**

**NB:** Not too sure, probably pretty much the same as it's been for the last decade. We are talking about only a few thousand sales per issue.

**JS: What's the current status of *Is It... Uncut?***

**NB:** The magazine has been on hold for the past few years, but hopefully will be back one day.

**JS: When did you start writing for the FAB mags?**

**NB:** From not long after Harvey started *Flesh & Blood*. I wrote for other

FOUNDED ON A CHORUS OF "IS IT UNCUT?"

magazines like *Delirium* and Stephen Thrower's *Eyeball*, too.

**JS: What was Harvey Fenton like to work with?**

**NB:** Harvey's great to write for. Laid back and always appreciative of one's efforts. He's one of the really "good guys" in the UK genre scene.

**JS: Did you ever have any contact with John Martin? I was a big fan of *Giallo Pages*.**

**NB:** I met him a couple of times. Nice guy, to my recollection.

**JS: He always seemed OK to me, but I can't help but bring up his "rant". I never quite understood why he lashed out like that.**

**NB:** I didn't either, at the time. But, the passage of years has proved him largely right in many ways on several people named in his article. Wish I'd taken him more seriously back then; it might have spared me some unpleasant dealings with certain individuals. No names from me!

**JS: One of the bigger mags in the UK was the *Dark Side*. What were your first impressions of it?**

**NB:** Never much cared for it. Even in the early days, it had the feel of a "slapped together to make money fast" production.

**JS: I was shocked when the plagiarism charges started popping up a few years ago. What was your reaction to that?**

**NB:** I had already fallen out with [editor/publisher Allan] Bryce prior to that (unsurprising to me) bombshell. It had been common knowledge on the ground that there had been plagiarism going on there for years. Some people are just users of others' skills and knowledge. I'll say no more.

**JS: Midnight Media is still putting out printed material; they should be applauded for that. How big of a market is there for A5 booklets?**

**NB:** The A5 booklets are very popular, both here and abroad. The Germans love such things! *Giallo Scrapbook* and *Slash Hits* have been the most popular, I believe. My personal favorite of the A5 booklets that I wrote for MM is *Hispanic Horrors*, which ironically hasn't sold well enough to guarantee a follow up. But, I'm very proud of it, and one day hope to be able to write further on Spanish language horror.

**JS: What are you working on now?**

**NB:** I'm planning an article for David Kerekes' *Headpress* on my recollections of being a big bootleg vinyl collector in the 1970s/1980s. I will also be interviewing other collectors and maybe even a few bootleggers themselves. Should be done by the end of 2012 at the very latest, given my sloth-like speed these days!

# Chapter Twenty-Eight

# Steve Green

## Fanzine Focus

By David Kerekes

Steve Green has read and reviewed a lot of fanzines. Probably more than most. His roots lie in the "archaic stencil duplicators" of British science fiction and fantasy fandom in the 1970s. But to horror fans he is best known for his regular "Fanzine Focus" column in the pages of the *Dark Side* magazine, which he maintained for an incredible fifty-one issues through the 1990s.

DS JAN/FEB 96 #53

FANZINE FOCUS

Steve Green waxes lyrical over QUEEN KONG and ZETA ONE, and finds time to review some fanzine as well...

MANSPLAT

ALIENS

EVERYTHING BUT THE NIPPLE

28

The Dark

PAGES FROM THE *DARK SIDE*'S "FANZINE FOCUS" COLUMN.

Fanzine Focus was an important voice for the small press in the UK, publicizing fledging and established zines free of charge. Many publishers relied on it, with some going so far as to say they would likely have folded without it. Fanzine Focus also brought a sense of, well, *focus* to the world of UK horror zines, hitherto sorely lacking in community spirit. It could be critical but it also offered gentle guidance from time to time.

Flicking through some of the Fanzine Focus columns over its six year span, one is struck by the sheer wealth of publications being produced over such a relatively short space of time. (The copies of FF I have date from July 1991 to sometime in 1996, but mine isn't an extensive collection.) Some zines remain familiar today and are somewhat legendary in their own right (*Shock Cinema*, *Flesh & Blood*, *Eyeball*, etc). But a good many more are otherwise forgotten (*Petrification*, *Hellfire*, *Read with Mummy*, the *Goblin* et al). Among those to have fallen by the wayside are efforts by adolescent creators. Steve points out that this juvenile element is one of the notable differences between the horror zines of the UK and others elsewhere in the world. It's a valid point, and one at odds with the general attitude.

So, while Fanzine Focus was a working platform for the small press of its day, now it exists as a record of a hidden history, a snapshot of a medium that was only ever viewed contemptuously by those outside of it. As for those within it, very few were taking notes.

Steve was.

This interview with Steve Green took place at his midlands home on the afternoon of May 24, 2012.

RECORDED & INDEXED

DRAFT

FANZINE FOCUS

Steve Green covers the fanzine scene...

DARK TERRORS

THE GOBLIN

MAGAZINES OF THE MOVIES

**DAVID KEREKES: What is your background in small press publishing?**

**STEVE GREEN:** I first encountered fanzines through the *Radio Times*. I heard about the Dr Who Fan Club. It was a bizarre little organisation, which a guy had somehow persuaded the BBC in the early 1970s to sponsor. That was one of my first contacts. Then I began reading *World of Horror* magazine, which at that point was carrying a fanzine news column and which I now know to have been written by Lee Kennedy. I ended up joining the British Science Fiction Association, and reading their stuff. But it all started pretty much with the fanzine column in *World of Horror*. That's the reason why I began doing Fanzine Focus all those years later.

**DK: *World of Horror* was a great magazine, wasn't it?**

**SG:** It was an exceptional magazine. It had a certain edge to it. It had some extraordinarily gory covers. I remember one of Sheila Keith with her eye almost hanging out [laughs]. It was printed on this incredibly cheap paper, 'cos, towards the end, they were obviously cutting the budget, so the paper was like toilet roll.

**DK: *World of Horror* inspired you to go into Fanzine Focus...**

**SG:** Well it certainly inspired me to get involved in fandom, and through it I encountered some of the more acerbic writers out there. There was an excellent fanzine called *Fantasy Trader*, which was a comic zine. It had loads of powerful letters from people arguing about various new comics; they'd rip the latest DC and Marvel stuff to shreds. It was really fun to read. I thought, this is something I want to get into. In 1977, at age sixteen, I joined the local science fiction group in Birmingham and got involved doing their fanzine. It was extremely dry and tedious. Then I got into doing my own fanzines. The first being at the end of '77. That was called *Astron*. I was

at college, I had a bit of income coming in, I was able to afford to print it myself and send it out. I did a few fanzines that had sort of fanzine review sections.

**DK: How did you get the gig with the *Dark Side* and Fanzine Focus?**

**SG:** I was originally a newspaper journalist and wanted to get back into writing after an awful office job, so went freelance at the start of 1991. I looked at the magazines that were out there at the time—*Shivers* and *Starburst*—and they were pretty bad payers. Then I was chatting to [the *Dark Side* editor/publisher] Allan Bryce. We moved in the same circles. I pitched the idea for some sort of fanzine column. And he went for it. At the time, *Dark Side* was bimonthly. Back in the early days [1990s], the first problem that hit was actually trying to find fanzines to review.

**DK: Okay.**

**SG:** There was a little word of mouth but it was very difficult to actually find anybody who was carrying any lists. A couple of exceptions was your own *Headpress* and Jim McLennan's *Trash City*, which did carry other people's zines and addresses. One of the things I've always liked about science fiction fanzines is that they tended to review each other. It was sort of a big community, and we obviously referred to each other's fanzines. This happened a lot in science fiction fanzines; didn't happen so much in comic fanzines, and it didn't happen much in horror zines, either. I suspect the comic and horror zines saw themselves as vaguely commercial, they carried a price tag. A lot of science fiction zines didn't carry a price tag; the usual way of getting a copy was to ask for one nicely, send them a copy of yours, and they'd send one back. Or, send them a stamped addressed envelope. They didn't expect to make money from it. Comic and film zines, on the other hand, did tend to carry a price tag. Obviously a minor one, but enough to cover the cost of producing the magazine. So, if you wanted to get a copy, you'd have to pay for it, and I think that's why they didn't particularly want to publicise rival publications. You think about it: The target audience was really teenage boys, and teenage boys don't have a massive disposable

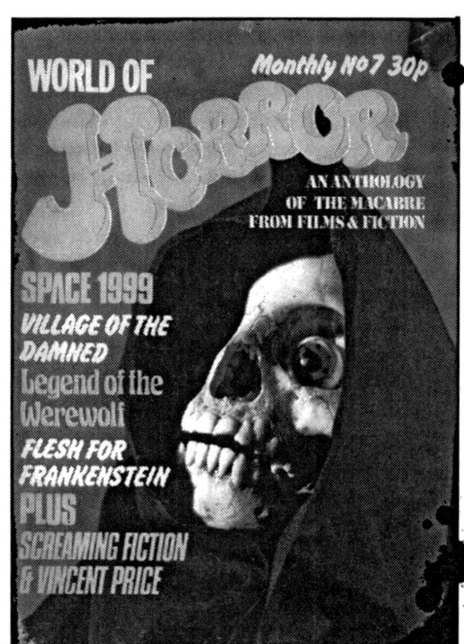

income. If it turns out they prefer some other fanzine, your own zine might come undone.

**DK: [Flicking through copies of the *Dark Side*.] Your earlier columns, such as this one from October 1991, give coverage to only a handful of fanzines. Here it's about five or six.**

**SG:** Because that was all I could find.

**DK: I'm assuming that situation changed very quickly.**

**SG:** It took a little while, but once I was about three or four columns in, then people began sending me stuff. I always used to make absolutely certain that my address was listed. Not Allan's address, otherwise I might not have received anything! I think when I first started working for *Dark Side*, it was owned by Robert Maxwell; it was part of his empire. And then, it became slightly looser, and Allan and his business partner [as Stray Cat Publishing] were able to sort of buy it out. His business partner had been a printer, which was quite useful for the *Dark Side*; he'd make sure they got cheap printing. But, for one horrifying period, I was technically working for Robert Maxwell [laughs].

**DK: Some of your Fanzine Focus introductory preambles offer guidance to aspiring zinesters, and you get a bit of flak for it. Most people shouldn't do a fanzine, you wrote at one point. They should probably find something else to do instead [laughs].**

**SG:** I'd probably have planned to say that there are some people who get into fanzines for the wrong reason. They aren't really there to express any real opinions; they just want to do it because it's a craze. And there were some bloody awful fanzines, let's be frank about it. The alternative would be, you do something which is not terribly good, which doesn't sell and that puts you off it forever. So, somebody who, may one day have become an interesting writer, or an interesting artist—suddenly they're out of the picture. They're probably not even going to be interested in fanzines, because they got burned.

Admittedly, I was trying to push people in certain directions, trying to encourage them to be better editors, to take more care over the stuff they produced.

**DK: Where you aware of cycles in specific types of subject matter?**

**SG:** Yes, very much so. A lot of the cheaper-looking magazines, a lot of the more one-man-band type efforts, were obviously done by younger people, and some were clearly still at school. And in those days—we're talking about the glorious days of the video nasty, and pirate videos, and nth generation copies of things being passed around—yeah, suddenly a particular film would be doing the rounds, because you would see the same films reviewed on a regular basis. Like, there'd be a new Dario Argento out, and everyone would be talking about this new Dario Argento film, which obviously wasn't available over the counter. Or, a Jörg Buttgereit film, something like *Nekromantik*. When *Nekromantik* came

# FANZINE FOCUS

**How can you avoid having your nasties grabbed? Steve Green covers this and other equally salubrious topics in his regular small press roundup...**

The relentless media hysteria over "video nasties" and the recent nationwide clampdown on the underground trade in uncertificated videos are unpleasant reminders that not all fanzine readers are sympathetic to the genre. Indeed, trading standards officers reportedly trawled the classified ads in one leading semi-pro title in search of unwary dealers (the absurdity of a law which dictates that a particular cassette can be legally possessed if bought in 1982, but mutates into a dangerous threat to society if re-sold a decade later, is obviously one they'd prefer to ignore, perhaps because such high-profile "swoops" help justify their department's budget applications).

What effect, if any, the current political climate will have upon the fanzine field remains to be seen. Undoubtedly, certain editors will become more cautious with the advertising they accept, whilst some pundits may adopt a less contemporaneous timeframe for reviews of pre-BBFC material. But it's a racing certainty that fanzines will continue to balk at the perceived injustice of the Video Recordings Act; fandom, after all, has always thrived on oppression.

## HEADPRESS

Speaking of unjust censorship, the ever-excellent HEADPRESS devotes one third of its fourth issue to the campaign by Manchester Chief Constable James Anderton and like-minded city magistrates to shut down Savoy Press; Anderton, now thankfully free to converse with God on a full-time basis, claimed the surreal novel LORD HORROR was anti-semetic, conveniently forgetting that the disputed passages are merely in-context statements by the central protagonist, an acknowledged racist, and that the wording was lifted from Anderton's own homophobic rantings, simply substituting the word "jew" for "gay". Co-editor David Kerekes submits a powerful argument against the authorities' attempts to silence the imprint's subversive voice, whilst partner David Slater reviews the career of Richard Baylor, a film-maker whose experimental shorts are unlikely to get legal distribution in the UK under the current regime; also well worth checking out is Chris Mikul's overview of the "Hookers for Jesus" phenomenon and Kerekes' encounter with "miracle healer" Melvin Banks.

## DIVINITY

Given David Flint's involvement with the launch of HEADPRESS, comparisons between that magazine and his new project, DIVINITY, are inevitable, though misguided; nor should it be viewed as a return to the psychosexual themes ploughed by the late SHEER FILTH!. That said, there are superficial similarities in the subject matter, even if Flint seems more likely to examine the personal motivations and leave the "bizarre culture" context for his former colleagues. Features in his first issue include a tribute to starlet Margaret Nolan (background gloss in such varied fare as WITCHFINDER GENERAL and the CARRY ON series), a profile of director Walerian Borowczyk (LA BETE, DOCTEUR JEKYLL ET LES FEMMES), interviews with porn star Hyapatia Lee ("I think sex is much healthier to explore explicitly than violence is"), and a Soho peepshow performer, an overview of the horror imprint, 'Creation' and an interview with resident artist Mike Philbin (currently collaborating with James Havoc on the graphic novel RAISM). DIVINITY promises to take its readers "from orgasm to obliteration", although its debut is striking enough to indicate its own obliteration should be some considerable time away.

# STEVE GREEN

## FANZINE FOCUS

brother Richard, has gathered together some cracking material on horror cinema's "golden age," including a fascinating examination of MARK OF THE VAMPIRE's box office battle with BRIDE OF FRANKENSTEIN in 1935 (the effective death knell for the careers of both Bela Lugosi and director Tod Browning), the conclusion of an extensive Val Lewton filmography and a welcome interview with 1960s scream queen turned producer Barbara Steele, recalled in her BLACK SUNDAY role on David Daniels' superb cover illustration and recently back on American tv screens in the DARK SHADOWS sequel. Triffic stuff.

### 1-SHOT

Curiously, whilst Britain was exporting Barbara Steele to Italy, our own movie industry was importing foreign starlets like Ingrid Pitt, Britt Ekland and Dahlia Lavi to add a touch of glamour. Tim Greaves' 1-Shot Publications made its debut last year with YUTTE STENSGAARD: A PICTORIAL SOUVENIR, which proved successful enough to spawn another two illustrated tributes. The first, YUTTE STENSGAARD: MEMORIES OF A VAMPIRE, unearths further rare photographs from the Danish actress' film and tv career, but where this showcase really finds its strength is when Greaves includes quotes from former colleagues and family members, even if Stensgaard herself remains curiously reluctant to discuss that period of her life. Noticeably less close-mouthed is the star of MADELINE SMITH: A CELLULOID RETROSPECTIVE, who discusses her work on such films as FRANKENSTEIN AND THE MONSTER FROM HELL and TASTE THE BLOOD OF DRACULA ("If the newspapers and the public chose to make me into a pin-up, I was more than happy to go along with it"), accompanied by a stack of stills from THE VAMPIRE LOVERS. It's obviously a labour of love (or perhaps lust) for Greaves, and I look forward to his planned volume honouring Veronica Carlson.

### DARK TERRORS

There are more Hammer highlights in issue five of Mike Murphy's DARK TERRORS, including in-depth critiques of the classic PLAGUE OF THE ZOMBIES and its "back to back" sibling, THE REPTILE, soundtrack reviews and a long-overdue profile of Hammer composer James Bernard, who reveals that SHE originally included a song from Christopher Lee and recalls that the grim PLAGUE offered little opportunity for "nice tunes." Murphy's continuing series on lost Hammer projects meanwhile exhumes VLAD THE IMPALER, which at one point would have starred Richard Burton and Richard Harris, with Ken Russell in the director's chair. Intriguingly, the success of Francis Ford Coppola's gothic BRAM STOKER'S DRACULA has helped place the original Bryan Hayles screenplay in the running as Hammer's re-launch production.

### INTERNATIONAL

Back across the Big Pond, Tim Paxton has been publishing his monthly newsletter MONSTER! since 1988, and has now launched a twice yearly spin-off magazine, MONSTER INTERNATIONAL. Some of the material is reprinted, such as Horacio Higuchi's trawl through "little known or poorly reported" foreign productions (his column in the second issue includes such obscure fare as Toho's GIANT MONSTER VARAN and Roger Corman's THE SAGA OF THE VIKING WOMEN AND THEIR VOYAGE TO THE WATERS OF THE GREAT SEA SERPENT). But the larger format also allows Paxton to include lengthier essays, such as a Jesus Franco "creature feature" filmography and Steve (PANICOS) Fronone's guide to Mexican [illegible], ranging from SANTO CONTRA LAS MUJERES VAMPIRO (a 1961 match for wrestling superhero Santo) to 1966's EL IMPERIO DE DRACULA, which [illegible] chunks of Hammer's DRACULA, PRINCE OF DARKNESS, a box-office smash down south the previous year.

out it was almost like watching dominoes fall over: one by one, all the magazines, all these people were mentioning *Nekromantik*.

**DK: The UK fanzine was driven a lot by the video nasties, of course.**

**SG:** To my mind, that's the major reason that they existed in the first place. Horror fandom is different to science fiction and comics fandom, in so much as people tend to be writing about other people's work. So, there's less actual creator material coming out; it's more review, critical material. But there's no getting around the fact that the moment the government began clamping down on so-called video nasties, the films suddenly became exciting, and people wanted to see these things and write about them. Then they wanted to brag that they'd seen these things. So, it was the fuel that kept a lot of the British movement going.

As the column progressed, I did extend the range and begin carrying information on magazines outside Britain. A lot of American fanzines were plugged in the column. Not a huge number of European magazines; they don't really have the same tradition. But in Britain, and to a small extent, Northern Ireland, you can't get around the fact that a huge number of those fanzines would not have existed had the government not tried to tell us we couldn't see those films.

**DK: Beyond the nasties being a creative impetus, how did the threat of the video clampdown and police raids affect zine publishers?**

**SG:** As I say, most of the people were doing the sort of "gosh, wow, guess what I saw last night?" kind of reviews. They were fairly young; they were mid- to late teens. I don't think they actually had much comprehension of what was going on. There wasn't any kind of political discussion inside the pages that I can recall—other than "Down with censorshit". But there was

no real sort of political context or political pressure. There's all these people who were really outraged. Most of them were below the age of voting. But they could have petitioned the fact. I remember when I was first involved in *Star Trek* fandom, back in the seventies, we actually had petitions to get the BBC to show four particular episodes. Of course, nowadays, two seconds later there'd be a Facebook group with 100,000 people joining it.

**DK: Whenever the mainstream approached the topic of zines, which wasn't at all often, it was invariably negative. The worst example, of course, was John Gullidge and *Samhain*.**

**SG:** John was running a youth group, or he was scout leader, or somesuch, and happened to publish a horror film fanzine. The local press went after him for that. It was just appalling. He's a guy who runs a magazine that talks about horror films. That doesn't mean he shouldn't be allowed to be near children; it's ridiculous. You wouldn't apply the same thing, say, to the editor of *Sight & Sound* for having reviewed Ken Russell's *The Devils*. There's a really irritating snobbishness inside certain elements of the media.

**DK: What shockwaves did the *Samhain* thing cause within the zines?**

**SG:** Sadly, not a huge amount. People didn't really pick up on it—some people did, some of the older editors commented on it, in passing. I'm pretty sure I commented on it at the time. As I say, there was no consensus: that is probably one of the major differences between horror fandom and comics fandom, or science fiction fandom. There doesn't seem to be a cohesive sense of a community. It's disparate people. You might get people collaborating on a fanzine, you might get two or three people together, because they happened to go to the same school, or go to the same college, or something; you might get that happening.

**DK: What would you say were the fundamental differences between the fanzines of the UK and the US and, indeed, elsewhere?**

**SG:** The US magazines tended to look more professional. They weren't always that much more professional inside, but they certainly looked more professional; a more professional ambience. Quite a lot of the American film fanzines were also fiction fanzines. There was less actual talking about film. For them, horror was the genre, horror was the writing. So, there were fewer horror cinema fanzines coming from the US. Considering that the US is six times larger than the UK in terms of population, their output was not anything like it was in Britain. [Flicking through issue 46, circa 1996.] I'm looking for foreign publications. *Shock Cinema*'s listed here, which was a good film magazine. But *Prohibited Matter* from Australia was basically fiction and comics, so was *Skin Tomb*—again, from Australia. The British fanzines at that point were coming out of the video nasty crap, I think it was getting a bit old hat. So, people were trying to make their fanzines more professional, maybe give them a bit more longevity. And very few of them actually survived. Many didn't get past issue two.

**DK: But, you were amassing a pile of fanzines; you wouldn't at any**

FROM BEYOND

FANZINE FOCUS

HELLFIRE

BOOK OF THE DEAD

HEADPRESS

COLD SWEAT

DARKNESS

**point have thought they were a disposable commodity?**

**SG:** Every fanzine that I was sent—every fanzine that I was sent during that period, I still have.

**DK: Oh, wow.**

**SG:** I still have them all. They're in crates upstairs in the attic, and the extension at the back of the kitchen, there are boxes and boxes and boxes of fanzines out there. I've got every fanzine I've ever had, I still have. To me, they are not disposable. I wasn't 100 per cent happy about some of the stuff that I was sent—and neither was my wife! Some of it was really quite dodgy. There was one—I can't think of the title offhand—that was essentially just pictures of autopsies. Whether or not it really even qualified, I included it in the column; I guess, if you count *Faces of Death* as a horror film, you could class this as a horror fanzine.

I was getting fanzines from Brazil; I think I got one from Venezuela. Stuff that was equally dodgy. Yeah, some of the stuff was a little odd, and sometimes you sensed that the people writing the reviews were taking a slightly unwholesome interest in elements of the horror film—particularly violence against women. But, I wasn't there to make moral judgements; occasionally, maybe I did go a little that way, but it wasn't my business to say "this is filth".

**DK: What kind of numbers of zines were you receiving when Fanzine Focus hit its stride?**

**SG:** I ceased doing Fanzine Focus after fifty-one editions of it—which is a terrifying period of time! It means I wrote more than 100,000 words. Final issues were getting crazy. You see, I made the promise to myself that I would not exclude a fanzine; I wouldn't put it back to the next issue. Every fanzine would get reviewed, or at least get plugged. But by the end of it, it was getting silly; I was getting twenty-five or thirty of the things to review. I think one issue it may even have been forty. And I've only got 2,000 words.

Well, you do the calculation—that gives me about fifty words per zine. I was only paid for 2,000 words an issue. But I used to write over that every time.

**DK: The latter zine heavy columns are effectively just a name check with contact details.**

**SG:** It's basically listings—and I'm trying to give a flavour of what was out there. [*Dark Side* number 59.] Good grief, how many are in that one? *Bubblegum* number one, for instance, that's not a review. Basically I'm just saying what's in it, because I just don't have the space.

**DK: When and why did Fanzine Focus stop?**

**SG:** It was a combination of things. I had less free time, and Stray Cat had been very, very slow in paying. That was happening to all of the *Dark Side* contributors.

**DK: If you had to sum up Fanzine Focus as one memorable element, what would that be?**

**SG:** I suppose it would be some pride in thinking that I helped give a push to a number of fanzine editors, at a time when there was literally nothing else around to help them. Yeah, I guess it would be that. I remember the thrill that I got, reading Lee Kennedy's fanzine column in *World of Horror*—reading *World of Horror* full stop. Well, I knew that there were people who were reading *Dark Side* the same way—they were thinking this was *our* magazine. So, when I read the fanzine column that Lee wrote, I had a real buzz from knowing that there were people out there publishing stuff. And when I sent off my 15p, or whatever, and got something back, it was a great thrill. After a while, I thought, if they can do this, I can do this; that was that buzz. I don't think that exists anymore for people; I think they aren't quite as interested in creating artefacts in that sense; paper artefacts. But there is a pleasure and a pride I can take in the fact that some of these people would never have got past their first issue, if it hadn't been for Fanzine Focus. I'm repaying that column in *World of Horror*. I felt I owed it a debt in a sense and this was how I was paying it back.

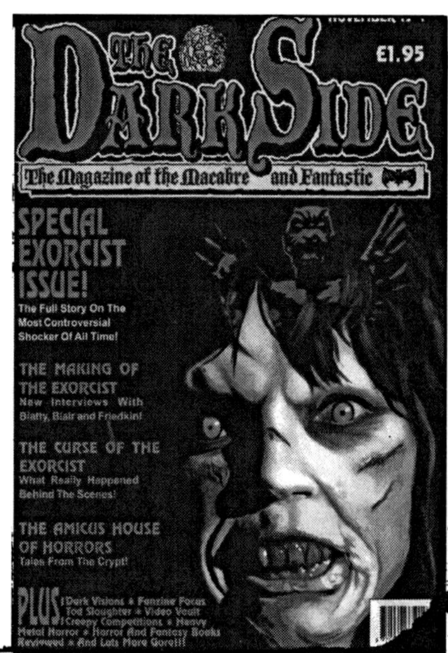

# CHAPTER TWENTY-NINE

# NATHAN MINER

## BITS N PIECES

BY CHRIS POGGIALI

NOTHING SO APPALLING IN THE ANNALS OF HORROR!
You'll Recoil and Shudder as You Witness the Slaughter and Mutilation of Nubile Young Girls — in a Weird and Horrendous Ancient Rite!
MORE GRISLY THAN EVER IN BLOOD COLOR!
Produced by David F. Friedman
Directed by Herschell G. Lewis

Back in the days when I was a full-time college student and a part-time fanzine editor, I attended two consecutive FANEX conventions in Baltimore—going solely by the video release dates of the movies Fred Olen Ray was there to promote, they were probably FANEX 4 (*Mob Boss*) and 5 (*Inner Sanctum*, *Evil Toons*)—where I had the pleasure of meeting Nathan Miner, a member of the Horror and Fantasy Film Society of Baltimore and the editor of its official fanzine, *Bits n Pieces*. I had been a fan of this zippy zine from the moment it rolled off the lot, although at the time I couldn't tell you why it appealed to me, since I was too concerned with keeping my own Winter rat on the road to give very much thought to what made someone else's vehicle purr so sweetly. Twenty-plus years later, I'm incapable of reading many of the reviews I penned for my zine and others, but I still find the articles in *Bits n Pieces* fresh and informative. The reason, I'm pretty sure, has a lot to do with this: Nathan was more concerned with history and facts than he was with opinions—his or anyone else's in the Horror and Fantasy Film Society of Baltimore.

Yes, there were reviews in each issue, but Nathan would never devote more than one or two pages to the negatives, while the positives were singled out in a column titled "Best of the Bunch," under a cute illustration of three or four bananas (Despite its editor's devotion to *The Texas Chain Saw Massacre* and the gore films of H.G. Lewis, *Bits n Pieces* was a family-friendly fanzine). The bulk of his publication was devoted instead to in-depth interviews with genre personalities (Gunnar Hansen, Clive Barker, Linnea Quigley) and meaty articles on subjects ranging from cheapo-cheapo video companies to the history of anthology horror films. The talented staff of writers included Gary and Sue Svehla of *Midnight Marquee*, John Freyer, video collector extraordinaire Lorne Marshall, Martin Rybicki, and John Clayton, who took over editorial control of *Bits n Pieces* when Nathan left for college shortly after completing issue 6.

His next zine focused on drive-in movie theatres and the years in which they thrived; the opinions in *Drive-In Theatre Newsletter* (1993–1995) were limited to reviews of any and all books and videos related to the subject of open air theatres. Nathan and co-editor Mark Bialek filled the pages with reader recollections, newspaper ads, frames from intermission films, a "Gone But Not Forgotten" column devoted to defunct drive-ins, and well-researched profiles of drive-ins that were still in operation. An entertaining piece on drive-in gimmicks appears in the debut issue, while the sophomore effort includes a reprint from a 1950s film exhibitor journal ("Franks Mean Sales: A Review of How to Merchandise and Increase Sales of Frankfurters at Outdoor Theatre Concession Stands") and an excellent original piece by Nathan titled "Filmack Studios: A Look at the Creators of the Snack Bar Trailers."

Because I saw Nathan in action and on his home turf at those two FANEX

## BITS N PIECES

RECORDED & INDEXED

conventions so many years ago, I can vouch for his dedication to the world of fandom and the time and energy he invested in those twelve very special issues; it seemed like every time I tried to dig through a box of pressbooks or a crate of one-sheets in the dealer rooms during those FANEX weekends, Nathan was already there with pen and paper in hand, flipping through pages and jotting down notes related to some horror or exploitation obscurity. I had those encounters in mind last September when a "Mystery Movie" blog post on *Temple of Schlock* was solved thanks to the information found in an issue of *Drive-In Theatre Newsletter*. Twenty years later, we're still learning from the bits and pieces uncovered by Nathan Miner.

The following interview was conducted via telephone on August 1, 2012.

---

**CHRIS POGGIALI: Although film bloggers and webmasters are frequently compared to the fanzine editors of twenty-five or thirty years ago, I don't think most of them realize just how good they've got it now.**

**NATHAN MINER:** You know the old cliché, we didn't have the internet, we didn't have these databases that list actors and everything they ever appeared in since the beginning of time. Back when we were doing this stuff, it was hard to find material—really hard to find material—but that made it interesting. It made it kind of a treasure hunt. I used the dealer's room at our own conventions to sift through and find pressbooks, which would give me some hints about the people involved in these things.

**CP: I used to do the same thing.**

**NM:** And that's what brought everybody together. All these fanzine editors, who were people like you and me who were hungry, they weren't happy just watching the movies, they wanted to know more, they wanted to know the behind-the-scenes. I've always been that way. Whatever I've gotten into, I want to take the next step. I'm not happy just being into it, I want to know the nuts and bolts, the behind-the-scenes, the who, what, where, and why. For so many of the people who were doing these zines, that's why they were doing it, because they had the same enthusiasm for it. It was kind of like a shared experience for all of us to trade the fanzines, like "Oh yeah! You saw this movie too?"

**CP: A lot of times, just finding the movies was no easy task!**

**NM:** Right, so you had your typed list of the videocassettes you had available and you would trade those with people and amass your library of sometimes hardly watchable, who-in-the-heck-knows-how-many-generations-removed copies of something, just to be able to see it! That was all part of the fun of it—discovering things. That's what made it fun. Now it's too easy. I can go on diabolik.com and order four or five DVDs of these super rare movies taken from the master negatives and have them

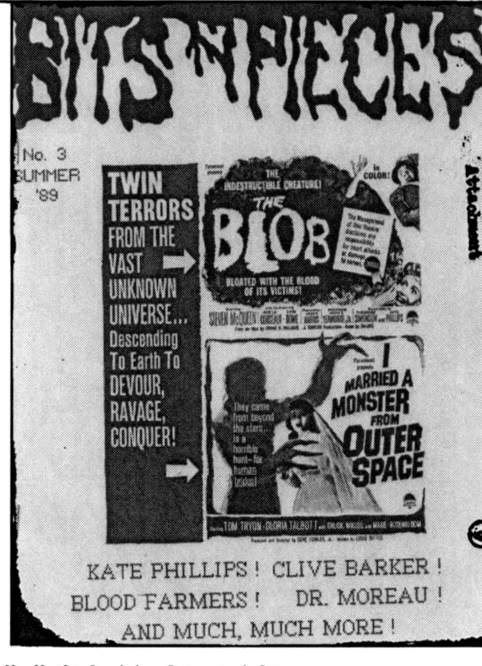


delivered to my door. It's still fun to see these films but you lose the reward of finally finding them. You really had to search for them, so when you finally found them, it meant a little bit more than just pulling up a website and clicking the "order" button.

**CP: How did you get interested in these crazy movies anyway?**

**NM:** I started off, I guess like anyone else, when we're young we flip through the TV guide and see all these incredible titles for these different movies and either try to stay up and watch them or, in the days of the VCR, we just set the VCR and taped all this ridiculous stuff off of television late at night.

**CP: Let me guess—you were a *Fangoria* reader?**

**NM:** Yup, I had a subscription to that. I've got all the *Fangoria*s upstairs still.

**CP: But not so much *Famous Monsters of Filmland*?**

**NM:** *Famous Monsters* is a little bit old for me. I liked it for the nostalgic, kitschy kind of value. The goofy pictures, and sometimes they'd draw the blood in there and the fangs on the black and white pictures.

**CP: Is your copy of the *Psychotronic Encyclopedia of Film* still in one piece?**

**NM:** Mine is filthy dirty on the edges and the cover is falling off. That's one of the only things we had to look up these films in during those days.

**CP: Were you the most popular kid in school?**

**NM:** Not at all. I'm sure a lot of us were not the most popular kid in the school. Isn't that weird how that happens? Why is that? Why is it always the oddballs who get into this stuff? One thing I think about is… y'know what? We probably identified with the killers! As mean as that seems, we saw Jason hacking up those jocks and thought, "Yeah, that's pretty cool!" Not that you want to say that out loud too much, or to too many people [laughs]! But there's definitely something to that, don't you think?

**CP: Yes, but let's not go there! What was the first horror movie you**

# NATHAN MINER

## BITS N PIECES

RECORDED & INDEXED

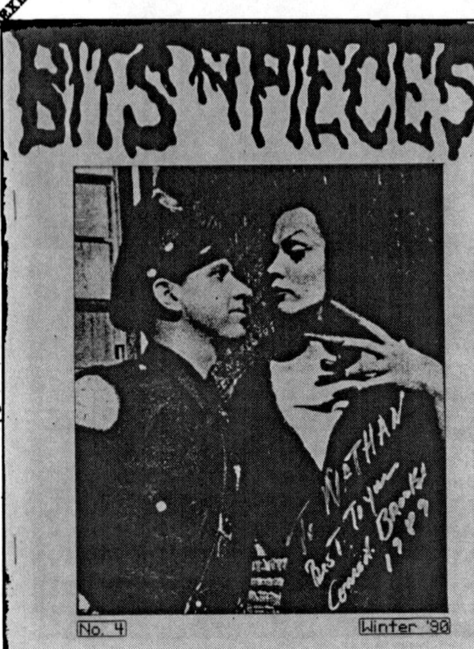


**rented on video?**

**NM:** Herschell Gordon Lewis' *The Wizard of Gore*. It was the Midnight Video big box, with that horrible illustration of the magician sawing the hell out of that lady on the front. After that, I was hooked. After seeing that monumental epic of sleaze and what-the-hell-is-this, I just had to have more. That started my journey, and it's still continuing. I still have that spark when I see something like that. When I see *Carnival of Blood*, I think yes, that hits the mark, that's the sweet spot right there! That's what I'm lookin' for!

**CP: Let's talk about your involvement with FANEX and the Baltimore fan community.**

**NM:** When the first FANEX convention was held in Baltimore, I didn't know it was going on until I saw a write-up in our local paper about it. That led me to Gary Svehla, who was at that time a member of a group that was called the Horror and Fantasy Film Society of Baltimore. I can't remember how I ever managed to get in touch with him but I did, found out about the group, and he said, "We meet once a month down at the wastewater treatment plant." One of their members worked there and he could get one of the meeting rooms for free, so I guess to make it more "official," they'd hold their meetings at another location. So I went over there and met everybody, and they had been talking about the next convention, because it takes the whole year to plan these things and kick them off. I really got involved in that, and it started the ball rolling for me.

**CP: It must've been exciting to find a group of likeminded people so close to you.**

**NM:** Baltimore was like this little hotbed of fan activity, which I never realized until I met Gary. He lived right down the street from where I

used to live, he was like two minutes away, and it really opened my eyes that there were all these other types of people just like me who liked all this weird stuff! So I owe a lot to him and that little group of film fans; that really opened a lot of avenues to me.

**CP: FANEX was a big part of the film society's existence?**

**NM:** Or pretty much the only part. I mean, that's really why we existed was to do those conventions, and they took a whole year, so we were practically planning the next one as soon as the last one wrapped up.

**CP: What were their meetings like?**

**NM:** Basically they'd talk about movies that were coming out in theaters and then they'd show a film. I always wanted a little bit more. I felt like "Why don't one of us pick a movie each time and then talk about it?"

**CP: More like a film discussion group.**

**NM:** Yeah, or a miniature convention for each meeting. I was always reaching for more information, more in-depth meat about the subject. A lot of the guys were there just to have a good time, joke around and watch the movies, but there was a core of us who really wanted to know more about the films.

**CP: Whose idea was it to start a fanzine?**

**NM:** I came up with the idea. I said "Hey, look, why don't we do a fanzine and all the members of this film society can contribute articles." Everyone was real enthusiastic about it, and they agreed that they were going to pay for it out of their budget. That's why—particularly with the first issue—you see a lot of articles that I would not really publish myself. There's one about Disney villains in there, and something about the different versions of *A Christmas Carol*, if I'm remembering correctly…

**CP: Yes, that was the "Yule Ghouls" article.**

**NM:** Yup! And they were all written by different members of

TERROR

# NATHAN MINER

## BITS N PIECES

RECORDED & INDEXED

this society. Because some of the wives that were members, they were into the fantasy films and some musicals even, but they weren't into the horror, so that's why it was the Horror and Fantasy Film Society of Baltimore. They really turned their nose up at the horror end of it. "Everybody is welcome," that's how I had to pitch my spiel, so they all contributed and wrote articles.

**CP: What was the next step?**

**NM:** I went out and bought a typewriter that could type two columns of text and align them as columns. I drew the *Bits n Pieces* logo myself, slapped that up there, and got the thing started. I would type everything out, cut the columns up, and then search frantically for some kind of illustrations, cos back then it was hard to find graphics for a lot of these movies. Especially when you were doing photocopies, you had to keep in mind the quality of what you were going to use. You couldn't use a lot of fancy color pictures.

**CP: Having been a fanzine editor myself, I know something must've gone wrong while you were putting together that first issue!**

**NM:** I had a big disaster with Kinko's. The first time I laid out the issue, I didn't realize you had to be within the boundaries of a certain line, because I was using some kind of printer's graph paper and I was outside the borders of an 8½ x 11 sheet. So when it came back from the printer, it was all too big and everything was cut off on the edges. I thought, "Oh my God…" And I was an extremely shy guy. I'm better now, but back then I was really shy and kept to myself. The idea of having to call Kinko's and complain that they messed up my magazine was horrifying to me! But I did, I called them back and surprisingly enough they said "Bring it in." So I hauled the big box of I-don't-know-how-many copies—I guess we made 300 copies or so at that time—back to the store and they reprinted it for me gratis. After that hurdle, I learned how to better lay out my product. I got very familiar with the White-Out tube. And I really enjoyed it. I had a ball, even though I had these little headaches and stumbling blocks with the first issue. Everybody seemed to be impressed with it, and it was a go after that. We tried to put two out a year, and have one out when the FANEX convention would roll around.

**CP: The sixth issue of *Bits n Pieces* doesn't seem much different from the previous five, which says to me that you knew from the start the kind of fanzine you wanted to publish.**

**NM:** I really did aim for some sort of quality. I didn't want to just put out a fanzine that had reviews. Who cares what I think about this movie? We had some reviews, because so many of these films people had never heard of, or they couldn't find, but after a while I get tired of that and I say "Where's the meat and potatoes? What can I do to make *Bits n Pieces* a little bit better, a little more memorable? What can I contribute that's going to be somehow meaningful or more worthwhile?" I tried to do that with the interviews, by finding people who actually have some history.

**CP: How did you land the Gunnar Hansen interview for your first**

**issue?**
**NM:** My mother had been a subscriber to *Yankee* magazine, and she said, "Hey Nate! Gunnar Hansen—isn't that the guy from one of your movies? Something about Texas?" I said, "Yeah, he's Leatherface!" She said, "Well, he has an article in *Yankee* magazine! Maybe you can talk to him." So I wrote to *Yankee* magazine, to the editors, and they were like, "Yeah, here's his home address." [laughs] This was a neat time to interview him, because it was right before he made *Hollywood Chainsaw Hookers*. He had been out of the scene. He wasn't doing conventions, he wasn't making movies. He was just this figure that not a lot of people really knew much about. I thought that was really cool to talk to him, but I was nervous as hell! Man, I was so nervous! I went to Radio Shack and bought that little thing that you hook up to a portable tape recorder that you can put into the phone jack and record phone conversations. And he was really so nice. "Do you have time to do an interview?" "Yeah, let's do it now." "Right now?! Oh–my–God!!" [laughs] I got out my notes and that was it! We did it! When I hung up I was sweaty and nervous, but so proud of myself, and I started transcribing it. It was a good feeling. I think I had some intelligent questions to ask. I tried to have some semblance of authority and professionalism about me.

**CP: It's much easier to set up interviews with people once you've had one or two published.**

**NM:** What's really funny is that Kate Phillips, who wrote *The Blob*, was in *Yankee* magazine also! I was like, "Damn, mom, you keep reading *Yankee* and bringing me these names! When you see Herschell Gordon Lewis in there, you be sure to tell me!" [laughs] Again, I wrote to *Yankee* magazine, told them I did this magazine, they said "OK, here's her address!" So I got in touch with her and talked about *The Blob* [in issue number 3].

He comes to Life to the sounds of
ROCK & HORROR
TEENAGE DRACULA
COLOR by DeLuxe
R RESTRICTED
an Independent-International picture


**CP: *The Blob* got a lot of coverage in *Bits n Pieces*. I know the first issue contains Bill Littman's negative review of the 1988 remake.**

**NM:** We also published a little tour that we did of the actual sites where *The Blob* was filmed in Pennsylvania. We knew this guy, Wes Shank, who was a friend of Gary's, who actually owns the original *Blob*. He keeps it in a roofing tar bucket, with its own little sign, "The Original Blob." He has some of the miniatures, too, like how they filmed the *Blob* coming up underneath the door of the freezer. It's a forced perspective cardboard miniature with a photograph of the set pasted onto it. Really cool stuff. Again, I'm really blown away that we got to do that. John Clayton, who would later edit *Bits n Pieces*, wrote a little article about that trip and we stuck some pictures in there to illustrate it.

**CP: You did an excellent interview with Sam Sherman in your second issue.**

**NM:** Gary was close with Sam, and when I heard he was going to be a guest [at FANEX], my jaw dropped open. That was like a milestone for me, to be able to talk to him. He's a really neat guy, but I had no idea that he loves to talk, and talk, and talk so much! The first time I met him, we were in the FANEX suite and he kept me up until four in the morning talking on and on and on! Everybody had gone to bed, and I had to go home and get some sleep, cos I had to be back early to start the convention, and he's talking and talking [laughs]! But I wouldn't have left for the world! He was so enthusiastic, sharing stories with this total stranger, this little twenty-two year old, like he'd known me forever. He is definitely a unique personality.

**CP: Were Baltimore fan-filmmakers like Don Dohler and George Stover members of the film society?**

**NM:** They weren't in the film society, per se. They didn't really attend the

VOL. 2 NO. 2

# GIANT SUMMER ISSUE!!

$1.50 Adults
- KIDDIES FREE -
(JUST KIDDING!)

## FANTASTIC 4TH!!

Welcome to the latest edition of what we hope is your most informative source of drive-in theater information. Memorial Day weekend is in full swing as I write this, and the Bengies Drive-In is helping to celebrate by holding it's traditional Memorial Day weekend "Dusk to Dawn" movie marathon. Last night I spent an enjoyable evening at the Bengies, tossing the frisbee, shooting pinball, and enjoying movies and vintage intermission advertisements on the largest screen in the state. I can't think of a more fitting way for the editor of this newsletter to kick off the summer of '94, and I hope that many of you also made the drive-in a part of your Memorial Day celebration.

If the May issue of Smithsonian magazine and the summer edition of Pennsylvania Heritage are any indication, there is an increasing awareness and interest in the open air theater. The Smithsonian ran a five page photo spread concerning freelance photographer Douglas Merriam and his intentions to "document as many drive-ins around the country as he could find." Included among the photos are a drive-in church service in Houlton, Maine and the impressive Moonlite Theater in Abingdon, Virginia.

"Moonbeams and B-Movies: The Rise and Fall of the Drive-In Theater" is the title of an article appearing in the summer Pennsylvania Heritage magazine. Although I haven't seen it yet, the color illustrated feature will no doubt be of interest to our readers. If you would like to get a copy, send a $5 check or money order payable to the Friends of the PHMC to: Pennsylvania Heritage, P.O. Box 1026, Harrisburg, PA 17108-1026. Tell 'em the newsletter sent ya! Special thanks to reader Bruce Clark for telling us about the article.

Just so everyone knows, our very own "Drive-In Theatre Fanatic Fan Club" is now official. Yes, the very first fan club devoted strictly to drive-ins is now a part of the National Association of Fan Clubs. So, if you've been holding off on joining, a bit sceptical of our authenticity, fear no more.

This is our first issue since we began offering subscriptions, and I'm relieved that we've gotten it out on schedule. Because the newsletter is put out only twice a year, Mark thought it would be a good idea to send an occasional "hello we're still alive" letter to our subscribers. I'm not exactly sure what we'll include in the letters, but rest assured that we'll try our best to come up with an informative supplement to the newsletter.

We sincerely appreciate your patronage and hope we have succeeded in bringing you an enjoyable evening of entertainment. When leaving, turn right on the ramp in front of you and exit at the marquee sign. Please drive home carefully, and come back again soon.

-Good Night.

DRIVE-IN THEATRE NEWSLETTER
c/o Nathan Miner
225 W. First St.
Frostburg, MD 21532

DRIVE-IN THEATRE VOLUME 2 NUMBER 2.

Attachment

meetings, but they were around. They were friends of Gary's who mainly helped out with the conventions. George Stover supplied a lot of prints for our conventions. I never really met Don Dohler, but I was aware of his movies, of course, being shot here in Baltimore. He had put out a science-fiction fanzine, *Cinemagic*, which dealt with how special effects were done, and for that time—the 1970s—there was not a lot of information on how to actually do that kind of thing.

**CP: George Stover had also done a few fanzines by that time, including *Black Oracle*, which he edited with Bill George, and *Cinemacabre*.**

**NM:** *Cinemacabre* was a slick little digest, taken to a professional printer. When I saw that, I thought, "Whoa, this guy really means business! He's spendin' some money!" And it was the same with his Cinemacabre Video. Back then, you got videotapes of questionable quality when ordering from some places, but George took his prints to a place that would use that wetgate process to fill in the scratches and make the print look a little bit better as it's being transferred to a master tape. He did all that and was really particular. He was a stickler for quality.

**CP: You mentioned in one of your emails that you attended screenings in Stover's basement...**

**NM:** Yeah, with Gary and Don Leifert, who was an actor in Don Dohler's movies. He was an English teacher at a local high school, and he was also in a theater group. We'd go over to George's house, like every Wednesday evening, and watch films in his basement. Those guys were really into the Universal, the Hammer, the older films, and I was the young punk who was into all the crazy gore films from the seventies. They would tolerate me, and just kind of laugh and shake their heads as I'd tell them about the latest Herschell Gordon Lewis epic I'd managed to locate on tape [laughs]. We'd bring tapes that we thought were interesting to watch before we got

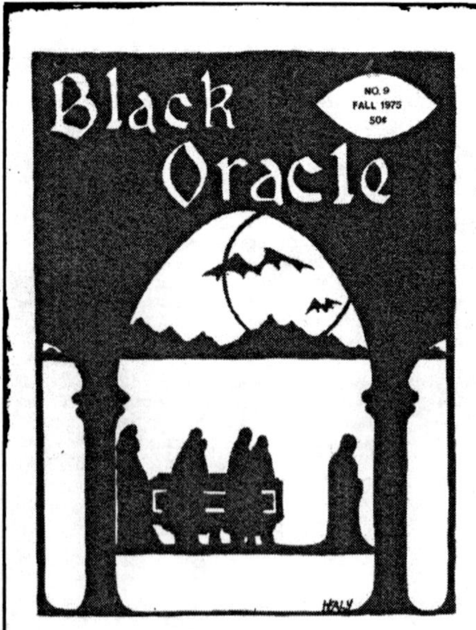


GEORGE STOVER'S *BLACK ORACLE* (NUMBER 9), THE WORLD'S SMALLEST FANZINE.

down to the main feature of the night, and we'd pop 'em in and watch vignettes and different things. So I'd bring along a *Sleazemania* compilation and show them trailers for some crazy—what was that one, I think it's a lost film, about a guy looking through a peephole?

**CP: *The Smut Peddler*?**

**NM:** *The Smut Peddler*! Yes, that one! I showed them that trailer and they were just, like, "Where the hell do you get this stuff?!" [laughs] I was the trash horror film guy, but they all took me under their wing. They felt I was kind of adorable, I guess. We got along well. Those guys are great, and I had a lot of good times with them.

**CP: I'm often asked why I bother documenting the history of films that so many people find worthless or beneath contempt. It's as if they assume *The Smut Peddler* just crawled out of a sewer instead of being made by someone someplace with a camera.**

**NM:** To enjoy a lot of these films, you have to have an artistic bent. You have to "get it." You have to enjoy and understand the time period that they were filmed in. The hairstyles, the cars, the music, the whole thing—it's not just "the film," it's a time capsule. That's what's so appealing to me.

**CP: I like Elvis Presley and Doris Day and Jerry Lewis movies, but at a certain point I get sick of watching a Hollywood set designer's idea of an American living room. I'm not saying H.G. Lewis or Andy Milligan or Doris Wishman movies are better, but—**

**NM:** They didn't have set designers! They just shot a film in somebody's house! They went in there, put plastic down, shot whatever, squirted blood all over the carpet and furniture and then they left! That's what you're seeing, these little time capsules that say "Here's the sixties." Here's the Suez Motel down in Florida. Here's Coney Island's spook house in

*Carnival of Blood*. I love seeing that stuff. People who don't have that bent just see a badly made film, but there are a lot of nuances that attract people like you and me to these films.

**CP: Getting back to the subject, what are some of the fanzines you traded with that you really admired?**

**NM:** Well, I had to laugh, I scanned through the first issue of *Bits n Pieces* a little while ago and noticed I gave *Temple of Schlock* kind of an "eh?" review [laughs]! I had to chuckle. I was like, "Uh-oh!"

**CP: Your review was pretty good considering some of the things that were written about us!**

**NM:** I really liked *Ecco*. That was one of the standards that I aspired to with *Bits n Pieces*. [Charles Kilgore] always came up with these really off-the-wall films and was able to talk to people and do these really cool interviews. I always admired him for what he was able to do. And he had it done offset. It always looked so nice. I was so jealous. That's one thing that I always wanted to do with *Bits n Pieces* was to be able to go offset and actually have some pictures in there that people could see.

**CP: I still revisit my issues of *Ecco* a few times a year. Another fanzine that has really held up is *Exploitation Retrospect*.**

**NM:** Dan [Taylor], yeah, he was funny. I'll always remember him as the college kid with the backpack full of beer! Remember that? Running around FANEX with a backpack full of alcohol? He was there for a good time. I'm happy to see that he's still involved and doing stuff on the internet.

**CP: We should also give a shout-out to *Subhuman* and its great stable of writers.**

**NM:** Yeah, and of course *Video Watchdog* was the magazine that everyone was blown away by. I know I was. Tim Lucas, I always thought he was top-notch. I envied him so badly because I could imagine him being able to watch movie after movie on laserdiscs that he would get for free probably, and spending a week going through all of the special features! Just picking

apart these films until there was nothing left [laughs]! So I always looked up to him, and got to meet him at one of the FANEX conventions. I think we gave him an award for Best Fanzine. We used to have award ceremonies at the conventions.

**CP: I remember! I attended a couple of those ceremonies. *Temple of Schlock* was even nominated one year, which shocked the hell out of me. I enjoyed the fanzine panel at FANEX 4, even though I was late getting to the room and didn't participate. Was that your idea?**

The Drive-In attracts young families with children, young people with aged parents, people with dogs they won't leave at home, teen-agers and college students. Assures deep refreshing entertainment for men, women and children of all ages.
Drive-Ins give you a healthier type of entertainment, a place where you can enjoy nature's air conditioning—come dressed as you please—even bring the children dressed for bedtime.

FROM *DRIVE-IN THEATRE NEWSLETTER*, VOLUME 3 NUMBER 1.

**NM:** It was, yeah. We would get together and pitch ideas for panels, and I said "Let's get all the fanzine editors together." Again, it was a real accepting atmosphere. As long as we weren't dong something too off-the-wall and they could fit it into a one-hour timeslot, you were good to go with it. So I started sending letters, "Hey, do you want to come to FANEX? We'll get you in for free! Just come over and do this panel!" I can't even remember what we talked about. I guess we were just shootin' the shit about the pros and cons of doing the zines, like we're doing now, twenty-five years later. That's what we're still talking about.

**CP: What was the last issue of *Bits n Pieces* that carried your name?**

**NM:** Number 6 was the last one I did, in Summer 1991. I went to college shortly after that, in Frostburg, Maryland, and was concentrating on my studies up there and that's kind of when I started parting ways with this life because I was three hours away and didn't really feel like driving back and forth too much to Baltimore, and I was up there in western Maryland studying wildlife and fisheries management. I thought I was going to be a forester, running around in the woods, but that never worked out. That was what I was going to school for, an outdoorsy type.

**CP: I fell out of the fanzine world around the same time, and didn't**

RECORDED & INDEXED
DRAFT

**know until recently that someone else had taken over *Bits n Pieces* after you left.**

**NM:** I knew I was going off to college full-time, and I said, "Hey, does anybody want to do this? Take over the reins of *Bits n Pieces*?" So John Clayton said, "Yeah, I'll do it." John was in the group. It was a real homegrown magazine, and it stayed within this film community. They changed the logo at that time. I thought, "There goes my hand drawn logo!" But they did go to a slick, glossy cover. I was so envious. "They went to offset with this issue! Boy, he gets to have all the perks now!"

**CP: So they kept you on the mailing list for a while?**

**NM:** They were kind enough to send me one. I don't think I wrote anything for it, unless I did a review or something.

**CP: What did you think of the content of that issue?**

**NM:** They did Hammer films, and I remember thinking "Okay, now we're back to the standard fanzine," because *Midnight Marquee* was always Hammer films and thirties Universal. But that's what Gary grew up with, and that was a big emphasis in that club, the older classic films.

**CP: They also added the ampersand and made it *Bits & Pieces*.**

**NM:** Well, Gary was an English teacher so maybe that was a little more correct, I don't know. Or maybe it shows they were a little more uptight, that bunch that was doing it then, and I was a little bit more of a free spirit kind of guy [laughs]! At that point, I pretty much did drop out of sight as far as being involved in their film society, and I don't think I saw any other issues after that one. There were no hard feelings or anything, I just got wrapped up in my school studies and didn't partake in the fanzine or the conventions very much anymore. I guess around '91 was the last convention that I did.

**CP: Clayton did three issues and then quit. After a two year hiatus the zine was resurrected by someone else and renamed *After Midnight*.**

**NM:** Again, I don't have those issues, so I'm a little bit foggy on how it all worked out, but somebody else did take it over. I think the Horror & Fantasy Film Society of Baltimore changed its name, too. I'm not even sure what it became. But I can't stress enough that I have really fond memories of that group of people. They came at a good time for me, and they let me explore this area of fandom—or filmdom, or whatever you want to call it—in ways that I would've never ever been able to otherwise. I especially owe a big tip of the hat to Gary for getting me involved in all of that, and letting me take a shot at doing a fanzine, and being there and encouraging me.

**CP: Less than two years after you gave up *Bits n Pieces*, you started another fanzine, *Drive-In Theatre Newsletter*. The first issue appeared in January 1993.**

**NM:** I had stayed really good friends with one particular member of the film group [Mark Bialek] whose favorite movie was *The Texas Chain Saw Massacre*, and it's kind of my favorite movie, too. We loved Paul Partain, who played Franklin, the guy in the wheelchair. We knew all of his lines

VOL. 2 NO. 1

$1 Adults - KIDDIES FREE - (JUST KIDDING!)

IT'S DRIVE-IN SHOWTIME AGAIN!

DRIVE-IN Theatre NEWSLETTER

THRILLING 3RD ISSUE!!

and we'd always mimic him. We were just crazy kids, y'know? But that's how I met [Mark] and we became really good friends. We also had an intense love of drive-in movie theaters. I've always enjoyed writing as a hobby, and this was another case where I was able to say, "Hey, let's do a fanzine!" I guess it's in my blood to be the one to chip away and find the meat and potatoes of any given thing that I'm interested in.

**CP: It was quite a departure from *Bits n Pieces*, in that it dealt with the theaters rather than the movies. What did you like most about doing this fanzine?**

**NM:** We would take excursions, little weekends to the various drive-ins that were either shut down or still operating in whatever State we were wandering off to, and we'd collect memorabilia and take pictures and I'd try to find the history behind each one. Sometimes we'd run into the owners at the property and get to talk to them. We met a lot of people that were into drive-ins, and we even did a dusk-to-dawn show at Bengies Drive-In here in Baltimore. We invited all of our readers and had a table set up with stuff we were selling. Quite a few people did show up who were readers of ours. Again, it takes that spark, that wanting to do more than just "I'm a fan of this" or "I like this." If you're willing to put effort into something, it can have big rewards.

**CP: What was your circulation?**

**NM:** We had 150 to 200 readers.

**CP: As with *Bits n Pieces*, you published six issues and then called it quits. What happened?**

**NM:** Mark and I had a little bit of a row later on, because I'm too serious at times. He was the "Gee whiz, I like the drive-in!" guy and I was more of the scholar. I wanted to do a serious study of the drive-ins: How many cars did this theater hold? When was it built? Who built it? When did it change to widescreen? And he was like, "I want to do a song about the hot dogs and

You'll SCREAM yourself into a state of SHOCK when you SEE-
BAT DEMONS!
CLAW CREATURES!
SNAKE MEN!
HUMAN VAMPIRES!
ALL NEW ALL COLOR
HORROR OF THE BLOOD MONSTERS
JOHN CARRADINE
ROBERT DIX
VICKI VOLANTE
Produced and Directed by AL ADAMSON
Executive Producers CHARLES McMULLEN and ZOE PHILLIPS
GP
Released by INDEPENDENT-INTERNATIONAL Pictures Corp.
COLOR by Spectrum X A New Dimension in Terror!


ANOTHER SAM SHERMAN MOVIE.

the popcorn and how great it is to go to the theater!"

**CP: One thing I like about the zine is that it does offer a mix of both styles.**

**NM:** It kind of worked for a while, a nice balance between the serious and the fun of the drive-in. It got really good responses. People would say to me, "You seem to be really serious and you have some good information about the history. Mark's good, too, taking pictures and writing fun little essays." That was his thing, fun little essays about going to the drive-in. He handled that end of it, the fun stuff, and I would do the more serious, in-depth reporting on the closure of the 202 Drive-In in West Chester, Pennsylvania.

**CP: Who was behind the Drive-In Theatre Fanatic Fan Club?**

**NM:** That was Mark also. He had this whole mail order thing going on. He made these little membership cards, and he would make prints of different architectural drawings he got from D. Edward Vogel, who runs Bengies Drive-In and whose father, Jack Vogel, built that drive-in and many others. Mark had all the sketches and drawings and would make fine color copies of these things and frame them and sell them. He started taking off with his fan club and not really doing the newsletter part, and I was getting kind of pissed at that. So we had a little row and stopped doing it.

**CP: You were out of the scene for a long time, but in the past few years I've seen your name resurface as an online reviewer. What brought you back to the fan community?**

**NM:** With the advent of DVD, that was a whole other renaissance for these films! We had stuff that we'd heard about but never thought we'd get to see, and from all over the world, all these obscure films that people were all of a sudden digging up and putting out on DVD. So this big explosion of stuff got me really excited again and got me into the movies once more.

**CP: And now computers have eliminated nearly all of the headaches that you had to deal with years ago as a fanzine editor.**

**NM:** I know! I find it so cool that I can now capture frames off a DVD on my computer and make my own stills! I mean, how easy is that? I don't have to go to a dealer's table and try to scare up a black and white still from some movie with a scene on it that I don't remember, or it's not even an exciting one. Now I can capture Ilsa topless whipping some guy into submission! Anything we want is right there for the capture!

VOL. 1 NO. 2

50c Adults — KIDDIES FREE —

We are back... with a New Season of Smash Hits!

DRIVE-IN Theatre NEWSLETTER

2ND ISSUE!!

Yes, we're back! Your "D.I.N." editors were a little apprehensive concerning the type of reception that this particular newsletter would receive, but happily, reader response has been enthusiastic. We've learned that there are indeed other "devoted ones" out there who feel the same sort of "mystical attachment" to what is basically a barren field with a building, hundreds of lopsided metal posts, and a large, obtrusive steel structure which is used as a movie screen (often referred to here at the "D.I.N." offices as "the monolith"). We appreciate the letters from select readers and hope that you will continue to fill our mailbox with those great clippings, stories, and just about any sort of drive-in related material that you'd care to provide us with.

Hey! It's mid-summer, the peak of drive-in activity. Time to load up the car with snacks, lawn chairs, blankets, and ETC, as you roll on over to your local (or nearest) oozone. Yes, it's unfortunate that the days of **Shriek of the Mutilated** and **Blood Drinkers** type double-bills are a thing of the past, but the drive-in still needs your support. There's bound to be some bone-headed action flicks out this summer, so pack up the kiddies, go early, toss the frisbee, and enjoy the show!

Here's a thought. How many of you own, or have access to a video camera? A few people I know have decided to film their trip to the drive-in, rolling the camera from the purchase of their ticket, all the way up to showtime. You could even capture the ten minute intermission if you are one of the fortunate few who still enjoy the old snack bar ads between double features. What I had in mind was a Drive-In Newsletter compilation tape featuring everyone's video clips. Imagine being able to experience trips to various drive-ins from various states that you'd otherwise never have the chance to attend! We here at the newsletter will edit your tapes together into two hours of ozone bliss. When winter time rolls around, and your favorite drive-in shuts down, you can sit back and relax with this tape. If this sounds like a good idea, go to it and send in those videos!

It's always a relief to complete an issue, and I'd like to thank Mark for providing photos for the hot dog and Filmack articles, as well as doing the complete layout for our intermission.

We're glad to have you with us this evening and hope you enjoy the feature. The snack bar will remain open all evening, ready to serve you with a wide variety of taste-tempting treats. And now - on with the show!

THE DRIVE-IN THEATRE NEWSLETTER
C/O NATHAN MINER
225 W. FIRST STREET
FROSTBURG, MD. 21532

**CP: Lately you've been writing about music for weirdomusic.com.**

**NM:** It's all about lounge exotica stuff—Martin Denny, Arthur Lyman, Esquivel!, what they call "elevator music" but a lot of it is quite advanced and very jazzy. Writing about music is a whole other ballgame. Writing about something that's visual is easier than writing about something that you're just hearing. There's a new vocabulary, a new way of having to describe things. They seem to like my reviews, so I have quite a few up there.

**CP: How did you hook up with the folks at [the website] *The Deuce: Grindhouse Cinema Database*?**

**NM:** I still enjoy writing about movies, and this might seem crazy, but I do my own little digest reviews, just for myself. So I was probably doing research for one of the movies when I came across the site. I thought, "It's really stupid if I'm writing all this stuff and nobody's seeing it." Again, I want to share with people. So I approached them about doing some reviews, and they wrote back and said sure. For one of the Paul Naschy movies I reviewed, I got something like thirty-two thumbs up responses! I thought that was pretty cool. You mean thirty-two people read this review? Hopefully they're getting something out of it. I'm still peppering the reviews with some history about the films and information about the actors. I'm still trying to include a little more meat.

# CHAPTER THIRTY

# KEITH CROCKER

## EXPLOITATION JOURNAL

GRATUITOUS APE AND GIRL PICTURE FROM "THE GREATEST BOOK I HAD EVER SEEN".

Keith Crocker is the man responsible for the *Exploitation Journal*, an excellent fanzine from Long Island, New York that first saw print in 1987. Featuring raucous film reviews and extensive interviews with the likes of Ingrid Pitt, Mel Welles, Diane Thorn, and Al Adamson, the *Exploitation Journal* quickly established itself as a trailblazer. Its features were very well-researched, and the *EXJ* boys brought with them a rough and rowdy attitude that was oftentimes irreverent and almost always hilarious.

Distribution woes forced the *Exploitation Journal* into a state of hibernation in 2005, but Keith Crocker did not sit still. His first feature film, *The Bloody Ape* (co-written by *EXJ* conspirator and *DVD Drive-In* editor George Reis), was a self-proclaimed "gore-soaked love letter to the sex and violence of the grindhouse era," and his follow up, *Blitzkrieg: Escape From Stalag 69*, is just as twisted as its title suggests.

Keith Crocker is currently at work on an Edgar Allan Poe anthology, *Three Slices of Delirium*, and he still runs Cinefear Video, the rare and out of print film catalog that he started in back in 1990. The *EXJ* itself is still in a state of hiatus, but as Crocker confirms, there's no telling what the future will bring...

The following interview was conducted via email, January–February 2013.

---

**KEITH CROCKER:** I came from a large family. It wasn't unusual for everyone to gather around the TV Saturday night for *Chiller Theater*—that was my first exposure to horror cinema. As a kid, the horror films scared the hell out of me. Later in life, they'd sooth and comfort me. But through *Chiller Theater*, I was exposed to the classic Universal monsters—*Frankenstein*, *Dracula*, *The Mummy*, and *The Wolfman*. Through Channel 13, I was exposed to the silent classics: *Nosferatu*, *Warning Shadows*, and the work of Lon Chaney, Sr. Many years later came cablevision and a station called Escapade...

**JOHN SZPUNAR: Why the attraction to exploitation and horror?**

**KK:** Escapade was a cablevision station that specialized in exploitation films. Literally, the movies came right off the drive-in screens to the station. It was there that my education began. Russ Meyer, Radley Metzger, Roger Corman. Really, I saw *Cherry, Harry and Raquel*, *Beneath the Valley of the Ultra Vixens*, Corman's *Nurse* series, and violent Italian gangster films like *Ricco* (they played it under the title *Cauldron of Death*). I learned more from that station than I did from college. As far as why I gravitate to horror and exploitation, I guess it's just artist angst, that well of anger that exists inside you. You can release that anger in positive ways and negative ways. For me, horror films were a positive experience that vacuumed out the anger.

DRAFT

RECORDED & INDEXED

KING OF CRAP. *EXPLOITATION JOURNAL* NUMBER 1.

# ANDY MILLIGAN: THE KING OF CRAP

By Keith J. Crocker

Andy Milligan is a name that all serious cinema student's should be familiar with.Better yet,all serious exploitation film lovers should be familiar with.This wonderful wizard of gore proudly proclaims that he has shot all his masterpieces for no more than $10,000 dollars,some for even under that.Milligan did not start out as a film director.Actually he was a garment worker in Manhatten. He made a short promotion reel for a short film idea that a friend suggested to him to try his hand at.This film,shot in 1964,later came to the attention of a New York distributer named William Mishkin,a fellow who told Milligan that if he would spice up his film with more nudity, he would distribute it.Milligan reluctantly agreed and the rest is history.

In 1968,tired of doing nudies,Milligan decided to make a horror film. This film,THE GHASTLY ONES,is a classic example of Milligan cinema. Milligan decided he would show nudity but that wouldn't be the premise. He decided to go for shock rather than titillation.So gore became the next area of experimentation with Milligan.As a matter of fact this is where Milligan showed his classic filmmaking ingreients.These would include a few seconds of shocking violence,about twenty minutes of dialouge, another few seconds of gore and so on. While Milligan's films are truly boring you can't say they are not unique.Milligan covers himself by making his films period pieces,because of his garment days he has constant costume disposal at his reach.

Milligan directs,writes,photographs & edits all his own films.He also does the bizarre make-ups as well.His make-up effects fluctuate between stupid and phoney looking to passable to at times very good.Milligan has often been mistakenly identified as being British because several of his films feature British performers and actually have some location footage that was done in England.Milligan was really a Staten Island resident.He had a friend who worked for cargo and this guy would often pass Milligan off as a currier and send him over to England with his camera. Milligan owned 16mm equipment and shot all his films in 16mm and would later have them blown up to 35mm for distribution.His films are grainy and poorly edited.However,this editing process proves worthwhile during gore scenes, with Milligan tricking us into believing we have seen more than he has really shown.His gore effects can be shocking,focusing on eyes being torn out , legs and arms being hacked off,bodies sawed in half and throats slashed.His themes deal with classic horror charecters.Werewolves, vampires,hunchbacks, deranged monks and murder for profit or desire are usually featured.Milligan,in interviews,has claimed that his relationship with Will Mishkin has been a shakey one.He calls Mishkin a "cheap man" and has called the producers son Lewis an "idiot".Yet,after these comments were reported, Milligan made a film for Mishkin's son.He never said he wouldn't work for them did he! So here then is a Milligan filmography.All his films are on video. (except his early softcore porn and later hardcore porn)so they are available for public viewing.

SADISTIC SUSPENSE!
SPINE-CHILLING!
MAN-EATING RATS and BLOOD-SUCKING WEREWOLVES!
THE RATS ARE COMING!
THE WEREWOLVES ARE HERE!
IN BLOOD-DRIPPING COLOR
HOPE STANSBURY with JACKIE SKARVELLIS and THE RATS of MOONEY MANOR
IF YOU DON'T HAVE THE GUTS —STAY AWAY!
Distributed by William Mishkin Motion Pictures Inc.
GP PARENTAL GUIDANCE SUGGESTED
* This film contains material which may not be suitable for pre-teenagers.

**JS: I'm curious about the movie theaters on Long Island.**

**KC:** The local theaters in my area played a lot of the same films that you would see on 42nd Street. On Long Island, we didn't have grindhouses per se simply because that expression would refer to a theater that operated twenty-four and seven. But we did have theaters that played any cheap piece of crap that came out. We had theaters that specialized in martial arts films. We had porno theaters (in neighborhoods that allowed them). Some theaters were grand and showed only Hollywood product. Most of these theaters are gone now; some have been plexed and multi plexed.

**JS: How about drive-ins?**

**KC:** We had drive-ins, and some damn good ones. It was at the Sunrise Drive-in in 1979 that I saw *Dawn of the Dead* and *Meatcleaver Massacre*, which really put the idea of being a filmmaker in my head. I saw Polanski's *The Tenant* at the movies. Saw a re-release of *The Exorcist* in a theater.

**JS: You mentioned porno theaters...**

**KC:** I had to travel into Queens, NY, just to see porn movies. The porn house in Hempstead (called the Fine Arts) was way too dangerous, and I was a coward. The other porn house, the Salisbury, cut the films to a single X rating, so we'd cross the border to the Queens Village Theater. I lived in movie theaters from 1980 through '85, but then the flicks started to suck and I went far less frequently.

**JS: What kind of books were influential to you?**

**KC:** I was a big collector of books on horror films. Those paperback Bounty Books from England fueled my imagination because they had nude photos and other such pictures from the European horror flicks that actually weren't too popular or seen in the States around that time. Denis Gifford had a book out at the time called *A Pictorial History of Horror Movies* which was just the greatest book I had ever seen. It covered so much ground, and made me realize what a smorgasbord of movies that was out there. I read *Famous Monsters of Filmland* and the very early *Fangoria*, which at one time was actually a good magazine, if you can believe that! Two other great magazines from that time were *HorrorFan* and *Slaughterhouse*. Both zines were crushed under the weight of the Fango publishers. *Slaughterhouse* had a sense of humor; they actually spoofed themselves by writing jokes within the context of an article.

**JS: Let's talk about fanzines.**

**KC:** Wherever there was a fanzine, I was a subscriber. Donald Farmer's *Splatter Times*. Ray Young and *Magick Theatre*. Rick Sullivan and the *Gore Gazette*. Barry Kaufman and his error-ridden *Demonique*. And of course, Bill Landis and *Sleazoid Express*. Usually I'd wonder in on these zines by accident, or a friend would lend me an issue. Guys sold fanzines out of the back of magazines like *Fangoria*, and I was the lunatic seeking them out. I was hooked. Zines were my drugs; movies as well, and for that reason, I'm still alive.

# KEITH CROCKER

## EXPLOITATION JOURNAL

RECORDED & INDEXED

DRAFT

**JS: What can you tell me about Rick Sullivan?**

**KC:** I loved Rick Sullivan. He shared my sense of humor. He didn't try to please people; in fact, he went in the opposite direction and really ruffled their feathers. He didn't hold back, he told you how it was. Honesty with a sense of humor.

**JS: How did you meet him?**

**KC:** I meet Rick Sullivan through Nathan Schiff, as they used to correspond—Schiff knew him through [screenings at] the Dive. During the early days of horror film conventions, Sullivan was the MC and was pissing everyone off at the early Chiller shows. I'd hear his announcements and I'd be laughing my balls off. We also exchanged zines. He caught a lot of heat over his writing, his cut and paste pictures, etc. Plus, he was selling videos of stuff that he shouldn't have been selling. I sorta followed in his footsteps. But he caught hell, hence his silence these days. Once burned, twice shy.

**JS: What are your memories of Bill Landis?**

**KC:** I also loved Bill. My relationship with him began much later though, more or less after he re-emerged from his own self-imposed exile. I had read *Sleazoid* in the late eighties—the issues I saw came from [my friend] Joe Parda, who was also a big Bill Landis fan. Landis was scholarly, took his subject seriously, and was funny without really trying to be. Sullivan was just plain nuts. I feel I patterned my writing style after both guys. I wasn't afraid to laugh, to be a wise ass, and to sorta tell things as they were. At other times, I took the subject very seriously and gave it the academic appreciation it deserved.

**JS: By all accounts, Bill Landis was a pretty complex character...**

**KC:** My relationship with Bill and his wife was at times volatile—one day they loved you, the next day they chewed your ass out. No provocation; they'd simply let you have it with both barrels. I had many a phone conversation, especially with Bill. He was a decent fellow with lots of troubles. I do miss him.

**JS: You started the *Exploitation Journal* in 1987...**

**KC:** Yes, indeed I did. It was the love child of both me and Joe Parda. In

fact, I believe it was Parda who proposed the idea of us doing a zine together. This was when he and I met in a film class in the Fall semester of 1986. I was thrilled with the idea, and by the next semester (Spring 1987), we had our first issue out. We gave it out for free at the college, and we had a very limited number of issues. The folks in the film department got a huge kick out of it, though I'm not quite sure what they really thought of the subject matter. Remember, the environment was not like it is now. Folks weren't so open about their interest in horror, exploitation, and porn films, but this was great because it put the spark of a revolutionary in you. You felt like you were doing something that others would never do.

**JS: So, the *Exploitation Journal* was originally the brainchild of you and Joe Parda?**

**KC:** Yes. Joe Parda and I started the *EXJ*. He was my co-editor until issue number 15. Some of my most inspired writing occurred during the Joe Parda years, but a lot of that had to do with being in college, full of vim and vigor. We had energy and humor back then; those issues are still a fun read.

**JS: Why did you and Joe part ways?**

**KC:** The biggest problem I had with Parda and the *EXJ* was that he wanted to make the zine semi-hardcore. Bear in mind that hardcore porn in a zine limited your distribution, and in the case of the college, it would have gotten us thrown out. Also, I wanted to make the zine a tad more accessible to women; I didn't want them to shut down if they came across the zine. It wasn't like it is today, you had to be careful. So that issue in point was one of our first big blowouts. I didn't mind covering porn flicks and using decrepit ad mats, but hardcore porn photos would have stopped us dead. Also, he developed a lack of interest by the time we got past issue 8. I wanted to go on, but he was losing the fire. *The Bloody Ape* ended up putting the kibosh on our friendship—we fought over the writing of the screenplay, so he ultimately ended up doing some camera work on that film and that was about it. The *EXJ* was our bastard child.

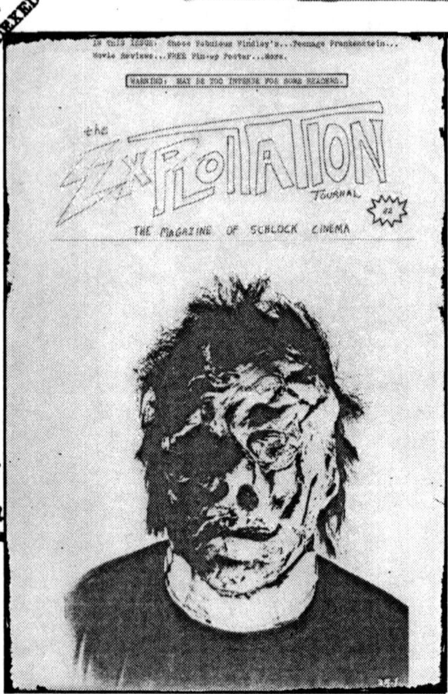


**JS: How were you laying out the early issues?**

**KC:** By typewriter, literally. Our first issue was oversized, 8½ x 14. Parda made the master on that size paper—he typed up the article, and left room for the ad mats, which came from our pressbook and still collections. This style of doing the *EXJ* continued until we hooked up with George Reis and he started laying out the *EXJ* on a word processor. I believe issue number 15 was the first done on a word processor, and even then George still had to leave space for the ad mats and such. Later in time, we got a scanner and were able to scan images onto the master page. I did the last three issues on a computer.

**JS: What was the initial cost of production?**

**KC:** In the beginning, it was none or close to it. Joe Parda printed up the very first issue of *EXJ* using a copy machine from a local library. So, you're talking about breaking the piggy bank open and using chump change. The big break came when I started printing them up at my night job. I used to sell mortgage insurance by phone. The office I worked in had the copy machine, so off I went. Issues 2 through 4 were printed for free—I believe issue 8 was, as well (I did that one at my girlfriend's job). The other issues were printed at Staples when they were new to Long Island. Believe it or not, Staples actually had guys experienced in printing manning the machines. Later, they decided to replace experience with inexperience because it was cheaper. All this was fairly inexpensive. And as the prices rose, both George Reis and I found a cheap printing company to do the *EXJ*s. Those were some of the best looking issues (issues volume 2, numbers 1–7). Those guys went out of business, so whenever I could get a friend in a print shop to do me a favor, I did. But, that's why the print quality of the issues often varied. When I finished in 2005, I was doing one-color covers. Interesting story: Cinefear Video was started to earn money to print up the *EXJ*s, and in the early days it did just that.

**JS: How did you distribute in the early days?**

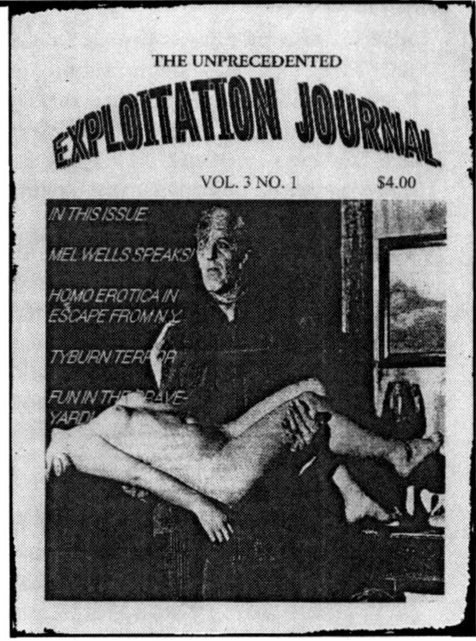


**KC:** Early on, we were the unofficial school paper of our college. Then we started taking ads in other zines and pro magazines and selling the *EXJ*s. Our college offered that we could use their copy machines provided we let other students in the film department write for the zine. But, we knew that by doing that we would become sell outs. Hence, we declined.

**JS: What eventually happened with distribution?**

**KC:** Believe it or not, I was contacted by Desert Moon Periodicals. The guy who ran it at the time was David Williams, and he was an honest, upstanding gentleman. They acted as our distributor for many years. It all went downhill when he sold the company to a real Jackass named Herschy. This guy blew the company wide open, and in doing so raised costs for the company, which they gladly took out of our earnings. By the time they went out of business, they had a reputation of being outright rip-offs. I departed a while before they went out. They technically would still owe me money, but they've been gone quite some time now and going after that money would be like pissing in the wind. The best distributor was Tower Records and Video. We were also with them for a great long time, and they paid you half up front for your zine run. Losing them was the straw breaker for me, that's when I decided to put the *EXJ* on hiatus.

**JS: You reviewed *Last House on Dead End Street* in issue number 2. How did you become aware of the film?**

**KC:** We were free advertising for video stores. We reviewed films that we saw in the theater, but more than anything, we were reviewing the video tapes we were renting. And there was no barter or exchange here; this was just us reviewing these films because we loved renting them. There was no motivation for anything like there is with the internet today. Anyhow, I ended up renting *Last House on Dead End Street* (on the Sun Video label) from Five Town Video, located in Inwood, Long Island. I had seen that horrific commercial for it back on TV in the late seventies, and now here was the film sitting on a video shelf. From that very same video store I saw *Loves of Irina*, *The Screaming Dead*, *Nazi Love Camp 27*, and *Dawn of the Mummy*—you name it, I saw it. Those were the days…

RECORDED & INDEXED

DRAFT

**JS: What was The First Annual Exploitation Film Festival?**

**KC:** We got a lot of attention for the first two issues of *EXJ* back at college. It was decided that we'd further our agenda by having an *Exploitation Journal* film festival at the school. We needed the permission of faculty, and our screenplay writing teacher came to bat and got us a room in the dairy barn—no joke, [New York Institute of Technology] was located on the grounds of an old farmland.

**JS: Did you screen actual prints?**

**KC:** We used video projection. We showed *Loves of Irina*, *Night of the Bloody Apes*, *Caged Heat*, and *Forbidden World*. The students who wandered in from the lunchroom had no clue what the fuck to make of all this. Except, of course, the teacher who gave us the permission to use the room. He came in for *Night of the Bloody Apes*. He brought a big hoagie sandwich in with him—he was laughing his ass off through the whole thing. It was great!

**JS: Was this a one-time event?**

**KC:** We both were close to graduation, so we never had the chance to get another one off the ground. But honestly, the world was a different place. The stuff we were showing was jaw-dropping at the time.

**JS: You mentioned [filmmaker] Nathan Schiff. Was he a part of your scene?**

**KC:** Yes. I was introduced to Nathan Schiff via a fellow named Kevin Radigan. He was the manager at a video store called Get With it Video. He was friendly with both Joe Marzano (*Cool it Baby*, *Venus in Furs*) and Nathan Schiff (*Long Island Cannibal Massacre*). I became friendly with both Schiff and Marzanno thanks to Kevin. Schiff did makeup effects for some of my short films, like *DeSade '88*. I was also friendly with a fellow named Howard Carson; he owned the Magic Shop on Long Island. That's where I got the ape costume for *The Bloody Ape*. I met Dennis Daniel through Howard Carson. So yeah, there was one of those "six degrees of separation" for all us Long Island guys. But as usual, familiarity breeds contempt. At the time though, it was wonderful knowing all these people.

**JS: How did you land your interview with John Waters?**

**KC:** I used to correspond with him through the mail. I was making a Super-8 film with my girlfriend's friends in the early eighties, and one of the dudes knew John Waters—he had been to his apartment in Baltimore. Anyhow, he gave me Waters' address and phone number. I never called him, but I did send him my early films, and we corresponded by mail. I finally met him in person several years later when he came to speak at the college (which happened as a direct suggestion from both Parda and myself to faculty). Anyhow, that's when we interviewed him for *EXJ* and the school paper.

**JS: What was he like in those days?**

**KC:** When we corresponded by mail, he was great. When we did the

interview, it was years later. He was on tour promoting *Hairspray*. Divine had just died, and Waters was quite miserable. He was short during the interview, somewhat distracted in thought, and one wished that perhaps we should all do this a different day. But the show went on, and we did it.

**JS: When did Cinefear Video come about?**

**KC:** Cinefear Video started in Spring of 1990. We thought it would be a great way to supplement the printing of the *EXJ*. It was a bigger success than we thought. In 1992, we starting transferring 16mm prints of rare films to video. We used to sell to Marshall Discount Video; they were a huge outfit (they used to advertise in *Fangoria* magazine all the time). That was also how I ended up with a killer VHS collection. All the stores were going out of business, and we were building a huge catalog for ultra cheap. The classic video labels were already out of print. We sold videos through the *EXJ*, and it in turn paid for *EXJ* printing. One hand washes the other. I've been running Cinefear Video for twenty-three years now.

**JS: Let's talk a little about the review style in the *Exploitation Journal*. I really liked the diversity.**

**KC:** Review style depended on who was writing—Parda was very different from myself. So was George Reis, and any of our guest writers. That's why it was a fun read—we didn't try to imitate each other. We were just ourselves. I wrote from the heart; passion was the name of the game. And I got a different kick out of working with the different co-editors. I wish not to compare my style with anyone

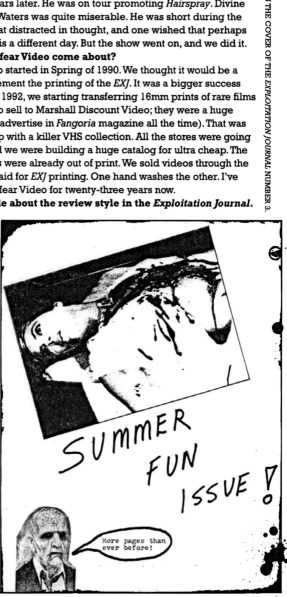

ON THE COVER OF THE *EXPLOITATION JOURNAL* NUMBER 3.

else's, but if I had to, I'd say it was a cross between Rick Sullivan (the edgy humor) and Bill Landis (with the introspective articles on particular films).

**JS: When did you start working with George Reis?**

**KC:** George was making contributions to issues from the early teens on, but he came to his own as a fill-in editor on number 15 and was finally fully in place by number 16. I met George sometime in '91. By Summer of '93 we were a team.

**JS: Why did you start renumbering the *Exploitation Journal* with volume 2?**

**KC:** To pull away from the Joe Parda years. It was really George Reis' decision to do so, He felt he could change the layout in such a way that it would create a different class of journal from what we had been doing. And, he did succeed in doing that. It was his way of proving himself as a very competent co-editor. The differentiation actually makes the various issues more collectable. The Joe Parda years were down and dirty. The George Reis years were almost prozine. His layouts were great!

**JS: I was just about to mention the layout change.**

**KC:** Yeah, George was more methodical in the way he laid it out. Using his words processor, it all got a lot more professional. I believe he wanted to turn us into a full-time zine that would move over to some color layouts, etc. But because I was coming from a more purist angle, I didn't work hard enough to get paying ads in the zine to help with its reproduction. Later I did, but it was way too late in the game and our publishing was erratic, which made it hard to sometimes tie ads in with product they were selling. We had always wanted *EXJ* to be ad free. We only wanted to push us and the zine, but that was a very unrealistic approach.

THE
LIMITED COLLECTOR'S ISSUE
EXPLOITATION JOURNAL
THE CONNOISSEUR'S GUIDE TO HORROR & EXPLOITATION IN THE CINEMA
Bloody British Special
Vol. 2, No. 2-3
$4.00
RICHARD GORDON INTERVIEW
PETE WALKER
NORMAN J. WARREN
THE AMICUS ANTHOLOGIES
PETER CUSHING
REVIEWS AND MORE


**JS: I'm curious about the column "Ricco Rates the Boob Bars." What can you tell me about it?**

**KC:** Like any zine trying to stay in the times, we wanted to expand coverage of things cultural that really weren't being covered elsewhere. Hence, "Ricco Rates the Boob Bars." That dude Ricco was a friend of mine at the time. He lived in Brooklyn, and frequented the topless bars all over the five boroughs and Jersey, so we figured we'd let

him loose to do a column. Those were fun reads and a very good idea. But, Ricco carried lots of bad with him, and he had to go. That simple. We were going to continue the column, but decided to can it after the Ricco experience. Really, it just boils down to not having enough time to do what you want to do, that's why you have other people do it.

**JS: In volume 3 number 1, you interviewed a few local porn theater projectionists. What can you tell me about the Fine Arts Theater?**

**KC:** It was a nasty porn theater located in the heart of Hempstead, which was suffering from serious urban decay. As I stated in the *EXJ* article on the theater, I was a coward. I never went to the Fine Arts. That area was very dangerous at the time, due to the crack epidemic and the fact that you had stray hookers roaming the place. It was a slice of 42nd Street on Long Island, and the films were raunchy enough to attest to that. Still, there was no comfort to be gained in attending that theater—I didn't want to be looking over my shoulder all night. We avoided it like the plague.

**JS: How about the Salisbury Adult Theater?**

**KC:** That was a safer area to go to; it was industrial, but not threatening like Hempstead. However, they cut the films down to a single X rating. You couldn't show XXX in Westbury, they had a law against it. So if you didn't mind blue balls, it was the place to go. But seeing hardcore with the hardcore cut out of it made no sense to me, hence we beat it over the border into Queens to go to the Queens Village Theater, which was a grand old movie house that was run by the mafia. It was located across the street from a Roman Catholic Church—the mafia didn't want any shit, so they kept the theater clean. For me, this was just the perfect porn film environment. All these theaters died off once video hit big. The Queens Village Theater is now a Baptist church. The Fine Arts is a mini mall. The Salisbury is a CVS [drugstore].

**JS: The *Exploitation Journal* gave Andy Milligan's films a lot of coverage.**

**KC:** Yeah. He's one of the biggest influences on me as a filmmaker, and he warranted two big articles in the *EXJ*. My thesis film in college was going

RECORDED & INDEXED
DRAFT

to be a documentary on Milligan. In fact, I got a hold of Lew Mishkin's phone number and was all set to interview him. But I was looking for Milligan, who had already moved to California. I was still in college; I had no money to go to California and look him up.

**JS: What became of the Mishkin interview?**

**KC:** Mishkin was set to go, but we got stuck in traffic on the 59th Street Bridge on our way to Manhattan to see him. He had to leave for the reading of a will, and we never rescheduled. I ended up making the short film *A Zombies Tale* instead. Milligan is still one of many cinematic gods to me. I simply loved his style, or lack of it.

**JS: As time went on, your publishing schedule started to become more erratic...**

**KC:** That usually happens when you try to juggle too many tasks at once. Filmmaking is really my calling and teaching film is very much my profession, so for the most part I engaged in a struggle between all the oars I needed to have in the waters when it came to making money. The *EXJ* almost always broke even—I never suffered as a result of it. But once I broke off from Desert Moon Periodicals (and once so many of the venues started closing down), the *EXJ* became less and less of a priority. This especially happened when I was doing the zine on my own in the early 2000s.

**JS: Why did you stop publishing altogether?**

**KC:** Tower Records and Video closing really did in my remaining distribution. Everything was aimed at the internet. I had already moved Cinefear Video to the internet (in 1999) and that had done very well. To me, the zine scene looked dead, so I threw the towel in. But, I never said the *EXJ* was dead. I simply said I put it on hiatus—for all I know, zines will rise from the dead and be granted broad distribution once again. I'll be there if it happens. In fact, George Reis and I have recently talked about the possibility of doing another *EXJ*, but once again, everything needs to be in alignment. We wouldn't attempt it unless the distribution and whatnot has been worked out.

**JS: Are you satisfied with what you accomplished?**

**KC:** The *EXJ* tells the tale of the end of the grindhouse era, the start and demise of the video store era, and broaches the DVD world. Honestly, I think twenty-five issues and eighteen years is more than enough time and dedication. I'm very proud of the whole three volumes of work.

**JS: Let's talk about your career as a filmmaker. You dedicated *The Bloody Ape* to Bill Landis...**

**KC:** You bet. Bill had just passed away prior to our DVD re-release of the film. Bill was a fan of the film, and I was a fan of his, so I dedicated the film to him.

**JS: You shot *The Bloody Ape* on Super-8.**

**KC:** Yeah. *Bloody Ape* was shot in 1992/93. Every jerk or bozo was shooting

stuff on video. I was trained on film, that was my background, hence I had no desire to shoot video. I thought it looked awful, and I still feel it does. So we bought up (at discount prices) expired Super-8 film stock, and off we went. To this day, the fact that I shot it on Super-8 film has been its best selling point. Folks like the cheap, washed out look. It reminds them of *Carnival of Blood*, another movie which inspired me, big time. Anyway, I took a big break after what was a very difficult shoot, and finally started to edit the film in '97. Got a color corrected transfer and had an analog re-edit done. It came out on video via Vanguard Distributors, who are still in business. It saw re-release on DVD in '99, via Wildeye Releasing.

A SEX-STARVED WILD BEAST
TRAPPED IN A CITY ROTTED TO HELL
HE RAPED AND KILLED IN THE BLOODIEST RAMPAGE EVER!
THE
BLOODY APE


**JS: What kind of budget were you working with?**

**KC:** Budget? What's that?! We had no budget; we shot until we ran out of film. I guess in the long run we may have dumped about $5,000 into it, but that was over the course of many years, so we never felt it. Yeah, we were the grass roots movement of cinema when it came to that film.

**JS: How long did it take to complete the film?**

**KC:** Technically, about a year and a few months. Mostly shooting weekends and some weeknights. I was trying to hold down a full-time day job while I did it. It was a great experience, but it was a grueling project. Dealt with lots of asshole non talents while making it. But, it was a great education. No regrets.

**JS: I wanted to ask you about some of the sets. Where did you shoot the carnival footage?**

**KC:** The carnival was 100 per cent authentic. We shot at a local carnival that comes to the same place every year around the fouth of July weekend. We went during the day, a weekday, and no one was really there yet. We improvised the whole thing, and the carnival was delighted to help out.

**JS: I'm assuming that you didn't have permits.**

**KC:** No permits. Nothing was done legally on either *Bloody Ape* or *Blitzkrieg*. We stole our locations. The video store we used was owned by a friend of mine. The police office was actually a middle school that we shot

RECORDED & INDEXED
DRAFT

in at night. I still don't know how we did this film...

**JS: Where was the protest footage shot?**

**KC:** At the same place the carnival was held, only in the parking lot. There was a Grateful Dead gig going on that night, and folks were flocking in. It was one of the last concerts Jerry Garcia ever did. Most of the patrons were very willing, others told us to get lost because they were dealing in illegal things! Lots of fun!

**JS: What led up to *Blitzkrieg: Escape From Stalag 69*?**

**KC:** Back in the day, I never released a film without advertising another upcoming film. So with the video release of *Bloody Ape*, we had shot the trailer for a nazispoitation film called *Schindler's Lust*. We shot that on black and white 16mm reversal film. It came out so well that I decided to make it into a feature in the 2000s. That trailer got downloaded so many times on my Cinefear site that I figured it couldn't fail, and it didn't. But like *Bloody Ape*, it was a grueling shoot that lasted over a year. However, the production values were completely different because I was working with completely different people. Different mindset. Different ideas. Hence, you get a very different film. It was the first thing I ever shot on digital video. I'm very proud of it, as well.

**JS: How did the experience differ from shooting *The Bloody Ape*?**

**KC:** Working with real actors from the NY scene—having a cameraman with 35mm experience, a guy doing the makeup effects—it freed me up to concentrate on direction. All in all, I felt like I got more of what I wanted on the screen. I had more competent help, which took some, but not all of the pressure off. It was a better experience, but a shoot is a shoot and it was still grueling.

**JS: What are you currently working on?**

**KC:** I finished the screenplay for a film called *Three Slices of Delirium*, a Poe anthology. We have a trailer for it up on YouTube. I'm still writing the screenplay for *Rasputin on Campus*, and we already shot the trailer for that (also up on YouTube). We are currently seeking financing for one or both films. They are both period pieces and would be a tad costly to make, hence we need outside money. I was recently hired as a director for a motion picture based on some recent killings that have occurred on Long Island. If the guy producing gets the financing we are good to shoot Summer 2013.

**JS: Do you have any final thoughts you'd like to share?**

**KC:** Yeah—if I was well paid for all the work and time I invested into my life, I'd be a very wealthy man. That said, I don't regret anything I've had involvement with. My life has been fuller because of it. If you have dreams, you can make them happen. It's all about discipline and devotion, and I have plenty of that...

# Chapter Thirty-One

## Shane M. Dallmann

## Hand it to Remo!

ART BY BRIAN MAZE.

# SHANE M. DALLMANN

## HAND IT TO REMO!

RECORDED & INDEXED

DRAFT

I'll venture that everyone present and accounted for has had some sort of a run in with Shane M. Dallmann. A regular contributor to *Video Watchdog* and *Screem*, Dallmann got his start in 1991 with a two-part article on Paul Naschy that appeared in the pages of *Fangoria*. Those very pages served as my introduction to Dallmann's work (as well as of that of the Hombre Lobo himself) and he followed through with another Naschy piece in Chas. Balun's *Deep Red*. In today's internet-driven world, it's sometimes difficult to remember a time when instant information wasn't just a click away. But those days did exist not very long ago, and Dallmann's research was not only responsible for putting Naschy's films back on the map, but for cataloging them, as well. *Deep Red* readers also knew Dallmann as "Remo D", the wisecracking hook-wielding lunatic who seemed to be on a crazy crusade to document every onscreen occurrence of hand amputation known to man. He even went to the trouble to rent and watch Bobby Suarez's *The One Armed Executioner* all the way through. A thankless task, indeed. Gotta like this guy.

In 2002, Dallmann tested the waters and tried his—ahem—hand as a horror host. *Remo D's Manor of Mayhem* has been going strong ever since, offering the denizens of Monterey County, California something different in a static sea of reruns and infomercials. In 2001, he co-directed the remake of Jack Curtis' *The Flesh Eaters*, a production that remains unreleased as of writing.

Today, Dallmann's work can be found in the pages of *Video Watchdog* and *Screem*. In the Summer of 2012, I decided to drop the man a line to see what makes him tick.

The following interview was conducted via email, June-July, 2012.

---

**JOHN SZPUNAR: Could you give me a little background on what attracted you to the horror genre?**

**SHANE M. DALLMANN:** Whenever I talk about my attraction to the genre, I always start with the same story: that of my very first "movie" memory—in my case, it involved watching *The Incredible Shrinking Man* with my father. Everybody remembers the scene with the "giant" spider, and plenty of people will tell you how they hid behind the sofa or at least covered their eyes. Not me. I was simply fascinated. I knew it wasn't "real" and I never worried that a giant spider was coming to get me, but I was captivated all the same by the spectacle. A black and white movie on a tiny television screen was showing me something I couldn't see anywhere else. Color me "hooked."

**JS: What kind of books were you hooked on when you were growing up?**

**SMD:** Believe it or not, I had quite the background in Shakespeare by the time I reached the first grade—again, thanks to my father, who had

the actual plays, condensed "storybook" versions for young readers and (best of all) a record collection supplied with read-along booklets. I even liked the plays without the ghosts and witches! My mother supplied the requisite fairy tale collections, Winnie-the-Pooh and the Narnia books, while I started in on the Oz books on my own courtesy of the local library. And my grandfather sparked my fascination with Greek mythology thanks to a story collection he gave me for Christmas. My father also had hardbound collections of classic newspaper comic strips (*Buck Rogers* in particular) and a wide array of superhero origin stories, so I was familiar with pretty much all of the classic comic book characters, though incidentally, the first book I started collecting in earnest (with no prompting from anybody else) was Marvel's *Power Man and Iron Fist*.

COLOR SHANE "HOOKED!" GET IT?

**JS: It sounds like your parents were supportive of your choices of entertainment.**

**SMD:** Absolutely—beyond *The Incredible Shrinking Man*, I always looked forward to watching WGN-Chicago's Saturday night creature features with my father, who told me all sorts of great things about the classic monsters and the people behind them (though it was more than frustrating when my parents started devoting Saturday nights to *The Carol Burnett Show*, *All in the Family*, *Mary Tyler Moore* and *Bob Newhart*, I actually learned a great deal about comedy watching those shows). Sure, there was the expected "you need to spend more time with your schoolwork and less with the monsters," but my parents never tried to suggest that monster and horror movies were "bad" in themselves. Of course, the plethora of weekend monster movie offerings eventually started including stronger material than the Universal, Hammer and AIP classics. I was dismayed when my father told me that we wouldn't be watching *Nightmare Castle* on creature features because it was too nasty... then again, he put the last fifteen minutes of the movie on *anyway*, and that's where most of the rough stuff took place! And unforgettably, he's the one who gave in and took me to see *Halloween* when I was too young to go on my own—that remains the most terrifying time I ever spent in a movie theatre…

**JS: *Halloween* really got to me as a kid, as well. Now, you're also a television horror host. How big of an impact did horror hosts have on you as a kid?**

**SMD:** A truly profound impact. Fuzzy VHF signals in the 1970s made me dimly aware of the original Svengoolie (Jerry G. Bishop) and I still remember watching The Ghoul (Ron Sweed) cutting up with Froggy during a screening of *The Crawling Eye*, but I didn't get to watch either show regularly. Summer trips to visit my grandparents in San Francisco allowed me to catch glimpses of the late, great Bob Wilkins (who supplied trivia, information and special guests as opposed to performing comic relief) and his eventual replacement John Stanley on KTVU's own creature features, so I filed those examples away for reference. By the time I was staying up late and watching additional horror movies on weekend television, there were no active horror hosts in Chicagoland, so I started improvising my own "host" segments during the commercial breaks. I didn't have a special name or a well-defined character for myself, but I tried to supply both movie information and comedy in the handfuls of tradition that I'd already seen. It took Rich Koz debuting as the Son of Svengoolie on Chicago's WFLD-32 to thoroughly galvanize me—I now had an out-and-out role model, and even though I undoubtedly drove him crazy with constant letters (the first one even serving as a type of audition/ plea to appear on the show—that didn't happen, but my joke *was* the first one he read out of his mailbag) and even the occasional phone call to the station, he never had anything but appreciation for his fans. Today, Rich is still going strong as Svengoolie himself while he and Bob Wilkins still comprise essential parts of my own host character, Remo D.

**JS: Back to magazines—*Famous Monsters of Filmland* made a big impact on a lot of kids from your generation. When did you discover it?**

**SMD:** Back when I was in the first grade… my father had exactly one issue stashed away and I eventually found it. It had a color rendition of a classic scene from *The Bride of Frankenstein* on the cover; I don't recall the exact issue number. I can't tell you how many times I read it from cover to cover—ads included! I kept an eye out for any and every movie cited in that issue to turn up on television. I especially remember a column called "The Crystal Ball" and Uncle Forry's declaration that "YOU'LL 'bawl' if you miss any of these!" I'm afraid that the only title I remember from that particular list was *Donovan's Brain*. It took me forever to catch up to that movie, but of course, I eventually did.

**JS: Did *Famous Monsters* fuel any creative juices?**

**SMD:** Oh, *FM* more than made me want to write… when the magazine finally started making itself available at my local stores, one of the very

# HAND IT TO REMO

## What Do You Say To A One-Armed Executioner?

by Shane Dallman

ENTER REMO D. *DEEP RED* NUMBER 7.

first issues I bought (1977) had Darth Vader on the cover and contained a Darth Vader essay contest: what do you like about Darth Vader and/or what would you like to see happen with him in future *Star Wars* installments? I answered both questions and obsessively counted my handwritten words to avoid going over the limit… and I was rewarded with one of 250 Darth Vader posters up for grabs. Needless to say, I was quite happy with my accomplishment!

**JS: What was your initial reaction to *Fangoria*?**

**SMD:** Ah, high school. The amazing magazine with all of the incredibly gory pictures—I became something of a sensation simply for carrying it around with me at school (the "dare you to look" thing). *Fango* became the newest and most valuable source for both historical articles and previews of films that I needed to see. You'll recall that my father *had* taken me to see *Halloween* (not to mention *Alien*), but *Dawn of the Dead* and *Friday the 13th* weren't going to happen, and something like *Zombie* (which graced the cover of the first issue I bought) wasn't even going to play locally. Ah, but *Fango* coincided with both our acquisition of cable TV and my eventual ability to see what I wanted on my own. The first film that I discovered through *Fango* (as opposed to Siskel and Ebert on *Sneak Previews*) and actually saw on the big screen was *The Howling*, and the first film that *Fango* lit a fire under me to see was *Videodrome*, which remains another huge influence on not only my writing, but the way I watch movies in general.

Attachment

## HAND IT TO REMO!

RECORDED & INDEXED

DRAFT

NASCHY GETS HIS DUE. *FANGORIA* NUMBER 104.

# PAUL NASCHY: THE HUMAN YEARS

By SHANE M. DALLMANN

**Part Two**

***Forgoing his famous werewolf character, the Spanish horror star turned director for a string of shockers, only some of which are available here.***

**Spanish lycanthropy met Japanese samurai mysticism in *La Bestia y la Espada Magica*.**

The first half of this article explored the horror career of Paul Naschy (Jacinto Molina Alvarez, a.k.a. Jacinto Molina) from 1968 through the first two of his four collaborations with director Carlos Aured, taking us to 1973. This point marked a transition for Naschy as an actor, as he began to concentrate less on monsters and more on normal human roles, while remaining firmly in the horror genre.

HOUSE OF PSYCHOTIC WOMEN [1973; [illegible] Video [uncut]; [illegible]]

Here's a title almost everyone knows, one which has been given plenty of contemptuous attention while the actual film has taken a back seat. Naschy's first non-supernatural film, originally titled *Los Ojos Azules de la Muñeca Rota* ("The Blue Eyes of the Broken Doll") casts him as a drifter looking for work. He finds it in the mansion of three bizarre sisters: a wheelchair-bound Maria Perschy; a red-haired nymphomaniac; and a repressed woman with a synthetic hand. At the same time that Naschy arrives in town, a

**In the unreleased-in-the-U.S. *La Bestia y la Espada Magica*, Naschy was a wolf in a sheepskin coat.**

50 FANGORIA #104

**JS: I kind of think of you as the Paul Naschy guy. When did you first become aware of his films?**

**SMD:** The first Paul Naschy film I ever saw was *Assignment Terror*, a "monster mash" thriller hugely influenced by *House of Frankenstein*. I caught that on a Sunday afternoon "Chiller Theatre" on Chicago's Channel 32 with no preparation whatsoever… hey, it had a vampire, a werewolf, a mummy and a monster that they couldn't quite get away with referring to as the "Frankenstein" monster. It had surprising gore, strange music and a terrific bit in which the werewolf jammed the mummy into a spinning wheel and set him on fire—it was "What's not to like?" At the time, of course, I had no idea that the fellow playing the werewolf (under the name "Paul Naschi") had also written the film (as Jacinto Molina Alvarez)—but the actor best known as Paul Naschy soon started turning up in all sorts of creature features (*Frankenstein's Bloody Terror*, *Horror Rises from the Tomb*, etc.) on my local channels. However, I have to give plenty of credit to my mother—had she not specifically forbidden me to watch *The Mummy's Revenge* (she caught the nastiest scene quite by accident when I wasn't around), I might not have become quite that obsessive about seeing it! Some of his films were terrific, some… not so much, but I automatically respected the Spanish actor who obviously had it in mind to pay tribute to all of the classic monsters he himself must have grown up watching.

**JS: A lot of Naschy films went through rotation on cable.**

**SMD:** When we got cable in the early 1980s, WOR-9 from New York made me aware of several more Naschy titles (the films they ran as *House of Doom* and *Horror of the Werewolf* are best known to us as *House of Psychotic Women* and *Night of the Howling Beast*). But it took Michael Weldon's invaluable *Psychotronic Encyclopedia of Film* to spell out just how much more Paul Naschy had to do with the films in which he appeared as an actor.

**JS: How did your *Fangoria* article about Naschy come about?**

**SMD:** *Fangoria* had started running some of the most interesting video-based articles I'd read to date, courtesy of Tim Lucas—particularly valuable to me was his two-parter on the films of Dario Argento and the state in which such films were seen in America. I'd been obsessively collecting movies on VHS in addition to compiling handwritten information in notebooks, and it suddenly hit me. (1) Paul Naschy was the *one* figure in cinematic horror history (judging by a comparable body of work, of course) that had *not* gotten his exhaustive due in a publication like *Fangoria* ; and (2) I had copies of every Naschy film available in the States. Someone needed to write that article, and I decided that someone would be me. The result: "The Mark Of Naschy" appeared in *Fangoria* numbers 103 and 104 as my first published work.

**JS: I believe you first met Naschy at a *Fangoria* convention…**

# SHANE M. DALLMANN

## HAND I[illegible] REMO!

COULDN'T RESIST… PAUL NASCHY FAN ART (UNCREDITED) FROM *DEMONIQUE* NUMBER 1.

**SMD:** Shortly after the *Fango* article was published, I was able to personally introduce myself to Tony Timpone and Michael Gingold at one of the magazine's LA conventions—I certainly couldn't afford to travel to all of them, but we stayed in touch. Naschy, at that time, had yet to actually visit America, and I suggested to Tony that he would make a terrific guest if such a thing could be worked out. It took a while, but it finally happened in January of 1998—Tony had alerted me to the event well ahead of time and I was able to swing a trip to New York for the sole purpose of meeting the man who had unknowingly kick-started my writing career. This meeting was immediately followed by my long-delayed arrival on the internet—thanks to that technology, I was able to stay in touch with my new friend for the rest of his life, even though I only met him once more in 2000, when I was able to introduce him to my daughter Rebecca.

**JS: Where did the moniker "Remo D" come from?**

**SMD:** The name "Remo" derives equally from the paperback action hero Remo Williams, aka "The Destroyer," whose books I was frequently seen carrying in the eighties and nineties—and from a lifetime weariness of "Come back, Shane" jokes, which inspired me to ditch my given name in favor of a nickname (not legally, strictly informally) when I moved to California to study film at San Francisco State University. The "D" is simply my last initial—when I signed on to perform comedy at a campus cantina, I simply scribbled "Remo D." as the host already knew who I was… but when he actually announced me by that name, I liked the sound of that. So there it is!

**JS: How did you come to start writing for *Deep Red*?**

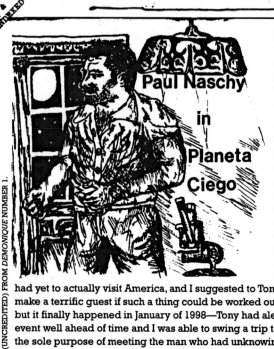

**SMD:** I had become aware of the various writings of Chas. Balun, through and including *Deep Red* by the time I started serious work on the Paul Naschy article and was very pleased to meet the man himself behind a

XERO
FEROX

table at an earlier LA *Fango* convention. I essentially introduced myself as a major fan and proceeded to snap up both movies and books from his table. Soon, Chas. knew me as the guy who was determined to buy out his entire catalog (the heyday of underground VHS trading had begun, and I simply had to have copies of everything he and his crew were writing about). I provided him with a copy of my Naschy manuscript at the same time I was waiting to hear back from *Fango*, and he asked me if I was interested in submitting it to *Deep Red*. Well, had *Fango* turned it down, that's where you would have seen it, but as that was *not* the case,

NIGHT TIME
IS NOT ALWAYS THE RIGHT TIME . .
You feel your Heart POUNDING,
You know It's out there,
You can't SCREAM,
NOW IT'S AT YOUR THROAT –
NIGHT of the HOWLING BEAST
starring PAUL NASCHY • GRACE MILLS
SILVIA SOLAR • LOUIS INDUNI
in GEVACOLOR
a CONSTELLATION FILMS INC.

Chas. was still good enough to ask that I write a different sort of Naschy piece for his publication—he also welcomed various capsule review contributions to the "Gore Score" column and, of course, my "Hand it to Remo" humor column (yep, the greatest and goriest hand removal scenes in cinema history).

**JS: What are your memories of Chas?**

**SMD:** The man had the most unfettered, boisterous personality and sense of humor I've known—he loved talking about the great "chunkblowers" and tearing apart the "timid" horror movies with equal gusto, but he was equally well-versed and enthusiastic about books, music—and yes, even animals (would you believe that one of his favorite films was *Ring of Bright Water*?). You could talk to the guy for hours without ever getting bored, and he was always ready with a great, sarcastic gibe if he heard the right cue. My favorite had to be his response to the collector's mania of finding *the* most complete print of any movie imaginable—he overheard me mentioning that I'd found a longer cut of something-or-other while waiting in line at a convention, and he came up with a big grin and said "Yeah, but you gotta find the Venezuelan videocassette… it's got three extra nanoseconds at the end of the second reel!" Perhaps "the adults-only Uncle Forry" wouldn't be terribly off-base to describe Chas. Balun,

RECORDED & INDEXED

Ironically, he was *not* a fan of Paul Naschy and made no bones about saying so in front of me, even though he did indulge his considerable artistic talents to provide me with an original "Many Faces of Naschy" painting at my request/commission. As it happened, Chas. Balun and Paul Naschy passed away within weeks of each other, and I paid them simultaneous tribute on an episode of the *Manor* in which I broke character and spoke as plain old Shane in their memories.

**JS: You've written for a lot of fanzines over the years.**

**SMD:** During my *Deep Red* tenure, the fanzine explosion was at its height. I also contributed to Louis Paul's *Blood Times* (reviews of the Naschy films available only through underground trading among other items), Michael Weldon's *Psychotronic* (my interview with the late, great action star Steve James, whom I'd met and befriended at a *Fango* Halloween party), and Tom Simmons' *Video Junkie* (elaborate defenses of both the post-*Chain Saw* career of Tobe Hooper and the Hammer films of the 1970s).

**JS: How did your gig with *Video Watchdog* begin? I think you started writing for it in 1998?**

**SMD:** As I'd always enjoyed reading the obsessively detailed "*Video Watchdog*" articles of Tim Lucas in *Fangoria* and *Gorezone*, it was a foregone conclusion that I'd subscribe to his solo magazine. I had a letter published in the eigth issue and earned a "Video Watchdog Informant" button for the effort, but as this was an "invitation only" publication as far as lengthier articles went, I wasn't expecting to turn up in its pages anytime soon (remember, this was still my "manual typewriter and no internet" phase). However, now and then I needed to call the *Watchdog* office with questions regarding my subscription, and one such call just happened to put me in touch with the man himself. Technical questions resolved, it was easy to segue into a conversation about missing footage in, for instance, *Frankenstein and the Monster from Hell* and various *Godzilla* films. It just so happened that Tim was planning some extensive *Godzilla* coverage for an upcoming *VW* special edition, and when he heard that I could account for no less than three different versions of *Terror of Mechagodzilla*, I got my invitation right then and there. I wound up covering both *Terror* and the Japanese and American variants of *Godzilla 1985*. And by the time *VW* expanded to a monthly publication rate, I was online and on Tim's mailing list, so I eagerly snapped up the opportunity to become a regular reviewer.

**JS: How did your gig with *Screem* come about?**

**SMD:** Literally out of the blue in my case. I had seen an issue or two of *Screem* in the past, but the book and magazine dealers in my area never carried it. However, Greg Goodsell (whom I'd met, befriended and shared space with in many an issue of *Deep Red*) wrote regularly for *Screem*, and when Darryl Mayeski was casting about for additional writers, Greg gave him my name and address (without tipping me off). So lo and behold, an

issue of *Screem* arrived in my mailbox with a personal letter attached—might I be interested in becoming a part of this publication? Do you think Darryl needed to ask twice?

**JS: *Screem* and *VW* cater to a similar audience but they each take a different approach. How difficult is it to switch gears when submitting work?**

**SMD:** I'd like to think that you'd recognize my writing "voice" no matter for whom I'm writing, but I certainly have to adjust to my surroundings. As mentioned earlier, my original *Fango*/Naschy articles were directly inspired by the Tim Lucas approach, so there's always been some of Tim in my writing and I found it quite easy to segue into *VW* (which is not to say that he didn't provide me with specific pointers and guidance when I needed them). When I write for *VW*, I have the impression that I'm writing for long-time enthusiasts whose experience matches or surpasses my own—that if I say, for example, *Soylent Green*, everyone reading that review will know exactly what I'm talking about and that I don't need to go into any further detail. As it happened, however, I reviewed *Soylent Green* not for *VW* but for *Screem*. Today they're still talking about the possibility of a remake, and it occurred to me that many *Screem* readers were quite a bit younger than me and might not even have seen *Soylent Green* (they might even have managed to avoid the famous catchphrase). So I reviewed the film exactly as the mystery it was supposed to be and I adopted a more conversational tone as a result. Only on two occasions have I reviewed the same film for both publications, and each time, of course, I wrote two separate reviews. The most notable example was the DVD release of *Don't Go in the House*. For *VW*, I concentrated on the film's place in early eighties psychothriller history, the DVD extras and how the disc compared to the out-of-print tape version, while in *Screem*, I described exactly what it was like to see the film in the middle of a drive-

# NASCHY 101

## *A User Friendly Guide*

by Shane M. Dallman

The fact that you're reading this book indicates that you are already aware that we, as fans of horror, have passed the point where the shockers of Europe were largely ignored in favor of our homegrown product. Argento, the Bavas, Fulci, and even Deodato and D'Amato have received their due recognition in these pages and others. So why has it taken so long for Paul Naschy to get his share of credit in these parts? The man's been making horror films practically non-stop since 1967, functioning as star, screenwriter (as Jacinto Molina Alvarez, which is his real name), and as producer/director since the late 1970's. His reputation in Europe, especially in his native Spain, is assured, so what's holding him back here?

The answer is easier than you might think. Argento, Fulci, and the other well-knowns command the attention of their audiences by virtue of their visual flair above all else — from eye-popping camerawork to creative gore. Their characters and stories, though rarely less than interesting, are secondary, and have a better chance of surviving the dubbing jobs imposed on them en route to America. Though Naschy's films feature many striking, atmospheric sets in the flavor of Hammer's gothic thrillers, these are used to create a feeling of absorption and familiarity and do not induce the viewer to keep his eyes open for offbeat surprises. Naschy entered show business as a screenwriter — even his acting career was an afterthought — and the emphasis in his films is on the strength of the characters, in keeping the role of the actor important. The sloppy dubbing routinely given to his films in the States makes his old-fashioned monster movies seem unduly wordy — and a social satire like [illegible] *Beasts* (1980) has no chance at all.

Getting into Naschy's work takes a bit of practice. It also takes getting hold of the

To destroy the Monster,
was to destroy the one she loved!!
Could she?
Could you?
DR. JEKYLL AND THE WEREWOLF

uncensored video versions, as the television prints rarely add up to anything worth watching. If you're interested in getting started, here are some suggestions as to good starting points for the various tastes of various horror fans.

For those who enjoy Spanish horror primarily for the rich, moody atmosphere and aren't bothered by leisurely pacing, the adventures of Naschy's most famous character, werewolf Waldemar Daninsky, have a lot to offer. 1980's *The Craving* is a remake of (and improvement on) 1970's

78

THE HOMBRE LOBO. *DEEP RED* NUMBER 7.

# SHANE M. DALLMANN

## HAND IT TO REMO!

SHANE M. DALLMANN AS REMO D.

in triple bill, what it was playing with, and how it holds up today.

**JS: You mentioned horror hosts and the *Manor*. Could you tell me a little about *Remo D's Manor of Mayhem*?**

**SMD:** From the day Rich Koz debuted as the Son of Svengoolile, I'd wanted to be a television horror host myself. Of course, by the time I was old enough (and had the right friends) to make that dream a reality, the face of late-night weekend television had irrevocably changed. Unless you *were* Svengoolie, Elvira, etc. and had a decades-long reputation backing you up, no local television station would even consider paying you to host their dusty old movies. Why should they, when the "infomercial" people happily paid *them* to advertise their junk night after night? Today, if you want to mount a "horror host" show, you need to avail yourself of online and/or public access television resources. Thankfully, our new public access station (AMP) was eagerly seeking new programming circa 2002, and I teamed up with two powerhouses in order to make the *Manor* happen.

**JS: You have quite a cast of characters on the show.**

**SMD:** We've had many, many semi-regulars and guest players over the years, but the core cadre has remained the same. In addition to playing Kato, the Black Hornet, Gregg Galdo has contributed countless hours to editing and behind-the-scenes production duties, and professional entertainer Dave Deacon (Dr. Montag) has given us the benefit of both his technical expertise and his (literal) bag of tricks for the ten-years-plus we've been on the air.

**JS: For those who haven't seen it, what's a typical show like?**

**SMD:** We combine the Svengoolie style of comic craziness (we've had various soap opera plots involving our continuing adventures, "season cliffhangers" included) with the Bob Wilkins/John Stanley informational approach (one segment of every episode is devoted to pure movie trivia which I deliver in a stand-up style), while I hand-pick the movies to mirror the classic "creature feature" experience I lived through myself.

**JS: I cut my teeth on the local creature features when I was growing up.**

**SMD:** If you regularly watched the weekend creature features (hosted or not), you got far more than the traditional Universal and Hammer classics (which *we* can't show, of course—we have to stick to public domain and/or otherwise unlicensed films, but there's plenty to choose from all the same). You got a crash course in Mexican horror. Spanish horror. German horror. Italian horror. Filipino horror. Crime dramas passed off as horror films. The list goes on and on. You didn't have to seek them out—they came to *you*, and if you were a fan, then you couldn't help but start to assemble all of these films into a sort of overwhelming historical context. The death of the weekend creature feature was one of the most devastating blows to young fandom—sure, you can find just about everything on DVD today, but how would you know to look for something in the first place if someone hadn't shown it to you to begin with? That's the gap I'm trying to fill, and that's why I was delighted to discover that I was by no means the only one filling it. Today I'm proud to call *Remo D's Manor of Mayhem* "a presentation of the Horror Host Underground!"

**JS: You've done some work in feature films yourself. Could you tell me a little bit about your unreleased remake of *The Flesh Eaters*?**

**SMD:** Back in 1999, my good friend and creative partner Christo Roppolo and I were talking about the remake phenomenon, and he was telling me all sorts of things he'd like to do with the *Invasion of the Body Snatchers* franchise. But the story he described didn't sound like *Body Snatchers* to me—it sounded more like *The Flesh Eaters*. And when I pointed that out, the look on Christo's face resembled that of Tex Avery's wolf as his jaw hit the floor. Within a few days, we were hammering out a screenplay. Sadly, Christo's father had just suffered a fatal automobile accident, and Christo chose to apply a portion of the resulting inheritance to shooting *Flesh Eaters* himself (I served as co-writer and co-director on set) with locally recruited talent filling out the cast and the effects crew. Our redux

RECORDED & INDEXED

DRAFT

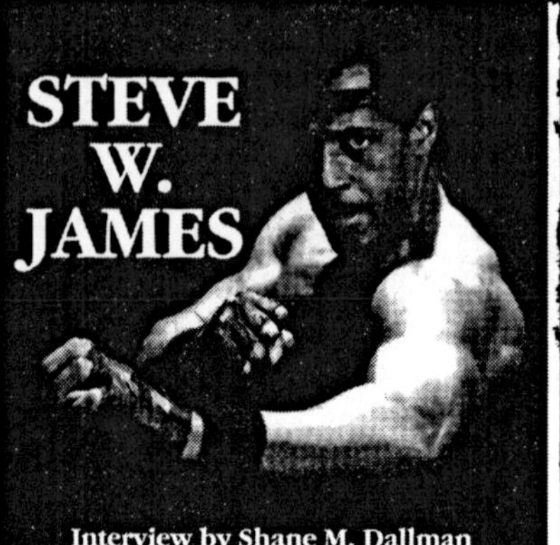

STEVE W. JAMES

Interview by Shane M. Dallman

Steve James was often a better actor and always a better martial arts fighter than whoever he was a sidekick to in his many action features. He was a knowledgeable movie fan who went to conventions, collected videos and even wrote to fanzines. He was trying to get away from sidekick roles and had recently had some success playing the lead hero, villains and even comedy roles. Fans of the friendly, muscular 6'1" actor were shocked when he died on Dec. 18, 93 at 41 due to pancreatic cancer.

An only child, Steve James was raised in the Bronx, the son of show business people. His father was a professional musician, his mother had been a chorus girl and his actor uncle James Wall was the first black man on the CAPTAIN KANGAROO show (as Mr. Baxter). James attended a Catholic school on 106th St., Power Memorial High School and entered C. W. Post College on Long Island in 1970 as an Arts and Film major. While in college he got a job as an extra in THE EDUCATION OF SONNY CARSON ('74). After graduating, he joined the South St. Seaport Theatre where he acted and was a stage manager. His first professional stage role was as the African harpooner in "Moby Dick." He got some work in TV commercials starting in 76 (for Wheaties, Budweiser and other products).

James also spent a lot of time on 42nd St., watching double bills in the 60s and 70s, and was a fan of Bruce Lee. He took Tae Kwon Do courses, learned the Southern Style of Tiger Claw Kung-Fu and became an expert at using traditional and non-traditional weapons.

He was a fan of horror movies too. "All of them.

PSYCHOTRONIC 49

PSYCHOTRONIC NUMBER 18.

SHANE WITH [LEFT] GREG GOODSELL.

was completed in 2001 (shortly before the *Manor* debuted—naturally, one of the earliest episodes featured interviews with Christo and the cast) and received kudos from such people as Fred Olen Ray, Jim VanBebber (who enthused that Dave Hoskins, our take on Dr. Bartel, was "the best bad guy EVER!") and even Uncle Forry (who graciously accompanied us to the screening at that year's *Fango* LA convention).

**JS: What was it about the original that attracted you to try your hand at a remake?**

**SMD:** The original *Flesh Eaters* surprised and shocked me when it surfaced amongst the typically "safe" (Universal, etc.) creature feature material to which I had become accustomed in the 1970s. Martin Kosleck was a terrific villain, and I never got over the scene in which he slipped Omar the Beatnik some "dormant" flesh eaters in a glass of water—and then recorded his dying screams with a tape recorder, the better to transform the victim into an effective decoy. Just thinking about the film again in the 1990s made me think that we could create something today that would have the exact same effect now that the original had in the 1960s. Unlike some of the classics from the era, this was something we could actually do, and we knew it.

**JS: What finally happened to the project?**

**SMD:** The aftermath, sadly, was a debacle of historic proportions. Our original research indicated that the original *Flesh Eaters* had lapsed into the public domain (it was being sold by several companies that specialized in such product) and we were unable to reach anybody involved in the original production until well after the fact (when a surprised Arnold Drake—writer/producer of the original—managed to get in touch with us after interviewer Tom Weaver personally handed him a copy of our version). The legal status of the film remained controversial when it transpired that Drake had sold the video rights to both Fred Olen Ray's Retromedia and to Dark Sky Entertainment simultaneously. We had made overtures to have our remake (fully acknowledged and credited as such—we were completely above-board and had never attempted to sneak this past anybody) included as a supplement, but the Retromedia release wound up being cancelled (after pressing), while our alleged "contact" person at Dark Sky (no longer affiliated with the label) turned out to be a shady character who told us that we had been turned down (for this *and* our subsequent original production *The Wooden Gate*, which featured cameos by Jeff Burr and Jim VanBebber)... years later, he laughingly admitted to a friend that he had actually thrown our discs away without letting anybody else see them!

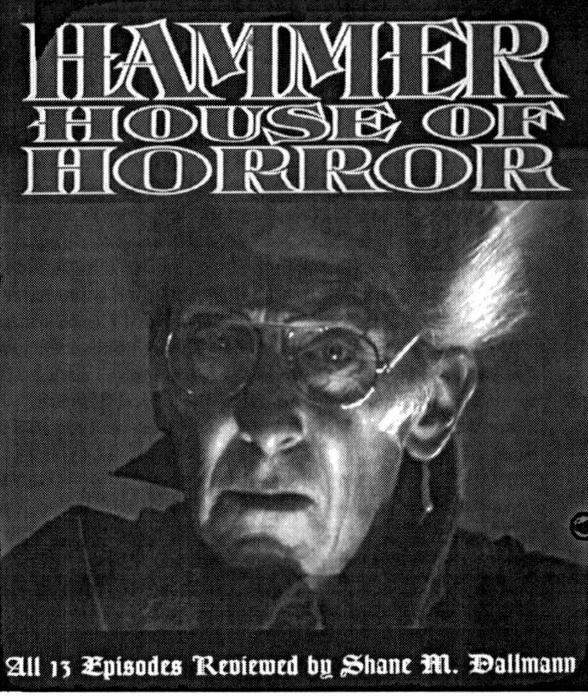

HAMMER
HOUSE OF
HORROR
All 13 Episodes Reviewed by Shane M. Dallmann


VIDEO WATCHDOG NUMBER 84.

Attachment

Drake has since passed away with all references to our remake stricken from his last published interviews; but we still hope that someone with the power to do so will clear the air and allow our sincere, credited tribute to

RECORDED & INDEXED
DRAFT

be seen properly.

**JS: I'd like to hear the story behind your commentary for *Don't Answer the Phone*. How did that come about? What was the experience like?**

**SMD:** Another example of pure luck. My friend Bruce Holecheck is a video supplement specialist, and he was in charge of BCI's debut of the uncut *Don't Answer the Phone* on DVD (the previous release was a bowdlerized TV print). He'd managed to get what turned out to be the final interview of star Nicolas Worth, but with the deadline looming, he was unable to travel to Northern California in time to record the desired feature audio commentary with director Bob Hammer. But as it happens, Bob Hammer lives within walking distance of me, so with mere days to spare, we were put in touch. I had almost no time for preliminary research, but I *was* well-versed on the film and its era, so our conversation (recorded while we watched the uncut film on Bob's old VHS copy) flowed easily and naturally. Incidentally, Bob and his wife Mira were the most gracious of hosts, and they even turned up later at the *Manor* (Mira in particular was a scream as fortune-teller "Madame Mira"). On a more sober note, Bob later returned to deliver farewell remarks after the passing of Nicolas Worth, and we received permission to run Bruce's interview with Worth on the show, as well.

**JS: As someone who is still very active in the genre, I'm curious about your thoughts on today's fanzines?**

**SMD:** I wish there were more of them. And I wish we still had bookstores that carried them. The two publications for which I continue to write today always impress me with their care and quality, and when I'm lucky enough to happen across *Rue Morgue*, *Shock Cinema*, *Ultra Violent*, and *HorrorHound*, I know I'm in for plenty of good reading, be it amusing, nostalgic or provocative. And of course, I'm proud of my contribution to *Fangoria* and am extremely pleased to see it continue to thrive to this day.

**JS: What do you think of the new generation of fans?**

**SMD:** We'll always be there. It's interesting to see that what today's young horror fans are experiencing as originals, my generation calls a spate of remakes, but that's really nothing new—what do you call the Hammer films of the fifties and sixties in comparison to the Universal classics of the thirties and forties? *Scream/Twilight* flame wars notwithstanding, there's plenty of enthusiasm, debate and dialogue continuing throughout the community. I'm still glad to be a part of it and I always look forward to seeing what happens next—and discovering just what I'm going to say about it.

# Chapter Thirty-Two

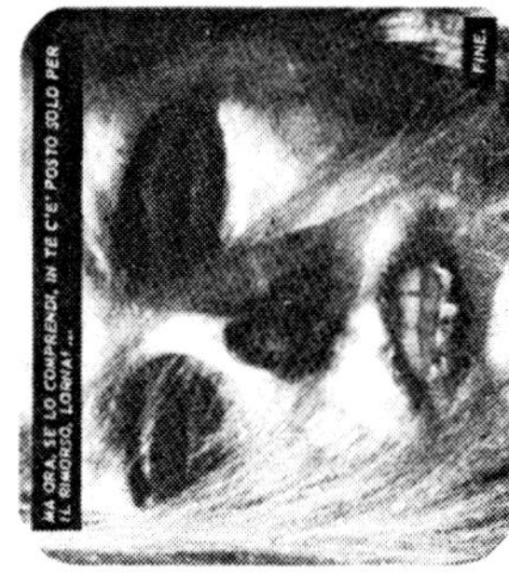


# Tim Lucas
## The Watchdog Barks!

## How to Read a Franco Film

LEAD ARTICLE AND IMAGES FROM THE DEBUT *VIDEO WATCHDOG*.

Photos courtesy Lucas Balbo/Nostalgia Archives

THE WATCHDOG BARKS!

RECORDED & INDEXED

DRAFT

# The Cutting Room Floor

## Videos Restored and Compared

In the Spring of 1990, word on the streets had it that Tim Lucas was about to launch a new magazine. I was already a fan of his work—the articles that he penned for *Fangoria* and *Gorezone* ranked among my favorites. Tim's eagle-eyed reports about what had been snipped and censored from Frank Henenlotter's *Brain Damage* and Dario Argento's *Opera* were real eye openers, and I was anxious to see what he would do with a magazine of his own. In June of that year, I settled down on my favorite movie-viewing couch and opened an issue of *Video Watchdog* for the first time. Little did I know that it was about to change my life.

Lucas had assembled an all-star cast of contributors for his maiden effort. Steve Bissette, Craig Ledbetter, and Jeff Smith were all present and accounted for, as well as the renegade newcomer, Lucas Balbo. And then, there was Tim Lucas himself. I'd been impressed with what the man had written before, but his work in *Video Watchdog* took things to an entirely new level. No longer shackled by the word-count restrictions (and, indeed, content restrictions) of *Fango* and *Gorezone*, Lucas kicked things off with a mammoth study of the films of Jess Franco. I hadn't given Uncle Jess much thought before, but once I finished reading "How to Read a Franco Film", I made it a point to investigate his work. I'm still watching and enjoying Franco films to this day, but I digress...

*Video Watchdog* turned out to be a hit, and Tim Lucas went on to change the world of home video. His obsessive eye seemed to be everywhere at once—he scoured the latest VHS and laserdisc releases, comparing and contrasting their picture quality and running times with previous (and oftentimes contemporaneous) editions. His contributors happily followed suit, and after a while *Video Watchdog* became the final word on the subject.

As the years went by, the contributors in the *Watchdog*'s kennel began to multiply. Soon, the likes of John Charles, Shane M. Dallmann, Douglas E. Winter, Ramsey Campbell, and Joe Dante showed up in its pages. Talented bunch that they are, the *Watchdog*'s star shone even brighter.

The highly intelligent film criticism in *Video Watchdog* cannot be overlooked, and neither can its presentation. Under the careful eye of art

director Donna Lucas, each and every issue is a beautiful thing to behold. Like many of the films that it covers, *Video Watchdog* can easily be regarded as a work of art.

In 2007, Tim Lucas self-published his magnum opus, *Mario Bava: All the Colors of the Dark*. Weighing in at over 1,000 pages, the book is the end result of his lifelong love affair with the films of its subject. Astonishing achievement that it was, one might think that Tim Lucas would want to rest for a while. If anyone deserved a little time off, surely it was he. To the contrary (and much to our benefit), it seems as if the man was just starting up.

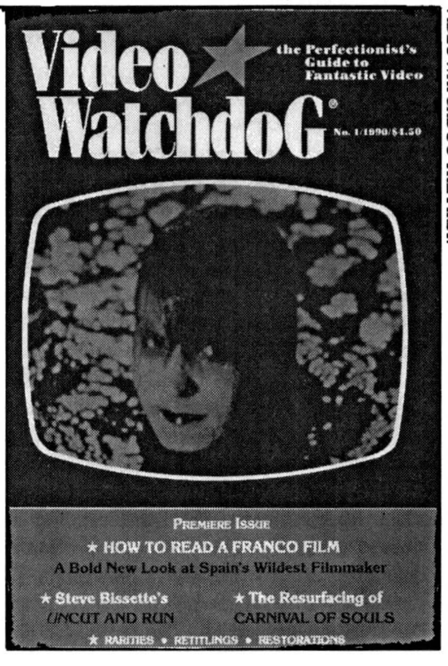

VIDEO WATCHDOG THE FIRST.

I have always admired Tim Lucas. I admire his tenacity, his knowledge, and his love and dedication to the genre that has been a part of my life since my childhood . I've always wanted to talk to him, to let him know how much his work has meant to me. Twenty-two years after I opened that first issue of *Video Watchdog*, I finally got my chance.

The following interview was conducted via email, April–November, 2012.

---

**JOHN SZPUNAR: When did movies come into your life?**

**TIM LUCAS:** My grandmother took me to my first movie when I was three or four years old. I was living then in the care of my grandmother, who lived in an apartment building with a basement that terrified me because whenever I opened the door, the light from the window behind me caused the cockroaches down there to scatter. I remember walking up Elm Avenue toward Montgomery Road, where the Plaza Theater stood, and her telling me what to expect, that the screen was going to be bigger than TV, that it would be dark inside, that I mustn't talk or disturb the other people, etc. I'm sure she must have intended to take me to the co-feature, maybe an Elvis movie because she loved Elvis Presley; anyway, we ended up seeing the end of *The Incredible Shrinking Man*. So as we entered the dark theater and

walked down the sloping aisle to our seats, the first thing I saw on this huge screen was a giant spider charging toward me, with a blast of brassy music! I let go of my Granny's hand and ran up the aisle screaming—and hearing a number of grown-ups chuckling in my wake. So my first impression of the movies was that it was like my granny's basement, only worse! I guess it's similar to what those Victorians experienced when they saw the first movie of a train pulling into a train station and thought it was going to come crashing through the screen! Anyway, I cowered at the concession stand till my grandmother came out to calm me down; she promised me that the spider was gone, it wasn't coming back. She finally convinced me, and we went back in... settled into our seats... and then the spider came back! And again, I ran back out into the lobby, but this time didn't I believe granny when she said it really was gone for good, this time. We didn't end up seeing whatever we were supposed to see, that night. I remember her being very cross with me as we walked back home.

**JS: I was the same way as a kid—horror films terrified me. It's interesting that so many of us bothered to stick with them.**

**TL:** I was initially repulsed and terrified by horror. I went through a period of sustained screaming at certain images on television, like the deformed doctors and nurses in *The Twilight Zone*'s "Eye of the Beholder" and the gremlin on the airplane wing in "Nightmare at 20,000 Feet." (Between that and *The Incredible Shrinking Man*, Richard Matheson had much to answer for in my household!) My mother and grandmother actually barred me from seeing *The Twilight Zone* for a couple of years after my first screaming fit. But I wanted to see it again and knew, in order to do that, I would have to master my emotions and my fears.

**JS: Can you tell me a little more about your childhood? I'm guessing that you were fan of comic books.**

**TL:** I was born to a woman who had buried her husband, who died from a genetic heart problem, early in her pregnancy. She had a nervous breakdown and there was later a suicide attempt, when I was about four years old. I was raised either by my grandmother, by other relatives, and later by foster families till I was eight. For the period when I was maybe five through eight, I was told that I couldn't live with my mother because she had a night job at the telephone company, but it's more likely she was institutionalized and was able to see me only on weekends. We had a ritual, that she would pick me up from whatever foster home I was at, then drive me to the pharmacy nearest the drive-in where we were going, where I would pick out a stack of comics to read in the car until night fell. I can remember reading funny animal comics, *Classics Illustrated*, various superhero titles—at first DC, but I became a complete Marvel snob in 1964. I started collecting *The Amazing Spider-Man* with number 13, the Mysterio cover. And the next one introduced the Green Goblin. I stared at Steve Ditko's art for hours; I couldn't get enough of him. I bought the Jack

Kirby titles as well, and he drew most of Marvel's covers in those days, but it was all about Ditko for me—at least until Steranko showed up. But this would have been around 1961, 1962… it was a great time to go to the drive-in, with all the AIP and Toho stuff happening.

**JS: Did your mother and grandmother ease up on their feelings toward your choices of entertainment as you got older?**

**TL:** I was the first and only grandson in the family, for many years, and I was adored and given most anything I wanted, at least for awhile. In some ways, being barred from watching *The Twilight Zone* for that period of time cultivated my imagination. I can remember lying in bed and hearing Marius Constant's end titles music, which I found scary in itself; I remember thinking that the pizzicato strings sounded like the Devil tiptoeing to my door. In retrospect, I must have been liable to hallucinations; I can remember sitting in my grandmother's kitchen one day when something burst out from under her sink. I still don't know what it was—a mouse, a rat, a cockroach—because what I believed I saw was some kind of a biomechanical monster, broken and bloody with metal parts sticking out. I screamed and my grandmother scolded me, saying it was nothing as she calmly dealt with it. I wouldn't step foot back into that kitchen for hours. As for my mother, she was also supportive and indulgent, but some might also say she was neglectful; she didn't know how to express affection other than by buying me things or giving me money or taking me to movies. Which, incidentally, were usually the movies I wanted to see. Later, after her attempt on her life, when I went to stay with other foster families, it was a real wake-up call; I had to abide by their rules, and sometimes these families had stern, censorious, backwards attitudes. I remember staying with one family who allowed their kids—and by extension, me—only one bottle of soda per week, as a Friday treat, and they also confiscated from me a copy of *Mad* magazine I'd brought into their house. They said it was Communist trash.

*VIDEO WATCHDOG*'S RETRO COLUMNIST JOE DANTE.

## THE WATCHDOG BARKS!

**JS: How deeply did the monster craze of the sixties affect you?**

**TL:** It gave me a place to belong. I was more intellectual than physical, more drawn to reading than to sports, to the full moon rather than the sun. And of course, I had scary skeletons in my closet: a father who died before I was born, a mother who was mysteriously absent a lot of the time, I moved around too frequently to make friends, and the sons of the houses I entered took me as a territorial threat and spread lies about me that won them favor and got me punished. So I had a lot of unprocessed psychological shit in my head, and the monster craze was helpful to me in terms of processing that. It's comparable in some ways to the popularity of men's pulp magazines like *Argosy* and *Men's Adventure* in the wake of the Korean war—those fantasies of sex and war and danger helped men disturbed by their war memories to process and compartmentalize what they'd been through, what they were going through.

**JS: When did you first become aware of *Famous Monsters of Filmland*?**

**TL:** It had to be sometime circa late 1962, early 1963. In one of the houses where I stayed, with a cousin of my late father and her slightly older son, there was a locked room we were forbidden to enter. One day I came upstairs and found the door open, and the lady of the house was looking for something in there. I stood in the doorway, trying to see amid all this attic-type stuff what was so verboten. I caught sight of a short stack of monster magazines, which had been taken away from the son as punishment for some trespass or other. I asked if I could look at them, probably begged a little, and was allowed to look at them until the room was locked again. Under those conditions, my pupils must have been fully dilated, and it was obviously an occasion I've never forgotten and which had great impact on my life.

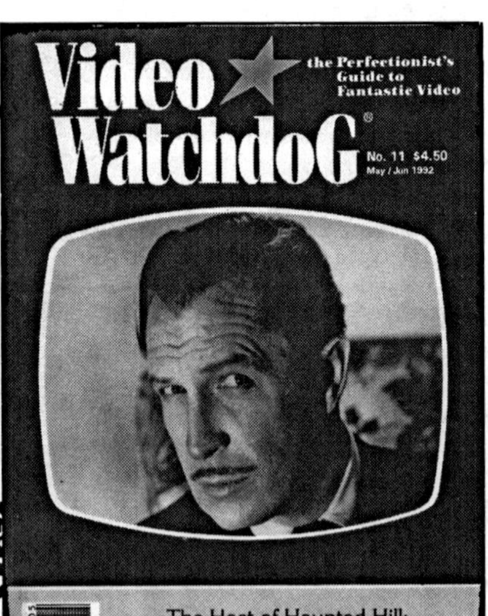

Video Watchdog
the Perfectionist's Guide to Fantastic Video
No. 11 $4.50
May / Jun 1992
The Host of Haunted Hill:
VINCENT PRICE
Interview Videography and More!
RARITIES • RETITLINGS • RESTORATIONS


I remember turning the pages as if spellbound, sometimes flinching with horror at some frightful image, looking away and then looking back. I remember looking at some images until I could begin to see past the monster makeup to the people beneath it. Suddenly I could see through

the *Frankenstein* monster to Boris Karloff beneath, and I could see in his eyes that the monster was misunderstood, a creature to be pitied. So, to continue my self-psychoanalysis a bit, I imagine I determined to know monsters better so that I could better understand them, and find ways of staying on their good side. In short, they were a means of learning how to deal with my mother (whose moods could swing violently, though she was never physically violent with me), and the outsiderly life my circumstances had imposed upon me.

**JS: How big of an influence was it on the films that you went to see?**

**TL:** Naturally I wanted to see the stories that went with the pictures. When I was living with this mother-and-son family I mentioned, I was again within walking distance of the Plaza Theater, and the son and I would sometimes go to matinees together. One weekend, I very much wanted to go and he was playing in a ballgame, so I was allowed to go alone. I couldn't have been more than six or seven years old, and the matinee was a reissue of *Frankenstein 1970*—and I can still hear the sounds of those teenage girls screaming whenever the bandaged monster appeared. It seems like a mild film today, but back in the day, with that crowd, it was pandemonium!

**JS: A lot of kids go through phases. Did your love for horror and science fiction ever diminish?**

**TL:** There was one year, 1966–67, a couple of years after I went back to live with my mother permanently, when we lost our income for a year and had to live in a public housing community. I had the good fortune to move in next door to a kid who had some Marvel comics older than the earliest ones I'd managed to collect, but monster magazines were not part of that environment, for some reason. But car culture was huge. So I drifted away from monsters for a year and became obsessed with building car models and reading magazines about funny cars, Lotuses and Chapparals. It was an odd diversion, because as an adult, I don't drive a car. When Social Security payments from my late father kicked in when

## THE WATCHDOG BARKS!

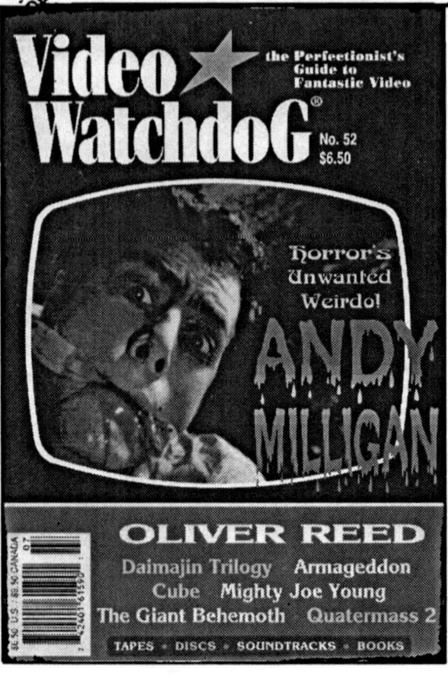


I was twelve, we moved back to my hometown of Norwood, Ohio. My mother gave me the Gigantic Frankenstein model kit as a kind of homecoming gift—I still have it. I had most of the early Aurora kits, but the Big Frankie is the only one I kept. Around that same time, while walking home from school one day, I saw a kid sitting on a curb, reading a copy of *Famous Monsters* (number 35) and I asked him where he got it. He told me about an independent grocery market that was selling bundles of three for a quarter, with the logo part of the covers cut off—which the store had returned to the distributors for credit, the crooks. But this chance discovery, which coincided with discovering *Dark Shadows* on television, got me back into active collecting.

**JS: I'm thirty-eight years old. By the time I started reading about horror films in magazines, *Fangoria* was already in full swing. Still, I looked back on early *Famous Monsters* issues with interest—even at a young age, they were amazing cultural artifacts to me. Even more so, today.**

**TL:** Even the most familiar stills they published were new then, and the magazine itself was beautifully produced up till their mid-thirties. They were printed on Rotogravure paper and smelled wonderful, and each new Basil Gogos cover was a masterpiece.

**JS: *Famous Monsters* played a major part in the whole monster kid phenomenon. What do you think the horror/science fiction world would be like today if Forrest J Ackerman had never set pen to paper?**

**TL:** With all due respect to Forry, I don't think his writing had any serious impact on the horror/science fiction world at all. (Well, that's not entirely fair; he did give me an appreciation of puns, and he stressed to me the importance of ascribing dates to titles. I've actually heard fans in conversation say things like, "I was watching *Dracula's Daughter* (1936), and..." So that is *some* impact.) I mean, to this day, there isn't much in *Famous Monsters* I can say I actually read. Forry's personality, on the other

hand, had a tremendous impact on the American monsters experience; he took something traditionally horrifying and made it fun and witty. He contextualized this interest in ways it might not have been otherwise. As an individual, he gave a lot of disenfranchised kids a model of a kind of grown-up we could grow up to be.

**JS: Were you active in any journalism programs in school?**

**TL:** I became my high school paper's first film critic on my first day in high school. At orientation, the senior class president, Randy Parsons, who was also the editor of the school paper the *Mirror*, encouraged us "frosh" to involve ourselves in school activities. So when the assembly let out, I followed him into the hall, chased him down and volunteered. I also cartooned for the paper and did some record reviews, too.

**JS: How did your taste in horror and science fiction change as you grew older?**

**TL:** I became less obsessed with Universal classic horror and much more fascinated with all kinds of European horror and fantasy. I realized I wasn't really into horror for the horror, but for a kind of dark, bizarre aesthetic that can only be found in horror films and surrealist paintings. Seriously, when I saw my first Salvador Dalì painting, or when I read my first Alain Robbe-Grillet novel, I felt the same excitement I felt for *Frankenstein's Daughter*.

**JS: Who was the first director that you actively followed, or claimed as your own?**

**TL:** The earliest behind-the-scenes names I collected were Roger Corman and Terence Fisher. I had no idea what a director was, but I came to understand his role must be tremendously important because it was the last name always onscreen before the fade-to-black as the story began. Then I began to look for their names on movie posters and newspaper ads, because I knew I could count on that movie to be a picture that delivered.

**JS: When did you first become aware of fanzines, be it science fiction, horror fiction, or otherwise?**

**TL:** While shopping for comics one day at a Neisner's five-and-dime store, I met an older kid

RECORDED & INDEXED

DRAFT

named Brad Balfour. We stayed in touch and he had a background in science fiction and everything else. He and a group of friends published a small-circulation ditto zine called *Advocates of the Infinite*, and this later spun off a small family of zines under the shared imprint of the Vergen Press. A group of us decided to pool our resources and buy a communally owned mimeograph machine; Brad did *Conglomeration*, Frank Johnson did *Schamoob*, both being science fiction zines, and Brad encouraged me—on the basis of a little appreciation of a scene from *Horror of Dracula* I had written—to do a horror film zine. That's what I did over a two-year period, using our mimeograph. The first I called the *Hydraulic Peanut Butter Sandwich* (its front cover was a blatantly stolen page from *Castle of Frankenstein*, its back cover was left over back pages printed for Brad's zine), the second was called *Apples Woofer* (its cover was someone's original art of a lobster monster, which I completely devalued by tracing it onto a stencil), but I kept the numbering sequential. The second issue contained an amusing overview of the contemporary horror film scene by a published author I'd befriended at Midwestcon, Andrew J. Offutt. I was fourteen or fifteen years old. There is some stuff in both issues that deeply embarrasses me, so I've suppressed them, not that they were ever seen by many people.

**JS: What are your memories of *Monster Mania*?**

**TL:** Russ Jones' *Monster Mania* was terrific because it leaned on Hammer product. Without it, I think that whole middle period of Hammer with *Dracula Prince of Darkness*, *Plague of the Zombies* and *Frankenstein Created Woman* would have been a lot less magical.

**JS: A lot of people cite *Castle of Frankenstein* as a turning point.**

**TL:** As I got older, it became my favorite magazine. It introduced me to the world beyond monsters—the worlds of Orson Welles, Jean Cocteau, Fantomas and Judex! *Famous Monsters* was my baby food, but *Castle of Frankenstein* became my meat and drink.

**JS: Did any of these publications make you want to start writing or creating yourself?**

**TL:** I drew. I drew monsters all the time. I related primarily to comics in those days, comics and monster magazines, so that was how I knew to express myself. I didn't really start reading fiction with any kind of passion till high school, even though I bought interesting looking paperbacks whenever I followed my mother to the thrift stores ("junk shops") she loved to frequent. When I was drawing, all the art I did was representative; I didn't invent my own monsters.

**JS: As you grew older, did you ever encounter any kind of peer backlash for being interested in fantasy films?**

**TL:** Not so much, because I'm in with the In Crowd. The people I've known who haven't understood the interest—or worse, who considered it sick—have always turned out to be the people with the most serious,

underlying problems. Those are the people who would have been burning witches in the days before movies.

**JS: How did you start writing for *Cinefantastique*? How did you discover it?**

**TL:** When I got to be old enough to be trusted to take the bus downtown by myself, I discovered a bookstore in Cincinnati called Kidd's. It was run by a very tall, friendly, even-tempered guy named Bernd Baierschmidt, who was like a living conduit between every artistic or pop culturally minded person in town. He hooked up untold dozens, maybe hundreds, of friends at this bookstore, which became our meeting place. I bought my first bootleg albums in Kidd's basement. I first heard the Velvet Underground there. And that's where I discovered *Cinefantastique*. I was checking out with a stack of magazines and Bernd, who then was just the guy behind the counter, said "If you're interested in this kind of thing, did you see that other magazine over there in that little alcove? *Cinefantastique*?" I didn't, but it was issue number 3. So after a quick flip through the interior, I added it to my stack. I was there that day with my friend Mike Hennel—I think we had gone downtown to see *Gimme Shelter*. And we went to a Frisch's Big Boy restaurant for lunch before the show began. I remember Mike saying to me, as we were waiting for our food to be delivered, "You must really like that magazine." "Why?" "Because that's the third time you've taken it out of the bag to look at it! Maybe you should try writing for them."

Jump forward a few months and Mike had committed suicide, hanged himself. He was only fifteen. I was numb and stayed home from school for two weeks... and, in that time, I undertook the self-therapy of writing some sample reviews and submitting them to Fred Clarke at *Cinefantastique*. One of them was a long review of *A Clockwork Orange*, which I actually saw the night Mike died, and I also submitted short reviews of *Godzilla vs The Swamp Monster* and *Horror on Snape Island*. I had actually forgotten I'd submitted them when I received a letter from Fred, accepting the *Snape Island* review. He also said he would

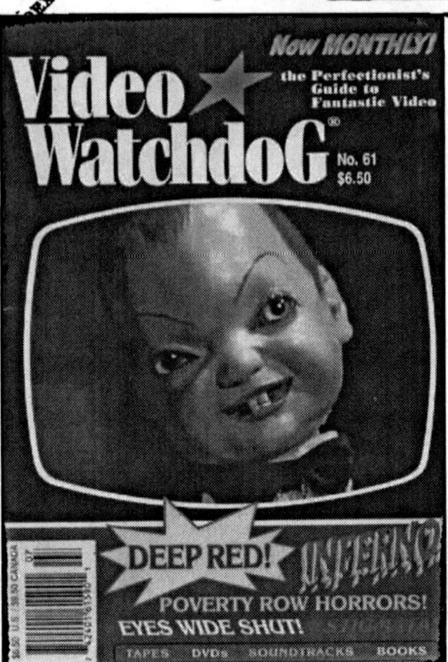

have accepted the *Clockwork Orange* review, but he had already promised it to another reviewer, Dale Winogura. I left home not long after this, and it was about two years later that I met someone who had some back issues of *CFQ*, one of which contained my review! I was astounded. I was then working as the film editor of a local entertainment paper, the *Queen's Jester*, which gave me access to certain promotional items, and when I called Fred to ask for a copy of the issue containing my review, I told him I had just come into some transparencies for this upcoming Warner Bros. release, *The Exorcist*. So I immediately became Fred's "Cincinnati bureau." When all is said and done, I was with *CFQ* for eleven years.

**JS: What kind of guy was Fred Clarke?**

**TL:** On a personal level, he was a strange mix of introverted and cocky; I later learned he was a very tortured individual, and I learned fairly early on that he could also be a terrible pain in the ass. I've written a lengthy essay about my years of working with him, called "Citizen Clarke," which *Little Shoppe of Horrors* plans to publish. Fred was like my Roger Corman: he got me started, he gave me a vision of what I ended up doing professionally and how my wife and I live; he encouraged me, he taught me the discipline of being definitive in my work, and he paid very little... but that was okay. He was exploiting me, and I was exploiting him, if you will. What wasn't okay, finally, was when he took almost two years' worth of my work on *Videodrome* and *The Dead Zone*, which were supposed to become a double issue and a single issue respectively, and had his assistant cut them down to fit into a single issue together—and I was paid by the word. They cut my work down to such an extent, it had to be paraphrased... and that was the end of our association.

**JS: How did you start writing for *Video Times*?**

**TL:** I think a friend told me about them, that he'd seen them on a newsstand. I checked it out and got in touch with the editor, who is still a friend. When I joined them, their writers were reviewing videotapes

no differently than they were reviewing movies shown in theaters. It was there that I told them videotapes needed to be reviewed differently, that people needed to be made aware of how they looked, how and if they were cropped, if they were missing footage, etc. My first "Video Watchdog" column grew out of these discussions, and the approach began to have an effect on the way all movies were reviewed there, and a number of other places besides, after that.

**JS: What was *Overview*?**

**TL:** *Overview* was a one-shot video magazine produced on videotape (VHS) by Michael Nesmith (formerly of the Monkees) for his Pacific Arts Corporation company. I was told—by the same friend who alerted me to *Video Times* (which later became *Video Movies*)—that this project was underway; I sent them a proposal. To my surprise and delight, they accepted and flew me out—it was my first-ever trip to Los Angeles. On my first day there, I wrote the script for my segment. On the second day, I recorded it in a sound studio. I remember being on the elevator going down, and the doors opening to Carly Simon, who was waiting to go up. That evening, a crew and I drove out to the industrial area of town and I starred in some wraparound footage shot on location in 35mm. My first trip to LA and I was starring in my own film! They test-marketed the end product in a few locations; the tape only cost $1 and they encouraged people to tape over it, if they liked... but there was never a second issue. My segment was one of a few singled out for special praise in industry reviews.

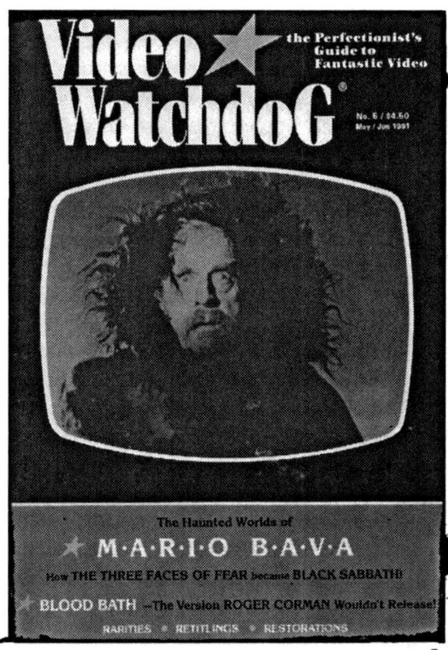

Video Watchdog
the Perfectionist's Guide to Fantastic Video
The Haunted Worlds of
M·A·R·I·O B·A·V·A
How THE THREE FACES OF FEAR became BLACK SABBATH!
BLOOD BATH —The Version ROGER CORMAN Wouldn't Release!
RARITIES • RETITLINGS • RESTORATIONS


**JS: I first became aware of your writing when I started reading *Gorezone*. How was your experience writing for it?**

**TL:** Fine, no complaints whatsoever. I had written a piece for *Fangoria* about how Dario Argento's films had been cut up for the US market, which was eye-opening for a lot of people, so it was a kind of "Watchdog" article. Both *Video Movies* and *Overview* had folded, so my "Video Watchdog" concept was without a home, and I pitched it to Tony Timpone. He liked the idea, but not for *Fango*... and that's when he told me about their plans to launch *Gorezone*. I appeared in all but the last issue.

Donna and I started *Video Watchdog* magazine during that time, and I didn't have the time to look after both responsibilities.

**JS: Come to think of it, I might have first read your work in *Fangoria*. What was your initial reaction to *Fango*?**

**TL:** I bought it from the very first issue and still have a complete run. That said, the emphasis on gore and makeup effects, it's not my interest, but there's usually a few things in each issue that grabs my attention. So it's always been a magazine I flip through, rather than read cover-to-cover.

**JS: A few other notables wrote for *Gorezone*—Steve Bissette and Chas. Balun, to name but two. Do you remember how you first met Steve?**

**TL:** Steve and I met when he sent me a fan letter, circa 1985, after I published a two-part article about Mario Bava in *Fangoria*. I had been researching my book then for quite awhile and decided it was time to stake a claim, so to speak. But Steve and I became fast friends, fast brothers really, and we were swapping tapes and having three-hour phone calls in no time. It has really been one of the most important relationships in my life, because Steve published my only work in comics and persuaded me to finish a graphic novel I'd undertaken as a traditional novel, which became *Throat Sprockets*.

**JS: What did you think of Chas. Balun's *Deep Red*?**

**TL:** I have great respect for Chas. and what he was able to accomplish with his own personality and material, but his passions weren't mine. He and I were like opposite sides of the same coin; he grabbed for the gusto of horror, and I savored the genre for its aesthetics and poetry. I know we had a mutual professional respect, but we didn't seek each other out for friendship. We never spoke, actually. Steve Bissette was a close friend of his, and he told me on a couple of occasions that we'd be great amigos if we ever met, but that didn't happen. When he died, I wrote a letter of sincere condolence to his widow, affirming what I felt were his role and accomplishment in our shared field, as I think he would have done for Donna, were our fortunes reversed. So let that stand as the thumbnail of our relationship.

**JS: When did the idea for *Video Watchdog* (as a magazine in itself) first hit you?**

**TL:** There was always too much material to fit into the *Gorezone* column, and as I became more and more immersed in home video, especially what was then happening with import and bootleg tapes, I found myself writing articles that were much too long to publish anywhere. So Donna and I began discussing the possibility of producing a newsletter supplement to the column, which also coincided with the things she had been learning about computers and desktop publishing at her day job. She was discovering she had a knack for it. As we continued to ruminate on it, various friends came forward who offered material, stills, etc., and the newsletter idea bloomed into a magazine in its own right.

Lon Chaney Jr. wrestled a bear in a deleted scene from MCA Video's THE *what* MAN?

woof.

THE WOLF MAN—That's right! Paramount Video has issued letterboxed S-VHS copies of the second sequel to RAIDERS OF THE LOST *what*?

arf.

Good boy! Most horror movies today have to be cut till the MPAA gives them *what* rating?

RRRRR....

You're *fantastic*, VIDEO WATCHDOG! I'm going to SUBSCRIBE right away!

...and pick up #1 while you still can!

Send your name and address along with Check, Cash or Money Order to:

**Video★ WatchdoG**
P.O. Box 5283
Cincinnati, OH 45205-0283

| 6 Issue Subscription — $18 |
|---|
| Outside USA — $24 |
| Outside USA 4th Class Air Mail — $31<br>Sample Issue — $4.60 / Outside USA — $6.60 |

U.S. funds only.
Subscriptions begin with next available issue.

Premiere Issue! Features Jess Franco essay and interview.

$6.00

SUBSCRIPTION AD FROM *VIDEO WATCHDOG* NUMBER 2.

## THE WATCHDOG BARKS!

*THROAT SPROCKETS*, THE NOVEL.

throat
sprockets
A NOVEL OF EROTIC OBSESSION
tim lucas
'Genuinely kinky and perverse and smart' Bret Easton Ellis


**JS: Why self-publish *Video Watchdog*?**

**TL:** It's every writer's dream to control how their work is published, and to profit from it to the fullest. Also, no one else was offering, but we had the means to do it ourselves, so we did.

**JS: How did you originally solicit contributors?**

**TL:** I turned to friends, people who were part of my video-trading circle, the few fellow writers I knew. Once the first issue came out, it was quickly recognized as something new, a place that encouraged free-thinking, open-ended writing; a place that would run a long feature on someone like Jess Franco or Ruggero Deodato's *Cut and Run*. So we got offers of material quickly.

**JS: You had a letters column in your first issue. How did that come about?**

**TL:** Those were letters we received in response to the ad for *Video Watchdog*, which we placed in *Fangoria*.

**JS: Lucas Balbo and Peter Blumenstock were two of my favorite early contributors to *VW*. How did you become aware of their work?**

**TL:** They were aware of my work and we became pen-pals, which I had more time for in those days. I don't think either of them had written in English before they wrote for me, so you couldn't really say I was aware of their work. It wasn't until Lucas visited us sometime in 1989 that I became aware of his history as a zine publisher in his own right, with *Nostalgia*.

**JS: One of my favorite books is the *Obsession: The Films of Jess Franco*. How did you get involved with that?**

**TL:** That was a project of Peter's and Christian Kessler's. Lucas had been compiling his own book about Franco—he carried this large green binder with him, which he called his "green Bible"—and they all decided to work together to produce and complete Lucas' work as best they could. I updated my "How To Read A Franco Film" essay from *Video Watchdog* number 1 as a foreword and they also used an essay about Soledad

XEROX FEROX

Miranda, which I had written for Craig Ledbetter's *European Trash Cinema*. They wanted to list me as a co-writer, but I did not feel like I was part of their venture from its conception. My work was tacked on at the beginning and end, so I requested the "Special Material By" credit instead.

**JS: *Fangoria* brought in a lot of small press zines in its wake. Were you buying any of them? What were some of your favorites?**

**TL:** Trading, moreso than buying. I remember particularly *Psychotronic*, *European Trash Cinema*, *Monterscene*, *Samhain*, *Blood and Black Lace*, *Eyeball* and *Delirious*, in addition to some long-running titles like *Midnight Marquee*. All of them had something important to offer. I think any writer who publishes their own magazine can't help but like what they do best, because it is literally what they want to see and read in a publication. I always got a kick out of *Delirious*, especially, because Steve Johnson ran certifiably insane, endless scratch-note analyses of films that weren't likely to get a second look anywhere else.

**JS: A lot of the UK zines took on a more "scholarly" or serious tone than their US counterparts. Why do you think that was?**

**TL:** The X certificate. You had to be an adult to see horror films in the UK. Kids can see horror films in the US, and truth be told, there are a lot of US writers about horror films who can't move beyond Universal, or can't move beyond Hammer. They want to stay close to their primal childhood experience with those films, and they don't venture beyond them and won't branch out. One of the basic philosophies behind *Video Watchdog* is the importance of seeing things like the influence of, say, Antonioni on Argento's first films—and to see that, you need to see some Antonioni. This is something I've carried over from *Castle of Frankenstein*, where you would see mention of films like *Children of Paradise* right alongside *Children of the Damned*.

**JS: You started working on your Mario Bava book at a very early age.**

**TL:** March of 1975. The book appeared in 2007.

**JS: How did working on that balance with your *VW* schedule?**

**TL:** I had been writing, off and on, since the beginning, and the job was somewhat less than half-done when I committed to finishing, sometime around 1997. *Video Watchdog* was a bimonthly for its first ten years, then became a monthly in 2000 and remained so for another ten years, when we reverted to bimonthly. But the book could

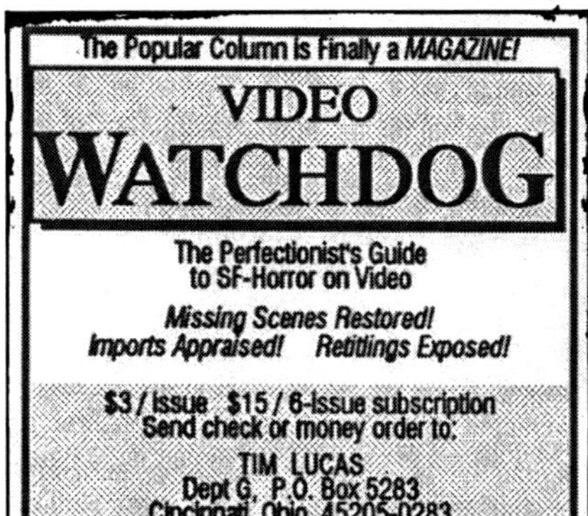
The Popular Column is Finally a MAGAZINE!
VIDEO WATCHDOG
The Perfectionist's Guide to SF-Horror on Video
Missing Scenes Restored!
Imports Appraised! Retitlings Exposed!
$3 / Issue $15 / 6-Issue subscription
Send check or money order to:
TIM LUCAS
Dept G, P.O. Box 5283
Cincinnati, Ohio 45205-0283

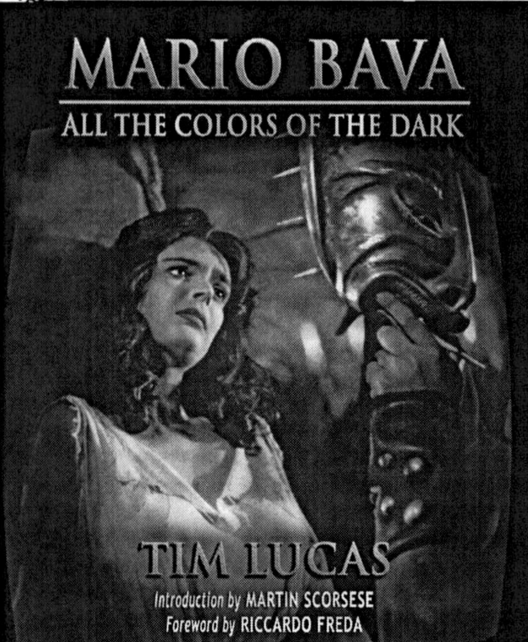


literally be moved forward only between issues of an eighty-page magazine, which I had to partly write as well as produce. When I finished my work, Donna commenced the layout, which took her another four years—between issues of a monthly magazine. Of course we were exhausted, but I also kept bringing new updated material to the book during that time, so it was continuing to grow. The index alone took us six months and is a particular circle of Hell neither of us wants to revisit.

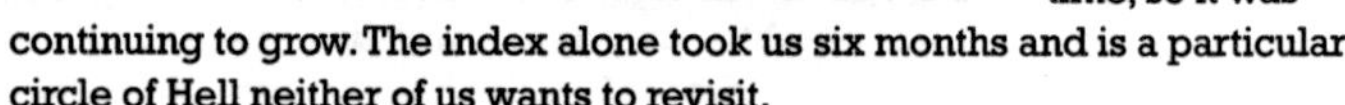

**JS: *Video Watchdog* has a critical eye peeled for mismatched running times and for discrepancies in the film transfers themselves. This takes a lot of work, but a lot of people seem to be listening. How big of an impact do you feel that *VW* has made on the way that films are being presented on DVD and blu-ray?**

**TL:** A whole group of our early readers have gone on to find work in the home video industry, founding companies, restoring films, digging up obscure movies we wrote about and giving them legitimate, subtitled releases. When we started in 1990, horror films were the most frequently abused kinds of films on video—they were habitually cut, retitled (!), badly cropped, you name it. And today, horror films are probably the most popular film genre in the world, and there is a strong collector's market for them—arguably stronger than any other genre following. I think this latter part was also true in 1990, because horror has always been the most collectible genre on home video, but now you can see that respect reflected on the production end. I think *Cinefantastique* was responsible for popularizing the interest in Making-Of articles, which has since become a form of documentation co-opted by production companies as a means of controlling their publicity.

I think *Video Watchdog* has had a comparable impact in regard to the seriousness with which the horror genre is now treated today.

**JS: I've often wondered how difficult it is to survive without outside advertising.**

**TL:** That all depends on your production costs. Donna and I work out of our home; the magazine is produced there and shipped out from there, very Mom and Pop. We laugh when we see movies set in magazine offices where you see editors assign five or six people to make one decision, or when you see an editor supervising the printing of a cover. Without going into a lot of personal detail, it's not all that difficult to survive without outside advertising… until it's not. But the economy is shaky and the internet has occupied a lot of people's reading time, so the worlds of professional print journalism are suffering across the board. We've recently hired an advertising director and are starting to accept a limited amount of outside advertising. We don't make and never have made a fortune from the magazine; *Video Watchdog* is not addressed to a popular market, but a connoisseur market. So the selling of a modest amount of ad space per issue will help us to cover our printing costs—which are considerable for a full-color magazine—and keep us going.

**JS: Has the access to online information hurt your sales?**

**TL:** That's open to debate, because there a number of factors involved. There is more online information now than when we started, but it doesn't tend to be the kind of information we publish; it's not all that different from the information you can read on the packaging of your DVD or blu-ray, because the industry we once policed has become much more responsible. What the companies tell us we're getting is pretty much what we're getting; the aspect ratios are there, the running times are there, and sometimes Jess Franco's name is above the freaking title! The days of trying to figure what movie *The Revenge of Dr. X* really is, are over. This is why I stress now that *Video Watchdog*, first and foremost, is "The Perfectionist's Guide to Fantastic Cinema." People read us because we present a gold standard of excellence in our writing and because our perception of these films is advanced and unique.

I think a source like *DVD Beaver* is valuable; they show frame grabs of different releases side by side, and they give you graphs that show, scientifically, how the values of one disc differ from another. But even though Gary Tooze writes well, I'm not convinced that people take the time to read what he has to say after they've checked out the frame comparisons for themselves; they see for themselves and they move on. It's the nature of the beast. I put a fair amount of free writing up online via my two blogs (*Video WatchBlog* and *Pause. Rewind. Obsess.*) and I promise you: just because people have access to online information doesn't mean they absorb it, not the same way people internalize and store what they read on paper, what they have physically sought out and purchased.

RECORDED & INDEXED

DRAFT

When you sit at a computer, your sitting stance says "Inform me." That's aggressive rather than receptive. You want to be informed in the least amount of time possible; you are not looking to be nourished or educated. I love YouTube, but if a video is longer than six minutes, I'll wait and watch it downstairs via my DirecTV connection.

**JS: You seem to be writing all the time. What kind of an outlet is "blogging" for you?**

**TL:** It's instant gratification for me and also a hook to attract internet browsers to the work we're doing in *Video Watchdog*, mainly. Blogging is also a vehicle that allows my editorial voice to comment on events that our readers need to process—like the deaths earlier this year [2012] of Lina Romay and Jonathan Frid, and by putting my rough draft thoughts out there, the feedback helps me to weed through that work as I rework it for the permanence of print. But there is always the hope, too, that the blogs will be discovered by some people who have never heard of *Video Watchdog* itself and might be tempted to order a subscription or sample copy.

**JS: What's your take on the way printed information is heading these day? I worry about the evolution of collected information a lot.**

**TL:** Everyone speaks about it as if the situation is dire, and it is in many ways, yet if you actually walk into a bookstore and check out the magazine displays, there have never been more horror and cult film-related magazines on the market at any one time. It's astounding—and it would be healthy, if not for a few facts—like the stranglehold that a monopoly distributor and retailers have on independent publishers, in terms of the colossal percentages they demand for simply making our hard work available in the visible marketplace. Furthermore, above and beyond those outrageous percentages, retailers insist that the publisher eat a certain amount of the product they ship; they call it "shrinkage," which is an industry term for stolen goods, and which basically insists they are not financially liable for any issues that get stolen from their stores. To a big magazine, that's dandruff, it's negligible, but for a smaller magazine, it hurts. And they tell you, if you don't like it, go elsewhere—and there is no elsewhere. So spiraling corporate greed is hurting print information as much as anything, and probably more than anything.

As for the magazine audience, I think the internet makes a lot of people feel they've reached an informational saturation point, even though they are scanning more than they actually read. Nobody remembers what they read online. If they do remember what they read, chances are they can't remember the source. I'm as addicted to Facebook as anybody, and I know that more and more people are more interested in communicating, sharing their lives and enthusiasms these days, than they are in solitary reading. Also, the Baby Boomer/Monster Kid generation that collects these kinds of magazines, they are now at that point in middle-age when they're

running out of room to house their collections, so they're either letting go or becoming more selective, and they also have other demands on their time, like grandchildren or their midlife crisis.

**JS: Will the monster magazines survive?**

**TL:** I'm not at all certain that magazines will survive—or books, or movies for that matter. Everything I see happening around me, technologically, suggests that we are being collectively lured away from independent learning and recreational autonomy into internet corrals where our thoughts and actions can be monitored. I do believe that some kind of monster appreciation will always be with us, but I imagine that the educative side of the monster magazine experience will fall by the wayside for most people, as indeed it does now for a lot of people who might consider themselves horror fans.

I am a firm believer that everything happens historically for a reason, and monster magazines are not exempt from this. Eventually, for them to have been at all successful in their mission, they must either die out or evolve. Given the way most people are, and the way the magazine market is changing, I don't see much interest or time left to us for further evolution. Besides, most monster magazines we see today are exercises in nostalgia, new product pacifiers for the eye and collector impulse, and the horror genre itself doesn't seem too interested or able to perpetuate monsters as a going concern—today's monsters rarely have the sort of individual identity that a makeup artist like Jack Pierce was able to invest in his work. Guillermo del Toro's films sometimes introduce a new monster with that sort of impact, but they are always fleeting characters in much larger stories. Today's storytellers have to pile it on, for commercial reasons, and to be compatible with the short attention spans sitting out there in the dark.

Perhaps the monsters have fulfilled their covenant with us. Within my lifetime, I have seen them teach people to be more sympathetic and tolerant toward other people who look strange, who stand outside society. With the world much better connected today technologically, young people may no longer need the same insights they needed when racism and superstition and other inbred suspicions ran rampant, as they did when I was a kid in the 1950s and sixties. Of course, the horror genre has long since stopped using monsters to such remedial ends, and today's monsters don't always have subtext, societal or otherwise.

What I feel is more important is that some form of serious criticism of the horror genre survive, because the genre has always commented obliquely on tendencies in our society that the mainstream is either not ready or not free to address directly. It's important—perhaps becoming increasingly important—for people to be more alert, more conscious, through discussion and deconstruction of our entertainment, of exactly what we are being told, how we as a society are mutating, so that whatever happens next won't take us too uncomfortably by surprise.

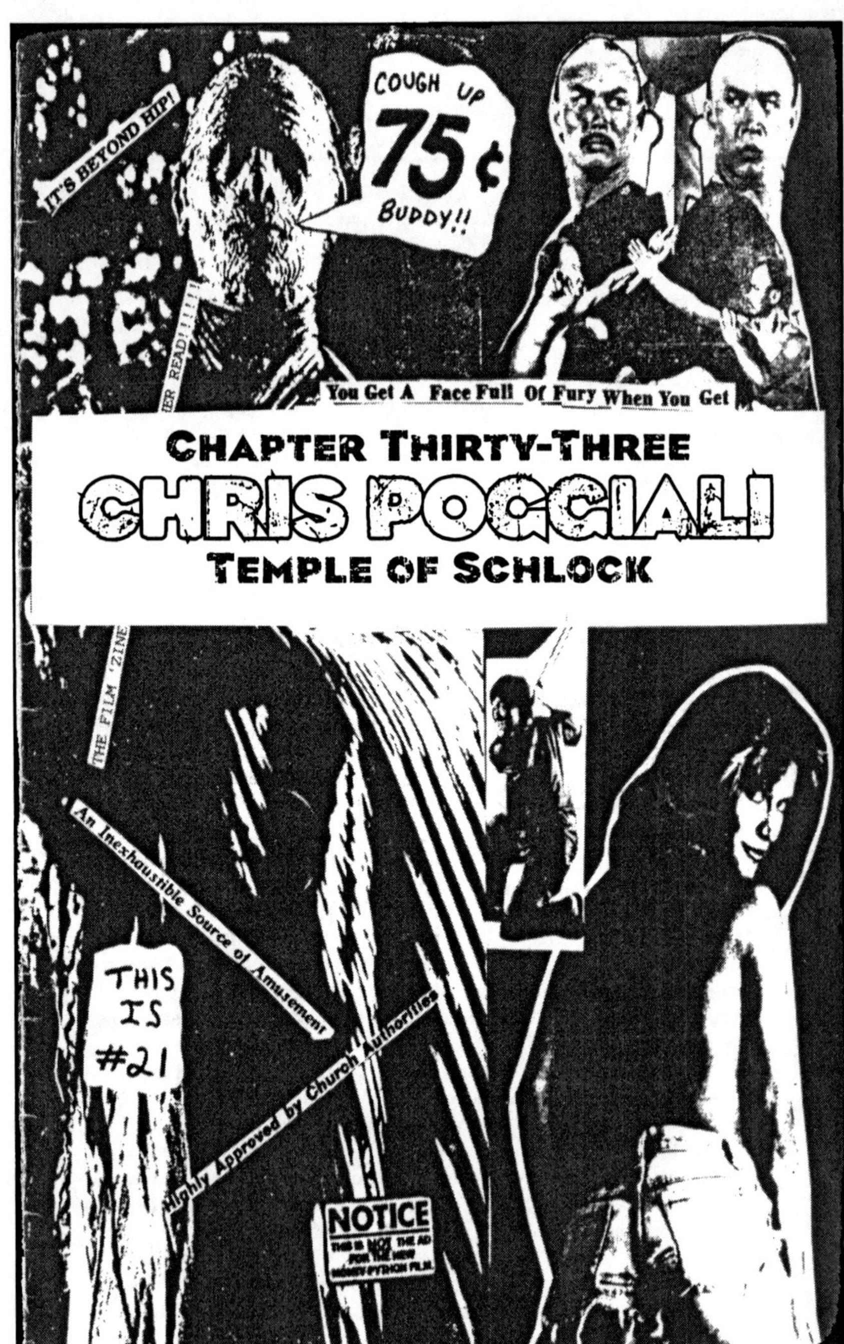


# Chapter Thirty-Three

# Chris Poggiali

## Temple of Schlock

Chris Poggiali began publishing *Temple of Schlock* in 1987, just shortly before I began collecting fanzines in earnest. The premiere issue proclaimed, "We do half-rate reviews for half-rate movies," but in my eyes, there was nothing half-rate about it. Poggiali and co-editor Paul DeCirce met the home video explosion of the eighties at the gate, and the result was an impressive (and ample) array of in-depth film reviews. The boys at *Temple of Schlock* cast their net wide—they seemed to be obsessed with each and every genre that fell under the wide shadow of the exploitation umbrella. The zine went on for a twenty-four issue run before sadly closing shop in 1991.

At some point in 2008, I ran into Chris Poggiali again while surfing the net. It seemed that the mighty *Temple* had opened its doors once again, this time as a blog (www.templeofschlock.blogspot.com). I bookmarked the thing on the spot, and promptly became a full-fledged fan addict.

Chris Poggiali was one of the first people I contacted when I began my research for *Xerox Ferox*. The man certainly knows his stuff, and he quickly became my go-to guy when I was putting this book together. Indeed, he conducted three outstanding interviews that grace these very pages.

When we finally spoke on the phone (in two marathon sessions), the combined conversations clocked in at over five hours. So, now that we've got the man on the line, let's dive in. Here he is, folks—Chris Poggiali, the Sultan of Schlock!

The following interview was conducted via telephone, June–July, 2012.

---

**JOHN SZPUNAR: When did you become aware of schlock films?**

**CHRIS POGGIALI:** I've been interested in movies for as long as I can remember. About the time my family moved from Pittsburgh to upstate New York, I started to notice that certain movies would play in certain theaters. In Pittsburgh they would've been the downtown theaters playing the horror and exploitation. I got to Syracuse when I was about seven, and the downtown theaters were on their way out or gone by that time, so we're talking really about drive-ins.

There were four or five drive-ins in Syracuse. The major releases would play three theaters a lot of times. But what I like to refer to as "outlaw movies" would get only one screen, usually a drive-in. They'd have titles like *Attack of the Killer Tomatoes*, *The Cars that Eat People*, and *Centerfold Girls*—sex and violence would always be the attraction. They played at one theater, and that was it. So, it was always kind of the outlaw image that drew me to these movies. It was like, "Here's something that's only playing there, but these other movies are playing at two or three more accessible theaters." *Close Encounters of the Third Kind*—yeah, I want to see it, but this other movie is only in one theater, and it's a drive-in theater. Why is that?

I guess it's the same way that some people are drawn to heavy metal and others are drawn to rap, or some people follow the lives of serial killers and mobsters. I just took to these "outlaw" movies.

**JS: Do you have any favorite directors from your formative years?**

**CP:** Steven Spielberg was definitely a favorite of mine. The fastest way to get me involved in any sort of online argument is if you downgrade *1941*. I'll jump in there swinging. Yeah, I loved *Jaws* and *Close Encounters of the Third Kind*, and I saw *Raiders of the Lost Ark* nine times in theaters, but *1941* really grabbed me. I remember all the talk about Steven Spielberg the wonder kid falling flat on his face with it. Really? I've always loved it, and pretty much everything else he did up to and including *The Color Purple*. I'd also heard about Peter Bogdanovich—again, another guy who fell flat on his face, supposedly with *Nickelodeon*, which I think is a great movie, also. And, *Saint Jack*, which was supposedly him slumming, was a very good movie. So, I knew about those guys. But, probably the first director that I discovered on my own was Jack Starrett. I'm working on a book with a friend of mine about Jack. I remember when *Race with the Devil* played on television. My mom ran out of the room when the snakes jumped out of the cabinets in the camper. I found out later that he had done *Cleopatra Jones* and *The Losers*, which I really liked. So, I started following directors, and by the time *Psychotronic* and the Leonard Maltin film guide entered my life, I knew about guys like Herschell Gordon Lewis, Al Adamson, and Ed Wood. And I was very lucky to have a father who knew a lot about directors. He introduced me to the films of John Ford, Alfred Hitchcock, Orson Welles, Sam Fuller—when *The Big Red One* came out, he told me all about *The Steel Helmet*, which he had seen as a kid and it had made a big impression on him. So, I knew Sam Fuller was a force to be reckoned with. It was something that my father got me interested in, and I just picked it up along the way. I was reading magazines and watching different movie shows like Siskel and Ebert. *That's Hollywood* was a show that 20th Century Fox produced in the seventies. I wouldn't miss an episode of it. I was always at the television whenever it was on.

**JS: What else was on TV?**

**CP:** Cartoons, old sitcoms, *Star Trek*, *Batman*, you name it. When I got to Syracuse, there was a show on Saturday afternoons called *Monster Movie Matinee*, hosted by Dr. Enoch Witty, who was never shown except for his hand. It was a creepy, bony hand with a big ring on it. The doctor would wave his hand and speak to his Igor-type assistant whose name was Epal. They were in a smoky haunted house setting, or in a dungeon. The exterior of the house was only shown at the beginning, and it was miniature house with smoke all around it. I found out much later that Epal was played by Bill Lape, who was also Salty Sam on the Saturday morning variety show for kids, *Salty Sam's Super Saturday*. Lape backwards is Epal. Speaking of words spelled backwards, on Sundays there was a show called *Eivom* that would

also run horror movies. It began with a cheesy computer generated title card of the word "Movie" gyrating and shaking until it became "Eivom" and a menacing voice in an echo chamber would say "EEEEEEEEE–VOMMMMMMMM!!!!" with wind howls and scary music in the background. There was no horror host, just this threatening opener. After the weird graphic, they would go into a Universal horror film or a giant monster movie from the fifties.

**JS: What kinds of things were you reading?**

**CP:** It was mostly age-appropriate fiction like Sid Fleischman, Judy Blume, Beverly Cleary, Daniel Pinkwater. I loved *The Three Investigators* mysteries, and not just because they hung out with Alfred Hitchcock [laughs]! It wasn't until *Starlog* came along that I would go into bookstores and read the movie magazines. Economy Books was a mini chain in upstate New York. They had a store in the mall nearby, with the new books and magazines on the first floor the used books and magazines in the basement. I'd spend a couple of hours in Economy—I'd take the bus over and read the movie magazines and the teen magazines. A lot of times, you would read about new movies in something like *16* or *Tiger Beat*. I remember when *Zapped!* came out. I didn't care about Scott Baio, but I wanted to read about *Zapped!* I would just work my way through all the new magazines and then I'd go to the basement and read a lot of back issues. They still had issues of *Creem* from the early and mid-seventies, usually with the covers torn off.

**JS: I really miss stores like that. You could spend hours going through things.**

**CP:** I'd read about the movies that were coming out. They'd play at the drive-in, and I'd clip out the movie ads, which was always something that I was interested in. There were times when I couldn't see the movie, but I'd clip out the ad and go to the store to buy the novelization. As long as I wasn't coming home with a porno

MONSTER "EIVOM" MATINÉE.

magazine, my parents didn't really question what I was reading. I could go and get the novelization of something that was R-rated and they wouldn't make a big deal out of it. I remember when *The Gauntlet* came out. I really wanted to see it, because of the Frank Frazetta poster and that great black and white photo of Eastwood and Sondra Locke on the chopper. The novelization is a lot nastier than the movie. So, I really didn't understand that—"You can't go see that movie, it's rated R." But I could read the book, where the opening chapter was X rated [laughs].

**JS: Were you buying monster magazines from the bookstore or just reading them there?**

**CP:** I didn't buy them. I would read them in the stores. I didn't have much of an allowance, and the allowance that I got would usually go toward other things like View-Masters, Matchbox cars and trading cards. I was a big collector of baseball cards and movie cards like *Star Wars*. I thought it was strange that trading cards aimed at kids were being produced for *Saturday Night Fever* and *Alien*, which were R-rated movies.

**JS: In retrospect, that is kind of weird.**

**CP:** *Saturday Night Fever* was R, but then Paramount cut a PG version because it was so popular and a lot of kids wanted to see it because of the music and the dancing. There was talk about Fox doing it with *Alien*, as well. That might account for why there were trading cards.

**JS: How did *Temple of Schlock* come about?**

**CP:** I had written a couple of reviews for *Slimetime*, which was a newsletter out of Syracuse that was done by Steve Puchalski.

**JS: What did you send him?**

**CP:** There were two that I remember. I sent him a review of *Ebony, Ivory, and Jade* and a review of a biker movie called *Angels Die Hard*. I knew that he liked biker movies and I thought, "He hasn't reviewed *Angels Die Hard* yet; let me do that." So, I wrote those reviews and

September, 1990 Number Twenty-three.
TEMPLE OF SCHLOCK
STILL ONLY 75¢!
(But since we're now badass "Hall of Shamers," we'll take your 75¢ and never send you issues, OK?)
THE FILM FANZINE THAT MADE IT INTO Factsheet Five's "HALL OF SHAME!"
#23
JEFF GAITHER ©1988

BIZARRE AND BARBARIC... MACABRE AND GRUESOME... BLOOD-STAINED AND SADISTIC...

Weirdos! Hippies! FOR PEOPLE WITH NERVES OF IRON ONLY!!! Kooks! Killers!

SLIMETIME

NUMBER NINE, JULY 1987 "WE SLEAZE TO PLEASE"

sent them to him. He didn't use the *Angels Die Hard* one but he put *Ebony, Ivory, and Jade* in his ninth issue. He didn't tell me he was publishing it, he just put it in and sent me that issue. This was July 1987.

**JS: Did you know Steve prior to this?**

**CP:** Not really. I think we had exchanged a letter or two shortly after I got the first issue. He ran the film program at Syracuse University, and showed *Night of the Living Dead* and *Dawn of the Dead* in October of 1986. The first issue of *Slimetime* was in a box on a table as I went into the auditorium. I grabbed one and instantly fell in love with it. I thought it was the greatest thing I'd ever read. It was exactly what I was interested in at that time. I was in high school but I hung around SU and downtown Syracuse because that's where all the record stores, comic books stores and big libraries were located. There was a store called Twilight Book and Game Emporium that always carried the latest issue of *Slimetime.* One day I just decided to review a couple of movies I had rented. I typed the reviews and sent them off to him with a cover letter, and he published *Ebony, Ivory and Jade* in number 9. I was really excited and I wanted to write more for him and other zines. I had a friend named Paul DeCirce, who was two grades behind me in school. I showed him *Slimetime* and said, "Come on, let's write some reviews and get them published! It's fun!" By that time, I had a pretty big pile of other fanzines. I showed them to Paul, and he went through every one of them. Half an hour later, he put the last one down and said, "You know what? I'm not impressed. We can do this. Let's just do our own fanzine." I wasn't really into that idea—it seemed like too big of a responsibility—but by the end of the day, he had talked me into it.

**JS: Who came up with the title *Temple of Schlock*?**

**CP:** That was Paul's idea. I had shown him *Schlock*, the John Landis movie, so he had the word rattling around in his head. We threw the first issue together very quickly, with a couple of friends, and there were some things that we did in there that we never did again.

**JS: Such as?**

**CP:** Paul wrote a piece of fiction for that issue, and I wrote a cereal review.

*SLIMETIME NUMBER 9*

3 Foxy Mama's Turned Loose...
They call 'em EBONY IVORY & JADE
They Can Whip Any Man Ever Made!
ROSANNE KATON • COLLEEN CAMP • SYLVIA ANDERSON
PG


At the time, Syracuse was a test market area for breakfast cereals. There was a fanzine called *Flake*—I don't know if you're familiar with it.

**JS: No, I'm not.**

**CP:** *Flake* was dedicated to breakfast cereals. Anyway, at the time that we were doing *Temple of Schlock*, there was a cereal out called Fruit Islands. A lot of people I've mentioned it to have never heard of it, but I reviewed it and it was horrible [laughs]. I remember that Craig Ledbetter wrote to us when we were picking up steam, around issue four or five. He said, "I don't have number one. The first issue you sent me was number two." We didn't want to send it to him for the longest time, but we finally did. He wrote back "I can see why you guys were hesitant about sending it out, but you've done a few good things since. First of all, you dropped the cereal reviews." [laughs]

**JS: What else was in the first issue?**

**CP:** We reviewed *The GI Executioner*, *Blood Sucking Freaks*, *Night of the Living Dead*. It was a mixture of well documented stuff with more obscure things. It's crude as hell, but it's funny.

**JS: How were you producing *Temple of Schlock*?**

**CP:** With the second issue, we realized that we could take the graphics that we had, put them on a piece of paper, and draw an outline around them. Then, we'd put the paper into the typewriter and type around the outline [laughs]. Even that sounds primitive, but that's something we didn't figure out until after the first issue. Looking at that first one would drive me crazy. I typed my reviews on a typewriter, and then I'd hand the copy to Paul. We'd cut out the art for a review and paste it on the paper, underneath the review. We put in some comics to fill up space, since we weren't typing directly on the page. And it was all different fonts, too. Paul would type up his thing on a computer, so we had a dot matrix review on one page, and the next page was done on my typewriter. Then, there'd be a comic strip of a cat by our friend Jeff Lewis. Then comes a *Night of the Living Dead* review—it takes up half a page, so we put in a newspaper ad

for *Night of the Living Dead*, but then a quarter of the page was empty. So we put in a drawing of a guy throwing up, and there were hands and arms and an octopus tentacles sticking out of his vomit. We did it that way for nine pages! We didn't even have a tenth page—the back cover was blank. It never occurred to us that we could put in another picture of someone throwing up [laughs].

The second issue looked completely different. Unfortunately, Paul went gunning for Steve Puchalski with that one. He decided that he didn't like Steve, for whatever reason. And he didn't even know the guy—he didn't know Steve at all. I guess he decided that Syracuse wasn't big enough for two fanzines. He did the layout right in front of me, for several pages, before I said, "Paul, this looks like *Slimetime*. It's isn't green and it's sloppy as hell, but you're doing *Slimetime*." And we got the nastiest letter back from Steve when we sent him the issue. He was furious. "I can plug you guys," he wrote, "But I'm going to tell it like it is. You guys really need to get your own style. You're ripping me off." After that, I said to Paul, "Listen, we've got to make this look like something else and not like the zine that's right across town!" We started to do our own thing with number three, but it wasn't until we started reducing *Temple of Schlock* and doing it as a digest that I really felt comfortable.

SPECIAL THANKS TO ARBY'S ON ERIE BLVD. FOR LETTING ME DO THE LAYOUT IN THEIR STORE

TEMPLE OF SCHLOCK #18 JUNE 1989

C/O PAUL DECIRCE, 409 HIXSON AVE., SYRACUSE, NY 13206

Hey hey, we're back! And only a month later, too (See, we really are back on schedule!). Chris is still in charge, Paul still sunbathing somewhere. Anyway, issues are still 75¢ each, subscriptions $4.50 for 6 issues. Overseas, a buck an issue, or free in trade for your fanzine. All aboard? Here we go....

Hammer HITS HORROR ON THE HEAD

AN IN-DEPTH SERIES BY JOHN P. FEENEY

PART 7

The source for THE VAMPIRE LOVERS was Joseph Sheridan LeFanu's story Carmilla. And as LUST FOR A VAMPIRE and TWINS OF EVIL grew out of this first film, LeFanu's work is the inspiration for the entire trilogy, a classic in erotic horror.

Referred to by Rev. Montague Summers as "the best of the English vampire stories," Carmilla was first published in the London magazine "The Dark Blue" in 1871. One of it's readers was Bram Stoker, then a young part-time newspaper reporter. It is fair to assume that LeFanu influenced Stoker's later classic, Dracula, and thus Carmilla is the well-spring for the modern Western tradition of the vampire.

Though Carmilla is the work for which he is best remembered, LeFanu was a successful journalist, editor of "Dublin University Magazine" and author of a number of acclaimed ghost stories. LeFanu had a morose nature exacerbated by the death of his sister at the age of twenty-seven and the premature death of his wife in 1858. Following the demise of the latter, he became a recluse in his home on Merrion Square, Dublin, earning the sobriquet "Invisible Prince." It was during these latter years, while LeFanu was given to walks in his secluded garden, tormented by nightmares, disposed to writing late at night and consuming vast quantities of tea, that Carmilla was published.

IF YOU DARE... taste the deadly passion of the BLOOD-NYMPHS!

CAUTION not for the mentally immature!

The Vampire Lovers

**JS: You were pretty young when you started *Temple of Schlock*. How much time did you put into the craft of writing?**

**CP:** Not a lot. Paul could be a much bigger wiseass in his reviews, but he was also a more serious writer when he wanted to be, so some of his reviews have aged better than a lot of mine. I write now pretty much the same that I wrote back then, but the only difference is, there's more thought put into it beforehand. I write on paper first, then I type it, and usually while I'm typing I do a revision. But I didn't start doing that until I got a correctable typewriter, which was probably around issue nine! After that, I went through a lot of correctable tape, let me tell you! And a

## TEMPLE OF SCHLOCK

RECORDED & INDEXED

DRAFT

lot of the reviews are still horrible. I saw one the other day that cracked me up. I had typed some mess of a statement, realized it was terrible halfway through, and because I was running out of correctable tape and didn't want to waste what I had left, I put in parentheses, "Wow, is that a poorly constructed sentence," and just kept typing to the end.

**JS: *Temple of Schlock* had a lot of great contributing writers.**

**CP:** At one point we had half the guys from *Hi-Tech Terror* writing for us: Dave Szurek, Roger Reus, Kris Gilpin, and Keith Hall, Jr. We had a guy called the Keeper of the Pit, who still writes for the blog. At the time, he was a movie poster dealer who advertised in *Fangoria*, "Send $2.00 for small but sleazy catalog." His business was called the Poster Pit. I wrote to him for his poster catalog in 1984, and I thought it was hilarious. Every movie title was followed by a silly pun and the price of the poster or pressbook. As an example, when the Roger Corman production *Cocaine Wars* came out, the catalog entry read, "John Schneider, fighting for what's white!" We started corresponding, and when I started the zine, I asked him if he wanted to write reviews. Other zine editors like Jeff Smith and Nathan Miner contributed some reviews, too. John Donaldson sent me the unfinished second issue of his fanzine *Damn-Fino* and told me I could use whatever I wanted from it, so I took almost all of his reviews and interspersed them throughout the last five issues of *Temple of Schlock*. A writer in New Mexico named Octavio Ramos, Jr. was one of our most faithful contributors, along with Szurek.

**JS: What are your memories of Dave Szurek?**

**CP:** I remember the first letter that we got from Dave. He wanted to contribute, and he asked to see an issue. I was really excited. I knew Dave's stuff from *Hi-Tech Terror* and *Wet Paint*, but what had really made a big impression on me was his "Detroit Grindhouse Blues" article that appeared in *Magick Theatre* number 7. That's his masterpiece, I think. When he wrote to us, I said to Paul, "We have to get this guy! Let's offer him a column!" We asked him if he wanted to submit something for every

issue and he thought that was great—and then came the letters. Thirty page letters, all handwritten.

**JS: Do you still have them?**

**CP:** I wish I'd kept them. I have one of them. When Paul left *Temple of Schlock*, he took half of the stuff with him, and I think he may have taken a lot of the correspondence. Paul wrote to the editors more than I did. If you look at issues of *Subhuman* or *Wet Paint* from that time, there's usually a letter from Paul in there. He probably has the angry letter that Steve Puchalski sent us. I went looking for it the other day—I wanted to include it in the book.

MAY/JUNE
STILL ONLY 75¢!
#22
TEMPLE OF SPINE SHATTERING SCHLOCK
FREE JEANNE BELL POSTERS TO FIRST 1000 PATRONS
SHE'S A ONE MAMA MASSACRE SQUAD!

YOU'VE MET 'GINGER' NOW MEET...
PEPPER
She was a secret agent

FOR ADULTS ONLY
by Phil M. Neas

Friday, May 11th, 7:30 p.m.---I was giving Velma a quick lesson in sword-swallowing when the phone rang. It was Ugly Louie. He was in tears. The video store he usually rented from went bust and wiped out their "Adult" section. I'm not talkin' porn here--TABOO, INSATIABLE, THE RESURRECTION OF EVE. They never carried that stuff to begin with. No, I'm talkin' "Adult" film of the R-rated variety. Y'know, the stuff we used to catch at the drive-ins--PETS, CHERRY HILL HIGH, TAKIN' IT OFF, and so on.

"Don't lose it, Louie," I said. "I'll pick you up in twenty and we'll skip past my video place." I hung up. Movies tonight. Why not? No more booze, nothin' on T.V., and I was gettin' sick of lookin' at the top of Velma's head. Yup, movies tonight.

After a lot of arguing and a little fisticuffs, we agreed that our best bet would be THE BIG BET, a 1985 teen romp directed by none other than Bert I. Gordon! A few chuckles and a lot of skin made this an all right rental, even if the plot was just a little too timeworn. A shy high school guy likes the new blonde in town, and bets a creepy rich kid that he can bed her down in ten days. Sylvia Kristel puts in a couple of appearances as the kid's sexy neighbor; she removes her blouse, of course. The highlight of THE BIG BET, though, is the elevator dream sequence, where Monique Gabrielle strips down to her au naturel and messes with the teen on the floor. Monique is quickly becoming the Queen of Softcore. Who can forget her nude walk through a museum in AMAZON WOMEN ON THE MOON, the sight of her and Michelle Bauer slipping out of their clothes at the same time in SCREEN TEST, or similar performances in DEATHSTALKER II and YOUNG LADY CHATTERLY II? We'll definitely be looking out for her in the upcoming SILK 2.

For a second feature we picked up PEPPER. This was first shown in theatres as CHECKMATE in '73, then re-released as PEPPER in 1975 to cash in on the popular GINGER movies. Forget it. Cheri Caffaro never had it so bad. Diana Wilson stars as Pepper Burns, a secret agent who wears hot pants and receives her orders from a talking vibrator. Pepper's latest assignment is to stop the evil Madame Chang, a direct descendant of Fu Manchu who plays chess and plans on destroying several major cities with a satellite beam. Her sidekick is the evil Mr. Snow, a creepy dude who wears Roger McGuinn style shades. Expect lots of nudity, horrible music, and misfire humor (Two characters named Wong and Thong are described as "Madame Chang's yellow pages." Mysterious). Carol Kaye (MR TUTOR) plays a secretary. Roberta Findlay was the director of photography. Well, the time has come for me to slip back into my office for a smoke session and a shot of mouthwash. See you next issue, when I

**JS: It could have been your introduction [laughs].**

**CP:** That's what I had in mind [laughs]! But yeah, Dave was a character. He was living in Detroit at the time he was writing for us. One of the letters he sent us had a list of every fanzine that he had written for. I wish I had kept that...

**JS: His name was everywhere.**

**CP:** He had these lists of alternate titles that he would send us, and they were not to be believed. First of all, if you look at some of the articles that he was writing around that time, they degenerate into lists after a while. He'd write, "During the sixties, the Adams Theater would show old favorites like..." and then there'd be a list of fifty movies. Then he'd write, "Meanwhile, the Fox Theater down the street would show chestnuts like..." and he'd list fifty more movies. It wasn't like any of the zines were paying him by the word, so I never understood why he would do this. I guess he was just really into making lists. So he had a list of funky alternate titles that he was sending around to everybody. No one had ever heard of any of these titles. At first, I didn't question it, but then Dave wrote to me about *Blood Sucking Freaks*, which he had a lot of aka's for, and one of them was *Blood Freak*. I knew that was another movie, but he said, "No, it played in Detroit at one point as *Blood Freak*." Then he started putting in these crazy alternate titles for things like *Evil Dead 2*—titles that nobody had heard of for movies that were really popular with horror fans. *Evil Dead 2* was something

like *Haunted House in the Woods*. Also, some major studio films with whacked out alternate titles. People were getting pissed and saying "Dave, where are you getting these things? Are you making up these titles?" He'd say, "No, it played in Detroit under this title." Finally, John Donaldson sent the list to Carl Morano, who was working for Troma at the time, I think in charge of the theatrical prints. Carl made a call and found out some sub-distributor in Michigan was changing the titles to get around the rental fees, and running the prints in drive-ins. Dave was only writing down these bogus titles.

**JS: So, Dave was right.**

**CP:** [laughs] He was, but if I had that list today, I wouldn't submit any of those titles to the IMDb!

**JS: I wanted to ask you about some of the artists that you had for *Temple of Schlock*. What can you tell me about the Evil Twin?**

**CP:** The Evil Twin was Barry Wooldridge. He designed two of our logos, and he did a lot of the little logos inside the magazine, like "The Szurek Zone" and "Letters from the Loonies." We did all of our logos for a while, until Barry contacted us and said, "Your zine would look a lot better if an artist helped you out with some of this stuff." I think that's how that happened.

**JS: He was doing some things for *Subhuman*.**

**CP:** He had a comic strip for *Subhuman*, but he did a lot of work for other editors and concert posters for different bands. He designed the second

Number 15, January 1989

TEMPLE OF SCHLOCK
Paul V. DeCirce
409 Hixson Ave.
Syracuse, N.Y. 13206

SUBSCRIPTIONS: $4.50 for 6 issues. $1 each over seas. Free in trade for your fanzine. Letters and contributions are always welcome.

HELLBOUND: HELLRAISER II (New World;1988) Reviewed by Octavio Ramos, Jr.

HELLBOUND: HELLRAISER begins where HELLRAISER [TOS#8] left off. Kirsty (Ashley Laurence), having survived the sadistic Cenobites' attack, awakens in an asylum. Instead of receiving a well-deserved vacation, Kirsty discovers that her dad is alive and well but living in hell. Kirsty decides to save him and in the process discovers that the Cenobites are the least of her problems.

It seems the psychiatrist taking care of Kirsty also happens to be obsessed with the beyond. When he hears Kirsty's story, the doctor obtains a mattress covered in blood, blood that once belonged to Julia (Clare Higgins). The doctor then feeds a patient to the mattress (the hospital cellar is full of insane patients that the doctor uses for experiments and food) and a skinless Julia returns.

Meanwhile, Kirsty and a kid doctor discover the doctor's insane plan. They enter the doc's room and discover three puzzle boxes. To throw a monkey wrench into the plot, a girl named Tifanny (Imogen Boorman) has a knack for puzzles. With all the fixin's set up, the descent to hell begins.

Up to this point, HELLBOUND had me captivated, although a little worried. The rest of the film confirmed my worries. It's in the decent into hell that things begin to fall apart. Kirsty's search for her father is abandoned with three lines, we discover that hell ain't such a bad place to be, and we get smatterings of philosophy that contradict each other.

In HELLRAISER, merely stepping into hell brought hoards of unspeakable nasties. In this sequel, however, only the Cenobites (all eliminated in an anti-climactic way) and a Lovecraftian-type "god" inhabit hell. The ending, which I won't give away, almost saves the film. Almost...

Although the plot suffers, there are some horrible moments in the film. The asylum cellar reminds one of a modern SNAKE PIT, there's a new Cenobite that will scare the hell out of even Temple Dwellers and

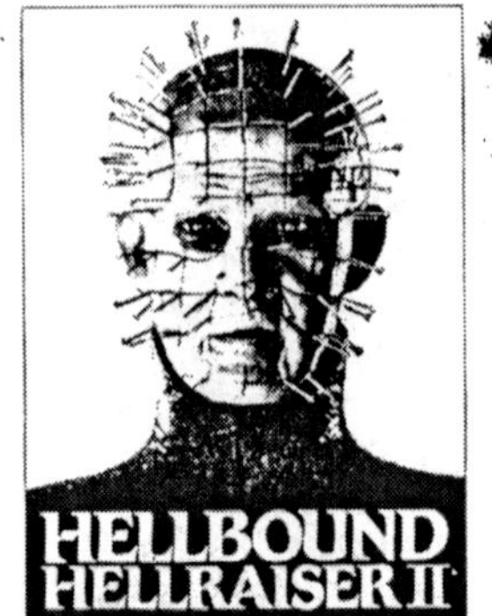

XEROX
FEROX

logo for the Poster Pit. He also did some stuff for *Wet Paint*.

**JS: Speaking of *Wet Paint*, what are your memories of Jeff Smith?**

**CP:** Jeff was a nice guy. I really liked him, and I wrote some reviews for *Wet Paint*. He reviewed a couple of things for us, also. His zine got more and more substantial. It seemed like he was always just about to go semi-pro, but he never really made the leap. One thing to mention is his artwork. He was a comic book artist and did most of the artwork for his zine. I have issue number 23 here, which has his rendering of the stabbing in the neck from *Suspiria*. He did another one that's a parody of a *Fangoria* cover. It says, "Exclusive: Jason Unmasked." It has a picture of Jason with his mask off, revealing the face of Alfred E. Neuman underneath.

SUPERB CRAFTSMANSHIP SOLID TERROR

TEMPLE OF SCHLOCK

NUMBER 2, DECEMBER 1987 WE PUT SANTIAGO TO SHAME!

Greetings, earthlings! Have we got an issue this time! Last ish, we were just foolin' around; getting a feel of writing our own rag. Well, we know just how hard it is. And I think you'll see a vast improvement from the last fun-filled issue! This time, we got reviews of classics like ALIEN and DAWN OF THE DEAD. We also got forgettable garbage like FAT GUY GOES NUTZOID and BLOODSUCKING FREAKS (both from our buddies, Troma). Plus we got a special treat: a review of the black Japanese comedy, THE CRAZY FAMILY. Us Temple dwellers have staggered around the mansion looking for some extra reviews here and there, and we're plum out of 'em! We need help! Become a schlockster!! Send us a review of a movie that is degrading, rude, crude, and immoral. We'd appreciate (and print) them! Also, back issues and present issues are available. Send for future issues and subscriptions at your own risk, please. If (due to continuity problems) we don't make an issue you've paid for, we'll gladly return your money. (Unless we wante it buying cheap twinkies at Wilson Farms; only kidding.) Issues are [illegible] each. Send comments, drawings, articles, and cash for trash to TEMPLE OF SCHLOCK, C/O LIZ WYATT, P.O. BOX 365, E. SYRACUSE, N.Y. 13057.

When there's
no more room in HELL
the dead will walk the EARTH
DAWN OF THE DEAD

DAWN OF THE DEAD (1979): Written and directed by George A Romero (MARTIN, KNIGHTRIDERS, SEASON OF THE WITCH, NIGHT OF THE LIVING DEAD, APARTMENT LIVING, DAY OF THE DEAD, THE CRAZIES, CREEPSHOW). Starring Ken Foree, Scott Reiniger, Gaylen Ross and Tom Savini (KNIGHTRIDERS, CREEPSHOW 2). DAWN OF THE DEAD is the second, and longest (126 min.) of the dead movies (NIGHT OF THE LIVING DEAD 1968) and DAY OF THE DEAD (1985) and many people consider this to be the strong point of the series. Two SWAT specialists (Peter and Roger) team with two television productionists (Steve and Fran) and head for the skies in search of safety from the millions of flesh eating zombies that [illegible] the world. The quartet lands on the top of a shopping center, where they make their home. This classic cult movie includes many famous gore scenes (thanks to fifth-star effect man Tom Savini) like the screwdriver in the ear, the hatchet in the head and numerous decapitations. Every horror fan must see this flick, and if you can sit through the zombie feast scene, you can handle anything. After watching it, you will understand when we say that no other horror movie has ever or will equal it. It is a must for any horror lover. The sequel is DAY OF THE DEAD (1985).
--Paul DeLiteo

**JS: You sent me a great picture of a lot of zine editors together at a convention.** **[See page 481.]**

**CP:** Nathan Miner sent me that. It was taken at a FANEX show in Baltimore, I think in 1990, when they had a fanzine panel. Nathan, Dan Taylor, Mike Gingold, Gary Svehla, Charlie Kilgore, Steve Puchalski and a couple of others were on it. Barry Wooldridge was there, too. I think Gary and Nathan got sort of irritated when I went up afterwards and introduced myself. They asked, "Why were you sitting out there? Why weren't you up on the panel?" As I recall, I was in the dealer room talking with Ron Harvey and the Keeper of the Pit and was late getting to the panel.

**JS: Let's talk a little about the home video boom.**

**CP:** I remember 1985 being the year that video really kicked in. A couple of years later we would review stuff that was playing in theaters, but we didn't have access to a lot of the lower budgeted stuff that somebody like Rick Sullivan had. He had a lot more urban theaters to go to. In Syracuse, we were stuck with more mainstream fare. If it wasn't playing at a drive-in, we had to go with what was on video. It's not accidental that 1985 was the last year that *Sleazoid Express* was around. Bill Landis was already writing about the way things were changing in New York. I don't think *Chicago Shivers* was around much later than 1985. *Scareaphanalia* started in '83,

and Mike eventually covered more videos, but he was mostly a theatrical guy. Luckily, what we lost on the theatrical front was gained 100 times over with the sudden access to so many older and international obscurities. I could finally see Herschell Gordon Lewis movies easily, after reading about them for so long. Prior to video, people had to keep their eyes on the local drive-ins to see if *Two Thousand Maniacs* would show some weekend. I remember it playing as late as 1977 or '78, but home video made it so much more accessible. So we could rent older movies that otherwise never would've been able to see, and also newer films that had played in some cities but bypassed other parts of the country—things like *Christmas Evil* and *The Black Room*. There were also direct-to-video movies that had screened at the Mifed or the Cannes festivals and were advertised in full-page *Variety* ads suddenly appearing on video shelves with almost no fanfare. So there was suddenly a great amount of movies at our fingertips, and the fanzines helped sort through and organize them to some extent. *Ecco* was one of the best of these zines. Charles Kilgore would find incredibly rare stuff on VHS, including some things I still haven't seen to this day. The first few issues of *Ecco* were dedicated solely to mondo movies.

**JS: You did some writing for *Fangoria*. How did that work come about?**

**CP:** I became good friends with Michael Gingold through fanzine trading. I was following *Scareaphanalia* before I started *Temple of Schlock*. We corresponded through the mail, and in the Summer of 1988, while Paul and I were visiting New York City, we met up with Mike and hung around with him for a few days. We wanted to watch Jackie Chan movies on 42nd Street, but he wasn't into that idea at all, so we helped him deliver issues of *Scareaphanalia* to his vendors around town. We went to Kinko's to pick up the issues, and then dropped off a bunch at the Sci-Fi Horror Emporium in Greenwich Village, which also carried *Gore Gazette*. The following Summer we were back in New York and Mike invited us to the *Starlog* offices on Park Avenue to meet Tony Timpone. This was just after Tony's appearance on *The Morton Downey, Jr. Show*, which was kind of

humiliating and not Tony's finest hour. But we dropped by *Fangoria* and met Tony and I got to know him pretty well after that. I moved back to New York City after college and at some point, I started writing for *Fangoria*. I wrote book reviews, features and interviews for them.

TEMPLE OF SCHLOCK

WARRIOR OF THE LOST WORLD

ROBERT GINTY

A FILM BY DAVID WORTH

**JS: Before I forget, what can you tell me about the Tony Timpone/Morton Downey, Jr. episode? He was on there with Rick Sullivan...**

**CP:** Sometime in 1989, Morton Downey did a show dedicated to horror films. He had Michael Berryman, Rick Sullivan, Tony Timpone, and someone no one had heard of who claimed to be a slasher movie director. He was a ringer, and not a convincing one. He had a list of credits that were all bogus. You could see Rick Sullivan smirking—he knew immediately that this guy was a plant to make the horror fans look like nuts. Rick gave a thoughtful explanation of why he liked horror movies and he talked about *Gore Gazette*. Michael Berryman was presented as the star of *The Hills Have Eyes*, and he was definitely lucid and well spoken. But for some reason, Tony—I don't know what he was thinking—made these statements that parents should let their kids watch whatever they want, at any age, and Morton Downey, Jr. just let him have it. As the show was about to cut to a commercial, Downey put his arm around Tony and said, "The moral of this story is, 'Don't let your kids take a bath with Uncle Barney here.' We'll be back after this commercial!" Paul and I couldn't stop laughing. When we met Tony, we had to bite our tongues. All the way up on the elevator Mike kept saying, "I want a job at *Fangoria*! Don't say anything about Uncle Barney!" [laughs] Anyway, that show set off a whole chain of unpleasant events in the fanzine community.

**JS: What happened?**

**CP:** The next issue of the *Gore Gazette* came out a few weeks later, and Rick Sullivan really ripped into Tony. He made a couple of good points, but then he resorted to insults and name calling. Shortly after that, Mike wanted to do an article for *Gorezone* about fanzines. He contacted all of the major fanzines that were around at the time, with two exceptions: *Psychotronic Video* and *Gore Gazette*. Mike sent out questionnaires to all of the zine editors, including Michael Weldon, who never responded for whatever reason. Maybe he didn't get it, or he forgot, who knows, but he didn't respond. However, Mike didn't send a questionnaire to the *Gore Gazette* because Tony wanted no mention of Rick Sullivan in the magazine. Frankly, after all the crap Rick wrote about Tony and the magazine, I would've done the same thing had I been in Tony's shoes. So Mike purposely omitted *Gore Gazette* from the article, and Rick called him out on it. "You've got until the next issue to come forward and explain yourself," Rick said. Mike never did, so Rick spent those last few years of *Gore Gazette*'s run ripping apart Mike, Tony, and anyone else connected to *Fangoria*. It was really unpleasant for a lot of us who were friends with Mike and Tony, but who also read *Gore Gazette*. Rick took no prisoners. He just slashed and burned.

**JS: I wrote to Michael Weldon a few times about this book, but he hasn't responded. What did you think of *Psychotronic*?**

**CP:** *Psychotronic* was one of the big influences on me, moreso than a lot of fanzines. I was unfamiliar with the *Psychotronic* newsletter from 1980, which was a weekly guide to movies that were being shown on TV in the New York area. I've actually never seen an issue of that. I first learned of Michael Weldon with the *Psychotronic Encyclopedia of Film*. I read about it in *Fangoria*, but it was probably about a year before I got the book, and it immediately became the most important film book in my collection. When Weldon started doing his "Psychotronic" column in *High Times* magazine, I'd pick it every month just to read the column. We sent him a copy of *Temple of Schlock* and he gave us a write-up in *High Times* that got brought us a lot of subscribers.

**JS: Why did *Temple of Schlock* come to an end?**

**CP:** We knocked out an issue a month for fifteen months, from December 1987 to February 1989. Some of them were eight or ten pages, but once we went to digest size, just as many were twelve or sixteen pages. Paul really liked doing sixteen pagers. I would lean toward twelve page issues,

TEMPLE OF SCHLOCK
Paul V. DeCi[illegible]e
409 Hixson Ave.
Syracuse, N.Y. 13206

SUBSCRIPTIONS: $4.50 for 6 issues. $1 each over seas. Free in trade for your fanzine. Letters and contributions are always welcome.

Faster,
PUSSYCAT!
KILL! KILL!
The SWEETEST KITTENS Have The SHARPEST CLAWS!


FASTER PUSSYCAT! KILL! KILL! (Meyer; 1986S) Reviewed by Chris Poggiali

Russ Meyer's classic has finally found its way into the pages of TOS! Yeah yeah, everyone knows this film is a) John Waters' all-time favorite movie and b) the inspiration for a lousy heavy metal band named Faster Pussycat, but is it really that incredible? It's something else, that's for sure.

Three crazy go-go girls have nothing better to do than race around the desert in their Porsches and read off laughably bad lines of "cool" dialogue. Of course, two of the three ruffian women drive convertibles, so you know right off the bat that they're not really driving because the clouds behind them are prefectly still. Anyway, they race this goofy hotshot and run him off the track, where the leader of the girls (Tura Satana) breaks his back and kills him. The two other girls stand in the background and cheer on their leather-clad, man-beating leader. Haji plays the Mexican go-go girl, and I could understand about every fifth word out of her mouth. Lori Williams is the third girl, a blonde in tight clothing who's just out for "kicks." This is a real motley assortment—Tura yells, screams, and karate chops everyone while Haji scowls and mutters and Lori drinks herself into a stupor.

The chicks grab the dead racer's girlfriend, drug her, and take off to "lose her" somewhere. At a gas station they discover that there's a rich old man living out in the desert with his two sons. This sparks the interest of Tura, who decides to hit the old timer's shack and grab the loot. First off, the old guy is a lecherous kook in a wheelchair who has a lot of money floating around around his ranch because of an insurance deal. One of his sons is a big, strong idiot called Vegetable. The other

but his were always sixteen, and once I went to college he did most of the typing, layout, correspondence, photocopying and mailing himself for five or six of those issues in a row, sixteen pagers, while he was still a junior in high school and writing for the school newspaper, acting in theater productions, working part-time at the Shoppingtown movie theater, studying for the SAT, etc. He burned himself out. I'd come home on weekends maybe once or twice a month, we'd talk on the phone, and I would send him my reviews and any ads and other graphics I could turn up, but I couldn't do much more when I was in Buffalo and he was in Syracuse. He told me in March of '89 that he needed a break, so when the semester ended for me I did issues 17 and 18, and he came back and did 19 in August. Halfway through that issue, I told him that I was sick of doing *Temple of Schlock* and I wanted to go off and start a zine called *Cormania*. I was really only kidding—I mean, I thought it would be a cool idea, but I didn't really want to be the one to do it. But I told him, "I think there should be a fanzine dedicated to Roger Corman, and I think I'm going to do it." Paul got really pissed We were in New York on the subway when I told him this, and he didn't talk to me for the rest of the day. We were hanging around with Mike Gingold later, I think the three of us went to the Quad to see *Carnival of Souls* and Mike had no idea what was going on between us—we covered it well. Anyway, Paul sensed that I was going to stick him with *Temple of Schlock*, so he bailed out first. I continued it for as long as I could, five or six more issues. What really pissed me off is that Paul didn't

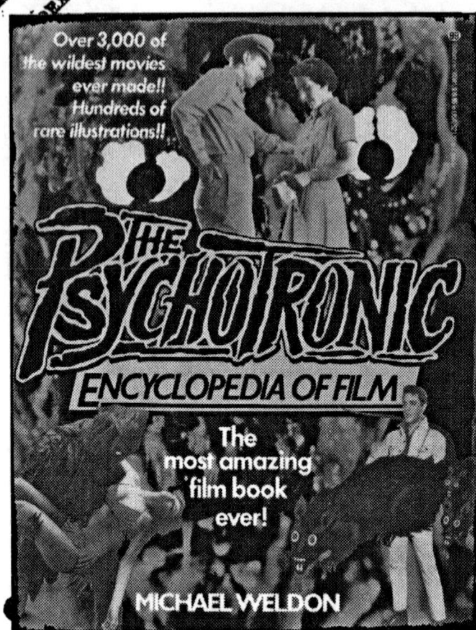

Over 3,000 of the wildest movies ever made!! Hundreds of rare illustrations!!
THE PSYCHOTRONIC ENCYCLOPEDIA OF FILM
The most amazing film book ever!
MICHAEL WELDON

THE SEMINAL *PSYCHOTRONIC ENCYCLOPEDIA.*

give me all of the subscriber information. A couple of people had sent him money, and he never bothered to write down their names and addresses. He certainly didn't give me the money. I started putting together the next issue, and it took longer than it should have. The next thing I know, I get this issue of *Factsheet 5*, and we're in the hall of shame. A couple of people had rightfully complained. They sent us money, and they never heard from us. So I got really upset and attacked Paul in the pages of *Temple of Schlock*. I wrote something nasty about *Factsheet 5* also, which was unfortunate because we'd had a good relationship with them up to that point. So I was getting soured on the whole thing.

**JS: How many more issues did you do after Paul left?**

**CP:** Five. I started a sixth issue but that never went beyond the cover and a couple of reviews.

**JS: *Temple of Schlock* was never distributed to the newsstands.**

**CP:** I really had no interest in that. I was happy for people like Charlie Kilgore and Tim Lucas and Steve Puchalski when they all got to that level, but it was never for me. To get to that level, you have to deal with advertisers, distributors, postal rates… After a while, I could barely deal with the staff at Kinko's! My heart wasn't in it. Now that I'm doing a blog, I'm tickled to death because I don't have to worry about any of that. I don't advertise on my blog because I don't need to. It's a hobby, not a source of income. I don't even like accepting review copies—I don't want to feel like I owe somebody a review, and I really don't want to review the same movie that forty-eight other blogs and magazines are reviewing. I'd rather give people something that they can't find anyplace else, even if it's something as simple as a cool newspaper ad or a scan of a rare soundtrack LP or one-sheet.

**JS: From being a young kid doing a fanzine to the present day, you've obviously stuck with it. My question for you is, why?**

**CP:** Well, I stopped *Temple of Schlock* when I was twenty-one or twenty-two, and brought it back as a blog when I was thirty-seven, so for a few years in between I didn't stick with it. I guess you could say it stuck

May,1988 "Has anyone ever seen this place? How do we know it's real?" Bog Schlocksto #7

Write to us-- if you dare! $3 for **6 issues** to: Paul DeCirce,409 Hixson Ave,Syracuse,N.Y. 13206

CYNTHIA'S GOT A GRAVE PROBLEM!
13 years ago, something terrifying almost killed her.
Now it's come back to finish the job.
BAD DREAMS


BAD DREAMS(20'th Century Fox,1988).Reviewed by Paul DeCirce.

It seems as if the modern horror movie, on a whole, is finally beginning to improve. Honestly, I think our brains are still sizzling from the meaningless FRIDAY THE 13'TH PART 6, JASON LIVES. I think genre-makers are beginning to understand that horror/gore lovers sometimes want to see both, not just one or the other. In the past, it's always been heavy **doses** of gore(MAKE THEM DIE SLOWLY[TOS#5] and DAWN OF THE MUMMY[TOS#6]) or overmilked doses of blood-less tripe(THE CHANGELING, PUFF THE MAGIC DRAGON)

BAD DREAMS puts an end to that. The mis-leading t.v. ads, that compare BAD DREAMS Harris to Jason, Leatherface and Freddie, don't do it justice. In the aspect of the "villain," Harris (played by the excellent Richard Lynch) outranks both Jason, Freddie, And L.F. Jason is an idiot who serves no other purpose than to rob snot-nosed-Fangoria-worshipping 12 year olds of $29.95 for a video. Freddie is the almighty blowhard of a revenge seeker, and Leatherface is **Gunnar** Hansen, the worst put-down of 'em all. Harris is none of these. He has a different outlook on life. He wants his soul to rest, thats all. In someone else's eyes, Harris wouldn't be evil at all.

See, our story starts in the mid-seventies (you know, the time also known as culture-hibernation thanks to disco, Elton John, and Dance Fever?), where Harris has rounded up some leftover hippies and brought them to a "Unity House," where they all commit a group **suicide,** Jennifer Rubin (the druggie from NIGHTMARE ON ELM ST.3), how-ever, survived. Now, 13 years later she comes out of her coma, only to find a very much changed world. She's committed to a happy house, which isn't really too good, because 1)she's not crazy, and 2)Harris (who **burned** up) has come back

page whun

with me. I worked a lot of jobs, mostly in publishing and libraries, got a Masters degree, and wrote about a dozen movie screenplays, none of which were produced. I just turned in a treatment for a horror film a couple of months ago, and worked on a Christian film last month. It was a rewrite job—my name's not going to be on it or anything. That was strictly for cash. I wrote a couple of scripts with William Grefé. I co-wrote a horror script called *Bleed* that Darin Scott, the producer of *Menace II Society* and *Tales from the Hood*, wanted to do for a long time.

**JS: When was this?**

**CP:** Darin optioned it in 2005, and tried for four years to set it up at studios. The last time we spoke, which was earlier this year, he said he still wants to make *Bleed* because he loves the script so much. But to answer your question about *Temple of Schlock*, I brought it back because I thought it could be revived cheaply and easily. I was not happy with the way it went out. I owed people money, and I thought if I brought it back as a blog, I could make it up to them. I still have a list of everybody who is still owed money. It's not a long list, and we're not talking about a lot of money, but the fact is we took it and didn't deliver the product. For a lot of people, it's only $2.75. I think there was one guy in Sweden who's still owed eight or nine dollars. But I've always had them in mind. Once I started writing for

*Fangoria* and *Shock Cinema*, I had in mind that I could bring back *Temple of Schlock*, either as a newsletter or as a one-shot, to settle my debts. When I realized that I could do it as a blog, I decided to go that route. I've been doing it for four years now, and I love it.

**JS: You mentioned that you've been scanning all of the pages of *Temple of Schlock*...**

**CP:** Yes, I'm compiling a book of all of the issues of *Temple of Schlock*. I'm scanning the pages and putting them together with some new material from Paul as well as the Keeper of the Pit, Kris Gilpin, Tim Ferrante, Don Guarisco and a few other writers. I wanted it out by the twenty-fifth anniversary of our first issue, but that date has come and gone already.

**JS: What is it like to look back at those old issues?**

**CP:** I'm a different person now than I was twenty-two years ago, but in many ways, I'm the same person. When I go back and read through things, sections of the reviews read exactly the same way—I'm concerned about the release dates and the distributors. In other ways, the reviews are completely different. I'm incredibly bored by plot synopsis. It kills me. That's the one thing that prevents me from writing more reviews. The only thing worse than reading a plot synopsis is writing it...

Sanctum series and, most importantly, an appreciation of l
maverick "Wild" Bill Wellman. Highly recommended! No trad
videos music/prints letters/submissions wanted. Price:$4.25. Su
for 6 issues. PhanMedia, P.O. Box 216, Ocean Grove, NJ 07756
standard/polished/ED)

**Psychotronic Video**

#26. Michael Weldon's publication remains the prototype fc
exploitation film fanatics. This issue boasts interviews with fe
pioneer Doris Wishman and a no-holds barred talk with Gregory
who, under various pseudonyms, has appeared in everything fr
tional films for Unicef to raunchy hardcore. Also included are
the schlockmeister Ormond family and of Ed "Kookie" Byrnes.
*Psychotronic* excels with its video reviews of the demented, the
the wonderful along with comprehensive obituaries of en
personalities, both famous and obscure. Still setting the standard
reviews zines books comics videos music/prints letters/submis
ed. Price:$5. Subs:$28 for 6 issues. Michael Weldon, 33
Narrowsburg, NY 12764-6126 (98 pages/standard/polished/E

**Shock Cinema**

***Guide to cult movies, arthouse oddities, and driv***

#11. Delightfully irreverent and eclectic reviews of cinema ob
range from the reflexive art fare of Robbe-Grillet's unfathom
*Europa Express* to the hopelessly dated '60s cult-drug film C
a French Jerry Lewis comedy (the mind boggles!) that than
made it to our shores, along with the usual assortment of Hon
and gore flicks. Moreover, there's an incisive article on so-call
dent films" that are really just another variation on Hollywooc
a capsule survey of ten truly offbeat foreign films that will pr
find their way to your local video store. Publisher Steve
commentary is idiosyncratic and intensely personal, bu
states, "If you're pissed off by my opinions, get y
magazine." Loves trading/reviews zines videos/prints
Subs:$12 for 3 issues. Steve Puchalski, P.O. Box 518
Station, New York, NY 10009 — Email: shockcin@ao
http://members.aol.com/shockcin/index.html (44 pages/st

**Spectrum**

#11, September '97. A glossy publication with a decide
proclaims itself the magazine of television, film, and
publicizes the recent release of *Kull the Conqueror* wit
star Kevin Sorbo and a historical overview of the cha
Howard scholar Charles Hoffman. There's also a det
noted comic book artist Barry Windsor-Smith in w
inherent superiority of film to comics. *Xena* is repre
summary of her second season episodes. No trades/re
letters. Price:$4.95. Subs:$25 for 4 issues. Craig Mille
tions, 1912 E. Timberview Ln., Arlington, TX
70473.2254@compuserve.com (40 pages/offset/standa

**Video Confidential**

***Specializing in U.S., European & Asian***

#37, Fall '97. VC takes a handful of the latest cult v
them a good shakedown. *Bordello* sounds like one
movies that is hard to forget, mixing Western come
violence, and sex. There's "chicken abuse," family s
daughters, and boyfriends who can't decide whether to ra
just marry them. This issue also takes on Jayne Mansfiel
*Primitive Love*, the rare *Bruce Lee: Lost Interview*, and a cou
releases from '76. No trades/reviews books videos/subm
Price:$2. Subs:$7 for 6 issues. Carl Morano, Morano Mo
8822 Second Ave., N. Bergen, NJ 07047-5280 — Emai
aol.com — Web site: http://www.digital-nation.com (4 pa
dard/DTPed/CWB)

**Wrapped in Plastic**

#31, October '97. A very polished magazine that is an al

TAKEN FROM *FACTSHEET 5* NUMBER 63 (MARCH 1998).

# Chapter Thirty-Four

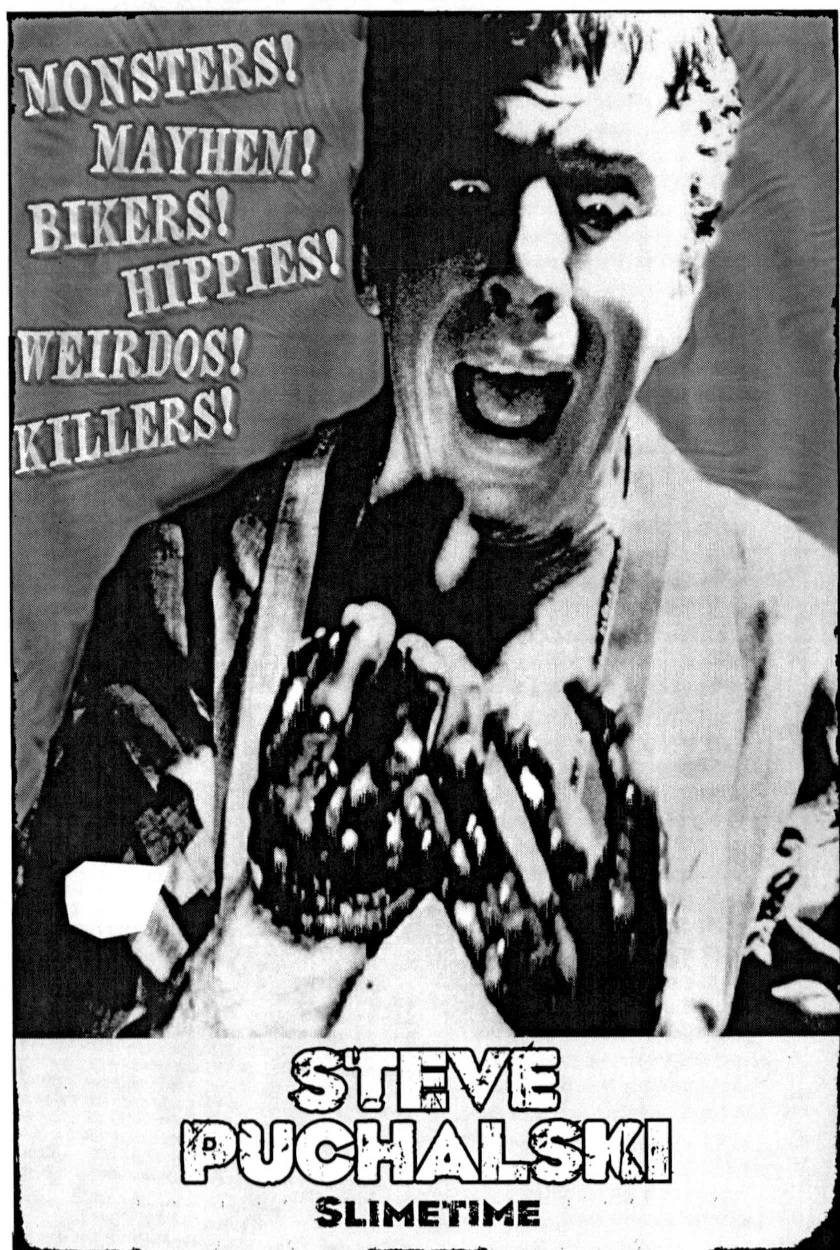

When I saw a copy of *Shock Cinema* on the shelves of a chain bookstore near my house in 1994, I couldn't believe my eyes. I'd been reading the zine since the third issue, but I'd never seen it for sale at a place like this before. At first, I figured that there had been a distribution glitch—that somehow a box of the things had ended up at the local Borders and they'd decided to sell them rather than ship them back to the printer. I bought the magazine and added it to my collection, curious as to whether I'd see it on the stands again.

Some months later, while casually browsing at Tower Records, I did another double take. There it was again, triumphantly sharing the shelf space with a handful of mainstream mags—its crude yellow cover stuck out like a sore thumb. I stood there with a devilish grin on my face. I knew that times were changing.

*Shock Cinema* is the brainchild of one Steven Puchalski. A few years earlier, he had made major waves with *Slimetime*, a zine that I'd heard a lot about but rarely had the opportunity to read. As I began my long-lasting love affair with *SC*, two things rang out loud and clear: (1) this Puchalski guy knew his shit, and (2) his reviews were hilarious as hell. And man… the movies he reviewed! Puchalski had a knack for tracking down some of the rarest films on the planet. With his guidance, my video library seemed to triple overnight.

Seeing that issue of *SC* on a major newsstand was a major revelation to me. Puchalski had somehow managed to infiltrate the system without changing one of his words. He had stealthily slithered through the cracks, staking his claim on a land that was almost overwhelmingly populated by the likes of *Premiere* and *Entertainment Weekly.* All these years later, I still get a charge out of walking up to the counter with the newest issue of *Shock Cinema* in my hands.

It was a no-brainer that should I interview Steve Puchalski for this book, and so interview him I did. The following conversation took place in the Summer of 2012. We made our introductions and chatted for a bit. And before long, we were wading knee-deep in a all things shocking and slimy…

The following interview was conducted via telephone on July 27, 2012.

---

**STEVEN PUCHALSKI:** I've been into film for a long time, starting from the age of twelve or thirteen. At first, it was really just the mainstream stuff that made it to central New York theaters, but I saw everything possible—the good, the bad, whatever was playing. Over time, I developed increasingly eclectic tastes and when I attended college, I ran the University Union Cinemas film program.

**JOHN SZPUNAR: Where was that?**

# Steve Puchalski

## Slimetime

SLIMETIME PRESENTS
SHOCK CINEMA
No. 1
$2 /
FILMS AND VIDEOS WITH TEETH!
Dennis Hopper
THE LAST MOVIE
NIGHT OF THE LEPUS
Herzog · Roeg · Jodorowsky
Rudy Ray Moore · Godzilla
Hippies · Vampires · Bikers
Cult Movies · Weird Music
Mindless Gore · And More

*SHOCK CINEMA* NUMBER 1.

**SP:** Syracuse University. I did all the programming for that organization. At the time, it was the largest 16mm college film series in the country. And by my senior year, we were showing over 300 different films a year.

**JS: What kind of films were you screening?**

**SP:** We showed all of the mainstream hits, but we also programmed a lot of classic films, as well as loads of cult and obscure arthouse fare—everything from Corman, Tarkovsky and Fassbinder, to Kenneth Anger and Nic Roeg. We also ran weekly midnight movies, plus all-night animation marathons. It gave me an opportunity to see a wide array of films on the big screen and with an audience for the first time, and expanded my interest in exploitation, underground and all-around fringe cinema. It was a real learning experience.

**JS: Where were you renting the prints from?**

**SP:** We rented them from non-theatrical distributors from all around the country. In the late seventies, 16mm film rentals was a huge business, with companies spread across the US.

**JS: Did you just have to pay a flat rental fee, or did you have to divvy up royalties?**

**SP:** It varied. The more obscure stuff was usually a flat rental—anywhere from $75 to several hundred bucks. For any new releases, the distributor would get a percentage of your box-office, similar to a theatrical distribution set-up. You'd pay up to $600 versus sixty per cent—whichever was higher. We had a pretty impressive operation, with screenings six nights a week, and at least ten different films every week. In addition to running the actual film showings and selling tickets, we also had to publicize the screenings—printing posters and writing reviews of our upcoming movies. I ended up penning a lot of those reviews myself, and I tried to make them as weird and funny and entertaining as possible. That basically inspired the style of film criticism that later went into *Slimetime* and *Shock Cinema*.

**JS: Was the film series well attended?**

**SP:** Oh, yeah. This was before cable TV was installed in the dorms, and a few years before the VHS boom. So U.U. Cinemas was one of the primary entertainment venues on campus. The theater held 400 people and we'd often sell out several shows a night. We once showed a softcore-X movie—Bill Osco's *Alice in Wonderland*—and even though a blizzard was dumping

two feet of snow on the area, we had a line of students stretched across campus, patiently waiting in the freezing cold to buy tickets.

**JS: What were the theaters in Syracuse like?**

**SP:** Most of the theaters were owned by one big corporate chain, so they were strictly mainstream. There were a handful of drive-ins still open, and that's where you'd have to go for the latest exploitation, plus in the middle of downtown Syracuse there was one gorgeous old theatre, the Loew's. As a little kid, I saw *Yellow Submarine* and the Adam West *Batman* movie there, but by the seventies, it became the sole venue for blaxploitation. There was also one lone arthouse theater, about ten miles outside of town, but if they got one really popular foreign film, they'd hold it over for months on end. So the only way to see a lot of the smaller releases was to head down to New York City, which I started doing on a regular basis once I was in college. I'd book a room at a seedy, old Times Square hotel—in those days, they were pretty fuckin' cheap and my favorite was the long-defunct Hotel Seymour on W. 45th—then see eight to ten films in forty-eight hours. I'd hit Times Square, the artsy theatres around Central Park South, and ultimately wind up in the Village for a midnight show of something like *Forbidden Zone* or *Basket Case*. There was nothing like that in Syracuse.

TRISTER KEANE'S
SLIMETIME
A GUIDE TO SLEAZY, MINDLESS ENTERTAINMENT.
Number One, October 1986 "All the Shit That's Shat to Shoot."

SLIMETIME NUMBER 1.

**JS: A lot of people kind of forget that before the age of video, if you didn't see a film theatrically, you might never see the thing again.**

**SP:** That's precisely why I used to buy those cheap movie novelizations when I was a young teenager. If you missed a film in the theater—or couldn't get in, because it was R-rated—you could read the shitty novelization instead.

**JS: How did *Slimetime* get started?**

**SP:** When I first started making my own zines in the mid-eighties, I wasn't really aware of the other film zines. After college, I happened to be working at a place that had an accessible copy machine, so I initially experimented with different types of zines. I did a couple different

RECORDED & INDEXED

DRAFT

"WE SLEAZE TO PLEASE."

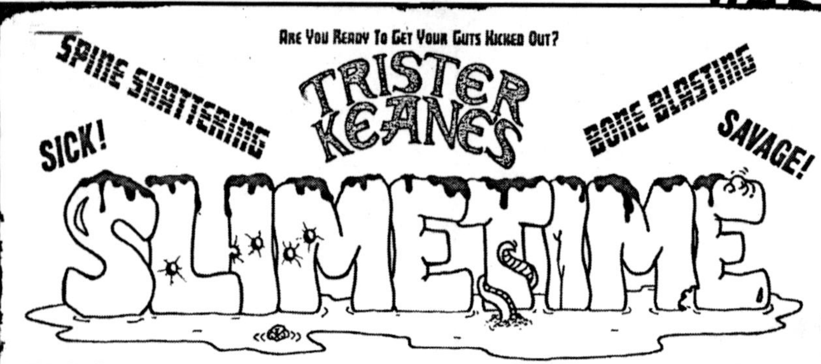

ARE YOU READY TO GET YOUR GUTS KICKED OUT?
SPINE SHATTERING
SICK!
TRISTER KEANE'S
BONE BLASTING
SAVAGE!
SLIMETIME


NUMBER FOUR, FEBRUARY 1987 "WE SLEAZE TO PLEASE."

It's snowing outside, cars are doing graceless pirouettes in the street, and a chilly forecast tells me that it's the perfect time to plop down at my typewriter and begin "SLIMETIME #4". Of course, I could always switch on the Christian Broadcasting Network and watch some hollow-headed born-again, slobbering about The Almighty Dollar (probably the most terrifying use of television I have ever seen)...But enough of my incoherent ramblings. Onto some incoherent film reviews, because we've got lots of oddities for this edition. Not much on the new release front (there was "The Kindred" and "Deadtime Stories", but I'm not gonna toss away $4.75 on them, since they'll probably hit the video stores in two months), but we do have a bunch of giant monsters, outer space nasties, wacky animation, unintentional laughs, and more morally objectionable violence than you can blast a double-barreled shotgun at...Remember to keep those cards and letters coming , folks, especially if you have fun suggestions for future issues, or opinions on any recent sleaze-flicks (not that we'll ever run out of trashy movies, that is). Once again, the address is SLIMETIME c/o S. Puchalski, 1108 East Genesee St. #103, Syracuse, NY 13210...

LAST HOUSE ON THE LEFT (1972):"It rests on 13 acres of earth over the very center of Hell" -ad line. ...We're starting out this issue with a real classic. And a vile one it is, too...Directed by first-timer Wes Craven and produced by Sean Cunningham (Mr. "Friday the 13th"); now that Wes is hotshit after "Nightmare on Elm St.", you can see how grimy he can get when he sets his mind to it. "Based on a true story", a pair of pretty teenagers, Mari and Phyllis, decide to go into town for a concert. But first, they try to score some grass, and fall prey to a quartet of wise-cracking geeks. City-cousins to the Texas Chainsaw Clan, they're heroin-addicted, child-molesting, nun-killing psychopaths who're wanted by every cop in the state. So, instead of an innocent night on the town, Mari and Phyllis get locked in the trunk of a car, taken out to the country, and are physically and mentally tortured by the shrieking sadists. They are forced to piss their pants, strip, beg, and finally, when they try to escape, they're carved up or blown away. But when the psycho's limo breaks down, they wind up at the doorstep of Mari's middle-class Mom and Pop, who end up taking revenge (shades of Wes' next feature, "The Hills Have Eyes"). Mom chews off one guy's dick during a blow job and spits it in the lake, while Dad takes on the leader with a chainsaw in the living room...Though amateurish (lots of portentous music, and unnecessary comic relief from two bone-headed sheriffs), it's still remarkably unsettling, and considering it was made 15 years ago, it's still up to the raunchiness of today's slasher

literary zines and a few collage-artwork digests—they were often viciously anti-Ronald Reagan. I'd test out whatever came to mind, then hand them out to friends and around campus. The one cult-film zine that I became aware of during my visits to New York City was Rick Sullivan's hilarious *Gore Gazette*. I absolutely loved it, and decided to put my own spin on the idea. But where Rick primarily reviewed recent Times Square releases, I delved into a wider range of schlock—old and new video releases, Late Show TV fodder, whatever low budget crap I could dredge up. This was long before the internet or the IMDb, of course, and these types of films were generally ignored by mainstream film publications. So I basically took the gonzo film criticism I'd been doing for the university film series, laid it out in an eight- to ten-page newsletter format and printed it up on green paper. Most importantly, if a film stunk, I certainly wasn't afraid to call it a rancid chunk of shit. And that was *Slimetime*.

**JS: What was the original print run for *Slimetime*?**

**SP:** The first *Slimetime*—and I think I even mentioned this in the first issue—could've easily been a one time thing, so there weren't many printed. Whether I'd continue doing it on a regular basis was dependent on the reaction I got from assorted readers and friends. Luckily, it was pretty positive... The first issue was maybe 300 copies tops. I ended up publishing a total of twenty-seven issues from 1986 to 1989. Near the end, I was printing around 750 each.

**JS: You were originally distributing locally...**

**SP:** I handed out the first issues for free at the film showings around Syracuse University. There were also a few local video stores where I would trade copies of the newsletter for free rentals. They'd put out a stack and sell them, or simply give 'em away. I really didn't think about making a profit—it was all about the love of these strange films and amusing a few similarly minded movie fans. After an issue or two, I started sending a bunch of copies to friends in New York City, and they'd take it around to record stores and See Hear, the East Village fanzine shop. It was slow for the first few months, but after word of mouth started to spread—particularly after *Slimetime* began popping up in Manhattan—I found myself getting more and more paid orders (as well as the occasional joint from a fan), a reporter from the city newspaper contacted me about doing an article on myself and *Slimetime* (it must've been an extremely slow day for news), plus I started receiving assorted film-zines and realized that there was this whole other subculture out there. I initially thought it was just the *Gore Gazette*, and that was it. I wasn't even aware of *Sleazoid Express* or all of the other homemade zines. But once I discovered that more and more people were reading *Slimetime* and I started to get letters from around the world, I quickly delved deeper into the zine scene.

**JS: What zines made an impact on you?**

**SP:** A lot of the early film zines that I encountered primarily focused

RECORDED & INDEXED

DRAFT

on horror and gore, but I'm personally more interested in B-movies, exploitation and cult films. So I was drawn to the more esoteric ones—Cecil Doyle's *Subhuman*, Dan Taylor's *Exploitation Retrospect* and, later on, Chris Poggiali's *Temple of Schlock*. Plus I really enjoyed a lot of the overseas zines, like *Crimson Celluloid*. Best of all, *Slimetime* led to my first paid writing assignments, courtesy of Stefan Jaworzyn from *Shock Xpress*. He contacted me out of the blue. He'd been reviewing and plugging *Slimetime* in *Shock Xpress*, and asked if I'd like to write for 'em. Of course, I jumped at the opportunity and not only reviewed several films for Stefan, but also contributed three feature articles—on blaxploitation, biker movies and LSD flicks... I was with friends when I received an envelope in the mail after my first article was printed. There was a crisp 100 dollar bill inside and I was like, "I just got $100 in cash for writing about Fred Williamson movies? That is damned cool [laughs]!"

**JS: You told me that you've been friends with Rick Sullivan off and on. How did you meet him?**

**SP:** From my trips to New York City. At the time, Rick was running the *Gore Gazette* film series at the Dive. I'd grab a few friends and we'd go see some sleazy film, pick up the latest *Gore Gazette*, and drink excessively. The first time I actually had contact with Rick was through the mail, though. Our college film series was preparing an all-night drive-in festival—*Hollywood Boulevard*, *Caged Heat*, *Three the Hard Way*—and I wrote Rick about renting some of the coming attractions that he showed at the Dive. He owned these huge reels of old horror and exploitation trailers, and they were perfect to run in between our features. He seemed cool with the idea, so I came down to NYC for one of his screenings. I was wandering around this dark, dank barroom. "Does anybody know where Rick is?" Someone pointed to a guy fiddling with a 16mm projector in the back. I walked up and asked, "Are you Rick Sullivan?" He replied, "No," not even bothering to look up from his work. "Well, I'd like to make him some money. I'm Steve Puchalski. I wanted to rent some of his movies." He spun around and said, "Hi, I'm Rick." Not surprisingly, he didn't want to be bothered by yet another idiotic, drunk-ass fanboy. We've been acquaintances ever since, and I even gave him an open offer to pen a column for *Shock Cinema*, after *Gore Gazette* went belly-up—whatever topics he chose, and even using a pseudonym, if he'd prefer. I really miss his acerbic writing, but it's always good to get a Christmas card from Rick and know that he and his family are doing well.

**JS: Did you have any kind of relationship with Bill Landis?**

**SP:** Not really. I talked to Bill on the phone a few times after we moved out to New Jersey. He somehow got hold of my number—he'd heard I'd recently relocated to Jersey City. He asked all about my neighborhood, or if we had mutual friends, but there was very little overlap. He seemed like a cool guy, but unfortunately, we never got to meet in person.

**JS: How did you go about selecting the contributing writers for *Slimetime*?**

**SP:** *Slimetime*'s primary contributors—Tavis Riker, Brian J. Edwards and Steve Shapiro—were longtime friends from my college days. We'd all written past reviews for the college film series and, more importantly, we all loved to get drunk and stoned and watch weird movies. I knew their various writing styles, they added a little more diversity to the zine—so it wasn't just me writing the whole damned thing—plus they could be really, really, funny. I figured that if I got a laugh out of their writing, everybody else would.

**JS: Didn't you work for Kim's Video for a time?**

**SP:** That's right. For five years, from 1990 to 1995. I moved to New York City in 1990—just after the demise of *Slimetime* and its rebirth as *Shock Cinema*—and my first job there was at Kim's Video in the East Village, at their long-defunct second-floor location on the corner of 2nd Avenue and St. Mark's. At the time, it was one of the premiere cult video stores in the city. Strangely enough, I owe my first promotion—only a couple weeks into the job—to Todd Phillips, the future director of *The Hangover*. Todd worked the early morning shift and had to open the store at 8 AM, but was promptly fired after he was caught sleeping on the counter by the store's owner, Mr. Kim. When I arrived for my shift a couple hours later, Kim tossed me Todd's keys and told me that I was now an assistant manager. Within a year, I became the buyer for that store, with Kim basically giving me carte blanche. As long as I stayed within my budget and made a solid profit, he didn't care what the hell I bought or where I bought it from. We stocked loads of gray market bootlegs, the latest Hong Kong releases straight from Chinatown, DIY underground efforts purchased from local filmmakers—just about anything you could imagine, and film fans travelled from all over the city to rent movies from Kim's. If a rare film wasn't available anywhere else, they knew that we might just have a copy of it.

**JS: Why did *Slimetime* cease publication?**

**SP:** It was a case of making the best out of a really horrible situation. While

# STEVE PUCHALSKI

## SLIMETIME

RECORDED & INDEXED

DRAFT

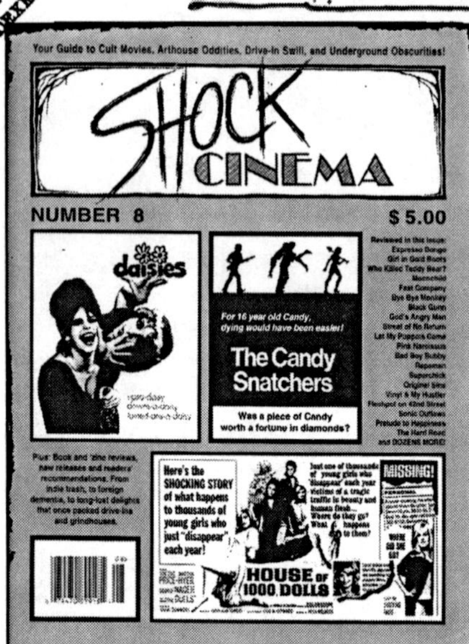


I was doing *Slimetime*, a friend of mine had a... breakdown, to put it mildly. He's been in prison since 1990 for second degree murder. But before that, he'd been a very close friend within our group. I knew the guy for over a decade. During his breakdown, he did a lot of bizarre things, one of which was trying to get me fired from my day job by ratting me out to my bosses—since I was photocopying *Slimetime* at my workplace. He didn't succeed though, because it turned out that everyone at my job used the copy machines for their own off-duty purposes. Even my superiors. So I just got a slap on the wrists. He, unfortunately, soon went off the deep end, brought a shotgun to his workplace and killed one of his bosses. And with so much upheaval in my life, I felt it was time to put *Slimetime* to rest. After a few months passed, I began to get that writing itch again though. But this time around I'd upgrade to a magazine format, invest some of my own savings—printing the first issue cost more than a month's rent, and I didn't even know if the thing would sell—and give it my best shot. Luckily, I happened to know a local printer who gave me a great price because I'd sent them a lot of business over the years. I changed the title to *Shock Cinema*, since *Slimetime* sounded a bit juvenile and lightweight—plus, if successful, I wanted the magazine to grow in a more serious direction. *Shock Cinema* was born out of the real-life chaos that had killed *Slimetime*.

**JS: I was completely shocked when I found issue number 6 at my local Borders.**

**SP:** *Shock Cinema*'s early distribution grew quickly and organically. I produced the first two issues in Syracuse, there were only 500 copies of each, and my first big distribution deal was with Tower. Tower Books was amazing when it came to embracing zines of every kind, and I think that later chains like Borders were simply emulating their strategy. Thanks to Tower, *Shock Cinema* was now available in stores across the nation for the first time. When it came to our early distribution, it was mostly due to a lot of hard work. I spent a lot of time on research, queried other publishers

on how they got their zines into various places, and sent copies of every new issue to potential distributors. Eventually, I got *Shock Cinema* into more and more stores. The Borders chain used a periodical distributor called Desert Moon, who got a huge number of zines into mainstream outlets back in the early nineties (unfortunately, they also went bankrupt years later and ripped-off those same zine publishers). That was probably around issue 4 or 5. By issue 6, *Shock Cinema*'s print run was over 3,000 copies and steadily growing.

SHOCK CINEMA
No. 2
$2 / $3(w/postage) $4(overseas)
The Medical Jungle doctors dont talk about!
OPENS THE DOOR TO SIGHTS YOU'VE NEVER SEEN BEFORE
Recommended FOR ADULTS
SHOCK CORRIDOR
More pages!
More reviews!
More trash!
SHOCK! SHOCK! SHOCK!
From Arthouses to Grindhouses
Dennis Hopper Vincent Price
Jim Brown Charles Bukowski
CULT FILMS and SCHLOCK CULTURE!

**JS: Were you able to gauge the reaction of a more mainstream audience?**

**SP:** The fact that distributors were requesting larger and larger draws with each issue convinced me that I must be on the right track, and I've never been concerned about tailoring the magazine towards a more mainstream audience. I was simply publishing the type of film magazine that I would want to read. And nowadays, I probably cover even more obscure movies than in the early issues of *Shock Cinema*. Besides, outside of occasionally running into fans of the mag at Kim's Video, I didn't have that much direct contact with my readers; that is, until issue number 8 in '96, when we decided to get a dealers table at a local convention to help promote the magazine. It was only then that I met a lot of longtime readers and got an inkling of the mag's wide appeal. I was a little taken aback, to be honest, but I also knew I should just continue going with my gut instinct.

**JS: When did people start sending you things to review?**

**SP:** Right off the bat. And particularly after *Shock Cinema* started up. Sometimes it would be homemade efforts from underground filmmakers, occasionally readers would send me rare titles from their own private collection, plus video distributors were always sending me their stuff—sometimes legit, more often bootleg. In fact, Mike Vraney was not only one of our earliest advertisers—purchasing an ad in issue number 2 for his brand new mail order business, Something Weird Video—but also sent me a bunch of VHS tapes out of the blue. I had no idea who he was at the time, but I checked out his tapes and immediately knew he had excellent taste in schlock. It wasn't until *Shock Cinema* upgraded a little bit, got a

# STEVE PUCHALSKI

## SLIMETIME

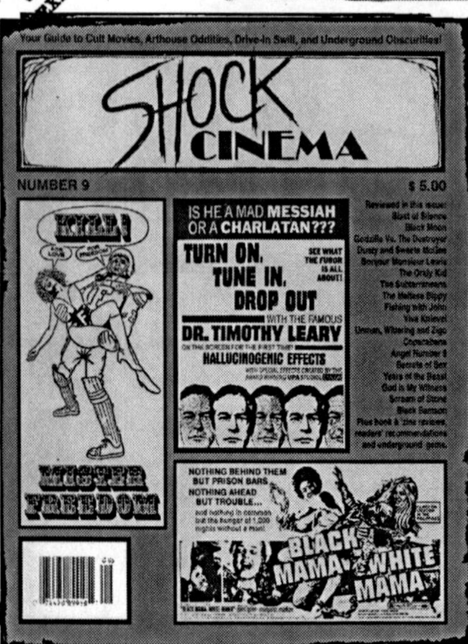


barcode and made it into the big chain bookstores that more mainstream distributors started contacting me and inundating me with screeners.

**JS: You introduced a slick cover with issue number 8...**

**SP:** That was yet another lucky coincidence. I got married right after issue 7, and my father-in-law happened to be in the printing business. Suddenly some slicker options opened up because of his contacts. My wife Anna had also done printing jobs with her dad, so she was familiar with the ins and outs of that business. I was soon introduced to different printers and got some really good prices from them—which allowed me to upgrade the mag. Over the years, I've established my own relationships with printing plants and wholesale paper distributors, and it manages to keep my costs incredibly low.

**JS: You started running interviews with issue number 12.**

**SP:** Yeah, that was 1998. The internet had really exploded in the previous couple years, with a lot of sites focusing on horror and exploitation film reviews, so I felt the need to take the magazine in a slightly different direction. The first interview was something that basically fell into my lap. Chris Poggiali—another ex-resident of snowy Syracuse, NY—penned our very first *Shock Cinema* interview with William Smith. I figured, "Let's give it a shot, run one interview and see what folks think." Well, the reaction was great, so the next issue we did two, then three, etc. And now, the interviews are just as important, if not more important, than the reviews. We've profiling a lot of actors and filmmakers who've never really had a chance to tell their story. It's a slice of cinematic history, and I'm proud to be able to highlight their amazing careers in the magazine.

**JS: How do you go about choosing an interview subject?**

**SP:** A lot of the time, it's simply whoever is willing to be grilled for a couple hours about their careers. It's not as easy as you might think, and a lot of my favorite actors have passed on the idea. They either don't want to spend an afternoon regurgitating the past, they're writing an autobiography and don't want to give away their best anecdotes, or in some rare instances—cough, Peter Fonda, cough—they actually wanted

to get paid for it. My writers are always searching for good interview candidates though, and they'll send me lists of names, then I pick the most intriguing possibilities—usually people who haven't been interviewed that often, or if they have been interviewed a lot, we try to find a new angle. A lot of character actors have been interviewed to death about their horror films, but you don't hear about their early struggles, or their stage work, or their most obscure gigs. We want to give them a chance to have their voice heard, which is why we maintain a simple Q&A format. I really like the fact that people can read it and it's almost as if you're sitting in a room with them.

**JS: I'd like to hear a little about the distribution collapse of the late nineties. How did you handle that?**

**SP:** You take a little bit of a hit. Tower didn't go under until a little after that. When Tower went under, it hurt a lot of zines, especially small ones. But the company I mentioned earlier, Desert Moon Periodicals—their collapse was the big one in the late nineties. They dealt with a lot of zines and owed a lot of small press publishers. In the end, everyone got ripped off. And when you lose thousands of dollars, which is what happened in my case, your immediate instinct is to simply toss in the towel. Screw it. Why the hell should I kill myself, if some assholes are going to fuck me over? Luckily, I didn't embrace that attitude. I kept going and instead looked for and quickly found alternate distributors. We were fortunate that *Shock Cinema* was pretty slick and well established at the time, so other distributors were eager to work with us. In the end, we weren't hurt that much, circulation-wise. It did kick our ass financially though.

**JS: Are you sustained mostly by subscribers or by distribution, at this point?**

**SP:** Distribution, mainly, but subscribers and assorted mail orders are also a huge amount. Plus I regularly get people ordering an entire run of back issues, which is always a pleasant windfall. It's a little from everywhere—our current subscription list is larger than ever before, but the major distributors still get a vast majority of the issues. You know, one of the main reasons

RECORDED & INDEXED

# STEVE PUCHALSKI

## SLIMETIME

DRAFT

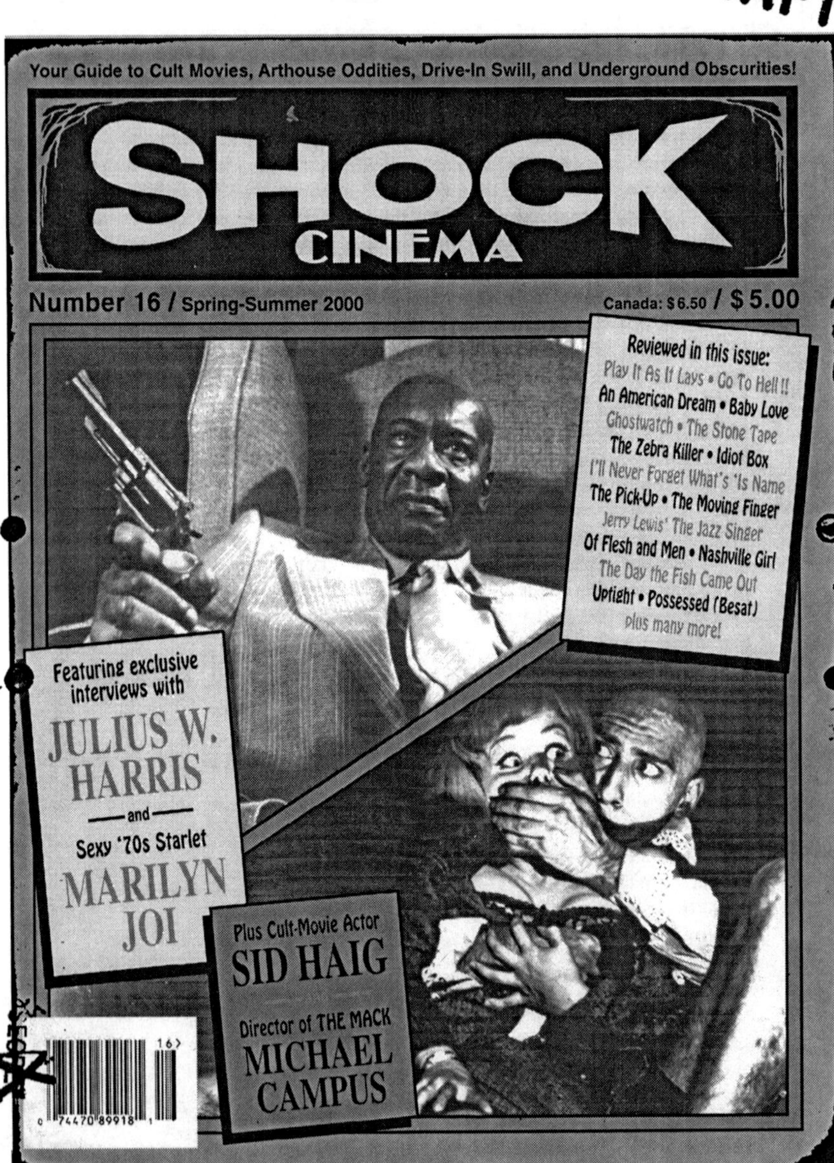

Your Guide to Cult Movies, Arthouse Oddities, Drive-In Swill, and Underground Obscurities!
SHOCK
CINEMA
Number 16 / Spring-Summer 2000
Canada: $6.50 / $5.00
Reviewed in this issue:
Play It As It Lays • Go To Hell !!
An American Dream • Baby Love
Ghostwatch • The Stone Tape
The Zebra Killer • Idiot Box
I'll Never Forget What's 'Is Name
The Pick-Up • The Moving Finger
Jerry Lewis' The Jazz Singer
Of Flesh and Men • Nashville Girl
The Day the Fish Came Out
Uptight • Possessed (Besat)
plus many more!
Featuring exclusive interviews with
JULIUS W. HARRIS
and
Sexy '70s Starlet
MARILYN JOI
Plus Cult-Movie Actor
SID HAIG
Director of THE MACK
MICHAEL CAMPUS
0 74470 89918 1
16

that *Shock Cinema* has survived so long is because of its loyal readers, who continue to search out the magazine in brick-and-mortar stores, shell out their hard-earned cash and keep the mag alive. I can't tell you how much I appreciate their loyalty.

**JS: How did your deal with Headpress come about for the *Slimetime* book?**

**SP:** Again, I was very fortunate. David Kerekes had read all of the *Slimetimes* as they came out—he had the total collection, and simply approached me with the idea. "Steve, what do you think about putting it all together as a book?" Of course, I jumped at the chance. Best of all, there was very minimal work for me to do, outside of minor editing. We cut a deal, signed the contract, put out the book, and soon I was getting a royalty check for crap that I'd written ten years earlier. How cool is that? Having the first edition published in 1996 was incredible; but then to have a completely revamped and overstuffed new edition released in 2002 only made the experience better.

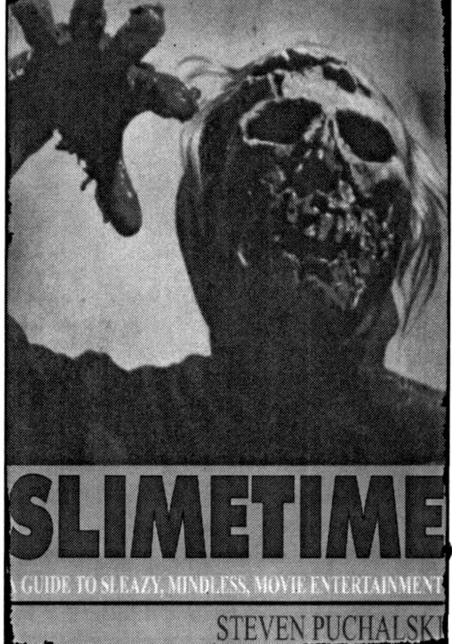

SLIMETIME
A GUIDE TO SLEAZY, MINDLESS, MOVIE ENTERTAINMENT
STEVEN PUCHALSKI


THE *SLIMETIME* BOOK, ORIGINAL PRINTING (HEADPRESS, 1996).

**JS: Were you surprised that he approached you about the project?**

**SP:** Yeah, very much so. I was thrilled by the whole idea.

**JS: You've done some freelancing for *Fangoria*. What was it like doing interviews for them?**

**SP:** One of the difficult things about interviewing people for *Fangoria*—or any corporate publication—is their space limitations. I'd get an assignment, then talk to some filmmaker for two hours. Then I'd have to whittle it down to the smallest possible article and edit out some of the best material. That happened *waayyyy* too often [laughs]. For example, I interviewed Ron Jeremy, when he was appearing in Troma's *Terror Firmer*. It was a fun interview, but the piece had to be chopped down to basically a sidebar in the end... Still, *Fangoria* was a good, regular writing gig, and Mike Gingold was always cool to deal with.

**JS: When did you start freelancing?**

**SP:** Well, I already mentioned the articles written for *Shock Xpress*. After that, I took on whatever writing gigs I could find—as any freelancer knows,

it's whatever pays the bills, right? I wrote for the *TV Guide* website, zines like *Asian Cult Cinema*, and it was a lot of fun co-penning *Fangoria*'s Dr. Cyclops video column for seventeen years. I even wrote an article for a wrestling magazine! It was about pro-wrestlers who eventually became actors, and I have no idea if it actually made it into print. But they did pay me for it. Plus I've cranked out some really mainstream crap as well. When you're asked to write a puff-piece on the careers of George Lucas or Steven Spielberg, it's hard to turn down a quick paycheck when it'll cover that month's rent. You take the work where you can get it. I'm also still writing for *Sci-Fi* magazine. The reviews are pretty basic, but their editors are easy to work with and it's a nice, regular paycheck. I've been doing that for nearly twenty years.

**JS: So, are you able to make a living off of writing at this point?**

**SP:** Yes. Ever since I left Kim's back in '95. It's not easy though. It's a lot of work, as anyone who's ever freelanced can tell you. Plus I supplemented it with ways to earn extra cash, like when we were doing conventions. It certainly feels like you're always working—always hustling. But whenever I'd start to whine, friends would set me straight with, "You're kidding, right? You don't have a fucking day job. You don't have to get up every morning." And they were right. I really have little to complain about.

**JS: What's your movie viewing schedule like?**

**SP:** It varies. I don't attend many theatrical screenings anymore—the audiences are horrible, even at invitation-only screenings—but there isn't a day when I'm not watching some movie. And when I really get focused on an upcoming issue, I'll crack a nice bottle of single malt whisky and watch three or four flicks a day. It's always good to get into a groove. When I'm reviewing potential *Shock Cinema* fare, I'll take pages of rambling, longhand notes as I watch 'em, with plenty of research afterward—looking for little details that'll make the eventual review stand out.

**JS: What's kept you motivated throughout the years?**

SHOCK CINEMA
Number 43
Serving the Film Fanatic since 1990
$5.00
CHRIS ELLIOTT
BRUCE DAVISON
STEVE RAILSBACK
IAN OGILVY
O-LAN JONES

ISSUE NUMBER 43 AND STILL GOING STRONG.

**SP:** That's a good question. My love of film, for one thing. The hunt for obscure films that have somehow fallen through the cracks. And nowadays, giving some long-overdue recognition to the amazing character actors that I grew up watching. Not to mention, the love of my wife, Anna, who's supported me through every hill and valley of this crazy career.

**JS: Do you still get the same thrill out of writing about film as when you started?**

**SP:** Yes, absolutely. That's the great thing. When it's all coming together, it feels the same as it did twenty-five years ago. But I've definitely gotten a lot harder on myself in terms of my writing. I'm much more self-critical. As you get older, you want everything to be better and better. When I did *Slimetime*, I was just spewing my opinions, while pounding down a six-pack of PBR's and getting it out there as fast as possible. There was a spontaneity to the process. Today, I probably think about everything a little more and plan it all out better—I think my readers have grown as well, and expect a certain level of professionalism nowadays. The fact that so many people tell me that they read each issue cover-to-cover is really high praise... You know, it's often a shitload of work and frustrations, but I've loved every minute of it.

COLUMBIA PICTURES presents
MATINEE ONLY
TODAY
The Magic World of Topo Gigio
in WONDER COLOR
Topo Gigio's FIRST Full-Length Movie!
ED SULLIVAN says:
"Anyone who saw Topo Gigio on my Sunday Night TV show will agree his first movie is really big entertainment!"
ALL 50¢ SEATS

# Chapter Thirty-Five
# Charles Kilgore
## The Ecco Chamber

WHY IS THIS WOMAN SCREAMING?
Find out inside!

Charles Kilgore was a hard man to track down. I had been given several leads, but they all inevitably ended up as dead ends. This was disturbing news to me—if there was one person that I wanted to talk to, that I needed to talk to, it was him.

Charles Kilgore published *Ecco* from 1988 to 1996. I got my hands on the very first issue after I saw a small ad for the thing in the premiere issue of *Slaughterhouse*. At this stage in the game, I was just beginning my journey into the strange world of the fanzines. Slowly but surely, I was picking them off, one by one, happily adding everything I came across to my ever growing library. Some of them were good, some of them were bad, and some of them were outstanding. From the very start, *Ecco* was one of the most fascinating zines that I'd ever laid eyes on.

Rewind for a second and think about it. There was once a time when information about the early mondo and sexploitation films was not easy to come by. Hell, the very films themselves seemed to have vanished. Every issue was filled with strange and fascinating stories about movies I'd never heard of. And the more I read about them, the more fascinated I became. I wanted to see them. I needed to see them. With *Ecco* by my side, I began my journey.

But where was Charles Kilgore today? He seemed to have vanished, much like the films that he once wrote about. I friended him on Facebook, but there was no response. Desperate to get in contact with him, I started digging deeper. I had a vague memory of Tim Lucas saying that he was friends with the man—that he had even spoken to him recently. I contacted Tim, inquiring about Kilgore's whereabouts and he wrote back, saying that he'd pass my request along. I sat back and waited.

A few days later, I got a letter from Charles Kilgore. He was up for an interview, and we made arrangements to speak on the phone. What follows is a transcription of our conversation...

The following interview was conducted via telephone on July 30, 2012.

---

**JOHN SZPUNAR: Where did you grow up?**
**CHARLES KILGORE:** In Norfolk, Virginia. The Navy is the big industry there and if you weren't in the Navy, the chances were that you worked for a business that catered to the Navy. The downtown area was what you might expect from a place that catered to sailors. It was pretty sleazy, with lots and lots of taverns, porn shops, adult theaters, and prostitution. At a horror film convention, I overheard Johnny Legend telling someone that it was the sleaziest town that he'd ever been in. I felt a little bit of pride there, because he lives in LA [laughs]. Of course, when I was really young, I didn't know anything about that—typically when you're a child, you're not exposed to that sort of thing. But early on, I sort of got an

RECORDED & INDEXED

DRAFT

interest in material that a lot of people might find disturbing.

**JS: Can you give me an example?**

**CK:** When I was five or six years old, my family vacationed at a little resort called White Lake, North Carolina. We rented a cabin, and the cabins were kind of like duplexes; there was another one next to the cabin that we were staying in. There was a family staying there and the husband had a men's adventure magazine. Like I said, I was five or six, but I fixated on the cover. There was a soldier and a woman and their clothes were in shreds. They were hiding in a cave from the Nazis or the Japanese; I can't remember which. And they were covered in scorpions—there were scorpions all over them! They couldn't scream, because if they did, the people that were looking for them would find them. I think the guy's wife saw me looking at that cover. I went out to play with their daughter, who was pretty close to my age, and when I came back, it was gone.

**JS: [laughs] What other things caught your attention as a child?**

**CK:** Like a lot of kids, I was really into dinosaurs. I had one of these projectors that was really popular; they were used in classrooms. There was a mirror inside of this plastic casing and a light—you would put it on top of a magazine and it would project the image of the magazine on the wall. There was an article in *LIFE* magazine about the movie *Journey to the Center of the Earth*. I remember projecting this big dinosaur image on the wall.

**JS: When did you become more aware of your seedy surroundings?**

**CK:** I remember a particular instance. There was a theater in downtown Norfolk. This was probably the first time I went to the sleazy area. It was called the Byrd Theater and I wanted to see this movie called *The Giant Behemoth*. My mother would always take me to the movies—we had this thing where she would take me to see the movies that I wanted to see. In exchange, I had to go see the movies that she wanted to see. She wouldn't go to the Byrd because she was uncomfortable going to a theater that catered to drunk sailors. My older brother volunteered to take me.

**JS: How old were you?**

**CK:** I was six years old. I liked dinosaurs, but I didn't know that this dinosaur gave off radiation waves that turned people into charcoal. It freaked me out. It was a lot more than I expected and I had to use

the bathroom. And it was the bathroom from hell, with a shit encrusted toilet. It was really, really nasty. I asked my brother if we could go home so I could use the bathroom there. He took me home, and on the way there, I learned from him (to my dismay) that we couldn't come back. That was it. I ended up not seeing the rest of *The Giant Behemoth* for something like fifteen years.

**JS: Hopefully with the comfort of a nicer bathroom.**

**CK:** With a clean toilet, absolutely [laughs]! The funny thing is that I was waiting for a bus out there many, many years later and the Byrd Theater was showing a double bill of *The Bloodthirsty Butchers* and *Torture Dungeon*, the Andy Milligan films. They had a quality theater there.

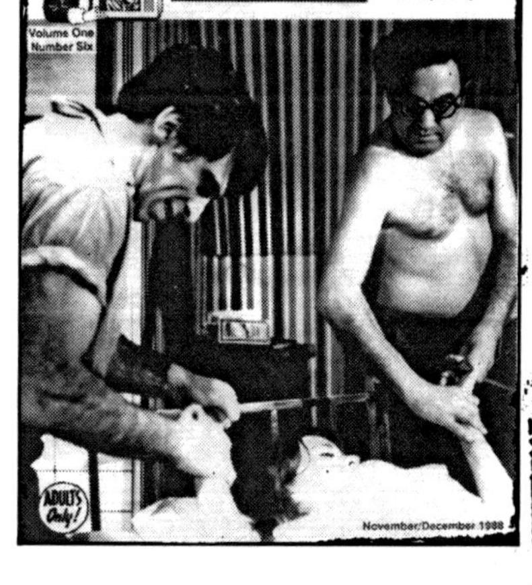


**JS: What other films do you remember seeing as a kid?**

**CK:** I saw *Santa Claus*, the K. Gordon Murray film. That was my first foreign film. Of course, I didn't know it was foreign at the time; I just thought there was something wrong with the film—their lips didn't match up to what they were saying.

**JS: That's a strange movie, weather you're aware of its origin or not! What was your initial impression of it?**

**CK:** It freaked me out. It was strange. I didn't ever think that I was being good all year round for any other reason other than to make sure that I got toys. The whole idea of Satan claiming my soul was just not something that occurred to me. The kids in the theater were really confused. They didn't know what the hell was going on.

**JS: Do you have any other early movie memories that stand out?**

**CK:** Well, another movie that I saw and enjoyed when I was young was *Gorgo*. I was around eight years old. But the dinosaur thing pretty much ended after I started to get into my teens. If I like any dinosaur movies now, they're probably closer to *Gorgo*—something where it's cheesy and fun, as opposed to Jurassic Park. I also remember watching Richard Cunha's *She Demons* on television. In Norfolk, we had a great presentation of late-night movies called *Shock Theater*. It was hosted by a local television personality in the guise of a character named Roland, who was a little bit like Lurch from *The Addams Family*. He had this big scar down his face. They showed some great films and I remember watching *She*

RECORDED & INDEXED

# CHARLES KILGORE

## THE ECCO CHAMBER

DRAFT

ART BY STEVE BISSETTE.

No. 15
ECCO
the world of bizarre video
$2.50
WARNING! THIS IS
SWAMP TRASH
WEIRD ADVENTURE!
SEE MOONSHINERS WHO PLAY FOR KEEPS AND ONLY THE LUCKY SURVIVE!
IF MOONSHINE AND LOVIN' DON'T KILL YOU . . . THERE'S ALWAYS THE SKEETERS, GATORS AND QUICKSAND!
SEE DEATH STRUGGLE IN QUICKSAND THAT SWALLOWS A MAN ALIVE!
A DANGEROUS GAME!
XXX
S. R. BISSETTE 7/91

*Demons* and being impressed with it.

**JS: Were you ever afraid of the films that you saw?**

**CK:** I managed to scare myself. One time a kid who lived in the house behind ours was going to spend the night over. I slept in an upstairs area that had been an attic. Part of it had been converted into a bedroom, but there was a door that opened and went into the attic. I convinced this kid that there was a monster in there. I still have this memory of looking out the window and seeing him running back to his house in his pajamas, leaping over the fence. And then I was scared—I scared myself. But I had some really scary things going on in my own life. My mother was an alcoholic and I would often look at my own life like a movie, which sort of helped me deal with it. I'm sure that had a lot of influence on my taste in films. Did you ever see a movie called *Flesh Eaters*?

**JS: Yeah.**

**CK:** Well, I saw that at the drive-in with my mother, a woman who was a friend of hers, and her son. I was probably around eleven or twelve years old. *Flesh Eaters* was on, and my mom had these tall-boys—she was drinking one after the other. By the end of the night, my mother would have melted a breathalyzer. The other woman didn't drive, and we were too young. We were like, "How are we going to get home?" So, my mother's driving us, and she makes a wrong turn. We were heading out to the country in this desolate area. There were fields on either side of us—we were going and going and going. The other kid was starting to freak out. I was sort of used to having these experiences, but he obviously wasn't. His mom managed to persuade my mother to turn around. She finally pulled into a desolate church parking lot to reverse course and we finally made it home. That sort of dovetailed with the film, because in *Flesh Eaters*, there's an actress character who's an alcoholic. She saves the day—not because she's a good person or anything, she just wants revenge because the mad scientist thought he killed and buried her. She pops up at the right moment, and two surviving characters are saved. So, I'm trying to process all of this in my mind; it was really kind of strange.

**JS: You mentioned that you were fascinated by things that other people might find disturbing...**

**CK:** I've always had an interest in macabre things. My mom would take me to see *Gorgo*, *Reptilicus*, or whatever I wanted to see. In exchange, I would go see what she wanted, which was *Auntie Mame* or Douglas Sirk's remake of *Imitation of Life*. I always fixated on the most bizarre aspects of those movies. One time, she took me to see Cecil B. DeMille's *Samson and Delilah*. The only scene that I remember from the whole film is when he's chained up in the coliseum and these dwarves are approaching him with jawbones and pinching his legs. That really stands out.

**JS: When did you start going to the movies on your own?**

**CK:** I went to a private school and the whole deal was, if you showed up

# CHARLES KILGORE

## THE ECCO CHAMBER

late, you got a demerit. They were really big on the demerit system—they sort of modeled themselves after an English prep school. When my mother was on one of her drinking binges, I would cut her alarm clock off so she wouldn't wake me up. She would wake up the next morning, not knowing that she hadn't actually set it. What I would also do was take ten or twenty dollars out of her purse. I would tell her, "You know, I really can't go to school late because I'll get a demerit. Why don't you write me a note saying I'm sick?" She would do this, and I would then take the bus downtown for the day and go to see movies. Downtown Norfolk wasn't 42nd Street, but because it was a Navy town, there were lots and lots of exploitation films playing. I saw *The Fiendish Ghouls* and *Horrors of Spider Island* on a double-bill. When I got a little bit older, I got a fake ID and I saw some films that I wasn't supposed to see, like *Succubus*. I used my fake ID to see *Blood Feast* and *Two Thousand Maniacs* when those two films were paired together. And least but not least, I saw *Ecco*, a primary influence. When my uncle found out that I saw that movie, he told my parents that I should not have seen it.

**JS: What was a typical day away from school like?**

**CK:** I had money, so I'd see a film. I'd go to Orange Julius and get a hot dog. But first I'd go to Henderson's Newsstand which was owned by a character named Bootsie Goldstein. Bootsie was always getting in trouble for selling porn. This was before any kind of porn was legal and he got busted over and over again. He would get out of prison and the next thing you know, he'd be arrested again. The guy would just not give up—he was determined. "This is what the sailors want and this is what we're gonna give 'em!" He also had all these underground papers like the *Berkeley Barb*, *Zap Comix*, and the *East Village Other*. I would buy all of those and have a great day out while the other kids were in school.

**JS: It was sort of an alternate education, in a way...**

**CK:** Yeah, it was. On the day I turned eighteen, I went to see a porn film in downtown Norfolk. It was of the genre known as a "white coater," and I saw it at the Colonial theater, a beautiful old art-deco film theater that had been a burlesque theater. Before that, it had been a vaudeville theater where Fred Astaire and Mae West had appeared.

**JS: Where else were you seeing films?**

**CK:** When I was old enough to drive, I went to the drive-in. The downtown area was really changing; they were trying to clean it up and everything like that. My friends and I would drive to Elizabeth City, North Carolina, to this liquor store that we knew would sell to anybody. We were high school students, and they would sell us cheap wine. We'd go to the drive-in and drink. I saw the *I Drink your Blood/I Eat your Skin* double bill there. We saw some really sicko films there such as *The Baby* and *Love Me Deadly*; the more twisted they were, the more we liked them.

**JS: Did you ever make it over to Times Square?**

**CK:** I only got there once to see films. That was back in 1984 and I saw this great triple bill. There was a mondo movie called *Sweet and Savage* playing with *Toxic Zombies* and *The Nesting*, which was about a haunted whorehouse. The audience was great. It was all of these street dudes, cab drivers, and me. They were selling weed out in the open in the audience and shit like that. Just unbelievable.

**JS: How did the New York crowd compare to Norfolk crowd?**

**CK:** Well, here's the thing. The Times Square audience was a little scarier than the audience that I was used to. There were occasional fights and disturbances in Norfolk, but it was all enlisted Navy guys and they knew that the MPs were out patrolling. They didn't want to create a stir. The odor in Norfolk's Granby Theater was unique—a blend of concession hot dogs and cheap cologne.

**JS: When did you become aware that people were actually writing about these kinds of films?**

**CK:** I read magazines like the *Eye* and others like that, but they really didn't write about exploitation films. They were more about independent American cinema, which was just as much my interest as the exploitation films. The first thing that I read was probably Michael Weldon's *Psychotronic* book. And shortly after I got that, I found out about *Sleazoid Express*. *Sleazoid Express* was and is my favorite of all of the fanzines. It had its own atmosphere and the perspective was totally unique. It was almost as if Bill

# CHARLES KILGORE

## THE ECCO CHAMBER

RECORDED & INDEXED

DRAFT

No. 8
$1.25
ECCO
the world of bizarre video
THIS ISSUE:
KLAUS KINSKI:
Saint Or Slut?
TEST TUBE BABIES
POSITIVELY ADULTS ONLY!
March/April 1989


Landis defined an aesthetic that no one else has touched since, or really can. Now, I never really wanted to do what he did—I mean, I think he was a computer programmer and became a porn projectionist and then appeared in some of the films. I never wanted to do that. But I don't think his zine would have been the same if he hadn't done it. It did more than just look at the films—it pulled you into that whole world. It was fascinating to me and I have to say that the demise of *Sleazoid* was probably the biggest influence in my putting out *Ecco*.

**JS: How so?**

**CK:** Well, I searched in vain for something like *Sleazoid Express*. I was in a shop in New York called Cinemabilia and I picked up a copy of Rick Sullivan's *Gore Gazette*. It was entertaining in its own way, but it wasn't *Sleazoid*. Every zine I picked up had something to recommend, but it wasn't the same thing—I felt there was a real hole created by its demise. I knew I couldn't fill that hole, but I did know that there was room for another perspective. Also, my confidence was bolstered by some really terrible fanzines that I picked up. There were several of them that were just pathetic. I thought, "Jesus, anybody can do this." That sort of made me feel a little more courageous about putting out my own. Also, I made friends with a guy who owned a video store in Alexandria, Virginia. It was called the Video Vault, and they specialized in really bad movies. As a matter of fact, their slogan was, "Guaranteed worst movies in town." They went for all the cult films. Most video stores at the time would just go through one particular distributor. The Video Vault would go to anybody, even buying from Rick Sullivan. Rick was selling ninth and tenth generation copies of hard to find titles. They would get anything from anybody, just to have it—they were really into it. Their whole "so good it's bad" thing got coverage in *Reader's Digest*, of all places. But anyway, I had access to this great store that had titles that other people probably couldn't find. And I also had access to the film library of the Library of Congress. That's where I did a lot of my research. They had the AFI guide to sixties films and I would go through

that, page after page. I learned about Roberta Findlay's films before I actually saw one.

**JS: Jimmy McDonough was telling me that he and Bill Landis used to do the same thing.**

**CK:** Yeah. I didn't know that they were doing that, of course—I just happened to find them. I'd be reading those things, and I'd be, "Oh my God, I have to see this!" I had the advantage of having great resources at a time before there was any internet.

**JS: What kind of reaction did *Ecco* initially get?**

**CK:** At first, not a lot. It didn't generate a lot of interest, locally. From day one, my goal was to get it into the newsstands, because when I was growing up, that's how you got everything. I just sort of pictured myself seeing *Ecco* at a newsstand and saying, "I've got to have that!" But, it didn't go over that well at first. It was really only after I started trading with a lot of people that the word of mouth went out. Eventually, some interest started being generated and my numbers went up and up, to the point where I was getting quite a lot of issues printed. The early magazine pretty much broke even.

**JS: How did you originally produce it?**

**CK:** I think the very first issue was probably only around 200 copies. I wound up reprinting the first couple of issues. It was not a xeroxed zine—from the very start, it was offset. It was printed on 11 x 17 inch paper and was folded over. I pretty much got that from *Sleazoid*—I liked the look of the magazine, and I tried to replicate it. It had its own, unique look.

**JS: I bought quite a few issues of *Ecco* from the newsstand. How did you get that sort of distribution?**

**CK:** I actually learned about the distributors from my friends Tim and Donna Lucas of *Video Watchdog*. I also sold independently to stores—there was one place in New York on St. Mark's Place called See Hear, a newsstand that specialized in fanzines. A number of places like that started picking it up.

**JS: I remember buying the Joel Reed issue from Borders.**

**CK:** That's the rarest issue. I think I only have one copy of it. You know, I did find out something interesting: Tower Records stopped selling *Ecco*. I met a guy who worked for Tower and he told me the reason was that they thought it was racist.

# CHARLES KILGORE

## THE ECCO CHAMBER

RECORDED & INDEXED

DRAFT

No. 18
$3.00
ECCO
the world of bizarre video
THIS ISSUE:
Over the Threshold with Barbet Schroeder
The Wild World of Doug Hobart, Part II
Plus More Bizarre and Unusual Home Video!


CONSIDERED RACIST.

**JS: Why would they think that?**

**CK:** You know, I really don't know. But, I thought it was hilarious that the store that sold *ANSWER Me!* thought that *Ecco* was racist.

**JS: *Ecco* was covering certain films and filmmakers that nobody else was touching at the time.**

**CK:** That's what I was trying to do. I was trying to be educational about the films that I had seen at the theaters and drive-ins in Norfolk and the tapes from the Video Vault, Something Weird, and other sources.

**JS: How did you go about doing research in the pre-internet days?**

**CK:** Well, like I said, a lot of it was done at the Library of Congress. And as much as I liked *Sleazoid*, I knew that they made errors—they made assumptions that were certainly not true. They identified *Shanty Tramp* and *Shantytown Honeymoon* as the same film. But, if you didn't see the film, you'd have no way of knowing—there was a lot of bad information out there. The one story that I would have loved to have been able to break was how the *Olga* films (that were made in New York by someone credited as Joseph Mawra) were connected to the films shot by K. Gordon Murray's group in Florida. They used the same pseudonym. Was it a just name that they liked and used? There was no internet at the time, and a lot of the people I talked to wouldn't talk about it.

**JS: Really?**

**CK:** I was trying to research an article on *Shanty Tramp*. Have you ever seen the film?

**JS: Yeah.**

**CK:** You know the young black man who punches out the greaser? That guy later starred in a television comedy series, and he became a pretty successful actor Off-Broadway. I called him up and mentioned *Shanty Tramp*, and he just freaked out. He thought I was trying to do an exposé on him, or something like that. I was trying to convince him—"No, I like the film!" He kept saying, "I didn't do anything wrong!" Later, Bill Rogers (who played the preacher in the film) told me that some of the actors got into trouble and lost their jobs for appearing in that film.

**JS: You did a lot of breakthrough interviews with people who would have otherwise have been ignored. How difficult was it to track them down?**

Carroll Baker: Her Life In Exploitation

No. 9

ECCO

the world of bizarre video

$1.25

Persons under 18 will positively not be admitted. I D CARD REQUIRED

May/June 1989

CK: Like who?

**JS: Well, how about [cinematographer] C. Davis Smith?**

**CK:** C. Davis Smith turned out to be a neighbor of my in-laws. I had driven past his street many times, and didn't know it. One of the things that I really liked to do was talk to people about the other aspects of their careers. I found out that Chuck did the little animated parrot in the Gillette commercials. He did a lot of industrial films—I love all of that stuff. To me, that's just as interesting as his exploitation work. I also thought his attitude toward the exploitation films was cool. We were at one of those horror movie conventions and Joe Sarno was there. We were all sitting around talking, and the subject of Roberta Findlay came up. I mentioned that I would have loved to interview her, but I understood that if you tried to talk to her, she'd hang up. Chuck said, "She was a lot more approachable when I knew her." Joe Sarno said, "Yeah, but you knew her a lot better than the rest of us did." He turned beet-red—they had had a thing, you know?

**JS: [laughs] But seriously, how did you track these people down?**

**CK:** A lot of it was just cold calls—digging out a phone directory and looking for names. I'd also get information from other people. I'd be talking to them and they'd say, "I happen to know where so-and-so is." That's the wonderful thing about doing fanzines—you're connected to other people. Someone else might not be interested in doing an Audrey (*Olga's House of*

RECORDED & INDEXED

# CHARLES KILGORE

## THE ECCO CHAMBER

DRAF

No. 20
ECCO
the world of bizarre video
$4.00
SPECIAL S&M ISSUE!
Bodies Racked by Unspeakable Tortures!
Sardu
Olga
SHOW BIZ AGENT LURES GIRLS
UNSUSPECTING BEAUTIES FORCED INTO SLAVERY
IMPORTS YOUNG GIRLS FOR LOVE
DOMESTIC JOB OFFERS FRONT FOR PROSTITUTION
WHIPS NUDE TEEN-AGE GIRL IN PUBLIC PARK
SADO MASOCHIST HIDEOUT RAIDED
SCORES ARRESTED: TORTURE EQUIPMENT CONFISCATED
SRB
Audrey "Olga" Campbell
Joel "Bloodsucking Freaks" Reed
Dancing Outlaw
Sixties Psychedelia
and Much More!

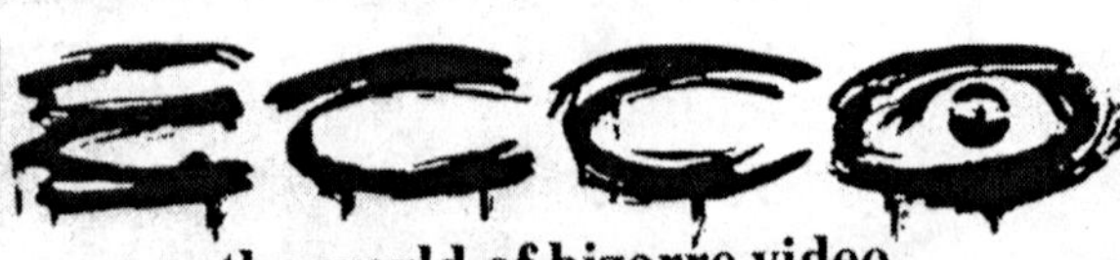

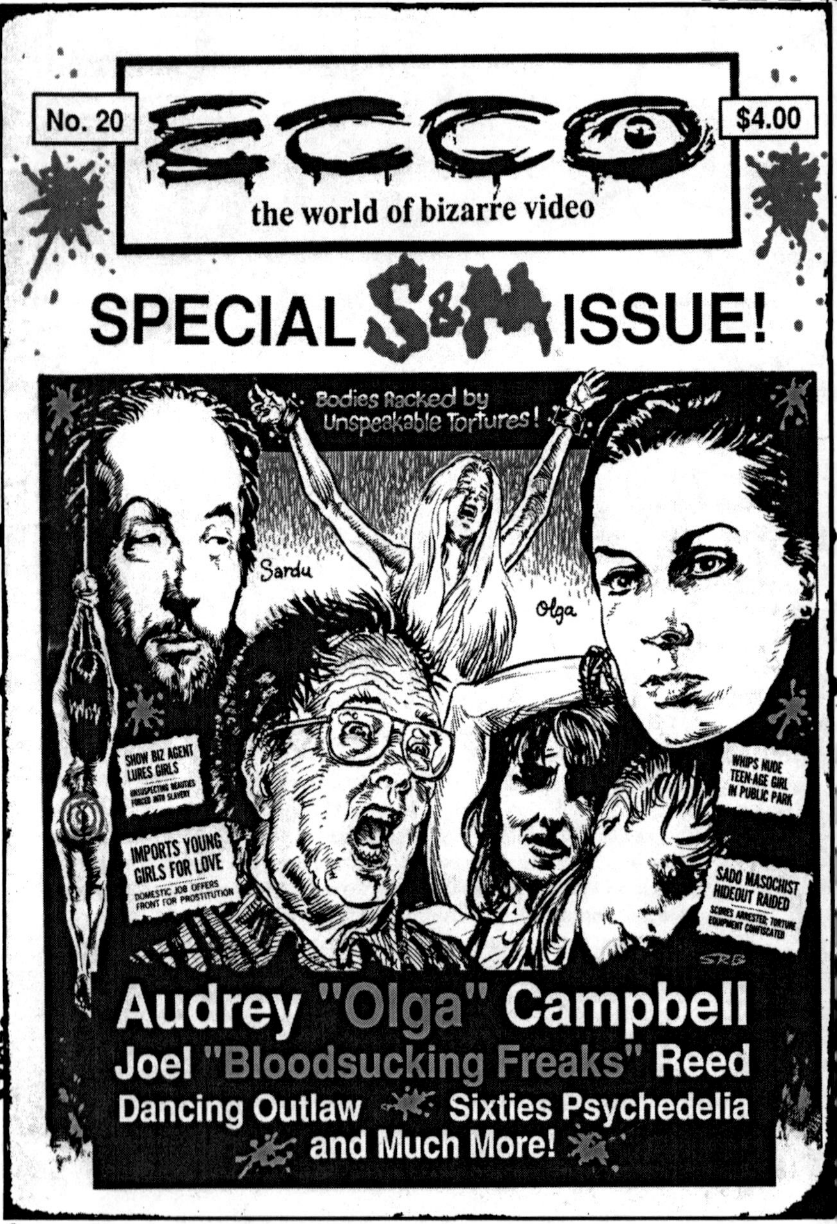

THE RARE ISSUE. ART BY STEVE BISSETTE.

*Shame*) Campbell interview, but they have her number.

**JS: What was she like?**

**CK:** She was wonderful. Just the chattiest person in the world. The interview only encompassed a small fraction of what we talked about. She would go off topic constantly. I had no idea that she had been a model for a cosmetics company in New York. Someone from the company happened to be driving through Times Square and saw her picture on a poster. She lost her job because of that—they couldn't have a model who was also in nudie films. But, she was really funny and she was curious about her earlier films, because she hadn't seen them in quite some time. She was a little shocked—I think she remembered them as being a little more tame than they actually were. But she didn't say, "I didn't realize that there was so much sadomasochism in them." It was the nudity aspect that she didn't remember.

**JS: Did you find that a lot of people were shocked or embarrassed by their past?**

**CK:** There was a lot of self-effacing humor, more so than embarrassment. And then you'd get somebody like Bill Rogers—he was such a ham. He was in *Shanty Tramp* and *A Taste of Blood*. He was doing little theater at the time that I talked to him. We sort of became friendly after the interview—he'd call me from time to time. He was not at all embarrassed by what he'd done. I'd say that for the most part, people weren't embarrassed, and the ones who were didn't want to participate.

**JS: Were people surprised that you were calling them?**

**CK:** Yeah. Absolutely. They were like, "Why do you want to talk to me?" They didn't really think that anybody would be interested, all these years later. There was definitely some amusement. I remember Chuck Smith telling me that he wanted to set the record straight—the exploitation films were very profitable for him and his family.

**JS: Why did you think it was important to document these people's lives?**

**CK:** Well, I realized that nobody else was doing it. I know that *Sleazoid Express* got into that a little bit with Toby Ross, and people like that. But at the time, the horror side of the story was being covered a lot more than the low budget sexploitation side. I wouldn't really go so far as to say that I'm a horror movie fan—I like the exploitation films a lot more. I haven't seen any of the *Saw* movies. To be honest, I don't want to sit for ninety minutes and watch somebody get tortured. That just doesn't appeal to me. I looked at the exploitation films as independent cinema. They were interesting because they weren't made by a big conglomerate of people, but were unique visions from people trying to tap into the social zeitgeist of the time. They would present an image of what they thought audiences wanted to see. And a lot of the time it really wasn't that at all—it was just the image in their mind. I think that makes things more interesting. So, that's who I wanted to talk to. I was never able to interview Doris Wishman, but I think it's fascinating that someone told her cameraman to get a close up of that ashtray [laughs].

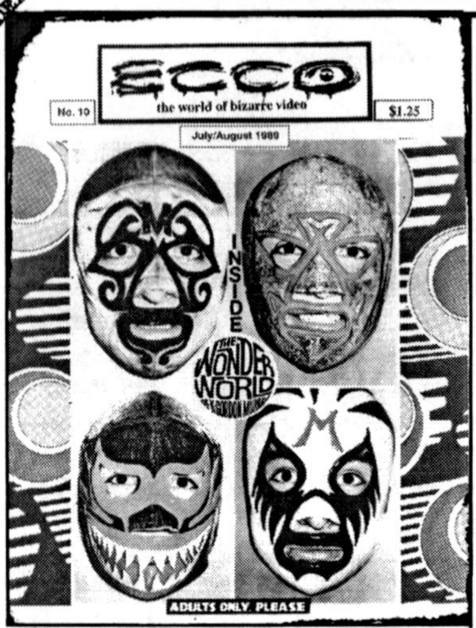


**JS: I loved your interview with Joel Reed.**

**CK:** I'll tell you something about that. The subject of Bill Landis came up, and he said lots and lots of things. I sent him the article, because I wanted to make sure that he was comfortable with what he said. He and Landis had issues—and I'm not going to pass judgment on anybody—but obviously there was bad blood between the two. Joel asked me to take a lot of the more scurrilous references out.

**JS: I meant to ask you how you assembled your staff of contributors.**

**CK:** Writers came out of the woodwork. One was a guy who worked with my wife. His background wasn't so much in hardcore exploitation movies as it was sixties pop and stuff. I liked his perspective. But that was part of the problem. When you've created an aesthetic and people want to write for you, you sort of have to bend the envelope a little bit. That was always a problem for me. And, I graduated from college with a major in English Literature. I'm very particular about grammar and sort of thing, so I was always editing my contributors. That got to be a problem—people don't like to be edited. You find that in the professional world, as well. People really object to having their work edited. On the plus side, I was very fortunate in that I had very good writers.

**JS: One of the contributors to *Ecco* was Steve Bissette. How did he get involved in things?**

**CK:** Steve was a big fan of the magazine, and he approached me with the idea of doing some covers. Of course, I'm not going to say no to a famous cartoonist [laughs]! He did such a great job with them. Some people liked my earlier covers better—they thought his covers made it look like they were buying a comic book, rather than a film magazine. That's not such a big issue if you're selling by mail, but on the newsstands, there is the possibility that some people will be confused. I never really worried about it—I thought the covers looked cool.

**JS: You mentioned that you were particular about *Ecco*'s content. Did you let your contributors run free, or did you give them specific assignments?**

**CK:** A little of both. Dom Salemi and I would talk about the articles, and he would always ask me, "How does this sound? Would you like an article

No. 7

ECCO

the world of bizarre video

$1.25

THIS ISSUE:
Mondo New York
David F. Friedman
"Pat" Patterson

January/February 1989

on this?" He was always carful to approach me with something that I would consider doing myself. With Bissette, I would take his suggestions, knowing that he'd come up with something that I was going to love. He wrote an article on Abel Gance's *J'accuse*. I think that any magazine would have been happy to accept it, and I was pleased to have it in mine.

**JS: When did you start freelancing?**

**CK:** When I got asked. I got a call out of the blue from the editor of *Slaughterhouse*. I wrote several articles for them. With *Filmfax*, it was the same thing—they called me up.

**JS: What was it like writing for *Filmfax*?**

**CK:** The managing editor at *Filmfax* was a piece of work. I had run part one of my K. Gordon Murray article in *Ecco*. She wanted to run it as an exclusive. She tried to get me to cancel part two, and I said, "I can't do that. I'll rewrite it for *Filmfax*, but there's no way that I'm not going to run it in *Ecco*."

**JS: What was your relationship with Something Weird Video like?**

**CK:** Those guys helped me out a lot. Our interests were along the same line. Many of the films that I covered in *Ecco* were from that company. It got a little uncomfortable at a certain point because I never really thought of myself as a modern incarnation of the Forty Thieves. I think they wanted good reviews to help sell their videos. I would ask for certain titles to review, and they would send me stuff that I wasn't interested in, such as Barry Mahon

THE ECCO CHAMBER

films. I didn't want to cover films so lacking in interest. But, they were very generous in sending films that I otherwise wouldn't have been able to see. And occasionally, they would send me an unfamiliar title and I'd be, "Oh, I've got to write about this!" Something Weird has done more for keeping those films alive than anyone I can think of.

**JS: Why did you stop publishing?**

**CK:** There were a number of reasons. I'd say the basic reason was it just got to where it was no longer any fun. I was also getting screwed by the distributors—every issue cost me money. And then, there were problems with some of the writers. One writer's family members were getting on my case, because I wasn't paying him. At the time, I didn't know anyone who wrote for fanzines who actually got paid. I was already losing money on every issue.

**JS: Were you aware of just how big of an impact you made with *Ecco*?**

**CK:** Well, I hoped everyone was interested and entertained. I liked the films, and I thought the background of the films was something that people should know about. I wanted to inspire people to see them and also try to save them. You have Martin Scorsese, who is donating money to resurrect Michael Powell films, but you don't have a lot of people trying to save these films. I was hoping to foster a wider appreciation for what I viewed as a somewhat disreputable form of folk art. I did my best.

ART BY SELWYN HARRIS.

# Chapter Thirty-Six

# Mike McPadden

## All's Swell in Happyland

# MIKE McPADDEN

## ALL'S SWELL IN HAPPYLAND

Mike McPadden was the publisher and editor of *Happyland*, one of the greatest sleaze-zines of the 1990s. In an era saturated by *ANSWER Me!* clones, *Happyland* was a refreshing (yet perverted) package that pulled no punches. Harkening back to the glory days of *Gore Gazette* and *Sleazoid Express*, McPadden (under the pen name Selwyn Harris) took the reader on a wild ride through the streets of Times Square—a ride that, in retrospect, seems all the more poignant today. As Mayor Giuliani was whitewashing the theater screens and back alley walls, McPadden vaulted the turnstiles at Port Authority with a nothing-to-lose attitude, giving a new generation of sleaze-freaks the final snapshot of an era that would soon be dead and buried.

These days, McPadden lives in Chicago, where he works as a writer for the popular website Mr. Skin. At the time of this interview, he was putting the finishing touches on *Heavy Metal Movies* and *If You Like Metallica*..., his first full-length book projects. For a moment, though, let's take a trip back to 1991 and have one last look at what once was one of the strangest, most dangerous, and... happiest places on earth.

The following interview was conducted via telephone on April 26, 2012.

---

**JOHN SZPUNAR: You've got a couple books in the works...**

**MIKE McPADDEN:** It's really funny. I've been writing professionally for twenty years, working on getting book deals. I got really close in the late nineties to do a book called *Teen Sex Comedies*, which would have been an encyclopedia of just that.

**JS: Why wasn't it published?**

**MM:** It fell apart. That was for St. Martin's. And then, a couple of years ago, Fantagraphics put out *Destroy All Movies*, which was an incredible punk movie book. I grew up as a heavy duty punk rocker; I was really into that. But, in my middle age, I found that I've moved far more toward heavy metal. So, I was like, "Oh. Somebody should do the metal version of this book." Then I thought, "Oh... It should be me."

**JS: How did the deal come about?**

**MM:** I'd had some casual contact with Ian Christie from Bazillion Points. I just loved the books that they put out and pitched it, and he said, "Great!" So, that book happened. Then, like a month later, a friend said, "I'm working for Hal Leonard Publishing. We have a Metallica book scheduled and we need somebody to write it." I was like, "Oh, fuck!" So, I had to write two books last year.

**JS: That's a pretty heavy workload.**

**MM:** [laughs] Dude, it was murder!

**JS: I'm feeling the pressure, and I'm only working on one!**

XERO
FEROX

**MM:** I mean, it was awesome, but…

**JS: [laughs] I'll get back into your current projects a in a bit, but I'd like to talk a little about fanzines. *Happyland* is often mentioned in the same breath as *Gore Gazette* and *Sleazoid Express*.**

**MM:** Yeah. Here's the thing—I was a *Gore Gazette* fanatic. I worshiped Rick Sullivan.

**JS: When did you first discover his stuff?**

**MM:** I think the *Daily News* did an article about *Gore Gazette* when I was twelve. I guess that was in 1980 or '81; it was shortly after it first came out. I would write in to him and get it—I just loved it.

**JS: Were you reading *Sleazoid Express*, as well?**

**MM:** I'd hear references to *Sleazoid Express*, but I could never find it anywhere. I guess it was because of my age. I was in high school from '82 to '86, which were the glory days of *Sleazoid Express*. I didn't find a copy until years later and when I did, it just blew my mind. When *Happyland* came out, that's what everyone compared it to.

**JS: I've always seen a kinship between the two.**

**MM:** I'm honored that anyone would compare them, but I had never seen an issue of *Sleazoid Express*. I didn't see it until those late nineties issues came out.

**JS: I'd seen a few odd issues of the original run before it came back again. I liked the new stuff, but it was like apples and oranges compared to what I'd seen earlier.**

**MM:** Yeah. I did it backwards. Obviously, the original stuff was what it was, but I still thought there was a lot of cracked genius in those later issues.

**JS: That's certainly true. I guess *Sleazoid Express* changed with the times. There was no Times Square scene anymore.**

**MM:** Have you talked with any people who had to deal with Landis personally?

**JS: Yeah. I never really talked to Bill, though. Michelle Clifford read me the riot act years ago when I was trying to get in touch with him. I was doing some research on Joel Reed and**

IF YOU
LIKE
METALLICA...
HERE ARE OVER 200 BANDS, CDS, MOVIES, AND OTHER ODDITIES THAT YOU WILL LOVE
MIKE MCPADDEN

**she really let me have it.**

**MM:** She is a nightmare. She is a complete fucking nightmare. I was working at *Celebrity Skin* in the early 2000s. There was freelance work, so I got in touch with them. They handed in some insane fucking crap that I had to edit, but was still an honor.

**JS: Didn't they complain about that job?**

**MM:** Yeah. I don't know if you've ever tried to write for porno mags in New York, but getting paid is a burden beyond belief. It's fucking hard. It takes months and months. They flipped the fuck out. Landis was calling me all the time, saying, "I know terrorist techniques! I could ruin your company's credit rating!" I was like, "Oh Jesus, God!" Everybody I have ever known who has ever dealt with them has the same story.

**JS: I never experienced the full brunt of their antics, but I was pretty young when Michelle chewed me out. It really confused me.**

**MM:** You step on this landmine, and it's like, BA–BOOM! The shrapnel keeps hurling at you. Bill was a genius, though. I don't want to toss the word around lightly, but in terms of what he did with *Sleazoid Express*, he got there first and he got there better than anybody.

**JS: He was an amazing talent. And the stuff he did with Jimmy McDonough was priceless.**

**MM:** The last issue—the "Quiet Man" issue—is not just the greatest zine of all time, it's one of the greatest pieces of writing that I've ever read in my life.

**JS: I agree completely. And almost all of those early New York zines were incredible. Speaking of which, do you remember a zine called *Grindhouse*?**

**MM:** Yeah. It was handwritten and it was crazy. The guy's name was J. Adler. I was such a nut that I went up to his address and started hanging around outside to figure out which guy he was. I never figured it out [laughs].

**JS: What inspired you to do *Happyland*?**

**MM:** I was in a bunch of shitty bands that never took off. I was like, "I'm just going to publish a fucking zine." This was in 1991. Actually, J. Adler wrote the funniest shit. He was talking about jacking off to *Cannibal Holocaust* or something. He said he blew a load on the screen—the line was, "I had to get the bitch in the booth to wipe that shit off." I was so inspired. I had to make a zine that was exactly like that sentence the whole way through. So, that's what I did. I tried to write the most offensive zine ever, while being true to myself. I wasn't into that early nineties serial killer shit.

**JS: What distanced you from that scene?**

**MM:** I was into drinking and fucking, seeing gross movies, and having a good time. I was really full of hate and anger, but murder isn't fun, it's a bummer. That's what it comes down to. And I picked a lot of fights in my zine, but to me, it was always like professional wrestling.

**JS: You called yourself Selwyn Harris. Why?**

**MM:** Those were two theaters on 42nd Street, the Selwyn and the Harris. By sheer coincidence, of the original grindhouses, those where the last two that were still standing. My girlfriend at the time was called Lyric Liberty—she was named after two other theaters.

GRINDHOUSE
where the blood hits the fun!
NUMBER 3
SPRING 1989

*GRINDHOUSE*—JACKING OFF TO *CANNIBAL HOLOCAUST*.

**JS: I've heard a lot about the Lyric.**

**MM:** The Lyric was the first grindhouse I ever went into. I saw *Humongous* there in 1982 when I was thirteen. I went with a cousin of mine.

**JS: How old was he?**

**MM:** About twenty or so. We were going to pick up his sister. This was the day after I graduated from eighth grade and she was taking a train down from Canada. We were going to pick her up at Grand Central Station and the train got delayed by a couple of hours. It was like, alright, let's go to the movies. We walked up 42nd Street and we saw *The Beast Within*. *Humongous* was the second feature; we saw a little bit of that, then split.

**JS: Times Square must have seemed crazy to a thirteen year old.**

**MM:** It was wild, but it wasn't as wild as when I started going there on my own. And when I started drinking and going on my own, forget it! I always wondered what those places were like. As a kid, I'd collect scrapbooks of exploitation movie ads from the newspaper. This was before VCRs. It was a big fucking deal for me to go see that movie. And of course, we didn't tell my parents or anything. The film was rated R—never mind the complete insane asylum that I saw it in!

# MIKE McPADDEN

## ALL'S SWELL IN HAPPYLAND

RECORDED & MIXED

DRAFT

TYPICAL NIGHT AT THE LYRIC. *HAPPYLAND* NUMBER 2.

LYRIC

THEY CALL HIM FLIPPER

(...Selwyn Harris' recounting of a 42ND Street Fright so intense, it had Fishe and him runnin for the relative-comfort and safety of Cinema Kings Highway...)

October 12th,1990/
Dateline:the Deuce.

It was the toughest call of the year. The setting couldn't have been more familiar-Fishel and I were in the midst of our weekly Friday night Forty-Second Street frolic - but a dilemma arose of unprecedented magnitude. We had been planning to see the just-released "Marked for Death" featuring the pre-bloat Steven Seagal going ponytail-to-dreads against Rastamen running wild in suburbia, but an amble up to 8th Avenue had revealed that Puerto Rican porn godess KEISHA would be at Show World in all her mega-mammaried magnificence. We had one serious fucking decision to make.

I was all in favor of the Lady (note the capital "L"; that denotes that she's got CLAAASS): we could drop a tenspot to get into the Triple Treat, watch the tropical tasty shake her mangos, and then each load a buck or two worth of tokens into a private booth and pop sackfuls of coconut milk all over the floor. No fuss, and just a little muss (and the mop-jockey would take care of that). Fishel, however, was tight on funds, so I made the concession: kicks-in-the-ass won out over tits-and-ass. We approached the Lyric theatre (where "Marked for Death" was playing) and within seconds the first omen of things to come was upon us.

You see, to reach the silver-haired (and gold-toothed) Negress in the ticket booth, we had to navigate our way through a cluster of young Latina pubescitas - who knew they were on line? (They could just as easily been Keisha's hometown booster club trying to figure out which way Show World was, for all I knew). It turned out, of course, that they WERE on line line and the littlest of them let my white ass know right properly; "Jew trah det sheet in MY neighbuhood", she informed me, "Motherfucka. jew would be sorry!" I was sorry anyway, and I told her and she said something back, but my Homegirlese was a little rusty so I have no idea what it was. Maybe she complimented me on the prompt politeness of my apology. Maybe.

What we should have taken as the second warning occured inside the theatre, when we saw that ther were virtually no seats left. Except for two. In the last row. Behind a pair of boisterous, hearty, well-muscled African American gents. We sat down right in back of them. This was a bad idea.

These new neighbors of ours, the substance-abusers of color, had been whooping it up and having a fine night out at the theatre. Bully for them! They were occupying the first three seats in from the aisle, leaving an empty chair between them, which they then utilized as a handy dumping ground for their empty 40-oz Malt Liquor bottles. How ingeneous! Eco-conscious, too! Thus far, they had made five deposits and were well into prepping numbers six and seven.

Fishel and I assumed, though Christ knows why, that even though our homeys were conversing throughout the opening credits, once the actors on-screen started talking, they would stop. Ha. Ha. Ha. The degenerate duo continued in their give-and-take as casually and melifluously as though they were on line for food stamps or under arrest or engaged in any other of their day-to-day activities, but with one minor adjustment: to be heard above the movie's war-whoops, flying limbs and artillery fire, the dreadful discoursers upped their volume. Considerably. Like beyond Sam Kinison, beyond the Reverb Motherfuckers, beyond Chinese New Year, and beyond Fishel in the bathroom on Saturday morning. My ears have never endured such a trial, and yours haven't either.

It's not as though their talk wasn't engaging
(STEPIN: "Yo! Hushmush muffusk shih huffmuckfuck! HA-ha-AHA!"
FETCHIT: "Ah heah DAT! Ha ha ha ha!"), but it was knocking plaster off of the ceiling. Still, though, what were we to do? Raise our index fingers to our puckered lips and say "Do you MIND!?!", punctuating each syllable with a tap, maybe? It probably wouldn't have worked. And so the Nasty Negroid Noise-a-Thon continued.

...And actually got LOUDER upon its taking a universally provocative direction: oh,the power of pussy! What implemented this was that the lilting Latinas that I had seemingly wronged outside were now inside and searching for seats. Within seconds, our heroes were searching the seats of the girls' pants. "LOOKIT DAT ASS!", the more vociferous of the two yelled to the other one who was not two feet away from him.

"YOU KNOW AH KNOWS IT! YOU KNOW AH KNOWS IT!", came the response. Considering the VOLUME of his words, all those lucky bastards up the block at Show World probably knew he knewed it, too.

They tried to slap each other five. They missed.

"JEW BETTER WATCH IT, NIGGA!", the lass with "DAT ASS" shouted back at our boyz. And, wow, it was none other than my bon-bon from the box office. What a firecracker!

But ever the verbal gamesman, the Mad Chatter turned her warning around by announcing, "YOU RIGHT, BITCH, I'LL WATCH IT! I'LL WATCH YO ASS ALL NIGHT! FUCK DA MUFFUCKIN MOOBIE!" What a display of one-upsmanship! He wasn't done yet, though -- oh no!

"AND IF YA'LL DOAN LIKE IT", he continued, "I'LL LOOKIT YO MAN'S ASS-FUCK YA'S ALL! WOOOOO-HAHAHAHAHAHAHA!!!!"

For that genuinely surprising declaration of sexual liberation, the brothers made good on the high five. The audience was pleased, too, showering the unexpected performer with laughter, applause, "HO SHITS!", and that annoying "HOO-HOO-HOO" sound. Fishel and I, in the meantime, were cement. We sat feigning fixation on a movie that we could neither hear for all the brouhahahahaha, nor could we see for all the darked-skinned limbs flailing in felicitaion. We were scared. Shitless.

We were spared true, unadulterated terror, however, until Super blurted to Fly, "AH GOTS TA PESS!". That meant he would be moving. HO SHIT!

His buddy gave him

**JS: What kind of asylum are we talking about?**

**MM:** Here's the reality of it: I grew up in Brooklyn in the seventies. And I took the train from Brooklyn to Manhattan from 1982 to 1986.

**JS: When you were in high school?**

**MM:** Yeah. I got mugged minimally once a year. New York was a fucking cesspool; it was dangerous and violent—your father got beat up regularly just going to work. It sucked. But at the same time, it was exciting and fun and crazy. There was a downside and an upside. There's a very romantic notion of that downside. Do you know the movie *The Goodbye Girl*?

**JS: With Richard Dreyfuss and Marsha Mason?**

**MM:** Yeah. They live in SoHo, right when it was gentrifying in the seventies. Marsha Mason is carrying groceries. A car pulls up, a guy jumps out and punches her, grabs her purse, and drives away. That's what New York was like when I was a kid. It sucked. At the same time, it sucks now. It's fucking heinous to go back there.

**JS: I didn't make it there until just before Giuliani had had his way with the place.**

**MM:** Giuliani had nothing to do with it. What killed Times Square was home video, crack, and AIDS.

**JS: The times and technology changed.**

**MM:** We don't go out to see porno movies anymore. We don't go out to see cannibal movies anymore. And then with crack and AIDS, there was a sense of real violent insanity and real death mixed in with all of the dangerous fun.

**JS: Didn't you see some shows at the Dive?**

**MM:** Yeah. It was weird. I was fifteen years old, and that was a time when you could walk into a bar in New York at age twelve and order a drink. Nobody batted an eye. I didn't start drinking until later—I wanted to go see the movies because I worshiped the *Gore Gazette*.

**JS: What was that scene like?**

**MM:** It was an older crowd. They were all drunk and yelling and cheering. I have to say, I was mildly annoyed because I just wanted to watch the movies. It wasn't like 42nd Street at all.

**JS: What was the difference?**

**MM:** On 42nd Street, when the audience was screaming and

RECORDED & INDEXED
DRAFT

participating, it was very different. They were having involuntary reactions to their reality.

**JS: Do you remember the 8th Street Playhouse?**

**MM:** I tried to see *Ilsa* there when I was fourteen. It was part of a *Sleazoid* festival, and I got turned away for being too young.

**JS: That's happened to the worst of us [laughs]. Hey, I meant to ask you this—it might sound kind of clichéd, but when did you decide that you wanted to write?**

**MM:** Well, I went to SUNY Purchase [Purchase College, State University of New York] to go to film school and I flunked out. I spent a couple of years not doing anything. That's when I started writing—I put it together in *Happyland*. A few months after the first issue, a friend of mine who had been working at the *New York Press* brought it in and they loved it. They offered me freelance and I've been writing for money ever since. Their art director had worked at *Hustler* and he sent *Happyland* out to them. I got a full-time gig working there for a few years.

**JS: You also worked for *Screw*. What was that like?**

**MM:** *Screw* was pretty great. There were a lot of the same people in the porno mags and in the zine world. David Aaron Clark was the editor at the time.

**JS: Josh Alan Friedman's one of my favorite writers. He did some work for *Screw*, as well.**

**MM:** Oh yeah. He's been out to Chicago a couple of times and I've done some readings with him. He's the salt of the earth. His brother and his father are giants in their fields and Josh is a brilliant guy. I just wish he'd write some more books!

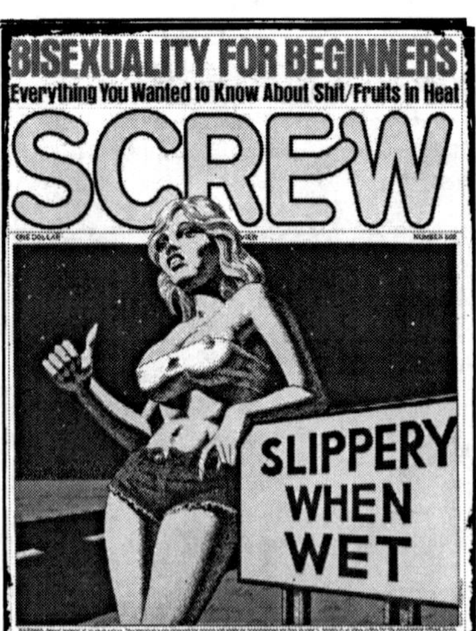


**JS: I'm curious—was your writing for *Happyland* alcohol-fueled?**

**MM:** Yeah. Well, no. I never wrote drunk because I couldn't do anything while I was drinking except drink. To go out and live, I had to drink. I've been clean for almost thirteen years. I'll tell you, I got clean in LA for a while. I came back to New York in October of '94 for the weekend or something. All the theaters on 42nd Street had closed, except for this one little shitbox multiplex up at the end of the block by the Port Authority. There was a 3 AM showing of *New Nightmare*.

**JS: The Freddy Krueger film?**

**MM:** Yeah. I showed up there sober

at 3 AM, which would have been the normal time that I went to a movie when I was drinking. I'm sitting there in this fucking theater, and the freaks come out at night. I got scared shitless! I was like, "What the fuck am I doing here?" I got up and ran out of the theater before the movie started. No wonder I was fucked up all the time! Jesus...

**JS: Where were you working when you were doing *Happyland*?**

**MM:** During the day, I had a job where I worked with retarded and autistic children. At night, I worked in the library at a Wall Street firm.

**JS: What was that like?**

**MM:** It was awesome, because I had computers, xerox machines, and paper.

**JS: I'll assume that Wall Street helped give birth to *Happyland*.**

**MM:** Yep. The only cost was reams of colored paper. That was very popular with the zinesters in the early nineties. The colors were things like Lift-off Lemon and Rocket Red. A ream of that was probably ten bucks or something. It didn't cost me anything. As often as I could, I stole postage from them, as well.

**JS: Didn't Matador Records have something to do with distribution?**

**MM:** For the first year, it was just out of my house. Then, Johan Kugelberg from Matador picked it up.

**JS: How did *Happyland* evolve over the years?**

**MM:** In the beginning, I wanted to meet girls. I drank at this bar called Downtown Beirut on First Ave and 10th Street. It was a punk bar, and I started writing this thing called "The Downtown Beirut Top 10 List" every week. It would be like ten stupid things that I liked, or whatever. I xeroxed them up and handed them out; I plastered them all over the bathroom and stuff. The zine kind of grew out of that. I started that in 1990—it was like the first version of *Happyland*. It gave me something to talk to girls about. And then, when I started the zine, I was like, "OK. I'm going to do a couple of things here. I'm going to emphasize what a drunk I am and I'm going to write that chicks really think I'm awesome and they want to fuck me." It wasn't true, but I wrote it and I swear to god it came true. So that was one thing. Then, I worked at *Hustler* and was in the porn business for a while. I

# MIKE MCPADDEN

## ALL'S SWELL IN HAPPYLAND

didn't do the zine for years. But then, the internet happened and I got sober—a lot of crazy things happened. 9/11 hit, and I thought it was the end of the world. I thought, "This is it. I better do some more *Happylands*." I put out three huge issues really fast. I think that those are as good as the original ones. They're different—they're not crazy and I'm not picking fights with anyone, but they're still pretty good.

**JS: Did punk zines influence you at all?**

**MM:** Absolutely. It all comes from punk, really. Music wise, *Conflict* was the big one.

**JS: Gerard Cosloy's zine?**

**MM:** Yeah. It was very nasty and cynical. I didn't agree with the guy's musical taste, but I loved it. He had a show on WFMU that I did a couple times, shitfaced drunk.

**JS: Is that archived?**

**MM:** I don't know. But, I just loved his writing. I'm trying to think of some other music zines. There was one called *Roessiger* that was pretty good—I think it was from Arizona. It had a word search that I was really jealous of. It just said, "Find these words: MASTURBATE, KILL." It was nothing but a grid of MASTURBATE and KILL. That whole aesthetic and mindset was really where I was coming from.

**JS: Before I forget, what kind of movies were you watching when you were growing up?**

**MM:** Monster movies. That's it. Monsters, horror, and sex. It never changed. I saw *Caddy Shack* and *Alien* in the theater—those are the first R-rated movies I saw. I was obsessed with *King Kong* on Chanel 9 in New York—they showed it all the time. The Vincent Price movies played on *The 4:30 Movie*. I was insane for *Mad Monster Party* when I was a little kid. And in terms of sex stuff, my neighbor was a film archivist. He collected all kinds of oddities. He would have these screenings at Brooklyn College where he'd show found footage and things like that. He had a blooper from a baby powder commercial. There were two girls in a bathroom and they have towels on. One girl's towel fell off and her tits came right out. The other girl panicked and threw her towel off, too. I saw that when I was seven years old. It blew my fucking mind—I couldn't believe it. I went out for intermission with my parents and I had to talk about anything but that. They showed the *King Kong*

MIKE MCPADDEN—HAPPY AFTER ALL THESE YEARS. PHOTO COURTESY MIKE MCPADDEN.

Volkswagen ad, and I was like, "Boy, I really liked that *King Kong* commercial." Which was true, but that wasn't what I was thinking about.

**JS: Were you into comics at all?**

**MM:** No, I was into *Mad* magazine. I was obsessive over *Mad*. And that's where it begins, really. I was six years old, and they had a flea-market at my school. I bought a shopping bag full of *Mads* for a quarter. That really rocked the universe for me. My father was a Green Beret, and he thought that *Mad* was very subversive, and correctly so. It would teach me to disrespect institutions and authority. So, there was always a lot of tension in my house over *Mad* magazine. I started fucking up in school when I was nine. He made me get all of my *Mad* magazines and we tore them up together. Years later, my very first tattoo (out of the hundreds that I have now) was Alfred E Neuman. So, make no mistake—if you want to fuck your kids up… [laughs]

**JS: Did *Fangoria* play a role in things?**

**MM:** Oh, yeah. I was kind of scared of it. It would freak me out to bring it home, but I would run to the supermarket to read it every month.

**JS: Now that we're back on the subject of magazines, what did you think about *Slimetime*?**

**MM:** I never saw *Slimetime*, I saw *Shock Cinema*. He seems like a good dude, Puchalski, but I always thought he was a terrible writer. I used to make fun of him a lot in *Happyland* and he fucking came to my house one day [laughs]. My insane old landlord and his giant German Sheppard didn't let him in. He wrote about that in *Shock Cinema*. I was like, "Oh… that kind of sucks!" But I thought it was pretty funny that he at least wrote about it. I mean, I've had contact with him and he's a good dude. And he does a valuable service, I have to say. That magazine alerted me to a lot of movies that I otherwise wouldn't have found on my own.

**JS: A lot of the New York guys seemed to have it in for one another.**

**MM:** It's like pro-wrestling. If you're a writer, it's like… you're a pussy. Some people go out on a limb and get into real fights, and the rest of us write about stuff. You start writing, and then you start writing really funny, ballsy stuff. It breeds a macho

RECORDED & INDEXED

DRAFT

mentality—it's like false machismo. I think that's kind of what it is. It's kind of like pro-wrestling; everyone's kind of boasting.

**JS: Speaking of fighting, you wrote an article in *Happyland* called "They Call Him Flipper" (about audience pandemonium at the Lyric theater). Was something like that a regular experience?**

**MM:** I'd have to say that it was a regular experience, but it wasn't constant. There were lots of fights because there were a lot of homeless people. A lot of people smoking crack. Hookers walking around offering blowjobs and crazies who were just there for the shelter. They'd be watching some fucking karate movie or something and they'd get emotionally overwhelmed by it. I saw guy beat the fuck out of a homeless woman. It really wasn't fun. It was kind of horrifying. A lot of bottles getting tossed against the screen or being dropped from the balcony. I walked downstairs once at the Harris, I think; it had this really steep staircase. There was a big drug deal going on in the men's room. I just fucking froze.

**JS: Things were pretty clean by the time I got to New York. Most of the adult bookstores were selling horror and schlock films in the front and XXX stuff in the back.**

**MM:** That was the 70–30 rule. That was the Giuliani thing that shut down what was left. It was either 70–30 or 80–20, but the overwhelming amount of a business had to be non-adult. They would just buy volumes of shit VHS tapes and dump them in the front of the store. It was pretty hilarious—I found a lot of cool stuff that way.

**JS: At the same time, a lot of these places had tapes like *Animal Farm* for sale.**

**MM:** Isn't it the craziest thing that the bestiality stuff was still just out in the open?

**JS: How much of that do you think was mob fueled?**

**MM:** I think roughly 100 per cent [laughs]! The crazy things that I got addicted to were the open window peepshows. It was a dollar to get the window open, and then for two bucks, you could squeeze some boobs and a butt. You got forty seconds of really good squeezing time.

**JS: What kind of people were waiting in line for that kind of thing?**

**MM:** You had the cross section of the world there. And some of the women were really heinous. But at the end, there was this explosion of women from the Soviet Union and the Eastern Bloc countries—they were fucking gorgeous. Hotter than any Hollywood movie star, and you could molest them for three bucks. A lot of my paychecks and a lot of my afternoons were wasted in those places.

**JS: What brought you to Chicago?**

**MM:** I got hired by Mr. Skin. I don't know if I'll stay here forever, but it's been good; I like it here. The Mr. Skin gig has been great. I've written two books under the Mr. Skin imprimatur—the *Mr. Skin Skincycopedia* and *Mr. Skin's Skintastic Video Guide*, which makes it all the more

# LAPPSAPOPPIN!

...SELWYN HARRIS lapdances around NYC.

(NOTE: Lo the perils of publishing behind schedule! This piece was written back in the sadly delusional days when I thought HAPPYLAND #4 would be hitting the street some time in April (remember *that* unfunny joke?). Bad news, kids: EVERY establishment described in the treatise below has either been shut down or beaten into "movies only" submission by the Orwellian Thought Thugs from the Times Square Redevelopement Program. Good thing I went on WFMU not long ago to declare the redevelopement utterly impotent and in no way capable of shutting down a single neon naked lady on the Deuce. Oops. I'm too fucking tired to whip up another manifesto on that particular topic; just consider the following a requiem. Some things truly are too good to last. Like this fanzine.)

Lap-dancing, Mardi Gras, Tease-n-Squeeze, Greasing Prettied-Up Puerto Rican Palms For the Pleasure of Having a Cottage-Cheese Caboose Booming Up & Down on Your Bone-On: call it what you will, it seems to be some sort of rage in the Bug Apple these days, a rage of which the borough of HAPPYLAND wholeheartedly approves. Our support is so enthusiastic (and costly), that we recently received yet another letter from The New York Savings Bank inquiring as to why we haven't added so much as a measly cent to the $8.73 that keeps our account open in over six months. HA--they'd be better off asking one (or a dozen) of the delightfully colorful seat-level entertainers who labor in these new lascivitoriums about the whereabouts of my finances: the *LADIES* don't seem to have any difficulty whatsoever in extracting cash from yours truly. In fact, the friggin' bank should be more concerned with keeping their mitts on the pittancely eight-bucks-&-change in the first place: certainly my newly beloved couch-cuties need it more than they do, and woe unto he who would ask me which of those parties (the bank or the bone-boomers) I need more.

How about you?

**************************

Cum-padres, cancer spread in our city this past Winter. Ugly cancer, vile cancer, misogynist cancer: the kind of cancer that forces women to starve themselves, to put plastic leukemia-bombs in their tits, to waste their money on pore-clogging war-paint---Hugh Hefner cancer. Among the tumors that cropped up in light of this infection were "Goldfingers", "Scores", "Stringfellows Pure Platinum" and a whole bunch of others that advertise in the Newsday sports pages. These loathsome pits are high-tech, Wall Street-sanitized versions of what pimple-dicks in $1200-dollar suits think a tit bar should be, complete with "carving board" buffet tables, walls of TV monitors beaming out every sports event going on on the planet at any given time (just to let the girls know that, sure, their tits are okay, but they ain't worth shit compared to Bobby Bonilla) and, of course, scads of brain-unencumbered bimbolines who brought their Barbie dolls to some quack plastic surgeon, so that he could use it as a model as he chipped away any part of their bodies that didn't look like it was manufactured by Mattel. In addition, these prick-palaces have lighting systems that could blow away the Hayden Planetarium's weekly "Laser Genesis" rockfest, but, still, as much as I despise such "Upscale Gentleman's Clubs", I must admit that you'd find me at "Flashdancers" a lot sooner than you'd ever see me surrounded by loose joint salesman in a museum auditorium with my head tilted toward the ceiling watching green trapezoids bounce off each other to "The Lamb Lies Down on Broadway". But that's just a funny sentence I felt like writing.

Scumigos (rhymes with "amigos", get it?), what I have cum to report to you on this day concerns a benevolent, counter-cancer that grew alongside the one described above. For a few weeks, there, it seemed that for every "Trump's Tush Mahol" that was opening up, some dank, sleazy, squirt toilet sprang to life for brief, but infinitely fruitful, lifespans. These foreboding-to-all-but-the-truest-of-believers holehells allowed women to really be women--in all their pudged-up, unshaven, odiferous glory--and allowed men to be the powerless, worshipful, slaves-to-punani cretins that we are (and that shitpits like "Scores" go all out to make it seem like we aren't). A little honesty, particularly on that level, goes a long way in my book, so believe me when I tell you that my intrepid travails to these establishments were purely for both anthropological and supportive purposes, as well as to inform you, my reading audience, about new and intriguing trends in the field of female-male relations; in short, purience was never a part of the equation. A lesser fanzine, now, would follow that preceding sentence above with the colloquialism, "Not". But we're better than that. And so are you.

Not.

**FANTASY IN MOTION (it was on the North side of 42nd Street before it burned down, then it moved south, then it changed its name to "Show Time Fantacy" (sic) and stopped offering Lap Dances)** Label me as you will, but I prefer my ladyfriends, both professional and otherwise, blobby and caucasoid (not that, in a pinch, I don't ravenously devour whatever's set out in front of me, but...). Imagine my delight, then, when after paying the weighty ten dollar entrance fee, I locked eyes inside with an even weightier blonde bouillelabasse spilling over the sides of a folding chair with my name practically written all over her cellulite. Excited, I shot her my finest little-boy-lost-in-the-big-city-with-only-his-fat-wallet-to-protect-him-and-his-hardon. Unimpressed, she shot back "I'm on break", which shot me right the hell down.

exciting to have two books with my own fucking name on the cover coming out [laughs].

**JS: What's a typical day like at Mr. Skin?**

**MM:** It's like any other place. There's a lot of laughing and joking; the site's really fun. And Mr. Skin himself is a really funny guy. We go in and we think of funny names for boobs. The guys in the back go through scenes with a microscope—our big find in recent years was Brigitte Bardot's ass hair in some movie. It's pretty awesome.

**JS: It sounds like a dream job, in a way.**

**MM:** Yeah, it is. I can't believe that this job exists and that I have it.

**JS: Let's get back to the stuff that you're working on now. What can we expect from *Heavy Metal Movies*?**

**MM:** Oh, dude, it's massive. It's 666 reviews with interviews and sidebars. It's fucking gigantic. I don't know how big this book is going to end up being.

**JS: Do you worry about that?**

**MM:** Yeah, I worry about it [laughs]! My original hope was to have this done by June, but I'm going to turn it in in December. So yeah, it's going to be a long, hot Summer. I'm going to be sitting and writing and writing and writing. But, I know that you'll be doing it, too.

**JS: Bazillion Points puts out some great stuff. I loved their *Touch and Go* book, and I can't wait to get my hands on *We Got Power*, not to mention *Heavy Metal Movies*. It's going to be a good year.**

**MM:** I'm completely honored to be working with them. I think they're the best publishing house going right now. No offense to Headpress—I love them, too [laughs].

**JS: I guess that's a good way to end things. I hope I've been coherent...**

**MM:** Yeah! And listen, if you have any follow ups, send them my way. Call me any time.

**JS: Sure thing. Hey—thanks a lot for the interview.**

**MM:** You got it, man. My pleasure.

# Chapter Thirty-Seven

## Devil Dolls and Blackest Hearts!

BLACKEST HEART NUMBER 3.

ARTWORK BY PASQUAL GONZALEZ.

# SHAWN "SMITH" LEWIS

## DEVIL DOLLS AND BLACKEST HEARTS!

Shawn "Smith" Lewis was the editor and publisher of *Blackest Heart*, an aptly named fanzine that reared its ugly head in the early 1990s. Its often misunderstood sense of humor and playful jabs at anything remotely resembling "good taste" soon gave it a reputation as the magazine you loved to hate—or hated to love. *Blackest Heart* lasted only three issues, but Lewis stayed in the publishing game, providing fans with a seemingly bottomless bag of bloody goods. If you were a horror fan in the nineties and early 2000s, it's safe to say that you purchased something from his mail order company, Blackest Heart Media.

Ever want to hear the music scores to *Zombie*, *House by the Cemetery*, and *Cannibal Ferox* in the comfort of your own home? Shawn "Smith" was the man to see. Ever wonder how some of Fulci's moistest and meatiest moments would play out in graphic novel form? Shawn was there, as well. Ever get nostalgic for the good old days of Chas. Balun's *Deep Red*? Shawn did, too and he published the last two issues of the master's mighty mag.

Today, Shawn Lewis runs Rotten Cotton Graphics, one of the finest genre T-shirt companies on the planet. He recently wrote and produced the notorious *Black Devil Doll*, an outrageous blaxsploitation puppet movie directed by his brother Jonathan. (A homage/satire of Charles Novell Turner's obscure 1984 *Black Devil Doll From Hell*.) As outspoken and as cavalier as ever, Shawn Lewis took a little time to talk to me on a fine afternoon in April. Let's get all old school and play back the tape to see what the man had to say...

The following interview was conducted via telephone on April 2, 2012.

---

**JOHN SZPUNAR: In the introduction to *Lucio Fulci: Beyond the Gates*, you thank your mother for raising you on horror films.**

**SHAWN LEWIS:** Yeah. It all goes back to when I was a kid. My mom's a horror fan. Not as much of a fan as I consider myself, but she was a casual one and we watched a Bay Area horror show that came on on Saturday night. It was called *Creature Features*. Bob Wilkins hosted it, and I grew up watching that from the time I was three. After Bob Wilkins left that show, John Stanley took over. It was on for years; I watched that for most of my childhood. I don't know—I don't let my kids watch half the things that my mom let me watch. She took me to see *Jaws* when I was seven. I saw *Zombie* at the drive-in when I was a little kid. She just thought it was fantasy; it was fun. She never looked at it as if it was dangerous for me. So, it's probably her fault that I'm into this [laughs]. But yeah, that's pretty much how things started for me.

**JS: What was it about horror films that grabbed you?**

**SL:** I don't know. I never really thought about it. I just always thought they were cool. I never had nightmares from watching them, and I was

never frightened by them when I was little. I just thought it was fun and exhilarating in the same way that some people enjoy rollercoasters or skiing. I liked horror movies for the same reasons, I guess.

**JS: How old were you when started going to the drive-in?**

**SL:** I was ten years old and my cousins and I would go. As I got older, I had to sneak into stuff that my mom didn't want to go see. But I distinctly remember seeing things like *Zombie* and *Gates of Hell*.

**JS: The Italians...**

**SL:** I knew they were Italian movies, but I didn't know who Lucio Fulci was. I didn't really pay attention to that stuff until I got older and I started reading Chas. Balun's stuff, like *Deep Red* and the *Connoisseur's Guide*.

**JS: I was in the dark about the origins of those films, as well.**

**SL:** When we were kids, there was no internet. You had to get magazines, you had to write letters—you had to really be into it to be a fan. I remember the big deal back then was the ad in *Fangoria* for FantaCo.

**JS: FantaCo was a real eye-opener for our generation.**

**SL:** I loved going through the catalogs and buying everything, from *Gore Shriek* to *Deep Red*. That's when I found out who Chas. was. I became pen-pals with him because I was a fan, and our relationship grew from there. But, that's pretty much what I was into. It started with the Italian stuff at the drive-in, and I saw all of the American stuff, too. I remember seeing *Scanners*, the *It's Alive* films, and things like that. I really dug that stuff.

**JS: I used to ride my bike to the corner store to pick up *Fangoria* when I could afford it. Were you aware of *Fango* from the get-go?**

**SL:** No. I didn't discover *Fango* from the first issue. I was in a Walden's bookstore when I saw an issue where they covered the movie *The Sender*. They showed a scene where somebody sort of knocked somebody's head off with their palm. That really blew me away and I subscribed. I got all of the back issues.

**JS: In my mind, *Deep Red* was to *Fangoria* what *Fango* was to *Famous Monsters*.**

RECORDED & INDEXED

**SL:** That's an excellent analogy. At the time, nobody was writing like Chas. His stuff just worked really well. He really got it. I enjoyed reading Uncle Bob's stuff in *Fango*, but there was something about Chas. He was one of us. He was a fan who was describing things from a fan's point of view, instead of some suit doing a set visit and trying to talk about a movie that he didn't really get. I was hooked on his writing style from the first day I read his stuff.

**JS: How did you get started writing?**

**SL:** I'm trying to remember how it came about. Chas. would sell things that were not available on tape through his mail order. I started trading with him and getting videos from other friends who were collecting. That was the way you got stuff back then. There wasn't a day that went by where I didn't get a copy of a Japanese laserdisc or something in the mail. It was big deal. And then, the people who didn't have anything to trade wanted stuff, so I started selling it. I started reviewing movies in my catalog. I think that led to me doing a magazine. That's how I started writing about movies.

**JS: When did the first issue of *Blackest Heart* come out?**

**SL:** If I'm not mistaken, we were writing in 1989 and I finally got it published in 1990. At that time, I was computer-illiterate. I didn't even have a computer. My co-editor Tim Patrick had some kind of a publishing program and he laid everything out. All we did was print it out and take it to the Kinko's. The first two issues were pretty much photocopied. I was going back to Kinko's and reprinting them so often that it was getting to be annoying. We'd go there and everyone was reading it—they gave us these weird looks. So for the third one, I found a printer that was local and had it offset printed there. That's why it has the card stock and is printed a little nicer. Actually, it's funny—I used that printer to do a couple of issues of the *Deep Red* magazines that I published. When we were doing the last issue of *Deep Red*, I went in to pick the magazine up and the building was boarded up. The printer

had been arrested for printing counterfeit money. I couldn't get the magazines—we were screwed. That's why there was a delay on that last issue. It finally came out six months later.

**JS: That's pretty crazy. Do you have any back stock of those old issues?**

**SL:** I might have some issues of the last *Deep Red*—the one with the *Cannibal Holocaust* image. The other one, with *The Beyond* cover, is long gone.

**JS: What other zines inspired you?**

**SL:** You know, the other thing that inspired *Blackest Heart* was Rick Sullivan. I loved Chas.' writing, but I remember reading the *Gore Gazette* and going, "Wow! This is like Chas. and Howard Stern put together!" It was fun, and I liked it. I was an angry teenager and I thought, "Let's do something that's like a tabloid of the horror genre—the Howard Stern of exploitation!" And that's why *Blackest Heart* was what it was. We were really crude just for the sake of being that way. We thought it was fun, but if you didn't know us, you would probably take it seriously. We always had that problem with our sense of humor. You'd either get it or you'd think, "Wow, these kids are just assholes!" There was always a fine line, and I really enjoyed that.

**JS: What was Rick Sullivan's take on *Blackest Heart*?**

**SL:** It was great. He really enjoyed what we were doing.

**JS: Did you ever meet him?**

**SL:** Yeah. I used to go to Chiller all the time when I was younger. He's another guy that you should interview. Nobody really knows why he stopped doing what he was doing. The main thing that I heard was that he pissed off a particular "editor" of a popular independent film magazine, which I can't name for legal reasons. Anyway, rumor has it, that this "editor" turned Sullivan in to the FBI for selling Tracy Lords videos. I guess Rick was driving kids to school on a bus—that's what he did for a living. They were going to mess with his job, so he had to basically bail out from the entire scene. That was the story that I heard. I don't know if that's true, but I almost believe it because I used to piss off this "editor", too. I remember going to my PO Box right after *Blackest Heart* number 3 came out, which featured a

BLACKEST HEART
THE MOST DANGEROUS MAGAZINE IN THE WORLD!
ISSUE #2 $6.00
CENSORED BANNED AND BURNED!
HORROR
GORE
SLEAZE
SEXPLOITATION
XXX - ADULTS ONLY!

# SHAWN "SMITH" LEWIS

## DEVIL DOLLS AND BLACKEST HEARTS!

RECORDED & INKED

THE MOST DISGUSTING MAGAZINE IN THE WORLD

BLACKEST HEART

ISSUE #1 $5.00

PETER JACKSON'S
BRAIN DEAD
JOHN WOO
LUCIO FULCI
CHRISTIAN GORE
(FUCKING PRICK)

UNDER-
GROUND
HORROR
FILM
AND
VIDEO

ANAL NUNS
SON OF CRUEL
SHOES
MEATMAN
FAMOUS
FUCKHEADS
BEER
DEATH METAL WITH
*CIRCUS OF FEAR*
REVIEWS:
HELLRAISER III
UNCUT RABID
GRANNIES

REVIEWS
FICTION
ARTWORK
EDITORIALS
SEXPLOITATION
SLEAZE
GORE

FOR ADULTS ONLY! (MUST BE OVER 18, DAMMIT!)

pretty nasty piece on this "editor", and with all my mail was a card from the MPAA! I called the number and the MPAA informed me that they were investigating me for selling copies of that shitty Kevin Costner film *Waterworld* at Chiller Theatre Convention in New Jersey. I had to prove that I was working that day to clear my name. I'm pretty sure this "editor" tried to set us up, but I can't prove it. But whatever, it was a long time ago, and I probably deserved it for being an asshole.

**JS: How did you go about choosing your staff for *Blackest Heart*?**

**SL:** It was basically just friends, if I remember correctly. I think Ken Kish (of Cinema Wasteland) used to write a piece in there. Just about everyone in there was a pen-pal. It's like today you have Facebook and all this shit, but back then you actually had to write a letter and get it stamped. When I think about how things are today, I'm blown away by how things have changed.

**JS: In such a short period of time, too. It's mind boggling.**

**SL:** It really is. I mean, even just with selling things. I had to make a catalog, put an ad in *Fangoria*, people had to send away for the catalog, I had to mail the catalog, they'd get the catalog, they had to write down what they wanted, they'd get a money order—it's unreal what you had to do to order a T-shirt back then. Now it's like, "Click, click, click." It's amazing.

**JS: How did you meet your co-editor, Timothy Patrick?**

**SL:** Timothy and I went to school together a Christian school, from first grade through eighth. We went to different high schools, but remained friends throughout high school and a few years into college.

**JS: What's he up to these days?**

**SL:** He is now a mechanical engineer and builds bombs for the government. He's also a born again Christian and he won't talk to me anymore. Go figure.

**JS: Do you mind if I ask you about Damon Foster (editor of *Oriental Cinema*)?**

**SL:** No, go ahead. You can ask me anything you want.

**JS: It seems like you really had a falling out with him.**

**SL:** Well, here's the thing. He wrote a couple things for *Blackest Heart*. He was a local dude who lived around here and I knew about him. I didn't have any friends who were into Asian cinema at the time—I was into it, but not comfortable enough to write about it. Naturally, I asked him and he wrote a couple of pieces for issues 1 and 2. I got an overwhelming amount of hate mail about him. People were complaining that they didn't like his writing style and they thought he was a tool. I was torn—should I be honest and print things about his writing and be a jerk? I didn't know what to do. Basically, I left it up to Tim, who was my co-editor. I said, "Look, Damon's not a huge friend of mine or anything, but this is what the fans of the magazine are saying."

**JS: I remember reading a pretty negative review of one of his films in *Blackest Heart*.**

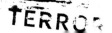

**SL:** It was a review of *Age of Demons*. That's what really pissed him off. We gave it a bad review, but we were honest. I guess when you do a magazine, you're supposed to lie and say your friends' movies are cool when they're not. We never did that. I remember being at a convention right after the magazine came out. It was in San Jose, and Damon Foster and his friend who was in the movie were there. They walked up to my table and they had this attitude like they were going to beat me up and kick my ass. It was almost like a bad kung fu movie. They were shaking. The short guy said, "You said I studied karate at McDonald's!" He was freaking out. I said, "First of all, I didn't write that. I published it, but I didn't write it. But it's an honest review. And besides, everything in the magazine is a joke. I make fun of myself—I'm sitting on the toilet on one page." I basically talked them out of wanting to beat me up. I saw Damon around five years ago at a concert and he said hi to me, so I guess he's not mad anymore. But, it wasn't one of those things where I had a falling out with this guy and was like, "Now I'm going to bash him!" It was an honest thing where the reviewer didn't like his movie. I think Tim said something negative about his writing in the editorial, too. But you know, we were kids. I'm an adult now and I've got two kids. I think differently about things. If I had chance to do that now, I wouldn't do it. When you're a dumb kid, you do dumb stuff.

**JS: I don't want to keep hitting on negative things, but I recall you having a falling out with Chris Gore as well. How did that whole falling out happen?**

**SL:** I really don't have anything against him anymore. I see him at shows and I think he's even on my Facebook page. Again, I was a dumb kid. But the thing with Chris Gore was that he attacked Chas. Chas. was our hero at the time, and you kind of just took a side. Who is this guy messing with Chas? We got pissed and we decided to write about him because of what he did.

**JS: For those who don't know the story, what did he do?**

**SL:** Chas. was selling copies of *Nekromantik*. I guess Chris Gore got the US rights. I mean, look—all he

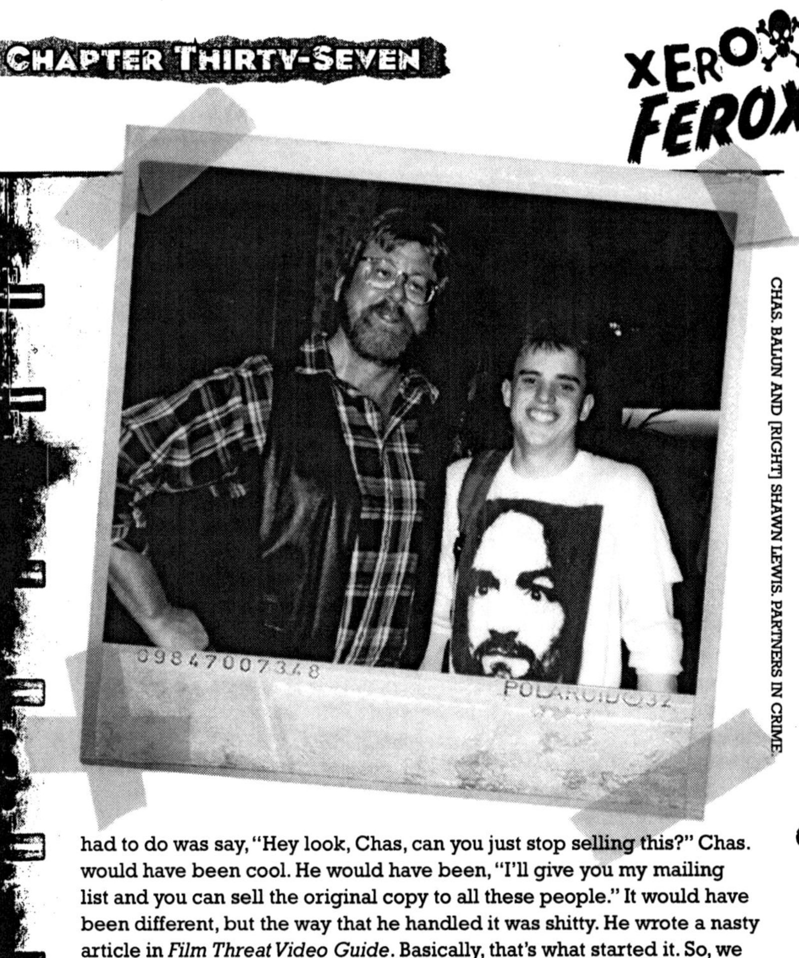

CHAS. BALUN AND [RIGHT] SHAWN LEWIS. PARTNERS IN CRIME.

had to do was say, "Hey look, Chas, can you just stop selling this?" Chas. would have been cool. He would have been, "I'll give you my mailing list and you can sell the original copy to all these people." It would have been different, but the way that he handled it was shitty. He wrote a nasty article in *Film Threat Video Guide*. Basically, that's what started it. So, we just had fun messing with him. Now I look back on it and I would never do something like that today. But I don't really regret doing it. It was a lot of fun. I never heard from him personally about what he thought of it. I was at a convention when issue 3 came out and this guy came up to the table and started flipping through it. We did this whole piece on Chris Gore in there and he sat there and read the whole thing. He said, "It's all true." I didn't know who the fuck this guy was, but I ended up seeing a picture of him later. It was David E. Williams, one of the guys who wrote for *Film Threat*. I thought that was funny.

**JS: *Blackest Heart* only lasted for three issues.**

**SL:** Yeah. There were supposed to be four. You know, I'm just going to be honest with you—issue four got put on the back burner, and by the time I got back to it, I was a different person. I had changed, and I didn't want to do it anymore. I was afraid that if I did the magazine, the fans wouldn't like it because it wouldn't be the same. I decided not to do another one. I still have

CD SOUNDTRACK BOOTLEGS.

that negative attitude, but it's not as bad as it used to be. Your thinking changes as you grow. And I'm not a religious person, but I kind of believe in karma, somehow. If you treat people shitty, people are going to treat you shitty. I've experienced that, and I don't like it. I decided, "You know… this is getting old. I'm not going to do this anymore." When I was going to do *Blackest Heart* number 4, it was going to be straight reviews and strait horror with a little attitude, but that wasn't the same thing anymore. I never did it.

**JS: I remember buying a lot of soundtrack CDs from you. I think the first one was the score to *Zombie* by Fabio Frizzi. How did you get into doing that?**

**SL:** Well, at the time, those things weren't available. It was kind of like the video thing. The only release of the *Zombie* soundtrack was a Japanese 45. One side of the record had the theme song from *Zombie* and the other had the calypso/island type song. That was the only way you could get the music. Well fuck, you know… let's put this on CD! We bootlegged it, and I had Chas. do the cover art for it. It was a learning experience; I had never done anything like it. It didn't sound very good, but it was fun and relatively inexpensive to produce. And it was popular—I sold out of that one really quickly. I think I only made 1,000 of them and they were gone, like BOOM!

**JS: I'm pretty sure that I got one from you at a *Fangoria* convention. Those CDs were cool. I really liked the *House by the Cemetery* CD that had an interview with Catriona MacColl.**

**SL:** Yeah. The other CDs were done the same way. There was one that we did with *Gates of Hell* and *Zombie*, and it was mastered from some LPs that I had. I had some Italian-pressed albums that were fucking awesome. That one sounded a little bit better because the quality of the LPs was better. We took them to a place that cleaned them up a little to get rid of the popping. You could still tell they were from LPs, but they sounded a lot better. By the time we started releasing the comic books and the CDs, I had met Stephen Romano and he had his own studio. We were able to mix the music in a twenty-four track studio and make it sound really fat. And by that point, everything was licensed.

**JS: What kind of a project was it to put out the *Lucio Fulci: A Symphony***

*of Fear* **CD?**

**SL:** That was a lot of work. It was really difficult. It was actually supposed to be longer—we still have a whole third disc of stuff that never made it on there.

**JS: Have ever you considered releasing it?**

**SL:** Nobody buys CDs anymore. I've been talking to Docion Alucarda, the guy who used to run Graveside Entertainment, because we produced it together. We've been talking about how to get all that crap on iTunes or something. We were contemplating re-releasing it with new packaging and putting some of the outtakes on there. But I don't think anyone's going to buy CDs anymore. Not like they used to, anyway.

**JS: I guess you could try a gimmick and release it as a record, but I don't know how many people are pressing vinyl these days.**

**SL:** Yeah. There's only a couple of places left that press vinyl. But it was fun doing it, and it was pretty inexpensive for us because we had all the bands produce their own music. I think we only ended up paying for a few tracks. So, it was really inexpensive to do, but it was a lot of work compiling it all and getting it all worked out.

**JS: A little while ago, you were talking about the graphic novels that you put out. I've got *Zombie* and *The Beyond*. Were you involved with Derek Rook's *Gates of Hell* comic book?**

**SL:** I didn't produce that one. See, *Zombie* sold really well. But at the time, *The Beyond* wasn't as popular as *Zombie* and I had trouble selling that one. The printer bill for that was outrageous, as you can imagine. Doing a comic book is very expensive. So, when it came time to do *Gates of Hell*, I just told the guy, "Man, I'm not doing it." It just wasn't worth it. By that time, I was about to get married and I had other bills. I just couldn't afford it. Steve Romano and Derek Rook published the first issue of *The Gates of Hell*, and it was amazing. Recently, those guys went back in and took the *Zombie* comic and colored it. It's all color now, and they're going to release it as a series. They're going to do that with *Gates of Hell*, too.

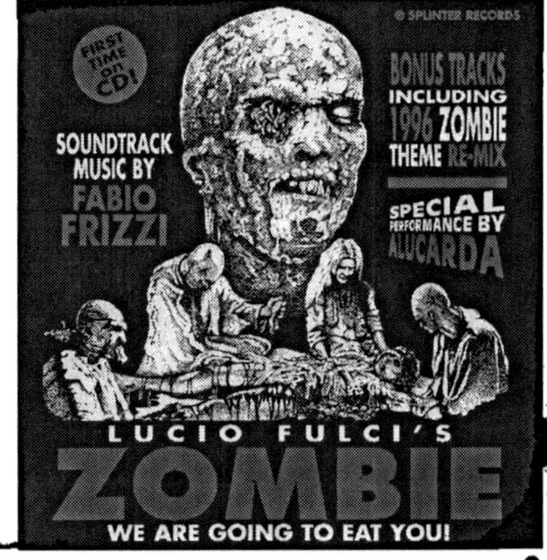


**JS: How did you come to publish the last two issues of *Deep Red*?**

**SL:** Well, the older Chas. got, the lazier he got. He didn't want to write anymore. He had this attitude of, "Nobody cares about my stuff." I said, "Dude, you're crazy! You have fans, you just

RECORDED & INDEXED

BLACKEST HEART NUMBER 2.

# THE GUYS WHO THROW THIS FUCKIN' THING TOGETHER

**TIMOTHY PATRICK**

I've been writing fiction for about four years, but that isn't my dream job. No, I want to appear on *Showtime at the Apollo* as a white comedian. My opening joke would be: *All I see is eyes and teeth.* I wonder if they'd laugh?

Seriously, I hope to have my novel, **FAMILY KILLERS**, published in the near future. I suspect that my writing may be too intense for most publishers, so I might do it myself and sell it through the mail. We'll see (let me know if you'd be interested in purchasing a copy--it's about 220 8-1/2" x 11" pages).

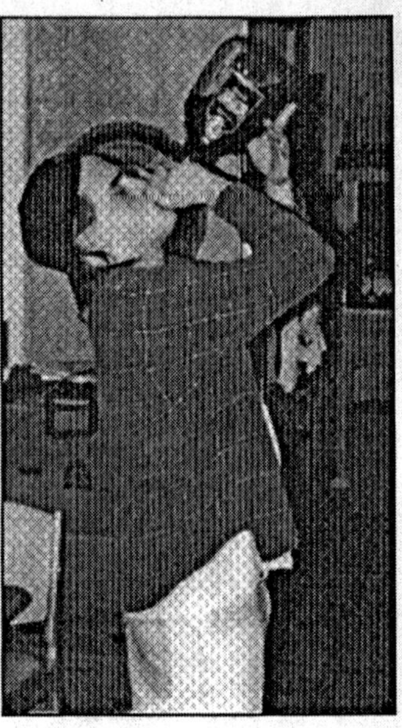

**SHAWN SMITH**

I'm sick and tired of bullshit, pussy, horror mags! I've had my own underground videotape business for the last six years, and I've seen a lot of shitty mags. My customers always complained that there were no magazines with balls. So a few years ago I started **Gore Connection.**

**Gore Connection** had the right intentions, but we didn't have the money or the help to make it a great mag. Once we started pimpin' 'ho's and saving our money, we could finally afford to make BLACKEST HEART!

don't get it!" I basically had to talk him into doing those *Deep Red*s. It was like pulling teeth trying to get him to do them. And you can notice that anything that he put out just got thinner and smaller; instead of being a book, it would be a pamphlet. That's just the way he was. And that's why the issue with *The Beyond* spider cover doesn't really have a voice. It's not like the old *Deep Red*s. I didn't like that one, personally. When we did the last one, I said, "Chas, we've got to really do something cool with this one and make it special." I think the last one is a lot better.

**JS: I think so, too. You also published a lot of Chas.' later books. How**

**many books did *Blackest Heart* put out?**

**SL:** Oh, man. I don't know. It was quite a bit just with *Blackest Heart* itself, and then the *Deep Red*s and the comic books. I mean, that's all I was doing. It seemed like I was always publishing something. I never counted, but I did a lot of it.

**JS: How did distribution work?**

**SL:** I pretty much self-distributed the majority of that stuff. I didn't have a problem, because I had so many people on my mailing list, from all over the world. When I got to *The Beyond* comic book, I had Diamond sell some of those for us. That was really my first distributor. Everything before that was self-distributed through my mail order. I liked it better that way because I made more money. It might have taken me a little longer to move that stuff, but in the long run, things turned out better. That's the way you did things back then. If you were doing a small market item, there wasn't a distributor who would carry it, anyway.

**JS: How did Rotten Cotton get started up?**

**SL:** The market for the bootleg tapes was dying quickly. I was like, "I can't continue to do this." At that time, I still had a day job.

**JS: What were you doing?**

**SL:** I was a baker. I made doughnuts and bread and cake. I was there for twelve years. Actually, I had to get up at two in the morning, so it wasn't a day job [laughs]. But, that's what I did. I was like, "I don't want to continue doing this shit and I can't continue doing videos." We were selling T-shirts through *Blackest Heart*, and I thought, "Well, maybe I can make that a better deal." Years ago, there was a company called Mutilation Graphics. They sold punk and drive-in movie T-shirts. I used to buy them when I was in high school. They were selling their company in the late eighties and I couldn't afford to buy the company. A good friend of mine bought it, and he changed the name to Ransom Note Graphics. I ended up buying some shirts

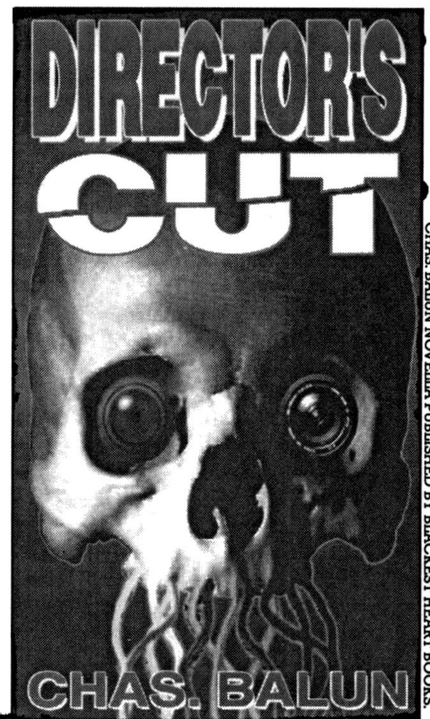


CHAS. BALUN NOVELLA PUBLISHED BY BLACKEST HEART BOOKS.

from him and putting them in the *Blackest Heart* catalog. He ended up selling Ransom Note Graphics right when I was trying to figure out how to get a T-shirt thing going. I ended up buying his T-shirt company. He taught me how to screen print, and I changed the name to Rotten Cotton. I fazed *Blackest Heart* out and just started doing the T-shirt thing. Once I did that, Chas. Balun became a full-time employee with me. He was the art director and all he did was design T-shirts. And, that was another reason why he wasn't doing books. Literally every week, he was designing a T-shirt for me. So, Rotten Cotton completely took over, I quit my day job, and I never looked back.

**JS: I'm interested in the mechanics of things. How do you go about producing and screening a shirt, especially with the amount of detail that Chas.' artwork had?**

**SL:** It's different now. Chas. was really old school. He didn't use a computer for anything! Towards the end, that got extremely frustrating because if you're not using a computer, you're behind. Basically, Chas. would draw the artwork by hand with a triple-O Rapidograph pen. He drew with dots. That artwork was just dot, dot, dot, dot, dot, dot, dot, dot with a fucking magnifying glass for hours. That's how he would do it. And then, he would take it to a place and have them shoot film. They'd roll the film up into a tube and ship it to me. I have screens that I coat with a light emulsion. You burn the image, and if there's more than one color, you have to burn each color in a separate plate. You have to burn all the images. Basically, screen printing, the way I do it, is all done by hand. You're running a squeegee over a screen with ink in it onto the shirt. You have to cure the shirt in an industrial dryer. It's a long process, and it's expensive.

**JS: How long did it take you to master that?**

**SL:** I'm really good at it now. If you bought a shirt from me twelve years ago, you might have gotten a really shitty shirt. It's a learning process, and I'm at the point now where I can do it in my sleep because that's all I've been doing for more than fifteen years. But now, it's different. Towards the end, Chas. finally got on board with the computer and got friendly with it to the point where he could draw and scan the image in. He'd manipulate it with the computer and email it to me. I have a printer here where I can output the film. We cut out the whole step of having the film shot and it made it a lot easier. But yeah, he was stubborn about wanting to use a computer. He was an old hippy; Chas. didn't even like the phone. He would rather just talk in person.

**JS: How big is your operation these days?**

**SL:** Well, I have two kids now. My daughter is seven and my son is three. When they were younger, I hired an employee to help me out because I couldn't take care of my kids and do the work. But now I've got my kids in school and daycare. And when the economy went bad, I had to let my employee go. So basically, it's just me. I do all the printing, folding,

*BLACK DEVIL DOLL*. HE'S A LOVER, HE'S A KILLER... HE'S A MOTHAFUCKIN' PUPPET!

packaging, shipping, and internet. I have a guy that does artwork and design, but as far as all the labor here, everything is me. I think we have around 500 designs and they're all hand done. So basically, I get up in the morning and work until I go to bed. It's not easy, but when you're working for yourself, it doesn't matter. If I was working those hours making doughnuts, I wouldn't be able to handle it.

**JS: As if you weren't busy enough, how did *Black Devil Doll* come about?**

**SL:** Well, I've always been a fan of those shitty Charles Band movies.

**JS: Empire Pictures?**

**SL:** Yeah. Stewart Gordon's *Dolls* is my favorite. I don't know what it is about that stuff. There's something about having a puppet reacting to actors that I've always enjoyed. I even liked the lame TV show *Alf* because of that. Kid stuff, like the Muppet movies—I don't know what it is, but I've always been really interested in that. I always thought that I'd missed my calling and I should have been a ventriloquist. *Black Devil Doll from Hell* is another favorite of mine. So, my brother was in college and started to make films. And another friend of mine made this cat-fight video called *Brawling Broads*. We were all hanging out one night, watching movies. I think we were watching *Puppetmaster* or something. I said, "We need to make a fucking puppet movie! We can do this—we have cameras, we have everything. Let's do this!" Literally within a month of me saying that, we were shooting. It happened that quick. The next weekend, we started writing a script. I was looking online for people who made ventriloquist dolls. I found this white doll, and I said, "Can you just send me the doll unpainted and unassembled? We're going to make our own thing." I bought a head, hands, and a torso. We started messing around with it, trying to come up with a look. That's how that started.

**JS: How long did it take to complete the film?**

**SL:** Well, we had a lot of problems because we all had day jobs. I was running Rotten Cotton, and I had kids. It was pretty hectic. Most of the cast were strippers who were unreliable. We were afraid that we'd shoot something with these girls and they'd have to come back for another scene and we'd never see them again. We were really terrified of that the whole time. I think it took a month to shoot everything on weekends. Then, you're talking about a lot of post—the Foley work was all done old school; we didn't use a computer for any of that stuff. The doll's voice had to be done in post and the editing took forever. We really didn't know what we were doing, and we were using this really crappy consumer-grade camera. When we were looking through the viewfinder, we thought, "OK, this is what we're framing." In actuality, it was like a few inches or so off. There were scenes that we shot that were perfect, but you could see my hand operating the doll. We were worried that we weren't even going to have a movie. It was pretty hectic. I think it took a month to shoot it and then another month to re-shoot the things that were fucked up. And it took a year or more to edit it. We were learning, and there were so many mistakes that we had to correct. But it was a learning experience. My brother actually went on to film school and we all know what we're doing now. When we make the next one, we'll be smarter.

**JS: Did you have any problems with the tone of the film?**

**SL:** You would think so, but not really. We had people complain here and there, but that's part of the fun. People have called me racist and everything, and I get it—but, my stepfather is black. He raised me from the time I was three. My brothers are half-black. I grew up in Oakland, and most of my friends are black, so I'm almost like a black guy trapped in a white guy's body. I've never looked at the film as being racist, because I've just had a different experience than other people. And anyone who knows me and knows my family doesn't look at it as being racist, either. But, I do understand a person who doesn't know what the deal is looking at it that way. We just made fun of stereotypes because stereotypes are fun. We don't take it too seriously. I can understand how somebody would, but that doesn't bother me.

**JS: So, has the film been received well for the most part?**

**SL:** Oh, yeah. The way we promoted that film and the way we sold it was really smart. I think it really worked. It's got tons of fans and we've sold more units than I thought we could ever sell. We got great distribution—Grindhouse distributed it—and we got it into just about every store you

can imagine. So yeah—for a movie that cost ten grand, it's amazing how well it's done.

**JS: When can we expect the next installment in the *Devil Doll* series to rear its head?**

**SL:** Well, it takes us a while to do these things, especially with this one. You'll know why it's taking so long when you see what we've come up with. I'd say in 2013—in the next year sometime. I defiantly want to make it happen next year. We've got an entire new way of promoting and selling this one. It's going to be completely different. Times are changing, and DVD sales are not what they used to be, so we've got a new plan. It's going to be an amazing new way to promote, sell, and release a movie. I can't really give anything away, but it's going to be awesome.

**JS: You've got a very strong work ethic. What do you credit that to?**

**SL:** My dad. He was really strict with me. It was one of those things where I'd get up on Saturday morning and I had chores that lasted until it got dark. I'm not as bad with my kids because I hated that. I see why my dad did it now, but I hated it back then. I feel that it made me responsible. I dropped out of college because I had this thing in my head—I can stay in college, get a corporate job, and be miserable or I can figure out how to make a living doing something that I want to do. And then, when you have a blue collar job like being a baker, all you do all day is think, "How the fuck can I get out of here?" I was working with guys who were sixty and had been there their whole life. There was no way in hell I was going to do that. I wanted to make a living doing what I wanted to do. I'd go to these conventions when I was a kid and I'd see everyone making a living doing what they liked. So, I credit my dad for teaching me how to work harder. You have to be self-disciplined. I could have easily given up with *Black Devil Doll*. It was hard. And learning how to screen print was harder than learning how to bake. For the first few years, it was the most frustrating and difficult thing. I can't tell you how many times I wanted to throw the towel in. You've got to work hard. That's what it is...

# OUR PERSONAL SHITLIST: A COLLECTION OF PEOPLE WHO SHOULD KILL THEMSELVES BECAUSE THEY ARE SUCH WORTHLESS PIECES OF SHIT

*BY: TIMOTHY PATRICK AND SHAWN SMITH*

# IN MEMORIAM: ANDY COPP

ON JANUARY THE 19TH, INDEPENDENT FILMMAKER, ACTOR, ARTIST AND WRITER, ANDREW COPP, TOOK HIS OWN LIFE. HE WAS 40 YEARS OLD.

ANDY AND I HAD BEEN ONLINE FRIENDS (AND BEFORE THAT, PEN-PALS THROUGH THE MAIL) FOR OVER 12 YEARS. WE WERE INTRODUCED BY A MUTUAL FRIEND, AND WE WERE BONDED BY OUR MUTUAL LOVE OF ODD AND UNUSUAL CINEMA. WE NEVER MET IN PERSON SINCE WE LIVE IN TOTALLY DIFFERENT SECTIONS OF THE CONTINENT, BUT THE AMOUNT OF MOVIE ZINES AND FILMS WE TRADED THROUGH THE MAIL MADE ANDY COPP'S NAME A WELL-KNOWN ONE IN MY HOUSEHOLD.

BACK IN THE LATE '90S AND EARLY 2000'S ANDY PUBLISHED A MOVIE ZINE CALLED NEON MADNESS. THE HIGHLIGHT OF THIS SERIES, IN MY OPINION, WAS AN EXCLUSIVE INTERVIEW THAT ANDY RAN IN ITS 8TH ISSUE WITH NOW DECEASED FILMMAKER ROGER WATKINS. AS THE PUBLISHER OF CINEMA SEWER ZINE, I WAS SO JEALOUS! SPEAKING OF WHICH, ANDY WROTE THE TERRIFIC "I WISH I'D TAPED THAT: THE ORIGINAL UNDERGROUND COMPILATION VIDEOS" ARTICLE IN CINEMA SEWER #23 -- EASILY THE HIGHLIGHT OF THAT ISSUE, AND A SMART PIECE OF JOURNALISM THAT REVEALED A DEEP KNOWLEDGE AND RESPECT FOR THE MOSTLY UNKNOWN HISTORY OF VIDEO EPHEMERA.

BUT IT WAS WITH HIS DEEPLY PERSONAL FILMMAKING THAT ANDY REALLY USED HIS CREATIVE VOICE. COPP LIVED IN DAYTON OHIO, AND WAS AN ABSOLUTE GODFATHER OF THE UNDERGROUND LOW-BUDGET HORROR/EXPLOITATION FILM SCENE, SEEMINGLY THERE FROM THE BEGINNING WHEN IT COMES TO THIS GENERATION OF INDEPENDENT FILMMAKERS. HIS MOVIES WERE ALWAYS CHALLENGING, BLOOD-SOAKED, AND NEVER BORING. THEY DEMANDED A REACTION, AND WEREN'T EASILY FORGOTTEN, AND WITH THE AMOUNT OF UTTERLY DERIVATIVE PABLUM GENRE FANS HAVE TO WADE THROUGH TO FIND MEANINGFUL WORK, I CAN THINK OF NO BETTER COMPLIMENT TO ANDY AND HIS FILMOGRAPHY.

REST IN PEACE, MY FRIEND. YOU WERE A WONDERFUL, INTELLIGENT PERSON WHO SEEMED TO ALWAYS HAVE TIME OR WORDS OF ENCOURAGEMENT FOR OTHERS IN NEED. YOUR UNWAVERING KINDNESS WAS AND WILL ALWAYS BE FUCKING LEGENDARY, AND I SO DEEPLY WISH I COULD TALK TO YOU NOW -- BUT THIS WILL HAVE TO DO.

-- ROBIN BOUGIE, JANUARY 21ST, 2013

I always admired the work of Andy Copp. I'll never forget seeing *The Mutilation Man* for the first time. Andy gave me a copy of the DVD at a Cinema Wasteland convention in Ohio, and it was the first thing I watched when I made it home.

I was immediately impressed by what he had done. I had been reading about the film in the underground press for quite a while, and I was happy to see that it more than lived up to my expectations. Shot on 16mm, Super-8, and VHS, *The Mutilation Man* was a striking vision. A lot of critics use the phrase "fever dream" to make a point. In this case, the words would be an understatement.

At the convention, Andy told me that he edited and published a fanzine called *Neon Madness*. I quickly amassed a collection of back issues, and kept my eyes peeled for his next film. The next thing that I saw was something called *Black Sun*. Andy told me that making the film had been an even more personal journey than making *The Mutilation Man*, and let me tell you, I was in no position to doubt him.

I followed Copp's career very closely over the following years. With every film he made, he seemed to tap deeper and deeper into his psyche. His unfinished epic, *The Church of the Eyes*, looked as if it would be his most intimate film yet.

At some point over the last year, I asked Andy if I could interview him for this book. I wanted to ask him a few questions about his work as an independent filmmaker. I wanted to know about his days as a fanzine editor. I wanted to get his story down. He responded within minutes, and we did this interview soon after.

We wrote back and forth many times in the months that followed, mostly about the films that we'd seen and the books that we'd read. Before long, I considered Andy Copp a friend.

Our correspondence went on until January 8, 2013. Andy wrote to me about something or other, and I wrote him back. I never received a reply. Eleven days later, I got the news. Andy Copp had taken his own life.

At first, I couldn't believe it. Why? Why? Why? I couldn't answer that question then, and I sure as hell can't answer it now. And truth be told, I really don't want to. I don't want to dig that deep.

There's not much more that I can say at the moment. Fare thee well, my friend. Hopefully, we'll meet again one day.

The following interview was conducted via telephone on February 8, 2012.

---

**JOHN SZPUNAR: How old were you when you first got into horror films?**

**ANDY COPP:** When I was growing up, there was a program on our local TV called *Shock Theater*. It was hosted by Dr. Creep, and I used to watch it a lot. Growing up, I had a very dysfunctional family. My father was a

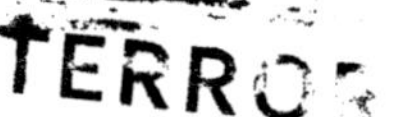

"I WISH I'D TAPED THAT!"

☆ THE ORIGINAL UNDERGROUND COMPILATION VIDEOS ☆ BY: ANDY COPP

ILLUSTRATIONS + LETTERING BY: BOUGIE

BLACK FAG !!!

*RE-ANIMATOR* AND—NOTHING TO DO WITH IT—ANDY COPP ARTICLE MASTHEAD IN *CINEMA SEWER* NUMBER 23. ART BY ROBIN BOUGIE.

raging alcoholic. The only time that my family "worked" was when *Shock Theater* was on. We would all come together as a family and watch that. There were no beatings, there was no screaming. We would watch it, and things were good. Through that, I really identified with horror films, from a very tiny age. Eventually my dad left and things got a lot better, but I kept that identification with the genre. It became a real safety mechanism thing.

**JS: It's interesting that horror films, which are usually pretty scary to little kids, could serve as a comfort zone.**

**AC:** Yeah. A lot of that came from Dr. Creep. He was like a big teddy bear type of a guy and he was very goofy and funny. Years later, I ended up becoming friends with him. I revived his show and directed it for ten years. Everything came full circle.

**JS: I'm skipping ahead a little bit, but what was that like?**

**AC:** Oh, it was awesome. I got to hang out with the guy from my childhood. I traveled the convention circuit with him. He was doing the same thing that I watched as a kid. It was a fortunate way to reconnect with all that.

**JS: Did you sneak into a lot of R-rated films as a kid?**

**AC:** No. Let me back up. My mom met my stepdad Gene Lowe, and he was a horror fanatic. An exploitation movie fanatic. They had no problems with me watching that kind of stuff. I remember my stepdad taking me to see *Re-Animator* when it came out. The theater didn't want to let me in and he threw a fit at them until they did. I had no issues with that stuff.

**JS: You were lucky.**

**AC:** Yeah. They would take me to that stuff. But at the same time, I wasn't really into the really crazy shit that I got into later. There was this weird period where I wasn't into that stuff. I was more into the science fiction fantasy stuff until I hit my early teens and really started diving into it. I missed a lot of stuff on its first run. But, my parents were going to see it. I remember them coming home saying, "Oh, we saw this zombie movie. It had blah, blah, blah, blah, blah!" Years later, I realized that they had seen a triple feature of *Zombie*, *Night of the Zombies*, and *Burial Ground*. I looked back and went, "Man, I love that stuff now but didn't then. I could have seen it!"

**JS: OK, let me get a frame of reference here. When were you born?**

**AC:** 1972.

**JS: I was born in '73, so we're about the same age. I remember seeing ads in the paper for things like *Burial Ground* and *The Gates of Hell*. I actually cut those out and taped them to my folders for school.**

**AC:** I did the same thing. Like I said, there was a period of time where I wasn't into horror movies for about three or four years. It probably had to do with my parents breaking up. I got back into it around 1984 or '85.

**JS: Video filled in a lot of gaps for me. I remember seeing the box for *Zombie* at the video store, thinking, "I can finally see this thing!" I remembered seeing the ad when it ran in the paper.**

**AC:** That's the thing. Even though I went through that period where I wasn't watching horror films, I was totally fascinated by the ad mats. Every Thursday, I'd get the paper and see what was opening the next day. I'd spend hours going through it. We had tons of drive-ins here in Dayton and they opened all of that sleaze and horror stuff. Even though I was scared of that stuff, I would always look to see what opened. My parents always went. My cousins, who lived down the street, always went. I always got the stories from them, even if I didn't go. I heard about *Basket Case*, the zombie movies, and *Blood Sucking Freaks*. And I totally remember those ads. When I got older, I spent a couple of years going through the microfilm at the local library finding those ads. I started collecting them; I have binders full of them.

**JS: *Evil Dead 2* came out when I was in eighth grade. I saw the ad with the smiling skull and snuck in to see it. I read that it was made by some guys from Michigan. They were older than me, but they were young. It got me thinking about filmmaking in a way that I hadn't before. When did you realize that you wanted to start making movies?**

RECORDED & INDEXED



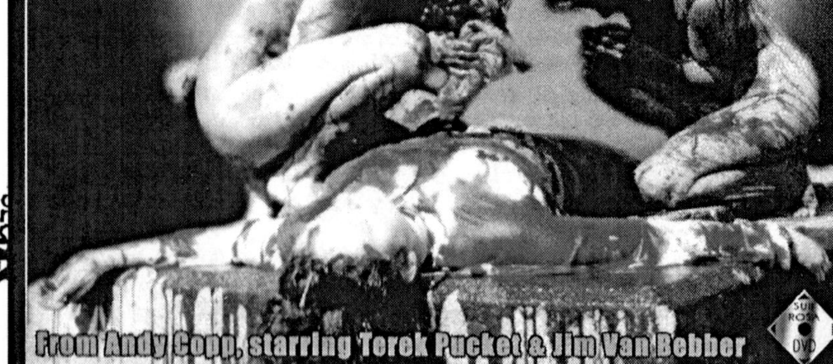

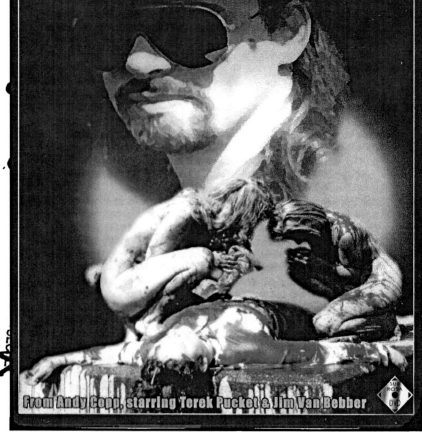

**AC:** When I was a kid, there were always movies in my house. The TV was always on and I was always going to the movies. My stepfather was around a lot when I was a kid, and to get me to stop being scared of horror movies (because he loved them so much), he explained to me about the special effects in *The Howling*. He sat me down one day—there must have been something on TV, an article in the paper, or something. I remember the conversation between us, more than anything. He was like, "This is how it's done. It's not real." That kicked it over for me. I was like, "Holy shit, that's awesome!" I decided that I wanted to be a special effects artist. I was obsessed with special makeup effects for years. I went through that typical kid phase where the house was filled with masks. I was like the kid from *Summer School*. For years, it was like that. And then, I saw a double-whammy on video of *Texas Chain Saw* and *The Evil Dead*. I distinctly remember watching those two films in high school. It all changed for me. It wasn't about special effects anymore; it was about making an audience feel the way that I felt when I was watching those movies.

**JS: What was it about those two films that made you feel that way?**

**AC:** I just remember being mesmerized at how terrifying and relentless they were. They just kept coming at you—a rollercoaster of fear. I took both of them back to the video store and rented them again. I watched them over and over for three or four days straight. Every time I watched them, they affected me the same way. I wanted to make movies that did the same thing. I no longer wanted to do special effects; I wanted to be the guy who orchestrated the whole package.

**JS: What kind of effects were you doing as a kid?**

**AC:** The typical stuff—latex scars and fake fingers. Freddy Krueger makeups; that was big in the eighties. From that, I did fake bodies and fake body parts. Lots of burn makeups. Nothing too sophisticated. I did a lot of intestines [laughs]. It was all good fun stuff. It progressed to me being able to do effects for my own movies.

**JS: What were the video stores like in your neighborhood?**

**AC:** We had great video stores in Dayton and I miss a lot of them. Dayton's got a lot of urban areas; it's kind of segmented. And that's a goldmine for exploitation video. I was at a good age to discover that. We had two or three of them that were in the more urban areas of town. One of them was called Video Castle. I went there as soon as I was able to drive. Over half of the store was this wall of horror movies and they got more horror movies all the time. It was in a black area of town, so it was a huge part of their stock. They had insane shit—they were getting stuff that no other stores had. It was one of the first places that was getting a lot of that shot on video crap that people now are paying huge amounts of money for. They were one of the first stores to get *Nekromantik*. I don't have any clue why they got it. It wasn't the Film Threat tape, either; it was the tape before the Film Threat tape.

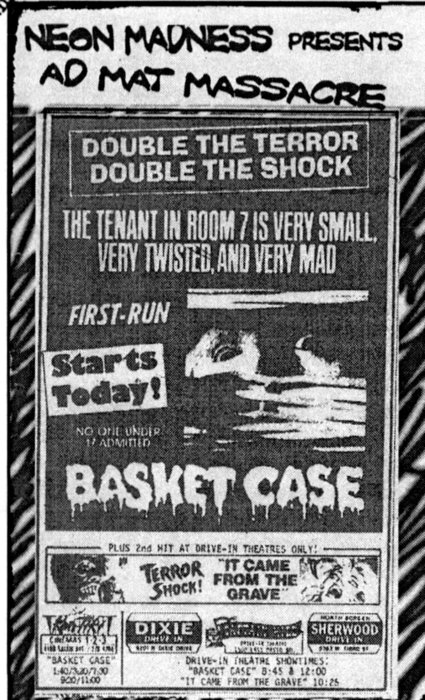
NEON MADNESS PRESENTS
AD MAT MASSACRE
DOUBLE THE TERROR
DOUBLE THE SHOCK
THE TENANT IN ROOM 7 IS VERY SMALL, VERY TWISTED, AND VERY MAD
FIRST-RUN
Starts Today!
NO ONE UNDER 17 ADMITTED
BASKET CASE
PLUS 2nd HIT AT DRIVE-IN THEATRES ONLY!
TERROR SHOCK!
"IT CAME FROM THE GRAVE"
DIXIE
SHERWOOD
"BASKET CASE"
DRIVE-IN THEATRE SHOWTIMES:
"BASKET CASE" 8:45 & 12:00
"IT CAME FROM THE GRAVE" 10:25

**JS: A store by my house had that, too.**

**AC:** Yeah. They had some of those Chuck Vincent directed horror flicks. They just had everything. It was crazy. They had all of the blaxsploitation flicks. They had the Albert Pyun action flicks. There were three or four video stores like that around Dayton. There was another one that was literally across the main street behind my house. I used to go there all the time, too. But that was the era where the 7-11s would rent videos. I remember going to the 7-11 by my house because it was the only place in Dayton that had *Rawhead Rex*.

**JS: There was one store by my house that, for some reason, had some Jean Rollin films. They weren't subtitled; they were all in French. I'm still trying to figure out why they had them and if anyone ever rented them besides me.**

**AC:** Right! [laughs]

**JS: OK, let's move on to magazines. I'm sure you were reading *Fangoria*.**

**AC:** Yeah. That's where everybody started. I was a nut about that kind of stuff. I read *Fangoria* and I read *Cinefantastique*. And I read *Gorezone*, of course. I have fond memories of reading *Gorezone*. Actually, I liked *Gorezone* better than *Fango*.

**JS: *Gorezone* had some great writers.**

**AC:** Yeah. That's what made it so good. Then, around that same time period, in the late eighties, there was *Slaughterhouse* and *HorrorFan*. I read both of those. I think I still have all of the issues. From what I understand, they were both forced off the newsstand by the Starlog Group. I'm almost positive that both of those mags were taking up shelf space, so Starlog started publishing this other magazine called *Toxic Horror*. Their sole reason to do that was to get rid of those other magazines. Once it happened, they quit publishing *Toxic Horror*.

**JS: *Slaughterhouse* introduced me to a lot of things that weren't being covered in *Fangoria*.**
**AC:** Absolutely. They were covering Japanese stuff, *Street Trash*—they were the first people to talk about Jim VanBebber and they covered the movie *Beware! Children at Play*.
**JS: Yeah. That was called *Goblins* at the time, wasn't it?**
**AC:** Yeah, I think you're right.
**JS: *Slaughterhouse* also covered a lot of the stuff that FantaCo was publishing. It was one of the first places where I read about *Gore Shriek* and *Deep Red*.**
**AC:** I think I'd already been reading *Deep Red* at that point. I had a couple issues of it—the publishing schedule was so sporadic.
**JS: What was your initial reaction to *Deep Red*?**
**AC:** That was the big one. For me, it was the introduction to all of the stuff that I wasn't seeing anywhere else. I already had Chas.' first two books, and I thought, "This is a whole new world that *Fangoria*'s not even talking about." That just opened up my world. It had an attitude that was much more in tune to how I was thinking about things. It opened my eyes. Chas. had an attitude of, "Hey, kid—you can come up and fucking do this."
**JS: I wanted to touch on that...**
**AC:** It's funny, because as he got older, he kind of regretted that later because there was so much bad stuff out there. But that was his attitude. It was him talking to the fans, saying, "Hey! I'm one of you guys. We don't have to put up with taking crap. You can do it yourself." That spoke to me and I know it spoke to a lot of other people. It made you feel like you were part of something. He was a real cheerleader for the genre and for young people. And it was a real important thing for him to do what he did. He was a very anti-corporate cheerleader—be independent. That was a really big deal for me in my life. I picked up a camera. I'm not saying that I wouldn't have done it without that, but I don't know if I would have done it quite as aggressively. *Deep Red* was a really important thing for me, and I certainly wouldn't have done my own fanzine without having read it.
**JS: When did you pick up a camera for the first time?**
**AC:** It would have been right before I went to film school. I didn't get my hands on a camera until a year before that. It's going to sound funny, but believe it or not, I went to church a lot in the couple of years before I went to film school. Of course, all of that's changed since I became an adult, but it was a good place to hang out and be a kid. My first films were done through church. I have these really weird church films that are really funny to look back on.
**JS: Were they shot on Super-8?**
**AC:** No, they were video. I didn't shoot on Super-8 until I went to film school.
**JS: What kind of video equipment were you using?**
**AC:** It was one of those ancient Super-VHS cameras that had a separate

RECORDED & INDEXED

DRAFT

deck that you had to carry around. And even those films were really weird action/horror films. Even though they were church films, they were very much influenced by the stuff that I liked.

**JS: What were those films like?**

**AC:** They were really bizarre things. They were based on church proverbs, but my friends and I were running around with toy guns [laughs]. They were totally inappropriate for what we were doing.

**JS: How did film school come about?**

**AC:** I wanted to become a filmmaker. Wright State University was right here in town. VanBebber had gone there, as well. It was the film school to go to, and I managed to get some grants together.

**JS: What was film school like?**

**AC:** It was not a good experience, really. The first couple of years were good, but they had some weird criteria and it became a little unpleasant. I went the year before Tarantino hit big. I was making horror films and I loved exploitation movies, but that school was really focused on documentaries and drama. I was just not a fit for there, and they were very vocal about that. They found ways for me to not go on with the program.

**JS: It's sort of strange that a place that's supposed to be harboring creativity would frown upon a creative act.**

**AC:** The weirdest thing is that once Tarantino became huge, he became a big deal. If I would have started school two years later, I would have been fine. All of that stuff became creatively acceptable.

**JS: What happened after film school?**

**AC:** That's when I dove into making *The Mutilation Man*. I started writing it immediately after film school and within a year and a half, I started shooting it.

**JS: What gave you the idea to make that film?**

**AC:** Being angry about film school was a huge part of it. I had also read *The*

*Hunger Artist* by Kafka recently, and it sort of got my brain thinking about somebody doing something to their own body out of protest. It sort of grew from there.

**JS: How did you get the project rolling?**

**AC:** It was one of those things where it was like, I'm either going to do it or I'm not going to do it. I spent a lot of time writing the script. I was friends with Jim [VanBebber] at the time, and I knew Terek Puckett and Mike King through him. I knew a lot of people who were willing to help, and through those guys, I was able to get equipment. I managed to save some money to get started. It was just one of those things. I started shooting on 16mm and those guys agreed to help—I just jumped in and did it.

**JS: How long did it take you to finish the film?**

**AC:** It ended up taking five years. It's the typical story that you always hear—you hear about Buddy G doing *Combat Shock* that way. You go so far and then you run out of money. You stop for a while and get a little money and then you shoot a little more.

**JS: Over all, was it an enjoyable experience?**

**AC:** It was exciting, because it was my first movie. I hadn't made anything except school films. So, yeah, it was an enjoyable experience. At the same time, it was a little nerve-wracking. It was five years, start and stop. People involved with it were moving away and coming back. I look back at the film and don't see the movie—I see those five years.

**JS: Are you happy with the finished film?**

**AC:** To a degree. I'm happier with it now than I was for a long time. But working at the level I work at, I'm never really happy with anything because all I see is what I don't have the means to do what I want to do.

**JS: I was really impressed with the mixed media in *The Mutilation Man*. Was that always essential to your vision?**

**AC:** Yeah. From the very beginning, I always wanted it to be shot on a couple of different formats. I wanted it to look fractured. That's something that I love doing; it comes from my love of experimental films. And visually, I really like the film, even though it's never been properly mastered. I had to edit it by sneaking into editing bays.

**JS: When did you start writing, as far as journalism goes?**

**AC:** I did a lot of critical writing for classes in college. I really enjoyed it. In the mid-nineties, I was working at a movie theater here in town called Neon Movies. I was put in charge of their midnight screenings and I brought in Hong Kong movies and horror films. I was one of the first people to screen *Meet the Feebles*. It didn't go over well, but I was proud that I did it. In doing that, I was doing a lot of local write-ups and I decided to do my own zine to coincide with the midnight screenings. That's when I launched *Neon Madness*. The first two issues were kind of tied into the midnight shows. That's where it all started.

**JS: How were you producing the magazine?**

# ANDY COPP

## NEON MADNESS

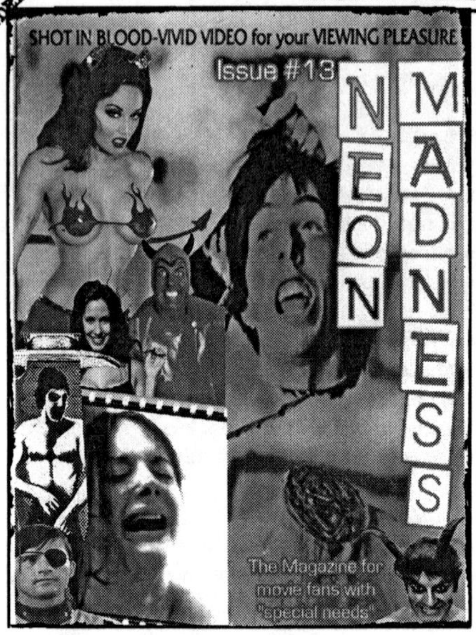

SHOT IN BLOOD-VIVID VIDEO for your VIEWING PLEASURE
Issue #13
NEON MADNESS
The Magazine for movie fans with "special needs"


**AC:** The first few issues were really simple—taking them to a local printer and getting them xeroxed. I was banging them out on an extremely primitive word processor. I didn't have a computer, I had a word processor that had one of those tiny orange-lit LCD screens. I typed it out on that and hand-cut everything. It was a real cut and paste thing. I printed them as I needed them. I'd do ten-, fifteen-, twenty copies at a time and take them to the local comic shops or the theater and go from there.

**JS: How big of an audience did you have?**

**AC:** It never went crazy. I never printed more than a couple hundred. It was never a huge thing, but the internet helped. And the conventions helped—that was really the big thing. I'd have them at the table and people started to buy them. Word of mouth got around and people started asking for them. Locally, it always did OK. There were several shops here that carried it.

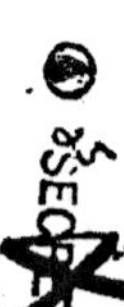

**JS: How many issues did you put out?**

**AC:** Fourteen.

**JS: How late in the game did you start doing *Neon Madness* shows on TV?**

**AC:** Well, I started working in public access a couple of years after that, in 1997. I probably started doing the show in '98. From 1998 until 2004, the show was just me in my living room. It was literally just that—me in my living room in front of a wall of video tapes. It was edited well; don't get me wrong—that was actually one of the best things about it. I'd pick five or six movies that I wanted to talk about, and that's what I'd do. I did a lot of episodes of that; I don't even know how many. It changed in 2005 when I met Michelle McLaughlin, who had been in a couple of my movies. She really wanted to get in on it and we completely changed the format. We were still talking about movies, but it became more of a sexy *Sneak Previews* kind of thing—we were going back and forth. She'd flash her tits to keep people awake. We started doing book reviews and stuff like that. It became a little more involved.

**JS: As a filmmaker, was it a little more gratifying to do the TV show?**
**AC:** No, because I did both. I never stopped the printed zine. They hit different parts for me. I'm weird that way—I'm the kind of person who really values my solitary time. The zine really fulfilled that. I could take time to zone out and write. And even when I got a computer, I still did it cut and paste. I spent a lot of time doing it that way; it was an artistic outlet. Doing the shows with Michelle was almost a lark. We'd just sort of goof off and have a good time with it. So, they sort of functioned as two different things.
**JS: Why did you stop doing the *Neon Madness* show?**
**AC:** Michelle moved away and I just kind of stopped doing it. I didn't do the video version again at all until I started doing the *Exploitation Nation* video blog recently.
**JS: Let's talk a little about that.**
**AC:** Well, I'd done *Neon Madness* for years but I kind of cleaned my slate for a year or two and focused on filmmaking. I had to finish *Quiet Nights of Blood and Pain*—I wanted to get that done and get it out into the marketplace. And another reason that I stopped doing *Neon Madness* was that I was getting way too much product to review. I was on a lot of screener lists from companies that I didn't even know anything about. I was getting stacks of stuff, and it got to where it was work. I wasn't doing it because I enjoyed it, I was doing it because I'd be like, "OK, I don't even know this company, but I've got to cover this movie." I was feeling really guilty because I was getting so much stuff. So, I took about a year to try and concentrate on my film work. But, I missed writing about movies and I missed talking about movies. I was like, "OK, I'm going to start doing this again. I need to do it." I opened *Exploitation Nation* as a blog as result of that. And then, I really missed doing a show. I just recently picked that up again.
**JS: The episodes that I've seen are really fun.**
**AC:** Yeah. And they're formatted different; it's not just me sitting there. And, I'm trying to incorporate a few different things. I talk about old bootlegs and VHS tapes.
**JS: I don't want to get off topic here, but do you want to talk about the bootleg scene in the nineties?**
**AC:** Sure. I think it's an important thing. A lot of the bootlegs in the nineties (that a lot of us traded) weren't available in any other form. The horror genre was a dead issue in the nineties; I think we can all agree on that. Though a lot of younger fans didn't live through that. So they don't know the wasteland the horror genre was at that time. But, it seems to me that when the DVD boom happened in '98 and '99, a lot of the DVD companies that sprung up would judge a title's worth by its status as a bootleg.
**JS: If it was in demand...**
**AC:** Well, you can answer this question because you had a DVD company. I know that as a consumer, that's how I was judging things. If I'd spent a lot of money on it as a bootleg, I was like, "Well, fuck! I'm going to go buy *The*

Attachment

RECORDED & INDEXED

# ANDY COPP

## Neon Madness

DRAFT

*Beyond* on DVD because I bought it six times before."
**JS: Oh yeah, of course. I'd say that the entire boom was built on that.**
**AC:** It seems like even now, the companies that have survived are still releasing stuff that was being passed around back then.
**JS: Yeah. And for a time there, the little companies were big. I mean, my company was never huge, but for a little while, there was an entire industry that was built on fanzine and tape trading culture.**
**AC:** Right. Those things were locked together. You would get the new issue of *Shock Cinema* and would read what were essentially bootleg reviews.
**JS: That's how I first saw a lot of that stuff.**
**AC:** Those were titles that eventually made their way over to legitimate DVDs. Not everybody's ethical—I can understand that. I sold bootlegs for a long time and I'm not ashamed of it. But at the same time, I was anal retentive and ethical about it. If I found out that somebody had gotten the rights to something, I got rid of it immediately. I tried to keep up on that. I can understand people getting pissed off at bootleggers if they had the rights to some gem title. I totally get that. At the same time, those titles weren't being kept alive on their own through the nineties. That's the thing. If Chas. Balun hadn't been championing those movies, if tape traders hadn't been trading them, if there hadn't been bootlegs of them from import laserdiscs, people wouldn't be talking about them.
**JS: A lot of those films would have been lost if they hadn't been made available. And who else but the fans would actually bother to examine them?**
**AC:** I taught a horror movie class at a local college for about five years. That was actually something I talked about. Horror went underground in the nineties, and the tape trading and fanzine culture kept it alive. People were trading tapes and they were trading foreign movies. Things like the *Evil Dead Trap* films were available—it was hand-to-hand culture. Fans were getting these movies and saying, "Hey, I've got this. Let me get it to you." Without that, the horror culture would have taken a serious blow.
**JS: Things would have been a lot different. On the subject of VHS, what do you think of the resurgence of interest in the format? Old VHS tapes are selling for crazy prices.**
**AC:** It's a rose-colored glasses thing, that's for sure. It's the same way that people looked back at eight-track tapes a few years ago; it's a nostalgia thing. I understand part of it because of the artwork on the boxes.
**JS: Those painted covers were beautiful...**
**AC:** I can definitely see the collectability of it. But at the same time, I think the collectors market has eaten itself. You said it—people are asking insane amounts of money for these old tapes.
**JS: Yeah. And we were trying to avoid some of those tapes by buying bootlegs. Who wants to see *Creepers* when you can see an uncut print of *Phenomena*?**

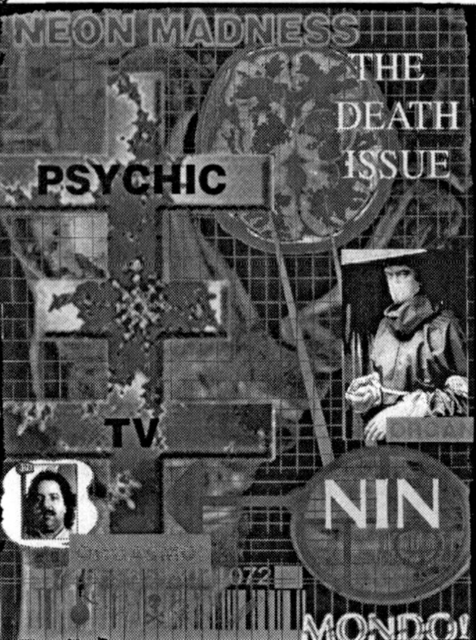


**AC:** That's exactly it. And you have people saying, "I have this tape of *The Twilight People*! I'll give it to you for ninety bucks." The fucking thing probably doesn't even play anymore. You're paying for a catalog number.

**JS: If I could go back in time and keep some of the tapes that I rented, I'd definitely do it. It's funny to me, though—a lot of the people who are buying the things were barely alive when I was renting them.**

**AC:** A lot of the younger guys just want to be a part of something that they weren't part of. And I guess that's OK. They just want to experience what you and I have been talking about—they want to go to one of those video stores and experience that stuff. But to do it at ninety bucks a pop is a little ridiculous.

**JS: What can you tell me about your new film, *Church of the Eyes*?**

**AC:** I've been working on that for a long time. It started as a music video with a guy from Indiana named Kevin Jones. He had a band called Swineburner. He was a fan of some of my work and we got together to do a crazy, experimental video piece to his music. Once we started throwing ideas around, it became a short film. And then, that short film became a feature film. It was just one of those things that grew and grew. Once it went from short film to feature film, it became intensely personal for me. My mother died in the interim, which was a big deal for me, obviously. And that's what the movie is dealing with—loss, pain, and coming to terms with those things. It became a huge project, and it was never meant to be.

**JS: What's the premise of the film?**

**AC:** The story is about a guy whose girlfriend dies in a car accident. In a fit of depression, he decides that he's going to find and kill God. It's very surreal and very much inspired by Jodorowsky. It's almost like a companion piece to *The Mutilation Man* and *Black Sun*.

**JS: What does "kill God" mean in the context of the film?**

**AC:** Well, in the film, it's not necessarily metaphorical. In the film he finds Him. The movie plays out like it's really happening. But if you're paying

attention and following along with the symbolism, maybe the whole thing is just the character coming to terms with the death of his girlfriend. Or maybe there's the subtext that he's killed himself. There are several layers going on and you're never sure what is what—none of that is explicitly spelled out.

**JS: There's a lot of subtext in your movies, and that's what I really enjoy about them. They're open to interpretation, and it's clear that you really think about what you're doing and that you put your heart into it.**

**AC:** This has turned to be the hardest movie that I've made, in a lot of ways. Not physically, but emotionally. It's been really draining.

**JS: A while back, you mentioned that you started out by making films for church. How much of an impact does your religious past have on you as a filmmaker?**

"Andrew Copp is the best motherf***ing filmmaker working in the underground today"
- Gates of Gore
"Well acted, good effects and a great ending"
- Cinema Wasteland
"Newcomer Telsa is beautiful and amazing...she draws you in...Michelle McLaughlin is gorgeous. A great revenge movie"
-Independent B-Movie
VENGEANCE IS MINE SAYETH THE LORD
THE ATROCITY CIRCLE


*THE ATROCITY CIRCLE* (2005), ANDY COPP'S THIRD FEATURE FILM.

**AC:** None. My religious views are pretty much the direct opposite of what they were when I was a teenager. I am basically agnostic with some heavy leanings towards some oddball spirituality at best. *That* influences my films. For example, *The Atrocity Circle*, my rape/revenge movie, is much more about how evil spreads and contaminates people. It is a metaphysical idea that resides under the surface. I've written a couple of scripts that are very anti-organized religion but they are too expensive to make. Right now, anyway.

**JS: When I interviewed Chas. Balun, he ended things by saying that genre would continue to grow and evolve through the work of the "true believers"...**

**AC:** He was right then, and still is. Watch a movie like *The Bunny Game* or *Life and Death of a Porno Gang*, and those are films clearly made my passionate, smart true believers. There are also a lot of jokers in the genre doing it because it almost always gets distribution and attention. Or people who think horror is just spraying blood on your brother's girlfriend's tits. A lot of crap gets made now, at all levels. But there is enough great stuff, stuff like *Martyrs* for example, that makes it all worthwhile.

## Chapter Thirty-Nine

# Scott Gabbey & Art Ettinger

## Ultra Violent!

SCOTT [RIGHT] AND ART AT THE UV TABLE AT CINEMA WASTELAND OCTOBER 2004. PHOTO COURTESY OF ART ETTINGER.

Ultra Violent is hands down one of the best horror zines on the market today. The brainchild of Mr. Scott Gabbey, *UV* hit the scene back in 1999. Featuring interviews with Nacho Cerda, Jörg Buttgereit, and Coffin Joe, *UV* quickly became one of my favorite things—it was refreshing to read a new magazine that catered to my strange and sleazy tastes.

The fourth issue brought with it the writing of Art Ettinger. His colossal interview with *Last House on Dead End Street* director Roger Watkins ran eighteen pages long, something almost unheard of in the underground press. Yes indeed, these boys were doing things right.

With each new issue, the interviews grew longer, and the films that they covered grew more extreme. Where else could you read a detailed set report on Fred Vogel's *August Underground's Mordum* or an interview with Johan (*Lucker the Necrophagous*) Vandewoestijne?

Art Ettinger went on to became *Ultra Violent*'s editor-in-chief with issue number 11. Scott Gabbey continues to publish the mag, and is now hard at work on an honest-to-goodness *book* about Coffin Joe. I decided that it was high time to talk to both men about the horror genre, *Ultra Violent*, and the winding road ahead of them.

The following interviews with Scott Gabbey and Art Ettinger were conducted via telephone on April 12, and February 20, 2012, respectively.

---

**JOHN SZPUNAR: You started *Ultra Violent* in 1999.**
**SCOTT GABBEY:** Yeah, 1999 was when the first issue was published. But in 1997, I published a zine called *Unsane*, which was just a stapled together digest size magazine that I put together on my own to give away at video stores. I spent a lot of time at the local video stores and renting obscure movies. I was basically trying to reach out to likeminded people.
**JS: Where were you living?**
**SG:** Southern Ohio. Appalachia—right on the border of West Virginia and Kentucky. I grew up in an area with characters like Jesco White, Hasil Adkins, and Mothman [laughs]. I was spending a lot of time watching obscure movies, and I wanted to do something with the knowledge that I was acquiring. When I was really young, my dad had a collection of video tapes. He had a lot of the Universal monster movies and I watched those pretty obsessively. And growing up in the eighties, the slasher movies were extremely popular. Back then, you could buy *Fangoria* at the grocery stores and gas stations.
**JS: I was really into slasher movies back then.**
**SG:** Yeah. A lot of the kids were into them. I remember doing projects in grade school where people were drawing Jason masks and things like that. As the years went by, a lot of the kids in school kind of grew out of it,

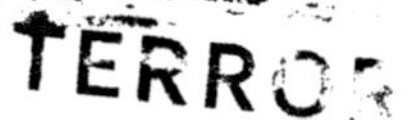

Recorded & Indexed

DRAFT

# Words of Wisdom, Caution, and Admiration:

Reviews of Ghastly and Astounding Cinema From Around the Globe

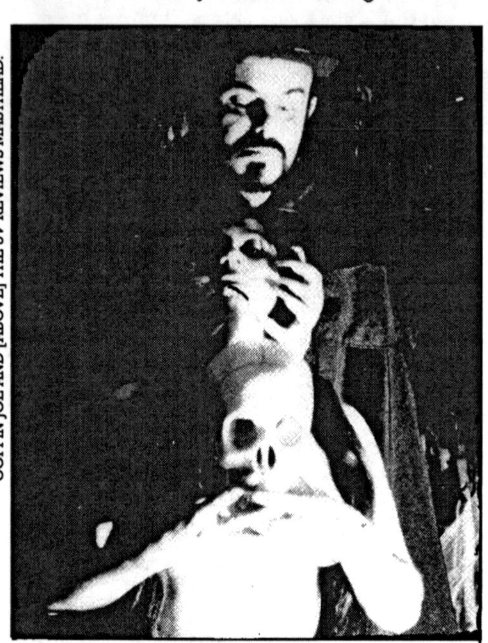

COFFIN JOE AND [ABOVE] THE *UV* REVIEWS MASTHEAD.

but I kind of grew more and more into it. I started reading everything that I could and kept watching as many movies as possible. There were three or four really great video stores that I used to rent from on a regular basis. They all knew me because I was a regular customer. They knew that I was really into horror movies, so they would always give me things like the Midnight Video and Blackest Heart Media catalogs. That was my gateway into a whole other world. Growing up in Appalachia, it was sort of an escape. There really wasn't much happening there.

**JS: You have just got back from Brazil...**

**SG:** Yeah, I spent six months there. It was a fantastic experience.

**JS: Did that have something to do with your Coffin Joe book?**

**SG:** Yes. I'm working with a translator who lives in Fortaleza, which is close to where I was staying. I was in a little fishing village called Cumbuco. My girlfriend's folks have a place down there, so that gave me the opportunity to work in a non-intrusive environment. It wasn't all work, though. We did a lot of traveling around Northeast Brazil. Coffin Joe lives in Sao Paulo, which is an amazing city, far from the area where we stayed. I've been to Sao Paulo several times specifically to do interviews for the book.

**JS: What's the status of the book?**

**SG:** My goal is to have it completed in 2013. The biggest obstacle that I've dealt with is the translations. I have around twenty hours of interview material with Coffin Joe on microcassettes, and it's all in Portuguese and broken English. Some of the interviews were conducted in his office and

the windows were open. You can hear cars going by in the background. Unfortunately, it's not the greatest audio. And you know what a pain in the ass it is just to transcribe something. Imagine translating and transcribing.

**JS: For the number of hours, it's got to be insane.**

**SG:** I've been quoted around $10,000. Obviously, I can't shell that out [laughs].

**JS: Have you ever had to use a translator for *Ultra Violent*?**

**SG:** I guess I've been pretty lucky, as far as that sort of thing goes. I've done interviews with people like Hideshi Hino. For that, Art Ettinger knew someone who was a professional Japanese-to-English translator. That was done over the phone. I would ask a question and she would translate his answers back to me. Most of the other foreign directors that I've interviewed could speak English. Jodorowsky was someone who had a really thick accent, and he talks 100 miles an hour. It was quite a task to transcribe everything.

ULTRA VIOLENT
Horror & Exploitation Cinema
Issue 1
$3.00 US / $5.00 WORLD
INTERVIEWS
Nacho Cerda
Reggie Bannister
Jim Van Bebber
Kyra Schon
Tom Savini
The Honeymoon Killers
George Romero
AND MUCH MORE!
Article by Antonella Fulci
Ein Zombie hing am Glockenseil
www.zombiebloodbath.com/uvm.html
The Sinful Nuns of Saint Valentine
Amando De Ossorio
Todd Sheets
Dario Argento's PHANTOM OF THE OPERA
ADULTS ONLY

ULTRA VIOLENT DEBUT.

**JS: What were some of your influences for *Ultra Violent*?**

**SG:** I'd say the two fanzines that made the biggest impression on me were *Deep Red* and *Dreadful Pleasures*. I don't remember how I wound up with a copy of *Dreadful Pleasures*. I might have picked it up at one of the video stores I used to go to. I really liked the layout. It was really slick and that was sort of what I was going for with *Ultra Violent*. There were a lot of magazines and fanzines that would print articles about death metal. I wanted to create a magazine that was strictly about film, and I wanted to make it look as neat and tidy as possible. I wanted it to look professional. I didn't want it to have all of those dripping fonts [laughs]. I used PageMaker to lay out the first issue. I was really obsessive compulsive and I wanted everything to be perfect. I spent a lot of time laying it out and making that happen.

**JS: How much of a time lapse was there between *Unsane* and *Ultra Violent*?**

**SG:** I guess about a year. I put out five issues of *Unsane*.

**JS: Can you tell me a little about that?**

**SG:** Well, it was monthly, and I did everything myself. Actually, I was working in a record store in the mid-nineties. Somebody came in and robbed the store. I was physically assaulted and punched in the face. I had a few weeks off of work and spent a lot of time watching movies. I had kicked around the idea of doing something, and that sort of gave me the

## ULTRA VIOLENT!

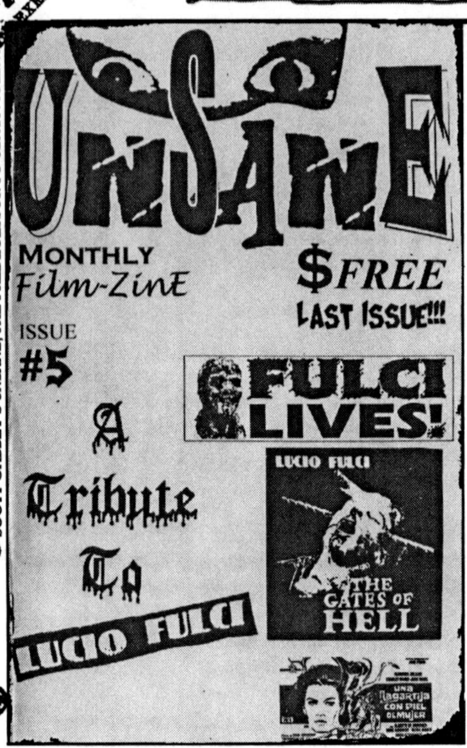


SCOTT GABBEY'S *UNSANE*, THE PREDECESSOR TO *ULTRA VIOLENT*

opportunity. I started to cut up old catalogs for the images, and I typed up the reviews on my computer. It was totally cut and paste. I'd hand them out for free in video stores, and I sent some to Shawn Lewis from Blackest Heart Media. He was doing a lot of conventions and that sort of thing. I'd send him ten or twenty issues, and that felt like a big deal to me [laughs].

**JS: What was the page count of those things?**

**SG:** Twelve pages, or something like that. They weren't very long, but it was hard work. My concept was to put it out every month, and I actually did it. That was probably the only time in my life that I met a deadline. I busted my ass to make sure that those things were out every month. I remember staying up for twenty-four or forty-eight hours to do everything that I had to do.

**JS: What made you want to start doing *Ultra Violent*?**

**SG:** Basically, with the advent of the internet, I made some new friends. One friend of mine had been in contact with Kyra Schon from *Night of the Living Dead*. He had her email address, so I emailed her, and asked to do an interview. Then, there was Monster Bash, the classic horror film convention in Pittsburgh. Tom Savini was going to be there. At that time, it was exciting for me to hear that Tom Savini was going to be at a convention [laughs]. It wasn't like it is now, where it's common for him to be at a show.

**JS: Who did you interview first?**

**SG:** Kyra was my first interview, ever. That was through email, and she was really sweet. She was at the convention that Savini was at, so I went there and met her in person. I remember feeling really nervous to meet Kyra. I remember approaching Tom Savini and doing a short interview with him at the show. From that point, I got in contact with Antonella Fulci. Lucio

Fulci was my gateway into the other world of horror. I grew up with the American slasher movies, but I really became obsessed with Fulci. Getting in contact with Antonella was very exciting. She agreed to give me an article that she had written. For the most part, I wrote the majority of the first few issues and conducted the interviews.

**JS: How did you decide that you had enough material to put out an issue?**

**SG:** I just started accumulating this material and I kind of ran with it from there. I basically had the idea that I wanted to put a magazine together, and I had been in contact with a guy who had put out a metal magazine of some variety. He put me in touch with Small Publishers, Inc., which is a print shop in Florida. They were printing a lot of zines, and I found out about their rates. I obviously had to pay for the first issue out of pocket. And I gave out all the ads in the first issue for free. They were basically places that I had been ordering from, like Video Wasteland, Blackest Heart, and Shocking Videos. The next issue, I went back to them and everybody returned the favor.

**JS: How did you get in touch with Nacho Cerda?**

**SG:** That was actually through Shawn Lewis. I bought my copy of *Aftermath* from Blackest Heart Media. I read his review and was like, "OK!" I was really into necrophilia movies at the time. I was obsessed with *Nekromantik* and all of that stuff. I got in touch with Shawn, and he ended up getting me in contact with Cerda. I think he got the information from Chas. Balun, actually. But, Nacho was a very cool guy to talk to and I was very excited. That was my first foreign director. He is actually one of the few directors that I kept in contact with over the years. I wrote the liner notes for the *Aftermath* DVD that was released by Unearthed Films.

**JS: You did a lot of distribution at horror conventions...**

**SG:** Yeah. I'd go to conventions and approach different dealers who were selling things that were related to what I was doing. There was

RECORDED & INDEXED
DRAFT

Damien Glonek and Ed Long with Unearthly Possessions, who are now doing Living Dead Dolls. They were selling *Cannibal Holocaust* T-shirts and things like that. I would wholesale it to them, and they would sell it at shows. The same thing with Ken Kish, who is now doing Cinema Wasteland. And pretty early on, I was in touch with Paul Brown from Midnight Media. I met him at a Chiller Theatre convention. He was publishing *Is it... Uncut?*, and I was in love with that. It was a funny moment, because I was standing there with an issue of *Uncut*, and he was standing there with an early issue of *Ultra Violent*. He would buy quite a few copies from me.

**JS: You're one of the few guys that I've talked to who started doing a zine at the dawn of the internet explosion. How did that affect what you were doing?**

**SG:** Oh man, it made all the difference, as much as I hate to admit it. If it weren't for the advent of the internet, I don't know if I would be doing it. Like I said, the first interview that I did was with Kyra, and that was because of the internet. I met Kate Hutchinson online. She's a brilliant writer, and she still writes for us.

**JS: What has your experience with distributors been like?**

**SG:** Dealing with distributors is much like dealing with the mob. I've had really terrible experiences with them. Tower Records went under while distributing *Ultra Violent*. They didn't owe me a fortune, but it was well over a grand. It was a lot of money for me. I remember getting a letter in the mail saying, "If you want to send in these documents, you can claim $500, and if you don't send us anything, you can claim $200." I claimed $200, because I'm not that organized, and they didn't even send me that [laughs]. I had the same experience with Desert Moon. That was another distributor that was distributing the magazine, early on. When you get a check from a distributor, it's kind of like a bonus. Advertising basically keeps *Ultra Violent* alive.

**JS: You said that you're not good with deadlines. Are you happy with your current publishing schedule?**

**SG:** I've learned to live with it. Like I said, when I started out, I was genuine about the deadlines. I've tried to do the same thing with *Ultra Violent*, but it never works, ever. I initially wanted to do it quarterly, and obviously that didn't happen. I tried to do it biannually, and that didn't happen. So, now it's annual, and that doesn't even exactly happen [laughs]. Over the years, I've learned to live with the fact that it comes out when it comes out. I've also learned from the collector's point of view. I'm sure you know this too, from being involved with Barrel Entertainment. People might bitch and moan when something doesn't come out when you say it's going to be out, but when it does come out, they get it and they forget that there was ever any delay. I always think about Grindhouse Releasing. For years people were bitching about the delay

ULTRA VIOLENT
Horror & Exploitation Cinema
Issue 3 Adults Only www.uv-magazine.com
Interviews
George Romero
Jose Mojica Marins
(aka Coffin Joe)
Andreas Schnaas
Ted V. Mikels
Claudio Simonetti of
Satan's Slave
Night of the Bloody Apes
The Nostril Picker
Necromaniac
Through Eyes of the Dead
Naked Blood
The Red Monks
and much more!

of *Cannibal Holocaust,* and then they put it out. It's like, "Oh, cool!" Nobody says anything more about it. It's over and done with. So, I just figure it comes out when it comes out.

**JS: Issue number 3 was the first time you were involved with Coffin Joe. Could you tell me a little bit about that?**

**SG:** Sure. I ended up getting in contact with Coffin Joe through Something Weird Video. I had ordered his movies through the Something Weird catalog, and I wanted to interview him. I talked to Lisa Petrucci, and she put me in contact with André Barcinski, who was his agent at the time. He's also the author of his biography and the director of the documentary about Coffin Joe that came out years ago. It was through him that I was able to do the first interview. It was entirely through email. It wasn't over the telephone. That was the beginning of my relationship with him, André, and that whole crew.

**JS: What kind of a guy is Coffin Joe?**

**SG:** [laughs] Very strange. He's a very strange and unusual character.

**JS: I kind of gathered that [laughs]!**

**SG:** He's actually a very endearing character because he's very childlike. When I visited his apartment, I was walking around and looking at everything. It's just ceiling to floor books. Then I noticed a theme—comic books, animation, Hitler, and pornography. That was basically it. And then, I noticed that they were in every language imaginable. His son told me, "My father cannot read all of these books, but he collects them." Coffin Joe is not really an educated man. He did not attend a university. In my opinion though, that's more of a testament to him as a filmmaker. He's basically self-taught, and he's done it all on his own.

**JS: His films are so unique. I've never seen anything quite like them.**

**SG:** They are, and that's exactly the way that I feel about him. I think it was Captain Beefheart who said, "If you want to be a different fish, you have to jump out of the school." That's his story. He's done it all in his own unusual

RECORDED & INDEXED
DRAFT

way.

**JS: How popular is he in Brazil these days?**

**SG:** Massively popular. He has his own television show. It was great living in Brazil for six months and being able to turn on the television and see Coffin Joe. He's a big deal down there. During Carnaval, a few years ago they had him on a giant float passing through the streets. It's crazy. When I was there in 2003 with Killjoy from [the band] Necrophagia, we were walking through the streets, and random people were approaching him—little kids running around saying, "Zé do Caixão! Zé do Caixão!" This lady came up to him and wanted him to hold her baby for a picture.

**JS: What can we expect from your book?**

**SG:** It's going to be a collection of interviews that I've conducted over the last ten years, compiled and printed in chronological order. It's the story of Coffin Joe, from his own perspective, and from the perspective of other actors, producers, and directors who have worked with him over the years. You can also expect a large collection of photographs, pressbooks, poster art, etc., that have never been seen outside of Brazil. It was never my intention to write a biography. I prefer interviews. I've always been that way. I would much rather get my information straight from the horse's mouth. That's why in *Ultra Violent*, the interviews really dominate the magazine.

**JS: *Ultra Violent* certainly lives up to its name.**

**SG:** When I started it, I was definitely at the height of my gore obsession. *Ultra Violent* was probably the most politically correct name that I had in a long list of ideas for a magazine title. That was at a point in time where I was really obsessed with Fulci and the *Guinea Pig* films. Throughout the years though, I feel that we've definitely broadened our horizons. There are things that I've published that certainly don't fit into the gore subgenre. I think that's a good thing, and I'm glad that we're able to do that. My interest in film has definitely evolved. It's all over the place.

**JS: How did you meet Art Ettinger?**

**SG:** I met Art through Bruce Holecheck. Bruce had talked about putting together a magazine called *Pages o' Filth*. Bruce was actually working with Shawn Lewis. I think Shawn was supposed to publish that. Anyway, Bruce and Art were the people who put me in touch with Roger Watkins when he announced that he was the director of *Last House on Dead End Street*. Art did the famous eighteen-page interview with Roger, which was originally supposed to be published in *Pages o' Filth*. That project basically went under, and the interview was offered to me. Of course I accepted it, and that was the beginning of my relationship with Art.

**JS: Art is now the editor of *Ultra Violent*...**

**SG:** After publishing the interview with Roger, Art has always been extremely enthusiastic and hard working. He's contributed to every issue since number 4. He and I started working very closely together.

**ULTRA VIOLENT**
**Issue 5**
**www.uvmagazine.com**

**Edited, Designed, & Published by**
Scott Gabbey

**Staff**
Art Ettinger
Lucifer Fulci
Damien Glonek
Bruce Holecheck
Killjoy
Jamie Summers
Trashboy
Bruce Weeden

**Contributing Writers**
Garrett Berry
John Coleman
Shane M. Dallmann
Scott Gabbey
Jose Luis Gonzalez
Greg Goodsell
Dave Kosanke
Bob Murawski
Allen Richards
Allana Sleeth
Shane Swenson
John Wheatman
David Zuzelo

**Webmaster**
Jamie Summers

**Main Office**
PO Box 110117
Palm Bay, Fl 32911-0117

**Email**
info@uvmagazine.com

**Front Cover Image**
Atsushi Muroga's *Junk*

UV Magazine © 2003 by Scott Gabbey

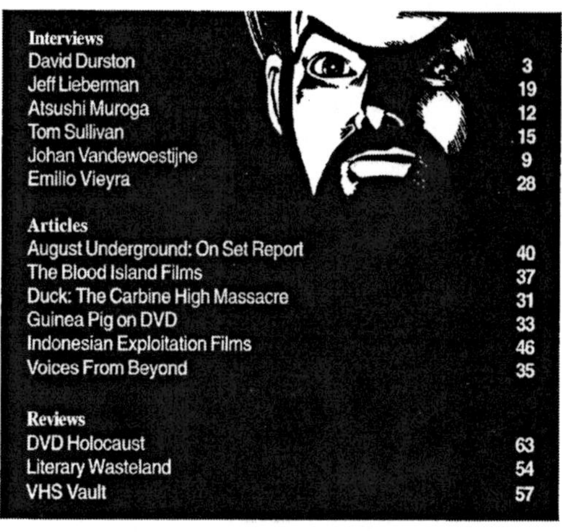


Better late than never, huh? I'm sure the majority of you are wondering why it took so long to get this issue out, which works out for the best because it gives us a chance to shamelessly self-promote our upcoming projects. Besides working around the clock to bring you the best in exclusive genre related knowledge and information, we're also in the process of compiling the definitive book / bible about Coffin Joe. We took a plane to South America a few months back and spent two weeks with Mojica (Coffin Joe) and his family. The book will be written almost entirely from Coffin Joe's point of view, referencing an incredibly long interview we conducted with him during the trip. We also took the time to talk to some of his cinematographers that have been working with him since the 60's, as well as a few modern day Brazilian horror directors, blah blah blah. We'll keep everyone posted. Aside from that, we also spent a few days with *Last House on Dead End Street* director Roger Watkins, working on a project entitled *Hobo Flats*. This one is completely off the beaten path. *Hobo Flats* is a screenplay that Watkins wrote almost 10 years ago, but has yet to see the light of day. Instead of a motion picture, we've decided to get this off the ground as a 2 CD spoken word album. Trust us, it's a mindfuckingly bizarre collection of words.

Issue 6 has already been started, so you'll have that soon....that's right, soon. Drop by the website for updates, or feel free to call or email us anytime. Thanks for your appreciation and support. ***- Scott Gabbey***

**Special thanks to:** Shayne Barker, Barrel Entertainment, Eric Bechtold, Steve Biro, Paul Brown, Eric Caiden, Vince Corkadel, Josh Davidson, Mike Felsher, Andy Gore, Horacio Higuchi, Debbie Hill, Matt Kennedy, Justin Kerswell, Ken & Pam Kish, Shawn Lewis, Hayden Milligan, Brad Napier, Mike Pascuzzi, Bo Paycheck, Lisa Petrucci, George Reis, Bob Sargent, Kevin Shaw, Kevin Simpson, Tony Simonelli, Pete Tombs, Edward Wong, the interviewees for their cooperation, friends, family and everyone who has went out of their way to support us!

FIRST MENTION OF SCOTT GABBEY'S COFFIN JOE BOOK. *ULTRA VIOLENT* NUMBER 5.

# SCOTT GABBEY & ART ETTINGER

## ULTRA VIOLENT!

RECORDED & INDEXED
DRAFT

I was always very territorial about *Ultra Violent*. I created it. It's my brainchild. Years ago, I never would have dreamed of even giving someone a co-editor position. I always wanted complete and total control. Basically, ten years of editing and publishing *Ultra Violent* started to wear on me, and I realized that in order for the magazine to survive, I need to pass the day-to-day editor duties on to someone who truly wants to do it. I love it, and I'm still involved as the publisher, and will continue to write and contribute, but I elected Art as the editor starting with issue 11. He and I have a lot in common in terms of what we feel is appropriate for the magazine, and rarely ever disagree about content or design, so working together is a pleasure.

---

**ART ETTINGER:** As far back as I can remember, I was obsessed with the movie pages in the *Buffalo News*, my hometown newspaper. I was also obsessed with *Sneak Previews* on PBS. From as far back as I can remember—I'm talking four or five years old—when people would ask me, "What do you want to be when you grow up?" I would say, "A movie critic." Everyone kind of laughed—"Oh, cute. He thinks he's going to be a movie critic." I remember horror ad mats that I must have seen in the 'paper when I was five years old. Also, it didn't seem weird, because that's where I grew up, but even up until the early nineties, the *Buffalo News* would run ads for the porn theaters in Niagara Falls, New York. They'd be on the same page as the regular movie ads. The *LA Times* and the *New York Times* stopped running adult ads very early on. There were also lots of midnight movies in my hometown. I remember always looking at the newspaper ads, and being interested in that. No one in my family likes

# BACK TO DEAD END STREET

Roger Watkins, 1972

THE ULTIMATE INTERVIEW WITH THE DIRECTOR OF THE ULTIMATE NIHILISTIC HORROR FILM

## Roger Watkins

(aka Victor Janos, Richard Mahler)

*by Art Ettinger*



horror movies. My parents don't like them, and my older sister doesn't like them. We got cable in 1982 or '83, and the first horror movie I remember seeing was *Poltergeist*. I also saw *Halloween III* when it premiered on cable. When we got our first VCR in 1985, I was allowed to rent whatever I wanted, even though I was only ten years old. By the following year, I had really delved deep into it. I would rent more obscure movies. That was the year that I started reading genre publications, too, which dovetails into the subject of your book.

**JOHN SZPUNAR: What were your video stores like?**

**AE:** Looking back on it now, I had no conception that video stores weren't that amazing everywhere. There was a locally owned chain called Video Factory. The guy who started it also started reel.com, one of the early web stores. He ended up being really rich. He had these video stores in Buffalo that were basically like unabridged movie libraries. I didn't know, for example, that Sun Video tapes were rare because you could easily rent them in my hometown. You could rent Wizard, Unicorn, and Super Video tapes everywhere. *Last House on Dead End Street* was right next to *Last House on the Left*. I had no idea that you could rent *Last House on the Left* everywhere, but *Last House on Dead End Street* was a rare tape. They had everything. Video stores were amazing in my hometown. Video Factory was the best one, but there were other good ones, too. That chain ended up being bought out by Blockbuster in 1996. Until Blockbuster bought Video Factory, Blockbuster could not penetrate the Western New York area. Nobody could really compete with Video Factory because they were so good. And when they opened multiple locations, their smaller stores would still have stuff like the *Ilsa* movies and *Make them Die Slowly*. You had twenty-six stores in a little tiny city where you could rent these movies everywhere. At the time, I didn't realize how great my childhood video stores were. I just thought that was what video stores were like. I would like to go back in time and walk through those aisles. They were amazing.

**JS: We had some great stores in my town, as well. I was renting everything I could get my hands on.**

**AE:** We're about the same age, right? What was amazing was that people our age (with time on our hands) were able to become super well-watched in a way that previously wasn't possible. You and I could go into these video stores and watch these movies that took older people decades to see. In a Summer, we could watch hundreds of movies. We got this great film education at a young age. By the time I was twenty-one years old, I'd seen a ton of movies. And I would also intentionally rent things that I hadn't read about. The more obscure, the better. One of my favorite video store memories is renting *Blood Couple* and *Black Vampire* on the same day. I came home and I watched one. I put the other one in and I said, "This is the same movie!" I thought it was awesome. I felt like I was a member of a secret society because I'd figured that out.

**JS: You mentioned that you were reading about films in magazines when you were very young.**

**AE:** Here's the way that went. It was all so fast. I was really into *Star Wars* figures when I was a kid. Looking back on it, I think I was just mentally into collecting them more than actually playing with them. My parents both grew up really poor. My mom's from another country, and my dad grew up really poor in this country. They went from being middle class to being upper middle class over the course of my childhood. They both wanted to give us as much as they could. Most people would probably describe me as being a spoiled kid. My parents would buy me tons of that stuff. Anyway, I would read *Starlog* here and there. Growing up in Buffalo, my family would get wings a lot. Right next door to this place that we used to get wings from was a comic store called Queen City Bookstore. I would go in there and buy *Starlog* a lot. I saw *Fangoria* in there when I was a little kid and I wasn't really interested. But in the Summer before sixth grade, I bought the issue with the *Poltergeist II* cover. That was in 1986. I loved *Poltergeist* and I knew I was going to see *Poltergeist II*. I ended up reading every issue of *Fangoria* since then. I read it to this day. This comic store ended up moving locations, and it had lot of cool stuff. Very shortly after starting with *Fangoria*, I delved much deeper into the other publications that were going on at that time. I remember exactly where I bought the *Gore Score* by Chas. Balun. I was with my family, visiting my aunt and uncle in Philadelphia, and I found it in a comic store. The *Gore Score* changed my life. I loved that book so much. As soon as *Deep Red* started coming out, I bought every issue

Issue 4 Horror & Exploitation Cinema www.uvmagazine.com

Chas. Balun
Chats with
Jack Ketchum

BEYOND THE LIMITS
Interview with Olaf Ittenbach

AT THE STROKE OF MIDNIGHT
Jean Rollin Talks About His Artistic Vision

BACK TO DEAD END STREET
An 18 Page Exclusive with Roger Watkins,
Director of Last House on Dead End Street

PLUS:
Black Mamba
The Freakmaker
Criminally Insane
Swamp of the Ravens
Mark of the Astro Zombies
DVD Reviews and much more!

Special Double Issue

RECORDED & INDEXED

DRAFT

when they were new. Queen City Bookstore had a little stash of back issues of *Sleazoid Express* and *Gore Gazette*. All at once, I got this great crash course. When the newer magazines started coming out, like *Video Watchdog*, *Psychotronic*, and *Shock Cinema*, I bought them all from issue one. I was already a hardcore fan. Also very influential to me was the trailer compilation tape *Mad Ron's Prevues from Hell*, which I got my hands on in the Summer after seventh grade. I would search for all of the movies featured on it. It was because of that tape that I rented things that I had avoided before, like *Three on a Meathook*.

**JS: Did you ever try writing as a kid?**

**AE:** Well, when I was a very little kid, I was obsessed with movie criticism and movie review books. Besides loving *At the Movies*, *Sneak Previews*, and the TV review shows, I had this awful book called *Rating the Movies*. Then I got Leonard Maltin's book and the other video guides. I would try to write my own reviews, and they were really shitty. I wish I had kept a list of everything I watched. I never really did that until later. Anyway, I dabbled in writing movie reviews when I was a little kid, but I didn't do any actual writing until years later. In 1999, I started writing for *Punk Planet*. I started listening to punk and hardcore at a very early age. There's a huge connection between horror zines and punk zines, at least for me. *Ultra Violent*'s distribution would have never become what it is today if it weren't for my having written for *Punk Planet*. *Punk Planet*'s editor, Dan Sinker, gave us many distribution tips.

**JS: Punk and horror films are both very anti-authority.**

**AE:** Exploitation movies are some of the most subversive movies out there. They definitely have that vibe to them. You get some of the same rushes out of exploitation movies as you do out of punk rock. But I would say that punk doesn't seem to be the favored musical style of horror fans. I'd say that their favorite musical style is probably metal, which I can't stand. I was never into metal. To me, it's like the antithesis of everything I like [laughs]. I remember that this one kid in school was trying to get me into metal. He was like, "Check out Iron Maiden!" But I hated it. It was stupid. They sang about wizards, and I couldn't relate to the guitar lines. I wanted to listen to the Meatmen.

**JS: When did you start reading music zines?**

**AE:** It wasn't until the tenth grade that I found *Maximum Rocknroll*, and that just opened it all up. There was this huge revelation that there was access to records from around the world. You could put three dollars in an envelope and get a seven-inch. It was fascinating to me.

**JS: Are you still a fan of *MRR*?**

**AE:** *MRR* has its critics, but I love it. I've read every issue since the first one I bought in 1990. I think it's the best way to find out about the subculture, whatever that even means anymore. Things have changed a lot, but I think *MRR* is vital in the history of music, and in the history of

ART ETTINGER AND BILL LANDIS FEBRUARY 2003

zines. It still reaches so many people all over the world.

**JS: Tell me a little about *Punk Planet*.**

**AE:** My "day job" is as a public defender, which I love. I went to law school in 1998, and I was living in Madison, Wisconsin, which is kind of a dead college town. I was going to a lot of basement punk shows and was reading magazines like *Flipside* and *MRR*. I remember I was in a bookstore, reading *Punk Planet*. There was an open call. They were like, "We've never done this before, but let us know why you should be a record reviewer for *Punk Planet*. We're trying to diversify. We don't want all of our reviewers to be people we know. We want different voices." I sent them a message via email, and for a long time, I never heard anything back. I checked my PO Box one day, and there was a package from *Punk Planet*. It was a box of records to review with a note: "Congratulations. Out of 2,000 people who responded, we've picked you. Here are the guidelines. The reviews are due on July 4th, 1999." It was super exciting to me! I couldn't believe it. It wasn't really like me to email them like I did, to say that I was interested. But for some reason I wrote them, and they accepted me. So, from 1999, until it went under in 2007, I was one of their longest running record reviewers. I learned a lot. I was

getting old for punk rock at that time. It is a youth subculture, and *Punk Planet* helped me stay connected to things. It was a really good experience, and it continues to be a really good experience. When *Punk Planet* folded in 2007, I started reviewing for *Razorcake*, where I continue to write record reviews to this day.

ROCK STARS · INSIDE THE 'NEW' ECONOMY · THE EXPLOSION · ABORTION ACCESS · MARY TIMONY
PUNK PLANET
MAGAZINE
$3.50
IN 1994
GREEN DAY MADE IT BIG.
JAWBREAKER, THE SMOKING POPES, JAWBOX, SAMIAM, FACE TO FACE, SCHLEPROCK, SENSE FIELD, TEXAS IS THE REASON AND COUNTLESS OTHER BANDS DIDN'T.
THIS IS THEIR STORY.

**JS: What's it like writing record reviews?**

**AE:** I take my record reviewing seriously. I've been on the receiving end of being in a band, putting out records, and waiting with baited breath for the reviews to come out. Record reviews are hard to keep up with, though. It's much harder than people would think. It's hard not to say the same things every time. You get burnt out on it very quickly. When *Punk Planet* got bigger, they were sending me twenty records at a time, six times a year. That's 120 record reviews a year, which is a lot. Punk rock is pretty diverse, but still. How do you write record reviews without comparing X number of bands to the Clash? You end up saying the same things over and over again.

**JS: How did you get involved with *Ultra Violent*?**

**AE:** I was keeping up with horror zines, but the heyday of horror zines was over. There wasn't any *Deep Red*. There was no *Sleazoid Express* or *Gore Gazette*. Those were the big three for me, growing up, and as much as I liked *Gore Gazette* and *Sleazoid Express*, they were older. I was mainly reading back issues at that point. I was still watching a shitload of horror and exploitation movies while I was in college, and I even taught a class called Sick Flicks, that other students could take for college credit. I was heavily into tape trading, including when I was living in Cleveland after college. I was trying to get my hands on as many weird movies as I could. I went to Fantasia Fest in 1998 in Toronto, the year that they had Fantasia in both Montreal and Toronto. I met Nacho Cerda and saw *Aftermath* in

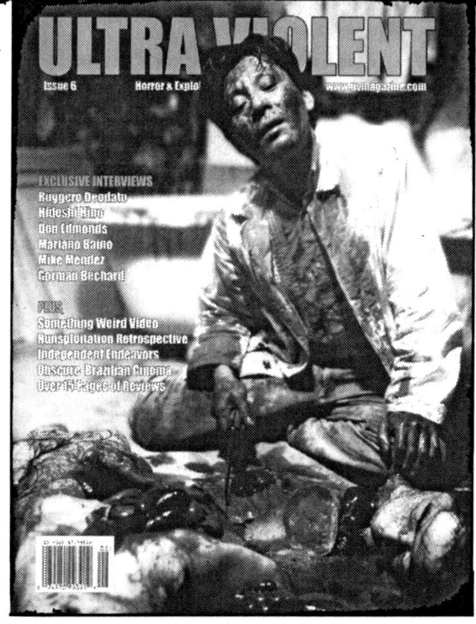


35mm. I had never gone to a convention before, other than a Ghoulardifest in Cleveland. Fantasia was a really big deal for me. We were only there for a couple days, but it was awesome. It was clear that after so many years, something was brewing. I wanted to do something beyond just being a fan who would post on internet message boards. I wanted to do something, but I didn't know what. I was very impressed with Dave Szulkin's *Last House on the Left* book. I still think it's one of the greatest film books ever written. There were a lot of good film books coming out at that time, which excited me. One of my first internet friends was Bruce Holecheck. He and I would trade videos and talk a lot online. I gave my first big interview to him. In the year 2000, Roger Watkins came out as having been the director of *Last House on Dead End Street*. That movie has always been one of my favorites. For years, if people asked me, "What's your favorite movie?" I'd say, "*Last House on Dead End Street*." It's still really important to me. One of the things that everybody loved about that movie was the huge mystery surrounding it. No one knew who made it. In 1989, there was a reference in Chas. Balun's *Deep Red Horror Handbook* to it having been made by a guy named Roger Watkins, but nobody really latched on to that. I remember reading that and thinking that maybe I could talk to Watkins someday. Anyway, Bruce Holecheck and I were talking to Roger Watkins online. It was awesome, but we didn't know if it was really the guy who made the movie that we were talking to. We had no clue. Bruce decided that he was going to start a zine called *Pages o' Filth*. He said to me, "I think you should interview Roger Watkins for it. You're the expert on that movie." I figured, why not? It would give me an excuse to talk to the guy on the phone. So, I gave Roger my phone number and he never called me. I was a little disappointed, but I wasn't really thinking much about it. Then, on Valentine's Day, February 14, 2001, I got a phone call. As soon as I heard Roger's voice and that laugh, I knew that it was the

RECORDED & INDEXED
DRAFT

guy from the movie.

**JS: Did you do the interview then and there?**

**AE:** I did my Roger Watkins interview in two sessions. The second time Roger called was when David Kerekes was in the US to meet him. A bunch of us talked to him at roughly the same time. Anyway, I did the interview, but *Pages o' Filth* never happened. I had read the first three issues of *Ultra Violent*. It was enthusiastic, and it was covering the same movies and filmmakers that I was interested in. Whoever was doing this magazine definitely had the same sensibilities as I did. Even though the magazines were fairly rudimentary, they were cool. When Bruce Holecheck's zine didn't happen, he said "Why don't you give Scott your interview?" I said, "It's eighteen pages long. No magazine's going to want to print it." Bruce suggested I try contacting Scott regardless, and I did. Scott loved the interview and decided to run it. Scott and I became fast friends. We have a lot of things in common. We're into the exact same movies, even small movies that people really don't give a shit about, like *My Friends Need Killing*. I've met three fans of that movie in my life, and he's one of them. Anyway, the Roger Watkins interview was really a big change for *Ultra Violent*. It was way longer than anything Scott had ever published up to that point.

**JS: You mentioned that Dan Sinker from *Punk Planet* had something do with distribution...**

**AE:** I told Scott, "Dan Sinker from *Punk Planet* seems like a good guy. He'd probably give you some distribution tips if you're interested in beefing up your distribution." I hooked Scott up with Dan, which ended up getting my first issue of *Ultra Violent*, issue 4, into Borders and Tower. We got picked up by Desert Moon, which at that time was the biggest distributor of specialty magazines. That was a slam bang start to my film writing, having my first published interview so widely distributed.

**JS: You were the**

**managing editor of *Ultra Violent* for quite a while.**
**AE:** Well, Scott and I really became very good friends. Even though I wasn't given editor credit on the next issue, I basically acted as managing editor for issue 5. I directed a lot of the content, and I line edited each article. I ended up officially becoming the managing editor with issue 6. It was a changing time for us. The more involved I became with *Ultra Violent*, the more opportunities arose for me outside of *Ultra Violent* as well, including contributing interviews to various DVD featurettes, writing DVD liner notes, and moderating audio commentaries.
**JS: You were on the set of *August Underground's Mordum*. How did you meet Fred Vogel?**
**AE:** I moved to Pittsburgh in 2001, and have lived here ever since. There was a video store in Pittsburgh called Incredibly Strange Video. I was in there one day and the owner said, "These guys made this movie called *August Underground*, and it's crazy. It's super sick. You have to see this thing. I'm going to ask the guy if I can lend it to you." Fred said yes, and I watched it. I really, really liked it. I thought that it worked for a gimmick movie. It was very smart and aggressive. I eventually met Fred, and he was surprisingly down to earth. When they started doing the second film, I thought it would be cool to do an on-set piece.
**JS: What was that like?**
**AE:** It's so hard to look at *Mordum* and compare it to what ToeTag has become. At that time, they were a bunch of maniacs. Not Fred, though. He was the most normal of them. But, Michael and Cristie were completely out of control. I awkwardly kind of revealed a bit too much in that article about some of the antics that transpired on set. A lot of the violence was real, and a lot of crazy things happened. They cast this one girl as a victim. They didn't know she was a junkie, and she started freaking out when she wanted heroin. It was wild. I don't want to sound tough, because I'm not, but

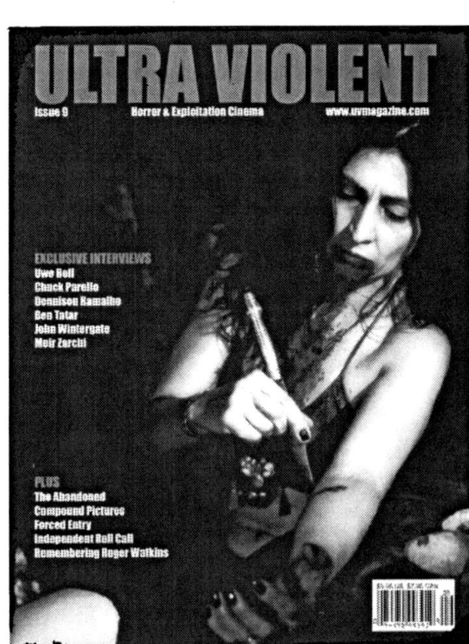

I've been exposed to a lot of craziness through punk rock. Nothing really seemed all that scary to me, whereas I think that to Fred, a lot of it really was. There was infighting between Michael and Fred, so the final movie is little bit of a mess. Their two visions clashed. And appearing in the movie was totally bizarre. There was this naked girl being raped on the ground. I'm standing there and I'm supposed to act like I'm shocked. It was fun, but they were a bunch of nuts at that time.

**JS: How do you think that your presence changed *Ultra Violent*?**

**AE:** My Roger Watkins interview became the style that is used to do interviews in *Ultra Violent*. We are now known for our over-the-top, in-depth, multi-page interviews. I did interviews with other people that were as long or even longer than my Watkins piece, including my interviews with Giovanni Lombardo Radice, Camille Keaton, and Meir Zarchi. If you took my Camille Keaton and Meir Zarchi interviews, each of those is a book-length interview. There actually is a Giovanni Lombardo Radice book, and it's way shorter than my *Ultra Violent* interview with him. The people who like and read the magazine now submit interviews to us in that style. In issue 11, my first issue as editor, we ran an interview with Ray Sager that is twenty pages long, or something crazy like that. Scott and I really hit it off, and he gave me a lot of control. He let me write whatever I wanted and he let me bring writers to the magazine. Scott started writing longer pieces himself. There aren't many short pieces in *Ultra Violent* anymore, and when there are, it's intentional.

**JS: How have things changed for you, now that you're the editor-in-chief?**

**AE:** I'm not doing anything different that I haven't already been doing for years. It's more that Scott is focusing on some other projects of his. He's not doing the layout of the magazine anymore. Ally Melling took over the layout and design of *Ultra Violent*. Scott will continue to contribute to *Ultra Violent*. Scott's still the publisher of the magazine and I'm the editor. It's really flattering that he entrusted me with *Ultra Violent*.

**JS: I'm glad that you're sticking with print.**

**AE:** I like reading magazines. Internet writing is very informal. I don't really consider it writing. Most of the web writing that I've read is done very quickly. I don't take it seriously. I like holding a magazine in my hand, sitting on the couch, and reading it. *Ultra Violent* is something that you can put on a shelf and use as a reference guide for years to come. You can read my interview with Camille Keaton twenty years from now, and it will still be an interesting read. Do you want to read it on a computer screen? I don't. I don't do much reading on the internet. People say, "Get Kindle or a Nook." I don't want a Kindle. I don't want a Nook. I don't watch movies on my laptop. And I'm not the only person who feels that way. There's a reason why print has survived. Reading ink on paper is an unmatchable experience...

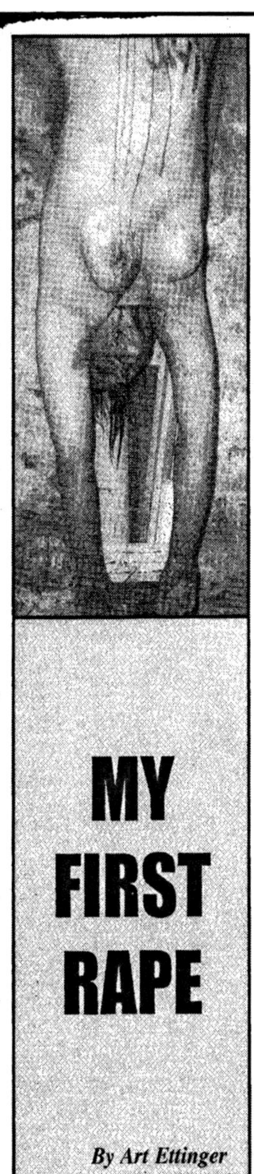


# August Underground's Mordum

## ON SET REPORT

*A fan of the original August Underground, I was excited about the chance to visit the set of the new follow-up feature, August Underground's Mordum. The film is in the same style as the original August (see sidebar), but with three killers appearing on screen instead of one. I had the pleasure of appearing in two scenes, and observing the shooting of the film's climax. It was an unforgettable experience to say the least. Hopefully the following diary entries successfully convey what I observed.*

**Friday, December 13, 2002**

Prior to completing *Mordum*, Toetag Pictures hosted a film festival after which they screened some early raw footage of *Mordum*. The event was well attended, one of the last at the D.I.Y. establishment The Rally Alley in Latrobe, Pennsylvania. Even though no punk bands were on the bill, the club's built-in crowd of decked-out teenage punks piled into the venue to see independent horror films and check out some metal bands.

I interviewed the young punks attending the festival as to what their first horror film experiences were and responses ranged from *Night of the Living Dead* to specific sequels in the major horror franchises to goofy flicks like *Dr. Giggles*. Besides a few people that had seen *Cannibal Holocaust*, *I Spit on Your Grave*, and *Last House on the Left*, pretty much no one there had any experience with extreme horror.

The raw *Mordum* footage screened to mixed reactions. One individual simply wanted to know if the feces in the film was an effect or the real deal. "Was that real shit?," he asked. He received no answer to his question by the filmmakers. Another young punk took a vow of celibacy as a result of the depraved footage: "I never want to have sex again. Simple as that."

Instead of talking to those that stayed and sat through the footage, I ran out and talked to some of those that walked out. One patron, incensed at what she had seen, said that *Mordum* was the "dumbest thing I have ever seen. It's not a horror film, it's stupid. I don't know what else to say." Her friend added that "it goes beyond the lines of an actual horror movie into just some guy with a camera running around acting stupid. I could do better. It sucked." Others that left the screening reacted in a more mild manner to the movie, including one individual that felt that the film "was pretty realistic but too drawn out."

One kid that walked out became introspective. "I think it's a bit pretentious and a bit artsy with no emotion or direction at all," he said. "It's definitely not realistic. It's put together well in the idea of if you had a bunch of memories and you saw them

"AT THAT TIME, THEY WERE A BUNCH OF MANIACS." *ULTRA VIOLENT* NUMBER 5.

# CHAPTER 39.5



# AN INTERVIEW WITH CINEMA SEWER'S ROBIN BOUCIE

COVER TO *CINEMA SEWER* NUMBER 20. ARTWORK BY VINCE RAURUS.

**ROBIN BOUGIE:** I've lived in Vancouver since 1997. I moved here because this is where my father's side of the family is and I wanted to be near them. I was raised by a single mom who was a teacher and moved a lot. I think I lived in ten different towns and cities in my first twelve years. Always the new kid. I love Vancouver though, probably my favourite place I've lived. I only wish it wasn't so expensive.

**JOHN SZPUNAR: What kinds of comics were you interested in as a kid?**

**RB:** Aside from being obsessed with comic magazines like *CARtoons* and *Heavy Metal*, I was a Marvel comics nerd. I loved John Romita, Jr.'s *X-Men*, Miller's *Daredevil*, *Secret Wars*, and all of the stuff that was big in the mid- to late eighties. It wasn't until my teens in the early nineties that I got into non-super hero comics like *Love and Rockets*, Otto Mesmer's *Felix*, and the new wave of underground stuff like *Hate*, *Eightball*, *Peep Show*, and *Yummy Fur*. Then I discovered the old undergrounds like Crumb, Rand Holmes, Jaxon, and it was over, man! Couldn't get enough of that. In my late twenties, I started getting really obsessed with classic 1960s DC stuff like *Lois Lane* and *Jimmy Olson*. Nowadays, my tastes are all over the place. I just like good entertaining comics.

**JS: When did you first start drawing?**

**RB:** Would have been in grade two. I liked to draw funny animal versions of comics I'd seen. Shit like "The Fantastikitty 4" and "Iron-Pup." [laughs] Kids just regurgitate stuff they like, I guess.

**JS: Were you encouraged?**

**RB:** By my friends, yeah. At recess, there would often be a few kids that would crowd around and shout out stuff for me to draw. I began realizing that other kids saw value in that, and I fostered it to some degree. Mostly I just did it because it was fun. My mom would encourage me, too. She's one of those moms that loves everything their kids do.

**JS: Did you ever go to art school?**

**RB:** Nope. Decided to open a store in a mall instead. A hand-painted T-shirt/comic shop. People would bring in a picture of something they wanted painted on a shirt or on the back of a jacket, and my wife and I (she's an artist as well) would paint it. We were nineteen, and we were there seven days a week for two years—we couldn't afford to hire anyone else. Got the whole "owning my own store" thing out of my system early, I guess. It was called Mind's Eye Artwear, and it was in the Wildwood Mall in Saskatoon, Saskatchewan.

**JS: How old were you when you first laid eyes on an underground comic?**

**RB:** Oh man, I remember that like it was yesterday! My mom is an old hippy from back in the day, and her dealer at the time was a hippy couple. I had no idea what was going on—I thought they were just family friends, but when we'd go over there, the adults would stay upstairs in the kitchen. They'd smoke up and have a grand time talking about adult stuff, and I'd be ushered into the basement to look at their comic collection. They knew I loved comics, so I'd stay out of their hair. This was when I was in grade four. Anyway, he had the old

## AN INTERVIEW WITH CINEMA SEWER'S

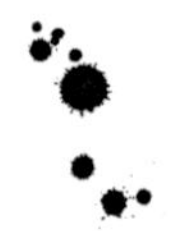

Barry Windsor-Smith *Conan* s, and all the other barbarian comics of the seventies, as well as some superhero stuff. I'd sit there and pore over them like they were important documents. Then, one time I discovered the box of undergrounds, and wow!

**JS: What comics were in the box?**

**RB:** The two that made the most lasting impression right out of the starting gate were *Bizarre Sex* (with a William Stout cover of a giant pussy-monster growling "EARTH MAAAN! GIVE MEEE YOUR SEEEED!") and an issue of *Young Lust*. with a couple from communist China. He's got her tit out and he's squeezing it right on the cover. They both have this vacant stare, and I was totally fascinated by those illustrations. Never saw anything like them before, and I was amazed.

**JS: When did you first become attracted to sleaze?**

**RB:** Well, I guess that would have been when, really. It all started there. But if you mean movies, then it probably started with an episode of *Miami Vice* called "Little Miss Dangerous" that I watched on my little black and white portable TV in my room. I did a comic about this in *Cinema Sewer*. It was an episode about a teenage prostitute who is a serial killer who murders her johns. Right around that time, I also watched a late-night movie screening of *Porky's* and masturbated for the first time while watching the girls shower scene near the beginning.

**JS: When did you start reading fanzines?**

**RB:** That would have been in 1991 or 1992, after my wife and I graduated and moved to Saskatoon. One night on TV, I saw a documentary by Ron Mann called *Comic Book Confidential*, and it changed my entire life. There was a single moment in that film where a New York artist named Sue Coe says something to the effect of, "You don't have to wait to be discovered as an artist. You don't need a publisher! You can publish your own comics, and stand on the street corner and sell them if you have to—anything to get them out there." It really struck a chord with Rebecca and me, and the next day we began work on our first photocopied mini-comic. We had no idea that other kids were doing them, but then I remembered that I'd seen

ROBIN TELLS IT LIKE IT IS. *CINEMA SEWER* NUMBER 13. ART AND TEXT BY ROBIN BOUGIE.

some when I'd visited Vancouver to see my dad a few years earlier. Everything came together in my mind. He'd taken me to this indie gallery called Smash on Cambie Street (it was in the same spot where Jackie Chan's uncle's grocery store is in *Rumble in the Bronx*) because they had a comic art show. There was a little box of photocopied comics on the counter made by this guy named Colin Upton. Flash-forward all these years later, and Colin is my downstairs neighbor. We've been friends for fifteen years now. But yeah, that was how it started, and from there I discovered *Factsheet 5*. That was the zine Bible back then. It was the internet before the internet, man. If you had an issue of that, you had the addresses and ordering info for thousands of zines, and that was fuckin' something else to a teenager. My tastes in music, movies and art were shaped by zines. Suddenly, Rebecca and I weren't alone in this shitty little Canadian prairie town. We were part of a zine army!

**JS: Did you put out any zines before *Cinema Sewer*?**

**RB:** I think I did about ninety comic zines before *Cinema Sewer*, but that was my first non-comic one. A friend of mine named Ricko did a zine called *Poopsheet*. It reviewed self-published comics. I was really getting into oddball drive-in movies by the mid-nineties—stuff like *Mondo Magic*, Russ Meyer's *Up!*, the women-in-prison movie *Sweet Sugar*, and all that amazing action stuff that was coming out of Hong Kong. I didn't think I was well-versed enough in things to do my own zine, so I asked him if I could have one or two pages in *Poopsheet* to review movies. That's where the first "Cinema Sewer" writing appeared. One issue later, he cancelled the zine, but I'd had such fun putting together the reviews and thinking about what I was going to review next that I had to put something together on my own. The seed had been planted.

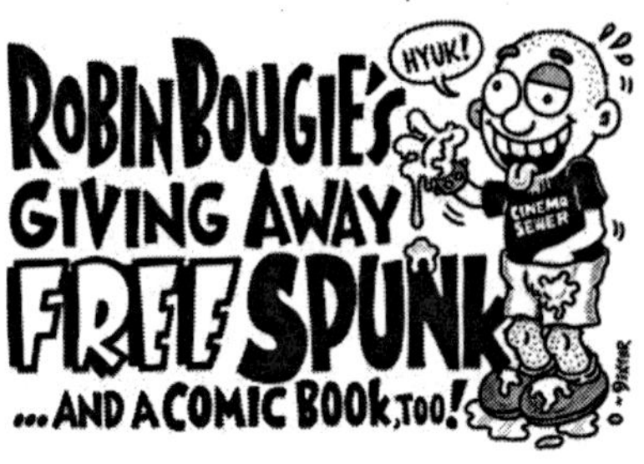

AN OFFER YOU CAN'T REFUSE.

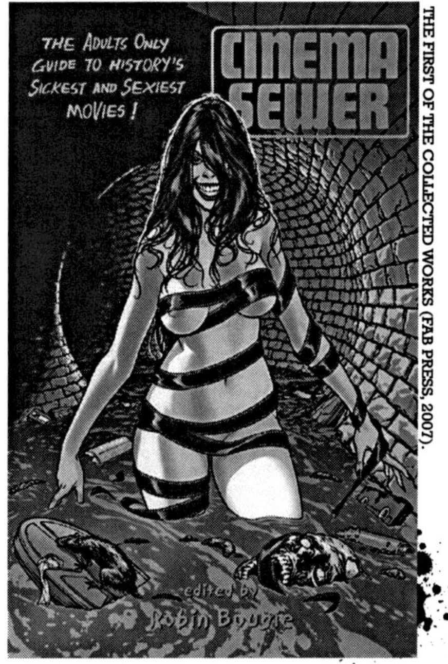

THE ADULTS ONLY GUIDE TO HISTORY'S SICKEST AND SEXIEST MOVIES!
CINEMA SEWER
edited by
Robin Bougie

THE FIRST OF THE COLLECTED WORKS (FAB PRESS, 2007).

**JS: Were you aware of John Holmstorm's *Punk*?**

**RB:** No I was not, but I was very familiar with his column in *Heavy Metal* where he used comics to review video games. I believe he was the very first video game reviewer, in fact. The graphics were so blocky and fragmented back then that he could simply replicate them in his cartoony drawing style and you knew what the game looked like! Brilliant. Holmstrom was great.

**JS: Were you inspired at all by *Sleazoid Express*?**

**RB:** I didn't discover that until the book came out in 2002. The zine had been cancelled by that time. I absolutely adore that book, though. Read it several times over. Then, I heard they were starting *Metasex*, and I was jazzed. I tried contacting Michelle and Bill to ask them about ordering or trading for it, and they quoted me this utterly outlandish $20 shipping cost to Canada. It was over and above the cost of a couple of magazines, and I won't lie to you—I was fucking offended by that. It's just some sheets of paper stapled together, not a coffee table book. I come from a zine background, not an eBay background, and that kind of thing is very uncool in that world. You charge a couple stamps, or a couple bucks, or whatever it is to pay for an envelope and the cost of getting it to the person. You don't look to make a 200 per cent profit on the shipping. I dunno, maybe they just didn't like me and wanted me to get lost. Anyway, Bill died, and I never really got to meet him or exchange zines or whatever. And that's sad because he was a movie-zine legend, you know? Would have been pretty sweet.

**JS: How long does it take you to put**

A BOUGIE FILM REVIEW FROM *CINEMA SEWER* NUMBER 25.

RAGE (1972) USA

GEORGE C. SCOTT GROWS SIDEBURNS AND PLAYS A CATTLE RANCHER WHOSE YOUNG SON IS POISONED BY A CHEMICAL AEROSOL WEAPON PERPETRATED (AND COVERED UP) BY THE MILITARY. GEORGEY DOESN'T LIKE IT WHEN HIS KIN ARE OFFED, SO HE GOES BUCKWILD. RAGE (1972) IS AN INTERESTING MOVIE WHEN YOU TAKE INTO CONTEXT WHEN AND WHERE IT WAS MADE. VIETNAM HAD JUST WRAPPED UP, AND SCOTT (HIMSELF A FORMER MARINE) USES THE FILM (WHICH HE ALSO DIRECTED) TO COMMENT ON THE DISILLUSIONMENT OF THE AMERICAN PEOPLE WITH THE US WAR MACHINE THAT HAD BEEN, UP UNTIL THEN, BEYOND REPROACH. IT'S NOT A PERFECT FILM, BUT IT WORKS.

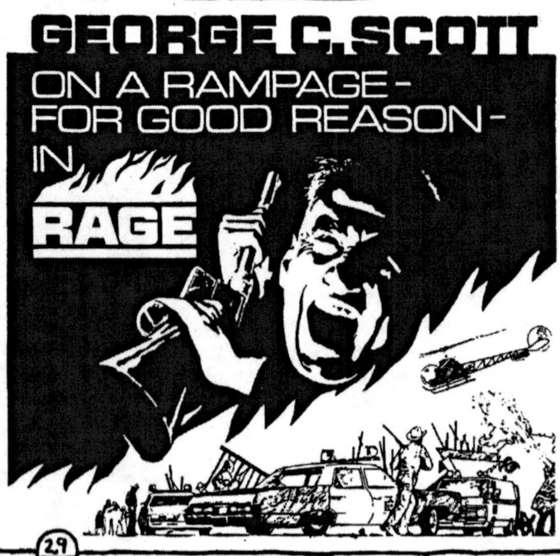
GEORGE C. SCOTT
ON A RAMPAGE -
FOR GOOD REASON -
IN
RAGE

29

**together an issue of *Cinema Sewer*?**
**RB:** About six months. I can only afford to print it once a year, though, because my printing costs are in the thousands and I only work at a video store.
**JS: What kind of work goes into the layout?**
**RB:** Well, everything is laid out by hand, using a glue stick and such. It's also all done same size as the final pages in the zine, which seems to surprise some people. They assume that I do it bigger and shrink it down.
**JS: What made you decide on the hand-printed approach?**
**RB:** Well, it's like comics. You do comics by hand. In the world of comics, it's considered very lame to use a computer for your lettering. Super lame. That's what you do if your lettering sucks, and you can't afford to hire a professional letterer to do it for you. I come from that background, and I letter pretty good, so I just started doing it that way. It's really 100 per cent an aesthetic choice, because I have to type everything out beforehand anyway. My spelling kind of sucks and I have to put it through a spellchecker. Sometimes if I think I can get away with it, I'll use a font that I made out of my hand lettering. That comes in handy now that I'm developing carpal tunnel syndrome. So far, people haven't caught on, and I've been using it for three years, on and off.
**JS: What kind of a pen do you use for your illustrations?**
**RB:** I use Staedtler Pigment Liners. I also use a pentel pocket brush pen. That is pretty much everything you need.
**JS: How much of your free time does *Cinema Sewer* eat up?**

*CINEMA SEWER* NUMBER 14. COVER ART BY DANNY HELLMAN.

**RB:** Pretty much all of it, if you consider that if I'm not making it, I'm watching movies to review, or social networking on Facebook in order to find new readers. If it weren't for the internet, *CS* would have gone under a long time ago. All of the magazine stores, music stores, and video stores that used to sell it have all gone under. So instead of packing up a dozen boxes to Tower Records (and all the other retailers I had before), I now pack up 1,000 individually addressed envelopes. What used to take an afternoon now accumulates to taking up weeks and weeks of my time. But you know what? I 'm certainly not complaining. Ninety-nine per cent of zines that were around when I started have gone under, never to be heard from again. I'm certainly

REQUEST A DRAWING FROM ROBIN BOUGIE.

not going to complain about having readers.

**JS: Is there an independent theater scene in BC?**

**RB:** It's very small—the BC liquor board has been trying to kill it. There's a theater called the RIO that has been fighting them for a year now, trying to sell beer and show rad movies. The city won't allow it. You can get stinking drunk anywhere else (like a hockey game or a bowling alley), but there is this old bylaw about showing movies and selling booze. The red tape is tough to get through. It's a giant clusterfuck, and it's very frustrating to see the city trying to kill a thriving local business when the economy is so cruddy. It's no wonder that we hardly have any indie theaters with this going on.

**JS: Are there any adult theaters left in Vancouver?**

**RB:** Yes. There's the Fox, which is a few blocks from my house. It still shows video projected DVDs. Up until 2003, it was the last remaining 35mm porn theater in North America still showing film prints on a regular rotating basis. They had a couple hundred prints of 1970s and early eighties XXX films that they owned, and they'd change them every week. I saw so many good movies, and really cherished it. I sometimes had *Cinema Sewer* launch parties in the lobby! Amazing times. It was like a tiny bit of the 42nd Street of the seventies picked up and dropped on the other side of the continent! Man, that is another loss I lament: The Fox switching to DVD. They just show regular new porn now. No real reason to go anymore, unless you want a blowjob. I doubt it'll be around much longer, as the hood is becoming gentrified, and the hipster clothing boutique next door has been complaining to the city about the whores going in and out of there.

**JS: What keeps you doing a print zine during the age of the internet?**

**RB:** I'm a print junky. I love everything about print. It speaks to me. It's how I want my work remembered. Besides, just because a new medium becomes popular doesn't mean every other existing medium should cease to exist. That is crazy, and there is no precedent for that in recorded history.

# THE UGLIEST CLASSIC ADULT MOVIE ADVERTISING EVER MADE

I'VE BEEN COLLECTING MOVIE ADVERTISING AND PRESSBOOKS FOR YEARS NOW, AND EVERY ONCE AND A WHILE I'M JUST MORTIFIED AT HOW POORLY DRAWN AND DESIGNED SOME OF THE X RATED STUFF WAS. HERE ARE SOME OF MY ALL TIME FAVORITES!

UUGAHGGH!! Soooo UGLY! THAT FLOATING DECAPITATED HEAD DRAWN WITH PENCIL CRAYONS BY AN 11 YEAR OLD GIRL IS AN AFRONT TO MY SENSES!

IF THIS ARTIST'S MOTHER COULD SEE HIM NOW! THIS INTER-RACIAL XXX SLEAZE FEST SPORTS SOME JIVE ASS PATHETIC ART WORK! I MEAN, WHAT'S THE DEAL WITH THOSE TWO BLACK DUDES?! THEY LOOK LIKE INBRED MUPPETS! THE FONT IS HARD TO READ, THE LAYOUT IS HEINOUS, AND THE ART IS GROUNDS FOR DISMISSAL! OVERALL, IT'S PROOF THAT THEY JUST **DIDN'T CARE**.

**HA HA HA HA!** OOH MAN, HOW FUCKIN' **LAME** IS THIS ONE? FROM THE "NEW NEW NEW" HASTILY DRAWN BY A RETARD WITH A MARKER, TO THE... WELL... WTF IS IT THAT SHE'S HOLDING?! THIS IS **SO** POORLY DONE, THE ONLY THING YOU CAN DO IS LAUGH... OR GO INSANE...

OOOOHHH... DARK AND SCARY! BUT EVEN MORE SCARY IS THAT THEY EXPECTED THIS CRAP TO ENTICE AN AUDIENCE! THE POEM PENNED BY SOME SIMPLETON IS ALSO QUITE UPSETTING. ·BARF·

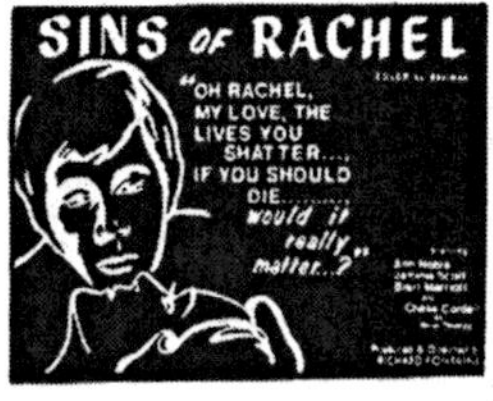

SINS OF RACHEL
"OH RACHEL, MY LOVE, THE LIVES YOU SHATTER..., IF YOU SHOULD DIE......... would it really matter..?"

GEORGINA SPELVIN in

ALL THE WAY

inEASTMAN COLOR

RATED X

MECCA TWIN

711 Pike St. 622-7711

WA-**HOO**! YOU KNEW I HAD TO SAVE "THE BEST" FOR LAST. THIS UN-NAMED ARTIST'S **RAD** RENDITION OF MISS GEORGINA SPELVIN SHOULD BE THE STUFF THAT BAD ADVERTISING ART LEGENDS ARE MADE OF! HA HA! FEAST YOUR EYES, MY FRIENDS!

FROM *CINEMA SEWER* NUMBER 17. ART AND TEXT: ROBIN BOUGIE.

IMAGE FROM *LIQUID CHEESE* NUMBER 29. ART BY PUTRID.

# CHAPTER FORTY

# DAVE KOSANKE

## LIQUID CHEESE

Dave Kosanke is the editor of *Liquid Cheese*, an excellent fanzine from Franklin, Wisconsin. Dave started *Liquid Cheese* in 1993, and as of this writing, has published thirty-three issues. "Movies and Music to Mangle your Mind!" is the magazine's motto, and that sure ain't false advertising. *Liquid Cheese* delivers the goods in every way, and the fact that it's still going strong is a testament to Kosanke's love for the printed page.

Through the years, *Liquid Cheese* has focused on everything from horror to porn. Dave's reviews and critiques are consistently on the mark, and his in-depth coverage of the horror convention scene is always fun and personal. Recent issues feature interviews with comic artist Mike Hoffman and Eric Caiden, the owner of Hollywood Book and Poster. Kosanke is currently in the process of updating the back catalog of *Liquid Cheese* to color.

I interviewed Dave last April. Before I knew it, we had talked for well over three hours. Subjects discussed in the following pages include the zine-scene of the 1990s, the golden years of VHS tapes and laserdiscs, and of course, the history and future of *Liquid Cheese*.

The following interview was conducted via telephone on April 21, 2012.

---

**DAVE KOSANKE:** I got introduced to horror and exploitation films through my parents. They would go to see anything that was horror, science fiction, or fantasy related. Anything from *At the Earth's Core* to *Food of the Gods* to *Laserblast*. I saw all kinds of oddball stuff, and I had a subscription to the *Monster Times* in the mid-seventies. It kind of just spiraled from there.

**JOHN SZPUNAR: Did television play a role in things?**

**DK:** Yeah. We had a horror host called TooLoose No-Neck. He played all kinds of oddball stuff—Larry Buchanan films and old Universal classics. I pretty much got the feel of everything, from the old films to the newer sixties and seventies type stuff. And besides that, I got hooked on all the TV shows, like *Outer Limits* and *The Twilight Zone*. I had a steady diet of TV, as well.

**JS: I just missed out on the big drive-in boom. The main theaters in my area had closed down by the time I was old enough to go the movies.**

**DK:** There were two drive-ins that were really close to my house. The main one was called the Forty-One Twin. Believe it or not, that only closed up a few years ago. They had four separate screens, so two screens were back to back. You could park on one end and watch a movie, and if you didn't like it, you could turn your head around and see what was happening on the screen behind you. That was kind of weird. But, we would see anything that was playing there. The earliest memories I have

ART BY MIKE HOFFMAN.

are from 1975 to '78—those were the years that we would see a lot of the movies that were playing.

**JS: Were you able to watch R-rated films when you were young?**

**DK:** My parents didn't take me to see anything that was R-rated, so I didn't see anything like that. Everything was rated PG. But again, it had monsters, or it had fantasy. I don't remember seeing any movie that wasn't related to genre. If I did see something that wasn't, I don't remember it.

**JS: What kind of things were you reading?**

**DK:** I remember reading all of the Warren titles. This would be right at the tail end of them. I started to buy *Eerie* and *Creepy*, but *Famous Monsters* was covering a lot of mainstream stuff—things like *ET*, *The Dark Crystal*, *Star Trek*, and *Star Wars*. I really wasn't into that as much as the monster stuff, so I never really bought an issue. But their comic stuff, yeah. I was definitely into that. And, *Fangoria* was more interesting than *Famous Monsters*, because they were covering the gore stuff that was starting to come out in the early eighties. They had one issue where they put Ozzy on the cover from the Bark At The Moon video. That sold me, because I was also into rock and metal music. Things kind of collided when I saw that issue. I'd always been looking at the magazine, but I'd never actually bought it. I kind of convinced my mom to buy that issue, because, hey, it had Ozzy on the cover. And once I read that issue, that was it. I think I subscribed two issues later, and I still subscribe to *Fangoria* to this day.

**JS: What else were you reading?**

**DK:** At the time, there really wasn't a lot else out there. There was mostly science fiction stuff like *Starlog*, and I never really cared for that. But once I got *Fangoria*, I started looking through the ads and I saw some of the other magazines that were out there. That's when I became more curious, and I started to investigate what some of the other titles were. You couldn't really find a lot of that stuff on the magazine rack, at least not in my neck of the woods. I was lucky to see what I did. I was always looking for something else. If we would go to a different store, I would go to the magazine rack and see what other titles there were. Specific stores carried specific magazines. It was pretty much the luck of the draw, depending on where I went.

**JS: When I was growing up, FantaCo's mail order was a big thing to me.**

**DK:** When I saw FantaCo's ad, it sparked my interest to seek out more of these titles. I got the original *Gore Score* by Chas. Balun, with the red cover. Then, I got the *Psychotronic Encyclopedia of Film*, Michael Weldon's first book. Those two things got me on a search for all this other stuff. *Psychotronic* opened the doors to different kinds of films that I never even would have considered as "cult", had I not read about them. And Chas. Balun's writing was an inspiration for me to see all these other movies that I'd never even heard of. So, that's what got the ball rolling. I bought *Splatter Movies* by John McCarty. That had a lot of cool stuff in it. I was still a teenager, like fourteen or fifteen, and I didn't really have a job yet, but I would get what I could.

# DAVE KOSANKE

## LIQUID CHEESE

PSYCHOHOLIC SLAG
COURTESY OF DAVE KOSANKE
ISSUE #5
MOVIES AND MUSIC TO MANGLE YOUR MIND!


*PSYCHOLIC SLAG—PRE-LIQUID CHEESE.*

**JS: How did the home video boom affect you?**

**DK:** That was big. We had one of the monster top-loader VCRs, and my parents started renting a lot of movies. And again, a lot of it was horror. *Creepshow* and John Carpenter's *The Thing* were two of our first rentals. And once they opened up a video store that I could actually walk or ride my bike to, I got a membership. It was amazing, because they would let kids rent anything. I even rented *Faces of Death*, because I was curious to see it.

**JS: That was the one thing that the guy at the store by my house wouldn't let me rent.**

**DK:** I got away with it, and I was pretty young [laughs]. There's no way that I would let kids rent that kind of thing, but back then, I guess they didn't care. But yeah, I rented that, *Dawn of the Dead*, *Evil Dead*—basically all of the stuff that was being released on VHS. Then, I found places that had sell-through titles for twenty bucks, and I started buying them. I also started getting blank video tapes and recording my own stuff, which I still have. I have box of stuff from the mid-eighties that I recorded. I even dated everything. The first tape that I have was dated January of '85, and I think the first movie that I recorded from cable was *Children of the Corn*.

**JS: What else is on the tapes?**

**DK:** I'd record anything that was horror—I didn't matter what it was. If it was on TV, I recorded it. I'd fill up tapes with six hours worth of stuff, and I did that for years. Like I said, I still have that box, and it kind of inspired me to go back and rewatch those tapes. I'm going to start doing a series of articles based on particular tapes. I've got so much weird stuff in there, and it would make for an interesting read. Saturday night was prime time viewing, and I'd sit in front of the TV with the remote in my hand. I'd be sure to hit Pause during the commercials. But, if a TV spot came on for *Hellraiser*, or something, I'd be sure to record it.

**JS: What got you interested in writing about films?**

**DK:** It was Chas. Balun. His writing was my number one influence. He had a column called "Piece o' Mind" in *Gorezone*.

**JS: I loved reading that column.**

**DK:** He did one that was called, "Faith, Fear, and Fanaticism." He was basically telling guys who were into this stuff to go out and do it on their own. Go make a movie. Go write a song, or go write a fanzine. That kind of stuck with me, because I was always into reading about this stuff. I thought, "I'd like to try my hand at writing, too." That article gave me the jumpstart to say, "I think I can do this."

**JS: How did you get started?**

**DK:** In the late eighties, I had a Commodore 64 computer at home, and I started writing my own stuff. I dubbed it *Gore Gazette*, but I had no idea that there actually was already a *Gore Gazette*. At the time, I was totally unaware of what Rick Sullivan was doing. I printed out a few things of my own, but it never went any further than a piece of paper. Once I got an upgrade on my computer, I started doing it cut and paste xerox. That was in the early nineties. I came up with the name *Psychoholic Slag*, which was based on a White Zombie song. I would hand draw the covers and clip out movie ads from the newspaper for the pictures. Basically, I would just review what I was watching at the movies or what I saw on TV.

**JS: How did you find your audience?**

**DK:** It was real basic. I would send a few issues out to certain key people, like Michael Weldon. I sent him an issue, and he actually printed the cover in an issue of *Psychotronic*. That was kind of cool; I wasn't expecting that. So, I was sending it out to some key guys, and I'd distribute copies at Nostalgia World, which was my local comic book store. In the early days, that's about as far as I went with it.

**JS: How many copies were you printing?**

**DK:** Barely any. I think

## Liquid Cheese

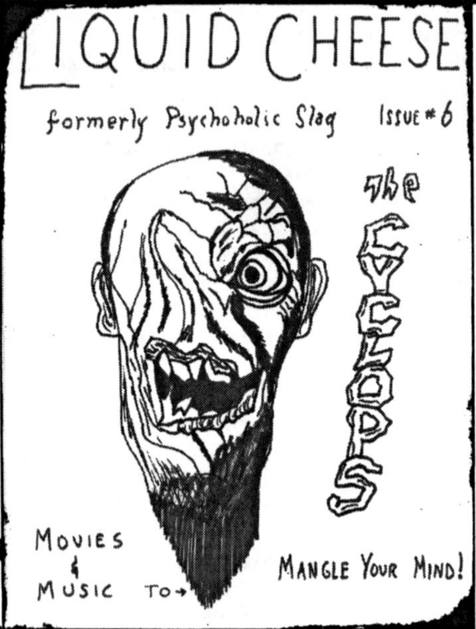


I ran off twenty or thirty copies of each one, and that was about it.

**JS: And how many issues did *Psychoholic Slag* run before you changed the name to *Liquid Cheese*?**

**DK:** Around five. I think I switched to *Liquid Cheese* with number 6. The first couple issues of *Liquid Cheese* were very similar to *Psychoholic Slag*. The layout and look was exactly the same. But then in '95, when I got my first PC, I redesigned everything. I was still calling it *Liquid Cheese*, but I kind of scratched everything that I'd done before. In 1996, I did *Liquid Cheese* number 1 to kind of say, "I'm starting from scratch." That was the official number one, at least in my eyes.

**JS: *Liquid Cheese* has covered a lot of diverse ground throughout the years...**

**DK:** I can look back at those early nineties issues, and there was a heavy Asian influence, with Hong Kong cinema, anime, and stuff like that. It's kind of like whatever was happening in fandom at the time. You'd read the other mags, and you'd see the influences creeping in. You're always looking for that next big thing. I would read all the different magazines, and somebody would mention a spaghetti western. I'd be intrigued by that, find the niche that I was interested in, and take it from there.

**JS: I was into anime for a little while, but it never really caught on with the horror audience.**

**DK:** I think a lot of it was because it wasn't specific to any one genre. It was kind of all over the place. You would focus on the horror stuff, and it was pretty extreme. Those films were interesting, but as a whole, it just had that flavor of "anything goes." It was a little too much for some people to take in. Even *Video Watchdog* was doing an anime column for a while, and that got zero feedback, as well. Some other magazines tried it, but it never caught on.

**JS: How are you producing *Liquid Cheese* these days?**

**DK:** I'm not doing anything that drastically different, to be honest. I now have

access to a color copier, but it's through my job. And I have access to xerox machines at my job, so I can do a heavier volume of printing there than what I was before. As far as the machines, it's still a xerox, so nothing's changed in that. It's just that now I can do more copies. That's pretty much what it boils down to, really.

**JS: What was the zine scene like in the early nineties?**

**DK:** It was pretty good. I was corresponding with a lot of other zine guys, like Craig Ledbetter from *European Trash Cinema*. I sent him an issue of *Liquid Cheese*, and he did a write up of it in one of his issues. The only thing was, he screwed up the state. Instead of putting WI, he put MI, meaning Michigan. So, I actually called him up and said, "I'm in Wisconsin." Then, we got into this big conversation, and I became really good friends with him. Michael Weldon and Steve Puchalski would always give me good reviews. And, I was meeting a lot of other zine guys through the mail. We were doing a lot of trading. I think the only issue I ever ran into was with this girl who did a zine called *Psychoholics Unanimous*. I traded zines with her, and she basically gave me a really bad review, saying that I came across as a sexist pig because I printed nude pictures of women. I was covering some pornography, and I think she was offended by that. I kind of had to go back at her a little bit and explain my stance. Aside from her, everybody else was really cool. Trading was great, and everyone was plugging each other's zines.

LIQUID CHEESE
Traci Lords
MOVIES AND MUSIC TO MANGLE YOUR MIND ISSUE # 1 SPRING 1996 $2.50


**JS: There was a point in time when magazines like *ETC* and *Ecco* were being sold in chain bookstores. Did you ever aspire to go that route?**

**DK:** There was a point where I was trying to distribute *Liquid Cheese* at local stores to see how that would go. The biggest obstacle I always ran into back then was the nudity. It would always turn people off. They didn't have a problem with it, per se, but they felt that some costumers might be offended by it. So, that was the biggest obstacle with making it a full distribution title. I never really wanted to compromise, and that's why I never made that leap.

# Dave Kosanke

## Liquid Cheese

DRAFT

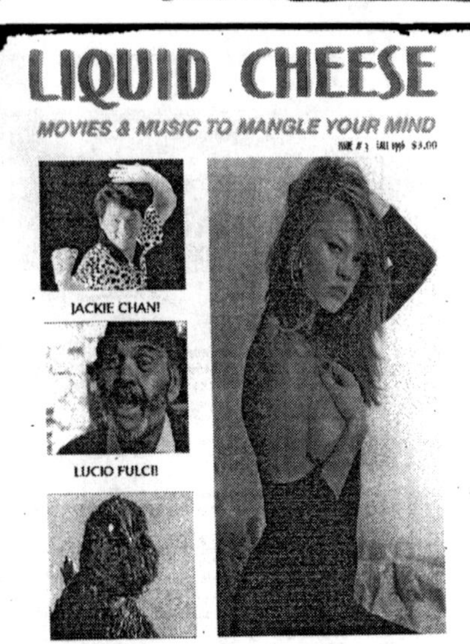

LIQUID CHEESE
MOVIES & MUSIC TO MANGLE YOUR MIND
JACKIE CHAN!
LUCIO FULCI!
G-CON 1996!
ANNA FALCHI!


**JS: After the DVD market implosion, I kind of drifted away from things for a while. Did you ever experience any kind of fatigue?**

**DK:** Yeah. After 2000, I stopped for four years. I wasn't doing anything with the magazine, and I wasn't as into it. People would ask me, "Are you going to bring back *Liquid Cheese*?" I was like, "I'm kind of burnt out." I just didn't have the passion at that time, for whatever reason.

**JS: Let's talk a little about conventions. What kind of a role did they play in things?**

**DK:** It was big. The first full-blown convention I went to was Chiller Theater in '96. It was mind blowing to see all of the stuff. I had been to a few shows in Milwaukee and Chicago, but nothing came even close to that first Chiller Theater show. Once I got that first big convention out of the way, I saw a way to push the zine that way. Not only to get people who were going to the conventions to read it, but to do some networking with some of the dealers and vendors. The biggest thing they had at Chiller was all the guys from England. You had Paul Brown and Trevor Barley from Midnight Media and Media Publications. Steve Midwinter was another one. Those were probably the three biggest guys who were doing the zine publishing over in England, and they had tables at Chiller Theater. And they always had the best stuff, magazine wise. I would buy whatever they had, and say, "Hey, are you guys interested in fanzines? I do one called *Liquid Cheese*." Each guy was blown away. They asked me to bring a box of them. "Can you run off fifty or 100 copies for us? We'll take them back to England and do the distribution thing over there." I said, "Absolutely." They said, "In return, we'll give you X amount of dollars in merchandise." So, I was doing that for a few years, which was great. I stopped going to the Chiller shows, and I think those guys stopped doing them as well. But for that brief moment, the convention thing was my main source of promotion. That's really how I got my name out there.

LIQUID CHEESE NUMBER 25. ART BY PUTRID.

**JS: What kind of guys were Paul Brown and Trevor Barley?**
**DK:** I became better friends with Paul, but he and Trevor always shared a table. They were really nice with everything they had to say—they loved American zines. I thought it was kind of funny. I said, "They're cool, but I love the British zines." You know, it was kind of like stroking each other's ego a little bit, but they were the nicest guys you'd ever want to meet. No pretense and no ego. They loved putting out all of that high quality stuff. I was floored at how good their publications looked—they were printed on the best paper stock, and everything about them was A class. And, they were talking about sleazy, nasty stuff, too, which was great. They didn't pander to any mainstream sensibilities.
**JS: I always wondered how they could afford to print such high quality stuff.**
**DK:** I don't know. I don't know what kind of print runs they had, either. They must have been doing really well. I had some of the Midnight Media catalogs, and would look at all the stuff that they had. It was great. And that was the stuff that they had at their table. They kind of had their hands in everything—they were doing CD soundtracks, as well. It was awesome.
**JS: A lot of the cover art for *Liquid Cheese* is amazing. I'm looking at a cover drawn by a guy called Putrid.**
**DK:** His real name is Matt Carr, but he goes by Putrid. His name is pretty well known in the underground horror and metal scene. He's a kid from Chicago who I met at a Flashback Weekend convention in 2007. He had a table set up there, and I saw his artwork. I was blown away—his stuff is amazing. We became really good friends. He was doing anything and everything, from album covers to zine articles and T-shirts. I asked him if he wanted to do a cover for *Liquid Cheese*, and he said yes. I didn't ask for anything specific, I said, "Just draw whatever," because I loved his artwork so much. He was doing covers from issue 23 through 31. The problem now

is that he's got so much work that he can't devote time to doing a full blown cover for me anymore. And, I knew that was going to happen. When I first saw his work, I knew that he would go big time. He's very well known today. In fact, he's doing his own zine right now called *Organ*.

**JS: Yeah. That looks like it's going to be really good.**

**DK:** He's actually handwriting the whole thing. He's drawing everything, and he's writing all the text by hand. The whole thing is going to be like *Cinema Sewer* and the metal mag *Slayer*. It's kind of a combination of the two. When it comes out, it's going to be incredible. The zine revolution lives on through guys like him. He worships all of the old stuff—VHS, fanzines, and cassette tapes.

**JS: That's an interesting phenomenon.**

**DK:** It's one of those generation things. They came in at the tail end of things—the video tape thing was starting to die down in the nineties, when these kids were growing up. They remember it, and now they want to relive that era.

**JS: I never would have dreamed that there would be a collector's market for old VHS tapes.**

**DK:** It's gone crazy. I go to all these conventions, and it's amazing the amount of video tapes that you see. These kids are going nuts for it. I shake my head—I get it, but I don't get it. I mean, I basically gave all of my videotapes away. Had I held on to them for a couple more years, I probably could have made some decent money with them. Once DVDs started coming out, I was like, "Why do I want videotapes? They look like crap, and they're cut."

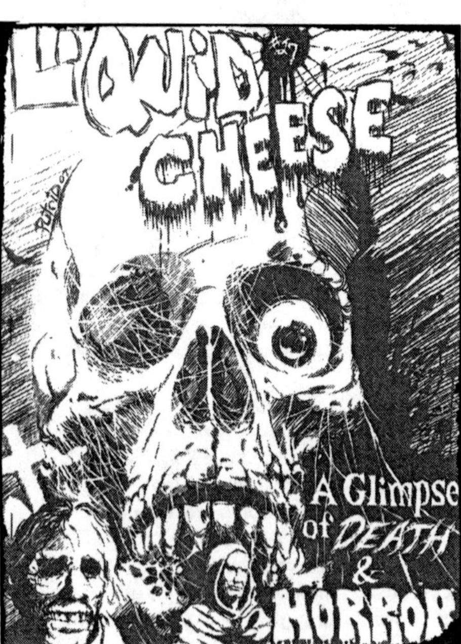


**JS: We used to have these stores called Video Liquidators over here. I would buy tapes from them for dirt cheap. Those kids would be in heaven if they were still around.**

**DK:** You know, one of the other things that ties into this is *HorrorHound*

magazine. They have a column in every issue written by Matt Moore. He's been doing a profile of all the old videotape companies. That really has taken off, too, as far as getting people interested in tapes. His articles have been really well received.

**JS: Were you into laserdiscs at all?**

**DK:** Yeah. In fact, they were a big part of the early issues of *Liquid Cheese*. It always had a laserdisc section. I was a huge, huge fan of them. That kind of came from *Video Watchdog*. They did two special issues, and one of them listed of all of these video retailers. I was looking for ads that were pertaining to laserdiscs, and I wrote to a handful of them. I said, "If you have a catalog, please send it to me."

**JS: Who did you write to?**

**DK:** I think Ken Crane's was one. I don't think I ever heard back from them, but another one I wrote to was Sight and Sound.

**JS: [laughs] I went to that store when I was driving through Massachusetts. It was insane.**

**DK:** They sent me a catalog, and that was it. I was putting in huge orders—I would drop hundreds of dollars. At one point, I had hundreds of laserdiscs.

**JS: I bought a laserdisc player when Elite released *Night of the Living Dead*. It's amazing to think that I was shelling out hundreds of dollars to feed my movie habit.**

**DK:** I bought my laserdisc player in '93, and the most I ever paid was for Criterion's *The Killer*. I think I paid around $125 for that. But again, I thought, "This is it. If you're a hardcore fan, this is the way to go." And, I was always into technology. If something came out that was "the next best thing", I had to have it.

**JS: I was the same way.**

**DK:** Yeah. I've always been one of those guys. That also tied into what I was writing about, because technology was rapidly changing, and I was trying to keep up. When CD-ROMs started coming out, I did a huge write-up

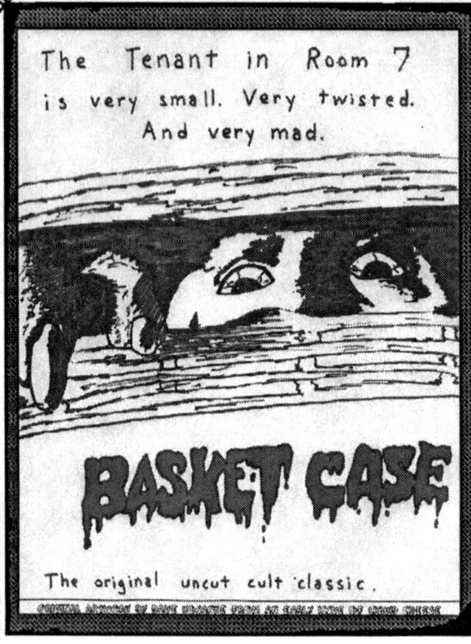
The Tenant in Room 7
is very small. Very twisted.
And very mad.
BASKET CASE
The original uncut cult classic.

EARLY ART BY DAVE KOSANKE.

about them. I was always writing about whatever the latest thing was. And I was always plugging Sight and Sound. It's funny, because one of the guys who worked for Sight and Sound is David Zuzelo. He wrote an article in *Deep Red Alert* number 2 about Lucio Fulci. I think he went by the name of David Quinn. It's funny how everything ties together when you start delving into all this stuff. Everybody is interconnected, in some sort of odd way.

**JS: It's a really small world, and the guys who are really into it tend to stick around forever.**

**DK:** It's crazy. It's like this small-knit community, but people are still into it, which I think is great.

**JS: Going back to your cover art, Mike Hoffman recently did a great drawing for *Liquid Cheese*.**

**DK:** Yeah. I first found out about him in some of the metal magazines back in the day. There was one called *S.O.D—Sounds of Death*, and he did a cover. There was also an interview with him in there. That's when I first became aware of his stuff. I had comic books that he was in, but I didn't think much about it until I read that interview. I put the connection together, and was like, "Holy crap! I've got some comics that he's done." And then I got interested, because he was a presence online. You could go to his eBay store or his website. I started writing to him. I said, "Hey, I do this publication. Could you send me a sample of one of your comics?" He ended up hooking me up with a box of stuff. There was one issue where I had a pretty decent amount of review space devoted to the publications that he sent me. So, we were corresponding a little bit, but then we lost touch.

**JS: What year would this have been?**

**DK:** This was in 2006 or 2007. Years and years went by, and I didn't really think much about him until one day when I was looking on Facebook. His

name popped up, and I was like, "It's Mike! I've got to get back in touch with him." I went to his page, and the location said Shorewood, Wisconsin. I couldn't believe it—that's very close to my house. So, I immediately got in contact with him and said, "How are things going? I see you're living in Shorewood." He said, "Yeah, we moved from South Carolina to Wisconsin." He wanted his kids to go to a better school. At that point, I was thinking, "I've got to see if I can go over to his house."

**JS: [laughs] That would have been my reaction.**

**DK:** I know that some artists are private, and I didn't think that he'd ever go for it. But I was like, "Screw it. What do I have to lose? He'll either say yes or he'll say no." So, I asked him if it would be cool if I could come over sometime. He said, "Yeah, absolutely."

**JS: What was he like?**

**DK:** He was great. He's the nicest guy—he's so laid back, and he's the ultimate independent artist, because he does everything himself.

**JS: What was his studio like?**

**DK:** It was really small. He sat in his chair and told me all these stories about the people he's met and worked with. I thought, "I've got to get an interview with him," because his stories were priceless. I came up with some questions, and I wrote down all of the titles that he's been involved with. Things like *Taboo*, Clive Barker's *Hellraiser*, and *Swamp Thing*. My goal was to ask him specific questions about those titles. He saw what I was going to ask him about, and kind of went off on his own. Rather than just asking questions, I let him talk about each title. As far as the cover for *Liquid Cheese*, he just came out about it. I wasn't going to ask him, because I thought it would be a big ordeal, but he said, "I'll draw a cover up for you." He sketched some ideas, and then I came over one day. He had a rough sketch, and he said, "What do you think of this?" I thought it looked awesome. Before I knew it, he got his drawing board out and he

started doing it, right there. He literally did the entire cover while I sat there and watched. It was one of those things that I never thought would happen.

**JS: I love it when zines have original artwork in them. Hey—what do you think of *Cinema Sewer*?**

**DK:** I love it. When I first got a copy, I thought it was really cool—there wasn't really anyone else doing anything like it. It was one of those things where I was so impressed that I had to write to Robin Bougie. We started corresponding, and his magazine kind of inspired me to do a sister publication to *Liquid Cheese* called *T.O.S.S.*

**JS: I was going to ask you about that...**

**DK:** It was totally devoted to XXX stuff. Robin reviews a lot of pornography in *Cinema Sewer*. That kind of got me thinking that I could do a side publication devoted to adult movies. When I got the first issue of that done, I sent it to him and he gave me a lot of constructive criticism.

**JS: Such as?**

**DK:** He said that I had too many pictures and not enough text. I definitely took that into consideration and said, "Yeah, he's right." Robin was really impressed with the next couple of issues. He said, "Why don't you send me twenty-five copies, and I'll distribute them up here in Canada. In turn, I'll send you X amount of copies of *Cinema Sewer*. You can do what you want with them." We were doing that for a while, but I only ended up doing six issues of *T.O.S.S.* It never really went that far. But for a while, he was my biggest supporter.

A HARD THING TO WRITE ABOUT.

**JS: How difficult is it to write about pornography?**

**DK:** It's kind of a hard thing to write about because a lot of the older stuff is really trashy. Robin was the first guy who was writing about it with intelligence. That kind of got me to say, "Well, I have this stuff that I'm

into, as well. Maybe I can do something similar."

**JS: I interviewed Robin for this book. *Cinema Sewer* is kind of hard to categorize. It's not really a horror zine, but he covers a lot of exploitation films. I'm trying to find a common thread. I guess it's all grindhouse stuff...**

**DK:** Pretty much. You can go back to the *Ilsa* movies and the *Olga* films. That kind of stuff doesn't really pertain to one genre. It's kind of a hybrid. The other thing, too, is when you talk about pornography... porno and horror have always been the two most ghettoized genres of film. They get the least respect. When most people find out that you're into that stuff, they think you're some kind of a nut. "Why would you like that? You're sick." So, I've always made that connection between the two. They get the least respect, but in turn, they probably have the most devoted fans. The two kind of go hand in hand. But, like you said, there's a fine line when you try to define it.

**JS: *Sleazoid Express* certainly startled both worlds. Were you a fan of Bill Landis?**

**DK:** Yeah. Unfortunately, I didn't get into his stuff until way later. *Sleazoid Express* was always a title that I heard about, but I never actually saw a copy until the late nineties. I went to his website, and he was offering the new incarnation of *Sleazoid Express*. I wrote to him and said, "Give me everything." And then, I obviously bought the book. I was fascinated, because he was a part of that that scene while it was happening. From there, I found some of the other people from that era, like 42nd Street Pete. He's another guy who has great stories. He actually wrote an article for me on Joe D'Amato in issue number 24 of *Liquid Cheese*. It was about one of his horror/porn hybrids, which kind of goes back to what we're talking about.

**JS: It's funny—we were just talking about fans who were born too late for the VHS boom. I really wish that I could have walked down 42nd Street in the seventies.**

**DK:** Yeah, it's the exactly same idea.

**JS: Do you think that print is a dying form of communication?**

**DK:** Well, it is to a certain degree, but I think that there's always going to be

# DAVE KOSANKE

## LIQUID CHEESE

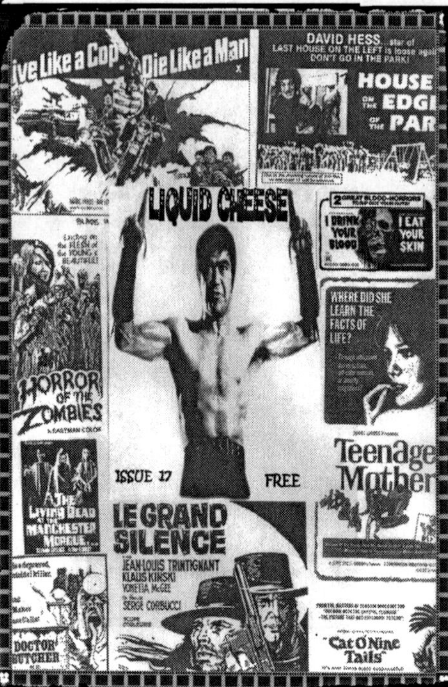


enough of an interest in it that it's still going to be around. I don't think it's ever going to go away. The magazine format especially seems to be doing OK. You've got a big influx of classic monster mags that are coming out. There's stuff like *Famous Monsters*, *Freaky Monsters*, and *Undying Monsters*. There are a lot of newer titles. There's got to be an interest, otherwise people wouldn't be publishing all of this stuff.

**JS: And, magazines like *Video Watchdog* and *Shock Cinema* are still alive and kicking. What's in the future for *Liquid Cheese*?**

**DK:** I'm still going to be doing the same thing I'm doing. I don't see it changing too much, although I want to get it out there even more. I'm doing it in color now, and I think that's the step that I needed to take in order to convince people it's something that I'm serious about. If somebody's going to pay $5 for *Liquid Cheese*, they're not going to feel cheated. That was always my biggest concern. People would say, "Why don't you charge money for it?" and I always felt self-conscious about it. I'd be, "Well, it's not professionally done, and I feel kind of guilty for asking someone to pay money for something that's on xeroxed paper." I've been fighting with that for years. But finally, when I saw how number 32 looked, I said, "I'm going to ask people to help support my fun so I can keep cranking stuff out in return." I think I'm going to go a little bit bigger with the page count. I'm going to start running ads now, too. I've been going to different companies and saying, "I've got cheap ad rates. Advertise your stuff." But, I'm only doing that with companies that I personally endorse. So, I kind of see it going from there. Being a little more available and professional, but with the same "anything goes" attitude where I can feel free to do whatever I want...

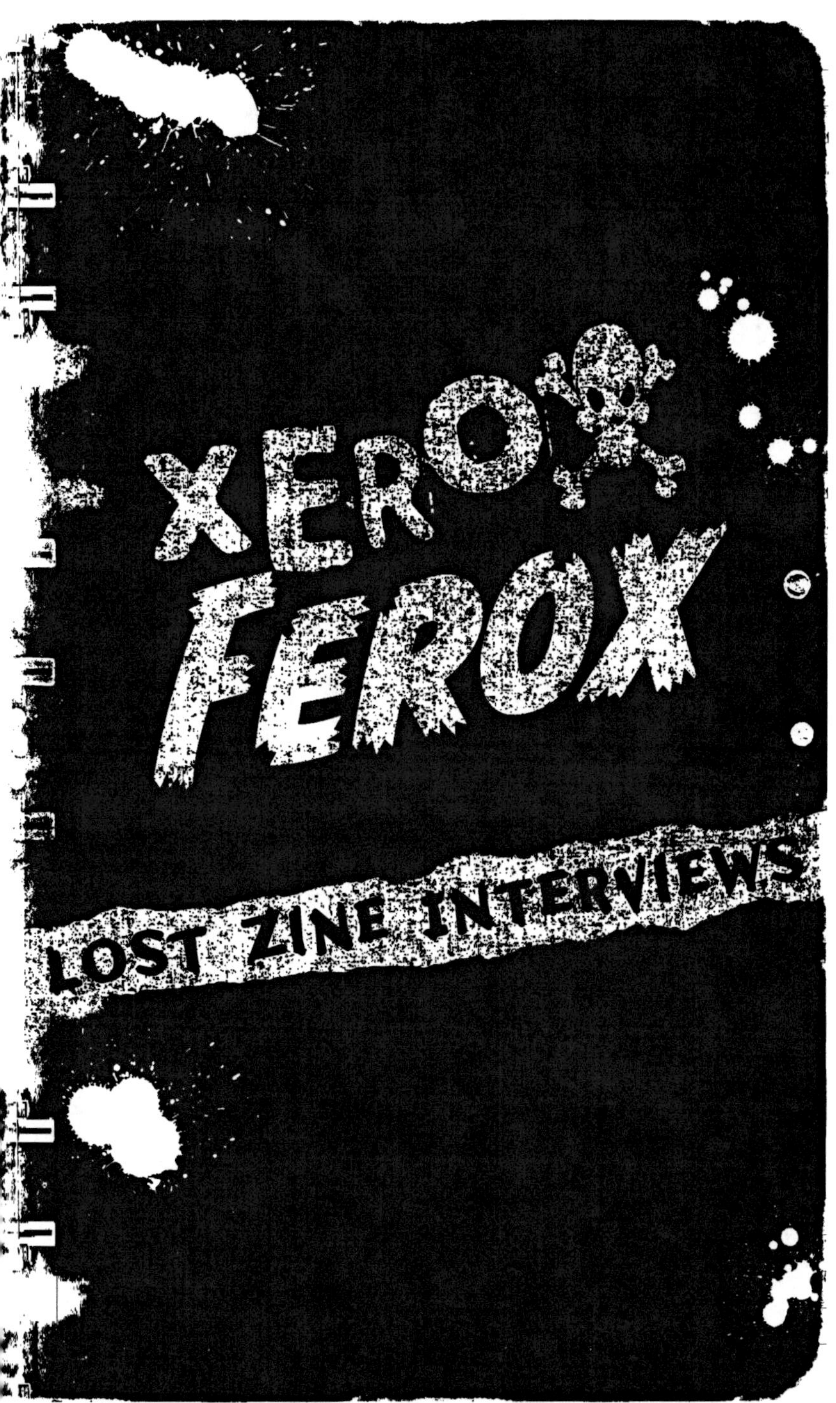
XEROX
FEROX
LOST ZINE INTERVIEWS

# JIM VANBEBBER

## MONSTER KID, SECOND GENERATION

JIM VANBEBBER AS SEEN IN *DEEP RED ALERT* NUMBER 1.

Jim VanBebber is the director of *Deadbeat at Dawn* and *The Manson Family*. I first read about both films in the *Deep Red Horror Handbook*. *Deadbeat* seemed like something that I'd enjoy—as Chas. Balun stated, "This one's really down-and-dirty and comes packed with killer fight scenes, splashy bullet hits, and nasty knifings. Hits like a jackboot to the nuts." OK... sold. *The Manson Family* (then known as *Charlie's Family*) had just started production and it sounded excellent, as well.

Getting my hands on *Deadbeat* was surprisingly easy—for some strange reason, one of the video stores near my house had the rare tape for rent. Rent it I did, and I instantly fell in love with the film. This VanBebber guy was something else—he wrote the screenplay, directed the movie, did the FX, and played the lead.

It took VanBebber years to complete *The Manson Family,* but when he finally did, it hit like an ARMY of jackboots. I was lucky enough to catch a rough cut of the film when it played at the Fantasia film festival in 1997. I sat there glued to my seat as the film unfolded.

*The Manson Family* finally got an official release in 2004, and I attended the Chicago premiere. I saw it three more times when it played Detroit. One of the strangest sagas in the history of independent filmmaking had come to a victorious conclusion, and I wanted to be there in the front row to share in the celebration.

So now, I invite you to enter a theater with me. The main attraction is VanBebber himself. Make yourself comfortable as he discusses his career as a filmmaker, the things that inspired him, and his latest project, *Gator Green*. And yeah... we'll talk about fanzines. After all, that's how most of us met the man...

# JIM VANBEBBER
## MONSTER KID, SECOND GENERATION

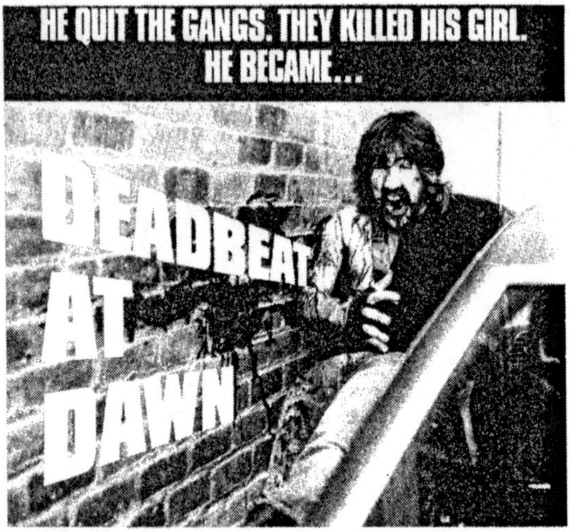

HE QUIT THE GANGS. THEY KILLED HIS GIRL.
HE BECAME...
DEADBEAT AT DAWN

**JOHN SZPUNAR: How long have you been living in Florida?**

**JIM VANBEBBER:** Oh, let's see... for a little more than a year.

**JS: And you're working on a film called *Gator Green*?**

**JVB:** Yeah. And this time around, I'm going back to the drawing board. I'll raise the money privately. I spent so much time in Los Angeles working on scripts, but nothing ever got done. After wasting a couple of years trying to get *Capone* up and running, only to have it yanked by Dark Sky, I was like, "Man... this is fucked." Most of my directing jobs were music videos, and most of them were outside of LA. I'll probably return to that weird fucking place someday, but I'm just going to try to go the independent route again. That's where I've always been the happiest—making stuff that is really near and dear to me, like *Deadbeat at Dawn* and *The Manson Family*.

**JS: I take it that you want to go with practical effects? No CGI?**

**JVB:** No fucking CGI, man. I can't stand it, even when it's used well. And unless you've got Industrial Light and Magic doing it, it always looks shitty. I mean, unless it's John Dykstra doing the fucking arms on Doc Ock [laughs]... Just look at any Sci-Fi network film. The shit is just laughable.

**JS: [laughs] I'll get back into *Gator Green* in a little while, but I want to start out with some general questions.**

**JVB:** Sure.

**JS: OK, first question: Your taste in film is all over the map. What puts "high art" and "low art" on an equal playing field?**

**JVB:** Well, I'm looking for passion. And a lot of great art films have the same passion as *The Texas Chain Saw Massacre*. You can tell that Fellini was fucking throwing himself full-bore into his greatest work, and the same can be said for Welles and the rest of the greats. I could give you the whole laundry list, but I consider *Texas Chain Saw* and *Evil Dead* as high art. And I think that the people who dismiss horror films as being base don't really have an open mind.

**JS: I feel the same way. And I really feel vindicated now that a lot of lowly "genre" films are finally becoming accepted. *The Beyond* recently played on TCM.**

**JVB:** Yeah. But it always comes too fucking late. I mean, *The Beyond* was originally butchered in its editing, and was released as *7 Doors of Death*.

**JS: That's the version I first saw.**

**JVB:** Yeah. And actually, *The Green Slime* recently played on Turner Classic Movies. I love it when that kind of shit happens, but it always takes decades.

**JS: Why do you think that is?**

**JVB:** Well, I think that the kids who stayed up past their bedtime to watch this stuff on the CBS midnight movie finally got jobs in these places. They're now in the position of power to say, "Hey, wait a minute. I loved this film as a kid." I mean, *Equinox* came out from Criterion…

**JS: That one really came out of left field.**

**JVB:** I know [laughs]! But it only happened after Dennis Muren and David Allen went on to bigger films. Dennis Muren's doing *Jurassic Park*, and all of the sudden, they're like, "Well, of course. This has to be a Criterion release!" The snobby-nosed people always have to have some kind of validation, other than the fact that it's just great shit. I'm not a film snob. If it's good film, it's freaking good—I don't care what genre it is. If it's made with passion and it's good filmmaking, that's all there is to it. I've seen some driver's ed films that I thought were incredibly well done. And there are some great anti-drug films that are fucking hilarious—they're classics in their own right. Mike Vraney from Something Weird Video knew what was going on. He was like, "This is not crap. This needs to be out on DVD."

**JS: The book that I'm writing is**

DEADBEAT AT DAWN

EARLY COVERAGE BY CHAS. BALUN IN THE *DEEP RED HORROR HANDBOOK*.

**DEAD BEAT AT DAWN**

1987/80 m/d: Jim Van Bebber

Muscular, exciting splatter actioneer transcends its gritty, 16mm look and micro-budget on the strength of Van Bebber's stylish, savvy direction. Keep an eye on this kid. He also wrote the screenplay, edited the film, handled the righteously gory FX and stars as a street gang leader attempting to rise above his grim and violent surroundings. This one's really down-and-dirty and comes packed with killer fight scenes, splashy bullet hits and nasty knifings. Hits like a jackboot to the nuts.

**about fanzines and fandom in general. Guys like you, Buddy Giovinazzo, and Jörg Buttgereit kind of got your "start", so to speak, from fanzine culture.**

**JVB:** Definitely. That's how people found out about the films. Fanzines were fucking great. And they certainly helped spread the word when you really had no publicity. People took notice. *Gore Gazette* was great. Rick Sullivan always wrote nice things about my work. And then, of course you had Chas.' *Deep Red*. It wasn't really a fanzine, per se; it was more of an honest to God mag. The *Deep Red Horror Handbook* certainly

# JIM VANBEBBER

## MONSTER KID, SECOND GENERATION

SCENE FROM *THE MANSON FAMILY*.

got my name out there, along with Jörg's and Buddy's. All of the sudden, you're being invited to film festivals in England.

**JS: Did you grow up in Dayton?**

**JVB:** No. I grew up in a small town in Ohio called Grenville, which is about an hour outside of Dayton. I moved to Dayton when I went to film school at Wright State. But, Dayton was an hour away, and it used to have a movie theater called the Kon-Tiki. That's where you'd to go to see *Mother's Day*, *Dawn of the Dead*, *Caligula*, or *Make them Die Slowly*. All of that great shit.

**JS: What was the scene in Greenville like?**

**JVB:** Greenville had two outstanding movie theaters, and I was at the movies every weekend—I didn't care what was playing. And I watched movies on TV, obsessively. That was back in the days of the horror hosts, and we had a great one out of Dayton called Dr. Creep.

**JS: He was the host of *Shock Theater*.**

**JVB:** Yeah. *Shock Theater* was a mainstay for me, from age five on. And there was another guy out of Bloomington, Indiana by the name of Sammy Terry. If the reception was coming in, he was always a good one to catch on Saturday nights. That's how I first saw *Equinox*, the Universal and Hammer horror films, and the shit that you'd never see anywhere else, like *The Eye Creatures*. Larry Buchanan stuff.

**JS: How do you account for the popularity of the horror hosts?**

**JVB:** Well, obviously, they were the most fun guys to watch on television. That was back when there were only three networks. You didn't have home entertainment, as far as films went—

VHS wasn't even around yet. So, when you were watching TV, you had your local news anchors, some dingbat kid's show that would run cartoons, and the horror hosts. The horror hosts worked for me, and they obviously worked for a lot of other people who were my age. And when the affiliates decided that they could make more money by showing infomercials, it was a terrible crime to the culture. After that, the kids didn't have horror hosts, they didn't have *Shock Theater*, and they didn't have drive-ins. It's like, man… you fuckers are missing out.

**JS: I was barely alive, but I was able to catch the last wave of horror hosts here in Detroit.**

**JVB:** That was a big part of my youth. I used to set my alarm clock and put it underneath my pillow when I was sent to bed. It'd go off at 11:15. I'd crawl to the top of the steps, listen to my parents watch the late news, and run back to my room when they were coming up the stairs. I'd give myself about ten minutes, then I'd creep downstairs like a freaking ninja to watch *The Black Scorpion*, *Gargoyles*, or whatever was on.

**JS: Did you ever get caught?**

**JVB:** I got caught many times, and I was always like, "But, it's a classic!"

**JS: [laughs] Let's hear a little more about the drive-ins.**

**JVB:** Oh, the drive-ins were great. We had two hardtop theaters, The Wayne and the State Theater, and they were both within walking distance. And then, we had the Speedway drive-in. Before I could even drive, I used to have my mom drive me out there with a lawn chair, so I could go watch *Phantasm* or a Bruce Lee movie. And then, as soon as I could drive, I was like, "I want to work at the drive-in."

**JS: Did you?**

**JVB:** I did. That was the greatest fucking job. Just going there on dates was a great part of my life. It should be part of every teenager's experience.

**JS: Were the drive-ins playing second-run stuff?**

**JVB:** During the Summer proper, they would play first-run films. But, when they first opened in the Spring—like from March up until mid-May—that's when the offbeat stuff was playing. They'd play that stuff again in the Fall, right up until they closed. And, that's when you would see stuff like *Last House on Dead End Street*, the European sex comedies, and the re-runs of Bruce Lee's first couple of films. For me, that was the best stuff. I'd much rather see *Don't Go in the House* than *Any Which Way but Loose*.

**JS: I agree, but then I have to say that *Any Which Way but Loose* is a pretty good movie [laughs].**

**JVB:** Oh yeah, it's aged beautifully.

**JS: What kind of a job did you have at the drive-in?**

**JVB:** I worked at the concession stand, and then, ultimately, I was a projectionist. But, that was only in the last year.

**JS: How long did you work there?**

**JVB:** I think I worked there for five years. I was the guy who you bought all of your candy, popcorn, and pizzas from. I'll tell you though, during the last eleven minutes of *The Road Warrior*—during the massive chase—nobody got served nothing! I was outside watching that every night, just taking it in. I was not believing what I was seeing.

# JIM VANBEBBER

## MONSTER KID, SECOND GENERATION

**JS: How old were you when you got your first camera?**

**JVB:** I was eleven. I bought a used Brownie windup. I still have it. It was great, man. It had a manual iris on it, so I could do fade-ins and fade-outs. Then, I got hip to running the film through the camera more than once and started doing split-screens and dissolves.

**JS: How would you do a split-screen?**

**JVB:** I'd take a piece of black poster board and cut out a little half-moon. I'd tape it right onto the lens and shot the lower half. I'd take notes on where the shot was on the footage meter and would run the film back to that point. Then, I'd put the half-moon on the other side. It's so easy to do that now, digitally. It's really taken for granted. But back then, it took some inventiveness. I still love to do that kind of shit.

**JS: Let's get back to monster mags. What kind of stuff were you reading?**

**JVB:** Well, I think I was five when I picked up my first *Famous Monsters*. Thank God there was a bookstore in town that sold it. And then when *Cinemagic* hit the scene, I was all over that. But when *Fangoria* came out, I was just like, "Here we go!"

**JS: Those early issues were something else.**

**JVB:** Uncle Bob Martin was the great voice of *Fangoria*. The tone certainly went more commercial and more Hollywood when Tony Timpone took over. I'm not even sure what to think of it these days. But, Bob Martin really liked the independent scene. He'd give *Basket Case* the kind of coverage that Timpone would give to *Nightmare 4*.

**JS: I've been meaning to ask you this—what attracted you to horror films as a kid?**

**JVB:** I don't know... the visceral jolt, I guess. For some reason, I loved being scared and freaked out. I was ten years old when I saw *Last House on the Left*, and for the next two days, I walked around thinking, "There ought to be a law. Nobody should be able to make something like that!" Then, around the third day, I was like, "Man, why is this film still freaking me out? Why am I still thinking about it? There must be some kind of genius at work." And up until I saw *Dawn of the Dead*, most of my 8mm films had a lot of stop-motion and were more Harryhausen-oriented. But after that, out came the red food dye and the blood! Rubber hands getting lopped off [laughs].

**JS: You eventually got a scholarship to Wright State University...**

**JVB:** Yeah. I had no money for college, and my parents certainly weren't rich. It was a question of, well... am I going to go to college? I knew that I wanted to learn sound, and that I wanted to learn 16[mm]. My guidance counselor said, "There's a film department at Ohio State, and there's one at Wright State." I went and checked out Ohio State, but they really didn't have their shit together, at all. The clincher was that Wright State was offering a scholarship. I went there and I showed them my 8mm film, *Into the Black*. I got the scholarship, and it paid for my first year of college.

**JS: What was the curriculum like over there?**

**JVB:** See, that's the thing. When I first went there, they weren't that big on production. They were trying to make everybody into a critic. It was all about film theory, which I could give a fuck

about. Fortunately, I had a good prof my first year, Jim Dolan.

**JS: Did you get to shoot anything?**

**JVB:** We started out shooting Super-8, and we got to do sound Super-8 in the last quarter. Then, Jim left. I didn't know if I was going to go back for a second year. I'd gotten a good job at the telecommunications center—they made local TV shows for the PBS channel and I had access to some good equipment.

**JS: Why did you decide to stay?**

**JVB:** The clincher for year two was that they hired Jim Klein and Julia Reichert, who were real honest to God filmmakers. They were a documentary team—they made the Academy Award nominated film, *Seeing Red*. They were the real deal, and they knew the nuts and bolts of filmmaking. So, I learned 16 from them, and said, "OK. I've got what I need to know. Now it's time to make *Deadbeat at Dawn*." I took out a student loan for my third year, but I didn't go. I spent it on getting *Deadbeat at Dawn* off the ground.

**JS: I first read about *Deadbeat at Dawn* in the fanzines.**

**JVB:** The *Deep Red Horror Handbook* and *Psychotronic* both gave it really good reviews. And then, Joe Bob Brigs had his newsletter, *We Are the Weird*. He gave it a great freaking review. And

No Room for the Damned:

The Last Days of John Martin

By S. R. Bissette

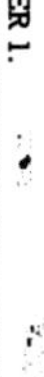

*DEEP RED ALERT* NUMBER 1.

Steve Bissette wrote one of the best reviews of *Roadkill: The Last Days of John Martin* that I've ever read.

**JS: How did he get a hold of that? Did you send it to him?**

**JVB:** I was at some convention, and he was there. He had a table, and I think I hooked him up with some tapes.

**JS: You wrote a couple of articles about the production of *The Manson Family* for *Deep Red Alert*. How did that come about?**

**JVB:** Chas. asked me if I'd write an article. He had a tape of the rough cut, and was like, "You need publicity. Why don't you write something?

# JIM VANBEBBER

DEEP RED ALERT
NUMBER 1 FALL 1991 4.95
The Return of LUCIO FULCI
Finally... THE FEEBLES
The Gutting of LEATHERFACE
All New!
SKINNY PUPPY
PIECE O'MIND
Jim Van Bebber
CHARLIE'S FAMILY

Maybe someone will give you some money." And Chas. was just the best. I was always glad that he liked my work, because he was so honest—if he didn't like your work, he had no bones about calling a dog a dog. And then, when I met him and hung out with him in California, he was just the nicest guy. A sweet and very intelligent film connoisseur who loved horror films. And he took on the thankless job of spreading the word. Nobody would have heard of *Combat Shock* or Jörg Buttgereit as early as they did, if it hadn't been for Chas. He went out of his way for the little guy, if he liked your work and saw some merit in it. He was one of the first champions of *Henry: Portrait of a Serial Killer*. There's nobody like him around anymore. He was taken way too early.

**JS: His "dog" reviews still crack me up.**

**JVB:** His stuff was just so fun to read. Joe Bob wrote well and was funny, but he wasn't funny like Chas. Chas. had some zingers. His writing style was like Lenny Bruce meets Hunter Thompson meets Lester Bangs, but about horror films.

**JS: Can you tell me a little about *Chunk Blower*?**

**JVB:** Sure. I got a call from this Canadian producer, Gary Blair Smith. He said, "I've got this film I want to make called *Chunk Blower*, and we're going to make a trailer for it first to help convince some company to give us a million dollars. That was a lot of money for an extreme splatter film, which is definitely what the script was. He had called Chas. and had asked for directors—he was considering John McNaughton, Buddy G, and me. Chas. sent him *The Last Days of John Martin*, and he decided on me. So, he flew me up to Vancouver. He paid me very little, but he put a lot of dough into that trailer. We shot it on 35 and blew up a car. I didn't have any say so in the casting—he cast this bouncer guy as the maniac, and the guy was terrible. But, I approached it with zeal, storyboarded the whole freaking thing, and had a lot of fun with it. We went around to four or five different companies and they were all nonplussed. It was a pretty bold idea, back at the time. A big budget splatter film doesn't seem like anything now after *Hostel* and the *Final Destination* films.

**JS: Chas. worked on the script...**

**JVB:** He worked on it. It was originally written by Gary and a guy named

The True Believers: Mike King, Jim VanBebber & Marcello Games

DEEP RED ALERT NUMBER 2. THE SAGA CONTINUES...

A FILMMAKER'S JOURNAL

THE CONTINUING STORY OF CHARLIE'S FAMILY BY JIM VANBEBBER

Attachment

Alan Zweig. Man, that script went through more passes—I think Chas. did like four or five drafts. I wrote a draft, just on spec. Gary could never find the financing for it. After a while, he became a family man and went back to being an assistant director. He couldn't get anywhere with it. A lot of people really trip out on that trailer. To me, it's OK, but I don't think it's anything great [laughs].

**JS: I really wanted to see the feature film.**

**JVB:** Oh, yeah. Same thing with *John Martin*, which was a short we made while trying to get that feature off the ground. I intend to make it someday. I took the original draft and updated it—you have to take into account all the stuff that has entered our lives since 1988.

**JS: Why do you think you never got the financing for *John Martin*?**

**JVB:** Well, when I was initially trying to get that off the ground, horror films were getting attacked. All of the gore was being shot for the *Friday the 13th* films, but then cut. The MPAA was a holy terror, threatening everything with an X rating. The producers were scared, and they were making bloodless movies. I mean, I think in *Nightmare 5* a character turns into a cartoon character and Freddy shreds him like paper. He bleeds paint. I'm like, "What the fuck?" Compared to the funnel of blood coming out of Johnny Depp's bed in the original, I'm like, "Man, you guys are really losing your focus here." But, it was all a reaction against this cry of, "Violence creates killers!" That's always been the lamest argument ever, for me. What horror film did Jack the Ripper watch? Don't give me that crap. It's a knee-jerk reaction, and the argument doesn't make sense or hold water. Film should have no limits, and art should have no limits. Literature should have no limits. If you don't fucking like it, don't read it or watch it. Unfortunately, there are more of those people than there are those like me and you. We're always going to be the sick minority.

**JS: As a filmmaker, what was your take on tape trading?**

**JVB:** Well, it was a necessary evil. I was trying to be a filmmaker, and as a filmmaker, you want that to be your source of income. That being said, so many people wouldn't have seen *Deadbeat* initially. There wouldn't have been the buzz about *Charlie's Family* if people weren't hooking up two VHS

EARLY AD FOR VANBEBBER'S FILMS.

JIM VANBEBBER
Promo Reel
complete & uncut

THE LAST DAYS OF
JOHN MARTIN

CHUNK
BLOWER
(trailer)

CHARLIE'S
FAMILY
(trailer)

$20 USA
$25 Foreign
*Postage
is included

73 Westpark Road
Dayton, OH 45459

This high quality, 20 minute promo tape has been struck directly from the original master. Each has been numbered and signed by the director.

decks in their basement and selling them in the back of some xeroxed fanzine. Ultimately, it was a good thing for the culture. As a filmmaker, it's piracy, but it's going to happen. There's not really anything you can do about it, so you best not sound like a pussy and bitch too much. Just accept it and be honored that people are caring enough about your stuff to want to dupe it and trade or sell it. A lot of the stuff had no chance of getting out there until *Film Threat Video Guide* started releasing VHS tapes. You know, Richard Kern's films, or whatever. Unless you lived in New York and went to some forum where it was being projected, you didn't get to see them.

**JS: What did you think about *Film Threat?***

**JVB:** I liked its anarchic approach. I always thought Chris Gore was a little too big for his britches, but at least he was getting the thing out there. David E. Williams was more my speed; I certainly like him better as a person. I was astounded by their hatchet job on Chas. It was unwarranted and unnecessary, and they lost some points forever in my book on that one. But, they treated me well with the release of *My Sweet Satan*. That was the first thing I made that actually made its money back for the investors.

**JS: Steve Bissette did some artwork for that film. How did that come about?**

**JVB:** Well, I was finishing it, and I was invited back to the Nothing Shocking Film Festival in London. It was put on by this guy named Spencer Hickman. The first year, I had shown *Deadbeat at Dawn*. Anyway, we kept in touch, and I told him that I was making a thirteen-minute teaser for *Charlie's Family*. I also told him that I was making this short, *My Sweet Satan*. He was like, "Bring copies. We'll have a table for you and you can sell it, and maybe make a little pub money." I called

Steve and said, "Hey man, could you try your hand?" He did it as a favor. He gave me a rough sketch—he didn't have any time to work on it any further. I busted out the color magic markers and gave it some color. That was the original cover for those tapes that were sold in England.

**JS: What was England like?**

**JVB:** England was awesome because they were still in the middle of their video nasties ban. The more you take something away from the kids, the more they want it. Their rabidness about horror films was an education to me. Everyone had their *Evil Dead* shirts and posters. The fans took it seriously—horror was to them what the freaking Beatles were to Americans in 1964. Going to the Nothing Shocking fest at the Scala theater in King's Cross in London with all these dudes lined up outside going, "What do you know about reality?" I was amazed. It was great. I was like, "There is an audience for this stuff. It's not just me that thinks it's worth doing." You know, Spencer Hickman had a horror zine with a glossy cover. It was called *Psychotic Reaction*.

**JS: I know it well. You know, the first time I ever saw *The Manson Family* was at the Fantasia festival in Montreal. You showed a rough cut.**

**JVB:** Yeah. That was a hell of a screening.

**JS: It was a great time. Everyone was there—Chas. Balun, Harvey Fenton from *Flesh & Blood*...**

**JVB:** Yeah. Nacho Cerda was there with *Aftermath*. Richard Stanley was there. Bob Murawski and Sage were there with *Cannibal Ferox*.

**JS: Chas. didn't like *Aftermath* at all.**

**JVB:** Yeah, I never understood that. He got offended—he took it as gore for gore's sake. I don't really think that's the case with *Aftermath*. It always amazed me that he loved *The Last Days of John Martin*, but he didn't like *Aftermath*. You know that those fuckers are out there. It's a valid film, and it's certainly no holds barred. It's so beautifully made that it's jaw dropping. You've got to give Nacho props on his directing. He's a real craftsman.

**JS: How do you feel about the way the mainstream press handled *The Manson Family*?**

**JVB:** Pretty good, for the most part. It's got a fresh tomato on Rotten Tomatoes. Certainly, Roger Ebert's confused review was the best ever. He's saying, "Don't go see it, but I give it three and a half stars." *Entertainment Weekly* dug it. For the most part, I think they got it. Of course, you've always got some people who say, "Amateur hour!" or whatever. The British press was pretty hard on it. But, at the same point, I don't care what they think. I don't make a film to get a good review. I make it for myself and for the audience—people like me and you. People who are going to enjoy it because it delivers what it promises.

**JS: What are your thoughts on Hollywood today?**

**JVB:** It's a tough racket. If you're trying to be innovative and trying to give people something new, it's not met with open arms. It's tricky. I don't understand why something like *Cabin Fever* is embraced and suddenly Eli's got the budget for *Hostel*. To me, while it's an OK film, *Cabin Fever* doesn't have the originality or the ferocity of *The Manson Family*. Yeah, we got some

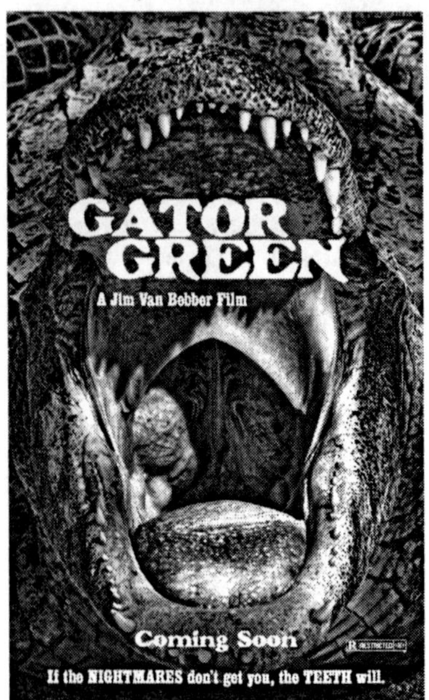


good reviews, but nobody was calling me up saying, "Hey, we want to make your next film." It's hard to be taken seriously. Unless you know somebody powerful or you've got your foot in the door some way, it's really hard to get anybody to pay attention to you. There are so many people killing themselves out there and never getting anywhere. It's a really depressing place to be if you're broke [laughs]. It's the worst! And, nobody has a fucking critical opinion. Everybody's so scared that if they diss something that makes money, somebody's going to find out about it and they won't work. Their only opinion is, if it made a lot of money, it must be good. Hollywood's the only place where you can find people talking favorably about the Michael Bay films. It doesn't make any sense. I met a lot of really cool people when I lived there, but after spinning my wheels, I just decided that if I'm going to get anything done, it's time to go back to the basics.

GATOR GREEN
A Jim Van Bebber Film
Coming Soon
If the NIGHTMARES don't get you, the TEETH will.

**JS: Are you still planning to make the *Capone* film one day?**

**JVB:** Oh, yeah. I love my *Capone* script. It's basically to Al Capone what *The Manson Family* was to Manson. It's like a damn history lesson. The story's never been done right. Screenwriters take liberties, and the truth is much more interesting than the crap they come up with. I'm really telling the story honestly for the first time—that's the attraction to me. So, I've got that and a lot of other scripts that may or may not see the light of day.

**JS: What can we expect from *Gator Green*?**

**JVB:** A real character-driven monster movie of sorts, only the monsters are alligators. I really don't want to say too much about it. It's one of my favorite things that I've ever written. I can't really compare it to anything. Maybe people will see a little bit of Tobe Hooper's *Eaten Alive* drifting around. Maybe a little bit of *Frogs*. But at the same time, it's more like if the Coen brothers made a nasty fucking horror film.

**JS: Nice.**

**JVB:** Yeah. I've got great hopes for it, and that's why I want to shepherd it all the way through. I want to have complete control over this mother because I'm tired of listening to false promises. I'm getting cynical in my old age, Johnny [laughs]. No, I've still got the fire. I've still got the spirit and I'm never going to stop…

THE
TIME
HAS
COME...

# CHARLIE'S FAMILY

a film by Jim VanBebber

Mercury Films presents a Jim VanBebber film:
**Charlie's Family** * *Starring* Marc Pitman, Leslie Orr, Maureen Allisse, Marcelo Games, Jim VanBebber, D'uan Edmonds, Charlie Goetz, Tina Martin, Geoff Burkman, Jim Sayer and Carl Day * *Music by* Download, Phil Anselmo, Superjoint Ritual, Down, Charles Manson, and Body and Blood * *Director of Photography* Mike King * *Edited by* Jim VanBebber and Michael Capone * *Associate Producer* Michael Capone * *Special Makeup Effects by* Jim Van Bebber and Andy Copp * *Produced by* Mike King * *Written and Directed by* Jim VanBebber * 95 minutes * Unrated

## REVIEW BY Chas Balun

Ohio filmmaker Jim VanBebber, whose previous short films *Roadkill: The Last Days of John Martin* (1988) and *My Sweet Satan* (1993) (Grand Prize Winner at the New York Underground Film Festival) and lone feature, *Deadbeat at Dawn* (1988), showed a ferocious, original and courageous talent of work, goes positively ballistic with *Charlie's Family*.

This is a genuinely frightening film experience. The murders, of course, are, indeed, horrifying. Shorn of all cinematic artifice, they are presented with all the stylish panache of a real snuff film. But it is not merely the bloodshed nor the hair-raising vicious knife attacks or frenzied, predatorial violence that proves the most troubling. That would be far too easy for a director of VanBebber's abilities. What *really* gets under your skin about *Charlie's Family* is the bleak, amoral landscape it explores, populated by soulless scavengers bound by blood to a messianic mad dog. This is an incendiary work, a devastating and profoundly disturbing glimpse into The Belly of the Beast. No prisoners are taken. No mercy asked.

34

# ROY FRUMKES

## FRUMKES ON FANZINES

STREET TRASH DIRECTOR JIM MURO (LEFT) AND PRODUCER ROY FRUMKES.

Roy Frumkes is the director of *Document of the Dead* and the writer/producer of *Street Trash*, two films that owe much of their cult status to the fanzine world. He readily admits that *Deep Red*'s coverage of his films helped put his name on the genre map. Frumkes is also the editor of *Films in Review*, the oldest film magazine in the United States. I got the idea to talk to him about his work in the horror genre, the impact that fanzines had on independent film, and *Films in Review*'s place in the age of the internet…

**JOHN SZPUNAR: To me, you always seemed like the intellectual "art-horror" guy.**

**ROY FRUMKES:** [laughs] They wanted to promote *Street Trash* as art-gore; they wanted to start a new genre. That was David Whitten—he was the head of PR at Lightning Films, which was a subdivision of Vestron Video in Connecticut. He got a lot of resistance from Vestron, but his ideas were all really smart. He thought that *Street Trash* should be part of a new subgenre called art-gore. They nixed all his ideas before *Street Trash* opened because they suddenly had a hit with *Dirty Dancing*—they suddenly became very anxious about not offending the critics. Much of *Street Trash*'s promotional campaign was about belittling the critics, so they killed all of his great ideas.

**JS: Whitten had a great track record in exploitation promotion.**

**RF:** He's the reason I went with Vestron. We had a much better financial offer from De Laurentiis. But De Laurentiis just didn't seem to know how to market a film like ours. Whitten was flowing with ideas, all of them very appropriate for

ROY FRUMKES WITH *STREET TRASH* SCULPTURES BY JAMIE CHIMINO.

the target audience. I have no false illusions about my films, including *The Substitute*. They're exploitation films. I think they're high class ones—they're done with integrity, and we raised enough money to support films that looked good and were what we wanted them to be.

**JS: Let's back up a little bit. What kind of films were you watching as a kid?**

**RF:** The ones that stuck out were the horror films. I was really scared of them, but I couldn't turn away. And when I say horror, I mean Disney films, as well. I don't know that there's a more terrifying film than *Pinocchio*, for the age group it's aimed at. That film was absurdly frightening.

**JS: What other films scared you?**

**RF:** We lived in a house in New Rochelle, New York. My folks would go out, and somewhere in the house was someone who was supposed to be looking after me, but I would be alone. In those days, the TV sets only had a couple of channels, and it was all black and white. They were running the Val Lewton films. I remember sitting in a chair in the living room and staring at the set. I was watching *Cat People*, and I was afraid to get off of the chair—I thought there was something under it. I have a brother who's five years older than me. He kind of took advantage of that kind of stuff. He would hide in the closet at night, and I'd go to bed, and he'd say "It's the black cat!" and scare the life out of me.

In terms of my actually becoming a part of that whole phenomenon, I blame that in part on my childhood, which was fraught with illness. I was a very sick kid—I had a handful of pretty dreadful illnesses and at times, the whole house might be quarantined. Everyone else would be somewhere in the back of the house, and I'd be lying there in pain with nothing to do. I would look out of this window across from my bed, and I'd just start inventing stories to keep myself occupied. My brother was afraid to come near me—he was told to stay away. The ideas that I was coming up with were twisted by the nature of what I was going through.

**JS: Did you come from a creative family?**

**RF:** I came from a theatrical family. My grandfather was Houdini's booking agent. He was a very colorful guy who hung out with people much younger than him. I loved listening to his stories; I was very hooked on that. I think that was also a very formative influence. I've still got Houdini's puppets sitting here. I have a friend who was at some kind of magician's

convention this week, and they said these things are priceless—there's no way to determine what they're worth. He carved them out of wood himself, and he created the costumes, all prior to going into magic. My grandfather also had some of Houdini's tricks—these beautiful things that he had created. I remember breaking them, not realizing what I was doing. I was too young. My mother acted in silent films, but my father was not creatively minded. He was a businessman. My brother pretty much took after him, and I took after my grandfather. When I was nine, I wrote a book. It took me a year—I typed with one finger on a manual typewriter. My father went and had it retyped and bound.

CREW T-SHIRT. FROM THE COLLECTION OF JAMIE CHIMINO.

**JS: What was the title?**

**RF:** It was called *The Phantom of Mesa Cove*, and it was kind of influenced by serials like *Flash Gordon*. Well, more like *Red Barry*, which was one of Buster Crabbe's lesser serials. I've still got it, and it's evidence to me that I had a fertile imagination and it was being stimulated somewhat by my isolation.

**JS: Did you ever make any films when you were growing up?**

**RF:** When I was thirteen, my father bought me a 16mm camera. He just bypassed the Super-8, so I was the only kid at my school actually making movies. This September is going to be my fiftieth high school reunion. I think they're going to want those movies, because I was shooting all the students. I was doing little stories—they weren't good, but they were in color. We were shooting Kodachrome, so they didn't fade; they still look beautiful today.

**JS: Is there any chance that they'll ever be released?**

**RF:** I didn't really understand film grammar that much—those films are not works of art. They're not going to appear on the supplements for

ON THE SET OF *STREET TRASH*. FROM THE COLLECTION OF JAMIE CHIMINO.

the *Street Trash* blu-ray or anything [laughs]. They remain in my closet, but I did them.

**JS: When did you realize that you wanted to make movies professionally?**

**RF:** I can't exactly remember when, but it was always there. I transitioned from writing stories to writing screenplays. I went to Tulane University in New Orleans, and kept trying to write stuff. I had approached the studios—my family had some contact there.

**JS: What did you major in?**

**RF:** I think I was misadvised. The studio contacts told me to major in anything except film, because I'd get that when I got out. So, I majored in English and creative writing. But, I think they were wrong. I think that they were trying to dissuade me or misguide me. To this day, I think it was bad advice. I think I would have done better taking film classes as well as writing classes.

**JS: What was New Orleans like?**

**RF:** New Orleans was an odd town. They didn't have much interest in film. They only were interested in Creole food, Cajun food, and jazz. Quite seriously—this was before Creole and Cajun food spread around the country. This was the only city where you could find it, and they were only interested in their own stuff. When films were being shot there, they would call the school and ask me if I wanted to come along. I was the entertainment editor of the *Tulane Hullabaloo!* I'd visit the sets, and I'd make friends with the publicists. I'd meet the stars who were there. When I'd come home to New York on vacation, I would try to follow up on some of the contacts I'd made. The most important ones were probably in the publicity departments.

LEGENDARY ARTICLE IN *DEEP RED* NUMBER 4.

## ROY FRUMKES: Filmmaker

# STREET TRASH

# DOCUMENT OF THE DEAD

With Photographs By K. S. KOLBERT And KAREN OGLE From The ROY FRUMKES Collection

### BY DENNIS DANIEL

Our story begins in the downstairs den of one Nathan Schiff, a recent acquaintance of mine, who is a lover of horror and science fiction films. Nathan is one of those lucky guys who has all the "right connections" when it comes to collecting obscure movies on videotape. Over the years, he has stuffed boxes upon boxes of juicy, rare, "how the fuck did you get that" videos in his little den of doom. Just waiting to show guys like me his collection because I'm one of the few people on Earth who gives a shit that he has the uncut, original Japanese version of GODZILLA... etc...etc...

As I feasted my eyes on this video banquet of the bizarre, I beheld such wonderous, seldom-seen titles as THE H MAN, THE TERROR BENEATH THE SEA, THE EXOTIC ONES, THE LAST HOUSE ON DEAD END STREET, THE UNDERTAKER AND HIS PALS...and a curious title I had heard of but never thought anyone would own...DOCUMENT OF THE DEAD!

"Nathan," I wheezed. "Surely, this can't be the infamous documentary about the making of DAWN OF THE DEAD!"

But, also, I had some freedom down there that I wouldn't have had up here, where they were more savvy. I remember being on the set of *The Cincinnati Kid*. They walked me up to Steve McQueen. "This is the entertainment editor!" I remember him looking at me like, "What the fuck am I being introduced to this kid for?" It was really funny, you know [laughs]? I was the only one they could get. So, that was that. When I came back, I took one year at NYU.

**JS: What was NYU like?**

**RF:** I had Haig Manoogian, who was one of Scorsese's favorite people. I also met a fellow named Harry Hurwitz. Harry was a frustrated filmmaker, and we became friendly. Some of his ideas were similar to mine, but he was a bit more advanced than me. He had already done some shorts that had been released non-theatrically. We both dropped out of college, I raised some money, and we made a film together called *The Projectionist*, with Chuck McCann. It was Rodney Dangerfield's first film. I was twenty-four, and that kind of launched my career. Harry and I did four films together. Only one of them really came out. One of them sort of came out, and two of them definitely did not come out [laughs]. But, it was a good, faltering start. We shot them in 35mm.

**JS: You were involved with a project called *Shriek Out*.**

**RF:** Yeah. We had gone over budget on *The Projectionist* for like the fourth time. Whenever that happened, I would be the guy who was called upon to go out and raise money. We hit on this scheme of making a cheap horror film—shooting it in ten days, editing it in two weeks, and then selling it and using the money to finish *The Projectionist*. So, I raised enough money to shoot this little horror film. It was called *Shriek Out*, and it starred Judd Hirsch. Before we

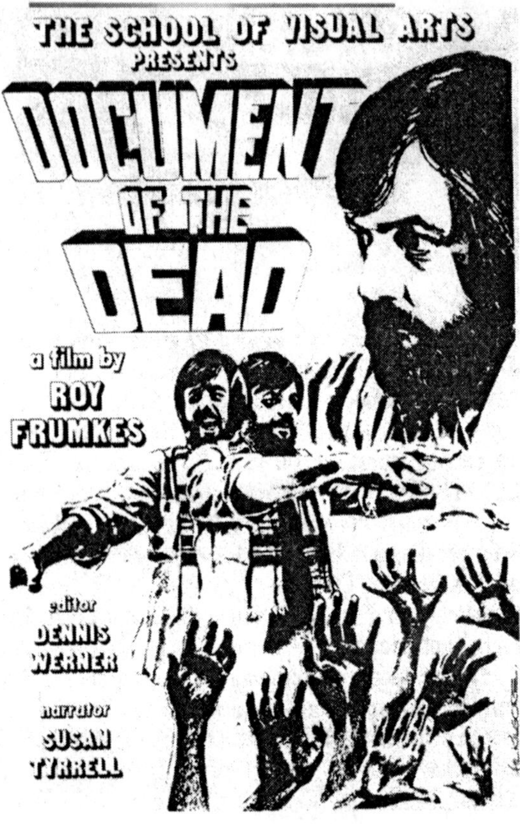
THE SCHOOL OF VISUAL ARTS
PRESENTS
DOCUMENT
OF THE
DEAD
a film by
ROY
FRUMKES
editor
DENNIS
WERNER
narrator
SUSAN
TYRRELL

started shooting, Harry Hurwitz and I said, "Let's go to Times Square and see what we're going to take!" We kind of boldly strolled down 42nd Street, and I said, "There's one—*Night of the Living Dead*." He said, "That looks great. Let's go in and see what kind of shit this is." Two hours later, we walked out thinking, "What the hell? We can't take that!" We had to pick that film [laughs]. We were so discouraged. Maybe a year later, George [A. Romero] was at the Museum of Modern Art. It had really become clear how special the film was. I attended his appearance, and he was backtracking about *Night*. "I'm not a horror filmmaker. I want to do other stuff. I don't understand why you're giving me all this attention." And for several years, as you know, he didn't do horror. That just didn't work, and he came back.

**JS: Do you think that George was destined to remain a horror director?**

**RF:** Yeah, I do. The correct mixture of whatever his gift was and the genre was ideal. I think *There's Always Vanilla* is just OK—it's got some intelligence and vision, but it doesn't jump at you the way his horror films do. And I think Richard Rubinstein really steered his career in a clear direction. The rest is history.

**JS: I know you've told the story a million times, but how did *Document of the Dead* come about?**

**RF:** Well, prior to teaching at SVA, I was teaching at SUNY Purchase. From the time I started teaching, I knew that there was something dishonest about what I was doing. This was pre-MTV, pre-DVD, pre-laserdisc, pre-VHS, pre-everything. There were only two hundred jobs out there for directors, and no one was letting go of them. There I was, teaching these kids to make movies, and honest to

God, there were no jobs. So, I said, "Well, the only stuff they're going to be doing is independent films. Let me see if I can finance a series of teaching films about independent filmmaking." At that time, there were documentaries about making films, but they were only about Hollywood blockbusters. The one for *Bonnie and Clyde* was great, but there was no way that students could relate to it. The independent scene and the Hollywood scene were kind of Ying and Yang. So, I pitched it to SUNY Purchase, but that was a big organization. I never heard back from them. When I went to SVA, I immediately pitched it again. I got a check a week later from the owner of the school, Silas Rhodes. He saw the promotional value of a series of films going out to high schools all over the country, saying, "Presented by SVA."

**JS: How did you wind up on the set of *Dawn of the Dead*?**

**RF:** At that time (1978), New York was what was known as a "union state." Not only could non-union people not shoot on a union film, you couldn't do non-union films. They would station all the union guys at the rental houses. If someone came in that they didn't recognize, they'd follow him and make sure that that set was "distracted." So, we had to look outside of New York to do the film. Earl Owensby was shooting *Wolfman* in the Carolinas, and George was doing *Dawn of the Dead*. I reached out to Richard Rubinstein. I'm told that there had never been a "making of" film about an independent feature before. Richard saw the value in it, and said, "Come on up." It's so strange, because when I was doing *The Definitive Document of the Dead*—when

ON THE SET OF *STREET TRASH*. FROM THE COLLECTION OF JAMIE CHIMINO. Attachment

I was doing the updates, let's say from *Diary of the Dead*, I'd get there and start setting up my shots. There would be three other documentary crews walking around. After I was done with my shots and walked away, they'd run over and get in my position because they figured, "Frumkes knows where to shoot from!" But back in '78, I was the only one there. It was really a very interesting situation.

**JS: How big of a crew did you have on *Document*?**

**RF:** I think it was seven people. We drove up in two cars. Sukey was my producer—she's the female zombie that gets the pie in her face. Reeves Lehmann, who's now the chairman of the film school, was my DP. James Callanan, who shot a ton of stuff for educational TV, was my second camera guy. He's the one who did the time lapse of me getting the makeup on.

Visually, I owe the success of *Document* to Reeves, because he had been a marine commando leader in the Tet Offensive in Vietnam. We had been told by Richard in no uncertain terms to, "Come out with long lenses, because you are not getting within 100 yards of George." Reeves started leading these commando raids on his stomach, and the crew would be crawling around the mall with the cameras. George would see this out of the corner of his eye. *Dawn* is a war film, and he really enjoyed what we were doing. He took down the barrier and said we could do whatever we wanted. That opened it up to really be more of a movie. It was incredible—we were at the right place at the right time. It was equally incredible that I sat on it for ten years. That was really a ballsy thing to do, but I wasn't getting the right offers. The film became kind of a myth... or a rumor.

**JS: I first read about *Document of the Dead* and *Street Trash* in Dennis Daniel's article for *Deep Red*. How did you two get in contact?**

**RF:** He called me. He said, "You know, I've been looking at films, and this name Frumkes keeps popping up in the weirdest places. I'd like to interview you for *Deep Red* magazine, but I'm not going to do it unless you're really frank and open." I said, "Well, judge for yourself." He did the interview, and Chas. really supported it. I have to tell you, to this day, the awareness of me in the genre is entirely due to *Deep Red*. I'm absolutely convinced of that—*Deep Red* coalesced all of the different and weird little things that I had done into one point. Amazing. So yeah, I'm very indebted to Dennis. And Dennis was along with me on the shoot for *The Definitive Document of the Dead*. He was really integral in that, and we've stayed friends after all these years.

**JS: Did you know Chas. Balun at all?**

**RF:** I never got close to Chas., but he was certainly an important person in the literary aspect of the horror genre. He always had that visceral passion that a lot of the other guys didn't quite rise to. He combined a number of elements of good writing together, and he seemed to understand the exact kind of writing that was appropriate for the genre. He was great at it.

**JS: A lot of independent filmmakers were championed in *Deep Red*.**

**RF:** You're absolutely right. I ended up traveling to England with John McNaughton and Buddy Giovinazzo. And that can't be coincidental. We were approached by a big horror convention (Splatterfest '90) in London, and they had to have pinpointed us because of *Deep Red*.

**JS: What are your memories of that convention?**

**RF:** A very nice guy put it together.

**JS: Justin Stanley.**

**RF:** Yeah. He pretty much pulled off a miracle. He somehow got it financed, got us all over there, and got us hotel rooms. And then, the thing started [laughs]. He froze—he just sat in the audience, paralyzed. I remember that I took over at some point, and was introducing people. Literally, the show ran itself. The inmates took over the asylum, and it went from there. It was a glorious event.

**JS: The UK had to put up with the whole video nasties thing.**

**RF:** Right. I mean, we had a thing over here about releasing R-rated versions

# TRASHING THE COMPETITION

## STREET TRASH

explodes onto Billboard's Chart of Top 40 video rentals.

| 31 | 30 | 25 | | | | | |
|---|---|---|---|---|---|---|---|
| 32 | NEW▶ | | STREET TRASH | Lightning Pictures<br>Lightning Video 9981 | R.L. Ryan<br>Vic Noto | 1987 | R |
| 33 | 31 | 25 | | | | | |

Released March 2, Lightning Video's cult classic, STREET TRASH, has already slimed its way in technicolor splendor to the top of home video rentals. Now through May 27th you can purchase STREET TRASH for only $69.98 list (regularly $79.98)! Check your inventory on this hot title and call your Advantage Distributor today!

VHS: LA 9981; BETA: LB 9981
91 MINUTES; ISBN: 0-8051-0493-3
UPC: 2848519981

LIGHTNING VIDEO

LIGHTNING PICTURES

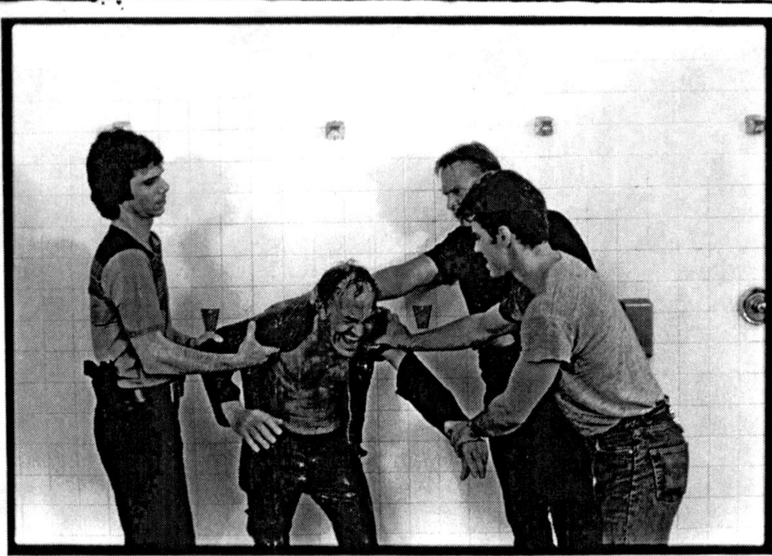

ON THE SET OF *STREET TRASH*. FROM THE COLLECTION OF JAMIE CHIMINO.

theatrically. Unfortunately, it made commercial sense to the studios. I remember when Wes Craven was doing *Shocker*. He told me there was what was known as a "Blockbuster clause" in the contract. In the Bible Belt of the United States, they wouldn't release anything stronger than an R. So, even though he had been given complete control on *Shocker*—and was so pleased with it—that part of the contract was waved in front of him at the eleventh hour. They had him make seven or nine cuts to satisfy Blockbuster, and they were the most important moments in the film. But even while that was happening, it seemed that director's cuts could sneak out—there were ways to see them. It wasn't as threatening to the genre, because somehow, the uncut version could be seen. We knew it. In England, that wasn't so. I believe that the act of championing these films was much more passionate over there.

**JS: I've always wondered how many prints you made of *Street Trash*.**

**RF:** We made ten prints. And by the way, ten minutes were cut out. Whitten believed that it needed to be ninety minutes. Jimmy Muro and I sat in the screening room with him, and we cut it together so we wouldn't be angry about it. He had to make ten prints of that version, and they'd play territory by territory. They'd do the east coast, they'd move down south, and then they'd move west. So, rather than spend all that money on 1,000 prints and advertising (which we would lose—and then the losses would be cross-collateralized into video, which was where we would ideally have been making all our profits), he had a very measured and conservative approach which would guarantee that people all over the country had heard of the film. A lot of people would see it and would be talking about it. It would make its money when it hit video—that was his concept. To explain it further, *Street Trash* opened in New York at the 8th Street Playhouse as a midnight show. This was in 1987. During the day and the evening, the film that was playing was *Full Metal Jacket.* Warner Brothers would pay for the entire ad, and there'd be a little space at the top or bottom that would say, "Midnight Only: *Street Trash*." So, we got our advertising for free. People who read the ads for *Full Metal Jacket* saw that the film was playing. Whitten was very canny about how he promoted the film. And then, when Vestron reneged on all of the ideas he had for promoting the film, he was so incensed that he resigned.

**JS: How did *Street Trash* initially do?**

**RF:** It didn't do well. I think it would have done well if all of his ideas had been implemented. I'm convinced of it. He asked me if I could get good quotes from people in the industry. I said, "Yeah, I can get some quotes from George, Wes, Jonathan Demme, John Waters, and Tom Savini." He said, "Get them." And then he designed this page for the *New York Times*. At the top, it said, "*Street Trash*." There was a line going down the page, and on the right were all the critics' reviews, which were just despicable. On the left, there were all these reviews from those guys, which were wonderful. And then it said, "Which side of the street are you on?" Well, that's the first thing they cut, because they didn't want to offend the critics. The *Village Voice* was capable of being a little more liberal and raunchy. He wanted a full page ad that just said, "*Street Trash*—Fuck you!" It goes on and

ON THE SET OF *STREET TRASH*. FROM THE COLLECTION OF JAMIE CHIMINO.

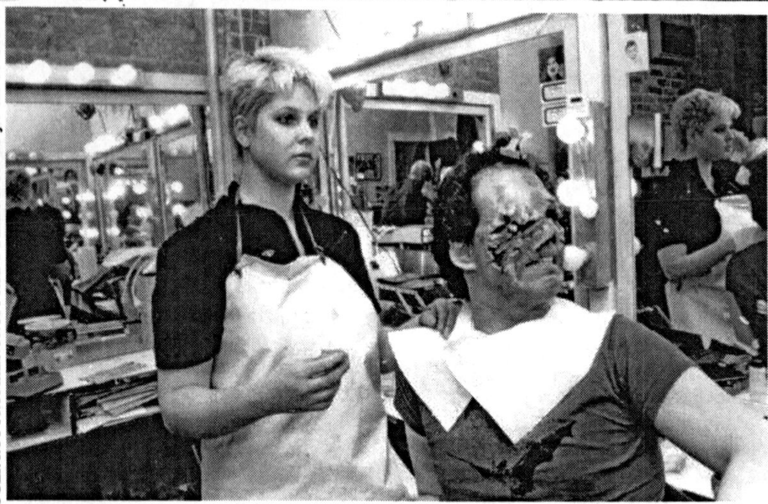

*STREET TRASH* MAKEUP ARTIST JENNIFER ASPINALL WITH PRODUCER ROY FRUMKES. FROM THE COLLECTION OF JAMIE CHIMINO.

on. He had this incredible campaign that would have paid off on home video. It really could have done gangbusters. They undercut him on everything. The only thing he ended up getting was the Lincoln Center premiere. We all rode in on dump trucks.

**JS: How did your peers at SVA react to the film?**

**RF:** We had our own premiere at the Ziegfeld in New York. The theater's never been the same since—there's just something about it that died that night [laughs]. The film had started, and I walked into the lobby and saw Reeves Lehmann and Jimmy Callanan. I said, "Guys, it's already on." They said, "We know that." They were leaving. And these guys were my friends [laughs]! The reaction was mixed. The film was so gorgeous looking that it kind of frustrated the critics who wanted to hate it, and they had plenty of reason to. I mean, in order to keep the audience off balance, we added that rape scene and the castration. Even the critics who were with it for the first forty minutes were suddenly going, "Oh, no! This is going too far!" It was a professional looking film, but my God—if there's a case for censorship in this country, maybe this is it.

**JS: Let's talk about your involvement with *Films in Review*.**

**RF:** I got out of college in 1966, and instantly joined the National Board of Review of Motion Pictures, which is the oldest film organization in the country. It started in 1909 as a reaction against censorship, which was already in full swing—civil and religious groups were breaking into booths and eviscerating films. And this was several years before features were being made. First they had the *National Board of Review* magazine and at some point in 1950, it turned into *Films in Review*. In '66, when I graduated, one of my friends' mothers belonged to the NBR and she

vouched for me. That's the only way you could join—someone had to bring you in. Soon after that, I started writing for them. I was their token young person. This was an old group, and the people in it were old. They'd screen a film, and someone would say, "Wow! When did they start using color?" I'm looking around—this is 1966 [laughs]! Now, of course, I'm one of the elders, but back then, I was the youngest person there, by a decade or more. Henry Hart was the editor. I liked him a lot, but he was very opinionated and against a lot of the stuff. When *2001* [*A Space Odyssey*] came out, I said to him, "Boy, that is a brilliant, breakthrough piece of footage." He patted me on the shoulder and said, "You'll learn," and just walked away. Anyway, I wrote for them for a long time. And then, in '96, when *The Substitute* came out (and I actually made some money), they were fazing *Films in Review* out. It was getting expensive to keep it in print, and they decided to let it go. I said, "You can't. It's really a part of history. I'll buy it from you." They looked at me and were kind of repressing their smiles. They said, "Go for it." They knew that I was doing something absolutely fool hearted [laughs]! So, I buy this magazine, and it's $25,000 an issue to put it out. And they had never, in all those years, taken advertising. It was a not-for-profit organization. So, I was stuck trying to turn this thing around. What little money I had put into it was quickly evaporating. We published it for a year. We changed the format and did some nice articles on Buddy G and independent film. Then, finally in 1997, I just gave up and brought it onto the internet. That's where it's been, ever since.

**JS: What do you think the future has in store for print magazines?**

**RF**: Well, I don't know. I've been getting calls from people to put out an LP of the score to *Street Trash*, and I thought LPs were long gone. I think things tend to rise and fall, and it's more than nostalgia. There's a certain pleasure you get from reading the printed page that you do not get reading on a screen. I'm in the minority now, but if someone in LA wants to read my latest script, they get a hard copy. I don't send them a file because it just doesn't read the same. It's too easy to stop and get distracted. So, I think those other mediums will make their comebacks, but *Films in Review*? Never. Even when it was doing its best, it had a niche market. I don't think it ever sold more than 12,000 copies, and we get a lot more readers than that on the internet. We have one writer, Victoria Alexander, who's very inflammatory. I'm very thankful for her, because she knows how to insult people everywhere on this planet. She's guaranteed to bring readers to *Films in Review*. What we would do in a month with the magazine, she can do for us in a day.

**JS: How did distribution work for a magazine like**

ORIGINAL PROP BOTTLE OF VIPER. FROM THE COLLECTION OF JAMIE CHIMINO.

***Films in Review?***

**RF:** I think it was done very much the way the others were. We would find a distributor who would get it to all the stores. I would see it in Grand Central Station, and I would see it in Borders and those places. It would appear in libraries, it would appear in Europe. But, the problem with that was, if at the end of three months they weren't all sold, they were returned. And the money had to be returned. So, it was misleading. We'd print all of these copies, and at the end, I'd have ten boxes (with several hundred copies per box) stored in the basement. And the stuff that I wanted to write about when I took over the magazine wasn't necessarily commercial. For instance, there was an NBR ceremony, which they do every year. They had Mel Gibson and Nicolas Cage. There was a shot of Nic Cage with a woman who was in that terrific film about R. Crumb. She was there to receive the award for *Crumb* because he was in Europe somewhere. They got a shot of her and Cage—it was a strange shot of the two of them. I said, "That's the one we're putting on the cover." I was advised by people, and I think correctly, to put Gibson on the cover. "You'll instantly sell 10,000 more issues." I said, "I know what you mean, but those shots of Mel are boring. This shot is really fun." So, I didn't necessarily always make commercially correct decisions with the magazine. I guess I had a certain vision.

**JS: Did accepting advertising ever pay off?**

**RF:** After five issues, we were getting enough advertising that it was only costing us $15,000 to put out an issue. But, we did a study, and it appeared that it would be another two or three years before we would break even and start making money. I just couldn't keep pouring that much into each issue. And really, my passion is screenwriting.

**JS: How do you fit that into your schedule?**

**RF:** Teaching is a good thing. At SVA, we get a four-month break. We get all of May, June, July, and August off. I really can get writing done. It's nice working at a job where you get that kind of time off. Plus, every seven years, you're entitled to a sabbatical, which is a paid year off. That's how I made *Street Trash*. Every seven years, I take a year off and do something.

**JS: What are you working on these days?**

**RF:** I recently optioned the remake rights to *Fiend Without a Face*. I wrote that, and I'm starting to have meetings. We'll see what happens. I also wrote a script and a book—a zombie noir story. Those are both going to go out momentarily to my agent. Rocco Simonelli and I just wrote something similar to *The Substitute* called *The Alternate*. That's out there already and they're getting it around.

**JS: Hopefully it will be a success.**

**RF:** I think it's very difficult and illusive… I've been in the biz for forty-four years, and I've only really had one hit—that's *The Substitute*. Luckily for me, I had a good lawyer and a good contract. They did three sequels, and they couldn't get rid of me. So, I almost have my retirement fund. I don't know if I can pull it off again. It's a very difficult market, but I'm grateful. I've had a very nice peripheral career…

# BUDDY GIOVINAZZO

## A FEW WORDS FROM BUDDY G...

A FEW WORDS FROM BUDDY G...

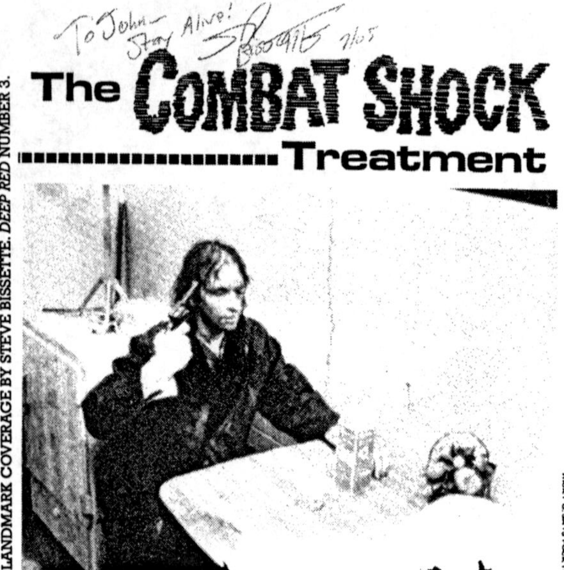


LANDMARK COVERAGE BY STEVE BISSETTE. *DEEP RED* NUMBER 3.

Director Buddy Giovinazzo is another filmmaker who first gained genre recognition within the pages of the fanzines. Nearly everyone I know can remember reading about *Combat Shock* for the first time. In my case, Steve Bissette made the introduction in *Deep Red* number 3. In *Deep Red* number 6, Buddy G joined Nathan Schiff (*Weasels Rip my Flesh*) and Pericles Lewnes (*Redneck Zombies*) in an engaging round table discussion about independent filmmaking with writers Chas. Balun and Dennis Daniel.

Buddy has since gone on to direct *No Way Home*, *The Unscarred*, *Life is Hot in Cracktown*, and a segment of the anthology film *The Theatre Bizarre*. In this interview, he generously took the time to answer a few questions about the zine scene of yore and his latest film, *A Night of Nightmares*.

**JOHN SZPUNAR: How long have you been living in Germany?**

**BUDDY GIOVINAZZO:** I've been living in Berlin for about twelve years now, with side trips to the US, mostly to LA, for filming. I shot *Life is Hot in Cracktown* in 2008/9 in LA, for instance. I was in LA for eighteen months straight for that film. I just shot *A Night of Nightmares* in LA in December of 2011. That lasted five months.

**JS: I'm guessing that *A Night of Nightmares* is a horror film.**

**BG**: Yes, it's a creepy horror film made on a low budget. It's got a tremendous cast in Marc Senter and Elissa Dowling.

**JS: How did the shoot go?**

**BG:** It was a difficult, because we were in the mountains about an hour north of Hollywood—it was another planet out there. We had all night shoots and it was freezing the whole time. The location itself was like a horror film. We shot on a farm that was once inhabited by Charlie Manson and his Family before they went to the Spahn ranch.

**JS: Wow...**

**BG:** The owner of the house where we shot told me that the Family was kicked off the farm because three days before Thanksgiving, they killed all the turkeys and ate them. The farmer, who was an ex-marine, threw them off the land. They went directly to Spahn ranch.

**JS: Unreal. You never know what kind of weird territory you're going to stumble across out there. Anyway, I'd like to talk to you about horror fanzines. Guys like you, Jim VanBebber, and Jörg Buttgereit got your "start" from fanzine culture...**

**BG:** That's right. Without the fanzines, you and I probably wouldn't be having this conversation right now.

**JS: I'd imagine that monster magazines gave you a pretty big kick as a kid.**

**BG:** Absolutely. *Famous Monsters* is probably the first film magazine I can remember as a kid. I remember seeing *Frankenstein* on the cover and it really freaked me out. So, I bought it and my mother made me bring it back.

**JS: A familiar story!**

**BG:** I was too embarrassed to bring it back to the candy store where I bought it, because the guy behind the counter kept asking me if I was sure I was allowed to buy it. So, what I did was lay it on top of a trash can in the hope that someone else would come by and pick it up. Share the poison's always been my view.

**JS: I hope it found a good home! Somewhat along the same line, I credit horror fanzines for introducing my generation to a lot of films that would have otherwise been discarded and forgotten. You must have seen a lot of that stuff first-hand.**

**BG:** I saw a triple bill that I'll never forget: *The Corpse Grinders*, *The Embalmer*, and *The Undertaker and his Pals*. I loved them all at the time. This is where I show my age, because I saw *The Horrors of Spider Island* in a theater when I was very young. Today, it's probably a horrible film, but at the time, I was traumatized by the sight of a dead body stuck in a giant spider web. The first time I saw brain matter on the big screen was a campy film with Joan Crawford called *Berserk! The Creeping Flesh* is another film I saw in the theater as a kid; when Peter Cushing lets his arm get chopped off because the monster wraps its tentacle around it—that was tattooed on my brain. Even to this day.

**JS: I probably first saw brain matter in *Fangoria*. How early were you reading that?**

**BG:** Probably the first year it came out, whenever that was. Late seventies, I'm guessing. It had a very "real" feel

# BUDDY GIOVINAZZO

## A FEW WORDS FROM BUDDY G...

BUDDY GIOVINAZZO -- (DEEP RED 3) wrote, produced and directed the much-acclaimed cult hit COMBAT SHOCK and penned the screenplay for the upcoming theatrical release, DEAD AND MARRIED (SHE'S BACK). Buddy has also written and produced several music videos and short films including JONATHAN OF THE NIGHT, SUBCONSCIOUS REALITIES and LOBOTOMY as well as directing the promotional reel for Joe (MANIAC) Spinell's proposed sequel, MANIAC 2: MISTER ROBBIE. Buddy is currently teaching a filmmaking class at a local university and has several scripts in various stages of production.

DIRECTORS' FORUM. *DEEP REED* NUMBER 6.

COMBAT SHOCK

**RED:** Why aren't horror films scary anymore? What's the deal with the new crop?

**BG:** I'll tell you the truth, I don't see 'em as much as I used to, primarily cause it's sequelization and bullshit. It's formularized. When I was a kid, horror films used to work as nightmares; they brought out all the fears you had as a kid. Nowadays, they play it too safe.

**NS:** They're making crappier movies now.

**BG:** Horror films to me today are like Stanley Kubrick's FULL METAL JACKET and CLOCKWORK ORANGE; they aren't trying to frighten you anymore. What they're trying to do is shock you, then make you laugh. There is no fright in today's hit; it's just shock. We know what Freddy Krueger is going to do; nobody's going to be afraid of him anymore. We go in to see the FX, to hear the funny lines.

**NS:** You ask anyone and they say Freddy Krueger's a hero; no one's afraid of him anymore. Every other line is a joke; he's doing jokes. There are no horror movies anymore; they're all horror-comedies. Even RE-ANIMATOR, which is a fantastic movie, was still a comedy. They blew it with the head being carried around. It's joke time.

**PL:** All of the movies coming out today are geared for kids, like big cartoons, and not very good cartoons. There haven't been many films that scared the shit out of me.

**NS:** Today, it's in the script; no

PERICLES LEWNES

BUDDY GIOVINAZZO

or $12 million for a film about a werewolf. And, they're not even good films.

**RED:** What have you seen recently that showed some merit?

**BG:** HELLRAISER--it was really great until the ending. The ending was typical of the kind of stuff they're

"We're being ripped off with films that were never released theatrically."

---

as a magazine. I never dreamed that it would become what it became. I'm glad that it did, because we needed something like that in the genre.

**JS: I'm guessing that you didn't have to leave your copy on a garbage can. Did it give you a jolt?**

**BG**: By the time I read my first *Fangoria*, I was almost beyond the stage of being shocked by most films. I remember liking the covers, and the way they put gore and special effects in the forefront. They made stars out of the special effects masters and that was definitely cool.

**JS: A lot of naysayers have been down on it throughout the years, but I'm glad it's still around.**

**BG:** It gives the genre legitimacy in the marketplace. The people who make the decisions on what gets made and what doesn't can see that horror is a viable and never-dying genre.

**JS: Let's talk about the fanzines that**

**came forth in its wake.**

**BG**: I read *Gore Gazette* all the time. I always loved Rick Sullivan's writing style—his no-bullshit approach to the genre. When someone tried to con us or play us for idiots, Rick Sullivan always called them out for it, and in a very funny way, too. I also read Steve Puchulski's *Slimetime*, Michael Gingold's *Scareaphanalia*, and of course *Deep Red*, which was probably the most intelligently written horror magazine that I can remember. Not to insult the others, but *Deep Red* approached the films in a more technical, analytical manner that I found surprising at the time. You just didn't read about horror films that way.

**JS: As I was saying earlier, I found out about a lot of films through the fanzines. How important were they to your discovery of films?**

**BG:** They weren't important to my discovery of films, per se. I lived in NYC and even as a young teenager, I was going to 42nd Street back in the late seventies and eighties at the heyday for exploitation. I was always interested or fascinated with the obscure, the darker side. I sought out whatever I wasn't supposed to be seeing at the time. I remember seeing *Saló* in a theater in NYC because the *New York Daily News* had a review from Rex Reed who wrote—I'm paraphrasing here—"You can almost smell the cat urine coming off the screen." Well, that's a recommendation for me!

**JS: A lot of the fanzines promoted what I'd consider a new renaissance of gritty low budget filmmakers. I was wondering—what gave you the bug to make your first feature?**

COMBAT SHOCK

1984-86/ d: Buddy Giovinazzo

The most obsessive and grueling independent horror film since THE EVIL DEAD. Angry, uncompromisingly bleak vision of life in the lower depths with a dishonorably discharged Vietnam vet suffering an impoverished existence with his burnout wife and hideous Agent Orange mutant infant in an absolute shithole apartment. Piecemeal memories of a war atrocity he may or may not have been responsible for finally drive him over the edge, culminating in an inevitable, almost unbearable climactic bloodbath of murder, suicide, and baby baking. Director Buddy Giovinazzo shot it for peanuts on Staten Island, but it's a brutal, brilliant film that pulls no punches. Nastiest sequence has a junkie cramming a fix into his vein with a fucking coat hanger...just a warm up for the final jolting movement of the film. Relentless, grim, terribly disturbing fare for those who can get into it. (SB)

COMBAT SHOCK REVIEW FROM THE *DEEP RED HORROR HANDBOOK*. Attachment

Ricky Giovinazzo in COMBAT SHOCK

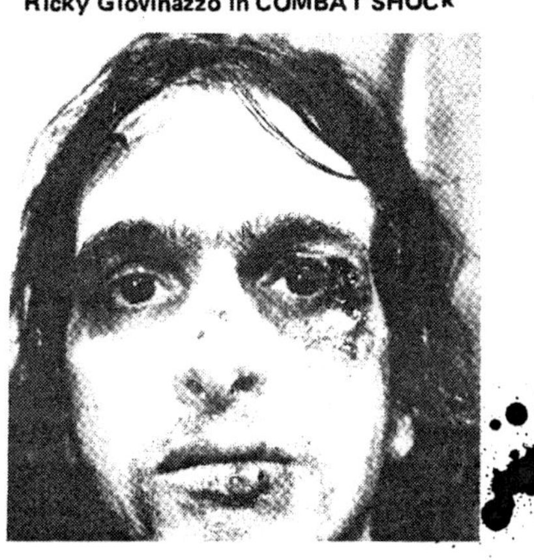

# BUDDY GIOVINAZZO

## A FEW WORDS FROM BUDDY G...

# INSIDE:

WIN *LITTLE SHOP OF HORRORS* AND *THE LAMP* ON VIDEO! FRANK HENENLOTTER INTERVIEWED! RICCARDO FREDA FILMOGRAPHY! BRIAN DE PALMA ON BEING UNTOUCHABLE! SHAUN HUTSON'S TOP TEN HORRORS! TOBE HOOPER ON CHAINSAWS! *FACES OF DEATH* EXPOSED! BRAD F. GRINTER REDISCOVERED! REVIEWS OF: *COMBAT SHOCK* . . . *NIGHT OF THE SORCERORS* . . . *THE OPENING OF MISTY BEETHOVEN* . . . *RIVER'S EDGE* . . . *BLOOD FREAK* . . . AND MANY MORE! HAMMER SEASON TRASHED! VIDEO REVIEWS! RABID CORRESPONDENCE! VILENESS! VITRIOL! VENOM! TOO MUCH!

Vol. 2 Issue 2. £1.25

ON THE COVER: ALAN JONES REVIEWS *COMBAT SHOCK* FOR *SHOCK XPRESS*.

**BG:** Believe it or not, my inspiration to become a filmmaker came primarily from John Waters. Now, my work is nothing like John's, but what I learned from him was that filmmaking is something you can do with your friends and have a blast doing it. You can make things that nobody else in their right mind would make. *Pink Flamingos* and *Female Trouble* made me look at filmmaking in a completely different way. These films were dirty and grimy, and there was no slickness to them whatsoever. And yet, to me, they were great films because they showed a slice of life that I'd never seen in film before. I realized that filmmaking doesn't have to cost millions. All it takes is a bad attitude, the stubbornness to persevere, and the desire to piss people off. I loved that and it was a lesson I've never forgotten.

**JS: Most people that I know of first became aware of *Combat Shock* by reading Steve Bissette's article in *Deep Red*...**

**BG:** That's right. If it wasn't for that article, I think *Combat Shock* would be gone right now. In fact, after its release, it died a fast yet painful death. I thought it was over, or at least my career was certainly over. Then, about three years later, I started getting calls from people all over the place. One guy in Finland called me up and wanted to talk to me about my film. I didn't know what he was talking about, until I read Steve Bissette's article. It made *Combat Shock* seem, for the first time, like a real movie.

**JS: Were you surprised that somebody wanted to put so much thought into the film?**

**BG:** I was shocked. Steve—and Chas. also—seemed to understand what was in my mind. And they also got the humor of *Combat Shock*, because I think *CS* is a very (okay, I'll admit, darkly) humorous film. At screenings, before I sold the film to Troma, people would be speechless, and not in a good way. I'd say to them, "But didn't you find it at all funny?" They would look at me like I'd just killed their dog. Steve really analyzed the film in a way that went behind the camera and tried to figure out what I was thinking, and why, and he achieved it.

**JS: *Deep Red* really gave up and coming filmmakers their due. What do you remember about the "Director's Forum" interview in *Deep Red*? You were there with Peri Lewnes and Nathan Schiff...**

**BG:** Roy Frumkes was there also, I believe—no wait! I think Roy missed the train or something. For some

reason, he couldn't make it (it would have been wild had he been there). Anyway, I remember Peri and Nathan. We sat in—I believe—Nathan's kitchen and did an interview together. Peri was someone I met when he worked at Troma and I think he'd just done his own film, *Redneck Zombies*. Nathan was someone I admired because he made his own films his own way, and he was a true independent filmmaker. Still is, I would think. I've lost touch with Peri and Nathan over the years. I'm still really good friends with Roy Frumkes, I'm sorry to say.

Fighting, killing, maiming, agent orange and torture cages were the easy part!...
LLOYD KAUFMAN and MICHAEL HERZ Present A TROMA TEAM Release
COMBAT SHOCK
R RESTRICTED


**JS: I talked to Roy the other day about the impact that *Deep Red* had on *Street Trash*. That magazine touched a lot of people. Any thoughts on Chas.' passing?**

**BG:** Horrible. I think he suffered, because he was sick for a while. I met Chas. a few times, once with his lovely wife, Pat. He was a giant in heart and in soul. I think the genre owes him a great deal of gratitude. He was a pioneer in bringing a higher level of discourse to horror. I think to Chas., there wasn't any difference between art films or horror films, both deserved respect and attention. It was his love and passion for the genre that touched anyone who knew him. He will be missed.

**JS: What can you tell me about the British reaction to *Combat Shock*? Their zine scene was really starting to take off.**

**BG:** There was *Samhain*, that I remember. But my biggest champion for *Combat Shock* at the time was the journalist Alan Jones. Alan wrote a tremendous review for *Combat Shock*; it was like he was also inside my head. His insights saw something that cast a new light on the film, and his support definitely brought attention to the film from the other side of the Atlantic. I felt an immediate kinship with him, too. He's such a great writer. Then, in the nineties, I got to go to England for a horror festival running at the Scala cinema, a wonderful cinema. I got to meet Alan. We've been great friends ever since.

# BUDDY GIOVINAZZO

## A FEW WORDS FROM BUDDY G...

[BOTTOM:] BOOTLEG OF THE DIRECTOR'S CUT OF *COMBAT SHOCK*, UNDER THE ORIGINAL TITLE *AMERICAN NIGHTMARES*.

**JS: That was at Splatterfest '90, right?**

**BG:** Yes. That was a tremendous experience. Justin Stanley set the whole thing up and he brought over John McNaughton, Scott Spiegel, Greg Nicotero, and Roy Frumkes. I met Richard Stanley there for the first time. Roy Frumkes and I visited the site of Jack the Ripper's last victim, but that's another interview.

**JS: By that time, tapes of *Combat Shock* were floating around.**

**BG:** I met a couple that came by train from Amsterdam to see *Combat Shock*. They told me they had seen the film twenty times, but wanted to finally see it in color. I was a bit puzzled. I told them, "But the film *is* in color!" They explained that the VHS copy they had bought had been copied so many times that the film they saw was in black and white.

**JS: You're still pretty much an outsider filmmaker. What are your thoughts on Hollywood today?**

**BG:** It's depressing, isn't it? I can't stand to see what's taken place in the industry. It's the same film over and over. Bigger, louder, and more stupid. I mean, I love mindless entertainment, I really do. But it seems that that's all they're making right now. Every film has to make 100 million in the first week or it's considered a disappointment. I know, I sound like a grumpy old man when I write this, but I miss the character-driven films of my youth. We've seen all the special effects that you can imagine and it always leaves me feeling nothing. Having said that, I regret never having made a Hollywood film, because I'd like to experience making a film on that level just once. But my friends who have done it have had heartbreaking, soul-crushing experiences and I would never want to

FUJI HQ HIGH QUALITY
Buddy G.'s
AMERICAN NIGHTMARES
BUDDY G ROCK VIDEOS + TRAILERS
VHS

go through that.

**JS: What are your thoughts on digital filmmaking?**

**BG:** We've lost something by going digital. I don't care what anyone says, it's not the equivalent of film. Not yet. I shot *Life is Hot in Cracktown* on 35mm, right up to the end. We finished on film and never went digital. During the festival run, I'd be in the theater with my wife Gesine, and we'd watch three, sometimes four films in a row. All shot on high-end HD cameras. There was no denying it, the second *Cracktown* came on the screen—in brilliant 35 film—the images were amazingly sharper and brighter; the color was vibrant. We've gotten used to the HD look, and we're accepting this new look without any resistance. Of course, on a low budget, it's absolutely cheaper to shoot, there's no argument. But, there's a trade off, and the trade off for me is image quality. Having just written that, I have to admit that my newest film *A Night of Nightmares* is shot on digital. It was the only way to get the film made; I could have never shot it on film with the money that we had. So, I put my focus and my energy into the story and the characters. I believe that a story well told, with great characters, will always be interesting.

BUDDY G WITH [LEFT] ROY FRUMKES. PHOTO COURTESY OF BUDDY GIOVINAZZO.

**JS: What can we expect from the film?**

**BG:** *A Night of Nightmares* is a sick little gem, a true horror film. Up until *The Theatre Bizarre*, I'd never made a true horror film before. My films all have elements of horror, but they're more character driven dramas than true horror films. That's always been my problem with the horror audience, they never knew what to make of my work—it's disturbing, yes, but it's not quite in the genre. Well, this film is completely in the genre and I loved making it. Hopefully it has all the elements that people who like my work would expect from me. It's twisted, realistic, and tries to fuck with your mind. Now, believe it or not, I have to go. I'm directing a German crime series here in Cologne, and if any of these companies here knew about my other films, I'd probably be thrown out of the country. So keep this interview a secret, okay?

# Index of Publications

# INDEX OF PUBLICATIONS

# Index of Publications

# Index of Publications

# Index of Publications

# INDEX OF PUBLICATIONS

# Index of Publications

# PUZZLE SOLUTION

| 1 E | 2 L | 3 A | 4 N | 5 D | ■ | 6 T | 7 H | 8 O | 9 R | ■ | 10 C | 11 H | 12 A | 13 P |
|---|---|---|---|---|---|---|---|---|---|---|---|---|---|---|
| 14 B | A | Y | O | U | ■ | 15 A | U | R | A | ■ | 16 H | A | L | E |
| 17 B | R | A | W | N | ■ | 18 K | E | R | N | ■ | 19 I | L | I | A |
| ■ | 20 S | H | A | G | G | 21 E | D | ■ | 22 S | 23 A | L | V | E | R |
| ■ | ■ | ■ | 24 Y | E | A | R | ■ | 25 M | O | R | D | A | N | T |
| 26 H | 27 A | 28 N | S | O | M | ■ | 29 F | E | M | U | R | ■ | ■ | ■ |
| 30 E | M | U | ■ | 31 N | U | 32 K | E | D | ■ | 33 M | E | 34 L | 35 O | 36 N |
| 37 R | O | T | 38 C | ■ | 39 T | O | T | A | 40 L | ■ | 41 N | O | N | E |
| 42 A | S | S | A | 43 M | ■ | 44 R | U | L | E | 45 R | ■ | 46 O | C | A |
| ■ | ■ | ■ | 47 L | A | 48 V | A | S | ■ | 49 P | U | 50 C | K | E | R |
| 51 A | 52 N | 53 T | I | G | E | N | ■ | 54 M | E | S | H | ■ | ■ | ■ |
| 55 M | E | A | G | E | R | ■ | 56 P | E | R | S | O | 57 N | 58 A | ■ |
| 59 B | A | B | U | ■ | 60 N | 61 O | E | L | ■ | 62 E | R | E | C | 63 T |
| 64 I | T | L | L | ■ | 65 A | N | T | E | ■ | 66 L | E | T | H | E |
| 67 T | H | E | A | ■ | 68 L | O | S | E | ■ | 69 L | A | T | E | D |

CLUES TO THE PUZZLE ON PAGE 359.

BACKGROUND: PAGES FROM *GRINDHOUSE* NUMBER 3.

**A HEADPRESS BOOK**
**First published by Headpress in 2013**

Headpress, Unit 365, 10 Great Russell Street, London, WC1B 3BQ, United Kingdom
*Tel* 0845 330 1844 *Email* headoffice@headpress.com

**XEROX FEROX**
**The Wild World of the Horror Film Fanzine**

Text copyright © John Szpunar and respective contributors
This volume copyright © Headpress 2013
Design, layout & Xerox Ferox logo: Mark Critchell
<mark.critchell@googlemail.com>
Cover: Stephen R. Bissette {*who dedicates his cover art to the memory of the late, great Chas. Balun, and his wife Pat*}
Headpress Diaspora: Thomas Campbell, Caleb Selah, Giuseppe, Dave T.

Special thanks from the publishers to Ian Richardson
for digital scanning & assist on the cover art.

Title page background from *Demonique: Journal of the Obscure Horror Cinema* number 1.

Images are reproduced in this book in the spirit of publicity and as historical illustrations to the text. Grateful acknowledgement is made to the respective artists, models and publishers.

The moral rights of the authors have been asserted.

All Rights Reserved. No part of this book may be reproduced, stored in a retrieval system, or transmitted, in any form or by any means, electronic, mechanical, photocopying, recording or otherwise, on earth or in space, this dimension or that, without prior permission in writing from the publisher.

**A CIP catalog record for this book is available from the British Library**

**ISBN 978-1-909394-10-0 (pbk)**
**ISBN 978-1-909394-11-7 (ebk)**
**NO-ISBN (hbk)**

*Headpress. The gospel according to unpopular culture.*

Headpress NO ISBN special editions are exclusive to World Headpress

WWW.WORLDHEADPRESS.COM

CPSIA information can be obtained at www.ICGtesting.com
Printed in the USA
BVOW01s0841201113

336663BV00001B/1/P